The Encyclopedia of American Religions:

Religious Creeds

The Encyclopedia of American Religions:

Religious Creeds

A Compilation of More Than 400 Creeds, Confessions, Statements of Faith, and Summaries of Doctrine of Religious and Spiritual Groups in the United States and Canada

VOLUME II

J. Gordon Melton

with

James Sauer

Gale Research Inc. • *DETROIT* • *WASHINGTON, D.C.* • *LONDON*

J. Gordon Melton

with James Sauer

Gale Research Inc. Staff

Amy Lucas, *Senior Editor*
Annette Piccirelli, *Project Coordinator*
Sara Burak, *Associate Editor*

Aided by:
Kristin Kahrs, Kathleen Lopez Nolan, Annette Novallo,
Christopher P. Scanlon, and Gwen E. Turecki

Benita L. Spight, *Data Entry Manager*
Gwendolyn S. Tucker, *Data Entry Supervisor*

Mary Beth Trimper, *Production Director*
Shanna Heilveil, *Production Assistant*

⊗™ The paper used in this publication meets the minimum requirements of American National Standard for Information Sciences--Permanence Paper for Printed Library Materials, ANSI Z39.48-1984.

♻ This book is printed on recycled paper that meets Environmental Protection Agency standards.

ISBN 0-8103-5491-8

Printed in the United States of America

Published simultaneously in the United Kingdom
by Gale Research International Limited
(An affiliated company of Gale Research Inc.)

Contents

RELIGIOUS CREEDS

Chapter 1: Ancient Creeds of the Christian Church

The Ecumenical Church

Chapter 2: Western Liturgical Family

Roman Catholic Church

Old Catholicism

Anglicanism

Independent Anglican Schools

Chapter 3: Eastern Liturgical Family

Orthodoxy

Contents

Contents

Acknowledgements

This volume could not have been completed without the assistance of Dr. James Sauer, Library Director at Eastern College, St. Davids, Pennsylvania. When the first volume of *Encyclopedia of American Religions: Religious Creeds* was published, Dr. Sauer contacted the Institute for the Study of American Religion and donated an extensive collection of doctrinal statements he had collected from Evangelical organizations and schools. These statements provided the groundwork for this second volume.

Again, I acknowledge my ever-growing debt to Joseph Boissé and his staff at the Donald C. Davidson Library at the University of California-Santa Barbara, with special thanks to David Tambo, director of the Special Collections Department. They have continued to go out of their way to assist on various institute projects and to house and care for the American Religions Collection. They have my personal thanks, and I am happy that their monumental efforts are being acknowledged by the larger community of scholars and researchers in American religious life.

Grateful acknowledgement is due to Sheed & Ward, Ltd. and Georgetown University Press for granting permission to reprint *Promulgations of the Council of Trent* (from *The Decree of the Ecumenical Council of Trent*, Sheed & Ward, Ltd. and Georgetown University Press, copyright © 1990).

Introduction

This second volume of *Encyclopedia of American Religions: Religious Creeds (EAR: Religious Creeds)* contains 400 creeds, confessions, and statements of belief for religious groups across North America. Not published in the first volume, these creeds represent Christian, Jewish, Islamic, Buddhist, Hindu, and other traditions with a following in the United States and Canada. In addition, historical notes and comments are provided to help researchers, librarians, students, and other information seekers understand the context in which creeds were written, revised, or discarded.

What is a Creed?

For the purpose of this book, "creeds" are defined as formal statements of belief to which members of a church are expected to give their intellectual assent. The writing of religious creeds is primarily an activity of Christian churches, but some other churches publish less rigid statements of belief that reflect a consensus of church teachings while recognizing some variance of belief among members (and even leaders). A number of religious groups publish statements with the understanding that such beliefs are secondary to the life of the group—greater emphasis is placed on piety, religious experience, liturgy, behavior (ethics), or ethnicity. Other churches are strictly anti-creedal. Nevertheless, even the most anti-creedal and experience-oriented groups usually have a small body of assumed intellectual content (a system of beliefs that can be put into words) and, on occasion, produce official group statements for members' use. Such statements fall within the scope of this work.

This Volume Complements and Expands Earlier Work

The first volume of *EAR: Religious Creeds*, published in 1988, was the first comprehensive compilation of the creeds, confessions, and statements of belief of American religious groups since the 1879 publication of Philip Schaff's landmark *The Creeds of Christendom*. The first volume of *EAR: Religious Creeds* contains more than 450 creedal texts, the authoritative doctrinal and belief statements of the religious groups described in Gale Research Inc.'s *Encyclopedia of American Religions (EAR)*. That first creedal volume filled a significant informational need, and the overwhelming response to it prompted the publication of this second companion title, designed to be used in conjunction with the first volume.

Newly Listed Religious Organizations. This volume of *EAR: Religious Creeds* contains the doctrinal statements of religious groups newly listed in the 1993 edition of Gale's *Encyclopedia of American Religions*, including many Canadian-based organizations. Additionally, this volume incorporates belief statements of religious groups listed in Gale's *Directory of Religious Organizations in the United States (DRO)*, also published in 1993. *DRO* profiles more than 2,400 non-church religious organizations, many of which promulgated their own doctrinal statements. *DRO* is especially important for its coverage of Evangelical Christian parachurch ministries. Evangelicals are scattered among hundreds of denominational bodies, many that are too small to form their own agencies for missionary work or have refrained from creating an expanded denominational structure. As an alternative, many Evangelicals support numerous independent nondenominational missionary and service organizations, which perform tasks traditionally undertaken by denominations. Doctrinal correctness being of utmost importance within the expanding world of Evangelicalism, almost every Evangelical organization has issued a doctrinal statement to assure supporters of the organization's orthodoxy.

Coverage Expanded to Include Educational Institutions. This volume includes doctrinal statements for more than 120 religiously based colleges and seminaries. Not all U.S. and Canadian religious institutions are represented because the majority of these schools use the same statement as their sponsoring church or denomination, most of which were included in the first volume of *EAR: Religious Creeds*. This volume focuses instead on institutions associated with noncreedal groups (i.e, those groups having no official statement of beliefs, such as the Plymouth Brethren). Although the noncreedal groups do not issue doctrinal statements themselves, many of the religious institutions associated with them, particularly Bible schools and colleges like the Plymouth Brethren's Emmaus Bible College, produce "official" summaries of their doctrinal position as a means of communicating the beliefs taught at the school to prospective students and donors. Specifically, this volume features statements of those schools that (1) are sponsored by a noncreedal church group and (2) have attempted to write a summary position statement for the group.

This volume also includes a sample of statements of independent religious schools, most serving the Pentecostal, Baptist, Fundamentalist, and Evangelical movements. These statements are frequently the most detailed and sophisticated summaries of differing positions held within the several movements. The texts selected for inclusion cover the range of positions held by the movements' leadership.

Emphasis on Independent Fundamentalist Creeds. Of the 400 creeds included in this volume of *EAR: Religious Creeds*, the largest number are found in the Independent Fundamentalist chapter. This emphasis is twofold. First, the largest number of independent religious organizations operating in America function in the Evangelical community. Second, while many non-Evangelical groups have been formed in recent years, only the Evangelical groups tend to produce a doctrinal statement as a matter of course. Roman Catholic-based religious organizations rarely write a doctrinal statement differing from the well-known position of the Roman Catholic Church. Liberal Protestant groups tend to be so theologically inclusive that they are unable to produce a consensus creedal statement or position paper; doctrinal agreement, however, is not a primary focus for these organizations. Finally, most Buddhist, Hindu, Jewish, and Muslim groups do not write doctrinal statements.

Contemporary Focus. This second volume of *EAR: Religious Creeds* retains the contemporary focus of the first volume. All of the creeds are currently operative for the groups and organizations under which they are listed. No attempt has been made to gather statements from defunct organizations; however, while compiling this volume it was discovered that both the Liberal Protestant Ecumenical Movement and the Evangelical Movement had produced a series of manifestos and creedal-like statements during the twentieth century that previously had been difficult to locate. These works are included in this volume because they still play a role in contemporary religious society.

Content and Arrangement

This volume of *EAR: Religious Creeds* is organized into the same 23 chapters as the first volume. These chapters are arranged according to the religious families classification schedule developed for Gale's *Encyclopedia of American Religions*. The material within each chapter is arranged alphabetically by the name of the group or organization, not by the name of the creed. Some material has been arranged to highlight those creeds and statements serving an entire religious family or groups of churches. In addition, statements that partially define religious families or subfamilies are placed at the beginning of the appropriate chapter or subchapter. (See the "Contents" pages for an overview of the arrangement of each of the 23 chapters.)

Creeds and statements presented in *EAR: Religious Creeds* contain the following elements:

Creed Title. The actual title, followed in parentheses by the name of the church or organization related to the statement. In those few cases where the statement has no title, a descriptive title has been assigned. Other groups or organizations that also subscribe to the creed or statement are mentioned in the notes following the text.

Text of Religious Creed or Statement. The full text of the creed in its authentic form. As with the first volume, the texts of creedal statements included in this volume have been reproduced in their authentic forms, although obvious typographical errors have been corrected. To insure accuracy, copies of the texts have been obtained in most cases directly from the headquarters of the group or organization. The authentic wording, grammar, and punctuation has been retained in all cases. No foreign material or explanatory notes have been introduced into the body of the text of the creeds.

Notes. Comments appear in italic type following the text of each individual creed or statement. When applicable, these explanatory notes provide information on the origin of the creed, call attention to the particular ideas and emphases covered (or in some cases omitted) by the text, discuss variant readings of the text as used by different churches, and point out relationships to other religious statements. Other religious groups that acknowledge the particular creed or statement are also covered here. For example, the statement originally issued by the National Association of Evangelicals has been adopted verbatim by a number of Evangelical organizations. Rather than reprinting the creed under the heading of each group, this volume refers readers to the explanatory notes following the statement of the National Association of Evangelicals to find a list of all of the groups that use that creed.

Cumulative Index Speeds Access to Both Volumes

To facilitate access to the material in both volumes of *EAR: Religious Creeds*, this second volume contains a cumulative Creed/Organization Name and Keyword Index. This index provides citations for the first and second volumes, including the full title of every creed and the names of all the religious traditions, individual churches, and religious organizations mentioned in the text and explanatory notes of both volumes. Important keywords in the creed titles and organization names are also indexed. Creed names appear in italic type to distinguish them from religious organizations. Citations refer users to the specific page where the indexed creed or religious group appears in the main body of the book. For ease in locating a specific citation in the main body of Religious Creeds, items are preceded by a "Vol I" or Vol II" designation as appropriate. Examples:

> Church of God (Abrahamic Faith)/Restoration Fellowship   Vol I: 586; Vol II: 395
> *Statement of Faith (Alpha and Omega Ministries)*   Vol II: 289
> Translators; Wycliffe Bible   Vol II: 357

Prominent Religion Expert Offers Unique Perspective

Dr. J. Gordon Melton, author of *EAR: Religious Creeds*, has been studying America's religious landscape for more than 20 years. A graduate of Garrett Theological Seminary in Evanston, Illinois, with a Ph.D. from Northwestern University, Dr. Melton is nationally recognized as a leading authority on religion, particularly small, recently established religious groups. Melton's current activities include teaching religious studies courses at the University of California-Santa Barbara, heading the Institute for the Study of American Religion, and writing articles and reference works on American religion. Among the many Gale titles authored by Melton are *Encyclopedia of America Religions*; *New Age Encyclopedia*; *National Directory of Churches, Synagogues, and Other Houses of Worship*; *Religious Leaders of America*; and the *Churches Speak Series*.

Suggestions Are Welcome

Users of *EAR: Religious Creeds* with inquiries, additional information, corrections, or other suggestions for improvements are invited to write the Institute for the Study of American Religion in care of its director. The institute is particularly interested in obtaining copies of statements missing from this volume for inclusion in future editions. Please contact:

> Dr. J. Gordon Melton, Director
> Institute for the Study of American Religion
> Box 90709
> Santa Barbara, CA 93190-0709

The
Encyclopedia
of American
Religions:
Religious
Creeds

Chapter 1

Ancient Creeds of the Christian Church

APOSTLES' CREED, ECUMENICAL VERSION

I believe in God, the Father Almighty,

> creator of heaven and earth.

I believe in Jesus Christ, his only Son, our Lord, who was

> conceived by the Holy Spirit,
> born of the Virgin Mary,
> suffered under Pontius Pilate,
> was crucified, died, and was buried;
> he descended to the dead.
> On the third day he rose again;
> he ascended into heaven,
> is seated at the right hand of the Father,
> and will come again to judge the living and the dead.

I believe in the Holy Spirit,

> the holy catholic church,
> the communion of saints,
> the forgiveness of sins,
> the resurrection of the body
> and the life everlasting. Amen.

Notes: *Typical of new versions of the Apostles' Creed that changed the common English text into a more contemporary English, this version from the United Methodist liturgy is a product of the process of liturgical reform during the last generation.*

*   *   *

The Ecumenical Church

FINAL REPORT [WORLD CONFERENCE ON FAITH AND ORDER (1927)]

PREAMBLE

Unanimously adopted by the full Conference

We, representatives of many Christian Communions throughout the world, united in the common confession of faith in Jesus Christ the Son of God, our Lord and Savior, believing that the Spirit of God is with us, are assembled to consider the things wherein we agree and the things wherein we differ. We now receive the following series of reports as containing subject matter for the consideration of our respective Churches in their common search for unity.

This is a Conference summoned to consider matters of Faith and Order. It is emphatically *not* attempting to define the conditions of future reunion. Its object is to register the apparent level of fundamental agreements within the Conference and the grave points of disagreements remaining; also to suggest certain lines of thought which may in the future tend to a fuller measure of agreement.

Each subject on the agenda was first discussed in plenary session. It was then committed to one of the sections, of more than one hundred members each, into which the whole Conference was divided. The report, after full discussion in subsection, was finally drawn up and adopted unanimously or by a large majority vote by the section to which it had been committed. It was twice presented for further discussion to a plenary session of the Conference when it was referred to the Churches in its present form.

Though we recognize the reports to be neither exhaustive nor in all details satisfactory to every member of the Conference, we submit them to the Churches for that deliberate consideration which could not be given in the brief period of our sessions. We thank God and rejoice over agreements reached; upon our agreements we build. Where the reports record differences, we call upon the Christian world to an earnest reconsideration of the conflicting opinions now held, and a strenuous endeavor to reach the truth as it is in God's mind, which should be the foundation of the Church's unity.

I. THE CALL TO UNITY

Unanimously adopted by the full Conference

God wills unity. Our presence in this Conference bears testimony to our desire to bend our wills to His. However we may justify the beginnings of disunion, we lament its continuance and henceforth must labor, in penitence and faith, to build up our broken walls.

God's Spirit has been in the midst of us. It was He who called us hither. His presence has been manifest in our worship, our deliberations, and our whole fellowship. He has discovered us to one another. He has enlarged our horizons, quickened our understanding, and enlivened our hope. We have dared and God has justified our daring. We can never be the same again. Our deep thankfulness must find expression in sustained endeavor to share the visions vouchsafed us here with those smaller home groups where our lot is cast.

More than half the world is waiting for the Gospel. At home and abroad sad multitudes are turning away in bewilderment from the Church because of its corporate feebleness. Our missions count that as a necessity which we are inclined to look on as a luxury. Already the mission field is impatiently revolting from the divisions of the Western Church to make bold adventure for unity in its own right. We of the Churches represented in this Conference cannot allow our spiritual children to outpace us. We with them must gird ourselves to the task, the early beginnings of which God has so richly blessed, and labor side by side until our common goal is reached.

Some of us, pioneers in this undertaking, have grown old in our search for unity. It is to youth that we look to lift the torch on high. We men have carried it too much alone through many years. The women henceforth should be accorded their share of responsibility. And so the whole Church will be enabled to do that which no section can hope to perform.

It was God's clear call that gathered us. With faith stimulated by His guidance to us here, we move forward.

II. THE CHURCH'S MESSAGE TO THE WORLD—THE GOSPEL

REPORT OF SECTION II

Received by the full Conference, *nemine contradicente*

The message of the Church to the world is and must always remain the Gospel of Jesus Christ. The Gospel is the joyful message of redemption, both here and hereafter, the gift of God to sinful man in Jesus Christ.

The world was prepared for the Coming of Christ through the activities of God's Spirit in all humanity, but especially in His revelation as given in the Old Testament; and in the fullness of time the eternal Word of God became incarnate, and was made man, Jesus Christ, the Son of God and the Son of Man, full of grace and truth.

Through His life and teaching, His call to repentance, His proclamation of the coming of the Kingdom of God and of judgment, His suffering and death, His resurrection and exaltation to the right hand of the Father, and by the mission of the Holy Spirit, He has brought to us forgiveness of sins, and has revealed the fullness of the living God and His boundless love

toward us. By the appeal of that love, shown in its completeness on the Cross, He summons us to the new life of faith, self-sacrifice, and devotion to His service and the service of men.

Jesus Christ, as the crucified and the living One, as Savior and Lord, is also the center of the world-wide Gospel of the Apostles and the Church. Because He Himself is the Gospel, the Gospel is the message of the Church to the world. It is more than a philosophical theory; more than a theological system; more than a programme for material betterment. The Gospel is rather the gift of a new world from God to this old world of sin and death; still more, it is the victory over sin and death, the revelation of eternal life in Him who has knit together the whole family in heaven and on earth in the communion of saints, united in the fellowship of service, of prayer, and of praise.

The Gospel is the prophetic call to sinful man to turn to God, the joyful tidings of justification and of sanctification to those who believe in Christ. It is the comfort of those who suffer; to those who are bound it is the assurance of the glorious liberty of the sons of God. The Gospel brings peace and joy to the heart, and produces in men self-denial, readiness for brotherly service, and compassionate love. It offers the supreme goal for the aspirations of youth, strength to the toiler, rest to the weary, and the crown of life to the martyr.

The Gospel is the sure source of power for social regeneration. It proclaims the only way by which humanity can escape from those class and race hatreds which devastate society at present into the enjoyment of national well-being and international friendship and peace. It is also a gracious invitation to the non-Christian world, East and West, to enter into the joy of the living Lord.

Sympathizing with the anguish of our generation, with its longing for intellectual sincerity, social justice and spiritual inspiration, the Church in the eternal Gospel meets the needs and fulfills the God-given aspirations of the modern world. Consequently, as in the past so also in the present, the Gospel is the only way of salvation. Thus, through His Church, the living Christ still says to men "Come unto me! . . . He that followeth me shall not walk in darkness, but shall have the light of life."

III. THE NATURE OF THE CHURCH

REPORT OF SECTION III

Received by the full Conference, *nemine contradicente*

God who has given us the Gospel for the salvation of the world has appointed His Church to witness by life and word to its redeeming power. The Church of the Living God is constituted by His own will, not by the will or consent or beliefs of men whether as individuals or as societies, though He uses the will of men as His instrument. Of this Church Jesus Christ is the Head, the Holy Spirit its continuing life.

The Church as the communion of believers in Christ Jesus is, according to the New Testament, the people of the New Covenant; the Body of Christ; and the Temple of God, built upon the foundation of the Apostles and Prophets, Jesus Christ Himself being the chief cornerstone.

The Church is God's chosen instrument by which Christ, through the Holy Spirit, reconciles men to God through faith, bringing their wills into subjection to His sovereignty, sanctifying them through the means of grace, and uniting them in love and service to be His witnesses and fellow workers in the extension of His rule on earth until His Kingdom come in glory.

As there is but one Christ, and one life in Him, and one Holy Spirit who guides into all truth, so there is and can be but one Church, holy, catholic, and apostolic.

The Church on earth possesses certain characteristics whereby it can be known of men. These have been, since the days of the Apostles, at least the following:

1. The possession and acknowledgment of the Word of God as given in Holy Scripture and interpreted by the Holy Spirit to the Church and to the individual. (Note A.)

2. The profession of faith in God as He is incarnate and revealed in Christ.

3. The acceptance of Christ's commission to preach the Gospel to every creature.

4. The observance of the Sacraments.

5. A ministry for the pastoral office, the preaching of the Word, and the administration of the Sacraments.

6. A fellowship in prayer, in worship, in all the means of grace, in the pursuit of holiness, and in the service of man.

As to the extent and manner in which the Church thus described finds expression in the existing Churches, we differ. Our differences chiefly concern:

1. The nature of the Church visible and the Church invisible, their relation to each other, and the number of those who are included in each. (Note B.)

2. The significance of our divisions past and present. (Note C.)

Whatever our views on these points, we are convinced that it is the will of Christ that the one life of the one body should be manifest to the world. To commend the Gospel to doubting, sinful, and bewildered men, a united witness is necessary. We therefore urge most earnestly that all Christians, in fulfillment of our Savior's prayer that His disciples may be one, reconsecrate themselves to God, that by the help of His Spirit the body of Christ may be built up, its members united in faith and love, and existing obstacles to the manifestation of their unity in Christ may be removed; that the world may believe that the Father has sent Him.

We join in the prayer that the time may be hastened when in the name of Jesus every knee shall bow and every tongue confess that Jesus Christ is Lord to the glory of God the Father.

Notes

(A) Some hold that this interpretation is given through the tradition of the Church; others through the immediate witness of the Spirit to the heart and conscience of believers; others through both combined.

(B) For instance

1. Some hold that the invisible Church is wholly in heaven; others include in it all true believers on earth, whether contained in any organization or not.

2. Some hold that the visible expression of the Church was determined by Christ Himself and is therefore unchangeable; others that the one Church under the guidance of the Holy Spirit may express itself in varying forms.

3. Some hold that one or other of the existing Churches is the only true Church; others that the Church as we have described it is to be found in some or all of the existing Communions taken together.

4. Some, while recognizing other Christian bodies as Churches, are persuaded that in the providence of God and by the teaching of history a particular form of ministry has been shown to be necessary to the best welfare of the Church; others hold that no one form of organization is inherently preferable; still others, that no organization is necessary.

(C) One view is that no division of Christendom has ever come to pass without sin. Another view is that the divisions were the inevitable outcome of different gifts of the Spirit and different understandings of the truth. Between these, there is the view of those who look back on the divisions of the past with penitence and sorrow coupled with a lively sense of God's mercy, which in spite of and even through these divisions has advanced His cause in the world.

IV. THE CHURCH'S COMMON CONFESSION OF FAITH

REPORT OF SECTION IV

Received by the full Conference, *nemine contradicente*

We members of the Conference on Faith and Order, coming from all parts of the world in the interest of Christian unity, have with deep gratitude to God found ourselves united in common prayer, in God our heavenly Father and His Son Jesus Christ, our Savior, in the fellowship of the Holy Spirit.

Notwithstanding the differences in doctrine among us, we are united in a common Christian Faith which is proclaimed in the Holy Scriptures and is witnessed to and safeguarded in the Ecumenical Creed, commonly called the Nicene, and in the Apostles' Creed, which Faith is continuously confirmed in the spiritual experience of the Church of Christ.

We believe that the Holy Spirit in leading the Church into all truth may enable it, while firmly adhering to the witness of these Creeds (our common heritage from the ancient Church), to express the truths of revelation in such other forms as new problems may from time to time demand.

FINAL REPORT [WORLD CONFERENCE ON FAITH AND ORDER (1927)] (continued)

Finally, we desire to leave on record our solemn and unanimous testimony that no external and written standards can suffice without an inward and personal experience of union with God in Christ.

Notes

1. It must be noted that the Orthodox Eastern Church can accept the Nicene Creed only in its uninterpolated form without the *filioque* clause; and that although the Apostles' Creed has no place in the formularies of this Church, it is in accordance with its teaching.

2. It must be noted also that some of the Churches represented in this Conference conjoin tradition with the Scriptures, some are explicit in subordinating Creeds to the Scriptures, some attach a primary importance to their particular Confessions, and some make no use of Creeds.

3. It is understood that the use of these Creeds will be determined by the competent authority in each Church, and that the several Churches will continue to make use of such special Confessions as they possess.

V. THE MINISTRY OF THE CHURCH

REPORT OF SECTION V

Received by the full Conference, *nemine contradicente*

We members of the Conference on Faith and Order are happy to report that we find ourselves in substantial accord in the following five propositions:

1. The ministry is a gift of God through Christ to His Church and is essential to the being and well-being of the Church.

2. The ministry is perpetually authorized and made effective through Christ and His Spirit.

3. The purpose of the ministry is to impart to men the saving and sanctifying benefits of Christ through pastoral service, the preaching of the Gospel, and the administration of the sacraments, to be made effective by faith.

4. The ministry is entrusted with the government and discipline of the Church, in whole or in part.

5. Men gifted for the work of the ministry, called by the Spirit and accepted by the Church, are commissioned through an act of ordination by prayer and the laying on of hands to exercise the function of this ministry.

Within the many Christian communions into which in the course of history Christendom has been divided, various forms of ministry have grown up according to the circumstances of the several communions and their beliefs as to the mind of Christ and the guidance of the New Testament. These communions have been, in God's providence, manifestly and abundantly used by the Holy Spirit in His work of enlightening the world, converting sinners, and perfecting saints. But the differences which have arisen in regard to the authority and functions of these various forms of ministry have been and are the occasion of manifold doubts, questions, and misunderstandings.

These differences concern the nature of the ministry (whether consisting of one or several orders), the nature of ordination and of the grace conferred thereby, the function and authority of bishops, and the nature of apostolic succession. We believe that the first step toward the overcoming of these difficulties is the frank recognition that they exist, and the clear definition of their nature. We therefore add as an appendix to our Report such a statement, commending it to the thoughtful consideration of the Churches we represent.

By these differences the difficulties of intercommunion have been accentuated to the distress and wounding of faithful souls, while in the mission field, where the Church is fulfilling its primary object to preach the Gospel to every creature, the young Churches find the lack of unity a very serious obstacle to the furtherance of the Gospel. Consequently the provision of a ministry acknowledged in every part of the Church as possessing the sanction of the whole Church is an urgent need.

There has not been time in this Conference to consider all the points of difference between us in the matter of the ministry with that care and patience which could alone lead to complete agreement. The same observation applies equally to proposals for the constitution of the united Church. Certain suggestions as to possible church organization have been made, which we transmit to the Churches with the earnest hope that common study of these questions will be continued by the members of the various Churches represented in this Conference.

In view of (1) the place which the episcopate, the councils of presbyters, and the congregation of the faithful, respectively, had in the constitution of the early Church, and (2) the fact that episcopal, presbyterial, and congregational systems of government are each today, and have been for centuries, accepted by great communions in Christendom, and (3) the fact that episcopal, presbyterial and congregational systems are each believed by many to be essential to the good order of the Church, we therefore recognize that these several elements must all, under conditions which require further study, have an appropriate place in the order of life of a reunited Church and that each separate communion, recalling the abundant blessing of God vouchsafed to its ministry in the past, should gladly bring to the common life of the united Church its own spiritual treasures.

If the foregoing suggestion be accepted and acted upon, it is essential that the acceptance of any special form of ordination as the regular and orderly method of introduction into the ministry of the Church for the future should not be interpreted to imply the acceptance of any one particular theory of the origin, character, or function of any office in the Church, or to involve the acceptance of any adverse judgment on the validity of ordination in those branches of the Church universal that believe themselves to have retained valid and apostolic Orders under other forms of ordination; or as disowning or discrediting a past or present ministry of the Word and Sacrament which has been used and blessed by the Spirit of God.

It is further recognized that inasmuch as the Holy Spirit is bestowed upon every believer, and each believer has an immediate access to God through Jesus Christ, and since special gifts of the Holy Spirit, such as teaching, preaching, and spiritual counsel, are the treasures of the Church as well as of the individual, it is necessary and proper that the Church should make fuller use of such gifts for the development of its corporate spiritual life and for the extension of the Kingdom of Jesus Christ, our Lord.

In particular, we share in the conviction, repeatedly expressed in this Conference, that pending the solution of the questions of faith and order in which agreements have not yet been reached, it is possible for us, not simply as individuals but as Churches, to unite in the activities of brotherly service which Christ has committed to His disciples. We therefore commend to our Churches the consideration of the steps which may be immediately practicable to bring our existing unity in service to more effective expression.

In conclusion, we express our thankfulness to Almighty God for the great progress which has been made in recent years in the mutual approach of the Churches to one another, and our conviction that we must go forward with faith and courage, confident that with the blessing of God we shall be able to solve the problem that lie before us.

Notes

1. The following is the view of the Orthodox Church, as formulated for us by its representatives.

    "The Orthodox Church, regarding the ministry as instituted in the Church by Christ Himself, and as the body which by a special *charisma* is the organ through which the Church spreads its means of grace such as the sacraments, and believing that the ministry in its threefold form of bishops, presbyters, and deacons can be based only on the unbroken apostolic succession, regrets that it is unable' to come in regard to the ministry into some measure of agreement with many of the Churches represented at this Conference; but prays God that He, through His Holy Spirit, will guide to union even in regard to this difficult point of disagreement.''

2. In western Christendom also there are conspicuous differences.

    One representative view includes the following points: (a) that there have always been various grades of the ministry, each with its own function; (b) that ordination is a sacramental act of divine institution, and therefore indispensable, conveying the special *charisma* for the particular ministry; (c) that bishops who have received their office by succession from the Apostles are the necessary ministers of ordination; (d) that the apostolic succession so understood is necessary for the authority of the ministry, the visible unity of the Church, and the validity of the sacraments.

On the other hand it is held by many Churches represented in the Conference (a) that essentially there is only one ministry, that of the Word and Sacraments; (b) that the existing ministries in these Churches are agreeable to the New Testament, are proved by their fruits and have due authority in the Church, and the sacraments ministered by them are valid; (c) that no particular form of ministry is necessary to be received as a

matter of faith; (d) that the grace which fits men for the ministry is immediately given by God, and is recognized, not conferred, in ordination.

Further we record that there are views concerning the ministry which are intermediate between the types just mentioned. For instance, some who adhere to an episcopal system of church government do not consider that the apostolic succession as described above is a vital element of episcopacy, or they reject it altogether. Others do not regard as essential the historic episcopate. Those who adhere to presbyterial systems of church government believe that the apostolic ministry is transmissible and has been transmitted through presbyters orderly associated for the purpose. Those who adhere to the congregational system of government define their ministry as having been and being transmitted according to the precedent and example of the New Testament.

VI. THE SACRAMENTS

REPORT OF SECTION VI

Received by the full Conference, *nemine contradicente*

We are convinced that for the purpose in view in this Conference we should not go into detail in considering Sacraments-by some called "Mysteries." The purpose therefore of this statement is to show that there may be a common approach to and appreciation of Sacraments on the part of those who may otherwise differ in conception and interpretation.

We testify to the fact that the Christian world gives evidence of an increasing sense of the significance and value of Sacraments, and would express our belief that this movement should be fostered and guided as a means of deepening the life and experience of the Churches. In this connection we recognize that the Sacraments have special reference to the corporate life and fellowship of the Church and that the grace is conveyed by the Holy Spirit, taking of the things of Christ and applying them to the souls through faith.

We agree that Sacraments are of divine appointment and that the Church ought thankfully to observe them as divine gifts.

We hold that in the Sacraments there is an outward sign and an inward grace, and that the Sacraments are means of grace through which God works invisibly in us. We recognize also that in the gifts of His grace God is not limited by His own Sacraments.

The Orthodox Church and others hold that there are seven Sacraments and that for their valid administration there must be a proper form, a proper matter and a proper ministry. Others can regard only Baptism and the Lord's Supper as Sacraments. Others again, while attaching high value to the sacramental principle, do not make use of the outward signs of Sacraments, but hold that all spiritual benefits are given through immediate contact with God through His Spirit. In this Conference we lay stress on the two Sacraments of Baptism and the Lord's Supper, because they are the Sacraments which are generally acknowledged by the members of this Conference.

We believe that in Baptism administered with water in the name of the Father, the Son, and the Holy Spirit, for the

FINAL REPORT [WORLD CONFERENCE ON FAITH AND ORDER (1927)] (continued)

remission of sins, we are baptized by one Spirit into one body. By this statement it is not meant to ignore the differences in conception, interpretation, and mode which exist among us.

We believe that in the Holy Communion our Lord is present, that we have fellowship with God our Father in Jesus Christ His Son, our Living Lord, who is our one Bread, given for the life of the world, sustaining the life of all His people, and that we are in fellowship with all others who are united to Him. We agree that the Sacrament of the Lord's Supper is the Church's most sacred act of worship, in which the Lord's atoning death is commemorated and proclaimed, and that it is a sacrifice of praise and thanksgiving and an act of solemn self-oblation.

There are among us divergent views, especially as to (1) the mode and manner of the presence of our Lord; (2) the conception of the commemoration and the sacrifice; (3) the relation of the elements to the grace conveyed; and (4) the relation between the minister of this Sacrament and the validity and efficacy of the rite. We are aware that the reality of the divine presence and gift in this Sacrament cannot be adequately apprehended by human thought or expressed in human language.

We close this statement with the prayer that the differences which prevent full communion at the present time may be removed.

Notes: *Motivated in large part by the scandal of divisions on the foreign mission fields, leaders of the larger Protestant church bodies in Europe and North America began to work toward the development of a united witness. The process would eventually lead to the formation of the World Council of Churches immediately after World War II. As the ecumenical dialogue heated up after World War I, it became focused on discussion around two categories: ''Life and Work'' and ''Faith and Order.'' Theological and creedal concerns fell largely under the latter. The First World Conference on Faith and Order became a symbol of the hope that the Protestant churches could find a united theological consensus.*

Delegates found some degree of theological consensus on a very abstract level, but quickly found significant disagreement on every specific topic under discussion. For example, the delegates soon discovered that different churches assigned vastly different levels of importance to creedal statements. The noncreedal churches did not use creedal statements, while other groups held to the Apostles Creed and the Nicene Creed as essential expressions of Christianity. In like measure, significant disagreements were highlighted on the issues of the nature of the church, the ministry, and sacraments. On the practical level, the question of sacrament and the sacramental nature of the ministry still remain the most important obstacle to any union between the older state churches with sacraments administered by priests, and the newer free churches that see the sacramental acts of baptism and the Eucharist as mere ordinances that require no minister with formal priestly authority.

The debates highlighted by the 1927 Faith and Order meeting set the agenda for a decade of discussions in numerous local gatherings and were continued at the second conference in 1937.

*   *   *

FINAL REPORT [WORLD CONFERENCE ON FAITH AND ORDER (1937)]

II. THE GRACE OF OUR LORD JESUS CHRIST

With deep thankfulness to God for the spirit of unity, which by His gracious blessing upon us has guided and controlled all our discussions on this subject, we agree on the following statement and recognize that there is in connection with this subject no ground for maintaining-division between Churches.

(i) The Meaning of Grace

When we speak of God's grace, we think of God Himself as revealed in His Son Jesus Christ. The meaning of divine grace is truly known only to those who know that God is Love, and that all that He does is done in love in fulfillment of His righteous purposes. His grace is manifested in our creation, preservation, and all the blessings of this life, but above all in our redemption through the life, death, and resurrection of Jesus Christ, in the sending of the holy and life-giving Spirit, in the fellowship of the Church and in the gift of the Word and Sacraments.

Man's salvation and welfare have their source in God alone, who is moved to His gracious activity towards man not by any merit on man's part, but solely by His free, outgoing love.

(ii) Justification and Sanctification

God in His free outgoing love justifies and sanctifies us through Christ, and His grace thus manifested is appropriated by faith, which itself is the gift of God.

Justification and Sanctification are two inseparable aspects of God's gracious action in dealing with sinful man.

Justification is the act of God, whereby He forgives our sins and brings us into fellowship with Himself, who in Jesus Christ, and by His death upon the Cross, has condemned sin and manifested His love to sinners, reconciling the world to Himself.

Sanctification is the work of God, whereby through the Holy Spirit He continually renews us and the whole Church, delivering us from the power of sin, giving us increase in holiness, and transforming us into the likeness of His Son through participation in His death and in His risen life. This renewal, inspiring us to continual spiritual activity and conflict with evil, remains throughout the gift of God. Whatever our growth in holiness may be, our fellowship with God is always based upon God's forgiving grace.

Faith is more than intellectual acceptance of the revelation in Jesus Christ; it is wholehearted trust in God and in His promises, and committal of ourselves to Jesus Christ as Savior and Lord.

(iii) The Sovereignty of God and Man's Response

In regard to the relation of God's grace and man's freedom, we all agree simply upon the basis of Holy Scripture and Christian experience that the sovereignty of God is supreme. By the sovereignty of God we mean His all-controlling, all-embracing will and purpose revealed in Jesus Christ for each man and for all mankind. And we wish further to insist that this eternal purpose is the expression of God's own loving and holy nature. Thus we men owe our whole salvation to His gracious will. But, on the other hand, it is the will of God that His grace should be actively appropriated by man's own will and that for such decision man should remain responsible.

Many theologians have made attempts on philosophical lines to reconcile the apparent antithesis of God's sovereignty and man's responsibility, but such theories are not part of the Christian Faith.

We are glad to report that in this difficult matter we have been able to speak with a united voice, so that we have found that here there ought to be no ground for maintaining any division between Churches.

(iv) The Church and Grace

We agree that the Church is the Body of Christ and the blessed company of all faithful people, whether in heaven or on earth, the communion of saints. It is at once the realization of God's gracious purposes in creation and redemption, and the continuous organ of God's grace in Christ by the Holy Spirit, who is its pervading life, and who is constantly hallowing all its parts.

It is the function of the Church to glorify God in its life and worship, to proclaim the gospel to every creature, and to build up in the fellowship and life of the Spirit all believing people, of every race and nation. To this end God bestows His Grace in the Church on its members through His Word and Sacraments, and in the abiding presence of the Holy Spirit.

(v) Grace, the Word and the Sacraments

We agree that the Word and the Sacraments are gifts of God to the Church through Jesus Christ for the salvation of mankind. In both the grace of God in Christ is shown forth, given, and through faith received; and this grace is one and indivisible.

The Word is the appointed means by which God's grace is made known to men, calling them to repentance, assuring them of forgiveness, drawing them to obedience and building them up in the fellowship of faith and love.

The Sacraments are not to be considered merely in themselves, but always as sacraments of the Church, which is the Body of Christ. They have their significance in the continual working of the Holy Spirit, who is the life of the Church. Through the sacraments God develops in all its members a life of perpetual communion lived within its fellowship, and thus enables them to embody His will in the life of the world; but the loving-kindness of God is not to be conceived as limited by His sacraments.

Among or within the Churches represented by us there is a certain difference of emphasis placed upon the Word and the sacraments, but we agree that such a difference need not be a barrier to union.

(vi) Sola Gratia

Some Churches set great value on the expression *sola gratia*, while others avoid it. The phrase has been the subject of much controversy, but we can all join in the following statement: Our salvation is the gift of God and the fruit of His grace. It is not based on the merit of man, but has its root and foundation in the forgiveness which God in His grace grants to the sinner whom He receives to sanctify him. We do not, however, hold that the action of the divine grace overrides human freedom and responsibility; rather, it is only as response is made by faith to divine grace that true freedom is achieved. Resistance to the appeal of God's outgoing love spells, not freedom, but bondage, and perfect freedom is found only in complete conformity with the good and acceptable and perfect will of God.

III. THE CHURCH OF CHRIST AND THE WORD OF GOD

(i) The Word of God

We concur in affirming that the Word of God is ever living and dynamic and inseparable from God's activity. ''In the beginning was the Word, and the Word was with God, and the Word was God.'' God reveals Himself to us by what He does, by that activity by which He has wrought the salvation of men and is working for their restoration to personal fellowship with Himself.

He calls and fashions His chosen people and speaks His Word to His prophets and apostles, interpreting to them the meaning of His action. In the fullness of time the Word, the Eternal Son of God, is manifested in Christ our Lord, the Incarnate Word, and His redeeming work, that is, in His words and deeds, in His life and character, in His suffering, death, and resurrection, culminating in the gift of the Spirit and in the life which He gives to the Church which is His body.

This divine revelation is addressed to man in the wholeness of his personality, and is apprehended by faith.

We are at one in asserting the uniqueness and supremacy of the revelation given in Christ, in whose Name alone salvation is offered to the world. But when we turn from this to the question whether we can come to know God through other and partial revelations we find differences which demand further study and discussion. None of us holds that there is a revelation *outside Christ* which can be put on the same level as the revelation in Christ. But while some are prepared to recognize *praeparatio evangelica* not only in Hebrew but also in other religions, and believe that God makes Himself known in nature and in history, others hold that the only revelation which the Church can know and to which it should witness is the revelation in Jesus Christ, as contained in the Old and New Testaments.

(ii) Holy Scripture and Tradition

A testimony in words is by divine ordering provided for the revelation uttered by the Word. This testimony is given in Holy

Scripture, which thus affords the primary norm for the Church's teaching, worship, and life. We discern a parallel, though an imperfect one, between the inspiration of Holy Scripture and the incarnation of the Word in Our Lord Jesus Christ: in each there is a union, effected by the Holy Spirit, between the divine and the human, and an acceptance, for God's saving purpose, of human limitations. "We have this treasure in earthen vessels." We are all convinced that this conception of the revelation cannot be shaken by scientific Bible research. But if it is conscious of its true nature, such research can render the Church important services in bringing about a right interpretation of the Scripture, provided that the freedom needed for carrying out its work is not denied to it.

Further, there is matter for fuller discussion in the problem of the tradition of the Church and its relation to Holy Scripture. By tradition is meant the living stream of the Church's life. Thus the Orthodox East, but not it alone, allows that there may be widespread opinions which, as being contrary to Scripture, cannot be considered to have the true authority of tradition, but it does not exclude from tradition some beliefs which do not rest explicitly on Scripture, though they are not in contradiction with it.

We are at one in recognizing that the Church, enlightened by the Holy Spirit, has been instrumental in the formation of the Bible. But some of us hold that this implies that the Church under the guidance of the Spirit is entrusted with the authority to explain, interpret, and complete the teaching of the Bible, and consider the witness of the Church as given in tradition as equally authoritative with the Bible itself. Others, however, believe that the Church, having recognized the Bible as the indispensable record of the revealed Word of God, is bound exclusively by the Bible as the only rule of faith and practice and, while accepting the relative authority of tradition, would consider it authoritative only in so far as it is founded upon the Bible itself.

We all agree that the Christian Church is constituted by the eternal Word of God made man in Christ and is always vitalized by his Holy Spirit. On the other hand, the divine task given to the Church is to proclaim and bear witness to this Word throughout the world by its preaching, its worship, and its whole life.

(iii) The Church: Our Common Faith

We are at one in confessing belief in the Holy Catholic Church. We acknowledge that through Jesus Christ, particularly through the fact of His resurrection, of the gathering of His disciples round their crucified, risen, and victorious Lord, and of the coming of the Holy Spirit, God's almighty will constituted the Church on earth.

The Church is the people of the new covenant, fulfilling and transcending all that Israel under the old covenant foreshadowed. It is the household of God, the family in which the Fatherhood of God and the brotherhood of man is to be realized in the children of His adoption. It is the body of Christ, whose members derive their life and oneness from their one living Head; and thus it is nothing apart from Him, but is in all things dependent upon the power of salvation which God has committed to His Son.

The presence of the ascended Lord in the Church, His Body, is effected by the power of the one Spirit, who conveys to the whole fellowship the gifts of the ascended Lord, dividing to every man severally as He will, guides it into all the truth and fills it unto all the fullness of God.

We all agree that Christ is present in His Church through the Holy Spirit as Prophet, Priest, and King. As Prophet He reveals the divine will and purpose to the Church; as Priest He ever liveth to make intercession for us, and through the eternal sacrifice once offered for us on Calvary, He continually draws His people to the Most High; and as King He rules His Church and is ever establishing and extending His Kingdom.

Christ's presence in the Church has been perpetual from its foundation, and this presence He makes effective and evident in the preaching of the Word, in the faithful administration of the Sacraments, in prayer offered in His name, and through the newness of life whereby He enables the faithful to bear witness to Himself. Even though men often prove faithless, Christ will remain faithful to the promise of His presence, and will so continue till the consummation of all things.

In their apprehension of this faith different persons lay a different emphasis on one or another aspect. Some lay greater stress on the perpetual and abiding Presence of Christ in His Body and with His people, while others lay greater stress on the fact that Christ is present only where His word is truly preached and received by faith.

A point to be studied is in what degree the Christian depends ultimately for his assurance that he is in vital touch with Christ upon the possession of the ministry and sacraments, upon the Word of God in the Church, upon the inward testimony of the Holy Spirit, or upon all of these.

(iv) The Church: Agreements and Differences

The Church, then, is the body of those on whom the call of God rests to witness to the grace and truth of God. This visible body was, before the Lord came, found in Israel and it is found now in the new Israel to which is entrusted the ministry of reconciliation. To this visible body the word "Ecclesia" is normally applied in the New Testament, and to it the calling of God belongs. It is the sphere of redemption. Apart from the Church man cannot normally attain full knowledge of God nor worship Him in truth.

Different Churches differ in their use of the term "church." Some would apply the term not only to the visible redeemed and redemptive community, but also to the invisible company of the fully redeemed; for only when the word is used in this sense would it be right to say, *"extra ecclesiam nulla salus."* But the invisible Church is no ideal Platonic community distinct from the visible Church on earth. The invisible Church and the visible Church are inseparably connected though their limits are not exactly coterminous. Others regard the use of the term "church" with reference to this invisible company of true Christians known only to God as misleading and unscriptural.

To speak of this invisible body as the true Church conveys the disastrous suggestions that the true Church need not be visible and that the visible Church need not be true. We will, however, recognize that the number of those whom God has brought into newness of life and joy in the Holy Ghost, and who have made personal response to the forgiving love of God, has limits hidden from human vision and known only to God.

Different Churches hold different views as to the basis of Church membership. Some would hold that all who have been baptized and have not by deed or word repudiated their heritage belong to the Church and are to be regarded as members. Others would confine membership to those who have made an open profession of faith in Christ and in whose lives some measure of the spirit of Christ may be discerned.

(v) The Church and the Kingdom of God

The Gospel of Jesus Christ bears witness to the reality both of the Church and of the Kingdom of God.

The Church rejoices in the Kingdom of God as present whenever man obeys the will of God. But the Church always looks with glad expectation to the consummation of the Kingdom in the future, since Christ the King, Who is present and active in the Church through the Holy Spirit, is still to be manifested in glory. The kingdom of God realizes itself now in a veiled form, until its full manifestation when God shall be all in all.

Agreeing in this faith we are not yet of one mind about (a) the relationship of the Church to the Kingdom, and (b) the extent to which the Kingdom is made known here and now.

Some stress the kinship between the Church and the Kingdom, others the distinction between them. Some lay emphasis on the actual presence of the Kingdom within the Church and the continuity of the two, holding that the coming of the Kingdom can be seen in the progress of the Church in this world and the work wrought through believers, or even through all men of good will the world over. Others lay emphasis on the Kingdom that is to come in glory; and others again think of the Kingdom as the ever-increasing reign of the righteousness and the love of God as manifested in Jesus Christ in every realm of life.

Again, some hold that the progress of the Kingdom can already be seen in this world; others hold that the Church knows the Kingdom by faith only, since the victory of Christ is still hidden from the world and is destined to remain hidden until the end of this age.

In some Churches these differing conceptions are felt to be of great moment, and act as a barrier to full intercourse, while in others they form no such obstacle but are held side by side without interfering with complete communion.

(vi) The Function of the Church

The function of the Church is to glorify God in adoration and sacrificial service and to be God's missionary to the world. She is to bear witness to God's redeeming grace in Jesus Christ in her corporate life, to proclaim the good news to every creature and to make disciples of all nations, bringing Christ's com-

mandments to communities as well as to individuals. In relation to those who belong to her fellowship or who are placed under her influence, the function of the Church is through the ministry of the Word and the Sacraments, and through Christian education, to make them into convinced Christians conscious of the reality of salvation. The needs of individual souls call for pastoral care and for a fellowship in the things of the Spirit through which the members provoke one another to good works, and to walk worthily of their calling, by true friendship, mutual help, and consolation, and the exercise of loving discipline. She is to intercede for all her members, especially for those who suffer for their faith, and for all mankind.

The Church must proclaim the righteousness of God as revealed in Jesus Christ and thus encourage and guide her members to promote justice, peace, and goodwill among all men and through the whole extent of life. The Church is thus called to do battle against the powers of evil and to seek the glory of God in all things, looking to the day when His Kingdom shall come in the fullness of its power.

(vii) The Gift of Prophecy and the Ministry of the Word

We are agreed that the presence and inspiration of the Holy Spirit are granted to His chosen instruments today, and especially to those called to be ministers of the Word of God. Not only in the corporate life and the teaching of the Church as a whole, but in each of its members according to His ability and calling, the Holy Spirit has come to dwell. Indeed, all perfect and abiding revelation given to us in Christ our Lord would certainly have perished from the world had there been no inspired men to record it and to preach it in every age. This revelation does not belong only to the past; it is also an ever-present word by which God speaks directly to the listening soul.

Moreover, all manifestations of the Spirit are manifestations of God's divine activity. It is here that prophecy finds its place in the Church's corporate life. In Christ all the truth of God's redemptive purpose for men is fully and sufficiently contained, but every age has its own problems and its own difficulties, and it is the work of the Spirit in every age to apply the one truth revealed in Christ to the circumstances of the time. Moreover, as past experience shows, these new applications bring to the Church a new understanding of the truth on which they rest. The Spirit may speak by whomsoever He wills. The call to bear witness to the Gospel and to declare God's will does not come to the ordained ministry alone; the Church greatly needs, and should both expect and welcome, the exercise of gifts of prophecy and teaching by laity, both men and women. When prophetic gifts appear it is for the Church not to quench the spirit or despise prophesyings but to test these prophesyings by their accordance with the abiding truth entrusted to it, and to hold fast that which is good.

(viii) "Una Sancta" and Our Divisions

Everything which the New Testament teaches concerning the Church presupposes its essential unity. But we, as we confess our faith in the one Church, are conscious of a profound cleavage between that faith and the conditions of the present time.

We acknowledge that all who accept Jesus Christ as Son of God and their Lord and Savior, and realize their dependence upon God's mercy revealed in Him, have in that fact a supernatural bond of oneness which subsists in spite of divergences in defining the divine mystery of the Lord. We rejoice that this sense of kinship is now drawing Christians nearer to each other, and that in many partial ways a foretaste of full fellowship between severed communions is even now being sought and found.

But we believe that the divisions of Christendom in every land are such as to hamper the manifestation of the unity of Christ's body. We deplore this with all our hearts; and we desire the Conference to summon members of the Churches to such penitence that not only their leaders, but the ordinary men and women who hear their message, may learn that the cause of Christian unity is implicit in God's word, and should be treated by the Christian conscience as an urgent call from God.

IV. THE COMMUNION OF SAINTS

Wherefore seeing we also are compassed about with so great a cloud of witnesses, let us lay aside every weight, and the sin which doth so easily beset us, and let us run with patience the race that is set before us, looking unto Jesus the author and finisher of our faith. Heb. xii, 1-2.

We use the term "communion of saints" as meaning that all who are "in Christ" are knit together in one fellowship through the Holy Spirit. This conception, which is found repeatedly in the Scriptures, occurs as a phrase of the Apostles' Creed, and gives expression to a precious truth for all Christians. With some, the phrase is regarded as synonymous with the Holy Catholic Church. For others, it expresses a quality of the Church which is realized only in so far as its members mutually share all the blessings which God bestows. For others, it is the description of a quality of life in those who are in grace. The communion of saints is not always regarded as co-extensive with the Church. For the Orthodox and certain other Churches and individual believers it means fellowship not only with living and departed Christians but also with the holy angels, and, in a very special sense, with the Blessed Virgin Mary.

In this connection the way in which we should understand the words "all generations shall call me blessed" was considered. No agreement was reached, and the subject requires further study.

The words "the communion of saints" expressed certain well-defined phases of the Christian Gospel and of the doctrine of the Church.

In the New Testament the word "saints" is applied to all the baptized. The term is further applied to the patriarchs, prophets, or martyrs of the Old Covenant and to those who, believing in Christ, laid down their lives for Him before they could receive baptism. In every case, the saints are those who are devoted to God, who yield themselves as instruments to His sovereign will. They are saints, not by virtue of their own merits, but through the forgiving grace and love of God.

There are Churches which hold that the communion is not as between individuals as such, but as between those who are being sanctified by God in His Church. Their unity is not merely the sum total of individuals, but it is a spiritual solidarity which has reality only in so far as they are in Christ, and thereby in His Church.

There are also those who interpret the word as neuter as well as masculine. For them the phrase means sharing in holy things, i.e. the means of grace. They emphasize right relations to holy things as the principal mark of the holiness of the faithful.

There are others who regard the Word of God and the Holy Spirit as the sole source of the communion of saints, and at the same time would emphasize righteousness and holiness of life. They would also stress the sacredness and value of the individual's personality. While doing so, they would guard against the evils resulting from an overemphasized individualism by insisting on the corporate nature of the fellowship in Christ. Since the term "saints" is almost always in the plural in the Scriptures, so it is believed that there is no true sainthood apart from the saintly community.

We are agreed that the communion of saints most certainly involves the mutual sharing of both spiritual and temporal blessings on the part of all living Christians. We believe that this mutual sharing should transcend all racial, political, social, and denominational barriers, in the spirit of Gethsemane and the Cross. Such, for example, is the fellowship of those associated in any truly Christian ecumenical movement. Therein we have experienced a very real, though not complete, communion of saints. Therein we humbly believe we experience the presence and power of the Holy Spirit.

Any conception of the communion of saints which is confined to the Church on earth alone is defective. Many further see in the communion of saints an affirmation of the unbroken communion between the living and departed in Christ. They believe themselves to be in communion with the departed and express this in their worship. They rejoice to think that there is a growing consciousness among Christians of nearness to the redeemed in the unseen world, refusing to believe that death severs the communion of those on earth with those departed.

For some, it is sufficient to leave their departed ones with God, being linked with them through Christ. Others regard it as a Christian privilege and duty to pray for the departed. Still others, conscious of the living presence, guardianship and help of the saints, ask their prayers before God.

We all agree that we ought to remember with thankfulness those who as followers of Christ witnessed a good confession in their day and generation, thereby winning victories for Christ and His Kingdom.

We wish to make it clear that "the communion which the saints have with Christ does not make them in any wise partakers of the substance of His Godhead, or to be equal with Christ in any respect." In no circumstances should the cherishing of this doctrine veil or shadow the sufficient and only mediatorship of Jesus Christ as our Lord and Redeemer. Neither must this honoring of the saints descend to superstition or abuse.

A right understanding of the doctrine of the communion of saints will help us to realize more vividly both that we are in this life members one of another, and that

"We are come unto mount Zion, and unto the city of the living God, the heavenly Jerusalem, and to an innumerable company of angels, to the general assembly and church of the firstborn, which are written in heaven, and to God the judge of all, and to the spirits of just men made perfect, and to Jesus the mediator of the new covenant."-Heb. xii, 22-24.

V. THE CHURCH OF CHRIST: MINISTRY AND SACRAMENTS

(i) The Authority for the Sacraments

1. We are agreed that in all sacramental doctrine and practice the supreme authority is our Lord Jesus Christ Himself.

2. All the Churches have based their sacramental doctrine and order upon their belief that, according to the evidence of the New Testament, the sacraments which they accept were instituted by Christ Himself. We are agreed that Baptism and the Lord's Supper occupied from the beginning a central position in the Church's common life, and take their origin from what was said and done by Jesus during His life on earth. Sacramental teaching and practice, therefore, are rightly founded upon the record of the New Testament.

3. The sacraments are Christ's gifts to His Church, which is not a static society but a living and growing organism and communion, guided by the Holy Spirit into all truth.

4. The Holy Spirit enables the Church, walking by faith in its risen Lord, to interpret Holy Scripture as expressing the living Word of God to every age, and to exercise a stewardship of its tradition concerning the sacraments.

5. All Church tradition regarding the sacraments ought to be controlled and tested by Scripture.

(ii) The Nature of the Sacraments

1. The sacraments are given by Christ to the Church as outward and visible signs of His invisible grace. They are not bare symbols, but pledges and seals of grace, and means whereby it is received.

2. Grace is bestowed in the sacraments within the fellowship of the Church by the personal action of Christ upon the believer. Faith is therefore a necessary condition for the effectual reception of grace.

3. God's gracious action is not limited by His sacraments.

4. It is our Lord Jesus Christ who through the Holy Spirit accomplishes every sacrament, and the action of the minister of the Church is only instrumental.

5. The sacraments are celebrated by the minister, not in virtue of any personal right of His own, but as minister of the Church.

6. Regarding the obligation of the sacraments and the questions whether and in what way they are to be deemed necessary to salvation there is divergence of doctrine among us. We think that some further mutual understanding and agreement on those points is required as a condition of full union.

(iii) The Number of the Sacraments

The Orthodox Church, the (Assyrian) Church of the East, the (Coptic) Egyptian-Orthodox Church, the Syrian Orthodox and Armenian Churches and the Old Catholic Churches, and many individual believers, as well as the Roman Catholic Church, hold that there are seven sacraments, but the Protestant Churches accept only two—Baptism and the Eucharist. The Anglican Church has never strictly defined the number of the sacraments, but gives a pre-eminent position to Baptism and the Lord's Supper as alone "generally necessary to salvation."

The Society of Friends and the Salvation Army observe no sacraments in the usual sense of that term. (cf.139)

The number of the sacraments largely depends upon the definitions of the term "sacraments" as given by various Churches. In most of the Protestant Churches there are such solemn religious acts as correspond more or less closely with some or all of the five other sacraments which are taught by the Roman, Orthodox, Old Catholic, and other Churches. And even though the name "sacrament" be refused, they are nevertheless *instituta Dei utilia*, as the second Helvetic Confession puts it.

Most of us agree that the question of the number of the sacraments should not be regarded as an insurmountable dividing line when we strive to attain to a united Church.

The divergence between the practice of the Society of Friends and the Salvation Army on the one hand, and that of other Churches on the other, admittedly presents serious difficulties, but we trust that even here the Holy Spirit will show us His will.

(iv) Validity

1. We agree that the sacraments practiced by any Christian Church which believes itself to be observing what Christ appointed for His Church are means of grace to those who partake of them with faith.

2. Confusion has sometimes been introduced by the use of the term "valid" in the two following senses:

   (a) It is sometimes used synonymously with "efficacious," so that the term "invalid" would imply that a sacrament has no spiritual value and is not a means of grace.

   (b) It is sometimes used to imply that the sacrament has been correctly performed.

In so far as Christians find themselves obliged by loyalty to Christ and to His Church to judge that the sacraments practiced by other Christians are invalid, or doubtfully valid, they should, in the cause of Christian truth and charity, do all in their power to see that the precise meaning of their judgement, and the grounds on which they are obliged to make it, are clearly understood.

Many of us are of the opinion, and desire to record our belief, that, although, it is the duty of a Church to secure that sacraments should be performed regularly and canonically, yet no judgment should be pronounced by any Church denying the "validity" of the sacraments performed by any Christian Church which believes itself to be observing what Christ appointed for His Church.

A special difficulty in regard to union arises from a great difference in doctrine which must not be underestimated. Those Churches which adhere to the doctrine of the Church from the age of the Great Councils to the Reformation regard it as one of the conditions for the validity of any sacrament except baptism (and in some cases, marriage) that it should be performed by a validly ordained or consecrated minister. Thus to them the validity of Holy Order is one of the indispensable conditions of the validity of other sacraments. On the other hand, some other Christians do not hold ordination to be a sacrament of Christ's institution, yet hold that an ordained minister is the proper minister of the Eucharist. Other Christians again hold that ordination is a sacrament, but do not hold it to be an essential condition of the validity of other sacraments, that they should be ministered by a validly ordained presbyter or bishop.

3. We believe that every sacrament should be so ordered that all may recognize in it an act performed on behalf of the universal Church.

4. To this end there is need of an ordained ministry recognized by all to act on behalf of the universal Church in the administration of the sacraments.

Note:-The Orthodox delegates submit the following statement:

Validity. As regards to the validity of sacraments the Orthodox delegates would like to confine themselves only to the following statement: According to the Orthodox doctrine valid sacraments are only those which are (1) administered by a canonically ordained and instituted minister and (2) rightly performed according to the sacramental order of the Church. They regard it therefore as unnecessary to accept any other document on this matter presented by the Conference.

(v) Baptism

Baptism is a gift of God's redeeming love to the Church; and, administered with water in the name of the Father, the Son, and the Holy Spirit, is a sign and seal of Christian discipleship in obedience to our Lord's command. It is generally agreed that the united Church will observe the rule that all members of the visible Church are admitted by Baptism.

In the course of discussion it appeared that there were further elements of faith and practice in relation to Baptism about which disagreement existed. Since the time available precluded the extended discussion of such points as baptismal regeneration, the admission of unbaptized persons to Holy Communion, and the relation of Confirmation to Baptism, we are unable to express an opinion as to how far they would constitute obstacles to proposals for a united Church.

(vi) The Eucharist

We all believe that Christ is truly present in the Eucharist, though as to how that presence is manifested and realized we may differ. Every precise definition of the presence is bound to be a limiting thing, and the attempt to formulate such definitions and to impose them on the Church has itself been the cause of disunity in the past. The important thing is that we should celebrate the Eucharist with the unfailing use of bread and wine, and of prayer, and of the words of institution, and with agreement as to its essential and spiritual meaning.

If sacrifice is understood as it was by our Lord and His followers and in the early Church, it includes, not His death only, but the obedience of His earthly ministry, and His risen and ascended life, in which He still does His Father's will and ever liveth to make intercession for us. Such a sacrifice can never be repeated, but is proclaimed and set forth in the eucharistic action of the whole Church when we come to God in Christ at the Eucharist or Lord's Supper. For us, the secret of joining in that sacrifice is both the worship and the service of God; corporate because we are joined to Christ, and in Him to each other (I Cor. 10:17); individual, because each one of us makes the corporate act of self-oblation his own; and not ceremonial only, but also profoundly ethical, because the keynote of all sacrifice and offering is "Lo! I come to do Thy will, 0 God." We believe also that the Eucharist is a supreme moment of prayer, because the Lord is the celebrant or minister for us at every celebration, and it is in His prayers for God's gifts and for us all that we join. According to the New Testament accounts of the institution, His prayer is itself a giving of thanks; so that the Lord's Supper is both a *verbum visible* of the divine grace, and the supreme thanksgiving *(eucharistia)* of the people of God. We are throughout in the realm of Spirit. It is through the Holy Spirit that the blessing and the gift are given. The presence, which we do not try to define, is a spiritual presence. We begin from the historical fact of the Incarnation in the power of the Holy Spirit, and we are already moving forward to the complete spiritual reality of the coming of the Lord and the life of the Heavenly City.

(vii) Ministry

A

I. The ministry was instituted by Jesus Christ, the Head of the Church, "for the perfecting of the Saints . . . the upbuilding of the body of Christ," and is a gift of God to the Church in the service of the Word and sacraments.

II.   This ministry does not exclude but presupposes the "royal priesthood," to which all Christians are called as the redeemed of Jesus Christ.

III.   Ordination to the ministry, according to New Testament teaching and the historic practice of the Church, is by prayer and the laying-on of hands.

IV.   It is essential to a united Church that it should have a ministry universally recognized.

It must be acknowledged, however, that even in connection with these statements, different interpretations are to be reckoned with.

For example, while all would agree that the ministry owes its origin to Jesus Christ and is God's gift to the Church, there are differences of judgment regarding the sense in which we may say that the ministry was "instituted" by our Lord.

Again, those who agree in accepting the lay-on of hands as the form of ordination differ on the meaning to be attached to the rite, or on the question by whom it should be administered.

Further fundamental differences of interpretation arise in connection with the doctrine of Apostolic Succession. In Episcopal Churches it has been thought of both as the succession of bishops in the principal sees of Christendom, handing down and preserving the Apostles' doctrine, and as a succession by laying-on of hands. From early times this double succession has been associated with the stewardship of the sacraments, and is regarded by certain Churches as constituting the true and only guarantee of sacramental grace and right doctrine. This view is represented by the statement formulated by the delegates of the Orthodox Church at Lausanne: Lausanne 44.

Substantially the same view finds another expression in the following statement offered on behalf of the Old Catholic Church:

"The Old Catholics maintain that Episcopacy is of apostolic origin, and that it belongs to the essence of the Church. The Church is the bearer of the ministry. The ministers act only by the commission of the Church. The ministry is received, administered, and handed on in the same sense and in the same way as the Apostles handed it down to the Church. The Apostolic Succession means the inseparability of Church and ministry and the continuity of both."

Certain other Churches of the East and some Anglicans would wish to be associated with one or other of the above statements. Other Anglicans would interpret the succession in a more general way to mean the transmission from generation to generation of the authority of ministerial oversight over both clergy and laity in the Church, and they regard it as both a symbol and a bond of unity.

In communions of the Presbyterian and Reformed tradition the view is held that the true Apostolic Succession is manifested in a succession of ordination by presbyteries duly constituted and exercising episcopal functions, and in the succession of presbyters in charge of parishes, with special emphasis on the true preaching of the Word and the right administration of the Sacraments. Thus the following statement was presented by Presbyterian delegates:

"Presbyterian delegates desire to have it noted that the conception of the ministry held by their Churches is founded on the identity of 'bishops' and 'presbyters' in the New Testament; that ordination is not by individual presbyter, nor by groups of presbyters, but only by 'presbyters orderly associated' in courts exercising episcopal functions; that a presbyterian succession in orders has been maintained unbroken; and that the functions of the diaconate in the New Testament have been performed not only by those named deacons, but also in some measure by the lay eldership, which in addition to a responsible share in the government and discipline of the Church in all its courts, assists in the dispensing of charity, the visitation of the people, and the distribution of the elements at Holy Communion."

Other communions, while unaccustomed to use the term "Apostolic Succession," would accept it as meaning essentially, or even exclusively, the maintenance of the Apostles' witness through the true preaching of the gospel, the right administration of the Sacraments, and the perpetuation of the Christian life in the Christian community.

In every case Churches treasure the Apostolic Succession in which they believe.

B

In its brief consideration of the form which the ministry might take in the united Church of the future, the Conference started from the following formula in the Report of the Lausanne Conference (See La 39).

The acceptance of the "historic Episcopate" carries with it the acceptance of the threefold ministry of bishops, presbyters, and deacons. Many would hold that such acceptance does not require any one dogmatic determination of the doctrine concerning the ministry, while for some this would be requisite. But all who value the "historic Episcopate" hold that it should not be interpreted apart from its historical functions.

In a united Church the intimate association of the presbyters in council with the bishop, and of the laity with both, in the government of the Church, should be conserved or restored. Thus the Episcopate would be both constitutional and representative of the whole Church.

If the ministry of the united Church should sufficiently include characteristic elements from the episcopal, presbyterial, and congregational systems, the present adherents of those systems would have recognized each others' places in the Church of God, all would be able to find a spiritual home in the united Church, and the doctrine of the Apostolic Succession would, upon a common basis of faith, attain to the fullness which belongs to it by referring at once to the Word, to the ministry and the sacraments, and to the life of the Christian community.

It should, however, be recognized that there are members of the Conference who are not persuaded that it is God's will that the one spiritual life of the undivided Church should be expressed through any one form of government, but would find place side by side for Churches of differing form of government, and within or beside the more formally organized body would include freer societies like the Friends and the Salvation Army.

The foregoing suggestions are put forward in the knowledge that they contain features which at the present stage may be unacceptable to some Churches on both wings of the Movement, but we are confident that, where the will to unite exists, the Holy Spirit will enable the Churches in the coming years to improve and develop these first tentative suggestions.

We are alike called of God to pray and to labor by every means for the promotion of this common aim, recognizing that the future or ultimate form to be assumed by the united Church must depend not only on the experience of the past, but above all, upon the continued direction of the Holy Spirit.

VI. THE CHURCH'S UNITY IN LIFE AND WORSHIP

(i) Our Premise and Our Goal

We take as the premise of our findings and our recommendations the already existing and growing spiritual unity, experienced by Christians as love of one another, understanding of one another, and respect for one another. We believe that no visible unity, acceptable to God and to the people of God, can be achieved save on the foundation of this spiritual unity. We believe that our common experience of spiritual unity derives from the fundamental faith that the Church is the body of Christ, and is, therefore, in principle and ideal, one. In trying to envisage the goal of our endeavors, we are not seeking to create something new; rather we are attempting to discover under the guidance of the Holy Spirit the full nature of the Church created by God in Christ.

Our goal is to realize the ideal of the Church as one living body, worshipping and serving God in Christ, as the fulfillment of our Lord's prayers and of our prayers.

(ii) The Several Conceptions of Church Unity

(a) CO-OPERATIVE ACTION

The unity which we seek may be conceived as a confederation or alliance of Churches for cooperative action.

In all areas where common purposes and tasks exist, such action is already widely possible without violation of conscience. Church "federations" are the most common expressions of such unity, and one of the most hopeful paths to understanding and brotherly relations. We believe federation, so construed, is a promising approach to more complete forms of unity. We do not share the fears, often expressed, that "federation" in this sense will obscure the goal of a fuller unity or postpone its attainment. The experience of many Churches in many lands forbids fears, since they run counter to the facts.

We recognize that federations for cooperative action should not be construed as examples of "federal union." Certain of our members wish to be recorded as believing that "federal

union" is not merely the most we can achieve, but also the most that we should desire.

We are agreed that cooperative action between Churches unable to achieve intercommunion or to look toward corporate union, and compelled by fidelity to conscience remain separate bodies with separate loyalties, is our final goal, since cooperative action in itself fails to manifest to the world the true character of the Church as one community of faith and worship, as well as of service.

(b) INTERCOMMUNION

A second aspect of Church unity is commonly indicated by the term *"intercommunion."* This is the fullest expression of a mutual recognition between two or more Churches. Such recognition is also manifested in the exchange of membership and ministrations.

We regard sacramental intercommunion as a necessary part of any satisfactory Church unity. Such intercommunion, as between two or more Churches, implies that all concerned are true Churches, or true branches of the one Church.

We think that it should be pointed out that the word "intercommunion" has at present several different connotations. In the fullest sense it means a relation between two or more Churches in which the communion of each is open to all members of the other at all times. This is to be distinguished from relations in which the communion of one Church is "open" to members of other Churches without complete reciprocal recognition, and still more from the occasional welcoming of members of other Churches by a Church whose normal rule would exclude them. We believe that "regularity" and "mutuality" belong to the full meaning of intercommunion. When this term "intercommunion" is used in discussion of Church unity, its meaning should be clearly defined.

We must note also the occasions on which at a gathering of Christian people united in a common enterprise, a Church has invited all who have full status in their own Churches to receive the Holy Communion according to the rite of the inviting Church. This has occurred both at Oxford and at Edinburgh during the Conference held this year. It is to be distinguished both from "intercommunion" and "open communion" as usually understood, and from such "joint celebration" as took place at Jerusalem in 1928.

(c) CORPORATE UNION

The third form in which the final goal of our movement may be expressed presents, from the standpoint of definition, the greatest difficulties. It is commonly indicated by such terms as "corporate union" or "organic unity."

These terms are forbidding to many, as suggesting the ideal of a compact governmental union involving rigid uniformity. We do not so understand them, and none of us desires such uniformity. On the contrary, what we desire is the unity of a living organism, with the diversity characteristic of the members of a healthy body.

The idea of "corporate union" must remain for the vast majority of Christians their ideal. In a Church so united the ultimate loyalty of every member would be given to the whole body and not to any part of it. Its members would move freely from one part to another and find every privilege of membership open to them. The sacraments would be the sacraments of the whole body. The ministry would be accepted by all as a ministry of the whole body.

Our task is to find in God, to receive from God as His gift, a unity which can take up and preserve in one beloved community all the varied spiritual gifts which He has given us in our separations. Such a living community, like all that live; cannot be a construction; life can come only from life; the visible unity of the Body of Christ can issue only from the Living God through the work of the life-giving Spirit.

While we do not conceive of the "corporate union," which we seek from God, as a rigid governmental unity, we find it difficult to imagine that unity, as it would exist between Churches within the same territory, without some measure of organizational union. At the same time, we can hardly imagine a corporate union which should provide for the relative autonomy of the several constituent parts in entire neglect of the "federal" principle.

In particular, and with immediate reference to the existing world situation, we do not believe that a Church, "corporately" united, could be an effective international community without some permanent organ of conference and counsel, whatever might be the authority and powers of that organ.

(iii) The Forms of Likeness Basic for Church Unity

1. LIKENESS IN FAITH OR CONFESSION AS A BASIS FOR UNITY.

(a) Likeness in faith or confession is not necessary for cooperative action, but we find that essential unity in faith or confession is a necessary basis for (b) full intercommunion and for (c) corporate union.

Such essential unity in faith would be sufficiently expressed for many of the Churches represented in this Conference by such a statement as the following:

> We accept as the supreme standard of the faith the revelation of God contained in the Holy Scriptures of the Old and New Testaments and summed up in Jesus Christ.

> We acknowledge the Apostles' Creed and the Creed commonly called the Nicene, as witnessing to and safeguarding that faith, which is continuously verified in the spiritual experience of the Church and its members remembering that these documents are sacred symbols and witnesses of the Christian faith rather than legalistic standards.

> We further affirm that the guidance of God's Holy Spirit did not cease with the closing of the canon of the Scripture, or with the formulation of the creeds cited, but that there has been in the Church through the centuries, and still is, a divinely sustained consciousness of the presence of the living Christ. (Note: Known in the Orthodox Church as the Holy Tradition.)

Finally, we are persuaded, in the classical words of one of the non-confessional communions, that "God has yet more light to break forth from His Holy Word" for humble and waiting Church. We Christians of this present age should therefore seek the continued guidance of the Spirit of the living God, as we confront our troubled time.

Some of the Churches represented in the Conference hold that Scripture is not only the supreme but the sole standard and source of Christian faith; they reject any suggestion of the equivalence of Scripture and tradition and any implication that the ancient creeds contain a sufficient interpretation of the Scriptural faith. Some of these Churches regard certain later confessions as possessing an importance and authority at least equal to that of the ancient creeds.

The Orthodox and certain other Churches can accept the Nicene Creed only in its uninterpolated form without the *filioque clause*, and those Churches and others hold that the "Holy Tradition" must be acknowledged as a standard and source of the faith complementary to, though wholly consonant with, the revelation in Scripture.

2. LIKENESS IN NON-SACRAMENTAL WORSHIP.

(a) Likeness in non-sacramental worship is not necessary for cooperative action.

(c) In the non-sacramental worship of God the Father, Son and Holy Spirit, we are agreed that there is little remaining occasion for maintaining the existing divisions between our Churches, and much common ground already exists for further unity.

We are all united, in such worship, in the use of the Holy Scriptures. We are further united in common prayer, which may be expressed in the spoken word, through silence or by employment of the sacred treasures of Christian literature, art, and music. In this worship we all stand before God in adoration of His Majesty, bringing to Him our own needs and the needs of our fellows. We wait for His grace in the forgiveness of our sins and for the restoration of our spirits through renewed communion with Him, and we dedicate ourselves to His service and the service of all mankind.

3. LIKENESS IN SACRAMENTAL FAITH AND PRACTICE.

(a) Cooperative activities do not require likeness in doctrine and administration of the sacraments.

(b) For Intercommunion.

   (i) Some of us hold that Churches which within their own order practice the two Gospel sacraments can freely allow intercommunion between their respective members.

   (ii) Others hold that no such intercommunion can take place until their Churches have agreed as to the validity of each other's ministrations of these, to them, essential sacraments.

(c) For full corporate union it will be necessary to reconcile the differences between Churches which insist, some upon two sacraments, some upon seven, and some upon no formal sacraments whatsoever.

The sacrament of the Lord's Supper (or Eucharist) is the Church's most sacred act of worship. Unity in sacramental worship requires essential unity in sacramental faith and practice.

The Society of Friends, in the silence of its meetings, seeks without formal sacraments the Real Presence of Him who suffered death that mankind might have life (cf. 75).

In this connection we find much cause for encouragement in (i) the liturgical movement on the Continent, and among the non-liturgical Churches in many other lands, and (ii) the increasing opportunities allowed for silence, and for spontaneity among those who use traditional liturgies. In this matter the distinction between liturgical and nonliturgical forms of worship is a diminishing occasion for division.

4. LIKENESS OF ORDERS AS A BASIS FOR UNITY.

(a) Lack of likeness of orders is no obstacle to cooperative action.

For (b) full intercommunion and (c) corporate union it will be necessary to reconcile the differences between Churches which hold (i) that a ministry in the threefold form of bishops, priests, and deacons was instituted in the Church by Christ; (ii) that the historic episcopate is essential for corporate union; (iii) that a ministry was instituted by Christ in which bishops as distinct from presbyters are not essential; (iv) that no specially ordained ministry whatsoever is required by the conception of the Church.

5. LIKENESS IN POLITY AS A BASIS FOR UNITY.

(a) Likeness in polity is not necessary for cooperative action.

(c) With reference to corporate union most of us endorse the following statement from the Lausanne Report (see La 39).

It will be noted that the above statements assume a substantial likeness, already existing or conceded in theory with respect to faith, confession, worship, polity.

It will be further noted that there is a marked unlikeness, whether as a matter of existing practice or as a matter of rival doctrines, when we are considering sacraments and orders.

(iv) Obstacles to Church Unity

1. OBSTACLES WHICH ARE RESTRICTED TO "FAITH" AND "ORDER"

We find that the obstacles most difficult to overcome consist of elements of "faith" and "order" combined, as when some form of Church government or worship is considered a part of the faith.

But we are led to the conclusion that behind all particular statements of the problem of corporate union lie deeply divergent conceptions of the Church. For the want of any more accurate terms this divergence might be described as the contrast between "authoritarian" and "personal" types of Church.

We have, on the one hand, an insistence upon a divine given in the Scriptures, in orders, in creeds, in worship.

We have, on the other hand, an equally strong insistence upon the individual experience of divine grace, as the ruling principle of the "gathered" Church, in which freedom is both enjoyed as a religious right and enjoined as a religious duty.

We are aware that between these extremes many variations exist, expressed as well in doctrine as in organization, worship, and types of piety. These variations are combinations of the two contrasted types of Church to which we have referred.

We do not minimize the difficulties which these contrasted types of Church present to our movement, nor are we willing to construe them as being due mainly to misunderstandings or to sin.

It is our hope and prayer that through the guidance of the Holy Spirit they may, in God's good time, be overcome.

Meanwhile it is our duty to attempt by study to enter still more sympathetically into the experience of others, and to "keep the unity of the Spirit in the bond of peace."

We suggest that the full range of the contrast between the two types of Church to which we have been referring, is in no wise covered by the antithesis of episcopal and non-episcopal orders.

This contrast may be expressed in many other terms. The problem of the authority of Scripture and the modes of its interpretation is the most classical instance,

2. OBSTACLES NOT RESTRICTED TO "FAITH" AND "ORDER"

(a) Obstacles which are, in part, theological or ecclesiastical, and, in equal part, sociological or political.

Such obstacles are met in the case of a national Church which hallows the common life of a given people, but is at the same time exposed to the perils of an exclusive provincialism or of domination by a secular state.

Frequently renewed testimony, given at this Conference, makes it plain that the Churches of the mission field are grievously hindered in their efforts to solve problems of this order so long as they remain unsolved in the "home" lands.

(b) Obstacles which are due mainly to historical factors.

We have, in Western Christendom, many separations which are the result of the divided secular history of Europe.

We have, in the Near and Middle East, certain conspicuous examples of religiously isolated communities, whose isolation is primarily due to their loyalty to an ancient heritage which goes back to earliest Christian times and often to lands far off from those in which they now exist.

(c) Obstacles which are of "cultural" origin.

In Churches which already enjoy substantial agreement upon matters of faith and order, and which may be said to stand upon common ground as representatives of one or other of the two contrasted types of Church, the prospect of corporate union is by no means clear or assured.

These Churches are not conscious of any obstacles to such union because of mutually exclusive doctrines. They are, however, kept apart by barriers of nationality, race, class, general culture, and, more particularly, by slothful self-content and self-sufficiency.

(v) What Can We Do to Move Toward the Unity We Seek?

The unity we seek is not simple but complex. It has two aspects: (a) the inner spiritual unity known in its completeness to God alone; and (b) the outward unity which expresses itself in mutual recognition, cooperative action and corporate or institutional unity. The concrete proposals here brought forward may be regarded as next steps toward the realization of the unity which the Churches should seek. Some of these proposals are of concern to individual communions, others of concern to groups of communions in certain countries or other areas, and still others may be considered as of ecumenical or worldwide range.

5. SPECIAL TIMES OF PRAYER.

The practice in some countries of setting apart one Sunday each year for special prayer for the ecumenical movement is worthy of wide observance. Since 1920 the worldwide observance of the eight days before Pentecost (Whitsunday) as a special time of prayer for the unity of Christ's Church has been fostered by the Faith and Order Movement. . . .

8. PRINCIPLES OF CO-OPERATION.

It is widely recognized that sound policies of co-operation in all spheres of Christian action have done much to facilitate the drawing together of the Christian Churches. Such co-operation between Christian bodies, if it is to be truly effective, must have regard to certain guiding principles and governing considerations drawn from experience already accumulated in many countries.

Among these attention is called to the following:

(1) In determining the sphere of cooperation due regard is paid to the objects to be achieved, namely:

(a) to meet real and recognized need;

(b) to obviate conflict and unnecessary waste;

(c) to accomplish important results which cannot be secured as well, if at all, by the co-operative agencies working separately.

(2) At the very beginning of the undertaking the various bodies joining in the co-operative arrangement enter into an understanding as to objectives, scope, direction, assignment of responsibilities, support, and all else vital to the success of the undertaking, and this understanding is set forth with clarity in writing.

(3) The co-operative agency possesses only such power as the cooperating bodies confer upon it.

(4) The plan of organization is made as simple as is compatible with achieving the desired results.

(5) Everything is done openly and in consultation.

(6) There is a sincere determination to understand the viewpoints and the distinctive characteristics of the different units, and willingness to accept what others have to give.

(7) Wherever co-operation is undertaken, it is carried through so thoroughly as to create the confidence on which further developments must depend.

(8) No large venture of co-operation can proceed to high success without adequate financial resources, but it is believed that those will be forthcoming if the other conditions here emphasized are met.

(9) The leaders are on their guard lest in their own lives there be manifested or tolerated those things which tend to destroy co-operation or to make impossible true Christian unity; for example, ignorance and prejudice, hazy thinking and vague statements, selfish ambition and jealousy, suspicion and lack of frankness, intriguing and disloyalty.

(10) The prime consideration to be borne constantly in mind by all engaged in the work of cooperation is that of rendering Christlike service. First and last in point of importance is the recognition of the Lordship of Jesus Christ, and the conviction that He Himself wills co-operation and unity.

13. PLANS FOR CHURCH UNION.

It is recommended that communions represented at the present Conference should consider the desirability of setting up effective standing commissions for the study of the ecumenical questions, for fostering mutually helpful relations with other communions, and for conducting conversations with other communions leading toward Church union.

It is highly desirable, in countries where conditions are favorable and the time seems ripe, that those communions which already enjoy a considerable measure of mutual understanding, fellowship, and co-operation should proceed without undue delay to the stage of official negotiations, or at least of conversations, and in particular should produce, as soon as may be, a preliminary or provisional draft scheme of union for submission to their constituencies.

15. TERRITORIAL AND ECUMENICAL UNITY.

A problem calling for far-sighted policy is that presented in areas where, when union is under discussion, it becomes necessary for a Church to choose between, on the one hand, entering into a unity with other denominations within the same national boundary, and, on the other hand, maintaining connections with other Churches of its own order throughout the world. Experience shows that the injury done to the Christian cause by the multiplicity of separate Churches within a given area is so great that the territorial unity of Churches should normally be regarded as desirable where it can be accomplished without violating the principles of the Churches concerned. It must, however, be recognized that the ideal of a territorially or nationally united Church is accompanied by certain dangers. Therefore we urge that in developing Church union on the territorial basis every care should be taken to preserve in nationally constituted Churches a sense of ecumenical relationship, and to maintain such relationship in every possible way. . . .

17. THE COUNCIL OF CHURCHES.

This Conference as well as the World Conference held at Oxford have approved in principle the proposal that the Churches should form a Council of Churches. Some members of this Conference desire to place on record their opposition to this proposal, but we are agreed that if the Churches should adopt it, the Council should be so designed as to conserve the distinctive character and value of each of the movements represented in the two Conferences. To this end it is desirable that, while freedom should be exercised in the formation of special committees, the Churches as such should come together on the basis of the doctrine of the Incarnation. The largest success of the plan depends upon securing adequate representation of every communion.

AFFIRMATION OF UNION IN ALLEGIANCE TO OUR LORD JESUS CHRIST

The Second World Conference on Faith and Order, held in Edinburgh in August, 1937, brought together four hundred and fourteen delegates from one hundred and twenty-two Christian communions in forty-three different countries. The delegates assembled to discuss together the causes that keep Christian communions apart, and the things that unite them in Christian fellowship. The Conference approved the following statement nemine contradicente:

We are one in faith in our Lord Jesus Christ, the incarnate Word of God. We are one in allegiance to Him as Head of the Church, and as King of kings and Lord of lords. We are one in acknowledging that this allegiance takes precedence of any other allegiance that may make claims upon us.

This unity does not consist in the agreement of our minds or the consent of our wills. It is found in Jesus Christ Himself, Who lived, died, and rose again to bring us to the Father, and Who through the Holy Spirit dwells in His Church. We are one because we are all the objects of the love and grace of God, and called by Him to witness in all the world to His glorious gospel.

Our unity is of heart and spirit. We are divided in the outward forms of our life in Christ, because we understand differently His will for His Church. We believe, however, that a deeper understanding will lead us toward a united apprehension of the truth as it is in Jesus.

We humbly acknowledge that our divisions are contrary to the will of Christ, and we pray God in His mercy to shorten the days of our separation and to guide us by His Spirit into fullness of unity.

We are thankful that during recent years we have been drawn together; prejudices have been overcome, misunderstandings removed, and real, if limited, progress has been made toward our goal of a common mind.

In this Conference we may gratefully claim that the Spirit of God has made us willing to learn from one another, and has given us a fuller vision of the truth and enriched our spiritual experience.

We have lifted up our hearts together in prayer; we have sung the same hymns; together we have read the same Holy Scriptures. We recognize in one another, across the barriers of our separation, a common Christian outlook and a common standard of values. We are therefore assured of a unity deeper than our divisions.

We are convinced that our unity of spirit and aim must be embodied in a way that will make it manifest to the world, though we do not yet clearly see what outward form it should take.

We believe that every sincere attempt to cooperate in the concerns of the kingdom of God draws the severed communions together in increased mutual understanding and goodwill. We call upon our fellow Christians of all communions to practice such co-operation; to consider patiently occasions of disunion that they may be overcome; to be ready to learn from those who differ from them; to seek to remove those obstacles to the furtherance of the gospel in the non-Christian world which arise from our divisions; and constantly to pray for that unity which we believe to be our Lord's will for His Church.

We desire also to declare to all men everywhere our assurance that Christ is the one hope of unity for the world in face of the distractions and dissensions of this present time. We know that our witness is weakened by our divisions. Yet we are one in Christ and in the fellowship of His Spirit. We pray that everywhere, in a world divided and perplexed, men may turn to Jesus Christ our Lord, Who makes us one in spite of our divisions; that He may bind in one those who by many worldly claims are set at variance; and that the world may at last find peace and unity in Him; to Whom be glory for ever.

Notes: *The Second International World Conference on Faith and Order made significant progress over the First Conference in defining the broad areas of essential agreement among the participating Protestant, Free Church, and Orthodox churches. It was able to find a formal consensus on issues such as the importance of grace, the nature of justification and sanctification, the sovereignty of God, the church, and the sacramental life. However, once it began to gain some depth in the understanding of the vital issues that had originally occasioned the split between the various denominational bodies, the old differences remained important. For example, in spite of broad agreement over the nature of the church, a significant disagreement remained over the relative impor-*

tance of the ministry and sacraments, the Word of God, and the inward testimony of the Holy Spirit to the life of the believer.

Underlying the Conference's deliberation was the hope of some form of church unity. The unity desired by some was organic union, a united church under a single governmental system. Others looked to a more loosely organized confederation of church bodies, whose unity would be expressed in common action in areas of agreement. In between these two ideas would be the establishment of intercommunion, in which separate churches would recognize and acknowledge the others' membership and ministry, and the members of one would be received at the communion table of the others. Both corporate unity and intercommunion imply an agreement on matters of faith, though confederation can be achieved apart from such agreement.

In the end, the Conference suggested the move to form a council of churches. The formation of that council was delayed as Christian Europe erupted into the blood bath known as the Second World War. However, soon after the war, many of the delegates led in the formation of the World Council of Churches. The initial unity was affirmed to be in the Lord, whom all Christians worshipped and secondarily in the more abstract theological consensus which the participating churches had been able to affirm. Delegates hoped that the future would provide the means of reconciling all of the continuing differences.

*   *   *

MESSAGE [WORLD COUNCIL OF CHURCHES (AMSTERDAM, 1948)]

The World Council of Churches, meeting at Amsterdam, sends this message of greeting to all who are in Christ, and to all who are willing to hear.

We bless God our Father, and our Lord Jesus Christ Who gathers together in one the children of God that are scattered abroad. He has brought us here together at Amsterdam. We are one in acknowledging Him as our God and Savior. We are divided from one another not only in matters of faith, order and tradition, but also by pride of nation, class and race. But Christ has made us His own, and He is not divided. In seeking Him we find one another. Here at Amsterdam we have committed ourselves afresh to Him, and have covenanted with one another in constituting this World Council of Churches. We intend to stay together. We call upon Christian congregations everywhere to endorse and fulfill this covenant in their relations one with another. In thankfulness to God we commit the future to Him.

When we look to Christ, we see the world as it is—His world, to which He came and for which He died. It is filled both with great hopes and also with disillusionment and despair. Some nations are rejoicing in new freedom and power, some are bitter because freedom is denied them, some are paralyzed by division, and everywhere there is an undertone of fear. There are millions who are hungry, millions who have no home, no country and no hope. Over all mankind hangs the peril of total war. We have to accept God's judgment upon us for our share in the world's guilt. Often we have tried to serve God and Mammon, put other loyalties before loyalty to Christ, confused the Gospel with our own economic or national or racial interests, and feared war more than we hated it. As we have talked with each other here, we have begun to understand how our separation has prevented us from receiving correction from one another in Christ. And because we lacked this correction, the world has often heard from us not the Word of God but the words of men.

But there is a word of God for our world. It is that the world is in the hands of the living God, Whose will for it is wholly good; that in Christ Jesus, His incarnate Word, Who lived and died and rose from the dead, God has broken the Power of evil once for all, and opened for everyone the gate into freedom and joy in the Holy Spirit; that the final judgment on all human history and on every human deed is the judgment of the merciful Christ; and that the end of history will be triumph of His Kingdom, where alone we shall understand how much God has loved the world. This is God's unchanging word to the world. Millions of our fellowmen have never heard of it. As we are met here from many lands, we Pray God to stir up His whole Church to make this Gospel known to the whole world, and to call on all men to believe in Christ, to live in His love and to hope for His coming.

Our coming together to form a World Council will be in vain unless Christians and Christian congregations everywhere commit themselves to the Lord of the Church in a new effort to seek together, where they live, to be His witnesses and servants among their neighbors. We have to remind ourselves and all men that God has put down the mighty from their seats and exalted the humble and meek. We have to learn afresh together to speak boldly in Christ's name both to those in power and to the people, to oppose terror, cruelty and race discrimination, to stand by the outcast, the prisoner and the refugee. We have to make of the Church in every place a voice for those who have no voice, and a home where every man will be at home. We have to learn afresh together what is the duty of the Christian man or woman in industry, in agriculture, in politics, in the professions and in the home. We have to ask God to teach us together to say No and to say Yes in truth. No, to all that flouts the love of Christ, to every system, every program and every person that treats any man as though he were an irresponsible thing or a means of profit, to the defenders of injustice in the name of order, to those who sow the seeds of war or urge war as inevitable; Yes, to all that conforms to the love of Christ, to all who seek for justice, to the peacemakers, to all who hope, fight and suffer for the cause of man, to all who—even without knowing it look for new heavens and a new earth wherein dwelleth righteousness.

It is not in man's Power to banish sin and death from the earth, to create the unity of the Holy Catholic Church, to conquer the hosts of Satan. But it is within the Power of God. He has given us at Easter the certainty that His purpose will be accomplished. But, by our acts of obedience and faith, we can on earth set up signs which point to the coming victory. Till the day of that victory our lives are hid with Christ in God, and no earthly disillusion or distress or Power of hell can separate us from Him. As those who wait in confidence and joy for their deliverance, let us give, ourselves to those tasks which lie to our hands, and so set up signs that men may see.

Now unto Him that is able to do exceeding abundantly above all that we ask or think, according to the power that worketh in us, unto Him be glory in the Church by Christ Jesus, throughout all ages, world without end.

Notes: *The World Council of Churches was formed at Amsterdam in 1948, amid the devastation of World War II. The formation of the Council was itself such a significant event that little further progress was made by Council members on any doctrinal issues previously highlighted by the Faith and Order conferences. The Message issued at the close of the Council's meeting skirts doctrinal issues and speaks more to the open wounds remaining from the war years. The Message is no less significant for that reason, as the Council would find that future deliberations on Faith and Order issues would offer very little resolution to the problems so clearly presented in the pre-World Council conferences. However, the continuing lack of theological agreement would not prevent the Council from sponsoring research, dialogue, and a united witness on various social issues.*

*　　*　　*

MESSAGE [WORLD COUNCIL OF CHURCHES (EVANSTON, 1954)]

To ALL our fellow Christians, and to our fellowmen everywhere, we send greetings in the name of Jesus Christ. We affirm our faith in Jesus Christ as the hope of the world, and desire to share that faith with all men. May God forgive us that by our sin we have often hidden this hope from the world.

In the ferment of our time there are both hopes and fears. It is indeed good to hope for freedom, justice, and peace, and it is God's will that we should have these things. But He has made us for a higher end. He has made us for Himself, that we might know and love Him, worship and serve Him. Nothing other than God can ever satisfy the heart of man. Forgetting this, man becomes his own enemy. He seeks justice but creates oppression. He wants peace, but drifts towards war. His very mastery of nature threatens him with ruin. Whether he acknowledges it or not, he stands under the judgment of God and in the shadow of death.

Here where we stand, Jesus Christ stood with us. He came to us, true God and true Man, to seek and to save. Though we were the enemies of God, Christ died for us. We crucified Him, but God raised Him from the dead. He is risen. He has overcome the powers of sin and death. A new life has begun. And in His risen and ascended power, He has sent forth into the world a now community, bound together by His Spirit, sharing

His divine life, and commissioned to make Him known throughout the world. He will come again as judge and King to bring all things to their consummation. Then we shall see Him as He is and know as we are known. Together with the whole creation we wait for this with eager hope, knowing that God is faithful and that even now He holds all things in His hand.

This is the hope of God's people in every age, and we commend it afresh today to all who will listen. To accept it is to turn from our ways to God's way. It is to live as forgiven sinners, as children growing in His love. It is to have our citizenship in that Kingdom which all man's sin is impotent to destroy, that realm of love and joy and peace which lies about all men, though unseen. It is to enter with Christ into the suffering and despair of men, sharing with them the great secret of that Kingdom which they do not expect. It is to know that whatever men may do, Jesus reigns and shall reign.

With this assurance we can face the powers of evil and the threat of death with a good courage. Delivered from fear we are made free to love. For beyond the judgment of men and the judgment of history lies the judgment of the King who died for all men, and who will judge us at the last according to what we have done to the least of his brethren. Thus our Christian hope directs us towards our neighbor. It constrains us to pray daily, "Thy will be done on earth as it is in heaven," and to act as we pray in every area of life. It begets a life of believing prayer and expectant action, looking to Jesus and pressing forward to the day of His return in glory.

Now we would speak through our member churches directly to each congregation. Six years ago our churches entered into a covenant to form this Council, and affirmed their intention to stay together. We thank God for His blessing on our work and fellowship during these six years. We enter now upon a second stage. To stay together is not enough. We must go forward. As we learn more of our unity in Christ, it becomes the more intolerable that we should be divided. We therefore ask you: Is your church seriously considering its relation to other churches in the light of our Lord's prayer that we may be sanctified in the truth and that we may all be one? Is your congregation, in fellowship with sister congregations around you, doing all it can do to ensure that your neighbors shall hear the voice of the one Shepherd calling all men into the one flock?

The forces that separate men from one another are strong. At our meeting here we have missed the presence of Chinese Churches which were with us at Amsterdam. There are other lands and churches unrepresented in our Council, and we long ardently for their fellowship. But we are thankful that, separated as we are by the deepest political divisions of our time, here at Evanston we are united in Christ. And we rejoice also that, in the bond of prayer and a common hope, we maintain communion with our Christian brethren everywhere.

It is from within this communion that we have to speak about the fear and distrust which at present divide our world. Only at the Cross of Christ, where men know themselves as forgiven sinners, can they be made one. It is there that Christians must pray daily for their enemies. It is there that we must seek deliverance from self-righteousness, impatience and fear. And those who know that Christ is risen should have the courage to expect new power to break through every human barrier.

It is not enough that Christians should seek peace for themselves. They must seek justice for others. Great masses of people in many parts of the world are hungry for bread, and are compelled to live in conditions which mock their human worth. Does your church speak and act against such injustice? Millions of men and women are suffering segregation and discrimination on the ground of race. Is your church willing to declare, as this Assembly has declared, that this is contrary to the will of God and to act on that declaration? Do you pray regularly for those who suffer unjust discrimination on grounds of race, religion, or political conviction?

The Church of Christ is today a world-wide fellowship, yet there are countless people to whom He is unknown. How much do you care about this? Does your congregation live for itself, or for the world around it and beyond it? Does its common life, and does the daily work of its members in the world, affirm the Lordship of Christ or deny it?

God does not leave any of us to stand alone. In every place He has gathered us together to be His family, in which His gifts and His forgiveness are received. Do you forgive one another as Christ forgave you? Is your congregation a true family of God, where every man can find a home and know that God loves him without limit?

We are not sufficient for these things. But Christ is sufficient. We do not know what is coming to us. But we know Who is coming. It is He who meets us every day and who will meet us at the end—Jesus Christ our Lord.

Therefore we say to you: Rejoice in hope.

Notes: *As with the previous Message in 1948, the Message from Evanston, Illinois, acknowledged the formal unity of the participating churches and centered its message on the problems of the world. It bemoaned the loss of direct communion with the Chinese Christian community, cut off by the rise of the Maoist government. With some degree of recovery from the Second World War evident, it turned to the more perennial problems of hunger, racism, religious discrimination, and political oppression. The Council called for a Church that would take responsibility for the world around it. A world-affirming view, as opposed to those Christian perspectives that prioritized the evangelism of individuals, would become characteristic of the Council and the focal point of criticism.*

*   *   *

MESSAGE [WORLD COUNCIL OF CHURCHES (NEW DELHI, 1961)]

The Third Assembly of the World Council of Churches, meeting in New Delhi, addresses this letter to the member churches and their congregations. We rejoice and thank God that we experience here a fellowship as deep as before and wider. New member churches coming in considerable numbers and strength both from the ancient Orthodox tradition of Eastern Christendom and from Africa, Asia, Latin America and other parts of the world visibly demonstrate that Christianity now has a home in every part of the world. In this fellowship we are able to speak and act freely, for we are all partakers together with Christ. Together we have sought to understand our common calling to witness, service and unity.

We are deeply grateful for the prayers of countless Christian people and for the study of our theme 'Jesus Christ the Light of the World' by which many of you have shared in our work. Now we return to our churches to do, with you, the things that have been shown to us here.

All over the world new possibilities of life, freedom and prosperity are being actively, even passionately, pursued. In some lands there is disillusionment with the benefits that a technically expert society can produce; and over all there hangs the shadow of vast destruction through war. Nevertheless mankind is not paralysed by these threats. The momentum of change is not reduced. We Christians share men's eager quest for life, for freedom from poverty, oppression and disease. God is at work in the opening possibilities for mankind in our day. He is at work even when the powers of evil rebel against him and call down his judgement. We do not know by what ways God will lead us: but our trust is in Jesus Christ who is now and always our eternal life.

When we speak to men as Christians we must speak the truth of our faith: that there is only one way to the Father, namely Jesus Christ his Son. On that one way we are bound to meet our brother. We meet our brother Christian. We meet also our brother man; and before we speak to him of Christ, Christ has already sought him.

Christ is the way and therefore we have to walk together witnessing to him and serving all men. This is his commandment. There is no greater service to men than to tell them of the living Christ and no more effective witness than a life offered in service. The indifference or hostility of men may check our open speaking but God is not silenced. He speaks through the worship and the sufferings of his Church. Her prayers and patience are, by his gracious acceptance of them, made part of the witness he bears to Christ.

We need to think out together in concrete terms the forms of Christian service for today and together act upon them. In no field has Christian cooperation been more massive and effective than in service to people in every kind of distress. There is no more urgent task for Christians than to work together for community within nations and for peace with justice and freedom among them, so that the causes of much contemporary misery may be rooted out. We have to take our stand against injustice caused to any race, or to any man on account of his race. We have to learn to make a Christian contribution to the service of men through secular agencies. Christian love requires not only the sharing of worldly goods but costly personal service. All over the world young people are giving an example in their spontaneous offering of themselves.

We must together seek the fullness of Christian unity. We need for this purpose every member of the Christian family, of Eastern and Western tradition, ancient churches and younger churches, men and women, young and old, of every race and every nation. Our brethren in Christ are given to us, not chosen by us. In some things our convictions do not yet permit us to act together, but we have made progress in giving content to the unity we seek. Let us therefore find out the things which in each place we can do together now; and faithfully do them, praying and working always for that fuller unity which Christ wills for his Church.

This letter is written from the World Council of Churches' Assembly. But the real letter written to the world today does not consist of words. We Christian people, wherever we are, are a letter from Christ to his world 'written not with ink but with the spirit of the living God, not on tablets of stone but on tablets of human hearts'. The message is that God in Christ has reconciled the world to himself. Let us speak it and live it with joy and confidence, 'for it is the God who said "Let light shine out of darkness" who has shone in our hearts to give the light of the knowledge of the glory of God in the face of Jesus Christ'.

1st Sunday in Advent 1961

The Assembly decided that the following affirmations, which were said by all in its closing service, should be sent to the churches with the message, so that they can be used in congregational worship and especially in united services.

''We confess Jesus Christ, Savior of men and the light of the world;

Together we accept his command;

We commit ourselves anew to bear witness to him among men;

We offer ourselves to serve all men in love, that love which he alone imparts;

We accept afresh our calling to make visible our unity in him; We pray for the gift of the Holy Spirit for our task.''

Notes: *The Message of the third World Council meeting in New Delhi, India, in 1961 was notable for the increased participation and membership in the Council by a significant number of Eastern Orthodox churches and newer churches based in Latin America, Africa, and Asia. Their entrance into the Council confirmed the efforts of the older member churches. The participation of these churches broadened the global perspective of the Council's deliberation and began to transform its dominant Western European/North American perspective on the world. The addition of other church bodies also highlighted the need to overcome the disunity within the Christian community.*

A persistent theme in the Council's deliberation and its final Message was the witness to Christ offered in Christian service. The most urgent task for the Christian community was action on the issues of war and racism. It also called attention to the possibilities for Christian action through secular agencies.*

*   *   *

MESSAGE [WORLD COUNCIL OF CHURCHES (UPPSALA, 1968)]

The excitement of new scientific discoveries, the protest of student revolts, the shock of assassinations, the clash of wars: these mark the year 1968. In this climate the Uppsala Assembly met first of all to listen.

We heard the cry of those who long for peace; of the hungry and exploited who demand bread and justice; of the victims of discrimination who claim human dignity; and of the increasing millions who seek for the meaning of life.

God hears these cries and judges us. He also speaks the liberating Word. We hear him say—''I go before you. Now that Christ carries away your sinful past, the Spirit frees you to live for others. Anticipate my Kingdom in joyful worship and daring acts.'' The Lord says, ''I make all things new.''

We ask you, trusting in God's renewing power, to join in these anticipations of God's Kingdom, showing now something of the newness which Christ will complete.

1. All men have become neighbors to one another. Torn by our diversities and tensions, we do not yet know how to live together. *But God makes new.* Christ wants His Church to foreshadow a renewed human community.

    Therefore, we Christians will manifest our unity in Christ by entering into full fellowship with those of other races, classes, age, religious and political convictions, in the place where we live. Especially we shall seek to overcome racism wherever it appears.

2. Scientific discoveries and the revolutionary movements of our time open new potentialities and perils for men. Man is lost because he does not know who he is. *But God makes new.* The biblical message is that man is God's trustee for creation, that in Christ the ''new man'' appears and demands decision.

    Therefore, with our fellow-men we accept our trusteeship over creation, guarding, developing and sharing its resources. As Christians we proclaim Jesus as Lord and Savior. God can transform us into Christ's new humanity.

3. The ever widening gap between the rich and the poor, fostered by armament expenditure, is the crucial point of decision today. *But God makes new.* He has made us see that Christians who in their acts deny dignity to their fellow men deny Jesus Christ, in spite of all that they profess to believe.

Therefore, with the people of all convictions, we Christians want to ensure human rights in a just world community. We shall work for disarmament and for trade agreements fair to fall. We are ready to tax ourselves in furtherance of a system of world taxation.

4. These commitments demand the worship, discipline and mutual correction of a world-wide community. In the World Council of Churches, and its regional, national and local counterparts, only the beginning of this community has been given to us. *But God makes new.* The ecumenical movement must become bolder, and more representative. Our churches must acknowledge that this movement binds us to the renewal.

Therefore, we re-affirm our covenant to support and correct one another. Present plans for church union call for decision, and we seek fuller communion with those churches which are not yet in full fellowship with us. We know that we never live the fullness of what we profess and we long for God to take over. Yet we rejoice that already we can anticipate in worship the time when God renews ourselves, all men, all things.

Notes: *The Message of the Fourth Assembly of the World Council gathered in Uppsala, Sweden, encountered not only the issues raised by the Civil Rights movement in the United States, but the racism evident in the relations between the churches controlled by white people of European extraction and the churches of the Third World. The critique of social relationships under the name of social ''revolution'' caught the attention of Christian leaders not only in the West, but in every part of the world. Thus it is not surprising to see that the situation dominated the deliberations and the issue of the unity of the member churches was pushed aside in the call for making the Council even more inclusive in its membership. Specifically, the Council needed to reach out to those churches that were not yet a part of it, nor its regional or national councils, which were emerging as component units of ecumenical community, i.e., those churches willing to engage in the dialogue to which the World Council had given focus.*

*　　　*　　　*

MESSAGE [WORLD COUNCIL OF CHURCHES (NAIROBI, 1975)]

As participants at the Fifth Assembly of the World Council of Churches, we send affectionate greetings to our sisters and brothers in our Lord Jesus Christ.

Representatives of many church traditions and cultures, we gathered together in Nairobi, Kenya. In a continent determined

to be free, and moved by the joy with which African Christians celebrate the Lord, we tried to respond to the needs of the world. We had more representatives of the six continents than before and also more women, young people and laity.

For eighteen days, we gathered under our common theme: Jesus Christ frees and unites. Listening to one another, we experienced the joy of unity across the barriers of culture and race, sex and class: we also experienced the pain of these deep divisions. Deliberation on our common witness in Bible study and prayer, in informal small groups and large formal meetings, brought us closer together. Ideology and sharp contrasts in opinion and commitment pulled us apart. The Assembly report gives the direction of our thoughts. It will reach you soon.

Now we bring you these prayers and ask you to pray with us:

God, Creator and Author of Life, warned anew of the threats to human survival, we confess that the way we live and order society sets us against one another and alienates us from your creation, exploiting as though dead things to which you have given life. Separated from you we live in emptiness. We long in our own lives for a new spirituality of intention, thought and action. Help us to struggle to conserve the earth for future generations, and free us to share together, that all may be free.

Kyrie eleison, Lord have mercy

God of Love, who through Jesus Christ shares our suffering, forgives our sins and delivers from the bondages of oppression . . . help us to desire and nourish in ourselves sustaining community with our brothers and sisters everywhere. Give us courage to share suffering when it comes. Restore to us the joy of resurrection, that in the midst of situations we can hardly bear we may sing out:

Hallelujah, Praise be to you, O Lord

God of Hope, whose Spirit gives light and power to your people, empower us to witness to your name in all the nations, to struggle for your own justice against all principalities and powers and to persevere with faith and humor in the tasks that you have given to us. Without you we are powerless. Therefore we cry together:

Maranatha, Come Lord Jesus

Grant that we may with one voice and one heart glorify and sing praise to the majesty of your Holy Name, of the Father, the Son and the Holy Spirit.

Amen.

Notes: *The brief Message from the World Council Assembly in Nairobi noted the expansive experience shared by those who gathered in the first African assembly meeting, which did more* *to present the problem of dealing with Christians in their many varied expressions than resolve issues of ideological expression.*

* * *

MESSAGE [WORLD COUNCIL OF CHURCHES (VANCOUVER, 1982)]

LIFE TOGETHER

Greetings in the name of Jesus Christ, from the Sixth Assembly of the World Council of Churches in Vancouver, Canada. We represent four hundred million people of three hundred member churches. Among us women, young people and persons with disabilities are participating in larger numbers than before. Thank you for your supporting prayers. We are filled with praise to God for the grace given to us since our last meeting. In many places churches have grown in numbers and depth of commitment. We rejoice in courage and faith shown in adversity. We are humbled by those newly called to be martyrs. The Holy Spirit has poured out these and many other gifts, so that we meet with thanksgiving.

This meeting comes in a succession which began at Amsterdam in 1948 with the commitment to stay together. Since then we have been called to grow together and to struggle together. Here under the theme ''Jesus Christ—the Life of the World'' we are called to live together. In the Assembly we taste that life. Our worship in a great tent which reminds us of the pilgrim people; the presence of Canadian Indians which has challenged us; our moving prayer and praise in many languages but one spirit of devotion; our struggles to face divisive issues; the songs of children—all are part of life together in the Christian family. The significant participation of guests from other faiths and of thousands of visitors speaks to us of the wider human community.

This engagement together in Vancouver underlines how critical this moment is in the life of the world, like the turning of a page of history. We hear the cries of millions who face a daily struggle for survival, who are crushed by military power or the propaganda of the powerful. We see the camps of refugees and the tears of all who suffer inhuman loss. We sense the fear of rich groups and nations and the hopelessness of many in the world rich in things who live in great emptiness of spirit. There is a great divide between North and South, between East and West. Our World—God's world—has to choose between ''life and death, blessing and curse''.

This critical choice compels us to proclaim anew that life is God's gift. Life in all its fullness reflects the loving communion of God, Father, Son and Holy Spirit. This is the pattern for our life, a gift filled with wonder and glory, priceless, fragile and irreplaceable. Only when we respond in a loving relationship with God, with one another and with the natural world can there be life in its fullness. The misery and chaos of the world

result from the rejection of God's design for us. Constantly, in public and private, fellowship is broken, life is mutilated and we live alone. In the life of Jesus we meet the very life of God, face to face. He experienced our life, our birth and childhood, our tiredness, our laughter and tears. He shared food with the hungry, love with the rejected, healing with the sick, forgiveness with the penitent. He lived in solidarity with the poor and oppressed and at the end gave his life for others. In the mystery of the Eucharist the resurrected Lord empowers us to live this way of giving and receiving. ''Unless a grain of wheat falls into the earth and dies, it remains alone; but if it dies it bears much fruit'' (John 12:24). Only the converting power of the Holy Spirit enables this way of life to be formed in us. Such a transformation is costly and means the willingness to risk even death in our Kingdom pilgrimage.

On that road we acknowledge our unfaithfulness. The division of the Church of at central points of its life, our failure to witness with courage and imagination, our clinging to old prejudice, our share in the injustice of the world—all this tells us that we are disobedient. Yet God's graciousness amazes us, for we are still called to be God's people, the house of living stones built on Christ the foundation. One sign of this grace is the ecumenical movement in which no member or church stands alone.

The Assembly therefore renews its commitment to the ecumenical vision. The Lord prays for the unity of his people as a sign by which the world may be brought to faith, renewal and unity. We take slow, stumbling steps on the way to the visible unity of the Church but we are sure the direction is essential to our faithfulness. Since the Nairobi Assembly there has been movement in many places, new united churches, acts of common witness, local ecumenical projects. There is new theological convergence which could enable decisive steps towards one eucharistic fellowship. We especially thank God for the hope given to us by the ''Baptism, Eucharist and Ministry'' document and seek widespread response to it.

We renew our commitment to mission and evangelism. By this we mean that deep identification with others in which we can tell the good news that Jesus Christ, God and Savior, is the Life of the World. We cannot impose faith by our eloquence. We can nourish it with patience and caring so that the Holy Spirit, God the Evangelist, may give us the words to speak. Our proclamation has to be translated into every language and culture. Whatever our context among people of living faiths and no faith, we remember that God's love is for everyone, without exception. All are invited to the banquet. Jesus Christ, the living bread, calls everyone who is hungry, and his food is unlimited.

We renew our commitment to justice and peace. Since Jesus Christ healed and challenged the whole of life, so we are called to service the life of all. We see God's good gift battered by the powers of death. Injustice denies God's gifts of unity, sharing and responsibility. When nations, groups and systems hold the power of deciding other people's lives, they love that power. God's way is to share power, to give it to every person. Injustice corrupts the powerful and disfigures the powerless. Poverty, continual and hopeless, is the fate of millions; stolen land is a cause of bitterness and war; the diversity of race becomes the evil imprisonment of racism. We urgently need a new international economic order in which power is shared, not grasped. We are committed to work for it. But the question comes back to us, what of the Church? Do we yet share power freely? Do we cling to the wealth of the Church? Do we claim the powerful as friends and remain deaf to the powerless? We have tasks near home.

Injustice, flagrant, constant and oppressive, leads to violence. Today life is threatened by war, the increase in armaments of all sorts, and particularly the nuclear arms race. Science and technology, which can do so much to feed, clothe and house all people, can today be used to terminate the life of the earth. The arms race everywhere consumes great resources that are desperately needed to support human life. Those who threaten with military might are dealing in the politics of death. It is a time of crisis for us all. We stand in solidarity across the world to call persistently, in every forum, for a halt to the arms race. The life which is God's good gift must be guarded when national security becomes the excuse for arrogant militarism. The tree of peace has justice for its roots.

Life is given. We receive God's gift with constant thankfulness. At the Assembly's opening worship a mother held up her baby at the Lord's Table. It was a sign of hope and of continuity of life. Sometimes we are almost overcome by the smallness and insignificance of our lives; then we feel helpless. But as we feed upon the bread of life in worship we know again and a gain God's saving act in Christ in our own lives. We are astounded and surprised that the eternal purpose of God is persistently entrusted to ordinary people. That is the risk God takes. The forces of death are strong. The gift of life in Christ is stronger. We commit ourselves to live that life, with all its risks and joys, and therefore dare to cry, with all the host of heaven: "O death, where is your victory? Christ is risen. He is risen indeed."

Notes: *The World Council Assembly meeting in Vancouver gathered after four years of reflection on the Nairobi Assembly. While the experience of even more new cultural and language groups within the context of the Assembly was noteworthy, the Council was ready to make some positive statements about developing insights. The Assembly circulated a document on key Christian practices and structures, "Baptism, Eucharist, and Ministry," and found a degree of unity in the willingness of member churches to discuss it. Overwhelmingly, the Assembly found its unity, however, in its mutual response to situations of injustice and war.*

The real accomplishment of the Assembly was the diversity of the various people present. Perhaps the Assembly was summarized best by anthropologist Margaret Mead who, speaking at one of the closing sessions, noted, "You people are a sociological impossibility. You have absolutely nothing in com-

mon—-except your extraordinary conviction that Jesus Christ is the Savior of the world."

*   *   *

MESSAGE [WORLD COUNCIL OF CHURCHES (CANBERRA, 1991)]

The Assembly adopted the following statement on "The Unity of the Church as Koinonia: Gift and Calling".

The purpose of God according to Holy Scripture is to gather the whole of creation under the Lordship of Christ Jesus in whom, by the power of the Holy Spirit, all are brought into communion with God (Ephesians 1).

The church is the foretaste of this communion with God and with one another. The grace of our Lord Jesus Christ, the love of God and the communion of the Holy Spirit enable the one church to live as sign of the reign of God and servant of the reconciliation with God, promised and provided for the whole creation.

The purpose of the church is to unite people with Christ in the power of the Spirit, to manifest communion in prayer and action and thus to point to the fullness of communion with God, humanity and the whole creation in the glory of the kingdom.

The calling of the church is to proclaim reconciliation and to provide healing, to overcome divisions based on race, gender, age, culture, color and to bring all people into communion with God.

Because of sin and the misunderstanding of the diverse gifts of the Spirit, the churches are painfully divided within themselves and among each other. Their scandalous divisions damage the credibility of their witness to the world in worship and service. Moreover, they contradict not only the church's witness but also its very nature.

We acknowledge with gratitude to God that in the ecumenical movement the churches walk together in mutual understanding, theological convergences, common suffering and common prayer, shared witness and service, and they draw close to one another.

This has allowed them to recognize a certain degree of communion already existing between them. This is indeed the fruit of the active presence of the Holy Spirit in the midst of all who believe in Christ Jesus and who struggle for visible unity now.

Nevertheless, churches have failed to draw the consequences for their life from the degree of communion they have already experienced and the agreements already achieved. They have remained satisfied to coexist in division.

The unity of the church to which we are called is a koinonia given and expressed in:

- the common confession of the apostolic faith;

- a common sacramental life entered by the one baptism and celebrated together in one eucharistic fellowship;

- a common life in which members and ministries are mutually recognized and reconciled;

- a common mission witnessing to all people to the gospel of God's grace and serving the whole of creation.

The goal of the search for full communion is realized when all the churches are able to recognize in one another the one, holy, catholic and apostolic church in its fullness.

This full communion will be expressed on the local and the universal levels through conciliar forms of life and action. In such communion churches are bound in all aspects of their life together at all levels in confessing the one faith and engaging in worship and witness, deliberation and action.

Diversities which are rooted in theological traditions, various cultural, ethnic or historical contexts are integral to the nature of communion; yet there are limits to diversity. Diversity is illegitimate when, for instance, it makes impossible the common confession of Jesus Christ as God and Savior the same yesterday, today and forever (Hebrews 13:8); salvation and the final destiny of humanity as proclaimed in Holy Scripture and preached by the apostolic community.

In communion diversities are brought together in harmony as gifts of the Holy Spirit, contributing to the richness and fullness of the church of God.

Many things have been done and many remain to be done on the way towards the realization of full communion.

Churches have reached agreements in bilateral and multilateral dialogues which are already bearing fruit, renewing their liturgical and spiritual life and their theology. In taking specific steps together the churches express and encourage the enrichment and renewal of Christian life, as they learn from

one another, work together for justice and peace and care together for God's creation.

The challenge at this moment in the ecumenical movement as a reconciling and renewing movement towards full visible unity is for the Seventh Assembly of the WCC to call all churches:

- to recognize each other's baptism on the basis of the BEM document;

- to move towards the recognition of the apostolic faith as expressed through the Nicene-Constantinopolitan Creed in the life and witness of one another;

- on the basis of convergence in faith in baptism, eucharist and ministry to consider, wherever appropriate, forms of eucharistic hospitality; we gladly acknowledge that some who do not observe these rites share in the spiritual experience of life in Christ;

- to move towards a mutual recognition of ministries;

- to endeavor in word and deed to give common witness to the gospel as a whole;

- to recommit themselves to work for justice, peace and the integrity of creation, linking more closely the search for sacramental communion of the church with the struggles for justice and peace;

- to help parishes and communities express in appropriate ways locally the degree of communion that already exists.

The Holy Spirit as the promoter of *koinonia* (2 Corinthians 13:13) gives to those who are still divided the thirst and hunger for full communion. We remain restless until we grow together according to the wish and prayer of Christ that those who believe in him may be one (John 17:21).

In the process of praying, working and struggling for unity, the Holy Spirit comforts us in pain, disturbs us when we are satisfied to remain in our division, leads us to repentance and grants us joy when our communion flourishes.

Notes: *The maturing vision of the ecumenical church, which had received the impact of the full participation of non-European Christians in the several previous World Council of Churches Assemblies, bore fruit at the 1991 Assembly at Canberra, Australia. Of all the World Council Messages, the 1991 statement gave the clearest vision of a united church and set a program for reaching it. It offered a platform that is not unlike the Chicago and Lambeth quadrilaterals (which appear elsewhere in this volume) proposed in the 1880s. A four-fold basis for union was projected in a common confession of faith (in the Bible and ancient creeds), a common sacramental life, a common mutually recognized ministry, and a common mis-*

sion. These four items build on the willingness of each church to honor the other church, in spite of its differences, as a member of the one body of Christ. A program to experience the united church was then spelled out in some detail.

Possibly, the most important accomplishment of the Canberra Assembly was the posing of the ultimate union of Christians as an eschatological vision, a reality to be fully realized only at the end of time. In the meantime, however, real steps toward that unity, both in restructuring and in the experience of one fellowship (koinonia), may be taken.

*   *   *

EVANGELISM TODAY (1976) (NATIONAL COUNCIL OF CHURCHES OF CHRIST IN THE U.S.A.)

One way of setting forth what evangelism means in the ecumenical experience today is to review the journey of the past twenty-five years of that experience—a period in which evangelism has been a central issue in American church life. During this period of changing concepts of evangelism, its fullness has never been totally disclosed at any one time or place, and this statement does not attempt a final or definitive description of it.

In the 1950s two major methods were utilized in evangelism: mass meeting campaigns and lay visitation programs, both inviting persons to make decisions for Jesus Christ. Although other factors probably contributed, these modes of sharing the Gospel coincided in the 1950s with a season of growth in church membership unparalleled in American church history.

However, growth in church membership and calling people to Christian discipleship were not necessarily the same. In the early 1960s it became apparent that for many people joining the church had not produced a significant change of attitude or behavior.

This failure of new church members to be enlisted in a pilgrimage toward fuller Christian discipleship called into question the effectiveness of the methods then being used. There followed an intense theological re-examination of what the demands of Christian discipleship should mean both for individuals and for society.

In the process of that re-examination, the practice of evangelism as a congregational function in which people are confronted with the Gospel and called to Christian discipleship was

minimized in those denominations which were working together in the National Council of Churches. Denominational attention was focused on social injustices, and efforts were made to mobilize church members to help rectify them. A false division resulted. Instead of social awareness and action being seen as natural expressions of Christian discipleship to which people are called by evangelism, social action was thought to be a contrast and corrective to evangelism. In this mistaken polarization between them, both—and the whole life of the church—were weakened.

Today we can see the futility of that polarization, but the churches still seem strangely bound by a reluctance to name the Name of Jesus as Lord and Savior. Christians seem to lack the facility today to exclaim with excitement, "Jesus loves me; therefore, I love you!" At this moment in history, there is great need for the churches to recover the ability to name the Name of Jesus Christ as Lord and Savior and bear witness to that Name in word and deed.

But naming the Name and bearing witness to it must be better understood: the commitment to Jesus Christ is a profound event. It is a *personal* event; by the power of the Holy Spirit sinners experience the divine forgiveness and commit themselves to live obediently to Christ the living Lord. It is a *social* event; relationship with friends, neighbors and family are radically altered by the revolutionary demands and allowances of divine love. It is a *community* event; it engrafts one into the community of believers, the church. It is a *public* event; new confrontations with the institutions of society occur, for the "principalities and powers" which impoverish and enslave humanity cannot go unchallenged by Christians!

Commitment to Jesus Christ must be made in the context of the issues posed for us by the moment of history in which we find ourselves—history in which God is at work, through us and sometimes in spite of us. That commitment to Jesus Christ must have an impact on the issues of social and economic justice through the stewardship, integrity and interdependence of Christian disciples. Thereby commitment to Jesus Christ is inescapably a personal, social, community, and public historical event which affects the world and the human beings in it for whom Christ died.

Commitment to Jesus Christ is not a once-for-all event. It is the beginning of one's spiritual pilgrimage of discipleship. Those who are disciples of Christ face continual turning-points which offer new experiences rooted in being "born anew to a living hope" (I Pet. 1:3). We never move beyond the need to hear the renewing call to "repent and believe in the gospel" (Mk. 1:15), in order to live more obediently to the word of the Lord in every area of life, turning from the dead values of self-centered living, acquisitive consumption and upward social striving.

Commitment to Jesus Christ means to embrace more completely in our *personal* lives the new way of life which God's

EVANGELISM TODAY (1976) (NATIONAL COUNCIL OF CHURCHES OF CHRIST IN THE U.S.A.) (continued)

grace initiates, manifesting the Spirit's fruit of love, joy, peace, goodness, meekness, gentleness and self-control. Commitment to Jesus Christ means in our *social* life to love others more deeply, even as Christ loves us and gave himself for us, a love which is giving, accepting, forgiving, seeking and helping. Commitment to Jesus Christ in *community* life means to be called out from the isolation of individualism, from conformity to the ways of the world into the fellowship of disciples which is the church, where by obedience we discover freedom, by humble service we are fulfilled, by sharing the suffering of others we are made whole. Commitment to Jesus Christ in our *public* lives means to be engaged more earnestly in the work not only of relieving the poor and hungry but removing the causes of poverty and hunger in the struggle to remedy both inequities and iniquities, in the liberation of the oppressed and the vindication of the deprived, in the establishment of God's rule in the affairs of humanity. Commitment to Jesus Christ brings confidence that, however dark the present hour, the ultimate victory is assured through Him who is the Lord.

The task of evangelism today is calling people to repentance, to faith in Jesus Christ, to study God's word, to continue steadfast in prayer, and to bearing witness to Him. This is a primary function of the church in its congregational, denominational and ecumenical manifestations. It challenges the most creative capabilities in the churches while at the same time depending upon the Holy Spirit to be the real evangelist.

Now, after the journey of the past twenty-five years, we can call upon people to confess the Name of Jesus Christ and to bear witness to that Name in their lives with a fuller understanding of Christian discipleship and a deeper commitment to share the Good News we have found.

Notes: *Of the many policy statements issued by the National Council of Churches of Christ in the U.S.A., Evangelism Today deals with a crucial issue between the member churches of the council and those of the emerging Evangelical Movement, an issue that has been exported to Protestant churches around the world. All of the larger Protestant groups in America had experienced the schism between those who placed a priority on evangelism, the calling of individuals to faith in Christ, as opposed to those who placed a priority on the church's acting to create a more just social order. The intent of Evangelism Today was to overcome that dichotomy. Its effect within the mainline Protestant churches during the 20 years since its appearance is highly debatable.*

Chapter 2
Western Liturgical Family

Roman Catholic Church

PROMULGATIONS OF THE COUNCIL OF TRENT

SESSION 3
4 February 1546

Acceptance of the creed of the catholic faith

In the name of the holy and undivided Trinity, the Father and the Son and the holy Spirit. This holy, ecumenical and general council of Trent, lawfully assembled in the holy Spirit, with the same three legates of the apostolic see presiding, has considered the tremendous nature of the matters to be treated, especially those which fall within the dual purpose on account of which the council was primarily brought together: the rooting out of heresy and the reform of conduct. The council recognizes with the Apostle that *we are not contending against flesh and blood, but against spiritual hosts of wickedness in the heavenly places;* with him, likewise, it exhorts each and everyone in the first place to *be strong in the Lord, in the strength of his might, in all things taking the shield of faith with which you can quench all the flaming darts of the evil one, and take the helmet of salvation with the sword of the spirit which is the word of God.* Consequently, that this loving care of the council may both begin and continue by the grace of God, it determines and decrees first of all to begin with a creed of the faith. In this if follows the example of the fathers of the more revered councils who, at the beginning of their proceedings, were accustomed to make use of this shield against all heresies, and in some cases by this means alone they have drawn unbelievers to the faith, defeated heretics and strengthened the faithful. Hence the council voted that the creed which the holy Roman church uses as the basic principle on which all who profess the faith of Christ necessarily agree as the firm and sole foundation against which *the powers of death shall never prevail,* should be expressed in the words in which it is read in all the churches. It runs as follows:

I believe in one God, the Father almighty, maker of heaven and earth, of all that is, seen and unseen. And in one Lord, Jesus Christ, the only Son of God, eternally begotten of the Father, God from God, light from light, true God from true God, begotten, not made, of one being with the Father. Through him all things were made. For us and for our salvation he came down from heaven: by the power of the holy Spirit he became incarnate from the virgin Mary, and was made man. For our sake he was crucified under Pontius Pilate; he suffered death and was buried. On the third day he rose again in accordance with the scriptures; he ascended into heaven and is seated at the right hand of the Father. He will come again in glory to judge the living and the dead, and his kingdom will have no end. I believe in the holy Spirit, the Lord, the giver of live, who proceeds from the Father and the Son. With the Father and the Son he is worshipped and glorified. He has spoken through the prophets. I believe in one holy catholic and apostolic church. I acknowledge one baptism for the forgiveness of sins. I look for the resurrection of the dead, and the life of the world to come. Amen.

SESSION 4
8 April 1546

First decree: acceptance of the sacred books and apostolic traditions

The holy ecumenical and general council of Trent, lawfully assembled in the holy Spirit, with the same three legates of the apostolic see presiding, keeps ever before its eyes this purpose: that the purity of the gospel, purged of all errors, may be preserved in the church. Our lord Jesus Christ, the Son of God, first proclaimed with his own lips this gospel, which had in the past been promised by the prophets in the scriptures; then he bade it to preached to every creature through his apostles as the source of the whole truth of salvation and rule of conduct. The council clearly perceives that this truth and rule are contained in written books and in unwritten traditions which were received by the apostles from the mouth of Christ himself, or else have come down to us, handed on as it were from the apostles themselves at the inspiration of the holy Spirit. Following the example of the orthodox fathers, the council accepts and venerates with a like feeling of piety and reverence all the books of both the old and the new Testament, since the one God is the author of both, as well as the traditions concerning both faith and conduct, as either directly spoken by Christ or dictated by the holy Spirit, which have been preserved in unbroken sequence in the catholic church.

PROMULGATIONS OF THE COUNCIL OF TRENT (continued)

The council has decided that a written list of the sacred books should be included in this decree in case a doubt should occur to anyone as to which are the books which are accepted by this council. They are as follows. The old Testament: the five books of Moses, namely Genesis, Exodus, Leviticus, Numbers, Deuteronomy; Joshua, Judges, Ruth, four books of Kings, two of Paralipomenon, Esdras I and II (which is also named Nehemiah), Tobit, Judith, Esther, Job, 150 Psalms of David, Proverbs, Ecclesiastes, Song of Songs, Wisdom, Ecclesiasticus, Isaiah, Jeremiah with Baruch, Ezechiel, Daniel; the twelve minor prophets, namely Hosea, Joel, Amos, Obadiah, Jonah, Micah, Nahum, Habakkuk, Zephaniah, Haggai, Zechariah, Malachi; two books of the Macabees, I and II. The new Testament: the four gospels according to Matthew, Mark, Luke and John; the Acts of the Apostles written by the evangelist Luke; fourteen letters of Paul the apostle, to the Romans, two of the Corinthians, to the Galatians, to the Ephesians, to the Philippians, to the Colossians, two to the Thessalonians, two to Timothy, to Titus, to Philemon, to the Hebrews; two letters of the apostle Peter; three of the apostle John; one of the apostle James; one of the apostle Jude; the Apocalypse of the apostle John.

If anyone should not accept as sacred and canonical these entire books and all their parts as they have, by established custom, been read in the catholic church and as contained in the old Latin Vulgate edition, and in conscious judgement should reject the aforesaid traditions: let him be anathema. Hence, let all understand the order and manner by which the council will proceed after laying down the foundation of the profession of faith, and what witnesses and supports it will especially use in strengthening its teachings and renewing conduct in the church.

Second decree: acceptance of the Latin Vulgate edition of the Bible; rule on the manner of interpreting sacred scripture etc.

Moreover, the same holy council considers that noticeable benefit can accrue to the church of the God if, from all the Latin editions of the sacred books which are in circulation, it establishes which is to be regarded as authentic. It decides and declares that the old well known Latin Vulgate edition which has been tested in the church by long use over so many centuries should be kept as the authentic text in public readings, debates, sermons and explanations; and no one is to dare or presume on any pretext to reject it.

The council further decrees, in order to control those of unbalanced character, that no one, relying on his personal judgment in matters of faith and customs which are linked to the establishment of christian doctrine, shall dare to interpret the sacred scriptures either by twisting its text to his individual meaning in opposition to that which has been and is held by holy mother church, whose function is to pass judgment on the true meaning and interpretation of the sacred scriptures; or by giving it meanings contrary to the unanimous consent of the fathers, even if interpretations of this kind were never intended for publication. Whoever acts contrary to this decision is to be publicly named by religious superiors and punished by the penalties prescribed by law.

In this regard, as is right, the council wishes to impose a restriction also on printers who, thinking they have a right to do what they wish without restraint and without the permission of ecclesiastical superiors, print the texts of sacred scripture with added notes and commentaries of anyone at all; and this they often do without stating the name or with a false name of the press and, what is more serious, without the name of the author; and they have books of this kind, printed in other places, on sale without permission. Hence the council decrees and determines that hereafter the sacred scriptures, particularly this ancient Vulgate edition, shall be printed after a thorough revision; that no one may print or have printed any books on sacred subjects without the name of the author, nor in future sell them or even keep them in his possession, unless they have first been examined and approved by the local ordinary, under pain of anathema and fine as determined in the regulation of the most recent Lateran council. If they are regulars, in addition to the above examination and approval, they must also obtain permission from their own superiors and have the books acknowledged by the latter, in accordance with the formula of their own institutes. Those who make written copies of or publish those books without their having previously been examined and approved, are liable to the same penalties as the printers. Those who process or read them; if they have not disclosed the author, are to be regarded as the author. The actual approval of such books is to be given in written form and should be authoritatively displayed at the front of a book, whether it be written or printed. All this, namely the approval and assessment, is to be done without fee, so that approval may be given to what deserves to be approved, and rejection to what has to be condemned.

In addition, the council wished to check the lack of discretion by which the words and sentiments of sacred scripture are turned and twisted to scurrilous use, to wild and empty fancies, to flattery, detraction, superstitions, godless and devilish magical formulae, fortune telling, lotteries, and also slanderous pamphlets. So as to banish this kind of irreverence and contempt, and so that no one may in future dare in any way to make use of the words of sacred scriptures for these or similar purposes, the council orders and prescribes that all persons in that category, violaters and profaners of the word of God, should be checked by the bishops by legal and imposed penalties.

SESSION 5
17 June 1546

Decree on original sin

The aim of the holy ecumenical and general council of Trent, lawfully assembled in the holy Spirit, with the same three legates of the apostolic see presiding, is that our catholic faith *without which it is impossible to please God* may, after it has been cleansed of errors, remain complete and unsoiled in its integrity, and that the christian people may not be *carried about with every wind of doctrine*. For, amid the many evils by which the church of God is troubled in our times that ancient serpent, the undying enemy of the human race, is stirring up not only new disagreements but also old ones about original sin and its remedy. The council now wishes to call back those who are going astray and to strengthen the hesitant. And so, following the witness of the sacred scriptures, of the holy fathers, and of the most authoritative councils, as well as the agreement and judgment of the church, it determines, confesses and declares as follows with regard to original sin.

1. If anyone does not acknowledge that the first man, Adam, when he acted against God's command in paradise, immediately lost that holiness and justice in which he had been created and, because of the sin of such a transgression, incurred the anger and displeasure of God and consequently death, with which God had previously threatened him, and with death a captivity under the power of him *who,* thenceforth, *had the power of death, that is, the devil;* and that the whole Adam, because of that sinful disobedience, was changed in body and soul for the worse: let him be anathema.

2. If anyone declares that the sin of Adam damaged him alone and not his descendants, and that the holiness and justice received from God, which he lost, he lost for himself alone and not for us; or that, while he was stained by the sin of disobedience, he transmitted only death and bodily pains to the whole human race, but not that sin which is the death of the soul: let him be anathema, for he contradicts the Apostle saying, *Sin came into the world through one man, and death through sin, and so death spread through the whole human race because everyone has sinned.*

3. If anyone asserts that this sin of Adam which, one by origin and passed on to all by propagation and not by imitation, inheres in everyone as something proper to each, is removed by human and natural powers, or by any remedy other than the merit of the one mediator, our lord Jesus Christ who has reconciled us to God in his own blood, being *made our righteousness and sanctification and redemption;* or if anyone denies that the actual merit of Christ Jesus is applied to both adults and infants through the sacrament of baptism duly administered in the form of the church: let him be anathema; for *there is no other name under heaven given among people by which we must be saved.* Hence that saying: *"Behold the Lamb of God, behold him who takes away the sins of the world. And that other: For as many of you as were baptized, have put on Christ.*

4. If anyone says that recently born babies should not be baptized even if they have been born to baptized parents; or says that they are indeed baptized for the remission of sins, but incur no trace of the original sin of Adam needing to be cleansed by the water of rebirth for them to obtain eternal life, with the necessary consequence that in their case there is being understood a form of baptism for the remission of sins which is not true, but false: let him be anathema. For the saying of the Apostle, *Sin came into the world through one man and death through sin, and so death spread through the whole human race because everyone has sinned,* must be understood not otherwise than as the catholic church in its entire extent has always understood it. For, according to the rule of faith transmitted from the apostles, even small children, who could not yet of themselves have committed any kind of sin, are truly baptized for the remission of sins in order that they contracted by generation may be cleansed in them by regeneration. For, *unless one is born again of water and of the holy Spirit, he cannot enter the kingdom of God.*

5. If anyone says that the guilt of original sin is not remitted through the grace of our lord Jesus Christ which is given in baptism, or even asserts that all which pertains to the true essence of sin is not removed, but declares it is only erased and not attributed: let him be anathema. For God hates nothing in the reborn, because there is no condemnation for those who are truly buried with Christ by baptism into death, *who do not walk according to the flesh* but, putting off the old person and putting on the new person created according to God, become innocent, stainless, pure, blameless and beloved children of God, *heirs indeed of God and fellow heirs with Christ,* so that nothing at all impedes their entrance into heaven. The holy council confesses and perceives that in the baptized, concupiscence or a tendency to sin remains; since this is left as a form of testing, it cannot harm those who do not give consent but, by the grace of Christ, offer strong resistance; indeed, *that person will be crowned who competes according to the rules.* This concupiscence the Apostle sometimes calls sin, but the holy council declares that the catholic church has never understood it to be called sin in the sense of being truly and properly such in those who have been regenerated, but in the sense that it is a result of sin and inclines to sin. If anyone holds a contrary view: let him be anathema.

6. The same holy council, however, also declares that it is not its intention to include in this decree, when it is dealing with original sin, the blessed and immaculate virgin Mary, mother of God, but rather that observance must be given to the constitutions of Pope Sixtus IV of happy memory, in accord with the penalties included in those constitutions, which the council renews.

Second decree: on instruction and preaching

1. The same holy council, loyal to the decision of popes and recognized councils, while embracing these and adhering to them, has decided to issue the following decree so as to prevent the heavenly treasure of the sacred books, which the holy Spirit in his supreme generosity has bestowed on us, from being left unnoticed: In those churches where an allowance or benefice or stipend under any other name exists for disposal to those who instruct in sacred theology, bishops, archbishops, primates and other local ordinaries are to oblige and compel, even by a reduction of their income, those who receive such an allowance, benefice or stipend, to give explanations and interpretations of sacred scripture personally if they are competent, and otherwise by a suitable substitute who is to be chosen by the bishops, archbishops, primates and other local ordinaries. In future, however, such an allowance, benefice or stipend is to be bestowed only on competent persons who can personally carry out that function. Any provision made otherwise shall be null and avoid.

PROMULGATIONS OF THE COUNCIL OF TRENT (continued)

2. In metropolitan or cathedral churches, however, if the region is of note and contains many people, and also in collegiate churches which exist in some well known town, even if not belonging to a particular diocese (provided clergy are present in some numbers), where no salaried post or benefice or stipend assigned for this purpose exists, let the salaried post which first becomes vacant, for whatever reason except by resignation, and to which no incompatible duty is attached, be understood to be for ever attached and allotted for that purpose. And if in such churches there should be no endowed post or one which is inadequate, the metropolitan or the actual bishop is to make provision for the required instruction in sacred scripture: this he will provide for, with the advice of his chapter, by assigning the revenue of some simple benefice (the obligations of the same, however, having been provided for), or by contributions from those enjoying privileges in the city or diocese, of from some other source as shall be more conveniently available. However, this has to be arranged so that any other forms of instruction, established by custom or on any other grounds, are in no way omitted.

3. But churches of which the annual income is slight, or where the clergy and people are so few in number that instruction in theology cannot conveniently be provided in them, should have at least a master, who is to be chosen by the bishop with the advice of his chapter, to teach grammar without fee to clerical and other poor students, so that later on, God willing, they will be able to transfer to formal studies in sacred scripture. Therefore, to that master of grammar there should be allotted the income from some simple benefice which he will enjoy so long as he remains in his teaching post (provided, however, that the actual benefice is not deprived of the services due to it); or some appropriate salary should be paid from the chapter's or the bishop's resources; or the bishop himself should enter into some agreement appropriate to his church and diocese, to prevent any neglect under whatever pretext of that pious, useful and beneficial arrangement.

4. In monasteries of monks, too, where it can conveniently be arranged, instruction in sacred scripture should take place. If the abbots are negligent in this matter, the local bishops, as delegates of the apostolic see in this connection, are to compel them to this course by appropriate remedies.

5. In convents of other regulars, however, in which studies can suitably flourish, instruction in sacred scripture is likewise to take place; and this instruction is to be assigned to the more suitably qualified masters by the general or provincial chapters.

6. In public schools where this instruction, so honorable and the most necessary of all, has not so far been established, let it be introduced by the devotion and charity of the most religious princes and governments for the defence and growth of the catholic faith and the preservation and spread of sound doctrine. And where, though once introduced it has been neglected, let it be restored.

7. To prevent impiety being spread under the guise of piety, the same holy council has decided that no one is to be admitted in either a public or a private capacity to this office of giving instruction who has not previously been tested and approved by the local bishop concerning his life, character and knowledge. This, however, is not to be understood as applying to instructors within monastic enclosures.

8. Those giving public teaching in the schools on sacred scripture, and students who attend these same schools, shall fully enjoy and benefit, in the case of absence, from all privileges granted common law with regard to the receipt of the revenues of their endowed posts and benefices.

9. But since the preaching of the gospel is no less necessary than instruction for a christian state, and this is the chief task of the bishops, the same holy council has decided and decreed that all bishops, archbishops, primates and all others who preside over the churches are personally bound, unless legitimately impeded, to preach the holy gospel of Jesus Christ.

10. But if it should happen that the bishops and others mentioned above are hindered by some legitimate restriction, they shall be bound, according to the provision of a general council, to appoint men who are capable of carrying out effectively this duty of preaching. But if anyone treats with contempt the fulfillment of this duty, he is to be subjected to severe penalties.

11. Archpriests also, ordinary priests and any others who have some control over parochial and other churches, and have the care of souls, are to feed with the words of salvation the people committed to their charge. This they should do either personally or, if they are legitimately impeded, through others who are competent, by teaching, at least on Sundays and solemn feasts, according to and their own their hearers' capacity, what it is necessary for all to know with a view to salvation, by proclaiming briefly and with ease of expression the vices they must avoid and the virtues they must cultivate so as to escape eternal punishment and gain the glory of heaven. If any of them fail to provide that teaching, even if for some reason he lays claim to be exempt from the bishop's jurisdiction, and even if the churches are said to be somehow exempt or perhaps attached or united to a monastery which lies outside the diocese, so long as they are actually within a diocese provision of pastoral care from the bishop is not to be lacking, lest that verse be fulfilled: *The children beg for food, and no one gives it to them.* Hence, after a warning from the bishop, if they have failed in their allotted task for a period of three months, they are to be brought under ecclesiastical or other censures at the discretion of the bishop, to the extent that, if it seems to be expedient, a fair compensation is to be paid from the revenues of the benefice to another who takes the respon-

sibility, until the incumbent mends his way and fulfills his own duty.

12. If, however, any parish churches are found subject to monasteries which are not in any diocese, and if the abbots and regular superiors are negligent in the aforesaid matters, they are to be compelled by the metropolitans in whose provinces these same dioceses are situated, who will be acting in this matter as delegates of the apostolic see. The execution of this decree cannot be impeded by any custom or exemption or appeal or protest or recourse, until a competent judge, who shall have proceeded summarily and examined only the truth of the case, shall have made an investigation and given a decision.

13. But regulars of any order may not preach even in the churches of their own order unless they have been tested and approved by their own superiors with respect to their life, moral character and knowledge, and gain their permission; and with that permission they are bound to come in person before the bishops and ask for their blessing before they begin to preach.

14. In churches, however, which do not belong to their own orders they are obliged, in addition to the permission of their own superiors, to have that also of the bishop, without which they may preach in any form in churches not belonging to their own orders. But the bishops are to grant this permission without a fee.

15. But if (which heaven avert) a preacher is sowing errors or scandals among the people, even if he is preaching in a monastery of his own or of another order, the bishop shall forbid him to preach. If he has been preaching heresies, the bishop shall take proceedings against him in accordance with the tenor of the law and the custom of the region, even though the preacher may claim that he is personally exempt by a general or particular privilege. In that case the bishop is to proceed by apostolic authority as delegate of the apostolic see. But bishops should take care that a preacher is not harassed either by false reports or by other calumnies, so that he may have reasonable grounds for complaint against the charges.

16. Moreover, bishops should take precautions not to allow as preachers in their city or diocese any who, though regular in name, are living outside the enclosure and obedience of their own religious institutes, or secular priests (unless they are known to them and of approved moral character and doctrine), even though some kind of privilege is claimed, until there is consultation on the matter with the holy apostolic see, from which it is unlikely that privileges of this kind are extracted by unworthy persons unless by deliberate lying and suppression of the truth.

17. Those soliciting alms (also commonly called fortune-hunters), whatever their status, may in no way claim the right to preach either personally or through another. Those who act against this ruling are to be totally restrained by bishops and local ordinaries making used of suitable preventives, all privileges whatsoever notwithstanding.

SESSION 6
13 January 1547

Decree on justification

Introduction

At this time there has been spread an erroneous doctrine about jurisdiction, with resulting loss of many souls and serious damage to the unity of the church. Because of this, the holy ecumenical and general council of Trent, lawfully assembled in the holy Spirit for the praise and glory of almighty God, the peace of the church, and the salvation of souls, sets down its intention: those presiding in the name of our father and lord in Christ, Paul III by divine providence pope, being John Mary bishop of Palestrina de Monte and Marcellus priest of the holy Cross in Jerusalem, cardinals of the holy Roman church and legates *a latere* of the holy see. Its intention is to set out for all the christian faithful the true and sound doctrine on justification which the sun of justice, Jesus Christ, pioneer and perfecter of our faith, taught, the apostles handed down, and the catholic church under the prompting of the holy Spirit has always retained. This it does by imposing a strict check on anyone who dares to believe, preach or teach otherwise than is defined and declared in the present decree.

Chap. 1. On the powerlessness of nature and law to justify

First of all, for a true and genuine understanding of the doctrine of justification, the holy council declares that everyone must acknowledge and confess that, since all lost their innocence in the sin of Adam, became unclean and (in the words of the Apostle) *by nature children of wrath,* as is set out in the decree on original sin, they were so far slaves of sin and under the power of the devil and death, that not only could the gentiles not be freed from or rise above it by the force of nature, but neither could the Jews even by the letter of the law of Moses, though their free will, for all it had been weakened and sapped in strength, was in no way extinct.

Chap 2. The ordering and the mystery of Christ's coming

Wherefore it came about the Father in heaven, *the Father of mercies and God of all comfort,* when that blessed fullness time came, sent Jesus Christ his Son, announced and promised both before the law and in the time of the law by many holy fathers, in order *to redeem* the Jews *who were under the law* and that *the gentiles who did not pursue righteousness might attain it,* so that all might receive adoption as sons. Him God *put forward as an expiation by his blood, to be received by faith, for our sins, and not for ours only, but also for the sins of the whole world.*

Chap. 3. Who are justified through Christ

But though *he died for all,* yet not all receive the benefit of his death, but only those to whom the merit of this passion is imparted. For just as men and women would not actually be born unjust if they were not bred and born from the seed of Adam, since by that descent they incur through him their own state of injustice while they are being conceived; so, if not reborn in Christ, they would never be justified, because by that rebirth there is granted to them, through the merit of his passion, his grace by which they become just. For this gift the Apostle enjoins on us always to give *thanks to the Father who has qualified us to share in the inheritance of the saints in light. He has delivered us from the dominion of darkness and transferred us to the kingdom of his beloved Son, in whom we have redemption, the forgiveness of sins.*

Chap. 4. Suggested description of the justification of a sinner and its character in the state of grace

By those words there is suggested a description of the justification of a sinner: how there is a transition from that state in which a person is born as a child of the first Adam to the state of grace and of adoption as children of God through the agency of the second Adam, Jesus Christ our savior; indeed, this transition, once the gospel has been promulgated, cannot take place without the waters of rebirth or the desire for them, as it is written: *Unless a person is born again of water and the holy Spirit, he cannot enter the kingdom of God.*

Chap. 5. On the need of preparation for justification in adults and its source

The council further declares that actual justification in adults takes its origin from a predisposing grace of God through Jesus Christ, that is, from his invitation which calls them, with no existing merits on their side; thus, those who had turned away from God by sins are disposed by God's grace inciting and helping them, to turn towards their own justification by giving free assent to and co-operating with this same grace. Consequently, though God touches a person's heart through the light of the holy Spirit, neither does that person do absolutely nothing in receiving that movement of grace, for he can also reject it; nor is he able, by his own free will and without God's grace, to move himself towards justice in God's sight. Hence, when scripture says, *Return to me and I will return to you,* we are being reminded of our freedom; when we answer, *Restore us to yourself, O Lord, that we may be restored,* we are admitting that we are forestalled by the grace of God.

Chap. 6. The manner of preparation

People are disposed for that justice when, roused and helped by divine grace and attaining the faith that comes from hearing, they are moved freely towards God and believe to be true what has been divinely revealed and promised, and in particular that the wicked are justified by God *by his grace through the redemption which is Christ Jesus.* At the same time, acknowledging that they are sinners, they turn from fear of divine justice, which profitability strikes them, to thoughts of God's mercy; they rise to hope, with confidence that God will be favorable to them for Christ's sake; and they begin to love him as the fount of all justness. They are thereby turned against sin by a feeling of hatred and detestation, namely by that repentance which must occur before baptism. Finally, when they are proposing to receive baptism, they are moved to begin a new life and to keep God's commandments. Of this attitude of mind, scripture says: *Whoever would draw near to God must believe that he exists and that he rewards those who seek him;* and, *Take heart, son, your sins are forgiven;* and, *Fear of the Lord drives out sin;* and, *Repent and be baptized every one of you in the name of Jesus Christ for the forgiveness of your sins, and you shall receive the gift of the holy Spirit;* and, *Go, therefore, and make disciples of all nations, baptizing them in the name of the Father, and of the Son, and of the holy Spirit, teaching them to observe all that I have commanded you;* finally, *Direct your hearts to the Lord.*

Chap. 7. What the justification of the sinner is and what are its causes

This disposition and preparation precede the actual justification, which consists not only in the forgiveness of sins but also in the sanctification and renewal of the inward being by a willing acceptance of the grace and gifts whereby someone from being unjust becomes just, from being an enemy becomes a friend, so that he is an heir *in hope of eternal life.* The causes of this justification are: final cause, the glory of God and of Christ, and eternal life; efficient cause, the God of mercy who, of his own free will, washes and sanctifies, placing his seal and anointing with the *promised holy Spirit who is the guarantee of our inheritance;* meritorious cause, his most beloved and only-begotten Son, our lord Jesus Christ who, when we were at enmity with him, *out of the great love with which he loved us,* merited justification for us by his most holy passion on the wood of the cross, and made satisfaction to God the Father on our behalf; instrumental cause, the sacrament of baptism, which is the sacrament of faith, without which justification comes to no one. Finally, the one formal cause is the justness of God: not that by which he himself is just, but that by which he makes us just and endowed with which we are renewed in the spirit of our mind, and are not merely considered to be just but we are truly named and are just, each one of us receiving individually his own justness according to the measure which the holy Spirit apportions to each one as he wills, and in view of each one's dispositions and co-operation. For though no one can be just unless the merits of the passion of our lord Jesus Christ are communicated to him; nevertheless, in the justification of a sinner this in fact takes place when, by the merit of the same most holy passion, the love of God is poured out by the agency of the holy Spirit in the hearts of those who are being justified, and abides in them. Consequently, in the process of justification together with the forgiveness of sins a person receives, through Jesus Christ into whom he is grafted, all these infused at the same time; faith, hope and charity. For faith, unless hope is added to it and charity too, neither unites him perfectly with Christ nor makes him a living member of his body. Hence it is very truly said that faith without works is dead and barren, and in Christ Jesus neither circumcision is of any avail nor uncircumcision, but faith *working through love.* From apostolic tradition, catechumens seek this faith from the church before the sacrament of baptism when they ask for the faith that gives eternal life; and this, without hope and charity, faith cannot give. Consequently, they immediately hear the word of Christ: *If you would enter life, keep the commandments.* Thus, receiving true and christian justness in exchange for that which Adam, by his disobedience, lost for himself and for us, the reborn are immediately ordered to preserve the justice freely granted to them through Jesus Christ in a pure and spotless state like a best robe, so that they may carry it before the tribunal of our lord Jesus Christ and possess eternal life.

Chap. 8. How justification of the sinner freely granted through faith is to be understood

When the Apostle says that a person is justified by faith and as a gift, those words are to be understood in the sense which the perennial consent of the catholic church has maintained and expressed, namely, that we are said to be justified by faith because faith is the first stage of human salvation, the foundation and root of all justification, without which it is impossible to please God and come to the fellowship of his children. And we are said to receive justification as a free gift because nothing that precedes justification, neither faith nor works, would merit the grace of justification, for if it is by grace, it is no longer on the basis of works; otherwise (as the same Apostle says) grace would no longer be grace.

Chap. 9. Against the vain confidence of the heretics

But though it is necessary to believe that sins are not forgiven, nor have they ever been forgiven, save freely by the divine mercy on account of Christ; nevertheless, it must not be said that anyone's sins are or have been forgiven simply because he has a proud assurance and certainty that they have been forgiven, and relies solely on that. For this empty and ungodly assurance may exist among heretics and schismatics, as indeed it does exist in our day, and is preached most controversially against the catholic church. Neither should it be declared that those who are truly justified must determine within themselves beyond the slightest hesitation that they are justified, and that no one is absolved from sin and justified except one who believes with certainly that he has been absolved and justified, and that absolution and justification are effected by this faith alone—as if one who does not believe this is casting doubts on God's promises and on the efficacy of the death and resurrection of Christ. For, just as no devout person ought to doubt the mercy of God, the merit of Christ and the power and efficacy of the sacraments; so it is possible for anyone, while he regards himself and his own weakness and lack of dispositions, to be anxious and fearful about his own state of grace, since no one can know, by that assurance of faith which excludes all falsehood, that he has obtained the grace of God.

Chap. 10. On the increase of justification received

So those justified in this way and made friends and members of the household of God, going from strength to strength, are (as the Apostle says) renewed from day to day by putting to death what is earthly in themselves and yielding themselves as instruments of righteousness for sanctification by observance of the commandments of God and of the church. They grow and increase in that very justness they have received through the grace of Christ, by faith united to good works, as it is written: *Let him who is holy become more holy;* and again, *Do not wait until death to be justified;* again, *you see that a person is justified by works and not by faith alone.* Indeed, holy church asks for this increase in justice when it prays, *Lord, give us an increase in faith, hope and charity.*

Chap. 11. The keeping of the commandments: its necessity and possibility

But no one, however much justified, ought to think that he is exempt from the observance of the commandments, nor should he use that rash statement, forbidden by the fathers under anathema, that the commandments of God are impossible of observance by one who is justified. For God does not command the impossible, but by commanding he instructs you both to do what you can and to pray for what you cannot, and he gives his aid to enable you; for his commandments are not heavy, his yoke is sweet and his burden light. Those who are children of God love Christ; and those who love him (as he himself bears witness) keep his words which, of course, they can do with the divine help. For in this mortal life men and women, however holy and just, will sometimes fall into sin, at least light and everyday sins which are also called venial, but they do not therefore cease to be just. For the voice that says, *Forgive us our trespasses,* is the voice of the just and it is humble and truthful. Hence it is the just who should feel themselves bound to walk in the path of justice all the more because, now that they are *set free from sin and are become slaves of God,* and are living *sober and upright lives,* they can make progress through Jesus Christ, through whom they had access to that state of grace. For God does not abandon those once justified by his grace, unless he is first deserted by them. Therefore, no one should yield to complacency in faith alone, thinking that by faith alone He has been established as an heir, and that he will obtain that inheritance even if he has not suffered with Christ so as to be glorified with him. For (as the Apostle says) even Christ himself, *though he was the Son of God, learned obedience through what he suffered, and being made perfect, he became the source of eternal salvation to all who obey him.* Consequently, the Apostle himself warns those who are justified saying, *Do you not know that in a race all the runners compete, but only one receives the prize; so run that you may obtain it. I do not run aimlessly, I do not box as one beating the air; but I pummel my body and subdue it, lest after preaching to others, I myself should be disqualified.* Likewise Peter, the prince of the apostles: *Be more zealous by good works to confirm your call and election, for if you do this you will never fall.* Hence it is certain that they are opponents of the orthodox teaching of religion who say that in every good work the just person sins at least venially; or (which is more intolerable), that he deserves eternal punishment; likewise, those who hold that the just sin in all their works if, when arousing their sloth and encouraging themselves to run in the race, in addition to the aim that above all God may be glorified, they are also looking to an eternal reward; since it is written: *I have inclined my heart to perform your statutes for the sake of the reward, and the Apostle said of Moses that he looked to the reward.*

Chap. 12. Rash presumption predestination must be avoided

In addition, no one, so long as he remains in the present life, ought so to presume about the hidden mystery of divine predestination as to hold for certain that he is unquestionably of the number of the predestined, as if it were true that one justified is either no longer capable of sin or, if he sins, may promise himself sure repentance. For, apart from a special revelation, it is impossible to know whom God has chosen for himself.

Chap. 13. On the gift of perseverance

Similarly, concerning the gift of perseverance, it is written: *He who endures to the end will be saved* (and, indeed the gift can have no other source save him who has the power to uphold one who stands so that hey may continue, and to restore him who falls). Even though all should place an unshaken hope in God's help and rest in it, let no one promise himself with absolute certainty any definite outcome. For, unless they themselves neglect his grace, as God has begun the good work, so he will bring it to completion, bringing about both the will and the performance. Nevertheless, let those who think themselves to stand, take heed lest they fall, and work out their own salvation with fear and trembling, in labors, watching, almsdeeds, prayers and offerings, in fastings and chastity. For, knowing that they are reborn to the hope of glory, and not yet to glory itself, they ought to tremble about the struggle with the flesh, with the world, with the devil, which still remains and in which they cannot be victors unless, with the grace of God, they do what the Apostle says: *We are debtors, not to the flesh, to live according to the flesh, for if you live according to the flesh you will die; but if by the Spirit you put to death the deeds of the body, you will live.*

Chap. 14. On the fallen and their restoration

Those who fall away by sin from the grace of justification which they had received, can again be justified when at God's prompting they have made the effort through the sacrament of penance to recover, by the merit of Christ, the grace which was lost. For this kind of justification is a restoration of the fallen, which the holy fathers suitably call a second plank for the grace shattered in a storm. It was for the sake of those who fall into sin after baptism that Jesus Christ instituted the sacrament of penance, when he said: *Receive the holy Spirit; if you forgive the sins of any, they are forgiven; and if you retain the sins of any, they are retained.* Hence it must be taught that the repentance of a Christian after a fall is very different from repentance at baptism: it includes not only ceasing from sins and detestation of them, or *a humble and contrite heart,* but also confession of them in the sacrament of penance, to be made at least in desire and in due season, absolution by a priest, and also satisfaction by fasting, almsgiving, prayers and other devout exercises of the spiritual life; these take the place, not indeed of eternal punishment which is remitted together with the guilt either by the sacrament or the desire of the sacrament, but of temporal punishment which (as scripture teaches) is not wholly discharged—as happens in baptism—by those who, lacking gratitude for the grace of God which they have received, have grieved the holy Spirit and not feared to violate the temple of God. Of this repentance it is written: *Remember, then, from what you have fallen; repent and do the works you did at first; and again, For godly grief produces a repentance that leads to salvation and brings no regret; and again, Repent; and, Bear fruit that befits repentance.*

Chap. 15. Grace, but not faith is lost by every mortal sin

It must be asserted, against the subtle modes of thinking of certain people, who *by fair and flattering words deceive the hearts of the simple-minded,* that the grace of justification once received is lost not only by apostasy, by which faith itself is lost, but also by any other mortal sin, though faith is not lost. Thus is defended the teaching of the divine law which excludes from God's kingdom not only unbelievers, but also the faithful if they are guilty of fornication, adultery, wantonness, sodomy, theft, avarice, drunkenness, slander, plundering, and all others who commit mortal sins from which, with the help of divine grace, they can refrain, and because of which they are severed from the grace of Christ.

Chap. 16. On the fruit of justification, namely merit from good works, and on the nature of that merit

Hence, to those justified by this means, whether they have continued to preserve the grace received or have recovered it once lost, the words of the Apostle should be addressed: *Always abound in the work of the Lord, knowing that in the Lord your labor is not in vain. For God is not so unjust as to overlook your work and the love which you showed for his sake. And, Do not throw away your confidence, which has a great reward.* Thus, to those who work well right to the end and keep their trust in God, eternal life should be held out, both as a grace promised in his mercy through Jesus Christ to the children of God, and as a reward to be faithfully bestowed, on the promise of God himself, for their good works and merits. This, then, is that crown of righteousness which the Apostle says is laid up for him after his fight and his race, and will be awarded by the righteous judge not only to him but to all who love his appearing. For Jesus Christ himself continually imparts strength to those justified, as the head to the members and the vine to the branches, and this strength always precedes, accompanies and follows their good works, and without it they would be wholly unable to do anything meritorious and pleasing to God; hence it must be believed that nothing more is needed for the justified to be considered to have fully satisfied God's law, according to this state of life, by the deeds they have wrought in him and to have truly deserved to gain eternal life in their time (provided they die in a state of grace). For Christ our savior says: *Whoever drinks of the water that I shall give him will never thirst, but it will become in him a spring of water welling up to eternal life.* Thus our own personal justice is not established as something coming from us, nor is the justice of God disregarded or rejected; what is called our justice, because we are justified by its abiding in us, is that same justice of God, in that it is imparted to us by God through the merit of Christ. However, it must not be overlooked that, though so much is attributed in scripture to good works (Christ indeed promises that anyone who gives a cup of cold water to one of the least of his little ones will not lack his reward; and the Apostle bears witness: *This slight momentary affliction is preparing for us an eternal weight of glory beyond comparison),* yet no Christian should ever either rely on or glory in himself and not in the Lord, whose goodness towards all is so great that he desires his own gifts to be their merits. And because *we all make many mistakes,* each of us ought to keep before his eyes the severity and judgment as much as the mercy and goodness; and even if he is not aware of anything in himself, a person ought not to pronounce judgment on himself, for our whole life must be examined and judged not by our judgment but by that of God, *who will bring to light the things now hidden in darkness and disclose the purposes of the heart; then everyone will receive his commendation from God, who, as it is written, will render to everyone according to his works.*

After this catholic teaching about justification—and unless each one faithfully and firmly accepts it, he cannot be justified—the holy council decided to attach these canons, so that all may know not only what they must hold and obey, but what they must totally avoid.

Canons concerning justification

1. If anyone says that a person can be justified before God by his own works, done either by the resources of human nature or by the teaching of the law, apart from divine grace through Jesus Christ: let him be anathema.

2. If anyone says that divine grace through Jesus Christ is given solely to enable a person to live justly and to merit eternal life more easily, as if each could be done through free will without grace, even though with a struggle and with difficulty: let him be anathema.

3. If anyone says that, without preceding inspiration of the holy Spirit and without his help, a person can believe, hope, love and repent, as he ought, so that the grace of justification may be granted to him: let him be anathema.

4. If anyone says that a person's free will when moved and roused by God, gives no co-operation by responding to God's summons and invitation to dispose and prepare itself to obtain the grace of justification; and that it cannot, if it so wishes, dissent but, like something inanimate, can do nothing at all and remains merely passive: let him be anathema.

5. If anyone says that, after the sin of Adam, human free will was lost and blotted out, or that its existence is purely nominal, a name without substance, indeed a fiction introduced into the church by Satan: let him be anathema.

6. If anyone says that it is not in human power to adopt evil ways, but that God is the agent for evil acts just as for good, not only by permitting them but also in a full sense and by personal act, so that the betrayal of Judas no less than the call of Paul is an act fully his: let him be anathema.

7. If anyone says that all acts be done prior to justification, no matter for what reason, are either truly sins or deserve God's hatred; or that the more earnestly one strives to dispose oneself for grace, the more gravely does one sin: let him be anathema.

8. If anyone says that the fear of hell, because of which we seek refuge in God's mercy by expressing sorrow for sins, or refrain from committing sin, is itself a sin or makes sinners worse: let him be anathema.

9. If anyone says that the sinner is justified by faith alone, meaning thereby that no other co-operation is required for

him to obtain the grace of justification, and that in no sense is it necessary for him to make preparation and be disposed by a movement of his own will: let him be anathema.

10. If anyone says that people are justified without the justice of Christ by which he gained merit for us; or that they are formally just by his justness itself: let him be anathema.

11. If anyone says that people are justified either solely by the attribution of Christ's justice, or by the forgiveness of sins alone, to the exclusion of the grace and charity which is poured forth in their hearts by the holy Spirit and abides in them; or even that the grace by which we are justified is only the good-will of God: let him be anathema.

12. If anyone says that the faith which justifies is nothing else both trust in the divine mercy, which pardons sins because of Christ; or that it is that trust alone by which we are justified: let him be anathema.

13. If anyone says that to secure pardon of his sins, everyone must believe, with certainty and without any hesitation about his own weakness and lack of dispositions, that his sins have been forgiven: let him be anathema.

14. If anyone says that a person is absolved from sins and is justified by the fact that he certainly believes he is absolved and justified; or that no one is truly justified except one who believes that he is justified, and that by that faith alone are forgiveness and justification effected: let him be anathema.

15. If anyone says that a person reborn and justified is bound to believe as a matter of faith that he is certainly in the number of the predestined: let him be anathema.

16. If anyone says with absolute and infallible certitude (unless he shall have learned this by special revelation) that he will certainly have that great gift of final perseverance: let him be anathema.

17. If anyone says that the grace of justification is the lot only of those predestined to life, but that all the rest who are called are indeed called, but do not receive the grace, as they are predestined to evil by God's power: let him be anathema.

18. If anyone says that the commandments of God are impossible of observance even by a person justified and established in grace: let him be anathema.

19. If anyone says that in the gospel nothing but faith is prescribed, while other matters are indifferent, neither described nor forbidden, but free; or that the ten commandments in no way apply to Christians: let him be anathema.

20. If anyone says that a justified person, of whatever degree of perfection, is not bound to keep the commandments of God and of the church but only to believe, as if the gospel were simply a bare and unqualified promise of eternal life

without the condition of observing the commandments: let him be anathema.

21. If anyone says that Jesus Christ was given to men and women by God as a redeemer to trust, and not also as a lawgiver to obey: let him be anathema.

22. If anyone says either that one justified can persevere in the justice received without the special help of God; or that, even with that help, he cannot: let him anathema.

23. If anyone says that a person, once justified, cannot sin any more or lose grace, and therefore that one who falls and sins has never been truly justified; or, on the other hand (apart from a special privilege from God such as the church holds in the case of the blessed Virgin), that he can avoid all sins, even venial sins, throughout his life: let him be anathema.

24. If anyone says that justice once received is neither preserved nor increased in the sight of God by good works, but that the works themselves are no more than the effects and signs of the justification obtained, and not also a cause of its increase: let him be anathema.

25. If anyone says that in any good work a just person sins at least venially, or (which is more intolerable) mortally, and thus deserves eternal punishments, and is not thereby damned only because God does not impute those works unto damnation: let him be anathema.

26. If anyone says that the just ought not, in return for good works wrought in God, to expect and hope for an eternal reward from God through his mercy and the merit of Jesus Christ, if by acting rightly and keeping the divine commandments they persevere to the end: let him be anathema.

27. If anyone says that there is no mortal sin save that of unbelief; or that grace, once received, is lost by no other sin, however serious and enormous, than that of unbelief: let him be anathema.

28. If anyone says that when grace is lost by sin, faith too is always lost; or that the faith that remains is not true faith, even if it is not a living faith; or that one who has faith without charity is not a Christian: let him be anathema.

29. If anyone says that one who has fallen after baptism cannot rise again by the grace of God; or that he can recover the lost justice by faith alone, and without the sacrament of penance as the holy Roman and universal church, taught by Christ and his apostles, has to this day professed, maintained and taught: let him be anathema.

30. If anyone says that once the grace of justification has been received, the fault of any repentant sinner is forgiven and the debt of eternal punishment is wiped out, in such a way that no debt of temporal punishment remains to be discharged, either in this world or later on in purgatory, before entry to the kingdom of heaven can lie open: let him be anathema.

31. If anyone says that a justified person commits sin when he does something good with a view to an eternal reward: let him be anathema.

32. If anyone says that the good deeds of a justified person are the gifts of God, in the sense that they are not also the good merits of the one justified; or that the justified person, by the good deeds done by him through the grace of God and the merits of Jesus Christ (of whom he is a living member), does not truly merit an increase in grace, eternal life, and (so long as he dies in grace) the obtaining of his own eternal life, and even an increase in glory: let him be anathema.

33. If anyone says that this catholic doctrine concerning justification, set out in this present decree by the holy council, detracts in any way from the glory of God or the merits of Jesus Christ our Lord, and does not rather make clear the truth of our faith, and the glory alike of God and of Jesus Christ: let him be anathema.

Decree on the residence of bishops and others of lower rank

Chapter 1

The same holy council, with the same presidents and legates of the apostolic see, desiring to gird itself to restore ecclesiastical discipline, which to a considerable extent has collapsed, and to correct depraved customs among both clergy and christian people, has decided to take as its starting point those who have control over the more important churches: *for the integrity of the rulers is the salvation of the subjects.* Consequently, the council trusts by the mercy of our Lord and God and the prudent skill of the vicar of God on earth that the governing of the churches (a task to be dreaded even for the shoulders of angels), in accord with the venerable ordinances of the blessed fathers, that those will surely be chosen who are most worthy and whose life hitherto, at every stage from early boyhood up till more mature years, gives witness of services to ecclesiastical discipline carried out in a praiseworthy manner. It warns, and wishes to consider under warning, all who by whatever name or title have charge of patriarchal, primatial, metropolitan and cathedral churches: they are to attend to themselves and to *all the flock in which the holy Spirit has placed them, to feed the church of God which he obtained with his own blood,* and, as the Apostle enjoins, to watch, to do their work in all things and to fulfil their proper ministry. They should know that they can never fulfil that duty if, like hirelings, they abandon the flocks committed to them and completely neglect the guardianship of their flocks, whose blood will be required at their hands by the supreme judge, since it is most certain that the shepherd's excuse is not accepted if the wolves devour the sheep and the shepherd knows it not. Nevertheless, at this time there are found (a fact much to be deplored) some who are forgetful of their own salvation and, preferring things of earth to those of heaven, and human to divine, wander around various courts, or keep themselves occupied in caring for temporal affairs (while the flock is abandoned and the sheep entrusted to them neglected). Hence the holy council has decided to renew, as it now renews by the present decree, the ancient canons (which by the disorder of the times and of people have all but fallen into disuse) promulgated against absentees; and further, for the more stable residence of the same and the reform of conduct in the church, to establish and decree in the following manner:

If anyone, no matter by what dignity, rank or preeminence he may be distinguished, is absent from a church—patriarchal, primatial, metropolitan or cathedral—committed to him by whatever title, cause, name or right, by dwelling without lawful impediment or just and reasonable explanation for six unbroken months outside his own diocese, he incurs immediately by law the forfeiture of a quarter of one year's revenue, to be applied by one of higher ecclesiastical rank to the church treasury and to the poor of the place. But if he continues in an absence of this kind for another six months, he will automatically lose another quarter of his revenue, to be disposed of in a similar manner. If, however, his obstinacy goes farther, he must be subjected to the more severe penalty of the sacred canons thus: the metropolitan with regard to absentee bishops, the oldest suffragan in residence with regard to an absent metropolitan, under penalty automatically incurred of being forbidden entry into the church, is obliged within three months to denounce them by letter or messenger to the Roman pontiff, so that he may take action by the authority of his supreme see against those absentees, as the degree of contumacy of each demands, and provide for those churches more useful shepherds according as he knows in the Lord is fitting for salvation.

Chapter 2

Those below the rank of bishop, when by title or favor they hold ecclesiastical benefices which by law or by custom demand personal residence, are to be compelled by their ordinaries by suitable legal measures to reside (according as shall seem expedient for the good ordering of the churches and the increase of divine worship, after due consideration of the condition of places and persons); and no one is to be favored by privileges or permanent indults with respect to non-residence or to the reception of revenue while absent. Temporary concessions and dispensations, however, granted only for true and reasonable causes and legally proved before the ordinary, will retain their force; nevertheless, in these cases it is the duty of the bishops (as delegates of the apostolic see in this matter (to ensure that the care of souls is in no way neglected, by assigning suitable substitutes and allotting them an appropriate part of the revenue; in this matter no privilege or exemption of any kind is to avail anyone.

Chapter 3

Those in charge of churches are to strive prudently and diligently to correct the infringements of their subjects; and no secular cleric under pretext of any personal privilege, or regular living outside his monastery even under pretext of a privilege of his order, is to be thought exempt, if he is at fault, from being able to be examined, punished and corrected, in accordance with canonical ordinances, by the ordinary of the place (as delegated in this matter by the apostolic see).

Chapter 4

Chapter of cathedrals and of other major churches, and the members of the same, are not able to protect themselves by any exemptions, customs, legal decisions, oaths, or agreements (which cover only those initially concerned and not their successors), from the possibility of being visited, corrected and emended, even by apostolic authority, as often as it shall be needful, in accordance with canonical ordinances, by their own bishops and other major prelates, personally by themselves, or by those they choose to attach to themselves.

Chapter 5

No bishop, under pretext of any privilege whatsoever, may lawfully carry out pontifical functions in another's diocese except with the express permission of the ordinary of the place, and only one persons subject to that ordinary; if it should be done otherwise, the bishop is automatically suspended from the exercise of a bishop's functions, and those so ordained by him from the exercise of their orders.

SESSION 7
3 March 1547

First decree [On the sacraments]

Introduction

For the completion of the doctrine of salvation concerning justification which was promulgated at the immediately preceding session by the unanimous consent of the fathers, there was general agreement to treat the most holy sacraments of the church by means of which all true justness either begins, or once received gains strength, or if lost is restored. Therefore the holy, ecumenical and general council of Trent, lawfully assembled in the holy Spirit, with the same legates of the apostolic see presiding, set as its aim the removal of errors and the rooting out of heresies, which have arisen at the present time concerning the most holy sacraments: some, which have revived, concern heresies condemned in the past by our fathers; others more recently devised greatly oppose the purity of the catholic church and the salvation of souls. By adhering to the teaching of the holy scriptures, the apostolic traditions, and the common opinion of other councils and of the fathers, this council has established and formally decreed the canons here set out; later (with the help of the divine Spirit) it will publish others which remain for the completion of the work begun.

Canons on the sacraments in general

1. If anyone says that the sacraments of the new law were not all instituted by our lord Jesus Christ; or that there are more or fewer than seven: namely, baptism, confirmation, eucharist, penance, last anointing, order, matrimony; or that one or other of these seven is not truly in the full sense a sacrament: let him be anathema.

2. If anyone says that those same sacraments of the new law are no different from the sacraments of the old law, except by reason of a difference in ceremonies and in external rites: let him be anathema.

3. If anyone says that these seven sacraments are so equal to each other that on no ground is one of greater dignity than another: let him be anathema.

4. If anyone says that the sacraments of the new law are not necessary for salvation but are superfluous, and that

people obtain the grace of justification from God without them or a desire for them, by faith alone, though all are not necessary for each individual: let him be anathema.

5. If anyone says that these sacraments have been instituted only to nourish faith: let him be anathema.

6. If anyone says that the sacraments of the new law do not contain the grace which they signify; or do not confer that grace on those who place no obstacle in the way, as if they were only external signs of grace or justice received by faith, and some kind of mark of the christian profession by which believers are distinguished from unbelievers in the eyes of the people: let him be anathema.

7. If anyone says that grace is not given by sacraments of this kind always and to all, as far as depends on God, even if they duly receive them, but only sometimes and to some: let him be anathema.

8. If anyone says that grace is not conferred by the sacraments of the new law through the sacramental action itself, but that faith in the divine promise is by itself sufficient for obtaining the grace: let him be anathema.

9. If anyone says that in the three sacraments, namely, baptism, confirmation and order, a character, namely a spiritual and indelible mark, is not imprinted on the soul, because of which they cannot be repeated: let him be anathema.

10. If anyone says that all Christians have the power to exercise the ministry of the word and of all sacraments: let him be anathema.

11. If anyone says that, when ministries effect or confer the sacraments, they do not need the intention of at least doing what the church does: let him be anathema.

12. If anyone says that a minister in a state of mortal sin, even if he observes all the essentials which belong to the effecting or administering of a sacrament, does not effect or administers it: let him be anathema.

13. If anyone says that the received and approved rites of the catholic church in customary use in the solemn administration of the sacraments may, without sin, be neglected or omitted at choice by the ministers, or can be changed to other new ones by any pastor whatever: let him be anathema.

Canons on the sacrament of baptism

1. If anyone says that the baptism of John had the same effect as the baptism of Christ: let him be anathema.

2. If anyone says that true and natural water is not a necessary element in baptism, and therefore twists those words of our lord Jesus Christ, *unless one is born of water and*

the holy Spirit, into some form of metaphor: let him be anathema.

3. If anyone says that in the Roman church (which is the mother and mistress of all the churches) there is not the true teaching on the sacrament of baptism: let him be anathema.

4. If anyone says that the baptism which is given by heretics in the name of the Father and of the Son and of the holy Spirit, with the intention of doing what the church does, is not a true baptism: let him be anathema.

5. If anyone says that baptism is optional, namely that it is not necessary for salvation: let him be anathema.

6. If anyone says that one who is baptized cannot, even if he wishes, lose grace however much he sins, unless he refuses to believe: let him be anathema.

7. If anyone says that those baptized are obliged to faith alone, but not to the observance of the whole law of Christ: let him be anathema.

8. If anyone says that those baptized are exempt from all the precepts of holy church, whether they are in writing or handed down, so that they are not bound to observe them, unless of their own free will they wish to submit themselves to them: let him be anathema.

9. If anyone says that people must be recalled to the memory of the baptism they received, thereby understanding that all vows made after baptism become of no effect by the force of the promise already made in their actual baptism, as if such vows detract from the faith they have professed and from the baptism itself: let him be anathema.

10. If anyone says that, solely by the remembrance of receiving baptism and of its faith, all sins committed after baptism are forgiven or become venial: let him be anathema.

11. If anyone says that, if anyone has denied the faith of Christ among unbelievers, his true and rightly conferred baptism must be repeated when he has turned back to repentance: let him be anathema.

12. If anyone says that no one should be baptized except at that age at which Christ was baptized, or at the point of death: let him be anathema.

13. If anyone says that little children, because they make no act of faith, should not after the reception of baptism be numbered among the faithful; and that, therefore, when they reach the age of discretion, they should be re-baptized; or that it is better than their baptism be omitted than that they be baptized while believing not by their own faith but by the faith of the church alone: let him be anathema.

14. If anyone says that, when they grow up, those baptized as little children should be asked whether they wish to ratify

what their godparents promised in their name when they were baptized; and that, when they reply that they have no such wish, they should be left to their own decision and not, in the meantime, coerced by any penalty into the christian way of life, except that they be barred from the reception of the eucharist and the other sacraments, until they have a change of heart: let him be anathema.

Canons on the sacrament of confirmation

1. If anyone says that confirmation of the baptized is an empty ceremony, and not rather a true and proper sacrament; or that at one time it was nothing but a form of religious instruction in which those approaching adolescence presented an account of their faith publicly to the church: let him be anathema.

2. If anyone says that they are slighting the holy Spirit who assign some special power to the holy chrism of confirmation: let him be anathema.

3. If anyone says that the ordinary minister of holy confirmation is not a bishop only but any simple priest: let him be anathema.

Second decree: On reform

The same holy council, with the same legates presiding, intending to follow up for the praise of God and the growth of the christian religion the work which had been begun concerning residence and reform, judged that what follows should be set down, subject always on all points to the authority of the apostolic see.

1. No one is to be accepted for the administration of cathedral churches unless he is of legitimate birth, of mature age, and endowed with sound moral character and education, in accordance with the constitution of Alexander III which begins *Cum in cunctis* and was promulgated at the Lateran council.

2. No one, no matter of what distinction of rank, status or preeminence, may presume, contrary to what is set down in the sacred canons, to accept and retain at the same time several metropolitan or cathedral churches by title or by gift or by any other claim, since that person must be thought very fortunate who is able to rule one church well and fruitfully and for the salvation of the souls entrusted to him. Those who now have possession of several churches, contrary to the sense of the present decree, after one at their choice has been retained, are obliged within a period of six months to resign from others if they are at the free disposal of the apostolic see, and from the rest within a year; otherwise the churches themselves (the one last obtained alone being excepted) are automatically to be reckoned vacant.

3. Lesser ecclesiastical benefices, especially those involving the care of souls, are to be conferred on worthy and competent persons such as can reside in the place and carry out personally the care of souls in accordance with

the constitution of Alexander III which begins *Quia nonnulli,* issued at the Lateran council, and that other of Gregory X which begins *Licet canon,* issued at the general council of Lyons. Any other appointment or provision made, however, is completely void; and let the ordinary who made the appointment know that he will be faced with the penalties of the general council's constitution which begins *Grave nimis.*

4. For the rest, whoever presumes to accept and to hold simultaneously several charges of otherwise incompatible benefices, either by way of union for life or as a perpetual gift or by any other name or title, in conflict with the design of the sacred canons, and especially of the constitution of Innocent III which begins *De multa,* shall now stand deprived in law of those benefices, in accordance with the terms of that constitution as well as by the force of the present canon.

5. Let local ordinaries strictly compel those who hold several charges or otherwise incompatible ecclesiastical benefices to show their dispensations, and in other situations proceed in accordance with the constitution of Gregory X issued at the general council of Lyons which begins *Ordinarii,* which this same holy council considers should be renewed, and now renews with the addition that the ordinaries themselves are unfailingly to provide, by a chosen group of competent vicars an assignment of an appropriate part the revenues, that the care of souls be in no sense neglected and the benefices themselves in no way deprived of the services due to them. In the matters just indicated, no one may claim support from appeals, privileges or exemptions of any kind, even with the appointment of special judges with powers of injunction.

6. Perpetual unions of benefices within the last forty years are liable for examination by the ordinaries as delegates of the apostolic see, and those which were obtained by stealth or deception shall be declared void. Those which were granted within the said period, but have not yet wholly or in part been given effect, shall be presumed to have been obtained by deceitful means, as well as any made in the future at the request of anyone, unless it is established that they have been created for lawful or otherwise reasonable causes, which are to be verified in the presence of the ordinary, after those who have an interest have been summoned. Therefore (unless a contrary decision shall have come from the apostolic see) they shall completely lack force.

7. Ecclesiastical benefices involving the care of souls, which are found to be permanently united with and linked to cathedral, collegiate and other churches or monasteries, benefices or colleges or holy places of any kind, are to be visited every year by the local ordinaries, who are to ensure that there is careful provision that the care of souls is carried out in a praiseworthy manner by means of competent vicars, even perpetual (unless the ordinaries judge it expedient to arrange otherwise for the good government of the churches), and these will be appointed by them with a portion of the revenues, even that destined for a particular purpose—a third or a greater or lesser part

as the bishops will decide. In the matters just indicated, no one may claim support from appeals, privileges or exemptions, even with the appointment of judges with powers of injunction of any kind.

8. Local ordinaries will be obliged to visit each year with apostolic authority churches, no matter how exempt, and by appropriate legal means to make provision that any repairs which are necessary are carried out, and that the churches are not deprived of the care of souls, if this applies to them, or of other services due to them: with a total exclusion of appeals, privileges, customs, even with prescription from time immemorial, or the appointment of judges with powers of injunction.

9. Those promoted to major churches are to receive the rite of consecration within the time fixed by law; and no one may claim support for a grant of delay beyond six months.

10. When a see is vacant it shall not be lawful for chapters of churches within a year from the day of vacancy to grant, either by terms of the common law or by force of any kind of privilege or custom, permission for ordination, or letters dimissorial or testimony (as some call them), to anyone not under pressure by reason of an ecclesiastical benefices received or about to be received. If contrary action be taken, the chapter contravening the law shall be subjected to ecclesiastical interdict; and those ordained on those terms, if they have been raised to minor orders, enjoy no privilege of clerics, particularly in criminal matters; but it so major orders, they are automatically suspended from the exercise of them according to the good pleasure of the future prelate.

11. There is to be no granting of faculties for promotion to orders by anyone except to those who have a legitimate reason why they cannot be ordained by their own bishops; this reason must be set down in writing, and then they shall not be ordained save by a bishop resident in his own diocese, or by one carrying out episcopal functions on his behalf, and after a careful examination.

12. Faculties concerning non-advancement shall be valid for one year only, except when granted in cases defined by law.

13. Those presented or elected or nominated by no matter which ecclesiastical persons, including nuncios of the apostolic see, shall not be established or confirmed in, or admitted to, any kind of ecclesiastical benefice, under pretext of some privilege or custom even with prescription from time immemorial, unless they have first been examined by the local ordinaries and found suitable; and no one shall be able to protect himself, by recourse to an appeal, from the obligation of undergoing the examination. Exceptions, however, are granted to those presented, elected or nominated by universities or colleges of general studies.

14. In cases of exempt persons, the constitution of Innocent IV which begins Volentes, issued at the general council of Lyons, is to be observed, and this same holy council judges it should be renewed, and does renew it. It makes the further addition that, in civil cases about wages and concerning needy persons, secular clerics, and regulars living outside their monasteries however exempt, even in cases where they have a definite judge of their case appointed by the apostolic see, and in other cases where they have no such judge, can be brought before local ordinaries, as delegated in this matter by the apostolic see, and can be constrained and compelled by lawful means to pay their debt. No force at all is to be given to privileges or exemptions, or bodies appointed to defend privileges, or their powers of injunction, that are opposed to the above directives.

15. Ordinaries shall take care that hospices of all kinds are managed by their administrators, by whatever name they may be called or in whatever manner exempt, with fidelity and diligence, observance being given to the terms of the constitution of the council of Vienne which begins *Quia contingit*. Indeed, this same holy council judged that constitution should be renewed, and does renew it with the limitations therein contained.

SESSION 13
11 October 1551

Decree on the most holy sacrament of the eucharist

The holy ecumenical and general council of Trent, lawfully assembled in the holy Spirit, and having as presidents the same legate and nuncios of the holy apostolic see, has come together under the special guidance and direction of the holy Spirit in order that it may set out the true and ancient teaching faith and the sacrament, and supply a remedy for all the heresies and other serious troubles by which the church is now miserably disturbed and torn apart in a great variety of divisions; yet it had among its chief aims right from the beginning to tear up root and branch the tares of those detestable errors and schisms which the enemy in these calamitous times has own in the teaching of faith in the most holy eucharist and its use and liturgy, the very sacraments which the Savior left in his church as a symbol of its unity and love, whereby he wished all Christians to be mutually linked and united. Consequently, the same most holy council, handing on that sound and uncontaminated teaching concerning this venerable and divine sacrament of the eucharist which the catholic church, instructed by our lord Jesus Christ himself and his apostles, and taught by the holy Spirit as he daily proposes to her all truth, has always retained and will preserve till the end of the world, prohibits all Christians from venturing to believe, teach or preach otherwise concerning the most holy eucharist than as has been explained and defined in this present decree.

Chap. 1. On the real presence of our lord Jesus Christ in the most holy sacrament of the eucharist

In the first place, the holy council teaches and openly and without qualification professes that, after the consecration of the bread and the wine, our lord Jesus Christ, true God and true man, is truly, really and substantially contained in the propitious sacrament of the holy eucharist under the appearance of those things which are perceptible to the senses. Nor are the two assertions incompatible, that our Savior is ever seated at the right hand of the Father in his natural mode of existing, and that he is nevertheless sacramentally present to us by his substance in many other places in a mode of existing which, though we can hardly express it in words, we can grasp with minds enlightened by faith as possible to God and must most firmly believe. For thus did all our forefathers, as many as were in the true church of Christ and treated of this most holy sacrament, most clearly profess: namely, that our Redeemer at the last supper instituted this so admirable sacrament when he bore witness in express and unambiguous words that, after the blessing of the bread the wine, he was offering to them his own body and his own blood. Since those words, recorded by the holy evangelists and afterwards repeated by St. Paul, bear that proper and very clear meaning, which the fathers understood them to have, it is surely a most intolerable and shameful deed for some base and argumentative persons to twist them to false and imaginary meanings that deny the reality of Christ's flesh and blood, against the universal understanding of the church which, *as the pillar and bulwark of the truth,* detests these contrived theories of evil people as the work of the devil, and constantly recalls and confesses with gratitude this outstanding favor of Christ.

Chap. 2. *The reason for the institution of this most holy sacrament*

Therefore, our Savior, about to depart from this world to the Father, instituted this sacrament in which he as it were poured out the riches of his divine love towards humanity, *causing his wonderful works to be remembered,* and he bade us cherish his memory as we partook of it and *to proclaim his death until he comes* to judge the world. He wished this sacrament to be taken as the spiritual food of souls, to nourish and strengthen them as they lived by his life who said, *he who eats me will live because of me,* and as an antidote to free us from daily faults and preserve us from mortal sins. He further wished it to be a pledge of our future glory and unending happiness, and thus a sign of that one body of which he is the head and to which he wished us all to be united as members by the closest bonds of faith, hope and love, so that we should all speak with one voice and there might be no division among us.

Chap. 3. *On the excellence of the most holy eucharist over the other sacraments*

There is indeed this which is common to the most holy eucharist along with the other sacraments: it is a sign of sacred reality and the visible form of invisible grace. But in there is found the excelling and unique quality that, whereas the other sacraments first have the force of sanctifying at the moment when one uses them, in the eucharist the author of holiness himself is present before their use. For the apostles had not yet received the eucharist from the hand of the Lord when he declared with all truth that it was his own body which he was offering. And it has at all times been the belief in the church of God that immediately after the consecration the true body of our Lord and his true blood exist along with his soul and divinity under the form of bread and wine. The body is present under the form of bread and the blood under the form of bread and the blood under the form of wine, by virtue of the words.

The same body, however, is under the form of wine and blood under the form of bread, and the soul under either form, by virtue of that natural link and concomitance by which the parts of Christ the Lord, who has now risen from the dead and will die no more, are mutually united. The divinity, too, is present by that marvelous hypostatic union with his body and soul. Hence it is entirely true that as much is contained under one of the forms as under both; for Christ exists whole and entire under the form of bread and under any part of that form, and likewise whole under the form of wine and under its parts.

Chap. 4. *On transubstantiation*

But since Christ our redeemer said that it was truly his own body which he was offering under the form of bread, therefore there has always been complete conviction in the church of God—and so this holy council now declares it once again—that, by the consecration of the bread and wine, there takes place the change of the whole substance of the bread into the substance of the body of Christ our Lord, and of the whole substance of the wine into the substance of his blood. And the holy catholic church has suitably and properly called this change transubstantiation.

Chap. 5. *On the worship and reverence to be shown to this most holy sacrament*

Hence there is no room for doubting that all Christians, by a custom always accepted in the catholic church, should reverently express for this most holy sacrament the worship of adoration which is due to the true God. For it is not less worthy of adoration because it was instituted by Christ the Lord in order to be consumed. For we believe that the same God is present therein of whom the eternal Father declared when introducing him into the created world, *Let all God's angels worship him;* he whom the Magi, falling down, worshipped; he who, finally, as the scriptures bear witness, was adored by the apostles in Galilee. The holy council further declares that it was with true religious devotion that the custom was introduced into the church of God whereby every year, on a special fixed day of festival, this sublime and venerable sacrament should be hailed with particular veneration and solemnity, and carried with reverence and honor in processions through streets and public places. For it is most reasonable that some days have been set aside on which all Christians may manifest, with some noteworthy and unusual tokens, their thoughts of gratitude and remembrance towards the Lord and redeemer they share, for a favor so much beyond words and clearly divine by which his victory and triumph over death are recalled. And thus indeed must truth, the victor, celebrate a triumph over falsehood and heresy so that, confronted with so much splendor and such great joy of the universal church, her enemies weakened and broken may fall into decline or, touched by shame and confounded, may in time come to repentance.

Chap. 6. *On reserving the sacrament of the holy eucharist and taking it to the sick*

The custom of reserving the eucharist in a sacred place is so ancient that even the age of the council of Nicaea recognized it. In addition, the practice of carrying the holy eucharist to the sick, and hence its careful reservation for that purpose in the

PROMULGATIONS OF THE COUNCIL OF TRENT (continued)

churches, is not only consonant with right and proper understanding, but can be shown to be enjoined in may councils, and has been observed by long-standing custom of the catholic church. And so this holy council rules that this salutary and necessary practice is to be universally retained.

Chap. 7. On the preparation to be observed for the worthy reception of the holy eucharist

If it is unfitting for anyone to approach any sacred functions except in a spirit of holiness, then surely the more the sacred quality and divinity of this heavenly sacrament are understood by a Christian, the more carefully ought he or she to be on guard against approaching to receive it without great reverence and holiness, especially since we read those awesome words of the Apostle: *anyone who eats and drinks unworthily without discerning the body of the Lord, eats and drinks judgement upon himself.* Consequently anyone desiring to communicate should be reminded of his injunction: *let a person examine himself.* The practice of the church declares that examination necessary, so that no one who is aware of personal mortal sin, however contrite he may feel, should approach the holy eucharist without first having made a sacramental confession. The holy council has decreed that this practice should always be retained by all Christians, even by those priests who may have the obligation to celebrate mass, so long as they do not lack an available confessor. But if a priest should celebrate in urgent need without previous confession, let him confess at the first opportunity.

Chap. 8. On the use of this wonderful sacrament

With respect to the use, however, our fathers rightly and wisely distinguished three types of reception of this holy sacrament. For they taught that some, being sinners, receive it only sacramentally; others receive only spiritually, namely those who have the desire to eat the heavenly food that is set before them, and so experience its effect and benefit by a lively *faith working through love;* the third group, who receive both sacramentally and spiritually, are those who so test and train themselves beforehand, that they approach this divine table clothed in a wedding garment. In the reception of the sacrament, there has always been a custom in the church of God that the laity receive communion from priests, but that priests, when celebrating, administer communion to themselves; this custom, coming down as from apostolic tradition, should rightly and deservedly be retained. Finally, the holy council with true paternal affection enjoins, exhorts, begs and entreats *through the tender mercy of our God* that each and all who are marked by the name of Christian should now, at long last, join together and agree in this sign of unity, this bond of love, this symbol of harmony; and that, mindful of the so great majesty and surpassing love of our lord Jesus Christ, who gave his own dear life as the price of our salvation and his own flesh for us to eat, they should believe and reverence these sacred mysteries of his body and blood with such constancy and firmness of faith, such dedication of mind, such devotion and worship, that they may be able to receive frequently that life-supporting bread, and that it may be for them truly the life of the soul and the unending health of the mind; thus, strengthened by its

force, may they be able after the journey of this wretched pilgrimage to reach the heavenly fatherland, there to eat without veil the same bread of angels which they now eat beneath the sacred veils.

But since it is not enough to declare the truth unless errors are exposed and refuted, it is the will of the holy council to affix these canons so that, with the catholic teaching already recognized, all may also understand which heresies they must guard against and avoid.

Canons on the most holy sacrament of the eucharist

1. If anyone denies that in the most holy sacrament of the eucharist there are contained truly, really and substantially, the body and blood of our lord Jesus Christ together with the soul and divinity, and therefore the whole Christ, but says that he is present in it only as in a sign or figure or by his power: let him be anathema.

2. If anyone says that in the venerable sacrament of the eucharist the substance of the bread and wine remains together with the body and blood of our lord Jesus Christ, and denies that marvelous and unique change of the whole substance of the bread into the body, and of the whole substance of the wine into the blood, while only appearance of bread and wine remains, a change which the catholic church most aptly calls transubstantiation: let him be anathema.

3. If anyone denies that the whole Christ is contained in the venerable sacrament of the eucharist under each of form, and under each part of each form when it is divided: let him be anathema.

4. If anyone says that the body and blood of our lord Jesus Christ are not present in the wondrous sacrament of the eucharist after the completion of the consecration, but only in its use, while it is being consumed, but not before or after; and that the true body of the Lord does not remain in the hosts or consecrated particles which are reserved or remain over after the communion: let him be anathema.

5. If anyone says either that the principal fruit of the most holy eucharist is the forgiveness of sins, or that other effects dot not result from it: let him be anathema.

6. If anyone says that Christ, the only-begotten Son of God, is not to be adored in the holy sacrament of the eucharist by the worship of adoration, including its outward expression; and therefore is not to be reverenced by the celebration of a special festival nor carried round solemnly in procession, as is the praiseworthy rite and custom everywhere of holy church; nor exposed publicly to the people that he may be adored; and that those who so adore are idolaters: let him be anathema.

7. If anyone says that it is unlawful to reserve the holy eucharist in a sacred place, but that it must of necessity be distributed to those present immediately after the consecration; or that it is unlawful for it to be carried with due honor to the sick: let him be anathema.

8. If anyone says that Christ, when presented in the eucharist, is consumed only spiritually, and not also sacramentally and really: let him be anathema.

9. If anyone denies that each and all of Christ's faithful of both sexes, when they have reached the age of discretion, are bound in accordance with the commandment of holy mother church to receive communion every year, at least at Easter time: let him be anathema.

10. If anyone says that it is unlawful for a priest, when celebrating, to give himself communion: let him be anathema.

11. If anyone says that faith alone is sufficient preparation for receiving the sacrament of the most holy eucharist: let him be anathema. And, in order that so great a sacrament may not be received unworthily, and hence unto death and condemnation, the holy council establishes and declares that, granted the availability of a confessor, those burdened by an awareness of mortal sin, however much they may feel themselves to be contrite, must first avail themselves of sacramental confession. But if anyone presumes to teach, preach or obstinately assert the contrary, or even defend it in public debate, by that very act he shall be excommunicated.

Decree on reform

The same holy council of Trent, lawfully assembled in the holy Spirit, having as presidents the same legate and nuncios of the holy apostolic see, intends to decide some matters concerning the jurisdiction of bishops in order that, accordance with a decree of the last session, they may reside with greater willingness in the churches committed to them, the easier and more convenient it is for them to govern those subjects to them and to preserve them in uprightness of life and behavior. First of all, the council judges they should be reminded that they are shepherds not oppressors, that they are to preside over their subjects but not lord it over them: they are to love them as children and brothers, and take pains by exhortation and counsel to deter them from what is unlawful so that they may not be obliged, when they do wrong, to restrain them by appropriate penalties. Concerning those, however, who through human frailty have chanced to fall into sin, that precept of the Apostle has to be keep: that they reprove, beseech and rebuke them in all goodness and patience since often *kindness towards those to be corrected is more effective than severity, exhortation more than threat, charity more than command.* But, since it is the duty of an attentive and kind shepherd first to apply gentle medicine to the ailments of the sheep, if there is need for the seriousness of the rod because of the wrong done, then strictness should be tempered with restraint, judgment with mercy, severity with lenity, so that the discipline which is salutary and essential for the people may be kept without harshness, and those who have been corrected may improve; or, if they refuse to repent, others may be deterred from faults by the salutary example of the punishment imposed. Later, when the seriousness of the malady may so demand it, it is for the shepherd to proceed further, to harsher and weightier remedies; and if even these measures are not effective, to ensure that those at fault are removed, so that he at least frees the other sheep from the danger of contagion. Since those

guilty of crimes, to avoid punishments and evade the judgments of bishops, frequently make pretext of complaints and hardships and, by taking refuge in an appeal, impede the judicial process; therefore the council, to prevent such persons perverting a remedy established to guard innocence into a defence of wickedness, and to counteract cunning and evasion of this kind, thus determined and decreed:

Canon 1

In cases concerning visitation and correction, aptitude or unsuitability, as also in criminal cases, there is to be no appeal prior to the definitive sentence from the bishop or his vicar general in spirituals, arising from interlocutory action or any other grievance whatever; the bishop or his vicar shall not be bound to a postponement by a frivolous appeal of this kind; but he shall be able to proceed further in spite of any inhibition emanating from the judge of the appeal as well as from any written document or custom, even immemorial, unless a grievance of this kind cannot be made good by the definitive sentence or there is no possible appeal from the same; in those cases, what has been laid down by the holy and ancient canons shall remain unimpaired.

Canon 2

In criminal cases, the case for an appeal from the sentence of a bishop or his vicar general in spirituals (where there is ground for an appeal), if it happens to have been remitted to that region by apostolic authority, may be entrusted either to the metropolitan or even to his vicar general in spirituals, or—if he should for some reason be under suspicion or is more than two legal days' journey away, or the appeal has been from his decision—to one of the neighboring bishops or their vicars, but not to judges of lower rank.

Canon 3

An accused, who is appealing in a criminal case from the bishop or his vicar general in spirituals, shall produce intact, in the presence of the judge to whom he has appealed, the acts of the first legal process and, unless the sees them, the judge may in no way proceed to his final resolution. The person from whom the appeal has been made shall produce those acts for the appellant without charge within thirty days; otherwise, the case of an appeal of this type shall be concluded without them, according as justice may indicate.

But since there are occasions when crimes of such gravity have been committed by ecclesiastical persons that, on account of their heinous nature, these persons have to be removed from sacred orders and handed over to the secular tribunal in which, according to the sacred canons, a stated number of bishops is required; and since, if it would be difficult to provide the full number of bishops, the appropriate legal procedure should be delayed; and since, even when they could come together, their residence would be interrupted; the council in consequence decided and decreed:

Canon 4

It shall be lawful for a bishop in person, or through his vicar general in spirituals, to proceed against a cleric in recognized orders, including those of the priesthood, even to his condemnation and verbal deposition, and when acting in person even to the actual and solemn reduction from the orders themselves and from ecclesiastical status, in cases in which the presence of other bishops to the number as defined in the canons is required; and he may act even without them, if he has present and supporting him a like number of abbots who have by apostolic privilege the use of mitre and crozier, if they can be found in the state or diocese and can conveniently be present; and failing even that, he may act if he has with him other persons of recognized ecclesiastical rank who are available, are of mature years and are commendable by their knowledge of the law.

And because it sometimes happens that some persons by false pleas, which however have some plausibility, wrest favors whereby penalties imposed on them by the just severity of bishops are either totally remitted or reduced; and since it is not to be borne that a lie, which displeases God so much, should not only go unpunished but obtain for the liar pardon of another fault; the council has therefore declared and decreed:

Canon 5

A bishop residing in his diocese shall, by his own authority as delegate of the apostolic see, even without full legal form, take cognizance of cheating over or theft of a favor procured by false pleas (concerning the pardon of some public crime or delinquency about which he had begun to make enquiry, or the remission of a penalty to which the accused had been condemned by him); and after he shall have lawfully established that it was obtained by means of a statement of what was false or a concealment of what was true, he shall not allow the favor in question.

But the subjects of a bishop, though they have been justly punished, are nevertheless prone to hate him intensely and, as though they had suffered an injustice, to bring false charges against him so as to cause him distress by any means in their power. Consequently, fear of such vexation frequently renders him very hesitant to enquire into and punish their faults. Therefore, lest with great harm to himself and to the church he be forced to abandon the flock entrusted to him and to wander about lowering the dignity due to a bishop, the council has declared and decreed:

Canon 6

A bishop, even if official proceedings are being taken against him by enquiry or denunciation or accusation or by any other method, shall in no case be cited or enjoined to present himself in person, except for a ground on which he could be deposed from or deprived of office.

Canon 7

Witnesses shall not be accepted for explanations or proofs in a criminal case or in an otherwise grave charge against a bishop, unless there are corroborative witnesses and they are of good standing, reputation and sound character; and if they make any

formal statements out of hatred, rashness or greed, they shall be dealt with by severe penalties.

Canon 8

Cases against bishops (when they have to appear in person because of the nature of the charge laid against them) shall be referred to the supreme pontiff and decided by him.

SESSION 14
25 November 1551

Teaching concerning the most holy sacraments of penance and last anointing

The holy, ecumenical and general council of Trent, lawfully assembled in the holy Spirit , with the same legate and nuncios of the holy apostolic see as its presidents, realizes that in the decree on justification a good deal about the sacrament of penance was introduced for a reason which seemed necessary, namely the close connection between the two subjects. Nevertheless, so great is the accumulation of errors about that sacrament during our time that no small public advantage will come from giving a more detailed and full definition concerning this sacrament in which, once the widespread errors have been disclosed and uprooted with the assistance of the holy Spirit, the catholic truth will become more clear and distinct. This holy council now lays before all Christians this truth to be for ever observed.

Chap. 1. On the need for the sacrament of penance and its institution

If thanksgiving to God in all the regenerated was such that they unfailingly preserved the justice received by his favor and grace in baptism, there would have been no need for a sacrament other than baptism to be instituted for the forgiveness of sins. But since God, *rich in mercy, knows our frame,* he has also bestowed a remedy of life on those who have subsequently surrendered to the slavery of sin and the power of the devil, namely the sacrament of penance by which the benefit of Christ's death is applied to those who have fallen away after baptism. Repentance, indeed, was necessary at all times for all who had stained themselves by some mortal sin so as to gain grace and justice, including those who had asked to be cleansed by the sacrament of baptism, in order that, rejecting and correcting their perversity, they might with a hatred of sin and a genuine sorrow of mind detest so great an offence against God. Hence the prophet says: *Repent and turn from all your transgressions lest iniquity be your ruin. The Lord also said: Unless you repent, you will all likewise perish.* And Peter, prince of the apostles, commending penance to those sinners about to be baptized, said: *Repent, and be baptized every one of you.* Moreover, before the coming of Christ penance was not a sacrament, nor after his coming does anyone receive it prior to baptism. But the Lord instituted the sacrament of penance at that particular moment when, after his resurrection from the dead, he breathed on his disciples, saying: *Receive that holy Spirit; if you forgive the sins of any, they are forgiven; if you retain the sins of any, they are retained.* The universal consent of the fathers has always understood that by this remarkable act and by these clear words the power to forgive and retain sins, and so to reconcile those who had fallen after baptism, was communicated to the apostles and to their lawful successors; and the catholic church with sound reason denounced and condemned the Novatians as heretics when they obstinately denied the power to forgive. Consequently this holy council, approving and accepting the literal and true meaning of those worlds of the Lord, condemns the fraudulent interpretation of those who, opposing the institution of this sacrament, falsely twist the words to mean the power of preaching the word of God and of proclaiming the gospel of Christ.

Chap. 2. *The difference between the sacraments of penance and baptism*

But in fact this sacrament is seen to differ in many respects from baptism. For, apart from the fact that the matter and form, by which the essence of a sacrament is constituted, are totally distinct, there is certainly no doubt that the minister of baptism ought not to be a judge, since the church exercises judgment on no one who has not previously entered it by the gate of baptism. *For what have I to do with judging outsiders?* says the Apostle. It is otherwise with those of the household of the faith whom Christ has once made members of his body by the font of baptism; for if these should afterwards defile themselves by some fault, the church does not wish them to be cleansed by a repetition of baptism (since this is under no circumstances lawful in the catholic church), but to stand as culprits before this tribunal in order that they may be set free through the decision of the priests, not once but as often as, in repentance of sins admitted, they have recourse to it. Besides, the fruit of baptism is something other than the fruit of penance. For by baptism we put on Christ and become in him an entirely new creature, gaining full and complete remission of all sins; this newness and wholeness, however, we can in no way reach by the sacrament of penance without great weeping and labor on our part, as the divine justice demands, and so penance has rightly been called by the holy fathers a laborious kind of baptism. But this sacrament of penance is necessary for salvation for those who have fallen baptism, just as baptism itself is for those not yet regenerated.

Chap. 3. *On the parts and fruit of this sacrament*

In addition, the holy council teaches that the form of the sacrament of penance, in which its effectiveness chiefly lies, is expressed in those words of the minister, *I absolve you etc.;* To these indeed, by a praiseworthy custom of holy church, some prayers are added, but they in no way affect the essence of the form, nor are they necessary for the administration of the sacrament. The acts of the penitent, namely contrition, confession, satisfaction, are as it were the matter of this sacrament. These are called parts of penance, in that, by God's institution, they are required in the penitent for the integrity of the sacrament, and for the full and complete forgiveness of sins. Of course, the meaning and fruit of this sacrament, so far as its force and efficacy are concerned, is reconciliation with God, which in devout persons who are receiving this sacrament with devotion is often followed by a peace and a serenity of conscience accompanied by an intense consolation of spirit. While handing on these teachings on the parts and effect of this sacrament, the holy council at the same time condemns the opinions of those who insist that the constituent parts of penance are the fears which afflict conscience and faith.

Chap. 4. *On contrition*

Contrition, which holds the first place among the above-mentioned acts of the penitent, is a grief and detestation of mind at the sin committed, together with the resolution not to sin in the future. This movement of sorrow has been necessary at all times to obtain the pardon of sins and, in a person who has fallen after baptism, it finally prepares for the forgiveness of sin if it is linked with trust in the divine mercy and the desire to provide all the other requirements for due reception of the sacrament. The holy council therefore declares that this contrition includes not only ceasing from sin, the resolve of a new life and a beginning of it, but also a hatred of the old in accordance with the words: *Cast away from you all the transgressions which you have committed against me, and get yourselves a new heart and a new spirit.* And certainly one who has pondered those exclamations of the saints, *Against you only have I sinned and done what is evil in your sight; I am weary with my moaning, every night I flood my bed with tears; in my bitterness of soul I recall all my years before you;* and others like them, will easily understand that they have sprung from an intense hatred of the past life and a very deep hatred of sins. The council further teaches that, though it sometimes happens that this contrition is made perfect by love, and a person is reconciled with God before this sacrament is actually received; nevertheless, the reconciliation is not to be attributed to the contrition without a desire for the sacrament being included in it. But of that imperfect contrition, which is called attrition since it is generally conceived either out for a consideration of the baseness of sin or from a fear of hell and punishments, as long as it excludes the will to sin and hopes for pardon, the council declares that not only does it not make a person a hypocrite and even more of a sinner, but that it is even a gift of God and an impulse of the holy Spirit, not yet actually dwelling in the penitent, but only moving him, helped by which he prepares for himself a path towards justice; and although it cannot of itself and without the sacrament of penance lead the sinner to justification, yet it disposes him to beg and obtain the grace of God in this sacrament of penance. For, struck to their advantage by this fear, the Ninivites at the terrifying preaching of Jonah did penance and obtained mercy from the Lord. For that reason some make false accusations against catholic writers, as if they have taught that the sacrament of penance confers grace without a good impulse on the part of its recipients, something which the church of God has never taught nor imagined. But they also teach falsely that contrition is wrested or forced from people, not freely willed.

Chap. 5. *On confession*

From the time of the institution of the sacrament of penance already explained, the universal church has always understood that there was also instituted by the Lord the complete confession of sins, and that this is necessary by divine law for all who have fallen after baptism. For our lord Jesus Christ, when about to ascend from earth to heaven, left priests as his own vicars, as overseer and judges, to whom all mortal sins into which Christ's faithful might have fallen were to be referred, so that by the power of the keys might declare the decision of

PROMULGATIONS OF THE COUNCIL OF TRENT (continued)

forgiveness or retention of sins. For it is clear that priests could not have exercised this judgment if the case were unknown, nor could they have preserved fairness in imposing penances if the faithful had declared their sins only in general, and not rather specifically and in detail. Hence it follows that all mortal sins that penitents are aware of after a careful self-examination have to be related in the confession, even if they are very private and committed only against the last two commandments of the Decalogue, since these may often quite seriously damage the soul and are more dangerous than those which are openly admitted. For venial sins, by which we are not cut off from the grace of God and into which we more frequently fall, although they may be admitted in confession (as the practice of devout persons shows), can nevertheless be passed over in silence without fault and expiated by many other remedies. But since mortal sins, even those of thought, make people children of wrath and enemies of God, it is essential to seek pardon of God by an open and humble confession of all of them. Thus, when Christ's faithful endeavor to confess all sins which come to mind, they are beyond doubt setting them before the divine mercy for all to be pardoned. Those, however, who do otherwise and knowingly hold some things back, are presenting nothing to the divine goodness for forgiveness through the priest; for if a sick man is ashamed to disclose his wound, the doctor does not heal with medicine what he is unaware of. It further follows that the circumstances which change the sin's nature must also be explained in confession because, without them, the sins themselves are not being completely revealed by the penitents nor made known to the judges, and it is impossible for the latter rightly to estimate the gravity of the faults and to impose on the penitents the penance appropriate to them. Hence it is completely unreasonable to teach that these circumstances have been thought out by idle minds or that only one circumstance need be confessed, namely a sin against a brother. And it is impious to say that confession according to these rules is impossible, or to call it a tormentor of consciences; for it is clear that the church requires nothing more of penitents than that, after each has examined himself diligently and explored all the nooks and crannies of his conscience, he confess those sins by which he recalls that he has mortally offended his Lord and God; but the other sins, which do not come to mind when he is carefully examining himself, are understood to have been included in a general form in the same confession; for those we say confidently with the prophet, *Lord, clear me from hidden faults.* The difficulty of this kind of confession and the shame at uncovering sins could seem to be burdensome, were it not lightened by so many advantages and consolations which will most certainly be granted through the absolution to all who approach the sacrament worthily. For the rest, with regard to the manner of confessing secretly to a priest alone, though Christ has not forbidden anyone to confess his sins publicly—is expiation for his offenses and in self-humiliation, both as an example to others and for the edification of the church which has been offended—yet this is not commanded by divine precept, nor would it be really well-considered to enjoin by human law that sins, especially secret ones, must be revealed by public confession. The fact that secret sacrament confession, which holy church has used from its beginning and still uses, has always been commended by

the most venerable and most ancient fathers with great and unanimous agreement, clearly refutes that empty calumny of those who do not fear to teach that it is a human invention foreign to the divine command, originating from the fathers assembled in the Lateran council; for the church did not establish through the Lateran council that Christ's faithful should confess, which it had understood to be a necessary institution of divine law, but that the precept of confession should be discharged by one and all at least once a year on their reaching the age of discretion. Hence, throughout the whole church, at the sacred and most acceptable season of Lent, the salutary custom of confessing is observed with very great fruit for the soul of the fruitful; and this custom the present holy council thoroughly approves and cherishes as holy and deserving to be retained.

Chap. 6. On the minister of the sacrament and on absolution

Concerning the minister of the sacrament, however, the holy council declares false and completely alien to the truth of the gospel all teachings which destructively extend the ministry of the keys to all persons indiscriminately, in addition to bishops and priests, and maintain against the institution of this sacrament that those words of the Lord, *Whatever you bind on earth shall be bound in heaven, and whatever you loose on earth shall be loosed in heaven, and, If you forgive the sins of any they are forgiven; if you retain the sins of any, they are retained,* were spoken to all Christ's faithful without distinction and discrimination, so that anyone has the power to forgive sins, public sins by reproof if the one reproved agrees to this, secret sins by a voluntary confession made to anyone. The council also teaches that even priests who are in mortal sin discharge as ministers of Christ the function of forgiving sins by the power of the holy Spirit conferred in ordination, and that those think wrongly who insist that bad priests do not have this power. And although a priest's absolution is a stewardship of another's gift, nevertheless it is not only a bare service, either of proclaiming the gospel or of declaring that sins have forgiven' but it is like a judicial act in which a verdict is pronounced by him as a judge; and therefore the penitent should not so flatter himself about his own faith that, even if he has no contrition or the priest has no intention of acting seriously and truly absolving, he may yet think he is truly absolved in the sight of God on the grounds of his faith alone. For faith without repentance would not secure any forgiveness of sins, nor would anyone be other than most careless of his salvation who, though aware that a priest was absolving jokingly, made no serious effort to find another acting with due care.

Chap. 7. On reservation of cases

Since the nature and meaning of the judicial process require that a verdict be passed only over those subject to it, the church of God has always maintained, and this council confirms its complete truth, that an absolution should be considered to have no value if pronounced by a priest over someone over whom he as neither ordinary nor delegated jurisdiction. Our most holy fathers judged that it was very important for the discipline of the christian people that certain more heinous and more serious offenses should be absolved, not by any priest whatever, but only by those of highest rank; hence popes in virtue of the supreme power committed to them in the universal church, could rightly reserve to their own particular decision some more serious classes of offence. And (since all that is from God is well ordered) there can be not doubt that this same procedure is lawful for all bishops, each in his own diocese, *for building up,* however, *not for destroying,* in virtue of that greater authority committed to them over their subjects than that of other priests of lesser rank, especially with regard to those offenses to which the penalty of excommunication is attached. It is in harmony with divine authority that this reservation of sins has force not only in external administration but also in the sight of God. Nevertheless, lest anyone perish on that account, it has always been most devoutly observed in the same church of God that there be no reservation in immediate danger of death, and so all priests may then absolve all penitents without distinction from every kind of sin and censure; outside this particular case, since priests have no power in reserved cases, their one endeavor should be to persuade the penitents to approach judges of higher rank who have legal power to grant absolution.

Chap 8. On the necessity and the fruit of satisfaction

Finally, there is satisfaction. Of all the parts of penance, it has at all times been commended to the christian people by our fathers; yet in our day it is the only thing particularly attacked under the lofty pretext of devotion by those who maintain the appearance of devotion but have denied its inner reality. The holy council consequently declares that it is completely false and alien to the word of God that a fault is never forgiven by God without all penalty being condoned as well: for manifest and famous examples are found in scripture which, apart from divine tradition, refute this error beyond all question. Surely the nature of divine justice itself demands that those who, prior to baptism, have failed through ignorance, should be received by God into grace in one manner; but in another manner those who, after once being, freed from slavery to sin and to the devil and after receiving the gift of the holy Spirit, have not feared knowingly to violate the temple of God and to grieve the holy Spirit. It also befits the divine clemency not to free us from sins without any satisfaction with the result that, given the opportunity and thinking sins of small importance, we become neglectful and insolent towards the holy Spirit and fall into more serious faults, storing up anger against ourselves in the day of wrath. For it is beyond doubt that penances imposed in satisfaction very much deter people from sin, hold them in check by a kind of rein, and make those doing penance more cautious and more watchful for the future; they also heal the remaining effects of sins and, by the practice of the contrary virtues, remove vicious habits acquired by evil living. Nor has any path ever been considered more secure in the church of God for removing the threat of punishment by the Lord than that people should make regular use of these works of penance with genuine sorrow of mind. Moreover, while by making, satisfaction we suffer for our sins, we become like Christ Jesus who made satisfaction for our sins, and from whom is all our sufficiency, and we also have a most sure pledge thereby that, if we suffer with him, we shall also be glorified with him. For this satisfaction which we offer in payment for our sins is not so much ours that it is not also done through Christ Jesus; for we can do nothing of ourselves as of ourselves; with his cooperation we can do everything in him who strengthens us.

Thus we have nothing of which to boast; but all our boasting is in Christ, in whom we live, in whom we merit, in whom we make satisfaction and *yield fruits that will benefit repentance,* which have their worth from him, are offered by him to the Father, and through him are accepted by the Father. The priests of the Lord, therefore, as the spirit of prudence shall suggest, must enjoin salutary and appropriate penances in keeping with the type of offence and the ability of the penitent, so as not to become sharers in the sins of others by imposing very light tasks for very serious faults, and perhaps thereby conniving at the sins by acting with too great indulgence towards the penitents. Let them rather bear in mind that the satisfaction they impose should not only be aimed at protecting the new life and at being a remedy against weakness, but also be for the atonement and punishment of past sins; for the ancient fathers believe and teach that the keys were granted to priests not only for releasing but also for binding. Nor for that reason did they think that the sacrament of penance is a forum of wrath or penalties, just as no Catholic ever supposed that the value of the merit and satisfaction of our lord Jesus Christ was either obscured or in some way diminished as a result of acts of satisfaction on our part. Because the innovators refuse to acknowledge this, they so emphasize that a new life is the best penance as to take away the whole force and practice of satisfaction.

Chap. 9. On the works of satisfaction

The council further teaches that the abundance of the divine generosity is so great that through Jesus Christ we are able to make satisfaction before the Father not only by penances voluntarily undertaken by us to atone for sin, or those imposed by the judgment of the priest according to the extent of the fault, but also (and this is the greatest proof of love) by the temporal afflictions imposed by God and borne by us with patience.

Teaching on the sacrament of last anointing

The holy council, however, decided to attach to the above teaching on penance the following points about the sacrament of last anointing, which was regarded by the fathers as the final complement not only of penance but also of the whole christian life, which ought to be an ever continuing penance. So, first of all, it states its teaching about that sacrament's institution's. Our most merciful Redeemer wished provision to be made for his servants of salutary remedies against all the darts of all enemies for every occasion in life. Just as he has prepared by other sacraments very important supports by which Christians may be able to keep themselves safe from all the more serious spiritual disquiets during their lifetime, so likewise by the sacrament of last anointing he has guarded the end of life by a very strong defence. For though our adversary seeks and seizes opportunities through the whole of life of finding ways to devour our souls, yet there is no time at which he draws more strongly on every shred of his skill to destroy us utterly, and to deprive us, if he can, of our confidence in the divine mercy, than when he sees that our departure from life is at hand.

Chap. 1. On the institution of the sacrament of last anointing

This holy anointing of the sick was instituted as a true and proper sacrament of the new Testament by Christ our Lord, as is suggested in Mark's gospel, and recommended and announced to the faithful through James, the apostle and brother of the Lord. He says: *Is anyone among you sick? Let him call for the elders of the church, and let them pray over him, anointing him with oil in the name of the Lord; and the prayer of faith will save the sick person and the Lord will raise him up; and if he has committed sins, he will be forgiven.* By these words, as the church has learned by an apostolic tradition that has been handed on, he is teaching the matter, the form, the official minister and the effect of this sacrament. The church has understood the matter to be oil blessed by a bishop, for anointing very fittingly manifests the grace of the holy Spirit by which the soul of the sick person is invisibly anointed; and, finally, that the form is the words, By this anointing etc.

Chap. 2. On the effect of this sacrament

Moreover the reality and effect of this sacrament is explained in the words: *And the prayer of faith will save the sick person, and the Lord will raise him up; and if he has committed sins, he will be forgiven.* For the reality is the grace of the holy Spirit, whose anointing takes away sins, if there are any still to be expiated, and the remains of sin, and comforts and strengthens the soul of the sick person, by arousing in him great trust in the divine mercy; supported by this the sick person bears more lightly the inconveniences and trials of his illness, and resists more easily the temptations of the devil who lies in wait for his heel, and sometimes he regains bodily health when it is expedient for the salvation of his soul.

Chap. 3. On the minister of this sacrament and the time at which it ought to be given

The words quoted above also give a very clear rule about those who should receive and those who should administer this sacrament. For they show that the proper ministers of this sacrament are ''presbyters'' of the church, and by this title in the text are to be understood, not the elders or leading figures among the people, but either bishops or priests duly ordained by them *by the laying on of hands of the presbyterate.* It is also stated that this anointing is to be used for the sick, in particular those who are so dangerously ill that they seem to be about to depart from life; and consequently it is also called the sacrament of the departing. If the sick persons should recover after receiving the anointing, they may be helped again by the support of this sacrament, when they incur another similar risk to life. Hence there is no reason to listen to those who teach, against the open and clear meaning of the apostle James, that this anointing is either a human fabrication or a rite received from the fathers which includes neither a command from God nor a promise of grace; nor to those who assert that it has now ceased, as though it belonged only to the grace of healings in the primitive church; nor to those who say that the rite and usage observed by the holy Roman church in the administration of this sacrament are at odds with the statement of the apostle James, and so should be changed to something else; nor, finally, to those who declare that this final anointing can, without sin, be treated as negligible by the faithful. For all these views are very clearly in conflict with the clear words of this leading apostle. Indeed, in administering this anointing the

Roman church, mother and mistress of all others, only does (in matters which constitute the substance of this sacrament) what the blessed James prescribed. Nor, indeed, could there be any slighting of so great a sacrament without immense impiety and an insult to the holy Spirit himself.

These are the truths concerning the sacraments of penance and last anointing which this holy ecumenical council openly confesses, teaches and proposes to all Christ's faithful to be believed and maintained. And it gives the following canons to be kept without alteration, condemning under anathema for all time those who hold the contrary.

Canons concerning the most holy sacrament of penance

1. If anyone says that in the catholic church penance is not truly and properly a sacrament instituted by Christ the Lord for the reconciliation of the faithful to God himself, as often as they fall into sins after baptism: let him be anathema.

2. If anyone confuses the sacraments, by saying that baptism is itself the sacrament of penance, as if these two sacraments were not distinct, and therefore penance is not rightly named a second plank after shipwreck: let him be anathema.

3. If anyone says that those words of the Lord and Savior, *Receive the holy Spirit; if you forgive the sins of any, they are forgiven; if you retain the sins of any, they are retained,* are not to be understood to refer to the power of forgiving and retaining sins in the sacrament of penance, as the catholic church has always from the beginning understood them; but in opposition to the institution of this sacrament, twists their meaning to authority to preach the gospel: let him be anathema.

4. If anyone denies that, for the full and complete forgiveness of sins, three acts are required in the penitent to form as it were the matter of the sacrament of penance: namely, contrition, confession and satisfaction, which are called the three parts of penance; or says there are only two parts of penance, namely, terrors afflicting the conscience once sin is acknowledged, and faith arising from the gospel or from the absolution, with which a person believes that his sins have been forgiven through Christ: let him be anathema.

5. If anyone says that contrition, prepared for by means of examination, recapitulation and formal renunciation of sins, in which one reflects over one's years in bitterness of soul, by weighing up the seriousness, great number and foulness of one's sins, the loss of eternal happiness and the onset of eternal damnation, while determining to lead a better life, is not true and useful sorrow and does not prepare for grace, but makes a person a hypocrite and even more of a sinner; and further, that such sorrow is forced and not freely willed: let him be anathema.

6. If anyone denies that the institution of sacramental confession or its necessity for salvation are from divine law; or asserts that the manner of confessing secretly to a priest

alone, which the catholic church has always observed from the beginning and still observes, is foreign to the institution and command of Christ and is a human invention: let him be anathema.

7. If anyone says that for the forgiveness of sins in the sacrament of penance it is not necessary by divine law to confess each and all mortal sins which are remembered after due and careful reflection, even secret sins and those against the last two commandments of the Decalogue, together with circumstances which change the character of the sin; but that confession of this kind is useful only for the instruction and consolation of the penitent, and was in past times observed only for the imposition of a canonical satisfaction; or says that those who make an effort to confess all their sins wish to leave nothing for the divine mercy to pardon; or, finally, that it is not permitted to confess venial sins: let him be anathema.

8. If anyone says that the confession of all sins, in the form the church preserves, is impossible and should be abolished by devout persons as a human tradition; or that each and all of Christ's faithful of either sex are not bound to it once a year, in accordance with the constitution of the great Lateran council; and that consequently Christ's faithful should be persuaded not to confess during the Lenten season: let him be anathema.

9. If anyone says that sacramental absolution by a priest is not a judicial act, but a mere ministry of pronouncing and declaring to the penitent that his sins are forgiven, so long as he simply believes that he is released from them; and this even when the priest does not absolve seriously but in jest; or says that confession is not required on the part of the penitent for a priest to be able to absolve him: let him be anathema.

10. If anyone says that priests who are in mortal sin have not the power of binding and loosing; or that priests are not the only ministers of absolution, because Christ said to each and all of the faithful: *Whatever you bind on earth shall be bound in heaven, and whatever you loose on earth shall be loosed in heaven;* and, *If you forgive the sins of any, they are forgiven; if you retain the sins of any, they are retained;* and that by these words anyone has power to absolve from sins, from public ones by reproof, provided that the reproved person consents, and from secret ones by a voluntary confession: let him be anathema.

11. If anyone says that bishops have no right to reserve cases to themselves, except for reasons of public order, and that therefore reservation of cases does not prevent a priest from truly absolving from reserved sins: let him be anathema.

12. If anyone says that the entire punishment is always remitted by God along with the sin, and that the satisfaction made by penitents is nothing else but the faith by which they grasp that Christ has made satisfaction on their behalf: let him be anathema.

13. If anyone says that, for temporal punishment for sins, no satisfaction at all is made to God, through the merits of Christ, by the sufferings imposed by God and patiently borne; or by the penances enjoined by a priest; or, further, by those voluntarily undertaken such as fasts, prayers, almsgiving or other additional works of devotion; and consequently that the best penance is only a new life: let him be anathema.

14. If anyone says that the satisfactions by which penitents atone for their sins through Jesus Christ are not acts of worship of God, but are human traditions which obscure the teaching on grace, the true worship of God and the very benefit of the death of Christ: let him be anathema.

15. If anyone says that the keys have been given to the church only for loosing and not also for binding; and that, consequently, when priests impose penalties on those who confess, they are acting contrary to the purpose of the keys and to the institution of Christ; and that it is a fiction that, after eternal punishment has been taken away by the power of the keys, there often remains temporal punishment to be discharged: let him be anathema.

Canons concerning the sacrament of last anointing

1. If anyone says that last anointing is not truly and properly a sacrament instituted by Christ our Lord and made known by blessed James the apostle, but is only a rite received from the fathers or a human invention: let him be anathema.

2. If anyone says that the holy anointing of the sick does not confer grace, nor remit sins, nor soothe sick persons, but has now ceased because it was only a grace of healing of a past age: let him be anathema.

3. If anyone says that the rite and usage of last anointing which the holy Roman church observes do not agree with what the blessed apostle James meant, and so ought to be changed; and that they can without sin be regarded as negligible by Christ's faithful: let him be anathema.

4. If anyone says that the presbyters of the church who, as blessed James enjoins, should be brought in to anoint the sick person, are not priests who have been ordained by a bishop, but the elders in any community; and that on that account the proper minister of last anointing is not exclusively a priest: let him be anathema.

Decree on reform

Introduction

Since it is properly the office of bishops to reprove the faults of all subjects, they must take particular care not to acquiesce if clerics, especially those appointed to the pastoral care of souls, are guilty of leading unworthy lives. For if they pass over their irregular and corrupt practices, how can they rebuke the laity for their vices when they could be confounded by one word from the latter for permitting clerics to be much worse than they? And how free will priests be to correct laity, when these can quietly answer that the priests have themselves behaved in the very way they are reproving? Bishops will therefore charge their clerics, of whatever rank they may be, to give a lead in their conduct, speech and learning to the people of God entrusted to them, and to be mindful of what scripture says: *Be holy, for I am holy.* And, as the Apostle says, let them put *no obstacle in anyone's way, so that no fault may be found with their ministry, but rather* commend themselves *in every way as servants of God,* lest that saying of the prophet find fulfillment in them: *The priests of God profane what is sacred and reject the law.* That the bishops may be able to carry this out more freely, and not be encumbered by any pretext whatever, the same holy ecumenical and general council of Trent, with the same legate and nuncios of the apostolic see presiding over it, has decided that the canons which follow should be set down and decreed.

Canon 1

It is more honorable and safe for a subject, by rendering due obedience to those in charge, to serve in a ministry of lower rank than to seek the dignity of higher ranks to the scandal of superiors. Hence, in the case of anyone who has been forbidden by his own prelate to advance to holy orders, for whatever reason, including some secret misdeed, and by whatever process even a non-judicial one; and of anyone who has been suspended from his ecclesiastical orders or grades or honors; no permission granted against the will of his prelate to have himself advanced to orders, or for restitution of previous orders or grades or honors or dignities, shall have any force.

Canon 2

Some bishops of churches which are in the territories of unbelievers, lacking any clergy or christian people, are in a sense wanderers with no fixed place of residence who are in search not of what belongs to Jesus Christ but of the sheep of another shepherd without his knowing it; and these see themselves forbidden by this holy council from exercising pontifical functions in another's diocese, except by the express permission of the local ordinary and only with regard to persons subject to the same ordinary. So, in deceit and in contempt of the law, they brazenly choose a fictitious episcopal seat in a place where there is no diocese, and then presume to mark with the character of a cleric and to advance to sacred orders, including even the priesthood, whoever approaches them, even if they have no commendatory. As a result it often happens that people are ordained, though unsuitable, untrained and ignorant, who have been rejected by their own bishop as incapable and unworthy, and they cannot correctly perform the divine office or administer the church's sacraments. In view of these facts, therefore, none of the bishops who are called titular, even if they reside or have spent some time in a place within no diocese, even if' the place is exempt, or in some monastery of an order, may validly advance or ordain to any sacred or minor orders, even first tonsure, in virtue of any temporary privilege of promoting whoever may come to them, the subject of another, even on the grounds of his being well known as one of their household, without the expressed consent or dimissorial letters of his own prelate. Anyone who acts contrary to this will be automatically suspended for a year from the exercise of episcopal functions, and the one so

promoted will be suspended from the exercise of the orders so received for as long as it seems good to his own prelate.

Canon 3

A bishop shall have power to suspend, for a period which he shall judge proper, from the exercise of the orders received, and to prohibit from carrying out any ministry either at the altar or any other, those he has found unsuitable and incompetent for the celebration of the divine office or the administration of the church's sacraments; this with respect to any of his clerics, especially those in holy orders, who have been promoted by any authority whatever without a previous examination by him and without commendatory letters, even though they were approved as fit by the person by whom they were ordained.

Canon 4

All prelates of churches ought to apply diligent attention to correcting the open faults of their subjects; and, by the statutes of this holy council, no clerics residing in their own churches are to be held immune, on the grounds of any privilege whatever, from the possibility of being visited, punished and reproved in accordance with the canonical ordinances. The prelates shall have the power, as delegates in this matter of the apostolic see, when and as often as need arises in or out of the time of visitation, to correct and impose penalties on all secular clerics no matter how exempt, who would otherwise be subject to their jurisdiction, for their misdeeds, open faults and delinquencies; and no exemptions, declarations, customs, decisions, oaths, agreements binding only their authors, made in favor of the clerics themselves or of their relations, chaplains, servants, agents and any others whatsoever, from consideration and in respect of the exempt clerics themselves, shall be valid.

Canon 5

Further, there are some who, on the grounds that a variety of wrongs and annoyances are being inflicted on them with regard to their property, possessions and rights, obtain by letters of protection the appointment of special judges to protect and defend them from wrongs and annoyances of that kind, and to keep and maintain them in actual or alleged possession of the property, possessions and rights and not permit them to be troubled in these matters, and they twist letters of that kind in many respects to a meaning which is false and contrary to the intention of the donor. Consequently, letters of protection, no matter what their clauses and stipulations, or what judges they appoint, or on whatever ground or title the were granted, shall not avail anyone of whatever dignity or status he may be, even if a chapter is involved, against the possibility of being accused, summoned, examined and proceeded against in criminal or mixed cases in the presence of his bishop or another ordinary superior, or of being freely summoned before an ordinary judge in those matters, even if rights are in some way due to him from a concession. In civil cases too no one, if he is the plaintiff, shall be permitted to bring anyone to judgment before his own conservatory judges. And, in cases in which he is the defendant, if the conservator chosen by him happens to be declared suspect by the plaintiff; or if a disagreement arises between the judges themselves, the conservator and the ordinary, with regard to the competence of the jurisdiction; then in no wise shall the case go forward, until a decision has been given by legally appointed arbitrators about the suspicion or the competence of the jurisdiction. But conservatory letters of this kind are not to be valid for members of his household, who are wont to protect themselves by such, only two being excepted and on condition that they have lived at his personal expense. And no one is to enjoy the benefit of similar letters be, and a period of five years. It shall also be illicit for conservatory judges to maintain an established tribunal. In cases affecting wages and needy persons, however, the decree of this holy council on this subject shall retain its full rigor. On the other hand, general universities and colleges of teachers and scholars, places belonging to regulars as well as hospices actually practicing hospitality, and persons attached to such universities, colleges, places and hospices, are in no way included in the present canon, but are to be completely exempt and understood to be so.

Canon 6

Though the habit does not make the monk, clerics must nevertheless always wear the clerical dress appropriate to their own order so that they may show by the suitability of their outward dress the interior uprightness of their characters. Yet, so great has grown the rashness of some and their contempt of religion at the present time that, giving little weight to personal dignity and clerical honor, they wear lay clothes even in public, a walking contradiction, with one foot among divine things and the other among those of the flesh. For that reason all ecclesiastical persons, however exempt, who are either in sacred orders or have obtained formal or informal dignities, offices or ecclesiastical benefices of any kind, if after warning by their own bishop, even by a public order, they do not wear the proper clerical dress befitting their order and dignity and in keeping with the regulation and command of their bishop, they can and should be restrained by suspension from their orders, office and benefice, and from the fruits, revenues and profits of those benefices; and if, after having once received correction they again fail in his matter, also by the deprivation of offices and benefices of this kind: this by a renewal and extension of the constitution of Clement V which begins *Quoniam,* published at the council Of Vienne.

Canon 7

Since someone who has killed his neighbor deliberately and by lying in wait for him ought to be removed from the altar, therefore anyone who has killed a person intentionally, even if the crime has not been proved by legal process nor otherwise made public, but has remained secret, cannot at any time be promoted to holy orders, nor shall it be lawful to grant him any ecclesiastical benefices, even if they do not include the official care of souls; rather he is to be cut off permanently from every ecclesiastical order, benefice and office. if, however, it is reported that he has killed someone not intentionally but by accident, or in repelling force by force as when one protects oneself from death, and for that reason a dispensation is needed by law in some way for holy orders and the ministry of the altar, and for any kind of benefices and dignities; then let the matter be committed to the local ordinary or, as the case may

be, to the metropolitan or the neighboring bishop, who shall be able to dispense only after studying the case and testing the petitions and reports, and not otherwise.

Canon 8

Moreover, since certain people, some of whom are true shepherds and have flocks of their own, seek to control other people's sheep as well, and sometimes so direct their attention to others' subjects that they neglect the care of their own; therefore no one, even if he enjoys episcopal rank, who has the privilege of punishing someone else's subjects, should in any circumstances take action against clerics who are not his own subjects, especially those in sacred orders, no matter how heinous the crimes of which they are guilty, except through the medium of the actual bishop of those clerics if he resides at his own church, or of someone deputed by that bishop; otherwise, the process and everything that depends on it shall be completely without validity.

Canon 9

And because by an excellent law dioceses and parishes have been made separate, and to each flock have been assigned their own shepherds and to less important churches their rectors, who each have responsibility for their own sheep, so that ecclesiastical order may not be confused, or one and the same church belong in some way to two dioceses, not without serious inconvenience to those who may be its subjects; therefore benefices of one diocese, whether they are parish churches, perpetual vicariates, simple benefices, prestimonies or prestimonial portions, are not to be joined permanently to a benefice or monastery or college or place, even pious, belong to another diocese, even on the plea of increasing divine worship or the number of the beneficiaries, or for any other reason: hereby is explained the decree of this holy council about unions of this kind.

Canon 10

Benefices belonging to regulars, which by custom have been assigned in title to professed regulars, when they happen to fall vacant by the death or resignation of the occupant, or on some other way, shall be conferred only on religious of that order or on those who are absolutely committed to take the habit and make profession, and on no others (so that they do not put on a garment woven in wool and linen together).

Canon 11

Because regulars who transfer from one order to another are able to obtain permission easily from their own superior to remain outside a monastery, and thereby have the opportunity to wander about and to desert religious life, no prelate or superior of any order shall be able, by virtue of any special power, to admit anyone to the habit or to profession except on the condition that he remain permanently in enclosure under the obedience of his superior in the order to which he is transferred; and one thus transferred, even if he belonged to the canons regular, remains entirely incapable of holding secular benefices, including those having the care of souls.

Canon 12

No one, whatever his ecclesiastical or secular dignity, should or shall be able to procure or hold the right of patronage for any reason whatever, unless he has founded and built from nothing a church, benefice or chapel, or has suitably endowed from his own personal and inherited possessions one already set up but with an insufficient endowment. In the case of such a foundation or endowment, however, the institution is reserved to the bishop, and to no other person of lower rank.

Canon 13

Further, it shall not be lawful for a patron, on the ground of some privilege, to present anyone in any way to the benefices within his legal patronage, except to the ordinary bishop of the locality, to whom the provision of or institution to this benefice would belong on the lapse of the privilege; otherwise any presentation and institution which may follow are to be and to be regarded as null.

The holy council further declares that in the next session, which it has already decreed should be held on 25 January of next year, 1552, it has to deal with the sacrifice of the mass as well as to treat of the sacrament of order, and to pursue the subject of reform.

SESSION 21
16 July 1562

Teaching on communion under both kinds and of children

Introduction

The holy ecumenical and general council of Trent, lawfully assembled in the holy Spirit, with the same legates of the apostolic see as presidents, seeing that various horrifying errors about the most awesome and holy sacrament of the eucharist are being spread in different places by the tricks of the most evil spirit, because of which many people in some provinces seem to have fallen away from the faith and obedience of the catholic church, has judged that the subjects of communion under both kinds and that of children should be set out here. It therefore forbids all the faithful to presume to believe or teach or preach on these matters otherwise than is explained and defined in these decrees.

Chap.1. Laity and non-consecrating clergy are not bound by divine command to communion under both kinds

Hence this holy council, taught by the holy Spirit, who is the Spirit of wisdom and understanding, the Spirit of counsel and piety and following the judgment and custom of the church itself, declares and teaches that laity, and clergy who are not consecrating, are under no divine command to receive the sacrament of the eucharist under both kinds; and that it can in no way be doubted (with integrity in faith) that communion under either kind is sufficient for their salvation. For, though Christ the Lord instituted this revered sacrament at the last supper and gave it to the apostles in the forms of bread and wine, this institution and gift do not mean that all the faithful are bound by a precept of the Lord to receive both forms. Nor is it correct to deduce from that saying in the sixth chapter of John that communion in both kinds was commanded by the Lord, however it may be understood from different interpretations of the holy fathers and doctors. For he who said, *unless you eat the flesh of the son of man and drink his blood, you have no life in you,* also said, *if anyone eats of this bread, he will live for ever.* And he who said, *he who eats my flesh and drinks my blood has eternal life,* also said, *the bread which I shall give for the life of the world is my flesh.* And finally, he who said, *he who eats my flesh and drinks my blood abides in me, and I in him,* said as well, *he who eats this bread will live for ever.*

Chap.2. The power of the church in administering the sacrament of the eucharist

The council further declares that the church always had the power in administering the sacraments of making dispositions and changes it judged expedient for the well-being of recipients, or for the reverence due to the sacraments themselves, provided their essentials remained intact, in view of changing affairs, times and places. This the Apostle seems to have indicated plainly enough when he said: *This is how one should regard us, as servants of Christ and stewards of the mysteries of God;* and it is surely clear that he himself used this power, not only in many other matters', but over this sacrament too, when after giving some instructions for its conduct he said: *About the other things I will give directions when I come.* Although from the beginning of christian worship the use of both kinds was common, yet that custom was very widely changed in the course of time; and so holy mother church, acknowledging her authority over the administration of the sacraments and influenced by good and serious reasons, has approved this custom of communicating in one form and has decreed this to be its rule, which is not to be condemned nor freely changed without the church's own authority.

Chap.3. Christ is received whole and entire under either kind, as is the true sacrament

The council also declares that, although our Redeemer instituted this sacrament at the last supper and gave it to the apostles in two forms, as was said above; it must nevertheless be asserted that Christ is also received whole and entire, as is the true sacrament, under either kind alone, and that therefore, as far as the effect is concerned, those who receive only one form are not cheated of any grace necessary for salvation.

Chap.4. Children are not bound to sacramental communion

Finally, the same holy council teaches that children under the age of discernment are not bound by any obligation to sacramental holy communion, seeing that after rebirth by the water of baptism and incorporation in Christ they are not at that age able to lose the grace they have received of being children of God. Nor are times past to be condemned if they sometimes observed that custom in some places. For those holy fathers had good reason for their practice in the situation of their time, and we must certainly believe without dispute that they did not do this for any necessity of salvation.

Canons on communion under both kinds and of children

1. If anyone says that all Christ's faithful should receive both forms of the most holy sacrament of the eucharist by command of God or as necessary to salvation: let him be anathema.

2. If anyone says the holy catholic church was not led by proper causes and reasons to communicate laity, and even clergy who are not consecrating, in the one form of bread alone, and has erred in the matter: let him be anathema.

3. If anyone says that Christ, the source and author of all graces, is not received whole and entire under the one form of bread, on the grounds that he is not then received under both forms according to Christ's institution, as some would falsely assert: let him be anathema.

4. If anyone says that eucharistic communion is necessary for children before they reach the age of discernment: let him be anathema.

Two other questions proposed, but not yet discussed, namely:

''Whether the reasons which led the holy catholic church to communicate the laity and even non-celebrating priests in the form of bread alone are so compelling that the chalice is not to be allowed to these for any reason''; and, ''Whether, if for reasons that are proper and according to christian charity it seems right to allow the chalice to an individual or nation or kingdom, this should be allowed on certain conditions, and what these are'': the same holy council reserves for examination and decision at another time, at the earliest opportunity.

Decree on reform

Introduction

The same holy ecumenical and general council of Trent, lawfully assembled in the holy Spirit, with the same legates of the apostolic see as presidents, has decided on this occasion to make the following enactments on the matter of reform, for the praise of almighty God and the enhancement of holy church.

Canon 1

As ecclesiastical rank should be free of every hint of greed, bishops and others who ordain and their officials may not on any grounds accept anything, even when it is freely offered, for the conferring of any orders even the clerical tonsure, nor for dimissorial or testimonial letters, nor for sealing documents, nor for any other reason. In places where the praiseworthy custom does not hold of their receiving nothing, and in these alone, scribes may only accept the tenth part of a gold piece for each dimissorial or testimonial letter, and then only if they are not paid a fixed salary for carrying out their function; nor may any part of the scribe's emoluments go directly or indirectly to the bishop concerned in conferring the order in question. The council decrees that they are strictly bound to give their services for nothing, wholly annulling and forbidding all taxes and customs to the contrary, however immemorial, in whatever places, as these can better be called abuses and corruptions supporting the evil of simony. Those who act otherwise by

either giving or accepting will automatically incur not only the divine judgment but also the penalties imposed by law.

Canon 2

It is not fitting that those enlisted for the service of God should bring disgrace on their order by begging or plying some mean trade, but it is public knowledge that many are admitted to holy orders with hardly any process of selection, who pretend by various tricks and deceits that they possess a church benefice or have sufficient means of their own. Hence the holy council lays down that in future no secular clerk should be advanced to holy orders, however suitable he may otherwise be in character, learning and age, until it is first legally established that he has unchallenged tenure of a church benefice sufficient for respectable living. And he may not resign that benefice without a declaration that he was ordained with that benefice as his title; his resignation is not to be accepted unless there is proof that he can live comfortably by other means, and without it his resignation is null. Henceforth those possessing a patrimony or pension may only be ordained if the bishop judges they should be accepted for the need and welfare of his churches, and has first ensured that they really possess a patrimony or pension and that these are sufficient to support them. And these incomes may not thereafter be alienated or cancelled or diminished without the bishop's permission, until they have acquired an adequate church benefice or have some other means of support; the penalties of the ancient canons about these matters being hereby renewed.

Canon 3

Church benefices were instituted to provide divine worship and other ecclesiastical offices. Hence, so that divine worship may in no way be weakened, but rather that due attention be paid to it in every way, the holy council enacts as follows. In both cathedral and collegiate churches where there are no daily allocations, or such small ones that they can really count for nothing, a third of the income and of all revenue and proceeds from higher dignities, canonries, minor dignities, portions and offices is to be set aside and converted into daily allocations; these are to be divided proportionally among those with dignities and others taking part in divine service according to shares laid down at the first partition of revenues by the bishop, acting even as delegate of the apostolic see; this without prejudice to the customs of those churches where those not resident or not officiating receive nothing or less than a third; and all exemptions and other customs, however immemorial, and appeals of all kinds, are to be overruled. And should any obstinacy persist on the part of those not officiating, proceedings may be taken against them according to the stipulations of the law and the holy canons.

Canon 4

In all churches of parish or baptismal status, where the people are so numerous that the rector cannot by himself meet the demands of administering the sacraments of the church and conducting divine worship, bishops acting even as delegates of the apostolic see are to compel rectors or others responsible to add to their staff as many priests as may be necessary to maintain the sacraments and celebrate divine worship. But in parishes where parishioners can only come to receive the sacraments and attend divine offices with great inconvenience, because of distance or inaccessibility, new parishes may be founded, even against the will of pastors, according to the form given in the constitution of Alexander III beginning *Ad audientiam*. And the priests who are for the first time assigned to the charge of newly erected churches must be allotted, at the discretion of the bishop, an adequate share of revenues belonging in any way to the mother church. And, if need be, the people must be compelled to provide sufficient for the support of these priests, notwithstanding any general or special reservation or attachment with regard to the said churches. Nor may such arrangements and foundations be canceled or impeded by stipulations of any kind, even those arising from resignation, or by any other abrogations or suspensions.

Canon 5

And so that the standing of churches in which God is served by the sacred offices may be maintained in due respect, bishops may, even acting as delegates of the apostolic see, and in legal form though without prejudice to the incumbents, create permanent unions of any churches whatsoever of parish or baptismal status, and of other benefices whether involving care of souls or not, together with their pastors, both by reason of their poverty and in other cases allowed by law, even when such churches or benefices are under a general or special reservation or attached in some way or other. And such unions may not be revoked or in any way infringed in virtue of any stipulation, even by reason of resignation or abrogation or suspension.

Canon 6

Some illiterate and incompetent rectors of parish churches are unsuitable for sacred ministries, and others destroy rather than build up by the immorality of their lives. Hence bishops, even acting as delegates of the apostolic see, may appoint, for those who are illiterate and incompetent, if they otherwise live good lives, temporary assistants or vicars, and assign them a part of the revenues sufficient for their support, or otherwise provide for them, setting aside all appeals and exemptions. Those, however, who live in a base and scandalous fashion should first be warned, then compelled by punishments; then, if they still persist incorrigibly in their evil ways, bishops have the power to deprive them of their benefices according to the provisions of the sacred canons, and to set aside any exemption or appeal.

Canon 7

Great care should be taken that what is dedicated to divine service should not fall into decay by the wastage of time and pass out of human memory. Hence bishops, even acting as delegates of the apostolic see, may on their own judgment transfer simple benefices, including those with the right of patronage, from churches which have fallen down with age and lack resources for their repair, appointing those concerned to mother churches or others of the same locality or neighborhood; and they should set up altars or chapels in these latter churches with the same dedications, or transfer the dedications to altars or chapels already built, together with all the emolu-

ments and obligations falling on the original churches. But they should take steps to restore and rebuild tumbledown parish churches, even those under the right of patronage, from any revenues and resources in any way belonging to the churches; and if these do not suffice they should put pressure for this purpose, by all suitable means, on all patrons and others who receive income from the said churches, or failing these on the parishioners, setting aside any appeal, exemption or opposition. But if all are too poor, then they should be transferred to mother or neighboring churches, with permission to turn over both the said parish churches and others that are in ruins to respectable secular uses, but with a cross set up in each.

Canon 8

It is right that the bishop should keep a watch on everything that concerns the worship of God and where necessary supply for any deficiencies. Hence those so-called commendatory monasteries, including abbeys, priories and provostries, in which there is no regular observance, as well as benefices both with and without the care of souls, both secular and regular, however held in trust and even exempted, should be visited annually by bishops, even acting as delegates of the apostolic see. And the bishops must also ensure by appropriate remedies, if necessary by the sequestration of revenues, that anything needing repair or restoration is put in order, and that any care of souls attached to them or dependent institutions, and all other duties, are properly carried out, notwithstanding any appeals, privileges, customs, including those of immemorial duration, writs of protection and deputations of judges with their injunctions. In institutions where there is regular observance, bishops should ensure by fatherly admonitions that their own regular superiors should observe a proper way of life according to the rules of their own institute, and see that it is observed, maintaining and directing their subjects in their obligations. If after being warned these superiors have not made a visitation and corrected abuses within six months, then the bishops, acting as delegates of the apostolic see, may themselves conduct the visitation and correction, just as the superiors would be able to do according to their rule, notwithstanding any appeals, privileges and exemptions, which are to be set aside.

Canon 9

Many remedies introduced by various earlier councils—of the Lateran of Lyons and of Vienne—against the evil practices of those collecting alms have become unavailing in more recent times. Rather has their malpractice been seen to grow all the time, to the great scandal and discontent of all the faithful, to such an extent that hope seems to have vanished. For these reasons the council enacts that henceforth in all places of the christian religion the very name and activity of collector be wholly abolished, and that people should be given no admittance whatever to exercise this role, notwithstanding any privileges granted to churches, monasteries, hospices, holy places, and persons of any rank, state or dignity, or any customs however immemorial. And the council decrees that any indulgences or spiritual favors, of which the faithful should not be deprived by this ruling, should henceforth be published to the people at the appropriate times by the local bishops through the agency of two members of their chapter, who will also be empowered to make an honest collection of alms and other offerings for charity, without receiving any payment for the task. And may all thereby understand that these treasures of the church are administered to increase devotion and not private gain.

SESSION 22
17 September 1562

Teaching and canons on the most holy sacrifice of the mass

In order that the ancient faith and the teaching on the great mystery of the eucharist may be retained in the holy catholic church unqualified and complete in every detail, and be preserved in its purity by the rejection of all errors and heresies; the holy ecumenical and general council of Trent, lawfully assembled in the holy Spirit, with the same legates of the apostolic see as presidents, and taught by the light of the holy Spirit, teaches and declares all that follows concerning the eucharist in so far as it is a true and unique sacrifice, and decrees that it is to be preached to the faithful.

Chapter 1

As there was no fulfillment under the old covenant because of the powerlessness of the levitical priesthood (as the apostle Paul testifies), it was necessary (God the Father of mercies thus ordaining) for another priest to arise according to the order of Melchisedech, our lord Jesus Christ, who was able to bring to completion all due to be sanctified and to lead them to perfection. And so he, our Lord and God, was to offer himself once to God the Father on the altar of the cross, a death thereby occurring that would secure for them eternal redemption. But his priesthood was not to be eliminated by death. So, in order to leave to his beloved spouse the church a visible sacrifice (as human nature requires), by which that bloody sacrifice carried out on the cross should be represented, its memory persist until the end of time, and its saving power be applied to the forgiveness of the sins which we daily commit; therefore, at the last supper on the night he was betrayed, as the catholic church has always understood and taught, he announced that he had been appointed for ever a second priest in the order of Melchisedech, offered his body and blood to God the Father under the forms of bread and wine, and handed them to the apostles under the same material symbols to be received by them (whom at that point he was making priests of the new covenant), and he commanded them and their successors in the priesthood to offer them by the words: *Do this in remembrance of me* etc. For after celebrating the old passover which the whole people of the children of Israel offered in memory of their departure from Egypt, he instituted a new passover, namely the offering of himself by the church through its priests under visible signs, in memory of his own passage from this world to the Father, when he redeemed us by the shedding of his blood, rescued us from the power of darkness and transferred us to his kingdom. And this is none other than that clean oblation that can be soiled by no unworthiness or evil on the part of those offering, which the Lord foretold through Malachy as being offered in purity in every place to his name, which would be great among the nations. And the apostle Paul indicates the same clearly enough in writing to the Corinthians, when he says that those contaminated by sharing in the table of demons cannot be sharers in the table of the Lord, by ''table'' meaning ''altar'' in both places. Finally this is the offering, prefigured by many images of sacrifice in the age of nature and the law, which was to embrace all the values signified by them, as the fulfillment and consummation of them all.

Chapter 2

In this divine sacrifice which is performed in the mass, the very same Christ is contained and, offered in bloodless manner who made a bloody sacrifice of himself once for all on the cross. Hence the holy council teaches that this is a truly propitiatory sacrifice, and brings it about that if we approach God with sincere hearts and upright faith, and with awe and reverence, *we receive mercy and find grace to help in time of need.* For the Lord is appeased by this offering, he gives the gracious gift of repentance, he absolves even enormous offenses and sins. For it is one and the same victim here offering himself by the ministry of his priests, who then offered himself on the cross: it is only the manner of offering that is different. For the benefits of that sacrifice (namely the sacrifice of blood) are received in the fullest measure through the bloodless offering, so far is this latter in any way from impairing the value of the former. Therefore it is quite properly offered according to apostolic tradition not only for the sins, penalties, satisfactions and other needs of the faithful who are living, but also for those who have died in Christ but are not yet fully cleansed.

Chapter 3

It has been the custom in the church to celebrate masses from time to time in honor and memory of the saints; the council, however, teaches that the sacrifice is not offered to them, but only to God who gave them their crown. So the priest does not say, ''Peter and Paul, I offer sacrifice to you'', but, thanking God for their triumph, he implores their patronage, *that they may deign to intercede for us in heaven, whose memory we recall on earth.*

Chapter 4

Holy things must be treated in a holy way, and this sacrifice is the holiest of all things. Hence, so that it might be offered worthily and with reverence, the catholic church has for many centuries fixed a venerable eucharistic prayer quite free from error, and containing only what savors in the highest degree of that holiness and devotion which raises the minds of those offering to God. For it contains both the Lord's very own words and elements from apostolic tradition and the devout enactments of saintly popes.

Chapter 5

And as human nature is such that it cannot easily raise itself up to the meditation of divine realities without external aids, holy mother church has for that reason duly established certain rites, such as that some parts of the mass should be said in quieter tones and others in louder; and it has provided ceremonial such as symbolic blessings, lights, incense, vestments and many other rituals of that kind from apostolic order and tradition, by which the majesty of this great sacrifice is enhanced, and the minds of the faithful are aroused by those visible signs of

PROMULGATIONS OF THE COUNCIL OF TRENT (continued)

religious devotion to contemplation of the high mysteries hidden in it.

Chapter 6

The holy council would certainly like the faithful present at each mass to communicate in it not only by spiritual devotion but also by sacramental reception, so that the fruits of this sacrifice could be theirs more fully. But, if this does not always happen, the council does not for that reason condemn as private and illicit masses in which only the priest communicates. Rather, it approves and commends them, for they too should be considered truly communal masses, partly because the people communicate spiritually in them, and partly because they are celebrated by an official minister of the church, not for his own good alone but for all the faithful who belong to the body of Christ.

Chapter 7

The holy council draws the attention of priests to the rule of the church that they should mix water with the wine to be offered in the chalice, both because Christ the Lord is believed to have done so, and because water came from his side together with blood and this sacred sign is recalled by this mixing. Further, when in the Revelation of blessed John the peoples are said to be waters the union of Christ the head with his faithful people is signified.

Chapter 8

Although the mass is full of instruction for the faithful people, the council fathers did not think it advantageous that it should everywhere be celebrated in the vernacular. Each church in its place should retain its ancient rite, approved by the holy church of Rome, mother and teacher of all the churches. At the same time, lest the sheep of Christ go hungry or the children ask for bread and there is no one to break it for them, the holy synod instructs the shepherds and all who have responsibility for souls frequently to explain during the celebration of mass, either personally or through another, some of what is recited in the course of the mass, and in addition to give some explanation of this mysterious and most holy sacrifice, especially on Sundays and feast days.

Chapter 9

But as in these days many errors are being spread abroad, and much is being taught or argued by many people against this ancient faith founded on the holy gospel, the traditions of the apostles and the teaching of the holy fathers; this holy council, after holding many weighty and mature discussions of these matters, has decided by unanimous agreement of the fathers to condemn and banish from holy church all that is contrary to this most pure faith and sacred teaching, by the canons which follow.

Canons on the most holy sacrifice of the mass

1. If anyone says that a true and proper sacrifice is not offered to God in the mass, or that the offering is nothing but the giving of Christ to us to eat: let him be anathema.

2. If anyone says that by the words, *Do this in remembrance of me,* Christ did not make the apostles priests, or did not lay down that they and other priests should offer his body and blood: let him be anathema.

3. If anyone says that the sacrifice of the mass is only one of praise and thanksgiving, or that it is a mere commemoration of the sacrifice enacted on the cross and not itself appeasing; or that it avails only the one who receives and should not be offered for the living and the dead, for their sins, penalties, satisfactions and other needs: let him be anathema.

4. If anyone says that by the sacrifice of the mass blasphemy is committed against the most holy sacrifice of Christ enacted on the cross, or that it devalues that sacrifice: let him be anathema.

5. If anyone says that it is an imposture for masses to be celebrated in honor of the saints and to secure their intercession with God, as is the mind of the church: let him be anathema.

6. If anyone says that the canon of the mass contains errors and should therefore be abolished: let him be anathema.

7. If anyone says the ceremonial, vestments and external signs used by the catholic church in the celebration of mass are incitements to impiety rather than instruments of devotion: let him be anathema.

8. If anyone says that masses in which only the priest communicates sacramentally are unlawful, and so should be abolished: let him be anathema.

9. If anyone says the rite of the Roman church, in which the words of consecration and parts of the eucharistic prayer are said in a low voice, should be condemned; or that mass should only be celebrated in the vernacular; or that water should not be mixed with the wine to be offered in the chalice, on the grounds that this is against Christ's institution: let him be anathema.

Decree on things to be observed and avoided in celebrating mass

Anyone can easily appreciate what great care must be taken to celebrate mass with full religious diligence and reverence, who reflects that in scripture the person who does the work of God with slackness is called accursed. We are bound to declare that no other work more holy or divine can be carried out by the christian faithful than this awesome mystery, in which the very life-giving victim by whom we have been reconciled to God the Father is daily offered by priests on the altar. It is equally evident that every effort and attention must be given to carrying it out, both with the greatest possible interior cleanliness and purity of heart, and in an outwardly devout and reverent manner. But many practices foreign to the dignity of so great a sacrifice appear to have crept in, either by the wear and tear of time or through human negligence and depravity. And so, to restore due honor and worship for the glory of God and the spiritual support of the faithful people, the holy council decrees that bishops in charge of dioceses should be greatly concerned and under obligation to forbid and root out anything that has been brought in, either by greed which is the service of idols, or by irreverence which can hardly be distinguished from impiety, or by superstition which is the counterfeit mimic of true devotion.

As far as greed is concerned, they must (to comprise much in a few words) absolutely forbid every element of trade of any kind, contracts and anything given for the celebration of new masses, and also demands and insistent requests for alms that are more like exactions, and similar practices which come close to the taint of simony or at least to money-grubbing.

To avoid irreverence, each bishop should publish a prohibition in his own diocese against permitting a wandering and unknown priest to celebrate mass. And they must not allow anyone whose guilt is public and notorious either to serve at the altar or to take part in divine worship. They must not allow this holy sacrifice to be celebrated by any secular or religious priests whatever in private houses, and wholly outside a church or the oratories dedicated exclusively to divine worship, which are to be designated and visited by the bishops; nor before those attending have made plain by the proper ordering of their dress that they are present not only bodily but with devout attention of mind and heart. And they should keep out of their churches the kind of music in which a base and suggestive element is introduced into the organ playing or singing, and similarly all worldly activities, empty and secular conversation, walking about, noises and cries, so that the house of God may truly be called and be seen to be a house of prayer.

Finally, to leave no room for superstition, they are to ensure by edict with accompanying penalties that priests do not celebrate at other than the proper times, nor use in the celebration of mass rites or ceremonies and prayers other than those approved by the church and traditional from long and praiseworthy usage. They should banish from the church any idea of a particular number of masses and candles which derives more from the cult of superstition than from true religion, and teach the people the nature and source of the very precious and heavenly effect of this most holy sacrifice. Let them also instruct their people to attend their parish churches frequently, at least on Sundays and greater feasts. These points are here brought to the attention of all local ordinaries in summary fashion that they may have an eye not only to them but to any other matters of the kind, and may, in virtue of the power given them by the holy council and acting even as delegates of the apostolic see, issue prohibitions, commands, corrections and ordinances, and compel the body of the faithful to absolute observance of them by ecclesiastical censures and other penalties which they may see fit to impose: and this notwithstanding any privileges, exemptions, appeals and customs of any kind.

Decree on reform

The same holy ecumenical and general council of Trent, lawfully assembled in the holy Spirit, with the same legates of the apostolic see as presidents, to ensure the matter of reform, has decided in this session to issue the following instructions.

Canon 1

There is nothing that more constantly trains others in devotion and the worship of God than the living example of those who have consecrated themselves to the divine service. For when these are seen to have raised themselves from worldly affairs to a higher level, others turn their eyes to them as to a mirror, and gather from them what to imitate. Hence it is most important for clergy called to share the Lord's portion so to fashion their whole life and habits that by dress, gesture, gait, speech and in every other way they express only what is serious, moderate and wholly devout. They must avoid even small faults, which in them would be great, so that their actions may command the respect of all. And the more these standards enhance and benefit the church of God, the more carefully must they be preserved. Hence the holy council decrees that all that has been fully and profitably enacted on other occasions by popes and councils about regulating the life-style, probity, conduct and teaching of clerics, and similarly all rules about loose living, feasting, dances, gambling, gaming and offenses of all kinds, as well as avoiding worldly commerce, should all be fully observed in the future subject to the same penalties, or even stricter ones, to be imposed by the judgment of the bishop. Nor may appeal suspend the execution of any penalty that concerns the correction of such conduct. And if bishops find that any of these rules have fallen into abeyance, they should revive them at once and see that they are kept strictly by all. And this notwithstanding any contrary customs, lest they themselves come to pay the penalty at the hands of God for neglecting the discipline of their subjects.

Canon 2

Anyone in the future who is to be appointed to a cathedral church must not only be fully qualified in terms of birth, age, conduct, life-style and other factors required by the holy canons, but must have already been in sacred orders for a period of at least six months. Information on these matters, if the diocesan office knows little or nothing about him, should be got from legates of the apostolic see or provincial nuncios, or his own bishop, and failing him from neighboring diocesan bishops. In addition, he must be equipped with sufficient learning to meet the requirements of the duties to be imposed on him; hence he should rightly have held the post of master or doctor or licentiate in sacred theology or canon law in a university, or be proved equipped to teach others by the public certificate of an academic institution. If he is a regular he must have an equivalent testimonial from the superiors of his own order. All the aforesaid referees, from whom information or attestation is to be derived, are bound to provide it honestly and free of charge; otherwise they must know that their consciences are heavily burdened and that God and their superiors will requite them.

Canon 3

Bishops, even acting as apostolic delegates, may take a third of all income and revenue of any kind from all higher dignities, minor dignities and offices that exist in cathedral or collegiate churches, and apportion them in shares to be fixed by their own judgment. This is to be done in such a way that, if those who receive shares have not carried out the responsibility personally assigned to them, according to a schedule published by the bishop, by whatever date is prescribed, they lose their share for that day and have no rights of ownership over it; it is to be applied at the discretion of the bishop to the church fabric, if

PROMULGATIONS OF THE COUNCIL OF TRENT (continued)

there is need, or to another place of devotion. If their obstinacy persists, bishops should take proceedings against them according to the regulations of the sacred canons. But if one of the aforesaid higher dignities in cathedral or collegiate churches entails by right or custom no jurisdiction, administration or ministry; and if there arises in the diocese outside the city a post involving the care of souls which the person holding the dignity would like to take up; then, for as long as he resides in the church with care of souls and serves it, he is to be regarded as present and taking part in divine worship in the cathedral and collegiate churches. These rules are to be regarded as applying only to those churches where there is no custom or statute that higher dignities which do not involve service lose a part of their income and revenues amounting up to one third. All this is notwithstanding even immemorial customs, exemptions and contracts, even those confirmed under oath and by any authority whatever.

Canon 4

Anyone appointed to divine service in cathedral or collegiate churches of seculars or regulars, who has not been ordained to the order of at least the subdiaconate, is to have no voice in the chapter of these churches, even if others would willingly grant it to him. Further, any who in these churches hold or in future shall hold higher dignities, minor dignities, offices, prebends, portions and any other benefices, to which are attached various duties (such as, for example, to say or sing masses or the gospel or epistles); and whatever distinction they may have in terms of privilege, exemption, prerogative or nobility of birth; these are all hereby bound, on the cessation of any lawful impediment, to receive the necessary orders within a year; other-wise they will incur the penalties of the constitution of the council of Vienne which begins with the words, Ut ii qui, which this council renews by this present decree. And bishops are to compel them to exercise these their orders on the stated days, and to fulfil all the other duties in divine worship to which they are bound, subject to the same penalties and even more severe ones to be imposed at their discretion. And in future such benefices are only to be assigned to those seen to possess in full the age and other necessary qualifications; otherwise the assignment shall be null.

Canon 5

Dispensations granted by any authority, if they are to be delivered outside the Roman curia, should be delivered to the diocesan bishops of those who have asked for them. Those that are graciously granted, however, do not take effect until they have first been examined by the same bishops as apostolic delegates in a summary fashion and without judicial process, to ensure that the requests as formulated are not flawed by deceit or fraud.

Canon 6

In commutations of last wills, which should not be made without a just and compelling reason, bishops as delegates of the apostolic see must ensure, by summary examination with-out a judicial process, that nothing is stated in the petition which conceals the truth or suggests falsehood, before such commutations are put into execution.

Canon 7

In appeals in any cases that are laid before them, apostolic legates and nuncios, patriarchs, primates and metropolitans are bound, both in allowing appeals and in granting injunctions after appeal, to adhere to the form and tenor of the sacred constitutions and in particular that of Innocent IV beginning Romana. And this notwithstanding any custom, even immemorial, or title or privilege to the contrary; otherwise the injunctions and procedures and all else that follows from them are legally null.

Canon 8

Bishops, acting even as delegates of the apostolic see, are to be executors in cases provided by law of all dispositions of goods for pious purposes, both by last will and between the living, and are to have the night of visiting hospices, colleges of any kind and lay confraternities, even those going by the name of ''school'' or any other name, but not those under the direct patronage of kings without their permission. According to the provisions of the sacred canons they are, in virtue of their office, to examine and regulate almshouses, charitable lending houses and all pious establishments of whatever name, even if the running of such establishments is in the hands of laity and they are protected by a privilege of exemption, and all premises founded for the worship of God, or the salvation of souls, or to support the poor. And all this notwithstanding even immemorial custom, privilege or statute.

Canon 9

Both ecclesiastical and lay administrators of the fabric of any church, even a cathedral, or of a hospice, confraternity, almshouse, charitable lending house or other pious establishments of any kind, are bound to give an account of their administration annually to the bishop of the diocese, all customs and privileges of any kind to the contrary being hereby withdrawn, unless it happens that the statutes of institution of such a church or premise expressly provide otherwise. But if provision is made by custom or privilege or local statute that the account is to be submitted to others assigned for the purpose, then the diocesan bishop is to be added to their number, and any releases conducted otherwise will not be valid for the said administrators.

Canon 10

Since many losses and occasions for litigation arise from the incompetence of notaries, the bishop, acting even as delegate of the apostolic see, may examine and check the ability of any notaries, even those appointed by apostolic, imperial or royal authority; and if he finds they are ill-equipped or have at times defaulted in their duty, he may forbid them perpetually or for a time to exercise their office in ecclesiastical and spiritual affairs, disputes and cases; nor shall any appeal from them suspend the bishop's prohibition.

Canon 11

If any cleric or lay person, whatever the splendor of his rank, even if it be imperial or royal, is so seized by greed, the root of all evils, as to presume to divert to his own use and to usurp, or to prevent from reaching those to whom they rightly belong, the jurisdictions, goods, rents and rights, even feudal and of emphyteusis, and the incomes, emoluments or any revenues, of any church or any secular or regular benefice or a charitable lending house or any other pious institution, which should be applied to the needs of the ministers and of the poor; and whether he does this personally or through others compelled by force or fear, or by subordinate clerical or lay persons, or by whatever device or on whatever manufactured title; then he is to remain under anathema until such time as he has restored in their entirety the jurisdictions, goods, things, rights, incomes and rents which he has seized or which have come to him by any means, even by the gift of a subordinate person, to the church and its administrator or beneficiary, and has further-more received absolution from the pope. But if he is the patron of that church, even holding patronage by law, he is automati-cally deprived of that right, in addition to the penalties men-tioned. Any cleric who has devised or connived at such iniquitous fraud and usurpation is to be subject to the same penalties, and in addition is to be deprived of any existing benefits and made ineligible for any further benefits, and is to be suspended from exercise of his orders at his bishop's discretion, even after full repayment and absolution.

Decree on the request for granting the chalice

At the previous session the same holy council reserved to a later occasion, when opportunity offered, examination and decision on two matters proposed from outside and not yet discussed, namely: ''Whether the reasons which led the holy catholic church to communicate the laity and even non-celebrating priests in the form of bread alone are so compelling that the chalice is not to be allowed to these for any reason;'' and, ''Whether, if for reasons that are proper and according to christian charity it seems right to allow the chalice to an individual or nation or kingdom, this should be allowed on certain conditions, and what these are''. Now the council, desiring the best solution for the salvation of those on whose behalf the petition was made, has decided to refer the whole matter to our most holy lord, and by this decree so refers it, so that in his unrivalled wisdom he may judge what will be best for the christian community and most salutary for those requesting the use of the chalice.

SESSION 23
15 July 1563

The true and catholic doctrine of the sacrament of order, to condemn the errors of our time

Chapter I

Sacrifice and priesthood are so joined together by God's foundation that each exists in every law. And so, since in the new covenant the catholic church has received the visible sacrifice of the eucharist from the Lord's institution, it is also bound to profess that there is in it a new, visible and external priesthood into which the old has been changed. The sacred scriptures show, and the tradition of the catholic church has always taught, that this was instituted by the same Lord our savior, and that power was given to the apostles and their successors in the priesthood to consecrate, offer and adminis-ter his body and blood, as also to remit or retain sins.

Chapter 2

But as the ministry of so holy a priesthood is a godly service, it was altogether fitting, so as to ensure its exercise in a more worthy and reverent manner, that in the careful organization of the church there should be other and varied orders of ministers to give official assistance to priests, so arranged that those already distinguished by the clerical tonsure should ascend through the minor to the major orders. For scripture not only speaks of priests but also of deacons, and teaches in weighty words what must chiefly be looked to in ordaining them. And from the very beginning of the church the names and proper functions of each of the following orders are known to have been in use (though not of equal rank), namely: subdeacon, acolyte, exorcist, reader and doorkeeper. For the subdiaconate is included among major orders by fathers and holy councils, and we often read in them of the other lower orders.

Chapter 3

As it is quite clear from the witness of scripture, apostolic tradition and the unanimous consent of the fathers, that grace is conferred in sacred ordination carried out by words and external signs, no one can doubt that in a proper and true sense order is one of the seven sacraments of holy church. For the apostle says: *I remind you to rekindle the gift of God that is within you through the laying on of my hands; for God did not give us a spirit of timidity but a spirit of power and love and self-control.*

Chapter 4

In the sacrament of order, as in baptism and confirmation, a character is imprinted, which cannot be deleted or removed. Hence the holy synod justifiably condemns the opinion of those who assert that priests of the new covenant have only temporary power, and when duly ordained can be made laity once more if they do not exercise the ministry of the word of God. And if anyone maintains that all Christians without distinction are priests of the new covenant, or that all are equally endowed with the same spiritual power, he appears to be openly overthrowing the church's hierarchy, which is *drawn up as a battle line,* just as if (against the teaching of blessed Paul) all were apostles, all prophets, all evangelists, all pastors, all teachers. The holy council further declares that, apart from the other ranks in the church, bishops in particular belong to this hierarchical order and (as the same apostle says) have been made by the holy Spirit *rulers of the church of God;* and that they are higher than priests and are able to confer the sacrament of confirmation, to ordain the ministers of the church and to fulfil many other functions, whereas those of lower order have no power to perform any of these acts. The holy council further teaches that in the ordination of bishops, priests and other ministers neither the consent nor calling nor authority of the people or of any secular power or functionary or so required that without it the ordination would be invalid. On the contrary, it declares that those who are raised to the

PROMULGATIONS OF THE COUNCIL OF TRENT (continued)

exercise of these ministries when called and appointed only by a secular power and functionary, and those who have the temerity to assume such office themselves, are to be regarded one and all, not as ministers of the church, but as thieves and robbers who have not entered by the sheepgate.

These are the general truths which the holy council has decided to teach to the christian faithful about the sacrament of order. But it has determined to condemn contrary teachings by certain appropriate censures in the following manner, so that all may use the rule of faith with Christ's help, and may more easily recognize and hold to catholic truth amid the darkness of so many errors.

Canons on the sacrament of order

1. If anyone says that in the new covenant there is no visible and external priesthood; or that there exists no power to consecrate and offer the true body and blood of the Lord, and to forgive or retain sins, but only a duty and a mere service of preaching the gospel; or that those who do not preach are simply not priests: let him be anathema.

2. If anyone says that apart from the priesthood there do not exist other orders in the catholic church, both major and minor, by which one reaches the priesthood as by successive steps: let him be anathema.

3. If anyone says that order or holy ordination are not a true and proper sacrament instituted by Christ; or that they are a human fabrication devised by men who know nothing of church affairs; or that they are simply a rite for choosing ministers of the word of God and of the sacraments: let him be anathema.

4. If anyone says the holy Spirit is not given through holy ordination, and so bishops say *Receive the holy Spirit in vain;* or that no character is imprinted by it; or that someone who was once a priest can become a layman again: let him be anathema.

5. If anyone says the sacred anointing which the church uses in holy ordination is not only unnecessary but despicable and destructive, as are the other ceremonies of holy order: let him be anathema.

6. If anyone denies that there exists in the catholic church a hierarchy consisting of bishops, priests and ministers, instituted by divine appointment: let him be anathema.

7. If anyone says that bishops are not of higher rank than priests, or have no power to confirm and ordain, or that the power they have is common to them and the priests; or that orders conferred by them are invalid without the consent or calling of the people or of secular authority; or that those are legitimate ministers of the word and sacraments who have neither been duly ordained nor commissioned by ecclesiastical and canonical authority, but have other origins: let him be anathema.

8. If anyone says that bishops who are elevated by the authority of the pope are not legitimate and true bishops, but a human fabrication: let him be anathema.

Decree on reform

The same holy council of Trent, pursuing the subject of reform, has decided and decreed to issue the canons which follow.

Canon 1

All to whom care of souls has been entrusted are subject to the divine command to know their sheep, to offer sacrifice for them, to nourish them by preaching God's word, by administering the sacraments and by the example of good works of every kind, to have fatherly care of the poor and of all others who are wretched, and to be devoted to other pastoral duties. As none of these roles can be fulfilled by those who do not stay with and watch their flock, but desert them like hirelings the holy synod charges and exhorts them to remember the divine commands and, being examples to the flock, to rule and feed them with faithful wisdom. The holy council has no wish that the holy and wise rules previously made about residence under Paul III of happy memory should be interpreted in a sense foreign to the intention of the council, as if permission were given by that decree for an absence of five continuous months. So, abiding by those rules, the holy synod declares that all by any name or title who are in charge of patriarchal, primatial, metropolitan and cathedral churches of any kind whatsoever, even if they are cardinals of the holy Roman church, are bound to reside personally in their church or diocese, and there to fulfil the duties of their office, nor may they be absent except to the degree and on the grounds that follow.

For, as christian charity, pressing need, due obedience and the evident benefit of church or state sometimes insistently requires the absence of some; the holy council decrees that these legitimate grounds of absence must be approved in writing by the pope or the metropolitan, or in the metropolitan's absence a senior suffragan bishop in residence who may also approve the absence of his metropolitan, except when the absence comes about because of some duty of state and responsibility attached to bishoprics, the grounds of which are so well known, and sometimes sudden in occurrence, that there is no need even to notify the metropolitan of them. It will, however, be for the latter to consider with his provincial council the permissions given by himself or his suffragan, to ensure that no one is abusing this right and to inflict canonical penalties on those offending. Those going away should meanwhile be careful to provide for their sheep so that as far as possible they suffer no harm by their absence. Those who are to be away for a short time are not considered by the ancient canons to be absent, as they are soon to return: but the holy council desires that the time of such absences each year, apart from the causes previously stated, should never exceed two or at the most three months, whether continuous or interrupted, and that care should be taken that this only happens for good reasons and without damage to the flock. Whether these conditions are fulfilled it leaves to the conscience of those absenting themselves, in the hope that they will be responsible and hesitant since human hearts lie open to God, whose work they are bound at their peril to conduct without fraud. Meanwhile it charges in the Lord and exhorts the same prelates not on any account to be away from their cathedrals during the time of Advent and Lent, and the days of the birthday and resurrection of the Lord, Pentecost and the body of Christ, unless episcopal duties summon them elsewhere in the diocese, for then their flocks need most of all to be renewed and to rejoice in the Lord at the presence of their pastor.

If, however, anyone (and may it never happen) is absent in contravention of this decree, the holy synod decrees that, in addition to the other penalties imposed against non-residents under Paul III and hereby renewed, and the guilt of mortal sin thereby incurred, such a one will not receive revenues in proportion to the length of the absence; nor can he in conscience retain these funds even if no claim is made on them, but he is obliged to dispose of them (or in his default it is to be done by a higher ecclesiastic) on the fabric of the churches or the poor of the locality; and any pact or arrangement is forbidden which allows appeal for funds wrongly accepted, whereby the aforesaid revenues would be paid to him in whole or in part. And this notwithstanding any privileges granted to any college or fabric fund.

The holy synod declares and decrees the same guilt and the same loss of revenues and penalties on incumbents of lower rank and on all persons whatsoever who possess any ecclesiastical benefice involving the care of souls. It does so on the understanding that, whenever they happen to be absent for a reason previously known and approved by the bishop, they will leave a suitable substitute, to be approved by the bishop, and assign him a due measure of payment. Their leave of absence is to be given in writing and free of charge, and may not exceed two months except for a serious reason. But if when recalled by edict, even if not personally, they remain obdurate, then the council wishes bishops to be free to compel them by ecclesiastical censures and by sequestration and subtraction of their revenues and other legal remedies, including even deprivation of the benefice; nor may the execution of such a remedy be suspended for any privilege, permission, friendship, exemption even by reason of any benefice, agreement, decree even under oath or confirmed by any authority, custom even if immemorial (which is rather to be considered an abuse), or appeal or injunction even in the Roman court or in virtue of the constitution of Eugenius.

Finally the holy synod orders this decree and that given under Paul III to be promulgated in provincial and episcopal councils. For it desires that matters closely touching the duty of shepherds and the salvation of souls may be so frequently dinned into the ears and minds of all that with God's help they may never fade in time to come through the wear and tear of time or human forgetfulness and neglect.

Canon 2

If those appointed to the charge of cathedral or greater churches of any title or designation, even if they are cardinals of the holy Roman church, have not received consecration to their office within three months, they are bound to restitution of revenues which they have received; if they have still neglected this for a further three months, then by law they are to be deprived of their churches. If the consecration takes place outside the Roman court, it should be celebrated in the church to which they have been appointed or in the province, if this can conveniently be done.

Canon 3

Bishops should confer orders personally. But if they are prevented by illness, they should send their subjects to another bishop for ordination only when they have been tested and approved.

Canon 4

The first tonsure should not be given to those who have not been confirmed and taught the basic truths of faith, or who cannot read or write, and only when there is sound evidence that they have chosen this form of life to give faithful service to God, and not to escape secular justice by fraud.

Canon 5

Those to be promoted to minor orders should have a good testimonial from their parish priest and the master of the school in which they are being educated. Those to be admitted to the successive major orders should approach the bishop during the month before their ordination: he will ensure through the parish priest or whoever he thinks fit that the names and intention of those wishing to be ordained should be published in the church; who will then enquire carefully about their origins, age, conduct and life-style befitting the faith, and will send as soon as possible to the bishop testimonial letters containing the results of his research.

Canon 6

No one who has received the first tonsure, or even one in minor orders, may be given a benefice before his fourteenth year. Nor does he share exemption from secular jurisdiction unless he holds an ecclesiastical benefice, or wears clerical dress and tonsure and serves a church by episcopal appointment, or lives in a seminary or by episcopal permission in a school or university with the intention of receiving major orders. In the case of married clerics, the constitution of Boniface VIII beginning *Clerici, qui cum unicis* is to be observed, provided that these clerics when appointed by a bishop to service and ministry at some church do in fact serve or minister at that church and wear clerical dress and the tonsure. No privilege or custom however immemorial is to avail anyone to the contrary.

Canon 7

The holy synod, following in the footsteps of the ancient canons, decrees that when a bishop arranges to hold an ordination, all wishing to join the sacred ministry are to be summoned to the city on the Wednesday before the ordination, or when the bishop chooses. For his part the bishop, with the help of priests and other men of judgment who are trained in divine law and experienced in ecclesiastical sanctions, is to make a thorough examination and enquiry into the family, personality, age, education, conduct, doctrine and faith of the ordinands.

Canon 8

Ordinations are to be celebrated publicly in the cathedral church at the times determined by law, when the canons of the church have been summoned for the purpose and are present. If they take place elsewhere in the diocese, one of the greater churches should if possible be chosen, and its clergy should be present. Everyone is to be ordained by his own bishop. If anyone asks to be raised to orders by another bishop, this permission should never be granted, even on grounds of some general or special rescript or privilege, and even during the legal times, unless his worthiness and conduct are commended by testimony of his own bishop. If this rule is contravened, the ordaining bishop is suspended from conferring orders for a year, and the person ordained is suspended from the exercise of the orders received as long as his own bishop shall judge fitting.

Canon 9

A bishop may not ordain a member of his household who is not one of his subjects, unless he has lived with him for three years and immediately confers an actual benefice on him, all deceit being set aside; and this notwithstanding any custom to the contrary however immemorial.

Canon 10

Henceforth abbots and others with whatever exemption, residing within the confines of any diocese, even if they are said to be "of no diocese" or exempt, may not henceforth confer the tonsure or minor orders on anyone who is not a regular subject to them; nor may these abbots or other exempt persons or any colleges or chapters, even those of cathedral churches, grant dimissorial letters to any secular clerics to be ordained by others; but the regulation of all such matters, when everything contained in the decrees of this holy synod has been observed, belongs to the bishops within whose diocesan territory the ordinands Eve; all this notwithstanding any contrary privileges, prescriptions or customs however immemorial. And the council orders the penalty imposed on those who obtain dimissorial letters from the chapter when the see is vacant, against the decree made by this holy council under Paul III, to be extended to those who obtain such letters not from the chapter but from any other persons succeeding, in place of the chapter, to the episcopal jurisdiction while the see is vacant. Those granting such letters against the provisions of the decree are automatically suspended for a year from their office and benefice.

Canon 11

Minor orders should be conferred at spaced intervals, on those who at least understand Latin, unless another arrangement seems best to the bishop, so that they can learn more clearly the gravity of this orderly progression. And they may thus train themselves in the responsibilities of each office under the bishop's control, and do so in the church to which they are attached, unless they happen to be absent for the purposes of study, and thus go up step by step with good living and greater learning growing with their age. This they will chiefly demon-strate by good example, faithful service in the church, greater respect for priests and those in higher orders, and a more frequent reception than before of holy communion. At the point of moving on to the higher steps and the sacred mysteries, no one should be advanced who has not shown himself by the promise of his learning to be fitted for major orders. And they are not to be advanced to holy orders until a year after they have received the last grade of minor orders, unless in the judgment of the bishop the need or advantage of the church requires otherwise.

Canon 12

Henceforth no one is to be advanced to the subdiaconate before his twenty-second, or to the diaconate before his twenty-third, or to the priesthood before his twenty-fifth year. But bishops must realize that not anyone of those ages should be advanced, but only those who are worthy and whose age is to be reckoned by good living. Regulars similarly are not to be ordained too young nor without careful examination by the bishop, and all privileges in this matter are wholly ruled out.

Canon 13

Those to be ordained subdeacons and deacons should be of good repute and already tested in minor orders. They should be well educated, trained in all that belongs to the exercise of their order and with hope that by God's help they can live a celibate life. They should serve the churches to which they are assigned and realize that it is highly desirable that they should receive holy communion at least on Sundays and greater feasts, when they minister at the altar. Those advanced to the holy order of the subdiaconate should not be allowed to proceed to a higher rank until they have spent a year as subdeacons, unless the bishop judges otherwise. Two holy orders should not be conferred on the same day, even on regulars, notwithstanding privileges and indults of any kind that have been granted.

Canon 14

Those to be advanced to the priesthood should be men who have conducted themselves devoutly and faithfully in the earlier ministries. They should be of good repute and be men who have not only served in the diaconate for at least a full year (unless the bishop judges otherwise for the need and benefit of the church), but have also been shown by careful examination to be equipped to teach the people what all need to know for their salvation and to administer the sacraments, and to be so outstanding in devotion and chaste conduct that they can be expected to give a fine example of good works and holy living. The bishop is to see that they celebrate mass at least on Sundays and solemn feasts, and if they have the care of souls as often as their responsibilities require. For a legitimate reason the bishop may grant a dispensation for omission of an order to those who have not served in it.

Canon 15

Although at their ordination priests receive the power to forgive sins, the holy council nevertheless decrees that no one, even a regular, may hear the confessions of seculars, even priests, nor be considered qualified to do so, until he has been judged by the bishops to be qualified by means of an examination if they deem one to be necessary, or in some other way, and has received their approval which is to be given free of charge: this notwithstanding any privileges or any custom however immemorial.

Canon 16

No one should be ordained unless his bishop judges that he will be useful or necessary for his churches. Hence the holy council, following the example of the sixth canon of the council of Chalcedon, decrees that no one is to be ordained henceforth without being assigned to the church or place of piety for the needs and advantage of which he is being advanced, and where he may fulfil his functions and not wander about in a homeless fashion. And if he deserts that post without the bishop's consent, he is to be banned from sacred ministry. And furthermore no wandering cleric is to be allowed by any bishop to celebrate the liturgy and administer the sacraments without commendatory letters from his own bishop.

Canon 17

The functions of holy orders from deacon to doorkeeper have been commendably accepted in the church since apostolic times, and though lapsing for a time in some places are now being brought back to use according to the sacred canons, and are not to be denounced by heretics as superfluous. Hence the holy council, desiring from its heart to restore early practice, decrees that henceforth these ministries are only to be exercised by those holding the appropriate orders; and it exhorts and commands in the Lord each and all who are in charge of churches, as far as can reasonably be done, to restore these functions in the cathedral and collegiate and parish churches of their diocese, if the number of people and the revenues of a church make this possible; and it bids them assign stipends from part of the revenues of some simple benefices, or of the church's fabric fund if its resources suffice, or of both, to those who carry out these functions, who can be fined or totally deprived of payment at the bishop's judgment if they are negligent. And if there are not enough celibate clerics to carry out the functions of the four minor orders, there can be added married clerics of worthy life, as long as they have not married twice, who will fulfil these tasks and wear the tonsure and clerical dress in the church.

Canon 18

If they are not rightly brought up, those of adolescent years tend to make for the world's pleasures and, unless trained to religious practice from an early age before habits of vice take firm hold on so many, they never keep to an orderly church life in an exemplary way without very great and almost extraordinary help from almighty God. Hence the holy council decrees that every cathedral, metropolitan and greater church is obliged to provide for, to educate in religion and to train in ecclesiastical studies a set number of boys, according to its resources and the size of the diocese: the boys are to be drawn from the city and diocese, or its province if the former do not provide sufficient, and educated in a college chosen for the purpose by the bishop near to these churches or in another convenient place. Those admitted to the college should be at least twelve years old, of legitimate birth, who know how to read and write competently,

and whose character and disposition offers hope that they will serve in church ministries throughout life. The council wishes the sons of poor people particularly to be chosen, but does not exclude those of the more wealthy provided they pay for their own maintenance and show an ambition to serve God and the church. The bishop will divide these boys into the number of classes he thinks fit, according to their number, age and progress in ecclesiastical learning; some he will assign to service of the churches when he considers the time is ripe, others he will keep for education in the college; and he will replace those withdrawn by others, so that the college becomes a perpetual seminary of ministers of God. So that they may be more appropriately grounded in ecclesiastical studies, they should always have the tonsure and wear clerical dress from the outset; they should study grammar, singing, keeping church accounts and other useful skills; and they should be versed in holy scripture, church writers, homilies of the saints, and the practice of rites and ceremonies and of administering the sacraments, particularly all that seems appropriate to hearing confessions. The bishop should ensure that they attend mass every day, confess their sins at least every month, receive the body of our Lord Jesus Christ as often as their confessor judges, and serve in the cathedral and other churches of the area on feast days. In consultation with two of the senior and more experienced canons of their choosing, bishops are to see to all these arrangements and any others useful or necessary for this enterprise, as the holy Spirit may prompt, and by constant visitation ensure that they are always kept in force. They will punish the difficult and incorrigible and those who spread bad habits with severity, and expel them if need be; and they will take the utmost care to remove all obstacles from such a worthy and holy foundation and promote all that preserves and strengthens it.

Steady revenues will be needed—over and above those already allotted in some churches and places to the education or maintenance of boys, which will naturally be applied to this seminary under the care of the bishop—for the construction of the college, payment to the teachers and servants, maintenance of the young people and other expenses. Hence the bishops in question should set up a council with two from the chapter, one chosen by the bishop and one by the chapter itself, and two from the city's clergy, one similarly chosen by the bishop and the other by the clergy. This council is to subtract a part or share from the revenues of the following: the bishop's table and that of the chapter; all major and minor dignities, offices, prebends, portions, abbacies and priorates of whatever order, even regular, or quality or condition they may be; all revenues of hospices given under title or for administration according to the constitution of the council of Vienne beginning *Quia contingit;* and every kind of benefice including those of regulars, even if they are in anyone's right of patronage, exempt or in no diocese, or attached to other churches or monasteries or hospices or any other pious institutions even if exempt; and from the treasuries of churches and other places, and any other ecclesiastical revenues or incomes, even of other colleges (if the seminaries of those learning and teaching for the general good of the church are not included in them, for the council wished these to be exempt except in respect of any revenues over and above those needed for the proper support of the seminaries) or associations or confraternities, which in some places are called schools, and of all monasteries except those of mendicants, but including those from tithes belonging for any reason to laity, from ,whom ecclesiastical subsidies are normally due, and to members of any militia or military order (the brothers of St John of Jerusalem alone being exempt). The bishop's council will assign and annex the share so subtracted to this college, together with simple benefices of whatever value or rank and also prestimonies or prestimonial portions as they are called, even before they become vacant, without prejudice to divine worship and the incumbents. And this is to take place even if the benefices are reserved or assigned, and the fusing and application of those benefices is not to be suspended or obstructed in any manner, but in all circumstances to take effect, notwithstanding any vacancy even in the bishop's curia or any constitution whatever. For the payment of this portion the local bishop shall use ecclesiastical censures and other legal means, even calling on the aid of the secular arm if need be, to compel the holders of benefices, major and minor dignities, and each and all the above mentioned, whether the revenues are for themselves or for the wages they may have to pay to others from the said sources, while retaining a portion equivalent to what they owe in wages; and this with regard to each and all of the above-mentioned enactments is notwithstanding any privileges, exemptions even those requiring special annulment, custom however immemorial, or appeal or plea that would delay execution. But should the situation arise that the seminary is found to be sufficiently endowed in whole or in part by the effective joining of benefices or by some other means, then the portion of each benefice subtracted as above by the bishop and annexed shall be repaid in whole or in part, as the case requires. And if the prelates of cathedrals and other major churches prove negligent in the construction and maintenance of this seminary, and remiss in paying their own share, then the archbishop is to give a sharp rebuke to the bishop, and the provincial council to an archbishop or higher prelate, and compel them to take all the above measures, and ensure with all zeal that this holy and religious work is put in hand wherever possible at the earliest opportunity. The bishop is to receive a yearly account of the revenues of this seminary in the presence of two of his chapter and two deputed by the clergy of the city.

Finally, so that provision may be made at minimum cost for setting up such schools, the holy council decrees that bishops, archbishops, primates and other local ordinaries should compel and oblige, even by withdrawing their salaries, those who occupy lectureships and others to whose office is attached the duty of reading or teaching, to teach those to be instructed in these schools, either personally or by suitable substitutes to be chosen by these instructors and approved by the bishops. And if in the opinion of the bishop the substitute is unsuitable, they must nominate another who is qualified; if they fail to do so, the bishop is to make the appointment himself. And these instructors are to teach what the bishop regards as appropriate.

Further, these posts and offices which are called lectureships are to be conferred only on doctors or masters or licentiates in holy scripture or canon law and on persons otherwise suitable who can fulfil the duty themselves; and any other provision

shall be null and invalid. And this notwithstanding any privileges whatever or customs however immemorial.

But if in any province there are churches so burdened with poverty that they cannot fully make provision for a college, the provincial synod or the metropolitan with two of his suffragan bishops will see to the founding of one or more colleges, as need requires, at the metropolitan church or another more convenient church of the province, where the boys from these churches can be educated; and will provide for them from the revenues of two or more churches where a college cannot conveniently be founded.

In the case of churches with extensive dioceses the bishop may have one or more seminaries in the diocese, as he thinks fit, but these should depend in all matters on the one founded and established in the city.

Finally, if any difficulty arises, either over the union of benefices or over the taxing or assigning or annexing of portions, such as would either hinder or disturb the establishment or maintenance of this seminary; then either the bishop and the deputies mentioned, or the provincial synod, as befits the character of the region and the quality of churches and benefices, has power to decree and provide in any way whatever that shall seem appropriate and necessary to ensure the successful future of this seminary, even by subtracting from or adding to the above directions, if need be.

SESSION 24
11 November 1563
[Teaching on the sacrament of marriage]

Inspired by the holy Spirit, the forefather of the human race pronounced marriage to be a perpetual and indissoluble bond when he said: *This at last is bone of my bones and flesh of my flesh. . . Therefore a man will leave his father and mother and cleave to his wife, and the two will become one flesh.*

Christ our Lord taught more openly that two alone are to be coupled and joined by this bond when, referring to the words just quoted as spoken by God, he said, So they are no longer two but one flesh, and went on at once to confirm the lasting nature of the same bond, previously declared only by Adam, with the words, *What therefore God has joined together, let no one put asunder.*

Christ himself, the instituter and perfecter of the most holy sacraments, merited for us by his passion the grace that would perfect natural love, strengthen the unbreakable unity and sanctify the spouses. This the apostle Paul indicated when he said, *Husbands love your wives, as Christ loved the church and gave himself up for her,* and went on to add, *This is a great mystery and I take it to mean Christ and the church.*

Since grace received through Christ raises marriage in the dispensation of the gospel above the unions of the old law, our holy fathers and councils and the universal tradition of the church have always taught that it is rightly to be counted among the sacraments of the new law. Against this teaching wicked and wild people of our time have not only thought basely about this revered sacrament but, as is their wont, smuggling in the license of the flesh on pretext of the gospel, they have said and written a great deal that is foreign to the mind of the catholic church and to custom from apostolic times, bringing great damage to the christian faithful. Desiring to confront their rash opinions, the holy and universal council as decided to root out the more glaring errors and heresies of these schismatics, so that their noxious infection may not spread, and to decree against these heretics and their errors the anathemas that follow.

Canons on the sacrament of marriage

1. If anyone says that marriage is not in a true and strict sense one of the seven sacraments of the gospel dispensation, instituted by Christ, but a human invention in the church, and that it does not confer grace: let him be anathema.

2. If anyone says that Christians may have more than one wife at once and that it is forbidden by no divine law: let him be anathema.

3. If anyone says that only the grades of consanguinity and affinity expressed in Leviticus pose an impediment to contracting marriage and make one contracted invalid; and that the church can neither dispense from any of them nor enact others that prevent marriage or make it null: let him be anathema.

4. If anyone says the church did not have the power to establish diriment impediments to marriage, or erred in doing so: let him be anathema.

5. If anyone says that the bond of marriage can be dissolved by a spouse on the grounds of heresy, or irksome cohabitation, or continued absence: let him be anathema.

6. If anyone says that a due marriage which is not consummated is not dissolved by the solemn religious profession of one of the spouses: let him be anathema.

7. If anyone says the church erroneously taught and teaches, according to evangelical and apostolic doctrine, that the bond of marriage cannot be dissolved by the adultery of one of the spouses; and that neither party, even the innocent one who gave no grounds for the adultery, can contract another marriage while their spouse is still living; and that the husband commits adultery who dismisses an adulterous wife and takes another woman, as does the wife dismissing an adulterous husband and marrying another man: let him be anathema.

8. If anyone says the church is in error in deciding that for a variety of reasons a separation between spouses from bed or from cohabitation may take place for a stated or an indefinite time: let him be anathema.

9. If anyone says that clerics in holy orders, or regulars who have made solemn profession of chastity, may contract marriage, and that such a contract is valid, in spite of church law and the vow, and that the opposite view amounts to a condemnation of marriage; and that all can contract marriage who do not consider they have the gift of chastity (even if they have vowed it): let him be anathema. For God would not deny the gift to those who duly ask for it, nor allow us to be tempted beyond our strength.

10. If anyone says the married state is to be preferred to that of virginity or celibacy, and that it is no better or more blessed to persevere in virginity or celibacy than to be joined in marriage: let him be anathema.

11. If anyone says that the prohibition against the solemn celebration of marriage at certain seasons of the year is a tyrannical superstition, arising from pagan superstition; or condemns the blessings and other ceremonies used in the church at such celebration: let him be anathema.

12. If anyone says that marriage cases are not the affair of ecclesiastical judges: let him be anathema.

Canons on the reform of marriage

Chapter I

There is no doubt that secret marriages, entered by free consent of the parties, are true and valid marriages as long as the church has not made them null. Hence those are worthy of condemnation, and the holy council condemns them under anathema, who deny that they are true and valid, and falsely assert that marriages contracted by children still at home without the consent of their parents are null, and that the parents can make them either valid or invalid. Nevertheless, the holy church of God has always detested and prohibited such marriages for the best of reasons. Now, the council recognizes that such prohibitions have been ineffective owing to human disobedience, and weighs up the serious sins that arise from these secret marriages, especially on the part of those who persist in a state of damnation in that they have deserted a first wife married in secrecy and have publicly contracted marriage with another woman and live with her in a permanent state of adultery. The church, in that it does not judge about what is not public, is unable to treat this evil unless it uses a more effective remedy. Hence, following in the footsteps of the holy council of the Lateran held under Innocent III, this council orders that henceforth, before a marriage is contracted, an announcement of those intending to marry shall be made publicly during mass by the parish priest of the contracting parties on three successive feast days. After these announcements have been made, and if no legitimate impediment is raised in objection, the celebration of the marriage must then take place in open church, during which the parish priest will, by questioning the man and woman, make sure of their consent and then say, *I join you together in marriage, in the name of the Father and the Son and the holy Spirit,* or use other words according to the accepted rite of each province. But if in some cases there are grounds for suspecting that the marriage will be maliciously obstructed if that number of announcements are made, then let there be only one announcement, or let the parish priest at least celebrate the marriage in the presence of two or three witnesses; then before its consummation the announcements are to be made in the church, so that any underlying impediments may more easily be detected, unless the ordinary considers it better for them to be omitted, which the holy council leaves to his wise judgment. The holy synod now renders incapable of

PROMULGATIONS OF THE COUNCIL OF TRENT (continued)

marriage any who may attempt to contract marriage otherwise than in the presence of the parish priest or another priest, with the permission of the parish priest or the ordinary, and two or three witnesses; and it decrees that such contracts are null and invalid, and renders them so by this decree. Further it orders that severe penalties be imposed at the ordinary's discretion on a parish priest or other priest who celebrates marriage with fewer witnesses, and on witnesses who assist at any marriage without a parish priest or appointed priest, and on the parties themselves. The holy synod also exhorts spouses not to live in the same house before they have received the priest's blessing in church. And it lays down that this blessing must be given by the couple's own parish priest, nor may permission for this blessing be given to any other priest except by the parish priest himself or the local ordinary, notwithstanding any custom however immemorial (which should rather be considered an abuse) or any privilege. But if any parish priest or other priest, whether he be secular or regular, even if he maintains he is permitted by privilege or immemorial custom, dares to join in marriage spouses of another parish without their parish priest's permission, or to impart the blessing, he will automatically be suspended until absolved by the ordinary of the parish priest who should have taken part in the marriage and from whom the couple should have received the blessing. The parish priest must have a book in which he records the names of the couple and of the witnesses, and the day and place of the marriage contracted, and must keep it safely by him.

Finally, the holy synod exhorts couples to make a careful confession of their sins and to approach the most holy sacrament of the eucharist with devotion before they marry, or at least three days before they consummate the marriage. The holy synod earnestly desires that, if any provinces have praiseworthy customs and ceremonies in this matter, over and above those here mentioned, these should by all means be retained. So that such salutary precepts may not escape anyone's notice, the council orders all local bishops to see that this decree is promulgated to their people as soon as they can, and is explained in all the parish churches of their dioceses; this should be done as soon as possible in the first year, and then again as often as they think expedient.

The council further determines that this decree shall begin to take effect in each parish after thirty days, to be counted from the first day of promulgation in that parish.

Chapter 2

Experience teaches that marriages are often unknowingly contracted in prohibited forms, because of the mass of prohibitions: and then they either continue in serious sin or are dissolved amid great scandal. The holy synod wishes to relieve this unsatisfactory situation and so deals first with the impediment arising from spiritual relationship. It therefore enacts, according to the provisions of the sacred canons, that one person alone, whether man or woman, or at most one man and one woman, should act as sponsors at a baptism. The impediment of spiritual relationship is then contracted: between them and the baptized person and his parents; and between the person baptizing and both the one baptized and his parents.

Before the parish priest proceeds to a baptism, he should carefully enquire from those concerned which person or persons they have chosen to receive the baptized person from the font, and should admit only this or these persons as sponsors, registering their names in the book and explaining the impediment they have contracted, so that they may not be excused by ignorance. Any others touching the baptized person contract no spiritual relationship whatever, all contrary rules notwithstanding. If matters are handled differently through the fault or negligence of the parish priest, he should be punished at the bishop's discretion. And the spiritual relationship contracted by confirmation does not go beyond the person confirming and the one confirmed together with his father and mother and sponsor; all other impediments between other persons arising from this spiritual relationship being hereby abolished.

Chapter 3

The holy council totally abolishes the impediment arising from public decency in cases where a betrothal is for some reason invalid; but in cases where the betrothal is valid, the impediment is not to go beyond the first degree, since a prohibition of this kind cannot be observed in further degrees without harm resulting.

Chapter 4

Further, the holy synod, for the same and other most serious reasons, restricts the impediment which is incurred by affinity contracted through fornication, and which nullifies a subsequent marriage, to those alone who are in the first and second degrees. It enacts that in further degrees such affinity does not invalidate a marriage subsequently contracted.

Chapter 5

If anyone knowingly has the presumption to contract marriage within the forbidden degrees, he must separate and realize he has no hope of a retrospective dispensation, all the more so in the case of one who has not only dared to contract the marriage but also to consummate it. If he did it in ignorance but neglected the solemn observances required for contracting marriage, he is to be subject to the same penalties. For, a person who rashly makes light of the church's saving precepts does not deserve to experience its ready compassion. if, however, all solemn observances were adhered to, and it later becomes known that there was an underlying impediment, of which he was very probably ignorant, then he may more easily be granted a dispensation, and free of charge. For marriages still to be contracted, either no dispensations should be given, or rarely, and then for a good reason and free of charge. No dispensation should be given in the second degree except in the case of great princes and for a public cause.

Chapter 6

The holy council decrees that no marriage can take place between one who carries off a woman and his victim, while she remains in his power. But if, after being separated from him and being settled in a safe and free place, she consents to take him as her husband, then let him have her as his wife; but all the same he and all who connived with him and gave support and assistance are automatically excommunicated, in public disrepute for ever and ineligible for high office. If they are clerics they are to lose their status. And the man is further bound to provide the woman he carried off with what the judge decides to be a proper dowry, whether he marries her or not.

Chapter 7

There are many men of no fixed abode who wander from place to place and, being of shiftless character, leave their first wife and marry another, and often several in different places, while the first is still alive. Wishing to cure this disease the holy council gives a fatherly warning to those concerned not to accept this kind of vagabond for marriage. It urges secular magistrates to restrict them severely; and it orders parish priests not to take part in their marriages without first making a careful enquiry and then, after sending a report to the bishop, securing his permission to proceed.

Chapter 8

It is a serious sin for unmarried men to have a concubine, and even more serious and a great act of contempt for the great sacrament when married men also live in this state of damnation, and even have the effrontery on occasion to keep and support them in their own homes together with their wives. In order to meet this great evil with appropriate remedies, the holy council decrees that if, after being admonished on the matter even officially three times by the ordinary, they have not ejected their concubines and disassociated themselves from them, they are to be sentenced to excommunication and not absolved from it until they obey in deed the admonition given them. But if they ignore the censures and continue in concubinage for a year, the ordinary should proceed against them with a severity measured to their offence. Women, whether married or unmarried, who publicly live in adultery or concubinage with men, if they do not obey after three admonitions, shall be punished severely by the local ordinary in virtue of his office and without any plaintiff according to the measure of their guilt, and even cast out of the town or diocese, if the ordinary so judges, calling on the secular arm if need arises; and other penalties against those guilty of adultery or concubinage are to remain in force.

Chapter 9

Worldly desires and greed so often blind the mental vision of temporal lords and officials that with threats and penalties they coerce men and women living under their jurisdiction, especially those who are wealthy or have the expectation of a rich inheritance, to contract marriages unwillingly with persons that these lords and magistrates have prescribed for them. As it is the height of wickedness to violate the freedom of marriage, and for injustices to be meted out by those from whom justice is expected, the holy council forbids all of whatever rank or dignity or state they may be, under pain of anathema automatically incurred, to use any pressure on their subjects or on anyone else to prevent them marrying freely.

Chapter 10

The holy council orders that, from the beginning of Advent till the feast of the Epiphany, and from Ash Wednesday until the octave of Easter inclusive, the ancient prohibitions against solemn celebrations of marriage are to be observed by all. At other seasons it allows such solemn celebrations, and bishops will ensure that they take place with becoming modesty and decency. For marriage is a holy matter to be conducted in a holy way.

Decree on reform

The same holy council, pursuing the subject of reform, has passed the following decrees in this present session.

Canon 1

If at any level of church office wise and prudent care is needed that nothing should be disorderly or distorted, then even greater effort is needed to ensure that no mistake is made in the choice of him who is set above all levels. For the orderly condition of the whole family of God will change, if what is required from the body is not found in the head; hence, though the holy synod has made other useful decrees about promotion to cathedral and other greater churches, it nevertheless considers this office to be of such importance that, if effort were given to it proportionate to its value, one would never seem able to take sufficient care. So the council determines that the moment an office falls vacant, prayers and supplications should be offered in public and private, and announced by the chapter throughout the city and diocese, so that clergy and people may beg from God the favor of a good shepherd. Without wishing to change any arrangements at the present time, the council exhorts and charges all who have any right under any title from the apostolic see in the appointment of prelates, or assist the process in any way, to have as their first consideration that they can do nothing more conducive to the glory of God and the salvation of the people than to have every concern to appoint good shepherds who are fitted to guide the church; and that they will sin mortally by sharing in the sins of others unless, disregarding requests or human affection or the prompting of the ambitious, they take the utmost care to have men advanced on the claim of their own merits, persons of legitimate birth whom they know to be endowed with virtue, age, learning and all the other qualities required by the sacred canons and by the decrees of this council of Trent. However, in view of the variety of nations, people and cultures, no single standard can be used in gathering serious and adequate evidence of all these qualities from men of virtue and wisdom. Hence the holy council enjoins that in each provincial synod held under the metropolitan's presidency, there should be drawn up a formula of examination or enquiry and information proper to each place and province, as seems most useful and appropriate for that place, to be approved by the holy Roman pontiff. And when this examination or enquiry about the person to be appointed has finally been completed, it should be drawn up as a public dossier including all the evidence and the profession of faith of the candidate, and sent at once in its entirety to the pope, so that with full knowledge of the matter and information about the persons, he may himself make the best provision for the churches, judging for the sake of the Lord's flock whether the nominees are shown to be suitable by the examination and enquiry. And all enquiries, information, testimonies and commendations of any kind about the qualities and standing in the church of the nominee, by whoever conducted even in the Roman curia, are to be carefully scrutinised by the cardinal who is to report to the consistory and three other cardinals: the report of the cardinal and three other cardinals, confirmed by their signatures, will affirm that each of the four cardinals, after detailed consideration, has found those to be appointed endowed with the qualities required by the sacred canons and this council, and has reached the sure judgment on peril of his eternal salvation that they are fit to be put in charge of churches. Then, when the report has been given in consistory, the decision is to be postponed to a further consistory, so that there may be more mature information about the enquiry itself, unless the pope thinks otherwise. And the holy council decrees that each and every requirement established by it already for the appointment of bishops in regard to their life, age, learning and other qualities, should also be observed in the creation of cardinals of the holy Roman church, even if they are deacons, all of whom the pope will choose from all christian nations, as far as reasonably possible, and as he finds men that are suitable. Finally the same holy council, in a time of such turmoil in the church, cannot fail to observe that nothing is more necessary to the church of God than that the most blessed bishop of Rome, in view of the care for all the church that his office carries, must make it his priority to choose as his aides only the most picked men as cardinals, and put the best and most suitable pastors in charge of each church; and this is all the more true in that our lord Jesus Christ will require from his hands the blood of Christ's sheep, who perish under the rule of sinfully negligent shepherds, heedless of their responsibility.

Canon 2

Wherever they have lapsed, provincial councils for the control of conduct, correction of abuses, settling disputes and other matters allowed by the sacred canons, are to be restored. Hence metropolitans should not omit to summon a council in their province, either personally or if legitimately hindered through their senior suffragan bishop, within one year at least from the end of the present council, and then at least every three years, after the octave of the Easter resurrection of our lord Jesus Christ, or at another time more convenient in the tradition of the province. At this all bishops and others who by law or custom should be present, with the exception of any who would incur immediate danger in crossing the sea, are absolutely bound to assemble. And in future the bishops of a province are not to be forced under pretext of any custom to go unwillingly to the metropolitan church. Bishops not subject to any archbishop should choose a neighboring metropolitan once and for all and are then obliged to take part with the others in his provincial synod, and to observe and to see to the observance of all decided at it. In all other matters their exemption and privileges remain safe and intact. Diocesan synods, too, should be held every year, and attendance at these is obligatory on all, even those who are exempt and would be bound to attend if their exemption ceased, and who are not subject to general chapters. For the sake of parochial or other churches of seculars, even those attached to another church, all who are in charge of them must attend the synod, whoever they are. And if metropolitans or bishops or others mentioned above are negligent in these matters, they will incur the penalties laid down in the sacred canons.

Canon 3

Patriarchs, primates, metropolitans and bishops must without fail visit their diocese personally or, if legitimately impeded, through their vicar general or visitor; and if because of its extent they cannot visit it every year, then they should cover the greater part of it, so that it is covered every two years by them or their visitors. Even after a full visitation of his own diocese, a metropolitan is not to visit the cathedral churches nor dioceses of other bishops of the province, except for a reason considered and approved at the provincial synod. Archdeacons, deans and others of lower rank should henceforth visit those churches which they have legitimately been accustomed to visit, only personally and with the help of a notary taken with the bishop's consent. Visitors to be appointed by a chapter, where the chapter has the right of visiting, must first be approved by the bishop; but the bishop is not thereby prevented, nor his visitor if he is impeded, from visiting the same churches separately; and archdeacons or others of lower rank are obliged to give him an account within a month of any visitation made and show him the depositions of witnesses and all the proceedings. This is notwithstanding any custom however immemorial and any privileges or exemptions of any kind. The chief aim of all these visitations will be to ensure sound and orthodox teaching and the removal of heresies, to safeguard good practices and correct evil ones, to encourage the people by exhortation and warning to the practice of religion, peace and blameless life, and to make any dispositions for the benefit of the people that place, time and opportunity may suggest to the wisdom of the visitors. That all this may the more easily and smoothly come about, each and all those mentioned above who are concerned in visitations are charged to embrace all with fatherly love and christian zeal: therefore, content with modest transport and service, they should endeavor to complete the visitation with all speed, though with due thoroughness. While it is in progress they must take care they are not a burden to anyone through unnecessary expenses, and that neither they nor any of their party accept anything for expenses during the visitation, even from money left for pious uses, except what is legally owed to them from wills made in favor of the church, and neither money nor gift of any kind or however offered: notwithstanding any custom however immemorial. They may, however, accept the meals served to them and their party in moderate style and necessary for the time and not beyond it. It is, however, for those visited to choose whether they prefer to pay the fixed sum they have hitherto been accustomed to pay, or to supply the meals just mentioned; but without prejudice to the force of old agreements entered into with monasteries and other places of devotion or non-parochial churches, which are to remain intact. However, in places or provinces where it is the custom that neither meals nor money nor anything else is accepted by the visitors, but all takes place free of charge, that should be observed. But if in any of the above cases anyone dares to accept anything more (which heaven forbid), he is not only to make twofold restitution within a month but also to be punished without any hope of pardon by the penalties enacted in the constitution of the general council of Lyons beginning *Exigit,* and any other penalties of the provincial synod at the judgment of that synod. Patrons are in no way to interfere with what concerns the administration of the sacraments, nor to intrude on the visitation of the church's ornaments, or the revenues from stable goods and funds, unless they have the right to do so from the foundation and establishment of the church; but bishops should conduct this themselves and see that the income of the funds is spent on necessary and beneficial purposes of the church, as they think best.

Canon 4

It is the desire of the council that the office of preaching, which particularly belongs to bishops, should be exercised as often as possible for the salvation of the people. Hence, accommodating the canons published elsewhere on this subject under Paul III of happy memory to the needs of the present time, it decrees as follows: Bishops are to announce the sacred scripture and the law of God in their own church either personally or, if they are legitimately prevented, through others whom they appoint to the office of preaching; in other churches this is to be done by the parish priest or, if these are prevented, by others appointed by the bishop at the expense of those who are obliged or are accustomed to pay the costs; this is to be done in the city or in any parts of the diocese that the bishop considers expedient, at least on every Sunday and solemn feast, and daily or at least three times a week during the seasons of fasting, namely Lent and Advent, if they consider this should be done, and as often at other times as they judge appropriate. And the bishop should carefully instruct the people that each of them is under obligation to attend their parish church, when they can reasonably do so, to hear the word of God. No secular or regular may presume to preach against the wish of the bishop, even in churches of his own order. The same priests will see that at least on Sundays and great feasts the children in every parish are taught the elements of the faith and obedience to God and their parents by those whose task it is, and if necessary compel them by church censures. This is notwithstanding privileges and customs. In other matters the decrees on the office of preaching enacted under Paul III retain their force.

Canon 5

The pope alone is to take cognisance of and decide on more serious criminal charges against bishops, even (which God forbid) of heresy, which could involve deposition or privation. But if a charge arises which of necessity has to be heard outside the Roman curia, it is not to be heard by anyone except metropolitans or bishops chosen by the pope. But such a hearing is of a special kind, firmly under the control of the pope, who never allows to it greater authority than to take cognisance of the fact and complete the procedure, which it will then send at once to the pope, who reserves to himself the definitive sentence. For the rest, the decrees on this subject made on another occasion under Julius III of happy memory, and the constitution made in a general council under Innocent III beginning *Qualiter et quando,* are to be observed by all.

Lesser criminal charges against bishops are to be heard and concluded only in the provincial synod or by those deputed by the provincial synod.

Canon 6

Bishops have power to dispense from all irregularities and suspensions arising from an offence that is not public, except in the case of voluntary homicide and in other cases which have been taken to court; and, after imposing a salutary penance, to absolve freely in the forum of conscience within their diocese those of their subjects who are guilty in any cases that are not public, even those reserved to the apostolic see; this they may do in person or through a substitute specially deputed for the purpose. The same permission is given to them alone in the same forum of conscience for the offence of heresy, but not to their deputies.

Canon 7

So that the faithful people may approach the reception of the sacraments with greater reverence and spiritual devotion, the holy council charges bishops not only to explain their power and benefit in a way that those receiving can grasp, before they themselves administer them to the people; but to ensure that the same is done by all parish priests with devotion and wisdom, even in the. vernacular tongue, where there is need and it can reasonably be done; and this is to be done according to the form laid down by the holy council for each sacrament, which bishops should take steps to have accurately translated into the vernacular and explained to the people by all parish priests. Similarly, during mass or the celebration of office on every feast or solemnity they should explain the divine commandments and precepts of salvation in the vernacular and should be zealous to implant them in the hearts of all (leaving aside useless questions) and educate them in the law of the Lord.

Canon 8

The Apostle warns that public sinners should be openly rebuked. When therefore someone commits a crime publicly and in the view of many, by which others are offended and scandalized and disturbed, then without a doubt a fitting penance for the crime in question should be publicly imposed on such a person, that one who has incited others to evil by his example should recall them to an upright life by the evidence of his penance. A bishop may, however, commute this kind of public penance into another one that is secret, when he considers this more profitable. And in all cathedral churches the bishop should establish a post of confessor to be united with the next prebend to fall vacant, to be held by a master or doctor or licentiate in theology or canon law, of forty years of age, or otherwise if someone is found more suitable for the character of the place; and while he hears confessions in the church he is to be counted as being present in choir.

Canon 9

The rules established on another occasion under Paul III of happy memory, and recently under our blessed lord Pius IV in this same council, about the care to be taken by ordinaries over the visitation of benefices, even those that are exempt, are also to be observed in those secular churches which are said to be of no diocese, in that they are to be visited by the bishop whose cathedral church is nearest, if that is agreed, and otherwise by the person chosen once and for all during the provincial synod by the prelate of that place, even acting as delegate of the apostolic see. And this notwithstanding privileges and customs of any kind however immemorial.

Canon 10

That bishops may more easily keep the people they govern in dutiful obedience, they have the right and power in all that concerns visitation and correction of their people, even acting as delegates of the apostolic see, to arrange, change, punish and carry out, according to canonical sanctions, anything they judge necessary for the correction of their subjects and the benefit of their diocese: nor in matters of visitation or emendation of conduct shall any exemption or injunction, appeal or complaint, even addressed to the apostolic see, in any way obstruct or suspend the execution of what they have commanded, decreed or judged.

Canon 11

Privileges and exemptions given to many people on various grounds are today seen to cause great disturbance of episcopal jurisdiction and to give occasion to the exempt for lax standards of living. Hence the holy council decrees that: if anyone on occasion, prompted by reasonable and serious and almost necessary reasons sees fit to decorate some persons in or out of the Roman curia with the honorary titles of protonotary, acolyte, count palatine, royal chaplain or other distinctions of this kind; or to appoint others as oblates or attached in some other way to any monastery, or as serving by name in military orders or monasteries or hospices or colleges, or under any other title; then, let it be understood that nothing in any of these privileges so detracts from the authority of the ordinaries that those to whom they have already been granted, or may in future be granted, are any the less subject fully and in all matters to the ordinaries as delegates of the apostolic see, as was enjoined for royal chaplains in the constitution of Innocent III beginning *Cum capella*. Those, however, are excepted who are actively serving in the places mentioned or the military orders, and reside within their confines and buildings, living under their obedience, or who have legally made profession according to the rule of these military orders, a fact of which the ordinary must have proof. And this is notwithstanding any privileges, even those of the order of St John of Jerusalem and other military orders. As to the privileges usually accorded to those living in the Roman curia by virtue of the constitution of Eugenius or of belonging to households of cardinals, such privileges are not to be understood as applying, by reason of the aforesaid benefices, to those holding church benefices but they remain subject to the jurisdiction of the ordinary. And this is notwithstanding any injunctions.

Canon 12

When dignities are established in churches, especially cathedral churches, in order to preserve and strengthen church discipline, in that those who occupy them should excel in religious devotion, be a good example to others and assist the bishop in his work and office, then clearly those who are called to fill them should be men able to rise to this responsibility. And so henceforth no one is to be promoted to any dignity involving the care of souls unless he has reached the twenty-fifth year of his age and is a person in clerical orders commended by the learning necessary to discharge his office and by

probity of life, according to the constitution of Alexander III promulgated at the Lateran council and beginning *Cum in cunctis*. Archdeacons, too, who are called the eyes of the bishop should in all churches as far as possible be masters in theology or doctors and licentiates in canon law. For other dignities and posts which do not involve the care of souls, suitable clerics should be recruited who are not less than twenty-two years of age. Those appointed to benefices of any kind involving the care of souls are obliged, within two months at most of the date of their taking possession, to make a public profession of their orthodox faith with their hands in those of the bishop or, if he is prevented, in the presence of his vicar general or official, and give their oath and promise that they will remain in the obedience of the Roman church. Those appointed to canonries and dignities in cathedral churches are bound to do the same not only in the presence of the bishop or his vicar, but in the chapter. Otherwise none of the appointees mentioned shall receive his salary nor shall his possession be valid. No one henceforth is to be received into a dignity, canonry or portion unless he has already received the holy order required by that dignity, prebend or portion, or is of such an -age that he may be validly inducted within the time laid down by law and by this holy council. And in all cathedral churches all canonries and portions are to have annexed to them the order of priest, deacon or subdeacon. The bishop jointly with the counsel of his chapter is to designate and assign, as seems expedient, to which of the holy orders each post is attached, but in such a way that at least half will be priests and the rest either deacons or subdeacons; and where the even more praiseworthy custom prevails that all or the majority should be priests, let it be observed. The holy council further urges that, where this can reasonably be done, all the dignities in provinces and at least half of the canonries in cathedral churches and distinguished collegiate churches should be conferred only on masters and doctors or even licentiates in theology or canon law. Further, those who hold dignities or canonries or prebends or portions in the same cathedral or collegiate churches may not, in virtue of any statute or custom, be absent from their churches for more than three months in a year, without prejudice to the constitutions of those churches which require a longer time of service; otherwise each offender is to be deprived in the first year of half the revenues which are his by reason of the prebend and residence. But if anyone repeats the negligence, he is to be deprived of all the income gained in that year; if obstinacy persists, proceedings should be taken against them according to the enactments of the sacred canons. Those, however, are to receive their shares of distributions who are present at the stated times; the rest are to go without them, all collusion and recuperation being excluded, according to the decree of Boniface VIII beginning Consuetudinem, which the holy council restores to force; notwithstanding any statutes and customs of any kind. All are obliged to attend the divine office personally and not through substitutes, and to assist and serve the bishop when he is celebrating mass or other pontifical rites, and when in choir for sung worship to praise the name of God reverently, distinctly and devoutly in hymns and canticles. Let them, moreover, wear becoming dress at all times, both in and out of church, and abstain from unlawful hunting, fowling, dances, taverns and games, and so excel in integrity of life that they may justly be called the church's senate. For other matters concerning the due ordering of the divine office, the provincial synod shall enjoin a precise rule in the light of the good and the customs of each province about the appropriate style of singing and chanting, about the determined manner of gathering and remaining in choir, and all that is necessary about church ministers and anything else of the kind. Until then the bishop may make provisions for all that seems expedient in consultation with not less than two canons, one chosen by himself and the other by the chapter.

Canon 13

As many cathedral churches are so poor and with such slender revenues that these in no way match episcopal dignity and church needs, the provincial council should summon those concerned and consider with them which churches it would be right to unite with neighboring ones because of their slim resources, and which they can strengthen with new revenues; they should then draw up a program and send it to the pope, so that he may be guided by it, as in his wisdom he thinks fit, to unite poor churches together or to build up others by increase in income. In the meantime, while these steps are being taken, the pope can make provision for such bishops who need increased resources because of the poverty of their dioceses, out of certain benefices, as long as they do not involve the care of souls and are not dignities or canonries and prebends, nor monasteries in which regular observance is in force or which are subject to general chapters and fixed visitors. In the case of parish churches whose resources are so meager that they cannot meet their obligations, the bishop will provide, if this can be done by the union of benefices, excluding those of regulars, so that by the allocation of first fruits or tithes, or by contributions and collections from parishioners, or by whatever means he finds reasonable, sufficient be put together to supply the decent support of the rector and parish. In all unions, however, whether made for these or other reasons, parish churches should not be combined with monasteries of any kind, nor abbacies, nor dignities or prebends of the cathedral or collegiate church, nor with other simple benefices or hospices or military orders; and those already so united should be reviewed by the local bishops in accordance with the decree made in this same council on another occasion under Paul III of happy memory, which is to be observed in the case of those united between that time and this. And this is notwithstanding any particular forms of words, which are to be regarded as adequately expressed in the above. Further, in future no cathedral churches whose revenue does not exceed a thousands ducats in true annual value are to be burdened with any pensions or reservations of income, nor parish churches whose revenue does not exceed a hundred ducats. In cities or other places where parish churches have no fixed boundaries, and the rectors have no congregation of their own to serve but administer the sacraments to all who come to ask at random, the holy council bids bishops, for the good spiritual state of the souls entrusted to them, to divide the people into separate and clear parishes and to assign to each their own proper and permanent parish priest, who will be able to know them and from whom alone they may licitly receive the sacraments; or he must provide in some other and better way, as the character of the place may require. And bishops must see that the same is done as soon as possible in cities and other places where there are no parish churches. This is notwithstanding any privileges whatever or customs however immemorial.

Canon 14

In many cathedral, collegiate and parochial churches, either from their constitutions or from reprehensible custom, the practice can be noted that in the election, presentation, nomination, institution, confirmation, collation or some other provision, or admission, to possession of some cathedral church or benefice, canonry or prebend, or to part of the revenues, or to the daily distributions, certain illicit conditions or deductions from the revenues, payments, promises or compensations are introduced, or even what in some churches are called mutual profits. In detestation of such practices the holy council commands bishops not to allow any such payments that are not applied to pious uses, or those dues that are suspect of the stain of simony or sordid greed; and they are to make a careful revision of their constitutions and customs in this matter and, excepting only those they approve as praiseworthy, to remove and abolish the rest as base and scandalous. And the council decrees that any who contravene in any way the contents of this decree shall be liable to the penalties published against those guilty of simony in the sacred canons and the constitutions of various popes, all of which it renews. And this is notwithstanding any statutes or constitutions whatever or customs however immemorial, even those confirmed by apostolic authority, of all of which the bishop may take cognisance as delegate of the apostolic see with regard to their fraud, by subtraction or addition, and to their defect of intention.

Canon 15

In some cathedral churches and those of distinguished colleges, the prebends and distributions are at once so many and so meager that they do not suffice to support the proper state of the canons, in view of the standing of the place and the persons. In these the bishop may with the consent of the chapter unite them with some simple benefices, though not those of regulars; or, if provision cannot be made in this way, he may reduce the number by suppressing some of them (with the consent of the patrons where laity have the right of patronage), and apply their income and revenues to the daily distributions of the prebends that remain; but in doing so he should ensure that sufficient remain to provide reasonably for the cerebration of divine worship and the standing of the church. This is notwithstanding any constitutions or privileges of any kind, or any general or special reservation or attachment; nor may the unions or suppressions aforesaid be set aside or obstructed by any stipulations even arising from resignation, or by any other qualifications or suspensions.

Canon 16

When a see falls vacant the chapter, when the duty falls to it of receiving revenues, should appoint one or more careful and reliable treasurers to take charge of church property and revenues, with the duty of giving an account to the person who is responsible. The chapter is strictly bound likewise within eight days of the bishop's death to appoint an official or vicar or to confirm the existing one in office; the appointee should be at least a doctor or licentiate in canon law, or otherwise qualified as far as possible; if such action is not taken, it will fall on the metropolitan to appoint the deputy; but if the church is itself the metropolitan cathedral or exempt and the chapter has been negligent (in the above action), then the senior of the suffragan bishops shall appoint a suitable treasurer and vicar for the metropolitan church, and the nearest bishop shall make the appointments for the exempt church. Further, the bishop appointed to that vacant see is to ask for an account in all matters of his concern regarding the official acts, jurisdiction, administration or any part of their responsibilities from the same treasurer, vicar and any other officials and administrators appointed in his place, during the vacancy, by the chapter or any others; and he may punish any who have failed in their administrative duties, even if these officials, after giving their report to the chapter, have obtained absolution and discharge from it or its deputies. And the chapter is obliged to give an account to the succeeding bishop of any documents belonging to the church that have come into their hands.

Canon 17

When one person occupies the posts of several clerics church order is upset, and so it was provided in a holy manner by the sacred canons that no one should be appointed to two churches. But many people nevertheless are not ashamed to evade sound laws by devious means and to occupy many benefices at once, deceiving themselves but not God through the base lust of greed. Hence the holy council, desiring to restore due order to the governing of churches, commands that the present decree is to be observed by all persons whatever, however distinguished their rank and even if it be that of cardinal. It decrees that henceforth only one church benefice may be conferred on each person; but allows that, if this does not suffice to support the incumbent in a reasonable fashion, another simple benefice may be granted him provided that both do not require residence. And these rules are to apply not only to cathedral churches, but to all other benefices of any kind, whether secular or regular, even commendatory, and whatever their title or quality. And those who at the present time occupy more than one parish church, or a cathedral benefice and a parish church, are strictly bound, notwithstanding any dispensations and unions made for life, to keep only one cathedral or parochial church and to relinquish the remaining parochial ones within six months. Otherwise all the benefices they occupy are to be considered vacant in law and can freely be conferred as vacant on others who are suitable, nor may those who previously occupied them retain their revenues in good conscience after this stated time. It is the wish of the holy council, however, that some reasonable provision should be made for the needs of those resigning benefices, as shall seem good to the pope.

Canon 18

It is of the highest import for the salvation of souls that parishes be governed by worthy and qualified men. That this may be achieved more carefully and accurately the holy council decrees that, when a parish church falls vacant by death or resignation, whether in the curia or in any other way, even if the care of the church is said to fall to the bishop and it is administered by one or more persons on his behalf, and even in

churches called patrimonial or receptive where the bishop is accustomed to give the care to one or more persons, all of whom the council orders to be bound to the examination set out below, and even if the parish church is reserved or generally or specially attached even in virtue of an indult or privilege in favor of the cardinals of the holy Roman church or abbots or chapters; then if necessary, as soon as he has heard of the vacancy, the bishop must appoint a suitable vicar to take on the duties of the church, and assign him what in his judgment is a suitable share of the revenues, until a rector is allocated to it. Next, the bishop and any person having the right of patronage must give to appointed examiners the names of some clerics suited to being rectors of the church, within ten days or any other period determined by the bishop. And it is to be open to others knowing men fitted for the post to put forward their names, so that there may then be a careful enquiry about the age, conduct and aptitude of each one. And, if it is found better by the bishop or the provincial synod in the light of local practice, men who wish to be considered may be so invited by public edict. When the dateline has passed, all whose names have been registered are to be examined by the bishop or, if he is prevented, by his vicar general and by not less than three other examiners: if their votes are equally divided, or each for different persons, the bishop or his vicar general may give a casting vote. Every year in the diocesan synod at least six examiners are to be proposed by the bishop or the vicar general, and these are to be approved as acceptable by the synod: when any vacancy occurs the bishop should choose three of these to carry out the examination with him; then at the next vacancy he is to choose the same or another three out of the six, as he prefers. These examiners are to be masters or doctors or licentiates in theology or canon law, or other clerics or regulars including mendicant friars, or even laity, who are seen to be more suitable for the task. All are to swear on the holy gospels of God that they will set aside every human attachment and carry out their responsibility faithfully. And they must take care not to accept anything by reason of the examination, either before or after; otherwise they and those giving to them will incur the sin of simony, from which they cannot be absolved until they have relinquished whatever benefices they have in any manner acquired, even previously, and they are made incapable of holding other benefices in the future. They must give an account of all these actions, not only before God, but at the provincial synod if need be, at whose judgment they may be seriously punished if it is discovered that they have done anything in conflict with their duty. On completion of the examination they are to report which men have been judged suited by age, conduct, doctrine, wisdom and in other ways appropriate to the government of the vacant church, and the bishop will choose the one he regards as the most suited, and on him and no other shall appointment to the church be conferred by him who has the duty of appointing. If an ecclesiastic has the right of patronage, and the bishop that of institution, then the person whom the patron considers most suited among those approved by the examiners is obliged to present himself to the bishop so as to be instituted by him. If, however, someone other than the bishop has the right of institution, then the bishop alone shall choose the most worthy of the approved candidates for the patron to present to the person who has the right of institution. But if patronage is in the hands of laity, anyone presented by the patron must be examined by the same board as above, and is not to be appointed unless judged suitable by them. In all the above cases, the church is not to be entrusted to anyone other than one examined and approved by the board according to the stated procedure: nor is the report of these examiners to be prevented or suspended from taking effect by any transference of authority or appeal, even made to the apostolic see or its legates, vice-legates or nuncios, or to bishops or metropolitans, primates or patriarchs. Otherwise the vicar whom the bishop previously appointed temporarily on his own judgment when the church fell vacant, or shall subsequently appoint, is not to be removed from care and administration of that church, until it is committed to the same person or to another person chosen and approved as above; and all other provisions or institutions made in any form other than the above are to be held fraudulent. And this is notwithstanding any exemptions from this decree, indults, privileges, impediments, attachments, new provisions or indults granted to any universities, even for a fixed payment, or any other impediments of any kind. But if the revenues of the said parish church are too small to support the whole procedure of examination, or no one offers himself for examination, or if serious strife and rioting could be stirred up in some places because of open factions and discord; then the ordinary, on the advice of the deputed examiners and if he considers it in conscience better, may omit this procedure and conduct a private examination of his own, but observing all the other procedures outlined above. And it shall be in the power of the provincial synod to make provision, if it considers anything should be added to or omitted from the above procedure of examination.

Canon 19

The holy council decrees that henceforth no mandates of provisions, or expectative graces as they are called, should be granted to anyone, even to colleges or universities or senates or any other individual persons, even under the title of indult or for a fixed payment, or on any other ground, and that it is not lawful to use those already granted. Nor are mental reservations or any other favors with regard to future vacancies, nor indults in regard to other churches or monasteries, to be granted to anyone, even to cardinals of the holy Roman church, and those hitherto granted are to be regarded as abrogated.

Canon 20

Cognisance of all cases in any way belonging to ecclesiastical jurisdiction, even those concerning benefices, is to be taken in the presence of the local ordinary alone in the first instance, and they must without fail be concluded within two years of the case being introduced. Otherwise, after that interval the parties, or one of them, shall be free to approach higher judges to take up the case at the point it had reached and see to its completion as soon as possible. But before that time cases are not to be committed to others or transferred, nor should appeals put in by the parties be accepted by higher judges of any kind, nor should any committal or injunction be made by the latter except upon a definitive sentence, or one having definitive force, when any grievance thus arising cannot be put right by appeal from the definitive sentence. Cases are excepted from these rules which according to canonical regulations are to be

handled by the apostolic see, or which on urgent and reasonable grounds the pope shall decide to commit or transfer under a specially sealed rescript to be signed by his holiness's own hand. In addition, matrimonial and criminal cases are to be left to the examination and jurisdiction of the bishop alone, not that of the dean or archdeacon or other lower judges even during their visitation, even if in a particular case some legal dispute is pending at the time between the bishop and the dean or archdeacon or lower judges over taking cognisance of that case; and if when the case is before the bishop one party shall truly prove poverty, he shall not be compelled to conduct the same matrimonial case outside the province in the second or third instance, unless the other party is willing to provide sustenance and legal costs. Legates even *a latere,* nuncios, church governors and others, whatever the force of their faculties, must not presume to obstruct bishops in the aforesaid cases, nor in any way usurp or disturb their jurisdiction, nor even take proceedings against clerics or any other ecclesiastical persons until they have first requested the bishop to do so and he has failed; otherwise their proceedings and rulings have no force and they are bound to repay any loss caused to the parties. Furthermore, if anyone appeals in cases permitted by law, or complains of any grievance, or otherwise has recourse to another judge because of the lapse of the two years above stated; then he is obliged to transfer all the acts of the case before the bishop to the appeal judge at his own expense, having first given notice to that bishop so that he may give any information about the case he thinks fit to the appeal judge. But if the defendant appears, he too is bound to pay his share of the costs of transferring the acts, if he wishes to use them, unless local custom provides otherwise, namely that the appellant bears all these costs. Further, the notary is obliged for a suitable fee to make a copy of the documents available to the appellant as soon as possible, and at the latest within a month; and if the notary practices deceit in producing a copy, he is to be suspended from the exercise of his office at the bishop's discretion and to pay a fine equal to twice the legal costs, to be divided between the appellant and the poor of the locality. The judge, too, if he is aware of and connives at or otherwise assists in preventing the complete documents reaching the appellant in time, is to be subject to the same double fine as above. And this is notwithstanding in any of the above matters any privileges, indults, agreements (which only bind their authors) or other customs whatever.

Canon 21

The holy council is anxious that in times to come no opportunity for doubt should arise from any of the decrees published by it, and in particular from the following words in the decree published in the first session under our most blessed lord Paul IV: ''Those steps which shall seem fitting and appropriate to the holy council, at the proposal of the legates and presidents, to ease the disasters of the present time, to abate religious controversies, to restrain deceitful tongues, to correct the abuses of depraved conduct, to bring true peace and christian reconciliation to the church.'' The council now explains them and declares that it was not its intention to change in any way by these words the usual way of handling business in general councils, nor to add or subtract anything by way of innovation and contrary to what has hitherto been determined by the sacred cannons or the formula of general councils.

SESSION 25
3-4 December 1563

Decree on purgatory

As the catholic church, instructed by the holy Spirit, has taught from holy scripture and the ancient tradition of the fathers in its holy councils and most recently in this ecumenical council that purgatory exists, and that the souls detained there are helped by the prayers of the faithful and most of all by the acceptable sacrifice of the altar; the holy council charges bishops to ensure that sound teaching on purgatory, handed down by the holy fathers and sacred councils, is believed and held by the christian faithful and everywhere preached and expounded. In homilies to uninstructed people the more difficult and subtle questions, which do nothing to sustain faith and give rise to little or no increase of devotion, should be excluded. They should not allow uncertain speculation or what borders on falsehood to be publicly treated. And they should prohibit all that panders to curiosity and superstition, or smacks of base gain, as scandalous stumbling-blocks to the faithful. Bishops should see to it that the offerings of the faithful who are living, namely masses, prayers, alms and other works of piety, customarily done by the faithful for those of the faithful who have died, should be performed piously and with devotion according to the laws of the church, and that whatever is due for these purposes from testamentary bequests or any other sources should be discharged by priests and ministers of the church and others bound to this duty in no perfunctory manner but with diligence and accuracy.

On invocation, veneration and relics of the saints, and on sacred images

The holy council charges all bishops and others with the office and responsibility of teaching, according to the practice of the catholic and apostolic church received from the earliest times of the christian religion, to the consensus of the holy fathers and to the decrees of the sacred councils, as follows: they are first of all to instruct the faithful carefully about the intercession of the saints, invocation of them, reverence for their relics and the legitimate use of images of them; they should teach them that the saints, reigning together with Christ, offer their prayers to God for people; that it is a good and beneficial thing to invoke them and to have recourse to their prayers and helpful assistance to obtain blessings from God through his Son our lord Jesus Christ, who is our sole redeemer and savior; and that those hold impious opinions who deny that the saints who enjoy eternal happiness in heaven should be invoked, or who say either that they do not pray for people, or that calling on them to pray for all of us is idolatry, or contrary to the word of God, or impugns the honor of the one mediator between God and humankind, Jesus Christ, or that it is foolish to invoke those reigning in heaven with mind and voice. And they should teach that the holy bodies of the blessed martyrs and others who live with Christ, in that they were living members of Christ and a temple of the holy Spirit, due to be raised by him to eternal and glorified life, are to be venerated by the faithful, and that through them many blessings are given to us by God: and hence that those are altogether to be condemned, as holy church has formerly condemned them and now condemns them again, who assert that no veneration or honor is owed to the relics of the saints, or that it is futile for people to honor them and other sacred memorials, and that they rehearse the memory of the saints in vain when seeking to gain their help.

And they must also teach that images of Christ, the virgin mother of God and the other saints should be set up and kept, particularly in churches, and that due honor and reverence is owed to them, not because some divinity or power is believed to lie in them as reason for the cult, or because anything is to be expected from them, or because confidence should be placed in images as was done by the pagans of old; but because the honor showed to them is referred to the original which they represent: thus, through the images which we kiss and before which we uncover our heads and go down on our knees, we give adoration to Christ and veneration to the saints, whose likeness they bear. And this has been approved by the decrees of councils, especially the second council of Nicaea, against the iconoclasts.

Bishops should teach with care that the faithful are instructed and strengthened by commemorating and frequently recalling the articles of our faith through the expression in pictures or other likenesses of the stories of the mysteries of our redemption; and that great benefits flow from all sacred images, not only because people are reminded of the gifts and blessings conferred on us by Christ, but because the miracles of God through the saints and their salutary example is put before the eyes of the faithful, who can thank God for them, shape their own lives and conduct in imitation of the saints, and be aroused to adore and love God and to practice devotion. If anyone teaches or holds what is contrary to these decrees: let him be anathema.

The holy council earnestly desires to root out utterly any abuses that may have crept into these holy and saving practices, so that no representations of false doctrine should be set up which give occasion of dangerous error to the unlettered. So if accounts and stories from holy scripture are sometimes etched and pictured, which is a help to uneducated people, they must be taught that the Godhead is not pictured because it can be seen with human eyes or expressed in figures and colors. All superstition must be removed from invocation of the saints, veneration of relics and use of sacred images; all aiming at base profit must be eliminated; all sensual appeal must be avoided, so that images are not painted or adorned with seductive charm; and people are not to abuse the celebration of the saints and visits to their relics for the purpose of drunken feasting, as if feast days in honor of the saints were to be celebrated with sensual luxury. And lastly, bishops should give very great care and attention to ensure that in this matter nothing occurs that is disorderly or arranged in an exaggerated or riotous manner, nothing profane and nothing unseemly, since holiness befits the house of God.

That these points may be carried out more faithfully, the holy synod lays down that no one may erect or see to the erection of any unusual image in any church or site, however exempt, unless it has been approved by the bishop. Nor are any new miracles to be accepted, or new relics recognized, without the bishop similarly examining and approving them. And as soon as he learns of something of this kind, he should consult with theologians and other devout men and decide as truth and devotion suggest. But if some doubtful or resistant abuse has to be rooted out, or some far more serious problem arises in these matters, then before deciding the issue the bishop should await the opinion of the metropolitan and his fellow bishops in the provincial synod, but ensuring that no new and unprecedented decree be passed in the church without the pope being consulted beforehand.

Decree on regulars and nuns

The same holy council, pursuing the subject of reform, has decided to decree what follows.

Chapter 1

The holy council is well aware how much grace and benefit arises in the church from monasteries which are devoutly founded and rightly administered. It considers that it is necessary for the ancient and regular discipline to be restored where it has collapsed, and to be pursued with greater constancy where it has been preserved. That this may come about sooner and more easily it has decided to enact, as by this decree it does enact, that all regulars both men and women should order and arrange their lives according to the provision of the rule they profess; and that above all they should faithfully observe what belongs to the perfection of their profession, such as the vows of obedience, poverty and chastity, and any other special precepts particular to any rule or order which belong to their essential nature and to the preservation of common life, food and clothing; and it enjoins superiors to exercise the utmost diligence in general and provincial chapters and in their visitations, which they must not omit to conduct at the proper times, that their subjects do not abandon these standards, since it is quite clear that they cannot relax rules which belong to the substance of religious life. For if the very bases and foundations of all religious discipline are not carefully preserved, the whole building will necessarily topple.

Chapter 2

No regular, therefore, whether man or woman, may possess or keep immovable or movable goods of whatever value or however acquired as their own or even in the name of their religious house, but they should at once be handed over to the superior and annexed to the property of the house. Nor may superiors henceforth allow religious to have any stable goods, even for use without ownership or for use or administration or in trust. Administration of the property of monasteries and religious houses is to belong solely to their officials, who may be removed from office at the superior's will. Superiors may, however, permit them the use of movable goods to a degree that befits the lowly state of poverty they have professed, and while there should be nothing superfluous in this, nor should anything necessary be denied them. But if anyone is found or convicted of possessing anything otherwise, he or she is to be deprived for two years of active and passive voice and further punished according to the constitutions of his or her rule and order.

Chapter 3

The holy council gives permission to all monasteries and houses of men and women and of mendicants (except the houses of the Capuchin friars of St Francis and those called Minors in observance), even to those whose constitutions forbid it or who have not had it granted by apostolic privilege, lawfully henceforth to possess immovable goods. If any of the aforesaid places have been permitted by apostolic authority to possess such goods, but have been robbed of them, the council decrees that these goods must all be restored to them. In the aforesaid monasteries and houses of men and women, whether possessing immovable goods or not, only the number of religious should be established and maintained in the future that can be reasonably supported either from revenues belonging to the monasteries or by accustomed alms. Nor are such places to be founded in future unless the permission of the bishop in whose diocese they are to be established is first obtained.

Chapter 4

The holy council forbids any regular, without the permission of his superior, on pretext of preaching or lecturing or any pious work, to submit himself to the obedience of any prelate, prince, community, or any other person or establishment; nor shall any privilege or faculty obtained from others in this matter avail him. If he acts otherwise, he is to be punished by his superior as disobedient. Nor may regulars leave their religious houses, even on pretext of approaching their superiors, unless sent or summoned by these superiors. Anyone found abroad without the aforesaid command given in writing is to be punished by the local ordinaries as a deserter from his institute. Those sent to study at universities should live only in religious houses, otherwise action should be taken against them by the ordinaries.

Chapter 5

Renewing the constitution of Boniface VIII which begins *Periculoso,* the holy council commands all bishops, calling the divine justice to witness and under threat of eternal damnation, to ensure that the enclosure of nuns-in all monasteries subject to them by ordinary authority, and in others by the authority of the apostolic see, should be diligently restored where it has been violated, and preserved most carefully where it has remained intact; they should coerce any who are disobedient and refractory by ecclesiastical censures and other penalties, setting aside any form of appeal, and calling in the help of the secular arm if need be. The holy synod exhorts all christian princes to provide such aid, and enjoins this on all magistrates on pain of excommunication automatically incurred. After religious profession no nun may go out of her monastery on any pretext even for a short time, except for a legitimate reason approved by the bishop, notwithstanding any indults and privileges whatever. And no one of any kind or condition or sex or age may enter within the confines of a monastery without the permission of the bishop or superior given in writing, under pain of excommunication automatically incurred. And the bishop or superior should give permission only in necessary cases, nor may anyone else give it in any way, even in virtue of some faculty or indult previously given or to be given in the future. And as monasteries of nuns are often to

PROMULGATIONS OF THE COUNCIL OF TRENT (continued)

be found outside the walls of a city or town, and are exposed often without any protection to the plunder of wicked people and to other crimes, bishops and other superiors are to see, if it seems expedient, that the nuns from them are moved to new or old monasteries inside cities or populous towns, calling on the aid of the secular arm if need be. Those obstructing or disobeying should be compelled to obey by ecclesiastical censures.

Chapter 6

That everything should be done correctly and without deceit in the election of any superiors, abbots and temporary and other officials, and of generals and abbesses and other women superiors, the holy council first and foremost strictly orders that all the above be elected by secret ballot, so that the names of individual voters are never disclosed. Nor in the future shall it be lawful to appoint titular provincials or abbots or priors or any other superiors for the purpose of holding an election, or to have proxies acting for the voices and votes of those absent. If anyone is elected against the rulings of this decree the election shall be invalid, and the person who allows himself to be made provincial or abbot or prior in such a way shall for the future be incapable of holding any office in religious life; all permissions granted in this matter are to be regarded as hereby abrogated, and any granted in the future as fraudulent.

Chapter 7

An abbess or prioress, or by whatever other name the superior or person in charge is called, shall be chosen who is not less than forty years of age and has lived in a praiseworthy manner for eight years since making her profession. If no one of these qualities can be found in the same monastery, she can be chosen from another house of the same order. If this seems to the superior conducting the election to be seriously inconvenient, then with the consent of the bishop or another superior let someone be chosen from the same monastery over thirty years of age who has lived a good life for at least five years since profession. No one is to be superior of two monasteries, and if anyone has by some means charge of two or more she must be obliged to resign all but one of them within six months. If she has not resigned after that time, then all automatically fall vacant. He who presides over an election, whether the bishop or another superior, is not to enter the monastery's enclosure, but should hear or receive the votes of each religious before the window of the grille. In other details the constitutions of each order or monastery are to be observed.

Chapter 8

All monasteries which are not subject to general chapters or bishops, and do not have their ordinaries as regular visitors, but are accustomed to be governed under the immediate protection and rule of the apostolic see, are to be bound within a year from the ending of the present council, and then every three years, to group themselves in congregations according to the form of the constitution Of Innocent III made in a general council and beginning *In singulis,* and there to appoint certain regulars to discuss and determine the manner and rules for setting up the

aforesaid congregations and for executing statutes for them. If they are negligent in this matter, the metropolitan in whose province these monasteries lie may, as delegate of the apostolic see, assemble them for these purposes. But if there are not sufficient of these monasteries within the boundaries of one province to form a congregation, the monasteries of two or three provinces may form one congregation. When the congregations are formed, their general chapters and the presidents or visitors elected by them shall have the same authority over the monasteries of their congregation and over the religious living in them as have the other presidents and visitors in other orders. They are obliged to visit the monasteries of their congregation frequently, to take steps to their reform and to observe the decrees of the sacred canons and of this council. If they do not carry out these instructions, even at the bidding of the metropolitan, they are to become subject to the bishops in whose dioceses they are situated, as to delegates of the apostolic see.

Chapter 9

Monasteries of nuns immediately subject to the holy apostolic see, even under the name of chapters of St. Peter or St. John or whatever other name they go by, are to be governed by bishops as delegates of the said see, anything to the contrary notwithstanding. Those, however, which are governed by persons appointed in general chapters or by other regulars, are to be left in their guardianship and care.

Chapter 10

Bishops and other superiors of monasteries of nuns should carefully see to it that the nuns are enjoined in their constitutions to make confession of their sins at least once a month, and to receive the most holy eucharist, so as to fortify themselves with this powerful protection to conquer with vigor all the attacks of the devil. In addition to their ordinary confessor, the bishop or other superiors should offer an extraordinary confessor two or three times a year who should hear the confessions of all. And the holy council forbids the most holy body of Christ to be reserved in the choir or in the precincts of the monastery and not in a public church, not-withstanding any indult or privilege.

Chapter 11

In monasteries or religious houses of men and women which have attached to them the spiritual care of lay persons over and above those belonging to the household of the monasteries or institutions, the persons both regular and secular who carry out this care are to be immediately subject in all that concerns the said care and the administration of the sacraments to the jurisdiction, visitation and correction of the bishop in whose diocese they are situated; nor in this matter should anyone be appointed, even if instantly replaceable, without the same bishop's examination and consent, to be carried out personally or through his vicar: with the exception of the monastery of Cluny and its territory, and also of those monasteries and houses in which abbots general or other superiors of regulars exercise episcopal and temporal jurisdiction over parish priests and parishioners, without prejudice however to the rights of those bishops who exercise major jurisdiction over the said places and persons.

Chapter 12

Censures and interdicts should at the bishop's command be published and kept by regulars in their own churches, not only those put out by the apostolic see but also those published by ordinaries. And feast days which a bishop orders to be kept in his diocese are to be observed by all those who are exempt, even regulars.

Chapter 13

The bishop is to decide without appeal and notwithstanding any considerations all disputes that arise about precedence between ecclesiastical persons, secular or regular, often with great scandal: these arise in public processions, in the rites for burying the bodies of the dead, in carrying the canopy and suchlike. All those who are exempt, both secular and regular clerics of any grade, including monks, are bound to attend public processions when summoned, those alone being excepted who live permanently in stricter enclosure.

Chapter 14

A regular who is not subject to the bishop, and who lives in monastic enclosure, but has notoriously deserted it and is a source of scandal to the people, must at the bishop's urging be severely punished by his own superior within the time fixed by the bishop, and the superior must inform the bishop of the punishment. If the superior does not comply, he is to be deprived of his office by his own superior, and the offender may be punished by the bishop.

Chapter 15

Profession in any religious institute, whether of men or women, must not be made until the completion of the sixteenth year, nor is anyone to be admitted to profession who has spent less than a year in a state of probation after receiving the habit' Profession made before these times shall be null, incurring no obligation to the observance of the rule of any religious institute or order, and shall not have any other effects whatever.

Chapter 16

No renunciation made or obligation undertaken, even with an oath or in favor of any pious cause, shall be valid unless made within the two months before profession and with the permission of the bishop or his vicar; nor is it to be understood to take effect until after profession. Otherwise it shall be invalid and of no effect, even if made with express renunciation of this condition and even under oath. When the time of the noviceship is completed, superiors should admit to profession those they find suitable but dismiss the others from the monastery. By these enactments the holy council does not wish to introduce any innovation or to prevent the religious institute of clerics of the Society of Jesus from serving the Lord and his church according to their constitution, which has been approved by the holy apostolic see. And, except for the food and clothing of novices, both men and women, for the time when they are in probation before profession, nothing whatever may be given to their monastery on any pretext whatever by their parents or relatives or guardians from the novices' possessions, lest they be unable to leave because the monastery holds the whole or part of their substance and they could not easily recover it if they left. The holy council orders instead under penalty of anathema to givers and receivers that this should never happen, and that all that belongs to them must be returned to those leaving before profession. The bishop is to ensure that this is properly done, using the coercion of censures if need be.

Chapter 17

With an eye to the freedom of virgins due to be dedicated to God, the holy council determines that if a girl more than twelve years of age wants to take the religious habit, she should not take it, nor should she or any other girl take her vows at a later stage, until the bishop or his vicar, if the bishop is absent or prevented, or someone appointed at their expense has carefully discovered whether the girl is free or forced or under immoral pressure, and whether she understands what she is doing; and if her intention is shown to be devout and free, and she fulfills the conditions required by that monastery and order, and is also suited to the monastery, then she may be free to make her profession. To make sure the bishop is aware of the time of her profession, the person in charge of the monastery is bound to inform him a month before. If the superior does not inform him, she is to be suspended from office for as long as the bishop sees fit.

Chapter 18

The holy council imposes an anathema on each and all persons, of whatever rank or condition they may be, both clerics and laity, secular and regular, and whatever high office they fill, if they in any way force a virgin or widow or any other woman to enter a monastery against her will, except in cases expressed in law, or to take the habit of any religious institute, or to make her profession; and on all who give advice, help or encouragement and know she is not freely entering the monastery, or taking the habit, or making profession; and this however these persons are party to the action by their presence or consent or authority. It imposes a similar anathema on those who in any manner and without good reason obstruct the holy desire of virgins or other women to take the habit or make profession. And each and all of these procedures which are obligatory before profession or at profession are to be observed, not only in monasteries subject to the bishop, but in all others whatsoever. From them are excepted women who are called penitents or converts, in whose cases their own constitutions are to be observed.

Chapter 19

A regular who maintains that he entered religion under duress and fear, or even says he was professed before the legal age, or something similar, and wishes for any reason to put off his habit, or even to depart in his habit without the permission of superiors, is not to be listened to unless it is within five years from the day of his profession; and even then, only if he lays the reason he is maintaining before his superior and ordinary. But if before this he puts off the habit of his own accord, he should not be allowed to put up any case, but be forced to return to his monastery and be punished as an apostate from religious life; and no privilege of his institute is meanwhile to avail him. No regular may be transferred to a less strict religious institute in virtue of any faculty; nor may permission be given to any regular to wear the habit of his institute in a concealed way.

Chapter 20

Abbots who are heads of orders and other superiors of the said orders, who are not subject to bishops and who have lawful jurisdiction over monasteries of lesser rank or priories, should visit those subject monasteries and priories each in its own place and order, in virtue of their office, even if these are commendatory. The holy council declares that these latter, since they are subject to the heads of their orders, are not included in what was elsewhere laid down about the visitation of commendatory monasteries, and those who are superiors of the monasteries of the aforesaid orders are obliged to receive the aforesaid visitors and carry out their instructions. The monasteries that are themselves heads of orders are to be visited according to the constitutions of the apostolic see and of the orders themselves, and as long as these commendams last, claustral priors, or subpriors in priories that have a convent, should be appointed by the general chapters or visitors of those orders, to exercise control and spiritual government. In all other matters the privileges and faculties of the above-mentioned orders which concern their persons, places and rights, are to remain firm and intact.

Chapter 21

Since many monasteries, including abbeys, priories and provostries, have suffered no small harm in both spiritual and temporal matters from the bad government of those to whom they were entrusted, the holy council desires to recall them absolutely to the fitting discipline of monastic life. But so hard and difficult is the state of the present times that no remedy can be applied to all at once, as the council would wish, nor the same remedy to all. But that it may overlook no step by Which provision can be made for this situation in due course, the council first of all entrusts to the pope to ensure by his devotion and wisdom, in so far as he sees that the times allow, that regulars who are expressly professed in the order in question and are able to lead and guide the flock should be put in charge of those monasteries which are now found to be held in commendam and to have their own convents. As they fall vacant in the future, they are to be conferred on regulars only of distinguished virtue and holiness'. In the case of monasteries which are heads and primates of orders, whether they are abbeys or are called daughter priories of the so-called head houses: then, those who now hold them in commendam are bound, unless they have made provision for a successor who is a regular, either to make solemn profession 'of the rule of those orders, or to give them up; otherwise the aforesaid commendams are to be regarded in law as vacant. And, lest any deceit may be employed in any or all of the aforesaid, the holy council commands that the standing of each person appointed to the aforesaid monasteries should be expressed by name: any appointment made otherwise is to be regarded as fraudulent and as not protected by any subsequent occupancy even for three years.

Chapter 22

The holy council commands that each and all of the directions in the above decrees be observed in all the convents and monasteries, colleges and houses, of any monks and regulars of any kinds, and of any nuns, virgins and widows, even those living under the government of military orders including that of Jerusalem, and by whatever name they are known, and under any and every rule and constitution, and under the guardianship or government or any form of subjection, attachment or dependency of or to any order, whether of mendicants or non-mendicants or any other regular monks or canons; notwithstanding the privileges of each and all of them, in whatever form of words they are framed and called Mare Magnum, even those obtained at their foundation, or any constitutions and rules even given under oath, and any customs or prescriptions, however immemorial. The holy council, however, does not intend to detach from their institute and observance any regulars, men or women, who live under a stricter rule or statutes (except for the faculty of holding stable goods in common). And because the holy council desires each and all of the above instructions to be put into effect as soon as possible, it commands all bishops to carry out the aforesaid immediately in the monasteries subject to them and in all others specially entrusted to them in the above decrees, and similarly all abbots and generals and other superiors of the above-mentioned orders. And if anything is not put into effect, provincial synods are to supply for the negligence of the bishops and force the matter. Provincial and general chapters of regulars should take the necessary steps, and where there are no general chapters then provincial councils formed by delegates of the same order. And the holy council exhorts all kings, princes, states and magistrates, and orders them in virtue of holy obedience, to be willing as often as they are requested to give their support and authority to the aforesaid bishops, abbots, generals and others in charge in the carrying out of the reform contained above, so that all the foregoing may duly be put into effect without any hindrance, to the praise of almighty God.

Decree on general reform

Chapter 1

It is desirable that those who accept the episcopal ministry should recognize what their function is, and realize that they have been called not to personal advantages, nor riches nor a life of luxury, but to toil and solicitude for the glory of God. For there can be no doubt that the rest of the faithful are more readily aroused to the practice of religion and innocence of life, if they see those set over them absorbed, not in what is of the world, but in the salvation of souls and their fatherland in heaven. As the holy council considers this matter to be crucial in restoring church discipline, it charges all bishops to meditate these truths often and to shape their deeds and lives to this responsibility, as this is a perpetual manner of preaching. In the first place they should order all their conduct in such a way that others may be able to look to them for an example of moderation, modesty, continence and of the holy humility which so much commends us to God. Wherefore, after the example of our fathers in the council of Carthage, the council bids bishops not only to be satisfied with modest furnishings and table and a frugal living standard, but to take care that in the rest of their lifestyle and their whole household there should be nothing discordant with this office and not showing simplicity, zeal for God and contempt for vanities. The council wholly forbids them to try to improve the living of their relatives and household from church revenues, since the apostolic canons' too forbid them to give to relatives the property of the church which is God's; but if these are poor they may give to them as to other poor people but not divert or scatter church property for their sake. Indeed the holy council exhorts them with all its power to lay aside all earthly human affection towards brothers, nephews and relatives, for it has been a seeded of many evils in the church. The council decrees that what is here said about bishops should not only be observed according to their rank and condition by all who occupy church benefices, secular and regular, of any kind, but also apply to cardinals of the holy Roman church seeing that the administration of the universal church rests on their advice to the pope, and it would be a great wrong if they were not such shining examples of the same virtues and discipline of life as to turn the eyes of all deservedly towards them.

Chapter 2

The disasters of the time and the aggressive growth of heresies demand that nothing should be left undone that can contribute to confirming peoples and supporting the catholic faith. Therefore the holy council enjoins on patriarchs, primates, archbishops, bishops and all others who are normally members of provincial councils by law or custom, that in the first provincial council held after the end of this council they should openly accept each and all of the decisions and instructions of this holy council, that they should vow and profess true obedience to the pope, and that they should publicly detest and anathematize all the heresies condemned by the sacred canons and general councils especially this one. And that all henceforth who are appointed as patriarchs, primates, archbishops and bishops should in detail observe the same procedure at the first provincial council at which they are present. But if, which God forbid, anyone of all those mentioned refuses to do so, the bishops of the same province are bound under pain of divine wrath to inform the pope at once, and shall meanwhile abstain from communion with that person. All others who at present hold or shall in the future hold church benefices, and are obliged to meet in a diocesan synod, shall observe and do the same in the first synod that is held; otherwise they are to be punished according to the form of the sacred canons. In addition, all concerned with the care, visitation and reform of universities and places of general studies should carefully ensure that these universities accept in full the canons and decrees of this holy council, and that the masters, doctors and others in the same universities teach and interpret the catholic faith according to the directions of these canons and decrees, and that they bind themselves by oath to this obligation at the beginning of each year. And if any other matters need correction and reform in the same universities, let them be put right and regulated by those whose concern it is, for the furtherance of religion and church order. The pope will ensure through his delegates that the universities immediately subject to his protection and visitation are visited and reformed to a healthy state in the same manner as above and as his judgment sees most fitting.

Chapter 3

Although the sword of excommunication is the chief instrument of church discipline and of great effect in keeping the people to their duty, yet it is to be wielded with great reserve and caution, since experience teaches that if it is inflicted rashly or for trivial reasons, it is despised rather than feared and breeds disorder rather than salvation. Wherefore the excommunications imposed after repeated warnings to produce a disclosure (as it is called), or lost or alienated property, are never to be decreed except by a bishop, and then on no ordinary matter and only after such a case, which arouses his special concern, has been examined with great care and thoroughness; nor should he be persuaded to use excommunication by the authority of any secular person, even a magistrate, but the whole matter must rest on his own judgment and conscience, when he personally judges for reasons of subject, place, person and time that excommunications should be decreed. All ecclesiastical judges. are commanded, whatever their rank, in all judicial cases, whenever effective sentence against property or person can be carried out on their own authority in any part of their jurisdiction, to abstain both in conducting and concluding the case from ecclesiastical censures or interdict; but, if it seems proper to them, in civil cases in any way belonging to the ecclesiastical forum, they may proceed against anyone, even laity, and determine cases, by monetary fines which by the very fact of their exaction must be assigned to pious places of the locality, or by the taking of pledges and distraint of persons to be carried out by their own executors or those of others, or even by the deprivation of benefices or other legal remedies. But if the carrying out of a sentence against property or persons is impossible through the contumacy of those guilty, then they may strike them with the sword of anathema in addition to other penalties, on their own judgment. In criminal cases, too, where execution of a sentence against property or persons is possible, as above, they must abstain from censures; but if it is not easy to see that the sentence is carried out, then the judge may use this spiritual weapon against delinquents, if the seriousness of the crime so requires and after at least two warnings, even by an edict, have been given. But it would be intolerable for any secular magistrate to prevent an ecclesiastical judge from excommunicating anyone, or order that an excommunication imposed should be revoked, on the grounds that the rulings of this present decree have not been observed: for cognisance of this belongs to ecclesiastical and not to secular judges. And if any excommunicated person has not recanted after the warnings laid down in law, he is not only to be barred from the sacraments and the fellowship and welcome of the faithful, but if he persists for a year in a rebellious spirit befouled by the tolls of censures, then proceedings may be taken against him as a person suspect of heresy.

Chapter 4

It may often come about that so great a number of masses to be celebrated has been imposed on some churches by the sums left by dead persons that the daily obligation to the wills of testators cannot be met; or that the alms left for their celebration is so meager that no one can easily be found to undertake the task. Hence the pious provisions of testators are neglected and the consciences of those concerned with these duties are

PROMULGATIONS OF THE COUNCIL OF TRENT (continued)

burdened. The holy council, desiring to honor the sums left for pious uses as fully and beneficially as it can, gives power to bishops in the diocesan synod, and likewise to abbots and general superiors of orders in their general chapters, when the matter has been thoroughly considered, to make in the aforesaid churches whatever arrangements they can in conscience, as seems best to promote the honor and worship of God and the advantage of the churches, but only so that some commemoration is always made of those of the dead who have left sums for the salvation of souls and for pious purposes.

Chapter 5

Reason demands that sound arrangements should not be upset by contrary rulings. When, therefore, certain qualities are required or certain duties imposed by the establishment or foundation of certain benefices or other articles of government, then there must be no defaulting from them in the appointment to such benefices or in any other provision made. The same is to be observed with regard to prebends for theologians, masters, doctors or priests, deacons and subdeacons, so that no appointment is made that falls short of the qualities or holy orders required; any appointment made otherwise shall be considered fraudulent.

Chapter 6

The holy council instructs that in all cathedral and collegiate churches there be observed the decree beginning *Capitula cathedralium* made under Paul III of happy memory, not only when the bishop makes his visitation but whenever, in virtue of his office or at the petition of someone, he proceeds against a person on the grounds of the contents of that decree. At the same time the council enjoins that when the bishop takes proceedings outside the time of visitation, all the following should take place: at the beginning of each year the chapter is to choose two of its members on whose advice and consent the bishop or his vicar is bound to proceed, both in instituting the process and in all other legal acts right to the end inclusive, but in the presence of the bishop's notary and in his house or in the accustomed court. The two of them, however, shall have only one vote, and one of them may side with the bishop. But if both disagree with the bishop over any act or an interlocutory or definitive sentence: then within six days they and the bishop together should choose a third person, and if they disagree even over this choice it is to fall on the nearest bishop, and the matter over which they disagree is to be decided by the opinion of this third-party; otherwise the whole process and its effects shall be null and it shall produce no legal results. In cases of crime arising from incontinence, treated in the decree on concubinage, and in more heinous transgressions requiring deposition or degradation, where there is danger of flight and so there is need of personal detention lest judgment be eluded: the bishop alone may at the outset proceed to summary cognisance and necessary detention, but the aforesaid procedure is to be observed for the rest of the case. But in all cases consideration must be given that delinquents be kept in decent custody according to the nature of the offence and the quality of the persons. Bishops should on all occasions be accorded the honor their rank requires, and in choir and chapter and in

processions and other public activities the first seat and place should be theirs at their choice, and the leading authority in conducting affairs. If they propose something to the canons for discussion, and the matter to be treated is not one concerning themselves or their welfare, the bishops should themselves convoke the chapter, ask for the votes and decide the matter in view of them. In the absence of the bishop this role is to be performed by those of the chapter to whom it falls by law or custom, and the bishop's vicar does not take his place. In other matters, any jurisdiction and power the chapter may have, or administration of property, is to be left altogether preserved and intact. Any who do not hold dignities and are not in the chapter are all to be subject to the bishop in ecclesiastical cases. And all of the above is notwithstanding privileges even arising from foundation, or customs however immemorial, sentences, oaths, agreements which bind only their authors; but without prejudice in all matters to the privileges granted to universities of general studies or their personnel. And each and all of these instructions do not apply in those churches where bishops or their vicars, from constitutions or privileges or customs or agreements or by any other right, have greater power, authority and jurisdiction than is covered by this present decree; from these the holy council does not intend to derogate.

Chapter 7

As anything that wears the appearance of hereditary succession to ecclesiastical benefices is offensive to the sacred constitutions and contrary to the decrees of the fathers, in future no accession to or reversal of an ecclesiastical benefice shall be granted to anyone, even by consent, whatever his rank; nor are those hitherto granted to be suspended, extended or transferred. This decree applies to all ecclesiastical benefices, even in cathedral churches, and to all persons even those distinguished by the rank of cardinal. The same is to apply henceforth to coadjutorships with the right of succession, and no one is to be allowed them in any ecclesiastical benefice whatever. But if in some cathedral church or monastery there arises an urgent need and evident benefit that a prelate should be given a coadjutor, this appointment should not be with right of succession unless the case has first been carefully considered by the pope and it is established that the person has all the qualifications required by law and the decrees of this council for bishops and prelates; any appointment of this kind made otherwise is to be considered fraudulent.

Chapter 8

The holy council charges all occupying ecclesiastical benefices, secular and regular, constantly to exercise the duty of hospitality frequently praised by the holy fathers, with promptness and kindness in so far as their resources allow) remembering that those who love hospitality receive Christ among their guests. The council, however, commands those who hold in commendam, or the administration of or any title to, or even as united to their churches, what are commonly called hospices, or other pious institutions principally established for the use of pilgrims, the sick, the old and the poor, or when parish churches are united to hospices or have been established as hospices and have their administration granted by the patrons: they are to discharge the task and duty laid on them and to give in practice the hospitality they owe from the revenues assigned for this purpose, according to the constitution of the council of Vienne, renewed at this present council on another occasion under Paul III, beginning *Quia contingit*. But if hospices were founded to receive a particular kind of pilgrims or sick or other persons, and such persons are not to be found in the locality where the hospices are situated, or very few of them, the council nevertheless orders that their revenues should be diverted to another pious purpose as close to the original one as possible, and a more beneficial one in view of the time and place, as shall be decided to be most suitable by the ordinary together with two of the chapter who are more experienced in such matters, chosen by him, unless other provision was made in their foundation and establishment, in which case the bishop will do his best to carry out what was laid down, or if unable to do so to make useful provision as above. And if each and all of the above persons, of whatever order and religious institute and rank they be, including laity, who administer hospices but are not subject to regulars fulfilling religious observance, have in fact ceased to exercise the duty of hospitality, though provided with all that is necessary to meet their obligations, and though warned by the ordinary: then, not only may they be compelled to do so by ecclesiastical censures and other legal remedies, but they may be permanently deprived of the care of that hospice, and others put in their place by those concerned, and nevertheless be bound in conscience to restitution of revenues they have received contrary to the proper purpose of these hospices, without any remission or composition being allowed them. Nor should the administration or government of places of this kind henceforth be entrusted to one and the same person for more than three years, unless it is otherwise provided in its constitution. And all the above is notwithstanding any union, exemption and custom however immemorial to the contrary, or any privileges or indults, whatsoever.

Chapter 9

It would not be right to remove the legitimate rights of patronage and to ride roughshod over the pious desires of the faithful in making foundations. At the same time, ecclesiastical benefices cannot be allowed to be reduced to servitude because of this claim, as in fact happens at the hands of many shameless persons. To keep a reasonable balance in all things, therefore, the holy council decrees that the claim to right of patronage arises from foundation or endowment when this is proved by an authentic document and other legal requirements, or from repeated gifts over a long period of time which goes beyond living memory, or otherwise by legal enactment. In the case, however, of persons, or communities or universities, when the right may be assumed to have been acquired rather by usurpation, a fuller and more detailed proof is needed to establish a true claim; nor shall evidence of immemorial time suffice unless, in addition to other requirements, it is established by authentic documents that continuous gifts were made over a period of not less than fifty years and that these were all in fact delivered. All other patronage over benefices, both secular and regular or parochial, or over dignities or any other benefices in a cathedral or collegiate church, or faculties and privileges granted as a right of patronage or under any other title to nominate or choose or present to them when they fall vacant (except for patronage covering cathedral churches, and for other rights of patronage belonging to the emperor or kings or those possessing kingdoms and other mighty and supreme princes who have imperial rights over their dominions, and those granted in favor of institutions of general studies): all of these are to be understood as abrogated and annulled together with any quasipossession following from them; and benefices of this kind may be conferred completely freely by those with power to confer them, and resulting appointments shall have their full effect. The bishop may reject unsuitable persons presented by patrons for these purposes. As far as appointments to lower offices are concerned, those presented must be examined by the bishop according to the enactments made elsewhere by this holy council; otherwise any appointment made by lower authority is null and void. Patrons of benefices, of whatever order or rank they may be, even if they are communities or universities, or colleges of clergy or laity of any kind, are for no reason or ground whatever to intervene in the receipt of incomes, revenues or subsidies of any benefices, even if their right of patronage is legally established by foundation or endowment; but they must leave these to be disbursed to the rector or incumbent, notwithstanding any custom; nor may they presume to transfer the said right of patronage to anyone else by sale or claim, against the canonical sanctions; if they act otherwise they are to be subjected to the penalties of excommunication and interdict, and are automatically deprived of the said right of patronage.

In addition, attachments made by way of union of free benefices to churches subject to the right of patronage, including that of laity, or to parish churches or to any other benefices, even simple ones, or dignities or hospices, such that the aforesaid free benefices take on the status of those to which they are attached and come under the right of patronage; all these, if they have not yet fully come into effect, or are made in the future at the instance of anyone and are granted by any authority whatever, even apostolic: all these together with the unions themselves are to be regarded as brought about by fraud, notwithstanding any form of words or derogation contained in them which is to be considered as expressed; nor are they any further to be put into execution, but the attached benefices once they fall vacant are to be freely conferred as before. Attachments made forty years ago or less, which have achieved their effect and full incorporation', are nevertheless to be reconsidered and examined by the ordinaries, as delegates of the apostolic see, and any acquired by fraud or evasion are to be declared invalid together with the unions in question; the benefices themselves are to be separated off and conferred on others. Similarly all patronage over churches and any other free benefices, even dignities, which have-been acquired within the last forty years, or are due to be acquired in the future, either by increase of endowment or by new building or for any other similar reason, are to be carefully examined by the same ordinaries, even with the authority of the apostolic see and acting as its delegates, as above, and they are not to be obstructed by the faculties or privileges of anyone; and they will wholly revoke any they find were not legitimately established for the quite evident need of the church or benefice or dignity; and they should restore such benefices to their original state of freedom, without loss to the incumbents and after restoring to the patrons whatever was given by them for this purpose, not-withstanding privileges, constitutions and customs however immemorial.

PROMULGATIONS OF THE COUNCIL OF TRENT (continued)

Chapter 10

Sometimes because of evilly intended suggestion on the part of plaintiffs, and sometimes because of the remoteness of places, it has hitherto been impossible to have adequate information about persons to whom local cases are entrusted, and as a result cases between parties are sometimes entrusted to persons not altogether suitable. Hence the holy council decrees that in all provincial or diocesan synods a certain number of persons should be designated having the qualities laid down in the constitution of Boniface VIII beginning Statutum and in other respects suitable, so that henceforth in addition to local ordinaries they too may be entrusted with hearing local cases that are ecclesiastical and spiritual and belong to ecclesiastical jurisdiction. If one of the designated persons dies, the local ordinary on the advice of his chapter is to appoint another person to take his place until the next provincial or diocesan synod, so that each diocese has four or more approved persons.who are qualified as above, to whom cases can be entrusted by any legate or nuncio and even by the apostolic see; 'and as soon as the designation has been made, of which bishops should at once notify the pope, all delegations of other judges made apart from these are to be considered fraudulent. The holy council henceforth charges both ordinaries and all other judges to make efforts to bring cases to conclusion with all possible speed, and to counter the tricks of litigants whether in disputing the law or in using all means to postpone sentence, either by fixing a term or by some other suitable means.

Chapter 11

It usually brings great damage to churches when their goods are leased to others for a present sum of money, to the prejudice of successors. Therefore all such leasings, if the payments are made in advance, are to be regarded as wholly invalid in their obligation on successors, notwithstanding any privilege or indult. Nor shall such leasings be ratified in the Roman curia or out of it. Nor is it lawful to hire out ecclesiastical jurisdiction or the power of nominating or designating substitutes in spiritual matters, nor for the lessees to exercise such powers personally or through others; all grants to the contrary, even by the apostolic see, are to be regarded as fraudulent. And the holy council decrees to be null all leasings of ecclesiastical property, even those confirmed by apostolic authority, made within the last thirty years on a long term basis or, as happens in some areas, for twenty-nine or twice twenty-nine years, which the provincial synod or persons deputed by it shall judge to have been contracted to the loss of the church and against canonical sanctions.

Chapter 12

They are not to be tolerated who by various obstructive devices contrive to withdraw tithes from churches, or who brazenly lay hold of tithes paid by others and annex them, since the payment of tithes is due to God, and those who refuse to pay them or prevent others from doing so are purloining the property of others. The holy council therefore orders all, of whatever rank and condition they may be, who are concerned with the payment of tithes, to pay henceforth those to which they are bound in law, in their entirety, to the cathedral or any other churches or persons to whom they are lawfully owed. Those who either subtract them or obstruct them are to be excommunicated and not absolved from that guilt until they have made full restitution. The council further exhorts each and all, for the sake of christian love and their due obligation to their pastors, not to cavil at giving generous help from the goods granted them by God to bishops and parish priests of poor churches, to the praise of God and the preservation of the status of the pastors who watch over them.

Chapter 13

The holy synod decrees that wherever it has been customary for forty years or more for what is called the quarter for funerals to be paid to the cathedral or parish church, and whenever the same right is in future granted by any privilege to monasteries, hospices or any other pious institutions of any kind: henceforth the same shall be paid to the cathedral or parish church as heretofore, under the same right and in the same proportion; not-withstanding any grants, favors or privileges, even those named in *Mare Magnum,* or other contrary considerations.

Chapter 14

How base a thing it is and unworthy of the name of clerics, who have dedicated themselves, to divine worship, to live in the mire of unchastity and the uncleanliness of concubinage, that state declares clearly enough of itself, with its general offence to all the faithful and its great dishonor to the ranks of the clergy. Therefore, to recall ministers of the church to the continence and purity of life which befits them, and to enable the people to respect them the more that it sees their standards of life are high, the holy council forbids clerics of all kinds to keep concubines in or outside their houses, or other women about whom suspicion might arise, or to consort with them at all in a brazen fashion. otherwise they are to be punished with the penalties imposed by the sacred canons or the decrees of the church. If after being warned by superiors they still have such relationships, they are automatically to be deprived of a third of the revenues, subsidies and allowances of all their benefices and pensions of any kind, and these are to be applied to the church treasury or some other pious institution at the bishop's discretion. If they persevere in the same sin with the same or another woman, and pay no heed to a second warning, not only shall they thereby lose all income and revenues from their benefices and all pensions, which are to be applied to the above causes, but also they are to be suspended from the administration of their benefices as long as the bishop, acting even as delegate of the apostolic see, shall think fit. If even when suspended they do not cast them out, or even return to them, they are to be deprived permanently of all ecclesiastical benefices, shares, offices and pensions of any kind, and are made incapable and unworthy of holding any rank, dignity, benefice and office in the future until such time as, after a clear reformation of life, their superiors see fit for a good reason to dispense them from these impediments. But if, after sending the woman away, they are so bold as to resume the interrupted relationship or to attach other such women of low reputation to them, then in addition to the previous penalties they are to be struck by the sword of excommunication, nor any appeal or exemption to prevent or postpone the carrying out of this sentence. Cognisance of all the above cases does not belong to archdeacons or deans or any other lesser officials, but to the bishops alone, who may proceed without the clamor and publicity of a judicial process and solely on examination of the true facts. Clerics who have no benefices or pensions may, according to the quality of their fault and their perseverance in contumacy, be punished by the bishop by imprisonment, suspension from holy orders, inability to hold benefices, and in other ways according to the sacred canons. If bishops too (which God forbid) do not abstain from this sin but persevere in it even after warning by the provincial synod, they are automatically suspended; if they still persevere, they are to be reported by the same synod to the pope, who will take measures against them in view of the extent of their guilt, even by depriving them of office if need be.

Chapter 15

As the memory of a father's sin should be kept away from places consecrated to God, where purity and holiness are most in place, the sons of clerics who are not born of lawful wedlock may not themselves hold any benefice, even a dissimilar one, in churches where their fathers occupy or previously occupied any ecclesiastical benefice, nor serve in those churches in any way, nor hold pensions from the revenues of benefices which their fathers occupy or have occupied elsewhere. But if at the present time father and son are discovered to occupy benefices in the same church, the son should be compelled to resign his benefice or to exchange it with another outside that church within three months; otherwise he is automatically deprived of it and any dispensation in the matter is to be considered fraudulent. In addition, if any reciprocal resignations made by clerics in favor of their sons henceforth occur, whereby each acquires the benefice of the other, they are to be held as made wholly in deceit of this decree and of canonical rules, nor shall any collations subsequently made in virtue of such resignations or of any others made in evasion of the law be valid for the said sons of clerics.

Chapter 16

The holy council enacts that secular ecclesiastical benefices, by whatever name they are called, which retain the care of souls from their original foundation or on any other grounds, are henceforth not to be turned into simple benefices, even by the Assigning of a fair share to a perpetual vicar. This is notwithstanding any concessions whatever which have not come fully into effect. In cases where the care of souls has in fact been transferred to a vicar, contrary to their establishment or foundation, even if found to have been in this state from immemorial time, if a fair share of the revenues has not in fact been assigned to the vicar of the church, by whatever name he is called, such a share is to be assigned as soon as possible and at least within a year of the ending of this council, as the ordinary shall see fit, according to the form of the decree passed under Paul III of happy memory. But if this cannot reasonably be done, or has not been done within the stated time, then as soon as a vacancy occurs by the resignation or decease of the vicar or rector, or one falls vacant by any manner, the benefice is to receive the care of souls and the

vicariate be extinguished, so that matters return to their original state.

Chapter 17

The holy council can only be deeply saddened on hearing that some bishops forget their standing and seriously dishonor pontifical dignity in that they behave with unfitting subservience towards royal ministers, rulers and batons, in church and out of it, and, as if they themselves were lowly altar servers, not only give them an undeserved precedence but even act personally as their servants. Taking great exception to this, the holy council renews all the sacred canons, general councils and other apostolic instructions pertaining to the decorum and importance of the episcopal dignity, and orders bishops to refrain from such conduct in future, bidding them remember that on all occasions they are fathers and shepherds, and to have regard to their rank and holy order both in church and outside it. And it charges others, both princes and all else, to treat them with the honor and respect due to fathers.

Chapter 18

Just as it is of public benefit to relax the rigidity of the law on occasion, to do fuller justice to emerging circumstances and needs for the common good; so to set aside the law too often, and to give in to requests by reason of precedent rather than by careful discernment of persons and conditions, is nothing other than to open the door to everyone to transgress the law. Wherefore all must recognize that the most sacred canons are to be observed exactly by all, and as far as possible without distinction of persons. Dispensations may be given in some cases, when pressing and good reasons and an occasional greater good so demand; they are to be given after the case has been examined, with great wisdom and free of charge, by those who have the power of dispensation; any dispensation granted otherwise is to be regarded as fraudulent.

Chapter 19

The detestable practice of duelling, brought in at the instigation of the devil to ensure that through bloody bodily death he might also secure the destruction of souls, must be wholly wiped off the christian world. The emperor, kings, dukes, princes, marquises, counts and temporal lords under any other title, who appoint a place in their lands for single combat between Christians, are by that very fact excommunicated, and deprived of the jurisdiction and dominion they have obtained from the church over the city, castle or site in which or at which they have allowed a duel to take place, and these rights if they are feudal are at once acquired by their immediate overlords. Those who engage in a duel, and those called their seconds, are to incur the penalty of excommunication and the sequestration of all their property and permanent infamy, and they should be punished as murderers according to the sacred canons, and if they die in the engagement they are to be permanently deprived of ecclesiastical burial. Those, too, who give advice in law and in fact in a case of duelling, or in any other way persuade anyone to this course, and all spectators, are to be bound by excommunication and perpetual malediction. This is notwithstanding any privilege or evil custom however immemorial.

PROMULGATIONS OF THE COUNCIL OF TRENT (continued)

Chapter 20

The holy council desires church discipline not only to be restored among the christian people but also to be perpetually protected and preserved safe from all obstructions. Hence, over and above its rulings about ecclesiastical persons, it has thought it right to warn secular princes too of their responsibility, trusting that they, as Catholics whom God has wished to be protectors of the holy faith and of the church, will not merely allow a restoration of the church's law, but will also recall their subjects to due reverence towards the clergy, both parish priests and those in higher ranks; and will not allow officials and magistrates of lesser degree to violate the immunity of the church and of ecclesiastical persons, which has been established by the ordinance of God and canonical rulings, for any motive of greed or by any act of contempt; but will see that together with the princes themselves they give due observance to the sacred constitutions of popes and councils. It therefore decrees and commands that the sacred canons and all general councils together with other apostolic rulings, that have been published in favor of ecclesiastical persons and the freedom of the church and against their violators, all of which it renews by this present decree, be rigorously observed by all. Wherefore it also charges the emperor, kings, republics, princes and each and all of whatever rank and dignity they may be, that the more amply they are endowed with temporal goods and with power over others, the more devoutly they should revere what is of ecclesiastical right, as the special care of God and protected by his patronage; and not allow them to be damaged by any barons, squires, stewards, rulers or other temporal lords or magistrates, and particularly by servants of these princes themselves; but severely punish any who obstruct the church's freedom, immunity and jurisdiction; and to all of these may they themselves be a model of devotion, religious practice and protection of the churches, in imitation of the best and most religious of their predecessors as princes, who were the first to advance the good state of the church by their authority and generosity, as indeed to avenge it of the injury caused by others. May each do his duty in this matter with exactness, so that divine worship is devoutly conducted, and prelates and other clergy are allowed to continue at peace and without obstacles in their residences and at their tasks, to the great profit and edification of the people.

Chapter 21

Finally the holy council declares that each and every matter that has been laid down in this council about reformation of conduct and ecclesiastical discipline, in whatever phrasing and form of words, both under popes Paul III and Julius III of happy memory and under the blessed Pius IV, are so decreed that the authority of the apostolic see is and is understood to be intact in all of them.

DECREES PUBLISHED ON THE SECOND DAY OF THE SESSION

On indulgences

As the power of granting indulgences was given by Christ to the church, and this divinely given power has been in use from the most ancient times; the holy council teaches and commands that the practice of indulgences should be retained in the church, very salutary as it is for the christian people and approved by the authority of holy councils; and it anathematizes those who assert they are useless or deny there is any power in the church to grant them. But it desires that moderation be used in granting them, according to the ancient and approved custom of the church, so that ecclesiastical discipline be not sapped by too easy conditions. Desiring, too, to correct and punish the abuses which have crept in and are the occasion for heretics to blaspheme this distinguished name of "indulgence": it enacts in general by this present decree that all base gain for securing indulgences, which has been the source of abundant abuses among the christian people, should be totally abolished. But as other abuses arising from superstition, ignorance, irreverence or any other source, because of the manifold corruptions of localities and provinces where they are committed, cannot be adequately specified and forbidden; the council enjoins all bishops to make a careful survey of such abuses in their churches and to report them to the first provincial synod, so that after being judged by the opinion of other bishops as well, they may at once be reported to the pope, and of his wisdom and authority he may decide what is best for the universal church, in order that the gift of sacred indulgences may be dispensed to all the faithful piously, holy and without corruption.

On the choice of foods, fasting and feast days

The holy council further exhorts all pastors, and beseeches them through the most holy coming of our Lord and Savior, that as good soldiers they assiduously commend to every one of the faithful all that the holy Roman church, mother and teacher of all churches, has laid down; and in particular all that has been laid down in this and other ecumenical councils; and that they take every care that they are obedient to all these things, particularly those concerning mortification of the flesh such as choice of foods and fasts, and all that goes to increase of devotion such as the devout and faithful celebration of feast days; exhorting their people often to obey those put in charge of them, for if they hear them they will hear God who rewards them, and if they despise them they will find God himself to be their avenger.

Index of books, the catechism, breviary and missal

The holy council, in the second session celebrated under our most holy lord Pius IV, entrusted to certain chosen fathers to consider what needed to be done about various censures and books that were either suspect or dangerous, and report back to it. Hearing from them now that they have exerted all their efforts in this matter, but that a clear judgment cannot reasonably be passed by the council because of the number and variety of the books, the council orders that all they have prepared should be presented to the pope and so by his wisdom and authority be completed and published. It gives similar orders in the matter of the catechism prepared by those commissioned, and of the missal and breviary.

The place of ambassadors

The holy council declares that by the places assigned to ambassadors, both ecclesiastical and secular, whether in their seating or in processions or by any other acts, no prejudice has been established against any of them, but all their rights and privileges, and those of their emperor, kings, republics and princes, are intact and safe and remain as they were before the present council.

Reception and observance of the council's decrees

This has been a time of such disaster, and the malice of heretics so obdurate, that there is nothing they have not infected with error, at the instigation of the enemy of the human race, even in what was clearest in our profession of faith or most certainly defined. Hence the holy council has mainly been concerned to condemn and anathematize the chief errors of the heretics of our age, and to hand on and teach the true catholic doctrine; according as it has now condemned, anathematized and taught. Since so many bishops, summoned from different provinces of the christian world, cannot be absent for so long from their churches without serious loss and widespread danger to the flock entrusted to them, and since no hope is left that the heretics, invited so often even under the safe-conduct they asked for and so long awaited, are ever going to come here, it has at last become necessary to close this holy council. It only remains for the council to charge all princes in the Lord, as it now does, to give their help and not allow the decrees here made to be abused or violated by heretics, but to see that they are devoutly received and faithfully observed by them and by all. But if any difficulty arises over the reception of these decrees, or any matters are raised as needing clarification (which the council does not believe to be the case) or definition, the council is confident that, in addition to other remedies it has put in hand, the pope will ensure that the needs of the provinces are met for the glory of God and the peace of the church, either by summoning persons who are suitable for dealing with the matter, particularly from the provinces where the difficulty has arisen, or even by holding a general council if he thinks this necessary, or by whatever means he thinks best.

Decree on reciting and reading in this session the decrees published in the same council under popes Paul III and Julius III

As many matters have been determined and defined in this holy council at different times under both Paul III and Julius III of happy memory about doctrine and reformation of conduct, the holy council now desires that they be recited and read.

Notes: *The sixteenth-century Council of Trent was the keystone of the Roman Catholic Church's response to the Protestant Reformation that had taken much of Northern and Western Europe from under Rome's hegemony. It was generally agreed, even by those who reject Martin Luther's and John Calvin's theology, that the church was in need of reform; however, for a variety of political reasons, the calling of a council was postponed for almost a quarter of a century after Luther issued his initial challenge in 1521. The full text of the promulgations are printed above, except for those housekeeping items that merely dealt with the scheduling of future sessions.*

When the council did meet, it took 18 years to complete its work. Delays were again caused by political maneuvers, though the war and the outbreak of plague in Trent contributed

to further delays. The final product, however, was to undergo broad changes in church life and set the pattern for Roman Catholicism until the sweeping reforms of Vatican II. The promulgations of Trent defined Roman Catholicism on all of the disputed points raised by the various phases of the Reformation. It is obvious that Rome took notice of the three major phases of dissenting: that of Martin Luther in Germany, John Calvin in Switzerland, and the radical free church Brethren (later to be known as Mennonites). Opinions of each are stated and refuted.

As the council proceeded, two separate but related discussions seemed to proceed side-by-side. First, a series of organization and discipline problems were considered. The fact that clerics at all levels had failed to remain true to their calling and had neglected the spiritual nurture of the people assigned to them helped fuel the Reformation. Thus, "cleaning house" was fundamental to any response and the majority of the promulgations amounted to self-cleaning regulations. These very necessary actions, and the resulting disciplinary action throughout the church, have less contemporary interest as they did not offer fundamental change to church life.

The doctrinal considerations did set some fundamental principles for the Roman Catholic Church in relation to competing Protestantism. The Roman Catholic Church is a sacramental liturgical body, and it received many of the Protestant theological questions as challenges to its sacramental thought and practice. The majority of its considerations took the form of anathemas on disputed points. Thus, in reading this lengthy set of promulgations, one can read the set of promulgations on reform of church life as one body of material, and the set on doctrines and sacraments as a second set. The comments immediately following will concentrate on the doctrinal and sacramental decrees.

The council opened with reaffirmation of the Nicene Creed, the single most universally accepted and definitive statement of Christian belief. It was a common base of agreement upon which the Roman bishops and the reformers could agree. However, the council quickly moved to the first issue that would begin to build a wall between the Roman Catholics and the Protestants; the definition of the books of the Bible. In its first decree at that first session, the council accepted the books of the Apocrypha as canonical. These books, such as Tobit, Judith, and Maccabees, were not acceptable to the reformers. In its second decree, the council designated the Latin Vulgate Bible as the accepted text to be used by the church, a refutation of Luther who had produced a new German Bible translated from the original Greek. It would be the twentieth century before Roman would move to a new biblical text based on Greek sources.

In the sixth session, the council took up the crucial issue of justification, the single most important doctrine uniting the reformers. Luther had championed the perspective that justification was the gift of God's grace and was received by faith alone. Reconciliation was possible, but a reconciling approach was not taken. Luther's idea of justification by grace through faith was attacked and the cooperative role of humans in the justifying process carefully delineated. In chapter 14 of the decree on justification, Calvin's understanding of predesti-

PROMULGATIONS OF THE COUNCIL OF TRENT (continued)

nation and the security of the believer was directly attacked. The reformers had emphasized the role of the sovereign God in justification/salvation, while the Roman Church retained its emphasis on the life-long cooperative process between God and the believer to produce salvation. At the sixth session, the council launched the reform of the bishops and the clergy in a effort to restore church discipline "which to a considerable extent has collapsed, and to correct depraved customs among both the clergy and christian people."

In session seven, the council considered the overall attack on the sacramental system inherent in the Reformation. Luther and Calvin agreed that there were only two sacraments and the Roman Catholic doctrine of transubstantiation was wrong, though their inability to agree on the nature of the sacrament was the formally the doctrine that separated them. The radical Brethren went even further. They did not believe in sacraments, ritual actions that carried God's grace to the persons participating. They believed only in two church ordinances, which they continued because the Bible commanded them to. The radicals also questioned infant baptism. Thus in the first decree of session seven, the council said that there were seven sacraments and any who disagreed were anathema. It went on to make a number of specific refutations of not only the reformers, but a variety of odd ideas that had been voiced by one or another persons in the past generation. During the thirteenth session the sacrament of the eucharist (Lord's supper) was given detailed consideration, during which the doctrine of transubstantiation was reaffirmed (chapter 4) and Calvin's idea of the spiritual reception of Christ was refuted.

At the fourteenth session, in the matter of internal reform, the council touched on a problem that would, over the centuries, increase with the continued breakdown of church control of religious matters in society as a whole, the problem of wandering bishops. There had always been bishops who for any number of reasons did not have a fixed diocese. When they set out in search of a flock, they became a challenge to church order, especially when they established themselves in an area where the church was weak or disorganized. Their continuance became the basis upon which the nineteenth century Old Catholic Church would be built and the Independent Catholic Movement would spread in the twentieth century.

In session 21, still further consideration of the sacraments led to a decree on the reception of communion. For some time the practice in the Roman church had been to give only the bread (not the wine) to the laity in the eucharist. This one element of communion had been a matter of considerable debate and criticism, and had become one of the Reformation issues. At Trent the Church set its policy of continuing to restrict the cup to the officiating priest during the eucharistic mass.

In session 22, buried within its lengthy further decree on the mass, the council legislated against saying the mass in the vernacular (chapter 8), a decree that had the effect of standardizing the Latin mass throughout the church internationally. The reformers had, of course, already moved to worship in the vernacular. However, only with the reforms following Vatican II in the last half of the twentieth century did the Roman

Church move to replace the Latin mass with worship in the language of the people. This caused considerable distress among many Roman Catholics and a number of schisms in the West, the most important being that led by Archbishop Marcel Lefebvre. Those groups that championed the cause of the Latin mass assumed the name "Tridentine" and hold the decrees of the Council of Trent (as opposed to those of Vatican II) as binding. They include the Ecclesia Catholica Traditionalis "Conservare et Praedicare," the Latin Rite Catholic Church, the Society of St. Pius V, the Society of St. Pius X, the Traditional Roman Catholic Church in the Americas, and the Tridentine Catholic Archdiocese in America.

With the decrees of the council in hand, the Counter-reformation could proceed in force, and many of the gains of the reformers in places such as Poland were taken away. All agree that the instituting of the internal reforms demanded by the council stopped the Reformation from spreading. The patterns instituted by the council stood for four hundred years. Vatican II can be seen as the first full scale reconsideration of those patterns and the controversies surrounding that council can be fruitfully seen as an attempt to alter deeply rooted forms (from the vernacular mass to the more reconciling language toward Protestants) that many believed had been set in concrete by the Council of Trent. It should also be noted that many of the decrees of the Council of Trent are still in force, and not being a matter of current controversy, were not revised or altered by subsequent council action or papal decree. It is a fruitful exercise to compare the above decrees of the Council of Trent with those of Vatican II, copies of which are readily available.

*   *   *

"INEFFABILIS DEUS," APOSTOLIC LETTER ON THE IMMACULATE CONCEPTION (1854)

The Ineffable God, whose ways are mercy and truth, whose is omnipotence, and whose wisdom reaches powerfully from end to end, and disposes all things sweetly, when he foresaw from all eternity the most sorrowful ruin of the entire human race to follow from the transgression of Adam, and in a mystery hidden from ages determined to complete, through the incarnation of the Word, in a more hidden sacrament, the first work of His goodness, so that man, led into sin by the craft of diabolical iniquity, should not perish contrary to His merciful design, and that what was about to befall in the first Adam should be restored more happily in the second; from the beginning and before ages, chose and ordained a mother for His only-begotten Son, of whom, made flesh, He should be born in the blessed plenitude of time, and followed her with so great love before all creatures that in her alone He pleased Himself with a most benign complacency. Wherefore, far before all the angelic spirits and all the Saints, He so wonderfully endowed her with the abundance of all heavenly gifts, drawn from the treasure of divinity, that she might be ever free from every stain of sin, and, all fair and perfect, should bear before her that plenitude of innocence and holiness than which, under God, none greater is understood, and which, except God, no one can reach, even in thought. And, indeed, it was most becoming that she should shine always adorned with the splendor of the most perfect holiness, and, free even from the stain of original sin, she should have the most complete triumph over the ancient serpent that Mother so venerable, to whom God the Father willed to give his only Son, begotten of His heart, equal to Himself, and whom He loves as Himself; and to give Him in such a manner that He is by nature one and the same common Son of God the Father and of the Virgin, and whom the Son chose substantially to be His Mother, and of whom the Holy Ghost willed that, by His operation, He, from whom He Himself proceeds, should be conceived and born.

Which original innocence of the august Virgin agreeing completely with her admirable holiness, and with the most excellent dignity of the Mother of God, the Catholic Church, which, ever taught by the Holy Spirit, is the pillar and ground of truth, as possessing a doctrine divinely received, and comprehended in the deposit of heavenly revelation, has never ceased to lay down, to cherish, and to illustrate continually by numerous proofs, and daily more and more by conspicuous facts. For this doctrine, flourishing from the most ancient times, and implanted in the minds of the faithful, and by the care and zeal of the Holy Pontiffs wonderfully propagated, the Church herself has most clearly pointed out when she did not hesitate to propose the conception of the same Virgin for the public devotion and veneration of the Faithful. By which illustrious act she pointed out the conception of the Virgin as singular, wonderful, and very different from the origin of the rest of mankind, and to be venerated as entirely holy, since the church celebrates by festivals only that which is holy. And, therefore, the very words in which the Sacred Scriptures speak of uncreated Wisdom and represent His eternal origin, she has been accustomed to use not only in the offices of the Church, but also in the holy liturgy, and to transfer to the origin of that Virgin, which was preordained by one and the same decree with the incarnation of Divine Wisdom.

But though all those things everywhere justly received amongst the faithful show with what zeal the Roman Church, the mother and mistress of all Churches, has supported the doctrine of the Immaculate Conception of the Virgin, yet the illustrious acts of this Church are evidently worthy that they should be reviewed in detail; since so great is the dignity and authority of the same Church so much is due to her who is the center of Catholic truth and unity, in whom alone religion has been inviolably guarded, and from whom it is right that all the Churches should receive the tradition of faith. Thus the same Roman Church had nothing more at heart than to assert, to protect, to promote, and to vindicate in the most eloquent manner the Immaculate Conception of the Virgin, its devotion and doctrine, which fact is attested and proclaimed by so many illustrious acts of the Roman Pontiffs, Our predecessors to whom, in the person of the Prince of the Apostles, was divinely committed by Christ our Lord the supreme care and power of feeding lambs and sheep, of confirming the brethren, and of ruling and governing the universal Church.

Indeed, Our predecessors have ever gloried in instituting in the Roman Church by their own Apostolic authority the Feast of the Conception, and to augment, ennoble, and promote with all their power the devotion thus instituted, by a proper Office and a proper Mass, by which the prerogative of immunity from hereditary stain was most manifestly asserted; to increase it either by indulgences granted, or by leave given to states, provinces, and kingdoms, that they might choose as their patron the Mother of God, under the title of the Immaculate Conception, or by approved sodalities, congregations, and religious families instituted to the honor of the Immaculate Conception; or by praises given to the piety of those who have erected monasteries, hospitals, or churches, under the title of the Immaculate Conception, or who have bound themselves by a religious vow to defend strenuously the Immaculate Conception of the Mother of God. Above all, they were happy to ordain that the Feast of the Conception should be celebrated through the whole Church as that of the Nativity; and, in fine, that it should be celebrated with an Octave in the universal Church as it was placed in the rank of the festivals which are commanded to be kept holy; also, that a Pontifical service in our Patriarchal Liberian Basilica should be performed yearly on the day sacred to the Conception of the Virgin; and desiring to cherish daily more and more in the minds of the Faithful this doctrine of the Immaculate Conception of the Mother of God, and to excite their piety in worshipping and venerating the Virgin conceived without original sin, they have rejoiced most freely to give leave that in the Litany of Loretto, and in the Preface of the Mass itself, the Immaculate Conception of the same Virgin should be proclaimed, and that thus the law of faith should be established by the very law of supplication. We ourselves, treading in the footsteps of so many predecessors, have not only received and approved what had been most wisely and piously established and appointed by them, but also mindful of the institution of Situs IV, We have appointed by our authority a proper Office for the Immaculate Conception, and with a most joyful mind have granted the use of it to the universal Church.

But since those things which pertain to worship are evidently bound by an intimate cord to its object, and cannot remain fixed and determined, if it be doubtful, and placed in uncertainty, therefore Our predecessors, the Roman Pontiffs, increasing with all their care the devotion of the Conception, studied most especially to declare and inculcate its object and doctrine; for they taught clearly and openly that the festival was celebrated for the Conception of the Virgin, and they proscribed as false and most foreign to the intention of the Church the opinion of those who considered and affirmed that it was not the Conception itself, but the sanctification, to which devotion was paid by the Church. Nor did they think of treating more indulgently those who, in order to weaken the doctrine of the Immaculate Conception, drawing a distinction between the first and second instant and moment of the Conception, asserted that the Conception was indeed celebrated, but not for the first instant and moment; for Our predecessors themselves thought it their duty to protect and defend with all zeal both the feast of the Conception of the Most Blessed Virgin, and the Conception from the first instant as the true object of devotion. Hence the words, evidently decretive, in which Alexander VII, declared the true intention of the Church, saying: "Certainly, it is the ancient piety of the faithful of Christ towards His Most Blessed Mother the Virgin Mary, believing that her soul, in the first instant of creation, and of infusion into the body, was by a special grace and privilege of God, in virtue of the merits of

"INEFFABILIS DEUS," APOSTOLIC LETTER ON THE IMMACULATE CONCEPTION (1854) (continued)

Jesus Christ her Son the Redeemer of mankind, preserved free from the stain of original sin, and in this sense they keep and celebrate with solemn rites the Festival of her Conception.''

And to the same, Our predecessors, this also was most especially a duty to preserve from contention the doctrine of the Immaculate Conception of the Mother of God, guarded and protected with all care and zeal. For not only have they never suffered that this doctrine should ever be censured or traduced in any way, or by any one, but they have gone much farther, and in clear declarations on repeated occasions they have proclaimed that the doctrine in which we confess the Immaculate Conception of the Virgin is, and by its own merit, held evidently consistent with Ecclesiastical worship, that it is ancient and nearly universal, and of the same sort as that which the Roman Church has undertaken to cherish and protect, and, above all, worthy to be placed in its sacred liturgy and its solemn prayers. Nor content with this, in order that the doctrine of the Immaculate Conception of the Virgin should remain inviolate, they have most severely prohibited the opinion adverse to this doctrine to be defended either in public or in private, and they have wished to crush it, as it were, by repeated blows. To which reiterated and most clear declarations, lest they might appear empty, they added a sanction; all which things Our illustrious predecessor, Alexander VII, embraced in these words—

''Considering that the Holy Roman Church solemnly celebrates the festival of the Conception of the Immaculate and Ever-Blessed Virgin, and has appointed for this a special and proper office according to the pious, devout, and laudable institution which emanated from Our predecessor, Sixtus IV, and wishing, after the example of the Roman Pontiffs, Our predecessors, to favor this laudable piety, devotion, and festival, and the reverence shown towards it, never changed in the Roman Church since the institution of the worship itself; also in order to protect the piety and devotion of venerating and celebrating the Most Blessed Virgin, preserved from original sin by the preventing grace of the Holy Ghost, and desiring to preserve in the flock of Christ unity of spirit in the bond of peace, removing offenses, and brawls, and scandals; at the instance and prayers of the said Bishops, with the Chapters of their churches, and of King Philip and his kingdoms, We renew the constitutions and decrees issued by the Roman Pontiffs, Our predecessors, and especially by Sixtus IV, Paul V, and Gregory XV, in favor of asserting the opinion that the soul of the Blessed Virgin, in its creation and infusion into the body, was endowed with the grace of the Holy Ghost, and preserved from original sin; likewise, also, in favor of the festival of the same Virgin Mother of God, celebrated according to that pious belief which is recited above, and We command that it shall be observed tinder the censures and punishments contained in the same constitutions.''

''And against all and each of those who try to interpret the aforesaid constitutions or decrees so that they may frustrate the favor shown through these to the said belief and to the festival or worship celebrated according to it, or who try to call into dispute the same belief, festival, or worship, or against these in any manner, either directly or indirectly, and on any pretext, even that of examining the grounds of defining it, or of explaining or interpreting the Sacred Scriptures or the Holy Fathers or Doctors: in fine, who should dare under any pretext or on any occasion whatsoever, to say either in writing or in speech, to preach, to treat, to dispute, by determining or asserting anything against these, or by bringing arguments against them and leaving these arguments unanswered, or by expressing dissent in any other possible manner; besides the punishments and censures contained in the constitutions of Sixtus IV, to which we desire to add, and by these presents do add, those: We will that they should be deprived *ipso facto,* and without other declaration of the faculty of preaching, of reading in public, or of teaching and interpreting, and also of their voice, whether active or passive, in elections; from which censures they cannot be absolved, nor obtain dispensation, unless from Us, or Our successors, the Roman Pontiffs; likewise, We wish to subject, and We hereby do subject, the same persons to other penalties to be inflicted at Our will, and at that of the same Roman Pontiffs, Our successors, renewing the constitutions or decrees of Paul IV, and Gregory XV, above referred to.''

''And We prohibit, under the penalties and censures contained in the Index of Prohibited Books, and We will and declare that they should be esteemed prohibited *ipso facto,* and without other declaration, books in which the aforesaid belief and the festival or devotion celebrated according to it is recalled into dispute, or in which anything whatever is written or read against these, or lectures, sermons, treatises, and disputations against the same, published after the decree of Paul V above mentioned, or to be published at any future time.''

All are aware with how much zeal this doctrine of the Immaculate Conception of the Mother of God has been handed down, asserted and propagated by the most distinguished religious Orders, the most celebrated theological academies, and the most eminent doctors of the science of Divinity. All know likewise how anxious have been the Bishops openly and publicly to profess, even in the ecclesiastical assemblies themselves, that the Most Holy Mother of God, the Virgin Mary, by virtue of the merits of Christ Our Lord, the Savior of mankind, never lay under original sin, but was preserved free from the original stain, and thus was redeemed in a more sublime manner. To which, lastly, is added this fact, most grave and, in an especial manner, most important of all, that the Council of Trent itself, when it promulgated the dogmatic decree concerning original sin, in which, according to the testimonies of the Sacred Scriptures, of the Holy Fathers, and of the most approved councils, it determined and defined that all mankind are born under original sin; solemnly declared, however, that it was not its intention to include in the decree itself, and in the amplitude of its definition, the Blessed and Immaculate Virgin Mary, Mother of God. Indeed, by this declaration, the Tridentine Fathers have asserted, according to the times and the circumstances of affairs, that the Blessed Virgin Mary was free from the original stain, and thus clearly signified that nothing could be justly adduced from the sacred writings, nor from the authority of the Fathers, which would in any way gainsay so great a prerogative of the Virgin.

And, in real truth, illustrious monuments of a venerated antiquity of the Eastern and of the Western Church most powerfully testify that this doctrine of the Immaculate Conception of the Most Blessed Virgin, every day more and more so splendidly explained and confirmed by the highest authority, teaching, zeal, science, and wisdom of the Church, and so wonderful propagated amongst all the nations and peoples of the Catholic world, always existed in the Church as received by Our ancestors and stamped with the character of a divine revelation. For the Church of Christ, careful guardian and defender of the dogmas deposited with her, changes nothing in them, diminishes nothing, adds nothing but, with all industry, by faithfully and wisely treating ancient things, if they are handed down from antiquity, so studies to eliminate, to clear them up, that these ancient dogmas of heavenly faith may receive evidence, light, distinction, but still may retain their fullness, integrity, propriety, and may increase only in their own kind—that is, in the same dogma, the same sense, and the same belief.

The Fathers and writers of the Church, taught by the heavenly writings, hard nothing more at heart, in the books written to explain the Scriptures, to vindicate the dogmas, and to instruct the faithful, than emulously to declare and exhibit in many and wonderful ways the Virgin's most high sanctity, dignity, and freedom from all stain of original sin, and her renowned victory over the most foul enemy of the human race. Wherefore, repeating the words in which, at the beginning of the world, the Almighty, announcing the remedies of his mercy, prepared for regenerating mankind, crushed the audacity of the lying Serpent, and wonderfully raised up the hope of our race, saying: "I will place enmity between thee and the woman, thy seed and hers," they taught that in this divine oracle was clearly and openly pointed out the merciful Redeemer of the human race—the only—begotten Son of God, Christ Jesus, and that his Most Blessed Mother, the Virgin Mary, was designated, and at the same time that the enmity of both against the Serpent was signally expressed. Wherefore, as Christ, the mediator of God and men, having assumed human nature, blotting out the handwriting of the decree which stood against us fastened it triumphantly to the Cross, so the Most Holy Virgin, bound by a most close and indissoluble chain with Him, exercising with Him and through Him eternal enmity against the malignant Serpent, and triumphing most amply over the same, has crushed his head with her immaculate foot.

This illustrious and singular triumph of the Virgin, and her most exalted innocence, purity, and holiness, her freedom from all stain of sin, and ineffable abundance and greatness of all heavenly graces, virtues, and privileges, the same Fathers beheld in that ark of Noah, which, divinely appointed, escaped safe and sound from the common shipwreck of the whole world; also in that ladder which Jacob beheld reaching from earth to heaven, by whose steps the Angels of God ascended and descended, on whose top leaned God himself; also in that bush which, in the holy place, Moses beheld blaze on every side, and amidst the crackling flames neither to be Consumed nor to suffer the least injury, but to grow green and to blossom fairly; also in that impregnable tower in front of the enemy, on which are hung a thousand bucklers and all the armor of the brave; also in that garden fenced round about, which cannot be violated nor corrupted by any schemes of fraud; also in that

brilliant city of God, whose foundations are in the holy mounts; also in that most august temple of God, which, shining with divine splendor, is filled with the glory of God; likewise in many other things of this kind which the Fathers have handed down, that the exalted dignity of the Mother of God and her spotless innocence, and her holiness, obnoxious to no blemish, have been signally preannounced.

To describe the same totality, as it were, of divine gifts, and the original integrity of the Virgin of whom Jesus was born, the same Fathers, using the eloquence of the Prophets, celebrate the august Virgin as the spotless dove, the holy Jerusalem, the exalted throne of God, the ark and house of sanctification, which Eternal Wisdom built for itself; and as that Queen who, abounding in delights and leaning on her beloved, came forth entirely perfect from the mouth of the Most High, fair and most dear to God, and never stained with the least spot. But when the same Fathers and the writers of the Church revolved in their hearts and minds that the Most Blessed Virgin, in the name and by the order of God himself, was proclaimed full of grace by the Angel Gabriel, when announcing her most sublime dignity of the Mother of God, they taught that, by this singular and solemn salutation, never heard on any other occasion, is shown that the Mother of God is the seat of all divine graces, and adorned with all the gift of the Holy Ghost—yea, the infinite storehouse and inexhaustible abyss of the same gifts; so that, never subjected to malediction, and alone with her Son partaker of perpetual benediction, she deserved to hear from Elizabeth, inspired by the Holy Ghost: "Blessed art thou amongst women, and blessed is the fruit of thy womb."

Hence it is the clear and unanimous opinion of the same that the most glorious Virgin, from whom He who is powerful has done great things, has shone with such a brilliancy of all heavenly gifts, such fullness of grace, and such innocence, that she has been an ineffable miracle of the Almighty, yea, the crown of all miracles, and worthy Mother of God; that she approaches as nearly to God as created nature can do, and is more exalted than all human and angelic encomiums.

And, therefore, to vindicate the original innocence and justice of the Mother of God, they not only compared her to Eve, as yet virgin, as yet innocent, as yet incorrupted, and not yet deceived by the most deadly snares of the most treacherous serpent, but they have preferred her with a wonderful variety of thought and expression. For Eve, miserably obeying the serpent, fell from original innocence, and became his slave, but the Most Blessed Virgin, ever increasing her original gift, not only never lent an ear to the serpent, but by a virtue divinely received utterly broke his power.

Wherefore, they have never ceased to call the Mother of God the lily amongst the thorns, earth entirely untouched, virgin, undefiled, immaculate, ever blessed, and free from all contagion of sin, from which was formed the new Adam, a reproachless, most sweet paradise of innocence, immortality, and delights, planted by God himself, and fenced from all snares of the malignant serpent, incorruptible branch that the worm of sin has never injured; fountain ever clear, and marked by the virtue of the Holy Ghost, a most divine temple, or treasure of immortality, or the sole and only daughter not of death but of life, the seed not of enmity but of grace, which by the singular providence of God has always flourished, springing from a corrupt and imperfect root, contrary to the settled and common laws. But if these encomiums, though most splendid, were not sufficient, they proclaimed in proper and defined opinions that when sin was to be treated of, no question should be entertained concerning the Holy Virgin Mary, to whom an abundance of grace was given, to conquer sin completely. They also declared that the most glorious Virgin was the reparatrix of her parents, the vivifier of posterity, chosen from the ages, prepared for himself by the Most High, predicted by God when he said to the serpent, "I will place enmity between thee and the woman," who undoubtedly has crushed the poisonous head of the same serpent; and therefore they affirm that the same Blessed Virgin was through grace perfectly free from every stain of sin, and from all contagion of body and soul and mind, and always conversant with God, and united with him in an eternal covenant, never was in darkness but always in light, and therefore was plainly a fit habitation for Christ, not on account of her bodily state, but on account of her original grace.

To these things are added the noble words in which, speaking of the Conception of the Virgin, they have testified that nature yielded to grace and stood trembling, not being able to proceed further; for it was to be that the Virgin Mother of God should not be conceived by Anna before grace should bear fruit. For she ought thus to be conceived as the first born, from whom should be conceived the first born of every creature. They have testified that the flesh of the Virgin, taken from Adam, did not admit the stains of Adam, and on this account that the Most Blessed Virgin was the tabernacle created by God himself, formed by the Holy Spirit, truly enriched with purple which that new Beseleel made, adorned and woven with gold; and that this same Virgin is, and deservedly is celebrated as she who was the first and the peculiar work of God, escaped from the fiery weapons of evil, and fair by nature, and entirely free from all stain, came into the world all shining like the morn in her Immaculate Conception; nor, truly, was it right that this vessel of election should be assailed by common injuries, since, differing very much from others, she had community with them only in their nature, not in their fault.

Moreover, it was right that, as the Only Begotten had a Father in heaven, whom the Seraphim proclaimed thrice holy, so He should have a Mother on the earth, who should never want the splendor of holiness. And this doctrine, indeed, so filled the minds and souls of our forefathers that a marvelous and singular form of speech prevailed with them, in which they very frequently called the Mother of God immaculate and entirely immaculate, innocent and most innocent, spotless, holy, and most distant from every stain of sin, all pure, all perfect, the type and model of purity and innocence, more beautiful than beauty, more gracious than grace, more holy than holiness, and alone holy, and most pure in soul and body, who has surpassed all perfectitude and all virginity, and has become the dwelling-place of all the graces of the Most Holy Spirit, and who, God alone excepted, is superior to all, and by nature fairer, more beautiful, and more holy than the cherubim and seraphim; she whom all the tongues of heaven and earth do

not suffice to extol. No one is ignorant that these forms of speech have passed, as it were, spontaneously into the monuments of the most holy liturgy, and the Offices of the Church, and that they occur often in them and abound amply; and that the Mother of God is invoked and named in them as a spotless dove of beauty, as a rose ever blooming and perfectly pure, and ever spotless and ever blessed, and is celebrated as innocence which was never wounded, and a second Eve who, brought forth Emmanuel.

It is no wonder, then, if the Pastors of the Church and the faithful people have daily more and more gloried to profess with so much piety and fervor this doctrine of the Immaculate Conception of the Virgin Mother of God, pointed out in the Sacred Scriptures, according to the judgment of the Fathers, handed down in so many mighty testimonies of the same, expressed and celebrated in so many illustrious monuments of a revered antiquity, and proposed, and with great piety confirmed by the greatest and highest judgment of the Church; so that nothing would be more dear, more pleasing to the same than everywhere to worship, venerate, invoke, and proclaim the Virgin Mother of God conceived without original stain. Wherefore, from the ancient times the Princes of the Church, Ecclesiastics, and even emperors and kings themselves, have earnestly entreated of this Apostolic See that the Immaculate Conception of the Most Holy Mother of God should be defined as a dogma of Catholic faith. Which entreaties were renewed also in these Our times, and especially were addressed to Gregory XVI, Our predecessor of happy memory, and to Ourselves, not only by Bishops, but by the secular clergy, religious Orders, by the greatest princes, and by the faithful people.

Notes: *Looking back from the 1990s to the sixteenth century, one can see several centuries of relative stability in the structure and intellectual life of the Roman Catholic Church. However this was followed by a century and a half of rather intense change. On a secular level, change began with the governmental disruptions that followed the American and French Revolutions and the revolutionary disruptions that swept Europe in 1830 and 1848. The initiation of a response by the Roman Catholic Church to these changes can be seen as beginning at the highest level with Ineffabilis Deus. The changes in Europe in the first half of the nineteenth century, which has accelerated decade by decade to the present day, has seen the Roman Catholic Church steadily stripped of its real power in the political processes of even the most Roman Catholic of countries. Included in the loss of power was the integration of the Papal States into a united Italy, and the reduction of the Pope's land to the present-day five-acre Vatican City.*

The church responded to its steady loss of temporal power by periodically strengthening the power of the hierarchy, especially the power and honor due the pope, within the Roman Church. At the same time, as the church lost its temporal power, it was also experiencing, at least in France and several European countries, a rebirth of devotion to the Blessed Virgin Mary. Beginning with Pius IX, papal blessing fell on Marian devotion and the popes enlisted that devotion in the cause of developing papal and hierarchial power. Thus Ineffabilis Deus, while important because it defined a new dogma, was equally important for the unique action of the pope stepping forward to assert his authority in defining the dogma without any formal backing of the church's bishops. In the future, assertions of papal authority would most often be accompanied with a statement about the Virgin.

The dogma that Pius IX defined was, of course, not a new idea. The Immaculate Conception, the idea that the Virgin Mary was born free of original sin, had been present in the church for centuries. Roman Catholic supporters would argue that the idea is biblical. Others would locate it in the Marian speculation following the definition of Mary as Theotokos (Mother of God) by the Council of Ephesus. All agree that by the Middle Ages it had received a level of acceptance. At the Council of Trent, it received passing reference in the decree on original sin. The council fathers specifically exempted the Virgin Mary from its statements about original sin.

It is the argument of Ineffabilis Deus that Mary was preserved from original sin so as to be a perfect vessel for the birth of Jesus. As such, she "approaches as nearly to God as created nature can do." Pius IX is merely responding to the testimony of the church through the centuries and the contemporary asking of the faithful to formally define the doctrine as a dogma (teaching) of the church. All Roman Catholics are expected to assent to this teaching.

*   *   *

DOGMATIC CONSTITUTION ON THE CATHOLIC FAITH (1871)

PIUS, BISHOP, SERVANT OF THE SERVANTS OF GOD, WITH THE APPROVAL OF THE SACRED COUNCIL, FOR PERPETUAL REMEMBRANCE

OUR LORD JESUS CHRIST, the Son of God, and Redeemer of Mankind, before returning to His heavenly Father, promised that He would be with His Church Militant on earth all days, even to the consummation of the world. Therefore, He has never ceased to be present with His beloved Spouse, to assist her when teaching, to bless her when at work, and to aid her when in danger. And this His salutary providence, which has been constantly displayed by other innumerable benefits, has been most manifestly proved by the abundant good results which Christendom has derived from Ecumenical Councils, and particularly from that of Trent, although it was held in evil times. For, as a consequence, the sacred dogmas of religion have been defined more closely and set forth more fully, errors have been condemned and restrained, ecclesiastical discipline has been restored and more firmly secured, the love of learning and of piety has been promoted among the clergy, colleges have been established to educate youth for the sacred warfare, and the morals of the Christian world have been renewed by the more accurate training of the faithful, and by the more frequent use of the sacraments. Moreover, there has resulted a closer communion of the members with the visible Head, an increase of vigor in the whole mystical body of Christ, the

multiplication of religious congregations and of other institutions of Christian piety, and such ardour in extending the kingdom of Christ throughout the world as constantly endures, even to the sacrifice of life itself.

But while we recall with due thankfulness these and other signal benefits which the divine mercy has bestowed on the Church, especially by the last Ecumenical Council, we cannot restrain our bitter sorrow for the grave evils, which are principally due to the fact that the authority of that sacred Synod has been contemned, or its wise decrees neglected, by many.

No one is ignorant that the heresies proscribed by the Fathers of Trent, by which the divine magisterium of the Church was rejected, and all matters regarding religion were surrendered to the judgement of each individual, gradually became dissolved into many sects, which disagreed and contended with one another, until at length not a few lost all faith in Christ. Even the Holy Scriptures, which had previously been declared the sole source and judge of Christian doctrine, began to be held no longer as divine, but to be ranked among the fictions of mythology.

Then there arose, and too widely overspread the world, that doctrine of rationalism, or naturalism, which opposes itself in every way to the Christian religion as a supernatural institution, and works with the utmost zeal in order that, after Christ, our sole Lord and Savior, has been excluded from the minds of men, and from the life and moral acts of nations, the reign of what they call pure reason or nature may be established. And after forsaking and rejecting the Christian religion, and denying the true God and his Christ, the minds of many have sunk into the abyss of Pantheism, Materialism, and Atheism, until, denying rational nature itself and every sound rule of right, they labor to destroy the deepest foundations of human society.

Unhappily, it has yet further come to pass that, while this impiety prevailed on every side, many even of the children of the Catholic Church have strayed from the path of true piety, and by the gradual diminution of the truths they held, the Catholic sense became weakened in them. For, led away by various and strange doctrines, utterly confusing nature and grace, human science and divine faith, they are found to deprave the true sense of the dogmas which our Holy Mother Church holds and teaches, and endanger the integrity and the soundness of the faith.

Considering these things, how can the Church fail to be deeply stirred? For, even as God wills all men to be saved, and to arrive at the knowledge of the truth; even as Christ came to save what had perished, and to gather together in one the children of God who had been dispersed: so the Church, constituted by God the mother and teacher of the peoples, knows its own office as debtor to all, and is ever ready and watchful to raise the fallen, to support those who are falling, to embrace those who return, to confirm the good and to carry them on to better things. Hence, it can never forbear from witnessing to and proclaiming the truth of God, which heals all things, knowing the words addressed to it: 'My Spirit that is in thee, and my words that I have put in thy mouth, shall not depart out of thy mouth from henceforth and for ever' (Isaias lix. 21).

DOGMATIC CONSTITUTION ON THE CATHOLIC FAITH (1871)
(continued)

We, therefore, following the footsteps of our Predecessors, have never ceased, as becomes our supreme Apostolic office, from teaching and defending Catholic truth, and condemning doctrines of error. And now, with the Bishops of the whole world sitting with us and judging with us, congregated by our authority in the Holy Spirit, in this Ecumenical Council, resting on the Word of God written and handed down, as We have received it inviolably preserved and truly expounded by the Catholic Church, We have determined to profess and declare the salutary teaching of Christ from this Chair of Peter and in sight of all, proscribing and condemning, by the power given to us of God, all errors contrary thereto.

CHAPTER I

OF GOD THE CREATOR OF ALL THINGS

The Holy Catholic Apostolic Roman Church believes and confesses that there is one true and living God, Creator and Lord of heaven and earth, Almighty, Eternal, Immense, Incomprehensible, Infinite in intellect, in will, and in all perfection; who, as being one, sole, absolutely simple and immutable spiritual substance, is to be declared as really and essentially distinct from the world, of supreme beatitude in and from Himself, and ineffably exalted above all things which exist, or are conceivable, except Himself.

This one only true God, of His own goodness and almighty power, not for the increase or acquirement of His own happiness, but to manifest His perfection by the blessings which He bestows on creatures, and with absolute freedom of counsel, created out of nothing, from the very first beginning of time, both the spiritual and the corporeal creature, to wit, the angelical and the mundane, and afterwards the human creature, as partaking, in a sense, of both, consisting of spirit and of body.

God protects and governs by His Providence all things which He hath made, 'reaching from end to end mightily, and ordering all things sweetly' (Wisdom viii. i). For 'all things are bare and open to his eyes' (Heb. iv. 13), even those which are yet to be by the free action of creatures.

CHAPTER II

OF REVELATION

The same Holy Mother Church holds and teaches that God, the beginning and end of all things, may be certainly known by the natural light of human reason, by means of created things, 'for the invisible things of Him from the creation of the world are clearly seen, being understood by the things that are made' (Rom. i. 20); but that it pleased His wisdom and bounty to reveal Himself and the eternal decrees of His will, to mankind by another and a supernatural way: as the Apostle says, 'God, having spoken on divers occasions, and many ways, in times past, to the fathers by the prophets; last of all, in these days, hath spoken to us by His Son' (Heb. i. I, 2).

It is to be ascribed to this divine revelation, that such truths among things divine as of themselves are not beyond human reason, can, even in the present condition of mankind, be known by every one with facility, with firm assurance, and with no admixture of error. This, however, is not the reason why revelation is to be called absolutely necessary; but because God of His infinite goodness has ordained man to a supernatural end, viz. to be a sharer of divine blessings which utterly exceed the intelligence of the human mind : for 'eye hath not seen, nor ear heard, neither hath it entered into the heart of man, what things God hath prepared for them that love Him' (I Cor. ii. 9).

Further, this supernatural revelation, according to the universal belief of the Church, declared by the Sacred Synod of Trent, is contained in the written books and unwritten traditions which have come down to us, having been received by the Apostles from the mouth of Christ Himself, or from the Apostles themselves, by the dictation of the Holy Spirit, have been transmitted, as it were, from hand to hand. And these books of the Old and New Testament are to be received as sacred and canonical, in their integrity, with all their parts, as they are enumerated in the decree of the said Council, and are contained in the ancient Latin edition of the Vulgate. These the Church holds to be sacred and canonical, not because, having been carefully composed by mere human industry, they were afterwards approved by her authority, nor merely because they contain revelation, with no admixture of error, but because, having been written by the inspiration of the Holy Ghost they have God for their author, and have been delivered as such to the Church herself.

And as the things which the Holy Synod of Trent decreed for the good of souls concerning the interpretation of Divine Scripture, in order to curb rebellious spirits, have been wrongly explained by some, We, renewing the said decree, declare this to be its sense: that, in matters of faith and morals, appertaining to the building up of Christian doctrine, that is to be held as the true sense of Holy Scripture which our Holy Mother Church hath held and holds, to whom it belongs to judge of the true sense and interpretation of the Holy Scripture; and therefore that it is permitted to no one to interpret the Sacred Scripture contrary to this sense, nor, likewise, contrary to the unanimous consent of the Fathers.

CHAPTER III

ON FAITH

Man being wholly dependent upon God, as upon his Creator and Lord, and created reason being absolutely subject to uncreated truth, we are bound to yield to God, by faith in His revelation, the full obedience of our intellect and will. And the Catholic Church teaches that this faith, which is the beginning of man's salvation, is a supernatural virtue, whereby, inspired and assisted by the grace of God, we believe that the things which He has revealed are true; not because of the intrinsic truth of the things, viewed by the natural light of reason, but because of the authority of God Himself who reveals them, and who can neither be deceived nor deceive. For faith, as the Apostle testifies, is the substance of things hoped for, the evidence of things that appear not,' (Heb. xi. 12).

Nevertheless, in order that the obedience of our faith might be in harmony with reason, God willed that to the interior helps of the Holy Spirit, there should be joined exterior proofs of this revelation; to wit, divine facts, and especially miracles and prophecies, which, as they manifestly display the omnipotence and infinite knowledge of God, are most certain proofs of His divine revelation, adapted to the intelligence of all men. Wherefore, both Moses and the Prophets, and most especially, Christ our Lord Himself, showed forth many and most evident miracles and prophecies; and of the Apostles we read: 'But they going forth preached everywhere, the Lord working with, and confirming the word with signs that followed' (Mark xvi. 20). And again, it is written: 'We have the more firm prophetical word, whereunto you do well to attend, as to a light shining in a dark place' (2 Peter i. I9).

But though the assent of faith is by no means a blind action of the mind, still no man can assent to the Gospel teaching, as is necessary to obtain salvation, without the illumination and inspiration of the Holy Spirit, who gives to all men sweetness in assenting to and believing in the truth.' Wherefore, faith itself, even when it does not work by charity, is in itself a gift of God, and the act of faith is a work appertaining to salvation, by which man yields voluntary obedience to God Himself, by assenting to and cooperating with His grace, which he is able to resist.

Further, all those things are to be believed with divine and Catholic faith which are contained in the word of God, written or handed down, and which the Church, either by a solemn judgment, or by her ordinary and universal magisterium, proposes for belief as having been divinely revealed.

And since without faith it is impossible to please God, and to attain to the fellowship of His children, therefore without faith no one has ever attained justification, nor will any one obtain eternal life, unless he shall have persevered in faith unto the end. And, that we may be able to satisfy the obligation of embracing the true faith and of constantly persevering in it, God has instituted the Church through His only begotten Son, and has bestowed on it manifest notes of that institution, that it may be recognized by all men as the guardian and teacher of the revealed Word ; for to the Catholic Church alone belong all those many and admirable tokens which have been divinely established for the evident credibility of the Christian Faith. Nay more, the Church by itself, with its marvelous extension, its eminent holiness, and its inexhaustible fruitfulness in every good thing, with its Catholic unity and its invincible stability, is a great and perpetual motive of credibility, and an irrefutable witness of its own divine mission.

And thus, like a standard set up unto the nations (Isaias xi.), it both invites to itself those who do not yet believe, and assures its children that the faith which they profess rests on the most firm foundation. And its testimony is efficaciously supported by a power from on high. For our most merciful Lord gives His grace to stir up and to aid those who are astray, that they may come to a knowledge of the truth; and to those whom He has brought out of darkness into His own admirable light He gives His grace to strengthen them to persevere in that light, deserting none who desert not Him. Therefore there is no parity between the condition of those who have adhered to the

Catholic truth by the heavenly gift of faith, and of those who, led by human opinions, follow a false religion; for those who have received the faith under the magisterium of the Church can never have any just cause for changing or doubting that faith. Therefore, giving thanks to God the Father who has made us worthy to be partakers of the lot of the Saints in light, let us not neglect so great salvation, but with our eyes fixed on Jesus, the author and finisher of our faith, let us hold fast the confession of our hope without wavering. (Heb. xii. 2, and 23.)

CHAPTER IV

OF FAITH AND REASON

The Catholic Church, with one consent has also ever held and does hold that there is a twofold order of knowledge, distinct both in principle and also in object: in principle, because our knowledge in the one is by natural reason, and in the other by divine faith; in object, because, besides those things to which natural reason. can attain, there are proposed to our belief mysteries hidden in God, which, unless divinely revealed, cannot be known. Wherefore the Apostle, who testifies that God is known by the gentiles through created things, still, when discoursing of the grace and truth which come by Jesus Christ (John i. 17) says : ' We speak the wisdom of God in a mystery, a wisdom which is hidden, which God ordained before the world unto our glory; which none of the princes of this world knew . . . but to us God hath revealed them by His Spirit. For the Spirit searcheth all things, yea, the deep things of God ' (I Cor. ii. 7-10). And the only-begotten Son Himself gives thanks to the Father, because He has hid these things from the wise and prudent, and has revealed them to little ones (Matt. xi. 25).

Reason, indeed, enlightened by faith, when it seeks earnestly, piously, and calmly, attains by a gift from God some, and that a very fruitful, understanding of mysteries; partly from the analogy of those things which it naturally knows, partly from the relations which the mysteries bear to one another and to the last end of man: but reason never becomes capable of apprehending mysteries as it does those truths which constitute its proper object. For the divine mysteries by their own nature so far transcend the created intelligence that, even when delivered by revelation and received by faith, they remain covered with the veil of faith itself, and shrouded in a certain degree of darkness, so long as we are pilgrims in this mortal life, not yet with God; 'for we walk by faith and not by sight' (2 Cor. v. 7).

But although faith is above reason, there can never be any real discrepancy between faith and reason, since the same God who reveals mysteries and infuses faith has bestowed the light of reason on the human mind, and God cannot deny Himself, nor can truth ever contradict truth. The false appearance of such a contradiction is mainly due, either to the dogmas of faith not having been understood and expounded, according to the mind of the Church, or to the inventions of opinion having been taken for the verdicts of reason. We define, therefore, that every assertion contrary to a truth of enlightened faith is utterly false. Further, the Church, which, together with the Apostolic office of teaching, has received a charge to guard the deposit of faith, derives from God the right and the duty of proscribing false science, lest any should be deceived by philosophy and vain fallacy (Coloss. ii. 8). Therefore all faithful Christians are not only forbidden to defend, as legitimate conclusions of science, such opinions as are known to be contrary to the doctrines of faith, especially if they have been condemned by the Church, but are altogether bound to account them as errors which put on the fallacious appearance of truth.

And not only can faith and reason never be opposed to one another, but they are of mutual aid one to the other; for right reason demonstrates the foundations of faith, and, enlightened by its light, cultivates the science of things divine; while faith frees and guards reason from errors, and furnishes it with manifold knowledge. So far, therefore, is the Church from opposing the cultivation of human arts and sciences, that it in many ways helps and promotes it. For the Church neither ignores nor despises the benefits to human life which result from the arts and sciences, but confesses that, as they came from God, the Lord of all science, so, if they be rightly used, they lead to God by the help of His grace. Nor does the Church forbid that each of these sciences in its sphere should make use of its own principles and its own method; but, while recognizing this just liberty, it stands watchfully on guard, lest sciences, setting themselves against the divine teaching, or transgressing their own limits, should invade and disturb the domain of faith.

For the doctrine of faith which God hath revealed has not been proposed, like a philosophical invention, to be perfected by human intelligence, but has been delivered as a divine deposit to the Spouse of Christ, to be faithfully kept, and infallibly declared. Hence also, that meaning of the sacred dogmas is perpetually to be retained which our Holy Mother the Church has once declared; nor is that meaning ever to be departed from, under the pretence or pretext of a deeper comprehension of them. Let, then, the intelligence, science, and wisdom of each and all, of individuals and of the whole Church, in all ages and all times, increase and flourish in abundance and vigor; but only in its own proper kind, that is to say, in one and the same doctrine, one and the same sense, one and the same judgement (Vincent. of Lerins, Common. n. 28).

CANONS

I

Of God the Creator of all things

1. If any one shall deny One true God, Creator and Lord of things visible and invisible; let him be anathema.

2. If any one shall not be ashamed to affirm that, except matter, nothing exists; let him be anathema.

3. If any one shall say that the substance and essence of God and of all things is one and the same; let him be anathema.

4. If any one shall say that finite things, both corporeal and spiritual, or at least spiritual, have emanated from the divine substance; or that the divine essence by the manifestation and evolution of itself becomes all things; or, lastly, that God is universal or indefinite being, which by determining itself constitutes the universality of things, distinct according to genera, species and individuals; let him be anathema.

5. If any one confess not that the world, and an things which are contained in it, both spiritual and material, have been, in their whole substance, produced by God out of nothing; or shall say that God created, not by His will, free from all necessity, but by a necessity equal to the necessity whereby He loves Himself; or shall deny that the world was made for the glory of God; let him be anathema.

II

Of Revelation

1. If any one shall say that the One true God, our Creator and Lord, cannot be certainly known by the natural light of human reason through created things; let him be anathema.

2. If any one shall say that it is impossible or inexpedient that man should be taught, by divine revelation, concerning God and the worship to be paid to Him; let him be anathema.

3. If any one shall say that man cannot be raised by divine power to a higher than natural knowledge and perfection, but can and ought, by a continuous progress, to arrive at length, of himself, to the possession of all that is true and good; let him be anathema.

4. If any one shall not receive as sacred and canonical the Books of Holy Scripture, entire with all their parts, as the Holy Synod of Trent has enumerated them, or shall deny that they have been divinely inspired; let him be anathema.

III

Of Faith

1. If any one shall say that human reason is so independent that faith cannot be enjoined upon it by God ; let him be anathema.

2. If any one shall say that divine faith is not distinguished from natural knowledge of God and of moral truths, and therefore that it is not requisite for divine faith that revealed truth be believed because of the authority of God,' who reveals it; let him be anathema.

3. If any one shall say that divine revelation cannot be made credible by outward signs, and therefore that men ought to be moved to faith solely by the internal experience of each, or by private inspiration; let him be anathema.

4. If any one shall say that miracles are impossible, and therefore that all the accounts regarding them, even those contained in Holy Scripture, are to be dismissed as fabulous or mythical; or that miracles can never be known with certainty, and that the divine origin of Christianity cannot be proved by them; let him be anathema.

5. If any one shall say that the assent of Christian faith is not a free act, but is inevitably produced by the arguments of human reason; or that the grace of God is necessary for

that living faith only which worketh by charity; let him be anathema.

6. If any one shall say that the condition of the faithful, and of those who have not yet attained to the only true faith, is on a par, so that Catholics may have just cause for doubting, with suspended assent, the faith which they have already received under the magisterium of the Church, until they shall have obtained a scientific demonstration of the credibility and truth of their faith; let him be anathema.

IV

Of Faith and Reason

1. If any one shall say that in divine revelation there are no mysteries, truly and properly so called, but that all the doctrines of faith can be understood and demonstrated from natural principles, by properly cultivated reason; let him be anathema.

2. If any one shall say that human sciences are to be so freely treated, that their assertions, even if opposed to, revealed doctrine, may be held as true, and cannot be condemned by the Church; let him be anathema.

3. If any one shall assert it to be possible that sometimes, according to the progress of science, a sense is to be given to dogmas propounded by the Church different from that which the Church has understood and understands; let him be anathema.

Therefore, fulfilling the duty of our supreme pastoral office, We entreat, by the mercies of Jesus Christ, and, by the authority of the same God and our Savior, We command all the faithful of Christ, and especially those who are set over others, or are charged with the office of instruction, that they earnestly and diligently apply themselves to ward off and eliminate these errors from Holy Church, and to spread the light of pure faith.

And since it is not sufficient to shun heretical privity, unless those errors also be diligently avoided which more or less nearly approach it, We admonish all men of the further duty of observing those constitutions and decrees, by which such erroneous opinions as are not here specifically enumerated, have been proscribed and condemned by this Holy See.

Given at Rome in Public Session solemnly held in the Vatican Basilica in the year of our Lord One thousand eight hundred and seventy, on the twenty-fourth day of April, in the twenty-fourth year of our Pontificate.

In conformity with the original.

Joseph, Bishop of St. Polten,

Secretary of the Vatican Council.

Notes: *The first Vatican Council opened on December 8, 1870, the feast of the Immaculate Conception. Many had called for such a council, the first since the sixteenth century. In its brief deliberations cut short by the outbreak of the Franco-Prussian War, two principle documents were passed. The first, the Dogmatic Constitution on the Catholic Faith reaffirmed some of the traditional doctrines of the church in light of the political and intellectual changes sweeping over the West. For example, against the first wave of modern critical approaches to the Bible, it declared that the church alone had the prerogative to interpret the Bible.*

Possibly the most important section of the document is chapter 4, ''On Faith and Reason,'' which included a discussion of the relation of church doctrines and the new body of scientific findings. This initial approach was to defend church teachings, no matter what science discovered. That approach had proved untenable and has since been replaced with more sophisticated methods of reconciling the two divergent sets of conclusions.

*   *   *

DOGMATIC CONSTITUTION ON THE CHURCH OF CHRIST (1871)

PIUS, BISHOP, SERVANT OF THE SERVANTS OF GOD, WITH THE APPROVAL OF THE SACRED COUNCIL, FOR A PERPETUAL REMEMBRANCE

THE Eternal Pastor and Bishop of our souls, in order to continue for all time the life-giving work of His Redemption, determined to build up the Holy Church, wherein, as in the House of the living God, all who believe might be united in the bond of one faith and one charity. Wherefore, before He entered into His glory, He prayed unto the Father, not for the Apostles only, but for those also who through their preaching should come to believe in Him, that all might be one even as He the Son and the Father are one. As then He sent the Apostles whom He had chosen to Himself from the world, as He Himself had been sent by the Father: so He willed that there should ever be pastors and teachers in His Church to the end of the world. And in order that the Episcopate also might be one and undivided, and that by means of a closely united priesthood the multitude of the faithful might be kept secure in the oneness of faith and communion, He set Blessed Peter over the rest of the Apostles, and fixed in him the abiding principle of this twofold unity, and its visible foundation, in the strength of which the everlasting temple should arise, and the Church in the firmness of that faith should lift her majestic front to Heaven. And seeing that the gates of hell with daily increase of hatred are gathering their strength on every side to upheave the foundation laid by God's own hand, and so, if that might be, to overthrow the Church: We, therefore, for the preservation, safe-keeping, and increase of the Catholic flock, with the approval of the Sacred Council, do judge it to be necessary to propose to the belief and acceptance of all the faithful, in accordance with the ancient and constant faith of the universal Church, the doctrine touching the institution, perpetuity, and nature of the sacred Apostolic Primacy, in which is found the strength and solidity of the entire Church; and at the same time to proscribe and condemn the contrary errors, so hurtful to the flock of Christ.

DOGMATIC CONSTITUTION ON THE CHURCH OF CHRIST
  (1871) (continued)

CHAPTER I

OF THE INSTITUTION OF THE APOSTOLIC PRIMACY IN BLESSED PETER

We therefore teach and declare that, according to the testimony of the Gospel, the primacy of jurisdiction over, the universal Church of God was immediately and directly promised and given to Blessed Peter the Apostle by Christ the Lord. For it was to Simon alone, to whom He had already said: 'Thou shalt be called Cephas,' that the Lord, after the confession made by him, saying: 'Thou art the Christ, the Son of the living God,' addressed these solemn words : 'Blessed art thou, Simon Bar-Jona; because flesh and blood have not revealed it to thee, but my Father who is in Heaven. And I say to thee that thou art Peter; and upon this rock I will build my Church, and the gates of hell shall not prevail against it. And I will give to thee the keys of the Kingdom of Heaven. And whatsoever thou shalt bind upon earth, it shall be bound also in heaven, and whatsoever thou shalt loose on earth, it shall be loosed also in heaven.' And it was upon Simon alone that Jesus after His resurrection bestowed the jurisdiction of Chief Pastor and Ruler over all His fold in the words: 'Feed my lambs: feed my sheep.' At open variance with this clear doctrine of Holy Scripture, as it has been ever understood by the Catholic Church, are the perverse opinions of those who, while they distort the form of government established by Christ the Lord in His Church, deny that Peter in his single person, preferably to all the other Apostles, whether taken separately or together, was endowed by Christ with a true and proper primacy of jurisdiction; or of those who assert that the same primacy was not bestowed immediately and directly upon Blessed Peter himself, but upon the Church, and through the Church on Peter as her Minister.

If anyone, therefore, shall say that Blessed Peter the Apostle was not appointed the Prince of all the Apostles and the visible Head of the whole Church Militant; or that he directly and immediately received from the same our Lord Jesus Christ a primacy of honor only, and not of true and proper jurisdiction; let him be anathema.

CHAPTER II

ON THE PERPETUITY OF THE PRIMACY OF BLESSED PETER IN THE ROMAN PONTIFFS

That which the Prince of Shepherds and great Shepherd of the sheep, Jesus Christ our Lord, established in the person of the Blessed Apostle Peter to secure the perpetual welfare and lasting good of the Church, must, by the same institution, necessarily remain unceasingly in the Church, which, being founded upon a Rock, will stand firm to the end of the world. For none can doubt, and it is known to all ages, that the holy and Blessed Peter, the Prince and Chief of the Apostles, the pillar of the faith and foundation of the Catholic Church, received the keys of the kingdom from our Lord Jesus Christ, the Savior and Redeemer of mankind, and lives, presides, and judges, to this day and always, in his successors the Bishops of the Holy See of Rome, which was founded by him, and consecrated by his blood. Whence, whosoever succeeds to

Peter in this See, does by the institution of Christ Himself obtain the Primacy of Peter over the whole Church. The disposition made by Incarnate Truth therefore remains, and Blessed Peter, abiding in the strength of the Rock that he received, has not given up the direction of the Church, undertaken by him. Wherefore it has at all times been necessary that every Church—that is to say, the faithful throughout the world should agree with the Roman Church, on account of its more powerful principality; that in that See, from which the rights of communion flow forth to all, being associated as members with the head, they may grow together unto one-compacted body.

If, then, anyone shall say that it is not by the institution of Christ the Lord, or by divine right, that Blessed Peter should have a perpetual line of successors in the Primacy over the Universal Church; or that the Roman Pontiff is not the successor of Blessed Peter in this Primacy; let him be anathema.

CHAPTER III

ON THE POWER AND NATURE OF THE PRIMACY OF THE ROMAN PONTIFF

Wherefore, resting on plain testimonies of the Sacred Writings, and adhering to the plain and express decrees both of our Predecessors, the Roman Pontiffs, and of the General Councils, We renew the definition of the Ecumenical Council of Florence, in virtue of which all the faithful of Christ must believe that the Holy Apostolic See and the Roman Pontiff possesses the primacy over the whole world, and that the Roman Pontiff is the successor of Blessed Peter, Prince of the Apostles, and is true Vicar of Christ, and Head of the whole Church, and Father and Teacher of all Christians; and that full power was given to him in Blessed Peter to feed, rule, and govern the Universal Church by Jesus Christ our Lord: as is also contained in the acts of the General Councils and in the Sacred Canons.

Hence we teach and declare that by the appointment of our Lord the Roman Church possesses a superiority of ordinary power over all other Churches, and that this power of jurisdiction of the Roman Pontiff, which is truly episcopal, is immediate; to which all, of whatever rite and dignity, both pastors and faithful, both individually and collectively, are bound, by their duty of hierarchical subordination and true obedience, to submit, not only in matters which belong to faith and morals, but also in those that appertain to the discipline and government of the Church throughout the world, so that the Church of Christ may be one flock under one supreme pastor through the preservation of unity both of communion and of profession of the same faith with the Roman Pontiff. This is the teaching of Catholic truth, from which no one can deviate without loss of faith and of salvation.

But so far is this power of the Supreme Pontiff from being any prejudice to the ordinary and immediate power of episcopal jurisdiction, by which Bishops, who have been set by the Holy Ghost to succeed and hold the place of the Apostles, feed and govern, each his own flock, as true Pastors, that this their episcopal authority is really asserted, strengthened, and protected by the supreme and universal Pastor; in accordance with the words of St. Gregory the Great: 'My honor is the honor of the whole Church. My honor is the firm strength of my brethren. I am truly honored, when the honor due to each and all is not withheld.'

Further, from this supreme power possessed by the Roman Pontiff of governing the Universal Church, it follows that he has the right of free communication with the Pastors of the whole Church, and with their flocks, that these may be taught and ruled by him in the way of salvation. Wherefore we condemn and reject the opinions of those who hold that the communication between this supreme Head and the Pastors and their flocks can lawfully be impeded; or who make this communication subject to the will of the secular power, so as to maintain that whatever is done by the Apostolic See, or by its authority, for the government of the Church, cannot have force or value unless it be confirmed by the assent of the secular power. And since by the divine right of Apostolic primacy, the Roman Pontiff is placed over the Universal Church, we further teach and declare that he is the supreme judge of the faithful, and that in all causes, the decision of which belongs to the Church, recourse may be had to his tribunal, and that none may re-open the judgment of the Apostolic See, than whose authority there is no greater, nor can any lawfully review its judgment. Wherefore they err from the right path of truth who assert that it is lawful to appeal from the judgments of the Roman Pontiffs to an Ecumenical Council, as to an authority higher than that of the Roman Pontiff.

If then anyone shall say that the Roman Pontiff has the office merely of inspection or direction, but not full and supreme power of jurisdiction over the Universal Church, not only in things which belong to faith and morals, but also in those which relate to the discipline and government of the Church spread throughout the world; or that he possesses merely the principal part, and not all the fullness of this supreme power; or that this power which he enjoys is not ordinary and immediate, both over each and all the Churches and over each and all the Pastors and the faithful; let him be anathema.

CHAPTER IV

CONCERNING THE INFALLIBLE MAGISTERIUM OF THE ROMAN PONTIFF

Moreover, that the supreme power of teaching is also included in the Apostolic primacy, which the Roman Pontiff, as the successor of Peter, Prince of the Apostles, possesses over the whole Church, this Holy See has always held, the perpetual practice of the Church confirms, and Ecumenical Councils also have declared, especially those in which the East with the West met in the union of faith and charity. For the Fathers of the Fourth Council of Constantinople, following in the footsteps of their predecessors, gave forth this solemn profession : The first condition of salvation is to keep the rule of the true faith. And because the sentence of our Lord Jesus Christ cannot be passed by, who said: 'Thou art Peter, and upon this Rock I will build my Church,' these things which have been said are approved by events, because in the Apostolic See the Catholic Religion has always been kept undefiled, and its holy doctrine proclaimed. Desiring, therefore, not to be in the least degree ,separated from the faith and doctrine of that See, we hope that we may deserve to be in the one communion, which

the Apostolic See preaches, in which is the entire and true solidity of the Christian religion.' And, with the approval of the Second Council of Lyons, the Greeks professed that the Holy Roman Church enjoys supreme and full primacy and preeminence over the whole Catholic Church, which it truly and humbly recognizes that it has received with the plenitude of power from our Lord Himself in the person of blessed Peter, Prince or Head of the Apostles, whose successor the Roman Pontiff is ; and as the Apostolic See is bound before all others to defend the truth of faith, so also if any questions regarding faith shall arise, they must be defined by its judgement. Finally, the Council of Florence defined: That the Roman Pontiff is the true Vicar of Christ, and the Head of the whole Church, and the Father and Teacher of all Christians ; and that to him in blessed Peter was delivered by our Lord Jesus Christ the full power of feeding, ruling, and governing the Universal Church.

To satisfy this pastoral duty our Predecessors ever made unwearied efforts that the salutary doctrine of Christ might be propagated among all the nations of the earth, and with equal care watched that it might be preserved genuine and pure where it had been received. Therefore the Bishops of the whole world, now singly, now assembled in Synods, following the long-established custom of Churches, and the form of the ancient rule, sent word to this Apostolic See of those dangers especially which sprang up in matters of faith, that the losses of faith might there be most effectually repaired where the faith cannot fail.' And the Roman Pontiffs, according to the exigencies of times and circumstances, sometimes assembling Ecumenical Councils, or asking for the mind of the Church scattered throughout the world, sometimes by particular Synods, sometimes using other helps which Divine Providence supplied, defined as to be held those things which with the help of God they had recognized as conformable with the Sacred Scriptures and Apostolic Traditions. For the Holy Spirit was not promised to the successors of Peter that by His revelation they might make known new doctrine, but that by His assistance they might inviolably keep and faithfully expound the revelation or deposit of faith delivered through the Apostles. And indeed all the venerable Fathers have embraced and the holy orthodox Doctors have venerated and followed their Apostolic doctrine; knowing most fully that this See of holy Peter remains ever free from all blemish of error according to the divine promise of the Lord our Savior made to the Prince of His disciples I have prayed for thee that thy faith fail not, and, when thou art converted, do thou confirm thy brethren.'

This gift, then, of truth and never-failing faith was conferred by Heaven upon Peter and his successors in this Chair, that they might perform their high office unto the salvation of all; that the whole flock of Christ kept away by them from the poisonous food of error, might be nourished with the pasture of heavenly doctrine; that the occasion of schism being removed the whole Church might be kept one, and, resting on its foundation, might stand firm against the gates of hell.

But since in this very age, in which the salutary efficacy of the Apostolic office is most of all required, not a few are found who take away from its authority, We judge it altogether necessary solemnly to assert the prerogative which the only-

DOGMATIC CONSTITUTION ON THE CHURCH OF CHRIST
   (1871) (continued)

begotten Son of God vouchsafed to join with the supreme pastoral office.

Therefore faithfully adhering to the tradition received from the beginning of the Christian faith, for the glory of God our Savior, the exaltation of the Catholic Religion, and the salvation of Christian peoples, the Sacred Council approving, We teach and define that it is a dogma divinely revealed: that the Roman Pontiff, when he speaks ex cathedra, that is, when in discharge of the office of Pastor and Doctor of all Christians, by virtue of his supreme Apostolic authority he defines a doctrine regarding faith or morals to be held by the Universal Church, by the divine assistance promised to him in blessed Peter, is possessed of that infallibility with which the divine Redeemer willed that His Church should be endowed for defining doctrine regarding faith or morals: and that therefore such definitions of the Roman Pontiff are irreformable of themselves, and not from the consent of the Church.

But if any one-which may God avert-presume to contradict this Our definition; let him be anathema.

Given at Rome in Public Session solemnly held in the
   Vatican Basilica in the year of Our Lord One thousand eight
   hundred and seventy, on the eighteenth day of July, in the
   twenty-fifth year of our Pontificate.
      In conformity with the original.
         Joseph, Bishop of St. Pollen,
            Secretary of the Vatican Council.

Notes: *The second, and by far more important, statement to arise from the First Vatican Council was the Dogmatic Constitution on the Church of Christ. This document has been the major building block of the contemporary assertion of papal authority. The document is a closely reasoned argument that concludes with the assertion of papal infallibility. The argument is based on biblical passages concerning the interaction of Jesus and Peter from which it is asserted that Peter was given a primacy among the apostles, a primacy that resulted in Peter becoming bishop of Rome and passing authority through the Roman pontiffs to the present day.*

Part of the primacy of the Papal Office is the supreme power of teaching. As the official teachings of the church have remained free from error, therefore, it is concluded that when the pope speaks ex cathedra, literally, from the chair, in his office as Pastor and Doctor of all Christians, and when defining a teaching on faith or morals as a dogma to be held by all Christians, he speaks infallibly. The council declared any who did not receive this conclusion to be anathema.

The declaration on infallibility was accepted by most Catholics. A small group in Europe saw it as a major innovation and broke to form the Old Catholic Church. Protestants in the United States decried the doctrine, but responded to it as another challenge to biblical authority. Conservative theologians at Princeton, adopting some of the language of the document, began to speak of the infallibility of the Bible.

It should be noted that only once since the definition of papal infallibility has the sitting pope chosen to speak with that authority, in 1950, when Pope Pius defined the dogma of the assumption of the Blessed Virgin Mary.

* * *

APOSTOLIC CONSTITUTION, THE ASSUMPTION OF THE BLESSED VIRGIN MARY (1950)

1. The most bountiful God, Who is Almighty, the plan of Whose Providence rests upon wisdom and love, tempers, in the secret purpose of His own mind the sorrows of peoples and of individual men by means of joys that He interposes in their lives from time to time, in such a way that, under different conditions and in different ways, all things may work together unto good for those who love Him.

2. Now, just like the present age, Our pontificate is weighed down by ever so many cares, anxieties, and troubles, by reason of very severe calamities that have taken place and by reason of the fact that many have strayed away from truth and virtue. Nevertheless We are, greatly consoled to see that, while the Catholic Faith is being professed publicly and vigorously, piety towards the Virgin Mother of God is flourishing and daily growing more fervent, and that almost everywhere on earth it is showing indications of a better and holier life. Thus, while the Blessed Virgin is fulfilling in the most affectionate manner her maternal duties on behalf of those redeemed by the blood of Christ, the minds and the hearts of her children are being vigorously aroused to a more assiduous consideration of her prerogatives.

3. Actually God, Who from all eternity regards Mary with a most favorable and unique affection has, "when the fullness of time came" put the plan of His providence into effect in such a way that all the privileges and prerogatives He had granted to her in His sovereign generosity were to shine forth in her in a kind of perfect harmony. And, although the Church has always recognized this supreme generosity and the perfect harmony of graces and has daily studied them more and more throughout the course of the centuries, still it is in our own age that the privilege of the bodily Assumption into heaven of Mary, the Virgin Mother of God, has certainly shone forth more clearly.

4. That privilege has shone forth in new radiance since Our predecessor of immortal memory, Pius IX, solemnly proclaimed the dogma of the loving Mother of God's Immaculate Conception. These two privileges are most closely bound to one another. Christ overcame sin and death by His own death, and one who through Baptism has been born again in a supernatural way has conquered sin and death through the same Christ. Yet, according to the general rule, God does not will to grant to the just the full effect of the victory over death until the end of time has come. And so it is that the bodies of even the just are

corrupted after death, and only on the last day will they be joined, each to its own glorious soul.

5. Now God has willed that the Blessed Virgin Mary should be exempted from this general rule. She, by an entirely unique privilege, completely overcame sin by her Immaculate Conception, and as a result she was not subject to the law of remaining in the corruption of the grave, and she did not have to wait until the end of time for the redemption of her body.

6. Thus, when it was solemnly proclaimed that Mary, the Virgin Mother of God, was from the very beginning free from the taint of original sin, the minds of the faithful were filled with a stronger hope that the day might soon come when the dogma of the Virgin Mary's bodily Assumption into heaven would also be defined by the Church's supreme teaching authority.

7. Actually it was seen that not only individual Catholics, but also those who could speak for nations or ecclesiastical provinces, and even a considerable number of the Fathers of the Vatican Council, urgently petitioned the Apostolic See to this effect.

8. During the course of time such postulations and petitions did not decrease but rather grew continually in number and in urgency. In this cause there were pious crusades of prayer. Many outstanding theologians eagerly and zealously carried out investigations on this subject either privately or in public ecclesiastical institutions and in other schools where the sacred disciplines are taught. Marian Congresses, both national and international in scope, have been held in many parts of the Catholic world. These studies and investigations have brought out into even clearer light the fact that the dogma of the Virgin Mary's Assumption into heaven is contained in the deposit of Christian faith entrusted to the Church. They have resulted in many more petitions, begging and urging the Apostolic See that this truth be solemnly defined.

9. In this pious striving, the faithful have been associated in a wonderful way with their own holy Bishops, who have sent petitions of this kind, truly remarkable in number, to this See of the Blessed Peter. Consequently, when We were elevated to the throne of the supreme pontificate, petitions of this sort had already been addressed by the thousands from every part of the world and from every class of people, from our beloved sons the Cardinals of the Sacred College, from our Venerable Brethren, Archbishops and Bishops, from dioceses and from parishes.

10. Consequently, while We sent up earnest prayers to God that He might grant to Our mind the light of the Holy Ghost to enable Us to make a decision on this most serious subject, We issued special orders in which We commanded that, by corporate effort, more advanced inquiries into this matter should be begun and that, in the meantime, all the petitions about the Assumption of the Blessed Virgin Mary into heaven which had been sent to this Apostolic See from the time of Pius IX, Our predecessor of happy memory, down to our own days should be gathered together and carefully evaluated.

11. And, since We were dealing with a matter of such great moment and of such importance, We considered it opportune to ask all Our venerable brethren in the episcopate directly and authoritatively that each of them should make known to Us his mind in a formal statement. Hence, on May 1, 1946, We gave them Our letter "Deiparae Virginis Mariae," a letter in which these words are contained: "Do you, Venerable Brethren, in your outstanding wisdom and prudence, judge that the bodily Assumption of the Blessed Virgin can be proposed and defined as a dogma of faith? Do you, with your clergy and people, desire it?"

12. But those whom "the Holy Ghost has placed as bishops to rule the Church of God" gave an almost unanimous affirmative response to both these questions. This "outstanding agreement of the Catholic prelates and the faithful," affirming that the bodily Assumption of God's Mother into heaven can be defined as a dogma of faith, since it shows us the concordant teaching of the Church's ordinary doctrinal authority and the concordant faith of the Christian people which the same doctrinal authority sustains and directs, thus by itself and in an entirely certain and infallible way, manifests this privilege as a truth revealed by God and contained in that divine deposit which Christ has delivered to His Spouse to be guarded faithfully and to be taught infallibly. Certainly this teaching authority of the Church, not by any merely human effort but under the protection of the Spirit of Truth, and therefore absolutely without error, carries out the commission entrusted to it, that of preserving the revealed truths pure and entire throughout every age, in such a way that it presents them undefiled, adding nothing to them and taking nothing away from them. For, as the Vatican Council teaches, "the Holy Ghost was not promised to the successors of Peter in such a way that, by His revelation, they—might manifest new doctrine, but so that, by His assistance, they might guard as sacred and might faithfully propose the revelation delivered through the Apostles, or the deposit of faith." Thus, from the universal agreement of the Church's ordinary teaching authority we have a certain and firm proof, demonstrating that the Blessed Virgin Mary's bodily Assumption into heaven—which surely no faculty of the human mind could know by its own natural powers, as far as the heavenly glorification of the virginal body of the loving Mother of God is concerned—is a truth that has been revealed by God and consequently something that must be firmly and faithfully believed by all children of the Church. For, as the Vatican Council asserts, "all those things are to be believed by divine and Catholic faith which are contained in the written word of God or in tradition, and which are proposed by the Church, either in solemn judgment or in its ordinary and universal teaching office, as divinely revealed truths which must be believed."

13. Various testimonies, indications, and signs of this common belief of the Church are evident from remote times down through the course of the centuries; and this same belief becomes more clearly manifest from day to day.

14. Christ's faithful, through the teaching and the leadership of their pastors, have learned from the sacred books that

the Virgin Mary, throughout the course of her earthly pilgrimage, led a life troubled by cares, hardships, and sorrows, and that, moreover, what the holy old man Simeon had foretold actually came to pass, that is, that a terribly sharp sword had pierced her heart as she stood under the cross of her divine Son, our Redeemer. In the same way, it was not difficult for them to admit that the great Mother of God, like her only begotten Son, had actually passed from this life. But this in no way prevented them from believing and from professing openly that her sacred body had never been subject to the corruption of the tomb, and that the august tabernacle of the Divine Word had never been reduced to dust and ashes. Actually, enlightened by divine grace and moved by affection for her, God's Mother and our own sweetest Mother, they have contemplated in an ever clearer light the wonderful harmony and order of those privileges which the most provident God has lavished upon this loving associate of our Redeemer, privileges which reach such an exalted plane that, except for her, nothing created by God other than the human nature of Jesus Christ has ever reached this level.

15. The innumerable temples which have been dedicated to the Virgin Mary assumed into heaven clearly attest this faith. So do those sacred images, exposed therein for the veneration of the faithful, which bring this unique triumph of the Blessed Virgin before the eyes of all men. Moreover, cities, dioceses, and individual regions have been placed under the special patronage and guardianship of the Virgin Mother of God assumed into heaven. In the same way, religious institutes, with the approval of the Church, have been founded and have taken their name from this privilege. Nor can We pass over in silence the fact that in the Rosary of Mary, the recitation of which this Apostolic See so urgently recommends, there is one mystery proposed for pious meditation which, as all know, deals with the Blessed Virgin's Assumption into heaven.

16. This belief of the sacred Pastors and of Christ's faithful is universally manifested still more splendidly by the fact that, since ancient times, there have been both in the East and in the West solemn liturgical offices commemorating this privilege. The holy Fathers and Doctors of the Church have never failed to draw enlightenment from this fact since, as everyone knows, the sacred liturgy, "because it is the profession, subject to the supreme teaching authority within the Church, of heavenly truths, can supply proofs and testimonies of no small value for deciding a particular point of Christian doctrine."

17. In the liturgical books which deal with the feast either of the Dormition or of the Assumption of the Blessed Virgin there are expressions that agree in testifying that, when the Virgin Mother of God passed from this earthly exile to heaven, what happened to her sacred body was, by the decree of divine providence, in keeping with the dignity of the Mother of the Word Incarnate, and with the other privileges she had been accorded. Thus to cite an illustrious example, this is set forth in that Sacramentary which Adrian I, Our predecessor of immortal memory, sent to the Emporer Charlemagne. These words are found in this volume. "Venerable to us, O Lord, is the festivity of this day on which the holy Mother of God suffered temporal death, but still could not be kept down by the bonds of begotten death, who has begotten Thy Son Our Lord incarnate from herself."

18. What is here indicated in that sobriety characteristic of the Roman liturgy is presented more clearly and completely in other ancient liturgical books. To take one as an example, the Gallican Sacramentary designates this privilege of Mary's as "an ineffable mystery all the more worthy of praise as the Virgin's Assumption is something unique among men." And, in the Byzantine liturgy, not only is the Virgin Mary's bodily Assumption connected time and time again, with the dignity of the Mother of God, but also with the other privileges, and in particular with the virginal motherhood granted her by a singular decree of God's providence. "God, the King of the universe, has granted thee favors that surpass nature. As He kept thee a virgin in childbirth, thus He has kept thy body incorrupt in the tomb and has glorified it by His divine act of transferring it from the tomb."

19. The fact that the Apostolic See, which has inherited the functions entrusted to the Prince of the Apostles, the function of confirming the brethren in the faith, has by its own authority, made the celebration of this feast ever more solemn, has certainly and effectively moved the attentive minds of the faithful to appreciate always more completely the magnitude of the mystery it commemorates. So it was that the feast of the Assumption was elevated from that rank which it had occupied from the beginning among the other Marian feasts to be classed among the more solemn celebrations of the entire liturgical cycle. And, when Our predecessor St. Sergius I prescribed what is known as the litany, or the stational procession, to be held on four Marian feasts, he specified, together, the feasts of the Nativity, the Annunciation, the Purification, and the Dormition of the Virgin Mary. Again, St. Leo IV saw to it that the feast, which was already being celebrated under the title of the Assumption of the Blessed Mother of God, should be observed in even a more solemn way when he ordered a vigil to be held of the day before it and prescribed prayers to be recited after it until the octave day. When this had been done, he decided to take part himself in the celebration, in the midst that a holy fast had been ordered from ancient times for the day prior to the feast is made very evident by what Our predecessor St. Nicholas I testifies in treating of the principal fasts which "the Holy Roman Church has observed for a long time, and still observes.

20. However, since the liturgy of the Church does not engender the Catholic faith, but rather springs from it, in such a way that the practices of the sacred worship proceed from the Faith as the fruit comes from the tree, it follows that the holy Fathers and the great Doctors, in the homilies and sermons they gave the people on this feast day, did not

draw their teaching from the feast itself as from a primary source, but rather they spoke of this doctrine as something already known and accepted by Christ's faithful. They presented it more clearly. They offered more profound explanations of its meaning and nature, bringing out into sharper light the fact that this feast shows, not only that the dead body of the Blessed Virgin Mary remained incorrupt, but that she gained a triumph out of death, her heavenly glorification after the example of her only begotten Son, Jesus Christ; truths that the liturgical books had frequently touched upon concisely and briefly.

21. Thus St. John Damascene, an outstanding herald of this traditional truth, spoke out with powerful eloquence when he compared the bodily Assumption of the loving Mother of God with her other prerogatives and privileges. "It was fitting that she, who kept her virginity intact in childbirth, should keep her own body free from all corruption even after death. It was fitting that she, who had carried the Creator as a child at her breast, should dwell in the divine tabernacles. It was fitting that the spouse, whom the Father had taken to Himself, should live in the divine mansions. It was fitting that she, who had seen her Son upon the cross and who had thereby received into her heart the sword of sorrow which she had escaped in the act of giving birth to Him, should look upon Him as He sits with the Father. It was fitting that God's Mother should possess what belongs to her Son, and that she should be honored by every creature as the Mother and as the Handmaid of God."

22. These words of St. John Damascene agree perfectly with what others have taught on this same subject. Statements no less clear and accurate are to be found in sermons delivered by Fathers of an earlier time or of the same period, particularly on the occasion of this feast. And so, to cite some other examples, St. Germanus of Constantinople considered the fact that the body of Mary, the Virgin Mother of God, was incorrupt and had been taken up into heaven to be in keeping, not only with her divine motherhood, but also with the special holiness of her virginal body. "Thou art she who, as it is written, appearest in beauty, and thy virginal body is all holy, all chaste, entirely the dwelling place of God, so that it is henceforth completely exempt from dissolution into dust. Though still human, it is changed into the heavenly life of incorruptibility, truly living and glorious, undamaged and sharing in perfect life." And another very ancient writer asserts: "As the most glorious Mother of Christ, our Savior and God and the giver of life and immortality, has been endowed with life by Him, she has received an eternal incorruptibility of the body together with Him Who has raised her up from the tomb and has taken her up to Himself in a way known only to Him."

23. When this liturgical feast was being celebrated ever more widely and with ever increasing devotion and piety, the Bishops of the Church and its preachers in continually greater numbers considered it their duty openly and clearly to explain the mystery that the feast commemorates, and to explain how it is intimately connected with the other revealed truths.

24. Among the scholastic theologians there have not been lacking those who, wishing to inquire more profoundly into divinely revealed truths and desirous of showing the harmony that exists between what is termed the theological demonstration and the Catholic faith, have always considered it worthy of note that this privilege of the Virgin Mary's Assumption is in wonderful accord with those divine truths given us in Holy Scripture.

25. When they go on to explain this point, they adduce various proofs to throw light on this privilege of Mary. As the first element of these demonstrations, they insist upon the fact that, out of filial love for His Mother, Jesus Christ has willed that she be assumed into heaven. They base the strength of their proofs on the incomparable dignity of her divine motherhood and of all those prerogatives which follow from it. These include her exalted holiness, entirely surpassing the sanctity of all men and of the angels, the intimate union of Mary with her Son, and the affection of preeminent love which the Son has for His most worthy Mother.

26. Often there are theologians and preachers who, following in the footsteps of the holy Fathers, have been rather free in their use of events and expressions taken from Sacred Scripture to explain their belief in the Assumption. Thus, to mention only a few of the texts rather frequently cited in this fashion, some have employed the words of the Psalmist: "Arise, O Lord, into thy resting place: thou and the ark, which thou has sanctified"; and have looked upon the Ark of the Covenant, built of incorruptible word and placed in the Lord's temple, as a type of the most pure body of the Virgin Mary, preserved and exempted from all the corruption of the tomb and raised up to such glory in heaven. Treating of this subject, they also describe her as the Queen, entering triumphantly into the royal halls of heaven and sitting at the right hand of the divine Redeemer. Likewise they mention the Spouse of the Canticles "that goeth up by the desert, as a pillar of smoke of aromatical spices, of myrrh and frankincense" to be crowned. These are proposed as depicting that heavenly Queen and heavenly Spouse who has been lifted up to the courts of heaven with the divine Bridegroom.

27. Moreover, the scholastic Doctors have recognized that Assumption of the Virgin Mother of God as something signified, not only in various figures of the Old Testament, but also in that Woman clothed with the Son, whom John the Apostle contemplated on the Island of Patmos. Similarly they have given special attention to these words of the New Testament: "Hail, full of grace, the Lord is with thee, blessed art thou amongst women," since they saw, in the mystery of the Assumption, the fulfillment of that most perfect grace granted to the Blessed Virgin and the special blessing that countered the curse of Eve.

28. Thus, during the earliest period of scholastic theology, that most pious man, Amadeus, Bishop of Lausanne, held that the Virgin Mary's flesh had remained incorrupt—for it is wrong to believe that her body has seen corruption—because it was really united again to her soul and, together with it, crowned with great glory in the heavenly courts.

"For she was full of grace and blessed among women. She alone merited to conceive the true God of True God, Whom as a virgin, she brought forth, to Whom as a virgin she gave milk, fondling Him in her lap, and in all things she waited upon Him with loving care."

29. Among the holy writers who at that time employed statements and various images and analogies of Sacred Scripture to illustrate and to confirm the doctrine of the Assumption, which was piously believed, the Evangelical Doctor St. Anthony of Padua holds a special place. On the feast day of the Assumption, while explaining the Prophet's words: "I will glorify the place of my feet," he stated it as certain that the divine Redeemer had bedecked with supreme glory His most beloved Mother from whom He had received human flesh. He asserts that "you have here a clear statement that the Blessed Virgin has been assumed in her body, where was the place of the Lord's feet. Hence it is that the holy Psalmist writes: 'Arise, O Lord, into thy resting place: thou and the ark which thou hast sanctified'." And he asserts that, just as Jesus Christ has risen from the death over which He triumphed and has ascended to the right hand of the Father, so likewise the ark of His sanctification "has risen up, since on this day the Virgin Mother has been taken up to her heavenly dwelling."

30. When, during the middle ages, scholastic theology was especially flourishing, St. Albert the Great who, to establish this teaching, had gathered together many proofs from Sacred Scripture from the statements of older writers, and finally from the liturgy and from what is known as theological reasoning, concluded in this way: "From these proofs and authorities and from many others, it is manifest that the most blessed Mother of God has been assumed above the choirs of angels. And this we believe in every way to be true." And, in a sermon which he delivered on the sacred day of the Blessed Virgin Mary's Annunciation, explained the words "Hail, full of grace," words used by the angel who addressed her, the Universal Doctor, comparing the Blessed Virgin with Eve, stated clearly and incisively that she was exempted from the fourfold curse that had been laid upon Eve.

31. Following the footsteps of his distinguished teacher, the Angelic Doctor, despite the fact that he never dealt directly with this question, nevertheless, whenever he touched upon it, always held together with the Catholic Church, that Mary's body had been assumed into heaven along with her soul.

32. Along with many others, the Seraphic Doctor held the same views. He considered it as entirely certain that, as God had preserved the most Holy Virgin Mary from the violation of her virginal purity and integrity in conceiving and in childbirth, He would never have permitted her body to have been resolved into dust and ashes. Explaining these words of Sacred Scriptures: "Who is this that cometh up from the desert, flowing with delights, leaning

upon her beloved." and applying them in a kind of accommodated sense to the Blessed Virgin, he reasons thus: "From this we can see that she is there bodily . . . her blessedness would not have been complete unless she were there as a person. The soul is not a person, but the soul, joined to the body, is a person. It is manifest that she is there in soul and in body. Otherwise she would not possess her complete beatitude."

33. In the Fifteenth Century, during a later period of scholastic theology, St. Bernardine of Siena collected and diligently evaluated all that the medieval theologians had said and taught on this question. He was not content with setting down the principal considerations which these writers of an earlier day had already expressed, but he added others of his own. The likeness between God's Mother and her divine Son, in the way of the nobility and dignity of body and of soul—a likeness that forbids us to think of the heavenly Queen as being separated from the heavenly King—makes it entirely imperative that Mary "should be only where Christ is." Moreover, it is reasonable and fitting that not only the soul and body of a man, but also the soul and body of a woman should have obtained heavenly glory. Finally, since the Church has never looked for the bodily relics of the Blessed Virgin nor proposed them for the veneration of the people, who have a proof on the order of a sensible experience.

34. The above-mentioned teaching of the holy Fathers and of the Doctors have been in common use during more recent times. Gathering together the testimonies of the Christians of earlier days, St. Robert Bellamaine exclaimed: "And who, I ask, could believe that the ark of holiness, the dwelling place of the Word of God, the temple of the Holy Ghost, could be reduced to ruin? My soul is filled with horror at the thought that this virginal flesh which had begotten God, had brought Him into the world, had nourished and carried Him, could have been turned into ashes or given over to be food for worms."

35. In like manner St. Francis of Sales, after asserting that it is wrong to doubt that Jesus Christ has Himself observed, in the most perfect way, the divine commandment by which children are ordered to honor their parents, asks this question: "What son would not bring his mother back to life and would not bring her into paradise after her death if he could?" And St. Alphonsus writes that "Jesus did not wish to have the body of Mary corrupted after death, since it would have redounded to His own dishonor to have her virginal flesh, from which He himself had assumed flesh, reduced to dust."

36. Once the mystery which is commemorated in this feast had been placed in its proper light, there were not lacking teachers who, instead of dealing with the theological reasoning that show why it is fitting and right to believe the Bodily Assumption of the Blessed Virgin Mary into heaven chose to focus their mind and attention on the faith of the Church itself, which is the Mystical body of Christ without stain or wrinkle and is called by the Apostle "the pillar and ground of truth." Relying on this common faith, they considered the teaching opposed to the doctrine of

Our Lady's Assumption as temerarious, if not heretical. Thus like not a few others, St. Peter Canisius, after he had declared that the very word "Assumption" signifies the glorification, not only of the soul but also of the body, and that the Church has venerated and has solemnly celebrated this mystery of Mary's Assumption for many centuries, adds these words of warning: "This teaching has already been accepted for some centuries, it has been held as certain in the minds of the pious people, and it has been taught to the entire Church in such a way that those who deny that Mary's body has been assumed into heaven are not be listened to patiently but are everywhere to be denounced as over-contentious or rash men, and as imbued with a spirit that is heretical rather than Catholic."

37. At the same time the great Suarez was professing in the field of Mariology the norm that "keeping in mind the standards of propriety, and when there is no contradiction or repugnance on the part of Scripture, the mysteries of grace which God has wrought in the Virgin must be measured, not by the ordinary laws, but by the divine omnipotence." Supported by the common faith of the entire Church on the subject of the mystery of the Assumption, he could conclude that this mystery was to be believed with the same firmness of assent as that given to the Immaculate Conception of the Blessed Virgin. Thus he already held that such truths could be defined.

38. All these proofs and considerations of the holy Fathers and the theologians are based upon the Sacred Writings as their ultimate foundation. These set the loving Mother of God as it were before our very eyes as most intimately joined to her divine Son and as always sharing His lot. Consequently it seems impossible to think of her, the one who conceived Christ, brought Him forth, nursed Him with her milk, held Him in her arms, and clasped Him to her breast, as being apart from Him in body, even though not in soul, after this earthly life. Since our Redeemer is the Son of Mary, He could not do otherwise, as the perfect observer of God's law, than to honor, not only His eternal Father, but also His most beloved Mother. And, since it was within His power to grant her this great honor, to preserve her from the corruption of the tomb, we must believe that He really acted in this way.

39. We must remember especially that, since the Second Century, the Virgin Mary has been designated by the holy Fathers as the new Eve, who, although subject to the new Adam, is most intimately associated with Him in that struggle against the infernal foe which, as foretold in the *protoevangelium,* would finally result in that most complete victory over the sin and death which are always mentioned together in the writings of the Apostle of the Gentiles. Consequently, just as the glorious resurrection of Christ was an essential part and the final sign of this victory, so that struggle which was common to the Blessed Virgin and her divine Son should be brought to a close by the glorification of her virginal body, for the same Apostle says: "when this mortal thing hath put on immortality, then shall come to pass the saying that is written: Death is swallowed up in victory."

40. Hence the revered Mother of God, from all eternity joined in a hidden way with, Jesus Christ in one and the same decree of predestination, immaculate in her conception, a most perfect virgin in her divine motherhood, the noble associate of the divine Redeemer who has won a complete triumph over sin and its consequences, finally obtained, as the supreme culmination of her privileges, that she should be preserved free from the corruption of the tomb and that, like her own Son, having overcome death, she might be taken up body and soul to the glory of heaven where, as Queen, she sits in splendor at the right hand of her Son, the immortal King of the Ages.

41. Since the Universal Church, within which dwells the Spirit of Truth Who infallibly directs it towards an ever more perfect knowledge of the revealed truths, has expressed its own belief many times over the course of the centuries, and since the Bishops of the entire world are almost unanimously petitioning that the truth of the bodily Assumption of the Blessed Virgin Mary into heaven should be defined as a dogma of divine and Catholic faith—this truth which is based on the Sacred Writings, which is thoroughly rooted in the minds of the faithful, which has been approved in ecclesiastical worship from the most remote times, which is completely in harmony with the other revealed truths, and which has been expounded and explained magnificently in the work, the science, and the wisdom of the theologians—We believe that the moment appointed in the plan of divine providence for the solemn proclamation of this outstanding privilege of the Virgin Mary has already arrived.

42. We, who have placed Our pontificate under the special patronage of the most holy Virgin, to whom We have had recourse so often in times of grave trouble, We who have consecrated the entire human race to her Immaculate Heart in public ceremonies, and who have time and time again experienced her powerful protection, are confident that this solemn proclamation and definition of the Assumption will contribute in no small way to the advantage of human society, since it redounds to the glory of the Most Blessed Trinity, to which the Blessed Mother of God is bound by such singular bonds. It is to be hoped that all the faithful will be stirred up to a stronger piety towards their heavenly Mother, and that the souls of all those who glory in the Christian name may be moved by the desire of sharing in the unity of Jesus Christ's Mystical Body and of increasing their love for her who shows her motherly heart to all the members of this august Body. And so we may hope that those who meditate upon the glorious example Mary offers us may be more and more convinced of the value of a human life entirely devoted to carrying out the heavenly Father's will and to bringing good to others. Thus, while the illusory teachings of materialism and the corruption of morals that follows from these teachings threaten to extinguish the light of virtue and to ruin the lives of men by exciting discord among them, in this magnificent way all may see clearly to what a lofty goal our bodies and souls are destined. Finally it is our hope that belief in Mary's bodily Assumption into heaven will make our belief in our own resurrection stronger and render it more effective.

43. We rejoice greatly that this solemn event falls, according to the design of God's providence, during this Holy year, so that We are able, while the great Jubilee is being observed, to adorn the brow of God's Virgin Mother with this brilliant gem, and to leave a monument more enduring than bronze of Our own most fervent love for the Mother of God.

44. For which reason, after We have poured forth prayers of supplication again and again to God, and have invoked the light of the Spirit of Truth, for the glory of Almighty God Who has lavished His special affection upon the Virgin Mary, for the honor of her Son, the immortal King of the Ages and the Victor over sin and death, for the increase of the glory of that same august Mother, and for the joy and exultation of the entire Church; by the authority of Our Lord Jesus Christ, of the Blessed Apostles Peter and Paul, and by Our own authority, We pronounce, declare, and define it to be a divinely revealed dogma: that the Immaculate Mother of God, the ever Virgin Mary, having completed the course of her earthly life, was assumed body and soul into heavenly glory.

45. Hence if anyone, which God forbid, should dare wilfully to deny or to call into doubt that which We have defined, let him know that he has fallen away completely from the divine and Catholic Faith.

46. In order that this, Our definition of the bodily Assumption of the Virgin Mary into heaven may be brought to the attention of the universal Church, We desire that this, Our Apostolic Letter, should stand for perpetual remembrance, commanding that written copies of it, or even printed copies, signed by the hand of any public notary and bearing the seal of a person constituted in ecclesiastical dignity, should be accorded by all men the same reception they would give to this present Letter, were it tendered or shown.

47. It is forbidden to any man to change this, Our declaration, pronouncement, and definition or, by rash attempt, to oppose and counter it. If any man should presume to make such an attempt, let him know that he will incur the wrath of Almighty God and of the Blessed Apostles Peter and Paul.

48. Given at Rome, at St. Peter's, in the year of the great Jubilee, 1950, on the first day of the month of November, on the Feast of All Saints, in the twelfth year of Our pontificate.

I Pius
Bishop of the Catholic Church,
have signed, so defining.

Notes: *Since the definition of papal infallibility in 1871, that authority has been used only once, in 1950, by Pope Pius XII, to define the doctrine of the assumption of the Blessed Virgin Mary. It culminated a century of growing attention to Marian devotion within the church in the century since the definition of the Immaculate Conception in 1854, and Marian devotees saw it as the logical extension of that doctrine. It was granted that she should overcome sin by her Immaculate Conception, so she was not subject to the law of remaining in the corruption of the grave and did not (as do the remainder of humankind) have to wait to the end of time for the redemption of her body.*

In this case, the doctrine is not traced to the Bible, but to the second century references to Mary as the new Eve. However, most attention is given to the increasing number of requests that have been received since the proclamation of the Immaculate Conception that the doctrine of the Assumption also be proclaimed.

*   *   *

Old Catholicism

STATEMENT (EVANGELICAL CATHOLIC CHURCH)

The Evangelical Catholic Church is not a new denomination which cam into existence ten years ago, or one hundred years ago in reaction to Vatican 1, or even some 450 years ago during The Reformation. She is a part of that Church which has existed ever since our ascended Lord commanded His Disciples to be His witnesses to the end of the age. Her faith, doctrine, and confessions are evidence of this link with the past. Her confessions repeatedly insist that in Her doctrine *there is nothing that varies from the Scriptures or from The Catholic Church,* and that She takes *most diligent care that no new doctrine should creep into our churches,* for a new doctrine would be neither Scriptural nor a universal Catholic doctrine. She believes and teaches the Faith of the ancient undivided Church, firmly holding to the mystery of The Holy Trinity and acknowledging Jesus as the one true God, the One Who is coming again to judge the living and the dead. As a testimony of Her preserving the wholeness of the full and true Faith of Jesus our God, The Evangelical Catholic Church espouses THE RULE OF SAINT VINCENT OF LERINS (434 A.D.):

Id teneasmus, quod ubique, quod semper, quod ab omnibus est; hoc est etenim vere propieque catholicum.

We maintain what everywhere and always by everyone has been believed, this being truly and actually Catholic.

Thus The Evangelical Catholic Church is not an interpretation of Christianity, not a party or a denomination; She is an integral part of that Body which Our Lord addressed when He said: *I am the vine, ye are the branches* and *Lo, I am with you always, even unto the end of the ages.* She believes and teaches the pure apostolic testimony of the Gospel, while at the same time being able to trace Her existence historically, through the consecration of Her Bishops, directly back to The Apostles (and through them to Our Lord).

The Synods of The Evangelical Catholic Church have consistently affirmed their acceptance of The Book of Concord and have adopted that polity which it espouses and prefers (the "emergency" long ago having ended). Thus the bond of The Evangelical Catholic Church with those first days in Nazareth and Galilee, both in the assurance of the proclamation of The Gospel in all its apostolic purity and in regular episcopal ordination by Bishops in Apostolic Succession, remains unbroken.

The Evangelical Catholic Church teaches that salvation can or must earn through works, for salvation is a gift freely given to us by our loving God. Whatever merit is required for salvation was earned by Christ Jesus! Our response to this free gift of salvation must be a living faith manifested by the way we live our lives (good works).

The Evangelical Catholic believes that The Holy Spirit is active in every aspect of the life of The Church, for The Church is constituted by The Spirit working through the Means of Grace and She is sanctified through The Word (the pure teaching) and Sacraments. The Spirit is not found apart from The Church, for He is found only wherever The Word is preached in Its truth and purity and The Holy Mysteries are rightly administered.

The Evangelical Catholic Church confesses one Baptism (for adults and infants), and insists that Baptism *is necessary to salvation.* This Sacrament of Holy Baptism incorporates one into The Body of Christ; to be baptized is to become a *full* member of The Church, to *put* on Jesus and became a living part of Him. By this precious mystery we receive salvation from sin and reconciliation with God by becoming participants in the Death and Resurrection of Christ Jesus. In Holy Baptism God engrafts the candidate into Jesus and raises him to New Life; God gives this Child the priceless gift of saving faith and the power of The Holy Spirit to fulfill his vocation in this world and to reign with Christ in His eternal kingdom.

Chrismation (confirmation) is seen as an part of Holy Baptism; here the candidate is sealed with The Sign of The Holy Cross and confirmed in The Faith with the gift of The Holy Spirit. There is no valid Biblical, historical, or theological reason for separating Chrismation from Baptism! It is naturally expected that the newly Baptized/Confirmed will immediately (as part of the very same Mass) join The Household of God at The Family Meal by fully participating in and receiving Holy Communion.

The Evangelical Catholic Church recognizes The Sacrament of The Holy Eucharist as the only form of public worship commanded by Our Lord Jesus Christ. The-Church has historically insisted that Masses are performed every Lord's Day and on the other festivals in which The Sacrament is offered to those who wish to use it. We affirm the Biblical teaching that The Bread and Wine become The Body and The Blood of Christ Jesus; we reject transubstantiation, consubstantiation, impanation, or any other effort to explain the mystery of Holy Communion. Each time we participate in The Holy Eucharist we are:

(1) reminding ourselves of all that God has done for us through His Son, Christ Jesus our Lord and Savior;

(2) publicly confessing our faith in Jesus as God and Savior;

(3) celebrating our unity with angels and archangels and all the hosts of Heaven, our oneness with all who have, do now, or will believe in Jesus as God and Savior;

(4) receiving, in the true, corporeal, physical body and blood of Jesus, the Medicine of Immortality;

(5) receiving the assurance that God does forgive all the sins of those who confess and repent;

(6) receiving the spiritual strength to endure and overcome all the temptations of Satan, the world, and even our old sinful nature (the Old Adam);

(7) offering and sacrificing to God—in thanksgiving for all that He has given us in love through Christ Jesus—all that we have and are (that is, me rededicate ourselves to God, reaffirm our Baptismal vows).

That is why Jesus said: This do often, as you do it, in remembrance of Me.

The Evangelical Catholic Church accepts the prophetic and apostolic Scriptures of The Old and New Testaments as the sole rule and standard according to which all doctrine and practice should be estimated and judged. We believe that The Holy Bible is the verbally inspired, inerrant, Spirit-breathed Word of God and that the other elements of Holy Tradition are in full accord with its contents. It is only with the consensus of The Church, guided by The Holy Spirit, that a proper interpretation of Holy Scripture is possible.

The Evangelical Catholic Church with The Council of Ephesus (431 A.D.), confesses Saint Mary as *THEOTOKOS*—God Bearer, a title affirmed in *The Formula of Concord.* We also consider Saint Mary ever virgin, a title affirmed in *The Smalcald Articles,* and recognize her as that most praiseworthy Virgin. We include in The Calendar the following feasts:
February 2: The Purification
March 25: The Annunciation
July 2: The Visitation
August 15: The Dormition
September 8: The Nativity of Mary

The Evangelical Catholic Church emphasizes Her Catholicity. It is important to do so. Without such an emphasis our vision of The Church is narrowed to one particular denomination, to one very limited period of time, to one locality, to one national or ethnic group. She claims as Her own the magnificent heritage and the worldwide scope that Christ has bestowed upon His Holy Bride; She is a contemporary manifestation of The Church of all times, of all people, of all places.

Notes: *The Evangelical Catholic Church is a small denomination founded in the 1970s by former members of the Lutheran Church-Missouri Synod, but affirms both Lutheran and Catholic roots. Its leadership has accepted Old Catholic orders.*

Lutheran influence sees its emphasis on salvation as the free gift of God and acceptance of only two sacraments, baptism and the Eucharist. It specifically denies confirmation as a separate sacrament. However, the Church denies both Catho-

STATEMENT (EVANGELICAL CATHOLIC CHURCH) (continued)

lic (transubstantiation) and Lutheran (consubstantiation) explanations of the nature of the Eucharistic sacrament. It affirms apostolic succession through a historic episcopacy.

* * *

STATEMENT OF UNION (INTERNATIONAL FREE CATHOLIC COMMUNION)

1. The Way of Salvation

Being created in the image and likeness of God, the human family has a glorious birthright which has become obscured through ignorance, doubt and sin resulting in a sense of alienation from God, from our true spiritual nature and from all of Creation. In the infinite compassion of God, Christ came forth from the heart of the Father, to take upon himself the fullness of our human estate, to liberate us and all Creation. By his incarnation, suffering, death, resurrection and ascension, a fully liberating and transforming grace was released into all Creation. In his love, He invites us to embrace this freedom and to participate in the work of redemption. By accepting and cooperating with this grace our lives are transfigured and Creation is transformed.

2. The Church

The Mystical Body of Christ consists of all who have consciously embraced the grace of Christ. A temple built with living stones, the Church is a sacrament of Christ and a dwelling place of the Holy Spirit. Referred to as the pillar and ground of truth, she has been entrusted with the care of Sacred Scripture and Tradition. However, the ultimate mission of the Church is to hold forth the message of Christ's eternal love and healing grace to all the world.

3. Scripture and Tradition

The principal guides for Christian faith and practice are found in Sacred Scripture and Tradition. Through the inspired writings of Sacred Scripture God has revealed the Word of Life. In addition to the Christian and Hebrew Scriptures, the Church has received oral, written and liturgical traditions which come to us from apostolic times. Through the working of the Holy Spirit in the life of the Church, Tradition is constantly nourished, renewed and expanded by the unique contributions of each generation and culture. Ever mindful that all people belong to God's Family, the Church must remain open to recognize the wisdom of the other great spiritual traditions of the world.

4. The Creeds

The principle doctrines of the Christian Faith are succinctly stated in what are commonly known as the Apostles' and Nicene Creeds. The Church looks to these ancient confessions as a standard and basis for Christian Unity.

5. The Law

Jesus said: "Hear, 0 Israel: The Lord our God is one Lord: You shall love the Lord your God with all your heart, and with all your soul, and with all your strength. The second is this, You shall love your neighbor as yourself. There is no other commandment greater than these."

Free Will is a fundamental and precious endowment given to all God's children. The Church must seek to cultivate and to protect individual freedom of thought, conscience and choice. While gently offering guidance, it is her duty to help God's People develop the faculty of discernment and take personal responsibility for their choices in life.

"You have been called to freedom, brothers and sisters, only do not use your freedom for self-indulgence, but through love serve one another."—St. Paul

6. The Sacraments

The sacraments are outward signs which confer the very grace they signify. These Mysteries, ordained by Christ, are seven in number, namely Baptism, Confirmation, Holy Eucharist, Reconciliation, Anointing the Sick, Matrimony, and Holy Orders.

- Baptism

  This Sacrament of Spiritual regeneration, administered by immersion or by the pouring on of water in the Name of the Father and of the Son and of the Holy Spirit, imparts sanctifying grace and constitutes initiation into the Mystical Body of Christ, the royal priesthood of believers and the sacramental life of the Christian community.

- Confirmation

  The grace of Pentecost, the anointing of the Holy Spirit, administered by the successors of the apostles with Chrism and the laying on of hands, empowers Christians to participate in the apostolic mission of the Church.

- Holy Eucharist

  The central act of worship of the People of God, in which we offer ourselves and our gifts in union with the eternal sacrifice of Christ and partake of His Real Presence under the forms of Bread and Wine, offers to us the privilege of direct Communion with our Lord Jesus Christ.

- Reconciliation

  The Sacrament in which Jesus Christ, through the ministry of the church, bestows the forgiveness of sins, heals broken fellowship and imparts grace for the amendment of life.

- Anointing the Sick

  The ministers of the Church anoint the sick with sacred oil, imparting the grace of Christ to those in need of healing for body or soul.

- Matrimony

  The Mystery of Marriage corresponds to the union of Christ and his Church. Through a voluntary, mutual commitment declared before God and the Church, the marital union becomes a channel of sacramental grace.

- Holy Orders

The Holy Spirit, though the laying on of hands and the consecratory prayer of the Bishop, ordains women and men, married or single, who are called to serve the Church, imparting to them special grace to administer the Sacraments and feed the flock of Christ.

Notes: *The International Free Catholic Communion is a new alignment of independent bishops and faithful who basically agree with Roman Catholicism, but exist independently of its administration. Its Statement of Union, adopted in 1991, accepts the Apostles and Nicene Creeds and the practice of the seven sacraments. Its bishops are not in communion with Rome but act as autonomous leaders of their assigned dioceses though existing in fellowship with other bishops of the Communion.*

* * *

Anglicanism

OUR THEOLOGICAL CONTEXT (ANGELICAN CHURCH OF CANADA/WYCLIFFE COLLEGE)

The Anglican evangelican tradition is one of the heirs of the Protestant Reformation of the sixteenth century, which aimed to be a "middle way" between the Church of the Western Middle Ages and the so-called "Radical Reformation". Standing between those who wanted to recycle medieval ecclesiastical tradition and those who presumed special revelations of the Holy Spirit, Protestants proclaimed the supremacy and sufficiency of Scripture as the rule of faith. Standing between those for whom a relationship with Christ depended on a sacramental system controlled by a mediatorial priesthood and those for whom it depended on obedience to a community discipline, Protestants proclaimed that it depended solely on the free grace of God. Standing between those who valued ordained or licensed vocations more than lay vocations and those for whom "everyone's private spirit and gift is the only bishop that ordaineth him to this ministry," Protestants recognized equal honor in all Christian vocations but judged that ministries should be exercised "decently and in order" according to Church discipline. Standing between those who (in Richard Hooker's words in 1594) superstitiously served "though the true God, yet with needless offices," and those who rationalistically stripped away "the beauty of holiness." Protestants affirmed a balanced and mature spiritually based on a strong confidence in the providence of God the Creator and Sustainer, the atoning work of Jesus Christ, and the guidance of the Holy Spirit. Wycliffe College stands consciously within this "middle way".

Our commitment to the Protestant tradition is expressed in six Principles which were initially set forth in the first Calendar of 1879-1880. Although their wording has changed, their message has not. Each student who joins our community is required to express his or her agreement with these Principles.

Not only (or even primarily) did the Reformation proclaim doctrines: it also inspired a renewal of theological scholarship and an application of new models of pastoral ministry. In Biblical studies, the Reformers aimed, not to re-demonstrate ancient dogmas, but to rediscover the intended meaning of the sacred authors. In historical scholarship, they returned to sources, debunked human traditions that claimed divine authority, and reconstructed the history of the Church. In their liturgical work, they re-thought the meaning of worship, purified the rites of the Church, and refashioned them into the vernacular. They constantly challenged their own faith with the questions: Is it true? Does it edify? Does it build up the Church? Their ideal pastor was someone who could help others do the same. Similarly, at Wycliffe, our goal is not simply to communicate an inert body of ancient thought to our students, but to teach the Reformation spirit of critical theological enquiry in a context of a committed Christian faith. Our objective is to teach the methods and resources of theological study and reflection; to help students integrate their faith, their intellect, their feelings, and their vocation: and to foster their capacity to recognize and to serve the living God at work in the world. We are not seeking students who want their preconceptions reinforced. Those who choose Wycliffe should be willing to be challenged and transformed.

Anglican evangelicalism is to be distinguished historically not only from other sixteenth-century options, but also from at least two later offshoots of the Protestant movement. In contrast to liberalism, Anglican evangelicals have affirmed that faith is not to be reduced to ethics, to religious experience, to pious feelings, or to other human or social phenomena, but stands apart as God's gracious gift. And in contrast to fundamentalism, Anglican evangelicals have affirmed that faith is not to be measured by its conformity to any kind of received doctrinal formulas, but that it must always be re-casting and reapplying the Gospel in new historical situations.

Notes: *Wycliffe College, Toronto, Ontario, is sponsored by the Anglican Church of Canada. Its statement summarizes the Anglican tradition in which it stands. The six "Principles" spell out key distinguishing ideas/practices that define the tradition.*

* * *

A COMMUNION OF COMMUNIONS (CHICAGO QUADRILATERAL) (EPISCOPAL CHURCH)

Whereas, many of the faithful in Christ Jesus among us are praying with renewed and increasing earnestness that some measures may be adopted at this time for the re-union of the sundered parts of Christendom ... we Bishops of the Protestant Episcopal Church in the United States of America, in Council assembled as Bishops in the Church of God, do hereby solemnly declare to all whom it may concern, and especially to our fellow Christians of the different Communions in this land, who, in their several spheres, have contended for the religion of Christ:

1. Our earnest desire that the Savior's prayer, 'That we all may be one', may, in its deepest and truest sense, be speedily fulfilled;

2. That we believe that all who have been duly baptized with water, in the name of the Father, and of the Son, and of the Holy Ghost, are members of the Holy Catholic Church;

3. That in all things of human ordering or human choice, relating to modes of worship and discipline, or to traditional customs, this Church is ready in the spirit of love and humility to forgo all preferences of her own;

4. That this Church does not seek to absorb other Communions, but rather, cooperating with them on the basis of a common Faith and Order, to discountenance schism, to heal the wounds of the Body of Christ, and to promote the charity which is the chief of Christian graces and the visible manifestation of Christ to the world;

But furthermore, we do hereby affirm that the Christian unity now so earnestly desired by the memorialists can be restored only by the return of all Christian communions to the principles of unity exemplified by the undivided Catholic Church during the first ages of its existence; which principle we believe to be the substantial deposit of Christian Faith and Order committed by Christ and his apostles to the Church unto the end of the world, and therefore incapable of compromise or surrender by those who have been ordained to be its stewards and trustees for the common and equal benefit of all men. As inherent parts of this sacred deposit, and therefore as essential to the restoration of unity among the divided branches of Christendom, we account the following, to wit:

1. The Holy Scriptures of the Old and New Testament as the revealed word of God.

2. The Nicene Creed as the sufficient statement of the Christian Faith.

3. The two Sacraments—Baptism and the Supper of the Lord—ministered with unfailing use of Christ's words of institution and the elements ordained by Him.

4. The Historic Episcopate, locally adapted in the methods of its administration to the varying needs of the nations and peoples called of God into unity of His Church.

Furthermore, Deeply grieved by the sad divisions which affect the Christian Church in our own land, we hereby declare our desire and readiness, so soon as there shall be any authorized response to this Declaration, to enter into brotherly conference with all or any Christian Bodies seeking the restoration of the organic unity of the, Church, with a view to the earnest study of the conditions under which so priceless a blessing might happily be brought to pass.

Notes: *In the 1880s, the Episcopal Church initiated discussions looking toward union with other denominations then operating in the United States. The results, promulgated in 1886, became known as the Chicago Quadrilateral, the four bases upon which a united church might be built: The Bible, the Nicene Creed, the sacraments of baptism and the eucharist, and the historic episcopate (bishops in apostolic succession). In future unity discussions, the fourth point almost always became the focus of contention.*

*   *   *

LAMBETH CONFERENCE (1888), RESOLUTION 343 (LAMBETH QUADRILATERAL) (EPISCOPAL CHURCH)

That, in the opinion of this Conference, the following Articles supply a basis on which approach may be by God's blessing made towards Home Reunion:—

(a) The Holy Scriptures of the Old and New Testaments, as 'containing all things necessary to salvation', and as being the rule and ultimate standard of faith.

(b) The Apostles' Creed, as the Baptismal Symbol; and the Nicene Creed, as the sufficient statement of the Christian faith.

(c) The two Sacraments ordained by Christ Himself—Baptism and the Supper of the Lord—ministered with unfailing use of Christ's words of Institution, and of the elements ordained by Him.

(d) The Historic Episcopate, locally adapted in the methods of its administration to the varying needs of the nations and peoples called of God into the Unity of His Church.

Notes: *The 1886 Chicago Quadrilateral was passed for consideration by the Lambeth Conference of 1888, an international gathering of bishops representing the Church of England and all of the churches of the Anglican tradition. In a slightly revised form, it was reissued as the Lambeth Quadrilateral. The primary additions were the references to the Apostles Creed and the needs of the text of the sacramental services following Christ's words of Institution.*

*   *   *

LAMBETH CONFERENCE (1968), RESOLUTION 43 (EPISCOPAL CHURCH)

The Conference accepts the main conclusion of the report of the Archbishop's Commission in Christian Doctrine entitled Subscription and Assent to the Thirty-Nine Articles (1968) and in furtherance of its recommendation suggests

(a) that each Church of our communion consider whether the Articles need be bound up with its Prayer Book;

(b) suggests to the Churches of the Anglican Communion at assent to the Thirty-Nine Articles be no longer required of ordinands;

(c) suggests that, when subscription is required to the Articles or other elements in the Anglican tradition, it should be required, and given, only in the context of a statement which gives the full range of our inheritance of faith and sets the Articles in their historical context.

Notes: *The Thirty-Nine Articles of Religion have been the traditional doctrinal statement of the Anglican tradition. Their content includes not only a positive statement of the Christian faith, but also numerous polemical statements reflective of the intense theological debates of the sixteenth century. In light of contemporary historical studies and ecumenical dialogues, the Church decided to back away from the Thirty-Nine Articles as a doctrinal standard.*

*　　*　　*

Independent Anglican Schools

STATEMENT OF FAITH (TRINITY EPISCOPAL SCHOOL FOR MINISTRY)

We recognize the need today for reaffirming the following beliefs:

ARTICLE I. The Holy Trinity

The mystery of the Holy Trinity, namely, that the one God exists eternally in the three persons: Father, Son and Holy Spirit; and has so revealed himself to us in the Gospel.

ARTICLE II. The Lord Jesus Christ

The full deity and full humanity of our Lord Jesus, God incarnate, who by reason of his birth of the Virgin Mary, sinless life, atoning death, bodily resurrection, glorious ascension and triumphant reign, is the only Mediator between God and man.

ARTICLE III. The Holy Scriptures

The trustworthiness of the canonical books of the Old and New Testaments as "God's Word written," which contain all things necessary for salvation, teach God's will for his world, and have supreme authority for faith, life and the continuous renewal and reform of the Church.

ARTICLE IV. Justification and Sanctification

The justification of the repenting and believing sinner as God's gracious act of declaring him righteous on the ground of the reconciling death of Christ, who suffered in our place and rose again for us; and sanctification as the gracious continuing activity of the Holy Spirit in the justified believer, perfecting his repentance, nurturing the new life implanted within him, transforming him into Christ's image, and enabling him to do good works in the world.

ARTICLE V. The Christian Church

The Church as the Body of Christ, whose members belong to the new humanity, are called to live in the world in the power of the Spirit, worshipping God, confessing his truth, proclaiming Christ, supporting one another in love and giving themselves in sacrificial service to those in need.

ARTICLE VI. Spiritual Gifts and Ministry

The calling of all Christians to exercise their God-given gifts in ministry, and to work, witness and suffer for Christ; together with the particular calling of ordained ministers, who, by preaching, teaching and pastoral care, are to equip God's people for his service, and to present them mature in Christ.

ARTICLE VII. The Gospel Sacraments

The sacraments of Baptism and Holy Communion as "visible worlds" which proclaim the Gospel, and are means of grace by which faith is quickened and strengthened;

In particular, the significance of the Lord's Supper as a communion in the Body and Blood of Christ, who offers himself to us in the action of this sacrament, so that by faith we may feed on him in our hearts and offer ourselves to him in gratitude for our salvation through his cross;

Also, the openness of the Lord's Table as the place where all baptized believers, being one in Christ, are free to celebrate their common salvation in the Lord, and to express their common their common devotion to his person and his service.

ARTICLE VIII. The Return of Christ

The personal return in glory of our Lord Jesus Christ at the end of this age for the resurrection of the dead, some to life, some to condemnation, for the glorification of his Church, and for the renewal of the whole creation.

Notes: *The Trinity Episcopal School for Ministry is an independent ministerial training school operating in the Anglican tradition. The school has assumed a conservative theological stance affirming the authority of Thirty-Nine Articles of Religion.*

Chapter 3
Eastern Liturgical Family

Orthodoxy

THEOLOGICAL POSITION (MERCIAN RITE CATHOLIC CHURCH)

We believe:

In one God, Father Almighty, Physician of our whole being, eternally existing in three persons: namely, the Father, the Son, and the Holy Ghost.

That Jesus Christ is the only begotten Son of the Father, conceived of the Holy Ghost, and born of the Virgin Mary.

That Jesus was crucified, died, and buried, and was raised from the dead and ascended into heaven to sit at the right hand of the Father Almighty.

We acknowledge that the Bible is in fact the inspired work of God.

We acknowledge that the rule of faith laid down by St. Vincent of Lerins: "Let us hold that which has been delivered everywhere, always and by all, for that is truly and properly Catholic" should be upheld by all within the Holy Church.

We repudiate all deviation or departure from the Primitive Faith of Christ, and we reject all innovations presented to the Church through Rome or other Churches, in whole or part, and bear witness to the essential principles and doctrines of the Undivided Church of Our Lord Jesus Christ.

We profess belief in the Nicene Creed, Apostle's Creed, and the Creed of St. Athanasius as having always been a part of the Christian Faith and Church Catholic.

We believe in Church and Apostolic Tradition which has come to us through the catholic bishops and doctors of the Primitive Church, and especially those defined by the Seven Ecumenical Councils of the Undivided Church, to the exclusion of all errors, ancient and modern.

We profess belief in seven Holy Sacraments: Baptism, Confirmation, Holy Eucharist, Holy Matrimony, Holy Orders, Pen-

ance, and Anointing of the Sick. We believe these to be outward and effective signs of Christ's continued presence within His Church, and means through which the believer may obtain grace from God. Furthermore, we believe in the "Real Presence."

We believe that only men may be advanced to the Ordination of Priest, following the example laid down by Christ, and preserved in the Primitive Church by the Apostles, and their successors.

We declare our sincere intentions to seek and investigate all possible avenues to achieve full sacramental communion and unity with other Christians who "worship the Trinity in unity," and who hold the Catholic and Apostolic Faith in accordance with the foregoing principles.

We believe that all human beings are Temples of the Trinity, and that every human being must be responsible for the good health and hygiene of their minds, bodies and spirits, and that God, through Nature and the Church, heals men of their ills. This does not say that medical or surgical care is not needed.

We believe that every human creature from the time of conception is a creature of God, made in His image and likeness, a precious soul; and all acts against this life which result in death shall be looked upon as sinful, if the act is unjustifiable or inexcusable.

Now, therefore, deeply aware of our duty to God and all who love and believe in the Faith of our Fathers, let us strive to love God and our neighbor with our whole mind, our whole body, and our whole spirit. Amen.

Notes: *The Mercian Rite Catholic Church continues the work of Bishop Joseph Sokolowski who, in 1970, left the Old Catholic Church in America to found the independent St. Paul's Monastery Old Catholic Church. However, the church considers itself to be in the lineage of Archbishop Joseph Rene Vilatte, founder of the American Catholic Church. Vilatte received his orders from the Malankara Syrian Orthodox Church.*

THEOLOGICAL POSITION (MERCIAN RITE CATHOLIC
  CHURCH) (continued)

The Mercian Rite Catholic Church is Orthodox in faith and practice and holds to "the essential principles and doctrines of the Undivided Christian Church." It acknowledges the Apostles, Nicene, and Athanasian Creed and affirms the Bible to be an inspired "work" of God. It celebrates seven sacraments—baptism, confirmation, holy Eucharist, marriage, holy orders, penance, and the anointing of the sick.

The Church sponsors the Holy Apostles Academy of Religion and Natural Health Sciences. Their concern for health is reflected in their belief that individuals are responsible for their health and that God heals through nature and through the church.

Chapter 4

Lutheran Family

DECLARATION OF FAITH (AMERICAN ASSOCIATION OF LUTHERAN CHURCHES)

I. A DECLARATION OF FAITH AND INTENTION OF BIBLICAL AND EVANGELICAL LUTHERANS WHO COVENANT TOGETHER TO FORM THE AMERICAN ASSOCIATION OF LUTHERAN CHURCHES

We covenant together in the Name of the Father, Son and Holy Spirit in order to form an association of Biblical and evangelical Lutheran congregations. As laity and pastors it is our desire to make clear testimony of our faith in Jesus Christ as Lord and Savior as revealed in the Bible—the divinely inspired, inerrant Word of God and the only infallible authority for Christian faith and life. (II Peter 1:19-21, II Timothy 3:14-17) (ALC Constitution 3.10)

Furthermore, we declare that we desire to be guided in our interpretation of the Word of God by the ecumenical creeds and the confessions of the Lutheran Church.

We also declare our intention to form the American Association of Lutheran Churches in which the authority of the congregation in all matters pertaining to its life and mission is not abrogated or diminished by any hierarchial church structure.

It is our intent to make a clear testimony to the Biblical emphasis that the new life in Christ is the life lived in thankful response to the grace of God in keeping with the moral imperatives which God declares in His Word (e.g. Galatians 5, Ephesians 5).

Our intention is to utilize the 1960 Constitution of the ALC as the format for the constitution of this American Association of Lutheran Churches.

It is, furthermore, our intention that this American Association of Lutheran Churches rejects the modernist practice of placing the method of science as an authority above Scripture. Furthermore, we acknowledge that there are "open questions" in theology and church practice.

Inasmuch, as it is the primary mission of the Church to win and hold people in a saving relationship with Jesus Christ, as mandated in the "Great Commission," the emphasis of this Association shall be to enable congregations in their evangelism, home and world mission outreach.

II. CONFESSION OF FAITH

The American Association of Lutheran Churches accepts all the canonical books of the Old and New Testaments as a whole and in all their parts as the divinely inspired, revealed, and inerrant Word of God, and submits to this as the only infallible authority in all matters of faith and life.

As brief and true statements of the doctrines of the Word of God, this Church accepts and confesses the following Symbols, subscription to which shall be required of all its members, both congregations and individuals:

a. The ancient ecumenical Creeds: the Apostolic, the Nicene, and the Athanasian.

b. The unaltered Augsburg Congression and Luther's Small Catechism.

As further elaboration of and in accord with these Lutheran Symbols, this Church also receives the other documents in the Book of Concord of 1580: the Apology, Luther's Large Catechism, the Smalcald Articles, and the Formula of Concord; and recognizes them as normative for its theology.

The American Association of Lutheran Churches accepts without reservation the symbolical books of the evangelical Lutheran church, not insofar as but because they are the presentation and explanation of the pure doctrine of the Word of God and a summary of the faith of the evangelical Lutheran church.

III. THE MISSION OF THE CHURCH

The primary mission of the Church is Christ's Great Commission (Matthew 28:19) . . . to go and make disciples of all nations, baptizing and teaching them to observe all that God has commanded . . . This task is a never ending one, not only in terms of reaching the unevangelized peoples of the world with the Gospel, but also in terms of evangelizing every generation. Until such time as the Association sends out missionaries, every congregation is encouraged to investigate possibilities of supporting missionaries through a variety of groups such as LAMP, World Mission Prayer League, World Confessional Lutheran Association, etc.

IV. EVANGELISM

We are called to be witnesses (Acts 1:8). This implies encouragement of and training for the members of each congregation in evangelism. This is not an option for Christians, but is part and parcel of the Great Commission (Matthew 28:19). There are several good training programs available. To be witnesses also implies starting new congregations in our own country. To this end we encourage congregations to be aware of possibilities in their own areas and with other congregations jointly to explore possible ways of starting mission congregations. Every congregation is encouraged to give prayer, personnel and monetary support for the starting of new congregations.

We are also concerned with renewal in our congregations. To this end we need to take seriously passages such as Ephesians, 4:7-16 and Article VII of the Augsburg Confessions. The goal of the Word of God (taught and preached) is to bring people into a saving relationship with Jesus Christ and to nature that relationship that it may grow and bear fruit to God's glory. Care must be exercised that local and national structures truly reflect this goal, for when this takes place then witnessing, evangelism and world mission will flourish.

V. STATEMENT ON CHRISTIAN/PARISH EDUCATION

One of primary ministries of the Church is nurturing or Christian/parish education. The Apostle Paul included the gift of teaching in His listing of the gift of the Spirit (I Corinthians 12). Luther say this as an urgent task and hence wrote His large and small catechisms (see also his introductions to these two documents in the Book of Concord). A number of Jesus' parables dealt with the need for growth (e.g. Matt. 13, Mark 4 and Luke 13) which implies nurturing and feeding the Christian life.

In thinking of Christian education, we want to affirm that the Bible is to remain the primary textbook at all levels—nursery school, Sunday School, confirmation and adult classes. Our goal should always be that every Christian will have a growing and working knowledge of the Bible (see Ephesians 4:8-16). All literature used for any study group should be judged on the basis of its use of and faithfulness to the Bible as set out in our Statement of Faith. We do not push any particular supply source, but will be responsible as a Church to share concerns and warnings about literature we know about that is not faithful to the Word of God.

Our Lutheran Confessions (as found in the Book of Concord) also need to receive attention in our Christian Education programs. These, along with the Word of God, are to be seen as a benchmark in evaluating all our teaching materials. We would encourage every congregation to have an overall Christian education plan; to emphasize adult education; and to share information with other congregations as to good Biblical materials that are faithful to our Lutheran heritage.

In our Christian/Parish education programs we need to remember and to teach accordingly, that education is not only "head knowledge," or in educational terms, must include the cognitive (knowledge) area, the affective (beliefs, attitudes, values, feelings) area, and the doing or skill (application to life) area. The Scriptures note favorably that Jesus "increased in wisdom and in, stature and in favor with God and man (Luke 2:52). James emphasizes the idea that true faith as opposed to simply claimed faith) expresses itself in action. Further, we need to recognize levels of growth in these areas. The saying is applicable here, that when we stop growing, we start dying. If our spiritual life is not growing in these three areas all of our life, then our spiritual life is in danger of dying.

VI. STATEMENT ON GIFTS OF THE SPIRIT

We recognize that Scripturally and historically every congregation will have unique aspects of ministry within the larger body of Christ, as the Holy Spirit wills and gives, just as individuals receive and manifest various gifts of ministry and service within the congregation, as the Holy Spirit wills and gives.

The AALC receives with joy this diversity of individuals and congregations. We urge upon congregations and their leadership (both clergy and lay) to also rejoice in this diversity and be diligent in exercising faithful and sound teaching, (as we confess in our Statement of Faith), guidance and correction as needed in all areas, always subject to the Scriptures, letting all things be done decently and in order, always governed by love.

We will attempt to provide study materials, guides and bibliographies to cover the Scriptures and various perspectives. As a beginning we suggest the following Scriptures: Mark 16:14-17; Romans 12:4-13; I Corinthians 12:13-14; Ephesians 4:11-16; I Peter 4:10-11.

VII. BIBLICAL STEWARDSHIP

We encourage Biblical Stewardship as an undergirding for the primary mission of the church (see such passages as I Peter 4:9-11, Luke 12:35-48 and II Corinthians 9). We need to refrain from constant haranguing about money and concentrate on solid teaching. When true and real Biblical needs are there, God's people will respond with their stewardship of time, talent and money. To this end the AALC will recommend solid Biblical teaching approaches and material, incorporated into the church's teaching ministry.

VIII. POLICY STATEMENT REGARDING THE SANCTITY OF LIFE AND ABORTION

February 24, 1987

In dependence upon God, with love for those who are fearful of bearing children and with charity toward those who hold differing opinions, regarding the sanctity of life and abortion, we of AALC:

1. Affirm that human life from conception is created in the image of God and is always sacred. Galatians 1:15, Jeremiah 1:5.

2. Understand that an induced abortion is a sin before God against mankind because it ends a unique human life for which God has a plan that would bring glory to Him and benefit to fellow human beings. Psalm 139:1,7,13.

3. Advocate the exercise of sexual and procreative act only within the framework of marriage in accordance with the teaching of God's Word so as to diminish temptation to turn to abortion.

4. Deplore the legal permissiveness that denies protection to the weakest and most defenseless of the human family, the unborn. We view this as an irresponsible and morally reprehensible neglect of God's gift of human life.

5. Reject the practice of induced abortion.

6. Acknowledge that there may be rare cases in which the mother's physical life is clearly and directly threatened and where all other possible alternatives to the lives of both mother and child have been exhausted, that abortion may be a tragic option.

7. Recognize that civil law is a significant factor in shaping the judgment of citizens concerning that which is right and wrong. The current legal climate of total permissiveness regarding abortion teaches that human life has diminished significance or value.

8. Urge that pastors, counselors and others dealing with the ''other victim'', mother herself, as well as fathers and others responsible for and involved in the practice of abortion, be knowledgeable and sensitive about profound guilt, remorse and shame that accompanies abortion and be diligent in ministering-the Gospel of forgiveness and new life through Christ Jesus to them.

9. Urge pastors to lovingly counsel women with problem pregnancies to avail themselves of options in dealing with the child other than abortion and that we strive to provide loving care, -guidance and means to facilitate such options for the mother.

10. Urge Christians everywhere to patiently strive through prayer, proclamation of God's Word regarding the sanctity of human life and all Christian and legal means to effect the changes in law necessary to provide full protection for all unborn and born children.

IX. AALC POSITION OF HOMOSEXUALITY

The AALC regards homosexual desires and behavior as sinful and contrary to God's intent for His children. It rejects the contention that homosexual desires, behavior and/or lifestyle are simply another form of sexuality equally valid with the God-given male-female pattern. We urge Pastors and Congregations to initiate Scriptural teaching in situations so as to counter the growing social approval of homosexual attitudes and mind set.

X. INTER-CHURCH COOPERATION AMERICAN ASSOCIATION OF LUTHERAN CHURCHES L.C.U.S.A.

That the AALC seeks cooperation, with Lutheran Church U.S.A. wherever it feels it is not comprising its stand.

A. Military Chaplaincy which already includes Lutheran Church Missouri Synod

B. Lutheran Immigration and Refugee Service (LIRS)

C. Lutheran World Relief

ALTAR FELLOWSHIP

We have officially inquired into pulpit and altar fellowship with the Lutheran Church, Missouri Synod, Wisconsin Association of Free Lutheran Congregations, Conservative Lutheran Association and the Evangelical Lutheran Synod. N.C.C. & W.C.C.

This association will not become a member of the above organizations and will not support by representation, money, or service, the above organizations.

LUTHERAN INDEPENDENT MINISTRIES

The AALC acknowledges and is supportive of the L.B.I. movement.

The AALC acknowledges and is supportive of the World Mission Prayer League.

The AALC acknowledges and is supportive of the Lutheran Evangelistic Movement.

The AALC acknowledges and is supportive of other conservative-Evangelical Lutheran independent organizations.

INTER-CHURCH COOPERATION

We do affirm the Lutheran position of ''Lutheran pulpits for Lutheran Pastors.'' We also recognize that while we use sound judgment with regard to Scriptural and doctrinal integrity, it will be appropriate at time to allow the witness of others in our pulpits.

We will cooperate with reformed Pastors in community events such as ministerial meetings, graduations and other celebrations.

Notes: *The American Association of Lutheran Churches was founded in 1987 by conservative members of the American Lutheran Church who rejected participation in the merger that led to the 1988 creation of the Evangelical Lutheran Church in America. At question in their separation, members who formed the Association rejected the theological divergences that had appeared in their parent body. First, they affirmed the inerrancy of the Scripture (referring to biblical teachings on matters of science and history) and the use of scientific methods to critique Scripture. The Association was also concerned with the spread of the Charismatic movement among members of the American Lutheran Church and tried to distance itself from some of the excesses of the movement. Finally, the*

DECLARATION OF FAITH (AMERICAN ASSOCIATION OF LUTHERAN CHURCHES) (continued)

Association has made very strong statements against abortion and homosexuality, in contrast to the acceptance of abortion (although some ambiguity remains on the issue of homosexuality) by the Evangelical Lutheran Church in America.

*   *   *

CONFESSION OF FAITH (CHURCH OF THE LUTHERAN BRETHREN OF AMERICA)

We believe that:

(1) The Bible, including both the Old and New Testaments as originally given, is verbally and plenarily inspired and free from error in the whole and in the part, and is therefore the final and authoritative guide for faith and conduct.

(2) There is one God eternally existent in three distinct persons in one divine essence, Father, Son, and Holy Spirit.

(3) God the Father has revealed Himself to us as the Creator of the world and its Preserver, to whom the entire creation and all creatures are subject.

(4) Man was originally created in the image and after the likeness of God to live in His fellowship. He fell into sin through the temptation of Satan and thereby lost fellowship with God, became totally depraved and is under the wrath of God.

(5) Jesus Christ, the Eternal Son, is the image of the invisible God. To accomplish our redemption He took upon Himself the form of man, being conceived of the Holy Spirit and born of the virgin Mary. By His perfect obedience and His substitutionary death on the cross He has purchased our redemption. He arose from the dead "for our justification" in the body in which He was crucified. He ascended into heaven, where He is now seated at the right hand of God, the Father, as our interceding High Priest. He will come a second time personally, bodily and visibly to gather the believers unto Himself, and to establish His millennial kingdom. Finally, He will judge the living and the dead and make eternal separation between believers and unbelievers.

(6) The Holy Spirit is a divine person eternally one with the Father and with the Son. His ministry is to call, to regenerate repentant sinners, to sanctify believers, and to preserve them in the one true faith. He guides and comforts the children of God, directs and empowers the Church in fulfillment of the great commission, and "convicts the world of sin, and of righteousness, and of judgment."

(7) The knowledge and benefit of Christ's redemption from sin is brought to man through the means of grace, namely the Word and the Sacraments. Through the Word, both the law and the Gospel, God convicts of sin and bestows His grace in Christ unto the forgiveness of sins to all who repent and believe. We believe that all men must have a conscious experience of sin and grace. In the Sacrament of Baptism God offers the benefits of Christ's redemption to all men, and graciously bestows the washing of regeneration and the newness of life to every believer. Because of the total depravity of human nature, and because the promise of God also includes little children, infants are to be baptized. In the Sacrament of Holy Communion, Christ gives to the communicants His body and His blood, declares the forgiveness of sins to all believers and strengthens their faith.

(8) The Church universal consists of all those who truly believe on Jesus Christ as their Savior. The local congregation is the communion of saints or true believers, "in which the Gospel is rightly taught and the Sacraments are rightly administered." Therefore, it follows that the membership of the local congregation shall comprise only those who by life and testimony show that they are living in fellowship with Jesus Christ.

(9) The Lutheran confession is a summary of Bible doctrines. We adhere to the following confessional writings: The Apostolic Creed, the Nicene and the Athanasian Creed, the Augsburg Confession, and Luther's Small Catechism.

Notes: *This confession of the Lutheran Brethren supplements the position taken in the Augsburg Confession, the traditional Lutheran statement. It shows the influence of twentieth-century fundamentalism in affirming the verbal and plenary inspiration of the Bible, Christ's substitutionary atonement, and the millennial kingdom. The confession further shows the influence of pietism in its demand for a conscious experience of sin and grace by the believer.*

*   *   *

CONFESSION OF FAITH [EVANGELICAL LUTHERAN CHURCH IN AMERICA (1988)]

Section 1. This congregation confesses Jesus Christ as Lord of the Church. The Holy Spirit creates and sustains the Church through the Gospel and thereby unites believers with their Lord and with one another in the fellowship of faith.

Section 2. This congregation holds that the Gospel is the revelation of God's sovereign will and saving grace in Jesus Christ. In Him, the World Incarnate, God imparts Himself to His people.

Section 3. This congregation acknowledges the Holy Scriptures as the norm for the faith and life of the Church. The Holy Scriptures are the divinely inspired record of God's redemptive act in Christ, for which the Old Testament prepared the way and which the New Testament proclaims. In the continuation of this proclamation in the Church, God still speaks through the Holy Scriptures and realizes His redemptive purpose generation after generation.

Section 4. This congregation accepts the Apostles', the Nicene, and the Athanasian creeds as true declarations of the faith of the Church.

Section 5. This congregation accepts the Unaltered Augsburg Confession and Luther's Small Catechism as true witnesses to the Gospel, and acknowledges as one with it in faith and doctrine all churches that likewise accept the teachings of these symbols.

Section 6. This congregation accepts the other symbolical books of the evangelical Lutheran church, the Apology of the Augsburg Confession, the Smalcald Articles, Luther's Large Catechism, and the Formula of Concord, as further valid interpretations of the confession of the Church.

Section 7. This congregation aims that the Gospel transmitted by the Holy Scriptures, to which the creeds and confessions bear witness, is the true treasure of the Church, the substance of its proclamation, and the basis of its unity and continuity. The Holy Spirit uses the proclamation of the Gospel and the administration of the sacraments to create and sustain Christian faith and fellowship. As this occurs, the Church fulfills its divine mission and purpose.

Notes: *The Evangelical Lutheran Church in America was formed in 1988 by the merger of the American Lutheran Church, the Lutheran Church in America, and the Association of Evangelical Lutheran Churches. Its brief Confession of Faith sets the Bible, the Augsburg Confession, and Luther's Small Catechism as its doctrinal standards. The Confession of Faith accepts the Book of Concord as secondary doctrinal interpretations. This position contrasts with the more conservative Lutheran bodies, such as the Lutheran Church—Missouri Synod, which accept all of the Book of Concord as their doctrinal standard.*

* * *

DOCTRINE (FROM CONSTITUTION AND BY-LAWS) (INTERNATIONAL LUTHERAN FELLOWSHIP, INC.)

Section 1. As an evangelical Christian fellowship in general, and as a Lutheran fellowship in particular, The International Lutheran Fellowship accepts and acknowledges the Holy Scriptures as the divinely inspired and revealed Word of God, inerrant and wholly reliable, and the only infallible rule and standard for faith and practice. The International Lutheran Fellowship is unreservedly and without compromise dedicated to the "holding fast the faithful Word" of the Holy Scriptures (Titus 1.9), and to the "contending earnestly for the faith once for all delivered to the saints," (Jude 3). It accepts and confesses not only the three oldest creeds of Christendom (The Apostolic, the Nicene, and the Athanasian) as faithful summaries of the central truths of Scriptures, but also the unaltered Augsburg Confession as a true exposition of the fundamental doctrines of Christianity together with the further development of these doctrines as contained in the Lutheran Confessions found in the Book of Concord in the sense that these confessions themselves declare in the Preface of the Formula of Concord.

Notes: *This recently formed Lutheran body adheres to the traditional Lutheran statement, the Augsburg Confession, but adds an emphasis on the inerrant and infallible Bible drawn from contemporary Christian fundamentalism.*

* * *

Independent Lutheran Schools

OUR FAITH COMMITMENT (LUTHERAN BIBLE INSTITUTE OF SEATTLE)

The Articles of Incorporation state, "This corporation accepts and acknowledges the Canonical Books of the Old and New Testament as the revealed Word of God and as the only sufficient and infallible rule and standard of faith and practice. It also accepts and confesses not only the three oldest symbols—The Apostolic, the Nicene, and the Athanasian—but also the unaltered Augsburg Confession, as a brief but true exposition of the fundamental doctrines of Christianity, said Confession being understood in accordance with the further development of these doctrines as contained in other Symbolical Books of the Lutheran Church, for instance the Apology, the Smalcald Articles, the Small and Large Catechism of Luther, and the Formula of Concord."

Notes: *The Lutheran Bible Institute of Seattle is one of a string of independent Bible institutes, the first of which was founded in Minneapolis in 1991. It and a sister institute in Anaheim, California, became an independent corporation in 1959. Its standard of faith is the books of the Book of Concord, the standard Lutheran doctrinal book compiled by Lutheran leaders in the sixteenth century.*

Chapter 5
Reformed-Presbyterian Family

Reformed

BASIS AND PRINCIPLES (CHRISTIAN REFORMED CHURCH IN NORTH AMERICA/CHRISTIAN SCHOOLS INTERNATIONAL)

The basis of Christian Schools International is the Scriptures of the Old and New Testaments, the infallible Word of God, as explicated in Reformed creedal standards. On this basis we affirm the following principles for Christian education:

THE BIBLE. That God, by His Holy Word, reveals Himself; renews man's understanding of God, of man himself, of his fellow men, and of the world. Directs man in all of his relationships and activities; and therefore guides His people also in the education of their children.

CREATION. That in their education, children must come to learn that the world and man's calling in it can rightly be understood only in relation to the Triune God who, by His creation, restoration, and governance, directs all things to the coming of His Kingdom and the glorification of His name.

SIN. That because man's sins brought upon all mankind the curse of God; alienates his from his Creator, his neighbor, and the world; distorts his view of the true meaning and purpose of life; and misdirects human culture; man's sin also corrupts the education of children.

JESUS CHRIST. That through our Savior Jesus Christ there is renewal of our educational enterprise because He is the Redeemer of, and the Light and the Way for, our human life in all its range and variety. Only through Him and the work of His Spirit are we guided in the truth and recommitted to our original calling.

SCHOOLS. That the purpose of the Christian school is to educate children for a life of obedience in their calling in this world as image-bearers of God; that this calling is to know God's Word and His creation, to consecrate the whole of human life to God, to love their fellow men, and to be stewards in their God-given cultural task.

PARENTS. That the primary responsibility for education rests upon parents to whom children are entrusted by God, and that Christian parents should accept this obligation in view of the covenantal relationship which God established with believers and their children. Parents should seek to discharge this obligation through school associations and school boards which engage the services of Christian teachers in Christian schools.

TEACHERS. That Christian teachers, both in obedience to God and in cooperation with parents, have a unique pedagogical responsibility while educating children in school.

PUPILS. That Christian schools must take into account the variety of abilities, needs, and responsibilities of young persons; that the endowments and calling of young persons as God's image-bearers, and their defects and inadequacies as sinners, require that such learning goals and such curricula will be selected as will best prepare them to live as obedient Christians; and that only with constant attention to such pedagogical concerns will education be truly Christian.

COMMUNITY. That because God's covenant embraces not only parents and their children but also the entire Christian community to which they belong, and because Christian education contributes directly to the advancement of God's Kingdom, it is the obligation not only of parents but of the entire Christian community to establish and maintain Christian schools, to pray for them, work for them, and give generously to their support.

EDUCATIONAL FREEDOM. That Christian schools, organized and administered in accordance with legitimate standards and provisions for day schools, should be fully recognized in society as free to function according to these principles.

Notes: *Christian Schools International, founded in 1920, is an association of Christian Reformed parochial schools that promotes religious elementary and high schools nationally, and fosters high standards for the continued improvement of such schools. Its Mission Statement begins with an affirmation*

BASIS AND PRINCIPLES (CHRISTIAN REFORMED CHURCH IN NORTH AMERICA/CHRISTIAN SCHOOLS INTERNATIONAL) (continued)

of the traditional creedal documents of the Christian Reformed Church, which are extended to cover the educational enterprise.

*　　*　　*

A BRIEF DECLARATION OF PRINCIPLES (PROTESTANT REFORMED CHURCHES IN AMERICA)

The Protestant Reformed Churches stand on the basis of Scripture as the infallible Word of God and of the Three Forms of Unity. Moreover, they accept the Liturgical Forms used in the public worship of our churches, such as:

Form for the Administration of Baptism, Form for the Administration of the Lord's Supper, Form of Excommunication, Form of Readmitting Excommunicated Persons, Form of Ordination of the Ministers of God's Word, Form of Ordination of Elders and Deacons, Form for the Installation of Professors of Theology, Form of Ordination of Missionaries, Form for the Confirmation of Marriage before the Church, and the Formula of Subscription.

On the basis of this Word of God and these confessions:

I. They repudiate the errors of the Three Points adopted by the Synod of the Christian Reformed Church of Kalamazoo, 1924, which maintain:

A. That there is a grace of God to all men, including the reprobate, manifest in the common gifts to all men.

B. That the preaching of the gospel is a gracious offer of salvation on the part of God to all that externally hear the gospel.

C. That the natural man through the influence of common grace can do good in this world.

D. Over against this they maintain:

1. That the grace of God is always particular, i.e., only for the elect, never for the reprobate.

2. That the preaching of the gospel is not a gracious offer of salvation on the part of God to all men, nor a conditional offer to all that are born in the historical dispensation of the covenant, that is, to all that are baptized, but an oath of God that He will infallibly lead all the elect unto salvation and eternal glory through faith.

3. That the unregenerate man is totally incapable of doing any good, wholly depraved, and therefore can only sin.

For proof we refer to Canons I, A, 6-8:

Art. 6. That some receive the gift of faith from God, and others do not receive it proceeds from God's eternal decree, "For known unto God are all his works from the beginning of the world," Acts 15:18. "Who worketh all things after the counsel of his will," Eph. 1:11. According to which decree, he graciously softens the hearts of the elect, however obstinate, and inclines them to believe, while he leaves the non-elect in his judgment to their own wickedness and obduracy. And herein is especially displayed the profound, the merciful, and at the same time the righteous discrimination between men, equally involved in ruin; or that decree of election and reprobation, revealed in the Word of God, which though men of perverse, impure and unstable minds wrest to their own destruction, yet to holy and pious souls affords unspeakable consolation.

Art. 7. Election is the unchangeable purpose of God, whereby, before the foundation of the world, he hath out of mere grace, according to the sovereign good pleasure of his own will, chosen, from the whole h an race, which had fallen through their own fault, from their primitive state of rectitude, into sin and destruction, a certain number of persons to redemption in Christ, whom he from eternity appointed the Mediator and Head of the elect, and the foundation of salvation.

This elect number, though by nature neither better nor more deserving than others, but with them involved in one common misery, God hath decreed to give to Christ, to be saved by him, and effectually to call and draw them to his communion by his Word and Spirit, to bestow upon them true faith, justification and sanctification and having powerfully preserved them in the fellowship of his Son, finally, to glorify them for the demonstration of his mercy, and for the praise of his glorious grace; as it is written, "According as he hath chosen us in him, before the foundation of the world, that we should be holy, and without blame before him in love; having predestinated us unto the adoption of children by Jesus Christ to himself, according to the good pleasure of his will, to the praise of the glory of his grace, wherein he hath made us accepted in the beloved." Eph. 1:4, 5, 6. And elsewhere: "Whom he did predestinate, them be also called, and whom he called, them he also justified, and whom he justified, them he also glorified." Rom. 8:30.

Art. 8. There are not various decrees of election, but one and the same decree respecting all those, who shall be saved, both under the Old and New Testament: since the Scripture declares the good pleasure, purpose and counsel of the divine will to be one, according to which he hath chosen us from eternity, both to grace and glory, to salvation and the way of salvation, which he hath ordained that we should walk therein.

Canons II, A, 5:

Art. 5. Moreover, the promise of the gospel is, that whosoever believeth in Christ crucified, shall not perish, but have everlasting life. This promise, together with the command to repent and believe, ought to be declared and published to all nations, and to all persons promiscuously and without distinction, to whom God out of his good pleasure sends the gospel.

The Canons in II, 5 speak of the preaching of the promise. It presents the promise, not as general, but as particular, i.e., as for believers, and, therefore, for the elect. This preaching of the particular promise is promiscuous to all that hear the gospel with the command, not a condition, to repent and believe.

Canons II, B, 6:

Art. 6. Who use the difference between meriting and appropriating, to the end that they may instill into the minds of the imprudent and inexperienced this teaching that God, as far as he is concerned, has been minded of applying to all equally the benefits gained by the death of Christ; but that while some obtain the pardon of sin and eternal life, and others do not, this difference depends on their own free will, which joins itself to the grace that is offered without exception, and that it is not dependent on the special gift of mercy, which powerfully works in them, that they rather than others should appropriate unto themselves this grace. For these, while they feign that they present this distinction, in a sound sense, seek to instill into the people the destructive poison of the Pelagian errors.

For further proof we refer to the Heidelberg Catechism III, 8 and XXXIII, 91:

Q. 8. Are we then so corrupt that we are wholly incapable of doing any good, and inclined to all wickedness?

Indeed we are; except we are regenerated by the Spirit of God.

Q. 91. But what are good works? Only those which proceed from a true faith, are performed according to the law of God, and to his glory; and not such as are founded on our imaginations, or the institutions of men.

And also from the Netherlands Confession, Art. 14:

Art. 14. We believe that God created man out of the dust of the earth, and made and formed him after his own image and likeness, good, righteous, and holy, capable in all things to will, agreeably to the will of God. But being in honor, he understood it not, neither knew his excellency, but willfully subjected himself to sin, and consequently to death, and the curse, giving ear to the words of the devil. For the commandment of life, which he had received, he transgressed; and by sin separated himself from God, who was his true life, having corrupted his whole nature; whereby he made himself liable to corporal and spiritual death. And being thus become wicked, perverse, and corrupt in all his ways, he hath lost all his excellent gifts, which he had received from God, and only retained a few remains thereof, which, however, are sufficient to leave man without excuse; for all the light which is in us is changed into darkness, as the Scriptures teach us, saying: The light shineth in darkness, and the darkness comprehende it not: where St. John calleth men darkness. Therefore we reject all that is taught repugnant to this, concerning the free will of man, since man is but a slave to sin; and has nothing of himself, unless it is given from heaven. For who may presume to boast, that he

of himself can do any good, since Christ saith, No man can come to me, except the Father, which hath sent me, draw him? Who will glory in his own will, who understands, that to be carnally minded is enmity against God? Who can speak of his knowledge, since the natural man receiveth not the things of the Spirit of God? In short, who dare suggest any thought, since he knows that we are not sufficient of ourselves to think anything as of ourselves, but that our sufficiency is of God? And therefore what the apostle saith ought justly to be held sure and firm, that God worketh in us both to will and to do of his good pleasure. For there is no will nor understanding, conformable to the divine will and understanding, but what Christ hath wrought in man; which he teaches us, when he saith, Without me ye can do nothing.

Once more we refer to Canons III and IV A, 1-4:

Art. 1. Man was originally formed after the image of God. His understanding was adorned with a true and saving knowledge of his Creator, and of spiritual things; his heart and will were upright; all his affections pure; and the whole man was holy; but revolting from God by the instigation of the devil, and abusing the freedom of his own will, he forfeited these excellent gifts; and on the contrary entailed on himself blindness of mind horrible darkness, vanity and perverseness of judgment, became wicked, rebellious, and obdurate in heart and will, and impure in his affections.

Art. 2. Man after the fall begat children in his own likeness. A corrupt stock produced a corrupt offspring. Hence all the posterity of Adam, Christ only excepted, have derived corruption from their original parent, not by imitation, as the Pelagians of old asserted, but by the propagation of a vicious nature.

Art. 3. Therefore all men are conceived in sin, and by nature children of wrath, incapable of saving good, prone to evil, dead in sin, and in bondage thereto, and without the regenerating grace of the Holy Spirit, they are neither able nor willing to return to God, to reform the depravity of their nature, nor to dispose themselves to reformation.

Art. 4. There remain, however, in man since the fall the glimmerings of natural light, whereby he retains some knowledge of God, of natural things, and of the differences between good and evil, and discovers some regard for virtue, good order in society, and for maintaining an orderly external deportment. But so far is this light of nature from being sufficient to bring him to a saving knowledge of God, and to true conversion, that he is incapable of using it aright even in things natural and civil. Nay further, this light, such as it is, man in various ways renders wholly polluted, and holds it in unrighteousness, by doing which he becomes inexcusable before God.

II. They teach on the basis of the same confessions:

A. That election, which is the unconditional and unchangeable decree of God to redeem in Christ a certain number of persons, is the sole cause and fountain of all our salvation, whence flow all the gifts of grace, including faith. This is the plain teaching of our confessions in the Canons of Dordrecht, I, A, 6, 7. See above.

And in the Heidelberg Catechism, XXI, 54, we read:

Q. 54. What believest thou concerning the "holy catholic church" of Christ?

That the Son of God from the beginning to the end of the world, gathers, defends, and preserves to himself by his Spirit and Word, out of the whole human race, a church chosen to everlasting life, agreeing in true faith; and that I am and forever shall remain a living member thereof.

This is also evident from the doctrinal part of the Form for the Administration of Baptism, where we read:

For when we are baptized in the name of the Father, God the Father witnesseth and sealeth unto us that he doth make an eternal covenant of grace with us, and adopts us for his children and heirs, and therefore will provide us with every good thing, and avert all evil or turn it to our profit. And when we are baptized in the name of the Son, the Son sealeth unto us, that he doth wash us in his blood from all our sins, incorporating us into the fellowship of his death and resurrection, so that we are freed from all our sins, and accounted righteous before God. In like manner, when we are baptized in the name of the Holy Ghost, the Holy Ghost assures us, by this holy sacrament, that he will dwell in us, and sanctify us to be members of Christ, applying unto us, that which we have in Christ, namely, the washing away of our sins, and the daily renewing of our lives, till we shall finally be presented without spot or wrinkle among the assembly of the elect in life eternal.

B. That Christ died only for the elect and that the saving efficacy of the death of Christ extends to them only. This is evident from the Canons II, A, 8:

Art. 8. For this was the sovereign counsel, and most gracious will and purpose of God the Father, that the quickening and saving efficacy of the most precious death of his Son should extend to all the elect, for bestowing upon them alone the gift of justifying faith, thereby to bring them infallibly to salvation: that is, it was the will of God, that Christ by the blood of the cross, whereby he confirmed the new covenant, should effectually redeem out of every people, tribe, nation, and language, all those, and those only, who were from eternity chosen to salvation, and given to him by the Father; that he should confer upon them faith, which together with all the other saving gifts of the Holy Spirit, he purchased for them by his death; should purge them from all sin, both original and actual, whether committed before or after believing; and having faithfully preserved them even to the end, should at last bring them free from every spot and blemish to the enjoyment of glory in his own presence forever.

This article very clearly teaches:

1. That all the covenant blessings are for the elect alone.

2. That God's promise is unconditionally for them only: for God cannot promise what was not objectively merited by Christ.

3. That the promise of God bestows the objective right of salvation not upon all the children that are born under the historical dispensation of the covenant, that is, not upon all that are baptized, but only upon the spiritual seed.

This is also evident from other parts of our confessions, as, for instance:

Heidelberg Catechism XXV, 65 and 66:

Q. 65. Since then we are made partakers of Christ and all his benefits by faith only, whence cloth this faith proceed?

From the Holy Ghost, who works faith in our hearts by the preaching of the gospel, and confirms it by the use of the sacraments.

Q. 66. What are the sacraments?

The sacraments are holy visible signs and seals, appointed of God for this end, that by the use thereof, he may the more fully declare and seal to us the promise of the gospel, viz., that he grants us freely the remission of sin, and life eternal, for the sake of that one sacrifice of Christ, accomplished on the cross.

If we compare with these statements from the Heidelberger what was taught concerning the saving efficacy of the death of Christ in Canons II, A, 8, it is evident that the promise of the gospel which is sealed by the sacraments concerns only the believers, that is, the elect.

This is also evident from Heidelberg Catechism XXVII, 74:

Q. 74. Are infants also to be baptized?

Yes: for since they, as well as the adult, are included in the covenant and church of God; and since redemption from sin by the blood of Christ, and the Holy Ghost, the author of faith, is promised to them no less than to the adult; they must therefore by baptism, as a sign of the covenant, be also admitted into the Christian church; and be distinguished from the children of unbelievers as was done in the old covenant or testament by circumcision, instead of which baptism is instituted in the new covenant.

That in this question and answer of the Heidelberger not all the children that are baptized, but only the spiritual children, that is, the elect, are meant is evident. For:

1. Little infants surely cannot fulfil any conditions. And if the promise of God is for them, the promise is infallible and unconditional, and therefore only for the elect.

2. According to Canons II, A, 8, which we quoted above, the saving efficacy of the death of Christ is for the elect alone.

3. According to this answer of the Heidelberg Catechism, the Holy Ghost, the author of faith, is promised to the little children no less than to the adult. And God surely fulfils

His promise. Hence, that promise is surely only for the elect.

The same is taught in the Netherlands Confession, Articles 33-35. In Article 33 we read:

Art. 33. We believe, that our gracious God, on account of our weakness and infirmities hath ordained the sacraments for us, thereby to seal unto us his promises, and to be pledges of the good will and grace of God toward us, and also to nourish and strengthen our faith; which he hath joined to the Word of the gospel, the better to present to our senses, both that which he signifies to us by his Word, and that which he works inwardly in our hearts, thereby assuring and confirming in us the salvation which he imparts to us. For they are visible signs and seals of an inward and invisible thing, by means whereof God worketh in us by the power of the Holy Ghost. Therefore the signs are not in vain or insignificant, so as to deceive us. For Jesus Christ is the true object presented by them, without whom they would be of no moment.

And from Article 34, which speaks of Holy Baptism, we quote:

Art. 34. We believe and confess that Jesus Christ, who is the end of the law, hath made an end, by the shedding of his blood, of all other sheddings of blood which men could or would make as a propitiation or satisfaction for sin: and that he, having abolished circumcision, which was done with blood, hath instituted the sacrament of baptism instead thereof; by which we are received into the Church of God, and separated from an other people and strange religions, that we may wholly belong to him, whose ensign and banner we bear: and which serves as a testimony to us, that he will forever be our gracious God and Father. Therefore he has commanded all those, who are his, to be baptized with pure water, ''in the name of the Father, and of the Son, and of the Holy Ghost''; thereby signifying to us, that as water washeth away the filth of the body, when poured upon it, and is seen on the body of the baptized, when sprinkled upon him; so doth the blood of Christ, by the power of the Holy Ghost, internally sprinkle the soul, cleanse it from its sins, and regenerate us from children of wrath, unto children of God. Not that this is effected by the external water, but by the sprinkling of the precious blood of the Son of God; who is our Red Sea, through which we must pass, to escape the tyranny of Pharaoh, that is, the devil, and to enter into the spiritual land of Canaan. Therefore the ministers, on their part, administer the sacrament, and that which is visible, but our Lord giveth that which is signified by the sacrament, namely, the gifts and invisible grace; washing, cleansing and purging our souls of all filth and unrighteousness; renewing our hearts, and filling them with all comfort; giving unto us a true assurance of his fatherly goodness; putting on us the new man, and putting off the old man with an his deeds.

Article 34 speaks of Holy Baptism. That all this, washing and cleansing and purging our souls of all filth and unrighteousness, the renewal of our hearts, is only the fruit of the saving efficacy of the death of Christ and therefore is only for the elect is very evident. The same is true of what we read in the same article concerning the baptism of infants:

Art. 34. And indeed Christ shed his blood no less for the washing of the children of the faithful, than for adult persons; and therefore they ought to receive the sign and sacrament of that, which Christ hath done for them; as the Lord commanded in the law, that they should be made partakers of the sacrament of Christ's suffering and death, shortly after they were born, by offering for them a lamb, which was a sacrament of Jesus Christ. Moreover, what circumcision was to the Jews, that baptism is to our children. And for this reason Paul calls baptism the circumcision of Christ.

If, according to Article 8 of the Second Head of Doctrine, A, in the Canons, the saving efficacy of the death of Christ extends only to the elect it follows that when in this article of the Netherlands Confession it is stated that ''Christ shed his blood no less for the washing of the children of the faithful than for the adult persons,'' also here the reference is only to the elect children.

Moreover, that the promise of the gospel which God signifies and seals in the sacraments is not for all is also abundantly evident from Article 35 of the same Netherlands Confession, which speaks of the Holy Supper of our Lord Jesus Christ. For there we read:

Art. 35. We believe and confess, that our Savior Jesus Christ did ordain and institute the sacrament of the holy supper, to nourish and support those whom he hath already regenerated, and incorporated into his family, which is his Church.

In the same article we read:

Further, though the sacraments are connected with the thing signified, nevertheless both are not received by all men: the ungodly indeed receives the sacrament to his condemnation, but he doth not receive the truth of the sacrament. As Judas, and Simon the sorcerer, both indeed received the sacrament, but not Christ who was signified by it, of whom believers only are made partakers.

It follows from this that both the sacraments, as well as the preaching of the gospel, are a savor of death unto death for the reprobate, as well as a savor of life unto life for the elect. Hence, the promise of God, preached by the gospel, signified and sealed in both the sacraments, is not for all, but for the elect only.

And that the election of God, and consequently the efficacy of the death of Christ and the promise of the gospel, is not conditional is abundantly evident from the following articles of the Canons.

Canons I, A, 10:

Art. 10. The good pleasure of God is the sole cause of this gracious election; which doth not consist herein, that out of all possible qualities and actions of men God has chosen some as a condition of salvation; but ,that he was pleased out of the common mass of sinners to adopt some certain persons as a peculiar people to himself, as it is written, ''For the children being not yet born neither having done any good or evil,'' etc., it was said (namely to Rebecca): ''the elder shall serve the younger; as it is written, Jacob have I loved, but Esau I hated.'' Rom. 9:11, 12, 13. ''And as many as were ordained to eternal life believed.'' Acts 13:48.

In Canons I, B, 2, the errors are repudiated of those who teach:

Art. 2. That there are various kinds of election of God unto eternal life: the one general and indefinite, the other particular and definite; and that the latter in turn is either incomplete, revocable, non-decisive and conditional, or complete, irrevocable, decisive and absolute. . .

And in the same chapter of Canons I, B, 3, the errors are repudiated of those who teach:

Art. 3. That the good pleasure and purpose of God, of which Scripture makes mention in the doctrine of election, does not consist in this, that God chose certain persons rather than others, but in this that he chose out of all possible conditions (among which are also the works of the law), or out of the whole order of things, the act of faith which from its very nature is undeserving, as well as its incomplete obedience, as a condition of salvation, and that he would graciously consider this in itself as a complete obedience and count it worthy of the reward of eternal life . . .

Again, in the same chapter of Canons 1, B, 5, the errors are rejected of those who teach that:

Art. 5. . . . faith, the obedience of faith, holiness, godliness and perseverance are not fruits of the unchangeable election unto glory, but are conditions, which, being required beforehand, were foreseen as being met by those who will be fully elected, and are causes without which the unchangeable election to glory does not occur.

Finally, we refer to the statement of the Baptism Form:

And although our young children do not understand these things, we may not therefore exclude them from baptism, for as they are without their knowledge, partakers of the condemnation in Adam, so are they again received unto grace in Christ. . .

That here none other than the elect children of the covenant are meant and that they are unconditionally, without their knowledge, received unto grace in Christ, in the same way as they are under the condemnation of Adam, is very evident.

C. That faith is not a prerequisite or condition unto salvation, but a gift of God, and a God-given instrument whereby we appropriate the salvation in Christ. This is plainly taught in the following parts of our confessions:

Heidelberg Catechism VII, 20:

Q. 20. Are all men then, as they. perished in Adam, saved by Christ?

No; only those who are ingrafted into him, and receive all his benefits, by a true faith.

Netherlands Confession, Art. 22:

Art. 22. We believe that, to attain the true knowledge of this great mystery, the Holy Ghost kindleth in our hearts an upright faith, which embraces Jesus Christ, with all his merits, appropriates him, and seeks nothing more besides him. For it must needs follow, either that all things, which are requisite to our salvation, are not in Jesus Christ, or if all things are in him, that then those who possess Jesus Christ through faith, have complete salvation in him. Therefore, for any to assert, that Christ is not sufficient, but that something more is required besides him, would be too gross a blasphemy: for hence it would follow, that Christ was but half a Savior. Therefore we justly say with Paul, that we are justified by faith alone, or by faith without works. However, to speak more clearly, we do not mean, that faith itself justifies us, for it is only an instrument with which we embrace Christ our Righteousness. But Jesus Christ, imputing to us all his merits, and so many holy works which he has done for us, and in our stead, is our Righteousness. And faith is an instrument that keeps us in communion with him in an his benefits, which, when become ours, are more than sufficient to acquit us of our sins.

Confer also Netherlands Confession, Articles 33-35, quoted above.

Again, confer Canons of Dordrecht II, A, 8, quoted above.

In Canons III and IV, A, 10, 14 we read:

Art. 10. But that others who are called by the gospel, obey the call, and are converted, is not to he ascribed to the proper exercise of free will, whereby one distinguishes himself above others, equally furnished with grace sufficient for faith and conversions, as the proud heresy of Pelagius maintains; but it must be wholly ascribed to God, who as he has chosen his own from eternity in Christ, so he confers upon them faith and repentance, rescues them from the power of darkness, and translates them into the kingdom of his own Son, that they may show forth the praises of him, who hath called them out of darkness into his marvelous light; and may glory not in themselves, but in the Lord according to the testimony of the apostles in various places.

Again, in the same chapter of Canons, Article 14, we read:

Art. 14. Faith is therefore to be considered as the gift of God, not on account of its being offered by God to man, to be accepted or rejected at his pleasure; but because it is in reality conferred, breathed, and infused into him; or even because God bestows the power or ability to believe, and then expects that man should by the exercise of his own free will, consent to the terms of salvation, and actually believe in Christ; but because he who works in man both to will and to do, and indeed all things in all, produces both the will to behave, and the act of believing also.

III. Seeing then that this is the clear teaching of our confession,

A. We repudiate:

1. The teaching:

a. That the promise of the covenant is conditional and for all that are baptized.

b. That we may presuppose that all the children that are baptized are regenerated, for we know on the basis of Scripture, as well as in the light of all history and experience, that the contrary is true.

For proof we refer to:

Canons I, A, 6-8;

The doctrinal part of the Baptismal Form:

The principal parts of the doctrine of holy baptism are these three:

First. That we with our children are conceived and born in sin, and therefore are children of wrath, in so much that we cannot enter into the kingdom of God, except we are born again. This, the dipping in, or sprinkling with water teaches us, whereby the impurity of our souls is signified, and humble ourselves before God, and seek for our purification and salvation without ourselves.

Secondly. Holy baptism witnesseth and sealeth unto us the washing away of our sins through Jesus Christ. Therefore we are baptized in the name of the Father, and of the Son, and of the Holy Ghost. For when we are baptized in the name of the Father, God the Father witnesseth and sealeth unto us, that he doth make an eternal covenant of grace with us, and adopts us for his children and heirs, and therefore will provide us with every good thing, and avert all evil or turn it to our profit. And when we are baptized in the name of the Son, the Son sealeth unto us, that he doth wash us in his blood from all our sins, incorporating us into the fellowship of his death and resurrection, so that we are freed from all our sins, and accounted righteous before God. In like manner, when we are baptized in the name of the Holy Ghost, the Holy Ghost assures us, by this holy sacrament, that he will dwell in us, and sanctify us to be members of Christ, applying unto us, that which we have in Christ, namely, the washing away of our sins, and the daily renewing of our lives, till we shall finally be presented without spot or wrinkle among the assembly of the elect in life eternal.

Thirdly. Whereas in all covenants, there are contained two parts: therefore are we by God through baptism, admonished of, and obliged unto new obedience, namely, that we cleave to this one God, Father, Son, and Holy Ghost; that we trust in him, and love him with all our hearts, with all our souls, with all our mind, and with all our strength; that we forsake the world, crucify our old nature, and walk in a new and holy life.

And if we sometimes through weakness fall into sin, we must not therefore despair of God's mercy, nor continue in sin, since baptism is a seal and undoubted testimony, that we have an eternal covenant of grace with God.

The Thanksgiving after Baptism:

Almighty God and merciful Father, we thank and praise thee, that Thou hast forgiven us, and our children, all our sins, through the blood of thy beloved Son Jesus Christ, and received us through thy Holy Spirit as members of thine only begotten Son, and adopted us to be thy children, and sealed and confirmed the same unto us by holy baptism; we beseech thee, through the same Son of thy love, that Thou wilt be pleased always to govern these baptized children by thy Holy Spirit, that they may be piously and religiously educated, increase and grow up in the Lord Jesus Christ, that they then may acknowledge thy fatherly goodness and mercy, which Thou hast shown to them and us, and live in all righteousness, under our only Teacher, King and High Priest, Jesus Christ; and manfully fight against, and overcome sin, the devil and his whole dominion, to the end that they may eternally praise and magnify thee, and thy Son Jesus Christ, together with the Holy Ghost, the one only true God. Amen.

The prayer refers only to the elect; we cannot presuppose that it is for all.

2. The teaching that the promise of the covenant is an objective bequest on the part of God giving to every baptized child the right to Christ and all the blessings of salvation.

B. And we maintain:

1. That God surely and infallibly fulfills His promise to the elect.

2. The sure promise of God which He realizes in us as rational and moral creatures not only makes it impossible that we should not bring forth fruits of thankfulness but also confronts us with the obligation of love, to walk in a new and holy life, and constantly to watch unto prayer.

All those who are not thus disposed, who do not repent but walk in sin, are the objects of His just wrath and excluded from the Kingdom of Heaven.

That the preaching comes to all; and that God seriously commands to faith and repentance, and that to all those who come and believe He promises life and peace.

Grounds:

a. The Baptism Form, part 3.

b. The Form for the Lord's Supper, under "thirdly":

All those, then, who are thus disposed, God will certainly receive in mercy. and count them worthy partakers of the table of his Son Jesus Christ. On the contrary, those who do not feel this testimony in their hearts, eat and drink judgment to themselves.

Therefore, we also, according to the command of Christ and the Apostle Paul, admonish all those who are defiled with the following sins, to keep themselves from the table of the Lord, and declare to them that they have no part in the kingdom of Christ; such as all idolaters, all those who invoke deceased saints, angels or other creatures; all those who worship images; all enchanters, diviners, charmers, and those who confide in such enchantments; all despisers of God, and of his Word, and of the holy sacraments; all blasphemers; all those who are given to raise discord, sects and mutiny in Church or State; all perjured persons; all those who are disobedient to their parents and superiors; all murderers, contentious persons, and those who live in hatred and envy against their neighbors; all adulterers, whoremongers, drunkards, thieves, usurers, robbers, gamesters, covetous, and all who lead offensive lives.

All these, while they continue in such sins, shall abstain from this meat (which Christ hath ordained only for the faithful), lest their judgment and condemnation be made the heavier.

c. The Heidelberg Catechism XXIV, 64; XXXI, 84; XLV, 116:

Q. 64. But doth not this doctrine make men careless and profane?

By no means: for it is impossible that those, who are implanted into Christ by a true faith, should not bring forth fruits of thankfulness.

Q. 84. How is the kingdom of heaven opened and shut by the preaching of the holy gospel?

Thus: when according to the command of Christ, it is declared and publicly testified to all and every believer, that, whenever they receive the promise of the gospel by a true faith, all their sins are really forgiven them of God, for the sake of Christ's merits; and on the contrary, when it is declared and testified to all unbelievers, and such as do not sincerely repent, that they stand exposed to the wrath of God, and eternal condemnation, so long as they are unconverted: according to which testimony of the gospel, God will judge them, both in this, and in the life to come.

Q. 116. Why is prayer necessary for Christians?

Because it is the chief part of thankfulness which God requires of us: and also, because God will give his grace and Holy Spirit to those only, who with sincere desires continually ask them of him, and are thankful for them.

Canons III and IV, A, 12, 16, 17:

Art. 12. And this is the regeneration so highly celebrated in Scripture, and denominated a new creation: a resurrection from the dead, a making alive, which God works in us without our aid. But this is in no wise effected merely by the external preaching of the gospel, by moral suasion, or such a mode of operation, that after God has performed his part, it still remains in the power of man to be regenerated or not, to be converted, or to continue unconverted; but it is evidently a supernatural work, most Powerful, and at the same time most delightful, astonishing, mysterious, and ineffable; not inferior in efficacy to creation, or the resurrection from the dead, as the Scripture inspired by the author of this work declares; so that all in whose heart God works in this marvelous manner, are certainly, infallibly, and effectually regenerated, and do actually believe. Whereupon the will thus renewed, is not only actuated and influenced by God, but in consequence of this influence, becomes itself active. Wherefore also, man is himself rightly said to believe and repent, by virtue of that grace received.

Art. 16. But as man by the fall did not cease to be a creature, endowed with understanding and will, nor did sin which pervaded the whole race of mankind, deprive him of the human nature, but brought upon him depravity and spiritual death; so also this grace of regeneration does not treat men as senseless stocks and blocks, nor takes away their will and its properties, neither does violence thereto; but spiritually quickens, heals, corrects, and at the same time sweetly and powerfully bends it; that where carnal rebellion and resistance formerly prevailed, a ready and sincere spiritual obedience begins to reign; in which the true and spiritual restoration and freedom of our will consist. Wherefore unless the admirable author of every good work wrought in us, man could have no hope of recovering from his fall by his own free will, by the abuse of which, in a state of innocence, he plunged himself into ruin.

Art. 17. As the almighty operation of God, whereby he prolongs and supports this our natural life, does not exclude, but requires the use of means, by which God of his infinite mercy and goodness hath chosen to exert his influence, so also the before mentioned supernatural operation of God, by which we are regenerated, in no wise excludes, or subverts the use of the gospel, which the most wise God has ordained to be the seed of regeneration, and food of the soul. Wherefore, as the apostles, and teachers who succeeded them, piously instructed the people concerning this grace of God, to its glory, and the abasement of all pride, and in the meantime, however, neglected not to keep the by the sacred precepts of the gospel in the exercise of the Word, sacraments and discipline; so even to this day, be it far from either instructors or instructed to presume to tempt God in the church by separating what he of his good pleasure hath most intimately joined together. For grace is conferred by means of admonitions; and the more readily we perform our duty, the more eminent usually is this blessing of God working in us, and the more directly is his work advanced; to whom alone all the glory both of means, and of their saving fruit and efficacy is forever due. Amen.

Canons III and IV, B, 9:

Art. 9. Who teach: that grace and free will are partial causes, which together work the beginning of conversion, and that grace, in order of working, does not precede the working of the will; that is, that God does not efficiently help the will of man unto conversion until the will of man moves and determines to do this. For the ancient Church has long ago condemned this doctrine of the Pelagians according to the words of the Apostle: "So then it is not of him that willeth, nor of him that runneth, but of God that hath mercy," Rom. 9:16. Likewise: "For who maketh thee to differ? and what hast thou that thou didst not receive?" I Cor. 4:7. And: "For it is God who worketh in you both to will and to work, for his good pleasure,'' Phil. 2:13.

Canons V, A, 14:

Art. 14. And as it hath pleased God, by the preaching of the gospel, to begin this work of grace in us, so he preserves, continues, and perfects it by the hearing and reading of his Word, by meditation thereon, and by the exhortations, threatenings, and promises thereof, as well as by the use of the sacraments.

Netherlands Confession, Article 24:

Art. XXIV. We believe that this true faith being wrought in man by the hearing of the Word of God, and the operation of the Holy Ghost, doth regenerate and make him a new man, causing him to live a new life, and freeing him from the bondage of sin. Therefore it is so far from being true, that this justifying faith makes men remiss in a pious and holy life, that on the contrary without it they would never do anything out of love to God, but only out of self-love or fear of damnation. Therefore it is impossible that this holy faith can be unfruitful in man: for we do not speak of a vain faith but of such a faith, which is called in Scripture, a faith that worketh by love, which excites man to the practice of those works, which God has commanded in his Word.

Which works, as they proceed from the good root of faith, are good and acceptable in the sight of God, forasmuch as they are all sanctified by His grace: howbeit they are of no account towards our justification. For it is by faith in Christ that we are justified, even before we do good works; otherwise they could not be good works, any more than the fruit of a tree can be good, before the tree itself is good.

Therefore we do good works, but not to merit by them, (for what can we merit?) nay, we are beholden to God for the good works we do, and not he to us, since it is he that worketh in us both to will and to do of his good pleasure. Let us therefore attend to what is written: When ye shall have done all those things which are commanded you, say, we are unprofitable servants; we have done that which was our duty to do. In the meantime, we do not deny that God rewards our good works, but it is through his grace that he crowns his gifts.

Moreover, though we do good works, we do not found our salvation upon them; for we do no work but what is polluted by our flesh, and also punishable; and although we could perform such works, still the remembrance of one sin is sufficient to make God reject them. Thus then we would always be in doubt, tossed to and from without any certainty, and our poor consciences continually vexed, if they relied not on the merits of the suffering and death of our Savior.

3. That the ground of infant baptism is the command of God and the fact that according to Scripture He establishes His covenant in the line of continued generations.

IV. Besides, the Protestant Reformed Churches: Believe and maintain the autonomy of the local church.

For proof we refer to:

The Netherlands Confession, Article 31:

Art. 31. We believe, that the ministers of God's Word, and the elders and deacons, ought to be chosen to their respective offices by a lawful election by the Church, with calling upon the name of the Lord, and in that order which the Word of God teacheth. Therefore every one must take heed, not to intrude himself by indecent means, but is bound to wait till it shall please God to call him; that he may have testimony of his calling, and be certain and assured that it is of the Lord. As for the ministers of God's Word, they have equally the same power and authority wheresoever they are, as they are all ministers of Christ, the only universal Bishop, and the only Head of the Church. Moreover, that this holy ordinance of God may not be violated or slighted, we say that every one ought to esteem the ministers of God's Word, and the elders of the Church, very highly for their work's sake, and be at peace with them without murmuring, strife or contention, as much as possible.

Church Order, Article 36:

Art. 36. The Classis has the same jurisdiction over the Consistory as the Particular Synod has over the Classis and the General Synod over the Particular.

Only the consistory has authority over the local congregation. Church Order, Article 84.

Art. 84. No church shall in any way lord it over other churches, no minister over other ministers, no elder or deacon over other elders or deacons.

The Form for the Installation of Elders and Deacons:

''. . . called of God's Church, and consequently of God himself. . .''

Notes: *The Protestant Reformed Church (PRC) was formed by former members of the Christian Reformed Church in the wake of the 1924 "Common Grace" controversy. The creedal formulations of the Protestant Reformed Church are the same as those of its parent body, because controversy did not concern them, but dealt with some additional points of doctrine affirmed by the Christian Reformed Church at its 1924 Synod meeting. In response, the founding members of the PRC issued a statement refuting the Christian Reformed Church position that the PRC found a deviation from its traditional Calvinist stance. This Declaration is published in the PRC's Book of Church Order.*

The controversy concerned the role of non-Christians and how grace appeared in the natural order. The Christian Reformed Church affirmed the existence of a "common grace" available to all persons, through which non-Christians could do "good." The PRC rejected the idea of common grace, and what they saw as the implications of common grace for the understanding of salvation. They affirmed that apart from regeneration, people can do no "good." Much of the argument was built on different uses of the word "good."

Presbyterian

THE ESSENTIALS (EVANGELICAL PRESBYTERIAN CHURCH)

All Scripture is self-attesting and being Truth, requires our unreserved submission in all areas of life. The infallible Word of God, the sixty-six books of the Old and New Testaments, is a complete and unified witness to God's redemptive acts culminating in the incarnation of the Living Word, the Lord Jesus Christ. The Bible, uniquely and fully inspired by the Holy Spirit, is the supreme and final authority on all matters on which it speaks.

On this sure foundation we affirm these additional Essentials of our faith:

1. We believe in one God, the sovereign Creator and Sustainer of all things, infinitely perfect and eternally existing in three Persons: Father, Son, and Holy Spirit. To Him be all honor, glory and praise forever!

2. Jesus Christ, the living Word, become flesh through His miraculous conception by the Holy Spirit and His virgin birth. He who is true God became true man united in one Person forever. He died on the cross a sacrifice for our sins according to the Scriptures. On the third day He arose bodily from the dead, ascended into heaven, where, at the right hand of the Majesty on High, He now is our High Priest and Mediator.

3. The Holy Spirit has come to glorify Christ and to apply the saving work of Christ to our hearts. He convicts us of sin and draws us to the Savior. Indwelling our hearts, He gives new life to us, empowers and imparts gifts to us for service. He instructs and guides us into all truth, and seals us for the day of redemption.

4. Being estranged from God and condemned by our sinfulness, our salvation is wholly dependent upon the work of God's free grace. God credits His righteousness to those who put their faith in Christ alone for their salvation, thereby justifies them in His sight. Only such as are born of the Holy Spirit and receive Jesus Christ become children of God and heirs of eternal life.

5. The true Church is composed of all persons who through saving faith in Jesus Christ and the sanctifying work of the Holy Spirit are united together in the body of Christ. The Church finds her visible, yet imperfect, expression in local congregations where the Word of God is preached in its purity and the sacraments are administered in their integrity; where scriptural discipline is practiced, and where loving fellowship is maintained. For her perfecting, she awaits the return of her Lord.

6. Jesus Christ will come again to the earth—personally, visibly, and bodily—to judge the living and the dead, and to consummate history and the eternal plan of God. "Even so, come, Lord Jesus," (Rev. 22:20).

7. The Lord Jesus Christ commands all believers to proclaim the Gospel throughout the world and to make disciples of all nations. Obedience to the Great Commission requires total commitment to "Him who loved us and gave Himself for us." He calls us to a life of self-denying love and service. "For we are His workmanship, created in Christ Jesus for good works, which God prepared beforehand that we should walk in them." (Eph. 2:10)

These Essentials are set forth in greater detail in the Westminster Confession of Faith.

Notes: *The Evangelical Presbyterian Church was founded in 1981 by some of the more theologically conservative members of the United Presbyterian Church in the U.S.A. and the Presbyterian Church in the United States, which were at the time in the process of merging to form the Presbyterian Church (U.S.A.). The Church affirms the traditional Reformed faith as expressed in the Westminster from which these Essentials have been derived. The Church is open to the Charismatic Movement and many of the founders (though not all) are involved in that movement.*

The Church is most committed to a missionary faith, a belief reflected in the seventh paragraph, concerning obedience to the Great Commission.

*　　　*　　　*

BASIS OF UNION (PRESBYTERIAN CHURCH IN CANADA)

(1) The Scriptures of the Old and New Testaments, being the Word of God, are the only infallible rule of faith and manners.

(2) The Westminster Confession of Faith shall form the subordinate standard of this Church: the Larger and the Shorter Catechisms shall be adopted by the Church and appointed to be used for the instruction of the people: If being distinctly understood that nothing contained in the aforesaid Confession or Catechisms, regarding the power or duty of the civil magistrate, shall be held to sanction any principles or views inconsistent with full liberty of conscience in matters of religion.

(3) The government and worship of this Church shall be in accordance with the recognized principles and practice of Presbyterian Churches, as laid down generally in the "Form of Presbyterian Church Government" and in "The Directory for the Public Worship of God."

The General Assembly of the year 1889 did further adopt, with the approval of Presbyteries, the following resolution:

"Subscription of the formula shall be so understood as to allow liberty of opinion in respect to the proposition, "A man may not marry any of his wife's kindred nearer in blood than he may of his own." (West. Cont., Chap. xxiv., Section 4).

Notes: *The Presbyterian Church in Canada was formed by those mostly conservative members of the Presbyterian Church* *in Canada who did not choose to join Canadian Methodists and Congregationalists in creating the United Church of Canada. The Presbyterian Church in Canada affirms traditional Presbyterian doctrinal standards, especially a strict allegiance to the Westminster Confession (I, p. 217). More liberal Presbyterians (i.e., those who had joined in the merger that created the United Church of Canada) have suggested that the Westminster Confession has become outdated in many respects.*

*   *   *

A BRIEF STATEMENT OF BELIEF (PRESBYTERIAN CHURCH IN THE UNITED STATES)

GOD AND REVELATION

The living and only true God has made himself known to all mankind through nature, mind, conscience, and history. He has especially revealed himself and his purpose for man in the variety of ways recorded in the Old and New Testaments. The Bible, as the written Word of God, sets forth what God has done and said in revealing his righteous judgment and love, culminating in Christ. The Spirit of God who inspired the writers of Scripture also illumines readers of Scripture as they seek his saving truth. The Bible calls men to an obedient response to the Gospel and is the supreme authority and indispensable guide for Christian faith and life.

God has revealed himself as the Creator, Sustainer, and Ruler of all that exists. In the exercise of his sovereign power in creation, history, and redemption, God is holy and perfect, abundant in goodness, and the source of all truth and freedom. He is just in his dealings with all the world; he requires that men live and act in justice; and he visits his wrath on all sin. He is gracious and merciful and does not desire that any should perish. Both his judgments and his mercies are expressions of his character as he pursues his redemptive purposes for man.

God is personal and he reveals himself as the Trinity of Father, Son, and Holy Spirit. It is the witness of the Scriptures, confirmed in Christian experience, that the God who creates and sustains us is the God who redeems us in Christ, and the God who works in our hearts as the Holy Spirit; and we believe that this threefold revelation manifests the true nature of God.

MAN AND SIN

God created man in his own image. As a created being, man is finite and dependent upon his Creator. Man can distinguish between right and wrong, and is morally responsible for his own actions. He reflects the image of God insofar as he lives in obedience to the will of God. A unique creature standing both within nature and above it, he is placed by God in authority over the world. It is, therefore, his responsibility to use all things for the glory of God. Although made in the image of

God, man has fallen; and we, like all mankind before us, sin in our refusal to accept God as sovereign.

We rebel against the will of God by arrogance and by despair. We thrust God from the center of life, rejecting divine control both of human life and the universe. From this perversity arises every specific sin, whether of negligence, perfunctory performance, or outright violation of the will of God.

Sin permeates and corrupts our entire being and burdens us more and more with fear, hostility, guilt and misery. Sin operates not only within individuals but also within society as a deceptive and oppressive power, so that even men of good will are unconsciously and unwillingly involved in the sins of society. Man cannot destroy the tyranny of sin in himself or in his world; his only hope is to be delivered from it by God.

CHRIST AND SALVATION

God, loving men and hating the sin which enslaves them, has acted for their salvation in history and especially through his covenant people. In the fullness of time, he sent his only, eternally begotten Son, born of the Virgin Mary. As truly God and truly man, Jesus Christ enables us to see God as he is and man as he ought to be. Through Christ's life, death, resurrection, and ascension, God won for man the decisive victory over sin and death and established his Kingdom among men. Through Christ, bearing on the cross the consequences of our sin, God exposed the true nature of sin as our repudiation of God. Through Christ, bearing on the cross the guilt of our sin, God forgives us and reconciles us to himself. By raising his Son from the dead, God conquers sin and death for us.

God has an eternal, inclusive purpose for his world, which embraces the free and responsible choices of man and everything which occurs in all creation. This purpose of God will surely be accomplished. In executing his purpose, God chooses men in Christ and calls forth the faith which unites them with Christ, releasing them from bondage to sin and death into freedom, obedience, and life. Likewise God in his sovereign purpose executes judgment upon sinful man.

Man cannot earn or deserve God's salvation but receives it through faith by the enabling power of the Holy Spirit. In faith, man believes and receives God's promise of grace and mercy in Christ, is assured of his acceptance for Christ's sake in spite of his sinfulness, and responds to God in grateful love and loyalty.

In repentance, man, through the work of the Holy Spirit, recognizes himself as he is, turns from his sin, and redirects his life increasingly in accordance with God's will. The Christian life is a continuing process of growth which reaches its final fulfillment only in the life to come.

THE CHURCH AND THE MEANS OF GRACE

The true Church is the whole community, on earth and in heaven, of those called by God into fellowship with him and with one another to know and do his will. As the body of Christ, the Church on earth is the instrument through which

God continues to proclaim and apply the benefits of his redemptive work and to establish his Kingdom.

The Church in the world has many branches, all of which are subject to sin and to error. Depending on how closely they conform to the will of Christ as head of the Church, denominations and congregations are more or less pure in worship, doctrine, and practice. The Presbyterian Church follows scriptural precedent in its representative government by elders (presbyters). These elders govern only in courts of regular gradation. The form of government of a church, however, is not essential to its validity. The visible church is composed of those who profess their faith in Jesus Christ, together with their children.

Through the Church, God provides certain means for developing the Christian mind and conscience and for maturing faith, hope, and love. Primary among these means are the preaching, teaching, and study of the Word; public and private prayer; and the sacraments.

The Bible becomes a means of grace through preaching, teaching, and private study, as the Holy Spirit speaks to human needs and reveals the living Word of God who is Jesus Christ. It illuminates man's thought and experience as it provides an occasion for the Holy Spirit's work of redemption and as it testifies to the working of God, but it is not intended to be a substitute for science and inquiry. In preaching and teaching, the Church proclaims and interprets the mighty acts of God in history and seeks to relate them to every phase of human life. The prayerful and diligent study of the Scripture guides the Christian in his relationships with God and his fellow man, and in his personal life.

Christian prayer is communion with God in the name of Jesus Christ through the inspiration and guidance of the Holy Spirit. In prayers, alone or with others, we acknowledge God's greatness and goodness, confess our sins, express our love to him, rejoice in his blessings, present our needs and those of others, receive from him guidance and strength, and joyfully dedicate ourselves to his will. To pray in the name of Christ, our Mediator, is not to repeat a formula, but to trust his redemptive work, to ask for his intercession, to depend upon his presence with us and to desire what he has taught us to value and believe.

Christ gave to the Church through his apostles the sacraments of Baptism and the Lord's Supper as visible signs and assurances of the Gospel. Baptism sets forth, by the symbolic use of water, the cleansing and regenerating love of God through the work of the Holy Spirit; in this sacrament we and our children are assured that we are members of the covenant family of God, and are publicly accepted into fellowship with Christ and his Church. The Lord's Supper sets forth, by the symbolic use of bread and wine, the death of Christ for our salvation; in this sacrament we have communion with the risen Christ, who gives himself to us as we receive in faith the bread and wine for the nourishment of our Christian life. Being assured of his forgiving and sustaining love, we renew our dedication and

enjoy fellowship with the whole people of God. The Lord's table is open to members of all churches who have publicly professed Jesus Christ as Savior and Lord and who come in penitence and faith.

CHRISTIAN LIFE AND WORK

Each Christian is called to be a servant of God in all of life, so that we must seek God's will for the work we do and for the manner in which we do it. Christian vocation may be found in any work where our own abilities and interests best meet the legitimate needs of God's world. The Church is charged under God with the obligation to seek out the most responsible and effective Christian leadership. It is the special role of the ordained ministry, including elders and deacons, to perform particular services in the life of the Church and to strengthen every Christian in the discharge of the responsibilities of the priesthood of all believers in the Church and the world. For the Christian, all life becomes significant as he does his daily work with dedication and diligence out of love for God and for his neighbor.

The range of Christian responsibility is as wide as human life. The Christian must recognize, but not accept as inevitable, the world as it is, distorted and torn by sin. Christians as individuals and as groups have the right and the duty to examine in the light of the Word of God the effects on human personality of social institutions and practices. As servants of the sovereign will of God, Christians are under obligation to their fellow men and to unborn generations to shape and influence these institutions and practices so that the world may be brought more nearly into conformity with the purpose of God for his creation. The Church's concern for the reign of God in the world is essential to its basic responsibility both for evangelism and for Christian nurture.

We believe that our destiny and that of the world are not subject to chance or fate, but to the just and loving sovereignty of God. In this assurance we face the problems of suffering and evil. Faith in the purpose and providence of God assures us of his presence in suffering and of his power to give it meaning. We are confident that no form of evil can separate us from the love of God, that God works in all things for good, and that evil will ultimately be overcome. Therefore, while we cannot fully understand the pain and evil of the present world, we can offer ourselves as active instruments of God's will in their conquest.

JUDGMENT AND THE LIFE TO COME

Eternal life is the gift of God. We are assured by the promises of the Gospel, by our relation to Christ, and by his resurrection that death does not put an end to personal existence, but that we too shall be raised from the dead. Those who have accepted the forgiving love of God in Christ enter into eternal life in fellowship with God and his people. This new life begins in the present world and is fulfilled in the resurrection of the body and the world to come. Those who have rejected the love of God bring upon themselves his judgment and shut themselves outside the fellowship of God and his people.

As Christ came once in humility, he will return in glory for the final judgment and for the consummation of his universal Kingdom. The work and promises of Jesus Christ give assurance that the age-long struggle between sin and grace will in God's good time have an end; all the power of evil will be destroyed, and God's holy, wise, and loving purposes will be accomplished.

Notes: *This statement was adopted in 1962 by the General Assembly of the Presbyterian Church in the United States. It was an attempt to provide a contemporary confession in modern language. It replaced a similar confession that had been adopted in 1913. In 1983 the Presbyterian Church in the United States merged with the United Presbyterian Church in the U.S.A. to form the Presbyterian Church (U.S.A.). While circulated in the merger materials, this Statement was not printed in the new church's Book of Confessions, but led to the United Church's adoption of a new Brief Statement of Faith in 1990.*

This Brief Statement of Belief affirms the well-known distinctives of the Reformed Faith, including the sovereignty of God, human depravity (corruption), and a church governed through presbyters (elders). Missing is any reference to predestination, which has been replaced by mention of the "free and responsible choices of man."

The Presbyterian Church in the United States had been deeply affected by the theological debates of the twentieth century, especially the fundamentalist-modernist controversy. Its alignment with the more modernist elements in the debate is most clearly reflected in the statement on the Bible, which can be compared with that of other contemporary Reformed/Presbyterian statements from more conservative bodies such as the Evangelical Presbyterian Church or of the various independent Evangelical organizations. Absent from this statement is any language about the inerrancy, infallibility, or verbal inspiration of the Bible, or even the Bible as the Word of God. Instead, the Statement speaks of the Bible as revealing the living Word of God, Jesus Christ.

*   *   *

A BRIEF STATEMENT OF FAITH [PRESBYTERIAN CHURCH (U.S.A.)]

In life and in death we belong to God.
    Through the grace of our Lord Jesus Christ,
        the love of God,
            and the communion of the Holy Spirit,
    we trust in the one triune God, the Hold One of Israel,
        whom alone we worship and serve.

We trust in Jesus Christ,
    fully human, fully God.
    Jesus proclaimed the reign of God:
        preaching good news to the poor
            and release to the captives,
        teaching by word and deed
            and blessing the children,
        healing the sick
            and binding up the brokenhearted,

eating with outcasts,
    forgiving sinners,
        and calling all to repent and believe the gospel.
Unjustly condemned for blasphemy and sedition,
Jesus was crucified,
    suffering the depths of human pain
        and giving his life for the sins of the world.
God raised this Jesus from the dead,
    vindicating his sinless life,
    breaking the power of sin and evil,
    delivering us from death to life eternal.

We trust in God,
    whom Jesus called Abba, Father.
    In sovereign love God created the world good
        and makes everyone equally in God's image,
            male and female, of every race and people,
        to live as one community.
    But we rebel against God; we hide from our Creator.
        Ignoring God's commandments,
        we violate the image of God in others and ourselves,
        accept lies as truth,
        exploit neighbor and nature,
        and threaten death to the planet entrusted to our care.
    We deserve God's condemnation.
    Yet God acts with justice and mercy to redeem creation.
        In everlasting love,
            the God of Abraham and Sarah chose a covenant people
                to bless all families of the earth.
        Hearing their cry,
            God delivered the children of Israel
                from the house of bondage.
        Loving us still,
            God makes us heirs with Christ of the covenant.
        Like a mother who will not forsake her nursing child,
        like a father who runs to welcome the prodigal home,
            God is faithful still.

We trust in God the Holy Spirit,
    everywhere the giver and renewer of life.
    The Spirit justifies us by grace through faith,
        sets us free to accept ourselves and to love God and neighbor,
        and binds us together with all believers
            in the one body of Christ, the church.
    The same Spirit
        who inspired the prophets and apostles
        rules our faith and life in Christ through Scripture,
        engages us through the Word proclaimed,
        claims us in the waters of baptism,
        feeds us with the bread of life and the cup of salvation,
        and calls women and men to all ministries of the church.
    In a broken and fearful world
        the Spirit gives us courage
        to pray without ceasing,
        to witness among all peoples to Christ as Lord and Savior,
        to unmask idolatries in church and culture,
        to hear the voices of peoples long silenced,
        and to work with others for justice, freedom, and peace.
    In gratitude to God, empowered by the Spirit,

A BRIEF STATEMENT OF FAITH [PRESBYTERIAN CHURCH (U.S.A.)] (continued)

we strive to serve Christ in our daily tasks
    and to live holy and joyful lives,
even as we watch for God's new heaven and new earth,
    praying, Come, Lord Jesus!

With believers in every time and place,
    we rejoice that nothing in life or in death
    can separate us from the love of God in Christ Jesus
    our Lord.

Glory be to the Father, and to the Son, and to the Holy Spirit. Amen.

Notes: *In 1990, the Presbyterian Church (U.S.A.) completed work on A Brief Statement of Belief. During the period prior to the 1983 merger, which produced the Presbyterian Church (U.S.A.), a copy of A Brief Statement of Belief that had been adopted by the Presbyterian Church in the U.S. was circulated but not accepted for inclusion in the new Book of Confessions of the united church. After its adoption in 1990, this revised Statement was added to the Book of Confessions.*

With an emphatic preface that the Statement is by no means complete, the Statement centers on the drama of creation. It emphasizes the sovereignty, faithfulness, and love of God toward humanity and the covenant God made with his people. It also reflects on some issues of contemporary importance including the equality of male and female and of races and people, the destruction of the environment, the admittance of women to the ministry, and the need to empower the oppressed.

Appended to the Statement is a lengthy cross-index to the Bible and the other confessions in the Book of Confessions.

*　　*　　*

MISSION STATEMENT (PRESBYTERIAN CHURCH (U.S.A.)/LOUISVILLE PRESBYTERIAN THEOLOGICAL SEMINARY)

Theologically, the Seminary is committed to the Lordship of Jesus Christ; to the Scriptures as unique and authoritative witness to Jesus Christ and, therefore, the standard by which faith and life are to be directed; and to the confessional standards of the Presbyterian Church (U.S.A.)

Notes: *This Mission Statement, prepared by one of the seminaries of the Presbyterian Church (U.S.A.), is typical of statements prepared by other seminaries of the church and of many seminaries of the larger denominations of liberal Protestantism. Louisville Presbyterian Theological Seminary is supported by the Presbyterian Church (U.S.A.) and charged with the task of training its next generation of ministers. It has also become a center for continued theological reflection and hence change in the church. It thus lives in a relationship of creative tension with the church as a whole. It is committed to*

the Confessions of the church while at the same time ''offering the church constructive criticism, thought, and planning for the communication of the Gospel in our time.''

Within liberal Protestantism, confessional standards are viewed not so much as documents or statements to which ascent or allegiance is given, but rather as mature statements of the faith from which a person learns and the contemporary Christian enters a vital dialogue.

*　　*　　*

OUR CREED (PRESBYTERIAN CHURCH (U.S.A.)/ PENIAL MISSION)

1. We believe in the one and only living God, creator of heaven and earth. Gen. 1:1; Isa. 42:5.

2. We believe that Yeshua (Jesus) who by His life, death, and resurrection fulfilled all the Messianic prophecies of the Old testament, is Israel's promised Messiah, and the Savior of the entire human race. Isa. 7:14; 9:6,7; 49:6; 53:1-12; Psa. 16:9-11.

3. We believe God made man in His own image and endowed him with a longing desire for intimate fellowship with God. Gen. 1:26; 2:7; 42:1,2.

4. We believe that man's disobedience to God's revealed will caused a separation between man and God. Gen. 2:16,17; Isa. 59-1,2.

5. We believe the only provision God made for reconciling man to Himself was through the atoning blood of the Messiah. Lev. 17:11; Isa. 53:5-8; 2 Cor 5-19.

6. We believe the Bible, both the Old and the New Testaments, to be God's Word and the only reliable and safe guide to faith and conduct. Num. 12:6-8; Isa. 8:20.

7. We believe that faith in Christ as the Mediator of the new covenant makes us real children of God through the new birth. Jer. 31:31-34; Ezek. 36:24-27; John 1:11-13.

8. We believe the Church to be the body of Christ, composed of all born again believers, both Jews and Gentiles, who constitute the living cells of Christ's body. 1 Cor. 12:12,13,27; Eph. 5:30-32.

9. We believe that the nation of Israel has been chosen of God to be a channel of blessing to all nations of the earth (Gen. 12:1-3; 22; 18); through their failure to keep the Law (Deut. 28:58, 63-66) and through their failure to recognize their true Messiah (Isa. 53:3; Matt. 23:37-39) they have been set aside as a nation (Hosea 3:4, 5) until the

second coming of Christ; then, they shall accept Him, and a nation will be born in a day. (Zech. 12:10; 13:1) (Isa. 66:6-9).

Notes: *The Penial Mission holds a unique place in the life of the Presbyterian Church (U.S.A.). It is the remnant of a once vital evangelistic mission that targeted Chicago's Jews for conversion to Christianity. However, it now exists in a church that has disowned that mission as the result of a lengthy dialogue with Jewish leaders during the last generation.*

The Mission's Creed reflects the older Jewish evangelistic endeavor. On the one hand, it presents a conservative faith based on the Bible as the Word of God. On the other hand, it develops that message especially for its Jewish audience. The statement speaks of God in Hebraic language (Yahweh) and of Jesus as the Messiah. It also reflects on the peculiar role of the nation of Israel.

* * *

STATEMENT OF FAITH (PRESBYTERIAN CHURCH (U.S.A.)/STERLING COLLEGE)

1. There is one God, who is infinitely perfect, existing eternally in three persons: Father, Son and Holy Spirit.

2. Jesus Christ is true God and true man. He was conceived by the Holy Spirit and born of the Virgin Mary. He died upon the cross, the Just for the unjust as a substitutionary sacrifice and all who believe in Him are justified on the ground of His shed blood. He arose from the dead according to the Scriptures. He is now at the right hand of the Majesty on high as our great High Priest. He will come again to establish His kingdom of righteousness and peace.

3. The Holy Spirit is a divine person, sent to indwell, guide, teach, empower the believer and convince the world of sin, of righteousness and of judgment.

4. The Old and New Testaments, inerrant as originally given, were verbally inspired by God and are a complete revelation of His will for the salvation of men. They constitute the divine and only rule of Christian faith and practice.

5. Man was originally created in the image and likeness of God; he fell through disobedience, incurring thereby both physical and spiritual death. All men are born with a sinful nature, are separated, from the life of God and can be saved only through the atoning work of the Lord Jesus Christ. The portion of the impenitent and unbelieving is existence forever in conscious torment; and that of the believer, in everlasting joy and bliss.

6. Salvation has been provided through Jesus Christ for all men: and those who repent and believe in Him are born again of the Holy Spirit, receive the gift of eternal life and become the children of God.

7. It is the will of God that each believer should be filled with the Holy Spirit and be sanctified wholly, being separated from sin and the world and fully dedicated to the will of God, thereby receiving power for holy living and effective service. This is both a crisis and a progressive experience wrought in the life of the believer subsequent to conversion.

8. Provision is made in the redemptive work of the Lord Jesus Christ for the healing of the mortal body. Prayer for the sick and anointing with oil are taught in the Scriptures and are privileges for the Church in this present age.

9. The Church consists of all those who believe on the Lord Jesus Christ, are redeemed through His blood and are born again of the Holy Spirit. Christ is the Head of the Body, the Church, which has been commissioned by Him to go into all the world as a witness, preaching the gospel to all nations.

   The local church is a body of believers in Christ who are joined together for the worship of God, for edification through the Word, for prayer, fellowship, the proclamation of the gospel and observance of the ordinances of baptism and the Lord's Supper.

10. There shall be a bodily resurrection of the just and of the unjust: for the former a resurrection unto life; for the latter, a resurrection unto judgment.

11. The second coming of the Lord Jesus Christ is imminent and will be personal, visible, and premillennial. This is the believer's blessed hope and is a vital truth which is an incentive to holy living and faithful service.

Notes: *Sterling College is affiliated with the Presbyterian Church (U.S.A.), but as is the case with many colleges and universities affiliated with liberal Protestant denominations, that relationship is very loose. The College serves not only Presbyterians in Arkansas and surrounding states, but also has many non-Presbyterians among the student body. It has a commitment to a Christian worldview, but offers no commitment to specifically Presbyterian approaches. This statement can be fruitfully compared with those of the independent Reformed/Presbyterian schools (reprinted below) who have more or less detailed statements of faith to which they are committed.*

* * *

Congregationalism

STATEMENT OF FAITH (UNITED CHURCH OF CANADA)

We are not alone, we live in God's world.

STATEMENT OF FAITH (UNITED CHURCH OF CANADA)
(continued)

We believe in God:
   who has created and is creating,
   who has come in Jesus, the Word made flesh,
     to reconcile and make new,
   who works in us and others by the Spirit.
We trust in God,
We are called to be the church:
   to celebrate God's presence,
   to love and serve others,
   to seek justice and resist evil,
   to proclaim Jesus, crucified and risen,
     our judge and our hope.
In life, in death, in life beyond death,
   God is with us.
We are not alone.
Thanks be to God. Amen.

Notes: *This Statement of Faith is designed for use in the weekly worship services in ways analogous to the Apostles Creed. Like many modern liberal Protestant creedal statements, it avoids mention of many traditional Christian doctrines, such as the Trinity, and allows a wide range of opinion concerning the nature of Jesus and his saving work. This text has been reprinted and used by other liberal Protestant denominations.*

*   *   *

Independent Reformed/Presbyterian Organizations

DOCTRINAL STATEMENT AND STATEMENT OF FAITH (PRESBYTERIAN EVANGELICAL FELLOWSHIP)

Doctrinal Statement:

This Fellowship stands firmly upon the whole Bible, the infallible, inerrant Word of God; and the doctrines of the Presbyterian and Reformed faith as expressed in The Westminster Confession of Faith and Catechisms. But this Fellowship is in no sense a separate denomination or church. It seeks merely to cooperate with and encourage all true churches and agencies in evangelism, seeking to promote the unity, purity, edification and growth of the churches through evangelism.

Statement of Faith:

We believe the Scriptures of the Old and New Testaments to be the inspired Word of God, the only infallible rule of faith and practice.

We believe that there is but one living sovereign and true God, existing eternally in three persons: Father, Son and Holy Spirit.

We believe in the deity of our Lord and Savior Jesus Christ, in His virgin birth, in His sinlessness, in His miracles, in His vicarious atonement by the shedding of His blood, in His bodily resurrection, in His ascension to the right hand of the Father, and in His personal return in power and glory.

We believe that all men are lost in sin apart from Jesus Christ, and that the only way of salvation is through faith in Jesus Christ by the work of the Holy Spirit.

We believe in the present ministry of the Holy Spirit who enables the Christian to live a life becoming to a follower of Christ.

We believe in the resurrection of both the believer and the unbeliever, that the believer will be raised up in everlasting glory and the unbeliever shall go away into everlasting punishment.

We believe that evangelism is the primary mission of the Church of Jesus, and is dependent upon the work of the Holy Spirit.

Notes: *The Presbyterian Evangelical Fellowship, founded in 1985, is a coalition of Evangelical organizations that function within the Presbyterian Church (U.S.A.). It represents the conservative membership that stayed within the Presbyterian church after many of the Fundamentalists left to found the Orthodox Presbyterian Church in the 1930s. It has called for a fairly literal approach to the Bible, and the Westminster Confession and Catechism, the traditional standards of Presbyterian doctrine.*

The Presbyterian Church (U.S.A.) passed a new Confession of Faith in 1967, and then placed it, the Westminster Confession and several other creedal statements into a book of Confessions. Many have interpreted that action as undermining the authority of the Westminster Confession by turning it into a mere historical artifact. This statement opposes any watering down of the essential position of the Westminster Confession on the most vital issues of God's sovereignty, Christ's saving activity, and human salvation.

*   *   *

DOCTRINAL BASIS (REFORMATION TRANSLATION FELLOWSHIP)

''The doctrinal basis of the organization shall be the Reformed or Calvinistic interpretation of Christianity as set forth in the Westminster Confession of Faith.''

Notes: *The Reformed Translation Fellowship is dedicated to the translation, publication, and distribution of Christian literature in the Chinese language. Its brief statement aligns* the Fellowship to the traditional standards of the Reformed faith.

* * *

Independent Reformed/Presbyterian Schools

DOCTRINAL STATEMENT (ATLANTA SCHOOL OF BIBLICAL STUDIES)

We stand firmly on the Bible, the infallible and inerrant Word of God written.

We sincerely receive and adopt the doctrine of the Historic Reformed Faith as expressed in the Westminster Confession of Faith and Catechisms and other Historic Reformed Confessions.

We sincerely receive and adopt the following brief statement of faith:

We believe the Scriptures of the Old and New Testaments to be the inspired Word of God, the only inerrant and infallible rule of faith and practice.

We believe that there is but one living, sovereign and true God, existing eternally in three persons, Father, Son and Holy Spirit.

We believe in the deity of our Lord and Savior Jesus Christ, in His virgin birth, in His sinlessness, in His miracles, in His vicarious atonement by the shedding of His blood, in His bodily resurrection, in His ascension to the right hand of the Father, and in His personal return in and glory.

We believe that all men are lost in sin apart from Jesus Christ, and that the only way of salvation is through faith in Jesus Christ enabled by the Holy Spirit.

We believe in the present ministry of the Holy Spirit who enables the Christian to live an obedient, fruitful life becoming to a follower of Christ.

We believe in the resurrection of both the believer and the unbeliever, that the believer will be raised up in everlasting glory and the unbeliever shall be sent away into everlasting punishment.

We believe that Evangelism at home and around the world is the primary mission of the Church of our Lord Jesus Christ. We are dependent on the work of the Holy Spirit and the Word for fruit.

We believe that the positive fruit of Evangelism should be carefully gathered into a body, biblically called the Church, for nurture, worshipping, and training in the things of God according to the Holy Scriptures.

Notes: *During the twentieth century, American Presbyterianism was deeply divided over the fundamentalist modernist controversy. When the modernists won control of the denominations and their seminaries in the 1930s, those who retained an allegiance to a more conservative theological approach had to form independent schools. The Atlanta School of Biblical Studies, Atlanta, Georgia, is an independent Evangelical Bible School supported by conservative Presbyterians. It maintains an allegiance to the Westminster Confession and the two Westminster Catechisms, the traditional Presbyterians doctrinal standards. In addition, the School has adopted the modern fundamentalist interpretation of those documents that includes the affirmation of the inerrancy and infallibility of the Bible.*

This statement can be fruitfully compared with the statements of the Presbyterian Church (U.S.A.), the organizational heir of the twentieth century modernist movement.

* * *

DISTINCTIVES (BIBLICAL THEOLOGICAL SEMINARY)

Biblical Theological Seminary is committed to the great Christian fundamentals and affirms, among equally biblical truths, the eternal deity of Christ, the virgin birth, the reality of the miracles of Christ, the substitutionary atonement of Christ to satisfy divine justice, and the bodily resurrection of Christ.

Theological liberalism, in its various forms, in the major departure from historic Christianity of this century. No person favorably inclined toward theological liberalism shall be appointed or retained as a board member, an administrator, or a faculty member, nor shall any person so inclined be considered as a chapel speaker or lecturer in special programs.

The General doctrinal position of the Seminary, to which all faculty and board members must adhere, is that of historic biblical Christianity in its reformed expression. Instruction is conducted within the framework of the system of doctrine contained in Scripture and expounded in the *Westminster Confession of Faith.*

The doctrinal distinctives of the school include an absolute loyalty to the authority and inerrancy of Scripture, a strong emphasis on biblical exegesis, a combination of thorough Christian scholarship with vital spiritual life and evangelistic passion, a firm commitment to the personal and premillennial return of Christ, and a stress upon the necessity of separation from unbelief and ungodliness.

Notes: *Biblical Theological Seminary, Hatfield, Pennsylvania, is an independent Reformed/Presbyterian seminary committed to the doctrinal position of the Westminster Confession*

DISTINCTIVES (BIBLICAL THEOLOGICAL SEMINARY)
(continued)

of Faith. Its statement of Doctrinal Distinctives commits it to a very conservative interpretation of the Confession with additional affirmations of the inerrancy of the Bible, the premillennial return of Jesus Christ, and separation from unbelief.

* * *

STATEMENT OF BASIS AND PRINCIPLES (REDEEMER COLLEGE)

Our supreme standard is the Bible. There Scriptures, both Old Testament and New, reveal some basic principles relevant to education, which we affirm:

Scripture. The Scriptures are the written and inspired Word of God, the infallible and authoritative rule of faith for the direction of the whole of life.

Creation. God created and structured the universe in all its many ways by His Word. The meaning of the creation is focused in man, God's image-bearer, with whom He has established a special covenant relationship in Jesus Christ.

Sin. Man's disobedience, which brought God's curse upon all mankind, alienated man from his Creator, himself, his fellow man, and the rest of the creation, distorted his view of the meaning and purpose of life; and misdirected human culture and learning.

Redemption. Christ, the Word of God incarnate, is the only Redeemer, the Renewer of our whole life. He restored man and the rest of the creation to God and calls man back to his God-appointed task in the world.

Human life. Man is by nature a religious being. All of human life, including educational work, must be understood as a response to the one true God. Consequently, man serves either the Lord or a god of his own making.

Knowledge. True knowledge of God, ourselves, and the rest of the creation is made possible only by means of a true faith in Jesus Christ, in whom are found all the treasures of wisdom and knowledge. True knowledge is attained only when the Holy Spirit enlightens men's hearts by the integrating Word of God and sets them in the truth. However, by God's gracious providence after the fall, those who reject the Word of God do provide many valuable insights into the structure of reality.

Teaching and Learning. In the context of their scholarship, the teachers of the College are called to lead students toward a deeper understanding of God's world and its history and to help them reach a cultural maturity grounded in Biblical faith. In order to carry out this calling, the teachers and students of the College should endeavor to discover God's laws and the structures of the creation so that the students may effectively

take up their specific responsibilities and vocations in a way that will further the coming of the Lord's Kingdom.

We believe that this Statement of Basis and Principles is wholly in harmony not only with Scripture but also with the historic creeds of the Reformation.

Notes: *Redeemer College is an independent conservative liberal arts college in the Reformed theological tradition. The school views itself as being in harmony with the historical creeds (Apostles, Nicene) of the Church and the confessions of the reformation (such as the Belgic and Second Helvetic), but has absorbed some modern Evangelical emphases reflected in its assertion of the infallibility of the Bible.*

* * *

STATEMENT OF FAITH (REFORMED BIBLE COLLEGE)

THE SCRIPTURES. We believe in the Scriptures of the Old and New Testaments as verbally inspired of God and inerrant in the original writings. We believe that this inspiration extends equally and fully to all parts of the supreme and final authority for faith and life (II Timothy 3:16; 11 Peter 1:21).

GOD. We believe in a personal God who has revealed Himself both in nature and Scripture, that He is one in essence and exists in three persons. This God is Sovereign, Loving and Living, and it is He who created the universe, upholds the same by His providence, and guides and rules all to His glory and His determined end.

JESUS CHRIST. We believe in the deity of the Lord Jesus Christ, in His virgin birth, in His sinless life, in His miracles, in His vicarious death and atonement through His shed blood, in His bodily resurrection, in His ascension to the right hand of the Father, and in His personal and visible return in power and glory.

THE HOLY SPIRIT. We believe in the person and present ministry of the Holy Spirit by Whose in dwelling the Christian is enabled to live a godly life, and by Whom the Church is empowered to carry out Christ's great commission.

MAN. We believe that man was created in the image of God, that he was tempted by Satan and fell, and that, because of the exceeding sinfulness of human nature, regeneration by the Holy Spirit is necessary for salvation.

SALVATION. We believe that all men are lost in sin through the fall and disobedience of Adam and Eve, that salvation is possible and real only through the shed blood and atonement of Jesus Christ on Calvary, appropriated through faith which is the gift of the Holy Spirit.

CHURCH. We believe that the church consists of all those whom Christ reconciles to the Father, that believers are to be faithful members of a local congregation, and that the church is God's agent for evangelization and missions.

FUTURE. We believe in the bodily resurrection of both the saved and the lost: those who are saved unto the resurrection of life and those who are lost unto the resurrection of damnation.

Notes: *Reformed Bible College is an independent conservative Bible school in the Reformed Presbyterian tradition. It affirms the fundamentalist affirmations concerning the authority of the Bible which it sees as inerrant, and verbally inspired. It also affirms the virgin birth, vicarious atonement, and visible second coming of Jesus.*

*   *   *

DISTINCTIVES (REFORMED THEOLOGICAL SEMINARY)

1. The Inerrancy of the Bible. Reformed Theological Seminary asserts the priority of Scripture alone over the life of the church. We believe that a loyal and reverent approach to the study of the Bible recognizes and affirms its plenary verbal inspiration and its absolute inerrancy as the divinely revealed and authoritative Word of God. Believing the Bible to be the "Word of God, the only infallible rule of faith and practice," Reformed Theological Seminary vigorously rejects any usurpation of biblical authority, whether in the form of church tradition, current decisions of church governing bodies, or theological trends.

   Reformed Theological Seminary seeks to develop men and women who have a burning desire both to know and to do the will of God as revealed in Scripture. Therefore, RTS is obligated to equip the student with the necessary skills to study the Scriptures and to practice the implicit and explicit teachings of Scripture.

2. The Reformed Theology of the Westminster Standards. The faculty teaches from a wholehearted commitment to the Westminster Confession of Faith and Catechisms. Fundamental to the Reformed theology contained therein is the belief that all doctrine, worship, faith and life must be conformed to the Bible, the Word of God. Hence, theological studies, both in form and content, must be biblical, fully reflecting the perspectives of Scripture as opposed to being primarily philosophical or historical.

3. The Biblical Form of Church Government. Reformed Theological Seminary asserts its confidence that God has ordained clear principles of church government for the ordering of His Church, and that conformity to these principles is essential to the well-being of the Church. Reformed Theological Seminary regards the biblical form of church government to be Presbyterian.

4. The Evangelical Mission of the Church. Scripture requires the Church to promote the glory of God and salvation of man through worship, evangelism, missions, Christian nurture, and the ministry of compassion. The Christian, individually and in association with others, has an obligation to develop and practice the full implications of both the great commission and the cultural mandate, under the Lordship of Christ.

To insure that these distinctives of the Seminary will be maintained each member of the Board of Trustees, faculty and ministerial advisors is required initially and annually to engage in and subscribe to a statement of belief and covenant as set forth in the Seminary's by-laws.

The Seminary recognizes that there are evangelical and Reformed brothers and sisters in Christ within various denominations and Christian organizations who hold views concerning doctrine, missions and evangelism different from its own distinctives. While committed to fulfilling its purpose and distinctives in these areas, the Seminary resolves to maintain openness to and appreciation for Christians in differing denominations and organizations in a loving spirit and thus contribute to the purity and the unity of the Christian community witness.

Notes: *The Reformed Theological Seminary, Jackson, Mississippi, is an independent theological training school that serves the needs of conservative Presbyterians in various denominations, some of which are too small to sponsor a seminary of their own. It is committed to the historical Presbyterian doctrinal standards as contained in the Westminster Confession of Faith and the two Westminster Catechisms. It also heir to the conservative side of the fundamentalist modernist controversy of the early twentieth century. As such, it affirms in the strongest terms the authority of the Bible as the inerrant and verbally inspired Word of God. In contrast to many Fundamentalist and Evangelical schools, it is firmly committed to a Presbyterian form of church government.*

Chapter 6

Pietist-Methodist Family

Scandinavian Pietism

STATEMENT OF FAITH (EVANGELICAL COVENANT CHURCH OF AMERICA/JESUS PEOPLE USA)

1. We believe that the Bible is the uniquely inspired and inerrant Word of God and is fully binding on all matters of faith, doctrine, and practice. We also accept the Chicago Statement of Biblical inerrancy.

2. We believe in the Christian doctrine of the Trinity, which says, specifically: that there is one and only one God—eternal, omnipotent, omniscient, omnipresent, triune; that within the unity of the Godhead there are three Persons, coequal, co-eternal, and consubstantial—God the Father, God the Son, and God the Holy Spirit; and that these three Persons are the one God.

3. We believe in the preexistence and full deity of the Lord Jesus Christ, who through the Incarnation became man without ceasing to be God, being at the same time both God and man, fully human and fully divine, in one Person.

4. We believe in the historic Virgin Birth of Jesus, the prophesied Messiah of the Old Testament, His sinless life, His death on the cross for our sins, His bodily resurrection from the dead, and His ascension into Heaven, according to the Scriptures.

5. We believe that as a result of the historic, space-time Fall in the Garden of Eden, man became a sinner and hopelessly separated from God; that Jesus Christ is the only provision for atonement for sin and reconciliation to God; that without the new birth no man will see the kingdom of God, and because of God's grace, not his own works, man is justified by faith alone in the finished work of Christ; and that on the coming Day of judgment all men will be resurrected bodily—the saved to enjoy eternal life with God, and the unsaved to face an eternal, righteous punishment in Hell.

6. We believe in and practice baptism by immersion, and we celebrate the Lord's Supper.

7. We believe in the Second Coming of Jesus Christ, in which He will personally and visibly return from Heaven to judge the living and the dead, and although no man can know the day, hour, or year, His return is imminent.

8. We believe in the ministry of the Holy Spirit, through whom all believers are justified, regenerated, and sanctified, Who is given to the Church to produce both fruit and gifts in its members, and that He makes it possible for a person who believes in Christ to live a godly life in this present fallen world.

9. We believe that all Christians are indwelt by the Holy Spirit upon their regeneration, and that the gifts of the Holy Spirit are valid for today's church.

10. We believe in the spiritual unity of all true believers in Christ; and that these believers, who are committed to Jesus Christ as Lord, are thus recognized as His Church.

Notes: *Jesus People USA is a community that grew out of the Jesus People Movement of the 1970s. In 1990, it united with the Evangelical Covenant Church, a relatively liberal denomination with a pietist background. The Jesus People are theologically a very conservative group and have inherited emphases from the traditionally antagonistic evangelical fundamentalism and pentecostalism. Jesus People USA affirms biblical inerrancy, baptism by immersion, and the contempo-*

141

rary validity of the gifts of the Spirit (speaking in tongues, healing, prophecy, etc.).

* * *

Episcopal Methodism

JUNALUSKA AFFIRMATION OF SCRIPTURAL CHRISTIANITY FOR UNITED METHODISTS (GOOD NEWS MOVEMENT WITHIN THE UNITED METHODIST CHURCH)

PREAMBLE

In a time of theological pluralism, Good News and other evangelicals within United Methodism have thought it necessary to reaffirm the historic faith of the Church. Our theological understanding of this faith has been expressed in the Apostles' Creed, Nicene Creed, and in John Wesley's standard *Sermons* and the *Explanatory Notes upon the New Testament.* We affirm in their entirety the validity and integrity of these expressions of Scriptural truth, and recognize them as the doctrinal standards of our denomination.

We also recognize that our situation calls for a contemporary restatement of these truths. The merging of two great traditions, the Evangelical United Brethren and the Methodist, with their two authentic witnesses to the historic faith, *The Confession of Faith* and *The Articles of Religion,* gives further occasion for such a statement. Moreover, we recognize the mandate which the doctrinal statement of the 1972 General Conference has placed upon "all its members to accept the challenge of responsible theological reflection."

Consequently, we offer to the United Methodist Church this theological affirmation of Scriptural Christianity.

THE HOLY TRINITY

Scriptural Christianity affirms the existence of the one Eternal God who has revealed Himself as Father, Son and Holy Spirit, three equal but distinct Persons, mysteriously united in the Godhead which the Church historically has described as the Holy Trinity.

GOD THE FATHER

Scriptural Christianity affirms that the first Person of the Holy Trinity, God the Father, is the Eternal One and reigns supremely. He has provided a covenant through which His creatures can be redeemed and through which His creation will be liberated from all evil and brought to final righteousness at the end of the age.

GOD THE SON

Scriptural Christianity affirms that the second Person of the Holy Trinity, the Eternal Son, became incarnate as Mary's virgin-born Child, Jesus of Nazareth, the Christ. In His unique Person, He revealed to us both the fullness of deity and the fullness of humanity. By His life, suffering, death, resurrection and ascension He provided the only way of salvation. His sacrifice on the cross once and for all was to reconcile the Holy God and sinners, thus providing the only way of access to the Father. Now He intercedes as High Priest before the Father, awaiting the day when He will return to judge every person, living and dead, and to consummate His Kingdom.

GOD THE HOLY SPIRIT

Scriptural Christianity affirms that the third Person of the Holy Trinity, the Holy Spirit, was active from the beginning in creation, revelation and redemption. It was through His anointing that prophets received the Word of God, priests became intermediaries between God and His people, and kings were given ruling authority. The Spirit's presence and power, measured in the Old Testament, were found without measure in Jesus of Nazareth, the Anointed. The Spirit convicts and woos the lost, gives new birth to the penitent, and abides in the believer, perfecting holiness and empowering the Church to carry out Christ's mission in the world. He came to indwell His Church at Pentecost, enabling believers to yield fruit and endowing them with spiritual gifts according to His will. He bears witness to Christ and guides God's people into His truth. He inspired the Holy Scriptures, God's written Word, and continues to illuminate His people concerning His will and truth. His guidance is always in harmony with Christ and the truth as given in the Holy Scriptures.

HUMANITY

Scriptural Christianity affirms that man and woman are fashioned in the image of God and are different from all of God's other creatures. God intends that we should glorify Him and enjoy Him forever. Since the Fall of Adam the corruption of sin has pervaded every person and extended into social relationships, societal systems, and all creation. This corruption is so pervasive that we are not capable of positive response to God's offer of redemption, except by the prevenient, or preparing, grace of God. Only through the justifying, regenerating and sanctifying work of the Triune God can we be saved from the corruption of sin, become increasingly conformed to the image of Christ, and restored to the relationships which God has intended for us.

THE HOLY SCRIPTURES

Scriptural Christianity affirms as the only written Word of God the Old and New Testaments. These Holy Scriptures contain all that is necessary for our knowledge of God's holy and sovereign will, of Jesus Christ the only Redeemer, of our salvation, and of our growth in grace. They are to be received through the Holy Spirit as the guide and final authority for the faith and conduct of individuals and the doctrines and life of the Church. Whatever is not clearly revealed in, or plainly established as truth by, the Holy Scriptures cannot be required as an article of faith nor be taught as essential to salvation. Anything contrary to the teachings of the Holy Scriptures is contrary to the purposes of God and must, therefore, be opposed. The authority of Scripture derives from the fact that God, through His Spirit, inspired the authors, causing them to perceive God's truth and record it with accuracy. It is evident that the Holy Scriptures have been preserved during the long process of transmission through copyists and translators, and we attribute such accurate preservation to the work of the Holy Spirit. These Scriptures are supremely authoritative for the Church's teaching, preaching, witness, identifying error, correcting the erring, and training believers for ministry in and through the Church.

SALVATION

Scriptural Christianity affirms that God offers salvation to a sinful humanity and a lost world through Jesus Christ. By His death on the cross the sinless Son propitiated the holy wrath of the Father, a righteous anger occasioned by sin. By His resurrection from the dead, the glorified Son raises us to newness of life. When we appropriate by faith God's atoning work in Jesus Christ we are forgiven, justified, regenerated by His Holy Spirit, and adopted into the family of God. By His grace He sanctifies His children, purifying their hearts by faith, renewing them in the image of God, and enabling them to love God and neighbor with whole heart. The fullness of God's great salvation will come with the return of Christ. This cosmic event will signal the resurrection of the saved to eternal life and the lost to eternal damnation, the liberation of creation from the Adamic curse, God's final victory over every power and dominion, and the establishment of the new heaven and the new earth.

THE CHURCH

Scriptural Christianity affirms that the Church of Jesus Christ is the community of all true believers under His sovereign Lordship. This Church, the Body of Christ, is one because it shares one Lord, one faith, one baptism. It is *holy* because it belongs to God and is set apart for His purposes in the world. It is *apostolic* because it partakes of the authority granted to the apostles by Christ Himself. It is *universal* because it includes all believers, both living and dead, in every nation, regardless of denominational affiliation. Its authenticity is to be found wherever the pure Word of God is preached and taught; wherever the Sacraments of Baptism and Holy Communion are celebrated in obedience to Christ's command; wherever the gifts of the Holy Spirit upbuild the body and bring spiritual growth; wherever the Spirit of God creates a loving, caring fellowship, and a faithfulness in witness and service to the world; and wherever discipline is administered with love under the guidance of the Word of God. The Church, as the Bride of Christ, will ultimately be joined with her Lord in triumphant glory.

ETHICS

Scriptural Christianity affirms that we are God's workmanship, created in Christ Jesus for good works. These works are the loving expressions of gratitude by the believer for the new life received in Christ. They do not earn one's salvation nor are they a substitute for God's work of redemption. Rather, they are the result of regeneration and are manifest in the believer as evidence of a living faith.

God has called us to do justice, to love kindness, and to walk humbly with Him. In the Scriptures are found the standards and principles that guide the believer in this walk. These ethical imperatives, willingly accepted by the believer, enable us to be a part of God's purposes in the world. Moreover, in this we are called to an obedience that does not stop short of our willingness to suffer for righteousness' sake, even unto death.

Our life in Christ includes an unstinting devotion to deeds of kindness and mercy and a wholehearted participation in collective efforts to alleviate need and suffering. The believer will work for honesty, justice and equity in human affairs; all of which witness to inherent rights and a basic dignity common to all persons created in the image of God. Such contemporary issues as racism, housing, welfare, education, Marxism, capitalism, hunger, crime, sexism, family relationships, aging, sexuality, drugs and alcohol, abortion, leisure, pornography, and related issues call for prayerful consideration, thoughtful analysis, and appropriate action from Christians, and must always be a matter of concern to the Church. Thus, we remember that faith without works is dead.

Notes: *The Good News Movement was founded in the mid-1960s to unite Evangelicals within the Methodist Church. The Methodist Church was at the time in the process of uniting with the Evangelical United Brethren to form the United Methodist Church (1968). The Good News Movement gained broad attention at first, but gradually lost much of its following through what many felt was an undue emphasis on faults within the Church, rather than concentrating on a positive program of evangelism.*

In 1968, the United Methodist Church began a rare period of theological reflection prompted by the necessity of reconciling the creedal statements of the former Methodist Church and the former Evangelical United Brethren. The problem of producing a new creedal statement became an impossible task due to the theological pluralism that existed within the Church. It is within that context that the leadership of the Good News Movement gathered at Lake Junaluska, North Carolina, where they released the Junaluska Affirmation. It is a conservative Evangelical statement of traditional affirmations most central to the Church's teachings.

Notable is the paragraph on The Holy Scriptures. The statement avoids the language of Princeton theology that speaks of infallibility and inerrancy, but nevertheless affirms the accuracy of the Bible. Unlike most Evangelical statements, this one points to major social ills and calls on supporters of the Movement to work together to address them.

The Good News Movement within the United Methodist Church is headquartered in Wilmore, Kentucky, near the campus of Asbury College. Asbury is an independent Holiness Methodist school. Though a cordial relationship exists between the

JUNALUSKA AFFIRMATION OF SCRIPTURAL CHRISTIANITY FOR UNITED METHODISTS (GOOD NEWS MOVEMENT WITHIN THE UNITED METHODIST CHURCH) (continued)

leadership of Asbury and the Good News Movement, this statement avoids affirming any distinct Holiness doctrines.

*   *   *

A STATEMENT OF FAITH OF THE KOREAN METHODIST CHURCH (UNITED METHODIST CHURCH)

We believe in the one God,
  creator and sustainer of all things, Father of all nations,
  the source of all goodness and beauty, all truth and love.
We believe in Jesus Christ,
  God manifest in the flesh,
  our teacher, example, and Redeemer, the Savior of the world.
We believe in the Holy Spirit,
  God present with us for guidance, for comfort, and for strength.
 We believe in the forgiveness of sins,
  in the life of love and prayer,
  and in grace equal to every need.
We believe in the Word of God
  contained in the Old and New Testaments
  as the sufficient rule both of faith and of practice.
We believe in the church,
  those who are united in the living Lord
  for the purpose of worship and service.
We believe in the reign of God
  as the divine will realized in human society,
  and in the family of God,
  where we are all brothers and sisters.
We believe in the final triumph of righteousness
  and in the life everlasting. Amen.

Notes: *The Korean Methodist Church is a product of the nineteenth-century missionary endeavor by Methodists in Korea. Over the twentieth century, as the mission matured and developed its own leadership, it became an autonomous church but retained fraternal relations with the United Methodist Church. The Korean Methodist Church's Statement of Faith is published in the hymnal of the United Methodist Church for use in that church's worship.*

*   *   *

THE WORLD METHODIST SOCIAL AFFIRMATION (UNITED METHODIST CHURCH)

We believe in God, creator of the world and of all people;
  and in Jesus Christ, incarnate among us,
who died and rose again;
and in the Holy Spirit,
  present with us to guide, strengthen, and comfort.

We believe;
God, help our unbelief.

We rejoice in every sign of God's kingdom:
  in the upholding of human dignity and community;
  in every expression of love, justice, and reconciliation;
  in each act of self-giving on behalf of others;
  in the abundance of God's gifts.
    entrusted to us that all may have enough;
  in all responsible use of the earth's resources.

Glory be to God on high;
and on earth, peace.

Notes: *The Methodist Church has been a prominent leader among Protestant churches for its commitment to social justice. At the beginning of the twentieth century they promulgated a social statement that has been regularly revised as new issues have emerged and opinions have developed. More recently, a confession of faith with a special emphasis social values was written. In 1992 it was published in the new edition of the Church's hymn book.*

*   *   *

Non-Episcopal Methodism

THEOLOGICAL POSITION (CONGREGATIONAL METHODIST CHURCH/WESLEY COLLEGE)

The church sets the school's standards and doctrines, which we believe to be Biblical. The Congregational Methodist Church supports the fundamental doctrines of the Bible. Among other statements these doctrines include belief in:

  The Unity and Trinity of the God-head, in God the Father, God the Son, and God the Holy Spirit, these three in one;

  The Bible to be the divinely inspired Word of God and that it contains the only way to salvation;

  The deity of Jesus Christ, that He is very God, and very man;

  The atonement of Christ through His death and resurrection from the dead;

  The personal, imminent, pre-millennial return of Jesus Christ;

  The creation of man by a definite act of God, and in the doctrine of the fall of man from original holiness;

  The doctrine of regeneration, or the new birth, by which the sinner becomes a child of God and is delivered from the power of sin;

The doctrine of entire sanctification as a second definite work of grace, by which the heart is cleansed by the Holy Spirit from all inbred sin;

The resurrection of both the saved and the lost—they that are saved unto the resurrection of life and they that are lost unto the resurrection of damnation;

The judgment of God upon the willful sinner and eternal punishment of the finally impenitent.

Notes: *The Congregational Methodist Church was formed in 1852 and has officially adopted the Articles of Religion common to Methodism as its doctrinal standard, with additional statements on sanctification, hell, and the premillennial return of Jesus Christ. This Theological Position statement of Wesley College, Florence, Mississippi, a liberal arts college affiliated with the Church, summarizes the Methodist perspective, but has included a definitive statement against the Pentecostal/Charismatic movement and the experience of speaking in tongues.*

*   *   *

DOCTRINAL STATEMENT (EVANGELICAL METHODIST CHURCH/JOHN WESLEY COLLEGE)

John Wesley College is a Christian College and is interdenominational in scope. It believes and teaches the fundamental doctrines of Evangelical Christianity, and it maintains a positive Wesleyan emphasis in its interpretation of doctrine. In accordance with this historic position of the church, the following statements are set forth:

1. We believe that there is but one living and true God, an eternally existent spiritual Being of absolute knowledge, power, and goodness; Creator and Preserver of all things visible and invisible; that in the unity of this Godhead, there are three persons of one substance, power and eternity — Father, Son, and Holy Spirit.

2. We believe that Jesus Christ is the second person of the triune Godhead; that He is eternally of one substance with the Father: that He became incarnated by the Holy Spirit; was born of the Virgin Mary, thus uniting in one perfect personality forever two whole and perfect natures, Godhood and manhood, very God and very man, the God-man, Jesus Christ.

3. We believe in the personality and deity of the Holy Spirit; that He did proceed from the Father and the Son and is the third person of the Godhead, of one substance, power and eternity with them; that He is present with and active in the church, convicting the whole world of sin and righteousness and judgment.

4. We believe that the 66 Books of the Old and New Testament, which the church has universally accepted as the Holy Scriptures, were given by Divine inspiration and constitute the revealed and infallible Word of God, as the only supreme, sufficient and authoritative rule of faith and practice, and that the Holy Spirit who motivated men of God to speak through the written word has providentially guarded, in its preservation, the integrity of the message, and continues to illumine the hearts of those who read, that they may understand God's redemptive plan.

5. We believe that man was a special creation by God but that he forfeited his first estate and is very far fallen from original righteousness: and because of the corruption of his nature, as received from Adam, he is inclined to evil and that continually.

6. We believe that Jesus Christ died for our sins, and by the shedding of His blood made atonement for the sins of all mankind, that this atonement is the only ground of salvation. We believe in Christ's bodily resurrection from the dead, that He ascended into Heaven to the right hand of the Father, and is there engaged in intercession for US.

7. We believe that penitent sinners are justified before God only by faith in Jesus Christ; that at the same time they are regenerated and adopted into the household of faith, the Holy Spirit bears witness with their spirit to this gracious work. This is sometimes called implicit or initial sanctification.

8. We believe that entire sanctification is that act of God by which believers are mace free from original sin and brought into a state complete devotion to God. We further believe that this work accomplished by the baptism with the Holy Spirit, Who also bears and witness. We also believe that while the approach may be more or less gradual, the actual experience is consummated in an instant and the life that follows should experience the fullness of the Holy Spirit and a continual maturing of the Christian graces.

9. We believe that Christians are called to be holy in all manner of living so that any conduct contrary to this rule of Scripture is not on repugnant to sight but is also inconsistent with a true Christian profession.

10. We believe in the holy universal Church: that it is composed of true believers in Jesus Christ; that it is for the maintenance worship, the edification of believers, and the proclamation of the Gospel to the whole world.

11. We believe in the imminent personal return of Jesus Christ to this world to establish His kingdom, to rule in righteousness. and to judge all men.

12. We believe in the bodily resurrection of the dead, that the bodies the just and unjust shall be reunited with their spirits: that everlasting life is assured to all who believe in. and all who follow Jesus Christ; and the finally impenitent shall go away into everlasting punishment in hell.

13. John Wesley College stands solidly within the Wesleyan-Arminian theological tradition and method of Biblical

DOCTRINAL STATEMENT (EVANGELICAL METHODIST CHURCH/JOHN WESLEY COLLEGE) (continued)

interpretation. The college does not promote the practice of speaking in ''tongues,'' but neither does it demean those who do believe in speaking ''tongues,'' nor does the school refuse to admit students who profess this gift. It does not, however, permit the practice or propagation this phenomenon on campus or in any public worship service related to the work of the college.

Notes: *John Wesley College, High Point, North Carolina, is affiliated with the Evangelical Methodist Church but has a broad Wesleyan Holiness theological stance. The College has composed its own theological Statement that reflects modern theological debates on the authority of the Bible, and affirms the Bible's infallibility. The Statement also affirms the Holiness doctrine, that believers may be sanctified in this life and thus be made free from original sin and brought into a state of entire devotion to God. It is also opposed to the modern Pentecostal/Charismatic movement and the related experience of speaking in tongues.*

*   *   *

DOCTRINAL STATEMENT (EVANGELICAL METHODIST CHURCH OF AMERICA/MANAHATH SCHOOL OF THEOLOGY)

We believe in the verbal inspiration and final authority of the Scriptures, Old and New Testament. We believe that the Bible reveals God, the fall of man, the only way of salvation and God's plan and purpose through the ages. We believe in the Trinity; Father, Son and Holy Spirit. We believe in the Deity and virgin birth of Jesus Christ. We believe in His vicarious atonement for the sins of man upon the cross of Calvary and in His physical resurrection from the tomb. We believe in His personal and pre-millennial return. We believe that salvation is by grace ''plus nothing''. We believe that men are justified by faith alone and are accounted righteous before God only through the merit of our Lord and Savior Jesus Christ. We believe in the everlasting conscious blessedness of the saved and the everlasting-conscious punishment of the lost. We believe and teach that we are not only saved by grace, but that we are, also, enabled by grace through faith to live a life that is pleasing and glorifying to Him through the empowering of His indwelling Spirit by which we are enabled to walk in His holy commandment, blameless and victorious.

Notes: *The Evangelical Methodist Church of America has been identified with fundamentalism during the years since its formation in 1952. Its official Articles of Religion, those common to Methodism, were written prior to the twentieth-century fundamentalist-modernist debates and do not reflect its arguments. However, these arguments are addressed in the Doctrinal Statement of the church's Manahath School of*

Theology, Hollidaysburg, Pennsylvania, which affirms verbal inspiration of the Bible and the vicarious atonement and the premillennial return of Jesus Christ.

*   *   *

DOCTRINAL STATEMENT (METHODIST PROTESTANT CHURCH/WHITWORTH COLLEGE)

Among other equally Biblical truths, we believe and maintain the following:

a. The plenary divine inspiration of the Scriptures in the original languages, their consequent inerrancy and infallibility, and, as the Word of God, the supreme and final authority in faith and life;

b. The Triune God: Father, Son, and Holy Spirit;

c. The essential, absolute, eternal deity, and the real and proper, but sinless, humanity of our Lord Jesus Christ;

d. His birth of the Virgin Mary;

e. His substitutionary, expiatory death, in that He gave His life ''a ransom for many'';

f. His resurrection from among the dead in the same body in which He was crucified, and the second coming of this same Jesus in power and great glory;

g. The natural depravity of man through the fall;

h. Salvation, the effect of regeneration by the Spirit and the Word, not by works but by grace through faith;

i. Sanctification, the indwelling of the Holy Spirit in His fullness subsequent to regeneration;

j. The everlasting bliss of the saved, and the everlasting suffering of the lost;

k. The real spiritual unity in Christ of all redeemed by His precious blood;

l. The necessity of maintaining, according to the Word of God, the purity of the Church in doctrine and life.

Notes: *The Methodist Protestant Church is one of several groups that stayed out of the 1939 merger of the larger*

Methodist churches. Officially, it has retained the common Articles of Religion of Methodism, but has adopted a conservative Holiness interpretation of those articles. The Doctrinal position of Whitworth College reflects the association of the church with contemporary Evangelicalism. The Statement affirms the inerrancy of the Bible, the Virgin Birth, and human depravity, and also affirms sanctification as an experience of the believer subsequent to regeneration.

*   *   *

German Methodism

DOCTRINAL STANCE (EVANGELICAL CONGREGATIONAL CHURCH/EVANGELICAL SCHOOL OF THEOLOGY)

Standing in the Reformation tradition, we hold to the principles of sola gratia (Grace alone), sola fide (Faith alone) and sola scriptura (Scripture alone). Grace, which is God's part, is extended to all men. Faith, without works, is man's response to God's offer of salvation. True faith will flower into a Spirit-directed life of obedience to God's Word. The School, in harmony with the denomination, believes the Holy Bible to be inerrant in the autographs.

The Evangelical Congregational Church subscribes to an evangelical interpretation of Christian faith expressed in Twenty Five Articles of Faith. Historically these articles were drawn from the Arminian-Wesleyan theology mediated through early American Methodism. The early leaders of the Evangelische Gemeinschaft (Evangelical Association)-Jacob Albright, John Seybert, and others—expressed these theological commitments in vigorous evangelism and a call to the full development of the Christian life in believers. The twenty-fifth article of faith declares the proper fruit of these theological persuasions in its challenge to world evangelization.

The Evangelical Congregational Church is a constituent member of the National Association of Evangelicals, and as such subscribes to the doctrinal position of the Association:

1. We believe the Bible to be the inspired, the only infallible authoritative Word of God.

2. We believe that there is one God, eternally existent in three persons, Father, Son, and Holy Spirit.

3. We believe in the deity of our Lord Jesus Christ, in His virgin birth, in His sinless life, in His miracles, in His vicarious and atoning death through His shed blood, in His bodily resurrection, in His ascension to the right hand of the Father, and in His personal return in power and glory.

4. We believe that for the salvation of lost and sinful man regeneration by the Holy Spirit is absolutely essential.

5. We believe in the present ministry of the Holy Spirit by whose indwelling the Christian is enabled to live a godly life.

6. We believe in the resurrection of both the saved and the lost; they that are saved unto the resurrection of life and they that are lost unto the resurrection of damnation.

7. We believe in the spiritual unity of believers in our Lord Jesus Christ.

Notes: *The Doctrinal Stance of the Evangelical Congregational Church's Evangelical School of Theology, Myerstown, Pennsylvania, reflects the two forces operating on the church—its Methodist heritage and modern Evangelicalism. The School is a member of the National Association of Evangelicals and subscribes to its articles of belief, which include an affirmation of the infallibility of the Bible.*

Chapter 7
Holiness Family

Nineteenth-Century Holiness

DOCTRINAL STATEMENT (CHRISTIAN AND MISSIONARY ALLIANCE/ALLIANCE THEOLOGICAL SEMINARY)

The seminary is committed to a thoroughly evangelical Christian view of man and the world. We believe:

There is one God, who is infinitely perfect, existing eternally in three persons: Father, Son and the Holy Spirit. Jesus Christ is true God and true man. He was conceived by the Holy Spirit and born of the Virgin Mary. He died upon the cross, the Just for the unjust, as a substitutionary sacrifice, and all who believe in Him are justified on the ground of His shed blood. He arose from the dead according to the Scriptures. He is now at the right hand of the Majesty on high as our great High Priest. He will come again to establish His kingdom of righteousness and peace. The Holy Spirit is a divine person, sent to indwell, guide, teach, empower the believer and convince the world of sin, righteousness, and of judgment.

The Old and New Testaments, inerrant as originally given, were verbally inspired by God and are a complete revelation of His will for the salvation of man. They constitute the divine and only rule of Christian faith and practice.

Man was originally created in the image and likeness of God; he fell through disobedience, incurring thereby both physical and spiritual death. All men are born with a sinful nature, are separated from the life of God, and can be saved only through the atoning work of the Lord Jesus Christ. The portion of the impenitent and unbelieving is existence forever in conscious torment; and that of the believer, in everlasting joy and bliss. Salvation has been provided through Jesus Christ for all men; and those who repent and believe are born again of the Holy Spirit, receive the gift of eternal life, and become the children of God.

It is the will of God that each believer should be filled with the Holy Spirit and sanctified wholly, being separated from sin and the world and fully dedicated to the will of God, thereby receiving power for holy living and effective service. This is both a crisis and a progressive experience wrought in the life of the believer subsequent to conversion. Provision is made in the redemptive work of the Lord Jesus Christ for the healing of the mortal body. Prayer for the sick and anointing with oil are taught in the Scriptures and are privileges for the church in this present age.

The church consists of all those who believe on the Lord Jesus Christ, are redeemed through His blood, and are born again of the Holy Spirit. Christ is the Head of the Body, the church, which has been commissioned by Him to go into all the world as a witness, preaching the gospel to all nations.

The local church is a body of believers in Christ who are joined together for the worship of God, for edification through the Word of God, for prayer, fellowship, the proclamation of the gospel, and observances of the ordinances of baptism and the Lord's Supper. There shall be a bodily resurrection of the just and the unjust; for the former, a resurrection unto life; for the latter, a resurrection unto judgment.

The second coming of the Lord Jesus Christ is imminent and will be personal, visible and premillennial. This is the believer's blessed hope and is a vital truth which is an incentive to holy living and faithful service.

Notes: *Alliance Theological Seminary, Nyack, New York, is the ministerial training school for the Christian and Missionary Alliance. The Seminary's statement of doctrine spells out the Holiness stance of the Alliance, which comes from the Keswick tradition, a British Holiness perspective that emphasizes the Holy Spirit's empowering the believer. Subsequent to salvation, the believer should seek sanctification in which the Holy Spirit separates the believer from sin and empowers him/ her for holy living. The Alliance was also a pioneer in the*

DOCTRINAL STATEMENT (CHRISTIAN AND MISSIONARY ALLIANCE/ALLIANCE THEOLOGICAL SEMINARY) (continued)

development of a divine healing ministry, a thrust that has continued to the present day.

*   *   *

DOCTRINAL STATEMENT [CHURCH OF GOD (ANDERSON, INDIANA)/ALBERTA BIBLE COLLEGE]

We believe:

1. the Scriptures, both Old and New Testaments, to be the inspired Word of God, the revelation of his will for the salvation of men, and the divine authority for all Christian faith and life;

2. in one God, Creator of all things, infinitely perfect and eternally coexisting in three Persons, Father, Son and Holy Spirit;

3. that Jesus Christ is the Son of God, truly divine and truly human, conceived of the Holy Spirit and born of the virgin Mary; that he died on the cross, a sacrifice for our sins; that he was resurrected bodily from the dead, ascended into heaven, where at the right hand of the Majesty on high, he is now our High Priest and Advocate;

4. that the ministry of the Holy Spirit is to glorify the Lord Jesus Christ at all times. He is working in the conviction and salvation of sinners and the sanctification of believers to indwell, instruct, and empower for godly living an Christian service;

5. that man was created in the image of God but through disobedience fell out of fellowship with God, and that only by salvation through the atonement of Jesus Christ can he be reconciled to God by faith;

6. that the true Church of God is composed of all redeemed persons, who through faith in Jesus Christ are united together in the body of Christ of which he is head. We believe in the royal priesthood of believers, in the exercise of divine healing and spiritual gifts in the church;

7. that the kingdom of God is a spiritual kingdom being established in the hearts and lives of believers as they acknowledge the lordship of Jesus Christ, and that this kingdom shall increase through the proclamation of the good news of salvation until the end of the age culminating in the Second Coming of Christ, the resurrection of the dead and the final Judgment.

Notes: *The Church of God (Anderson, Indiana) is a noncreedal church and has no official doctrinal statement, although there*

is a well-recognized doctrinal consensus of Holiness teachings. Over the years, a number of individuals have attempted to put that consensus into writing, but the closest document to an officially accepted statement is printed in the catalogue of the Church's Alberta Bible Institute. The statement is a brief summary of Evangelical Protestantism. The essential sentence is contained in the fourth paragraph, which affirms the world of the Holy Spirit in the conviction and salvation of sinners, and the sanctification of believers to indwell, instruct, and empower for godly living and Christian service, the distinctive teaching of the Holiness movement.

*   *   *

WE BELIEVE [CHURCH OF GOD (ANDERSON, INDIANA)/ANDERSON COLLEGE SCHOOL OF THEOLOGY]

WE BELIEVE that the gospel of Christ has the power to transform all persons who are willing to repent, believe in its promises and obey its commands.

a. Persons are justified before God on the basis of the free and universal offering of divine grace which is made effective by faith, expressed publicly through baptism and nourished by the Holy Spirit and the Word of God. "Therefore, since we are justified by faith, we have peace with God through our Lord Jesus Christ" (Rom. 5:1).

b. Persons are sanctified by the cleansing and empowering work of the Holy Spirit who establishes the lives of believers in perfect love and enables those lives to be lifted above the domination of sin. "For this reason I bow my knees before the Father . . . that . . . he may grant you to be strengthened with might through his Spirit in the inner man and . . . that you may be filled with all the fullness of God" (Eph. 3:14-19).

c. Jesus taught his disciples to lead disciplined and sacrificial lives of prayer, witness and service. He washed the feet of his disciples as an action symbol of the servant life appropriate for all. He taught his disciples to act with courage and compassion in the face of evil and disease. He demonstrated the healing dimension of God's will for the body, mind and spirit. "By this all men will know that you are my disciples, if you have love for one another" (John 13:35). "And he [Jesus] sent them out to preach the kingdom of God and to heal" (Luke 9:2).

d. Persons justified before God, sanctified by God and serving in God's name willingly submit to the lordship of Christ in all areas of life. They are thus present citizens of the Kingdom of God and they anticipate the glorious consummation of that Kingdom at the return of Christ. "Unless one is born of water and the Spirit, he cannot enter the kingdom of God" (John 3:5). "For the kingdom of God is not food and drink, but righteousness and peace and joy in the Holy Spirit" (Rom. 14:17).

We are convinced that the Christian life is both intensely personal and compellingly social. It begins in God's grace, leads to God's service and is fulfilled in God's eternity.

WE BELIEVE in a cluster of biblical teachings which form a vision of the church. Specifically:

a. God's church is the community of redeemed persons. It is not to be understood primarily as any or all of the humanly designed and historically conditioned organizations of Christians. It is a divinely ordered fellowship of all persons in harmonious relationship with God. A local congregation, then, is best understood as a local manifestation of the church universal. (Eph. 2:14-21; 1 Cor. 1:2).

b. God's church is a community of divine-human partnership with Christ as Head. The church is all of God's redeemed children. It is the people of God made members one of another under the headship of Christ (Eph. 2:19-22). It is that unique body chosen for purposeful partnership in accomplishing the will of God on earth. Persons who are admitted to membership in the church by the grace of God (Acts 2:47) and equipped service by the gifting of God (1 Cor. 12:4-7) are the Spirit-led persons who guide the life and work of the church, just as that Christian council at Jerusalem made strategic decisions in light of what "seemed good to the Holy Spirit and to us" (Acts 15:28).

c. God's church is a holy community. Its holiness does not center in its possession of sacraments as means of saving grace or in its being historically in line with a hierarchically conceived "apostolic succession." It is the "Body of Christ." Through the atoning work of Christ and the sanctifying work of the Holy Spirit, the church, through the individual lives of its members, is privileged to participate in and demonstrate that holiness. (1 Cor. 1:2, 3:17; Eph. 5:25-27).

d. God's church is intended to be a unified community. The dividedness among Christian people today is not just unfortunate; it is inappropriate and wholly unacceptable. Unity is clearly God's will for the church. Participation in the Lord's Supper dramatizes the intended unity of Christians as they celebrate their one Lord, one salvation, and one mission. But that unity, symbolized in worship, must find visible expression in the life and witness of the church. The goal is less a contrived peace treaty among deeply divided church organizations and more a radical reconsideration of what is an appropriate network of relationships among brothers and sisters in Christ. (Luke 22:14-19; John 17:20-21; Rom. 12:4-5; Gal. 3:28; Eph. 4:4).

We have committed ourselves to the implications of this vision of God's Church. A unified life and witness among brothers and sisters in Christ is not optional. It is a natural outcome of the experience of grace and membership in the body of Christ. It is a crucial factor in the effectiveness of the church on mission!

WE BELIEVE that God calls his people to mission. All Christians are mandated to bear witness to God's saving activity in Jesus Christ (Acts 1:8; Luke 24:48) and to "make disciples of all nations" (Matt. 24:48. In this regard it is important to note that:

a. There is an unalterable gospel which transcends all denominational boundaries and controversies. Its essence is found in St. Paul's great statement: "God was in Christ" (2 Cor. 5:19), and in its corollary: "Jesus is Lord" (1 Cor. 12:3). In these statements we have a sufficient basis and reason for the Christian mission to all the world. The Holy Spirit bears witness to Jesus as Christ and Lord and those who are filled with the Spirit will do the same John 15:26-27).

b. Accomplishment of the Christian mission requires that Christians rise above private prejudices and party spirits to their sacred privilege and urgent obligation as members of the church. The grace of God in Christ should find embodiment in the life of the church and expression through the evangelical witness and sacrificial service of the church. Only in this way will the world come to know that the reconciling love of God is real and greatly to be desired.

c. Proper theological perspective is essential. We preach Christ! And in light of Christ we know that holiness of life and the "bond of perfectness" in the church are foundational for the all important mission of the church. The church is on mission as the "Elect from every nation, Yet one o'er all the earth, Her charter of salvation—One Lord, one faith, one birth. One holy name she blesses, Partakes one holy food; And to one hope she presses, With every grace endued."

We are committed to God's Church on mission. Christ is central. Love, holiness and unity are crucial. A needy world is waiting!

WE BELIEVE in the principle of openness to all affirmations of the Christian faith which are expressions of the biblical revelation (John 16:13). This is a necessary stance for Christians who would venture on mission to the world with a desire to foster honest and growing relationships with fellow Christians from many cultural and creedal backgrounds.

The intended unity among Christians is not based on the achievement of full agreement on all theological questions. Rather, it is based on a common membership in the church through the grace of God and is anchored by a common commitment to the centrality of Christ and the authority of the Word of God.

As individuals, we seek to remain humble and open to the daily instruction and leadership of the Holy Spirit. As a movement, the Church of God seeks always to allow itself to be reformed so that, by avoiding any development of the stagnation of rigid creed or inflexible structure, it can remain a pliable instrument in the hands of God.

We are privileged to have received the basic truth of Christ in the biblical revelation, but we realize that our understanding and application of that truth are always subject to the continuing ministry of the Holy Spirit in our midst. The nature of the church requires that our theological understandings and church-related organizations be used to build bridges of hope to the world and not walls of division among Christians.

WE BELIEVE [CHURCH OF GOD (ANDERSON, INDIANA)/ ANDERSON COLLEGE SCHOOL OF THEOLOGY] (continued)

Notes: *Of several attempts to summarize the distinctive doctrinal position of the noncreedal Church of God (Anderson, Indiana), that of the members of the faculty and staff of the Church's School of Theology is most significant. It was prepared at the time of the Church's centennial both as a tool for assisting outsiders to understand the Church and as a stimulus for reflection and thought for the Church's members.*

The Church of God is a conservative church in the Holiness tradition. Its statement affirms the definitive Holiness idea that believers can be sanctified by the Holy Spirit and thus established in perfect love and dominion over sin. The church has also championed a divine healing ministry.

Much of the School's statement concerns the nature of the church, a concern utmost in the thought of the founders. The Church of God has been one of the few conservative churches that has championed the cause of church unity and has not seen it based strictly on doctrinal unity. The church has interacted with modern Evangelicalism but has resisted accepting its definitions of the faith, especially its language about the authority of the Bible.

*   *   *

STATEMENT OF BELIEF (CHURCH OF THE NAZARENE/MID-AMERICA NAZARENE COLLEGE)

We believe in the Lord God Almighty, the Creator, and that in Him is perfect love, forgiveness and justice. Jesus Christ is His Son and in coming to earth provided for salvation and demonstrated the qualities of moral perfection for all humanity. The Holy Spirit reveals the truth of Christ's redemptive work, leads and directs in all our patterns of living, purifies our hearts, and empowers us for service.

Individuals are of infinite worth because they are creations of God. They are integrated and complex spiritual, physiological, psychological, and social beings. Their highest sense of achievement and satisfaction arises from a personal relationship to God and a comprehensive stewardship of life.

The Bible is God's inspired Word and provides the final authority for instruction and guidance in Christian living. Christ taught us to love God and love our neighbor as ourselves. Our concept of service to God and humanity is based on this belief. We further believe in the doctrine of entire sanctification and the dynamic life of perfect love as reflected in Wesleyan theology.

We believe that people function in a society and that laws are needed for the society to operate efficiently. The form of government and the laws developed in the society are important to the individual and the church. We believe that the American form of democratic government is the finest yet achieved. and fully support its ideals. The importance of the individual, the right of all persons to achieve, and the belief in guaranteed civil liberties are central to American heritage, and are in line with the teachings of the Bible.

We believe Christian education provides a foundation for leadership based on a sound philosophy of life, a personal relationship with God and responsible citizenship. We accept the importance of personal inspiration in the educative process and believe that models based on Christ as the master teacher are important in Christian education.

The goals and objectives of education at Mid-America Nazarene College are designed to harmonize with this statement of belief.

Notes: *Mid-America Nazarene College, Olathe, Kansas, is one of the schools sponsored by the Church of Nazarene. Its Statement of Belief summarizes the lengthy Articles of Religion of the Church but adds a lengthy statement on the Christian and society and on democratic government.*

*   *   *

STATEMENT OF BELIEF (CHURCH OF THE NAZARENE/NAZARENE THEOLOGICAL SEMINARY)

We believe:

1. In one God—the Father, Son, and Holy Spirit.

2. That the Old and New Testament Scriptures, given by plenary inspiration, contain all truth necessary to faith and Christian living.

3. That man is born with a fallen nature, and is, therefore, included to evil, and that continually.

4. That the finally impenitent are hopelessly and eternally lost.

5. That the atonement through Jesus Christ is for the whole human race; and that whosoever repents and believes on the Lord Jesus Christ is justified and regenerated and saved from the dominion of sin.

6. That believers are to be sanctified wholly, subsequent to regeneration, through faith in the Lord Jesus Christ.

7. That the Holy Spirit bears witness to the new birth, and also to the entire sanctification of believers.

8. That our Lord will return, the dead will be raised, and the final judgment will take place.

Notes: *The Nazarene Theological Seminary, Kansas City, Missouri, is the ministerial training school for the Church of* *the Nazarene. This brief statement summarizes the lengthy Articles of Religion of the Church.*

*   *   *

ARTICLES OF FAITH [EVANGELICAL CHRISTIAN CHURCH (WESLEYAN)]

I. THE HOLY TRINITY.

There is but one living and true God; the Maker and Preserver of all things visible and invisible. In unity in this Godhead there are three Persons of one substance, power and eternity: God, the Father; Jesus Christ, the Son; and the Holy Spirit (Holy Ghost). 1 Cor. 8:4-6; I John 5:6-8; John 15:26.

1. God, the Father: The Father is the supreme Person in the Godhead. He sent the Son and the Holy Spirit into the world. The penitent sinner is reconciled to the Father, and to Him pertains the worship of every believer. Gen. 1:26; Isa. 45:5, 6.

2. God, the Son: Jesus Christ, the only begotten Son of the Father, was conceived by the Holy Spirit, born of the Virgin Mary, very God and very Man. He suffered, died by crucifixion and was buried, becoming a sacrifice for both original depravity and sins committed, that He might reconcile mankind to God. Luke 1:27-35; Acts 4:12; Acts 13:23-39. Christ did truly rise from the dead. He ascended into heaven and at the right hand of the Father. He now is High Priest and Advocate. Matt. 28: 1-10; I Cor. 15:3-20; Acts 2:23, 24; Heb. 6:20.

3. God, the Holy Spirit: The Holy Spirit proceeding from the Father and sent by the Son, is of one substance, majesty and glory with the Father and the Son, very and eternal God. His work is to reprove and convict the world of sin, of righteousness, and of judgement; to regenerate those who repent of their sins and believe in the Lord Jesus Christ; to cleanse the children of God and endue them with power; to establish, comfort and lead them into all truth. Matt. 28:19; John 15:26; 16:8, 3:5-9; 16:13; Acts 1:8, 15:8, 9.

II. THE HOLY SCRIPTURES.

4. We believe the Scriptures of the Old and New Testaments to be verbally inspired of God, inerrant in the originals. They are the Word of God and the final authority for faith and conduct. II Tim. 3:15-17; Acts 17:11; II Peter 1:19-21.

III. MAN.

5. Man was created by God, in His own image and holiness and did not evolve from matter or from lower forms of life. Through wilful disobedience, Adam brought upon himself physical and spiritual death, thereby passing on to all posterity a sinful nature (Rom. 3:11-18), for which man becomes personally responsible to God at the age of accountability. Gen. 1:27; 2:17; 3:19; Rom. 3:10-12; 5:12-18.

IV. FREE WILL.

6. Man cannot save himself by his own will or works (Ephesians 2:8,9). God graciously employs the means of awakening his mind to a sense of sinfulness and extends the invitation "Whosoever will may come and take of the water of life freely" (Rev. 22:17; John 6:44, 65). God enables all who willingly turn from sin unto Him, to find pardon and cleansing. Rev. 3:20.

V. REGENERATION.

7. A sinner can, through God's grace, become a "new creature" III Cor. 5:17) in Christ Jesus. There are two steps: repentance and faith (Acts 20:21; Mark 1:15). Repentance (Luke 13:3; 5:32; Acts 3:19) is a godly sorrow for sin (II Cor. 7:9), a confession of sins (I John 1:9), a voluntary turning from sin (Isa. 55:7), a cease from sinning (I John 3:6, 9) and includes where necessary, restitution (Lk. 19:8). Faith (Heb. 11:1) means to place complete trust not in our own works of righteousness (Titus 3:5), but in the atonement of Christ (Isa. 53:5), our adequate and only means of salvation (Heb. 2:3).

8. God, by His gracious act of justification (Rom. 4:25), grants full pardon (Rom. 3:24), releasing us of all guilt and penalty of sins committed (Psa. 103:'12). In an act of regeneration, the believer is born again (John, 3:3), quickened (Eph. 2:1) and made to pass from death unto life (John 5:24). By divine adoption (Rom. 8:15), the believer becomes a child of God. This work of grace becomes a conscious reality and is an instantaneous experience, for God's Spirit bears witness with our spirit that we are the children of God (Rom. 8:16).

VI. ENTIRE SANCTIFICATION.

9. Every child of God (John 17:19, 20; Luke 11:13), is commanded to be sanctified wholly (1 Thess. 4:3-7). Entire sanctification is an instantaneous work of grace, subsequent to regeneration (John 17:9-17), obtained by faith in God's promise (Acts 1:8; 2:1-4; 15:8, 9). The experience is wrought by the baptism of the Holy Spirit (Acts 1:5) at which time the believer is cleansed from original sin (depravity) (I John 1:7, 9; Rom. 6:22; 11 Cor. 7:1; Roms. 6:6), filled with perfect love (Malt. 5:48; I Cor. 13; 1 John 4:17, 18), empowered for service (Acts 1:8), established spiritually and enabled to live a holy life (Heb. 12:14; 11 Tim. 2:21). Jesus provided for our sanctification (Heb. 13:12); we may experience it now (I Cor. 6:11); the Holy Spirit will bear witness to it (John 14:15-17) and spiritual growth results from it (II Peter 3:18).

VII. THE GIFTS OF THE SPIRIT.

10. Gifts are selected by the Holy Spirit (Rom. 12:6-8) and bestowed upon the believer (I Cor. 12) at His direction (I Cor. 12:11). These must be distinguished from the Gift of the Holy Spirit, Himself, Who is given in the experience of sanctification (Luke 11:13; Acts 2:38; 19:2).

The purpose of such spiritual gifts is that the believer may function as a true child of God in fulfilling his duties both within the Church and the world (Luke 24:49; I Peter 4:10, 11). They are not given for personal enjoyment, exhilaration or exploitation (Eph. 4:11-16). When present, these gifts must be carefully exercised in faith and love. The gifts of the Holy Spirit are many and work through the natural abilities and interests of the Christian. No one gift will be found in every believer (1 Cor. 12:28-30).

VIII. SECURITY IN CHRIST.

11. There is security for those who walk in the light (I John 1:7). God keeps those who trust in Him (Isaiah 26:3; 40:31; John 10:27-29). A consistent, established, victorious life is possible and should be the desired goal of every Christian. Our relationship to Christ is conditional (John 15:4-6) and is retained by faith (Gal. 3:11) and obedience (Matt. 7:21; I John 2:4, 5).

God's Word clearly rejects the practice of sin in the life of the believer (I John 3:8, 9; 5:18). We are commanded to live a holy life (Heb. 12:14; II Pet. 3:11, 14). Throughout our earthly existence, there is the possibility of falling or turning away from God (I Cor. 10:12; Ezek. 18:24-26; 1 Cor. 3:17; Heb. 2:1-3; 3:12-14). We need not fail of God's grace; but, by faith, prayer and humble obedience we may enjoy moment by moment cleansing and maintain a victorious relationship with God.

If a believer sins, he has an Advocate (I John 2:1). God has an abundance of mercy and will fully pardon and restore the repentant backslider (Psalm 51; Hosea 14:4; Jer. 3:22; Rev. 2:5).

IX. THE CHURCH.

12. The church is a divine institution (Matt. 16:18), a living organism (Eph. 2:14-22) and was inaugurated at Pentecost (Acts 2). It is composed of the body of believers, who have manifested faith in Christ as their Savior, and who have separated themselves from the world (John 17:6-19; II Cor. 6:14-18). Christ is the head (Col. 1:18). He loved the church and gave Himself for it (Eph. 5:25-27). The church is described as the Bride of Christ (Rev. 19:7-9; 21:9), a building or temple (Eph. 2:21), and a body (Eph. 1:22, 23). The mission of the church is the proclamation of the gospel (Acts 1:8) throughout the world (Mark 16:15).

The organized church is for the perfecting of saints, the work of the ministry, edifying and unity of the body (Matt. 16:18; Eph. 4:11-16; 5:25-27).

X. THE ORDINANCES.

13. Baptism. Water baptism is a Christian sacrament, not essential to salvation from sin or a test of membership. It follows conversion (Acts 2:38) and is an outward witness or sign that one has truly decided to follow Christ and be His disciple. Single immersion, in the Name of the Father, the Son, and the Holy Spirit, is the recommended mode.

Each new convert should be encouraged to identify himself with his Lord (Matt. 3:13-15) publicly in Christian baptism. (Matt. 3:13-17; Acts 8:36-39; Romans 6:3, 4).

14. The Lord's Supper. This sacrament was instituted by Christ (Matt. 26:26-29; Luke 22:17-20). It should be observed periodically (I Cor. 10:16, 17) in remembrance of Jesus, who suffered and died to bring salvation. Those who participate should examine their hearts, lest they partake unworthily (I Cor. 11:27-29). Each time a person keeps this ordinance, he shows forth the Lord's death until He comes again. (I Cor. 11:26).

15. Other Observances, Christian practices like, ''washing the saints' feet'' (John 13:1-17; I Tim. 5:10), ''breaking of bread'' (Luke 24:35, Acts 2:42, 46) and ''fasting'' (Mark 2:18-20), may be observed when appropriate. Participation should be voluntary, in humility and love, in the Spirit of Christ, and for the edification of the saints.

XI. DEDICATION OF CHILDREN.

16. Children under the age of accountability are saved in the vicarious atonement of Jesus Christ, and they need neither water baptism nor the sacraments. However, we believe that parents should present their children, in their state of innocency, to the Lord in dedication, to show concern for the child's spiritual well-being (I Sam. 1:21-28; Luke 2:21, 22; 18:15-17). Parents thereby obligate themselves to rear their children in the nurture and admonition of the Lord (Eph. 6:4). The church will share in concern through prayer.

XII. DIVINE HEALING.

17. The privilege to seek divine intervention for the healing of physical ailments is scriptural (James 5:14-16). The disciples engaged in the ministry of healing (Mark 6:13), and the Apostle Paul refers to it (1 Cor. 12:9). The purpose of divine healing is to exalt Christ and glorify God. Many Christians have shown the sufficiency of God's grace in the patient bearing of physical handicaps and illnesses, when in certain instances the desired healing had been withheld. (11 Cor. 12:7-10).

XIII. THE SUPPORT OF THE CHURCH.

18. God's plan for the support of the church is through the systematic giving of tithes and offerings (Mal. 3:8-10). This method should be taught and practiced in the church. As God prospers and blesses him, the Christian should give proportionately, even above the tithe, as faithful stewards (11 Cor. 9:6, 7; Luke 6:38; 1 Cor. 9:14). Christians should be encouraged to include the church in their wills.

XIV. THE FAMILY.

19. The family is the foundation of our society, established by God, through the sacred rite of marriage (Gen. 2:24). Christians should sincerely seek God's guidance before entering into marriage, heeding the Biblical admonition ''Be ye not unequally yoked together with unbelievers'' (11 Cor. 6:14). God intends that marriage be for life (Mark

10:2-9). Only in the event of sexual sin is there Biblical allowance for divorce (Matt. 5:32, I Cor. 6:9-11; Gal. 5:19; Matt. 19:3-9). Christians should be charitable toward those who have become involved in marital or family breakdown.

XV. THE CHRISTIAN LIFE.

20. The Christian life is governed by two commandments: (a) to love the Lord our God with all the heart; and, (b) to love our neighbor as ourself (Ex. 20:3-6; Mark 12:28-31; Romans 13:8-10; Luke 10:27). In the outworking of these laws, we are expected to do good to all men, especially to those who are of the household of faith (Gal. 6:10). Good works characterized the Christian life, but do not merit salvation, for we are saved by grace (James 2:14-26; Eph. 2:1-9).

21. Self denial is a requirement for mature Christian living. To be "temperate in all things" (I Cor. 9:25), includes total abstinence from that which is wrong, either in fact or in appearance, and moderation in things themselves right or useful (1 Thess. 5:22; I Cor. 10:31).

22. God's Word teaches us to respect His Name (Ex. 20:7) and His Day (Ex. 20:8-10). We believe it to be the duty of Christians to use their influence in favor of a more complete recognition of laws recognizing and protecting the Lord's Day, and to avoid activities which do not contribute to the moral or spiritual ends of the holy day (Mark 2:27; Isa. 58:13, 14; Rev. 1:10).

23. The Christian Life is enlarged by participation in every means of grace, including: public worship (Heb. 10:25); family prayer (Gen. 18:19); Bible study and research (II Tim. 2:15), and other spiritual activities (Deut. 6:7; Acts 2:42; 17:11).

24. Any conformity to "the spirit of this age" must be discouraged. It is therefore necessary that dress be in accordance with the standards of modesty that properly portray an adornment of a meek and quiet spirit (Prov. 29:23; 1 John 2:15-17; 1 Pet. 3:3, 4; I Tim. 2:9, 10) that we refrain from membership in secret, oath-bound societies (Matt. 5:34-36; II Cor. 6:14-17; James 5:12; John 18:20); and that we avoid any participation in practices relating to Satanism, spiritism or any form of occultism (I Tim. 4:1; 1 Cor. 10:20; Eph. 6:10-13; Lev. 20:6). It is vitally important that we apply ourselves to careful use of our time and talents, engaging in the edification of one another (Eph. 2:18-22; 4:1-3; 4:11-16; 1 Pet. 2:9-10).

XVI. SOCIAL CONCERN.

The Christian is a citizen of two worlds and therefore exhibits Godly wisdom in influencing secular society toward an acceptance of the principles taught by Jesus Christ (Phil. 3:20).

25. The Bible recognizes lawful civil authority and ordinance, and encourages everyone to faithful obedience to such authority in the state, the church and the home, unless in direct conflict with the teachings of the Word (1 Tim. 2:1, 2).

26. The manufacture, sale and use of alcoholic beverages, tobacco or harmful drugs is in opposition to Scriptural teaching. Therefore each Christian should cleanse himself from all such filthiness of the flesh and spirit, perfecting holiness in the fear of God (11 Cor. .7:1; Prov. 20:1; Eph. 5: 18).

27. We recognize the dignity of equality inherent to all persons, and oppose material or spiritual restriction based on factors such as race, sex, color, national origin, and the like (James 2:1-9; Acts 17:26).

28. National differences should be settled by arbitration, for war results only in economic catastrophe, in personal tragedy, and in national humiliation. We urge holy men everywhere to pray for peace (Psa. 34:14; Isa. 2:4; Romans 12:18). It is sometimes necessary to answer the call of the nation to military service, but where this is in conflict with personal conviction and conscience (Acts 5:29), we support the effort of the individual to serve his country in a non-combatant capacity (I Pet. 2:13, 14).

29. As occasion arises, we "affirm" to the veracity of our statements rather than resort to non-scriptural types of oath-taking (Matt. 5:33-37; James 5:12).

XVII. THE CALL TO THE MINISTRY.

30. We believe a divine call is necessary for entry into the ministry of the Gospel. In this sense, a "call" is a summons from God to engage in the service of His choosing. In harmony with such a divine call, it is the responsibility of the individual to plan personal preparation and continual self-improvement (II Tim. 2: 1 5), in order to labor effectively for His cause, to prosper His church, and to be successful in winning souls to Him (Matt. 10; Romans 10:14, 15). It is the duty of each church to "Pray ye the Lord of the harvest, that He will send forth laborers into His harvest" (Luke 10:2; Acts 13:1-3).

XVIII. THE SECOND COMING OF THE LORD.

31. Jesus Christ will come again (Zech. 14:1-4; John 14:3). His return will be personal and pre-millennial; it may occur any moment (Matt. 24:32-34; Acts 1:9-11; Matt. 25:13). At His appearing, the church will be raptured. All who sleep in Jesus will be resurrected and all living saints translated, caught up to meet the Lord in the air (I Thess. 4:13-18). While the church is at the marriage supper of the Lamb (Rev. 19:7-9), great tribulation will be on earth (Matt. 24:21). After this, the Son of Man will appear with His saints to reign in righteousness and peace, one thousand years (Rev. 20:2-4; Isa. 2:2-4; Micah. 4:1-7). There will be a general resurrection of the unjust dead and all will appear for the great white throne judgement (Rev. 20:11-15; Matt. 25:31-46). After these things, "we, according to His promise, look for a new heaven and a new earth wherein dwelleth righteousness" (11 Pet. 3:13).

XIX. HELL.

32. Hell is a place and state of the damned (Psa. 9:17). It was prepared for the devil and fallen angels (Matt. 8:29; 25:41;

ARTICLES OF FAITH [EVANGELICAL CHRISTIAN CHURCH (WESLEYAN)] (continued)

11 Pet. 2:4; Jude 6). Men, who by personal choice, refuse or neglect God's provision of salvation, will go there (Luke 16:24; 13:3, 5; Rev. 21:8). Punishment and torment, without end, await those who are lost. (Isa. 33:14; Matt. 8:12; 25:46; Rev. 14:11; 19:20; 20:10).

XX. HEAVEN.

33. Heaven is the abode of the Godhead (Psa. 11:4; Matt. 6:9), the holy angels (Malt. 24:36), and the future home of those made righteous and holy through the blood of Jesus Christ (John 14:1-3; Heb. 12:14; Rev. 7:9-14). It is a holy place (Isa. 57:15), a better country (Heb. 11:16; 1 Cor. 2:9), a place of peace and happiness (Rev. 21:3, 4). The spirits of those who died in the faith are now in the presence of God (Luke 23:43), but we who are alive look steadfastly towards heaven (Heb. 11:10, 13; II Cor. 5:1-4; Matt 5:12), our desired and eternal home.

Notes: *The Evangelical Christian Church (Wesleyan), originally known as the Heavenly Recruit Association, was founded in 1884. It is one of the older Holiness churches. Its Articles of Faith are a concise statement of Evangelical Protestant Faith with a lengthy paragraph on Entire Sanctification, the distinctive teaching of the Holiness movement. The Church believes in divine healing, tithing, and the premillennial return of Jesus. The Church practices two ordinances, baptism and the Lord's Supper. Children are not baptized, but are presented by their parents to be dedicated to the Lord. Foot washing is an optional practice.*

*   *   *

ALDERSGATE COLLEGE BELIEVES (FREE METHODIST CHURCH OF NORTH AMERICA/ ALDERSGATE COLLEGE)

Aldersgate College accepts the Twenty-Two Articles of Religion found in The Book of Discipline of the Free Methodist Church. Within these articles, along with other matters of importance, we express our belief in:

• One God in Trinity

• Jesus Christ as the only Savior

• The person and work of the Holy Spirit

• The Authority of the Holy Scriptures

• Salvation through grace by faith

• The entire sanctification of believers

• The return of Christ in triumph

Notes: *This brief statement from a college sponsored by the Free Methodist Church summarizes the lengthy Articles of Religion of the Church.*

*   *   *

STATEMENT (FREE METHODIST CHURCH OF NORTH AMERICA/GREENVILLE COLLEGE)

The educational philosophy of the college includes, among others, statements about the nature of God, human life, and the universe, and is shaped by Biblical revelation. God is understood to be personal, the creator and ruler of an orderly emerging universe, through which He expressed his eternal purposes, meaning, creativity, and loving care. We learn about the universe through observation and thought but perceive its ultimate meaning from our understanding of God. The fullest information concerning God and his purposes comes from the revelation of Himself in redemptive acts—both in human history and in his incarnation in Jesus Christ—recorded and interpreted in the Bible. Knowledge of God is also discovered in man's scholarly and disciplined search for truth. One also learns about God through one's experience in Christian conversion and through the Holy Spirit as the divine presence in human life.

We are estranged from God and neighbor and must be reconciled to both through Faith in Jesus Christ in order to reach wholeness of being. We have rational faculties; we desire to know and find satisfaction in knowing. We are social in nature and circumstance and thus ought to live meaningfully as a functional part of society. At the same time, we ought to live redemptively, seeking to effect commitment to Christ and to the Christian world view.

Proceeding from these assumptions are the objectives sought by Greenville College. They include both spiritual and academic aims to be achieved in a unified process ministering to the whole person. As an institution cooperating in the work of the Church, Greenville College is urgently concerned to point all under its influence to Christ, to Foster in them a sound and fervent Christian life, and to summon them to participation in the redemptive mission of Jesus Christ. As an institution of learning, it recognizes that all of its instructional disciplines and campus programs, while reviewed from within the framework of Christian belief, are to contribute to the achievement of its objectives. The college resolves that the quality of its instruction shall be rigorous, scholarly, humane, and pedagogically sound. The college recognizes that as faith without works is dead, so knowledge without personal and social application is inert and unproductive of human good.

Notes: *Greenville College, Greenville, Illinois, is sponsored by the Free Methodist Church. This statement attempts to* *relate the theology of the Church to the school's educational mission.*

* * *

DEFINING OUR CHRISTIAN MISSION (FREE METHODIST CHURCH OF NORTH AMERICA/ SEATTLE PACIFIC UNIVERSITY)

In affirming the great tenets of the Christian faith, Seattle Pacific stands unequivocally for (1) the inspiration of the Old and New Testaments, (2) the deity of Christ, (3) the need and efficacy of the atonement, (4) the new birth as a divine work carried out in the repentant heart by the Holy Spirit, (5) the necessity and glorious possibility for the Spirit-filled Christian to live a life of victory over sin, and (6) the personal return of the Lord Jesus Christ.

Notes: *Seattle Pacific University, Seattle, Washington, is sponsored by the Free Methodist Church. Its mission statement attempts to relate the church's key beliefs to the school's educational task.*

* * *

STATEMENT (FREE METHODIST CHURCH OF NORTH AMERICA/SPRING ARBOR COLLEGE)

The college is thoroughly committed to evangelical Christian doctrine and standards of conduct. In accepting the fundamentals of the Christian faith, the college stands unequivocally for the inspiration of the Old and New Testaments, the deity of Christ, the need and efficacy of the atonement, the new birth as a divine work wrought in the repentant heart by the Holy Spirit, the need and glorious possibility of the born-again Christian being so cleansed from sin and filled with the love of God by the Holy Spirit that one can and should live a life of victory over sin.

Notes: *This brief statement by Spring Arbor College, Spring Arbor, Michigan, summarizes the position of its sponsor, the Free Methodist Church.*

* * *

DOCTRINAL STATEMENT [MISSIONARY CHURCH, INC. (U.S.)/FORT WAYNE BIBLE COLLEGE]

In order to maintain unity in the College and to hold consistently to the distinctive teaching to which the Bible College is committed, it is required that all full-time teachers and staff members subscribe to the following articles of faith:

1. The plenary inspiration of the Holy Scriptures, which results in their being God's written word to men and therefore of divine authority and without error in the original manuscripts. 1 Thess. 2:13; 11 Tim. 3:16; 11 Peter 1:20, 21.

2. The eternal existence of one God in three Persons: Father, Son, and Holy Spirit. Deut. 6:4, 5; Matt. 28:19; 11 Cor. 13:14. Cf. Matt. 3:16, 17 and John 14:16, 17.

3. The deity, the virgin birth, the sinless humanity, and the miracles of Jesus Christ. John 1:1, 3; 2:11; Luke 1:35; Matt. 1:20-23; Heb. 4:15.

4. The personality of the Holy Spirit and His present ministry of convicting and regenerating sinful man and of indwelling and empowering believers for service. John 3:5-8; 16:7-15; Rom. 8:9; Acts 1:8.

5. The fall of man by voluntary transgression in the Garden of Eden, by which he became depraved and plunged the entire race of man into a state of sin from which he can be saved only by the grace of God. Gen. 3:1-6; Rom. 3:9-18; 5:12-19; Eph. 2:1-3, 8, 9.

6. The substitutionary death, the bodily resurrection, and the ascension of Jesus Christ. Mark 10:45; Luke 24:39; Acts 1:9-11; 1 Peter 2:24.

7. The necessity of the new birth for entrance into the Kingdom of God and for receiving eternal life. John 3:3-7; Titus 3:5-7.

8. The conditioning of salvation solely upon repentance toward God and faith in the Lord Jesus Christ. Luke 13:3; Acts 16:31; 17:30; Eph. 2:8-1 0.

9. The filling with the Holy Spirit as a crisis experience after the new birth, conditioned upon entire yieldedness and faith and resulting in sanctification, victorious living, and more fruitful service. Acts 1:8; 2:4; Rom. 6:12, 13, 19; 12:l; Eph. 5:18.

10. Practical holiness and the maintenance of good works. Rom. 6:11; 12:2; Gal. 5:22, 23; Eph. 2: 1 0; 4:22-32; James 2:1 7, 18, 26.

11. The provision in the atonement for the divine healing of the body to be appropriated on the basis of believing prayer. Isa. 53:4, 5; Matt. 8:16, 17; James 5:13-18.

12. The invisible and universal church as an organism composed of all believers in the Lord Jesus Christ who have been called out from the world and have been vitally united by faith to Christ, its living Head and sovereign Lord. Matt. 16:18; 1 Cor. 12:12-27; Eph. 1:22, 23.

13. The visible and local church as an organized body of believers in Christ who are voluntarily joined together and who meet at regular times for teaching in the Word,

DOCTRINAL STATEMENT [MISSIONARY CHURCH, INC. (U.S.)/ FORT WAYNE BIBLE COLLEGE] (continued)

fellowship with the saints, observance of the ordinances, administration of discipline, exercise in prayer, and participation in public worship and evangelism. Acts 2:41, 42, 47.

14. The reality and personality of Satan. Job 1:6-14; Matt. 4:1-11; 11 Cor. 11:14. I Peter 5:8; Rev. 20:1-3, 7-10.

15. The degenerating course of this age and this world under the power of Satan. John 16:11; 11 Cor. 4:3, 4; Eph. 2:2. Cf. Eph. 6:12.

16. The duty of the church to give the gospel to all men whose salvation is dependent upon personal faith in Christ. Matt. 28:18-20; Acts 1:8; 4:12; 16:31.

17. The apostasy of the latter times culminating in the Great Tribulation and the second coming of Jesus Christ. Matt. 24:15-31; 1 Tim. 4:1.3; II Tim. 4:1 -4; II Thess. 2:3-1 0.

18. The future resurrection and immortality of the bodies of believers. Rom. 8:23; I Cor. 15.

19. The personal, bodily, and premillennial return of Jesus Christ to this earth. Matt. 24:27-31; Matt. 24:37-51; 25:31-46; Acts 1:10, 11; I Thess. 4:16, 17.

20. The literal and personal reign of Christ together with His saints on this earth during the millennium. I Cor. 15:23-28; Rev. 5:9, 1 0; 20:1-7.

21. The establishment of a new heaven and a new earth in which the righteous and righteousness will abide forever. Isa. 65:17; 66:22; 11 Peter 3:13; Rev. 21:1-22:7.

22. Eternal life for believers and eternal punishment for unbelievers. Dan. 12:1, 2; Matt. 25:46; Mark 9:43-48; Rev. 20:11-15; 21; 22:1-7.

Notes: *Fort Wayne Bible College, Fort Wayne, Indiana, is sponsored by the Missionary Church. Its lengthy Doctrinal Statement reflects the influence of both the Holiness movement and modern Evangelicalism. The school, as does the Missionary Church, believes in sanctification, a second special work of the Holy Spirit in the life of a believer by which s/he is filled with the Holy Spirit. The school also affirms the inerrancy and plenary inspiration of the Bible.*

*   *   *

PURPOSE EXPRESSED IN CREED (SALVATION ARMY/CATHERINE BOOTH BIBLE COLLEGE)

Administrative personnel and instructional faculty members of the Catherine Booth Bible College are committed to empha-

sizing a Christian life-style of faith, service, scholarship and lifelong development. While the College is open to and welcomes students of any denomination who profess a personal faith in Jesus Christ, students should understand that the College's emphasis reflects the theological position of the sponsoring denomination, the Salvation Army, and that its doctrinal beliefs will have implications on the academic, social, and spiritual activities of the College. Catherine Booth Bible College administrative and instructional faculty are:

Christians who

—believe that the Scriptures of the Old and New Testaments were given by inspiration of God; and that they only constitute the divine rule of Christian faith and practice;

—believe there is only one God, who is infinitely perfect - the Creator, Preserver and Governor of all things - and who is the only proper object of religious worship;

—believe that there are three persons in the Godhead - the Father, the Son and the Holy Ghost - undivided in essence and coequal in power and glory;

—believe that in the person of Jesus Christ the divine and human natures are united so that He is truly and properly God and truly and properly man;

—believe that our first parents were created in a state of innocency but, by their disobedience, they lost their purity and happiness; and that in consequence of their fall all men have become sinners, totally depraved, and as such are justly exposed to the wrath of God;

—believe that the Lord Jesus Christ has, by His suffering and death, made an atonement for the whole world, so that whosoever will may be saved;

—believe that repentance toward God, faith in our Lord Jesus Christ and regeneration by the Holy Spirit are necessary to salvation;

—believe that we are justified by grace, through faith in our Lord Jesus Christ. and that he that believeth hath the witness in himself;

—believe that continuance in a state of salvation depends upon continued obedient faith in Christ;

—believe that it is the privilege of all believers to be 'wholly sanctified', and that their 'whole spirit and soul and body' may 'be preserved blameless unto the coming of our Lord Jesus Christ' (I Thessalonians 5:23);

—believe in the immortality of the soul; in the resurrection of the body; in the general judgement at the end of the world; in the eternal happiness of the righteous; and in the endless punishment of the wicked.

Notes: *The Catherine Booth Bible College, Winnipeg, Manitoba, is sponsored by the Salvation Army, a Holiness denomination most known for its strong social vision and activity on behalf of the less fortunate. The school's statement summa-*

rizes the church's basic doctrinal stance. It does not mention the Army's most unique opinion concerning the nonobservance of the sacraments.

*   *   *

DOCTRINAL STATEMENT (WESLEYAN CHURCH/ BARTLESVILLE WESLEYAN COLLEGE)

WE BELIEVE:

1. That the Bible, composed of the Old and New Testaments, is the inspired and inerrant Word of God and is the supreme and final authority in faith and life.

2. That there is one God, eternally existing in three Persons: Father, Son and Holy Spirit.

3. In Jesus Christ as truly God and truly man, and in His virgin birth, His vicarious death, His bodily resurrection and His promised second coming.

4. In the personality of the Holy Spirit, and that His ministry is to reveal Christ unto man.

5. That God created man and the universe by special operation of divine power.

6. In the fall of man and the consequent sinful nature of all mankind which necessitates a divine atonement.

7. In justification by grace through faith and in regeneration by the Holy Spirit, who makes the penitent believer a new creature in Christ. The believer may through disobedience fall from grace, and unless he repents, be eternally lost.

8. That entire sanctification is an act of divine grace wrought in the believer through an act of the Holy Spirit whereby He takes full possession, cleanses, and equips for service on condition of total surrender and obedient faith.

9. That the gifts of the Spirit are given to believers as God wills for the purpose of edifying and strengthening believers, and are not in any sense the evidence of the Spirit's fullness nor are they necessary for salvation. Speaking or praying in an unknown tongue is a questionable practice and is often divisive to the Body of Christ.

10. In the personal existence of Satan.

11. That the Scriptures plainly teach the bodily resurrection of the just and the unjust, the everlasting happiness of the saved, an the everlasting and conscious suffering of the lost.

12. That all true Christians, assisted by the Holy Spirit, give evidence of a true faith by their good works and social concern.

Notes: *Bartlesville Wesleyan College, Bartlesville, Oklahoma, is sponsored by the Wesleyan Church. Its Doctrinal Statement affirms the Church's stance on entire sanctification. It also manifests some influence of the modern Evangelical movement in its affirmation of the inerrancy of the Bible.*

*   *   *

DOCTRINAL STATEMENT (WESLEYAN CHURCH/ CENTRAL WESLEYAN COLLEGE)

WE BELIEVE:

The Holy Scriptures contain all things necessary to salvation; so that whatsoever is not read therein, nor may be proved thereby, is not to be required of any man, that it should be believed as an article of faith, or be thought requisite or necessary to salvation. We do understand the books of the Old and New Testaments to constitute the Holy Scriptures. These Scriptures we hold to be the inspired and infallibly written Word of God, fully inerrant in their original manuscripts and superior to all human authority.

That there is one God, eternally self-existent, and in the Unity of this Godhead there are three Persons: the Father, the Son, and the Holy Spirit.

That Jesus Christ is the only begotten Son of God, conceived by the Holy Spirit, born of the Virgin Mary, very God and very man; and the only and sufficient mediator between God and man, who by the sacrifice of Himself provides atonement for the whole human race, and that whosoever believeth in Him shall be saved.

That man was created in the image of God, but through transgression fell from that holy state, incurred spiritual death, became depraved, and is inclined to do evil and that continually. But by the grace of God working in man and with man, he may by faith in the merit of our Lord and Savior Jesus Christ be justified and regenerated in nature, so that he is delivered from the power of sin and thus through the grace of God enabled to love and serve Him with the will and affections of the heart. All who reject the grace of God are lost.

That the Holy Spirit is a Divine Person, the Executive of the God-head, whose mission is to reveal Christ to man and to administer the Estate of Grace to all who truly believe; and that His special mission to the believer is to cleanse the heart from all sin, whether inherited or acquired, thus enabling him to love God with all his heart and his neighbor as himself.

That Jesus Christ rose from the dead, appeared on earth in a glorified bodily form; that He ascended to the right hand of God to occupy the Mediatorial Throne; that He will return to earth at God's appointed time; and that the blessed hope of His

DOCTRINAL STATEMENT (WESLEYAN CHURCH/ CENTRAL WESLEYAN COLLEGE) (continued)

return is a powerful incentive to holy living and to world evangelism.

That there is a conscious existence after death; everlasting happiness for the saved and everlasting woe for the lost.

Notes: *Central Wesleyan College, Central, South Carolina, is sponsored by the Wesleyan Church, and this Doctrinal Statement is generally in accord with the Articles of Religion of the Wesleyan Church. The Statement also shows the influence of the modern Evangelical movement in its affirmation of the inerrancy of the Bible.*

*　　*　　*

DOCTRINAL STATEMENT (WESLEYAN CHURCH/ HOUGHTON COLLEGE)

We believe that the Scriptures of the Old and New Testaments are fully inspired of God, and inerrant in the original writings, and that they are of supreme and final authority for faith and practice.

We believe that there is one God, eternally existing in three persons: Father, Son and Holy Spirit.

We believe that God created man and the entire universe by special operation of divine power.

We believe in the fall of man and the consequent sinful nature of all mankind which necessitates a divine atonement.

We believe in Jesus Christ as truly God and truly man, and in His virgin birth, His matchless teachings, His vicarious death, His bodily resurrection, and His promised second coming.

We believe in justification by grace through faith and in regeneration by the Holy Spirit, who makes the penitent believer a new creature in Christ and commences His lifelong sanctifying work.

We believe that the Christian may be filled with the Holy Spirit, or sanctified wholly, as a definite act of divine grace wrought in the heart of the believer to take full possession, cleanse and equip for service on condition of total surrender and obedient faith.

We believe in the personal existence of Satan.

We believe in the bodily resurrection of the dead—of the saved to everlasting blessedness and of the lost to everlasting punishment.

Notes: *Houghton College, Houghton, New York, is sponsored by the Wesleyan Church, and this Doctrinal Statement is generally in accord with the Articles of Religion of the Wesleyan Church. It also shows the influence of the modern Evangelical movement in its affirmation of the inerrancy of the Bible.*

*　　*　　*

Twentieth-Century Holiness

DOCTRINE (CHURCHES OF CHRIST IN CHRISTIAN UNION/CIRCLEVILLLE BIBLE COLLEGE)

We believe in one God; self-existent in three Persons, co-equal and co-eternal; Father, Son, and Holy Spirit.

We believe in the Bible, God's infallible Word, fully inspired by the Holy Spirit, the supreme authority for faith and practice.

We believe in the deity of Jesus Christ, who became man, being conceived of the Holy Spirit and born of a virgin. He lived in a sinless life and died a substitutionary death as a complete sacrifice for the sins of all mankind. He arose bodily from the dead and ascended to the right hand of the Father where He is now our interceding High Priest.

We believe that the Holy Spirit is a Divine Person who reveals Christ, both in a ministry to the world by restraining evil and by convicting of sin, and in a ministry to the Church by indwelling, empowering, guiding, teaching all Christians.

We believe that man was made in the image and likeness of God and by transgression incurred guilt before God, depravity of soul, and spiritual death.

We believe in the universal atonement Christ provided for all mankind and that they who do repent and believe on Him are justified and regenerated from the guilt and practice of sin.

We believe in entire sanctification as a definite crisis experience subsequent to regeneration. It is wrought on the basis of faith and consecration through the infilling of the Holy Spirit by which the believer is cleansed from all sin and to which the Spirit testifies.

We believe in the progressive growth in grace toward Christian maturity through a consistent Christian life of good works which springs from faith in God and obedience to His Word. This growth we believe to be a necessary complement to the above mentioned crisis experience.

We believe in the true universal Church as the Body of Christ and Temple of the Holy Spirit. It is composed of all true believers in Christ. It was created by Him for worship and fellowship and is commissioned by Him to publish the Gospel to all the world.

We believe in the personal return of Christ who shall come with power and great glory to gather the Church to Himself, to establish His millennial kingdom, and to judge the quick and the dead.

We believe in the resurrection of the just, who shall enter into an actual eternal heaven, and the resurrection of the unjust, who shall go away into an actual and eternal hell.

Notes: *Circleville Bible College, Circleville, Ohio, is sponsored by the Churches of Christ in Christian Union, a Holiness church. Its statement of Doctrine reflects this Holiness perspective in its affirmation of entire sanctification as a filling of the Holy Spirit leading to the believer being cleansed from sin.*

*   *   *

Glenn Griffith Movement

DOCTRINAL STATEMENT (BIBLE MISSIONARY CHURCH/BIBLE MISSIONARY INSTITUTE)

The doctrines taught in the Bible Missionary Institute are given in the Manual of the Bible Missionary Church and may be summarized thus:

1. That the Holy Scriptures were given by divine inspiration and are the Word of God and contain all things necessary to man's salvation.

2. That God the Father is the supreme Person in the Godhead, to Whom the Son and Holy Ghost, though of equal essence, are subordinate in office.

3. That Jesus Christ, the only begotten Son of God, the Second Person of the Trinity, was eternally one with the Father; that He was conceived by the Holy Ghost and was born of the Virgin Mary; that He died for our sins both actual and original, arose from the dead and ascended into Heaven, where He is making intercession for us.

4. That the Holy Ghost, the Third Person of the Trinity, proceeds from the Father and the Son as the true and eternal God, of one substance, majesty and glory with the Father and Son.

5. That all are born with the carnal mind which continues to exist after regeneration until destroyed by the Baptism with the Holy Ghost.

6. That justification, regeneration, and adoption are simultaneous in the experience of seekers after God and are obtained upon the condition of faith in the merits of the shed blood of Jesus, preceded by repentance; and that to this work the Holy Spirit bears witness.

7. That entire sanctification is provided by the blood of Jesus; is wrought instantaneously by faith, preceded by entire consecration; and to this work and state of grace the Holy Spirit bears witness.

8. That the Coming of Christ for His saints will be premillennial.

9. That there will be a resurrection both of the just and unjust and a future judgment according to the deeds done in this life.

10. That the first day of the week should be observed as the Christian Sabbath.

11. That the two sacraments of Christian Baptism and the Lord's Supper should be observed by the Church until Jesus comes again.

12. That the Bible teaches the doctrine of divine healing.

Notes: *The Bible Missionary Institute is a school sponsored by the Bible Missionary Church. Its Doctrinal Statement summarizes the lengthy statement of the Church. It affirms sanctification as an instantaneous work of the Holy Spirit in the life of the believer, the premillennial second coming of Jesus Christ, and divine healing.*

*   *   *

DOCTRINAL STATEMENT (PILGRIM HOLINESS CHURCH OF NEW YORK AND WESLEYAN HOLINESS ASSOCIATION OF CHURCHES/GOD'S BIBLE SCHOOL)

1. We believe that the Bible is the Word of God. We believe that "holy men of old spoke as they were moved by the Holy Ghost," so that what they wrote was under direct inspiration of the Holy Spirit and therefore is the inerrant, infallible Word of God, which is the only and sufficient guide to life, belief and conduct.

2. We believe in one eternal, almighty God who exists in a trinity of persons: the Father, the Son, and the Holy Ghost.

3. We believe in the deity of Jesus Christ, the second Person of the Divine Trinity, who became incarnate to provide an atonement for sin through His death on the cross. We believe that He arose from the dead and ascended into heaven where He ever lives to make intercession for those who come unto God by Him.

4. We believe that the atoning work of Jesus Christ has provided salvation for the lost human race and that this salvation is for whosoever will come to Him.

In appropriating this salvation, the person who believes in Jesus Christ with truly repentant heart is justified from his past sins and is made a new creature in Christ Jesus, thereby being enabled to live above the practice of sin.

We also believe there is a second crisis in the provision of salvation whereby the person who has been justified may also be sanctified by faith. This experience of entire sanctification is wrought instantaneously by the baptism with the Holy Ghost whereby the heart of the believer is cleansed from all inner sin.

DOCTRINAL STATEMENT (PILGRIM HOLINESS CHURCH OF NEW YORK AND WESLEYAN HOLINESS ASSOCIATION OF CHURCHES/GOD'S BIBLE SCHOOL) (continued)

We believe that the evidence of this experience is not any supernatural gift, but an inner witness that the heart has been purified from sin. We believe this experience of entire sanctification can only be maintained by a walk of obedience and faith.

5. We believe that there are certain duties and privileges which accompany the experience and the life of salvation.

    a. We believe that the person who belongs to Christ ought to show a transformation of life by separation from all evil and from worldly attitudes and practices which would prove to be impediments to his testimony and detrimental to spiritual life.

    b. We believe that it is the responsibility of all Christians to earnestly pray and labor for the salvation of the lost. Such missionary concern reaches out in soul-saving efforts at home and in passion for the salvation of those in distant lands.

    c. We believe in the Christian duty and privilege of prayer. The prayer life includes intercession for the lost, petition for the supply of needs for the individual and for the progress of the work of God, and thanksgiving and praise for blessings received from God. We also believe that God heals the physical body in response to the prayer of faith as promised in James 5.

6. We believe that Christ will personally return to this earth to reign according to His purpose. We believe that the rapture of His church will precede His second coming and can take place at any time. We also believe that His second coming will be pre-millennial.

Notes: *God's Bible School is a Holiness Bible college sponsored by several conservative Holiness groups including the Pilgrim Holiness Church of New York and the Wesleyan Holiness Association of Churches. Its Doctrinal Statement reflects a traditional Holiness perspective. There is also a strong statement on the inerrancy of the Bible.*

*　　*　　*

Holiness Organizations

DOCTRINAL STATEMENT (JAPAN EVANGELISTIC BAND)

Faith in our crucified, risen and ascended Lord Jesus Christ, the eternal Son of God who saves His people from their sins

(Matt. 1:21), baptizes with the Holy Spirit (John 1:33), is their present Advocate in heaven (Heb. 8:6), and is coming again for His waiting people (Phil. 3:20).

The above is based on the following scriptural truths:

a. The plenary inspiration of the Old and New Testaments as originally given, and their authority and sufficiency in all matters of faith and conduct.

b. A new birth by the Holy Spirit, received by faith on the ground of Christ's atonement (John 3:3,5; Titus 3:5,7).

c. A full salvation from sin and separation unto God, and a true union with Him through faith in our Lord and Savior Jesus Christ.

d. Sanctification as a work of grace in the heart of the believer (I Thess. 5:23; Rom. 6:6, 10-15), embracing heart cleansing (Acts 15:9), the filling of the Holy Spirit (Eph. 5:18), the indwelling of Christ (Eph. 3:17), and the perfecting of holiness in the fear of God (II Cor. 7:1).

Notes: *The Japan Evangelistic Band, founded in 1903, is a foreign mission sending agency operating within the Holiness tradition. Its brief Doctrinal Statement affirms the unique Holiness position of sanctification as a second experience of the Holy Spirit that brings internal cleansing and a perfection in holiness.*

*　　*　　*

ARTICLES OF FAITH (LONG FORM) (OMS INTERNATIONAL)

1. THE WORD OF GOD

The Bible is the fully and uniquely inspired Word of God written (2 Tim. 3:16; 2 Pe. 1:20-21). It is in its entirety the Word of God, given by men inspired by God. The divine initiative, activity, and superintendence in the process of inspiration imparts inerrancy to the original documents (Mt. 5:18). By God's supernatural providence the sixty-six books of the Old and New Testament canon were preserved with such integrity that for all intents and purposes our translations today are based upon an adequate equivalent to the autographs of Scripture. It constitutes for us today the revealed will of God in written form Ps. 119:11; Mt. 4:4) and the words of Scripture are for us the Word of God (He. 3:7).

The Bible is our sufficient and final authority for faith and practice (Is. 8:20; Mt. 24:35; Jn. 12:48). Through it the Holy Spirit, Who inspired its writing, continues to illumine (Ps. 119:18; 105; 130), instruct (2 Tim. 3:16-17), convict (He. 4:12-13), regenerate (Ja. 1:18; 1 Pe. 1:23), and sanctify (Jn.

17:17; Ep. 5:26). Whatever is not revealed in or established by the Scriptures cannot be made an article of faith essential to salvation (2 Tim. 3:15-17).

2. THE TRIUNE GOD

The one true and living God (1 K. 8:60; Is. 43:10-11; Mk. 12:29, 32; 1 Th. 1:9) is the eternal, personal Spirit. He is infinite and unchangeable in power, wisdom, holiness, and love (Is 6:3; Ja. 1:17). He is the Creator, Sovereign Ruler, and Preserver of all things whether visible or invisible (1 Pe. 4:19; Ps. 103:19; He. 1:3). In the divine unity of His Godhead there eternally exist three Persons of one essence, perfection, and power: the Father, the Son, and the Holy Spirit (Mt. 3:16-17; 28:19; 2 Co. 13:14).

3. JESUS CHRIST

Jesus Christ is the eternally begotten Son, the second person of the Triune Godhead. He was eternally one with the Father (Jn. 1:1; 10:30) and by the conception of the Holy Spirit was born of the virgin Mary (Lu. 1:27, 35; Mt. 1:20). Thus, two whole and perfect natures were forever united in one perfect personality in Jesus Christ. He is the eternal Word made flesh, the only begotten Son of the Father, and the Son of Man (Jn. 1:14; Jn. 3:16; Mt. 16:13). He is the God-man, truly and fully God and truly and fully man. He was sinless in life (1 Jn. 3:5). He and He alone was qualified to be our substitute, our Savior (1 Tim. 2:5; Jude 25).

He arose bodily from the dead (1 Co. 15:17, 20, 23; Ph. 3:21). He ascended into heaven to the right hand of the Father, the Majesty on high (Ac. 1:9, 11; He. 1:3; 8:1), where He is now enthroned. He will return from heaven in a second personal advent prior to His millennial kingdom (Ac. 1:11; He. 9:28; Re. 20:6). He will be the judge of all men (Ac. 10:42; 2 Tim. 4:1). He will reign in righteousness and will consummate His redemptive mission (Re. 11:15; 22:12-13). This blessed hope of the Christian inspires us to holy living, to missionary witness, and to sacrificial service (Tit. 2:13; Lu. 19:13; Mt. 16:27).

4. THE HOLY SPIRIT

The Holy Spirit is the third person of the Triune Godhead. He is of one substance with the Father and the Son, from Whom He has proceeded (Jn. 15:26) and is co-equal with Them in eternity, grace, and power. It is His ministry to glorify Jesus Christ (Jn. 16:14), and He is ever present and active in the Church of Christ (Jn. 14:16-17). He convicts the world of sin (Jn. 16:7-8), regenerates those who repent and believe (Jn. 3:7-8), and sanctifies and empowers the believers for godly living and service (Ro. 15:16; Ac. 1:8).

The Holy Spirit sovereignly bestows and distributes His gifts within His Church (I Co. 12:11, 18). No one gift of the Spirit is distributed to all believers (I Co. 12:29-30). Individual members of the Church receive a gift of the Spirit for the purpose of ministry and the upbuilding of the Church (Ep. 4:12). Sample lists of some of the gifts are listed in Ro. 12:6-8 and 1 Co. 12:8-10. The Holy Spirit places priority on grace and the fruit of the Spirit above the gifts of the Spirit (1 Co. 12:31; 14:1, 12), and among the gifts He places priority on the gifts of prophecy and teaching (1 Co. 12:28; 14:1-5). Men of God thus gifted by the Spirit (apostles, prophets, evangelists, pastors, and teachers are named) become God's gift to His Church (Ep. 4:11). The Holy Spirit gives detailed restrictions for the use of only one gift—speaking in tongues (1 Co. 12-14).

5. MAN, FREE-WILL, AND SIN

Man was created in the image of God (Ge. 1:27) and was innocent and pure (Ro. 5:12). God-likeness included his ability to choose between right and wrong, and he was thus morally responsible (Ge. 3:3; De. 30:19; Ro. 2:15). By his sinful free choice Adam rebelled against God, fell from his original innocence and purity, and received a fallen and sinful nature (Ro. 5:12). Each human being today is born with this sinful nature (Ps. 51:5; Ga. 3:22), and by his own sinful deeds has become guilty before God (Ro. 3:11-23). Apart from the regenerating work of God, man today is lost in sin, is dead in his trespasses and sins, and is without God and without hope (2 Co. 4:3; Ep. 2:1-3, 12).

The grace of God through Jesus Christ is freely bestowed upon all men, enabling all who will to turn from sin to righteousness and through believing on Christ receive pardon and cleansing from sin (Jn. 1:4, 9; Ro. 5:17-18; 1 Jn. 1:9). We therefore have a gospel for all the world so that whoever will may come (Re. 22:17), whoever is thirsty may come (Jn. 7:37), and whoever will can believe and have everlasting life (Jn. 3:16).

The believer is securely kept by the power of God as he abides in vital fellowship with Christ. However, since he continues to be morally responsible to God after his conversion and continues to have free will, it is possible for a Christian to fall away and rebel against God. If he does not return or seek restoration through repentance but persists in his sin and dies in this rebellious state, he will eternally lost (Eze. 33:12, 13, 18; 18:24; 3:20; Ro. 11:22; He. 3:6, 14).

6. ATONEMENT

Jesus Christ made a full atonement for the sins of the whole world (1 Jn. 2:2) by shedding His own blood upon the cross as a perfect and sufficient sacrifice (He. 9:13, 14, 26). His sacrifice need never be repeated or anything added to it, for He accomplished salvation once and for all (He. 10:10, 14, 15; Jn. 19:30). His vicarious death is the only ground for our salvation (Ac. 4:12; 1 Co. 3:11; 15:3). It is a sufficient atonement for the sins of the whole world (1 Tim. 2:6; 4:10). This atonement is efficacious for the salvation of little children in their innocency and for those irresponsible (Ro. 2:15; 5:13; Mt. 19:13-15). It is efficacious for those who have reached the age of accountability only when they repent and believe the gospel (Ac. 3:19).

7. THE NEW BIRTH

Repentance is that godly sorrow for sin which results from the convicting work of the Holy Spirit (Jn. 16:7-11; 2 Co. 7:9). It involves a sensing of personal guilt before God (Ps. 51:4), a voluntary turning away from sin (Ac. 26:20; Is. 55:7), and the confessing of sin and making restitution where possible (Pr. 28:13; 1 Jn. 1:9; Eze. 33:15; Lu. 19:8). It is the essential

ARTICLES OF FAITH (LONG FORM) (OMS INTERNATIONAL)
(continued)

preparation (Mk. 1:15; Mt. 3:8; Ac. 3:19; 20:21; 26:20) for saving faith—the simple trust in Christ for salvation (Jn. 20:31; Ro. 1:16; Ep. 2:8).

In the moment of the new birth the person is justified (Ro. 5:1), regenerated (Tit. 3:5), adopted into the family of God (Ep. 1:5; Ga. 4:6-7), and baptized by the Spirit into the body of Christ (1 Co. 12:13). From that moment the believer has the Holy Spirit as his helper and witness (Jn. 14:26; Ro. 8:9, 15, 16).

Justification is the gracious judicial act of God fully acquitting the repenting and believing sinner (Ro. 3:24-26; 5:1). God grants full pardon of all guilt, release from the penalty of sins committed, and acceptance as righteous, not on the basis of the merits or efforts of the sinner, but upon the basis of the atonement by Jesus Christ and the faith of the sinner (Ro. 3:28; Ga. 2:16; Tit. 3:7).

Regeneration or the new birth is the gracious work of God changing the moral nature of the repentant believer from darkness to light, from nature to grace, from death to life, from bondage of sin to liberty in Christ (Ac. 26:18; Ro. 6:22; Ep. 2:1; Tit. 3:5). The believer becomes a new creature in Christ Jesus, is born of the Spirit, and enters into a life of peace with God, obedience to the will of God, and love for all (2 Co. 5:17; Ro. 5:1; 6:13, 18, 19).

Adoption is the gracious act of God by which the justified and regenerated believer is constituted a son of God with the privilege of access to the Father, membership in the family of God, and inheritance with Christ (Jn. 1:12; Ro. 8:15, 17). Justification, regeneration, and adoption are simultaneous in the heart of the repentant believer.

The Holy Spirit is the witness to salvation by the inner assurance He imparts to the child of God (Ro. 8:16; 1 Jn. 3:24, 4:13; 5:6, 10; Ro. 8:9), and by the fruit of His life within the soul: peace with God (Ro. 5:1; 8:1), love for the children of God (1 Jn. 3:14; 4:12), joy in Christ (Ro. 15:13; Ga. 5:22; 1 Th. 1:6), the guidance of the Spirit (Ro. 8:14), and righteous conduct (1 Jn. 2:3-5; 3:9-10). Good works are the visible fruit of a life lived in Christ; they are not the condition of salvation but the result of salvation (Ep 2:8; Jn. 15:8, 16).

8. THE FULLNESS OF THE SPIRIT

The fullness of the Spirit is one of several terms used in the Bible to describe that work of grace in the heart of the believer subsequent to the new birth by which he is cleansed from sin and empowered for holy life and service (Ac. 2:4; 15:9; 1:8). It has been termed entire sanctification because there is an initial cleansing of the defilement of committed sins in the new birth (Tit. 3:5), because of the wholeness of the commitment necessary for one who would be Spirit-filled (Ro. 12:1-2; 6:13), and because of the wholeness of the cleansing from the defilement of the inner nature which results (1 Th. 5:23-24). The Spirit-filled person is enabled by the indwelling Holy Spirit to love God with his whole being Mt. 22:37-38; Ro. 5:5), and his neighbor as himself (Mt. 22:37-38; Ro. 5:5), and is enabled to

live in true holiness of life (Lu. 1:75; Ep. 5:25-27; Mt. 5:8; Tit. 2:12).

The infilling of the Spirit (entire sanctification, heart purity, the enduement of the Spirit, and other terms have also been used) is a definite experience of cleansing and empowering subsequent to the new birth. In responding to God's grace the believer experiences thirst for God's fullness (Jn. 7:37-39), humbles himself (Is. 6:3-7; Ro. 7:24-25), and makes a total consecration (Ro. 6:13, 16, 19). In this moment of total commitment (Ro. 12:1-2) and faith (Ac. 26:18), the Holy Spirit cleanses the inner nature of the believer (Ac. 15:9), and clothes him with His power (Lu. 24:49; Ac. 1:8). Christ thus baptizes with the Holy Spirit (Jn. 1:33; Ac. 1:4-5), fulfilling the great "promise of the Father" which is available to every Christian (Lu. 24:49; Ac. 1:4; 2:39).

The progressive aspect of sanctification is that process of growth in Christian maturity, Christlikeness, and practical godliness which results from walking obediently in the light (1 Jn. 1:7), from spiritual nurture and discipline (Ro. 12:2; 2 Co. 3:17-18), and from repeated infillings of the Holy Spirit and His continuing ministry in the cleansed and yielded believer (Ac. 4:31; Ep. 3:19; 5:18; Ro. 8:26).

The Holy Spirit is His own witness in the soul (Ro. 8:16; He. 10:14-15). He evidences His holy presence primarily by imparting His holiness to the life of the believer (Eze. 36:26-27; Ga. 5:16; Ep. 1:4 with Ro. 5:5) and producing within the believer the abundant fruit of the Spirit (Ga. 5:22-25). The evidence of the Spirit-filled and Spirit-empowered life is not the presence of any one gift or manifestation (1 Co. 12:4, 5, 11).

9. DIVINE HEALING

It is the privilege of the believer to ask God to heal those who are sick (Ja. 5:15), for the Lord is interested in our body (1 Co. 6:13). It may not always be God's will to heal (Ga. 6:11; 2 Co. 12:7-9).

10. RESURRECTION, HEAVEN, AND HELL

There will be a resurrection of the body for both the saved and unsaved dead (1 Co. 15:16-17, 42-44; Jn. 5:29). There will be eternal life and blessedness in heaven for the saved (Jn. 14:2-3; Jn. 3:16) where they will be in the immediate presence of God (Re. 22:3-4) and will share His eternal reign (Re. 22:5). There will be eternal death and punishment for the unsaved in hell, the lake of fire (Re. 20:15), where they shall consciously share the company of the damned (Re. 21:8) in eternal separation from God (2 Th. 1:9), under the punishing wrath of God (Jn. 3:36) which will be as eternal for the unsaved as life will be for the saved (Mt. 25:46).

11. THE CHURCH AND ITS UNITY

The Church is the universal body of Christ composed of all true believers in Christ, with Christ as its head (Col. 1:18). All who are born again are baptized into this one Church by the Holy Spirit (1 Co. 12:12-13). Christ builds His own Church

(Mt. 16:18). This Church does not become fractured by the fact that there is more than one denomination, nor does it become one through church union, for there never can be more than one true body of Christ (Ep. 4:4) and its membership record is in heaven, not on earth (He. 12:23). All true Christians are members of one another (1 Co. 12:12-27; Ep. 4:25). It is the responsibility of this Church and of each of its members to obey Christ's great commission to it and reach the whole world with the gospel of Christ (Mt. 28:18-20; Mk. 16:15; Lu. 24:47-49; Jn. 20:21-22; Ac. 1:8).

Notes: *OMS International (formerly the Oriental Mission Society) is a foreign missionary sending agency founded in 1901. It was one of the first independent missionary agencies serving the new Holiness denominations that were founded at the end of the nineteenth century. OMS has a conservative Holiness doctrine. It avoids the use of the popular Evangelical language that speaks of the Bible's infallibility and inerrancy, but nevertheless strongly affirms the Bible's inspiration and authority. Most importantly, OMS affirms the distinctive Holiness teaching concerning sanctification, the work of the Holy Spirit in the life of a believer by which the inner self is cleansed and empowered to live a holy life.*

*　　*　　*

ARTICLES OF FAITH (SHORT FORM) (OMS INTERNATIONAL)

Biblical doctrines emphasized by the Society are: 1) the full and unique inspiration of the Holy Bible as the divine Word of God, the only infallible, sufficient, and authoritative rule of faith and practice; 2) one God, eternally existent in three persons: the Father, the Son, and the Holy Spirit; 3) deity of our Lord Jesus Christ, His virgin birth, His sinless life, His vicarious death, His bodily resurrection, His ascension, His mediatorial intercession, and His personal premillennial second coming in power and glory; 4) the fall of man, his moral depravity, and the necessity of the New Birth; 5) substitutionary atonement through the shed blood of Christ; 6) justification by faith through regeneration by the Holy Spirit; 7) sanctification by faith (the infilling of the Spirit) subsequent to regeneration, wrought by the Holy Spirit in the act of total commitment, resulting in purity of heart and enduement of power for holy living and service; 8) security of the believer as he abides in vital fellowship with Christ; 9) resurrection of the body unto eternal life for the saved, and unto eternal punishment for the lost; 10) spiritual unity of all believers who comprise the Church, the Body of Christ.

Notes: *This brief form of the OMS International Articles of Faith is actually a revised form of the National Association of Evangelicals' Articles of faith with items concerning the unique Holiness perspective on entire sanctification added. This statement includes affirmation of the infallibility of the Bible and moral depravity, language not used in the longer form of the OMS International doctrinal statement, and reflec-*

tive more of modern Evangelicalism than of the Holiness tradition.

*　　*　　*

Independent Holiness Schools

STATEMENT OF FAITH (ASBURY COLLEGE)

As an independent liberal arts college, Asbury strives to offer an education of academic excellence in a thoroughly Christian context by maintaining a synthesis of the liberal arts tradition and the Christian faith as set forth specifically in the doctrines of Wesleyan Arminianism.

Christian education places supreme confidence in divine revelation. This is not to say that the results of human learning and discovery are in any way devalued. It is to say that all truth must be evaluated in the light of God's truth. In that light, we believe the Bible is the divinely inspired and infallible Word of God and is the final authority for truth and life. We hold sacred such classical Christian doctrines as Justification by Faith, Regeneration, Witness of the Spirit, and Entire Sanctification.

We believe that humanity is the fallen object of God's infinite love. Though created in the image of God, human beings fell through disobedience to God and stand in need of conversion. By faith in Jesus Christ, a person is reconciled to God and restored to fellowship with Him. Likewise by faith, the human heart may be cleansed from all sin through the Holy Spirit. Since we recognize this as the human race's deepest need and as the ultimate answer to its problems, we make every effort to lead each student to Jesus Christ as personal Savior and Sanctifier.

We believe that a call to life in Christ is a call to service. Thus a basic principle in our philosophy of education is to help each student see and accept his/her role as a servant-disciple in the world for which Christ died. While we elevate without apology the spiritual needs of humanity over political, social and economic concerns, we are dedicated to teaching our students the relevance of truth and love in God's redemptive plan for all aspects of life and society.

We are a multi-denominational college, and all students may participate fully in the spiritual life of the campus. However, the institution maintains its commitment to an evangelical Wesleyan Arminian perspective. The emphasis on holiness and the ministry of the Holy Spirit does not imply approval of, nor participation in, all doctrines or practices associated with groups which share our emphasis upon the work of the Spirit. In particular the College does not permit public ''speaking in tongues.'' This prohibition, like that against the teaching of the doctrine of eternal security, expresses an institutional responsibility to the heritage of the college and not an attempt to assess the validity of differing convictions.

Notes: *In the generation after the break of the Holiness movement with the Methodist Church and the retirement of*

STATEMENT OF FAITH (ASBURY COLLEGE) (continued)

Holiness professors from the Methodist colleges and seminaries, independent Holiness schools began to appear. Asbury College, Wilmore, Kentucky, became one of the most important of these schools. The school's statement of faith reflects a commitment to conservative Holiness themes in a Wesleyan-Arminian (John Wesley, Jacob Arminus) tradition.

The school is opposed to the modern Pentecostal/Charismatic movement (with is accompanying emphasis on speaking in tongues). It is also opposed to Calvinist theological perspectives such as that represented by the doctrine of the eternal security of the believer. The Wesleyan-Arminian tradition suggests the possibility that a believer can backslide and deny the faith thus moving into a lost condition.

* * *

STATEMENT OF FAITH (ASBURY THEOLOGICAL SEMINARY)

WE BELIEVE:

God

In the one God, creator and sustainer of all things, infinite in love, perfect in judgments, and unchanging in mercy. God exists eternally in three persons—Father, Son, and Holy Spirit;

Scripture

In the divine inspiration, truthfulness. and authority of both the Old and New Testaments, the only written Word of God, without error in all it affirms. The Scriptures are the only infallible rule of faith and practice. The Holy Spirit preserves God's Word in the church today and by it speaks God's truth to peoples of every age;

Humankind

That human beings were created in the image of God. This image was marred in every part through the disobedience of our first parents, and fellowship with God was broken. God, by His prevenient grace, restores moral sensibility to all humankind and enables all to respond to His love and to accept His saving grace, if they will;

Jesus Christ

That Jesus Christ is God's Son incarnate. born of the Virgin Mary. He died for the sins of all, taking on Himself on the behalf of sinful persons, God's judgment upon sin. In His body He rose from the grave and ascended to the right hand of the Father where He intercedes for us;

Holy Spirit

That the Holy Spirit is God present and active in the world. The Holy Spirit was given to the church in His fullness at Pente-

cost. By the Spirit, Christ lives in His church, the gospel is proclaimed, and the kingdom of God is manifested in the world;

Justification

That God graciously justifies and regenerates all who trust in Jesus Christ. Believers become children of God and begin to live in holiness through faith in Christ and the sanctifying Spirit;

Entire Sanctification

That God calls all believers to entire sanctification in a moment of full surrender and faith subsequent to their new birth in Christ. Through sanctifying grace the Holy Spirit delivers them from all rebellion toward God, and makes possible wholehearted love for God and for others. This grace does not make believers faultless nor prevent the possibility of their falling into sin. They must live daily by faith in the forgiveness and cleansing provided for them in Jesus Christ;

Assurance of Believers

That believers are assured that they are children of God by the inward witness of God's Spirit with their spirits, by faith in the gracious promises of God's Word. and by the fruit of the Spirit in their lives;

Christians in Society

That Christians are called to live in daily witness to the grace which comes to us in Jesus Christ, to preach the gospel to every person according to the command of Christ, and to declare God's insistence upon righteousness and justice in all relationships and structures of human society;

The Church

That the church is the people of God composed of all those who believe in Jesus Christ as Savior and Lord. The church is Christ's body: it is visible in the world wherever believers, in obedience of faith, hear the Word, receive the sacraments, and live as disciples;

Return of Christ

In the personal return of Jesus Christ, in the bodily resurrection of all persons, in final judgment, and in eternal reward and punishment;

God's Ultimate Victory

In God's ultimate victory over Satan and all evil and the establishment of His perfect kingdom in a new heaven and a new earth.

Notes: *Asbury Theological Seminary, Wilmore, Kentucky, emerged as a graduate ministerial training school on a campus adjacent to Asbury College. Its Statement of Faith attempts to summarize the Wesleyan-Arminian (John Wesley, Jacob*

Arminius) theological tradition within which it operates. It offers a detailed consideration of the definitive Holiness doctrine of entire sanctification. It also affirms an Evangelical doctrine of the inerrancy and infallibility of the Bible.

* * *

DOCTRINAL STATEMENT (HOBE SOUND BIBLE COLLEGE)

The theological statement to which Hobe Sound Bible College subscribes and to which it expects all members of faculty and staff to affirm yearly their allegiance is that of the conservative Wesleyan-American position and embraces the following:

1. The Bible, both Old and New Testaments, is the inspired Word of God and is infallible and inerrant in the original autographs.

2. There is one eternal God existing in three persons—God the Father, God the Son, and God the Holy Spirit.

3. Jesus Christ is the eternal Son of God. He was born of the virgin Mary, died for the sins of mankind on the cross, was buried, and on the third day rose again. He is now seated at the right hand of the throne of God in heaven from whence He is coming again to receive the Church as His bride.

4. The Holy Spirit is the Third Person of the Holy Trinity, and is the operating agent in the redemption of mankind, the superintendent of the Church, and the abiding Comforter of the children of God.

5. Man was created by the direct act of God and was made in the image and likeness of God, but through transgression fell and became depraved in nature and sinful in conduct.

6. Salvation is by faith in the atoning sacrifice of Jesus Christ

7. Regeneration is the act of the Holy Spirit whereby the penitent, trusting sinner is renewed in nature, changed in conduct, and brought into the family of God.

8. Entire sanctification is a second work of divine grace, subsequent to regeneration, wrought in the heart of the fully yielded, trusting child of God; whereby the heart is purified by faith and filled with the Holy Spirit.

9. There will be a resurrection of the dead, both of the saved and the unsaved, the saved to eternal bliss in the presence of God, and the unsaved to everlasting damnation.

Notes: *Hobe Sound Bible College, Hobe Sound, Florida, is an independent Holiness college. Its Doctrinal Statement is a summary of the Holiness doctrinal position, which that is most defined by its doctrine of entire sanctification as a second work*

of grace whereby the believer's heart is purified and filled with the Holy Spirit.

* * *

FAITH STATEMENT (HOLMES THEOLOGICAL SEMINARY)

1. We believe the school is God's work.

2. It is for His glory.

3. We believe it is pleasing to Him to direct and provide for His work.

4. We believe it honors God to rest upon Him for everything—Faith honors God.

5. We believe it strengthens the worker to be dependent entirely upon God. He looks for God's strength, instead of human.

6. We believe that God is calling out those who are willing to trust Him as witnesses, and examples, of faith.

7. We believe that God wants to teach His servants to trust Him for all things.

8. It is according to the promise of the Master. 'Seek ye first the kingdom of God, and His righteousness; and all these things shall be added unto you.'''

Notes: *Holmes Theological Seminary, Atlanta, Georgia, is an independent Holiness school that began 1898 as the Altamont Bible and Missionary Institute. The Statement outlines its basis as an independent school operating as a ''faith'' ministry.*

* * *

STATEMENT OF FAITH (MOUNTAIN VIEW BIBLE COLLEGE)

We believe that the one and only true God is Spirit; Creator and Sustainer of all things visible and invisible; eternally existent in three persons, one in substance and co-equal in power and glory-Father, Son and Holy Spirit.

We believe in the deity of the Lord Jesus Christ; in His eternal generation from the Father; in His Incarnation in which He was conceived by the Holy Spirit and born of the Virgin Mary; in His sinless life and miraculous works; in His vicarious death to make atonement for the sins of the world; in His bodily resurrection and ascension; in His imminent coming in power and glory.

We believe that the Holy Spirit is the third person of the Trinity; is of one substance, majesty, and glory with the Father and the Son, very and eternally God. His office and work is to

STATEMENT OF FAITH (MOUNTAIN VIEW BIBLE COLLEGE)
 (continued)

reprove and convict the world of sin, righteousness and judgement, and to dwell in the hearts of true believers, cleansing them from sin and imbuing them with spiritual power, stability, energy and to lead them into all truth.

We believe that the Bible, consisting of the sixty-six books of the Old and New Testaments, is the word God given by divine inspiration, inerrant in the original manuscripts, and is the unchanging authority in matters of Christian faith and practice.

We believe that man was created by an immediate act of God and not by the process of evolution. He was created in the image and likeness of God, possessing personality and holiness; the purpose of his creation being that he might glorify God and enjoy Him forever. Man having been created in the likeness of God is a self-conscious personality capable of free and rational choice.

We believe that our first parents did not remain in the happy state of their original creation, but, being deluded through the subtlety of Satan, voluntarily disobeyed the positive command of God, and thus were alienated from God and incurred upon themselves and their posterity the sentence of death both physical and spiritual. In consequence of this act of disobedience, the entire human race has become so corrupted that in every heart there is by nature that evil disposition which eventually leads to responsible acts of sin and to just condemnation.

We believe that since all men are sinners and guilty before God and are dead in trespasses and sin, and therefore are unable to save themselves, God has, out of His infinite love given His Son, the Lord Jesus Christ, to become man's Savior.

We believe that genuine repentance is a necessary attitude and act of man that makes it possible for a holy and just God to forgive man's sins. Faith must accompany repentance and is the act of the will whereby man embraces the promises of God and appropriates to himself personally the provisions of God's grace.

We believe that this great salvation provides for the forgiveness of man's sins and a restoration to divine favor.

We believe that salvation also includes sanctification which is the ministry of the Holy Spirit in the heart of the believer when he consecrates his life totally to God, subsequent to his conversion experience. This in turn must be followed by a life of disciplined obedience, that the believer may become more Christlike in his daily life.

We believe that the church is a divine institution composed of all true believers in Jesus Christ. We believe that the visible and local church is an organized body of believers in Christ who are voluntarily joined together and who meet at regular times for worship and fellowship.

We believe the Lord's Day is of divine origin. God has commanded that one day in seven shall be a day of rest and worship. With other Christians since apostolic times, we set apart the first day of the week as the Lord's Day, and exhort that with great care and Godly fear we should observe this day.

We believe the Christian ordinances are two in number, baptism and the Lord's Supper. They are the outward rites appointed by Christ to be administered in each local church, not as a means of salvation, but as visible signs and seals of its reality.

Notes: *Mountain View Bible College is an independent Holiness school. Its Statement of Faith is a detailed summary of Protestant faith and the Holiness position. The Statement affirms entire sanctification as a second work of the Holy Spirit in the heart of the believer. The college also affirms the inerrancy of the Bible.*

*　　*　　*

ASSUMPTIONS (TAYLOR UNIVERSITY)

1. Loving God and being accountable to Him are the primary motivations for Christian relationships and behavior.

2. The Bible is our authority; it provides the essential teachings and principles for personal and community conduct.

3. God, through the Holy Spirit, places in every believer the inner resources and attributes to minister to others through supportive relationships.

Notes: *Taylor University, Upland, Indiana, is an independent Holiness university. These brief underlying assumptions proposed by Taylor are to be understood as operating within a Wesleyan Holiness theological context. They call for a life of accountability to God, acknowledge the authority of the Bible, and the need for mutual concern for one another.*

Chapter 8
Pentecostal Family

White Trinitarian Holiness Pentecostal

DOCTRINAL STATEMENT [CHURCH OF GOD (CLEVELAND, TENNESSEE)/EAST COAST BIBLE COLLEGE]

We Believe

1. In the verbal inspiration of the Bible.

2. In one God eternally existing in three persons; namely, the Father, Son and Holy Ghost.

3. That Jesus Christ is the only begotten Son of the Father, conceived of the Holy Ghost and born of the Virgin Mary. That Jesus was crucified, buried, and raised from the dead. That He ascended to heaven and is today at the right hand of the Father as the Intercessor.

4. That all have sinned and come short of the glory of God and that repentance is commanded of God for all and necessary for forgiveness of sins.

5. That justification, regeneration, and the new birth are wrought by faith in the blood of Jesus Christ.

6. In sanctification subsequent to the new birth, through faith in the blood of Christ; through the Word, and by the Holy Ghost.

7. Holiness to be God's standard of living for His people.

8. In the baptism with the Holy Ghost subsequent to a clean heart.

9. In speaking with other tongues as the Spirit gives utterance, and that it is the initial evidence of the baptism of the Holy Ghost.

10. In water baptism by immersion, and all who repent should be baptized in the name of the Father, and of the Son, and of the Holy Ghost.

11. Divine healing is provided for all in the atonement.

12. In the Lord's Supper and washing of the saints' feet.

13. In the premillennial second coming of Jesus. First, to resurrect the righteous dead and to catch away the living saints to Him in the air. Second, to reign on the earth a thousand years.

14. In the bodily resurrection; eternal life for the righteous, and eternal punishment for the wicked.

Notes: *East Coast Bible College is sponsored by the Church of God (Cleveland, Tennessee), a Holiness Pentecostal denomination. The school's statement of faith summarizes the Holiness Pentecostal doctrine describing a process of salvation that begins with justification by faith and sanctification, and continues with the baptism of the Holy Spirit, evidenced by speaking in tongues. The Holiness Pentecostal perspective differs from most Pentecostal beliefs by suggesting that the baptism of the Holy Spirit is reserved for the sanctified believer.*

*　　*　　*

White Trinitarian Pentecostal

STATEMENT OF FAITH (ASSEMBLIES OF GOD/ ASSEMBLIES OF GOD THEOLOGICAL SEMINARY)

The Assemblies of God Theological Seminary is an integral part of The General Council of the Assemblies of God and adheres to the Statement of Fundamental Truths of the Assemblies of God as indicated in Article V of the Constitution and Bylaws. In summary, we believe:

. . . the Bible is the inspired and only infallible and authoritative Word of God.

. . . there is one God, eternally existent in three persons: God the Father, God the Son, and God the Holy spirit.

. . . in the deity of our Lord Jesus Christ, in His virgin birth, in His sinless life, in His miracles, in His vicarious and atoning

STATEMENT OF FAITH (ASSEMBLIES OF GOD/ ASSEMBLIES OF GOD THEOLOGICAL SEMINARY) (continued)

death, in His bodily resurrection, in His ascension to the right hand of the Father, in His personal future return to this earth in power and glory to rule a thousand years.

. . . in the Blessed Hope—the Rapture of the Church at Christ's coming.

. . . the only means of being cleansed from sin is through repentance and faith in the precious blood of Christ.

. . . regeneration by the Holy Spirit is absolutely essential for personal salvation.

. . . the redemptive work of Christ on the cross provides healing of the human body in answer to believing prayer.

. . . the baptism in the Holy Spirit, according to Acts 2:4, is given to believers who ask for it.

. . . in the sanctifying power of the Holy Spirit by whose indwelling the Christian is enabled to live a holy life.

. . . in the resurrection of both the saved and the lost, the one to everlasting life and the other to everlasting damnation.

Notes: *The Assemblies of God Theological Seminary, Springfield, Missouri, is the ministerial training school of the General Council of the Assemblies of God. Its Statement of Faith summarizes the Assemblies' Statement of Fundamental Truths.*

*   *   *

DOCTRINAL STATEMENT (ASSEMBLIES OF GOD/ BETHANY BIBLE COLLEGE)

Bethany Bible College accepts without reservation the "Statement of Fundamental Truths" of the General Council of the Assemblies of God. Specifically, Bethany's statement of faith is as follows:

1. The Bible is the Word of God, the infallible rule of faith and practice for all. It is superior to conscience and reason, although not contrary to reason.

2. There are three persons in the Godhead—Father, Son, and Holy Spirit. These three are One as to nature. They are each coeternally self-existent, yet none can exist without the other.

3. The Son of God, who was in the beginning God with God, for the sake of man, became man and was called Emmanuel—that is "God with man."

4. "By one man sin entered into the world and (death by sin; and so death passed upon all men, for that all have sinned."

5. Jesus Christ, the Lord of Glory, being crucified, tasted death for all men: he arose from the dead, and ascended to the Father, that whosoever repents and believes in Him may have eternal life.

6. Man is justified by faith in Jesus Christ, apart from works.

7. The Son of God baptizes believers with the Holy Spirit for life and service according to Acts 2:4.

8. Holiness of life is the result of the believer's identification with Christ in His death, resurrection, and present thronelife in Glory. It is attained by faith in the Lord Jesus Christ as the Sanctifier, through the power of the Holy Spirit.

9. Jesus Christ is the Physician of His people. By His atonement He purchased deliverance from every sickness, and His Spirit effects perfect healing as men believe.

10. The imminent return of Christ out of heaven to this earth is the blessed and living hope of all believers.

11. The subjugation to Christ of all rule and all authority is the ultimate purpose of the revelation of Jesus Christ.

12. "They which are written in the Lamb's book of life" shall enter the holy city, Jerusalem. But "whosoever was not found written in the book of life was cast into the lake of fire."

Notes: *Bethany Bible College, Santa Cruz, California, is sponsored by the General Council of the Assemblies of God. Its Doctrinal Statement summarizes the Assemblies' Statement of Fundamental Truths.*

*   *   *

STATEMENT OF FAITH (ELIM FELLOWSHIP)

1. We believe the Bible to be the inspired and only infallible, authoritative Word of God.

2. We believe in the triune Godhead as eternally existent in three persons: Father, Son and Holy Spirit.

3. We believe in the deity of Jesus Christ, in His virgin birth, in His sinless life, in His miracles, in His vicarious death and atonement through His shed Blood, in His bodily resurrection, in His ascension to the right hand of the Father, and in His present priestly ministry,

4. We believe in evangelistic and missionary fervor and endeavor.

5. We believe that for the salvation of lost and sinful man, regeneration by the Holy Spirit is absolutely essential. We further believe in the keeping power of God.

6. We believe that sanctification, holiness and the overcoming life is God's design for the Church, which is the Bride of Christ.

7. We believe that Baptism is for believers in the Lord Jesus Christ and is to be administered by immersion, thus bearing witness to the gospel of Christ's death, burial and resurrection for us, and our own new life in Him.

8. We believe that Communion, when shared by believers, witnesses to the saving power of the gospel, to Christ's presence in His church, and looks forward to His victorious return.

9. We believe in the Baptism in the Holy Spirit as on the day of Pentecost and in the continuing ministry of the Holy Spirit as evidenced in charismatic gifts and ministries, and in the fruit of the Holy Spirit in the life of the believer.

10. We believe that divine healing is obtained on the basis of the Atonement.

11. We believe in Christ's imminent personal return in power and great glory, and in His present and everlasting dominion.

12. We believe in the resurrection of both the saved and the lost: they that are saved unto the resurrection of eternal life and they that are lost unto the resurrection of eternal punishment.

Notes: *Elim Fellowship began as an independent Bible school in the early days of the Pentecostal movement before the new Pentecostal denominations had established training facilities. It developed into a denomination as its graduates formed a loose affiliation. Formally, its doctrine is like that of the Assemblies of God, but it is distinguished from the Assemblies in its acceptance and promotion of the Latter Rain Revival, a revival movement that swept through the Pentecostal movement in the late 1940s. The Assemblies denounced what it saw as excesses in the Latter Rain movement, which was centered on matters not treated in the Statement of Faith.*

*   *   *

DOCTRINAL STATEMENT (OPEN BIBLE STANDARD CHURCHES/OPEN BIBLE COLLEGE)

We believe that:

1. The Bible is the inspired Word of God and the only infallible guide and rule of faith and practice.

2. God, the personal creator of the universe, eternally exists in three persons: Father, Son, and Holy Spirit.

3. Man, who was divinely created in the image of God, willfully transgressed God's law and incurred both physical and spiritual death as a result. Henceforth, all of mankind is born with a sinful nature and is subject to the same penalty at the age of accountability.

4. The Lord Jesus Christ submitted Himself as a substitutionary sacrifice for the sins of mankind.

5. The Lord arose from the dead, ascended into heaven and is interceding for mankind as High Priest and Advocate in His present life.

6. Jesus Christ will return to earth as Savior and Lord imminently and premilliennially. Mankind will be resurrected bodily, the just to eternal happiness and security with God, and the unjust to everlasting punishment in hell.

7. Since man is unable to save himself, salvation comes by grace alone received through faith in Christ as Savior on the basis of godly repentance.

8. The Baptism of the Holy Spirit is a definite experience subsequent to conversion provided by the Lord for every believer for purposes of Christian witness, holiness and edification.

9. Divine healing, provided for in the atonement, is available to mankind in every age and is granted according to God's will in answer to believing prayer.

10. The great commission of Christ is literal and imperative today. To carry out a program of world evangelism is both the duty and supreme privilege of the Church.

Notes: *The Open Bible College is sponsored by the Open Bible Standard Churches, and its Doctrinal Statement summarizes the Articles of Faith of that church. It emphasizes belief in the baptism of the Holy Spirit and divine healing.*

*   *   *

STATEMENT OF FUNDAMENTAL AND ESSENTIAL TRUTHS (PENTECOSTAL ASSEMBLIES OF CANADA AND PENTECOSTAL ASSEMBLIES OF NEWFOUNDLAND)

PREAMBLE

The Pentecostal Assemblies of Canada stands firmly in the mainstream of historical Christianity. It takes the Bible as its all-sufficient source of faith and practice, and subscribes to the historic creeds of the universal church. In common with historical, evangelical Christianity, it emphasizes Christ as Savior and Coming King. It also presents Christ as Healer and it adopts the distinctive position that speaking in tongues is the initial evidence when Christ baptizes in the Holy Spirit. (See Section VI, 3).

I. HOLY SCRIPTURES

All Scripture is given by inspiration of God by which we understand the whole Bible to be inspired in the sense that holy men of God were moved by the Holy Spirit to write the very words of Scripture. Divine inspiration extends equally and fully to all parts of the original writings. The whole Bible in the original is, therefore, without error and as such is infallible,

STATEMENT OF FUNDAMENTAL AND ESSENTIAL TRUTHS
   (PENTECOSTAL ASSEMBLIES OF CANADA AND
   PENTECOSTAL ASSEMBLIES OF NEWFOUNDLAND)
   (continued)

absolutely supreme and sufficient in authority in all matters of faith and practice.

The Bible does not simply contain the Word of God, but is in reality the complete revelation and very Word of God inspired by the Holy Spirit. Christian believers today receive spiritual illumination to enable them to understand the Scriptures, but God does not grant new revelations which are contrary or additional to inspired biblical truth.

II. THE GODHEAD

The Godhead exists eternally in three persons: the Father, the Son, and the Holy Spirit. These three are one God, having the same nature and attributes and are worthy of the same homage, confidence and obedience.

1. THE FATHER

The Father exists eternally as the Creator of heaven and earth, the Giver of the Law, to whom all things will be subjected, so that He may be all in all.

2. THE SON

The Lord Jesus Christ, the Eternal and only Begotten Son of the Father, is true God and true man. He was conceived of the Holy Spirit, born of the Virgin Mary, and by His sinless life, miracles and teaching, gave full revelation of the Father.

He died upon the cross, the Just for the unjust, as a substitutionary sacrifice. He rose from the dead. He is now at the right hand of the majesty on high as our great High Priest. He will come again to establish His kingdom in righteousness and peace.

3. THE HOLY SPIRIT

The Holy Spirit is also God, performing actions and possessing the attributes of Deity. His personality is shown by the fact that He has personal characteristics and that individuals may relate to Him as a person.

III. ANGELS

1. CLASSIFICATION

Angels were created as intelligent and powerful beings to do the will of God and worship Him. However, Satan, the originator of sin, fell through pride and was followed by those angels who rebelled against God. These fallen angels or demons are active in opposing the purposes of God.

Those who remained faithful continue before the throne of God and serve as ministering spirits.

2. THE BELIEVER AND DEMONS

Demons attempt to thwart God's purposes. However, in Christ the believer may have complete liberty from the influence of demons. He cannot be possessed by them because his body is the temple of the Holy Spirit in which Christ dwells as Lord.

IV. MAN

Man was originally created in the image and likeness of God. He fell through sin and as a consequence, incurred both spiritual and physical death. Spiritual death and the depravity of human nature has been transmitted to the entire human race 14 with the exception of the Man Christ Jesus. Man can be saved only through the atoning work of the Lord Jesus Christ.

V. SALVATION

1. ATONEMENT OF CHRIST

Salvation has been provided for all men through the sacrifice of Christ upon the cross. It is the only perfect redemption and substitutionary atonement for all the sins of the world, both original and actual. His atoning work has been proven by His resurrection from the dead. Those who repent and believe in Christ are born again of the Holy Spirit and receive eternal life. Furthermore, in the atonement, divine healing was provided for all believers.

2. REPENTANCE AND FAITH

Man can only be born again through faith in Christ. Repentance, a vital part of believing, is a complete change of mind wrought by the Holy Spirit, turning a person to God from sin.

3. REGENERATION

Regeneration is a creative work of the Holy Spirit by which man is born again and receives spiritual life.

4. JUSTIFICATION

Justification is a judicial act of God by which the sinner is declared righteous solely on the basis of his acceptance of Christ as Savior.

VI. THE CHRISTIAN EXPERIENCE

1. ASSURANCE

Assurance of salvation is the privilege of all who are born again by the Spirit through faith in Christ, resulting in love, gratitude and obedience toward God.

2. SANCTIFICATION

Sanctification is dedication to God and separation from evil. In experience it is both instantaneous and progressive. It is produced in the life of the believer by his appropriation of the power of Christ's blood and risen life through the Person of the Holy Spirit. He draws the believer's attention to Christ, teaches him through the Word and produces the character of Christ within him. Believers who sin must repent and seek forgiveness through faith in the cleansing blood of Jesus Christ.

3. BAPTISM IN THE HOLY SPIRIT

The Baptism in the Holy Spirit is an experience in which the believer yields control of himself to the Holy Spirit. Through this he comes to know Christ in a more intimate way, and receives power to witness and grow spiritually. Believers should earnestly seek the Baptism in the Holy Spirit according to the command of our Lord Jesus Christ. The initial evidence of the Baptism in the Holy Spirit is speaking in other tongues as the Spirit gives utterance. This experience is distinct from, and subsequent to the experience of the new birth.

4. THE GIFTS OF THE SPIRIT

The gifts of the Spirit are supernatural abilities given by God through the exercising of which believers are enabled to minister effectively and directly in particular situations. They serve the dual function of building up the Church, and of demonstrating the presence of God within His Church.

5. DIVINE HEALING

Divine Healing provided in the atonement of Christ is the privilege of all believers. Prayer for the sick and gifts of healing are encouraged and practiced.

VII. THE CHURCH

1. THE UNIVERSAL CHURCH

All who are born again are members of the universal church which is the body and bride of Christ.

2. THE LOCAL CHURCH

A. Purpose

The local church is a body of believers in Christ who have joined together to function as a part of the universal church. The local church is ordained by God and provides a context in which believers corporately worship God, observe the ordinances of the church, are instructed in the faith and are equipped for the evangelization of the world.

B. Ordinances

a. The Lord's Supper

The Lord's Supper is a symbol, memorial and proclamation of the suffering and death of our Lord Jesus Christ. This ordinance of communion is to be participated in by believers until Christ's return.

b. Water Baptism

Water Baptism signifies the believer's identification with Christ in His death, burial and resurrection and is practiced by immersion.

c. Ministry

A divinely called and ordained ministry is the provision of the Lord to give leadership to the church as it fulfills its purposes.

VIII. THE END OF TIME

1. THE PRESENT STATE OF THE DEAD

At death the souls of the believers pass immediately into the presence of Christ, and these remain in constant bliss until the resurrection of the glorified body.

The souls of the unbelievers remain after death conscious of condemnation until the final bodily resurrection and judgment of the unjust.

2. THE RAPTURE

The rapture, the blessed hope of the Church, is the coming of the Lord in the air to receive to Himself His own, both the living who shall be transformed, and the dead in Christ who shall be resurrected. For this event the believer should be constantly looking. Believers will appear before the judgment seat of Christ to be judged according to faithfulness in Christian service.

3. THE TRIBULATION

The rapture of the Church will be followed by the tribulation, the fulfillment of Israel's seventieth week, during which the Church is with the Lord. The tribulation will be a time of judgment on the whole earth. The latter half of this period will be the time of Jacob's trouble, which our Lord calls the great tribulation.

4. THE SECOND COMING OF CHRIST

The return of Christ to earth in power and great glory will conclude the great tribulation with the victory at Armageddon, the defeat of antichrist and the binding of Satan. He will introduce the millennial age, restore Israel to her own land, lift the curse which now rests upon the whole creation, and bring the whole world to the knowledge of God.

5. THE FINAL JUDGMENT

There will be a final judgment in which the unbelieving dead will be raised and judged at the great white throne, according to their works.

The beast and false prophet, the devil and his angels, and whoever is not found in the Book of Life shall be cast into the lake of fire, not to annihilation but to everlasting punishment, which is the second death.

6. THE ETERNAL STATE OF THE RIGHTEOUS

The righteous will share the glory of God in the new heaven and the new earth for eternity.

Notes: *The Pentecostal Assemblies of Canada was formed in the 1920s by the Canadian districts of the American-based Assemblies of God and as might be expected, its statement is similar to that of the parent body. Similarly, the Pentecostal Assemblies of Newfoundland is a body whose congregations are concentrated in the Maritime provinces. It was once a part of the Pentecostal Assemblies of Canada, but separated in 1925. The Canadian groups retain strong fraternal relations with the Assemblies of God and they agree doctrinally in all essential issues.*

This statement is a conservative affirmation of Pentecostal faith. It affirms a belief in the gifts of the Spirit, divine healing,

STATEMENT OF FUNDAMENTAL AND ESSENTIAL TRUTHS (PENTECOSTAL ASSEMBLIES OF CANADA AND PENTECOSTAL ASSEMBLIES OF NEWFOUNDLAND) (continued)

and a premillennial eschatology (second coming). There are strong doctrines against divorce and in favor of tithing.

* * *

STATEMENT OF FAITH (PENTECOSTAL ASSEMBLIES OF CANADA/CENTRAL PENTECOSTAL COLLEGE)

We believe the Holy Scriptures to be the divinely inspired, infallible, inerrant and authoritative Word of God.

We believe there is one God, eternally existent in the three Persons of the Holy Trinity.

We believe in the virgin birth of the Lord Jesus Christ, His unqualified deity, His sinless humanity and perfect life, His all-sufficient atoning death, His bodily resurrection, His ascension to the Father's right hand, and His personal return at His second advent.

We believe that justification is a judicial act of God on the believer's behalf solely on the merits of Christ, and that regeneration by the power of the Holy Spirit is essential for personal salvation.

We believe in the present day reality of the baptism in the Holy Spirit according to Acts 2:4, the gifts of the Holy Spirit, and the Lord's supernatural healing of the body.

We believe in the Lordship of Christ over the Church, the ordinances of Christian baptism by immersion for believers and the Lord's Supper.

We believe in the imminent, personal return of Jesus Christ and in the eternal blessedness of the redeemed in heaven.

Notes: *Central Pentecostal College, Saskatoon, Saskatchewan, is sponsored by the Pentecostal Assemblies of Canada. Its brief Statement of Faith summarizes the Statement of Fundamental and Essential Truths of the Assemblies.*

* * *

STATEMENT OF FAITH (PENTECOSTAL ASSEMBLIES OF CANADA/WESTERN PENTECOSTAL BIBLE COLLEGE)

We believe. . .

. . . the Holy Scriptures are the divinely inbreathed, infallible, inerrant and authoritative Word of God.

. . . that there is one God, eternally existent in the Persons of the Holy Trinity.

. . . in the virgin birth of the Lord Jesus Christ, His unqualified deity, His sinless humanity and perfect life, the eternal all-sufficiency of His atoning death, His bodily resurrection, His ascension to the Father's right hand, and His personal coming again at His second advent.

. . . that justification is a judicial act of God on the believer's behalf solely on the merits of Christ, and that regeneration by the power of the Holy Spirit is absolutely essential for personal salvation.

. . . in holy living, the present day reality of the baptism in the Holy Spirit according to Acts 2:4, the gifts of the Holy Spirit, and the Lord's supernatural healing of the human body.

. . . in Christ's Lordship of the Church, the observance of the ordinances of Christian baptism by immersion for believers and the Lord's Supper.

. . . in the eternal blessedness of the redeemed in heaven and the eternal doom of the unregenerate in the lake of fire.

Notes: *Western Pentecostal Bible College, Clayburn, British Columbia, is sponsored by the Pentecostal Assemblies of Canada. The College's brief Statement of Faith summarizes the Statement of Fundamental and Essential Truths of the Assemblies.*

* * *

Deliverance Pentecostal

SUGGESTED ARTICLES OF FAITH (FULL GOSPEL FELLOWSHIP OF CHURCHES AND MINISTERS INTERNATIONAL)

I. THE SCRIPTURES INSPIRED

The Bible is the inspired Word of God, a revelation from God to men; the infallible rule of faith and conduct, and is superior to conscience and reason, but not contrary to reason (II Tim. 3:15, 16; 1 Pet. 2:2).

II. THE ONE TRUE GOD

The one true God has revealed Himself as the eternally self-existent, self-revealed "I AM"; and has further revealed Himself as embodying the principles of relationship and association, i.e., as Father, Son and Holy Ghost (Deut. 6:4; Mark 12:29; Isa. 43:10, 11; Matt. 28:19).

III. MAN, HIS FALL AND REDEMPTION

Man was created good and upright—for God said, "Let Us make man in Our Image, after Our likeness." "But man, by voluntary transgression fell and his only hope of redemption is in Jesus Christ, the Son of God." (Gen. 1:26-31, 3:1-7; Rom. 5:12-21).

IV. THE SALVATION OF MAN

(a) Conditions to salvation. The Grace of God, which bringeth salvation, hath appeared to all men, through the preaching of repentance toward God and faith toward the Lord Jesus Christ; Man is saved by the washing of regeneration and renewing of the Holy Ghost, and, being justified by grace through faith, he becomes a heir of God according to the hope of eternal life. (Titus 2:11; Ram. 10:13-15; Luke 24:47; Titus 3:5-7).

(b) The evidences of salvation. The inward evidence, to the believer of his salvation, is the direct witness of the Spirit (Rom. 8:16); the outward evidence to all men is a life of righteousness and true holiness.

V. BAPTISM IN WATER

The ordinance of baptism by burial with Christ should be observed as commanded in the Scriptures, by all who have really repented and in their hearts they have truly believed on Christ as Savior and Lord. In so doing, they have the body washed in pure water as an outward symbol of cleansing, while their heart has already been sprinkled with the blood of Christ as an inner cleansing; thus they declare to the world that they have died with Jesus and that they have also been raised with Him to walk in newness of life. (Matt. 28:19; Acts 10:47, 48 Rom. 6:4; Acts 20:21; Heb. 10:22).

VI. THE LORD'S SUPPER

The Lord's Supper, consisting of the elements, bread and fruit of the vine, is the symbol expressing our sharing the divine nature of our Lord Jesus Christ (2 Pet. 1:4); a memorial of His suffering and death (1 Cor. 11:26); and a prophecy of His coming (1 Cor. 11:26); and is enjoined on all believers "until He comes."

VII. THE PROMISE OF THE FATHER

All believers are entitled to, and should ardently expect, and earnestly seek, the promise of the Father, the Baptism in the Holy Ghost and fire, according to the command of the Lord Jesus Christ. This was the normal experience of all in the early Christian church. With it comes the enduement of power for life and service, the bestowment of the gifts and their uses in the work of the ministry (Luke 24:49, Acts 1:4; 1 Cor 12:1-31). This wonderful experience is distinct from and subsequent to the experience of the new birth (Acts 10:44-46; 11:14-16; 15:7-9).

VIII. THE EVIDENCE OF THE BAPTISM IN THE HOLY GHOST

The Baptism of the believers in the Holy Ghost is witnessed by the physical sign of speaking with other tongues as the Spirit of God gives them utterance (Acts 2:4). The speaking in tongues in this instance is the same in essence as the gift of tongues (1 Cor. 12:4 10, 28), but different in purpose and use.

IX. ENTIRE SANCTIFICATION

The Scriptures teach a life of Holiness without which no man shall see the Lord. By the power of the Holy Ghost we are able to obey the command, "Be ye Holy, for I am Holy," Entire Sanctification is the will of God for all believers, and should be earnestly pursued by walking in obedience to God's Word (Heb. 12:14; 1 Pet. 1:15, 16; 1 Thess. 5:23, 24; 1 John 2:6).

X. THE CHURCH

The Church is the body of Christ, the habitation of God through the Spirit, with divine appointments for the fulfillment of her great commission. Each believer, born of the Spirit, is an integral part of the General Assembly and Church of the First-born, which are written in heaven (Eph. 1:22, 23; 2:22; Heb. 12:23).

XI. THE MINISTRY AND EVANGELISM

A divinely called and scripturally ordained ministry has been provided by our Lord for a two fold purpose: (1) The evangelization of the world, and (2) The edifying of the body of Christ (Mark 16:15-20; Eph. 4:11-13).

XII. DIVINE HEALING

Deliverance from sickness is provided for in the atonement, and is the privilege of all believers. (Isa. 53:4, Matt. 8:16,17).

XIII. THE SECOND COMING OR BLESSED HOPE

The resurrection of those who have fallen asleep in Christ and their translation together with those who are alive and remain unto the coming of the Lord is the blessed hope of the Church. (1 Thess. 4:16-18; Rom. 8:23; Titus 2:13; 1 Cor. 15:51-52; Rev. 11:15).

XIV. THE MILLENNIAL REIGN OF JESUS

The revelation of the Lord Jesus Christ from heaven, the salvation of national Israel, and the millennial reign of Christ on the earth is the scriptural promise and the world's hope (2 Thess. 1:7; Rev. 19:11-14; Rom. 11:26-27; Rev. 20:1-7).

XV. THE LAKE OF FIRE

The devil and his angels, the beast and the false prophet, and whosoever is not found written in the Book of Life, shall be consigned to everlasting punishment in the lake which burneth with fire and brimstone, which is the second death. (Rev. 19:20; Rev. 20:10-15).

XVI. THE NEW HEAVENS AND NEW EARTH

We, "according to His promise, look for new heavens and a new earth wherein dwelleth righteousness" (2 Pet. 3:13; Rev. 21:22).

Notes: *The Full Gospel Fellowship of Churches and Ministers International is a loosely connected fellowship of churches and ministers who were originally brought together by their alignment with the work of Gordon Lindsey, a prominent Pentecostal minister in the great healing crusades of the 1950s and 1960s, initiated by William Marrion Branham. Lindsey parted with Branham, in part over the latter's denial of the Trinity. Lindsey was a former member of the Assemblies of God, as were many of those who originally affiliated with the Full Gospel Fellowship, and this statement is excerpted from*

SUGGESTED ARTICLES OF FAITH (FULL GOSPEL FELLOWSHIP OF CHURCHES AND MINISTERS INTERNATIONAL) (continued)

that of the Assemblies of God (I, p. 357), with a few additional phrases added.

The Fellowship is made up of autonomous congregations and the Articles of Faith are ''suggested'' for adoption by the local church, although there is no demand that they do so.

*   *   *

STATEMENT OF FAITH (KENNETH HAGIN MINISTRIES)

WE BELIEVE. . .

THE SCRIPTURES. The Bible is the inspired Word of God, the product of holy men of old who spoke and wrote as they were moved by the Holy Spirit. The New Covenant, as recorded in the New Testament, we accept as our infallible guide in matters pertaining to conduct and doctrine (2 Tim. 3:16; 1 Thess 2:13; 2 Peter 1:21).

THE GODHEAD. Our God is one, but manifested in three persons - the Father, the Son, and the Holy Spirit, being co-equal (Phil. 2:6). God the Father is greater than all; the sender of the Word (Logos) and the Begetter (John 14:28; John 16:28; John 1:14). The Son is the Word flesh-covered, the One Begotten, and has existed with the Father from the beginning (John 1:1; John 1:18; John 1:14). The Holy Spirit proceeds forth from both the Father and the Son and is eternal (John 15:26).

MAN, HIS FALL AND REDEMPTION. Man is a created being, made in the likeness and image of God, but through Adam's transgression and fall, sin came into the world. ''All have sinned, and come short of the glory of God.'' ''As it is written, There is none righteous, no, not one.'' Jesus Christ, the Son of God, was manifested to undo the work of the devil and gave His life and shed His blood to redeem and restore man back to God (Rom. 5:14; Rom. 3:10; Rom. 3:23; 1 John 3:8).

Salvation is the gift of God to man, separate from works and the law, and is made operative by grace through faith in Jesus Christ, producing works acceptable to God (Eph. 2:8).

ETERNAL LIFE AND THE NEW BIRTH. Man's first step toward salvation is godly sorrow that worketh repentance. The New Birth is necessary to all men, and when experienced produces eternal life (2 Cor. 7:10; 1 John 5:12; John 3:3-5).

WATER BAPTISM. Baptism in water is by immersion, is a direct commandment of our Lord, and is for believers only. The ordinance is a symbol of the Christian's identification with Christ in His death, burial, and resurrection (Matt. 28:19; Rom. 6:4; Col. 2:12; Acts 8:36-39).

The following recommendation regarding the water baptismal formula is adopted; to wit: ''On the confession of your faith in the Lord Jesus Christ, the Son of God, and by His authority, I baptize you in the Name of the Father, and the Son, and the Holy Ghost. Amen.''

BAPTISM IN THE HOLY GHOST. The Baptism in the Holy Ghost and fire is a gift from God as promised by the Lord Jesus Christ to all believers in this dispensation and is received subsequent to the New Birth. This experience is accompanied by the initial evidence of speaking in other tongues as the Holy Spirit Himself gives utterance (Matt. 3:11; John 14:16,17; Acts 1:8; Acts 2:38,39; Acts 2:38,39; Acts 19:1-7; Acts 2:4).

SANCTIFICATION. The Bible teaches that without holiness no man can see the Lord. We believe in the Doctrine of Sanctification as a definite, yet progressive work of grace, commencing at the time of regeneration and continuing until the consummation of salvation at Christ's return (Heb. 12:14; 1 Thess. 5:23; 2 Peter 3:18; 2 Cor. 3:18; Phil. 3:12-14; 1 Cor. 1:30).

DIVINE HEALING. Healing is for the physical ills of the human body and is wrought by the power of God through the prayer of faith, and by the laying on of hands. It is provided for in the atonement of Christ, and is the privilege of every member of the Church today (Mark 16:18; James 5:14-25; 1 Peter 2:24; Matt. 8:17; Isa. 53:4,5).

RESURRECTION OF THE JUST AND THE RETURN OF OUR LORD. The angels said to Jesus' disciples. ''This same Jesus shall so come in like manner as ye have seen him go into heaven.'' His coming is imminent. When He comes, ''. . . the dead in Christ shall rise first; then we which are alive and remain shall be caught up together with them in the clouds, to meet the Lord in the air. . .'' (Acts 1:11; 1 Thess 4:16, 17). Following the Tribulation, He shall return to earth king of kings, and Lord of lords, and together with His saints, who shall be kings and priests. He shall reign a thousand years (Rev. 20:6).

HELL AND ETERNAL RETRIBUTION. The one who physically dies in his sins without accepting Christ is hopelessly and eternally lost in the Lake of Fire and, therefore, has no further opportunity of hearing the Gospel or repenting. The Lake of Fire is literal. The terms ''eternal'' and ''everlasting,'' used in describing the duration of the punishment of the damned in the Lake of Fire, carry the same thought and meaning of endless existence as used in denoting the duration of joy and ecstasy of saints in the presence of God (Heb. 9:27; Rev. 19:20).

Notes: *Kenneth Hagin is a popular television minister whose work has led to the foundation of a Bible school in Tulsa, Oklahoma, and among its graduates who have started churches, a new denomination. Their statement is a basic statement of Pentecostalism in the Assemblies of God tradition. It is noteworthy that while affirming a conservative biblical faith, the statement does not mention the ideas and doctrines with which Hagin is most identified: the confession of faith, the understanding that a child of God can publicly confess (or claim) something from God and expect to receive it. The statement is also known for its acceptance of an Eastern Orthodox doctrine of the Trinity, which professes that the Holy Spirit proceeds from both the Father and the Son, not just the Father. (See the discussion on the Nicene Creed in I, p. 1-2.)*

* * *

Apostolic Pentecostal

ARTICLES OF FAITH (AFRICAN UNIVERSAL CHURCH)

I. The Scriptures

We believe that the Holy Bible was written by men divinely inspired, and is a perfect treasure to heavenly instruction; that it has God for its author, salvation for its end, and truth without any mixture of error for its matter; that it reveals the principles by which God will judge us; and therefore is, and shall remain to the end of the world, the true center of Christian union and the supreme standard and authority by which all human conduct and opinion should be tried.

II. The True Universal God

We believe the Scriptures teach that there is one, and only one, living and true universal God, an infinite, intelligent Spirit, whose name is JEHOVAH, the Maker and Supreme Ruler of Heaven and Earth; Father of all Races of Mankind; that in the unity of the God-head there are three persons, the Father, the Son, and the Holy Ghost; equal in every divine profection, and executing distinct but harmonious offices in the great work of redemption.

III. Original Sin

We believe the Scriptures teach that man, was created in holiness, under the law of His Maker; but by voluntary transgression fell from that holy and happy state, in consequence of which all mankind are now sinners not by constraint but choice; being by nature utterly void of that holiness required by the law of God, positively inclined to evil; and therefore under just condemnation, without defence or excuse.

IV. Salvation

We believe the Holy Scriptures contain all things necessary to salvation; so that whatsoever is not read therein, nor may be proved thereby, is not to be required of any man that it should be believed as an article of faith, or be thought requisite or necessary to salvation.

V. Justification

We believe the Scriptures teach that we are accounted righteous before God only after the merit of our lord and Savior Jesus Christ by faith, and not of our own works and deservings; wherefore, that we are justified by faith only, is a most wholesome doctrine, and very full of comfort, that it brings us into a state of most blessed peace and favor with God, and secures every other blessing needful for time and eternity.

VI. Freeness of Salvation

We believe the Scriptures teach that the blessings of salvation are made free to all by the gospel; that it is the immediate duty of all to accept them by a cordial, penitent and obedient faith; and that nothing prevents the salvation of the greatest sinner on earth but his own determined depravity and voluntary rejection of the gospel; which rejection involves him in an aggravated condemnation.

VII. Regeneration

We believe that the Scripture teach that in order to be saved, men must be regenerated, or born again; that it is effected in a manner above our comprehension by the Holy Spirit in connection with the Divine Truth, so as to secure our voluntary obedience to the gospel; and that its proper evidence appears in the holy fruits of repentance, faith and newness of life.

VIII. Repentance

We believe the Scriptures teach that repentance and faith are sacred duties, and also inseparable graces, wrought in the soul by the regenerating Spirit of God; whereby being deeply convinced of our guilt, danger and helplessness, and of the way of salvation by Christ, we turn to God with unfeigned contrition, confession, and supplication for mercy; at the same time heartily receiving the Lord Jesus as our Prophet, Priest and King, and relying on him alone as the only and all-sufficient Savior.

IX. Sin After Justification

We believe the Scripture teach that not sin willingly committed after justification is sin against the Holy Ghost, and unpardonable. Wherefore, the grant of repentance is not to be denied to such as fall into sin after justification. After we have received the Holy Ghost we may depart from grace given, and fall into sin and by the grace of God, rise again and amend our lives. And therefore they are to be condemned who say that they can no more sin as long as they live here; or deny the place of forgiveness to such as truly repent.

X. Sanctification

We believe the Scriptures teach that sanctification is the process by which, according to the will of God, we are made partakers of His Holiness; that it is a progressive work; that it is begun in regeneration; that it is carried on in the hearts of believers by the presence and power of the Holy Spirit, the Sealer and Comforter, in the continual use of the appointed means —especially by the Word of God—self-examination, self-denial, watchfulness, and prayer; and in the practice of all godly exercise and duties.

XI. The Church

The Visible Church of Christ is a congregation of faithful men in which the Pure Word of God is preached, and the Sacraments duly administered, according to Christ's ordinance, in all those things that of necessity are requisite to same; that a congregation may hold services in a house, outdoors, as was done by the Lord's Apostles, or may, as conditions and circumstances will permit, acquire an edifice for convenience and accommodation.

XII. The Sacraments

The sacraments ordained of Christ are not only badges or tokens of Christian men's profession, but rather they are certain signs of grace, and God's will toward us, by which He doth work invisibly in us and doth not only quicken, but also strengthen and confirm our faith in Him. There are two Sacraments ordained of Christ our Lord in the Gospel; that is to say, Baptism and the Supper of our Lord. We believe that only such as worthily receive the same are approved of Christ, and they that receive them unworthily, purchase to themselves condemnation, as Saint Paul saith,(I Cor. 11:29)

XIII. Baptism

We believe the Scriptures teach that Baptism is not only a sign of profession and mark of difference, whereby Christians are distinguished from others that are not Baptised, it is also a sign of regeneration or the new birth.

We believe that the form of Baptism whether by immersion, sprinkling or pouring on of water, is a matter purely to the choice and desire of the individual to be so baptized, and it is the duty of the Church to so comply with such request as circumstances, conveniences and local conditions will allow. Where no other choice is made known, the Missionary African Universal Church shall baptize at a convenient river, by immersion, excepting where circumstances, shall make it imperative to Baptize otherwise.

XIV. The Blessing of Infants

We believe the Scriptures teach that the Blessing of Infants is an institution of Christ's Church, Jesus having commanded His Church: "Suffer little children to come unto me, for of such is the Kingdom of Heaven. . . . One He took them up in His arms, put His hands upon them and blessed them."

The Blessing of Infants, however, is by no means to be accepted as a sign or profession of faith in the crucified, buried and risen Savior, with its effect, in death to sin and resurrection to a new life. Only persons who have reached their years of discretion, or are over the customary 12 years, upon regeneration and profession of faith in Jesus Christ as their personal Savior, and having satisfied the Church of the forgiveness of their sins in the new birth, are to be received into the Church for Christian Baptism in the Name of the Father, the Son and the Holy Ghost.

XV. The Lord's Feast

We believe the Scriptures teach the Lord's Feast to be a mandate of Christ to His Church and is a necessary institution as a moral and spiritual contribution to the welfare of the true believer and of the Christian Church; the Lord's Feast being a provision of bread and wine, representing Christ's body and blood, partaken of by all faithful Christians assembled for the purpose, in commemoration of the death of their Lord, showing their faith in the merits of His sacrifice, their dependence on Him for spiritual nourishment, and their hope of life eternal through His resurrection from the dead; its observance to be preceded by faithful self-examination.

XVI. The Lord's Day

We believe the Scriptures teach that one day of the week shall be set aside by the Church as the Lord's Day, and is to be kept sacred to religious purposes by abstaining from all secular labor, except works of mercy and necessity; by the devout observance of all the means of grace, both private and public; and by preparation for that rest that remaineth for the people of God.

XVII. On Universal Brotherhood

We believe that the Scripture teach that God made of one blood all races and nations of mankind for to dwell upon the face of the earth according to nations and countries; that it was never intended for individuals of one race to lose their identity into another race, but through the Word of God and the Gospel of our Lord Christ Jesus, each ethnic group would accept God's Plan of Salvation thereby causing cooperation one with the other to the end that His Kingdom come on Earth; His Will be done on Earth as it is in Heaven.

XVIII. On Civil Authority

We believe the Scripture teach that civil government is of divine appointment, for the interest and good order of human society; and that civil authorities are to be prayed for, conscientiously honored, and obeyed; except only in things opposed to the will of our Lord Jesus Christ, who is the only Lord of the conscience and the PRINCE OF THE KINGS OF THIS EARTH.

XIX. The World to Come

We believe the Scripture teach that the end of the world is approaching and a New Jerusalem from above as seen by Saint John the Divine is about to be established; that at the last day, Christ will descend from heaven, and raise the dead from the grave for final retribution; that a solemn separation will then take place; that the wicked will be adjudged to endless sorrow, and the righteous to endless joy; and that this judgment will forever fix the final state of men in heaven or hell on principles of righteousness.

Notes: *The African Universal Church was an early Pentecostal church in the African-American community. Its Articles present an Evangelical Trinitarian faith. It calls people to repentance and faith. Sanctification is a gradual process as the believers are made partakers of His Holiness. Two sacraments, rather than ordinances, are practiced. Through baptism and the Lord's Feast, God works invisibly in the believer.*

Baptism is for people who have reached an age (12 or above) at which they can make a profession of faith. Infants are blessed, but baptism is reserved for youth and adults.

* * *

THE ARTICLES OF THE CHURCH (APOSTOLIC OVERCOMING HOLY CHURCH OF GOD)

I. Of The Inspired Word Of God

We believe that the Bible is the inspired Word of God and that every part of scripture should be adhered to. The Scriptures of both the Old and New Testaments provide the prescription for the infallible, authoritative rule of Christ in our lives (II Timothy 3:16; II Peter 1:21; 68 Psalm 11; Daniel 7:13,14; John 3:35; Phil. 2:9-11).

II. Of The One True God

The one true God has revealed Himself as the eternally self-existent, "I AM," the Creator of heaven and earth and the Redeemer of mankind. (Exodus 3:14; John 8:58).

"Jesus is God" is the basis of our teachings (Exodus 34:6; I Kings 18:37-39; Deut. 4:35; Isa. 45:6; Mark 12:29; Acts 2:36; 9:5). The one true God who spoke to Israel through Moses and the prophets appeared among men in His Son Jesus who represents the fullness of the Godhead bodily (Col. 2:9). (Deut. 6:4; II Samuel 7:22; I Chron. 17:20; 83 Psalm 18; Isa. 43: 10; 13; 44:6; I Cor. 8:4; Eph. 4:5; I Tim. 2:5).

We believe that there are three that bear record in heaven—the Father, the Word and the Holy Ghost. These three are ONE manifested in the person Jesus Christ who being in the image of the Invisible God is the Creator of all things. He is Alpha and Omega, the beginning and the end (Isa. 9:6; John 14:8-11; Rev. 1:8 and John 10:30;38.

III. Of Faith

We believe in justification by faith according to Romans 5:1 and that no man is justified with God as long as he is doing what God says not to do (Hab. 2:4; Gal. 3:11, 12; Heb. 10:38).

We believe that faith consists with receiving what God has revealed and with receiving and trusting Jesus Christ as Lord and Savior; thusly impels the believer to loving obedience and good works (John 1:12; James 2:14-20).

IV. Of The Holy Ghost

We believe in the baptism of the Holy Ghost as it was on the day of Pentecost. We believe that those who receive the Holy Ghost will speak in other tongues. Acts 2:1-4; 19:5; 10:43-46; Luke 11:13).

V. Of Water Baptism

We believe in immersing in the water according to Acts 2:38; 8:12 and 10:47, baptizing in the Name of Jesus, the one who commissioned and gave authority to baptize. The commission given by Jesus in Matthew 28:19 was carried out by the Apostles (Acts 2:38; Acts 10:48; Acts 19:5).

VI. Of Sanctification And Holiness

We believe that Jesus Christ shed His blood to sanctify the people according to Hebrews 13:12, I John 1:7; 9 Thessalonians 5:23, St. John 17:17, and Acts 26:18.

We believe that sanctification does affect the whole man, even the innermost being according to Matthew 23:26 and I Thessalonians 5:23. We believe that this act is instantaneous and is carried on into holiness. (Leviticus 11:44).

Sanctification is a work of Grace. It begins in regeneration by the application of the blood of Jesus; read I John 1:7, Hebrews 9:14; 13:12, I Peter 1:8-20 and Revelations 7:14, John 1:12-13; 17:19, 2 Corinthians 5:17.

We understand that the word sanctification means separation and consecration (John 17:17; I Cor. 1:30; Eph. 5:25-26; 2 Timothy 2:21; I Pet. 1:2; Acts 20:32). The church of God in the early dispensations were sanctified. Scriptures which support our belief are Deut. 14:2; 7:6, Ez. 36:23; Jer. 1:5; 1 Cor. 1:2; 6:11, and Hebrews 2:11.

Godly living should characterize the life and work of all saints according to the pattern and example of Jesus and His Apostles. We should cleanse ourselves from all filthiness of the flesh and spirit, perfecting holiness in the fear of God. We must live a life of purity and abstain from all appearance of evil. Read I Thess. 5:22, 2 Cor. 7:2, 2 Peter 1:3-4, Rom. 8:5-9, Gal. 5:16-21, Phil. 3:12-16, Lev. 10:10 and 11:44.

VII. Of Women Preachers

The church believes that a woman has a right to preach or teach. God said He would pour out His Spirit upon all flesh, and sons and daughters shall prophesy. The word "prophesy" means to utter predictions, to make declarations of events to come, and to instruct in religious doctrine. Read Acts 2:17, Joel 2:28, Acts 21:9, Romans 16:1-2 and Philippians 4:3. When God made man, He also made woman to help man (Gen. 2:19-23).

VIII. Of Communion And Feet Washing

Saints of this faith shall observe the Lord's Supper using natural emblems—bread and wine. We use wine because we are under the Melchizedek Priesthood which gave to Abraham bread and wine—Gen. 14:18.

We believe that the Lord's Supper is a sign of the love that saints ought to have one for another.

We believe that feet washing should follow Communion. Jesus Christ himself instituted Feet Washing in St. John 13:5-9.

We believe that the modest order to feet washing is that brothers shall wash brothers' feet and sisters' shall wash sister's feet. This seems appropriate as Paul said, "Let all things be done decently and in order."

THE ARTICLES OF THE CHURCH (APOSTOLIC OVERCOMING HOLY CHURCH OF GOD) (continued)

Abraham washed the feet of the angels and Jesus washed his disciples' feet (St. John 13:1-17 and 18:4). Mary washed the feet of Jesus (Luke 7:44). Feet washing was continued in the New Testament Church (I Timothy 5:10).

Jesus gave his disciples sacrament (Matthew 26:29). He gave them the fruit of the vine (no water). I Cor. 11:20-30. Paul gave instructions as to how the Lord's Supper should be carried out.

IX. Of The Second Coming Of Christ

We believe in the second coming of Jesus Christ to this earth in a glorified body because we believe Him to be glorified and to be coming in the power of the Spirit to rule and judge the earth.

We believe that his coming win bring forth the dead in Christ. The saints of God shall rise first. And when He shall have come, the saints which are alive shall be changed from mortality to immortality. We shall reign with Him on this earth a thousand years. After the thousand years, we believe that there will be a White Throne Judgment in which the rest of the dead who knew not God shall rise from the dead and shall think to possess this earth again in wickedness. The Fire will be rained down out of Heaven before them and they shall be destroyed. This is the Last Death and Last Judgment. (Ref. John 14:1-3; Heb. 9:28; Acts 1:11; Rev. 1:7; Matt. 16:27; I Cor. 15; Col. 3:4; 2 Tim. 4:8; Rev. 21:8).

X. Of Divine Healing

We believe that this is a divine instruction upon the foundation of the Apostles and Prophets, Jesus Christ Himself is the Chief Corner Stone. It is the Christian's right and privilege to trust God for the healing of the body when one is sick or afflicted (James 5:14, Mark 11:22, Mark 9:23, Hebrews 11:6, and Acts 3:6, Verse 16).

We do not condemn those who are weak in the faith for using medicine, but we exhort and nourish and cherish them until they become strong. For the Bible says, "He that is weak in faith receive ye, but not with doubtful disputations" (Rom. 14:1).

The Scripture says that there will be some who use herbs, but we who do not use herbs must not judge those who do, (Rom. 14:2-4).

XI. Of Equal Morals And Duties

We believe in the equality of all mankind and that every man's duty toward God is the same. "Have we not all one Father? Hath not God created us. Why do we deal treacherously every man against his brother by profaning the covenant of our Father?" (Mal. 2: 10)

"And hath made of one blood all nations of men, for to dwell on the face of the earth, and hath determined the times before appointed and the bounds of their habitation." (Acts 17:26).

He fashioned their hearts alike: He considered all their works. (Psalm 33:15)

"Hear this, all ye people: give ear, all ye inhabitants of the world." (Psalm 49:1; "Both low and high, rich and poor, together." (Psalm 49:2)

XII. Of Laws Of The Land

We believe the civil magistrates are ordered for peace, safety and the welfare of all people. Therefore, it is our duty to be in obedience to all of the laws of the land so long as they are not contrary to the Word of God. We do not believe in war or going to war, for God is not the author of confusion, but of peace. (Romans 13:1;7)

XIII. Of The Holy Covenant

Having been led by the Spirit of Divine profession to receive the Lord Jesus Christ as a Savior and the supreme standard of our faith and love, we do now in the presence of God and His angels in solemn and joyful worship of the saints, testify together as ONE BODY IN CHRIST.

We, with a prayerful knowledge, tarry for the Holy Ghost. We promise to walk together as saints in holiness and in love to advance the cause of Christ and the Church. We dedicate ourselves to promote the spiritual growth of the Church, to sustain its worship, ordinances, discipline and doctrine, to give freely to its cause, to support the gospel and expense of the church, the relief of the poor and to spread the Apostolic message throughout all nations.

We wholly testify and promise to hold family and sacred devotion to provide religious education for our children and to educate relatives and friends to the principles of the Apostolic Overcoming Holy Church of God. We shall be resolved to walk as saints before mankind; to be just in our dealings, faithful in our engagements, cautious or watchful on all sides in our deportment. We shall submit ourselves to discipline from our homes and worship services with prayers, testimonies, songs and sermons.

We shall abstain from the sale and use of intoxicating drinks, from the use of tobacco, snuff, and other filthiness of the flesh. We shall abstain from the appearance of evil.

We shall read adequately and hold the sayings of 2 Peter 1:3-7 and be loyal at all times to the presiding bishop of the Apostolic Overcoming Holy Church of God.

We promise to watch over one another in brotherly love, to remember each other in prayer, to aid each other in sickness and distress; to cultivate sympathy and Apostolic feelings for one another; to respond freely to the church, the bishops, overseers, elders and saints; to be courteous in speech, to be slow to take offense, but always ready to forgive, being mindful to the rules of our Savior to secure it without delay. (St. Matthew 18:20-22)

We promise to look forward to "One Lord, One Faith, One Baptism," and to do as saints with God helping us. "If ye know these things, happy are ye if ye do them." (St. John 13:17)

XIV. Supportive Scripture of the Tithing System

The Bible is right and we should consider what was said of old and what Jesus said to his disciples—"O fools and slow of heart to believe all that the prophets have said", Luke 24:25. Read Leviticus 27:30 where the prophets of God said all the tithes belong to the Lord, and the Lord has given them to the Levi for his support. Malachi 3:6-10 says all who fail to pay tithes are robbers. The scriptures tell us to pay tithes, to pray and not faint, to wash one another's feet, to be baptized in Jesus' name, receive the Holy Ghost. If we believe it is right to do one, then it is right to do the other. Matthew 23:23 records the words of Jesus—"These things ought ye have done and not left the others undone." Paul said if we belong to Christ, then we are Abraham's seed. A Child should be like his father. Abraham paid tithes; therefore, to be like him we must pay ours.

Abraham was a friend to God and the tithing system began with him. Read Isaiah 41:8, Genesis 14:18-20. Tithes are not under the law. Abraham paid tithes 430 years before the law came into being. In his teachings Jesus said, If you were the children of Abraham, you would do the works of Abraham. Abraham was called a friend of God because he was honest with God.

Tithes should be paid by each member to the local pastor who shall pay his tithes to the district bishop. The bishops shall pay their tithes into a Relief Fund which shall be for the sick, orphans, widows and retired pastors and executives. (Genesis 14:20, 28:22, Leviticus 27:30, Numbers 18:29, 1 Chronicles 31:5, Malachi 3:8-18, Luke 18:12).

The Lord gave the tithes to take care of the pastoral work. It began as far back as the Melchizedek Priesthood and Moses later approved of this doctrine and ordered it to be carried out.

Notes: *The Apostolic Overcoming Holy Church of God is a non-Trinitarian church whose distinctive perspective has given voice in the second item of its Articles, which identifies Jesus as the one God who manifests as Father, Word, and Spirit, as opposed to Jesus as the second entity of the Trinity. As a result of this teaching, the Church practices baptism only in the name of Jesus, and not in the name of the Trinity. In addition, the Church has a strong statement in favor of women in the ministry, practices foot washing, believes in divine healing, and teaches abstinence from habits such as the use of intoxicants and tobacco. Members of the church are urged to tithe.*

*   *   *

STATEMENT OF FAITH (FULL GOSPEL ASSEMBLIES INTERNATIONAL/FULL GOSPEL BIBLE INSTITUTE)

1. Verbal inspiration of the accepted Canon of the Sacred Scriptures as originally given (2 Tim. 3:16; 1 Cor. 2:13).

2. The Tri-Unity of the Godhead (Matt. 28:19; Gal. 3:20).

3. The creation. test and fall of man, as recorded in Genesis; his total spiritual depravity and inability to attain to divine righteousness (Rom. 5:12, 18).

4. The Savior of men, the Lord Jesus Christ, conceived of the Holy Spirit, born of the Virgin Mary, very God and very man (Luke 1:30-35; John 1:18; Isa. 9:6).

5. The Gospel of the Grace of God, how that Christ died for our sin, was buried and rose again the third day for our justification (1 Cor. 15:1-4; Rom. 4:25).

6. The salvation of sinners by Grace alone, through faith in the perfect and sufficient work of the cross of Calvary', by which we secure remission of our sins (Eph. 2:8, 9; Heb. 9:12, 22; Rom. 5:1).

7. The bodily ascension of Jesus to Heaven. His exaltation and His personal coming for His Church (John 14:2, 3; 1 Thess. 4:13-18), and His rule of the Nations of the earth for one thousand years (Zech. 14:4, 5, 9; Isa. 11:1-4; Rev. 20:6).

8. Water Baptism of Believers by immersion in the Name of our Lord Jesus Christ (Acts 19:5; 10:47, 48; 8:37, 38).

9. The Baptism with the Holy Spirit as an experience subsequent to Salvation, with the Scriptural evidence namely, speaking in tongues (Acts 8:14-17: 10:44-46; 2: 1-4; Ga. 3:4, 15).

10. The Gifts of the Spirit as enumerated in 1 Corinthians, chapters 12-14 being exercised and practiced as manifest in the early Church.

11. The Spirit-filled life, a life of separation from the world, and the perfecting of holiness in the fear of God as an expression of Christian faith (Eph. 5:18; 2 Cor. 6:14; 2 Cor. 7:1).

12. The healing of the body by Divine Power, or Divine Healing in its many aspects as practiced by the early Church (Acts 4:30; Rom. 8:11; 1 Cor. 12:9; James 5:14).

13. The Lord's Supper as a Memorial for Believers (1 Cor. 11:23-32).

14. The Eternal Life of the Believer (John 5:24; 10:28), and the Eternal Punishment of the Unbeliever (Mark 9:43, 48; 2 Thess. 1:9; Rev. 20: 10-15).

15. The Reality and Personality of Satan (Job 1:7; 2 Cor. 11:14).

Notes: *The Full Gospel Bible Institute, Eston, Saskatchewan, is an independent Pentecostal Bible school in the Apostolic or "Jesus Only" tradition. Its Doctrinal Statement is a summary of the Apostolic position that emphasizes the One God and*

STATEMENT OF FAITH (FULL GOSPEL ASSEMBLIES INTERNATIONAL/FULL GOSPEL BIBLE INSTITUTE) (continued)

water baptism in the name of ''our Lord Jesus Christ'' rather than with the traditional Trinitarian formula. The Institute also affirms the verbal inspiration of the Bible, total human depravity, the baptism of the Holy Spirit evidenced by speaking in tongues, and divine healing.

* * *

Black Trinitarian Pentecostal

THE HOLINESS CREDENDA: TENETS OF THE HOLINESS FAITH AND DOCTRINE (CHURCH OF THE LIVING GOD, THE PILLAR AND GROUND OF THE TRUTH, INC.)

CREDENDUM I

We believe in God the Father, God the Son and God the Holy Ghost and that these Three are one in a holy estate of power of the God-head.

CREDENDUM II

We believe God the Father, God the Son and God the Holy Ghost are three powers of the Holy Union of Heaven being expressly called us !, God coming from Teman and the Holy One from Mount Paran; and that the Son of God was begotten of the Father.

CREDENDUM III

We preach and do firmly believe that Jesus Christ is the Son of the Living God, and that He was born of the Virgin Mary; that He was spiritually conceived and brought forth of the Virgin Mary thus taking upon Himself the likeness of sinful flesh and for sin condemned sin in the flesh that the righteousness of the Law might be fulfilled in those of us who walk not after the flesh but after the Spirit by which He was conceived in the Virgin Mary and brought forth in the likeness of every man in order to convince man of the very fact that human flesh can live in this world free from sin and condemnation.

CREDENDUM IV

We believe and do firmly preach that Jesus Christ the Son of the Living God was possessed of the full nature and disposition of humanity, but through obedience to the Father, He took on the whole armor of faith as an example to others of the same nature in order to be able and He was thus made able to resist the devil and to overcome the world.

CREDENDUM V

We believe that all who follow in His footsteps and example will likewise do no sin, but shall be able to overcome the world

as He did, who is the Way, the Truth, and the Life of all men spiritually.

CREDENDUM VI

We preach and do firmly believe that Jesus Christ was born in the world through the Virgin Mary for a purpose and that purpose was and is to save His people from their sins; that in Him is no sin and if we abide in Him we will commit no sin; that he that commiteth sin is of the devil; that no sin is or can be of God; and that those who commit sin are plainly made manifest that they are of their father, the devil.

CREDENDUM VII

We believe and do firmly preach that Jesus Christ is the Way and our example giver; that He was baptized and filled with the Holy Ghost and thereby was made able to resist the temptation of the devil; and that He spoke with unknown tongues.

CREDENDUM VIII

We believe that all Christian followers must be filled with the same Spirit in order to be able to resist the temptations of the devil and to overcome the world and to live free from sin in this world.

CREDENDUM IX

We believe and do firmly preach that the gospel of Jesus Christ is the power of God unto salvation unto every one that believeth it; that the gospel remits sins; that the gospel began in and with the Apostles at Jerusalem by the Holy Ghost which was given unto them; and that the Holy Ghost Is the power of God and is the Gospel.

CREDENDUM X

We believe and do firmly preach that the Bible evidence of receiving the baptism of the Holy Ghost and Fire is speaking with tongues as men of God giveth utterance as on the day of Pentecost and as mentioned in Acts 2:1 to 4; that the tongue spoken in through the utterance given by the Spirit may not be understood by man and may be unknown to men, but is understood of God; that the unknown tongue is a sign of God's victory over sin and the wicked purposes of vain men and their wicked imaginations; and that the unknown and devious tongues have always served to frustrate and stop the sinful purposes and attempts of wicked men and to establish the purpose and will of God. Wherefore, tongues are for a sign, not to them that believe, but to them that believe not.

CREDENDUM XI

We believe and firmly preach that people are justified and made clean through faith and by the words of Christ; that we are glorified and made wholly sanctified by receiving the baptism of the Holy Ghost and Fire with Bible evidence; that there are two stages of sanctification—first, self sanctification; and secondly complete or wholly sanctification which is also glorification of the body through the Spirit of the Living God—and that Christ died to save His people from sin and that His blood cleanseth us from all sin.

CREDENDUM XII

We believe that Jesus is the foundation of the Church, and that such a foundation was finished when He said on the cross "It is finished."

CREDENDUM XIII

We believe that God created man, male and female, man in his own image and likeness and that man being in the image and likeness of God was perfect, pure and holy, and free from all sin so long as he remained and abided in the image and likeness of God; that for the experience of sin and appreciation of righteousness man was permitted to be his own moral agent of decision and acception of life through righteousness or death through sin and disobedience; that man disobeyed, transgressed, sinned and died; and that through the fall of Adam from righteousness into sin through disobedience that death reigned for a time over all men even unto all.

CREDENDUM XIV

We believe that through the disobedience of one man, many were made sinners and that through the obedience of one, even Christ, many shall be made righteous and that in and through Christ we have access again to the Tree of Life to live again in the image and likeness of God, perfect, pure and free from sin without the purposed experience and worry of sin and with the acceptance and high appreciation of salvation from sin through Christ the Lord from heaven and the Tree of life. Amen.

COROLLARIES (Ordinances)

1. We believe in baptism of water by emersion, that is, by being carried under the water, conceived and brought forth which is the token of the real baptism of the Holy Spirit of God. We believe that water is a type of the good conscience which is the Holy Ghost and Fire. We believe water points to salvation but it is not in itself salvation nor can it wash away sin.

2. We believe that baptism is a necessary ordinance to be observed with all others, yet we know that it is the baptism of the Holy Spirit of God that puts us into the name of Jesus and into Jesus Himself. And that it is God's Spirit that saves us from sin and washes away our sins and keeps them washed away continually,

3. We believe and really know according to the words of Christ that it is necessary to observe and keep the commandments of Christ by washing one anothers feet the way He did for an example.

4. We believe it is right and necessary to observe the Lord's Supper or Passover as He did with His disciples before He was crucified by using unleavened bread as a token of His body and by using pure unadulterated water as a token and agreement of his blood as nothing except water will agree with his blood.

5. We believe in praying; We believe in keeping the Sabbath with the Covenant which is God, Christ and the Holy Ghost instead of types and shadows which was fulfilled by the coming of Christ. We believe that to cease from our own works is to cease from sin.

Notes: *The Church of the Living God, the Pillar and Ground of the Truth was established during the first decade of the twentieth century by Mary Magdalena Tate and a predominantly African-American Holiness movement. Soon after its founding, Tate led the church in the acceptance of the Pentecostal experience of speaking in tongues and the other gifts of the Spirit. This statement is in most respects a straightforward statement of Trinitarian Pentecostal faith.*

Of interest are the first two statements covering the belief in the Trinity. They speak of the Father, Son, and Holy Spirit as powers in the godhead rather than as persons, though their personhood is by no means denied. Also unusual among Christian churches, God's power is connected to specific places, such as Teman (see Jer. 49:7 and Ezek. 25:13) and Mount Paran (see Deut. 33:2).

The Church is decidedly perfectionist and affirms that those who follow Jesus do not sin. It follows in a Baptist tradition of seeing baptism as an ordinance (not a sacrament) and its method is by immersion. Foot washing is also practiced.

*   *   *

Latter Rain Pentecostal

FAITH (BETHESDA MISSIONARY TEMPLE)

1. We believe that the Bible is a supreme revelation from God, superior to conscience and reason, though not contrary to reason: and is therefore our infallible rule of faith and practice. II Tim. 3:16,17.

2. We believe that Jesus Christ came into the world to reveal the Father and was the brightness of His glory and the express image of His person, that Jesus Christ was the Creator of all things, for by Him the worlds were made. We further believe that in Christ dwelt all the fullness of the God—head bodily, and that it is impossible to know the Father without knowing the Son. John 14; Heb. 1: Col. 2.

3. Wherefore we acknowledge the Lordship of Jesus Christ over all things in heaven and in earth and under the earth. Phil. 2:9,10.

4. We believe that man, by transgression, fell from a state of righteousness and holiness in which he was first created into a state of death in trespasses and sins, in which he is held as slave of sin and an enemy of God until he is delivered by the power of the Gospel. Rom. 5:12-21.

5. We believe that each believer must lay a foundation of Biblical truth and experience upon which he builds his life. These foundation stones are: repentance from dead works, faith toward God, doctrine of baptism, laying on of hands, resurrection of the dead and eternal judgment. Heb. 6:1,2.

6. We believe that repentance toward God and faith toward our Lord Jesus Christ produces the work of justification in the believer. Through faith in he shed blood of Christ, he is brought on to the grounds of the New Covenant and made a partaker in the death of Christ. This is the initial step of salvation and is not to be considered synonymous with the complete "new birth." Rom. 5:1,9; Luke 22:20.

7. We believe that water baptism is an essential and necessary part of regeneration or the "new birth" and is to be performed only upon repentant believers, in the Name of the Lord Jesus Christ (which we believe is to be the fulfillment of the Father, Son and Holy Ghost) and for the remission of sin. Acts 2:38. This act is to be done by immersion, and we further believe that it is the means whereby we receive the Covenant Seal of Circumcision upon the heart. Col. 2:9-13. This work of baptism must be performed before the believer is entitled to partake of the Lord's Supper. Exod. 12:43-51. Water baptism is to be administered only to adult believers who have reached the age of at least 12 years.

8. We hold that all believers may speak in other tongues as the Spirit gives utterance (Acts 2:4) and is the receiving of the "new spirit" promised in the New Covenant. Ezek. 36:26. We believe that the speaking in tongues, as the Spirit gives utterance, is the initial physical sign of the baptism of the Holy Spirit and afterward has a continual two-fold aspect, viz: speaking to God and speaking to men.

9. We believe that each believer should speak in tongues and then covet to prophesy so that he might edify the whole church. I Cor. 14:1-5. We further believe that prophecy in the church is a sign of the end—time visitation of God (Joel 2. Acts 2), for the "testimony of Jesus is the spirit of prophecy," Rev. 19:10.

10. We believe in the doctrine of the laying on of hands for: (1) The confirmation and ordination of ministries by the laying on of hands by the presbytery. Acts 13:1,3. (2) The impartation of spiritual gifts when accompanied by prophecy and the laying on of hands by the presbytery. I Tim. 4:14; II Tim 1:6. (3) The impartation of the gift of the Holy Ghost. Acts 8:17,18. (4) The ministry of healing to the sick. Mark 16:16. (5) The confirming of believers in the faith. Acts 14:22. (6) The blessing and dedication (setting apart) of children. Mark 10:16.

11. We believe in the five-fold ministry given to the church at the ascension of Jesus Christ, and that they continue to be needed and should be expected today—the ministries of apostles, prophets, evangelists, pastors and teachers. Working with these ministries will be elders, deacons and deaconesses and the gifted men and women of the church.

12. We believe and teach the rite of foot washing for all New Covenant believer-priests, as the means of removing the defilement of this world from one another. We further believe that all are instructed to do so by the Lord Jesus Christ. John 13:14.15.

13. We believe "that by grace are ye saved through faith, and that not of ourselves; not works lest any man should boast." We further believe that the emphasis for a continuous walk in grace should be the emphasis of heart righteousness and purity and not in a particular custom of outward dress or adornment. Rom. 4;1-5.

14. We believe that the nine gifts of the Spirit (I Cor. 12) should be and must be operative in the church today in order for the church of enjoy the fullness of God. Also that these gifts are imparted by the sovereignty of the Holy Spirit and only work or are operated by this one and selfsame Spirit. I Cor. 12:11.

15. We hold that healing for the body is provided in the sacrificial death of our Lord Jesus Christ for "by His stripes we are healed." I Peter 2;24,25.

16. We believe that we are one body, being members one of another, and that the basis of our fellowship is in Christ in the power of the Spirit. Eph. 2:13-22; 4:3-6.

17. We believe in the imminent, personal return of our Lord and the restitution of all things spoken by the mouth of all the prophets since the world began. Matt. 24:42-44; Acts 1:11; 3:19-21.

18. We believe that the fearful, unbelieving, abominable, whoremongers, sorcerers, idolaters and liars shall have their part in the lake which burneth with fire and brimstone which is the second death. Rev. 21:8.

19. We believe that there shall be a new heaven and a new earth wherein dwelleth righteousness. II Peter 3:13; Rev. 21:1.

Notes: *The Bethesda Missionary Temple is a megachurch congregation located in the suburbs of Detroit, Michigan. It was a key center in the 1950s for the dissemination of the Latter Rain Movement. The Latter Rain followed all the traditional affirmations of the Assemblies of God, with which the Bethesda Temple was formerly affiliated, but emphasized the role of laying on of hands for the reception of the Holy*

Spirit and the role of prophecy, and advocated the establishment of a fivefold ministry (Ephesians 4:11-12) with a key role assigned to apostles who founded congregations and assumed some spiritual authority over those local churches.

* * *

BASIC BELIEFS OF THE OVERCOMER (HOUSE OF PRAYER CHURCH)

WE BELIEVE Mark 16:15-16 ... that we are commanded and commissioned by the Lord Jesus to preach the Gospel throughout the world to save men's souls. Those who believe not will be damned, and we have a burden to prevent that from being their destiny. We believe in sacrificing for foreign missions.

WE BELIEVE Titus 2:12 ... that we must live holy lives in this present world if we intend to see the Lord (Heb 12:14) and be a part of His body. We believe (II Cor 7:1) that we must cleanse ourselves from all filthiness of the FLESH (such as tobacco, liquor-wine-beer, narcotics, etc) and of the SPIRIT (such as hate, fear, unbelief, lust, etc). Holiness pleases our God!

WE BELIEVE I Cor 3:4 ... that the Church should enjoy the benefit of God's plan of plural ministry in the Body of Christ. We believe that every local church should have a plurality of ministry and government anointed by the Holy Spirit, and that there should be no sectarian walls between any of God's people throughout the world. We deplore the spirit of sectarianism, and believe that the system of denominationalism is an artificial invention of man, and was never ordained by God, and that Christ will destroy it so He can have one glorious Church on the earth without spot or wrinkle.

WE BELIEVE Acts 1:11 ... that Jesus will return to this earth, literally, physically, and visibly to set us His Kingdom, and to rule and reign.

WE BELIEVE Eph 4:11 ... that God set apostles and prophets in the Church, as well as pastors, and that these foundation ministries will continue to be a part of the true Church until we all come to the measure of the stature of the fullness of Christ. We believe that these ministries are used by the Holy Spirit as tools to perfect the saints until the end of this age, when they are replaced by the Melchizedek order of King-Priests.

WE BELIEVE I Cor 14:12 ... that we are to seek God for gifts of the Spirit that will enable us to edify the church. We believe the nine gifts of the Spirit of I Cor 12 should be found in each local assembly, and that they will come into greater use and with more anointing and results, as the saints walk with the Lord and yield themselves to Him. We believe that the gifts should be in subjection to the guidance and discipline of the Holy Spirit as He works through anointed leadership in the local assembly.

Notes: *The House of Prayer Church is one of the prominent fellowships to emerge out of the Latter Rain Revival. It was headed by Bill Britten (1918-1986) of Springfield, Missouri, and consists of various independent congregations affiliated by their acceptance of the Latter Rain teachings. The Latter Rain followed all the traditional affirmations of the Assemblies of God, but emphasized the role of laying on of hands for the reception of the Holy Spirit, and the role of prophecy, and advocated the establishment of a fivefold ministry (Ephesians 4:11-12) with a key role assigned to apostles who founded congregations and assumed some spiritual authority over those local churches.*

This statement denounces denominationalism and affirms the organization of the church under apostles and prophets. It also advocates a strict personal code of conduct.

* * *

Pentecostal/Charismatic Organizations

STATEMENT OF FUNDAMENTAL TRUTHS (CHRIST FOR THE NATIONS)

Christ For The Nations considers certain truths as being fundamental to an understanding of and a relationship to the one true and living God.

1. The One True God.

The one true God has revealed Himself as the eternally self-existent I Am, the Creator of the universe and the Redeemer of mankind (Deut. 6:4; Ex. 3:14; Isa. 43:10,11). God has further revealed Himself as a triune being manifested as Father, Son and Holy Spirit (Isa. 48:16; Matt. 28:19; Luke 3:22).

2. The Scriptures Inspired.

The Scriptures, both Old and New Testaments, are verbally inspired of God and are the revelation of God to man; the infallible, authoritative rule of faith and conduct (II Tim. 3:15-17; I Thess. 2:13; II Pet. 1:21).

3. The Deity of the Lord Jesus Christ.

The Lord Jesus Christ is the eternal Son of God and as such shares in the Divinity and Deity of God (Matt. 1:23; John 5:22,23: 11 John 3: Heb. 1:1-13).

4. Original Sin and the Fall of Man.

Man was created good and upright; for God said, "Let us make man in our image, after our likeness" (Gen. 1:26,27). The first man, Adam, through disobedience fell from the grace of God, and thus sin entered into the world, and death by sin. Adam's transgression incurred not only physical death for man but also spiritual death, which is eternal separation from God (Gen. 2:17; 3:6-24). Man's propensity to sin because of his sinful nature necessitates salvation from the power of sin and a Savior to provide that salvation (Rom. 7:13-25).

5. The Salvation of Man.

Man's only hope of redemption and salvation from the power of sin is through the shed blood of the Lord Jesus Christ (Acts 4:12; Rom. 5:8-13; 10:9; Jas. 1:21; Eph. 2:8).

6. Christ the One Shepherd.

Jesus Christ is the Good Shepherd.(John 10:11) and the Great Shepherd (Heb. 13:20). There is only one spiritual shepherd referred to in the New Testament and Jesus Christ is that one (John 10:16).

7. The Church and Its Mission.

The Church is the Body of Christ, the habitation of God through the Holy Spirit, with divine appointments for the fulfillment of her great commission. Each believer, born of the Spirit, is an integral part of the general assembly and the church of the firstborn, which was written in heaven (Eph. 1:22,23; 2:22; 12:23).

Since God's purpose concerning man is to seek and to save that which is lost, to be worshiped by man, and to build a body of believers in the image of His Son, the responsibility of the Church is:

a. To be an agency of God for evangelizing the world (Acts 1:8; Matt. 28:19,20: Mark 16:15,16).

b. To be a corporate body in which man may worship God (I Cor. 12:13)

c. To be a channel of God's purpose to build a body of saints being perfected in the image of His Son (Eph. 4:11-16: 1 Cor. 12:28: 14:12).

8. The Ordinances of the Church.

a. Baptism in water.

The ordinance of baptism by immersion in water is commanded in the Scriptures. All who repent of their sins and believe in Christ as Savior and Lord are to be baptized. This is a declaration to the world that they identify with Christ in His death and have been raised with him in newness of life (Matt. 28:19; Mark 16:16; Acts 10:47.48: Rom. 6:4).

b. The Lord's Supper or Holy Communion.

The Lord's Supper consisting of the, elements—bread and the cup of the fruit of the vine—is the symbol

expressing our sharing the divine nature of our Lord Jesus Christ (II Pet. 1:4), a memorial of His suffering and death (I Cor. 11:26), and a prophecy of His second coming (I Cor. 11:26) and is enjoined on all believers till He comes!

9. The Baptism in the Holy Spirit.

The baptism of believers in the Holy Spirit is evidenced by the initial physical sign of speaking with other tongues as the Spirit of God gives utterance (Acts 2:4). With the baptism in the Holy Spirit comes the enduement of power for life and service, the bestowment of the gifts or enablements of the Holy Spirit and their uses in the ministry of the body of Christ (Luke 24:49; Acts 1:4,8; 1 Cor. 12:1-31). This experience is distinct from and subsequent to the experience of the new birth (Acts 8:12-17; 10:44-46; 11:14,15; 15:7-9).

10. Divine Healing.

Divine healing was provided for in the Old Testament (Ex. 15:23-26; Ps. 103:1-3; Isa. 53:4-5) and is an integral part of the Gospel (Matt. 8:16,17; Acts 5:16; Jas. 5:14-16).

11. The Second Advent of Christ

The Second coming of Christ includes the catching away of the church (I Thess. 4:16,17) followed by the actual visible return of Christ with His Saints (the church) to reign with him on Earth for one thousand years (Zech. 14:5; Matt. 24:27, 30; Rev. 1:7; 19:11-14; 20:1-6). This millennial reign will bring the salvation of national Israel (Ezek. 39:28, 29; Zeph. 3:19,20; Rom. 11:26,27) and the establishment of universal peace (Isa. 11:6-9; Ps. 72:3-8; Mic. 4:3,4).

12. The Final Judgment

There will be a final judgment in which the wicked dead will be raised and will be judged according to their works. Whosoever is not found written in the Book of Life, together with the devil and his angels, the beast and the false prophet will be consigned to everlasting punishment in the lake which burns with fire and brimstone, which is the second death (Matt. 25:46; Mark 9:43-48; Rev. 19:20; 20:11-15; 21:8).

13. The New Heavens and the New Earth.

"We, according to His promise, look for new heavens and a new earth, wherein dwelleth righteousness" (II Pet. 3:13 Rev. 21:1).

Notes: *Christ for the Nations was founded in 1948 and emerged as an expression of the great Pentecostal healing revival of the early 1950s. It also served to expand the effects of that revival overseas to other countries. Closely related to Christ for the Nations is the Full Gospel Fellowship of Churches and Ministers International, which in turn drew its statement from that of the Assemblies of God. The statement is* *closely related to both organizations and is in essential doctrinal harmony.*

*　　　*　　　*

DOCTRINAL STATEMENT (FULL GOSPEL BUSINESSMEN'S FELLOWSHIP, INTERNATIONAL)

1. We believe in one God, Maker of all things and being in Trinity of Father, Son and Holy Spirit.

2. We believe that the Son of God, Jesus Christ, became incarnate, was begotten by the Holy Spirit, born of the Virgin Mary, and is true God and true man.

3. We believe the Bible, in its entirety, to be the inspired Word of God and the only infallible rule of faith and conduct.

4. We believe in the resurrection of the dead, the eternal happiness of the saved, and the eternal punishment of the lost.

5. We believe in personal salvation of believers through the shed blood of Christ.

6. We believe in sanctification by the blood of Christ, in personal holiness of heart and life, and in separation from the world.

7. We believe in Divine healing, through faith, and that healing is included in the Atonement.

8. We believe in the baptism of the Holy Ghost, accompanied by the initial physical sign of speaking with other tongues as the Spirit of God gives utterance, (Acts 2:4) as distinct from the new birth, and in the nine gifts of the Spirit, listed in I Corinthians 12, as now available to believers.

9. We believe in the Christian's hope—the imminent, personal return of the Lord Jesus Christ.

10. We believe in intensive world-evangelization and missionary work in accordance with the Great Commission, with signs following.

Section 3. The acceptance of the ten doctrinal points stated above in Section 2 of this article is essential to membership in the International and in the Chapters, and while we recognize the obligation of maintaining spiritual love and union toward all true Christians who may not accept all of these doctrinal points, and welcome them to our fellowship gatherings, they are not permitted any voice in the conduct of our activities and

are ineligible to membership in the International or in the Chapters.

Notes: *The Full Gospel Businessmen's Fellowship, International, founded in 1953, was one of the initial organizations promoting what became known as the Charismatic Movement. That movement, in basic theological agreement with Pentecostalism, spread the teachings of the contemporary operation of the Holy Spirit, finding expression through the exercise of the gifts of the Spirit in the Roman Catholic and mainline Protestant denominations. This brief Doctrinal Statement attempts to affirm a traditional Evangelical faith with a Pentecostal emphasis, while avoiding the various issues that have separated the various denominations. Its key affirmations are in divine healing and the baptism of the Holy Spirit evidenced by speaking in tongues.*

*　　　*　　　*

DOCTRINAL STATEMENT (MISSIONARY REVIVAL CRUSADE)

We Believe:

1. In the plenary and verbal inspiration of the Bible as originally given; that it is the only infallible Word of God, and the supreme and final authority in all matters of faith and conduct;

2. That there is only one true God, eternally existing in three Persons: Father, Son, and Holy Spirit;

3. In Jesus Christ, God the Son, the world's only Savior; in His preincarnation, virgin birth, sinless life, vicarious death, burial and bodily resurrection, and personal visible and premillennial return;

4. In God the Holy Spirit, Who convicts the world of sin, regenerates, indwells and empowers the believers; "the Baptism of the Holy Ghost is a blessed and definite experience apart from regeneration that should be diligently sought after and obtained, as the necessary enduement for effective service." This experience can take place simultaneously with or subsequent to salvation.

5. That all men are sinful and lost and can be saved only by grace through faith in the shed blood of Christ;

6. That deliberate willful disobedience to the revealed will of God brings any person, regardless of prior experience, under God's condemnation and judgment which can only be removed by thorough repentance, restitution, confession, and cleansing in the blood of Christ.

7. In the resurrection of the dead, the believer to life everlasting, and the unbeliever to eternal condemnation;

DOCTRINAL STATEMENT (MISSIONARY REVIVAL CRUSADE)
(continued)

8. That the church is the body of Jesus Christ, for which He will return, comprised of all who have accepted the redemption provided by Him;

9. That Christians are called to a life of separation from worldliness, sacrifice, discipleship, and surrender to the full will of God, and that this experience is made possible through the indwelling of Jesus Christ by His Spirit, in the lives of all those who are born again.

10. That water baptism by immersion and the Lord's supper are the ordinances to be practiced by saved people in accordance with the word of God.

Notes: *Missionary Revival Crusade, founded in 1959, is a Pentecostal foreign missionary organization operating primarily in Europe and Latin America. Its Doctrinal Statement offers a strong affirmation with a Pentecostal perspective on the baptism of the Holy Spirit as a necessary experience to empower believers for effective service.*

* * *

Independent Pentecostal Schools

DOCTRINAL STATEMENT (INTERNATIONAL BIBLE COLLEGE)

International Bible College is a Full Gospel, non-sectarian institution. Its doors are open to all sincere Christian young people irrespective of denominational connection. We maintain that God's people are ONE because of Calvary and therefore fellowship must be based on the Blood rather than on doctrinal interpretation or sectarian ties. It is our loyalty to Christ rather than our opinions about Him that should bind us together.

Since some will want to know, however, how we stand, we submit the following in brief. We believe in One God manifested as Father, Son, and Holy Ghost; Salvation by faith in the Atonement; Water Baptism by immersion for the believer; Sanctification and separation from worldliness; the Baptism of the Spirit for service; the nine Gifts of the Spirit and the five-fold ministry gifts as recorded in I Corinthians 12 and Ephesians 4; Divine healing; the lost estate of man; the command to evangelize all nations; the Second Coming of Christ; and the Future Judgment and eternal destruction of the wicked.

Our position is best summed up by the statement: In things essential—UNITY; in things non-essential—LIBERTY; in all things—CHARITY.

Notes: *International Bible College, San Antonio, Texas, is an independent Holiness Pentecostal school. Its Doctrinal Statement emphasizes the three experiences of the Christian life: justification, sanctification and the baptism of the Holy Spirit.*

* * *

WE BELIEVE (JIMMY SWAGGART BIBLE COLLEGE)

We Believe

. . . the Bible is the inspired and only infallible and authoritative written Word of God.

. . . there is one God, eternally existent in three persons: God the Father, God the Son, and God the Holy Ghost.

. . . in the deity of our Lord Jesus Christ, in His virgin birth, in His sinless life, in His miracles, in His vicarious and atoning death, in His bodily resurrection, in His ascension to the right hand of the Father, in His personal future return to this earth in power and glory to rule a thousand years.

. . . in the Blessed Hope—the rapture of the Church at Christ's coming.

. . . the only means of being cleansed from sin is through repentance and faith in the precious blood of Christ.

. . . regeneration by the Holy Spirit is absolutely essential for personal salvation.

. . . the redemptive work of Christ on the cross provides healing of the human body in answer to believing prayer.

. . . the baptism in the Holy Spirit, according to Acts 2:4, is given to believers who ask for it,

. . . in the sanctifying power of the Holy Spirit by whose indwelling the Christian is enabled to live a holy life.

. . . in the resurrection of both the saved and the lost, the one to everlasting life and the other to everlasting damnation.

Notes: *Prior to his split with the Assemblies of God in the late 1980s, evangelist Jimmy Swaggart's school, while independent, met with denominational approval. The split involved no doctrinal issues. Teachings of the Assemblies continue to be taught by Swaggart and the Jimmy Swaggart Bible School, Baton Rouge, Louisiana. The school's brief statement of belief* *summarizes the Assemblies' lengthy Statement of Fundamental Truths.*

* * *

STATEMENT OF FAITH (KINGSWAY CHRISTIAN COLLEGE AND SEMINARY)

1. We believe the Bible to be the inspired and infallible Word of God.

2. We believe in the eternal, omnipotent, omniscient, omnipresent, and immutable triune God; God the Father, God the Son, and God the Holy Spirit.

3. We believe that Christ was the Lamb of God, foreordained from the foundation of the world, and by the shedding of His blood on the cross, made provision for salvation for ALL men.

4. We believe that salvation is by God's grace alone; is received through sincere godly repentance, and a wholehearted acceptance of Jesus Christ as his personal Savior; through being born again.

5. We believe that having been cleansed by the blood, and quickened by the Spirit, it is God's will that we should be sanctified daily, and be made partakers of holiness; walking not after the flesh but after the Spirit; forsaking the very appearance of evil, such as: worldly dress, worldly amusements, worldly conversation, worldly habits, etc.

6. We believe that water baptism by immersion, in the name of the Father, Son, and Holy Ghost, is commanded by God; that it is subsequent to conversion, that it is not a saving ordinance, but an outward sign of an inward work.

7. We believe in the commemoration of the Lord's Supper as a type of the broken body and shed blood of our Lord Jesus Christ, and as an ordinance showing forth the death, burial and resurrection of our Lord, and a looking forward to the marriage supper of the Lamb.

8. We believe the baptism of the Holy Spirit is a definite experience, not identical with conversion and that the initial evidence of this experience is the speaking in other tongues as the Spirit gives utterance.

9. We believe that for the edification of the saints and the upbuilding of the church of Jesus Christ, the Holy Spirit has the following gifts to bestow upon the individual believer: the word of wisdom, the word of knowledge, faith, gifts of healing, working of miracles, prophecy, discerning of spirits, and divers kinds of tongues, and the interpretation of tongues, dividing to every man severally as He will.

10. We believe that the fruit of the Spirit is: love, joy, peace, longsuffering, gentleness, goodness, faith, meekness, temperance; against such there is no law. These should be cultivated in the life of every believer.

11. We believe that divine healing is the power of God to heal the sick and the afflicted in answer to believing prayer, and is provided for in the atonement. We believe that God is willing to, and does, heal the sick today.

12. We believe that the second coming of Christ is personal, imminent, and pre-millennial.

13. We believe that every born-again child of God should identify himself with the visible church of Jesus Christ, and should labor diligently, and contribute his temporal means toward the spreading of the Gospel here on earth. We believe that tithes should be given into the storehouse of the Lord.

14. We believe that government is ordained of God, and all Christians should be subject to the laws of the land, except those contrary to the revealed will of God. We pledge allegiance and moral and spiritual support to the United States of America.

15. We believe in the final judgment of the wicked at the great white throne, when the dead, both small and great, shall be resurrected to stand before God to receive the reward of their deeds done in the flesh.

16. We believe hell is a literal place of outer darkness, bitter sorrow remorse, and woe, prepared by God for the devil and his angels, and that there, into a lake that burns with fire and brimstone, shall be cast the unbelieving, the abominable, the murderers, sorcerers, idolaters, and all liars, and those who have rejected Jesus Christ, whose names are not written in the Lamb's book of life.

17. We believe that heaven is the habitation of the living God, where Christ has gone to prepare a place for all His children, where they shall dwell eternally, in happiness and security with Him.

18. We believe that the great commission of our Lord Jesus Christ to carry the Gospel message to the entire world in literal, imperative, and binding today; and that it is the supreme privilege and duty of the church of Jesus Christ to stress the cause of world wide missions.

Notes: *Kingsway Christian College and Seminary is an independent Pentecostal college. Its Statement of Faith is a summary of the Pentecostal theological perspective with its unique affirmation of the baptism of the Holy Spirit evidenced by the experience of speaking in tongues. The school also affirms the infallibility of the Bible, divine healing, and the premillennial return of Jesus Christ.*

Chapter 9

European Free-Church Family

Russian Mennonites

DOCTRINE (BRETHREN IN CHRIST/MESSIAH COLLEGE)

Messiah College was founded by educators with strong denominational concerns, but it has never been narrowly sectarian. Students are welcome without regard to denominational affiliation. The College follows the historical Christian position and adheres to the following doctrines;

The inspiration of the Holy Scriptures as the revelation of God, and their reliability as a guide to faith and conduct.

The self-existent, triune God-Father, Son, and Holy Spirit.

The deity and humanity of Christ, His death as atonement for our sins, His resurrection from the dead, His headship of the church, and His personal, visible, and imminent return.

The ministry of the Holy Spirit in guiding the church, convicting the sinner, regenerating the penitent and empowering the believer.

The church as the context of God's redeeming activity, the community of the redeemed, the new society.

Evangelism as a primary mission of the church.

Observance of the ordinances.

Justification as forgiveness of sins.

Sanctification as heart-cleansing and empowering for service.

The development and manifestation of the Christian graces in the believer as evidence of discipleship.

And the resurrection of the dead, with reward of punishment for all people according to their faith in Christ.

Notes: *Messiah College, Grantham, Pennsylvania, is sponsored by the Brethren in Christ Church, a denomination out of* *the Mennonite tradition. This brief statement summarizes the Doctrinal Statement of the Brethren in Christ Church.*

*   *   *

STATEMENT OF FAITH (CHORTITZER MENNONITE CONFERENCE)

We Believe:

1. in the one living eternal and true God who is the Creator of all things.

2. in the deity of Jesus Christ who became the propitiation for all sinners.

3. in the person of the Holy Spirit, sent from God and indwelling in every believer.

4. in the trinity of the Godhead—God, the Father; God, the Son; and God, the Holy Spirit.

5. in the virgin birth of Jesus Christ.

6. that the Scriptures of the Old and New Testaments are wholly inspired by God and are infallible and the final authority in faith and life

7. man is a sinner by nature.

8. man is a free moral agent.

9. in the church as the body of Christ and its mission is to fulfill the Great Commission'' of preaching, teaching and discipling.

10. that every repentant sinner should be baptized with water upon confession of his faith.

11. the Lord instituted the ordinance of communion as remembrance of his suffering.

STATEMENT OF FAITH (CHORTITZER MENNONITE CONFERENCE) (continued)

12. the church has the obligation to keep pure the Body of Christ by disciplining those who have fallen into gross sin.

13. to walk in love towards God and man, refraining from carnal strife and contentions in all areas of life.

14. that God instituted marriage as a permanent bond between male and female of the same faith.

15. all governments are instituted by God and therefore are to be respected as such.

16. the literal resurrection of the body, both of the just and the unjust.

17. in the everlasting blessedness of the saved, and the everlasting punishment of the lost.

18. in the personal and bodily return of the Lord Jesus Christ as King of Kings and Lord of Lords.

Notes: *The Chortitzer Mennonite Church is a small conservative Mennonite body that has absorbed emphases from modern Evangelicalism. Its Statement of Faith affirms the infallibility of the Bible, the literal resurrection of the body, and the personal and bodily return of Jesus Christ. The Church also practices strict discipline on members who have fallen from the church's behavioral standards (an aspect of church life that is typically dropped by the older Mennonite bodies).*

*   *   *

STATEMENT OF FAITH (EVANGELICAL MENNONITE CONFERENCE)

I. OF THE WORD OF GOD

We believe that the whole Bible is the inspired and infallible Word of God; that it is the supreme and final authority in all matters of faith and conduct (II Peter 1:21; Matt. 5:18; 24:35; II Tim. 3:16).

II. OF THE EXISTENCE AND NATURE OF GOD

We believe that there is but one God, eternal, infinite, and unchangeable, who exists and reveals Himself in three persons—Father, Son and Holy Spirit (Deut. 6:4, Psa. 90:2; Gen. 17:1; Psa. 147:5, 139:7-12, Isa. 40:28, 57:15; Mal. 3:6; Heb. 1:8, 12).

III. OF THE CREATION

We believe that God is the Creator and Originator of all things according to the Genesis account (Gen. 1:2; Ex. 20:11; Mk. 10:6; Heb. 11:3).

IV. OF THE FALL OF MAN

We believe that man was created by an immediate act of God, in His own image and after His own likeness, that by one act of disobedience he became sinful in nature, spiritually dead, subject to physical death, and from this fallen condition he was unable to save himself (Gen. 1:26, 27; 2:7 16, 17; Eph. 2:1-3, 12; Rom. 5:6; John 6:44).

V. OF JESUS CHRIST

We believe that Jesus Christ is the eternal Son of God; that He was conceived the Holy Spirit, and born of the virgin Mary; that He was without sin; that by His death He provided the only atonement for sin by the shedding of His blood, the divinely appointed substitute, thus reconciling man to God; that He rose again from the dead, ascended to glory, and lives to make intercession for His own (John 1:1, 14; Lk. 1:35; Isa. 7:14; Matt. 1:20-23; Isa. 53:5f; Rom. 5:8-10; Matt. 28:5; I Cor. 15:20; Acts 1:11; Heb. 7:25; Acts 4:12).

VI. OF SALVATION

We believe that the only way of salvation for man is by grace through faith in Jesus Christ; that man is justified from all sin on the ground of Christ's shed blood and resurrection; that when a person receives the new birth it is evidenced by a transformed life which is devoted to good works and a daily striving for holiness (John 3:15; Eph. 2:8; John 1:12, 13; Acts 4:12: James 2:24)

VII. OF THE HOLY SPIRIT

We believe that the Holy Spirit exists eternally as the third Person in the Trinity; that he convicts the world of sin and of righteousness and of judgement to come; that He indwells and comforts the believer, guides him into truth, empowers for service and enables him to live a life of righteousness (Acts 5:3, 4; 1:8; Matt 28:19; John 16:7f, 13:1 Cor. 3:16; II Cor. 3.3, 17; Rom. 8:1-4; Gal.4:6).

VIII. OF ASSURANCE

We believe that it is the privilege of every believer to know he has passed from death to life, that God is able to keep him from falling, and that faith and obedience are essential to the maintenance of one's assurance and growth in grace (1 John 3:14; Gal. 3:11; John 8:31f:I Peter 1:5-11; Rom. 8:14-17).

IX. OF THE CHURCH

We believe that the Church is the body of Christ, composed of all those who through repentance toward God, and faith in the Lord Jesus Christ, have been born again and have been baptized by one Spirit into one body; that the Church is the fellowship of those who are in the kingdom of Christ, the assembly of those who believe in Him, the brotherhood of the saints; that it is Church's divinely appointed mission to preach the Gospel to every creature; to conform to the will and image of Christ in full discipleship and to teach obedience to the will of God (Matt. 16:18; Eph. 1:23; Col. 1:18; Acts 20:21; Lk. 24:47; Acts 17:30; 16:31; Gal. 3:25; 1 Cor. 12:13; Matt. 28:19f, Acts 1:8; Rom. 8:20; Gal. 4:19; Col. 3:1-4).

X. OF SATAN AND HIS KINGDOM

We believe in the personality of Satan, The prince of the powers of darkness. The devil is the father of lies and a murderer from the beginning. We believe that Satan and his hosts seek to delude and lead astray the child of God by coming as an ''angel of light'' or as a ''roaring lion.'' The devil and his host blind the minds of the unbelievers, snatch away the Word of Truth at times, inflict illness, and oppress anyone who permits the evil powers entrance. The devil is uses any wiles imaginable in obstructing the advance of the Kingdom of God. The Christian therefore is engaged in a spiritual warfare with powers much greater than he has by himself. These evil powers can only be overcome through faith in the blood of Christ and the Word of God and the power of the Holy Spirit. Therefore Christians must test the spirits, resist the devil, draw nigh unto God, put on the whole armor of God, and continually consider themselves dead to sin and alive unto God (John 8:39-47; 1 Tim. 4:1-5; 1 John 4:1-6; 1 Peter 5:6-9; James 4:7; Eph. 2:1ff, 6:1ff).

XI. OF DISCIPLESHIP AND NON-CONFORMITY

We believe that there are two opposing kingdoms to which men give their spiritual allegiance, that of Christ and that of Satan. Those who belong to Satan's kingdom live for sin and self, and refuse the obedience of faith (Eph. 2:1-10).

Those who belong to the kingdom of Christ seek

1. To live holy lives and regard their bodies as temples of the Holy Spirit and crucify their flesh with its affections and lusts (Titus 2:11-14; If Thess. 3:6; Rom. 13:14).

2. To avoid any unequal yoke with unbelievers (11 Cor. 6:14-18; Rom. 12:1, 2; Eph. 5:11).

3. To walk in love towards God and man, refraining from carnal strife and contentions in all areas of life, from war (Rom. 12:14-21) and from swearing oaths (Matt. 5:33-37; James 5:12); to exercise proper stewardship of time, possessions and abilities (I Cor. 16:1, 2; II Cor. 8 and 9). Their daily Christian walk should manifest complete allegiance to Christ (I John 2:15-17; II Thess. 3:6; I Peter 2:9).

XII. OF ADMINISTRATION

We believe that the Lord has given the Church authority

1. To choose officials (Acts 6:1-6; Tit. 1:5, 6).

2. To regulate the observance of ordinances (Matt. 28:19, 20; John 12).

3. To exercise wholesome discipline (Tit. 3:15; Matt. 18:15-18).

4. To organize and conduct her work in a manner consistent with her high calling and essential to her highest efficiency (Matt. 28:19f; Eph. 4:11-16).

XIII. OF ORDINANCES

We believe in the administration of water baptism upon the confession of a personal faith in the Lord Jesus Christ, in the observance of the Lord's Supper, and in the believer's feetwashing.

XIV. OF THE RESURRECTION

We believe that Christ Jesus was raised bodily from the dead, and that all men also shall be resurrected bodily, both the just and the unjust, the just to the resurrection of life and the unjust to the resurrection of condemnation (John 20:20, 24-29; 5:28-29; 1 Cor. 15; Dan. 12:2; Rom. 8:11; Acts 24:15).

XV. OF THE COMING OF CHRIST

We believe in the personal return of our Lord Jesus Christ as the blessed hope of the believers, that ''we which are alive and remain,'' together with the dead in Christ, who will be raised first, shall be caught up to meet the Lord in the air and thus we shall be with the Lord forever (John 14:2f; Acts 1:11; Matt. 24:44; Heb. 10:37; Tit. 2:11-14; I Thess. 4:13-18).

XVI. OF THE INTERMEDIATE STATE

We believe that in the interval between death and resurrection, the righteous will be with Christ in a state of conscious bliss, but the unrighteous will be in a state of conscious suffering (Lk. 16:19-31; 23:43; Phil. 1:23; II Cor. 5:1-8; II Peter 2:4-9).

XVII. OF THE FINAL STATE

We believe that hell is the place of torment prepared for the devil and his angels, where with them the unrighteous will suffer the vengeance of eternal fire forever and ever and that heaven is the final abode of the righteous, where the righteous will dwell in the fullness of joy forever and ever (Matt. 25:41-46; Jude 7; Rev. 14: 8-11; 20:10, 15; II Cor. 5:1; Rev. 21:3-8; Rev. 22:1-5).

Notes: *Founded in Russia in the early nineteenth century and migrating to America in the 1870s, the Evangelical Mennonite Conference has been affected by the larger world of conservative Protestantism, whose concerns, more than those of the traditional Mennonite community, are reflected in their Statement of Faith. Thus the Conference affirms the infallibility of the Bible, the literal truth of the Genesis creation story, justification by grace through faith, and the personality of Satan. The Conference does affirm the traditional Mennonite distinctives of pacifism, swearing oaths, and adult baptism. It also practices foot washing.*

*   *   *

STATEMENT OF FAITH (MENNONITE BRETHREN CHURCH OF NORTH AMERICA/BETHANY BIBLE INSTITUTE)

Bethany Bible Institute acknowledges and confesses:

1. That the whole Bible is the inspired and infallible Word of God, and is the supreme and final authority in all matters of faith and conduct. (2 Peter 2:21, 2 Timothy 3:16.)

STATEMENT OF FAITH (MENNONITE BRETHREN CHURCH
OF NORTH AMERICA/BETHANY BIBLE INSTITUTE)
(continued)

2.   That there is one God, eternally existing in three persons: Father, Son and Holy Spirit. (2 Corinthians 13:14.)

3.   That Jesus Christ was begotten by the Holy Spirit, born of the Virgin Mary, and is true God and true man. (John 1:1,2,4; Matthew 1:18; Philippians 2:5-8.)

4.   That the Holy Spirit is a person, is God and is co-equal with the Father and the Son; convicts the world of sin, righteousness and judgement; regenerates and indwells the believer, is his constant guide and teacher. and the enabling power for victorious living and dedicated service. (John 15:26; John 16:7,8; Titus 3:5; John 3:5; John 16:13; Acts 1:8.)

5.   That man was created in the image of God, that he sinned, and thereby incurred for himself and the whole human race not only physical death, but also spiritual death, which is separation from God. (Romans 5:12,19; Genesis 1:26,27.)

6.   The Lord Jesus Christ died for man's sins, according to the Scriptures, and that all who believe on Him have the forgiveness of sins through His blood. (1 Corinthians 15:3, Ephesians 1:7.)

7.   That Christ arose bodily from the dead and ascended into heaven where He is now the believer's High Priest and Advocate. (1 Corinthians 15:4; Hebrews 7:25.)

8.   That the imminent return of Christ from heaven will be personal and visible, and that He will judge the living and the dead. (Acts 1:11; John 5:28,29.)

9.   That an individual becomes a child of God by being born of the Holy Spirit by the Word of God through a personal faith in Jesus Christ. (John 1:12,13; Titus 3:5.)

10. That the church, instituted by Christ, consists of all true believers, and that the Great Commission to make disciples of all nations is the supreme mission of the church in this age. (1 Corinthians 12:12,13; Matthew 28:19,20.)

11. That the ordinances of the church are water baptism by immersion, upon personal confession of faith and the Lord's Supper in remembrance of Christ. (1 Corinthians 11:23-26; Romans 6:4.)

12. That there will be a bodily resurrection of both the just and the unjust with a state of everlasting blessedness for believers, and a state of eternal punishment for all unbelievers. (1 Thessalonians 4:13-18; Revelation 20:11-15.)

13. That the Christian life is separated unto God, conforming to the teachings of the Word, and dedicated to the service of Christ. (Romans 12:1,2.)

Notes: *Bethany Bible Institute, in Hepburn, Saskatchewan, is a school of the Mennonite Brethren Church of North America. This Statement of Faith summarizes the longer Confession of Faith of the Mennonite Brethren, and affirms a consensus Mennonite evangelical faith.*

*   *   *

OUR CONFESSION OF FAITH (MENNONITE BRETHREN CHURCH OF NORTH AMERICA/ MENNONITE BRETHREN BIBLICAL SEMINARY)

The Mennonite Brethren Biblical Seminary is in full agreement with the Confession of Faith of the Conference of Mennonite Brethren Churches. The following confession is an article by article summary of that Confession of Faith.

1.   God. We believe in one God, eternally existing in three persons: Father, Son and Holy Spirit.

(a) We believe in God the Father, the Creator and Sustainer of this universe, who in infinite wisdom and love planned the redemption of mankind and accomplished it through Jesus Christ.

(b) We believe in Jesus Christ, truly God and truly human, who was born of the virgin Mary, lived a perfect life, was crucified for our sins, rose from the dead and was exalted to the right hand of God.

(c) We believe in the Holy Spirit who effects redemption in the lives of those who believe in Christ. He convicts, guides, teaches, rebukes, indwells, empowers, comforts, intercedes, unites believers into one body, and glorifies Christ.

2.   The Revelation of God. We believe that God has made His power and deity known in creation. He revealed Himself also in word and deed in the Old Testament. God revealed Himself supremely and finally in the Lord Jesus Christ, as recorded in the New Testament. We believe that all Scripture is inspired by God as people of God were moved by the Holy Spirit. We accept the entire Bible as the infallible Word of God and as the authoritative guide for the faith and life of Christian discipleship.

3.   Man and Sin. We believe that humanity was created in the image of God, sinless and in fellowship with God, with a free will to make moral choices. Man and woman chose sin and thus brought death upon the whole human race. As a consequence all people are sinful by nature, guilty before God and in need of forgiveness and restoration.

4.   Salvation by Grace. We believe that there is one God and Mediator between God and humanity, Jesus Christ, who

by his substitutionary death has redeemed humanity from the power of sin, death and eternal punishment. We are saved by God's grace through faith in Christ. Those who repent receive forgiveness of sins and by the power of the Holy Spirit are born into the family of God and, as faithful disciples, joyfully obey God's Word.

5. The Christian Life. We believe that the Holy Spirit indwells every believer and transforms him/her into the image of Christ and enables him/her to witness to Christ in daily life. The Christian lives in fellowship with God and other believers and joins a local church at baptism. The believer contributes to the building of the body of Christ with his/her material and spiritual gifts. By the means of grace provided by Christ, the believer seeks to grow to maturity, as this is expressed particularly in the ''fruit of the Spirit.'' Since the Christian's body is a ''temple of the Holy Spirit'' believers refrain from those things which harm the body and the mind. In striving for perfection the believer recognizes his/her complete dependence on God and the constant need for God's forgiving and cleansing grace.

6. The Church of Christ. We believe that the Church was established through Christ's redemptive work in history, and that it is comprised of all who put their faith in Him and who are baptized by the Spirit into one body, regardless of nation, race or social class. Despite the diversity in congregations and denominations, the Holy Spirit creates unity among all the people of God. The local church is an association of baptized believers. Mennonite Brethren churches, whose polity is in agreement with the constitution of the General Conference of Mennonite Brethren Churches, work together in a spirit of interdependence, love and submission one to another under the Lordship of Christ. Believers manifest loving concern for each other and submit to mutual admonition and discipline. Those who fail and refuse to be corrected are excluded from the fellowship of the church; those who repent are forgiven and restored.

7. The Mission of the Church. We believe that the Gospel is ''the power of God unto salvation,'' and that the command to make disciples of all nations is the primary task of the Church. Every member of the Church is called to participate in the mission of the Church as he/she is enabled by God's grace.

8. The Christian Ministries. We believe that God through the Holy Spirit has endowed all believers with gifts for Christian ministries. Some members of the Church, however, are called to lead, to preach, to teach, to evangelize, to nurture; others perform deaconal ministries. The Church commissions or ordains people for such ministries and loves, respects, and supports those who serve faithfully. Those in leadership are to live exemplary Christian lives.

9. Christian Baptism. We believe that Christians should be baptized in water upon confession of their faith in Christ. The Mennonite Brethren Church practices baptism by immersion, although it receives into fellowship those who have been baptized on confession of their faith by another mode. By baptism a believer enters into the fellowship of the local church and commits him/herself to a life of discipleship and service.

10. The Lord's Supper. Believers who have been baptized observe the Lord's Supper. In preparation every believer is to examine him/herself so as to partake in a worthy manner. Those who are at peace with God and their fellows are invited to the Lord's Table.

11. Marriage and the Christian Home. We believe that God instituted marriage. Believers who marry should have a common Christian commitment; a believer should not marry an unbeliever. We believe that divorce constitutes a violation of God's intention for marriage. Christian parents should nurture their children through exemplary living, prayer, worship, instruction in God's Word, and godly discipline.

12. The Lord's Day and Work. We believe that God has called us to work and that work is honorable. However, the Christian also needs to have time for worship, instruction in the faith and fellowship. Therefore, following the example of the New Testament Church, Mennonite Brethren gather on the Lord's Day for spiritual upbuilding and limit their labors on that day to work of necessity and deeds of mercy.

13. Christian Integrity. Christians are obligated to speak the truth at all times. As a witness to our integrity we refuse the making of oaths, in keeping with what Jesus taught in the Sermon on the Mount. Also, we avoid holding membership in lodges and secret societies, but seek rather to foster fellowship among believers.

14. The State. We believe that God has instituted the state. Our chief concern and primary allegiance, however, is to Christ's kingdom. We pray for our government, respect those in authority, pay taxes, obey all laws not in conflict with the Word of God, and witness against corruption and injustice in society.

15. Love and Nonresistance. We believe that Christians should live by the law of love and practice forgiveness of enemies as taught and exemplified by Jesus. We hold that it is not God's will that Christians take up arms in military service, but that they perform alternate service in time of war, and seek to alleviate suffering and bear witness to the love of Christ.

16. Christ's Final Triumph. We believe that God will some day bring His purposes to a final consummation. When Christ returns the dead in Christ will be raised and together with the living believers they will be transformed and they shall be forever with the Lord. In the end all evil powers will be defeated, and whereas the ungodly shall suffer eternal punishment, the saints shall enjoy eternal bliss in the presence of God.

OUR CONFESSION OF FAITH (MENNONITE BRETHREN CHURCH OF NORTH AMERICA/ MENNONITE BRETHREN BIBLICAL SEMINARY) (continued)

Notes: *The Mennonite Brethren Biblical Seminary, Fresno, California, is a ministerial training school of the Mennonite Brethren Church of North America. Our Confession of Faith summarizes the Confession of Faith of the Mennonite Brethren.*

*   *   *

STATEMENT OF FAITH (MENNONITE BRETHREN CHURCH OF NORTH AMERICA/WINKLER BIBLE INSTITUTE)

We believe in one God, eternal existing in three persons: Father, Son and Holy Ghost.

We believe that Jesus Christ was begotten by the Holy Spirit, born of the virgin Mary, and is true God and man.

We believe that man was created in the image of God: that he sinned, and thereby incurred, not only physical but also spiritual death which is separation from God.

We believe that the Lord Jesus died for our sins as a substitutionary sacrifice, and that all who believe in Him are justified on the ground of His shed blood.

We believe in the bodily resurrection of our Lord, in His ascension into heaven, and in His present life for us as High Priest and Advocate.

We believe in the bodily resurrection of the just and the unjust, the everlasting blessedness of the saved, and the eternal punishment of the wicked.

We believe that the individual who lives in sin and does not repent cannot inherent the Kingdom of God.

We believe that each individual must experience regeneration, being born again of the Holy Spirit by faith in the Lord Jesus Christ, in order to become a child of God.

We believe in the plenary verbal inspiration of the Bible and that it is the final authority for faith and life.

We believe that the Church is a body of believers whose responsibility it is to witness by life and word to the truth and to proclaim the gospel to all nations.

We believe in the premillennial return of Jesus Christ.

Notes: *Winkler Bible Institute, Winkler, Manitoba, is a ministerial training school of the Mennonite Brethren Church of North America. Its Statement of Faith briefly summarizes the Confession of Faith of the Mennonite Brethren.*

*   *   *

Brethren

COVENANT OF FAITH (FELLOWSHIP OF GRACE BRETHREN CHURCHES/GRACE COLLEGE/ GRACE THEOLOGICAL SEMINARY)

The Holy Scriptures . . .

We believe in the Holy Scriptures, accepting fully the writings of the Old and New Testaments as the very Word of God, verbally inspired in all parts and therefore wholly without error as originally given of God, altogether sufficient in themselves as our only infallible rule of faith practice (Matt. 5:18, John 10:35, 16:13, 17:17, 2 Tim. 3:16, 2 Pet. 1:21).

The One Triune God . . .

We believe in the One Triune God, who is personal, spirit, and sovereign (Mark 12:29, John 4:24, 14:9, Psa. 135:6); perfect, infinite, and eternal in His being, holiness, love, wisdom and power (Psa. 18:30, 147:5 Deut. 33:27); absolutely separate and above the world as its Creator, yet everywhere present in the world as the upholder of all things (Gen. 1:1 Psa. 104); self-existent and self-revealing in three distinct Persons—the Father, the Son, and the Holy Spirit (John 5:26, Matt, 28:19, 2 Cor. 13:14) each of whom is to be honored and worshiped equally as true God (John 5:23. Acts 5:3-4).

The Lord Jesus Christ . . .

We believe in the Lord Jesus Christ, who is the Second Person of the Triune God, the eternal Word and Only Begotten Son, our great God and Savior (John 1:1 3:16, Tit. 2:13, Rom 9:5); that, without any essential change in His divine Person (Heb. 13:8). He became man by the miracle of Virgin Birth (John 1:14, Matt. 1:23). thus to continue forever as both true God and true Man, one Person with two natures (Col. 2:9, Rev. 22:16); that as Man, He was in all points tempted like as we are, yet without sin (Heb. 4:15, John 8:46); that as the perfect Lamb of God He gave Himself in death upon the Cross, bearing there the sin of the world, and suffering its full penalty of divine wrath in our stead (Isa. 53:5-6, Matt 20:28, Gal. 3:13 John 1:29); that He rose again from the dead and was glorified in the same body in which He suffered and died (Luke 24:36-43, John 20:25-28); that as our great High Priest He ascended into heaven, there to appear before the face of God as our Advocate and intercessor (Herb. 4:14, 9:24, 1 John 2:1).

The Holy Spirit . . .

We believe in the Holy Spirit, who is the Third Person of the Triune God (Matt. 28:19, Acts 5:3-4), the divine Agent in nature, revelation and redemption (Gen. 1:2, Psa. 104:30, 1 Cor. 2:10, 2 Cor. 3:18); that He convicts the world of sin (John 16:8-11), regenerates those who believe (John 3:5), and indwells, baptizes, seals, empowers, guides, teaches, and sanctifies all who become children of God through Christ (1 Cor. 6:19, 12:13, Eph. 4:30, 3:16, Rom. 8:14, John 14:26, 1 Cor. 6:11).

The Creation and Fall of Man . . .

We believe in the creation and fall of man; that he was the direct creation of God, spirit and soul and body, not in any sense the product of an animal ancestry, but made in the divine image (Gen. 1:26-28, 2:7, 18-24, Matt. 19:4, 1 Thess. 5:23); that by personal disobedience to the revealed will of God, man became a sinful creature and the progenitor of a fallen race (Gen. 3:1-24, 5:3), who are universally sinful in both nature and practice (Eph. 2:3, Rom. 3:23, 5:12), alienated from the life and family of God (Eph. 4:18, John 8:42-44) under the righteous judgment and wrath of God Rom. 3:19, 1:18), and have within themselves no possible means of recovery or salvation (Mark 7:21-23, Matt. 19:26, Rom. 7:18).

Salvation by Grace Through Faith . . .

We believe in salvation by grace through faith, that salvation is the free gift of God (Rom. 3:24, 6:23), neither merited nor secured in part in whole by any virtue or work of man (Tit. 3:5, Rom. 4:4-5, 11:16), but received only by personal faith in the Lord Jesus Christ (John 3:16, 6:28-29, Acts 16:30-31 Eph. 2:8-9), in whom all true believers have as a present possessions the gift of eternal life, a perfect righteousness, sonship in the family of God, deliverance and security from all condemnation, every spiritual resource needed for life and godliness, and the divine guarantee that they shall never perish (1 John 5:13, Rom 3:22, Gal. 3:26, John 5:24, Eph. 1:3, 2 Pet. 1:3, John 10:27-30); that this salvation includes the whole man, spirit and soul and body (1 Thess. 5:23-24); and apart from Christ there is no possible salvation (John 14:6, Acts 4:12).

Righteous Living and Good Works . . .

We believe in righteous living and good works, not as the procuring cause of salvation in any sense, but as its proper evidence and fruit (1 John 3:9-11, 4:19, 5:4 Eph. 2:8-10, Tit. 2:14, Matt 7:16-18 1 Cor. 15:10); and therefore as Christians we should keep the word of our Lord (John 14:23), seek the

things which are above (Col. 3:1), walk as He walked (1 John 2:6), be careful to maintain good works (Tit. 3:8), and especially accept as our solemn responsibility the duty and privilege of bearing the Gospel to a lost world in order that we may bear much fruit (Acts 1:8, 2 Cor. 5:19, John 15:16); remembering that a victorious and fruitful Christian life is possible only for those who have learned they are not under law but under grace (Rom. 6:14), and who in gratitude for the infinite and undeserved mercies of God have presented themselves wholly to Him for His service (Rom. 12:1-2).

The Existence of Satan . . .

We believe in the existence of Satan, who originally was created a holy and perfect being, but through pride and unlawful ambition rebelled against God (Ez. 28:13-17, Isa. 14:13-14, 1 Tim. 3:7); thus becoming utterly depraved in character (John 8:44), the great Adversary of God and His people (Matt. 4:1-11, Rev. 12:10), leader of all other evil angels and spirits (Matt. 12:24-26, 25:41). the deceiver and god of this present world (Rev. 12:9, 2 Cor. 4:4); that his powers are supernaturally great but strictly limited by the permissive will of God, who overrules all his wicked devices for good (Job 1:1-22, Lk. 22:31-32); that he was defeated and judged at the Cross, and therefore his final doom is certain (John 12:31-32, 16;11, Rev. 10:10); that we are able to resist and overcome him only in the armor of God and by the Blood of the Lamb (Eph. 6:12-18, Rev. 12-11).

The Second Coming of Christ . . .

We believe in the second coming of Christ, that His return from heaven will be personal, visible and glorious a Blessed Hope for which we should constantly watch and pray, the time being unrevealed but always imminent (Acts 1:11, Rev. 1:7, Mark 13:33-37, Tit. 2:11-13, Rev. 22:20); that when He comes He will first by resurrection and translation remove from the earth His waiting Church (1 Thess. 4:16-18), then pour out the righteous judgments of God upon the unbelieving world (Rev. 6:1-18:24), afterward descend with His Church and establish His glorious and literal kingdom over all the nations for a thousand years (Rev. 19:1-20:6, Matt. 13:41-43), at the close of which He will raise and judge the unsaved dead (Rev. 20:11-15), and finally as the Son of David deliver up His Messianic Kingdom of God the Father (1 Cor. 15:24-28), in order that as the Eternal Son He may reign forever with the Father in the New Heaven and the New Earth (Luke 1:32:33. Rev. 21:1-22:26).

Future Life, Bodily Resurrection and Eternal Judgment . . .

We believe in future life, bodily resurrection and eternal judgment, that the spirits of the saved at death go immediately to be with Christ in heaven (Phil. 1:21-23, 2 Cor. 5:8), where they abide in joyful fellowship with Him until His second coming, when their bodies shall be raised from the grave and changed into the likeness of His own glorious body (Phil. 3:20-21, 1 Cor. 15:35-38, I John 3:2), at which time their works

COVENANT OF FAITH (FELLOWSHIP OF GRACE BRETHREN CHURCHES/GRACE COLLEGE/ GRACE THEOLOGICAL SEMINARY) (continued)

shall be brought before the Judgment Sea of Christ for the determination of rewards, a judgment which may issue in the loss of rewards but not the loss of the soul (1 Cor. 3:8-15), that the spirits of the unsaved at death descend immediately into Hades where they are kept under punishment until the final day of judgment (Luke 16:19-31, 2 Pet. 2:9 ASV), at which time their bodies shall be raised from the grave, they shall be judged according to their works and cast into the place of final and everlasting punishment (Rev. 20:11-15, 21:8, Mark 9:43-48, Jude 13)

One True Church . . .

We believe in the One True Church, the mystical Body and Bride of the Lord Jesus (Eph. 4:4, 5:25-32), which He began to build on the day of Pentecost (Matt. 16:18, Acts 2:47) and will complete at His second coming (1 Thess. 4:16-17), and into which all true believe of the present age are baptized immediately by the Holy Spirit (1 Cor. 12:12-13 with 1:2); that all the various members of this one spiritual Body should assemble themselves together in local churches for worship prayer, fellowship, teaching, united testimony, and the observance of the ordinances of our Lord (Heb. 10:25, Acts 2:41-47), among which are the following. The Baptism of believers by Triune Immersion (Matt. 28:20), the Laying on of Hands (1 Tim. 4:14, 2 Tim. 1:6), the Washing of the Saints' Feet (John 13:17), the Lord's Supper or Love-feast (1 Cor. 11:17-22, Jude 12 ASV), the Communion of the Bread and Cup (1 Cor. 11:23-24), and Prayer and Anointing for the Sick (Jas. 5:13-18).

Separation from the World . . .

We believe in separation from the world, that since our Christian citizenship is in heaven, as the children of God we should walk in separation from this present world, having no fellowship with its evil ways (Phil. 3:20 ASV. 2 Cor. 6:14-18. Rom. 12:2, Eph. 5:11), abstaining from all worldly amusements and unclear habits which defile mind and body (Luke 8:14, 1 Thess. 5:22, 1 Tim. 5:6 1 Pet. 2:11 Eph. 5:3-11 Col. 3:17, Eph. 5:3-5, 18, 1 Cor. 6:19-20), from the sin of divorce and remarriage as forbidden by our Lord (Matt. 19:9), from the swearing of any oath (Jas. 5:12), from the use of unbelieving courts for the settlement of disputes between Christian (1 Cor. 6:19), and from taking personal vengeance in carnal strife (Rom. 12:18-21), 2 Cor. 10:3-4).

Notes: *Grace College and Grace Brethren Theological Seminary, sponsored by the Fellowship of Grace Brethren Churches, are located amidst the collection of Evangelical churches and organizations (including the Fellowship headquarters) in Winona Lake, Indiana. The Grace Brethren have been among the most conservative groups within the Brethren tradition and the schools' Doctrinal Position reflects that conservatism. The Position affirms the inerrancy of the Bible, the existence of Satan, the personal and visible return of Jesus Christ, and separation from evil. Brethren refrain from swearing oaths,*

taking fellow Christians to court, and "taking personal vengeance in carnal strife." This statement forms the framework for instruction at Grace, but is not required to be accepted fully by students.

*　　　*　　　*

Quakers (Friends)

STATEMENT OF FAITH (NORTHWEST YEARLY MEETING OF FRIENDS CHURCH AND ROCKY MOUNTAIN YEARLY MEETING/GEORGE FOX COLLEGE)

1. We believe there is one God, eternally existent in three persons—Father, Son, and Holy Spirit.

2. We believe in the deity of our Lord Jesus Christ, in His virgin birth, in His sinless life, in His miracles, in His vicarious and atoning death through His shed blood, in His bodily resurrection, in His ascension to the right hand of the Father as the only mediator between God and man, and in His personal return in power and glory.

3. We believe that for the salvation of lost and sinful man, regeneration by the Holy Spirit is absolutely essential.

4. We believe the Bible to be the only inspired, infallible. authoritative Word of God.

5. We reverently believe that as there is one Lord, and one faith, so there is one baptism, whereby all believers are baptized in the one Spirit into the one body.

6. We believe the true supper of the Lord is observed when the believer partakes spiritually and inwardly.

7. We believe in the ministry of the Holy Spirit, who fills and indwells the consecrated believer and enables him to live a godly life.

8. We believe all war is utterly incompatible with the plain precepts of our divine Lord and Lawgiver.

9. We believe in the resurrection of both the saved and the lost; they that are saved unto the resurrection of life and they that are lost unto the resurrection of damnation.

Notes: *George Fox College, Newberg, Oregon, is sponsored by two independent conservative Friends churches, the Northwest Yearly Meeting of Friends Church and the Rocky Mountain Yearly Meeting. The College espouses the most Evangelical orthodox elements of the Society of Friends and affirms the Trinity, the atoning work of Jesus Christ, and the infallibility of the Bible. True to its Quaker heritage, the Statement of Faith holds to a spiritual observance of the Lord's Supper and pacifism.*

Chapter 10
Baptist Family

MESSAGE (1923) (BAPTIST WORLD ALLIANCE)

We are, first and always, Christians, acknowledging in its deepest and broadest sense the Lordship of Jesus Christ, and devoted to Him as the Son of God and Savior of the world. We rejoice that the spiritual unity of all believers is a blessed reality, not dependent upon organization or ceremonies. We pray that by increasing obedience to Christ's will, this unity may be deepened and strengthened among Christians of every name.

THE LORDSHIP OF JESUS CHRIST

There are various ways of stating the fundamental Baptist principle. If we indicate the source of our knowledge, we say the scriptures of the Old and New Testaments are divinely inspired, and are our sufficient, certain, and authoritative guide in all matters of faith and practice. As to the nature of the Christian religion, we affirm that it is personal and spiritual. We believe in the direct relation of each individual to God, and the right of everyone to choose for himself in all matters of faith. A Christian's religion begins in the soul when personal faith is exercised in Jesus Christ, the divine Redeemer and Lord, As the Revealer of God to men and the Mediator of salvation, Jesus Christ is central for Christian faith. His will is the supreme law for the Christian. He is Lord of the conscience of the individual and of the Church. Hence, the Lordship of Jesus Christ is a cardinal teaching of Baptists. It excludes all merely human authorities in religion.

THE NATURE OF BAPTIST UNITY

We desire to impress upon our Baptist brethren in every part of the world the importance of Baptist unity at the present time. Accepting the voluntary principle in religion and regarding the nature of Christianity as a spiritual relation between man and God, we inevitably take the same attitude on questions of faith and conduct as they arise within the churches. We hold fast to the freedom with which Christ has set us free, and this principle implies that we must be willing to love and to work with those who, agreeing with us on the main things and in loyalty to our distinctive Baptist principles, have their own personal convictions upon non-essentials. All Baptist organizations are formed on the voluntary principle. None of these possesses authority over any other. All enjoy equal rights and autonomy within the limits of their own purposes.

CHRISTIAN UNITY

Baptists have ever held all who have communion with God in our Lord Jesus Christ as our Christian brethren in the work of the Lord, and heirs with us of eternal life. We love their fellowship, and maintain that the spiritual union does not depend upon organization, forms, or ritual. It is deeper, higher, broader, and more stable than any or all externals. All who truly are joined to Christ are our brethren in the common salvation, whether they be in the Catholic communion, or in a Protestant communion, or in any other communion, or in no communion. Baptists, with all evangelical Christians, rejoice in the common basic beliefs; the incarnation of the Son of God, His sinless life, His supernatural works, His Deity, His vicarious atonement and resurrection from the dead, His present reign and His coming kingdom, with its eternal awards to the righteous and unrighteous.

To Baptists it is entirely clear that the direct relation of the soul to God, or the universal priesthood of believers, is the basis of the New Testament teaching as to the church and the ministry. Christian unity, therefore, as Baptists understand the New Testament, is a result of the operation of the Holy Spirit arising from a common faith in Christ, enlightened by a common understanding of His teachings, inspired by a common vision of the ends of the Kingdom of God, and issuing in a free and voluntary cooperation in the execution of the will of Christ. Christian unity is thus a flexible principle, adapting itself to every situation. It admits cooperation so far as there is agreement, and abstains from all coercion.

The implications of the voluntary principle based upon the universal priesthood of believers in their bearing upon Christian unity are clear. Baptists cannot consent to any form of union which impairs the rights of the individual believer. We cannot unite with others in any centralized ecclesiastical organization wielding power over the individual conscience. We cannot accept the sacerdotal conception of the ministry which involves the priesthood of a class with special powers for transmitting grace. We cannot accept the conception of ordination made valid through a historic succession in the ministry. As Baptists understand the New Testament, all believers being priests unto God, ministers can possess no further sacerdotal powers. They are called to special tasks of preaching and teaching and administration. They remain the spiritual equals of other believers in the church. Again, the principle of the universal priesthood of believers involves the direct authority of Jesus Christ, our Great High Priest. Christian unity, therefore, can only come through obedience to the will of Christ as revealed in the New Testament, which Baptists must ever take as their sole, sufficient, certain, and authoritative guide.

THE BAPTIST FAITH AND MISSION

As Baptists view it, the Christian religion finds its central truth in the incarnation of God in Jesus Christ, whose sinless life and heavenly wisdom, whose Deity, atoning death, resurrection from the dead, and whose second coming and lordship in the Kingdom of God constitute and qualify him for his work as its Founder and Mediator. God calls all men to salvation through him, in whom they are freely justified by grace through faith, and regenerated by the operation of the Holy Spirit. Regeneration, or the new birth, is a necessary condition of church-membership, since in this way alone can the churches be kept spiritual and responsive to the will of Christ. Church-membership of believers only is a fundamental Baptist principle. Each church, as made up of the regenerate, is competent to conduct its own affairs. It is, therefore, by its nature and constitution, a spiritual democracy, free and self-governing, and answering to Christ alone as its ultimate authority.

The New Testament recognizes nothing as baptism but the immersion in water of the believer upon profession of faith. In the Lord's Supper it recognizes no sacerdotal authority in those who administer it, and no sacramental quality in the bread and wine, by virtue of which it conveys grace through any change in the elements.

In the matter of the polity, the officers, and the ordinances of a church, Baptists seek to preserve the spirituality and simplicity of the New Testament, and at the same time the proper proportion of emphasis. A group of great spiritual principles underlies their conception of a church at all points. As a self-governing spiritual democracy, a church recognizes the spiritual competency and freedom of the individual members. Since it requires a personal profession of faith as a condition of baptism, it eliminates the proxy element in faith and respects the rights of personality. Hence, infant baptism is utterly irreconcilable with the ideal of a spiritual Christianity. Voluntary and not compulsory baptism is a vital spiritual principle of the New Testament.

The officers of a church are teachers and leaders, not ecclesiastical authorities. Thus at all points a church of Christ is the outward expression of great spiritual principles; the supreme value of personality, the inalienable rights of free choice and of direct access to God, the equality of all believers, and their common spiritual priesthood. No charge, therefore, can be

more groundless than that Baptists are ceremonialists or sacramentalists. They are the exact opposite of these things.

In harmony with the above principles, Baptists conceive their mission to the world to be moral and spiritual. Primarily, their duty is to make known the will of Christ and secure the willing submission of men to him, as set forth in the gospel of the grace of God. Evangelization and missions thus become prime factors in the program of Baptists. The command of Christ to preach the gospel to every creature is of permanent binding force. The necessity for education, philanthropy, and civic and social righteousness in manifold forms arises inevitably out of evangelizing and missionary activity.

RELIGIOUS LIBERTY AND ITS APPLICATIONS

Baptists from the beginning of their history have been the ardent champions of religious liberty They have often been persecuted, but they could never persecute others save in defiance of their own principles. Religious liberty is an inherent and inalienable human right. It arises out of the direct relation of the soul to God. Man is constituted in God's image. He is a free personality. Moral responsibility is based upon this freedom. This is a fundamental axiom of ethics as well as of religion.

Religious liberty, in its broadest significance, implies the following elements: First, no human authority of any kind, in society at large, in church or state, has any right to repress or hinder or thwart any man or group of men in the exercise of religious belief or worship. Second, the right of every man and group of men to complete freedom in the search for, the worship of, and obedience to God. Third, freedom to teach and preach those beliefs and truths which men may hold as committed to them from God to be made known to others.

Religious liberty is inconsistent with any union of church and state, because the church rests upon the spiritual principle of free choice, while the state rests upon law with an ultimate appeal to physical force. It is inconsistent with special favor by the state towards one or more religious groups and toleration towards others, because equality of privilege is a fundamental and inalienable religious right of all men. It is inconsistent with priestly and episcopal authority and with infant baptism, because free choice and voluntary obedience to Christ are essential to the Christian religion.

Thus Baptists stand for the rights of the individual versus the close ecclesiastical corporation, the direct relation of the soul to God versus the indirect, free grace versus sacramental grace, believers's baptism versus infant baptism, personal versus proxy faith, the priesthood of all believers versus the priesthood of a class, democracy in the church versus autocracy or oligarchy or other forms of human authority. Religious liberty is not license. It gives no right to the indulgence of lust or sin in any form. It confers no exemption from the authority of the state in its own sphere. It implies and requires loyalty to Christ on the part of every Christian. For non-Christians it implies responsibility to God alone for religious beliefs, and freedom from all coercion in matters of religious opinion. Baptists have ever insisted upon religious freedom for unbelievers and atheists, as well as Christians. However deplorable their unbelief, they are responsible not to human authorities but to God.

RELIGION AND ETHICS

Our religion is not only for the salvation of the individual, it is also ethical and social. The new life in Christ creates a new moral character and a new sense of social responsibility. The Christian ideal is God's Kingdom. He is to reign in all realms of life. His will is to rule in the family, in the church, in industry, in society, in the arts, in the state, and in international relations.

FAMILY LIFE

Family life of high quality is fundamental to all human progress. Here especially should personality, its needs, its discipline and development, control. Here Christ's law of mutual love and service should rule. Children are free personalities to be reared in the nurture and admonition of the Lord. The will is not to be broken, but disciplined and trained. The home should be a living fountain of religious life, where prayer and study of the Scriptures should not be shifted to the school or to any other agency. Divorce on unscriptural grounds is one of the greatest evils of the day in many parts of the world. The duty of all Christians everywhere is to resist this evil. Christ's teaching on the subject should be respected, and every proper means employed to resist and correct the tendency to divorce. The sacredness of the marriage vow, and the purity of home life should be safeguarded in all possible ways.

CHRISTIANITY AND SOCIAL QUESTIONS

There is widely apparent in the churches today the growth of a new conscience in relation to social problems and a new quest for the will of God in modern society. We are realizing afresh that the purpose of Christianity is the purification of the entire life of humanity, its end a community truly and completely Christian. The noble and self-sacrificing work of caring for the social wreckage of our time, the poverty-stricken and the outcast, must not cease. But our duty does not end there. Not simply by doing an honest day's work, or by cultivating relations of brotherhood with one's fellow-workers, important as these are, can the Christian obligation be fully met. We must strive also to the end that the organization of society itself shall accord with Christ's will, as well as that one's calling within society shall be conformable thereto.

Baptists gladly recognize the Christian duty of applying the teaching and spirit of our Lord to social, industrial, and family relations. While not committed to any of the varied and conflicting theories of economics, we affirm the Christian conception of industrial relations to be cooperation rather than competition. Life is a stewardship held for the enrichment of all, and not simply for personal gain.

We stand for world peace through international courts of justice, industrial peace through obedience to the rule of Christ, " Do unto others as ye would they should do unto you,'' domestic peace by acceptance of the sanctity of the marriage bond and the parental responsibility to train children in the nurture and love of the Lord.

CHRISTIAN STEWARDSHIP

Christian Stewardship rests upon the foundation of God's ownership of ourselves and our possessions. " Ye are not your own. Ye have been bought with a price,'' is the divine declaration. All wealth is to be held in trust as God's gift. It is to be used as He commands. The right of private ownership of property by the Christian does not mean the right to do as he wills with his own, but rather as God wills. The mere accumulation of wealth is not the aim of the Christian business man, but rather the use of wealth in the service of God and men. Under the old dispensation the Jews gave at least one-tenth of their income to the service of God. Christians are not under law but under the gospel. But surely their obligation requires giving upon a scale equal to that of Jews. One tenth, however, does not exhaust the Christian's obligation. All that he has belongs to God, and his giving should be in proportion to the needs and requirements of the Lord's work and his own ability, whether it be one-tenth or nine-tenths or even more of his income.

THE SABBATH

We recognize and reaffirm with vigor the sanctity of the Sabbath; all work, except works of necessity and mercy, should be avoided on the Sabbath day. God has appointed one day in seven as a day of rest and worship, and it should be observed by all men in accordance with the divine command. We condemn as unchristian the commercialization of the Sabbath day in the interest of business or amusement of any kind. As a civil institution, one day in seven, observed as a day of rest, has proved to be in the highest degree promotive of human welfare. The religious observance of the Sabbath as a day of worship is a matter for free and voluntary action. Laws to compel such observance are opposed to religious liberty. But laws to protect the Sabbath as a civil institution are right and should be enforced.

TEMPERANCE

We record our conviction that the modern movement to curb traffic in strong drink for beverage purposes is of God. We believe that governments should recognize the movement and that instead of deriving support from it through taxation, should abolish this traffic.

BAPTISTS AND LOYALTY TO STATE

Baptists have always been a loyal and patriotic people. This attitude arises out of their fundamental principles. It is a necessary result of their submission to the will of God as revealed in Jesus Christ. It is seen clearly in the light of their view of the State and of the Church. Baptists believe that the State is ordained of God. It is established to restrain and punish the evildoer and for the protection of human rights. It is, therefore, essential to human welfare. It is not to be used in the interest of any group or class, but to promote the common good. Its duty is to safeguard the personal, economic, civic and religious rights of all.

It thus appears that the work of the church and the work of the State. lie in different spheres. In the one case it is a spiritual, in the other a political task. There is no antagonism, and there should be no conflict. Each should freely pursue its own tasks in its own department of life by its own means and methods. Neither should seek to thwart or hinder the other. The members of the churches should obey the laws of the State as loyal

MESSAGE (1923) (BAPTIST WORLD ALLIANCE) (continued)

citizens or subjects. The State should protect the rights of all men of various religious beliefs. The supreme loyalty of all men is to God. Disobedience to the State, therefore, is never justified except when the State usurps the place of God in trying to compel the conscience in religious matters, or when it becomes a transgressor of the law of God in requiring what is in violation of Divine commands.

INTERNATIONAL RELATIONS

Nations are morally bound to each other. The State, like the individual, must be regarded as a member of a larger community in which other members possess rights similar to its own. This implies that in an orderly world there can be no real conflict of interests between various governments. Secret, selfish diplomacy and intrigue are crying sins before God. National selfishness is a terrible evil.

We record our profound conviction against war. It is destructive of all economic, moral and spiritual values. A war of aggression is a direct contradiction of every principle of the Gospel of Christ. It violates the ideals of peace and brotherhood and is inconsistent with the law of love. It alienates nations which Christ seeks to unify in bonds of friendship. It enthrones hate and dries up the fountains of sympathy. It sets power above right. It creates burdensome debts. It is prodigal in its waste of life.

The true remedy for war is the Gospel of Christ. The new birth by God's Spirit creates divine love within the soul of the individual. The law of God is thus written upon the heart. The greatest need of the world is acceptance of the Lordship of Christ, by men everywhere, and practical application of His law of love.

We favor cooperation among the nations of the world to promote peace. No nation can live an isolated life. To attempt to do so inevitably gives rise to complicated problems and leads to conflict in many forms. The good of all is the good of each, and the good of each is the good of all. Christ's law of service is the key to all human progress. Nations as well as individuals are bound by that law. By obedience to it shall we hasten the complete realization of God's will among men and the fulfillment of the ideals of the great prayer which the Master taught us to pray: "Thy Kingdom come. Thy will be done on earth as in heaven."

We believe that the world has come to a parting of the ways. It is another coming of the Son of Man. It is another Day of the Lord. The question is whether the world will pass along the way of order and peace and goodness and faith, or whether it will go down into skepticism and materialism. We believe that the simple message of the Baptists with its union of gospel and ethics, of faith and practice, with its note of freedom, democracy, spirituality, will find an answering chord in this new world.

Notes: *The Baptist World Alliance, founded in 1905, is an international fellowship of Baptist denominations. Notoriously unable to agree on doctrinal statements, in 1923 the Baptists*

were able to form a statement reflecting a Baptist consensus; this concensus remains a helpful document in defining the Baptist position relative to other denominational families. The 1923 Message emphasizes the voluntary nature of Baptist life, the affirmation of salvation in Christ, the necessity of believer's baptism by immersion, the sovereignty of the local church, religious liberty, and the voluntary observance of the Sabbath.

*   *   *

CHURCH COVENANT (SUGGESTED CONSTITUTION FOR BAPTIST CHURCHES)

Having been led, as we believe, by the Spirit of God, to receive the Lord Jesus Christ as our Savior, and on the profession of our faith, having been baptized in the name of the Father, and of the Son, and of the Holy Spirit, we do now in the presence of God and this assembly, most solemnly and joyfully enter into covenant with one another, as one body in Christ.

We engage, therefore, by the aid of the Holy Spirit, to walk together in Christian love: to strive for the advancement of this church in knowledge, holiness and comfort; to promote its prosperity and spirituality; to sustain its worship, ordinances, discipline and doctrines to contribute cheerfully and regularly to the support of the ministry, the expenses of the church, the relief of the poor and the spread of the Gospel through all nations.

We also engage to maintain family and secret devotions; to teach our children the Christian truths; to seek the salvation of our kindred and acquaintances; to walk circumspectly in the world; to be just in our dealings, faithful in our engagements, exemplary in our deportment; to avoid all tattling, backbiting and excessive anger; to abstain from the sale and use of intoxicating drink as beverage; and to be zealous in our efforts to advance the Kingdom of our Savior.

We further engage to watch over one another in brotherly love; to remember each other in prayer; to aid each other in sickness and distress; to cultivate Christian sympathy in feeling and courtesy in speech; to be slow to take offense but always ready for reconciliation, and mindful of the rules of our Savior to secure it without delay.

We moreover engage that when we remove from this place, we will as soon as possible unite with some other church where we can carry out the spirit of the covenant and principles of God's Word.

Notes: *The Baptists place the essence of church life in the sovereign local church; hence denominational associations and conventions have no power to force a structure on congregations. However, a number of suggestions for the organization of the local congregation have been widely* *circulated and local churches encouraged to adopt them as a means of bringing some uniformity to local churches. These suggested constitution elements frequently include a brief doctrinal statement.*

In 1957 Ralph M. Johnson and R. Dean Goodwin circulated such a constitution in their book, Faith and Fellowship of American Baptists. That constitution, which was offered for American Baptist Churches congregations to use, included a Church Covenant as a doctrinal statement. The Covenant centers on the elements of the Christian life—living together in love, evangelism, family life, and exemplary behavior in the community.

* * *

Calvinist Missionary Baptist

DOCTRINAL STATEMENT (AMERICAN BAPTIST CHURCHES IN THE U.S.A./JUDSON COLLEGE)

We believe that the Bible, composed of the Old and New Testaments, is inspired of God, inerrant, and the supreme and final authority in faith and life.

We believe in one God eternally existing in three Persons—Father, Son, and Holy Spirit.

We believe that Jesus Christ was begotten of the Holy Spirit and born of the Virgin Mary, and that he is true God and true man, and is the only and sufficient Mediator between God and man.

We believe in the personality of the Holy Spirit and that his ministry is to reveal Christ to men in the regeneration and sanctification of their souls.

We believe that God created all things that exist, and that man was created in the image of God, and that he sinned and thereby incurred spiritual death.

We believe in the vicarious death of the Lord Jesus Christ for our sins, in the resurrection of his body, his ascension into Heaven, and his personal and visible future return to the earth; and that salvation is received only through personal faith in him.

We believe that the church is the body of Christ, composed of all believers; and that the local church is to be engaged in worship, education, service and the spread of the gospel, and is to observe the ordinances of Baptism and the Lord's Supper.

Notes: *Judson College, Elgin, Illinois, is sponsored by the American Baptists Churches in the U.S.A. Its Doctrinal State-*

ment is a conservative Baptist statement that includes an affirmation of the inerrancy of the Bible, the vicarious death of Jesus Christ, and the role of the local church.

* * *

STATEMENT OF FAITH (AMERICAN BAPTIST CHURCHES IN THE U.S.A./NORTHERN BAPTIST THEOLOGICAL SEMINARY)

The doctrinal basis of Northern Baptist Theological Seminary is and shall be:

The Bible is the revealed Word of God, given by the Holy Spirit through chosen men, and so is fully inspired, authoritative, and the sufficient rule of faith and practice for the believer.

God exists eternally in three persons who are revealed in Scripture as Father, Son, and Holy Spirit. While these three are one, each has special office and activity: God, the Father, is the source, support, and end of all things; God, the virgin born Son, is the medium of revelation and redemption by virtue of his incarnation, life, and death; God, the Holy Spirit, is the one who inspires divinely chosen persons, reproves the world because of sin, regenerates and sanctifies the believer, and now represents the Son on earth.

Creation is the act of God by which he brought the universe and all that it contains into existence; the universe is preserved by natural law which is an expression of God's will; at the same time, God's miraculous working is not excluded from nature, as a means of making known his plan and purpose according to the pleasure of his will.

Humanity was made in the image of God and originally sinful Men and women are fallen in Adam, the head of the race, and are now by nature and choice sinners, living in revolt against their Creator, and are unable to escape from their sinful state on their own.

God's only way of reconciling sinful humanity to himself is provided in the work of Christ, the incarnate Son, fully human and fully divine; in his sinless life, his sacrificial death on the cross, his resurrection, his ascension, and his present intercession he reveals at the same time God's grace and his loving provisions for his creatures. Humans are reconciled unto God only as they by faith appropriate for themselves the salvation provided in Christ.

The Church is that universal and spiritual body which includes all the redeemed of which Christ the Redeemer is the head; the church in the local and visible sense is a group of believers, immersed on profession of faith in Christ, united under the direct, personal, undelegated lordship of Christ, voluntarily joined together for worship of God, service to others, and for carrying out the work of the Great Commission as given by Christ. Each local church is an autonomous body under Christ, cooperating with other churches of like faith and order in the work of evangelizing the world and advancing the interest of the Kingdom of God.

The ordinances are two in number. Baptism is the immersion of the believer in water in the name of the Father, Son, and Holy Spirit, following his confession of faith in Jesus Christ as his Lord and Savior; baptism symbolizes the death of the old life and the rising of the new. The Lord's Supper is a memorial instituted by Christ to be kept by believers as a symbol of his atoning death, and of himself as the Bread of Life, the one through whom we have spiritual life and vitality.

The second advent of Christ is his personal return by which the present age will be terminated. The ultimate hope of the believer is not in history but in that great eschatological event by which the present age is brought to its conclusion. The culmination of history takes place in the final judgement in which the unredeemed will be punished through eternal separation from God, and the redeemed will enter into a state of eternal peace and righteousness with him.

Notes: *The Northern Baptist Theological Seminary is sponsored by the American Baptist Churches in the U.S.A. and reflects the denomination's liberal Protestant stance. Its Statement of Faith avoids any mention of the inerrancy and infallibility of the Bible and its statement on creation is compatible with scientific opinion on the evolution of life. The statement has been revised in light of contemporary feminist concerns and has dropped the generic use of ''man.'' Otherwise, the statement continues traditional Baptist concerns for adult believer's baptism by immersion and the importance of the local church.*

*   *   *

DOCTRINAL STATEMENT OF TORONTO BAPTIST SEMINARY [ASSOCIATION OF REGULAR BAPTIST CHURCHES (CANADA)]

I. Of the Scriptures

We believe that the Holy Bible was (a) written by men supernaturally inspired; (b) that it has truth without any admixture of error for its matter; and (c) therefore is, and shall remain to the end of the age, the only complete and final revelation of the will of God to men; the true center of Christian union, and the supreme standard by which all human conduct, creeds and opinions should be tried.

(Explanatory)

(1) By ''The Holy Bible'' we mean that collection of sixty-six books, from Genesis to Revelation, which, as originally written, does not only contain and convey the word of God, but is the very Word of God.

(2) By ''Inspiration'' we mean that the books of the Bible were written by holy men of old, as they were moved by the Holy Spirit, in such a definite way that their writings were supernaturally inspired and free from error, as no other writings have ever been or ever will be inspired.

II. Of the Trinity

(1) We believe that there is (a) one, and only one, living and true God, an infinite, intelligent Spirit, the maker and supreme ruler of heaven and earth; (b) inexpressibly glorious in holiness, and worthy of all possible honor, confidence and love; (c) that in the unity of the Godhead there are three persons, the Father, the Son, and the Holy Ghost, equal in every divine perfection, and executing distinct but harmonious offices in the work of redemption.

(2) We believe (a) that Jesus Christ was begotten of the Holy Ghost in a miraculous manner, (b) born of Mary, a virgin, as no other man was ever born or can ever be born of woman and (c) that He is both the Son of God and God the Son.

(3) We believe that the Holy Spirit is a divine person; (a) equal with God the Father and (b) God the Son and (c) of the same nature; (d) that He was active in the creation; (e) that in His relation to the unbelieving world He restrains the Evil One until God's purpose is fulfilled; (f) that He convicts of sin, of righteousness, and of judgment; (g) that He bears witness to the truth of the gospel in preaching and testimony; (h) that He is the Agent in the New Birth; (i) that He sanctifies, and assures to us all the benefits of salvation.

III. Of the Devil, or Satan

We believe that Satan is a person and was once (a) holy, and enjoyed heavenly honors; but through pride and ambition to be as the Almighty, fell and (b) drew after him a host of angels; that he is now (c) the malignant prince of the power of the air, and the unholy god of this world. (d) We hold him to be man's great tempter, (e) the enemy of God and His Christ, (f) the accuser of the saints, (g) the author of all false religions, and the inspirer of all apostasy; (h) the chief of all the powers of darkness—destined however (i) to a final defeat at the hands of God's Son, and (j) to suffer eternal punishment in a place prepared for him and his angels.

IV. Of the Creation

We believe in the Genesis account of creation, and (a) that it is to be accepted literally, and not allegorically or figuratively; (b) that man was created directly in God's own image and after His own likeness; (c) that man's creation was not by evolution or evolutionary change of species or development through interminable periods of time from lower to higher forms; (d) that all animal and vegetable life was affected by special creation, and God's established law was that they should bring forth only ''after their kind''.

V. The Fall of Man

We believe (a) that man was created in innocence under the law of his Maker, but (b) by voluntary transgression fell from his sinless and happy state, (c) in consequence of which all mankind are now sinful, and are sinners not by constraint but of choice; and (d) therefore under just condemnation without defence or excuse; and (e) that man in his natural state is in a condition of total depravity, by which we mean his natural utter incapacity to receive the things of the Spirit of God apart from the quickening grace of the Holy Spirit.

VI. Of the Atonement for Sin

We believe (a) that the salvation of sinners is wholly of grace; (b) through the mediatorial offices of the Son of God, Who by the appointment of the Father, freely took upon Him our nature, yet without sin, honored the divine law by His personal obedience, and by His death made a full and expiatory atonement for our sins; (c) that His atonement consisted not in setting us an example by His death as a martyr, but was the voluntary substitution of himself in the sinner's place, bearing the penalty of God's Holy Law, the just dying for the unjust, Christ, the Lord, bearing our sins in His own body on the tree; (d) that having risen from the dead, He is now enthroned in the heaven and uniting in His person the tenderest sympathies with divine perfection. He is every way qualified to be a suitable, a compassionate and an all-sufficient Savior.

VII. Of Grace in the New Creation

We believe (a) that in order to be saved, sinners must be born again; (1) that the new birth is a new creation in Christ Jesus; (c) that it is instantaneous and not a process; (d) that in the new birth the one dead in trespasses and in sins is made a partaker of the divine nature and receives eternal life as the gift of God; (e) that such are kept by the power of God through faith unto eternal salvation and shall never perish; (f) that the new creation is brought about in a manner above our comprehension, not by culture, not by character, nor by the will of man, but wholly and solely by the power of the Holy Spirit in connection with divine truth, so as to secure our voluntary obedience to the gospel; (g) that its proper evidence appears in the holy fruits of repentance and faith and newness of life.

VIII. Of Justification

We believe that the great gospel blessing which Christ secures to such as believe in Him is Justification; (a) that Justification includes the pardon of sin, and the gift of eternal life on principles of righteousness; (b) that it is bestowed not in consideration of any works of righteousness which we have done, but it is the imputation of the righteousness of Christ on the ground of His perfect life and expiatory death.

IX. Of the Local Church

We believe that a church of Christ is a congregation of baptized believers (a) associated by a covenant of faith and fellowship of the gospel; (b) observing the ordinances of Christ; (c) governed by His laws; and (d) exercising the gifts, rights and privileges invested in them by His word; (e) that its officers are pastors (or elders or bishops) and deacons, whose qualifications, claims, and duties are clearly defined in the Scriptures; (f) we believe that the true mission of the church is found in our Lord's commission: First, to teach, or disciple, all nations, i.e., to preach the gospel in all the world, to make individual disciples, second to baptize, third, to teach and instruct as He has commanded, and thus to build up the church; (we do not believe in the reversal of this order); (g) we hold that the local church has the absolute right of self-government free from the interference of any hierarchy of individuals or organizations; and that the one and only superintendent is Christ, through the Holy Spirit; (h) that it is scriptural for true churches to cooperate with each other in the furtherance of the gospel and in contending for the faith, and that every church is the sole and only judge of the measure and method of its cooperation; (i) on all matters of membership, of polity, of government, of discipline, of benevolence, the will of the local church is final.

X. Of Baptism and The Lord's Supper

We believe that Christian baptism is (a) the immersion in water of a believer, (b) into the name of the Father, the Son and the Holy Ghost; (c) to show forth our union with the crucified, buried, and risen Christ, and our death to sin and resurrection to a new life; (d) that it is a condition of church membership and of the observance of the Lord's Supper (e) in which the members of the church by the sacred use of bread and wine are to commemorate together the love of Christ, preceded always by solemn self-examination.

(Explanatory)

By the statement that baptism is a condition of church membership and of the observance of the Lord's Supper, we take the same position as all evangelical believers, differing only from our brethren in our insistence that scriptural baptism consists only in the Immersion of the believer in water in the name of the Father, Son, and Holy Ghost; and since the Scripture requires that baptism shall follow immediately upon faith in Christ, and that this was the invariable practice of the apostolic church, we conceive it to be an obligation involved in our Lord's Commission to teach men to observe all things whatsoever He has commanded them, to maintain a testimony to the authority of New Testament precept and practice; and we further believe that to take any other than the position stated in this article would be to reverse the scriptural order of the ordinance, and to magnify the importance of the Supper above that of Baptism, and would involve the taking of a position at variance with that taken by all other bodies of evangelical believers in respect to the order of the ordinance. This statement is intended to ensure a clear testimony to the supreme authority of Christ as His will is revealed in the Scripture (1 Cor. 11:26).

XI. Of the Righteous and the Wicked

We believe that (a) there is a radical and essential difference between the righteous and the wicked; (b) that such only as through faith are justified in the name of the Lord Jesus and sanctified by the Spirit of our God, are truly righteous in His esteem; (c) while all such as continue in impenitence and unbelief are in His sight wicked, and under the curse; (d) and this distinction holds among men both in and after death, in the everlasting felicity of the saved and the everlasting penal suffering of the lost.

DOCTRINAL STATEMENT OF TORONTO BAPTIST SEMINARY [ASSOCIATION OF REGULAR BAPTIST CHURCHES (CANADA)] (continued)

XII. Of Civil Government

We believe that civil government is (a) of divine appointment, for the interests and good order of human society; (b) that magistrates are to be prayed for, conscientiously honored and obeyed; (c) except only in things opposed to the will of our Lord Jesus Christ; (d) Who is the only Lord of the conscience, and the coming Prince of the kings of the earth.

XIII. Of the Resurrection, Return of Christ and Related Events

We believe in the literal bodily resurrection of Christ, that He rose again the third day according to the Scriptures, that after manifesting Himself for forty days to His disciples, He ascended to His Father's right hand, where, as our Great High Priest, He ever liveth to make intercession for His own. We believe that according to His promise He will come again without sin unto salvation, that His coming will be personal, visible and glorious, as it is written in Titus 2:13-14:

"Looking for that blessed hope, and the glorious appearing of the great God and our Savior Jesus Christ; who gave himself for us, that he might redeem us from all iniquity, and purify unto himself a peculiar people, zealous of good works."

Notes: *The Association of Regular Baptist Churches emerged from the same controversies that produced the General Association of Regular Baptist Churches (GARBC). The Association's Toronto Baptist Seminary espouses a Statement of Faith that is very similar to that of the GARBC. It is a fundamentalist affirmation of Christian essentials, including the inerrancy of the Bible, the Trinity, the personality of Satan, the literal truth of the Genesis account of creation, and the everlasting suffering of the wicked in hell. It is based in part on the New Hampshire Confession of Faith (I, 492) and affirms Baptist emphases on the local church, adult baptism by immersion, two ordinances (not sacraments), and the perseverance of the saints by the power of God.*

*　　　*　　　*

DOCTRINAL STATEMENT (CANADIAN BAPTIST FEDERATION/UNITED BAPTIST CONVENTION OF THE ATLANTIC PROVINCES)

(1) THE SCRIPTURES. The Holy Scriptures of the Old and New Testaments have their authority from God alone, and are given to us by divine inspiration. They are the only perfect, supreme, infallible and sufficient standard of faith and practice.

(2) GOD. There is one true and living God; He is an infinite Spirit; self-existent, omnipresent, omniscient, omnipotent, good, wise, just and merciful. He is the creator, preserver and sovereign of the universe; He is inexpressibly glorious in holiness, and worthy of all honor, confidence and love. In the Godhead there are three persons in one—the Father, the Son and the Holy Spirit, who are equal in every divine perfection, and who execute distinct but harmonious offices in the great work of redemption.

(3) JESUS CHRIST. Jesus Christ, the Son of God, is the person of the Trinity who, by virtue of His sacrificial work, is the world's Redeemer and the Savior of all who believe. He is at present the intercessor of all His people at the right hand of the Father, and is to be the Judge of all men.

(4) THE HOLY SPIRIT. The Holy Spirit is the third person of the Trinity, by whom all saving, comforting and sanctifying power is exerted upon human hearts.

(5) STATE AND FALL OF MAN. Man was created sinless. By his own disobedience he fell into sin. Through his fall into sin, an evil nature was transmitted to the whole race, revealing itself in actual transgression, and bringing all under the reign of condemnation and death.

(6) ATONEMENT. The perfect life, vicarious death and resurrection of Jesus Christ, have removed the obstacles in the way of the Holy Spirit's regenerating power and of the Father's forgiving grace being extended to the sinner, and constitute for every believing soul an all-prevailing plea and sufficient ground for righteousness before God.

(7) REGENERATION. In regeneration a new life principle is begotten in the soul of man by the Holy Spirit through the word of truth, producing a disposition to joyful obedience to Christ and to holy conduct in life.

(8) REPENTANCE. In repentance the sinner, having seen his sin, being moved by the energy of the Holy Spirit, is led to grieve for and hate it as an offence against God, and apprehending the grace of our Lord Jesus Christ, he lovingly returns to God to walk in the way of His commandments.

(9) FAITH. Faith is a conviction of the intellect that God will perform all that He has promised and an implicit trust of the heart in Christ as a personal Savior. It includes a hearty concurrence of the will and affections with the whole plan of salvation as revealed in the gospel, and is a condition of justification and of cleansing from the pollution of sin and of all subsequent gospel blessings.

(10) JUSTIFICATION. Justification is an act of God wherein He accepts as righteous the sinner, to whom is imputed the perfect righteousness of Christ on the condition of faith alone.

(11) SANCTIFICATION. The Scriptures teach that sanctification is the process by which, according to the will of God, Christians are made partaker of His holiness; that it has its beginning in regeneration, and that it is carried on in the hearts of believers by the presence and power of the Holy

Spirit, in the continual use of the appointed means—the Word of God—self-examination, self-denial, watchfulness and prayer.

(12) THE CHRISTIAN SABBATH. We believe that the first day of the week is the Lord's day or Christian Sabbath and is to be kept sacred to religion purposes by abstaining from all secular labor and sinful recreations, by the devout observance of all means of grace, both private and public, and by preparation for that rest that remaineth for the people of God.

(13) A GOSPEL CHURCH. We believe that a Church of Christ is a congregation of baptized believers, associated by covenant in the faith and fellowship of the gospel; observing the ordinances of Christ, governed by His laws; and exercising the gifts, rights and privileges invested in them by His word. In more general sense the word Church is used to designate all whose names are written in the Lamb's Book of Life. The only scriptural officers are bishops or pastors, and deacons, whose qualifications, claims and duties are defined in the epistles of Timothy and Titus.

(14) BAPTISM. This is the immersion of believers in water into the name of the Father, Son and Holy Spirit, in which are represented their death to the world, the washing of their souls from the pollution of sin, their resurrection to newness of life, the burial and resurrection of Christ, their resurrection at the last day, and their engagement to serve God.

(15) THE LORD'S SUPPER. The Lord's Supper is an ordinance of Christ, to be observed by the churches in the manner indicated by Him in Matthew xxvi:26-30.

(16) DEATH. At death our bodies return to dust, our souls to God who gave them. The righteous being then perfected in happiness are received to dwell with God, awaiting the full redemption of their bodies. The wicked are cast into Hades reserved unto the judgment of the great day.

(17) RESURRECTION. There will be a general resurrection of the bodies of the just and of the unjust; the righteous in the likeness of Christ, but the wicked to shame and everlasting contempt.

(18) GENERAL JUDGMENT. There will be a judgment of quick and dead, of the just and unjust, on principles of righteousness, by our Lord Jesus Christ, at His second coming. The wicked will be condemned to eternal punishment, and the righteous received into the fullness of eternal life and joy.

Notes: *The Canadian Baptist Federation was formed in 1944 as a fellowship of regional Baptist associations in Canada. The federation has no common creed, but some of its constituent parts have written creedal statements. The 1905 Agreed Principles emerged when two Baptist associations (now part of the Canadian Baptist Federation) in the Maritime Provinces merged. The Principles affirm the infallibility of the*

Bible, Sunday as the proper Sabbath day, the local church, and believer's baptism by immersion.

* * *

DOCTRINAL POSITION (CONSERVATIVE BAPTIST ASSOCIATION/DENVER CONSERVATIVE BAPTIST SEMINARY)

1. We believe in the verbal, plenary inspiration of the Bible.

2. We believe in the unity and the trinity of the Godhead.

3. We believe in Jesus Christ, God's only begotten Son, our sole Mediator; we believe further in His pre-existence, His incarnation, His virgin birth, His sinless life, His substitutionary atonement, His bodily resurrection from the grave, His personal, visible, imminent, premillenia], return from heaven.

4. We believe in the Holy Spirit, His personality and His activity in regeneration, sanctification, and preservation.

5. We believe that man was created in the image of God, that he sinned in Adam, and that he is now a sinner by nature and by choice.

6. We believe in salvation by grace through faith in Jesus Christ, apart from human merit, works, or ceremonies.

7. We believe that the church is the spiritual body of which Christ is the Head and that there is a twofold aspect to the church, the universal and the local. We believe that the ordinances of the local church are two in number: baptism being the immersion of the believer in water; and the Lord's supper, a memorial of the atoning death of Christ until He comes.

8. We believe that the local church is autonomous in function, being free from interference by any ecclesiastical or political authority.

9. We believe in the resurrection of the human body; the eternal existence of all men either in heaven or hell; in divine judgments, rewards, and punishments.

10. We believe that we are under obligation to contend earnestly for the faith once delivered unto the saints.

At the beginning of each fiscal year all members of the Board of Trustees, administration, faculty, and staff are required to affirm and sign the Seminary's doctrinal statement without mental reservation.

Notes: *Denver Conservative Baptist Seminary, Denver, Colorado, is sponsored by the Conservative Baptist Association (CBA). Its Doctrinal Position summarizes and is in accord with CBA beliefs and emphasizes the verbal inspiration of the Bible, believer's baptism by immersion, the autonomy of the local church, and the need to defend orthodox Christianity.*

The Doctrinal Position must be reaffirmed by the faculty and staff annually.

*   *   *

STANDARD OF FAITH AND PRACTICE (CONSERVATIVE BAPTIST ASSOCIATION/ WESTERN CONSERVATIVE BAPTIST SEMINARY)

We believe that the Bible is the final standard of faith and practice for the believer in Jesus Christ and for His Church. While recognizing the historical value of creedal statements made throughout the history of the Church, we affirm the Bible alone as the infallible and final authority. Creedal formulations are of value in terms of the interpretive insights they afford and the cautionary guidelines they suggest as we constantly seek the mind of the Lord in refining our understanding of His Word.

With this in mind, we, the faculty of Western Conservative Baptist Seminary, recognize a solemn responsibility to give a contemporary confession of our faith. In so doing we acknowledge the formal statement of faith made by the founders of the Seminary as God's instrument in establishing His work and providing the Scriptural guidelines for that day. We also acknowledge that with the passing of time there is need to refine and restate our faith in terms of the critical and more exacting demands made upon us. Recognizing this twofold allegiance, first to the Word of God and, secondly, to the convictions of our forebears who bequeathed to us these challenges, we set forth our teaching position in the following abbreviated form.

CONCERNING THE SCRIPTURES

Revelation and Inspiration: We believe that God has revealed Himself and His truth by both general and special revelation. Whereas general revelation points to His existence, power, and glory, only special revelation describes His character of grace and His program of redemption for man. This special revelation has been given in various ways, preeminently in the incarnate Word of God, Jesus Christ, and in the inscripturated Word of God, the Bible. We affirm that the sixty-six books of the Bible are the written Word of God given to man by the Holy Spirit. (Ps. 19:1-6; John 1:1-5, 14, 18; 20:30, 31; Acts 14:17; Rom. 1:19, 20; 2:14, 15; I Thess. 2:13; Heb. 1:1, 2; 4:12).

These books were written by a process of dual authorship in which the Holy Spirit so superintended the human authors that, through their individual personalities and different styles of writing, they composed and recorded God's Word to man without error in the whole or in the part. These books, variously written but propositionally stated, constitute the written word of God and are the believer's only infallible rule of faith and practice. (Ps. 119:160; John 10:35; 17:17; I Cor. 2:13; II Tim. 3:16, 17; II Pet. 1:20, 21).

Illumination and Interpretation: Whereas there may be several applications of any given passage of Scripture, there is but one true interpretation and it is to be found as one diligently applies the grammatical-historical method of interpretation under the enlightenment of the Holy Spirit. This procedure gives due consideration to the various literary modes such as narrative, poetry, figures, etc., thus facilitating the proper understanding of the native meaning of each passage. (John 7:17; 16:12, 13; I Cor. 2:14, 15; I John 2:20).

CONCERNING GOD

The Triune God: We believe there is but one living and true God who is infinite, eternal, and unchangeable in His being, wisdom, power, holiness, justice, goodness, and truth. He is absolutely separate from and above the world as its Creator, yet everywhere present in the world as the upholder of all things. We further believe that God is one in essence, but eternally existent in three persons, Father, Son and Holy Spirit, each having precisely the same nature, attributes, and perfections, and each worthy of precisely the same worship, confidence, and obedience. (Gen. 1:26; Deut. 6:4; Ps. 139:8; Isa. 45:5-7; Matt. 28:19; Mark 10:18; John 4:24; Acts 17:24-29; II Cor. 13:14; Eph. 4:6).

God the Father: God the Father, the first Person of the Trinity, orders and disposes all things according to His own purpose and grace. As the absolute and highest Ruler in the universe He is sovereign in creation, providence, and redemption. He created the universe apart from pre-existing materials and without means. He has decreed for His own glory all things that come to pass, and continually upholds, directs and governs all creatures and events. This He does, so as in no way to be the author or approver of sin nor to abridge the accountability of morally intelligent creatures. He has graciously chosen from all eternity those whom He would have as His own; He saves from sin all who come to Him through Jesus Christ; and He relates Himself to His own as their Father. (Ps. 145:8, 9; I Chron. 29:11; Ps. 103:19; John 1:18; Rom. 11:33; 1 Cor. 8:6; Eph. 1:3-6; Heb. 4:13; I Pet. 1:17).

God the Son: Jesus Christ, the second Person of the Trinity, is the Son of God and the virgin-born Son of Man who was incarnated as the God-Man to reveal God, redeem man, and rule over God's kingdom. (Ps. 2:7-9; Isa. 7:14; 9:6; John 1:1, 3, 18, 29; 10:36; I John 1:3).

We believe that in the incarnation He surrendered nothing of the divine essence, either in degree or kind, all the while voluntarily limiting the manifestation of the divine attributes forming the essence. Although He was fully man, since He was also fully God, He was without sin as to nature, unable to sin in principle, and did not sin in fact. (John 1:14, 29; 8:46;II Cor. 5:21; Phil. 2:5-11; Col. 2:9; Heb. 4:15; 7:26; I Peter 2:21-24).

By His sinless life, miraculous ministry, and substitutionary death, He satisfied divine justice concerning sin. (Matt. 11:2-6;12:28; Rom. 3:24-26; II Cor. 5:19; Heb. 1-3; 10:5-10; I John 2:2;4:10).

In the resurrection of Christ from the grave God confirmed both the deity of Christ and His acceptance of the atoning work of Christ on the cross, raising Him bodily as a guarantee of the future resurrection to life of all believers. (Matt. 28:6; John 14:19; Acts 2:30, 31; Rom. 1:4; 4:25; 6:5-10; I Cor. 15:20).

After His ascension to the Father's right hand, He sent the Holy Spirit at Pentecost as a like-Companion to Himself to assume the care and keeping of His own. Throughout this age Christ is seated at the Father's side performing the intercessory aspect of His High Priestly work for believers. (John 15:26; Acts 2:33; Heb. 7:25; 10:12; 12:2; I Pet. 3:22).

Related to man, Christ is the only Mediator between God and man: the Head of His body, the Church; the coming universal King who will reign on the throne of David; and the final Judge of all who fail to place their trust in Him as their Savior from sin. (Isa. 53:10; Luke 1:31-33; John 5:27-29; Eph. 1:22; 23; Col. 1:18; I Tim. 2:5; Heb. 7:25; Rev. 20:11-15).

God the Holy Spirit: It is the work of the Holy Spirit, the third Person of the Trinity, to execute the divine will with relation to the world of men. We affirm this sovereign activity in creation, the incarnation, the written revelation, and the work of salvation. (Gen. 1:2; Matt. 1:18; John 3:5-7; II Pet. 1:20-21).

His work in this age began at Pentecost when He came from the Father, as promised by Christ, to initiate and complete the building of the body of Christ which is the church. The broad scope of this special divine activity includes convicting the world, glorifying the Lord Jesus and transforming believers into the likeness of Christ. (John 14:16-17; 15:26; 16:7-9; Acts 1:5; 2:4; I Cor. 12:13; II Cor. 3:18; Eph. 2:22).

This work in believers involves that of regeneration, baptism into the body of Christ, indwelling, sanctifying, instructing, empowering for service, and preserving to the day of Christ. We believe that He alone administers spiritual gifts to the church, not to glorify Himself for the gifts by ostentatious displays, but to glorify Christ and implement His work of redeeming the lost and building up believers in the most holy faith. (John 3:5-7; 16:14-15; Rom. 8:2; I Cor. 6:19; 12:4-13; Eph. 1:13-14; II Thess. 2:13).

CONCERNING ANGELS

Their Origin: The angels were all created simultaneously by God as a great host of sinless spirit-beings, most of whom kept their first estate of holiness and presently worship God and serve His purposes. (Ps. 148:2-5; Matt. 26:53; Col. 1:16; Heb. 1:14).

The Fall of Some: One of the angels fell through the sin of pride and influenced a large company of angels to follow him, who thereby became demons. Scripture usually refers to this angel as the Devil or Satan. (James 2:19; II Pet. 2:4; Rev. 12:9; and possibly Isa. 14:12-14; Ezek. 28:12-19).

Satan's Work: The work of Satan and the demons is the attempted subversion and supplanting of the work of God. By a subtle suggestion, Satan accomplished the moral fall of the progenitors of the human race, subjecting them and their posterity to his own power. (Ge. 3:1-7; Job 1:12; 2p; Ezek. 28:13-15; Zech. 3:1,2; John 8:44; II Cor. 4:3-4; Eph. 2:2).

Satan continues as the enemy of God and the accuser of God's people and persistently seeks to counterfeit the works and truth of God. (II Cor. 2:10-11; 11:13-15; Eph. 6:12, 16; I Pet. 5:8; Rev. 12:10).

Satan's Judgment: Satan was judged at the cross, though the sentence was not then executed, and he will finally be consigned to the lake of fire at the end of the Millennium. (Gen. 3:15; Isa. 14:12; Matt. 25:41; Luke 10:18; John 12:31; 16:11; I Tim. 3:6; Heb. 2:14; Rev. 12:9; 20:10).

CONCERNING MAN

His Original Nature: Apart from any natural processes man as male and female was created in the image of God, free from sin. He was created with a rational nature, great intelligence, and moral responsibility of God. (Gen. 1:26-28; 2:15-25; I Thess. 5:23; James 3:9).

His Original Purpose: He was originally created with the divine intention that he should glorify God, enjoy His fellowship, and fulfill His will and purposes on the earth. (Gen. 1:26-30; Isa. 43:7; Col. 1:16; Rev. 4:11).

His Subsequent Sin: Man subsequently fell into sin by a voluntary act of personal disobedience to the revealed will of God. (Gen. 2:16-17; 3:1-19; I Tim. 2:13-14).

His Present Condition: As a consequence man became subject to the wrath of God, inherently corrupt, and incapable of choosing or doing that which is acceptable to God apart from divine grace. Thus he is hopelessly lost apart from the salvation which is in the Lord Jesus Christ. (John 3:36; Rom. 3:23; 6:23; I Cor. 2:14; Eph. 2:1-3; I John 1:8).

The fall of man was an historical and non-repeatable act, the effects of which are transmitted to all men of all ages, Jesus Christ excepted. All men thus are sinners by divine pronouncement, nature, and deed. (Ps. 14:1-3; Jer. 17:9; Rom. 3:23; 5:12-19; James 2:10).

CONCERNING SALVATION

Its Elements: The salvation of man consists in the satisfaction of divine justice, the forgiveness of sins and reconciliation with God, the imputation of righteousness of Jesus Christ, the gift of eternal life, every spiritual resource needed for life and godliness, and the guarantee that those thus saved shall never perish. (Jonah 2:9; Isa. 53:6,10; John 10:27-29; Rom. 3:24; 5:8-9; 8:38-39; II Cor. 5:18, 19, 21; Gal. 2:16; Eph. 1:7; II Pet. 1:3; 1 John 4:10).

Its Attainment: This salvation is based upon the elective grace of God, was purchased by Christ on the cross, and is received by grace through faith, apart from any virtue or work of man, through the instrumentality of the Word of God as applied by the Holy Spirit. (John 1:12; 3:16; Acts 16:31; Rom. 8:29-30; 9:14-24; 10:8-13; Eph. 1:4-5; 2:8-10; II Thess. 2:13-14; Heb. 11:6).

Its Results: This salvation results in righteous living and good works as its proper evidence and fruit and will be experienced to the extent that the believer submits to the control of the Holy Spirit in his life through interaction with the Word of God. This is accomplished by conformity of the believer to the image of Christ, culminating in his glorification at Christ's coming. (John 5:24; 10:28; Rom. 8:35-39; I Cor. 6:19-20; II Cor. 3:18; Eph. 2:10; 5:17-21; Phil. 2:12-13; Col. 3:16; II Pet. 1:4-10; I John 3:2-3).

CONCERNING THE CHURCH

Its Nature: All who have placed their faith in Christ are united together immediately by the Holy Spirit in one spiritual body, the church, of which Christ is the Head. This body began on the day of Pentecost and will be completed at the coming of Christ for His own. In addition to the spiritual union and communion which extends to the entirety of the body of Christ, the members of this one spiritual body are directed to associate themselves together in local assemblies. (Matt. 16:18; Acts 1:4-5; 11:15; 2:46-47; I Cor. 12:13; Eph. 1:22-23; 2:19-22; 3:4-6; 5:25-27; Col. 1:18; Heb. 10:25).

Its Relationship: We believe that the individual members of this body and these local assemblies are priests before God having the privilege and responsibility of offering prayer and spiritual sacrifices to Him. Because God alone is Lord of the conscience, He has left it free from those doctrines or commandments of men which are in anything contrary to His Word. For this reason, separation of church and state should be maintained. Since civil magistrates are ordained of God, subjection in all lawful things commanded by them should be yielded by the believer in the Lord. (Matt. 22:15-22; Rom. 12:4-21; I Pet. 2:5-9; Rev. 1:6; Rom. 13:1-7; I Pet. 2:13-17).

Its Organization: These local assemblies have been given the needed authority for administering that order, discipline, and worship which Christ the sovereign Head has appointed. The Biblically designated officers serving under Christ and over the assembly are pastors (elders/bishops) and deacons. (Matt. 18:15-18; Acts 6:1-6; I Cor. 14:40; Eph. 4:11-12; I Tim. 3:1-13; Titus 1:5-9; I Pet. 5:1-5).

Its Mission: The mission of the church is to glorify God by worshipping corporately, building itself up in the faith by instruction of the Word, by fellowshipping and observing the ordinances, and by communicating the gospel to the entire world. (Matt. 28:19; Acts 2:41-42; Rom. 15:6, 9; Eph. 1:6, 12, 14; 3:10; 4:11-16; Heb. 10:25; 1 Pet. 2:9, 10).

Its Gifts: To fulfill its God-ordained mission of edification and evangelism the church has been given spiritual gifts. One class of gifts is that of gifted believers, who are given for the equipping of the saints for the work of this ministry. The other class of gifts is that of spiritual abilities, and each member of the body of Christ receives at least one such gift, which is sovereignly bestowed by the Lord. It is essential that each member develop and employ spiritual gifts for the church to accomplish its task. (Rom. 12:3-8; I Cor. 12:4-11; 27-31; 14:1-40; Eph. 4:8-13; I Tim. 4:14; II Tim. 1:6; I Pet. 4:10-11).

Since these gifts are bestowed by the Lord in order to fulfill specific purposes in God's program we believe that when the

purpose of any gift is fulfilled, that particular gift is terminated. (I Cor. 12:11; 13:8-10; 14:21-22; II Tim. 4:20 with Acts 19:11-12; Heb. 2:3-4).

Its Ordinances: Two ordinances have been committed to the local church—baptism and the Lord's Supper. Christian baptism is the immersion of a believer in water into the name of the triune God. This ordinance, being a command of Christ, is recognized as a prerequisite for membership in the local assembly. Likewise, the Lord's Supper was instituted by Christ for commemoration of His atoning death. These two ordinances are to be observed until the return of the Lord Jesus Christ. (Matt. 28:16-20; Luke 22:19-20; Acts 2:41; 10:47-48; I Cor. 11:23-29).

CONCERNING LAST THINGS

The Intermediate State: At death, the redeemed pass immediately into the presence of Christ and there remain in joyful fellowship until the first resurrection, that is, their bodily resurrection unto life. The unsaved at death descend immediately into Hades where they are kept under punishment until the second resurrection, that is, their bodily resurrection unto damnation. (Luke 16:22-23; 23:43; II Cor. 5:8; Phil. 1:21-26; 3:10, 11, 21; Rev. 20:11-15).

The Rapture of the Church: The next great event in the fulfillment of prophecy is the personal, bodily, return of the Lord to remove from the earth His waiting church and to reward them according to their works. (John 14:2-3; Rom. 14:10-12; I Cor. 3:11-15; 15:51-53; II Cor. 5:10; I Thess. 4:15-17; Titus 2:11-13; Rev. 3:10).

The Tribulation Period: After this removal from the earth the righteous judgments of God will be poured out upon the unbelieving world during the seven year period of tribulation, known as the seventieth week of Daniel. These judgments will be climaxed by the return of Christ in glory to the earth, at which time the Old Testament and tribulation saints will also be raised and the living will be judged. (Dan. 9:27; 12:1; Jer. 30:7; Matt. 24:15-31; 25:31-46; II Thess. 2:7-12; Rev. 16:1-19, 21).

The Millennium: After the judgment Christ will establish His Messianic Kingdom in which the resurrection saints will reign with Him over Israel and all the nations of the earth. (Deut. 30:1-10; Isaiah 11:1-16; 65:17-25; Ezek. 37:21-28; Rev. 19:11, 14; 20:1-6).

The Eternal State: At the close of the millennial reign the unsaved dead will be raised and committed to eternal punishment and the saved will enter the eternal state of glory with God. Having fulfilled His redemptive and kingdom missions as the Son of Abraham and the Son of David, Christ will deliver up the kingdom to God the Father that the Triune God may reign forever in all spheres. (Mark 9:43-48; I Cor. 15:24-28; II Thess. 1:9; II Pet. 3:10-13; Rev. 20-11-15; 21:1-4; 22:5;11).

Notes: *Western Conservative Baptist Seminary, Portland, Oregon, is sponsored by the Conservative Baptist Association (CBA) and its Standard of Faith and Practice is in accord with that of the CBA. The Western faculty of the school has presented a rather detailed statement of their position, including the role of creedal statements in light of the authority of the Bible. The Standard affirms the inerrancy of the Bible, the work of angels including the fallen angel Satan, total depravity (corruption), the authority of local congregations, believer's baptism by immersion, and the premillennial return of Jesus Christ.*

*　　*　　*

CONFESSION OF FAITH (GENERAL ASSOCIATION OF REGULAR BAPTIST CHURCHES/BAPTIST BIBLE COLLEGE OF PENNSYLVANIA)

We Believe. . .

In the verbal and plenary inspiration of the original manuscripts of the Old and New Testaments, which constitute the inerrant Word of God.

In the Trinity of the Godhead; one God eternally existing in three equal Persons—Father, Son and Holy Spirit.

In the deity, virgin birth, sinless life, substitutionary death, bodily resurrection and imminent premillennial coming of Christ.

In the personality of the Holy Spirit by Whom believers are called, regenerated, baptized into Christ, indwelt, sealed and filled for service.

In the direct creation of the universe and man by God apart from any process of evolution.

In the fall, total depravity and guilt of the race in Adam which for man's salvation necessitates the sovereign divinely-initiated deliverance of the sinner by the grace of God in Christ.

In God's sovereign election whereby in eternity past He chose some to be recipients of His grace in Christ.

In the eternal salvation of all individuals who put their faith in Christ, Whose blood was shed for the remission of sins.

In the unity of all true believers in the Church which is the body of Christ of which He is the sole Head.

In the local church as a company of baptized believers, independent and self-governing, which should fellowship with other churches of like faith and order. It is the responsibility of the local church to observe the ordinances baptism and the Lord's Supper, edify itself, and evangelize the world. We believe that the only biblical mode of believer's baptism is that of immersion, and that is to be administered in the name of the Father, Son and Holy Spirit. The ordinance of baptism is for believers only and it is a prerequisite for church membership. The officers of a New Testament church are pastors and deacons.

In the priesthood of all believers and the right of every individual to have direct dealings with God.

In the obedience to the biblical command to separate entirely from worldliness and ecclesiastical apostasy unto God.

In the separation of church and state with each believer having responsibilities to both.

In the personal existence of angels, demons and Satan.

In the bodily resurrection, immortality and pretribulation rapture of all believers at Christ's imminent coming.

In the sovereign selection of Israel as God's eternal covenant people, now dispersed because of her rejection of Christ and later to be regathered in the Holy Land, and saved as a nation at the second advent of Christ.

In the distinction between the nation Israel as God's earthly covenant people and the church as the spiritual Body of Christ.

In the bodily resurrection and judgment of unbelievers after the millennial reign of Christ.

In the eternal life and blessedness of all believers in heaven and the eternal existence and punishment of all unbelievers in the lake of fire.

Notes: *Baptist Bible College of Pennsylvania, located in Clarks Summit, is sponsored by the General Association of Regular Baptist Churches (GARBC). Its Confession of Faith summarizes and is in accord with that of the GARBC, a fundamentalist Baptist fellowship. It affirms the inerrancy of the Bible, believer's baptism by immersion, the priesthood of all believers, and the premillennial return of Jesus Christ. The school espouses the Calvinist theological tradition and affirms the total human depravity and the election by a sovereign God of those who will receive His grace.*

*　　*　　*

STATEMENT OF BELIEF (GENERAL ASSOCIATION OF REGULAR BAPTIST CHURCHES/FAITH BAPTIST BIBLE COLLEGE)

The Bible

We believe in the verbal-plenary inspiration by God of the original manuscripts of the Old and New Testament Scriptures, thus making them inerrant in all matters of which they treat.

The Trinity

We believe the one true and living God is one in essence, possessing three eternal, personal distinctions which are revealed to us as Father, Son and Holy Spirit, equal in every divine perfection, yet executing distinct but harmonious offices.

Jesus Christ

We believe that Jesus Christ was conceived by the Holy Spirit and born of the virgin Mary; that He is One Person possessing two natures and thus is true God and true man; that He lived a sinless life and gave Himself as a perfect substitutionary sacrifice for the sins of all men; that He arose bodily from the grave, ascended into Heaven where He is seated on the right hand of God interceding for His people and will return to the earth in keeping with His promises.

The Holy Spirit

We believe that the Holy Spirit is the third Person of the Triune Godhead; that He has been and will continue to be active throughout eternity; that, in gracious dealing with mankind, He has inspired the writing of the Scriptures; that He is in the world today convincing men of sin, of righteousness, and of judgment; that He is calling out a people for God among the Jews and Gentiles; that He regenerates those who believe, places them into the Body of Christ, indwells them and produces in them the fruit of the Spirit; and that He calls individuals to Christian service and empowers and directs them in that service.

Creation

We accept the Genesis account as being a historical record of creation and believe that the universe with all that is in it was created by God, not produced by some process of evolution.

The Spirit Realm

We believe that God created an innumerable company of sinless beings known as angels; that many of these continue in their holy state and are the ministers of God; that Lucifer (now known as Satan or the Devil) and many others rebelled against God; that these fallen angels, though defeated in the cross of Christ, still continue to oppose God and His work; that they will ultimately be judged by God and cast into the Lake of Fire to suffer everlasting punishment, which is their righteous due.

Man

We believe that man was originally created in the image and after the likeness of God; that through uncoerced disobedience Adam fell from his original state, became totally depraved in nature, was separated from God and came under condemnation and the sentence of death; that, because of the unity of human race and the natural headship of Adam, all men (Jesus Christ, only excepted) are born with sin natures and have come under the same consequences of sin.

Salvation

We believe that salvation is all of grace through the substitutionary work of Jesus Christ Who said the full redemptive price, fully satisfied God's righteous demands by suffering the death penalty for man's guilt and imputed to man His righteousness reconciling him to God; that salvation is made effective to man only upon his exercise of personal faith in Jesus Christ, which faith is not a meritorious work but possible only by the grace of God.

We believe that salvation includes justification, regeneration, adoption into the family of God, sanctification (positional, progressive and final) and glorification; that one who is truly born again will, by the grace of God, persevere and be kept saved forever.

Sanctification

We believe that every saved person is positionally in Christ, completely set apart for God. that in experience the saved person retains his sin nature. which is not eradicated in this life. and thus his present state is no more perfect than his daily experience: that there is a progressive sanctification wherein the saved person is to grow in grace and into Christlikeness by the unhindered power of the Holy Spirit, that when Christ appears the saved person will be fully sanctified so that his state will conform to his standing.

We believe that progressive sanctification involves separation not only from ungodly living but also from ungodly teaching; that though we love all men and seek their salvation, there are areas in which we cannot have fellowship with unbelievers; that, in areas of ecclesiastical fellowship, it may be necessary to separate even from our brethren in Christ, if they in turn maintain fellowship with unbelievers.

Dispensations

We believe that the dispensations are not ways of salvation. which has always been by grace through faith, but are stewardships by which God administers His purpose on earth through man under varying responsibilities; that changes in dispensational dealings depend upon changed situations in which man is found in relation to God due to man's failures and God's judgments: that, though several dispensations cover the entire history of mankind, only three of these are the subject of extended revelation in Scripture; that these three (Mosaic law, grace and millennial kingdom) are distinct and are not to be intermingled or confused.

The Church

We believe the Church which is Christ's body is composed of all true believers (those who have been born again through a personal acceptance of Christ as Savior) from Pentecost to the rapture; that this Church was brought into being on the day of Pentecost by the Holy Spirit's baptizing into one body all who were believers at that time; that on the day of Pentecost and since that time others have been and are being added to Christ as Savior; that at the rapture this Church will be complete and will be caught up to be united with Christ as His Bride, never to be separated from Him.

We believe that local churches are gatherings of professing believers in given communities, organized for the purposes of united worship, fellowship, administration of the ordinances (baptism and Lord's Supper), edification, discipline and effective promotion of the work of Christ throughout the world; that such local churches should be limited in membership to those who are born again, desire to follow Christ in obedience and have been immersed; that Christ is the supreme Head and every member has direct access to Him and is responsible to seek His will; that the only offices recognized in such New Testament churches are those of pastor (bishop, presbyter, elder) and deacon; that government is democratic with every member responsible to vote in keeping with his understanding of the will of Christ; that each local church is responsible directly to Christ and not to some other local church or organization; that there is value in fellowship and cooperation with other local churches of like convictions.

Civil Government

We believe that civil government was instituted by God and is still His means of maintaining peace and order among men; that believers here on earth are responsible in the area of civil government and should participate in it to promote and preserve good order in human society; that civil governments and churches (and fellowships of churches) are distinct from each other, must be organizationally separated from each other and neither must seek to control the other.

Things to Come

We believe that the Scriptures foretell certain future events among which are the following: Rapture of the Church. We believe that Jesus Christ will return to the atmosphere of this earth; that the dead in Christ will rise first, then believers who are still living will be caught up together with them to meet the Lord in the air and to ever be with the Lord; that the rapture is the next event on the revealed calendar and that no prophecy need be fulfilled before this occurs.

Tribulation. We believe that the rapture of the Church will be followed on earth by Israel's seventieth week; that, though there will be salvation, this will be a time of great judgments, the latter part being known as the great tribulation.

Second Coming. We believe that following the tribulation Christ will return to the earth with His glorified saints to establish the millennial kingdom; that during the 1,000 years of peace and prosperity Satan will be bound and Christ will reign with a rod of iron; that at the end of millennium Satan will be released for a short time, deceive many and lead them in final rebellion, but be destroyed with his armies.

Eternal State. We believe that the unsaved men of all ages will be resurrected and together with the evil angels will be finally judged and condemned to everlasting conscious punishment in hell; that all saved of all ages in glorified bodies will enjoy everlasting blessing in the presence of God.

Notes: *Faith Baptist Bible College, Ankeny, Iowa, is sponsored by the General Association of Regular Baptist Churches (GARBC), and its Statement of Belief summarizes and is in accord with that of the GARBC, a fundamentalist Baptist fellowship. The Statement affirms the inerrancy of the Bible, the existence of angels, the authority of the local church, believer's baptism by immersion, and a premillennial dispensational eschatology. Dispensationalism teaches that human history can be divided into a series of periods or dispensations—in each, God works in a slightly different manner toward humanity. Humanity now lives in the dispensa-*

tion of grace. In the near future Christ will return to take the members of the church to heaven prior to a period of tribulation, during which those remaining on earth will suffer. After the tribulation, Jesus will return to establish His kingdom on earth.

*   *   *

STATEMENT OF FAITH (GENERAL ASSOCIATION OF REGULAR BAPTIST CHURCHES/GRAND RAPIDS BAPTIST COLLEGE)

1. The Bible, verbally and plenarily inspired, is God's Word; infallible, inerrant, and authoritative in all matters of which it speaks.

2. There is one God, personal, infinite, perfect, and eternally existing as Father, Son and Holy Spirit, and each person is equal in every divine perfection.

3. The Holy Spirit is a divine person and works in conviction of men and in the regeneration, sanctification, and preservation of the believer.

4. Satan is a fallen. created personality. opposed to all that is holy and is destined for eternal punishment.

5. God directly created the universe from no pre-existing substance. We reject both naturalistic and theistic evolution.

6. Man was made in God's own image and fell into sin in Adam and is now a sinner both by nature and choice. and can be restored to God's favor only by God's provision in Christ as applied by the Holy Spirit.

7. Jesus Christ was conceived of the Holy Spirit. was born of the Virgin Mary, and He is true God and true man.

8. Salvation comes to man only by grace through faith in Jesus Christ, apart from any human merit through His substitutionary atoning sacrifice.

9. Jesus Christ rose bodily from the grave, ascended into heaven, and daily intercedes on our behalf as our High Priest.

10. In order to be saved, sinners must experience a new spiritual birth wrought by a sovereign God through the power of His Word and the ministry of the Holy Spirit. This birth is instantaneous and not a process, and is evidenced by newness of life.

11. Justification is an act of God in which He declares the believer to be righteous on the bases of faith in Christ and the imputation of Christ's righteousness to the believing sinner.

12. Sanctification is the setting apart of a believer unto God as His purchased possession through the work of the Holy Spirit and the power of His Word.

STATEMENT OF FAITH (GENERAL ASSOCIATION OF
REGULAR BAPTIST CHURCHES/GRAND RAPIDS BAPTIST
COLLEGE) (continued)

13. Every believer is eternally secure, being "kept by the power of God."

14. All those who have experienced salvation are members of the "church which is His body" and thus are eligible for baptism and membership in the local church. Jesus Christ is the Head of the church and every local church has the right under Christ to govern itself.

15. Baptism by immersion and the Lord's supper are ordinances of the church.

16. The Bible commands believers to be separated unto God and to be separated from worldliness and ecclesiastical apostasy.

17. Civil government exists by Divine appointment, and separation between it and the church should be maintained.

18. Israel is God's covenant people now dispersed because of unbelief but yet to be regathered and saved as a nation at the Second Advent of Christ.

19. The return of Christ includes both the Rapture of the Church and His return in glory. The first is for His church which is personal, pretribulational, premillennial and may occur at any moment. The second is His return to earth to establish His righteous reign over the earth. The coming is visible, personal, premillennial and in power and great glory.

20. All persons will experience resurrection, believers to a state of eternal felicity and unbelievers to eternal punishment.

Notes: *Grand Rapids Baptist College, in Grand Rapids, Michigan, affirms the inerrancy of the Bible, the personality of Satan, the eternal security of the believer, believers baptism by immersion, separation of believers from worldliness, unbelief in other churches, and a premillennial return of Jesus Christ.*

*   *   *

STATEMENT OF FAITH (GENERAL ASSOCIATION OF REGULAR BAPTIST CHURCHES/WESTERN BAPTIST COLLEGE)

We believe in. . .

The plenary verbal inspiration of the Scriptures;

The trinity of the Godhead: Father, Son and Holy Spirit, eternally coexistent personalities of the same essence;

The deity and virgin birth of Christ, His vicarious death, His bodily resurrection, His present high priestly ministry and mediatorship, and His personal, visible, premillennial return;
The personality of the Holy Spirit, and his ministry of convict-ing and regenerating sinners, and indwelling, anointing, sealing and empowering believers;

The fall of man from the state of innocency in which he was created to one of total depravity in which he is devoid of spiritual life, and incapable, apart from divine grace, of pleasing God;

The justification of the sinner by grace through faith plus nothing;

The election of the believer, "unto obedience and sprinkling of the blood of Jesus Christ," and the eternal indestructible character of his salvation in Christ;

The universality of the Church as the spiritual body of Christ, uniting all believers in organism, whose destiny it is to be caught up to be with Christ, the glorified head of "the Church, which is His body;"

The independence of the local church as an autonomous company of baptized believers, and as the divinely created agency through which the Church universal is to function in keeping the ordinances, enjoying fellowship, and evangelizing the lost;

The reality and personality of Satan, of fallen angels, and of demon spirits;

The bodily resurrection of the saved in immortality, and the conscious, eternal suffering of the lost.

Notes: *Western Baptist College, Salem, Oregon, is sponsored by the General Association of Regular Baptist Churches (GARBC), and its Statement of Faith summarizes and is in accord with that of the GARBC, a fundamentalist Baptist fellowship. It affirms the verbal inspiration of the Bible, the autonomy of the local church, believers baptism, and the premillennial return of Jesus Christ.*

*   *   *

DOCTRINAL POSITION (LIBERTY BAPTIST FELLOWSHIP/LIBERTY UNIVERSITY)

We affirm our belief in one God, infinite Spirit, creator, and sustainer of all things, who exists eternally in three persons, God the Father, God the Son, and God the Holy Spirit. These three are one in essence but distinct in person and function.

We affirm that the Father is the first person of the Trinity and the source of all that God is and does. From Him the Son is eternally generated and from Them the Spirit eternally proceeds. He is the designer of creation, the speaker of revelation, the author of redemption, and the sovereign of history.

We affirm that the Lord Jesus Christ is the second person of the Trinity. Eternally begotten from the Father, He is God. He was conceived by the virgin Mary through a miracle of the Holy Spirit. He lives forever as perfect God and perfect man: two distinct natures inseparably united in one person.

We affirm that the Holy Spirit is the third person of the Trinity, proceeding from the Father and the Son and equal in deity. He is the giver of all life, active in the creating and ordering of the universe; He is the agent of inspiration and the new birth; He restrains sin and Satan; and He indwells and sanctifies all believers.

We affirm that all things were created by God. Angels were created as ministering agents, though some, under the leadership of Satan, fell from their sinless state to become agents of evil. The universe was created in six historical days and is continuously sustained by God; thus it both reflects His glory and reveals His truth. Human beings were directly created, not evolved, in the very image of God. As reasoning moral agents, they are responsible under God for understanding and governing themselves and the world.

We affirm that the Bible, both Old and New Testaments, though written by men, was supernaturally inspired by God so that all its words are the written true revelation of God; it is therefore inerrant in the originals and authoritative in all matters. It is to be understood by all through the illumination of the Holy Spirit, its meaning determined by the historical, grammatical, and literary use of the author's language, comparing Scripture with Scripture.

We affirm that Adam, the first man, willfully disobeyed God, bringing sin and death into the world. As a result, all persons are sinners from conception, which is evidenced in their willful acts of sin; and they are therefore subject to eternal punishment, under the just condemnation of a holy God.

We affirm that Jesus Christ offered Himself as a sacrifice by the appointment of the Father. He fulfilled the demands of God by His obedient life, died on the cross in full substitution and payment for the sins of all, was buried, and on the third day He arose physically and bodily from the dead. He ascended into heaven where He now intercedes for all believers.

We affirm that each person can be saved only through the work of Jesus Christ, through repentance of sin and by faith alone in Him as Savior. The believer is declared righteous, born again by the Holy Spirit, turned from sin, and assured of heaven.

We affirm that the Holy Spirit indwells all who are born again, conforming them to the likeness of Jesus Christ. This is a process completed only in Heaven. Every believer is responsible to live in obedience to the Word of God in separation from sin.

We affirm that a church is a local assembly of baptized believers, under the discipline of the Word of God and the lordship of Christ, organized to carry out the commission to evangelize, to teach, and to administer the ordinances of believer's baptism and the Lord's table. Its offices are pastors and deacons, and it is self-governing. It functions through the ministry of gifts given by the Holy Spirit to each believer.

We affirm that the return of Christ for all believers is imminent. It will be followed by seven years of great tribulation, and then the coming of Christ to establish His earthly kingdom for a thousand years. The unsaved will then be raised and judged according to their works and separated forever from God in hell. The saved, having been raised, will live forever in heaven in fellowship with God.

Notes: *Liberty Baptist Fellowship was founded in 1981 by independent Baptist minister Jerry Falwell. Falwell had founded what became Liberty University in 1971, and it became the training ground for Baptist ministers who eventually left the school to found churches following the pattern set by Thomas Road Baptist Church, the congregation pastored by Falwell. Falwell had formerly been a member of the Baptist Bible Fellowship, with whom he had no doctrinal problems at the time he left it.*

This statement, the positional statement of the University, is an affirmation of a fundamental Protestant Christianity. Besides the acceptance of the traditional teachings of the ancient Christian creeds, it affirms the inerrancy of the Bible and a Baptist doctrine of the church as the local assembly of believers.

*   *   *

STATEMENT OF BELIEFS (NORTH AMERICAN BAPTIST CONFERENCE)

PREFACE

Baptists, since their beginnings, repeatedly have composed confessions which expressed the doctrinal consensus among related churches. In principle, however, Baptists always have insisted that no statement of faith can be considered creedally binding even upon concurring congregations. The purpose of their doctrinal summaries was to explain to other Christians and to the larger society what Baptists believed and practiced. Within and among Baptist churches, statements of faith also provided a standard for instruction, counsel and fellowship.

We, as North American Baptists, presently feel the need to state more fully our Baptist understanding of the Christian faith. The purpose that guided us in writing and the use that we intend for this declaration are

1. To further the sense of identity and the spirit of unity within our North American Baptist Conference by declaring our common doctrinal understandings;

2. To provide a basis for doctrinal instruction within our Conference;

3. To provide a basis for doctrinal discussions in the hiring of Conference personnel;

4. To serve as a reference point when opinions differ;

5. To provide a basis for doctrinal discussion in admitting new churches and new pastors into our various associations;

6. To provide a doctrinal guide for new churches; and

7. To give a doctrinal witness beyond our Conference.

In continuity with our immediate forefathers and the larger fellowship of Baptists throughout history, we seek to practice and propagate by God's grace the following convictions:

1. We believe the Bible is God's Word given by divine inspiration, the record of God's revelation of Himself to humanity (II Timothy 3:16). It is trustworthy, sufficient, without error—the supreme authority and guide for all doctrine and conduct (I Peter 1:23-25; John 17:17; II Timothy 3:16-17). It is the truth by which God brings people into a saving relationship with Himself and leads them to Christian maturity (John 20:31; I John 5:9-12; Matthew 4:4; I Peter 2:2).

2. We believe in the one living and true God, perfect in wisdom, sovereignty, holiness, justice, mercy and love (I Timothy 1:17; Psalm 86:15; Deuteronomy 32:3-4). He exists eternally in three coequal persons who act together in creation, providence and redemption (Genesis 1:26; I Peter 1:2; Hebrews 1:1-3).

   a. The Father reigns with providential care over all life and history in the created universe; He hears and answers prayer (I Chronicles 29:11-13; Matthew 7:11). He initiated salvation by sending His Son, and He is Father to those who by faith accept His Son as Lord and Savior (I John 4:9-10; John 3:16; John 1:12; Acts 16:31).

   b. The Son became man, Jesus Christ, who was conceived of the Holy Spirit and born of the virgin Mary (John 1:14; Matthew 1:18). Being fully God and fully man, He revealed God through His sinless life, miracles and teaching (John 14:9; Hebrews 4:15; Matthew 4:23-24). He provided salvation through His atoning death in our place and by His bodily resurrection (I Corinthians 15:3-4; II Corinthians 5:21; Romans 4:23-25). He ascended into heaven where He rules over all creation (Philippians 2:5-11). He intercedes for all believers and dwells in them as their everpresent Lord (Romans 8:34; John 14:23).

   c. The Holy Spirit inspired men to write the Scriptures (II Peter 1:21). Through this Word, He convicts individuals of their sinfulness and of the righteousness of Christ, draws them to the Savior, and bears witness to their new birth (James 1:18; John 16:7-11; I Thessalonians 1:5-6; Romans 8:16). At regeneration and conversion, the believer is baptized in the Holy Spirit (I Corinthians 12:13). The Spirit indwells, seals and gives spiritual gifts to all believers for ministry in the church and society (Romans 8:9-11; Ephesians 1:13-14; Romans 12:5-8; I Peter 4:10). He empowers, guides, teaches, fills, sanctifies and produces the fruit of Christlikeness in all who yield to Him (Acts 4:31; Romans 8:14; I Corinthians 2:10-13; Ephesians 5:18; II Thessalonians 2:13; Galatians 5:16, 22-23).

3. We believe God created an order of spiritual beings called angels to serve Him and do His will (Psalm 148:1-5; Colossians 1:16). The holy angels are obedient spirits ministering to the heirs of salvation and glorifying God (Hebrews 1:6-7, 13-14). Certain angels, called demons, Satan being their chief, through deliberate choice revolted and fell from their exalted position (Revelation 12:7-9). They now tempt individuals to rebel against God (I Timothy 4:1; I Peter 5:8). Their destiny in hell has been sealed by Christ's victory over sin and death (Hebrews 2:14; Revelation 20:10).

4. We believe God created man in His own image to have fellowship with Himself and to be steward over His creation (Genesis 1:26-28). As a result, each person is unique, possesses dignity and is worthy of respect (Psalm 139:13-17). Through the temptation of Satan, Adam chose to disobey God; this brought sin and death to the human race and suffering to all creation (Genesis 3; Romans 5:12-21; 8:22). Therefore, everyone is born with a sinful nature and needs to be reconciled to God (Romans 3:9-18, 23). Satan tempts people to rebel against God, even those who love Him (Ephesians 4:27; II Corinthians 2:11; Matthew 16:23). Nonetheless, everyone is personally responsible to God for thoughts, actions and beliefs and has the right to approach Him directly through Jesus Christ, the only mediator (Romans 14:12; I Timothy 2:5).

5. We believe salvation is redemption by Christ of the whole person from sin and death (II Timothy 1:9-10; I Thessalonians 5:23). It is offered as a free gift by God to all and must be received personally through repentance and faith in Jesus Christ (I Timothy 2:4; Ephesians 2:8-9; Acts 20:21). An individual is united to Christ by the regeneration of the Holy Spirit (Galatians 2:20; Colossians 1:27). As a child of God, the believer is acquitted of all guilt and brought into a new relationship of peace (Romans 5:1). Christians grow as the Holy Spirit enables them to understand and obey the Word of God (II Peter 3:18; Ephesians 4:15; I Thessalonians 3:12).

6. We believe the Church is the body of which Christ is the head and all who believe in Him are members (Ephesians 1:22-23; Romans 12:4-5). Christians are commanded to be baptized upon profession of faith and to unite with a local church for mutual encouragement and growth in discipleship through worship, nurture, service and the proclamation of the Gospel of Jesus Christ to the world (Acts 2:41-42, 47; Luke 24:45-48). Each church is a self-governing body under the lordship of Christ with all members sharing responsibility (Acts 13:1-3; 14:26-28). The form of government is understood to be congregational (Matthew 18:17; Acts 6:3-6; 15:22-23).

The ordinances of the church are baptism and the Lord's Supper. Baptism is the immersion of a believer in water in the name of the Father, and of the Son, and of the Holy Spirit (Matthew 28:18-20). It is an act of obedience symbolizing the believer's identification with the death, burial and resurrection of the Savior Jesus Christ (Romans

6:3-5). The Lord's Supper is the partaking of the bread and of the cup by believers together as a continuing memorial of the broken body and shed blood of Christ. It is an act of thankful dedication to Him and serves to unite His people until He returns (I Corinthians 11:23-26).

To express unity in Christ, local churches form associations and a conference for mutual counsel, fellowship and a more effective fulfillment of Christ's commission (Acts 15; I Corinthians 6:1-3).

7. We believe religious liberty, rooted in Scripture, is the inalienable right of all individuals to freedom of conscience with ultimate accountability to God (Genesis 1:27; John 8:32; II Corinthians 3:17; Romans 8:21; Acts 5:29). Church and state exist by the will of God. Each has distinctive concerns and responsibilities, free from control by the other (Matthew 22:21). Christians should pray for civil leaders, and obey and support government in matters not contrary to Scripture (I Timothy 2:1-4; Romans 13:1-7; I Peter 2:13-16). The state should guarantee religious liberty to all persons and groups regardless of their religious preferences, consistent with the common good.

8. We believe Christians, individually and collectively, are salt and light in society (Matthew 5:13-16). In a Christlike spirit, they oppose greed, selfishness and vice; they promote truth, justice and peace; they aid the needy and preserve the dignity of people of all races and conditions (Hebrews 13:5; Luke 9:23; Titus 2:12; Philippians 4:8-9; I John 3:16-17; James 2:1-4).

We affirm the family as the basic unit of society and seek to preserve its integrity and stability (Genesis 2:21-25; Ephesians 6:1-4).

9. We believe God, in His own time and in His own way, will bring all things to their appropriate end and establish the new heaven and the new earth (Ephesians 1:9-10, Revelation 21:1). The certain hope of the Christian is that Jesus Christ will return to the earth suddenly, personally and visibly in glory according to His promise (Titus 2:13; Revelation 1:7; 3:11; John 14:1-3). The dead will be raised, and Christ will judge mankind in righteousness (John 5:28-29). The unrighteous will be consigned to the everlasting punishment prepared for the devil and his angels (Matthew 25:41, 46; Revelation 20:10). The righteous, in their resurrected and glorified bodies, will receive their reward and dwell forever with the Lord (Philippians 3:20-21; II Corinthians 5:10; I Thessalonians 4:13-18).

Notes: *In 1982, the North American Baptist Conference adopted a lengthy Statement of Beliefs to meet formal needs and practical concerns. It provides a statement of doctrinal consensus to guide the hiring of personnel, and as a point of reference in further doctrinal discussions within the Conference. It is a traditional Baptist statement that affirms adult baptism by immersion, two church ordinances (not sacraments), congregational church government, and religious liberty. It also reflects contemporary religious controversies in its affirmation of the Bible as "without error," the occurrence of baptism of the Spirit at the time of conversion (rather than*

subsequent to conversion as advocated by the Pentecostal movement), and the centrality of the nuclear family.

* * *

CONFESSION OF FAITH (SOUTH CAROLINA BAPTIST FELLOWSHIP/TENNESSEE TEMPLE UNIVERSITY)

1. We believe in the verbal inspiration and authority of the Scriptures. We believe that the Bible reveals God, the fall of man, the way of salvation and God's plan and purpose in the ages.

2. We believe in God the Father, God the Son and God the Holy Spirit.

3. We believe in the deity, virgin birth and bodily resurrection of Jesus Christ.

4. We believe that salvation is "by grace" plus nothing and minus nothing. The conditions to salvation are repentance and faith.

5. We believe that men are justified by faith alone and are accounted righteous before God only through the merit of our Lord and Savior Jesus Christ. Justification is an eternal relationship that can never be broken.

6. We believe in the visible, personal and premillennial return of Jesus Christ.

7. We believe in the everlasting conscious blessedness of the saved and the everlasting conscious punishment of the lost.

Every student who expects to graduate from Tennessee Temple University will be required to sign a statement indicating agreement with the Confession of Faith.

Notes: *Tennessee Temple University, Chattanooga, Tennessee, is an independent Baptist school that has received the approval of the South Carolina Baptist Fellowship with which it is in doctrinal accord. the University and the school are representative of the fundamentalist Baptist tradition. All students are required to assent to the university's brief Statement of Faith, which briefly covers the fundamentals of evangelical Christianity from a premillennial perspective.*

* * *

GENERAL STATEMENT OF PHILOSOPHY (SOUTHERN BAPTIST CONVENTION/CRISWELL COLLEGE)

1. The privilege and duty of every Christian is to share in the evangelization of the world and to participate in the work of the church to that end.

2. In order to serve the Lord Jesus Christ, every Christian should equip himself as thoroughly as his gifts and opportunities allow.

3. The supreme Teacher is the Holy Spirit. This divine Teacher has various ways of working. He works as the believer prayerfully studies the Scriptures on his own. However, other ways in which He works must not be neglected. In particular, the ascended Saviour has given to His church men who are gifted to teach, and He wants His people individually and His church as a whole to benefit from their ministry (Eph. 4:7-14).

4. The sphere in which Christians are trained for service must have the following characteristics:

   a. The Bible must be the supreme textbook.

   b. The great gospel doctrines of the Bible must be taught clearly, forcibly, and as truths that inflame the heart.

   c. Those who teach must all be in wholehearted agreement with the essential doctrines of "the faith which was once delivered to the saints" (Jude 3).

   These doctrines include the sole authority, verbal inspiration, and inerrancy of the Holy Scriptures; the Father, the Son and the Holy Spirit as three Persons, but one God; the full deity and full humanity of the Lord Jesus Christ; His virgin conception, His penal substitutionary atonement, His death, bodily resurrection, and visible return; justification by grace alone through faith alone; the eternal bliss of the believer, and the eternal punishment of the unconverted.

   d. Learning in the classroom must go hand in hand with actual Christian service, especially in evangelism.

   e. Evangelism at home and evangelism abroad must never be divorced, but must be seen together as one task. Its concern for mission work in foreign countries must be encouraged.

5. The views of The Criswell College concerning the church and the ordinances are unequivocally Baptist. In these matters we freely submit to the New Testament as the sole rule of faith and practice. The local church is therefore a gathered community of those who have confessed their faith in the Lord Jesus Christ, independent of all external human control in order to be free to obey the Lord. Baptism is the immersion in water of those who have professed repentance and faith in the Lord Jesus Christ.

Notes: *Criswell College and Graduate School of the Bible, in Dallas, Texas, grew out of the lengthy ministry of R. A. Criswell, pastor of First Baptist Church in Dallas, Texas, the largest Baptist Church in America. The College functions independently, but operates within the larger fellowship of the Southern Baptist Convention that for the last generation has gone through an intense debate between conservatives and moderates. Criswell represented the conservative side of the*

debate and the founding of the school carried an implied criticism of many of the schools Southern Baptist schools as having moved into the moderate camp.

Much of the debate within the Southern Baptist Convention centered on the nature of the authority of the Bible. Conservatives tended to affirm the verbal inspiration and inerrancy of the Bible, and doctrinal uniformity within the fellowship over the essentials of the faith. This conservative position is spelled out in the General Statement of the school and should be read in the context of the Baptist Faith and Message passed by the Convention in 1963.

*   *   *

ARTICLES OF FAITH (SOUTHERN BAPTIST CONVENTION/DALLAS BAPTIST UNIVERSITY

I. THE SCRIPTURES

The Holy Bible was written by men divinely inspired and is the record of God's revelation of Himself to man. It is a perfect treasure of divine instruction. It has God for its author, salvation for its end, and truth, without any mixture of error, for its matter. We believe in the Scriptures of both the Old and New Testaments as verbally inspired by God and inerrant in the original writing, and that they are of supreme and final authority in faith and life. The Bible reveals the principles by which God judges us; and therefore is, and will remain to the end of the world, the true center of Christian union, and the supreme standard by which all human conduct, creeds, and religious opinions should be tried. The criterion by which the Bible is to be interpreted is Jesus Christ.

II. GOD

There is one and only one living and true God. He is an intelligent, spiritual, and personal Being, the Creator, Redeemer, Preserver, and Ruler of the universe. God is infinite in holiness and all other perfections. To Him we owe the highest love, reverence, and obedience. The eternal God reveals Himself to us as Father, Son, and Holy Spirit, with distinct personal attributes, but without division of nature, essence, or being.

   A. God the Father

   God as Father reigns with providential care over His universe, His creatures, and the flow of the stream of human history according to the purposes of His grace. He is all powerful, all loving, and all wise. God is Father in truth to those who become children of God through faith in Jesus Christ. He is fatherly in His attitude toward all men.

   B. God the Son

   Christ is the eternal Son of God. In His incarnation as Jesus Christ He was conceived of the Holy Spirit and born of the Virgin Mary, Jesus perfectly revealed and did the will of God, taking upon Himself the demands and necessities of human nature and identifying Himself completely with mankind, yet without sin. He honored the divine law by His personal obedience, and in His death on the cross He made provision for the redemption of men from sin. He was raised from the dead with a glorified body and appeared to His disciples as the person who was with them before His crucifixion. He ascended into heaven and is now exalted at the right hand of God where He is the One Mediator, partaking of the nature of God and of Man, and in whose Person is effected the reconciliation between God and man. He will return in power and glory to judge the world and to consummate His redemptive mission. He now dwells in all believers as the living and ever present Lord.

C. God the Holy Spirit

The Holy Spirit is the Spirit of God. He inspired holy men of old to write the Scriptures. Through illumination He enables men to understand truth. He exalts Christ. He convicts of sin, of righteousness, and of judgement. He calls men to Savior and effects regeneration. He cultivates christian character, comforts believers, and bestows the spiritual gifts by which they serve God through His church. He seals the believer unto the day of final redemption. His presence in the Christian is the assurance of God to bring the believer into the fullness of the stature of Christ. He enlightens and empowers the believer and the church in worship, evangelism, and service.

III. MAN

Man was created by the special act of God, in His own image, and is the crowning work of His creation. In the beginning, man was innocent of sin and was endowed by His Creator with freedom of choice. By his free choice, man sinned against God and brought sin into the human race. By this statement, we affirm our belief that man was created by a direct act of God in His image, not from previously existing creatures, and that all of mankind sinned in Adam and Eve, the historical parents of the entire human race. Through the temptation of Satan, man transgressed the command of God and fell from his original innocence; whereby his posterity inherits a nature and an environment inclined toward sin, and as soon as they were capable of moral action become transgressors and are under condemnation. Only the grace of God can bring man into His holy fellowship and enable man to fulfill the creative purpose of God. The sacredness of human personality is evident in that God created man in His own image, and in that Christ died for man; therefore every man possesses dignity and is worthy of respect and Christian love.

IV. SALVATION

Salvation involves the redemption of the whole man, and is offered freely to all who accept Jesus Christ as Lord and Saviour, who by His own blood obtained eternal redemption for the believer. In its broadest sense salvation includes regeneration, sanctification, and glorification.

A. Regeneration, or the new birth, is a work of God's grace whereby believers become new creatures in Christ Jesus. It is a change of heart wrought by the Holy Spirit through conviction of sin, to which the sinner responds in repentance toward God and faith in the Lord Jesus Christ. Repentance and faith are inseparable experiences of grace. Repentance is a genuine turning from sin toward God. Faith is the acceptance of Jesus Christ and commitment of the entire personality to Him as Lord and Saviour. Justification is God's gracious and full acquittal upon principles of His righteousness all sinners who repent and believe in Christ. Justification brings the believer into a relationship of peace and favor with God.

B. Sanctification is the experience, beginning in regeneration, by which the believer is set apart to God's purposes, and is enabled to progress toward moral and spiritual perfection through the presence and power of the Holy Spirit dwelling in him. Growth in grace should continue throughout the regenerate person's life.

C. Glorification is the culmination of salvation and is the final blessed and abiding state of the redeemed.

V. GOD'S PURPOSE OF GRACE

Election is the gracious purpose of God, according to which He regenerates, sanctifies, and glorifies sinners. It is consistent with the free agency of man, and comprehends all the means in connection with the end. It is a glorious display of God's sovereign goodness, and is infinitely wise, holy, and unchangeable. It excludes boasting and promotes humility.

All true believers endure to the end. Those whom God has accepted in Christ, and sanctified by his spirit, will never fall away from the state of grace, but shall persevere to the end. Believers may fall into sin through neglect and temptation, and sanctified by His Spirit, will never fall away from the state of grace, but shall persevere to the end. Believers may fall into sin through neglect and temptation, whereby they grieve the Spirit, impair their graces and comforts, bring reproach on the cause of Christ and temporal judgments on themselves, yet they shall be kept by the power of God through faith unto salvation.

VI. THE CHURCH

A New Testament church of the Lord Jesus Christ is a local body of baptized believers who are associated by covenant in the faith and fellowship of the gospel, observing the two ordinances of Christ, committed to His teachings, exercising the gifts, rights, and privileges invested in them by His word, and seeking to extend the gospel to the ends of the earth.

This church is an autonomous body, operating through democratic processes under the Lordship of Jesus Christ.

In such a congregation members are equally responsible. Its Scriptural officers are pastors and deacons.

The New Testament speaks also of the church as the body of Christ which includes all of the redeemed of the ages.

ARTICLES OF FAITH (SOUTHERN BAPTIST CONVENTION/
DALLAS BAPTIST UNIVERSITY (continued)

VII. BAPTISM AND THE LORD'S SUPPER

Christian baptism is the immersion of a believer in water in the name of the Father, the Son, and the Holy Spirit. It is an act of obedience symbolizing the believer's faith in a crucified, buried and risen Saviour, the believer's death to sin, the burial of the saviour, old life, and the resurrection to walk in newness of life in Christ Jesus. It is a testimony to his faith in the final resurrection of the dead. Being a church ordinance, it is prerequisite to the privileges of church membership and to the Lord's Supper.

The Lord's Supper is a symbolic act of obedience whereby members of the church, through partaking of the bread and the fruit of the vine, memorialize the death of the Redeemer and anticipate His second coming.

VIII. THE LORD'S DAY

The first day of the week is the Lord's Day. It is a Christian institution for regular observance. It commemorates the resurrection of Christ from the dead and should be employed in exercises of worship and spiritual devotion, both public and private, and by refraining from worldly amusements, and resting from secular employments, work of necessity and mercy only being excepted.

IX. THE KINGDOM

The Kingdom of God includes both His general sovereignty over the universe and His particular kingship over men who willfully acknowledge Him as King. Particularly the Kingdom is the realm of salvation into which men enter by trustful, childlike commitment to Jesus Christ. Christians ought to pray and to labor that the Kingdom may come and God's will be done on earth. The full consummation of the Kingdom awaits the return of Jesus Christ and the end of this age.

X. LAST THINGS

God, in His own time and in His own way, will bring the world to its appropriate end. According to His promise, Jesus Christ will return personally and visibly in glory to the earth; the dead will be raised; and Christ will judge all men in righteousness. The unrighteous will be consigned to Hell, the place of everlasting punishment. The righteous in their resurrected and glorified bodies will receive their reward and will dwell forever in Heaven with the Lord.

XI. EVANGELISM AND MISSIONS

It is the duty and privilege of every follower of Christ and of every church of the Lord Jesus Christ to endeavor to make disciples of all nations. The new birth of man's spirit by God's Holy Spirit means the birth of love for others. Missionary effort on the part of all rests thus upon a spiritual necessity of the regenerate life, and is expressly and repeatedly commanded in the teaching of Christ. It is the duty of every child of God to seek constantly to win the lost to Christ by personal effort and by all other methods in harmony with the gospel of Christ.

XII. STEWARDSHIP

God is the source of all blessings, temporal and spiritual; all that we have and are we owe to Him. Christians have a spiritual debtorship to the whole world, a holy trusteeship in the gospel, and a binding stewardship in their possessions. They are therefore under obligation to serve Him with their time, talents, and material possessions; and should recognize all these as entrusted to them to use for the glory of God and for helping others. According to the Scriptures, Christians should contribute of their means cheerfully, regularly, systematically, proportionately, and liberally for the advancement of the Redeemer's cause on earth.

XIII. COOPERATION

Christ's people should, as occasion requires, organize such associations and conventions as may best secure cooperation for the great objects of the Kingdom of God. Such organizations have no authority over one another or over the churches. They are voluntary and advisory bodies designed to elicit, combine, and direct the energies of our people in the most effective manner. Members of New Testament churches should cooperate with one another in carrying forward the missionary, educational, and benevolent ministries for the extension of Christ's Kingdom. Christian unity in the New Testament sense is spiritual harmony and voluntary cooperation for common ends by various groups of Christ's people. Cooperation is desirable between the various Christian denominations, when the end to be attained is itself justified, and when such cooperation involves no violation of conscience or compromise of loyalty to Christ and His Word as revealed in the New Testament.

XIV. THE CHRISTIAN AND THE SOCIAL ORDER

Every Christian is under obligation to seek to make the will of Christ supreme in his own life and in human society. Means and methods used for the improvement of society and the establishment of righteousness among men can be truly and permanently helpful only when they are rooted in the regeneration of the individual by the saving grace of God in Christ Jesus. The Christian should oppose in the spirit of Christ every form of greed, selfishness, and vice. He should work to provide for the orphaned, the needy, the aged, the helpless, and the sick. Every Christian should seek to bring industry, government, and society as a whole under the sway of the principles of righteousness, truth, and brotherly love. In order to promote these ends Christians should be ready to work with all men of good will in any good cause, always being careful to act in the spirit of love without compromising their loyalty to Christ and His truth.

XV. PEACE AND WAR

It is the duty of Christians to seek peace with all men on principles of righteousness. In accordance with the spirit and teachings of Christ they should do all in their power to put an end to war.

The true remedy for the war spirit is the gospel of our Lord. The supreme need of the whole world is the acceptance of His teachings in all the affairs of men and nations, and the practical application of His law of love.

XVI. RELIGIOUS LIBERTY

God alone is Lord of the conscience, and He has left it free *from* the doctrines and commandments of men which are contrary to His Word or not contained in it. Church and state should be separate. The state owes to every church protection and full freedom in the pursuit of its spiritual ends. In providing for such freedom no ecclesiastical group or denomination should be favored by the state more than others. Civil government being ordained of God, it is the duty of Christians to render loyal obedience thereto in all things not contrary to the revealed will of God. The church should not resort to the civil power to carry on its work. The gospel of Christ contemplates spiritual means alone for the pursuit of its ends. The state has no right to impose penalties for religious opinions of any kind. The state has no right to impose taxes for the support of any form of religion. A free church in a free state is the Christian ideal, and this implies the right of free and unhindered access to God on the part of all men, and the right to form and propagate opinions in the sphere of religion without interference by the civil power.

XVII. EDUCATION

The cause of education in the Kingdom of Christ is co-ordinate with the causes of missions and general benevolence, and should receive along with these the liberal support of the churches. An adequate system of Christian schools is necessary to a complete spiritual program for Christ's people.

Notes: *Dallas Baptist University is sponsored by the Southern Baptist Convention. Its Articles of Faith is based on the Baptist Faith and Message adopted by the convention in 1963, with additions by the faculty. For example, it adds the affirmation of the verbal inspiration and inerrancy of the Bible to the opening article on the Scriptures. The College also removed a paragraph from the article on Education and moved the remaining article to the end of its statement.*

*　　*　　*

ARTICLES OF RELIGIOUS BELIEF (SOUTHERN BAPTIST CONVENTION/NEW ORLEANS BAPTIST THEOLOGICAL SEMINARY

Article I

Sole Authority of Scriptures. We believe that the Bible is the Word of God in the highest and fullest sense, and is the unrivalled authority in determining the faith and practice of God's people; that the sixty-six books of the Bible are divinely and uniquely inspired, and that they have come down to us substantially as they were under inspiration written. These Scriptures reveal all that is necessary for us to know of God's plan of redemption and human duty. We deny the inspiration of other books, ancient or modern, and exalt the Bible to an unchallenged throne in our confidence. These Scriptures do not require the authorized interpretation of any church, or council, but are divinely intended for personal study and interpretation, under the guidance of the Holy Spirit.

Article II

One Triune God who is Father, Son and Holy Spirit. We believe in one only true and living God, the Creator and Sustainer of all things, who is infinite, eternal and unchangeable in every spiritual excellence, and who is revealed to us as Father, Son and Holy Spirit, three in one and one in three, as the essential mode of His existence.

The Father is the Head of the Trinity, into whose hands finally the Kingdom shall be given up. The Son is the promised Messiah of the Old Testament, Jesus Christ, who was born of the Virgin Mary, given to reveal God, died to redeem man, rose from the dead to justify the believer, is now at the right hand of God as our Advocate and Intercessor, and at the time the Father keeps in His own power, He will return in visible, personal and bodily form for the final overthrow of sin, the triumph of His people and the judgment of the world.

The Holy Spirit is a Person who has been sent from God to convict the world of sin, of righteousness and of judgment, to regenerate and cleanse from sin, and to teach, guide, strengthen and perfect the believer.

Article III

Satan and Sinful Man. We believe that man was created innocent, but that being tempted by Satan, he sinned, and thereafter all men have been born in sin, and are by nature children of wrath. The original tempter was Satan, the personal devil, who with his angels has been since carrying on his work of iniquity among the nations of the earth. The essence of sin is non-conformity to the will of God, and its end is eternal separation from God.

Article IV

Christ, God's Way of Atonement. We believe that a way has been provided whereby men born in sin may be reconciled to God. That Way is Jesus Christ, whose death atoned for our sin, and through union with Him we become partakers of His merits, and escape the condemnation of God's holy law. The atonement becomes personally effective through the foreordination and the grace of God, and the free choice and faith of man.

Article V

Christ, the only Savior from Sin, Without Whom Men are Condemned. We believe that apart from Jesus Christ there is no salvation. He is the only and all-sufficient Savior of sinners, irrespective of natural talents, family connection, or national distinction. All men are under condemnation through personal sin, and escape from condemnation comes only to those who hear and accept the gospel. The heathen, then, are under condemnation just as well as those who hear and reject the gospel, for they are sinners by both nature and practice. The pressing and inviolable obligation rests upon every church and

ARTICLES OF RELIGIOUS BELIEF (SOUTHERN BAPTIST CONVENTION/NEW ORLEANS BAPTIST THEOLOGICAL SEMINARY (continued)

individual to present the gospel to all men, that to all men may come the means of eternal life. Unless we proclaim the gospel we shall suffer loss, not only in this life, but in the day when we render to God the account of our stewardship.

Article VI

Conversion Includes Repentance, Faith, Regeneration and Justification. We believe that the Christian life begins with conversion. Conversion has several aspects, including repentance, faith, regeneration and justification. Repentance implies a deep and sincere change of thinking, feeling and willing toward sin and God, and faith is the surrender of the entire personality, thought, feeling and volition to Jesus Christ as Savior and Lord. Regeneration is the act of the Holy Spirit by which the sinner is born again, and his whole being is radically changed so that the believer becomes a new creation in Christ Jesus. Justification is the judicial act of God by which the sinner is declared forgiven and freed from the condemnation of his sin, on the ground of the perfect righteousness of Christ, imputed by grace through faith. The life begun in regeneration is never lost, but by the grace and power of God, and the faith and cooperation of the believer is constantly brought nearer to that state of perfect holiness which we shall experience finally in heaven.

Article VII

Final Resurrection of all Men. We believe in the final resurrection of all men, both the just and the unjust; and that those who here believe unto salvation shall be raised to everlasting life, while those who here disbelieve shall be raised to everlasting condemnation.

Article VIII

A New Testament Church a Body of Baptized Believers, Observing, Ordinances of Baptism and Lord's Supper. We believe that a New Testament Church is a voluntary assembly, or association of baptized believers in Christ covenanted together to follow the teachings of the New Testament in doctrine, worship, and practice. We believe there are only two Church ordinances—baptism and the Lord's Supper, and that a church as a democratic organization, is served by only two types of officers—pastors or bishops, and deacons. We believe that saved believers are the only scriptural subjects of baptism, and that immersion, or dipping, or burial, in water, and resurrection therefrom is the only scriptural act of baptism. We believe that the Lord's Supper is the partaking by the church of bread and wine, as a memorial of the Lord's death, and our expectation of His return. The bread typifies His body; the wine typifies His blood. We deny the actual presence of His body and blood in the bread and wine.

Article IX

Lord's Day and Christian Support of Civil Government. We believe that the Christian Sabbath, or Lord's Day, should be observed as a day of rest and Christian service in memory of

the resurrection of Christ, and as a means of Christian development and usefulness. We believe in civil government as of divine appointment, in the complete separation of church and state; and in the universal right to civil and religious liberty.

Article X

Baptist Loyalty to Distinctive Baptist Doctrines. We believe that Baptists stand for vital and distinctive truths, to many of which other denominations do not adhere, and that we cannot compromise these truths without disloyalty to the Scriptures and our Lord. We believe that we should cooperate with other denominations in so far as such cooperation does not affect these truths, but no union with them is possible, except on the basis of acceptance in full of the plain teachings of the Word of God.

Notes: *The faculty of the New Orleans Baptist Theological Seminary, a seminary of the Southern Baptist Convention, wrote their own statement of faith to which the members of the faculty subscribe. It affirms the authority of the Bible as the Word of God but avoids the use of such terms as infallible and inerrant. It also affirms the personality of Satan, believer's baptism by immersion, the role of the local church, the observance of the Sabbath, and the separation of church and state.*

*   *   *

ABSTRACT OF PRINCIPLES (SOUTHERN BAPTIST CONVENTION/SOUTHERN BAPTIST THEOLOGICAL SEMINARY)

I. The Scriptures.

The Scriptures of the Old and New Testaments were given by inspiration of God, and are the only sufficient, certain and authoritative rule of all saving knowledge, faith and obedience.

II. God.

There is but one God, the Maker, Preserver and Ruler of all things, having in and of Himself, all perfections, and being infinite in them all; and to Him all creatures owe the highest love, reverence and obedience.

III. The Trinity.

God is revealed to us as Father, Son and Holy Spirit each with distinct personal attributes, but without division of nature, essence or being.

IV. Providence.

God from eternity, decrees or permits all things that come to pass, and perpetually upholds, directs and governs all creatures and all events; yet so as not in any wise to be the author or approver of sin nor to destroy the free will and responsibility of intelligent creatures.

V. Election.

Election is God's eternal choice of some persons unto everlasting life—not because of foreseen merit in them, but of His mere mercy in Christ—in consequence of which choice they are called, justified and glorified.

VI. The Fall of Man.

God originally created Man in His own image, and free from sin; but, through the temptation of Satan, he transgressed the command of God, and fell from his original holiness and righteousness; whereby his posterity inherit a nature corrupt and wholly opposed to God and His law, are under condemnation, and as soon as they are capable of moral action, become actual transgressors.

VII. The Mediator.

Jesus Christ, the only begotten Son of God, is the divinely appointed mediator between God and man. Having taken upon Himself human nature, yet without sin, He perfectly fulfilled the law, suffered and died upon the cross for the salvation of sinners. He was buried, and rose again the third day, and ascended to His Father, at whose right hand He ever liveth to make intercession for His people. He is the only Mediator, the Prophet, Priest and King of the Church, and Sovereign of the Universe.

VIII. Regeneration.

Regeneration is a change of heart, wrought by the Holy Spirit, who quickeneth the dead in trespasses and sins enlightening their minds spiritually and savingly to understand the Word of God, and renewing their whole nature, so that they love and practice holiness. It is a work of God's free and special grace alone.

IX. Repentance.

Repentance is an evangelical grace, wherein a person being by the Holy Spirit, made sensible of the manifold evil of his sin, humbleth himself for it, with godly sorrow, detestation of it, and self-abhorrence, with a purpose and endeavor to walk before God so as to please Him in all things.

X. Faith.

Saving faith is the belief, on God's authority, of whatsoever is revealed in His Word concerning Christ; accepting and resting upon Him alone for justification and eternal life. It is wrought in the heart by the Holy Spirit, and is accompanied by all other saving graces, and leads to a life of holiness.

XI. Justification.

Justification is God's gracious and full acquittal of sinners, who believe in Christ, from all sin, through the satisfaction that Christ has made; not for anything wrought in them or done by them; but on account of the obedience and satisfaction of Christ, they receiving and resting on Him and His righteousness by faith.

XII. Sanctification.

Those who have been regenerated are also sanctified by God's word and Spirit dwelling in them. This sanctification is progressive through the supply of Divine strength, which all saints seek to obtain, pressing after a heavenly life in cordial obedience to all Christ's commands.

XIII. Perseverance of the Saints.

Those whom God hath accepted in the Beloved, and sanctified by His Spirit, will never totally nor finally fall away from the state of grace, but shall certainly persevere to the end; and though they may fall through neglect and temptation, into sin, whereby they grieve the Spirit, impair their graces and comforts, bring reproach on the Church, and temporal judgments on themselves, yet they shall be renewed again unto repentance, and be kept by the power of God through faith unto salvation.

XIV. The Church.

The Lord Jesus is the Head of the Church, which is composed of all His true disciples, and in Him is invested supremely all power for its government. According to His commandment, Christians are to associate themselves into particular societies or churches; and to each of these churches He hath given needful authority for administering that order, discipline and worship which He hath appointed. The regular officers of a Church are Bishops or Elders, and Deacons.

XV. Baptism.

Baptism is an ordinance of the Lord Jesus, obligatory upon every believer, wherein he is immersed in water in the name of the Father, and the Son, and of the Holy Spirit, as a sign of his fellowship with the death and resurrection of Christ, of remission of sins, and of giving himself up to God, to live and walk in newness of life. It is prerequisite to church fellowship, and to participation in the Lord's Supper.

XVI. The Lord's Supper.

The Lord's Supper is an ordinance of Jesus Christ, to be administered with the elements of bread and wine, and to be observed by His churches till the end of the world. It is in no sense a sacrifice, but is designed to commemorate His death, to confirm the faith and other graces of Christians, and to be a bond, pledge and renewal of their communion with Him, and of their church fellowship.

XVII. The Lord's Day.

The Lord's Day is a Christian institution for regular observance, and should be employed in exercises of worship and spiritual devotion, both public and private, resting from worldly employments and amusements, works of necessity and mercy only, excepted.

XVIII. Liberty of Conscience.

God alone is Lord of the conscience; and He hath left it free from the doctrines of commandments of men, which are in anything contrary to His word, or not contained in it. Civil magistrates being ordained of God, subjection in all lawful

ABSTRACT OF PRINCIPLES (SOUTHERN BAPTIST CONVENTION/SOUTHERN BAPTIST THEOLOGICAL SEMINARY) (continued)

things commanded by them ought to be yielded by us in the Lord, not only for wrath, but also for conscience sake.

XIX. The Resurrection.

The bodies of men after death return to dust, but their spirits return immediately to God—the righteous to rest with Him; the wicked, to be reserved under darkness to the judgment. At the last day, the bodies of all the dead, both just and unjust, will be raised.

XX. The Judgment.

God hath appointed a day, wherein He will judge the world by Jesus Christ, when every one shall receive according to his deeds; the wicked shall go into everlasting punishment; the righteous, into everlasting life.

Notes: *Southern Baptist Theological Seminary, Louisville, Kentucky, is sponsored by the Southern Baptist Convention. Its Articles of Religious Belief is a brief statement of evangelical Protestantism and Baptist distinctives. The latter include the affirmation of the authority of the local church, believers' baptism by immersion, and individual liberty of conscience.*

*   *   *

DOCTRINAL DISTINCTIVES (WORLD BAPTIST FELLOWSHIP/ARLINGTON BAPTIST COLLEGE)

1. The Word of God is that collection of 66 books known as the Holy Bible, is verbally inspired, providentially preserved, and is therefore our only rule of faith and practice.

2. God is spirit, at the same time Father, Holy Spirit, and Son, and became incarnate through a virgin birth.

3. The Son of God, Jesus Christ, died to save sinners, providing for the justification, sanctification, and glorification of all believers.

4. Jesus Christ rose from the dead and ascended into heaven where he intercedes for us as our only high priest.

5. The privileges and benefits of salvation are free to all sinners only by the new birth in which confession of sin is made and faith is exercised.

6. Truly born again believers publicly declare their faith by baptism, immersion in water symbolizing the death, burial, and resurrection of Jesus Christ.

7. The church is a local congregation of baptized believers who have covenanted together to obey Christ as their head, to proclaim the gospel to the lost of the world, and to teach discipleship to such as believe.

8. The Holy Spirit directs believers in their lives and works through the Word of God to the end that Christ may be glorified.

9. Jesus Christ is coming again personally to set up a kingdom and the end of the world will be marked by the resurrection of the just and unjust.

10. The hope of the second coming of Christ encourages the pure and separated living of His disciples while they engage in fulfilling the Great Commission.

A Fundamental Baptist believes in a supernatural Bible, which tells of a supernatural Christ, who had a supernatural birth, who spoke supernatural words, who performed supernatural miracles, who lived a supernatural life, who died a supernatural death, who rose in supernatural power, who intercedes as a supernatural priest, and who will one day return in supernatural glory to establish a supernatural kingdom on the earth.

Notes: *World Baptist Fellowship grew out of the ministry of fundamentalist Baptist pastor J. Frank Norris. Members of the faculty of the Arlington Baptist College, Arlington, Texas, is a summary of Baptist essentials including the verbal inspiration of the Bible, believer's baptism by immersion, the authority of the local church, and the personal return of Jesus Christ at the end of time.*

*   *   *

Black Baptist

DOCTRINAL STATEMENT (NATIONAL BAPTIST CONVENTION OF THE U.S.A., INC./AMERICAN BAPTIST COLLEGE OF ABT SEMINARY)

1. We believe that there is one God, eternally existing in three persons, Father, Son, and Holy Spirit.

2. We believe the Bible to be the inspired, the only infallible, authoritative Word of God.

3. We believe in the deity of our Lord Jesus Christ, in His virgin birth, in His sinless life, in His miracles, in His vicarious death and atonement through His shed blood, in His bodily resurrection, in His ascension to the right hand of the Father, and in His personal and visible return in power and glory.

4. We believe that man was created in the image of God, that he was tempted by Satan and fell, and that, because of the

exceeding sinfulness of human nature, regeneration by the Holy Spirit is absolutely necessary for salvation.

5. We believe in the present ministry of the Holy Spirit by whose indwelling the Christian is enabled to live a godly life, and by Whom the Church is empowered to carry out Christ's great commission.

6. We believe in the bodily resurrection of both the saved and the lost; those who are saved unto the resurrection of life and those who are lost unto the resurrection of damnation.

Notes: *The American Baptist College, Nashville, Tennessee, was founded as a joint project of the National Baptist Convention of the U.S.A. and the Southern Baptist Convention to serve African American students. Its Doctrinal Statement is derived from that of the American Accrediting Association of Bible Colleges. It affirms a consensus Evangelical theology and does not include any of the Baptist distinctives.*

*   *   *

General Baptist

DOCTRINAL POSITION (BAPTIST GENERAL CONFERENCE/BETHEL THEOLOGICAL SEMINARY)

Since its inception, theological studies at Bethel Theological Seminary have been set within the framework of historic evangelical theology, such as the reliability of the Scriptures as the authority for Christian living and church order; the depravity of man, necessitating divine redemption through personal regeneration: the virgin-born Christ as the incarnate Redeemer; the vicariously atoning death of Jesus Christ; the historicity of the Resurrection; and the certainty of the return of Christ.

While there has always been positiveness in teaching the essentials of Christian theology, Bethel has maintained an atmosphere of broad tolerance for divergent views in the peripheral areas of theological interpretation.

Theological education at Bethel has never been static. Today, as in the past, the theological position of the seminary combines the continuing foundational truths of evangelicalism with the best insights of contemporary thought. While Bethel, true to its heritage, preserves its own distinctive theology, there is healthy interaction of faculty and students with the larger ecumenical world of theological discussion.

Notes: *This brief statement of Bethel Theological Seminary, St. Paul, Minnesota, assumes "An Affirmation of Our Faith," the statement passed by the Baptist General conference in 1951. It assumes the an affirmation of essential conservative evangelical beliefs.*

*   *   *

Seventh-Day Baptist

STATEMENTS OF BELIEF (GERMAN SEVENTH DAY BAPTIST CHURCH)

STATEMENT 1. We believe that all Scripture given by inspiration in the Old and the New Testaments is the Word of God, and is the only rule of Faith and Practice. II Tim. 3:16; II Peter 1:19, 20, 21; Mark 7:13; I Thes. 2:13; Acts 4:29, 30, 31.

STATEMENT 2. We believe that unto us there is but one God, the Father; and one Lord, Jesus Christ, who is the Mediator between God and mankind, and that the Holy Ghost is the Spirit of God. I Cor. 8:6; I Tim. 2:5; II Tim. 3:16; II Peter 1:21; John 14:26.

STATEMENT 3. We believe that the Ten Commandments which were written on two tables of stone by the finger of God, continue to be the rule of righteousness for all mankind. We further believe that active participation in war by military service is in violation of the sixth commandment and the teachings of Jesus Christ. Ex. 20; Matt. 5:17, 18, 19; Mal. 4:4; Isaiah 1:25 and 2:10; Rom. 3:31; 7:25; 13:8, 9, 10; Eph. 6:2.

STATEMENT 4. We believe that all persons ought to be baptized in water by triune immersion in a forward position after confession of their faith in Jesus Christ as the Son of God. Matt. 28:18-20; Acts 2:38 and 8:36, 37; Rom. 6:3, 4; Col. 2:12.

STATEMENT 5. We believe that the Lord's Supper ought to be administered and received in all Christian Churches, accompanied with the washing of one another's feet previous to the breaking of the bread. Luke 22:19, 20; I Cor. 11:23, 24, 25, 26; John 13:4-17.

STATEMENT 6. We believe in the anointing of the sick with oil in the name of the Lord. James 5:13, 14, 15.

STATEMENT 7. We believe in the invocation of Infant Blessing. Matt. 19:13, 14, 15; Mark 10:13, 14, 15, 16; Luke 18:15, 16.

STATEMENT 8. We believe that all Christian Churches should have Elders and Deacons. Titus 1:5; Acts 6:3.

STATEMENT 9. We believe that the duties of the Deacons are: To provide for the Communion Service of the Church, and officiate thereat when necessary; to seek out and report to the church all cases of destitution or suffering within bounds of the church, especially such as arise from sickness; to provide necessary relief in behalf of the Church. They shall also be deemed co-worker in the ministry and counsellors in spiritual matters. They shall continue in office for life or during good behavior.

STATEMENT 10. We believe in observing the Seventh Day (Sabbath). He whom we worship was its first observer. Gen 2:1-3; Ex. 20:8-11; Ex. 16:23, 25, 29; Lev. 23:32: Nehemiah 9:14; Nehemiah 13:15, 16, 21; Isaiah 56:2-6; Matt. 28:1; Mark 2:27, 28; Luke 13:10; Acts 13:42; Acts 16:13; Acts 18:4; Heb. 4:4.

Notes: *The German Seventh Day Baptists date to the eighteenth century and the spread of the sabbatarian belief among German Baptists. As with the sabbatarian Baptists of British origin, the German Baptists emphasize the continuing role of the Ten Commandments, but differ by advocating baptism by triune immersion in a forward position, preaching foot washing, anointing the sick, and blessing infants (in the place of infant baptism).*

*   *   *

Baptist Organizations

DOCTRINAL STATEMENT (ASSOCIATION OF BAPTISTS FOR WORLD EVANGELISM)

I. Concerning the Scriptures

We believe that the Scriptures of the Old and New Testaments as originally written were both verbally and plenarily inspired and were the product of Spirit-controlled men and are, therefore, wholly without error. We believe the Bible is the supreme revelation of God's will for man and is our only rule of life and practice. (II Timothy 3:16; II Peter 1:19-21)

II. Concerning the True God

We believe in one God, the Creator of heaven and earth, manifesting Himself in three persons, the Father, Son and Holy Spirit, equal in power and glory and executing distinct and harmonious offices in the great work of redemption. (Exodus 2:2, 3; I Corinthians 8:6)

III. Concerning the Holy Spirit

We believe that the Holy Spirit is a divine person possessing all the attributes of personality and of deity. He is equal with the Father and with the Son and is of the same nature. His relation to the unbelieving world is that He convicts of sin, righteousness and judgment. His work among believers is that He baptizes into Christ, seals, indwells, infills, guides, and teaches them the ways of righteousness. We believe that there is a distinction between the ministry of the Holy Spirit in the Old Testament and the ministry of the Holy Spirit in the New Testament. There is, therefore, a new and unique work of the Holy Spirit in relation to the Body of Christ. (John 14:16, 17, 26; John 7:39; Hebrews 9:14; Ephesians 1:13, 14; Acts 1:5; I Corinthians 12:13)

IV. Concerning the Lord Jesus Christ

We believe that the Lord Jesus Christ was conceived by the Holy Spirit and born of the Virgin Mary; He is very God of very God, being "God manifest in the flesh"; He lived a life of absolute sinlessness and in His death He made a full and vicarious atonement for our sins, dying not a martyr's death, but as a voluntary substitute in the sinner's place. He rose again from the dead on the third day and ascended bodily into heaven. He is coming again to rapture His saints, and to set up the throne of David and establish His kingdom. His coming is imminent and will be personal, pre-tribulational, and pre-millennial. (Isaiah 7:14; John 1:1; I Peter 3:18; Matthew 28:6; Acts 15:16; Matthew 1:18-25; I Peter 2:22; John 14:3; I Thessalonians 4:16; II Thessalonians 2:6-8)

V. Concerning Man

We believe the Scriptures teach that man was created by a direct act of God and not from any previously existing form of life. By voluntary transgression he fell from his state of innocence, in consequence of which all men are now sinners by nature and by choice, being utterly devoid of that holiness required by law, positively inclined to evil, and therefore under just condemnation to eternal ruin without defense or excuse. (Genesis 1:27; Romans 5:12-19; Isaiah 53:6; Romans 3:23)

VI. Concerning Salvation

We believe the Scriptures teach that salvation of sinners is divinely initiated and wholly of grace through the mediatorial work of the Son of God; it is wholly apart from works and is upon the sole condition of repentance and faith in the Lord Jesus Christ; that in order to saved the sinner must be born again, being regenerated by the power of the Holy Spirit through faith in God's Word and becoming the recipient of a new nature; that the great gospel blessing which Christ secures to such as believe in Him is justification, which includes both pardon of sin and the imputation of divine righteousness solely through faith in the Redeemer's blood; that having exercised personal faith in the Lord Jesus Christ, the believer is completely justified and is in possession of a salvation which is eternally secure. (Ephesians 2:8-10; II Peter 1:4; John 10:28, 29; John 3:3-6; Acts 13:39; I Peter 1:18-23; Hebrews 4:2)

VII. Concerning the Church

We believe the Scriptures teach that the Church of Jesus Christ was inaugurated at Pentecost and must be considered in two aspects: the local church and the "church which is His body." The local church is a congregation of baptized believers, associated by a covenant in the faith and fellowship of the gospel, observing the ordinances of Christ, governed by His laws, and exercising the gifts, rights, and privileges invested in them by His Word; that its scriptural officers are pastors, sometimes called bishops or elders, and deacons; whose qualifications, claims, and duties are defined in the epistles of Timothy and Titus. The "church which is His body" is the entire company of believers in Christ, whether Jew or Gentile, regardless of denominational affiliation and present position in heaven or on earth. (Matthew 28:19, 20; Titus 1; Acts 2:41, 42; Ephesians 1:22, 23; Hebrews 12:23)

VIII. Concerning Baptism and the Lord's Supper

We believe the Scriptures teach that Christian baptism is the single immersion of a believer in water, in the name of the Father, Son, and Holy Spirit, to show forth in a solemn and beautiful emblem his identification with the crucified, buried, risen Savior; thus illustrating the believer's death to sin and his resurrection to a new life; that it is pre-requisite to membership and privileges in a local church. We believe that the Lord's Supper is the commemoration of His death until He comes and should be preceded by solemn self-examination. (Acts 8:36-39; I Corinthians 11:23-28; Romans 6:3-5)

IX. Concerning the Eternal State

We believe the Scriptures teach the bodily resurrection of the just and the unjust. All those who through faith are justified in the name of the Lord Jesus Christ will spend eternity in full enjoyment of God's presence and those who through impenitence and unbelief refuse to accept God's offer of mercy will spend eternity in everlasting punishment. (Psalm 16:11; Matthew 25:46; John 14:2; John 5:28, 29)

X. Concerning Satan

We believe the Scriptures teach that there is a personal devil who is "the god of this age," "the prince of the power of the air," who is full of all subtlety, who seeks continually to frustrate the purposes of God and to ensnare the sons of men, and who was conquered by Christ on the cross and is condemned to everlasting punishment. (Ephesians 2:2; Revelation 12:9; II Corinthians 4:4; II Corinthians 11:13-15; Hebrews 2:14)

XI. Concerning Christian Life

We believe the Scriptures teach that every believer, by the aid of the Holy Spirit, should walk in Christian love and holiness, exhibiting qualities of honesty, integrity, forgiveness, lovingkindness and spirituality. We further believe that any achievement in these characteristics will be evidenced by sincere humility and genuine zeal for the advancement of the cause of Christ. (II Corinthians 7:1; I Thessalonians 4:7; Philippians 4:8; Ephesians 4:32; Ephesians 5:1, 2; Ephesians 5:7-10; Ephesians 5:15-20; I Peter 5:5, 6; Proverbs 15:33; Galatians 5:22-25)

XII. Concerning Biblical Separation

We believe the Scriptures teach that the believer should be separated unto God from the world and from apostasy as exemplified in ecclesiastical organizations such as the National and World Councils of Churches. This doctrine is based upon God's eternal principle of division between truth and error and His specific command to be separate from unbelievers and disobedient brethren. This truth is to be practiced with an attitude of devotion, humility, compassion, and yet with conviction, to create the proper condition and atmosphere for the main objective, i.e. the salvation of the lost through the gospel of God. (Matthew 10:34-39; II John 9-11; Galatians 1:8, 9; I Corinthians 5:7-13; II Corinthians 11:4; II Corinthians 6:14; Matthew 18:15; I Timothy 6:3-6; II Timothy 2:16-18; Romans 16:17; Titus 3:10)

Notes: *The Association of Baptists for World Evangelism is one of several independent missionary agencies approved by the fundamentalist General Association of Regular Baptist Church (GARBC), upon whose Articles of Faith this Doctrinal Statement is based. The GARBC statement is in turn based on the New Hampshire Confession of Faith, the historical statement of faith for American Baptists. This statement contains a paragraph on "Biblical Separation" not contained in the GARBC Articles (but generally held by Regular Baptists).*

*   *   *

DOCTRINAL STATEMENT (BAPTIST INTERNATIONAL MISSIONS, INC.)

A. The Inspiration of the Bible. We believe the Bible is the verbally inspired Word of God.

B. The Person of God. We believe God is supreme in His person, eternal in His being, absolute in His attributes, glorious in His perfection. We believe in the Trinity.

C. The Person of Jesus Christ. We believe in the virgin birth of Christ, His deity and sinless life, His vicarious death, His bodily resurrection and ascension, and in His personal, premillennial return.

D. The Person of the Holy Spirit. We believe the Holy Spirit is the executive of the Godhead. We believe that He executes the plan of God for our conviction and salvation. Christians are partakers of the Holy Spirit and empowered for service by Him.

E. The Fall of Man. We believe that man was created in the image of God and by choice fell into sin and death. Hence, every person is sinful and under condemnation to eternal judgment.

F. The Salvation of Sinners. We believe that the salvation of sinners is wholly of grace, and that Jesus Christ is the only way of salvation.

G. The Freeness of Salvation. We believe that the blessings of salvation are made free by the Gospel, that nothing prevents the salvation of the greatest sinner but his own inherent depravity and voluntary rejection of the Gospel.

H. The Security of the Believer. We believe that those who receive Jesus Christ as Savior are eternally secure. Our Security rests on the finished work of Jesus Christ: as a result, we have assurance.

I. The Doctrine of the Church. We believe that the visible church is a congregation of baptized believers, practicing New Testament principles, believing its doctrines, observing its ordinances and exercising its autonomy.

J. The Doctrine of Heaven and Hell. We believe in the eternal blessedness of the saved in heaven and the eternal punishment of the lost in Hell.

DOCTRINAL STATEMENT (BAPTIST INTERNATIONAL MISSIONS, INC.) (continued)

CURRENT TRENDS OF THEOLOGY—As a fundamental agency, BIMI takes a separatist stand regarding the current trends that lead to discrediting the Bible and undermining the fundamentals of the faith.

Neo-orthodoxy—This theological persuasion is the result of a futile attempt to reconcile "Higher Scientific Biblical Criticism" with true Biblical interpretation. Such an approach to Biblical revelation is based upon half-truths and as such is false and deceptive. We utterly reject this method and position.

Neo-evangelicalism—This movement, while claiming to be fundamental in theology, has actually compromised the underlying principles of the Christian faith. It questions inspiration, rejects literal interpretation, accept liberals as Christians, takes a new attitude toward the ecumenical movement, promotes ecumenical evangelism, denies both ethical and ecclesiastical separation, restructures eschatology, and overstresses the social aspects of the Gospel. We hold this stance to be un-Scriptural.

Ecumenical Movement—The attempt to unite the different faiths today on the basis of the least common denominator of doctrine is a betrayal of the true unity of believers based upon the sound doctrine of the historic Christian faith. Its dialogue with other religions is dialectical. Its method of operation is subversive and shows a tendency of totalitarianism. Its concept of an ecclesiastical kingdom are not supported by Scripture. We reject all cooperation with this movement.

Neo-Pentecostalism—Recent years have seen an upsurge in interest in the sign gifts prevalent during the apostolic age. This has resulted in the growth of the charismatic movement which has infiltrated nearly every major denomination and has served as a cause of division in some fundamental churches. The movement has also become a catalyst for ecumenism and, as such, is a contradiction of all that is true and spiritual. BIMI rejects this movement as having no Biblical basis for existence. This Board will not aid or abet the charismatic movement on any of its fields.

Notes: *Baptist International Missions is a fundamentalist Baptist missionary agency. Its brief statement is derived from the New Hampshire Confession of Faith with an addenda specifically condemning Pentecostal and neo-Evangelical forms of conservative Protestantism and the liberal theological trends of neo-Orthodoxy and Ecumenism.*

*   *   *

ARTICLES OF FAITH (BAPTIST MID-MISSIONS)

We believe that the sixty-six books of the Old and New Testaments are verbally inspired of God and inerrant in the original writing and that they are of supreme and final authority in faith and life. (II Timothy 3.16-17; II Peter 1:19-21)

We believe in one God, eternally existing in three persons: Father, Son and Holy Spirit, equal in essence, while distinct in personality and function. (Exodus 20:2-3; Matthew 28:19; I Corinthians 8:6)

We believe in God's direct creation of the universe without the use of pre-existent material and apart from any process of evolution whatever, according to the Genesis account. (Genesis 1:1-31; Exodus 20:11; Colossians 1:16-17; Hebrews 11:3)

We believe that Jesus Christ, the eternal Son of God, was conceived by the Holy Spirit and born of Mary, a virgin, and is true God and true man. (John 1:1,14; Luke 1:35; Isaiah 7:14; Galatians 4:4)

We believe in the resurrection of the crucified body of our Lord, in His ascension into heaven, and in His present life there as High Priest and Advocate. (Matthew 28:1-7; Acts 1:8-11; I Corinthians 15:4-9; Hebrews 4;14-16)

We believe that the Holy Spirit is the agent of the new birth through conviction and regeneration and that He seals, indwells and baptizes every believer into the Body of Christ at the moment of conversion. We believe that the Holy Spirit fills, empowers and distributes service gifts to believers, but that sign gifts were restricted to the Apostolic Period. (John 3:5; Ephesians 1:13; Romans 8:9; I Corinthians 12:13; Ephesians 5:18; 4:11-12; Romans 12:6-8; Hebrews 2:3-4; Ephesians 2:20; Corinthians 13:8-13)

We believe that man was created in the image of God, that he sinned and thereby incurred not only physical death but also that spiritual death which is separation from God, and that all human beings are born with a sinful nature and are sinners in thought, word and deed. (Genesis 1:26-27; 3:1-6; Romans 5:12,19; 3:10-13; Titus 1:15-16)

We believe that the Lord Jesus Christ died as the substitutionary sacrifice for all men. The blood atonement He made was unlimited in its potential. It is limited only in its application, effectively saving those who are brought by the Holy Spirit to repentance and faith. (Isaiah 53:4-11; II Corinthians 5:14-21; I John 2:1-2; II Peter 2:1; I Timothy 4:10; John 3:5-8; 16:8-13)

We believe that all who receive by faith the Lord Jesus Christ are born again of the Holy Spirit and thereby become children of God. (John 1:12-13; 3:3-16; Acts 16:31; Ephesians 2:8-9)

We believe in the eternal security of the believer, that it is impossible for one born into the family of God ever to be lost because he is forever kept by the power of God. (John 6:39,49; 10:28-29; Romans 8:35-39; Jude 1: I Peter 1:5)

We believe in "that blessed hope"—the personal, premillennial, pretribulational and imminent return of our Lord and Savior Jesus Christ, when the Church will be "gathered together unto Him." (Titus 2:13, John 14:1-3; I Thessalonians 4:13-18; I Corinthians 15:51-58; II Thessalonians 2:1-13)

We believe in the literal fulfillment of the prophecies and promises of the Scriptures which foretell and assure the future regeneration and restoration of Israel as a nation. (Genesis 13:14-17: Jeremiah 16:14-15; 30:6-11; Romans 11)

We believe in the bodily resurrection of the just and the unjust, the everlasting blessedness of the saved, and the everlasting punishment of the lost. (Matthew 25:31-46: Luke 16:19-31; I Thessalonians 4:13-18: Revelation 21:1-8)

We believe that the Church which is Christ's body is the spiritual organism consisting of all born-again believers of this New Testament dispensation. (Ephesians 1:22-23; I Corinthians 12:13)

We believe that the local church is the agency through which God has chosen to accomplish His work in the world. A New Testament Baptist church is an organized body of baptized believers, immersed upon a credible confession of faith in Jesus Christ, having two offices (pastor and deacon), congregational in polity, autonomous in nature, and banded together for work, worship, edification, the observance of the ordinances and the worldwide fulfillment of the Great Commission. We believe that the local church, under Christ's headship, is to be free from any external hierarchy and should not associate itself with any ecumenical endeavor, neo-orthodoxy, new-evangelicalism, or any such efforts to compromise the Truth. (Acts 2:41-47; Ephesians 3:10; Matthew 28:18-20, I Timothy 3; I Peter 5:1-3; Ephesians 1:22; Romans 16:17; II Corinthians 6:14-17; I Timothy 6:3-5)

We believe that the scriptural ordinances of the church are baptism and the Lord's supper and are to be administered by the local church; that baptism, by immersion, should be administered to believers only as a symbol of their belief in the death, burial and resurrection of our Lord and Savior Jesus Christ and as a testimony to the world of that belief and of their death, burial and resurrection with Him; and that the Lord's supper should be partaken of by baptized believers to show forth His death ''till He come.'' (Matthew 28:18-20; Acts 2:41-47; 8:26-39; I Corinthians 11:23-28; Colossians 2:12)

Notes: *Baptist Mid-Missions is a fundamentalist Baptist missionary agency that works in close cooperation with the General Association of Regular Baptist Churches (GARBC). Its Articles of Faith are quite similar to those of the GARBC, but more condensed. Like the GARBC, there is a strong statement on the inerrancy of the Bible and the premillennial return of Christ. There is also a statement on the fulfillment of scriptural prophecies concerning Israel. Baptist Mid-Missions actively supports the Christian evangelization of Jews.*

* * *

DOCTRINAL STATEMENT (BEREAN MISSION)

THE TRINITY—We believe in one God, Creator of all things, infinitely perfect and eternally existing in three persons; Father, Son, and Holy Spirit.

THE VERBAL INSPIRATION—We believe the Holy Scriptures, both Old and New Testaments, to be the verbally inspired Word of God, without error in the original writings, the complete revelation of God's will for the salvation of man, and the divine and final authority for all Christian faith, life, and conduct.

TOTAL DEPRAVITY—We believe that man was directly created by God in His own image and likeness, but that he fell into sin. The entire human race became alienated from God, and is therefore eternally lost. The natural man of himself is utterly unable to remedy his lost condition.

SATAN—We believe in the personality of Satan; that he is the author of sin and the cause of man's fall; that he is the avowed enemy of God and man; that he is doomed and shall be eternally punished in the lake of fire.

VIRGIN BIRTH—We believe that Jesus Christ was conceived by the Holy Spirit, born of the Virgin Mary; that He died on the cross, a perfect and complete sacrifice for the sins of all mankind; that He arose bodily from the dead, and ascended into heaven, where He is now seated on the right hand of the Majesty on high, and ever lives to intercede as our High Priest and Advocate.

BLOOD ATONEMENT—We believe that without the shedding of blood there is no atonement for sin; that Christ in shedding His blood on Calvary's cross made atonement for the sins of all mankind.

RESURRECTION—We believe that Jesus Christ rose bodily from the grave and that the resurrection provides the only ground of justification and salvation for all who believe.

JUSTIFICATION BY FAITH—We believe that men are justified on the single ground of faith in the shed blood of Jesus Christ, and that only by regeneration of the Holy Spirit can salvation and eternal life be obtained.

PERSON AND WORK OF THE HOLY SPIRIT—We believe that the Holy Spirit is a Person, who convicts the world of sin, and regenerates, indwells, enlightens, guides and empowers the believer for godly living and service.

ETERNAL SECURITY OF THE BELIEVER—We believe that all born again believers, regenerated by the Holy Spirit, are eternally secure in Christ, and shall never come into condemnation for sin. While it is the believer's privilege to rejoice in the assurance of his salvation, this is not cause for license or liberty as an occasion to the flesh.

GIFTS OF THE SPIRIT—We believe that God gives spiritual gifts to all believers; that the apostolic age of signs, including tongues, ceased with the ministry of the apostles chosen by Christ in Person, but that the gifts of evangelists, pastors and teachers are sufficient for the ministry and perfecting of the church today.

We believe that God does hear and answer the prayer of faith, according to His own will, for the sick and afflicted.

THE CHURCH—We believe that the Church, which is a spiritual organism made up of all born again believers of this present age, is the body of Christ of which He is the Head. Its purpose is to bear witness and testimony to the whole world.

DOCTRINAL STATEMENT (BEREAN MISSION) (continued)

We believe in the establishment of the local church as clearly revealed and defined in the New Testament Scriptures.

SEPARATION FROM THE WORLD—We believe that all redeemed ones are called into a life of separation from all worldly and sinful practices.

TWO NATURES—We believe that all who are born again possess two natures, with provision made for the new nature to be victorious over the old nature through the power of the indwelling Holy Spirit.

We believe that all claims to the eradication of the old nature in this life are unscriptural.

SECOND COMING OF CHRIST—We believe in the personal, pre-tribulational, pre-millennial, and imminent return of our Lord Jesus Christ for His redeemed ones; that the blessed hope has a vital influence on the personal life and service of the believer; and that He will subsequently return to earth with His saints to establish His Millennial Kingdom.

MISSIONS—We believe that it is the obligation of every born again believer to bear witness by life and word to the truths revealed in the Word of God, and to proclaim the Gospel to all the world.

DISPENSATIONALISM—We believe in the dispensational view of Bible interpretation, but we reject the extreme teaching known as ''Hyper-dispensationalism,'' which opposes the ordinances of the Lords Table and water baptism for this age.

THE ORDINANCES—We believe that water baptism by immersion and the Lord's Supper are ordinances to be observed by the church during this present age. They are, however, not to be regarded as a means of salvation.

Notes: *The Berean Mission, founded in 1938, is a sending agency that supports missionaries in various parts of the world. It is fundamentalist in doctrine with a Baptist heritage, supporting the idea of two ordinances (not sacraments), one of which is baptism by immersion. It is opposed to certain current theological trends, including Pentecostalism and speaking in tongues, neo-Orthodoxy, neo-Evangelicalism, and the ecumenical movement.*

*　　*　　*

ARTICLES OF FAITH (EVANGELICAL BAPTIST MISSIONS)

I. CONCERNING THE SCRIPTURES

We believe that the Old and New Testament Scriptures as originally written by holy men of God who were borne along by the Holy Spirit, were God-breathed both equally and fully in all parts. We believe these Scriptures are completely without error and are therefore the final authority in all matters. We believe the Bible is the only infallible guide for faith and practice. (Matthew 5:17,18; Mark 12:36; Acts 1:16; Romans 15:4; I Corinthians 10:11; II Timothy 3:16, 17; Hebrews 5:12; II Peter 1:19-21, 3:15, 16)

II. CONCERNING THE TRUE GOD

We believe in one God. We believe in the unity of the Godhead. There are three eternal and coequal persons: the Father, Son, and Holy Spirit, who execute distinct and harmonious offices in the great work of redemption. (Genesis 1:1; Deuteronomy 4:35, 6:4; Isaiah 46:9; Matthew 3:16, 17, 28, 19, 20; John 1:1-3, 14; Acts 5:3, 4; Romans 1:19, 20; I Corinthians 8:6; Ephesians 1:3-14; 4:4-6; Hebrews 1:1-3; Revelation 1:4-6)

III. CONCERNING THE LORD JESUS CHRIST

We believe the Lord Jesus Christ, the eternal Son of God, was conceived by the Holy Spirit and born of the virgin Mary. He is fully God and fully man, yet without sin. He voluntarily laid down His life on the cross of Calvary as a substitute in the sinner's place to make full atonement for our sins. He rose from the dead on the third day, and after forty days. He ascended bodily into heaven. He is coming again, first to rapture His saints and then to establish His earthly kingdom of the throne of David. The rapture is imminent and will be personal, pre-tribulation, and pre-millennial. (Isaiah 7:14: 9:6, 7; Matthew 1:18-25; 28:6; John 1:1, 14; 14:3; Acts 1:9-11; 15,16; II Corinthians 5:20, 21: I Thessalonians 4:16, 17; I Peter 2:22-24, 3:18)

IV. CONCERNING THE HOLY SPIRIT

We believe the Holy Spirit is a Person of the Godhead because He possesses all the attributes of personality and of deity. He is equal with the Father and the Son and is of the same nature. He convicts unbelievers of sin, righteousness, and judgment. He is the agent of the new birth who immediately places the new believer into the Body of Christ. He seals, indwells, infills, guides, and teaches believers the ways of righteousness. We believe there is a distinction between the ministry of the Holy Spirit in the Old Testament and His ministry in the New Testament. There is a new and unique work of the Holy Spirit in relation to the Body of Christ. We believe that the Holy Spirit endues believers with service gifts upon conversion. We believe the Bible disavows the authenticity of the sign gifts (prophecy, speaking in tongues, interpretation of tongues, miracles, and healing) for today and repudiates the experience-oriented theology and ecumenically-oriented practice of the charismatic movement. (John 3:6, 7:39; 14:16,17, 26; 16:7-11; Acts 1:5, 4:8; Romans 8:9; 12:3-8; I Corinthians 6:19, 12:4-13, 28-31; 13:8-13; Ephesians 1:13, 14, 4:7-11, 30; Titus 3:4-7; I John 2:20-27)

V. CONCERNING MAN

We believe the Scriptures teach that man was created by a direct act of God and not from any previously existing form of life. By voluntary transgression man fell from his state of innocence, in consequence of which all men are now sinners by nature and by choice, are utterly devoid of the holiness required by God's standard, are positively inclined to evil, and therefore are without defense or excuse under just condemnation to eternal punishment and to everlasting existence separated from God. (Genesis 1:26, 27; 6:5; Psalm 14:1-3; 51:5; Jeremiah 17:9; John 5:25-30; Romans 3:10-12, 23; 5:12-9; Revelation 20:11-15)

VI. CONCERNING SALVATION

We believe the Scriptures teach the salvation of sinners is divinely initiated, wholly by grace, and accomplished only through the shed blood of the Son of God, that it is wholly apart from works and comes only through faith in the Lord Jesus Christ; that in order to be saved the sinner must be born again, being regenerated by the power of the Holy Spirit through faith in God's Word and becoming the recipient of a new nature; that the believer who has exercised personal faith in the Lord Jesus Christ is completely justified and possesses a salvation which is eternally secure. (Matthew 26:28; John 1:12, 13, 3:3-18, 36; 5:24; 6:29; 10:28, 29; Acts 13:39, 16:31; Romans 1:16, 17; 3:26; 4:5; 5:1, 9-11; 10:9-13; Galatians 6:15: Ephesians 2:8-10: I Timothy 2:5, 6; Titus 3:5; Hebrews 4:2; I Peter 1:18-23; II Peter 1:4)

VII. CONCERNING THE CHURCH

We believe the Scriptures teach the Church of Jesus Christ was inaugurated at Pentecost and must be considered in two aspects: the local church and the ''church which is His body.'' The local church is a congregation of baptized believers, associated by a covenant in the faith and fellowship of the Gospel, observing the ordinances of Christ, governed by His laws, and exercising the gifts, rights, and privileges invested in them by His Word. Its Scriptural officers are pastors, sometimes called bishops or elders, and deacons, whose qualifications, claims, and duties are defined in the epistles to Timothy and Titus. This definition of the local church leads to these Scriptural distinctives:

1. Sole authority of the Scriptures for faith and practice;

2. Autonomy of the local church;

3. Believer's baptism by immersion before church membership;

4. Two offices: pastor (elder, bishop) and deacon;

5. Two symbolic ordinances; baptism and the Lord's supper;

6. Individual priesthood of the believer and soul liberty;

7. Separation of church and state.

The ''church which is His body'' is the entire company of believers in Christ in this age, whether Jew of Gentile, regardless of denominational affiliation and present position in heaven or on earth. (Matthew 28:19,20; Acts 1:5; 2:1-4, 41:42; 10:44-48; I Corinthians 12:12,13; Ephesians 1:22,23; I Timothy 3:1-13; Titus 1:5-9)

VIII. CONCERNING BAPTISM AND THE LORD'S SUPPER

We believe the Scriptures teach Christian baptism in the name of the Father, Son, and Holy Spirit is the single immersion of a believer in water to show forth in a solemn and beautiful emblem his identification with the crucified, buried, risen Savior and to illustrate the believer's death to sin and his resurrection to a new life. It is prerequisite to membership and privileges in a local church. We believe the Lord's supper is the commemoration of His death until He comes and should be preceded by solemn self-examination. Observance of the Lord's supper is for believers only. The ordinances of baptism and the Lord's supper must be observed under the discipline of the local church. They do not have any saving merit. (Acts 2:41-47; 8:36-39; Romans 6:3-5; I Corinthians 11:23-28)

IX. CONCERNING THE RETURN OF OUR LORD JESUS CHRIST

We believe that the personal return of our Lord Jesus Christ to rapture His people, meeting them in the air, is imminent and will precede the tribulation (Daniel's seventieth week). We believe in the literal, personal, and bodily return of our Lord Jesus Christ to set up His kingdom on earth and that this will take place at the end of the tribulation. Therefore, the rapture is pre-tribulational and pre-millennial. (Daniel 9:25-27; Matthew 24:29-31; I Thessalonians 4:16:17; II Thessalonians 2:6-8; Revelation 20:1-4,6)

X. CONCERNING THE ETERNAL STATE

We believe the Scriptures teach the bodily resurrection of the just and the unjust. All those who are justified through faith in the name of the Lord Jesus Christ will spend eternity in full enjoyment of God's presence, and those who refuse to accept God's offer of mercy and grace will spend eternity in everlasting punishment in the lake of fire. We believe that the terms heaven and hell refer to literal and distinct places and not to a condition or state. (Luke 16:19-26; Johns 5;28,29; 14:2,3; Philippians 1:23; II Thessalonians 1:7-9; Revelation 20:11-15, 21:1-4)

XI. CONCERNING SATAN

We believe the Scripture teach there is a personal devil who is ''the good of this age'' and ''the prince of the power of the air,'' who is full of all subtlety, who continually seeks to frustrate the purposes of God and to ensnare the sons of men, and who was conquered by Christ on the cross and condemned to everlasting punishment. (John 16:11; II Corinthians 4:3,4; 11:13-15; Ephesians 2:2; 6:10-12; Colossians 2:15; Hebrews 2:14; I Peter 5:8; Revelation 12:9; 20:1-3,10)

XII. CONCERNING PERSONAL SEPARATION

We believe the Scriptures teach that every believer should be separated unto God from the world and should walk by the aid of the Holy Spirit in Christian love and holiness, exhibiting qualities of honesty, integrity, forgiveness, and loving-kindness. We further believe that any achievement in these characteristics will be evidenced by sincere humility and genuine zeal for the advancement of the cause of Christ. We also believe the Scriptures admonish every believer not to love the world or the things in the world, but rather to flee evil desires, avoid every kind of evil, and refrain from questionable practices which destroy one's testimony, offend one's brother, and fail to glorify God. (Romans 6:11-13; 14:19-21; I Corinthians

6:18-20; 8:9-13; 10:23,31-33; II Corinthians 7:1, Galatians 5:22-25; Ephesians 4:22-32; 5:1-21; Philippians 4:8; I Thessalonians 4:7; I Peter 1:14-16; 5:5,6; I John 2:15-17)

XIII. CONCERNING ECCLESIASTICAL SEPARATION

We believe the Scriptures teach that the believer should be separated from apostasy of ecclesiastical organizations made up of radicals, liberals, and those who sanction theological compromise. This doctrine is based upon God's eternal principle of division between truth and error and upon His specific command to be separate from unbelievers and disobedient brethren. This truth is to be practiced with an attitude of devotion to God, humility, compassion, and conviction so as to create the proper condition and atmosphere for the salvation of the unbeliever through the Gospel of God and for the restoration of the disobedient brother. We believe ecumenical evangelism which involves apostates violates the principles taught in God's Word. (Romans 16:17,18; I Corinthians 5:9-13; II Corinthians 6:14-18; Galatians 1:8,9; II Thessalonians 3:6,14,15; I Timothy 6:3-5; Titus 3:10,11; II John 9-11)

Notes: *Evangelical Baptist Missions is a fundamentalist Baptist missionary agency that has the approval of the General Association of Regular Baptist Churches upon whose Articles of Religion this statement is based. The GARBC ''Articles'' is based on an older Baptist statement known as the New Hampshire of Faith. Of interest is the additional paragraph ''Concerning Ecclesiastical Separation,'' which denounces a number of recent theological tendencies and calls for separation from theological compromise and liberalism.*

* * *

DOCTRINAL STATEMENT (GOSPEL FURTHERING FELLOWSHIP)

The Gospel Furthering Fellowship stands unequivocally for the following beliefs:

SCRIPTURES:

We believe in the verbal plenary inspiration of the 66 books comprising the Old and New Testament, inspired by God and inerrant in the original writing. We believe that they are of supreme and final authority in faith and life. Psa. 19:7, 119:9; Matt. 5:18; John 16:12,13; Rom. 15:4; 2 Tim. 3:16,17; 2 Pet. 1:20,21; 3:2.

GODHEAD:

We believe in one Triune God, eternally existing in three persons—Father; Son, Holy Spirit; co-equal in being, co-identical in nature, co-equal in power and glory, and having the same attributes and perfections. Deut. 6:4; Matt. 28:19; John 4:24; 10:30; 17:1,3; Acts 5:3, 4; 2 Cor. 13:14.

CHRIST'S PERSON AND WORK:

a. We believe that Jesus Christ was begotten by the Holy Spirit, born of the Virgin Mary, and is true God and true Man. John 1:1-18; Luke 1:26-35.

b. We believe that the Lord Jesus Christ died for our sins, according to the Scriptures, as a representative and substitutionary sacrifice; and, that our justification is made sure by His literal, physical resurrection from the dead. Rom. 3:24,25; 8:3; Eph. 1:7; 1 Pet. 1:3-5:24.

c. We believe in the resurrection of the crucified body of our Lord, in His ascension into heaven, and in His present life there for us, as High Priest and Advocate. Acts 1:9,10; Rom. 8:34; Heb. 7:15; 1 John 2: 1,2.

HOLY SPIRIT'S PERSON AND WORK:

a. We believe that the Holy Spirit is a person; that He is God, that He convicts the world of sin, of righteousness, and of judgment, and that He is the Supernatural Agent in regeneration, baptizing all believers into the body of Christ, indwelling and sealing them unto the day of redemption. John 3:5-7; 16:7-11; Acts 1:8; Rom. 1:9, 1 Cor. 6:19-20; 12:12-14; 2 Cor. 3:6; Gal. 5:16; Eph. 1:13, 14; 4:30.

b. We believe that He is the Divine Teacher who guides believers into all truth; and, that it is the privilege and duty of all the saved to be filled with the Spirit. John 16:13; 1 John 2;20,27; 1 Cor. 2:10-13; Eph. 5:18.

c. We believe that God is sovereign in the bestowment of gifts, for the perfecting of the saints, and that speaking in tongues, and the working of miracles ceased as the New Testament Scriptures were completed, and their authority established. We are not sympathetic to the present day tongues movement. We believe its tendencies are contrary to God's Word and, therefore, neither cooperate with those who practice tongues, nor retain as members any who participate in this movement. I Cor. 12:4-11; 2 Cor. 12:12; Eph. 4:7-12.

MAN:

We believe that man was created in the image of God; that he sinned in Adam and thereby incurred, not only physical death, but also spiritual death, which is separation from God; that all human beings are born with a sinful nature, and are totally depraved, and that they must be born again to be accepted of God. John 3:1-21; Rom. 3:9-20, 22, 23; 5:12; Eph. 2:1-3, 12.

SALVATION:

a. We believe that salvation is the gift of God brought to man by grace and received by personal faith in the Lord Jesus Christ whose blood was shed for the forgiveness of sins. Eph. 2:8-10; John 1:12; Eph. 1:7; 1 Pet. 1:17,19.

b. We believe that all who receive Christ by faith become children of God; that they are indwelt and sealed by the Holy Spirit and so secured in Christ forever. John 1:12,13; 1 Cor. 6:19,20; Eph. 1:13,14; 4:30.

c. We believe that every saved person possesses two natures with provision made for victory of the new nature over the old nature through power of the indwelling Holy Spirit; that all claims to eradication of the old nature in this life are Unscriptural. Rom. 6:13; 8:12, 13; Gal. 5:16-25; Eph. 4:22-24; Col. 3: 10; I Pet. 1: 14-16; 1 John 3:3-9.

CHURCH:

a. We believe that the Church of Jesus Christ was begun at Pentecost; is composed solely of born again believers of this age; is the Body and Bride of our Lord and is distinct from Israel. Acts 2:1-4; 1 Cor. 12:12-14; 2 Cor. 11:2; Eph. 1:22, 23; 4:11-13; 5:23-32.

b. We believe that the establishment and continuance of local churches is clearly defined and taught in the New Testament Scriptures. Acts 14:27; 20:17, 28-32; 1 Tim. 3:1-13; Titus 1:5-11.

ORDINANCES:

a. We believe that the Lord Jesus Christ ordained water baptism by immersion as a testimony portraying the believer's union with Christ in His death, burial and resurrection. Mark 1:8; Rom. 6:3, 4; Gal. 3:27; Col. 2:11-13.

b. We believe our Lord instituted the Lord's Supper to commemorate His death till He comes. 1 Cor. 11:23-26.

c. Moreover, we believe that neither Water Baptism nor the Lord's Supper has any saving merit.

SEPARATION:

a. We believe that all the saved should live in such a manner as not to bring reproach upon their Savior and Lord; that separation from all religious apostasy, all worldly, sinful pleasures, practices, and association is commanded of God. Rom. 12:1, 2; 14:13; 2 Cor. 6:14; 7:1; 2 Tim. 3:1-5; 1 John 2:15-17; 2 John 9-11.

b. We believe that any ecumenical movement or mass evangelism effort which attempts to unite believers with unbelievers is not of God; and that the philosophies of neo-evangelicalism and reprobate believers are unscriptural and therefore separate ourselves from those who practice these errors. Eph.5:11; Col.3:16; l John 5:2,3; 2 John l0; Jude 3,4.

SATAN:

We believe that Satan is a personal being, a fallen angel, the prince of demons, the great enticer and deceiver, the god of this age, and the adversary of Christ and His Church, and that his destiny is eternal punishment. Job 1:6,7; Isa. 14:12-17; Matt. 4:2-11; 25:41; 2 Cor. 4:3,4; 11:14; 1 Pet. 5:8; Rev. 20:10.

SECOND ADVENT OF CHRIST:

We believe in that "Blessed Hope", that personal, imminent, pre-tribulational and premillennial coming of the Lord Jesus Christ for His redeemed ones; and in His subsequent return to the earth, with His saints, to establish His Millennial Kingdom. Zech. 14:4-11; 1 Thess. 1:10; 4:13-18; 5:9; Rev. 3: 10; 19:11-16; 20:1-6.

ETERNAL STATE:

a. We believe in the bodily resurrection of all men, the saved to eternal life, and the unsaved to judgment and everlasting punishment. Matt. 25:46; John 5:28,29; 11:25,26; Rev. 20:5,6,12,13.

b. Saints at death are consciously present with the Lord awaiting the reunion of the spirit, soul and body at the first resurrection to be glorified forever with the Lord. Luke 23:43; 2 Cor. 5:8; Phil. 1:23; 3:21; 1 Thess. 4:16, 17; Rev. 20:4-6.

c. Souls of unbelievers remain in conscious misery after death until the second resurrection, when with soul and body united they shall appear at the Great White Throne Judgment and shall be cast into the Lake of Fire to suffer everlasting conscious punishment. Matt. 25:41-46; Mark 9:43-48; Luke 16;19-26; 2 Thess. 1:7-9; Jude 6, 7; Rev. 20:11-15.

MISSIONS:

We believe that it is the obligation of the saved to witness by life and by word to the truth of Holy Scripture and to seek to proclaim the Gospel to all mankind. Ezek. 3:18,19; Mark 16:15; Acts 1: 18; 2 Cor. 5:19,20; John 10:21.

POSITION:

G.F.F. is a fundamental Mission serving the independent Bible and Baptist churches, believing strongly in the centrality of the local church. Our cooperation with others is on a doctrinal basis.

Notes: *The Gospel Furthering Fellowship is a fundamentalist Baptist home missionary agency. Its Doctrinal Statement is derived from the New Hampshire Confession of Faith, but has added a strong statement on the verbal plenary inspiration and inerrancy of the Bible, and on separation from unapproved personal practices and erroneous theological trends.*

*   *   *

BIBLICAL PRINCIPLES (RUSSIAN GOSPEL MINISTRIES)

Since its formation in Russia in 1867, the brotherhood of Evangelical Baptist churches has stood firmly on the foundation of seven fundamental Biblical principles:

• the absolute authority of the Bible in all matters of life and faith.

• absolute freedom of conscience.

BIBLICAL PRINCIPLES (RUSSIAN GOSPEL MINISTRIES)
(continued)

- local church membership composed only of born-again believers.

- believers' baptism.

- autonomy of the local church.

- priesthood of the believers.

- separation of church and state. ·

Notes: *Russian Gospel Ministries, founded in 1980, is an independent fundamentalist missionary agency. Its brief statement of Biblical Principles includes a reference to Baptist distinctives of believers' baptism, the autonomy of the local church, and separation of church and state.*

*   *   *

ARTICLES OF FAITH (SHEPHERDS BAPTIST MINISTRIES)

I. Of The Scriptures

We believe in the authority and sufficiency of the Holy Bible, consisting of the sixty-six books of the Old and New Testaments, as originally written; that it was verbally and plenarily inspired and is the product of Spirit-controlled men, and therefore is infallible and inerrant in all matters of which it speaks.

We believe the Bible to be the true center of Christian unity and the supreme standard by which all human conduct, creed and opinions shall be tried. 2 Tim. 3:16, 17:2; Pet. 1:19-24.

II. The True God

We believe there is one and only one living and true God, an infinite Spirit, the Maker and supreme Ruler of Heaven and earth, inexpressibly glorious in holiness, and worthy of all possible honor, confidence and love; that is the unity of the Godhead there are three persons, the Father, the Son and the Holy Spirit, equal in every divine perfection and executing distinct but harmonious offices in the great work of redemption. Exod. 20:2,3; 1 Cor. 8:6; Rev. 4:11.

III. The Holy Spirit

We believe that the Holy Spirit is a divine person, equal with God the Father and God the Son and of the same nature; that He was active in the creation; that in His relation to the unbelieving world He restrains the evil one until God's purpose is fulfilled; that He convicts of sin, of righteousness and of judgment; that He bears witness to the truth of the gospel in preaching and testimony; that He is the Agent in the new birth; that He seals; endues, guides, teaches, witnesses, sanctifies and helps the believer. John 14:16, 17; Matt. 28:19; Heb. 9:14; John 14:26; Luke 1:35; Gen. 1:1-3; John 16:8-11; Acts 5:30-

32; John 3:5, 6; Eph. 1:13, 14; Mark 1:8; John 1:33; Acts 11:16; Luke 24:49; Rom. 8:14, 16, 26, 27.

IV. The Devil, or Satan

We believe in the reality and personality of Satan, the Devil; and that he was created by God as an angel but through pride and rebellion became the enemy of his Creator; that he became the unholy god of this age and the ruler of all the powers of darkness and is destined to the judgment of an eternal justice in the lake of fire. Matt. 4:1-11; 2 Cor. 4:4; Rev. 20:10.

V. Creation

We believe the Biblical account of the creation of the physical universe, angels, and man; that this account is neither allegory nor myth, but a literal, historical account of the direct, immediate creative acts of God without any evolutionary process; that man was created by a direct work of God and not from previously existing forms of life; and that all men are descended from the historical Adam and Eve, first parents of the entire human race. Gen. 1, 2; Col. 1:16, 17; John 1:3.

VI. The Fall of Man

We believe that man was created in innocence (in the image and likeness of God) under the law of his Maker, but by voluntary transgression Adam fell from his sinless and happy state, and all men sinned in him, in consequence of which all men are totally depraved, are partakers of Adam's fallen nature, and are sinners by nature and by conduct, and therefore are under just condemnation without defense or excuse. Gen. 3:1-6; Rom. 3:10-19; 5:12, 19; 1:18, 32.

VII. The Virgin Birth

We believe that Jesus was begotten of the Holy Spirit in a miraculous manner, born of Mary, a virgin, as no other man was ever born or can be born of woman, and that He is both the Son of God and God, the Son. Gen. 3:15; Isa. 7:14; Matt. 1:18-25; Luke 1:35; John 1:14.

VIII. Salvation

We believe that the salvation of sinners is divinely initiated and wholly of grace through the mediatorial offices of Jesus Christ, the Son of God, Who, by the appointment of the Father, voluntarily took upon Himself our nature, yet without sin, and honored the divine law by His personal obedience, thus qualifying Himself to be our Savior; that by the shedding of His blood in His death He fully satisfied the just demands of a holy and righteous God regarding sin; that His sacrifice consisted not in setting us an example by His death as a martyr, but was a voluntary substitution of Himself in the sinner's place, the Just dying for the unjust. Christ the Lord bearing our sins in His own body on the tree; that having risen from the dead He is now enthroned in Heaven, and uniting in His wonderful person the tenderest sympathies with divine perfection. He is in every way qualified to be a suitable, a compassionate and an all-sufficient Savior.

We believe that faith in the Lord Jesus Christ is the only condition of salvation. Repentance is a change of mind and purpose toward God prompted by the Holy Spirit and is an integral part of saving faith. Jonah 2:9; Eph. 2:8; Acts 15:11; Rom. 3:24, 25; John 3:16; Matt. 18:11; Phil. 2:7, 8; Heb. 2:14-17; Isa. 53:4-7; 1 John 4:10; 1 Cor. 15:3; 2 Cor. 5:21; 1 Pet. 2:24.

IX. Resurrection and Priesthood of Christ

We believe in the bodily resurrection of Christ and in His ascension into Heaven, where He now sits at the right hand of the Father as our High Priest interceding for us. Matt. 28:6, 7; Luke 24:39; John 20:27; 1 Cor. 15:4; Mark 16:6; Luke 24:2-6, 51; Acts 1:9-11; Rev. 3:21; Heb. 8:6; 12:2; 7:25; 1 Tim. 2:5; 1 John 2:1; Heb. 2:17; 5:9, 10.

X. Grace and the New Birth

We believe that in order to be saved, sinners must be born again; that the new birth is a new creation in Christ Jesus; that it is instantaneous and not a process; that in the new birth the one dead in trespasses and in sins is made a partaker of the divine nature and receives eternal life, the free gift of God; that the new creation is brought about by our sovereign God in a manner above our comprehension, solely by the power of the Holy Spirit in connection with divine truth, so as to secure our voluntary obedience to the gospel; that its proper evidence appears in the holy fruits of repentance, faith and newness of life. John 3:3; 2 Cor. 5:17; 1 John 5:1; Acts 16:20-33; 2 Pet. 1:4; Rom. 6:23; Eph. 2:1, 5; Col. 2:13; John 3:8.

XI. Justification

We believe that justification is that judicial act of God whereby He declares the believer righteous upon the basis of the imputed righteousness of Christ; that it is bestowed, not in consideration of any work of righteousness which we have done, but solely through faith in the Redeemer's shed blood. Rom. 3:24; 4:5; 5:1, 9; Gal. 2:16; Phil. 3:9.

XII. Sanctification

We believe that sanctification is the divine setting apart of the believer unto God accomplished in a threefold manner: first, an eternal act of God, based upon redemption in Christ, establishing the believer in a position of holiness at the moment he trusts the Savior; second, a continuing process in the saint as the Holy Spirit applies the Word of God to the life; third, the final accomplishment of this process at the Lord's return. Heb. 10:10-14; 3:1; John 17:17; 2 Cor. 3:18; 1 Cor. 1:30; Eph. 5:25-27; 1 Thess. 4:3, 4; 5:23, 24; 1 John 3:2; Jude 24, 25; Rev. 22:11.

XIII. The Security of The Saints

We believe that all who are truly born again are kept by God the Father for Jesus Christ. Phil. 1:6; John 10:28, 29; Rom. 8:35-39; Jude 1.

XIV. The Church

We believe that a local church is an organized congregation of immersed believers, associated by covenant of faith and fellowship of the gospel; observing the ordinances of Christ; governed by His laws; and exercising the gifts, rights and privileges invested in them by His Word; that its officers are pastors and deacons, whose qualifications, claims and duties are clearly defined in the Scriptures. We believe the true mission of the church is the faithful witnessing of Christ to all men as we have opportunity. We hold that the local church has the absolute right of self-government free from the interference of any hierarchy of individuals or organizations; and that the one and only Superintendent is Christ through the Holy Spirit; that it is Scriptural for true churches to cooperate with each other in contending for the faith and for the furtherance of the gospel; that each local church is the sole judge of the measure and method of its cooperation; that on all matters of membership, of polity, of government, of discipline, of benevolence, the will of the local church is final. I Cor. 11:2; Acts 20:17-28; 1 Tim. 3:1-13; Acts 2:41, 42.

We believe in the unity of all New Testament believers in the Church which is the Body of Christ. I Cor. 12:12, 13; Eph. 1:22, 23; 3:1-6; 4:11; 5:23; Col. 1:18; Acts 15:13-18.

XV. Baptism and the Lord's Supper

We believe that Christian baptism is the single immersion of a believer in water to show forth in a solemn and beautiful emblem our identification with the crucified, buried and risen Savior, through Whom we died to sin and rose to a new life; that baptism is to be performed under the authority of the local church; and that it is prerequisite to the privileges of church membership.

We believe that the Lord's Supper is the commemoration of His death until he come, and should be preceded always by solemn self-examination. We believe that the Biblical order of the ordinances is baptism first and then the Lord's Supper, and that participants in the Lord's Supper should be immersed believers. Acts 8:36, 38, 39; John 3:23; Rom. 6:3-5; Matt. 3:16; Col. 2:12; 1 Cor. 11:23-28; Matt. 28:18-20; Acts 2:41, 42.

XVI. Separation

We believe in obedience to the Biblical commands to separate ourselves unto God from worldliness and ecclesiastical apostasy. 2 Cor. 6:14-7:1; 1 Thess. 1:9, 10; 1 Tim. 6:3-5; Rom. 16:17; 2 John 9-11.

XVII. Civil Government

We believe that civil government is of divine appointment for the interests and good order of human society; that magistrates are to be prayed for, conscientiously honored, and obeyed; except in those things opposed to the will of our Lord Jesus Christ Who is the only Lord of the conscience, and the coming King of kings. Rom. 13:1-7, 2 Sam. 23:3; Exod. 18:21, 22; Acts 23:5; Matt. 22:21; Acts 5:29; 4:19,20; Dan. 3:17, 18.

XVIII. Israel

We believe in the sovereign selection of Israel as God's eternal covenant people, that she is now dispersed because of her disobedience and rejection of Christ, and that she will be regathered in the Holy Land and, after the completion of the Church, will be saved as a nation at the second advent of Christ. Gen. 13:14-17; Rom. 11:1-32; Ezek. 37.

ARTICLES OF FAITH (SHEPHERDS BAPTIST MINISTRIES)
(continued)

XIX. Rapture and Subsequent Events

We believe in the premillennial return of Christ, an event which can occur at any moment, and that at that moment the dead in Christ shall be raised in glorified bodies, and the living in Christ shall be given glorified bodies without tasting death, and all shall be caught up to meet the Lord in the air before the seven years of the Tribulation. 1 Thess. 4:13-18; 1 Cor. 15:42-44, 51-54; Phil. 3:20, 21; Rev. 3:10.

We believe that the Tribulation, which follows the Rapture of the Church, will be culminated by the revelation of Christ in power and great glory to sit upon the throne of David and to establish the millennial kingdom. Dan. 9:25-27; Matt. 24:29-31; Luke 1:30-33; Isa. 9:6, 7; 11:1-9; Acts 2:29, 30; Rev. 20:1-4, 6.

XX. The Righteous and the Wicked

We believe that there is a radical and essential difference between the righteous and the wicked; that only those who are justified by faith in our Lord Jesus Christ and sanctified by the Spirit of our God are truly righteous in His esteem; while all such as continue in impenitence and unbelief are in His sight wicked and under the curse; and this distinction holds among men both in and after death, in the everlasting felicity of the saved and the everlasting conscious suffering of the lost in the lake of fire. Mal. 3:18; Gen. 18:23; Rom. 6:17, 18; 1 John 5:19; Rom. 7:6; 6:23; Prov. 14:32; Luke 16:25; Matt. 25:34-41; John 8:21; Rev. 20:14, 15.

Notes: *Shepherds Baptist Ministries is a fundamentalist Baptist missionary agency. Its statement of belief is derived from the New Hampshire Confession of Faith and the Articles of Religion of the General Association of Regular Baptist Churches. There is a strong statement on the verbal plenary inspiration, the inerrancy, and infallibility of the Bible. The Ministries also engages in evangelism to the Jews, as is indicated by the statement on Israel.*

*　　　*　　　*

DOCTRINAL STATEMENT (UNITED MISSIONARY FELLOWSHIP)

THE HOLY SCRIPTURES

We believe the Holy Scriptures of the Old and New Testaments to be the verbally inspired word of God, the final authority for faith and life, inerrant in the original writings, infallible and God-breathed (2 Tim. 3:16,17; 2 Peter 1:20,21; Matt. 5:18; John 16:12,13).

THE GODHEAD

We believe in one Triune God, eternally existing in three persons—Father, Son, and Holy Spirit—co-eternal in being, co-identical in nature, co-equal in power and glory, and having the same attributes and perfections (Deut. 6:4; 2 Cor. 13:14).

THE PERSON AND WORK OF CHRIST

a. We believe that the Lord Jesus Christ, the eternal Son of God, became man, without ceasing to be God, having been conceived by the Holy Spirit and born of the Virgin Mary, in order that He might reveal God and redeem sinful man (John 1:1, 2:14; Luke 1:35).

b. We believe that the Lord Jesus Christ accomplished our redemption through His death on the cross as a representative, vicarious, substitutionary sacrifice; and, that our justification is made sure by His literal, physical resurrection from the dead (Romans 3:24,25; 1 Peter 2:24; Eph. 1:7; 1 Peter 1:3-5).

c. We believe that the Lord Jesus Christ ascended to heaven, and is now exalted at the right hand of God, where, as our High Priest, He fulfills the ministry of Representative, Intercessor, and Advocate (Acts 1:9,10; Heb. 9:24; 7:25; Rom. 8:34; 1 John 2:1,2).

THE PERSON AND WORK OF THE HOLY SPIRIT

a. We believe that the Holy Spirit is a person who convicts the world of sin, of righteousness, and of judgment, and, that He is the Supernatural Agent in regeneration, baptizing all believers into the body of Christ, indwelling and sealing them unto the day of redemption (John 16; 8-11; 2 Cor. 3:6; 1 Cor. 12:12-14; Romans 8-9; Ephesians 1: 13-14).

b. We believe that He is the Divine Teacher who guides believers into all truth; and, that it is the privilege and duty of all the saved to be filled with the Spirit (John 16:13; 1 John 2:20,27; Ephesians 5:18).

THE TOTAL DEPRAVITY OF MAN

We believe that man was created in the image and likeness of God, but that in Adam's sin the race fell, inherited a sinful nature, and became alienated from God; and, that man is totally depraved, and, of himself, totally unable to remedy his lost condition (Gen. 1:26, 27; Rom. 3;22,23; 5:12; Ephesians 2: 1-3, 12).

SALVATION

We believe that salvation is the gift of God brought to man by grace and received by personal faith in the Lord Jesus Christ whose precious blood was shed on Calvary for the forgiveness of our sins (Eph. 2:8-10; John 1:12; Eph. 1:7; 1 Peter 1: 17,19).

THE TWO NATURES OF THE BELIEVER

We believe that every saved person possesses two natures, with provision made for victory of the new nature over the old nature through the power of the indwelling Holy Spirit; and, that all claims to the eradication of the old nature in this life are unscriptural (Rom. 6:13; 8:12,13; Gal. 5:16-25; Eph. 4: 22-24; Col. 3:10; 1 Peter 1:14-16; 1 John 3:5-9).

THE ETERNAL SECURITY AND ASSURANCE OF BELIEVERS

a. We believe that all the redeemed, once saved, are kept by God's power and are thus secure in Christ forever (John 6:37-40; 10: 27-30; Romans 8: 1,38, 39; 1 Cor. 1:4-8; 1 Peter 1:5).

b. We believe that it is the privilege of believers to rejoice in the assurance of their salvation through the testimony of God's Word; which, however, clearly forbids the use of Christian liberty as an occasion to the flesh (Rom. 13:13,14 Gal. 5:13; Titus 2: 11-15).

THE CHURCH

a. We believe that the church, which is the body and espoused bride of Christ, is a spiritual organism made up of all born-again persons of this present age. (Eph. 1:22,23; 5:25-27; 1 Cor. 12:12-14; 2 Cor. 11:2).

b. We believe that the establishment and continuance of local churches is clearly taught and defined in the New Testament Scriptures. (Acts 14:27; 20:17; 28-32; 1 Tim. 3:1-13; Titus 1:5-11).

ORDINANCES

We believe in the two church ordinances; Water Baptism by Immersion for Believers, and the Lord's Supper. (1 Cor. 11:23-34; Acts 8:35-37; 10:47,48; 1 Cor. 1:14; Acts 8:12.

SEPARATION

We believe that all the saved should live in such a manner as not to bring reproach upon their Savior and Lord; and, that separation from all religious apostasy, all worldly and sinful pleasures, practices and associations is commanded of God (2 Tim. 3:1-5; Rom. 12: 1,2; 14: 13; 1 John 2:15-17; 2 John vvs. 9-11; 2 Cor. 6:14; 7:1).

MISSIONS

We believe that it is the obligation of the saved to witness by life and by word to the truths of Holy Scripture and to seek to proclaim the Gospel to all mankind. (Mark 16:15; Acts 1:8; 2 Cor. 5:19,20).

THE MINISTRY AND SPIRITUAL GIFTS

a. We believe that God is sovereign in the bestowment of all His gifts; and, that the gifts of evangelists, pastors, and teachers are sufficient for the perfecting of the saints today; and, that speaking in tongues and the working of sign miracles gradually ceased as the New Testament Scriptures were completed and their authority became established (1 Cor. 12:4-11, 2 Cor. 12:12; Eph. 4:7-12).

b. We believe that God does hear and answer the prayer of faith, in accord with His own will, for the sick and afflicted (John 15:7; 1 John 5:14,15).

DISPENSATIONALISM

We believe in the dispensational view of Bible interpretation but reject the extreme teaching known as "Hyper Dispensationalism", such as that teaching which opposes either the Lord's table or water baptism as a Scriptural means of testimony for the church in this age. (Matt. 28:19,20; Acts 2:41,42; 18:8; 1 Cor. 11:23-26).

THE PERSONALITY OF SATAN

We believe that Satan is a person, the author of sin and the cause of the fall; that he is the open and declared enemy of God and man; and, that he shall be eternally punished in the Lake of Fire. (Job 1:6,7; Isa. 14:12-17; Matt. 4:2-11; 25:41; Rev. 20:10).

THE SECOND ADVENT OF CHRIST

We believe in that "Blessed Hope", the personal, imminent, pre-tribulation and premillennial coming of the Lord Jesus Christ for His redeemed ones; and in His subsequent return to the earth, with His saints, to establish His Millennial Kingdom (I Thes. 4:13-18; Zechariah 14:4-11; Rev. 19:11-16; 20:1-6; 1 Thes. 1:10; 5:9; Rev. 3:10).

THE ETERNAL STATE

a. We believe in the bodily resurrection of all men, the saved to eternal life, and the unsaved to judgment and everlasting punishment. (Matt. 25:46; John 5:28,29; 11:25,26; Rev. 20:5,6,12,13).

b. We believe that the souls of the redeemed are, at death, absent from the body and present with the Lord, where in conscious bliss they await the first resurrection, when spirit, soul and body are reunited to be glorified forever with the Lord. (Luke 23:43; Rev. 20:4-6; 2 Cor. 5-8; Phil. 1:23; 3:21; 1 Thes. 4:16,17).

c. We believe that the souls of unbelievers remain after death, in conscious misery until the second resurrection, when with soul and body reunited they shall appear at the Great White Throne Judgement, and shall be cast into the Lake of Fire, not to be annihilated, but to suffer everlasting conscious punishment. (Luke 16:19-26; Matt. 25:41-46; 2 Thess. 1:7-9; Jude vvs. 6,7; Mark 9:43-48; Rev. 20:11-15).

Notes: *The United Missionary Fellowship is a fundamentalist Baptist missionary organization. Its Doctrinal Statement affirms the inerrancy of the Bible, total human depravity, the eternal security of believers, and premillennial return of Jesus Christ. It also includes such Baptist distinctives as believers' baptism by immersion and the authority of the local church.*

*　　*　　*

STATEMENT (WORLD WIDE MISSIONARY CRUSADER, INC.)

STANDING FOR: The Verbal Inspiration of the Holy Scriptures, the Virgin Birth of Christ, His Atoning Death, His Literal Resurrection and His Coming Again.

STANDING AGAINST: Satan, sin, modernism, pagan religions, pseudo-Christian religions and all cults.

Notes: *World Wide Missionary Crusader, founded in 1942, is an independent fundamentalist Baptist missionary agency specializing in the production of religious literature for distribution overseas.*

* * *

Independent Baptist Schools

CONVICTIONS (CALVARY BIBLE COLLEGE)

Calvary is:

SOLIDLY BIBLICAL—The Bible is the heart and core of every educational program at Calvary Bible College. Theologically, Calvary Bible College can be described as fundamental, premillenial, dispensational, and moderately Calvinistic. Each year, every faculty member and trustee must affirm his wholehearted acceptance of the Bible as the verbally inspired Word of God.

SEPARATED—Our ecclesiastical position is one of being loyal to Biblical separation. We have historically repudiated the National Council of Churches and the World Council of Churches. We reject ecumenical evangelism, neo-orthodoxy, and the neo-evangelical movements. It is our conviction that the College should have no embarrassing ties which would keep its faculty from exposing apostasy, heresy, or sin. It is our desire to be separated to God from worldliness, whether in personal behavior or in world church programs.

EVANGELISTIC—We believe that the "Great Commission" defines the primary mission of the Church. Calvary seeks to incorporate the spirit of evangelism and discipleship into the whole school family whether in the classroom, in chapel, or in extracurricular activities and projects.

A FRIEND OF BIBLE-BELIEVING CHURCHES—Calvary stands with all who love Christ and preach His Word. The attitude throughout the school is non-sectarian. Calvary is unaffiliated with any denomination or association so we can be unreservedly loyal to all fundamental churches faithful to Christ and the Bible. We are glad to maintain a good relationship with denominational churches and individuals which uncompromisingly hold the fundamentals of the faith.

NON-CHARISMATIC—Calvary Bible College does not foster, teach, or provide a hospitable atmosphere for the

"tongues" movement. If one of tongues persuasion desires to enter Calvary as a student and is willing to study with an open mind, he is welcomed. However, he is definitely prohibited from practicing or propagating his belief concerning the tongues doctrine and is carefully helped to understand the College's position on this important issue. The College position is clear. Tongues is not a part of our ministry, nor is it beneficial or necessary to our Christian life. It is neither sought nor encouraged. We are non-charismatic. Furthermore, each entering student should realize that Calvary Bible College will graduate only those who are in full agreement with its doctrinal position.

NURTURING CHARACTER AND TRUTH—We are persuaded that the Scripture teaches that what we are is as important as what we know. Ephesians 4:15 clearly states that we are to speak the truth (doctrine) in love (Christ-like character). This is the reason we put much effort in developing Christ-like character and a servant's heart while communicating God's Word. In all matters we endeavor to display the "excellent spirit" (Daniel 6:3) of the prophet Daniel. This man of God refused to compromise and yet he constantly displayed an attitude which endeared him to his superiors. He was neither vindictive nor self-righteous and by his dedicated life made a profound impact upon the kings of Babylon and Persia.

WILLING TO SERVE—It is our position that Bible education and Christian service training are essential in serving our Lord Jesus Christ and in achieving His global goals for His Church. We exist to serve you for these ends.

THE SCRIPTURES—We believe the Holy Scriptures of the Old and New Testaments to be the verbally and plenarily inspired Word of God (Matt. 5:18; 2 Tim. 3:16-17). We hold the Bible to be inerrant in the original writings, infallible, God-breathed, and the complete and final authority for faith and practice (2 Pet. 1:20-21).

We believe that the Scriptures, interpreted in their normal, literal sense, reveal divinely distinguishable economies in the outworking of God's purposes. These dispensations are not ways of salvation but rather divinely ordered stewardships by which God directs man according to His purposes. Three of these . . . the age of law, the age of the church, and the age of the millennial kingdom . . . are the subjects of detailed revelation in Scriptures (Gen. 12:1-3; Jn. 1:17; 2 Cor. 3:9-18; Gal. 3:13-25; Eph. 1:10; Col. 1:24-25; Heb. 7:19; Jn. 1:17; Rev. 20:2-6).

THE GODHEAD—We believe in one Triune God, Creator of all (Deut. 6:4; Col. 1:16), eternally existing in three distinct persons . . . Father, Son, and Holy Spirit (2 Cor. 13:14), yet one in being, essence, power, and glory, having the same attributes and perfections (Jn. 10:30).

THE PERSON AND WORK OF CHRIST—We believe in the deity of the Lord Jesus Christ. He is very God, the express image of the Father, who, without ceasing to be God, became man in order that He might reveal God and redeem sinful man (Matt. 1:21; Jn. 1: 18; Col. 1: 15).

We believe that God the Son became incarnate in the person of Jesus Christ; that He was conceived of the Holy Spirit; and He was born of the Virgin Mary; that He is truly God and truly man; that He lived a perfect, sinless life; that all His teachings and utterances are true. (Isa. 7:14; Matt. 1:23).

We believe that the Lord Jesus Christ died on the cross for all mankind (I Jn. 2:2) as a representative, vicarious, substitutionary sacrifice (Isa. 53:5-6). We hold that His death is efficacious for all who believe (Jn. 1:12; Acts 16:31), that our justification is grounded in the shedding of His blood (Rom. 5:9; Eph. 1:17), and that it is attested by His literal, physical resurrection from the dead (Matt. 28:6; 1 Pet. 1:3).

We believe that the Lord Jesus Christ ascended to heaven (Acts 1:9-10) in His glorified body and is now seated at the right hand of God as our High Priest and Advocate (Rom. 8:34; Heb. 7:25).

THE PERSON AND WORK OF THE HOLY SPIRIT—We believe in the deity (Acts 5:3-4) and the personality of the Holy Spirit.

We believe that the Holy Spirit convicts the world of sin, righteousness, and judgment (Jn. 16:8-11). He regenerates sinners (Titus 3:5) and indwells believers (Rom. 8:9). He is the agent by whom Christ baptizes all believers into His body (1 Cor. 12:12-14). He is the seal by whom the Father seals believers unto the day of redemption (Eph. 1: 13-14). He is the divine teacher who illumines believers' hearts and minds as they study the Holy Scriptures (Rom. 12:2; 1 Cor. 2:9-12).

We believe it is the duty and privilege of all the saved to be continually filled with the Holy Spirit (Acts 4:31). This filling is commanded (Eph. 5:18). Conditions for being filled are yielding to the Spirit's control (Rom. 8:14), victory over sin, and a dependent life (Gal. 5:16). The results of filling are Christ-like character, worship, submissiveness and service (Gal. 5:22-23).

We believe that the Holy Spirit gives gifts to each member of the body of Christ (I Cor. 12:11; Eph. 4:7). The Son of God sovereignly assigns the place of the ministry of the gifts in the body, and the Father provides the energy in the outworking of the gifts (1 Cor. 12:4-6). Each believer is to exercise his spiritual gift(s) for the common good to the building up of the body of Christ (Eph. 4:7-12).

We believe that the gift of speaking in tongues, which was a sign to the nation of Israel, and the other sign gifts gradually ceased as the New Testament was completed, and its authority was established (I Cor. 13:8; 14:21-22; 2 Cor. 12:12; Heb. 2:4).

ANGELS, GOOD AND EVIL—We believe in the reality and personality of angels. We believe that God created an innumerable company of these sinless, spiritual beings who were to be His messengers (Neh. 9:6; Psa. 148:2; Heb. 1:14).

We believe in the personality of Satan. He is a fallen angel who led a great company of angels into rebellion against God (Isa. 14:12-17; Eze. 28:12-15; Rom. 12:14). He is the great enemy of God and man, and his angels are his agents in the prosecution of his unholy purposes. He shall be eternally punished in the Lake of Fire (Matt. 25:41; Rev. 20:10).

MAN—We believe that man came into being by direct creation of God and that man was made in the image and likeness of God (Gen. 1:26-27).

SIN—We believe that the human race sinned in Adam (Rom. 5:12), that sin is universal in man (Rom. 3:23), and that it is exceedingly heinous to God. We believe that man inherited a sinful nature, that he became alienated from God, that he became totally depraved, and that of himself, he is utterly unable to remedy his lost estate (Eph. 2:1-5, 12). We believe that all men are guilty and in a lost condition apart from Christ (Rom. 2:1).

SALVATION—We believe that salvation is a gift of God's grace through faith in the finished work of Jesus Christ on the cross (Eph. 2:8-9). Christ shed His blood to accomplish justification through faith, propitiation to God, redemption from sin, and reconciliation of man. "Christ died for us" (Rom. 5:8-9) and "bore our sins in His own body on the tree" (I Pet. 2:24).

We believe that all the redeemed, once saved, are kept by God's power and are secure in Christ forever (Jn. 6:37-40; 10:27-30; Rom. 8:1, 38-39; 1 Cor. 4-8; I Pet. 1:5; Jude 24).

We believe that it is the privilege of all who are born again to rejoice in the assurance of their salvation through the testimony of God's Word (Rom. 8:16; 2 Tim. 1:12; 1 Jn. 5:13). We also believe that Christian liberty should never serve as an occasion to the flesh (Gal. 5:13).

We believe that the Scriptures disclose several aspects of sanctification. In addition to God's work of bringing a sinner to Christ (2 Tim. 2:13), one is set apart to God. This is positional sanctification and refers to his standing. He then undergoes a process, whereby the Holy Spirit quickens his affections, desires, and attitudes, enabling him to respond in faith to live a life of victory over sin. This is progressive sanctification and refers to his state (2 Cor. 3:18;7:1; Gal. 5:16-25; Eph. 4:22-29; 5:25-27; Col. 3:10). Some day his standing and his state will be brought into perfect accord. This is prospective or ultimate sanctification. (I Thess. 5:23; 1 Jn. 3:2).

THE CHURCH—We believe that the Church, which is the body and the espoused bride of Christ, began at Pentecost and is a spiritual organism made up of all born-again persons of this present age (I Cor. 12:12-14; 2 Cor. 11:2; Eph. 1:22-23; 5:25-27).

We believe that the establishment and continuance of local churches is clearly taught and defined in the New Testament Scriptures (Acts 14:27; 20:17; 28:32, 1 Tim. 3:1-13; Titus 1:5-11).

We believe in the autonomy of the local church free of any external authority or control (Acts 13:1-4; 15:19-31; 28:28; Rom. 16:1,4; 1 Cor. 3:9; 16; 5:4-7, 13; 1 Pet. 5:1-4).

We believe in the ordinances of believers' water baptism by immersion as a testimony and the Lord's Supper as a remembrance in this age of Christ's death for the church (Matt. 28:19-20; Acts 2:41-42; 18:8; I Cor. 11:23-26).

CONVICTIONS (CALVARY BIBLE COLLEGE) (continued)

We believe that the saved should live in such a manner as to not bring reproach upon their Savior and Lord, and that separation from religious apostasy, sinful pleasures, practices, and associations is commanded by God (Rom. 12:1-2; 2 Cor. 6:14-7:1; 2 Tim. 3:1-5; I Jn. 2:15-17; 2 Jn. 9-11).

We believe in the Great Commission as the primary mission of the church. It is the obligation of the saved to witness, by word and life, to the truths of Holy Scripture. The gospel of the grace of God is to be preached to all the world (Matt. 28:19-20; Acts 1:8; 2 Cor. 5:19-20). Converts are to be taught to obey the Lord and to testify concerning their faith in Christ as Savior in water baptism and to honor Christ by holy living and observance of the Lord's Supper (Matt. 28: 19; 1 Cor. 11:23-29).

THINGS TO COME—We believe in that "blessed hope" (Titus 2:13), the personal, imminent, pretribulational and premillennial coming of our Lord Jesus Christ to rapture His saints and receive His Church unto Himself (I Thess. 4:13-18).

We believe in the subsequent, visible return of Christ to the earth, with His saints, to establish His promised millennial kingdom (Zech. 14:4-11; I Thess. 1:10; Rev. 3:10; 19:11-16; 20:1-6).

We believe in the physical resurrection of all men, the saints to everlasting joy and bliss, the wicked to conscious and eternal torment (Matt. 25:46; Jn. 5:28-29; 11:25-26; Rev. 20:5-6, 12-13).

We believe that the souls of the redeemed are, at death, absent from the body and present with the Lord, where in conscious bliss they await the first resurrection when spirit, soul, and body are reunited to be glorified forever with the Lord (Luke 23:43; 2 Cor. 5:8; Phil. 1:23; 3:21; 1 Thess. 4:16-17; Rev 20:4-6).

We believe that the souls of unbelievers remain, after death, in conscious misery until the second resurrection when, with soul and body reunited, they shall appear at the Great White Throne judgment and shall be cast into the Lake of Fire, not to be annihilated but to suffer everlasting conscious punishment (Matt. 25:41-46; Mark 9:43-48; Luke 16:19-26; 2 Thess. 1:7-9; Jude 6-7; Rev. 20:11-15).

Notes: *Calvary Bible College, Kansas City, Missouri, is an independent fundamentalist Bible school out of the Baptist tradition. Its Convictions affirm the Baptist distinctives of believer's baptism by immersion and the authority of the local church. Its fundamentalist convictions have led to an affirmation of separation from doctrinal heresy, especially of liberal Christianity, the inerrancy of the Bible, the personality of Satan, total human depravity, and a premillennial dispensational eschatology. Dispensationalism teaches that human history can be divided into a series of periods or dispensations during which God works in a slightly different manner toward humanity. Humanity now lives in the dispensation of grace. In the near future Christ will return to take the members of the church to heaven prior to a period of tribulation through* which those remaining on earth will suffer. After the tribulation, Jesus will return to establish His kingdom on earth.

* * *

CONFESSION OF FAITH (LEXINGTON BAPTIST COLLEGE)

To set forth in order a declaration of those things which are most surely believed among usthat thou mightest know the certainty of those things wherein thou hast been instructed, we send forth the commonly believed confession of faith, as follows:

I. Of the Scriptures

We believe that the Holy Bible was written by men supernaturally inspired; that it has truth without any admixture or error for its matter; and therefore is, and shall remain to the end of the age, the only complete and final revelation of the will of God to man; the true center of Christian union and the supreme standard by which all human conduct, creeds, and opinions should be tried.

1. By "The Holy Bible" we mean that collection of sixty-six books, from Genesis to Revelation, which, as originally written does not only contain and convey the Word of God, but IS the very Word of God.

2. By "inspiration" we mean that the books of the Bible were written by holy men of old, as they were moved by the Holy Spirit, in such a definite way that their writings were supernaturally and verbally inspired and free from error, as no other writings have ever been or ever will be inspired.

II. Of the True God

We believe that there is one, and only one, living and true God, an infinite, intelligent Spirit, the maker and supreme ruler of heaven and earth; inexpressibly glorious in holiness and worthy of all possible honor, confidence and love; that in the unity of the Godhead there are three persons, the Father, the Son and the Holy Ghost, equal in every divine perfection, and executing distinct but harmonious offices in the great work of redemption.

III. Of the Holy Spirit

That the Holy Spirit is a divine person; equal with God the Father and God the Son and of the same nature, that He was active in this creation; that in His relation to the unbelieving world He restrains the Evil one until God's purpose is fulfilled; that He convicts of sin, of judgment and of righteousness; that He bears witness to the Truth of the Gospel in preaching and testimony; that He is the agent in the New Birth; that He seals, endues, guides, teaches, witnesses, sanctifies and helps the believer.

IV. Of the Devil, or Satan

We believe that Satan was once holy, and enjoyed heavenly honors; but through pride and ambition to be as the Almighty, fell and drew after him a host of angels; that he is now the malignant prince of the power of the air, and the unholy god of this world. We hold him to be man's great tempter, the enemy of God and His Christ, the accuser of the saints, the author of all false religions, the chief power back of the present apostasy; the lord of the anti-Christ, and the author of all the powers of darkness—destined, however, to final defeat at the hands of God's, Son, and to the judgment of an eternal justice in hell, a place prepared for him and his angels.

V. Of the Creation

We believe in the Genesis account of creation and that it is to be accepted literally, and not allegorically or figuratively; that man's creation was not matter of evolution or evolutionary change of species, or development through interminable periods of time from lower to higher forms; that all animal and vegetable life was made directly, and God's established law was that they should bring forth only ''after their kind.''

VI. Of the Fall of Man

We believe that man was created in innocence under the law of his Maker, but by voluntary transgression fell from his sinless and happy state, in consequence of which, all mankind are now sinners, not by constraint, but of choice; and therefore under just condemnation without defense or excuse.

VII. Of the Virgin Birth

We believe that Jesus Christ was begotten of the Holy Ghost in a miraculous manner; born of Mary, a virgin, as no other man was ever or can ever be born of woman, and that He is the Son of God, and God, the Son.

VIII. Of the Atonement for Sin

We believe that the salvation of sinners is wholly of grace; through the mediatory offices of the Son of God who by the appointment of the Father, freely took upon Him our nature, yet without sin, honored the divine law by His personal obedience, and by His death made a full and vicarious atonement for our sins; that His atonement consisted not in setting us an example by His death as a martyr, but was the voluntary substitution of Himself in the sinner's place, the Just dying for the unjust, Christ, the Lord, bearing our sins in His own body on the tree; that, having risen from the dead, He is now enthroned in heaven, and uniting in His wonderful person the tenderest sympathies with divine perfection, He is every way qualified to be a suitable, a compassionate and all-sufficient Savior.

IX. Of Grace in the New Creation

We believe that in order to be saved, sinners must be born again; that the new birth is a new creation in Christ Jesus; that it is instantaneous and not a process; that in the new birth the one dead in trespasses and in sins in made a partaker of the divine nature and receives eternal life, the free gift of God; that the new creation is brought about in a manner above our comprehension, not by culture, not by character, nor by will of man, but wholly and solely by the power of the Holy Spirit in connection with divine truth, so as to secure our voluntary obedience to the gospel; that its proper evidence appears in the holy fruits of repentance and faith and newness of life.

X. Of the Freeness of Salvation

We believe in God's electing grace that the blessings of salvation are made free to all by the gospel; that it is the immediate duty of all to accept them by a cordial, penitent, and obedient faith; and that nothing prevents the salvation of the greatest sinner on earth but his own inherent depravity and voluntary rejection of the gospel; which rejection involves him in an aggravated condemnation.

XI. Of Justification

We believe that the great gospel blessing which Christ secures to such as believe in Him is Justification; that Justification includes the pardon of sin and the gift of eternal life on principles of righteousness; that it is bestowed not in consideration of any works of righteousness which we have done; but solely through faith in the Redeemer's blood, His righteousness is imputed unto us.

XII. Of Repentance and Faith

We believe that Repentance and Faith are solemn obligations, and also inseparable graces, wrought in our souls by the quickening Spirit of God; thereby, being deeply convicted of our guilt, danger, and helplessness, and of the way of salvation by Christ, we turn to God with unfeigned contrition, confession, and supplication for mercy; at the same time heartily receiving the Lord Jesus Christ and openly confessing Him as our only and all-sufficient Savior.

XIII. Of the Church

We believe that a church of Christ is a congregation of baptized believers associated by a covenant of faith and fellowship of the gospel; observing the ordinances of Christ; governed by His laws; and exercising the gifts, rights, and privileges invested in them by His Word; that its officers of ordination are pastors or elders and deacons whose qualifications, claims, and duties are clearly defined in the scriptures; we believe the true mission of the church is found in the Great Commission; First, to make individual disciples; Second, to baptize the saved; Third, to teach and instruct as He has commanded. We do not believe in the reversal of this order; we hold that the local church has the absolute right of self government, free from the interference of any hierarchy of individuals or organizations; and that the one and only superintendent is Christ through the Holy Spirit; that it is scriptural for the true churches to co-operate with each other in contending for the faith and for the furtherance of the gospel; that every church is the sole and only judge of the measure and method of its co-operation; on all matters of membership, of policy, of government, of discipline, of benevolence, the will of the local church is final.

CONFESSION OF FAITH (LEXINGTON BAPTIST COLLEGE)
(continued)

XIV. Of Baptism and the Lord's Supper

We believe that Christian baptism is the immersion in water of a believer; in the name of the Father, of the Son, and of the Holy Ghost, with the authority of the local church, to show forth in a solemn and beautiful emblem our faith in the crucified, buried and risen Saviour, with its effect in our death to sin and resurrection to a new life: that it is pre-requisite to the privileges of a church relation and to the Lord's Supper; in which the members of the church, by the sacred use of bread and "fruit of the vine" are to commemorate together the dying love of Christ; preceded always by solemn self-examination.

XV. Of the Perseverance of the Saints

We believe that such only are real believers as endure unto the end; that their persevering attachment to Christ is the grand mark which distinguishes them from superficial professors; that a special Providence watches over their welfare; and that they are kept by the power of God through faith unto eternal salvation.

XVI. Of the Righteous and the Wicked

We believe that there is a radical and essential difference between the righteous and the wicked; that such only as through faith are justified in the name of the Lord Jesus, and sanctified by the Spirit of our God, are truly righteous in His esteem; while all such as continue in impenitence and unbelief are in His sight wicked, and under the curse, and this distinction holds among men both in and after death, in the everlasting felicity of the saved and the everlasting conscious suffering of the lost.

XVII. Of Civil Government

We believe that civil government is of divine appointment, for the interests and good order of human society; that magistrates are to be prayed for, conscientiously honored and obeyed; except only in things opposed to the will of our Lord Jesus Christ; who is the only Lord of the conscience, and the coming Prince of the kings of the earth.

XVIII. Of the Resurrection and Return of Christ and Related Events

We believe in and accept the sacred Scriptures upon these subjects at their face and full value. Of the Resurrection, we believe that Christ rose bodily "the third day according to the Scriptures"; that He ascended "to the right hand of the throne of God"; "that this same Jesus which is taken up from you into heaven shall so come in like manner as ye have seen Him go into heaven"—bodily, personally, and visibly; that the "dead in Christ shall rise first"; that the living saints "shall all be changed in a moment, in the twinkling of an eye, at the last trump"; "that the Lord God shall give unto Him the throne of His Father David"; and that "Christ shall reign a thousand years in righteousness until He hath put all enemies under His feet."

XIX. Of Missions

The command to give the gospel to the world is clear and unmistakable and this Commission was given to the churches.

Matt. 28:18-20, "And Jesus came and spake unto them saying, All power is given unto me in heaven and in earth. Go ye therefore, and teach all nations, baptizing them in the name of the Father, and of the Son, and of the Holy Ghost: Teaching them to observe all things whatsoever I have commanded you and lo, I am with you always, even unto the end of the world. Amen."

Mark 16:15, "And he said unto them, Go ye into all the world, and preach the gospel to every creature."

John 20:21, "As my Father hath sent me, even so send I you."

Acts 1:8, "But ye shall receive power, after that the Holy Ghost is come upon you; and ye shall be witnesses unto me both in Jerusalem, and in all Judea, and in Samaria, and unto the uttermost part of the earth."

Rom. 10:13,14,15, "For whosoever shall call upon the name of Lord shall be saved. How then shall they call on him in whom they have not heard? and how shall they hear without a preacher? And how shall they preach, except they be sent? as it is written, How beautiful are the feet of them that preach the gospel of peace, and bring glad tidings of good things."

XX. Of the Grace of Giving

Scriptural giving is one of the fundamentals of the Faith.

II Cor. 8:7, "Therefore as ye abound in everything, in faith, and utterance, and knowledge, and in all diligence, and in your love to us, see that ye abound in this grace also."

We are commanded to bring our gifts into the storehouse (common treasury of the church) upon the first day of the week.

1 Cor. 16:2, "Upon the first day of the week let every one of you lay by him in store, as God hath prospered him, that there be no gatherings when I come."

Under grace we give, and do not pay, the tithe—"Abraham GAVE a tenth part of all"—"Abraham GAVE the tenth of the spoils"—Hebrews 7:2,4—and this was four hundred years before the law, and is confirmed in the New Testament; Jesus said concerning the tithe, "These ye ought to have done"—Matt. 23:23.

We are commanded to bring the tithe into the common treasury of the church.

Lev. 27:30, "The tithe is the Lord's."

Mal. 3:10, "Bring ye all the tithes into the storehouse, that there may be meat in mine house, and prove me now herewith, saith the Lord of hosts, if I will not open you the windows of heaven, and pour you out a blessing, that there shall not be room enough to receive it."

In the New Testament it was the common treasury of the church.

Acts 4:34,35,37, "And brought the prices of the things that were sold and laid them down at the apostles' feet. Having land, sold it, and brought the money, and laid it at the apostles' feet.

Notes: *Lexington Bible College, Lexington, Kentucky, is an independent fundamentalist Bible school in the Baptist tradition. Its Confession of Faith affirms the inerrancy of the Bible and that the events of creation described in the Book of Genesis are to be taken as literally true. It also affirms the Baptist distinctives of believer's baptism by immersion and the authority of the local church.*

* * *

ARTICLES OF RELIGIOUS BELIEF (MID-AMERICA BAPTIST THEOLOGICAL SEMINARY)

Article I: The Bible

We believe that the Bible is the verbally inspired Word of God, wholly without error as originally given by God, and is sufficient as our only infallible rule of faith and practice. We deny that other books are inspired by God in the same way as the Bible.

Article II: God

We believe in the one true and living God, the creator and sustainer of all things. He is infinite, eternal, unchangeable, and is revealed to us as Father, Son, and Holy Spirit. The Father is the head of the Godhead, and into His hands the kingdom shall be delivered. The Son is the promised Messiah of the Old Testament, Jesus Christ, who was born of the Virgin Mary, hence the God-Man. He died on the cross to redeem man, rose again from the dead to justify the believer, ascended to the right hand of God where He intercedes for us, and in the Father's own time will return in visible, personal form to overthrow sin and judge the world. The Holy Spirit is the one sent from God to convict the world of sin, of righteousness, of judgment, to regenerate and cleanse from sin. He is the resident guide, teacher, and strengthener of the believer.

Article III: Satan and Sinful Man

We believe that man was created innocent, that he was tempted by Satan and sinned; because of this men have been born in sin since that time and are by nature the children of wrath. We believe that Satan is a personal devil who with his angels carries on the work of iniquity in this world. Sin is basically rebellion against God, and the end of sin is eternal separation from God.

Article IV: Salvation

We believe that Jesus Christ is the only Savior from sin. He atoned for our sins on the cross and rose again for our justification. Apart from Jesus Christ there is no salvation. All men are under condemnation through personal sin, and escape from condemnation comes only through the righteousness of Jesus Christ. This righteousness is imputed to the believer by grace through faith. The Holy Spirit regenerates the one who makes the life commitment to Jesus, and the life begun in regeneration is never lost.

Article V: Resurrection

We believe in the final resurrection of all men, just and unjust. We believe that those who commit their lives to Jesus Christ during this life will be raised to everlasting life, but those who are not committed to Jesus Christ in this life will be raised to everlasting condemnation.

Article VI: The Church

We believe that a New Testament church is a voluntary association of baptized believers in Christ who have covenanted together to follow the teachings of the New Testament in doctrine, worship, and practice. We believe the only two church ordinances are baptism and the Lord's Supper. We likewise believe that only those who are committed to Jesus Christ as Lord are Scriptural subjects for baptism and that immersion is the only proper mode of baptism. We believe that the Lord's Supper is a memorial to the Lord's death. The bread symbolizes His body which was given for us. The fruit of the vine symbolizes His blood which was shed for us. We believe that a church is a democratic organization served by two types of officers, pastors or bishops and deacons.

Article VII: Civil Government

We believe that God established civil government. We likewise believe in the complete separation of church and state.

Article VIII: Baptist Distinctives

We are Baptists because we believe that Baptists stand for distinctive truths to which other denominations do not adhere. We believe that we cannot compromise these truths without being disloyal to our Lord and to His Word. We do seek to cooperate with all others who are committed to Jesus Christ as Lord.

Notes: *Mid-America Baptist Theological Seminary, Memphis, Tennessee, is an independent Baptist school representative of the more conservative wing of the Southern Baptist Convention. Its Articles of Religious Belief, which must be signed by the faculty, affirms the inerrancy of the Bible, the personality of Satan, and the Baptist distinctives of believer's baptism by immersion, the authority of the local church, and the separation of church and state.*

* * *

OUR BELIEFS (PIEDMONT BIBLE COLLEGE)

THE SCRIPTURES

We believe that the Holy Bible was written by men divinely inspired, and is a perfect treasure of heavenly instruction; that it has God for its author, salvation for its end, and truth, without any mixture of error, for its matter; that it reveals the principles by which God will judge us; and therefore is, and will remain to the end of the world, the true center of Christian union, and the supreme standard by which conduct, creeds, and religious opinions should be tried.

THE GODHEAD

There is one and only one living and true God, an intelligent, spiritual and personal Being, the Creator, Preserver, and Ruler of the universe, infinite in holiness and all other perfections, to whom we owe the highest love, reverence and obedience. He is revealed to us as a Father, Son, and Holy Spirit, each with distinct personal attributes, but without division of nature, essence or being.

GOD THE SON

We believe that the Lord Jesus Christ was begotten of the Holy Spirit without a human father, born of a virgin and is truly God and truly man, that His deity is absolute, wholly unique and singular.

GOD THE HOLY SPIRIT

We believe in the personality and deity of the Holy Spirit, the third person of the Trinity, who is the divine interpreter of the infallible Word, who convicts the world, regenerates and indwells every true believer, testifying of Christ, energizing, enlightening and constraining in the way of holiness.

THE FALL OF MAN

We believe, according to the teachings of Scripture, that man was created a moral being in the image of God after His likeness, but man by voluntary transgression fell from his original sinless state. In consequence, the whole human race was involved in guilt making all mankind now sinners, depraved in nature, spiritually dead, subject to the powers of evil, void of holiness, positively inclined to evil, and hopeless apart from divine grace.

THE RESURRECTION OF CHRIST

We believe in the resurrection of the crucified body of Christ; that this body which was raised from the dead according to the Scriptures was a literal body consisting of flesh and bone and that He ascended into Heaven and sitteth on the right hand of God as the believer's High Priest and Advocate.

THE WAY OF SALVATION

We believe that salvation, according to the Scriptures, is wholly by grace through faith plus nothing. This salvation of the ill-deserving sinner is based upon the finished work of the Lord Jesus Christ who became the sinner's substitute before God and died a propitiatory sacrifice for the sins of the whole world.

Since the natural man is dead in trespasses and sins, at enmity against God and blinded by sin and Satan to his own condition, it is only through the operation of the Holy Spirit using the Word that man is brought to repentance and faith. No degree of reformation however great, no attainment in morality, however refined, no culture however attractive, no ordinance or ceremony however ancient and sacred, no feeling however satisfying, no sincerity however approved, no church membership however authenticated, can in the least degree add to the value of the precious blood, or to the merits of that finished work wrought for us by the Lord Jesus Christ.

JUSTIFICATION

Justification is God's gracious and full acquittal upon principles of righteousness of all sinners who believe in Christ. This blessing is bestowed, not in consideration of any work of righteousness which we have done, but as a state of most blessed peace and favor with God, and secures every other needed blessing.

THE FREENESS OF SALVATION

The blessings of salvation are made free to all by the gospel. It is the duty of all to accept them by penitent and obedient faith. Nothing prevents the salvation of the greatest Sinner except his own voluntary refusal to accept Jesus Christ as Teacher, Saviour, and Lord.

THE SECURITY OF THE BELIEVER

We believe that all born-again persons are eternally secure in Christ since the Scripture teaches that our justification before God alone rests upon the finished work of Christ and forever remains the unchanging grounds of the believer's faith. This security is further guaranteed by the continuous High Priestly work of Christ in Heaven itself, and by the work of the Holy Spirit who wrought regeneration in the believer and performs an unceasing ministry within his soul.

THE CHURCH

We believe that the church, the body of Christ, is composed of all those who have true faith in the Lord Jesus Christ. The visible church, or assembly, is a congregation of baptized believers associated by covenant in the faith and fellowship of the gospel, observing the ordinances of Christ, the true head of the church; looking to the Holy Spirit, the administrator, for guidance in exercising the gifts, rights, and privileges invested in the believer by His Word.

THE OBLIGATION TO HOLINESS

We believe that all believers in the Lord Jesus Christ are called into a life of separation from the world to which they have been crucified by the death of Christ, and should abstain from worldly lust and such practices and habits as will retard spiritual growth or cause others to stumble and thus bring reproach upon the cross of Christ. The believer is called upon to walk worthily keeping himself unspotted from the world, zealous of good works.

THE EVANGELIZATION OF THE WORLD

We believe in the evangelization of the world, placing emphasis upon the task of reaching the individual with the gospel and its implications and that no humanitarian and philanthropic schemes may be substituted for the preaching of the Cross.

BIBLE INTERPRETATION

We believe in accepting the literal teaching of the Word. "When the plain sense of Scripture makes common sense, seek no other sense:" Therefore, every declaration is to be taken in its primary, ordinary literal and its most obvious meaning unless the facts of the context and the well-defined laws of language clearly indicate the terms either to be symbolic or figurative and not literal. Whatever is not literal must be explained in the light of other passages which are literal.

CREATION

We believe in the Genesis account of creation which teaches that all things found their origin in God Who created by His own fiat instantaneously every living thing after its kind.

THE RETURN OF CHRIST

We believe according to Scripture, in the sure return of the Lord Jesus Christ, that this second coming will be a literal, bodily, personal return; that His coming for His bride, the Church, constitutes the "Blessed Hope" set before us, for which we should be constantly looking. We believe that His coming will be premillennial.

ESCHATOLOGY

(1) The righteous dead. We believe that the souls of those who trusted in Christ for salvation at death will go immediately into His presence and there remain in conscious bliss until the day of resurrection of the righteous dead at the second coming when soul and body shall be reunited to ever be with the Lord in glory.

(2) The unrighteous dead. We believe that the souls of the lost remain after death in conscious misery until the final judgment of the great white throne when the soul and body will be reunited in resurrection to be arraigned before God in judgment and then cast "into the lake of fire which is the second death" to be "punished with everlasting destruction from the presence of the Lord and the glory of his power."

SATAN

We believe in the reality of the person of Satan, "that old serpent, called the Devil and Satan, which deceiveth the world."

Notes: *Piedmont Bible College, Winston-Salem, North Carolina, is an independent fundamentalist Baptist school. Its statement of belief affirms the inerrancy of the Bible, total human depravity, the security of the believer, the literal interpretation of the Bible, the Genesis account of creation, and the premillennial return of Jesus Christ.*

* * *

Christian Church

STATEMENT OF FAITH (CHRISTIAN CHURCHES AND CHURCHES OF CHRIST/DALLAS CHRISTIAN COLLEGE)

That the Bible, or Holy Scriptures, alone is the divinely inspired Word of God, and therein is contained the revelation of the deity of Jesus Christ, the plan of salvation for mankind, and the faith and work of the New Testament Church; furthermore, that the testimony of such Scriptures testifies to prophecy concerning His advent, virgin birth, miraculous life, blood atonement, bodily resurrection, and ascension into heaven, and final return, and is expressly and historically true in the commonly accepted meaning of the terms; in addition that the Church of the New Testament ought everywhere to be restored with its divine plan of admission: faith, repentance, and baptism, with consequent godly life; and finally, that the New Testament Scriptures are wholly sufficient to build the kingdom of God.

Notes: *Dallas Christian College, Dallas, Texas, is an independent school sponsored by the Christian Churches and Churches of Christ, one branch of the Restoration Movement that began in the early nineteenth century around the work of Barton Stone and Thomas and Alexander Campbell. It is a noncreedal movement, but various affiliated organizations have created statements that reflect its doctrinal position. The Dallas Christian College affirms a New Testament faith consisting of belief in the Bible as the Word of God, salvation in Jesus Christ, and the restoration of the New Testament church.*

* * *

WE TEACH (CHRISTIAN CHURCHES AND CHURCHES OF CHRIST/KENTUCKY CHRISTIAN COLLEGE)

WE TEACH

THAT GOD is not only the omnipotent, omniscient and omnipresent Creator of the universe, but also the loving Father, Provider of all life, and righteous Judge.

THAT THE BIBLE is God's divinely inspired revelation to man. These Holy Scriptures are not to be added to, nor subtracted from, by anyone.

THAT JESUS IS THE CHRIST, the Son of God, Who came to earth in the fullness of time, as Savior and as Messiah. This same Jesus is recognized as the only begotten Son of God, born

WE TEACH (CHRISTIAN CHURCHES AND CHURCHES OF CHRIST/KENTUCKY CHRISTIAN COLLEGE) (continued)

of the virgin Mary, crucified on the Cross after a sinless life on earth, raised bodily as Lord from the tomb, ascended into heaven as King of Kings, and coming again to reclaim those who are His own.

THAT THE CHURCH is the divine institution by which God has provided for the preaching of the Gospel and the salvation of the world. This Church, the Body of Christ, has divinely given ordinances, which are Christian baptism, the immersion of the penitent believer for the remission of sins and the gift of the Holy Spirit, and the Lord's Supper, observed weekly in remembrance of Him.

THAT THE UNITY of all followers of Christ can be realized on basis of a return to the primitive pattern for the Church doctrine—in practice, in polity and in life—as seen in the New Testament.

Notes: *Kentucky Christian College, Grayson, Kentucky, is an independent school sponsored by the Christian Churches and Churches of Christ, one branch of the Restoration Movement that began in the early nineteenth century around the work of Barton Stone and Thomas and Alexander Campbell. Its brief statement attempts to summarize the basic principles of the Restoration Movement, including the authority of the Bible, salvation in Christ and the unity of the church through allegiance to New Testament patterns.*

*　　*　　*

WHAT WE BELIEVE (CHRISTIAN CHURCHES AND CHURCHES OF CHRIST/LINCOLN CHRISTIAN COLLEGE)

WHAT WE BELIEVE ABOUT THE CHURCH

We believe that the church is a unique institution, and that its singular character is manifest in every aspect of its being. It is unique in its origin. Conceived in the mind of God, planned by the Son of God, and established by His authority and under the guidance of the Holy Spirit, it breathes the atmosphere of its heavenly beginnings.

It is unique in its nature; it is divine. It is divine in its beginnings, in the life that it lives, in the truth that it teaches, in the faith that it holds, and in the destiny to which it looks forward. It defies comparison with any body of men on the face of the earth because of the quality of its life.

It is unique in its constituency. It alone is composed of those who have been "washed in the blood of the Lamb," who have seen the "city which hath foundations, whose maker and

builder is God." Only the church can boast a membership of those who are sons of God through faith in the son of God and obedience to His commands.

It is further unique in that it is the body of Christ, a living, functioning, purposive organism, which has as its head the divine Son of God. Always subservient to Him and subject always to His will, the church is the instrument of Christ for the accomplishment of His continuing mission on the earth.

WHAT WE BELIEVE ABOUT CHRIST

We believe that Jesus is the only begotten Son of God, that He was born of the virgin Mary. He was crucified by sinful men, buried, and the third day God brought Him forth from the grave. In Him rests all authority in heaven and on earth. He is the living, reigning King, the Savior of the world. To Him we must yield our allegiance. This we believe without any mental reservation.

WHAT WE BELIEVE ABOUT CHRISTIAN UNITY

Lincoln Christian College believes in the practicality of Christian unity because it sees Christians being made one with Christ every day. We are aware of the necessity of bringing the individual to oneness with Christ, through conversion to Christ and baptism into Christ, before that person may have any part in a union that could properly be called Christian.

When we think of Christian unity, our sights are not fixed upon the denomination as the unit, nor upon local congregations throughout the land as the unit, nor upon the individual in his relationship to other individuals as the unit, but upon the relationship of every individual who would be called a Christian to the Lord Jesus Christ. We believe that if one person can be united to Him, then two can and three and a hundred and as many as will. In doing this, of course, the individuals are united to each other in a true Christian fellowship, without which unity could never be Christian.

We despair of ever achieving Christian unity through submission to an earthly authority, be that authority a single individual or an organization composed of several individuals, but we believe that Christian unity may be achieved through the submission of us all to the authority and Lordship of Jesus Christ through a complete restoration of the Christianity of the New Testament.

WHAT WE BELIEVE ABOUT THE CHRISTIAN LIFE

"Wherefore if any man is in Christ, he is a new creature: the old things are passed away; behold, they are become new." The life of the Christian is a new life, beginning with the new birth, centered around a new core, with a new knowledge of God and of His Son, Jesus Christ, a new forgiveness of sin, a new redemption, and a new hope. It is a life of obedience to the will of Christ as Lord and Master, a life of stewardship, fellowship, worship, fruit-bearing, and love.

The life of the Christian begins with his faith in Jesus Christ and the beginning of his obedience to Him, and finds issue in that eternity where God will reign supreme over those who have chosen Him to be their God.

WHAT WE BELIEVE ABOUT THE IMPORTANCE OF EVANGELISM

We are committed to evangelism because by this means people are brought to Christ and nurtured in Christ. We are committed to evangelism because we believe in Christ and cannot obey Him unless we evangelize. Every class that is taught, every sermon that is preached, every song that is sung at Lincoln Christian College is for the purpose of inspiring the students to win souls to Christ. This is our only reason for existence.

WHAT WE BELIEVE ABOUT CHRISTIAN BAPTISM

Lincoln Christian College holds strictly to the original design and practice of Christian baptism. We believe that it is a command of the Lord Jesus Christ given to His apostles and carried out by them, and that it was His intention that it be continued in practice in every age of the church.

We understand it to be significant and necessary in the bringing of one who desires to be a Christian into Christ and unto remissions of sins, because of statements from Jesus Christ and His apostles to that effect and because it is the climax of every conversion in the New Testament. We submit that it would not have been so carefully attended to had Jesus and His apostles not thought it of the foremost significance in the evangelization of the world.

We regard it as extremely unfortunate that the world was transliterated and never translated into the English language. That this has created a world of confusion must be admitted by those who think carefully about it. We regard it as essential to world evangelism and necessary to the unity of Christians that all men everywhere restore baptism to its original design and practice as a complete immersion in water of one who truly believes in Jesus Christ as the Son of God, for the remission of sins.

WHAT WE BELIEVE ABOUT DIVINE AUTHORITY

Lincoln Christian College believes that God is the seat of authority. God is the Creator; we are the creatures of His creation. We, therefore, must obey Him.

God, our Heavenly Father, entrusted His authority to Jesus His only begotten Son. Have you not read that God said, "This is my beloved son in whom I am well pleased. Hear ye Him!" Jesus spoke to His disciples saying, "All authority hath been given unto me."

God is our Father; we are His children. Children do not make the rules to govern children. The Father has that responsibility. Jesus is the good Shepherd, we are the sheep of His fold. Sheep do not legislate for other sheep. Jesus is our Lord. We are His servants. Servants do not rule.

We must obey God rather than man.

WHAT WE BELIEVE ABOUT THE BIBLE

As is outlined in the Purpose and Policy of Lincoln Christian College, we believe and teach that the Scriptures of the Old and New Testaments are, in a unique sense, the revelation from God. The compass of this statement includes the origin of the Bible, both the Old Testament and the New Testament, and their basic nature as the revelation from God in a unique sense.

In stating these things there are no mental reservations, evasions, or equivocations whatsoever. We believe exactly what this statement above proclaims without any reservation of any kind. We believe that all the good of the life of man, all the hope that he has for his life, and all the expectation he has for an eternal destiny are to be found in the Bible. It is the source of his knowledge of God, of the hope and means of salvation, and of the hope of eternity. In it man finds God revealed, as well as His will for man. In it he finds the means of salvation, the divine pattern for the church, the pattern for the Christian life, and the promise of the deepest things for which the soul of man can hunger.

WHAT WE BELIEVE ABOUT HUMAN ORGANIZATIONS

The church of Christ is an organism with Jesus the Christ the head of the body. This body as well as all bodies needs only enough organization to make it function, and all this organization must be under the direction of the head. For this reason all organizations devised by mankind, which include colleges, missionary organizations, societies, and the like, are not true expedients when they hinder the work of Christ, and in that case they must be abolished.

Only those organizations that serve and help the church of Jesus Christ carry out the purpose of the Christ as it is outlined in His Word should be supported. Therefore, every human organization must be examined in the light of the Scriptures that it might be proved to be in keeping with the Scriptures. If it cannot meet God's standard, it must not be supported. This we believe. This we teach.

WHAT WE BELIEVE ABOUT CHRISTIAN FELLOWSHIP

We believe that there is a "togetherness," a common care of Christians for each other which triumphs over every earthly barrier and brings the individual Christian into sympathetic, unselfish, genuine comradeship with those of like, precious faith. This aspect of the Christian life was present long ago, caused the non-Christian of that age to marvel at "how the Christians love one another," and prompted those early Christians not to consider that anything they had was their own, but to be willing to surrender it to meet the needs of others of the truth.

Christian fellowship is the "cradle-to-the-grave" concern of the people of God for one another which begins with the passion of the Christian for the salvation of the sinner and continues after he has been won to Christ until he passes to his eternal reward. This fellowship is the sweetest possession on earth and will find its fruition only in the fuller life of the new Jerusalem.

WHAT WE BELIEVE ABOUT THE LORD'S SUPPER

Lincoln Christian College contends that the Lord's supper is an important element in Christian fellowship and in the maintenance of the highest privileges of our relationship to Jesus Christ. We believe that the apostles, acting under the directives

**WHAT WE BELIEVE (CHRISTIAN CHURCHES AND
CHURCHES OF CHRIST/LINCOLN CHRISTIAN COLLEGE)**
(continued)

of Christ, instituted its observance upon the first day of every week, as the central act of Christian worship.

We believe that there is considerably more in observing the Lord's supper than the mere recitation of certain words or the simple recognition of certain symbols. The words used by our Lord in describing the loaf and the cup and the emphasis placed upon it in the New Testament persuade us to this position. We regard it to be an essential mark of the identity of the church of Christ.

We reject the theory of transubstantiation, as well as the theory of consubstantiation and the theory of simple symbolism, but we hold that we may, with the scriptural exactness and safety, go as far in our descriptions of the supper and its observance as do our Lord and His apostles. We believe that the Christian should far less fail to meet his Lord at the hour of the Lord's supper than he would fail to meet a dinner engagement previously accepted.

It is our position that the weekly observance of the Lord's supper is not only scriptural, but that the restoration of that practice is the only answer to the problems that have risen regarding the frequency of its observance.

WHAT WE BELIEVE ABOUT MISSIONS

Just as Lincoln Christian College believes in, teaches, and practices evangelism, so it seeks to promote the missionary cause at every opportunity. It looks upon missions as the complement of evangelism, or, viewed from another perspective, the equivalent of evangelism as practiced upon a field at a distance from the local field. Strictly speaking, missions is evangelism in every essential. It should include all that evangelism includes.

Conceived as such it must never be confined to a program of social service on a foreign field. All too many times the missionary program has degenerated to a program of medical care and of teaching home economics, agriculture, hygiene, carpentry, and other disciplines of modern civilized life. It may at times and on some fields be advantageous to the cause of Christ to care for some of the more urgent physical requirements of the peoples among whom the missionary evangelist goes. But when the missionary program is chiefly composed of teaching the refinements of western civilization to the continuous neglect of the cultivation of a people of God through preaching and teaching the Word in order to win men to Christ and nurture them in Him, that program ceases to be missions.

The large percentage of the student body of the college who are taking training specifically for the mission field and the number of students who spend each summer on a home mission field testify to the interest of this college in that important function of the church. In the future every energy will be expended to bring about continuous improvement in the type of training offered and the number of students who volunteer for the work of evangelism on the needy fields away from the home front.

WHAT WE BELIEVE ABOUT THE FUTURE

Lincoln Christian College has a sincere and zealous confidence in the future. Our forefathers in the faith beheld the evils of the divisions among those who called themselves Christian and joined with a great host of those down through the ages who saw clearly that denominationalism is sin and that the only hope of the progress of that Kingdom is the taking of the New Testament and the New Testament alone as a guide to the faith, practice, and life of the Christian. A century ago it seemed that the great rallying cry of the return to the faith of the New Testament church would triumph in America. Denominational churches by the hundreds were swept into the Restoration Movement, the movement to restore New Testament order to the churches.

At the very height of this movement men began to lose confidence in the "faith once for all delivered to the saints" and began to want to compromise the Gospel to make it more agreeable with the message of denominational groups. The entrance of this trend marked the beginning of the decline of the hopeful possibility of a return to the power of the church of the New Testament, and the past half century has marked a tragic decline all along the line. Despite colorful attempts to convince the rank and file of the brethren in the churches, the statistics indicate a regrettable retreat and retrenchment in every aspect of the work of the churches. Evangelism declined. Missionary work dwindled and failed on many fields. Churches at home were closed and on the mission field station after station was abandoned.

But a new day has struck. There is rustling and bustling among those who would return to the old fires of faith, a new surge of evangelism, a return to an earnest confidence in the Bible as the revealed Word of God and of the power and importance of the apostolic order of things. Churches are being reopened, new churches are being established, new mission fields are being opened and are being reopened and the work of the Lord once more established. A great host of young men and young women of big purpose and determined zeal are flooding Bible colleges. Everywhere there is new life. There are new Christian camps, new Bible colleges, a wave of enthusiasm and interest in the work of the Lord manifested in many rallies, conferences, and other meetings which stress various areas of Christian work.

We do not believe that the plea for the restoration of the New Testament order of things has seen its day. Our great scandal has been that for many years our people who might have made one of the greatest contributions in the history of the church were willing for so long to trade their rich heritage for a mess of pottage. There is a new day for New Testament Christianity. We are lending every energy at our command to bring it about. We have confidence in the future and invite all others of like conviction to join with us in a great campaign to advance the cause of Christ and His Kingdom over all the world.

Notes: *Lincoln Christian College, Lincoln, Illinois, is an independent school sponsored by the Christian Churches and Churches of Christ, one branch of the Restoration Movement that began in the early nineteenth century around the work of Barton Stone and Thomas and Alexander Campbell. The Movement is noncreedal but several of its representative* *institutions have produced statements, that of Lincoln Christian College being among the most complete. It affirms most Restoration distinctives such as Christian unity, baptism by immersion for the remission of sins, the authority of the Bible, and the celebration of the Lord's supper weekly.*

* * *

STATEMENT OF FAITH (CHRISTIAN CHURCHES AND CHURCHES OF CHRIST/NEBRASKA CHRISTIAN COLLEGE)

Nebraska Christian College shall teach and advocate:

1. That God is the Creator; Jesus, His Son, is the Christ; and that the Holy Spirit is our Comforter and Guide.

2. That the Bible consisting of Old and New Testament Scriptures was given through the inspiration of God and that the New Testament Scripture constitutes the complete and final authority of the church.

3. That Jesus Christ, God in the flesh, was born of the Virgin Mary; that He lived, walked, and talked on this earth; that He was tempted like as we are, yet was without sin; that He was betrayed, condemned. crucified and died for the sins of mankind; that He was buried, and after three days rose again, according to the Scriptures. and that after forty days ascended to the Father and now sits at His right hand in glory, making intercession for the saints.

4. That Jesus Christ will come again; that the dead will be raised; and that God through Him shall judge the just and the unjust, each man according to his works.

5. That the terms of salvation are these: that a man shall believe on Jesus as the Christ and Lord, and as the only begotten Son of God; that he shall repent of his sins; that he shall confess Jesus' name before men; that he shall be buried with Him in Christian baptism to arise and walk in newness of life, to be a loyal and faithful steward of Christ in all things until death; thus working out his own salvation with fear and trembling: for "There is none other name given under heaven among men, whereby we must be saved.

6. That love of the brethren is the mark of discipleship. "In essentials unity. In non-essentials liberty. In all things love."

7. A congregational form of church government. The autonomy (right of self-government) of the local Churches of Christ. That the local church and her ministry are free and subject only to Christ and His Word.

8. A strict weekly observance of the Lord's Supper.

9. That the terms of salvation and church membership are one and the same.

10. That God still answers prayer, when approached in the name of the Lord Jesus.

11. That the Great Commission: "Go ye therefore and teach all nations, baptizing them in the name of the Father, and the Son, and of the Holy Spirit, teaching them to observe all things whatsoever I have commanded you" was given first to the Apostles and to every Christian. That the church of Christ was revealed in the New Testament, and has from the beginning been intensely evangelistic and that men today should use every means at their disposal to fulfill the Great Commission.

Notes: *Nebraska Christian College, Norfolk, Nebraska, is an independent school sponsored by the Christian Churches and Churches of Christ, one branch of the Restoration Movement that began in the early nineteenth century around the work of Barton Stone and Thomas and Alexander Campbell. Its Statement of Faith highlights Restoration Movement distinctives such as the authority of the New Testament, congregational church polity, and the weekly observance of the Lord's supper.*

* * *

CMF AND THE MOVEMENT (CHRISTIAN MISSIONARY FELLOWSHIP)

"In him all things hold together." Colossians 1:17

We understand the Restoration Ideal as a return to biblical Christianity in order to rediscover our oneness in Christ as a means to worldwide evangelism. The trilogy of "The Whole Gospel, the Whole Church, the Whole World" is true to the sacred scriptures and to our heritage as a people. We believe this ideal to be as relevant as truth, as necessary as mission and as enduring as time.

IN ESSENTIALS, UNITY. The New Covenant Scriptures reveal the meaning of the gospel and the marks of the church without which there is no valid faith, no continuing body. The essentials of unity are described as ONE BODY, ONE SPIRIT, ONE HOPE, ONE LORD, ONE FAITH, ONE BAPTISM, ONE GOD AND FATHER OF ALL (Ephesians 4:4-6). Our incorporation and by-laws reflect this commitment and bind us to the New Testament Scriptures in doctrine and to believer's baptism (immersion) in practice (Articles I & II: Doctrinal Position and Policy.)

IN NON-ESSENTIALS, LIBERTY. We understand inter-congregational agencies to be allowed by scripture, to be dictated by reason and to be supported by merit. No such agency should be confused with church or made a test of fellowship or brotherhood. As different gifts require different services, so different needs call forth varying agencies

IN ALL THINGS, LOVE, Because Christ is greater than all our differences, we have covenanted to love one another—

CMF AND THE MOVEMENT (CHRISTIAN MISSIONARY FELLOWSHIP) (continued)

beyond institutional affiliations, agency preferences, party loyalties and factional identities. Actually and ultimately, it is only in Him that all things hold together.

Notes: *The Christian Missionary Fellowship is an independent missionary agency working among the churches of the Restoration Movement that began in the early nineteenth century around the work of Barton Stone and Thomas and Alexander Campbell, primarily the Christian Church (Disciples of Christ) and the Christian Churches and Churches of Christ. Its brief statement affirms several distinctives of the Restoration movement including the unity of the Church based on New Testament principles, congregational autonomy, and believer's baptism by immersion.*

*　　　*　　　*

BASIC COMMITMENTS [CHURCHES OF CHRIST (NON-INSTRUMENTAL)/HARDING UNIVERSITY, GRADUATE SCHOOL OF RELIGION]

The Graduate School attempts to achieve its primary purpose within a framework of basic commitments:

1. To GOD, as the Creator of the world and the loving Father of humanity;

2. To JESUS of Nazareth, as the Incarnate Word, the only Son of God, and the risen Christ;

3. To SCRIPTURE, as the Word of God given by the inspiration of the Holy Spirit to be the infallible guide in religious matters;

4. To TRUTH, honestly and openly sought through resources past and present;

5. To the RESTORATION PRINCIPLE, rich with potential for insuring the presence of Christians attempting to be today what the first Christians were to be in their day;

6. To the WELFARE OF STUDENTS, as the institution seeks to deepen their faith, to increase their commitment

to Christ and his church, and to inspire them to minister to their contemporary world.

Notes: *Harding University, Searcy, Arkansas, is an independent school supported by the congregations of the Churches of Christ, one branch of the Restoration Movement that began in the early nineteenth century around the work of Barton Stone and Thomas and Alexander Campbell. The Movement is noncreedal, but the University's Graduate School of Religion has put together a statement of basic commitments that includes some of the basic beliefs of the Churches of Christ including the sole authority of Scripture as the Word of God.*

*　　　*　　　*

DOCTRINAL STATEMENT [CHURCHES OF CHRIST (NON-INSTRUMENTAL)/SAN JOSE COLLEGE]

The Articles of Incorporation of San Jose Bible College state the doctrinal position of the college in the following terms:

''To uphold the standards of the church of Christ as revealed in the New Testament Scriptures and the Deity of Christ (which includes—the Virgin Birth, His Miraculous Life, the Blood Atonement, His Bodily Resurrection from the grave, His Ascension into heaven and His personal Coming Again), to teach the plan of salvation as recorded in the Book of Acts which includes, God's grace, faith repentance, confession, baptism and a Godly life, to contend for the restoration of the early church in life, teaching, name and organization and purpose.''

Notes: *San Jose College, in San Jose, California, is an independent school supported by the congregations of the Churches of Christ, one branch of the Restoration Movement that began in the early nineteenth century around the work of Barton Stone and Thomas and Alexander Campbell. The Movement is noncreedal, but San Jose College, has produced a brief statement that includes the prime Restoration distinctive: the restoration of the New Testament church's life, teachings, name (Church of Christ), and organization (congregational).*

Chapter 11

Independent Fundamentalist Family

Fundamentalism/Evangelicanism

STATEMENT OF FAITH (NATIONAL ASSOCIATION OF EVANGELICALS)

1. We believe the Bible to be the inspired, the only infallible, authoritative Word of God.

2. We believe that there is one God, eternally existent in three persons: Father, Son and Holy Spirit.

3. We believe in the deity of our Lord Jesus Christ, in His virgin birth, in His sinless life, in His miracles, in His vicarious and atoning death through his shed blood, in His bodily resurrection, in His ascension to glory.

4. We believe that for the salvation of lost and sinful man, regeneration by the Holy Spirit is absolutely essential.

5. We believe in the present ministry of the Holy Spirit by whose indwelling the Christian is enabled to live a godly life.

6. We believe in the resurrection of both the saved and the lost; they that are saved unto the resurrection of life and they that are lost unto the resurrection of damnation.

7. We believe in the spiritual unity of believers in our Lord Jesus Christ.

Notes: *Founded in 1942, the National Association of Evangelicals (NAE) is the major cooperative structure for Evangelical denominations and missionary organizations. This brief statement covers only the essential theological topics at issue in the development of Evangelicalism as the next phase of Fundamentalism, which occurred at the end of the 1930s. Fundamentalism and Evangelicalism grew out of a crisis in authority occasioned by the rise of critical approaches to the Bible and scientific/historical challenges to the accuracy of the biblical text. Thus, the primary issue for Fundamentalists/Evangelicals has been the nature of the authority of the Bible, and typical of Evangelical statements of faith, the NAE begins with the assertion of belief in the Bible.*

As discussion of the nature of biblical authority proceeded within Fundamentalism and Evangelicalism, a set of technical terms had emerged. All assumed the Bible to be the Word of God, but some wished to spell out the meaning of that assertion in more detail. The primary terms that have emerged are infallibility, inerrancy, and plenary inspiration. Infallibility refers to the Bible's sufficiency and completeness in matters of God's revelation of truth concerning theological and moral concerns. This use is close to the Roman Catholic definition of the authority of the Pope as being infallible when speaking on matters of faith and morals. Inerrancy, in contrast, concerns the accuracy of the Bible when speaking on any issue, including science and history. Inerrancy is usually affirmed despite attacks on its accuracy by scholars who weight biblical statements in favor of their independent research findings, and textual critics who see the Bible as an edited book containing a variety of internal inconsistencies.

Plenary inspiration means that the very words of the Bible, not just its thoughts and ideas, are inspired, and hence, have the authority of revelation. The assertion of plenary inspiration presents its own problem in that no original copies of the books of the Bible exist, and all of the presently existing texts have differences. The problem of creating an authoritative text is a matter of intense debate. Also, the Bible was written in archaic languages. Modern forms of Hebrew and Greek differ considerably from those forms spoken in biblical times. While believing that a relatively accurate text has been preserved, many Fundamentalists/Evangelicals assert that complete plenary authority rests only with the original manuscripts, an assertion that protects the present text against the minor errors that are occasionally uncovered from the examination of the ancient manuscripts.

The Statement of Faith by the NAE avoids going into detail on the nature of biblical authority, an acceptable position that allows those Evangelicals who do not use the technical language concerning the Bible to freely participate without doctrinal reservations. It also avoids the other issues that divide Evangelicals, most importantly the specifics on the nature and work of the Holy Spirit as an indwelling presence in the life of the believer.

STATEMENT OF FAITH (NATIONAL ASSOCIATION OF EVANGELICALS) (continued)

This brief statement has been adopted by a number of Evangelical organizations. Those that have adopted it word for word include: Cityteam Ministries, Compassion International, Evangelical Council for Financial Responsibility, Evangelical Press Association, Evangelical Foreign Missions Association, Far East Broadcasting Company, Food for the Hungry, Link Care Center, Teen Missions International, World Vision, and Youth for Christ. Among those who have adopted it, but modified it to meet their specific needs or concerns include: Bible Literature International, Christian Literature Crusade, Christian Literature International, Christian Outreach International, Christians in Action, Eastern European Mission, Greater Europe Mission, Global Outreach Mission, Living Bibles International, Mission Aviation Fellowship, Spiritual Counterfeits Project, Steer, Inc., and the United World Mission. These modified statements are presented below in their proper order.

The NAE statement is a concise presentation of the bare essentials of conservative Evangelical free church Protestantism. It attempts to unite conservative Protestants in opposition to liberal ecumenical Protestantism (represented by the larger Protestant churches who are members of the National Council of Churches). It does not deal with those concerns that are a matter of difference between Evangelicals of differing denominational traditions. Those issues include total human depravity (affirmed by those of a Calvinist theological heritage, such as Presbyterians, and denied by the Methodists), the designation of baptism and the Lord's Supper as ordinances (Baptists) rather than sacraments (Presbyterians and Methodists), and the primacy of the local church (Baptists). The nature of the second coming of Jesus is a matter of intense debate among Evangelicals. There has been a growing acceptance of the premillennial return of Jesus to earth, (i.e., prior to the establishment of his thousand-year reign), as opposed to postmillennialism, the dominant Evangelical position in the nineteenth century.

*   *   *

CONFESSION OF FAITH (INTERDENOMINATIONAL FOREIGN MISSION ASSOCIATION)

The member missions do affirm and declare their belief in and defense of the historic Christian faith as set forth in the following:

1. We believe that the Bible, consisting of Old and New Testaments only, is verbally inspired by the Holy Spirit, is inerrant in the original manuscripts, and is the infallible and authoritative Word of God.

2. We believe that the one triune God exists eternally in three persons: Father, Son and Holy Spirit.

3. We believe that Adam, created in the image of God, was tempted by Satan, the god of this world, and fell. Because of Adam's sin, all men have guilt imputed, are totally depraved, and need to be regenerated by the Holy Spirit for salvation.

4. We believe that Jesus Christ is God, was born of a virgin, died vicariously, shed His blood as man's substitutionary sacrifice, rose bodily, and ascended to heaven, where He is presently exalted at the Father's right hand.

5. We believe that salvation consists of the remission of sins, the imputation of Christ's righteousness, and the gift of eternal life received by faith alone, apart from works.

6. We believe that the return of Jesus Christ is imminent, and that it will be visible and personal.

7. We believe that the saved will be raised to everlasting life and blessedness in heaven, and that the unsaved will raised to everlasting and conscious punishment in hell.

8. We believe that the church, the body of Christ, consists only of those who are born again, who are baptized by the Holy Spirit into Christ at the time of regeneration, for whom He now makes intercession in heaven and for whom He will come again.

9. We believe that Christ commanded the church to go into all the world and preach the gospel to every creature, baptizing and teaching those who believe.

Notes: *The Interdenominational Foreign Mission Association of North America, founded in 1917, is a cooperative network serving numerous independent Evangelical missionary organizations that sponsor missionaries in countries outside of North America. These missionary organizations have traditionally been called ''Faith'' missions and they are independent of regular denominational support. It differs from the Evangelical Foreign Missions Association, which includes both denominational mission boards and independent missionary organizations in its network. The Interdenominational Foreign Mission Association has a detailed statement of biblical authority, affirms all of the issues at stake in the Fundamentalist/Modernist controversy (the Trinity, virgin birth and vicarious atonement, and the second coming of Christ), and exalts the missionary enterprise. This statement has been adopted ''as is'' by several other Evangelical groups primarily concerned with world missions, including Frontiers, and the United Center for World Mission.*

*   *   *

NIAGARA CREED (1878)

I. We believe ''that all Scripture is given by inspiration of God,'' by which we understand the whole of the book called the Bible; nor do we take the statement in the sense in which it is sometimes foolishly said that works of human genius are inspired, but in the sense that the Holy Ghost gave the very words of the sacred writings to holy men of old; and that His Divine inspiration is not, in different degrees, but extends equally and fully to all parts of these writings, historical, poetical, doctrinal and prophetical, and to the smallest word, and inflection of a word, provided such word is found in the original manuscripts: 2 Tim. 3:16, 17; 2 Pet. 1:21; 1 Cor. 2:13; Mark 12:26, 36; 13:11; Acts 1:16; 2:4.

II. We believe that the Godhead eternally exists in three persons, the Father, the Son, and the Holy Spirit; and that these three are one God, having precisely the same nature, attributes and perfections, and worthy of precisely the same homage, confidence, and obedience: Mark 12:29; John 1:1-4; Matt. 28:19, 20; Acts 5:3, 4; 2 Cor. 13:14; Heb. 1:1-3; Rev. 1:4-6.

III. We believe that man, originally created in the image and after the likeness of God, fell from his high and holy estate by eating the forbidden fruit, and as the consequence of his disobedience the threatened penalty of death was then and there inflicted, so that his moral nature was not only grievously injured by the fall, but he totally lost all spiritual life, becoming dead in trespasses and sins, and subject to the power of the devil: Gen. 1:26; 2:17; John 5:40; 6:53; Eph. 2:1-3; 1 Tim. 5:6; 1 John 3:8.

IV. We believe that this spiritual death, or total corruption of human nature, has been transmitted to the entire race of man, the man Christ Jesus alone excepted; and hence that every child of Adam is born into the world with a nature which not only possesses no spark of Divine life, but is essentially and unchangeably bad, being in enmity against God, and incapable by any educational process whatever of subjection to His law: Gen. 6:5; Psa. 14:1-3; 51:5; Jer. 17:9; John 3:6; Rom. 5:12-19; 8:6, 7.

V. We believe that, owing to this universal depravity and death in sin, no one can enter the kingdom of God unless born again; and that no degree of reformation however great, no attainment in morality however high, no culture however attractive, no humanitarian and philanthropic schemes and societies however useful, no baptism or other ordinance however administered, can help the sinner to take even one step toward heaven; but a new nature imparted from above, a new life implanted by the Holy Ghost through the Word, is absolutely essential to salvation: Isa. 64:6; John 3:5, 18; Gal. 6:15; Phil. 3:4-9; Tit. 3:5; Jas. 1:18; 1 Pet. 1:23.

VI. We believe that our redemption has been accomplished solely by the blood of our Lord Jesus Christ, who was made to be sin, and made a curse, for us, dying in our room and stead; and that no repentance, no feeling, no faith, no good resolutions, no sincere efforts, no submission to the rules and regulations of any church, or of all the churches that have existed since the days of the Apostles, can add in the very least to the value of that precious blood, or to the merit of that finished work,

wrought for us by Him who united in His person true and proper divinity with perfect and sinless humanity: Lev. 17:11; Matt. 26:28; Rom. 5:6-9; 2 Cor. 5:21; Gal 3:13; Eph. 1:7; 1 Pet. 1:18, 19.

VII. We believe that Christ, in the fullness of the blessings He has secured by His obedience unto death, is received by faith alone, and that the moment we trust in Him as our Savior we pass out of death into everlasting life, being justified from all things, accepted before the Father according to the measure of His acceptance, loved as He is loved, and having His place and portion, as linked to Him, and one with Him forever: John 5:24; 17:23; Acts 13:39; Rom. 5:1; Eph. 2:4-6, 13; 1 John 4:17; 5:11, 12.

VIII. We believe that it is the privilege, not only of some, but of all who are born again by the Spirit through faith in Christ as revealed in the Scriptures, to be assured of their salvation from the very day they take Him to be their Savior; and that this assurance is not founded upon any fancied discovery of their own worthiness, but wholly upon the testimony of God in His written Word, exciting within His children filial love, gratitude, and obedience: Luke 10:20; 12:32; John 6:47; Rom. 8:33-39; 2 Cor. 5:1, 6-8; 2 Tim. 1:12; 1 John 5:13.

IX. We believe that all the Scriptures from first to last center about our Lord Jesus Christ, in His person and work, in His first and second coming; and hence that no chapter even of the Old Testament is properly read or understood until it leads to Him; and moreover that all the Scriptures from first to last, including every chapter even of the Old Testament, were designed for our practical instruction: Luke 24:27, 44; John 5:39; Acts 17:2, 3; 18:28; 26:22, 23; 28:23; Rom. 15:4; 1 Cor. 10:11.

X. We believe that the Church is composed of all who are united by the Holy Spirit to the risen and ascended Son of God, that by the same Spirit we are all baptized into one body, whether we be Jews or Gentiles, and thus being members one of another, we are responsible to keep the unity of the Spirit in the bond of peace, rising above all sectarian prejudices and denominational bigotry, and loving one another with a pure heart fervently: Matt. 16:16-18; Acts 2:32-47; Rom. 12:5; 1 Cor. 12:12-27; Eph. 1:20-23; 4:3-10; Col. 3:14, 15.

XI. We believe that the Holy Spirit, not as an influence, but as a Divine Person, the source and power of all acceptable worship and service, is our abiding Comforter and Helper, that He never takes His departure from the Church, nor from the feeblest of the saints, but is ever present to testify of Christ, seeking to occupy us with Him, and not with ourselves nor with our experiences: John 7:38, 39; 14:16, 17; 15:26; 16:13, 14; Acts 1:8; Rom. 8:9; Phil. 3:3.

XII. We believe that we are called with a holy calling to walk, not after the flesh, but after the Spirit, and so to live in the Spirit that we should not fulfill the lusts of the flesh; but the flesh being still in us to the end of our earthly

NIAGARA CREED (1878) (continued)

pilgrimage needs to be kept constantly in subjection to Christ, or it will surely manifest its presence to the dishonor of His name: Rom. 8:12, 13;13:14; Gal. 5:16-25; Eph. 4:22-24; Col. 3:1-10; 1 Pet. 1:14-16; 1 John 3:5-9.

XIII. We believe that the souls of those who have trusted in the Lord Jesus Christ for salvation do at death immediately pass into His presence, and there remain in conscious bliss until the resurrection of the body at His coming, when soul and body reunited shall be associated with Him forever in the glory; but the souls of unbelievers remain after death in conscious misery until-the final judgment of the great white throne at the close of the millennium, when soul and body reunited shall be cast into the lake of fire, not to be annihilated, but to be punished with everlasting destruction from the presence of the Lord, and from the glory of His power: luke 16:19-26; 23:43; 2 Cor. 5:8; Phil. 1:23; 2 Thess. 1:7-9; Jude 6, 7; Rev. 20:11-15.

XIV. We believe that the world will not be converted during the present dispensation, but is fast ripening for judgment, while there will be a fearful apostasy in the professing Christian body; and hence that the Lord Jesus will come in person to introduce the millennial age, when Israel shall be restored to their own land, and the earth shall be full of the knowledge of the Lord; and that this personal and premillennial advent is the blessed hope set before us in the Gospel for which we should be constantly looking: Luke 12:35-40; 17:26-30; 18:8; Acts 15:14-17; 2 Thess. 2:3-8; 2 Tim. 3:1-5, Tit. 2:11-15.

Notes: *In 1869, a group of conservative Protestant ministers, primarily Baptist, Congregationalist, and Presbyterian, began to meet annually. These meetings were later moved to Niagara Falls, Ontario, and became known as the "Niagara Conferences on Prophecy." Their concerns included the departure from traditional Protestant affirmation by many church leaders, and a discussion of the nature of biblical prophecy. Among the most important documents to come out the conferences was the 1878 Niagara Creed. It publicly announced the issues around which, a generation later, Fundamentalism would coalesce, including the verbal inspiration of the Bible, the Trinity, total human depravity, Jesus atoning work, the personality of the Holy Spirit, and the premillennial return of Christ to establish his thousand year reign.*

*   *   *

WHEATON DECLARATION (1966)

What urgency has prompted one thousand representatives and servants of the Church of our Lord Jesus Christ to convene this Congress on the Church's Worldwide Mission? What contemporary situation has compelled us to meet together to engage in serious study and consultation? What warrants the audacity that directs a comprehensive Declaration from ourselves to our constituencies, to fellow believers beyond our boundaries, and to a non-believing world? What challenges, what issues confronting Christians everywhere necessitate this kind of reaction and response?

In answer to these questions we make earnest and detailed reply. We are constrained to speak out of a love for Christ, a jealous regard for His glory in the Church, and a deep concern for man's eternal welfare. Indeed, our response to God's calling leaves no alternative. WE MUST SPEAK.

CERTAINTY IS NEEDED. . .

Many evangelical Christians are anxious and uneasy. Some are uncertain about the validity of biblical affirmations in this age of change. Why should we put heart, strength, and resources into the proclamation of Christ to every tribe, tongue, and nation of this burgeoning generation? This uncertainty demands that we make a Declaration to bring the biblical mission of the Church back into focus. WE MUST REITERATE OUR CERTAINTY.

COMMITMENT IS NEEDED. . .

Disturbing secular forces are at work in the hearts of Christians, eroding their commitment to Christ and His missionary purpose. We increasingly shrink from a "tough world growing tougher," turn deaf ears to appeals for costly advance, and rationalize: "Why not be content with past gains? After all, the Church is now worldwide. Let the younger churches finish the job." We need honest self-criticism and ruthless exposure of our heart attitudes in the light of Holy Scripture. Self-examination must be followed by application of the correctives. The situation demands deep renewal of our commitment to Christ's Lordship and willingness to pay any price and suffer, if need be, that this may be accomplished by the Holy Spirit in us and in His Church. WE MUST ISSUE AND HEED THIS CALL.

DISCERNMENT IS NEEDED. . .

Protestantism is afflicted with doctrinal uncertainty, theological novelties, and outright apostasy. Satan is active, sowing tares among the wheat, energizing false witnesses to propagate doubt and destroying true faith. Christians need the will and ability to "discern the spirits whether they be of God." The Church needs the courage to implement the New Testament disciplinary process to guard its purity, its peace, and its unity. God's people need the prophetic voice, calling for a separation from sin and error. WE MUST LIFT THAT VOICE.

HOPE IS NEEDED. . .

The world is in upheaval. Forces inimical to the Christian faith are growing stronger and more aggressive. Political movements, especially communism, call for the worship of collective man. They boast that man, unaided by any "god," will perfect society. They often lock step with ancient ethnic religions, resurgent and militant in outreach. Pseudo-Christian cults multiply and grow, feeding on man's innate desire for spiritual authority. A new challenge faces the Church loyal to biblical Christianity. What of the abiding sufficiency of Jesus Christ in this context of struggle and mounting hostility to His people? A declaration of hope is urgently needed. WE MUST PROCLAIM THAT HOPE.

CONFIDENCE IS NEEDED...

God is sovereign in our times. We believe in Him, in the progress of His gospel and in His triumph in history. We see abundant evidence of His gracious working in the Church and among the nations. We rejoice that we can speak of the Church's universality. We believe there are witnesses to Christ and His gospel in every nation, pointing to the certainty of God's ultimate triumph. "This gospel of the kingdom shall be preached in all the world for a witness unto all nations; and then shall the end come." (Matthew 24:14). The Scriptures emphatically declare that Christ will return when the gathering out of His true Church is completed. All human history shall be consummated in Him (Ephesians 1:10, Phillips). WE MUST AFFIRM THIS CONFIDENCE.

CONFESSION IS NEEDED...

Acknowledging our unworthiness, we address the worldwide household of faith, our brothers and sisters in Christ throughout the nations. Although we, like them, are the objects of God's grace, having been "washed . . . sanctified . . . justified in the name of the Lord Jesus, and by the Spirit of our God," we nonetheless feel the shortcomings of our service in the Church.

We have sinned grievously. We are guilty of an unscriptural isolation from the world that too often keeps us from honestly facing and coping with its concerns. In our Christian service we depend too much on promotion and publicity, too little on importunate prayer and the Holy Spirit. We frequently fail to communicate the gospel in a relevant, winsome fashion. We do not consistently develop Christians of outgoing evangelistic witness and high ethical concern. We ask our God and our brethren to forgive us.

But our confession must be more specific. When we make an honest, objective appraisal of our past ministry in the light of the Scriptures, we find that we have often failed:

To stress sufficiently the blessed hope of our Lord's return as an incentive to personal holiness and missionary passion.

To discern in any adequate fashion the strategic significance of the task of multiplying churches in receptive populations,

To trust fully the Holy Spirit's leadership in newly planted congregations, thereby perpetuating paternalism and provoking unnecessary tensions between national churches and missionary societies.

To apply Scriptural principles to such problems as racism, war, population explosion, poverty, family disintegration, social revolution, and communism.

To encourage that form of cooperation that would eliminate costly, inefficient duplication of administrative structures and increase the extent of our outreach.

These failures, which we recognize with contrition, require of us this objective appraisal, and an obedient response to the corrective authority of Scripture. WE MAKE THIS CONFESSION.

EVANGELICAL CONSENSUS IS NEEDED...

In addition to examining and rectifying our failures, we have an obligation to examine religious movements that challenge the uniqueness and finality of biblical Christianity. This Congress has been convened because of our concern for deeper insight and more balanced thinking about the peculiar threat they pose to our biblical faith.

The Roman Catholic Church, its outward stance and internal organization altered by Vatican II and its previous intolerance tempered by an apparent desire for open dialogue, requires our careful assessment and response.

Contemporary Protestant movements that boldly contend for the non-existence of the Gospel revealed by God, that propagate a neo-universalism denying eternal condemnation, that substitute inter-church reconciling service for aggressive evangelism, that blur the biblical distinction between "Church" and "Mission" between Romanism and Protestantism, and that create ecclesiastical organizations moving in the direction of a worldwide religious monopoly, likewise demand a careful assessment and response.

Pseudo-Christian cults that feed on man's innate desire for spiritual authority, in their intensive efforts to subvert the faith of untaught Christians and in their deceitful parading of themselves as the true followers of Christ, likewise demand a careful assessment and response.

Non-Christian religious systems, such as Islam, Hinduism, and Buddhism in their new missionary vigor, pose an oppressive threat to the growth of the Church and likewise demand careful assessment and response.

WE MUST DEFINE THIS CONSENSUS

OUR AUTHORITY...

In line with apostolic precedent, we appeal in the many issues that confront us to the Bible, the inspired, the only authoritative, inerrant Word of God. The Scriptures constitute our final rule of faith and practice. With the Apostle Paul, "we also believe, and therefore speak" (II Corinthians 4:13). Furthermore, the New Testament gives us the apostolic norm for balance between proclamation (kerygma) and service (diakonia). We ask only that those of like faith ponder our words in the light of Scripture, and thereby ascertain their truthfulness.

THE GOSPEL...

We regard as crucial the "evangelistic mandate." The gospel must be preached in our generation to the peoples of every tribe, tongue, and nation. This is the supreme task of the Church. We accept the New Testament description of "the gospel." By it we have entered into spiritual life. The gospel concerns the God-man, Jesus of Nazareth, who appeared in time and through whom God acted in a unique fashion. Though crucified and put to death, He was resurrected bodily by God's power. Christ died for us, shedding His blood as an atonement for our sins. In and through Him all men can be reconciled to God, made fit for His presence and His fellowship.

In Him has been made possible a new type of life, a Christ-centered, Christ-controlled life. Through the crucified and risen Lord Jesus Christ, we call every man, wherever he may be, to a change of heart toward God (repentance), personal faith in Jesus Christ as Savior, and surrender to His Lordship. The proclamation of this ''good news'' has at its heart the explicit imperative, ''Ye must be born again,'' (John 3:7). God says He will judge the world by His crucified, risen Son. We believe that if men are not born again they will be subject to eternal separation from a righteous, holy God. ''Except ye repent, ye shall all likewise perish'' (Luke 13:3).

WE NOW ADDRESS OURSELVES TO THOSE CRUCIAL ISSUES PARTICULARLY RELATED TO THE CHURCH'S WORLDWIDE MISSION IN OUR DAY . . .

MISSION—AND SYNCRETISM

The Underlying Issues

On this shrinking planet, with all human affairs moving toward an age of universality never previously witnessed, many voices call for a religion that has universal validity. The gospel of Jesus Christ is the message that has this validity. Syncretism, for our purposes, is the attempt to unite or reconcile biblically revealed Christian truth with the diverse or opposing tenets and practices of non-Christian religions or other systems of thought that deny it. Alarming are the deviant and heretical views within Christendom advocating a depersonalized theism acceptable to religions of East and West. Such syncretism denies the uniqueness and finality of Christian truth.

Since syncretism readily develops where the gospel is least understood and experienced, great clarity must be sought in presenting the uniqueness of Jesus Christ and the precise message of His saving work as revealed in the Bible. For effective, relevant communication of the gospel across cultural and religious barriers, we must first divest our presentation of those cultural accretions which are not pertinent to essential gospel truth. The truth should then be communicated in the context of the meaningful and pertinent linguistic and cultural terms of people that they may also come to a decisive understanding of the gospel.

We must resist syncretism in spite of any opposition we may encounter, and we must bear our testimony with humility and dignity.

The Witness of the Scriptures

The Old Testament prophets were unrelenting in their witness against the syncretistic practices of Israel. The New Testament apostles likewise combatted the syncretistic tendencies of their age, such as Gnosticism, in their defense of the gospel. Our dominant thrust is that the one and only true God has disclosed Himself in Jesus Christ, the incarnate Word, and in the Scriptures, the written Word. Biblical faith is unique because it

is revealed. To add to it or to change it is to pervert it. ''God, who . . . spake in time past unto the fathers by the prophets, hath in these last days spoken unto us by his Son. . .'' (Hebrews 1:1,2).

WE THEREFORE DECLARE

THAT, while seeking greater effectiveness in the communication of the Christian faith and acknowledging the uniqueness and finality of Jesus Christ, we will expose the dangers of syncretism.

THAT in the communication of our faith we must avoid unbiblical cultural accretions and emphases that may tend to obscure Christian truth.

THAT we will acquaint our total leadership more carefully with the religious beliefs and thought forms of the peoples among whom they live and serve, relative to syncretistic tendencies.

MISSION—AND NEO-UNIVERSALISM

The Underlying Issues

During the first nineteen centuries of the history of the Church, any teaching suggesting that all men ultimately would be redeemed was vigorously rejected as heretical. In our day, universalism is rapidly coming into the mainstream of teaching acceptable to some leading Protestant and Roman Catholic theologians. Many prominent church leaders increasingly champion this viewpoint. The new universalism is based upon a fragmented usage of Scripture, not on an exposition of the Scriptures in total wholeness and context.

The teaching of universalism, which we reject, states that, because Christ died for all, He will sovereignly and out of love bring all men to salvation. It proclaims the essential and final unity of the human race, which will never be broken-now or in the future-by God or by man. All mankind is ''reconciled''; those who have met Christ have an advantage above those who have not, but it is a difference in degree, not in principle. If men do not believe the gospel in this life-even if they reject it-their guilt and punishment will ultimately be removed. They are simply not conscious of the riches they possess.

The issue with universalism is not simply one of elevating human reason above the clear witness of the Scriptures and biblical Christianity. The whole mission of the Church is affected. The universalist merely proclaims a universal Lordship of Christ and summons men to acknowledge it in their lives. This can readily lead to syncretism and the eventual abandonment by the Church of its missionary calling. Christ is being betrayed by those calling themselves His friends.

The Witness of the Scriptures

We fervently accept the universal character of the claims of Scripture: God loves the world (John 3:16); Christ is the propitiation for the sins of the whole world (I John 2:2); all things have been reconciled to God through Christ (Colossians 1:20). God desires all men to be saved (I Timothy 2:4), and to unite all things in Christ (Ephesians 1: 9, 1 0) so that every knee should bow and every tongue confess His Lordship (Philippians 2: 10, 11), ''that God may be all in all'' (I Corinthians 15:28). Scripture, however, must explain Scripture. Christ taught eternal punishment as well as eternal life. He spoke of the cursed as well as the blessed (Matthew 25:34, 41, 46). Paul taught eternal destruction and exclusion from the presence of the Lord of all who obey not the gospel of our Lord Jesus (II Thessalonians 1:8, 9). Although God's claims are universal and His triumph will be universal, yet His saving grace is effective only in those who believe on Christ (John 1:12). There is a heaven and a hell; there are the saved and the lost. Scriptures gives us no other alternative; we must take seriously all it says of the wrath and judgments of the God and Father of our Lord Jesus Christ.

WE THEREFORE DECLARE

THAT we will, ourselves, be more forthright and thorough in our preaching and teaching of the testimony of the Bible on the awful reality of eternal loss through sin and unbelief.

THAT we shall encourage all evangelical theologians to intensify their exegetical study of the Scriptures relating to eternal punishment and the call to redemption and reconciliation.

THAT, since the mission of the Church inescapably commits us to proclaim the gospel which offers men the forgiveness of sins only through faith in Jesus Christ, our verbal witness to Him should accompany our service to the poor, the sick, the needy, and the oppressed.

THAT the repudiation of universalism obliges all evangelicals to preach the gospel to all men before they die in their sins. To fail to do this is to accept in practice what we deny in principle.

MISSION—AND PROSELYTISM

The Underlying Issues

The word ''proselytism'' means ''the making of a convert, especially to some religious sect, or to some opinion, system, or party.'' Recently the word has also been used as a charge against evangelistic effort, especially among those who are members of any denomination or other ecclesiastical body. In reaction to the dynamic witness of evangelicals, some religious groups and nationalistic forces have demanded that ''proselytism can and should be controlled.''

The proselytism that includes forced conversion or the use of unethical means (material and/or social) is contrary to the gospel of Christ and should be distinguished from that which is biblical and genuine.

The Witness of the Scriptures

Throughout the New Testament the apostles and other Christians ceaselessly proclaimed Christ and persuaded men to accept Him, renouncing their old religious allegiances and joining the Christian church (Acts 5:29; 8:4; 13:15-41; 18:4-11; 19:8). The Jews through whom the revelation of God was transmitted and the idol-worshipping Gentiles alike were exhorted to repent, believe, and be baptized; they then became members of a church.

WE THEREFORE DECLARE

THAT all followers of Christ must disciple their fellowmen. From this obligation there can be neither retreat nor compromise.

THAT we shall urge church and government leaders throughout the world to work for the inalienable right of full religious liberty everywhere. This means freedom to propagate and to change one's faith or church affiliation, as well as the freedom to worship God.

THAT we shall obey God rather than men in resisting the monopolistic tendencies both within and without Christendom that seek to stifle evangelical witness to Jesus Christ.

THAT we shall not use unbiblical, unethical methods of persuading people to change their religious allegiance. However, when we seek the conversion of unregenerate men, even though they may be attached to some church or other religion, we are fulfilling our biblical mandate.

MISSION—AND NEO-ROMANISM

The Underlying Issues

Some remarkable changes have taken place within the Roman Catholic Church that have introduced a new climate in its relations with Protestantism, Orthodoxy, Judaism, and the secular world. Differences that were once clearly etched have now become blurred. In this revolutionary age, churchmen increasingly call for Catholic and Protestant renewal in order to solve cooperatively the human problems of our era.

Vatican II has accelerated this desire for renewal. New emphases on biblical research have created formidable problems for Roman Catholic leaders.

Catholic Church authorities have never been so vocal in calling for an intensification of worldwide missionary activity. Many of their theologians display great interest in speculative universalism and existentialism. They also consider Protestants as ''separated brethren'' and desire friendly relations with them. And yet, whereas Roman Catholic practices may change, they say their dogmas are unchangeable. According to the Roman Catholic view, reunion of the churches must be on papal terms.

Though the Roman Catholic Church has a high view of Scripture, tradition continues to have a determinative authority. Its reform of the Mass is only a reform of the liturgy of the Mass. It has not abandoned any of its unbiblical dogmas concerning Mary, papal infallibility, etc.

The Witness of the Scriptures

The Word of God pronounces its own judgment upon the sacerdotalism and sacramentalism of the Roman Catholic Church. The Scriptures teach:

- The Bible as the infallible revelation from God (*sola scriptura*) (II Timothy 3:15-17)

- There is ''one mediator between God and men, the man Christ Jesus''(I Timothy 2:5)

- The finished work of Christ with no re-presentation of that sacrifice (Hebrews 10:14)

- Justification by faith alone, apart from works (*sola fide*) (Romans 1:17; 3:20-26)

- The universal priesthood of all believers (I Peter 2:5, 9; Hebrews 10:19-22)

- Mary herself needed a Savior (Luke 1:46-48)

- In the celebration of the Lord's Supper the elements remain, in form and essence, bread and wine (I Corinthians 11:25, 26 with I Corinthians 10:17)

- Jesus Christ is the only Head of the Body which is His Church (Ephesians 1:20-23)

WE THEREFORE DECLARE

THAT we rejoice in the wider use of the Scriptures among Roman Catholics.

THAT we shall pray that all those who study the Scriptures may be led by the Holy Spirit to saving faith in Christ.

THAT we shall urge evangelicals to seize today's unique opportunities for witness among Roman Catholics.

THAT we recognize the danger of regarding the Roman Catholic Church as "our great sister Church," even as we reaffirm the abiding validity of the Scriptural principles of the Reformers, that salvation is through faith in Christ alone and that the Bible is the only rule of faith and practice.

MISSION-AND CHURCH GROWTH

The Underlying Issues

The Church's work is to preach the gospel and plant congregations in every community. The implementation of this mission is being retarded by:

- Too little sensitivity to the authority and strategy of the Holy Spirit

- Too much missionary control

- Too much dependence on paid workers

- Too little training and use of the great body of laymen

- Complacency with small results long after a larger response could have been the norm

- Failure to take full advantage of the response of receptive peoples

- Over emphasis on institutionalism at the expense of multiplying churches

In today's world vast untouched areas are still to be found near existing churches. Huge sections of cities containing but a few congregations are increasingly responsive to the gospel. It is God's will that churches be multiplied. Thus the missionary still has an essential place in the dynamism of church growth even as he continues to exercise a spiritual ministry in the churches already established. But his particular ministry will be in the vanguard of planting new congregations.

The Witness of the Scriptures

In the Acts of the Apostles local congregations were God's primary agents for the widespread dissemination of the gospel. The total mobilization of the people and resources of the churches in effective, continuous evangelistic outreach is indispensable to the evangelization of the world (Acts 17:1-4 with I Thessalonians 1:8, 9; Ephesians 4:16). Church planting has the priority among all other missionary activities, necessary and helpful though they may be.

Apostolic procedures point to a confidence in the local church under the control of the Holy Spirit (Acts 14:23; Romans 15:14). True, on occasion, local churches experienced spiritual failure, but despite such setbacks the church moved on and outward. From the beginning the churches governed, supported, and reproduced themselves (Acts 19:10, 20).

WE THEREFORE DECLARE

THAT we reaffirm our confidence in and dependence on the Holy Spirit and call on the church to pray for that revival which is indispensable for its growth and outreach.

THAT we call upon all churches, mission societies, and training institutions to study diligently the nature, ministry, and growth of the church as set forth in the Scriptures.

THAT we urge that research be carried on by nationals and missionaries in all parts of the world to learn why churches are or are not growing and make such knowledge available.

THAT we urge the missionary enterprise to evaluate church growth opportunities now overlooked and to review the role, methods, and expenditures of our agencies in the light of their significance to evangelism and church growth.

THAT we should devote special attention to those people who are unusually responsive to the gospel and will reinforce those fields with many laborers.

THAT we must pray earnestly that the Holy Spirit will bring the less responsive fields to early harvest. We will not leave them untended.

MISSION—AND FOREIGN MISSIONS

The Underlying Issues

In this day of unprecedented missionary activity, urgent questions are being asked. What is the role of the missionary? What is his relation to the national church? Is his allegiance primarily to the church that sent him or to the newly established national church with which he serves? Who is to administer funds coming from the sending churches? How should such funds be used? Should the churches be fully self-supporting? Should church and mission organizations remain separate and distinct, or should the latter lose their identity? The issue is whether missionary service as presently conducted is in accord with Scripture.

Currently many claim it is impossible to maintain on biblical grounds the concept of the missionary society as a sending agency distinct from any national organization of churches on the field. Such thinking tends to obliterate the distinctive ministry of "foreign missionary." This kind of emphasis may diminish interest in missionary vocation on the part of Christian youth.

The Witness of the Scriptures

In obedience to the Great Commission, the Church has the continuing responsibility to send missionaries into all the world (Matthew 28:18-20; Acts 13:1-4).

The New Testament says many went forth according to our Lord's command. As a result believers were added to the Body of Christ. (Acts 8:12; 11:21, 24). New converts were gathered into congregations where they found fellowship and grew in grace (Acts 2:42; 9:31).

God gave to the churches apostles, prophets, evangelists, and teaching pastors (Ephesians 4:11). The apostles founded churches; they taught and functioned as advisors in the selection of local leadership (Titus 1:5) ; they strengthened and exhorted the churches (Acts 14:22; 15:41) ; they charged leaders with specific responsibilities of office (I Timothy 1:18: 3: 1-14) ; they also gave guidance in matters of discipline and doctrine (I Corinthians; Acts 15). The Holy Spirit works similarly through missionaries today.

In the New Testament no clearly defined structure for church-mission relationships can be adduced.

WE THEREFORE DECLARE

THAT we encourage church and mission leaders to define the role and to enlarge the vision of those called to pastoral or missionary service.

THAT the proper relationship between churches and missions can only be realized in a cooperative partnership in order to fulfill the mission of the Church to evangelize the world in this generation.

THAT the mission society exists to evangelize, to multiply churches, and to strengthen the existing churches. Therefore we recognize a continuing distinction between the church established on the field and the missionary agency.

MISSION—AND EVANGELICAL UNITY

The Underlying Issues

The unity of the Church of Jesus Christ is directly and significantly related to her worldwide mission. Our Lord's earnest petition to the Father on behalf of His Church (John 17) was for her essential spiritual unity and its visible expression in the world. His concern "that they all may be one" was in order "that the world may know that thou hast sent me."

Today many voices call for organizational church union at the expense of doctrine and practice (faith and order). Denominational divisions are seen as the great "scandal" of our day. Union becomes a major objective. However, organizational

church union of itself has seldom released a fresh missionary dynamism or an upsurge of missionary recruitment.

Christians having been regenerated by the Holy Spirit and who agree on the basic evangelical doctrines can experience a genuine biblical oneness, even if they belong to different denominations. Such biblical oneness cannot exist among those who have not been regenerated or among those who disagree on the basic evangelical doctrines, even if they belong to the same denomination. Evangelicals, however, have not fully manifested this biblical oneness because of carnal differences and personal grievances; and thus missionary advance and the fulfillment of the Great Commission have been hindered.

The Witness of the Scriptures

Concerning the nature of the unity of the Church we learn from Scripture:

* It is a unity given by God, to be preserved (John 17:21; Ephesians 4:3-6)

* It is a unity of essence, a new regenerate society whose individual members have been given a new nature—life in the Spirit (John 3:6; I Corinthians 12:13; II Corinthians 5:17; II Peter 1:4)

* It is a unity of belief, centered in the Person and work of Jesus Christ (I Corinthians 15:1-4 with Galatians 1:8; Ephesians 4:12-16; Colossians 1:27-20)

* It is a unity intrinsic to the fulfillment of God's missionary purpose for the world (John 17:20, 21, 23; Ephesians 4:16; Philippians 1:27)

WE THEREFORE DECLARE

THAT we are one in Christ Jesus, members of His Body, born again of His Holy Spirit, although we may be diverse in our structured relationships.

THAT we will endeavor to keep the unity of the Spirit in the bond of peace so that the world may believe.

THAT we will encourage and assist in the organization of evangelical fellowships among churches and missionary societies at national, regional, and international levels.

THAT we will encourage evangelical mission mergers when such will eliminate duplication of administration, produce more efficient stewardship of personnel and resources, and strengthen their ministries.

THAT we caution evangelicals to avoid establishing new churches or organizations where existing groups of like precious faith satisfactorily fill the role.

MISSION—AND EVALUATING METHODS

The Underlying Issues

A new age of intellectual advance has brought with it radical changes that require a new appraisal of missionary methodology. We are faced with new masses of humanity, we have developed new means of mass communication, we have been caught up in the maelstrom of new learning in the social sciences, and we sense man's frightening estrangement from God, himself, and society.

Churches and missions have been influenced by this ferment. Some have profited greatly from the insights of psychology, anthropology, sociology, and business management. Others regard the use of such insights as a wrong invasion of the religious by the secular. They question evaluating personal and organizational activity in the light of such procedures.

The best results come when, under the Holy Spirit, good principles of communication are combined with clear understanding of cultural and social patterns and applied to the proclamation of the Gospel. The great danger arises when there is an overdependence on techniques and learning that minimizes or leaves out the Holy Spirit.

Missionary methodology cannot be evaluated only in terms of anthropological and sociological relevance. Two realms are involved: the Church, as it reflects the holiness and redemptive purpose of God; and culture, as it reflects finite and sinful man. Hence, while the social sciences afford considerable insights for missionary methods, yet these must be subjected to the corrective judgment of Scripture.

The Witness of the Scriptures

Christ left us His example of evaluating one's life and service (John 17). His disciples knew themselves to be God's men, doing God's work in God's way; and they called on Christians to follow their example (I Corinthians 4:17; 11:1; Philippians 3:17; II Timothy 1:8, 13, 2:2, 7; 3:10-15). Their communication of the gospel was culturally relevant among Jews, barbarians, and intellectual Greeks (Acts 13:14-43; 14:8-18; 17:22-31; I Corinthians 9:19-23).

The Scriptures approve organization and the delegation of authority (Acts 6:2-4). They do not detail methods of organization and ministry, but they emphasize our dependence upon the Holy Spirit to produce spiritual results in the lives of people (I Corinthians 2:1-5).

Christ thoroughly instructed and trained His disciples in personal conduct and in methods of evangelism. He also taught them their need of the Holy Spirit's ministry (Luke 24:49; John 15:5, 26, 27; 16:7-15).

WE THEREFORE DECLARE

THAT we acknowledge our utter dependence upon the Holy Spirit in every aspect of our missionary calling.

THAT God's primary method for evangelism and church planting is the ministry of Spirit-gifted and empowered men and women preaching and teaching the Word of God.

THAT we will engage in periodic self-criticism in the light of the Scriptures and contemporary insights and seek more effective ways to attain our objectives.

THAT we urge extensive reading and research in the field of cross-cultural communication in order to propagate the gospel better.

THAT we will make the best use of all means for communicating the gospel, carefully guarding ourselves against overdependence upon mass media at the expense of personal witness.

THAT we encourage all missionaries and candidates to study in such areas as mass communication, anthropology, and sociology, while recognizing the priority of Bible knowledge and spiritual preparation.

THAT we will seek more effective means to evangelize and bring to spiritual maturity the masses of youth in the world today.

THAT we need to improve our missionary recruiting techniques, upgrade missionary educational preparation, and reduce our drop-out rates.

MISSION—AND SOCIAL CONCERN

The Underlying Issues

Whereas evangelicals in the eighteenth and nineteenth centuries led in social concern, in the twentieth century many have lost the biblical perspective and limited themselves *only* to preaching a gospel of individual salvation without sufficient involvement in their social and community responsibilities.

When theological liberalism and humanism invaded historic Protestant churches and proclaimed a ''social gospel,'' the conviction grew among evangelicals that an antithesis existed between social involvement and gospel witness.

Today, however, evangelicals are increasingly convinced that they must involve themselves in the great social problems men are facing. They are concerned for the needs of the whole man, because of their Lord's example, His constraining love, their identity with the human race, and the challenge of their evangelical heritage.

Evangelicals look to the Scriptures for guidance as to what they should do and how far they should go in expressing this social concern, without minimizing the priority of preaching the gospel of individual salvation.

The Witness of the Scriptures

The Old Testament manifests God's concern for social justice (Micah 6:8). Our Lord, by precept and example, stressed the importance of ministering to the physical and social, as well as spiritual needs of men (Matthew 5-9). His dealings with the Samaritans involved Him in racial and social issues (Luke 9:51-56; John 4:1-30; Luke 10:25-37).

His disciples followed His example (Galatians 2:10; Colossians 3:11; James 1:27;2:9-11). They taught and respected the role of government in promoting civil justice (Romans 13 and I Peter 2). The two great commandments are: ''Love the Lord thy God . . . and thy neighbor as thyself'' (Mark 12:29-31).

WE THEREFORE DECLARE

THAT we reaffirm unreservedly the primacy of preaching the gospel to every creature, and we will demonstrate anew God's concern for social justice and human welfare.

THAT evangelical social action will include, wherever possible, a verbal witness to Jesus Christ.

THAT evangelical social action must avoid wasteful and unnecessary competition.

THAT when Christian institutions no longer fulfill their distinctively evangelical functions they should be relinquished.

THAT we urge all evangelicals to stand openly and firmly for racial equality, human freedom, and all forms of social justice throughout the world.

MISSION—AND A HOSTILE WORLD

The Underlying Issues

The world is hostile to the Church because it is hostile to God. His Church is at war, not at rest. True to the prophecy of the Lord, the faithful Church has always experienced hostility.

In our age, however, this hostility has been intensified by the rise of atheistic communism, extreme nationalism, resurgent ethnic religions, secularism, and corrupted forms of Christianity. The ultimate source of hostility is the ''Prince of this world.'' He has even infiltrated some churches, whose apathy, indifference, selfishness, and failure to fulfill their mission disclose only too well Satan's opposition.

The Church is often rent asunder. Suffering defeat, crowded and buffeted, it seeks to understand the paradox of the promise of the Lord that the gates of hell shall not prevail against it. However, we need not despair of the Church for we believe in its final triumph.

The Witness of the Scriptures

Christ witnessed to the personality, purpose and power of Satan (Matthew 4:1-11; Luke 8:12; 11: 1:4-26). The apostles recognized Satan's ceaseless opposition to the propagation of the gospel and the growth of the Church (Ephesians 6:10-18; II Corinthians 4:4; I Thessalonians 2:18).

Satan's strategy is varied (II Corinthians 2:11), subtle (II Corinthians 11:3, 4), and relentless (I Peter 5:8). He inspires false christs (Matthew 24:5), false preachers (II Corinthians 11: 13:15), false prophets and teachers (II Peter 2:1-3), and false doctrines (I Timothy 4:1-3).

Christians are called to follow Christ, to believe and to suffer, to witness and to bear the cross (John 20:21; Philippians 1:29; Luke 9:23-26). In love for God and man, they suffer to effect the calling out and perfection of the Church (Colossians 1:24). Faithful Christians strive together in persevering prayer (Acts 4:24-31).

WE THEREFORE DECLARE

THAT we reaffirm our trust in the sovereign God, His triumph in history, and the victory of His Church.

THAT we will seek to recognize Satan's devices in the light of Scripture and resist him in the power of the Holy Spirit and on the basis of the finished work of Christ.

THAT we should meet persecution by obeying the Lord's command to love our enemies, bless those who curse us, do good to those who hate us, and pray for those who despitefully use us.

THAT our supreme loyalty is to Jesus Christ and all of our racial, cultural, social, and national loyalties are to be in subjection to Him. We will particularly encourage all Christian workers in churches and missions to discern and remove the tensions among themselves.

THAT we are deeply moved by the courageous witness of suffering Christians in many lands; that we will sustain them more faithfully by prayer; and that we will trust God for grace, should we be called upon to suffer for His sake.

THAT we call all believers to persistent prayer in the Spirit, believing that prayer and the proclamation of the gospel are the weapons of our warfare.

IN THE SUPPORT OF THIS DECLARATION

WE

the delegates here assembled in adoration of the Triune God, with full confidence in Holy Scripture, in submission to the Lord Jesus Christ, and looking for His coming again,

DO COVENANT TOGETHER.

for God's eternal glory, and in response to the Holy Spirit, with renewed dedication, and in our oneness in Christ as the people of God,

TO SEEK

under the leadership of our Head, with full assurance of His power and presence,

THE MOBILIZATION OF THE CHURCH

its people, its prayers, and resources,

FOR THE EVANGELIZATION OF THE WORLD IN THIS GENERATION

so, help us God!
AMEN.

Notes: *Following the establishment of the Evangelical Movement among a broad range of conservative Protestant believers from many denominations, conferences were periodically called to offer direction to the rather diverse movement. Among the early conferences was the meeting of the Congress on the Church's Worldwide Mission, which met in Wheaton, Illinois, from April 9 to 16, 1966, and was attended by over 1,000 delegates. The Congress released a lengthy document responding to what the delegates saw as major challenges to the Church's progress. While the forces of secularization remained a major concern, the challenges of what would eventually be called ''pluralism'' took center stage.*

WHEATON DECLARATION (1966) (continued)

The Congress called for an Evangelical consensus in response to selected competing religious movements—especially Roman Catholicism, liberal Protestantism, cults, and the major non-Christian religious traditions. Judaism was noticeably missing from the list. Specific issues included the aggressive worldwide missionary efforts of Roman Catholics, and the tendencies to seek a universalist religion, and to relinquish the missionary task to the indigenous churches established in foreign countries by liberal Protestants. In response, the conference reaffirmed the essentials of Evangelical faith, and called on Evangelicals to renew their commitment to the missionary task and to support it with study, the use of the best contemporary means for communicating with the masses, and develop missionary educational efforts.

The Wheaton Declaration raised the issue of social concern, the major agenda for liberal Protestants, and the item that would find the least response among Evangelicals. Finally, running through the document was the experience of the Cold War and the necessity to fight Communism.

*   *   *

THE CHICAGO DECLARATION ON SOCIAL CONCERN (1973)

As evangelical Christians committed to the Lord Jesus Christ and the full authority of the Word of God, we affirm that God lays total claim upon the lives of his people. We cannot, therefore, separate our lives in Christ from the situation in which God has placed us in the United States and the world.

We confess that we have not acknowledged the complete claims of God on our lives.

We acknowledge that God requires love. But we have not demonstrated the love of God to those suffering social abuses.

We acknowledge that God requires justice. But we have not proclaimed or demonstrated his justice to an unjust American society. Although the Lord calls us to defend the social and economic rights of the poor and the oppressed, we have mostly remained silent. We deplore the historic involvement of the church in America with racism and the conspicuous responsibility of the evangelical community for perpetuating the personal attitudes and institutional structures that have divided the body of Christ along color lines. Further, we have failed to condemn the exploitation of racism at home and abroad by our economic system.

We affirm that God abounds in mercy and that he forgives all who repent and turn from their sins. So we call our fellow evangelical Christians to demonstrate repentance in a Christian discipleship that confronts the social and political injustice of our nation.

We must attack the materialism of our culture and the maldistribution of the nation's wealth and services. We recognize that as a nation we play a crucial role in the imbalance and injustice of international trade and development. Before God and a billion hungry neighbors, we must rethink our values regarding our present standard of living and promote more just acquisition and distribution of the world's resources.

We acknowledge our Christian responsibilities of citizenship. Therefore, we must challenge the misplaced trust of the nation in economic and military might—a proud trust that promotes a national pathology of war and violence which victimizes our neighbors at home and abroad. We must resist the temptation to make the nation and its institutions objects of near-religious loyalty.

We acknowledge that we have encouraged men to prideful domination and women to irresponsible passivity. So we call both men and women to mutual submission and active discipleship.

We proclaim no new gospel, but the gospel of our Lord Jesus Christ, who, through the power of the Holy Spirit, frees people from sin so that they might praise God through works of righteousness.

By this declaration, we endorse no political ideology or party, but call our nation's leaders and people to that righteousness which exalts a nation.

We make this declaration in the biblical hope that Christ is coming to consummate the Kingdom and we accept his claim on our total discipleship till he comes.

Notes: *In November 1973, a group of Evangelical leaders gathered in Chicago to face the charge that Evangelicals had so prioritized evangelism that they had neglected their own heritage of social concern. The final product is somewhat like the Evangelism Today document produced by the National Council of Churches in 1967 that also attempted to redress liberal Protestantism's neglect of evangelism.*

The Chicago Declaration called on Evangelicals to affirm God's claim over all of life and to become socially active especially in defending the rights of the poor and oppressed and eradicating the structures that perpetuate racism. It also raised the issue of the redistribution of wealth and the need to challenge the trust often placed in the West's military and economic power.

While the Chicago Declaration was respectfully received by the Evangelical community, and some Evangelical leaders have prioritized social concerns, social issues remain a sec-

ondary agenda for the Evangelical Movement with the exception of activism on the issues of temperance and abortion.

* * *

THE LAUSANNE COVENANT (1974)

INTRODUCTION

We, members of the Church of Jesus Christ, from more than 150 nations, participants in the International Congress on World Evangelization at Lausanne, praise God for his great salvation and rejoice in the fellowship he has given us with himself and with each other. We are deeply stirred by what God is doing in our day, moved to penitence by our failures and challenged by the unfinished task of evangelization. We believe the gospel is God's good news for the whole world, and we are determined by his grace to obey Christ's commission to proclaim it to all mankind and to make disciples of every nation. We desire, therefore, to affirm our faith and our resolve, and to make public our covenant.

1. THE PURPOSE OF GOD

We affirm our belief in the one-eternal God, Creator and Lord of the world, Father, Son and Holy Spirit, who governs all things according to the purpose of his will. He has been calling out from the world a people for himself, and sending his people back into the world to be his servants and his witnesses, for he extension of his kingdom, the building up of Christ's body and the glory of his name. We confess with shame that we have often denied our calling and failed in our mission, by becoming conformed to he world or by withdrawing from it. Yet we rejoice that even when borne by earthen vessels the gospel is still a precious treasure. To the task of making that treasure known in the power of the Holy Spirit we desire to dedicate ourselves anew.

(Isa. 40:28; Matt. 28:19; Eph. 1:11; Acts 15:14; John 17:6, 18; Eph. 4:12; I Cor. 5:10; Rom. 12:2; II Cor. 4:7)

2. THE AUTHORITY AND POWER OF THE BIBLE

We affirm the divine inspiration, truthfulness and authority of both Old and New Testament Scriptures in their entirety as the only written word of God, without error in all that it affirms, and the only infallible rule of faith and practice. We also affirm the power of God's word to accomplish his purpose of salvation. The message of the Bible is addressed to all mankind. For God's revelation in Christ and in Scripture is unchangeable. Through it the Holy Spirit still speaks today. He illumines he minds of God's people in every culture to perceive its truth freshly through their own eyes and thus discloses to the whole church ever more of the many-colored wisdom of God.

(II Tim. 3:16; II Pet. 1:21; John 10:35; Isa. 55:11; I Cor. 1:21; Rom. 1:16; Matt. 5:17,18; Jude 3; Eph. 1:17,18; 3:10,18)

3. THE UNIQUENESS AND UNIVERSALITY OF CHRIST

We affirm that there is only one Savior and only one gospel, although there is a wide diversity of evangelistic approaches. We recognize that all men have some knowledge of God through his general revelation in nature. But we deny that this can save, for men suppress the truth by their unrighteousness. We also reject as derogatory to Christ and the gospel every kind of syncretism and dialogue which implies that Christ speaks equally through all religions and ideologies. Jesus Christ, being himself the only God-man, who gave himself as the only ransom for sinners, is the only mediator between God and man. There is no other name by which we must be saved. All men are perishing because of sin, but God loves all men, not wishing that any should perish but shall all should repent. Yet those who reject Christ repudiate the joy of salvation and condemn themselves to eternal separation from God. To proclaim Jesus as "the Savior of the world" is not to affirm that all men are either automatically or ultimately saved, still less to affirm that all religions offer salvation in Christ. Rather it is to proclaim God's love for a world of sinners and to invite all men to respond to him as Savior and Lord in the whole-hearted personal commitment of repentance and faith. Jesus Christ has been exalted above every other name; we long for the day when every knee shall bow to him and every tongue shall confess him Lord.

(Gal. 1:6-9; Rom. 1:18-32; I Tim 2:5,6; Acts 4:12; John 3:16-19; II Pet. 3:9; II Thess. 1:7-9; John 4:42; Matt. 11:28; Eph. 1:20,21; Phil. 2:9-11)

4. THE NATURE OF EVANGELISM

To evangelize is to spread the good news of that Jesus Christ died for our sins and was raised from the dead according to the Scriptures, and that as the reigning Lord he now offers the forgiveness of sins and the liberating gift of the Spirit to all who repent and believe. Our Christian presence in the world is indispensable to evangelism, and so is that kind of dialogue whose purpose is to listen sensitively in order to understand. But evangelism itself is the proclamation of the historical, biblical Christ as Savior and Lord, with a view to persuading people to come to him personally and so be reconciled to God. In issuing the gospel invitation we have no liberty to conceal the cost of discipleship. Jesus still calls all who would follow him to deny themselves, take up their cross, and identify themselves with his new community. The results of evangelism include obedience to Christ, incorporation into his church and responsible service in the world.

(I Cor. 15:3,4; Acts 2:32-39; John 20:21; I Cor. 1:23; II Cor. 4:5; 5:11,20; Luke 14:25-33; Mark 8:34; Acts 2:40,47; Mark 10:43-45)

5. CHRISTIAN SOCIAL RESPONSIBILITY

We affirm that God is both the Creator and the Judge of all men. We therefore should share his concern for justice and reconciliation throughout human society and for the liberation of men from every kind of oppression. Because mankind is made in the image of God, every person, regardless of race, religion, colour, culture, class, sex or age, has an intrinsic dignity because of which he should be respected and served, not exploited. Here too we express penitence both for our neglect and for having sometimes regarded evangelism and social concern as mutually exclusive. Although reconciliation with man is not reconciliation with God, nor is social action evangelism, nor is political liberation salvation. Nevertheless, we affirm that evangelism and socio-political involvement are both part of our Christian duty. For both are necessary expressions of our doctrines of God and man, our love for our neighbor and our obedience to Jesus Christ. The message of salvation implies also a message of judgement upon every form of alienation, oppression and discrimination, and we should not be afraid to denounce evil and injustice wherever they exist. When people receive Christ they are born again into his kingdom and must seek not only to exhibit but also to spread its righteousness in the midst of an unrighteousness world. The salvation we claim should be transforming us in the totality of our personal and social responsibilities. Faith without works is dead.

(Acts 17;26,31 Gen. 18;25; Isa. 1:17; Psa. 45:7; Gen. 1:26,27; Jas. 3:9; Lev. 19:18; Luke 6:27,35; Jas. 2:14-26; John 3:3,5; Matt. 5:20; 6:33; II Cor. 3:18; Jas. 2:20)

6. THE CHURCH AND THE EVANGELISM

We affirm that Christ sends his redeemed people into the world as the Father sent him, and that this calls for a similar deep and costly penetration of the world. We need to break out of our ecclesiastical ghettos and permeate non-Christian society. In the church's mission of sacrificial service evangelism is primary. World evangelization requires the whole church to take the whole gospel to the whole world. The church is at the very center of God's cosmic purpose and is his appointed means of spreading the gospel. But a church which preaches the cross must itself be marked by the cross. It becomes a stumbling block to evangelism when it betrays the gospel or lacks a living faith in God, a genuine love for people, or scrupulous honesty in all things including promotion and finance. The church is the community of God's people rather than an institution, and must not be identified with any particular culture, social or political system, or human ideology.

(John 17:18; 20:21; Matt. 28:19,20; Acts 1:8; 20:27; Eph. 1:9,10; 3:9-11; Gal. 6:14,17; II Cor. 6:3,4; II Tim. 2:19-21; Phil. 1:27)

7. COOPERATION IN EVANGELISM

We affirm that the church's visible unity in truth is God's purpose. Evangelism also summons us to unity, because our oneness strengthens our witness, just as our disunity undermines our gospel of reconciliation. We recognize, however, that organizational unity may take many forms and does not necessarily forward evangelism. Yet we who share the same biblical faith should be closely united in fellowship, work and witness. We confess that our testimony has sometimes been marred by sinful individualism and needless duplication. We pledge ourselves to seek a deeper unity in truth, worship, holiness and mission. We urge the development of regional and functional cooperation for the furtherance of the church's

mission, for strategic planning, for mutual encouragement, and for the sharing of resources and experience.

(John 17:21,23; Eph. 4:3,4; John 13:35; Phil. 1:27; John 17:11-23)

8. CHURCHES IN EVANGELISTIC PARTNERSHIP

We rejoice that a new missionary era has dawned. The dominant role of western missions is fast disappearing. God is raising up from the younger churches a great new resource for world evangelization, and is thus demonstrating that the responsibility to evangelize belongs to the whole body of Christ. All churches should therefore be asking God and themselves what they should be doing both to reach their own area and to send missionaries to other parts of the world. A re-evaluation of our missionary responsibility and role should be continuous. Thus a growing partnership of churches will develop and the universal character of Christ's church will be more clearly exhibited. We also thank God for agencies which labor in Bible translation, theological education, the mass media, Christian literature, evangelism, missions, church renewal and other specialist fields. They too should engage in constant self-examination to evaluate their effectiveness as part of the Church's mission.

(Rom. 1:8; Phil. 1:5; 4:15; Acts 13:1-3: I Thess. 1:6-8)

9. THE URGENCY OF THE EVANGELISTIC TASK

More than 2,700 million people, which is more than two-thirds of mankind, have yet to be evangelized. We are ashamed that so many have been neglected; it is a standing rebuke to us and to the whole church. There is now, however, in many parts of the world an unprecedented receptivity to the Lord Jesus Christ. We are convinced that this is the time for churches and para-church agencies to pray earnestly for the salvation of the unreached and to launch new efforts to achieve world evangelization. A reduction of foreign missionaries and money in an evangelized country may sometimes be necessary to facilitate the national church's growth in self-reliance and to release resources for unevangelized areas. Missionaries should flow ever more freely from and to all six continents in a spirit of humble service. The goal should be, by all available means and at the earliest possible time, that every person will have the opportunity to hear, understand, and receive the good news. We cannot hope to attain this goal without sacrifice. All of us are shocked by the poverty of millions and disturbed by the injustices which cause it. Those of us who live in affluent circumstances accept our duty to develop a simple life-style in order to contribute more generously to both relief and evangelism.

(John 9:4; Matt. 9:35-38; Rom. 9:1-3; I Cor. 9:19-23; Mark 16:15; Isa. 58:6,7; Jas. 1:27; 2:1-9; Matt. 25:31-46; Acts 2:44,45; 4:34,35)

10. EVANGELISM AND CULTURE

The development of strategies for world evangelization calls for imaginative pioneering methods. Under God, the result will be the rise of churches deeply rooted in Christ and closely related to their culture. Culture must always be tested and judged by Scripture. Because man is God's creature, some of his culture is rich in beauty and goodness. Because he is fallen, all of it is tainted with sin and some of it is demonic. The gospel does not presuppose the superiority of any culture to another, but evaluates all cultures according to its own criteria of truth and righteousness, and insists on moral absolutes in every culture. Missions have all too frequently exported with the gospel an alien culture, and churches have sometimes been in bondage to culture rather than to the Scripture. Christ's evangelists must humbly seek to empty themselves of all but their personal authenticity in order to become the servants of others, and churches must seek to transform and enrich culture, all for the glory of God.

(Mark 7:8,9,13; Gen. 4:21,22; I Cor. 9:19-23; Phil. 2:5-7; II Cor. 4:5)

11. EDUCATION AND LEADERSHIP

We confess that we have sometimes pursued church growth at the expense of church depth, and divorced evangelism from Christian nurture. We also acknowledge that some of our missions have been too slow to equip and encourage national leaders to assume their rightful responsibilities. Yet we are committed to indigenous principles, and long that every church will have national leaders who manifest a Christian style of leadership in terms not of domination but of service. We recognize that there is a great need to improve theological education, especially for church leaders. In every nation and culture there should be an effective training program for pastors and laymen in doctrine, discipleship, evangelism, nurture and service. Such training programmes should not rely on any stereotyped methodology but should be developed by creative local initiatives according to biblical standards.

(Col. 1:27,28; Acts 14:23; Tit. 1:5,9; Mark 10:42-45; Eph. 4:11,12)

12. SPIRITUAL CONFLICT

We believe that we are engaged in constant spiritual warfare with the principalities and powers of evil, who are seeking to overthrow the church and frustrate its task of world evangelization. We know our need to equip ourselves with God's armour and to fight this battle with the spiritual weapons of truth and prayer. For we detect the activity of our enemy, not only in false ideologies outside the church, but also inside it in false gospels which twist Scripture and put man in the place of God. We need both watchfulness and discernment to safeguard the biblical gospel. We acknowledge that we ourselves are not immune to worldliness of thought and action, that is, to a surrender to secularism. For example, although careful studies of church growth, both numerical and spiritual, are right and valuable, we have sometimes neglected them. At other times, desirous to ensure a response to the gospel, we have compromised our message manipulated our hearers through pressure techniques, and become unduly preoccupied with statistics or even dishonest in our use of them. All this is worldly. The church must be in the world; the world must not be in the church.

(Eph. 6:12; II Cor. 4:3,4; Eph. 6:11,13-18, II Cor. 10:3-5; I John 2:18-26; 4:1-3; Gal. 1:6-9; II Cor. 2:17; 4:2; John 17:15)

13. FREEDOM AND PERSECUTION

It is the God-appointed duty of every government to secure conditions of peace, justice and liberty in which the church may obey God, serve the Lord Christ, and preach the gospel without interference. We therefore pray for the leaders of the nations and call upon them to guarantee freedom of thought and conscience, and freedom to practice and propagate religion in accordance with the will of God and as set forth in The Universal Declaration of Human Rights. We also express our deep concern for all who have been unjustly imprisoned, and especially for our brethren who are suffering for their testimony to the Lord Jesus. We promise to pray and work for their freedom. At the same time we refuse to be intimidated by their fate. God helping us, we too will seek to stand against injustice and to remain faithful to the gospel, whatever the cost. We do not forget the warnings of Jesus that persecution is inevitable.

(I Tim. 1:1-4; Acts 4:19; 5:29; Col 3:24; Heb. 13:1-3; Luke 4:18; Gal. 5:11; 6:12; Matt. 5:10-12; John 15:18-21)

14. THE POWER OF THE HOLY SPIRIT

We believe in the power of the Holy Spirit. The Father sent his Spirit to bear witness to his Son; without his witness ours is futile. Conviction of sin, faith in Christ, new birth and Christian growth are all his work. Further, the Holy Spirit is a missionary spirit; thus evangelism should arise spontaneously from a Spirit-filled church. A church that is not missionary church is contradicting itself and quenching the Spirit. Worldwide evangelization will become a realistic possibility only when the Spirit renews the church in truth and wisdom, faith, holiness, love and power. We therefore call upon all Christians to pray for such a visitation of the sovereign Spirit of God that all his fruit may appear in all his people and that all his gifts may enrich the body of Christ. Only then will the whole church become a fit instrument in his hands, that the whole earth may hear his voice.

(I Cor. 2:4; John 15:26,27; 16:8-11; I Cor. 12:3; John 3:6-8; II Cor. 3:18; John 7:37-39; I Thess. 5:19; Acts 1:8; Psa. 85:4-7; 67:1-3; Gal. 5:22,23; I Cor. 12:4-31; Rom. 12:3-8)

15. THE RETURN OF CHRIST

We believe that Jesus Christ will return personally and visibly, in power and glory, to consummate his salvation and his judgment. This promise of his coming is a further spur to our evangelism, for we remember his words that the gospel must first be preached to all nations. We believe that the interim period between Christ's ascension and return is to be filled with the mission of the people of God, who have no liberty to stop before the End. We also remember his warning that false Christs and false prophets will arise as precursors of the final Antichrist. We therefore reject as a proud, self-confident dream the notion that man can ever build a utopia on earth. Our Christian confidence is that God will perfect his kingdom, and we look forward with eager anticipation to that day, and to the new heaven and earth in which righteousness will dwell and God will reign for ever. Meanwhile, we rededicate ourselves to the service of Christ and of men in joyful submission to his authority over the whole of our lives.

THE LAUSANNE COVENANT (1974) (continued)

(Mark 14:62; Heb. 9:28; Mark 13:10; Acts 1:8-11; Matt. 28:20; Mark 13:21-23; John 2:18: 4:1-3; Luke 12:32; Rev. 21:1-5; II Pet. 3:13; Matt. 28:18)

CONCLUSION

Therefore, in the light of this our faith and our resolve, we enter into a solemn covenant with God and with each other, to pray, to plan and to work together for the evangelization of the whole world. We call upon others to join us. May God help us by his grace and for his glory to be faithful to this our covenant! Amen, Alleluia!

Notes: *By the early 1970s, the identity of Evangelicals was firmly established in the United States and there was an emerging awareness of their worldwide impact. This transnational aspect of the movement was most evident when delegates from over 150 countries gathered at Lausanne, Switzerland, for a conference on worldwide mission. Out of this conference came one of the most influential documents determining the course of Evangelical life.*

*   *   *

THE HARTFORD APPEAL: AN APPEAL FOR THEOLOGICAL AFFIRMATION (1975)

The renewal of Christian witness and mission requires constant examination of the assumptions shaping the Church's life. Today an apparent loss of a sense of the transcendent is undermining the Church's ability to address with clarity and courage the urgent tasks to which God calls it in the world. This loss is manifest in a number of pervasive themes. Many are superficially attractive, but upon closer examination we find these themes false and deliberating to the Church's life and work. Among such themes are:

Theme 1: *Modern thought is superior to all past forms of understanding reality, and is therefore normative for Christian faith and life.*

In repudiating this theme we are protesting the captivity to the prevailing thought structures not only of the twentieth century but of any historical period. We favor using any helpful means of understanding: ancient or modern, and insist that the Christian proclamation must be related to the idiom of the culture. At the same time, we affirm the need for Christian thought to confront and be confronted by other world views, all of which are necessarily provisional.

Theme 2: *Religious, statements are totally independent of reasonable discourse.*

The capitulation to the alleged primacy of modern thought takes two forms: one is the subordination of religious statements to the canons of scientific rationality; the other, equating reason with scientific rationality, would remove religious statements from the realm of reasonable discourse altogether.

A religion of pure subjectivity and nonrationality results in treating faith statements as being, at best, statements about the believer. We repudiate both forms of capitulation.

Theme 3: *Religious language refers to human experience and nothing else, God being humanity's noblest creation.*

Religion is also a set of symbols and even of human projections. We repudiate the assumption that it is nothing but that. What is here at stake is nothing less than the reality of God: We did not invent God; God invented us.

Theme 4: *Jesus can only be understood in terms of contemporary model of humanity.*

This theme suggests a reversal of "the imitation of Christ"; that is, the image of Jesus is made to reflect cultural and countercultural notions of human excellence. We do not deny that all aspects of humanity are illumined by Jesus. Indeed, it is necessary to the universality of the Christ that he be perceived in relation to the particularities of the believers' world. We do repudiate the captivity to such metaphors, which are necessarily inadequate, relative, transitory, and frequently idolatrous. Jesus, together with the Scriptures and the whole of the Christian tradition, cannot be arbitrarily interpreted without reference to the history of which they are part. The danger is in the attempt to exploit the tradition without taking the tradition seriously.

Theme 5: *All religions are equally valid; the choice among them is not a matter of conviction about truth but only personal preference or life style.*

We affirm our common humanity. We affirm the importance of exploring and confronting all manifestations of the religions quest and of learning from the riches of other religions. But we repudiate this theme because it flattens diversities and ignores contradictions. In doing so, it not only obscures the meaning of Christian faith, but also fails to respect the integrity of other faiths. Truth matters; therefore differences among religions are deeply significant

Theme 6: *To realize one's potential and to be true to oneself is the whole meaning of salvation.*

Salvation contains a promise of human fulfillment, but to identify salvation with human fulfillment can trivialize the promise. We affirm that salvation cannot be found apart from God.

Theme 7: *Since what is human is good, evil can adequately be understood as failure to realize potential.*

This theme invites false understanding of the ambivalence of human existence and underestimates the pervasiveness of sin. Paradoxically, by minimizing the enormity of evil, it undermines serious and sustained attacks on particular social or individual evils.

Theme 8: *The sole purpose of worship is to promote individual self realization and human community.*

Worship promotes individual and communal values, but it is above all a response to the reality of God and arises out of the fundamental need and desire to know, love and adore God. We worship God because God is to be worshiped.

Theme 9: *Institutions and historical traditions are oppressive and inimical to our being truly human; liberation from them is required for authentic existence and authentic religion.*

Institutions and traditions are often oppressive. For this reason they must be subjected to relentless criticism. But human community inescapably requires institutions and traditions. Without them life would degenerate into chaos and new forms of bond age. The modern pursuit of liberation from all social and historical restraints is finally dehumanizing.

Theme 10: *The world must set the agenda for the Church. Social, political, and economic programs to improve the quality of life are ultimately normative for the Church's mission in the world.*

This theme cuts across the political and ideological spectrum. Its form remains the same, no matter whether the content is defined as upholding the values of the American way of life, promoting socialism, or raising human consciousness. The Church must denounce oppressors, help liberate the oppressed, and seek to heal human misery. Sometimes the Church's mission coincides with the world's programs. But the norms for the Church's activity derive from its own perception of God's will for the world.

Theme 11: *An emphasis on God's transcendence is at least a hindrance to, and perhaps incompatible with, Christian social concern and action.*

This supposition leads some to denigrate God's transcendence. Others, holding to a false transcendence, withdraw into religious privatism or individualism and neglect the personal and communal responsibility of Christians for the earthly city. From a biblical perspective, it is precisely because of confidence in God's reign over all aspects of life that Christians must participate fully in the struggle against oppressive and dehumanizing structures and their manifestations in racism, war, and economic exploitation.

Theme 12: *The struggle for a better humanity will bring about the Kingdom of God.*

The struggle for a better humanity is essential to Christian faith and can be informed and inspired by the biblical promise of the Kingdom of God. But imperfect human beings cannot create a perfect society, The Kingdom of God surpasses any conceivable utopia. God has his own designs which confront ours, surprising us with judgment and redemption.

Theme 13: *The question of hope beyond death is irrelevant or at best marginal to the Christian understanding of human fulfillment.*

This is the final capitulation to modern thought. If death is the last word, then Christianity has nothing to say to the final questions of life. We believe that God raised Jesus from the dead and are ''. . . convinced that there is nothing in death or life, in the realm of spirits or superhuman powers, in the world as it is or in the world as it shall be, in the forces of the universe, in heights or depths-nothing in all creation that can separate us from the love of God in Christ, Jesus our Lord'' (Romans 8:38 f.)

Notes: *In January 1975, a group of Evangelicals and others Christians not identified with the Evangelical movement gathered at Hartford, Connecticut, to deal with a broad set of theological issues. In the end, the group did not make any theological affirmations, but did reach a high level of consensus on a number of contemporary theological notions that they opposed and to which they called the attention of the Christian church worldwide.*

They focused their attack on a variety of ideas that have found a following in liberal Protestant thought, often as unspoken assumptions of theological discourse. Some of these ideas have tended to undermine specific theological affirmations, such as the reality of a personal deity, while others tended to deny the possibility of the theological task, such as the notion that religious statements are outside the realm of reasonable discourse. This document continues to find the acceptance of Evangelicals, but most liberal Protestants would affirm one or more of the opinions that it attacks.

*　　　*　　　*

THE CHICAGO CALL: AN APPEAL TO EVANGELICALS (1977)

Prologue

In every age the Holy Spirit calls the church to examine its faithfulness to God's revelation in Scripture. We recognize with gratitude God's blessing through the evangelical resurgence in the church. Yet at such a time of growth we need to be especially sensitive to our weaknesses. We believe that today evangelicals are hindered from achieving full maturity by a reduction of the historic faith. There is, therefore, a pressing need to reflect upon the substance of the biblical and historic faith and to recover the fullness of this heritage. Without presuming to address all our needs, we have identified eight of the themes to which we as evangelical Christians must give careful theological consideration.

A Call to Historic Roots and Continuity

We confess that we have often lost the fullness of our Christian heritage, too readily assuming that the Scriptures and the Spirit make us independent of the past. In so doing, we have become theologically shallow, spiritually weak, blind to the work of God in others and married to our cultures.

Therefore we call for a recovery of our full Christian heritage. Throughout the church's history there has existed an evangelical impulse to proclaim the saving, unmerited grace of Christ, and to reform the church according to the Scriptures. This impulse appears in the doctrines of the ecumenical councils, the piety of the early fathers, the Augustinian theology of grace, the zeal of the monastic reformers, the devotion of the practical mystics and the scholarly integrity of the Christian humanists. It flowers in the biblical fidelity of the Protestant

THE CHICAGO CALL: AN APPEAL TO EVANGELICALS (1977)
(continued)

Reformers and the ethical earnestness of the Radical Reformation. It continues in the efforts of the Puritans and Pietists to complete and perfect the Reformation. It is reaffirmed in the awakening movements of the 18th and 19th centuries which joined Lutheran , Reformed, Wesleyan and other evangelicals in an ecumenical effort to renew the church and to extend its mission in the proclamation and social demonstration of the Gospel. It is present at every point in the history of Christianity where the Gospel has come to expression through the operation of the Holy Spirit: in some of the strivings toward renewal in Eastern Orthodoxy and Roman Catholicism and in biblical insights in forms of Protestantism differing from our own. We dare not move beyond the biblical limits of the Gospel; but we cannot be fully evangelical without recognizing our need to learn from other times and movements concerning the whole meaning of that Gospel.

A Call to Biblical Fidelity

We deplore our tendency toward individualistic interpretation of Scripture. This undercuts the objective character of biblical truth, and denies the guidance of the Holy Spirit among his people through the ages.

Therefore we affirm that the Bible is to be interpreted in keeping with the best insights of historical and literary study, under the guidance of the Holy Spirit, with respect for the historic understanding of the church.

We affirm that the Scriptures, as the infallible Word of God, are the basis of authority in the church. We acknowledge that God uses the Scriptures to judge and to purify his Body. The church, illumined and guided by the Holy Spirit, must in every age interpret, proclaim and live out the Scriptures.

A Call to Creedal Identity

We deplore two opposite excesses: a creedal church that merely recites a faith inherited from the past, and a creedless church that languishes in a doctrinal vacuum. We confess that as evangelical we are not immune from these defects.

Therefore we affirm the need in our time for a confessing church that will boldly witness to its faith before the world, even under threat of persecution. In every age the church must state its faith over against heresy and paganism. What is needed is a vibrant confession that excludes as well as includes, and thereby aims to purify faith and practice. Confessional authority is limited by and derived from the authority of Scripture, which alone remains ultimately and permanently normative. Nevertheless, as the common insight of those who have been illumined by the Holy Spirit and seek to be the voice of the ''holy catholic church,'' a confession should serve as a guide for the interpretation of Scripture.

We affirm the abiding value of the great ecumenical creeds and the Reformation confessions. Since such statements are historically and culturally conditioned, however, the church today needs to express its faith afresh, without defecting from the

truths apprehended in the past. We need to articulate our witness against the idolatries and false ideologies of our day.

A Call to Holistic Salvation

We deplore the tendency of evangelicals to understand salvation solely as an individual, spiritual and otherworldly matter to the neglect of the corporate, physical and this-worldly implication of Gods saving activity.

Therefore we urge evangelicals to recapture a holistic view of salvation. The witness of Scripture is that because of sin our relationships with God, ourselves, others and creation are broken. Through the atoning work of Christ on the cross, healing is possible for these broken relationships.

Wherever the church has been faithful to its calling, it has proclaimed personal, salvation, it has been a channel of God's healing to those in physical and emotional need; it has sought justice for the oppressed and disinherited; and it has been a good steward of the natural world.

As evangelicals we acknowledge our frequent failure to reflect this holistic view of salvation. We therefore call the church to participate fully in God's saving activity through work and prayer, and to strive for justice and liberation for the oppressed, looking forward to the culmination of salvation in the new heaven and new earth to come.

Call to Sacramental Integrity

We decry the poverty of sacramental understanding among evangelicals. This is largely due to the loss of our continuity with the teaching of many of the Fathers and Reformers and results in the deterioration of sacramental life in our Churches. Also, the failure to appreciate the sacramental nature of God's activity in the world often leads us to disregard the sacredness of daily living.

Therefore we call evangelicals to awaken to the sacramental implications of creation and incarnation. For in these doctrines the historic church has affirmed that God's activity is manifested in a material way. We need to recognize that the grace of God is mediated through faith by the operation of the Holy Spirit in a notable way in the sacraments of baptism and the Lord's Supper. Here the church proclaims, celebrates and participates in the death and resurrection of Christ in such a way as to nourish her members. throughout their lives in anticipation of the consummation of the kingdom. Also, we should remember our biblical designation as ''living epistles,'' for here the sacramental character of the Christian's daily life is expressed.

A Call to Spirituality

We suffer from a neglect of authentic spirituality on the one hand, and an excess of undisciplined spirituality on the other hand. We have too often pursued a superhuman religiosity rather than the biblical model of a true humanity released from bondage to sin and renewed by the Holy Spirit.

Therefore we call for a spirituality which grasps by faith the full content of Christ's redemptive work: freedom from the guilt and power of sin, and newness of life through the indwelling and outpouring of his Spirit. We affirm the centrality of the preaching of he Word of God as a primary means by which his Spirit works to renew the church in its corporate life as well as in the individual lives of believers. A true spirituality will call for identification with the suffering of the world as well as the cultivation of personal piety.

We need to rediscover the devotional resources of the whole church, including the evangelical traditions of Pietism and Puritanism. We call for an exploration of devotional practice in all traditions within the church in order to deepen our relationship both with Christ and with other Christians. Among these resources are such h spiritual disciplines as prayer, meditation, silence, fasting, Bible study and spiritual diaries.

A Call to Church Authority

We deplore our disobedience to the Lordship of Christ as expressed through authority in his church. This has promoted a spirit of autonomy in persons and groups resulting in isolationism and competitiveness, even anarchy, within the body of Christ. We regret that in the absence of godly authority, there have arisen legalistic, domineering leaders on the one hand and indifference to church discipline on the other.

Therefore we affirm that all Christians are to be in practical submission to one another and to designated leaders in a church under the Lordship of Christ. The church, as the people of God, is called to be the visible presence of Christ in the world. Every Christian is called to active priesthood in worship and service through exercising spiritual gifts and ministries. In the church we are in vital union both with Christ and with one another. This calls for community with deep involvement and mutual commitment of time, energy and possessions. Further, church discipline, biblically based and under the direction of the Holy Spirit, is essential to the well-being and ministry of God's people. Moreover, we encourage all Christian organizations to conduct their activities with genuine accountability to the whole church.

A Call to Church Unity

We deplore the scandalous isolation and separation of Christians from one another. We believe such division is contrary to Christ's explicit desire for unity among his people and impedes the witness of the church in the world. Evangelicalism is too frequently characterized by an ahistorical, sectarian mentality. We fail to appropriate the catholicity of historic Christianity, as well as the breadth of the biblical revelation.

Therefore we call evangelicals to return to the ecumenical concern of the Reformers and the later movements of evangelical renewal. We must humbly and critically scrutinize our respective traditions, renounce sacred shibboleths, and recognize that God works within diverse historical streams. We must resist efforts promoting church union-at-any-cost, but we must also avoid mere spiritualized concepts of church unity. We are convinced that unity in Christ requires visible and concrete expressions. In this belief, we welcome the development of encounter and cooperation within Christ's church. While we seek to avoid doctrinal indifferentism and a false irenicism, we encourage evangelicals to cultivate increased discussion and cooperation, both within and without

their respective traditions, earnestly seeking common areas of agreement and understanding.

Notes: *In May 1977 a group of Evangelical leaders, primarily of a Reformed/Presbyterian background, gathered in Chicago to deal with a series of issues surrounding the Evangelical task. They called for more depth in Evangelical theology, attention to the authority of the creedal statements of the early church and Reformation, and the role of church authority in guiding biblical interpretation and evangelical efforts.*

This document was largely ignored by the Evangelical Movement as a whole because it represented only a narrow element of the Movement and attacked the larger noncreedal and nonsacramental segments of that Movement.

*   *   *

THE CHICAGO STATEMENT ON BIBLICAL INERRANCY (1978)

A Short Statement

1. God, who is Himself Truth and speaks truth only, has inspired Holy Scripture in order thereby to reveal Himself to lost mankind through Jesus Christ as Creator and Lord, Redeemer and Judge. Holy Scripture is God's witness to Himself.

2. Holy Scripture, being God's own Word, written by men prepared and superintended by His Spirit, is of infallible divine authority in all matters upon which it touches: it is to be believed, as God's instruction, in all that it affirms; obeyed, as God's command, in all that it requires; embraced, as God's pledge, in all that it promises.

3. The Holy Spirit, Scripture's divine Author, both authenticates it us by His inward witness and opens our minds to understand its meaning.

4. Being wholly and verbally God-given, Scripture is without error or fault in all its teaching, no less in what it states about God's acts in creation, about the events of world history, and about its own literary origins under God than in its witness to God's saving grace in individual lives.

5. The authority of Scripture is inescapably impaired if this total divine inerrancy is in any way limited or disregarded, or made relative to a view of truth contrary to the Bible's own; and such lapses bring serious loss to both the individual and the Church.

Articles of Affirmation and Denial

Article I

We affirm that the Holy Scriptures are to be received as the authoritative Word of God.

THE CHICAGO STATEMENT ON BIBLICAL INERRANCY (1978)
(continued)

We deny that the Scriptures receive their authority from the Church, tradition, or any other human source.

Article II

We affirm that the Scriptures are the supreme written norm by which God binds the conscience, and that the authority of the Church is subordinate to that of Scripture.

We deny that Church creeds, councils, or declarations have authority greater than or equal to the authority of the Bible.

Article III

We affirm that the written Word in its entirety is revelation given by God.

We deny that the Bible is merely a witness to revelation, or only becomes revelation in encounter, or depends on the responses of men for its validity.

Article IV

We affirm that God who made mankind in His image has used language as a means of revelation.

We deny that human language is so limited by our creatureliness that it is rendered inadequate as a vehicle for divine revelation. We further deny that the corruption of human culture and language through sin has thwarted God's work of inspiration.

Article V

We affirm that God's revelation in the Holy Scriptures was progressive.

We deny that later revelation, which may fulfill earlier revelation, ever corrects or contradicts it. We further deny that any normative revelation has been given since the completion of the New Testament writings.

Article VI

We affirm that the whole of Scripture and all its parts, down to the very words of the original, were given by divine inspiration.

We deny that the inspiration of Scripture can rightly be affirmed of the whole without the parts, or of some parts but not the whole.

Article VII

We affirm that inspiration was the work in which God by His Spirit, through human writers, gave us His Word. The origin of Scripture is divine. The mode of divine inspiration remains largely a mystery to us.

We deny that inspiration can be reduced to human insight, or to heightened states of consciousness of any kind.

Article VIII

We affirm that God in His Work of inspiration utilized the distinctive personalities and literary styles of the writers whom He had chosen and prepared.

We deny that God, in causing these writers to use the very words that He chose, overrode their personalities.

Article IX

We affirm that inspiration, though not conferring omniscience, guaranteed true and trustworthy utterance on all matters of which the Biblical authors were moved to speak and write.

We deny that the finitude or fallenness of these writers, by necessity or otherwise, introduced distortion or falsehood into God's Word.

Article X

We affirm that inspiration, strictly speaking, applies only to the autographic text of Scripture, which in the providence of God can be ascertained from available manuscripts with great accuracy. We further affirm that copies and translations of Scripture are the Word of God to the extent that they faithfully represent the original.

We deny that any essential element of the Christian faith is affected by the absence of the autographs. We further deny that this absence renders the assertion of Biblical inerrancy invalid or irrelevant.

Article XI

We affirm that Scripture, having been given by divine inspiration, is infallible, so that, far from misleading us, it is true and reliable in all the matters it addresses.

We deny that it is possible for the Bible to be at the same time infallible and errant In its assertions. Infallibility and inerrancy may be distinguished, but not separated.

Article XII

We affirm that Scripture in its entirety is inerrant, being free from all falsehood, fraud, or deceit.

We deny that Biblical infallibility and inerrancy are limited to spiritual, religious, or redemptive themes, exclusive of assertions in the fields of history and science. We further deny that scientific hypotheses about earth history may properly be used to overturn the teaching of Scripture on creation and the flood.

Article XIII

We affirm the propriety of using inerrancy as a theological term with reference to the complete truthfulness of Scripture.

We deny that it is proper to evaluate Scripture according to standards of truth and error that are alien to its usage or purpose. We further deny that inerrancy is negated by Biblical phenomena such as a lack of modern technical precision, irregularities of grammar or spelling, observational descriptions of nature, the reporting of falsehoods, the use of hyperbole and round numbers, the topical arrangement of material, variant selections of material In parallel accounts, and of the use of free citations.

Article XIV

We affirm the unity and internal consistency of Scripture.

We deny that alleged errors and discrepancies that have not yet been resolved vitiate the truth claims of the Bible.

Article XV

We affirm that the doctrine of inerrancy is grounded in the teaching of the Bible about inspiration.

We deny that Jesus' teaching about Scripture may be dismissed by appeals to accommodation or to any natural limitation of His humanity.

Article XVI

We affirm that the doctrine of inerrancy has been integral to the Church's faith throughout its history.

We deny that inerrancy is a doctrine invented by Scholastic Protestantism, or is a reactionary position postulated in response to negative higher criticism.

Article XVII

We affirm that the Holy Spirit bears witness to the Scriptures, assuring believers of the truthfulness of God's written Word.

We deny that this witness of the Holy Spirit operates in isolation from or against Scripture.

Article XVIII

We affirm that the text of Scripture is to be interpreted by grammatico-historical exegesis, taking account of its literary forms and devices, and that Scripture is to interpret Scripture.

We deny the legitimacy of any treatment of the text or quest for sources lying behind it that leads to relativizing, dehistoricizing, or discounting its teaching, or rejecting its claims to authorship.

Article XIX

We affirm that a confession of the full authority, infallibility, and inerrancy of Scripture is vital to a sound understanding of the whole of the Christian faith. We further affirm that such confession should lead to increasing conformity to the image of Christ.

We deny that such confession is necessary for salvation. However, we further deny that inerrancy can be rejected without grave consequences, both to the individual and to the Church.

EXPOSITION

Our understanding of the doctrine of inerrancy must be set in the context of the broader teachings of the Scripture concerning itself. This exposition gives an account of the outline of doctrine from which our summary statement and articles are drawn.

Creation, Revelation, and Inspiration

The Triune God, who formed all things by his creative utterances and governs all things by His Word of decree, made mankind in His own image for a life of communion with Himself, on the model of the eternal fellowship of loving communication within the Godhead. As God's image-bearer, man was to hear God's Word addressed to him and to respond in the joy of adoring obedience. Over and above God's self-disclosure in the created order and the sequence of events within it, human beings from Adam on have received verbal messages from Him, either directly, as stated in Scripture, or indirectly in the form of part or all of Scripture itself.

When Adam fell, the Creator did not abandon mankind to final judgment but promised salvation and began to reveal Himself as Redeemer in a sequence of historical events centering on Abraham's family and culminating in the life, death, resurrection, present heavenly ministry, and promised return of Jesus Christ. Within this frame God has from time to time spoken specific words of judgment and mercy, promise and command, to sinful human beings so drawing them into a covenant of relation of mutual commitment between Him and them in which He blesses them with gifts of grace and they bless Him in responsive adoration. Moses, whom God used as mediator to carry His words to His people at the time of the Exodus, stands at the head of a long line of prophets in whose mouths and writings God put His words for delivery to Israel. God's purpose in this succession of messages was to maintain His covenant by causing His people to know His Name—that is, His nature—and His will both of precept and purpose in the present and for the future. This line of prophetic spokesmen from God came to completion in Jesus Christ, God's incarnate Word, who was Himself a prophet—more than a prophet, but not less—and in the apostles and prophets of the first Christian generation. When God's final and climactic message, His word to the world concerning Jesus Christ, had been spoken and elucidated by those in the apostolic circle, the sequence of revealed messages ceased. Henceforth the Church was to live and know God by what He had already said, and said for all time.

At Sinai God wrote the terms of His covenant on tables of stone, as His enduring witness and for lasting accessibility, and throughout the period of prophetic and apostolic revelation He prompted men to write the messages given to and through them, along with celebratory records of His dealings with His people, plus moral reflections on covenant life and forms of praise and prayer for covenant mercy. The theological reality of inspiration in the producing of Biblical documents corresponds to that of spoken prophecies: although the human writers' personalities were expressed in what they wrote, the words were divinely constituted. Thus, what Scripture says, God says; its authority is His authority, for He is its ultimate Author, having given it through the minds and words of chosen and prepared men who in freedom and faithfulness ''spoke from God as they were carried along by the Holy Spirit'' (1 Peter 1:21). Holy Scripture must be acknowledged as the Word of God by virtue of its divine origin.

THE CHICAGO STATEMENT ON BIBLICAL INERRANCY (1978)
(continued)

Authority: Christ and the Bible

Jesus Christ, the Son of God who is the Word made flesh, out prophet, Priest, and King, is the ultimate Mediator of God's communication to man, as He is of all God's gifts of grace. The revelation He gave was more than verbal; He revealed the Father by His presence and His deeds as well. Yet His words were crucially important; for He was God, he spoke from the Father, and His words will judge all men at the last day.

As the prophesied Messiah, Jesus Christ is the central theme of Scripture. The Old testament looked ahead to Him; the New Testament looks back to his first coming and on to his second. Canonical Scripture is the divinely inspired and therefore normative witness to Christ. No hermeneutic, therefore, of which the historical Christ is not the focal point is acceptable. Holy Scripture must be treated as what it essentially is—the witness of the Father to the incarnate Son.

It appears that the Old Testament canon had been fixed by the time of Jesus. The New Testament canon is likewise now closed inasmuch as no new apostolic witness to the historical Christ can now be borne. No new revelation (as distinct from Spirit-given understanding of existing revelation) will be given until Christ comes again. The canon was created in principle by divine inspiration. The Church's part was to discern the canon which God had created, not to devise one of its own.

The word *canon,* signifying a rule or standard, is a pointer to authority, which means the right to rule and control. Authority in Christianity belongs to God in His revelation, which means, on the one hand, Jesus Christ, the living Word, and, on the other hand, Holy Scripture, the written Word. But the authority of Christ and that of Scripture are one. As our Prophet, Christ testified that Scripture cannot be broken. As our Priest and King, He devoted His earthly life to fulfilling the law and the prophets, even dying in obedience to the words of Messianic prophecy. Thus, as He saw Scripture attesting Him and His authority, so by His own submission to Scripture He attested its authority. As He bowed to His Father's instruction given in His Bible (our Old Testament), so He requires His disciples to do—not, however, in isolation but in conjunction with the apostolic witness to Himself which He undertook to inspire by His gift of the Holy Spirit. So Christians show themselves faithful servants of their Lord by bowing to the divine instruction given in the prophetic and apostolic writings which together make up our Bible.

By authenticating each other's authority, Christ and Scripture coalesce into a single fount of authority. The Biblically-interpreted Christ and the Christ-centered, Christ-proclaiming Bible are from its standpoint one. As from the fact of inspiration we infer that what Scripture says, God says, so from the revealed relation between Jesus Christ and Scripture we may equally declare that what Scripture says, Christ says.

Infallibility, Inerrancy, Interpretation

Holy Scripture, as the inspired Word of God witnessing authoritatively to Jesus Christ, may properly be called *infallible* and *inerrant.* These negative terms have a special value, for they explicitly safeguard crucial positive truths.

Infallible signifies the quality of neither misleading nor being misled and so safeguards in categorical terms the truth that Holy Scripture is a sure, safe, and reliable rule and guide in all matters.

Similarly, *inerrant* signifies the quality of being free from all falsehood or mistake and so safeguards the truth that Holy Scripture is entirely true and trustworthy in all its assertions.

We affirm that canonical Scripture should always be interpreted on the basis that it is infallible and inerrant. However, in determining what the God-taught writer is asserting in each passage, we must pay the most careful attention to its claims and character as a human production. In inspiration, God utilized the culture and conventions of his penman's milieu, a milieu that God controls in His sovereign providence; it is misinterpretation to imagine otherwise.

So history must be treated as history, poetry as poetry, hyperbole and metaphor as hyperbole and metaphor, generalization and approximation as what they are, and so forth. Differences between literary conventions in Bible times and in ours must also be observed; since, for instance, non-chronological narration and imprecise citation were conventional and acceptable and violated no expectation in those days, we must not regard these things as faults when we find them in Bible writers. When total precision of a particular kind was not expected not aimed at, it is no error not to have achieved it. Scripture is inerrant, not in the sense of being absolutely precise by modern standards, but in the sense of making food its claims and achieving that measure of focused truth at which its authors aimed.

The truthfulness of Scripture is not negated by the appearance in it of irregularities of grammar or spelling, phenomenal descriptions of nature, reports of false statements (*e.g.,* the lies of Satan), or seeming discrepancies between one passage and another. It is not right to set the so-called "phenomena" of Scripture against the teaching of Scripture about itself. Apparent inconsistencies should not be ignored. Solution of them, where this can be convincingly achieved, will encourage our faith, and where for the present no convincing solution is at hand we shall significantly honor God by trusting His assurance that His Word is true, despite these appearances, and by maintaining our confidence that one day they will be seen to have been illusions.

Inasmuch as all Scripture is the product of a single divine mind, interpretation must stay within the bounds of the analogy of Scripture and eschew hypotheses that would correct one Biblical passage by another, whether in the name of progressive revelation or of the imperfect enlightenment of the inspired writer's mind.

Although Holy Scripture is nowhere culture-bound in the sense that its teaching lacks universal validity, it is sometimes culturally conditioned by the customs and conventional view of a particular period, so that the application of its principles today calls for t different sort of action.

Skepticism and Criticism

Since the Renaissance, and more particularly since the Enlightenment, world-views have been developed which involve skepticism about basic Christian tenets. Such are the agnosticism which denies that God is knowable, the rationalism which denies that He is incomprehensible, the idealism which denies that He is transcendent, and the existentialism which denies rationality in His relationships with us. When these and un- and anti-biblical principles seep into men's theologies at presuppositional level, as today they frequently do, faithful interpretation of Holy Scripture becomes impossible.

Transmission and Translation

Since God has nowhere promised an inerrant transmission of Scripture, it is necessary to affirm that only the autographic text of the original documents was inspired and to maintain the need of textual criticism as a means of detecting any slips that may have crept into the text in the course of its transmission. The verdict of this science, however, is that the Hebrew and Greek text appear to be amazingly well preserved, so that we are amply justified in affirming, with the Westminster Confession, a singular providence of God in this matter and in declaring that the authority of Scripture is in no way jeopardized by the fact that the copies we possess are not entirely error-free.

Similarly, no translation is or can by perfect, and all translations are an additional step-away from the *autographa*. Yet the verdict of linguistic science is that English-speaking Christians, at least, are exceedingly well served in these days with a host of excellent translations and have no cause for hesitating to conclude that the true word of God is within their reach. Indeed, in view of the frequent repetition in Scripture of the main matters with which it deals and also of the Holy Spirit's constant witness to and through the Word, no serious translation of Holy Scripture will so destroy its meaning as to render it unable to make its reader "wise for salvation through faith in Christ Jesus" (2 Tim. 3:15).

Inerrancy and Authority

In our affirmation of the authority of Scripture as involving its total truth, we are consciously standing with Christ and His apostles, indeed with the whole Bible and with the main stream of church history from the first days until very recently. we are concerned at the casual, inadvertent, and seemingly thoughtless way in which a belied of such far-reaching importance has been given up by so many in our day.

We are conscious too that great and grave confusion results from ceasing to maintain the total truth of the Bible whose authority one professes to acknowledge. The result of taking this step is that the Bible which God gave loses it authority, and what has authority instead is a Bible reduced in content according to the demands of one's critical reasoning and in principle reducible still further once one has started. This means that at bottom independent reason now has authority, as

opposed to Scriptural teaching. If this is not seen and if for the time being basic evangelical doctrines are still held, persons denying the full truth of Scripture may claim an evangelical identity while methodologically they have moved away from the evangelical principle of knowledge to an unstable subjectivism, and will find it hard not to move further.

We affirm that what Scripture says, God says. May He be glorified. Amen and Amen.

Notes: *Within both Fundamentalism and Evangelicalism, the defense of the Bible and the definition of the nature of its authority are of major concern. Both of those concerns meet in the arguments over the inerrancy of the Bible. Inerrancy refers to the Bible's being free from error about any matter on which it speaks. A second term, infallible, generally refers to the Bible's trustworthiness when its speak on matters of faith and morals. While Fundamentalists uniformly affirm both the Bible's infallibility and inerrancy, Evangelicals, while affirming the infallibility, have argued about its inerrancy. (Some Evangelicals, especially those out of a Methodist heritage have refused to participate in the debates over biblical authority focused around the terms "infallible" and "inerrant.")*

In the light of this ongoing debate, a number of Evangelical scholars committed to the inerrancy of the Bible gathered in Chicago, on October 26-28, 1978, to reaffirm the doctrine. The statement, that defined the doctrine and built a careful argument for its correctness, was published with the intent of solidifying the doctrine within the Evangelical movement and has been widely circulated, especially among Evangelical scholars. It was the opinion of the authors that the doctrine was necessary if the authority of the Bible was not to be impaired. The International Council of Biblical Inerrancy was established as a continuing organization to focus the dialogue that might grow out of the statement.

Inerrancy is viewed by many Evangelicals as a key element in a broad argument with liberal Protestants over the nature of revelation. Evangelicals believe that God reveals not just Himself, but uses language as a means of revealing His will to humankind. Thus God inspired human writers to communicate His Truth in the form of the words of the Bible. The Chicago statement succinctly presents how inerrancy fits into the overall picture of biblical authority.

*   *   *

THE CHICAGO STATEMENT ON BIBLICAL HERMENEUTICS (1982)

Article I.

WE AFFIRM that the normative authority of Holy Scripture is the authority of God Himself, and is attested by Jesus Christ, the Lord of the Church.

WE DENY the legitimacy of separating the authority of Christ from the authority or Scripture, or of opposing the one to the other.

Article II.

WE AFFIRM that as Christ is God and Man in Person, so Scripture is, indivisibly, God's Word in human language.

WE DENY that the humble, human form of Scripture entails errancy any more than the humanity of Christ, even in His humiliation, entails sin.

Article III.

WE AFFIRM that the Person and work of Jesus Christ are the central focus of the entire Bible.

WE DENY that any method of interpretation which rejects or obscures the Christ-centeredness of Scripture is correct.

Article IV.

WE AFFIRM that the Holy Spirit who inspired Scripture acts through it today to work faith in its message.

WE DENY that the Holy Spirit ever teaches to any one anything which is contrary to the teaching of Scripture.

Article V.

WE AFFIRM that the Holy Spirit enables believers to appropriate and apply Scripture to their lives.

WE DENY that the natural man is able to discern spiritually the biblical message apart from the Holy Spirit.

Article VI.

WE AFFIRM that the Bible expresses God's truth in propositional statements, and we declare that biblical truth is both objective and absolute. We further affirm that a statement is true if it represents matters as they actually are, but is an error if it misrepresents the facts.

WE DENY that, while Scripture is able to make us wise unto salvation, biblical truth should be defined in terms of this function. We further deny that error should be defined as that which willfully deceives.

Article VII.

WE AFFIRM that the meaning expressed in each biblical text is single, definite and fixed.

WE DENY that the recognition of this single meaning eliminates the variety of its application.

Article VIII.

WE AFFIRM that the Bible contains teachings and mandates which apply to all cultural and situational contexts and other mandates which the Bible itself shows apply only to particular situations.

WE DENY that the distinction between the universal and particular mandates of Scripture can be determined by cultural and situational factors. We further deny that universal mandates may ever be treated as culturally or situationally relative.

Article IX.

WE AFFIRM that the term hermeneutics, which historically signified the rules of exegesis, may properly be extended to cover all that is involved in the process of perceiving what the biblical revelation means and how it bears on our lives.

WE DENY that the message of Scripture derives from, or is dictated by, the interpreter's understanding. Thus we deny that the "horizons" of the biblical writer and the interpreter may rightly "fuse" in such a way that what the text communicates to the interpreter is not ultimately controlled by the expressed meaning of the Scripture.

Article X.

WE AFFIRM that Scripture communicates God's truth of us verbally through a wide variety of literary forms.

WE DENY that any of the limits of human language render Scripture inadequate to convey God's message.

Article XI.

WE AFFIRM that translations of the text of Scripture can communicate knowledge of God across all temporal and cultural boundaries.

WE DENY that the meaning of biblical text is so tied to the culture out of which they came that understanding of the same meaning in other cultures is impossible.

Article XII.

WE AFFIRM that in the task of translating the Bible and teaching it in the context of each culture, only those functional equivalents which are faithful to the content of biblical teaching should be employed.

WE DENY the legitimacy of methods which either are insensitive to the demands of cross-cultural communication or distort biblical meaning in the process.

Article XIII.

WE AFFIRM that awareness of the literary categories, formal and stylistic, of the various parts of Scripture is essential for proper exegesis, and hence we value genre criticism as one of the many disciplines of biblical study.

WE DENY that generic categories which negate historicity may rightly be imposed on biblical narratives which present themselves as factual.

Article XIV.

WE AFFIRM that the biblical record of events, discourses and sayings, though presented in a variety of appropriate literary forms, corresponds to historical fact.

WE DENY that any event, discourse or saying reported in Scripture was invented by the biblical writers or by the traditions they incorporated.

Article XV.

WE AFFIRM the necessity of interpreting the Bible according to its literal, or normal, sense. The literal sense is the grammatical-historical sense, that is, the meaning which the writer expressed. Interpretation according to the literal sense will take account of all figures of speech and literary forms found in the text.

WE DENY the legitimacy of any approach to Scripture that attributes to it meaning which the literal sense does not support.

Article XVI.

WE AFFIRM that legitimate critical techniques should be used in determining the canonical text and its meaning.

WE DENY the legitimacy of allowing any method of biblical criticism to question the truth or integrity of the writer's expressed meaning, or of any other scriptural teaching.

Article XVII.

WE AFFIRM the unity, harmony and consistency of Scripture and declare that it is its own best interpreter.

WE DENY that Scripture may be interpreted in such a way as to suggest that one passage corrects or militates against another. We deny that later writers of Scripture misinterpreted earlier passages of Scripture when quoting from or referring to them.

Article XVIII.

WE AFFIRM that the Bible's own interpretation of itself is always correct, never deviating from, but rather elucidating, the single meaning of the inspired text. The single meaning of a prophet's words includes, but is not restricted to, the understanding of those words by the prophet and necessarily involves the intention of God evidenced in the fulfillment of those words.

WE DENY that the writers of Scripture always understood the full implications of their own words.

Article XIX.

WE AFFIRM that any preunderstandings which the interpreter brings to Scripture should be in harmony with scriptural teaching and subject to correction by it.

WE DENY that Scripture should be required to fit alien preunderstandings, inconsistent with itself, such as naturalism, evolutionism, scientism, secular humanism, and relativism.

Article XX.

WE AFFIRM that since God is the author of all truth, all truths, biblical and extrabiblical, are consistent and cohere, and that the Bible speaks truth when it touches on matters pertaining to nature, history, or anything else. We further affirm that in some cases extrabiblical data have value for clarifying what Scripture teaches, and for prompting correction of faulty interpretations.

WE DENY that extrabiblical views ever disprove the teaching of Scripture or hold priority over it.

Article XXI.

WE AFFIRM the harmony of special with general revelation and therefore of biblical teaching with the facts of nature.

WE DENY that any genuine scientific facts are inconsistent with the true meaning of any passage of Scripture.

Article XXII.

WE AFFIRM that Genesis 1-11 is factual, as is the rest of the book.

WE DENY that the teachings of Genesis 1-11 are mythical and that scientific hypotheses about earth history or the origin of humanity may be invoked to overthrow what Scripture teaches about creation.

Article XXIII.

WE AFFIRM the clarity of Scripture and specifically of its message about salvation from sin.

WE DENY that all passages of Scripture are equally clear or have equal bearing on the message of redemption.

Article XXIV.

WE AFFIRM that a person is not dependent for understanding of Scripture on the expertise of biblical scholars.

WE DENY that a person should ignore the fruits of the technical study of Scripture by biblical scholars.

Article XXV.

WE AFFIRM that the only type of preaching which sufficiently conveys the divine revelation and its proper application to life is that which faithfully expounds the text of Scripture as the Word of God.

WE DENY that the preacher has any message from God apart from the text of Scripture.

Notes: *Four years after the gathering of scholars who created the Chicago Statement on Biblical Inerrancy, a similar group of scholars gathered under the aegis of the International Council on Biblical Inerrancy to consider related question of hermeneutics. Hermeneutics is the science and art of interpretation, and given their view of the authority of the Bible, Evangelicals place a high priority on hermeneutical questions. The consultation held in Chicago, November 10-13, 1982, led to a set of affirmations and denials concerning scriptural interpretation.*

The primary affirmation of this statement concerns the Bible's role in expressing God's truth in propositional statements and that through it God communicates truth and the knowledge across all temporal and cultural boundaries. The Bile is for all time and all peoples. The Bible should be interpreted according to its normal literal sense, and with questionable passages, it is its own best interpreter. Appropriate critical tools are helpful in interpreting the Bible, and while the Church's

THE CHICAGO STATEMENT ON BIBLICAL HERMENEUTICS
(1982) (continued)

people should not ignore the accomplishments of biblical scholars, no one is ultimately dependent on it.

Moving from the general to the particular, the gathering affirmed the factual nature of the most controversial passages of the Bible, Genesis 1-11.

*   *   *

THE AMSTERDAM AFFIRMATIONS (1983)

We, evangelists assembled in Amsterdam from over 130 countries for the *International Conference for Itinerant Evangelists,* give thanks to God for the outpouring of His Spirit upon us as we have gathered in the name of Jesus. The Lord Himself has been in our midst to instruct us by His servants, to refresh us by His Spirit, and to revive us by His Word.

Before the Lord and one another, we affirm to the Church and to the world our ministry of evangelism.

I.   We confess Jesus Christ as God, our Lord and Savior, who is revealed in the Bible, which is the infallible Word of God.

II.   We affirm our commitment to the Great Commission of our Lord, and we declare our willingness to go anywhere, do anything, and sacrifice anything God requires of us in the fulfillment of that Commission.

III.   We respond to God's call to the biblical ministry of the evangelist, and accept our solemn responsibility to preach the Word to all peoples as God gives opportunity.

IV.   God loves every human being, who, apart from faith in Christ, is under God's judgment and destined for Hell.

V.   The heart of the biblical message is the Good News of God's salvation, which comes by grace alone through faith in the risen Lord Jesus Christ and His atoning death on the Cross for our sins.

VI.   In our proclamation of the Gospel we recognize the urgency of calling all to decision to follow Jesus Christ as Lord and Savior, and to do so lovingly and without coercion or manipulation.

VII.   We need and desire to be filled and controlled by the Holy Spirit as we bear witness to the Gospel of Jesus Christ, because God alone can turn sinners from their sin and bring them to everlasting life.

VIII.   We acknowledge our obligation, as servants of God, to lead lives of holiness and moral purity, knowing that we exemplify Christ to the Church and to the world.

IX.   A life of regular and faithful prayer and Bible study is essential to our personal spiritual growth, and to our power for ministry.

X.   We will be faithful stewards of all that God gives us, and will be accountable to others in the finances of our ministry, and honest in reporting our statistics.

XI.   Our families are a responsibility given to us by God, and are a sacred trust to be kept as faithfully as our call to minister to others.

XII.   We are responsible to the Church, and will endeavor always to conduct our ministries so as to build up the local body of believers and serve the Church at large.

XIII.   We are responsible to arrange for the spiritual care of those who come to faith under our ministry, to encourage them to identify with the local body of believers, and seek to provide for the instruction of believers in witnessing to the Gospel.

XIV.   We share Christ's deep concern for the personal and social sufferings of humanity, and we accept our responsibility as Christians and as evangelists to do our utmost to alleviate human need.

XV.   We beseech the body of Christ to join with us in prayer and work for peace in our world, for revival and a renewed dedication to the biblical priority of evangelism in the Church, and for the oneness of believers in Christ for the fulfillment of the Great Commission, until Christ returns.

Notes: *In 1983 a group of evangelists, Christians leaders who work full-time in traveling and engaging in mass evangelistic activities, gathered in Amsterdam, The Netherlands, for an International Conference for Itinerant Evangelists. American Baptist evangelist Billy Graham was among the prominent leaders of the conference. The Affirmations spoke to a number of criticisms of the evangelists, and they responded by pledging themselves to refrain from using manipulative methods in their evangelistic meetings, to lead lives of personal holiness and piety, to be upright in their use of financial resources, to work in conjunction with the local church, and to accept responsibility for the nurture of those converted by their ministry.*

*   *   *

LAUSANNE II: TWENTY-ONE AFFIRMATIONS (1989)

1.   We affirm our continuing commitment to the Lausanne Covenant as the basis of our cooperation in the Lausanne movement.

2.   We affirm that in the Scriptures of the Old and New Testaments God has given us an authoritative disclosure

of his character and will, his redemptive acts and their meaning, and his mandate for mission.

3. We affirm that the biblical gospel is God's enduring message to our world, and we determine to defend, proclaim, and embody it.

4. We affirm that human beings, though created in the image of God, are sinful and guilty, and lost without Christ, and that this truth is a necessary preliminary to the gospel.

5. We affirm that the Jesus of history and the Christ of glory are the same person, and that this Jesus Christ is absolutely unique, for he alone is God incarnate, our sin-bearer, the conqueror of death and the coming judge.

6. We affirm that on the cross Jesus Christ took our place, bore our sins and died our death; and that for this reason alone God freely forgives those who are brought to repentance and faith.

7. We affirm that other religions and ideologies are not alternative paths to God, and that human spirituality, if unredeemed by Christ, leads not to God but to judgment, for Christ is the only way.

8. We affirm that we must demonstrate God's love visibly by caring for those who are deprived of justice, dignity, food, and shelter.

9. We affirm that the proclamation of God's kingdom of justice and peace demands the denunciation of all injustice and oppression, both personal and structural; we will not shrink from this prophetic witness.

10. We affirm that the Holy Spirit's witness to Christ is indispensable to evangelism, and that without his supernatural work neither new birth nor new life is possible.

11. We affirm that spiritual warfare demands spiritual weapons, and that we must both preach the word in the power of the Spirit, and pray constantly that we may enter into Christ's victory over the principalities and powers of evil.

12. We affirm that God has committed to the whole church and every member of it the task of making Christ known throughout the world; we long to see all lay and ordained persons mobilized and trained for this task.

13. We affirm that we who claim to be members of the Body of Christ must transcend within our fellowship the barriers of race, gender, and class.

14. We affirm that the gifts of the Spirit are distributed to all God's people, women and men, and that their partnership in evangelization must be welcomed for the common good.

15. We affirm that we who proclaim the gospel must exemplify it in a life of holiness and love; otherwise our testimony loses its credibility.

16. We affirm that every Christian congregation must turn itself outward to its local community in evangelistic witness and compassionate service.

17. We affirm the urgent need for churches, mission agencies and other Christian organizations to cooperate in evangelism and social action, repudiating competition and avoiding duplication.

18. We affirm our duty to study the society in which we live, in order to understand its structures, values and needs, and so develop an appropriate strategy of mission.

19. We affirm that world evangelization is urgent and that the reaching of unreached peoples is possible. So we resolve during the last decade of the twentieth century to give ourselves to these tasks with fresh determination.

20. We affirm our solidarity with those who suffer for the gospel, and will seek to prepare ourselves for the same possibility. We will also work for religious and political freedom everywhere.

21. We affirm that God is calling the whole church to take the whole gospel to the whole world. So we determine to proclaim it faithfully, urgently, and sacrificially, until he comes.

Notes: *From July 11 to 20, 1989, over 3,000 delegates gathered in Manila, the Philippines, for what was hailed as the second Lausanne conference, called to assess the accomplishments of the world Evangelical Movement in the fifteen years since the first conference. Conferees noted, among other accomplishments, that during those fifteen years over 100 regional consultations had been held and 25 occasional papers published under the sponsorship of the Lausanne Committee for World Evangelism.*

Lausanne II cut little new ground, but like the assemblies of the World Council of Churches was notable for its inclusion of delegates of a host of cultures and backgrounds from 168 countries.

The conference issued a lengthy document, the Manila Manifesto. It included as its preamble the Twenty-One Affirmations, authored by theologian John Stott. The Affirmations are a reiteration of those contained in the Lausanne Covenant.

*　　　*　　　*

THE WILLOWBANK DECLARATION ON THE CHRISTIAN GOSPEL AND THE JEWISH PEOPLE (1989)

PREAMBLE

Every Christian must acknowledge an immense debt of gratitude to the Jewish people. The Gospel is the good news that Jesus is the Christ, the long-promised Jewish Messiah, who by his life, death and resurrection saves from sin and all its consequences. Those who worship Jesus as their Divine Lord and Savior have thus received God's most precious gift through the Jewish people. Therefore they have compelling reason to show love to that people in every possible way.

THE WILLOWBANK DECLARATION ON THE CHRISTIAN GOSPEL AND THE JEWISH PEOPLE (1989) (continued)

Concerned about humanity everywhere, we are resolved to uphold the right of Jewish people to a just and peaceful existence everywhere, both in the land of Israel and in their communities throughout the world. We repudiate past persecutions of Jews by those identified as Christians, and we pledge ourselves to resist every form of anti-Semitism. As the supreme way of demonstrating love, we seek to encourage the Jewish people, along with all other peoples, to receive God's gift of life through Jesus the Messiah, and accordingly the growing number of Jewish Christians brings us great joy.

In making this Declaration we stand in a long and revered Christian tradition, which in 1980 was highlighted by a landmark statement, "Christian Witness to the Jewish People," issued by the Lausanne Committee for World Evangelization. Now, at this Willowbank Consultation on the Gospel and the Jewish People, sponsored by the World Evangelical Fellowship and supported by the Lausanne Committee, we reaffirm our commitment to the Jewish people and our desire to share the gospel with them.

The Declaration is made in response to growing doubts and widespread confusion among Christians about the need for, and the propriety of, endeavors to share faith in Jesus Christ with Jewish people. Several factors unite to produce the uncertain state of mind that the Declaration seeks to resolve.

The holocaust, perpetrated as it was by leaders and citizens of a supposedly Christian nation, has led to a sense in some quarters that Christian credibility among Jews has been totally destroyed. Accordingly, some have shrunk back from addressing the Jewish people with the gospel.

Some who see the creation of the state of Israel as a direct fulfillment of biblical prophecy have concluded that the Christian task at this time is to "comfort Israel" by supporting this new political entity, rather than to challenge Jews by direct evangelism.

Some church leaders have retreated from embracing the task of evangelizing Jews as a responsibility of Christian mission. Rather, a new theology is being embraced which holds that God's covenant with Israel through Abraham establishes all Jews in God's favor for all times, and so makes faith in Jesus Christ for salvation needless so far as they are concerned.

On this basis, it is argued that dialogue with Jews in order to understand each other better, and cooperation in the quest for socioeconomic shalom, is all that Christian mission requires in relation to the Jewish people. Continued attempts to do what the Church has done from the first, in seeking to win Jews to Jesus as Messiah, are widely opposed and decried, by Christian as well as Jewish leaders.

Attempts to bring Jews to faith in Jesus are frequently denounced as proselytizing. This term is often used to imply dishonest and coercive modes of inducement, appeal to unworthy motives, and disregard of the question of truth that is being disseminated.

In recent years, "messianic" Jewish believers in Jesus, who as Christians celebrate and maximize their Jewish identity, have emerged as active evangelists to the Jewish community. Jewish leaders often accuse them of deception on the grounds that one cannot be both a Jew and a Christian. While these criticisms may reflect Judaism's current effort to define itself as a distinct religion in opposition to Christianity, they have led to much bewilderment and some misunderstanding and mistrust.

The Declaration responds to this complex situation and seeks to set directions for the future according to the Scriptures.

THE DECLARATION

I. THE DEMAND OF THE GOSPEL

Article I.1. We affirm that the redeeming love of God has been fully and finally revealed in Jesus Christ. We deny that those without faith in Christ know the full reality of God's love and of the gift that he gives.

Article I.2. We affirm that the God-given types, prophecies and visions of salvation and shalom in the Hebrew Scriptures find their present and future fulfillment in and through Jesus Christ, the Son of God, who by incarnation became a Jew and was shown to be the Son of God and Messiah by his resurrection. We deny that it is right to look for a Messiah who has not yet appeared in world history.

Article I.3. We affirm that Jesus Christ is the second person of the one God, who became a man, lived a perfect life, shed his blood on the cross as an atoning sacrifice for human sins, rose bodily from the dead, now reigns as Lord, and will return visibly to this earth, all to fulfill the purpose of bringing sinners to share eternally in his fellowship and glory. We deny that those who think of Jesus Christ in lesser terms than these have faith in him in any adequate sense.

Article I.4. We affirm that all human beings are sinful by nature and practice, and stand condemned, helpless and hopeless, before God, until the grace of Christ touches their lives and brings them to God's pardon and peace. We deny that any Jew or Gentile finds true peace with God through performing works of law.

Article I.5. We affirm that God's forgiveness of the penitent rests on the satisfaction rendered to his justice by the substitutionary sacrifice of Jesus Christ on the cross. We deny that any person can enjoy God's favor apart from the mediation of Jesus Christ, the sin-bearer.

Article I.6. We affirm that those who turn to Jesus Christ find him to be a sufficient Savior and Deliverer from all the evil of sin; from its guilt, shame, power, and perversity; from blind defiance of God, debasement of moral character, and the dehumanizing and destructive self-assertion that sin breeds. We deny that the salvation found in Christ may be supplemented in any way.

Article I.7. We affirm that faith in Jesus Christ is humanity's only way to come to know the Creator as Father, according to Christ's own Word: "I am the Way and the Truth and the Life; no one comes to the Father except through me" (John 14:6).

We deny that any non-Christian faith, as such, will mediate eternal life with God.

II. THE CHURCH OF JEWS AND GENTILES

Article II.8. We affirm that through the mediation of Jesus Christ, God has made a new covenant with Jewish and Gentile believers, pardoning their sins, writing his law on their hearts by his Spirit, so that they obey him, giving the Holy Spirit to indwell them, and bringing each one to know him by faith in a relationship of trustful gratitude for salvation. We deny that the blessings of the New Covenant belong to any except believers in Jesus Christ.

Article II.9. We affirm that the profession of continuing Jewish identity, for which Hebrew Christians have in the past suffered at the hands of both their fellow Jews and Gentile church leaders, was consistent with the Christian Scriptures and with the nature of the Church as one body in Jesus Christ in which Jews and non-Jews are united. We deny that it is necessary for Jewish Christians to repudiate their Jewish heritage.

Article II.10. We affirm that Gentile believers, who at present constitute the great bulk of the Christian Church, are included in the historically continuous community of believing people on earth which Paul pictures as God's olive tree (Rom. 11:13-24). We deny that Christian faith is necessarily non-Jewish, and that Gentiles who believe in Christ may ignore their solidarity with believing Jews, or formulate their new identity in Christ without reference to Jewishness, or decline to receive the Hebrew Scriptures as part of their own instruction from God, or refuse to see themselves as having their roots in Jewish history.

Article II.11. We affirm that Jewish people who come to faith in Messiah have liberty before God to observe or not observe traditional Jewish customs and ceremonies that are consistent with the Christian Scriptures and do not hinder fellowship with the rest of the Body of Christ. We deny that any inconsistency or deception is involved by Jewish Christians representing themselves as ''Messianic'' or ''completed'' or ''fulfilled'' Jews.

III. GOD'S PLAN FOR THE JEWISH PEOPLE

Article III.12. We affirm that Jewish people have an ongoing part in God's plan. We deny that indifference to the future of the Jewish people on the part of Christians can ever be justified.

Article III.13. We affirm that prior to the coming of Christ it was Israel's unique privilege to enjoy a corporate covenantal relationship with God, following upon the national redemption from slavery, and involving God's gift of the law and of a theocratic culture; God's promise of blessing to faithful obedience; and God's provision of atonement for transgression. We affirm that within this covenant relationship, God's pardon and acceptance of the penitent which was linked to the offering of prescribed sacrifices rested upon the foreordained sacrifice of Jesus Christ. We deny that covenantal privilege alone can ever bring salvation to impenitent unbelievers.

Article III.14. We affirm that much of the Judaism in its various forms of contemporary Israel and today's Diaspora is development out of, rather than an authentic embodiment of, the faith, love and hope that the Hebrew Scriptures teach. We deny that modern Judaism with its explicit negation of the divine person, work, and Messiahship of Jesus Christ contains within itself true knowledge of God's salvation.

Article III.15. We affirm that the biblical hope for Jewish people centers on their being restored through faith in Christ to their proper place as branches of God's olive tree from which they are at present broken off. We deny that the historical status of the Jews as God's people brings salvation to any Jew who does not accept the claims of Jesus Christ.

Article III.16. We affirm that the Bible promises that large numbers of Jews will turn to Christ through God's sovereign grace. We deny that this prospect renders needless the active proclamation of the gospel to Jewish people in this and every age.

Article III.17. We affirm that anti-Semitism on the part of professed Christians has always been wicked and shameful and that the Church has in the past been much to blame for tolerating and encouraging it and for condoning anti-Jewish actions on the part of individuals and governments. We deny that these silent failures, for which offending Gentile believers must ask forgiveness from both God and the Jewish community, lessen their responsibility to share the gospel with Jews today and for the future.

Article III.18. We affirm that it was the sins of the whole human race that sent Christ to the cross. We deny that it is right to single out the Jewish people for putting Jesus to death.

IV. EVANGELISM AND THE JEWISH PEOPLE

Article IV.19. We affirm that sharing the Good News of Jesus Christ with lost humanity is a matter of prime obligation for Christian people, both because the Messiah commands the making of disciples and because love of neighbor requires effort to meet our neighbor's deepest need. We deny that any other form of witness and service to others can excuse Christians from laboring to bring them to faith in Christ.

Article IV.20. We affirm that the Church's obligation to share saving knowledge of Christ with the whole human race includes the evangelizing of Jewish people as a priority: ''To the Jew first'' (Rom. 1:16). We deny that dialogue with Jewish people that aims at nothing more than mutual understanding constitutes fulfillment of this obligation.

Article IV.21. We affirm that the concern to point Jewish people to faith in Jesus Christ which the Christian Church has historically felt and shown was right. We deny that there is any truth in the widespread notion that evangelizing Jews is needless because they are already in covenant with God through Abraham and Moses and so are already saved despite their rejection of Jesus Christ as Lord and Savior.

Article IV.22. We affirm that all endeavors to persuade others to become Christians should express love to them by respecting their dignity and integrity at every point, including parents' responsibility in the case of their children. We deny that coercive or deceptive proselytizing, which violates dignity and integrity on both sides, can ever be justified.

Article IV.23. We affirm that it is unchristian, unloving, and discriminatory to propose a moratorium on the evangelizing of any part of the human race, and that failure to preach the gospel to the Jewish people would be a form of anti-Semitism, depriving this particular community of its right to hear the gospel. We deny that we have sufficient warrant to assure or anticipate the salvation of anyone who is not a believer in Jesus Christ.

Article IV.24. We affirm that the existence of separate churchly organizations for evangelizing Jews, as for evangelizing any other particular human group, can be justified pragmatically, as an appropriate means of fulfilling the Church's mandate to take the gospel to the whole human race. We deny that the depth of human spiritual need varies from group to group so that Jewish people may be thought to need Christ either more or less than others.

V. JEWISH-CHRISTIAN RELATIONS

Article V.25. We affirm that dialogue with other faiths that seeks to transcend stereotypes of them based on ignorance, and to find common ground and to share common concerns, is an expression of Christian love that should be encouraged. We deny that dialogue that explains the Christian faith without seeking to persuade the dialogue partners of its truth and claims is a sufficient expression of Christian love.

Article V.26. We affirm that for Christians and non-Christian Jews to make common cause in social witness and action, contending together for freedom of speech and religion, the value of the individual, and the moral standards of God's law is right and good. We deny that such limited cooperation involves any compromise of the distinctive views of either community or imposes any restraint upon Christians in seeking to share the gospel with the Jews with whom they cooperate.

Article V.27. We affirm that the Jewish quest for a homeland with secure borders and a just peace has our support. We deny that any biblical link between the Jewish people and the land of Israel justifies actions that contradict biblical ethics and constitute oppression of people-groups or individuals.

Notes: *Among the continuing controversial issues among Evangelicals has been the legitimacy of targeting Jews for evangelistic efforts. This debate has been fueled by the establishment of the state of Israel, which many Evangelicals see as a sign of the near approach of the return of Jesus, and the withdrawal from any evangelization of Jews among the larger liberal Protestant churches. During the 1970s, some North American Evangelicals opened a dialogue with Jewish leaders who were very much opposed to their continuing to target the Jewish community. Meanwhile, some Jewish converts launched a whole new evangelistic effort built around what became known as "Messianic Judaism." They argued that Jewish Christians could retain their Jewish culture, and they began to form ethnic parishes, which they termed "Messianic synagogues." In light of the call for world evangelism made by the Lausanne Covenant, and the new situation created by dialogue and Messianic Judaism, several consultations had been held in-*

cluding one in 1980 sponsored by the continuing Lausanne Committee for World Evangelism.

Then, in 1989 a group of Evangelicals interested in Jewish mission gathered under the sponsorship of the World Evangelism Fellowship and the Lausanne Committee. Arguing that it was un-Christian, unloving, and discriminatory to exclude anyone from the evangelization efforts, the assemblage issued a call for a continuing Jewish mission. In calling for that continued evangelism, the consultation also denounced anti-Semitism and specifically denied that the Jews were singularly responsible for sending Christ to the cross. The consultation also gave its blessing to the Messianic synagogues and denied any deception in Jewish converts who described themselves simply as "completed" or "fulfilled" Jews, a favorite self-description of Messianic Jews.

*   *   *

Plymouth Brethren

DOCTRINAL STATEMENT [CHRISTIAN BRETHREN (OPEN OR PLYMOUTH BRETHREN)/ EMMAUS BIBLE COLLEGE]

The teaching of Emmaus Bible College is based on the statement of faith which follows:

1) The Bible is inspired of God, inerrant in the original documents and of final authority in all matters of faith and practice.

2) There is one God, eternally existent in three Persons— Father, Son and Holy Spirit.

3) The Lord Jesus Christ is fully God, born of a virgin, sinlessly perfect. His sacrifice is substitutionary and representative. He rose bodily from the dead and ascended to His Father's right hand, where He now ministers as our Great High Priest. He will come to rapture His Church and subsequently return to reign over the earth.

4) Each member of the human race is fallen, sinful and lost, and regeneration by the Holy Spirit is absolutely essential for the salvation of man. Redemption is wholly by the blood of Christ, and salvation is by grace, through faith in our Lord Jesus Christ.

5) The Holy Spirit indwells the believer who is thus empowered to live a godly life.

6) There will be a resurrection of the saved and of the lost, of the saved unto eternal life, and of the lost unto eternal and conscious judgment.

7) The Church began with the descent of the Holy Spirit at Pentecost and is composed of all true believers in the Lord Jesus Christ. These believers are united to Him and to one another by the indwelling Spirit. The Church's calling,

hope and destiny are heavenly, and its chief functions are to glorify God and to witness for Christ until His return.

8) Christ, our risen Head, is the Giver of gifts, such as evangelists, pastors and teachers, and these men are responsible to Him for their service. They are given "for the perfecting of the saints unto the work of the ministry, for the edifying of the Body of Christ."

9) There are two Christian ordinances, baptism and the Lord's Supper. Baptism by immersion signifies that the believer, having died with Christ, is buried with Him in baptism and also is risen with Christ to walk in newness of life. The Lord's Supper is a memorial feast, instituted by the Lord Himself exclusively for His own.

10) Every true child of God possesses eternal life and being justified, sanctified and sealed with the Holy Spirit is safe and secure for all eternity.

11) The personal imminent return of the Lord Jesus Christ to translate His Church will be followed by the Tribulation and the inauguration of Christ's reign over the earth; He will then deliver up the Kingdom to God, the Father, that the Triune God may be all in all.

The teaching of Emmaus follows the historic, evangelical interpretation of the Scriptures which has, in general, been accepted by the Christian Church since its inception. It recognizes no sectarian barriers and seeks to declare the whole counsel of God without over-stressing any one line of truth.

Notes: *The Christian Brethren, like all groups that have emerged from the Plymouth Brethren tradition, is noncreedal and has no official statement of belief. However, Emmaus Bible College, Lombard, Illinois, a school sponsored by Christian Brethren congregations, has found it expedient to issue a Doctrinal Statement that summarizes the perspective of the college. It affirms the inerrancy of the Bible and a consensus theological statement. It assumes a free church stance regarding baptism and the Lord's Supper, which are considered ordinances rather than sacraments. It also prescribes the mode of baptism to be believer's baptism by immersion.*

*   *   *

Fundamentalists/Evangelicals

STATEMENT OF FAITH (ASSYRIAN EVANGELICAL CHURCH OF TURLOCK)

1. We believe that all scripture is given by inspiration of God. By this, we understand that the whole Bible is inspired in the sense that holy men of God "were moved by the Holy Spirit" to write the very words of scripture. We believe that this divine inspiration extends equally and fully to all parts of the writings historical, poetical, doctrinal, and prophetical as appeared in the inerrant, original manuscripts to all carts of the writings historical, poetical doctrinal, and prophetical as appeared in the inerrant, original manuscripts.

2. We believe the Godhead eternally exists in three persons—The Father, The Son, and The Holy Spirit.

3. We believe that Jesus Christ was conceived by the Holy Spirit, born of the Virgin Mary, and received a human body and a sinless human nature; yet, He retained His absolute deity, being at the same time truly God and truly man.

4. We believe in the deity and personality of the Holy Spirit, who indwells every true believer.

5. We believe that man was created in the image of God; that he sinned and thereby incurred not only physical death, but also that spiritual death which is separation from God; and that all human beings are born with a sinful nature.

6. We believe that the Lord Jesus Christ died for our sins according to the Scriptures as a representative and substitutionary sacrifice, and that all who believe in Him are justified on the ground of His shed blood.

7. We believe in the bodily resurrection and ascension of Jesus Christ and His present intercession in heaven for His saints.

8. We believe that the Church, the body of Christ, is composed of all those who personally receive Jesus Christ as Savior and Lord.

9. We believe in the real existence and personality of Satan.

10. We believe in "That Blessed Hope", the personal, premillennial, and imminent return of our Lord and Savior, Jesus Christ.

11. We believe in the bodily resurrection of the just and of the unjust; the everlasting blessedness of the saved; and the everlasting, conscious punishment of the lost.

12. We believe that upon salvation, we are divinely reckoned to be related to this world as strangers and pilgrims, ambassadors and witnesses, and that our purpose in life should be to make Christ known to the whole world.

Notes: *The Assyrian Evangelical Church of Turlock, California, is an independent Evangelical congregation composed predominantly of believers of Assyrian ethnic heritage. It affirms the consensus statement of Evangelical belief includ-*

ing the inerrancy of the Bible, the Trinity, the personality of Satan, and the imminent premillennial return of Jesus Christ.

*   *   *

TENETS OF FAITH (EVANGELICAL CHURCH ALLIANCE)

The Evangelical Church Alliance was founded by Godly men who were moved to band together for the purpose of promoting Evangelical Christianity throughout the world. They were motivated by a strong persuasion that the Bible, consisting of the sixty-six books of the Old and New Testaments, is the divinely inspired and inerrant Word of God, that the men who wrote it were moved by the Holy Ghost, that in its original manuscripts and languages it is without error, without contradiction, that it is historically accurate and scientifically correct, and that it is man's only and final word of authority in matters of faith and practice. They rejected the theory of organic evolution and affirmed that the opening chapters of the Book of Genesis contain the true account of creation and the beginning of life on the earth. They declared their belief in the virgin birth of Jesus Christ, His death and bodily resurrection, His ascension into heaven, that the shedding of His blood on the Cross provides man's only remedy for sin, and they looked forward to His coming again to rule on earth as King of Kings and Lord of Lords.

This is and shall continue to be the persuasion of the Evangelical Church Alliance, and all churches applying for membership, and all individuals applying for license, ordination, or membership must be so persuaded in order to be received into this Alliance.

All churches applying for membership, and all individuals applying for license, ordination or membership, shall subscribe to the following Tenets of Faith, which can never be repealed, changed, varied, altered, amended or modified:

A. We believe that both Old and New Testaments constitute the Divinely Inspired Word of God in the original languages and manuscripts.

B. We believe in one God existing eternally in three Persons: Father, Son, and Holy Spirit.

C. We believe that the Lord Jesus Christ, the Son of God, became man without ceasing to be God, in order that he might reveal God and redeem sinful men.

D. We believe that the Holy Spirit came forth from the Father and the Son to convict the world of sin, of righteousness, and of judgement; and to regenerate, sanctify, comfort and seal those who believe in Jesus Christ.

E. We believe that man is totally depraved in that of himself he is utterly unable to remedy his lost condition.

F. We believe that salvation is the gift of God brought to man by grace and received by personal faith in the Lord Jesus Christ, whose atoning blood was shed on the cross for the forgiveness of sins.

G. We believe in the water baptism of believers. symbolizing the believer's union in the death and resurrection of Jesus Christ.

H. We believe in the observance of the Lord's Supper, commemorating the sacrifice of our Savior for all mankind.

I. We believe the life of tile believer is to be separated from the world by consistent conduct before God and man, and is to be in the world as life-giving light.

J. We believe in the personal, and visible, and bodily return of the Lord Jesus Christ.

Notes: *The Evangelical Church Alliance, founded in 1928, is a fellowship of Evangelical congregations and ministers. Its Tenets of Faith affirm the Bible as the inspired Word of God, total human depravity, believer's baptism by immersion, and the separated life.*

*   *   *

Grace Gospel Movement

DOCTRINAL STATEMENT (GRACE MINISTRIES INTERNATIONAL)

''I therefore, the prisoner of the Lord, beseech you that ye walk worthy of the vocation wherewith ye are called, with all lowliness and meekness, with long-suffering. forbearing one another in love; endeavoring to keep the unity of the Spirit in the bond of peace. There is one body, and one Spirit, even as ye are called in one hope of your calling; one Lord, one faith, one baptism, one God and Father of all, who is above all, and through all, and in you all. But unto every one of us is given grace according to the measure of the gift of Christ'' (Eph. 4:1-7).

We affirm that the seven-fold unity expressed in this passage Is the Holy Spirit's doctrinal statement for the Church, which is the Body of Christ. We believe that all the expressions of doctrinal position and requirement for this Dispensation of the Grace of God must be in⁻ full accord with the Holy Spirit's outline. We recognize other doctrinal unities for other dispensations, but we affirm that Ephesians 4:4-6 stands alone as the doctrinal unity for this dispensation.

Desiring to be in full accord with the Mind of the Spirit, we hold and require the following doctrinal beliefs:

THE BIBLE

The entire Bible in its original writings is inerrant, being verbally inspired of God and is of plenary authority (2 Tim. 3:16, 17; 2 Pet. 1:2 1).

THE GODHEAD

There is one God, eternally existing in three Persons: Father, Son, and Holy Spirit (Deut. 6:4; 1 Tim. 2:5; Eph. 4:4-6; Matt. 28:19, 2 Cor. 13:14).

THE PERSON OF CHRIST

Jesus Christ was begotten by the Holy Spirit and born of the Virgin Mary and is true God and true man (1.K. 1:35; Phil. 2:6-9; Rom. 1:3, 4).

TOTAL DEPRAVITY

All men by nature are dead in trespasses and sins and are, therefore, totally unable to do anything pleasing to God (Eph. 2:1-3; Rom. 3:9-12).

REDEMPTION

God justifies ungodly sinners by His grace upon the ground of the blood of Christ through the means of faith. This complete salvation is bestowed as the free gift of God apart from man's works (Rom. 3:24-28; 5:1,9; Eph. 2:8,9).

ETERNAL SECURITY

All of the saved are eternally secure in Christ (Col. 3:1-4; Phil. 1:6; Rom 8:1; 8:29-34; Rom 8:38,39; John 10:27-29; Eph. 1:13-14).

PERSONALITY AND WORK OF THE HOLY SPIRIT

Holy Spirit is a Person, Who convicts the world of sin and Who regenerates, baptizes, indwells, enlightens, and empowers (John 16:8; Tit. 3:5; 1 Cor. 12:13; Eph. 3:17, 18; 3:16).

THE CHURCH

In the present dispensation there is only one true Church, which is called the Body of Christ (I Cor. 12:13; Eh. 1:22, 23; 3:6). The historical manifestation of the Body of Christ began with the Apostle Paul before he wrote his first epistle (I Thess. 2:14-16 cf. Acts 13:45,46; Phil. 1:5, 6 cf. Acts 16; 1 Cor. 12:13,27 cf. Acts 18).

GIFTS

The ministry gifts for the Body of Christ are enumerated in Ephesians 4:7.11; Romans 12:6-8; 1 Corinthians 12:1-31. Some of these gifts were permanent in nature and some were to pass away; some were of the nature of ministers given to the Church and some were individual enablements for spiritual services. Since the New Testament canon was completed through the ministries of Apostles and Prophets, we believe these two offices have been fulfilled and no longer exist. Likewise the sign gifts, such as tongues, miracles, and healing, which were addressed primarily to the nation of Israel (I Cor. 14:22) have fulfilled their purpose and have passed away according to I Corinthians 13:8-11.

WALK

By reason of Christ's victory over sin and of His indwelling Spirit, all of the saved may and should experience deliverance from the power of sin by obedience to Romans 6:11; but we deny that man's nature of sin is ever eradicated during this life (Rom. 6:6-14; Gal. 5:16-25; Rom. 8:37; 2 Cor. 2:14; 10:2-5).

LORD'S SUPPER

The communion of the Lord's Supper as revealed through the Apostle Paul in I Corinthians 11:23-26 is for members of the Body of Christ to observe "until He comes."

There is no place in Scripture where the Lord's supper and water baptism are linked together either as ordinances or as sacraments for the Church.

RESURRECTION

Jesus Christ was resurrected bodily from the dead (Luke 24:39-43). Therefore (1 Cor. 15:21), all men will have a bodily resurrection (Acts 24: 15): The saved to everlasting glory and the unsaved to everlasting punishment (John 5:29; Rev. 20:11-15).

BAPTISM

All saved persons have been made members of the Body of Christ by one divine baptism (I Cor. 12:13). By that one baptism every member of the Body of Christ is identified with Christ in His death, burial, and resurrection. In the Light of the statement concerning the one baptism in Ephesians 4:5, the statements concerning baptism in Colossians 2:12 and Romans 6:3, 4, and Paul's statement in I Corinthians 1:17 that "Christ sent me not to baptize, but to preach the gospel," we conclude that water baptism his no place in God's spiritual program for the Body of Christ in this Day of Grace.

SECOND COMING OF CHRIST

The rapture of the Church and the second coming of Christ will be pre-millennial. He will come first to receive the Church unto Himself (I Thess. 4:13-18; Phil. 3:20, 21) and then come to receive His Millennial Kingdom, over which He will reign (Zech. 14:4, 9; Acts 1: 10,11; Rev. 19;11-16; 20:4-6). Because of the nature of the Body of Christ, the resurrection and rapture of the Church, which is His Body, will take place before the Great Tribulation (Jet. 30:7; Matt. 24:15-31) at His appearing in the air (I Thess. 4:13-18; Phil. 3:20, 21; Tit, 2:13, 14; 1 Cor. 15:51-53). The resurrection of the other saved dead will occur after the Tribulation (Rev. 20:4-6).

STATE OF THE DEAD

Nowhere does Scripture extend the hope of salvation to the unsaved dead but instead reveals that they will ever continue to exist in a state of conscious suffering (Luke 16:23-28; Rev. 14:11; 20:14, 15; Col. 3:6-; Rom. 1:21-32; John 3:36; Phil. 3:19; 2 Thess. 1:9). The teachings of Universalism, of probation after death, of annhiliation of the unsaved dead, and of the unconscious state of the dead, saved or unsaved (Luke 16:23-28; PhiL 1:23; 2 Cor. 5:6;8). are opposed by us as being thoroughly unscriptural and dangerous doctrines.

DOCTRINAL STATEMENT (GRACE MINISTRIES INTERNATIONAL) (continued)

MISSION

The mission and commission of the Church, which is His body, is to proclaim the message of reconciliation (2 Cor. 5:14-21) and endeavor to make all men see what is the Dispensation of the Mystery (Eh. 3:8, 9). In this, we should follow the Apostle Paul (I Cor. 4:16; 11:1; Phil. 3:17; 1 Tim. 1:11- 16). That distinctive message which the Apostle or the Gentiles (Rom. 11:13; 15:16) calls "my gospel" (Rom. 2:16; 16:25) is also called the "gospel of the grace of God" (Acts 20:24). We, like Paul, must preach the entire Word of God in the light of this Gospel (2 Tim. 4:2; Gal 1:8, 9) and strive to reach those in the regions beyond where Christ is not yet named (Rom. 15:20; 2 Cor. 10:16).

Notes: *Grace Ministries International is a missionary sending agency. Its belief, as revealed in its Doctrinal Statement, is fundamentalist Christianity with one point of deviation. The Grace Gospel perspective assumes that the message of the church is best exemplified in the writings of Paul, through which the rest of the New Testament and the Bible must be understood. In light of the message of one baptism in I Corinthians 12 and Ephesians 4, the Grace Gospel followers do not practice water baptism, but rather believe in a spiritual baptism. This unique idea is termed the Dispensation of the Mystery.*

*   *   *

DOCTRINAL STATEMENT (THINGS TO COME MISSION)

INTRODUCTORY

"I therefore, the prisoner of the Lord, beseech you that ye walk worthy of the vocation wherewith ye are called, with all lowliness and meekness, with long suffering, forbearing one another in love; endeavoring to keep the unity of the Spirit in the bond of peace. There is ONE BODY, and ONE SPIRIT, even as ye are called in ONE HOPE of your calling; ONE LORD, ONE FAITH, ONE BAPTISM, ONE GOD and FATHER of all, who is above all, and through all, and in you all. But unto every one of us is given grace according to the measure of the gift of Christ." (Eph. 4:1-7.)

We affirm that the seven-fold unity expressed in this passage is the Holy Spirit's DOCTRINAL STATEMENT for the Church which is the Body of Christ. We believe that all expressions of doctrinal position and requirements for this Dispensation of the Grace of God must be in full accord with the Holy Spirit's outline. We recognize other doctrinal unities for other dispensations, but we affirm that Eph. 4:4-6 stands alone as the Doctrinal Unity for this dispensation.

Desiring to be in full accord with the Mind of the Spirit, we hold and require the following doctrinal beliefs.

THE BIBLE

The entire Bible in its original writings is verbally inspired of God, and is of plenary authority. (2 Tim. 3:16, 17; 2 Pet. 1:21.)

THE GODHEAD

There is ONE God, eternally existing in three Persons: Father, Son and Holy Spirit. (Deut. 6:4 Jn. 4.24; 10:30; Eph. 4:6.)

THE PERSON OF CHRIST

Jesus Christ was begotten by the Holy Spirit, and born of the Virgin Mary, and is true God and True Man. (Lk. 1:35; Phil. 2:6-9; Rom. 1:3, 4.)

TOTAL DEPRAVITY

All men by nature are dead in trespasses and sins, and are therefore totally unable to do anything pleasing to God. (Eph. 2:1-3; Rom. 8:7, 8.)

REDEMPTION

God justifies ungodly sinners by His grace, upon the ground of the blood of Christ, through the means of faith. This complete salvation is bestowed as the free gift of God apart from man's works. (Rom. 3:24-28; 5:1, 9; Eph. 2:8, 9.)

ETERNAL SECURITY

All the saved are eternally secure in Christ. (Col. 2:9; 3:1-4; Phil. 1:6.)

PERSONALITY AND WORK OF THE HOLY SPIRIT

The Holy Spirit is a Person who convicts the World of sin, and who, regenerates, baptizes, seals, indwells, enlightens, and empowers the saved. (Jn. 16:8; Tit. 3:5; I Cor. 12:13; Eph. 1:13, 17, 18; 3:16.)

THE CHURCH

In the present dispensation there is only ONE Bible Church, which is called the Body of Christ, having a membership composed of all of the saved. (I Cor. 12:13; Eph. 1:22, 23; 3:6.)

GIFTS

The only gifts necessary for the ministry of the Body of Christ are those enumerated in Eph. 4:7-16.

WALK

By reason of Christ's victory over sin and of His indwelling Spirit, all of the saved may and should experience deliverance from the power of sin by obedience to Rom. 6:11, but we deny that man's nature of sin is ever eradicated during his life. (Rom. 6:6-14; Gal. 5:16-25; Rom. 8:37; II Cor. 2:14; 10:2-5.)

LORD'S SUPPER

The communion of the Lord's Supper as revealed through the Apostle Paul in I Cor. 11:23-26 is for members of the Body of Christ to observe "until He comes."

There is no place in Scripture where the Lord's Supper and water baptism are linked together either as ordinances or as sacraments for the Church.

BAPTISM

All saved persons have been made members of the Body of Christ by ONE Divine baptism. By that ONE baptism every member of the Body of Christ is identified with Christ in His death, burial, and resurrection. In the light of the statement concerning the ONE baptism in Eph. 4:5, and the statement concerning baptism in Col. 2:12, and Paul's statement in I Cor. 1:17 that "Christ sent me not to baptize but to preach the gospel," we affirm that water baptism has no place in God's Spiritual program for the Body of Christ in this day of grace.

RESURRECTION

Jesus Christ was resurrected bodily from the dead, and at His coming He will raise all of the saved to everlasting glory, and at the end He will raise all of the lost to everlasting condemnation. (Luke 24:39; 1 Cor. 15:22-24; Rev. 20:11-15.)

SECOND COMING OF CHRIST

The second coming of Christ will be personal and pre-millennial. He will come first to receive the Church unto Himself. and then to receive His Millennial Kingdom over which He will reign. (I Thess. 4:13-18; Phil. 3:21; Rev. 19:11-20:10.)

STATE OF THE UNSAVED DEAD

"The Scripture in no place extends the hope of salvation to the unsaved dead, but instead reveals that they will ever continue to exist in a state of conscious suffering. The teachings of Universalism, of probation after death, of annihilation of the unsaved dead, and of the unconscious state of the dead are opposed by us as being thoroughly unscriptural and dangerous doctrines. (Lk. 13:23-28; Rom. 1:21-32; Jn. 3:36; Eph. 5:5; Phil. 3:19; Col. 3:6; II Thess. 1:9; II Cor. 5:6-8; 12:3, 4; Phil. 1:23; Rev. 14:11; 20:14, 15.)

Notes: *Things to Come Mission is a Grace Gospel missionary agency. Its belief is fundamentalist in content with the one exception of the unique Grace Gospel idea. The Grace Gospel perspective assumes that the message of the church is best exemplified in the writings of Paul through which the rest of the New Testament and the Bible must be understood. In light of the message of one baptism in I Corinthians 12 and Ephesians 4, the Grace Gospel followers do not practice water baptism, but rather believe in a spiritual baptism. This unique idea is termed the Dispensation of the Mystery.*

*　　*　　*

Evangelical Ministries

WHAT WE BELIEVE (ACCENT PUBLICATIONS)

1. We believe in THE HOLY SCRIPTURE: accepting fully the writings of the Old and New Testaments as the inerrant Word of God, verbally inspired in all parts and therefore altogether sufficient as our only infallible and authoritative rule of faith and practice. Psalm 119:160; Proverbs 30:5a; II Timothy 3:16,17; II Peter 1:19-21.

2. We believe in THE ONE TRUE GOD: who is an intelligent, sovereign, spiritual and personal Being; perfect, infinite, and eternal in His being, holiness and love, wisdom and power; absolutely separate from and above the world as its Creator, yet everywhere present in the world as the Upholder of all things. He is revealed to us as Father, Son and Holy Spirit, three distinct persons but without division of nature, essence or being, and each having a distinct ministry in God's relation to His creation and people. Genesis 1:1; Exodus 15:11; Psalm 83:18; 139:7-9, Matthew 28:19; John 10:30; 15:26.

3. We believe in THE LORD JESUS CHRIST: who is the second Person of the Triune God, the eternal Word and Only Begotten Son; that without any change in His divine Person, He became man by miracle of the Virgin Birth, thus to continue forever as both true God and true Man, one Person with two natures; that as Man He was tempted in all points as we are, yet without sin; that as the perfect Lamb of God He gave Himself in death upon the cross, bearing there the sin of the world, and suffering its full penalty of divine wrath in our stead; that He arose from the grave in a glorified body; that as our great High Priest He ascended into Heaven, there to appear before the face of God as our Advocate and Intercessor. John 1:1,14; 3:16; Matthew 1:18-25; Galatians 4:4,5; Philippians 2:6-10; 1 Corinthians 15:3-7; Hebrews 4:14-16 I John 2:1,2.

4. We believe in THE HOLY SPIRIT: who is the Third Person of the Trinity, and the divine Agent in nature, revelation and redemption; that He convicts the world concerning sin, righteousness and judgment; that He regenerates, indwells, baptizes, seals and anoints all who become children of God through Christ; that he further empowers, guides, teaches, sanctifies and fills believers who daily surrender to Him. John 3:5; 14:16,17,26; 16:7-14; Romans 8-9; I Corinthians 12:13; II Corinthians 3:18; Ephesians 1:13; 5:18.

5. We believe ALL MEN ARE BY NATURE AND CHOICE SINFUL AND LOST: that man was the direct creation of God, made in His image and likeness; that by personal disobedience to the revealed will of God, man become a

sinful creature, the father of a fallen race which is universally sinful in both nature and practice, thus alienated from the life and family of God, under the righteous judgment and wrath of God, and has within himself no possible means of salvation. Genesis 1:27; 3:6; Psalm 51:5; Romans 3:23; 5:12,19; Galatians 3:11.

6. We believe in SALVATION BY GRACE THROUGH FAITH: that salvation is the free gift of God, neither merited nor secured in part or in whole by any virtue or work of man, but received only by personal faith in the Lord Jesus Christ, in whom all true believers have as a present possession the gift of eternal life, a perfect righteousness, sonship in the family of God, deliverance and security from all condemnation, every spiritual resource needed for life and godliness, and the divine guarantee that they shall never perish; that this salvation affects the whole man; that apart from Christ there is no possible salvation. Ephesians 2:8,9; Titus 3:5; John 1:12, 3:14; 10:28,29; Romans 8:1; Philippians 1:6.

7. We believe in RIGHTEOUS LIVING AND GODLY WORKS: not as a means of salvation in any sense, but as its proper evidence and fruit; and therefore as Christians we should obey the Word of our Lord, seek the things which are above, walk as He walked, accept as our solemn responsibility the duty and privileges of bearing the gospel to a lost world; remembering that a victorious and fruitful Christian life is possible only for those who in gratitude for the infinite and undeserved mercies of God have presented themselves wholly to Christ. Ephesians 2:10; Romans 12:1,2; Philippians 2:16.

8. We believe in THE EXISTENCE OF SATAN: who originally was created a holy and perfect being, but through pride and wicked ambition rebelled against God, thus becoming utterly depraved in character, the great adversary of God and His people, leader of all other evil angels and wicked spirits, the deceiver and god of this present world: that his powers are vast, but strictly limited by the permissive will of God who overrules all his wicked devices for good; that he was defeated and judged at the cross, and therefore his final doom is certain; that we are able to resist and overcome him only in the armor of God, by the blood of the Lamb and through the power of the Holy Spirit. Isaiah 14:12-15; Ephesians 6:12; I Peter 5:8; I John 3:8; Revelation 12:9-11; 20:10.

9. We believe in THE SECOND COMING OF CHRIST: that His coming in the air to rapture His church, which is our blessed Hope, is always imminent; that when He has first by resurrection of the dead and translation of the living removed from the earth His waiting Church, He will then pour out the righteous judgments of God upon the unbelieving world and afterwards descend with His Church and establish His glorious and literal kingdom over all the nations for a thousand years. I Thessalonians 4:13-18; James 5:8; Hebrews 10:37; Jude 14,15; Revelation 19:11-16; 20:4-7.

10. We believe in FUTURE LIFE, BODILY RESURRECTION AND ETERNAL JUDGMENT: that the spirits of the saved at death go immediately to be with Christ in Heaven, that their works shall be brought before the Judgment Seat of Christ for the determination of rewards which will take place at the time when Christ comes for His own; that the spirits of the unsaved at death descend immediately into Hades where they are kept under punishment until the final day of judgment, at which time their bodies shall be raised from the grave, that they shall be judged and cast into Hell, the place of final and everlasting punishment. I Corinthians 15; II Corinthians 5:8-10; Luke 16:19-23; Revelation 20:11-15.

11. We believe in THE SEPARATION OF CHURCH AND STATE, with each having definite and distinct spheres of responsibility. Matthew 22:21; Romans 13:1-7.

12. We believe in THE PRIESTHOOD OF ALL BELIEVERS: that Christ is our Great High Priest and through Him every born-again person has direct access into God's presence without the need of a human priest; that the believer has the right and responsibility to personally study and interpret the Scriptures guided by the Holy Spirit. John 14:6; Hebrews 4:16; II Timothy 2:15; I Peter 2:1,5,9.

13. We believe in THE LORDSHIP OF JESUS CHRIST: that He alone is Head of the Body of Christ, into which all true believers are immediately baptized by the Holy Spirit; that all members of this one spiritual body should assemble and identify themselves in local churches. I Corinthians 12:13; Ephesians 1:22,23; 4:11-15; Galatians 1:22.

14. We believe in THE IMPORTANCE OF THE LOCAL CHURCH: that a New Testament church is a local assembly of born-again baptized believers united in organization to practice New Testament ordinances, to meet together for worship, prayer, fellowship, teaching and a united testimony, and to actively engage in carrying out the Great Commission. Acts 2:41,42; I Corinthians 11:2; Matthew 28:19,20.

15. We believe in THE INDEPENDENCE AND AUTONOMY OF THE LOCAL CHURCH: that each new Testament church is free to govern itself without ecclesiastical interference, and should cooperate with other New Testament churches as the Holy Spirit leads; that it is responsible to follow the pattern of the New Testament church and is directly accountable to God. Matthew 18:17; Acts 6:1-5; 13:1-3; 15:22-23.

16. We believe THE ORDINANCES GIVEN TO THE LOCAL CHURCH ARE TWO, BAPTISM AND THE LORD'S SUPPER: that Baptism is by immersion of believers, thus portraying the death, burial, and the resurrection of Jesus Christ; that the Lord's Supper is the partaking of the bread and cup by the believer as continuing memorial of the broken body and shed blood of Christ. Matthew 28:19,20; Acts 2:41; 8:38,39; Matthew 26:26-30; I Corinthians 11:23-34.

Notes: *Accent Publications, founded in 1947, is an Evangelical publishing house. Its statement of belief affirms the inerrancy of the Bible and a consensus Evangelical theological perspective. It affirms the importance of the local church and the two ordinances of the Lord's supper and believer's baptism by immersion.*

*   *   *

WHAT DOES ACTION BELIEVE? (ACTION INTERNATIONAL MINISTRIES)

Among other equally Biblical truths, we believe in:

A. The Bible, the Word of God; in its divine verbal, plenary inspiration; its inerrancy and infallibility in the original languages; and its supreme and final authority in faith and life. (II Tim. 3:16; II Pet. 1:20,21);

B. One God, eternally existing in three distinct persons: Father. Son and Holy Spirit (Deut. 6:4; Matt. 28:19; II Cor. 13:14);

C. The Lord Jesus Christ:

    1. His essential, absolute and eternal Deity (Phil. 2:6; John 1:4, Heb. 1:8);

    2. His true and sinless humanity (I Pet. 2:22; 1 John 3:5)

    3. His virgin birth (Isa. 7.14; Matt. 1:20);

    4. His substitutionary, propitiatory death (Matt. 20:28; Mark 1:45; I. Tim. 2:6);

    5. His bodily resurrection (John 20:19,20);1

    6. His ascension to the right hand of the Father (Mark 16:19; Luke 24:51); and

    7. His personal, visible and bodily coming again with power and great glory (Titus 2:13; John 14:2, 3; Rev. 19:11-16);

D. The Holy Spirit who shows the redeeming purpose of God to the world by convincing the world of sin, of righteousness and judgment (John 16:7-11), and by regenerating (Titus 3:5), uniting to Christ (I Cor. 12:13), indwelling (Eph. 1:13; 5:18), sanctifying (Gal. 5:16; I Cor. 6:11), illuminating (John 16:13) and empowering for service (I Cor. 12:4-11), all who place complete faith in the Lord Jesus Christ (Gal. 5:5);

E. The total depravity of Man because of the Fall (Gen.3:10-24);

F. Salvation by grace through faith in Jesus Christ apart from works (Eph. 2:8);

G. The everlasting bliss of the saved and the eternal suffering of the lost (Dan. 12:2; Luke 16:24-26; John 5:28; Rev. 20:14);

H. The real spiritual unity in Christ of all redeemed by His precious Blood (I Cor. 12:13; Eph. 1:4-6; 4:11-15; 5:25, 26); and

I. The necessity of maintaining, according to the Word of God, the purity of the Church in doctrine and life (I Cor. 6:19-20; and I Thess. 4:3)

Notes: *Action International Ministries, founded in 1970, is an independent Evangelical sending agency. Its statement of belief includes a strong position on biblical authority and a detailed understanding of the work of Christ and the Holy Spirit. Based in a Calvinist theological tradition, it affirms the doctrine of human depravity.*

*   *   *

OUR BASIS OF FAITH (AFRICA EVANGELICAL FELLOWSHIP)

1. The Scriptures: The divine inspiration by the Holy Spirit of the Old and New Testaments, thus guaranteeing that this revelation as originally given was without error; and their supreme authority in faith and practice.

2. The Trinity: The Trinity, the deity and the personality of the Father, of the Son and of the Holy Spirit, each having precisely the same divine nature and attributes: these three being one God.

3. Jesus Christ: The incarnation, including the divine conception, virgin birth and true humanity without sin; death, bodily resurrection, ascension and visible second advent of the Lord Jesus Christ; the universal sufficiency of His substitutionary atonement for the sins of the whole world, and the free justification by faith in Him alone of every sinner who repents, believes in, and receives Him as the personal Savior; our present Advocate with the Father.

4. The Holy Spirit: The Holy Spirit who convicts men of sin, regenerates them, baptizing them into the body of Christ at their conversion; who seals, indwells and fills believers, producing in them the fruit of the Spirit and who bestows power and gifts for service.

5. Satan: The personality of Satan, the arch-enemy of God: who seeks to usurp the authority of God and to deceive mankind, who shall ultimately be cast into the lake of fire for eternity.

6. Man: Man's original creation in innocency by God; his rebellion in Adam; the depravity of man's fallen nature and his inability of himself to please God; the necessity of the Holy Spirit's work as the only means of the regeneration and the sanctification of the believer.

7. Salvation: Holiness of heart and life and the full provision for this in Christ Jesus, good works as the proof and result of saving faith, the eternal salvation of the saved and the eternal punishment of the lost, present conscious assur-

OUR BASIS OF FAITH (AFRICA EVANGELICAL FELLOWSHIP)
(continued)

ance of salvation, absolution through Christ our High Priest alone and the joyful anticipation of His return; the believer's resurrection in a spiritual body to live in eternal fellowship with God.

Notes: *The Africa Evangelical Fellowship, founded in 1889, is a missionary agency operating primarily in southern Africa. Its statement of faith emphasizes biblical authority and the traditional Evangelical concerns for the Trinity, the work of Christ and the Holy Spirit, and salvation.*

*   *   *

STATEMENT OF DOCTRINE AND FAITH BASIS (AFRICA INLAND MISSION)

The members of this Mission declare their belief in:

SECTION I

The unity and trinity of God, eternally existing in three co-equal Persons, the Father, the Son, and the Holy Spirit.

SECTION 2

God the Creator and Preserver of all things, who created man, male and female, in His own image, and gave them dominion over the earthly creation.

SECTION 3

The deity and humanity of God the Son, the Lord Jesus Christ, who, being very God, also became man, being begotten by the Holy Spirit, born of the Virgin Mary, was crucified, dead and buried, was raised bodily from the dead, and ascended to the right hand of the Father; whose two natures continue eternally and inseparably joined together in one Person.

SECTION 4

The deity and personality of God the Holy Spirit, and the necessity of His work to make the death of Christ effective to the individual sinner, leading him to repentance toward God and faith in the Lord Jesus Christ; and in His ministry, dwelling permanently within and working through the believer for godly life and service.

SECTION 5

The divine, verbal inspiration and infallibility and inerrancy of the Scriptures of the Old and New Testaments as originally given, and their absolute and final authority in all matters of faith and conduct.

SECTION 6

The universal sinfulness and guilt of human nature since the fall, rendering man subject to God's wrath and condemnation.

SECTION 7

The sacrificial death of our Representative and Substitute, the Lord Jesus Christ, the incarnate Son of God, by the shedding of whose blood atonement was made for the sins of the whole world and whereby alone men are redeemed from the guilt, penalty and power of sin.

SECTION 8

The necessity of the new birth as the work of God the Holy Spirit, to be obtained only by receiving the Lord Jesus Christ as Savior; that men are saved by grace through faith, not by works.

SECTION 9

The security of the believer, based entirely on the atoning work of the Lord Jesus Christ, whereby, as a born-again child of God, he has assurance of salvation and has the right to all the privileges of the sons of God.

SECTION 10

The responsibility of the believer to maintain good works, and to obey the revealed will of God in life and service, through which eternal rewards shall be received.

SECTION 11

The True Church, whose Head is the Lord Jesus Christ, and whose members are all regenerate persons united to Christ and to one another by the Holy Spirit.

SECTION 12

The observance of the ordinances of Baptism and the Lord's Supper as appointed by the Lord Jesus Christ.

SECTION 13

The supreme mission of the Church as being to glorify God and to preach the gospel to every creature.

SECTION 14

The personal and visible return of the Lord Jesus Christ.

SECTION 15

The resurrection of the body.

SECTION 16

The eternal blessedness of the saved, and the eternal punishment of the lost.

Notes: *The Africa Inland Mission International, founded in 1895, oversees missionary activity in Africa and the urban United States. Its lengthy and, for Evangelicals, detailed Statement of Doctrine comes from its constitution. It affirms* *both the infallibility and inerrancy of the Bible, the Trinity, and the deity of Christ.*

*   *   *

STATEMENT OF FAITH (ALPHA AND OMEGA MINISTRIES)

We believe the Bible to be the written revelation of God, complete and sufficient in all respects. We believe the Scriptures to be "God-breathed" and therefore fully authoritative in and of themselves; they rely for their authority upon no church, council, or creed, but are authoritative simply because they are the Word of God. The Scriptures, as they embody the very speaking of God, partake of His authority, His power.

We believe in one true and eternal God, unchanging, unchangeable. We believe God is the Creator of all that exists in heaven and in earth. The God who is described in the Bible is unique; He is unlike anyone or anything else in all the universe. God has all power, all knowledge, all wisdom, and is due all glory, honor and praise. All that comes to pass does so at the decree of God. All things will, in the end, result in the glory of God.

We believe the Bible teaches that there is but one being of God, yet there are three Persons who share this one being of God: the Father, the Son, and the Spirit. Each Person is fully and completely God, each is described in Scripture as possessing the attributes of God. The Father, Son, and Spirit have eternally existed in the relationship described by term "Trinity."

We believe that man was created in the image of God. Man rebelled against His Creator, and fell into sin. As a result, man became spiritually dead, totally unwilling and indeed incapable of seeking after God. God, from eternity past, having foreordained all things, joined a certain people to Christ Jesus, so that He might redeem them from their sin and in so doing bring glory to Himself. Jesus Christ, the Son of God, died in the place of this elect people, providing full and complete forgiveness of sins by His death upon the cross of Calvary. No other work can provide for forgiveness of sins, and no addition can be made to the completed and finished work of Christ.

We believe that God, in His sovereign grace and mercy, regenerates sinful men by the power of the Holy Spirit, not by any action of their own, bringing them to new life. God grants to them the gifts of faith and repentance, which they then exercise by believing in Christ and turning from their sins in love for God. As a result of this faith, based upon the sacrifice of the Lord Jesus Christ, God justifies or makes righteous the one who believes. God's gift of faith, and the continuing work of the Holy Spirit in the lives of the elect, results in good works. These good works flow from true, saving faith; they are a necessary result of faith, but are not to be considered necessary to the gaining of justification, which is by God's grace through faith alone, so that no man can boast.

We believe Jesus Christ established His Church, which is made up of all the elect of God. His Church, as an obedient bride, listens to His Word as found in the Bible. All who believe in Christ are placed in His body, the Church. The local expressions of the Church are very important, and each believer should be actively involved in such a fellowship.

We believe that Christ is coming again to judge the living and the dead. This promise is found throughout the inspired Scriptures. Till His return, believers are to live lives that bring glory to God through Jesus Christ. The Church is to be busy doing the work of evangelism and discipleship, proclaiming the pure, uncompromised Gospel of Christ by teaching the Word of God.

Notes: *Alpha and Omega Ministries, founded in 1983, is an Evangelical Christian counter-cult group with special emphasis on countering the teachings of the Church of Jesus Christ of Latter-Day Saints, the Jehovah's Witnesses, and the Roman Catholic Church. Its Statement of Faith includes a strong statement on the authority of the Bible (though avoiding the language of infallibility, inerrancy, and plenary inspiration) and sets its position against all others. It affirms the Trinity, as opposed to the Jehovah's Witnesses, who deny the Trinity, and emphasizes the finished work of Christ, as opposed to Roman Catholics, who some feel implicitly deny the doctrine of transubstantiation in Mass.*

*   *   *

STATEMENT OF FAITH (AMERICAN ACCREDITING ASSOCIATION OF THEOLOGICAL INSTITUTIONS)

American Accrediting Association of Theological Institutions holds the following Doctrinal view:

We believe in the verbal inspiration of the 66 books of the Bible in its original writings and that it is without error and is the sole authority in all matters of faith and practice.

We believe there is only one true God, existing in three persons, Father, Son and Holy Spirit. These three, are co-eternal and co-equal from all eternity, each with distinct personalities but of one essence.

We believe that Adam was created without sin but fell by disobedience and thus the whole race fell and is by nature spiritually dead and lost.

We believe that Jesus Christ is the Son of God, co-existent with the Father and the Holy Spirit and that He came to the world, born of a virgin, shed His blood on Calvary, as a vicarious substitute for all sin that He was buried and rose again bodily and ascended to the right hand of the Father.

We believe in the personal work of the Holy Spirit which includes conviction of sin regeneration of sinners, and indwelling believers, as well as other ministries,

STATEMENT OF FAITH (AMERICAN ACCREDITING ASSOCIATION OF THEOLOGICAL INSTITUTIONS) (continued)

We believe that a soul is saved when He repents of his sins, and Christ is accepted as personal Savior and Lord and the Holy Spirit imparts eternal life.

We believe in the Premillennial Second Coming of the Lord Jesus, in the bodily resurrection of the righteous dead at His coming, and in an endless Heaven for all the redeemed and an endless punishment for the lost.

We hold to the conservative, fundamental, evangelical interpretation of the scriptures and the Christian faith and Non-Charismatic in doctrine.

The primary doctrinal qualification for those seeking accreditation by the American Accrediting Association of Theological Institutions is to believe in the following;

1. Verbal Inspiration of the original writings of the 66 books of the Bible.

2. Virgin Birth of the Lord Jesus Christ.

3. The Vicarious atonement and substitute of Jesus Christ on behalf of lost sinners.

4. The bodily resurrection of Jesus Christ.

5. The second coming of Jesus Christ.

6. The New Birth experience.

Notes: *The American Accrediting Association of Theological Institutions, founded in 1983, set standards for Bible college and other conservative Evangelical institutions of higher education. It includes under its supervision only those fundamentalist schools that operate from an acceptance of the inerrancy of the Bible. The Association is also specifically opposed to any accommodation to Pentecostalism.*

*　　　*　　　*

TENETS OF FAITH (AMERICAN ASSOCIATION OF BIBLE COLLEGES)

According to the Constitution of the American Association of Bible Colleges, the following statement of faith is to be subscribed to annually by each member school through the signature of the president or of a board official.

1. We believe that there is one God, eternally existing in three persons, Father, Son, and Holy Spirit.

2. We believe the Bible to be the inspired, the only infallible, authoritative Word of God.

3. We believe in the deity of our Lord Jesus Christ, in His virgin birth, in His sinless life, in His miracles, in His vicarious death and atonement through His shed blood, in His bodily resurrection, in His ascension to the right hand of the Father, and in His personal and visible return in power and glory.

4. We believe that man was created in the image of God, that he was tempted by Satan and fell, and that, because of the exceeding sinfulness of human nature. regeneration by the Holy Spirit is absolutely necessary for salvation.

5. We believe in the present ministry of the Holy Spirit by whose indwelling the Christian is enabled to live a godly life, and by Whom the Church is empowered to carry out Christ's great commission.

6. We believe in the bodily, resurrection of both the saved and the lost; those who are saved unto the resurrection of life and those who are lost unto the resurrection of damnation.

Notes: *Founded in 1947, American Association of Bible Colleges is the national accrediting agency for Bible colleges. Its brief Tenets of Faith affirm the infallibility of the Bible and an Evangelical theological consensus.*

*　　　*　　　*

DOCTRINAL STATEMENT (AMERICAN BOARD OF MISSIONS TO THE JEWS, INC.)

1. The American Board of Missions to the Jews, Inc. believes in the verbal, plenary inspiration of the Scriptures and that they are inerrant, infallible and authoritative.

2. We believe in the Triune nature of the one true God, and in the Deity of the Lord Jesus Christ, the only begotten Son of God, born of a virgin.

3. We believe that all mankind is separated from God because of sin and therefore in need of reconciliation through the Messiah of Israel, the Lord Jesus.

4. We believe in His sacrificial blood atonement at Calvary, His bodily resurrection from the dead, and His premillennial second coming.

5. We believe in presenting the Gospel *"to the Jew first and also to the Gentile"* so that lost mankind might be saved.

Notes: *The American Board of Missions to the Jews is one of the older organizations pursuing Christian evangelism in*

Jewish communities. This brief statement emphasizes the biblical authority for the Board's ministry.

*   *   *

A JEWISH CONFESSION OF FAITH (AMERICAN BOARD OF MISSIONS TO THE JEWS, INC./SAR SHALOM CONGREGATION)

ARTICLE I

I BELIEVE with all my heart in the God of Abraham, Isaac, and Jacob; as it is written, "Hear, O Israel: The Lord our God is one Lord." These Three are One: Father, Son, and Holy Spirit, one God. (Det. 6:4; Mark 12:29.)

ARTICLE 2

I believe with all my heart in the Lord Jesus Christ, the Son of God. I believe that He was born of the Virgin Mary, by the Holy Spirit, and through His death on the cross became an innocent and pure sacrifice for my sins. (Isaiah 7:14; Psalms 2:7; Luke 1:31.)

ARTICLE 3

I believe with all my heart that the Lord Jesus Christ after His death on the cross for my sins, rose again from the dead on the third day and ascended into heaven and is now seated on the right hand of the Father in heaven. (Psalms 16:10.)

ARTICLE 4

I believe with all my heart that the Lord Jesus Christ will come again to judge the living and the dead and to rule the world in righteousness and peace, and of His kingdom there shall be no end. (Daniel 12:2; Isaiah 9:6,7; 2 Tim. 4:1)

ARTICLE 5

I believe with all my heart in the Holy Spirit of God our Comforter, who dwells in my heart because of my faith in the Lord Jesus Christ. (John 14:16, 17, 26.)

ARTICLE 6

I believe with all my heart that the Lord Jesus Christ will gather unto Himself all true believers when the Church, His glorious Body, has been completed, and that all believers will be saved from the Tribulation and "the time of Jacob's trouble." I believe in the return of the Lord Jesus Christ with His saints and that we will reign with Him a thousand years here on the earth. (Jer. 30:7; I Thess. 4:16, 17; Dan. 2:44; 7:13, 14; Zech. 14:4, 9; Jude 14; Matt. 25:31; Rev. 3:10.)

ARTICLE 7

I believe with all my heart that the Old Testament, the Law, the Prophets, and the Writings, is the Word of God. (Exodus 20:1.)

ARTICLE 8

I believe with all my heart that the New Testament is the fulfillment of the Old Testament and that both together are one book, the inspired Word of the living God. (Matt. 1:22; Rev. 22:18, 19.)

ARTICLE 9

I believe with all my heart that all have sinned and cannot be counted righteous in God's sight without a sacrifice. I believe that the Lord Jesus Christ is the only sacrifice for our sins and that the Gospel of Christ is the power of God unto salvation to every one that believeth, to Jew and Gentile. (Gen. 6:5; Romans 1:16; 3:10; Psalms 14:1.)

ARTICLE 10

I believe with all my heart that all Jews will some day accept the Lord Jesus Christ as their Messiah and Savior, when God the Father shall pour upon the House of David the spirit of grace and supplications and they shall look upon Him whom they have pierced. (Zech. 12:10; Romans 11:26.)

THEREFORE:

I believe that I should try, with God's help; to read daily His Holy Word, meditate thereon, and pray daily unto our heavenly Father in the name of our Lord Jesus Christ; and to proclaim the good tidings of Jesus our Messiah to others that they, through the Holy Spirit, may be saved.

Notes: *This more complete Confession of Faith provides additional content to the very brief statement printed above. It is unique for its adaptation to particularly Jewish concerns. For example, the statement on the authority of the Old Testament (the Jewish Bible) is separated from that of the New Testament. In addition, the confession acknowledges that Christians and Jews worship the same God, speaks of Jesus' atoning work as sacrifice, and emphasizes the hope for the eventual conversion of the Jews.*

*   *   *

DOCTRINAL STATEMENT (AMERICAN COUNCIL OF THE RAMABAI MUKTI MISSION)

1. The Bible is the Word of God—the only Infallible rule of faith and practice.

2. There is one God eternally existing in three persons—Father, Son, and Holy Spirit.

3. The Lord Jesus Christ is the eternal Son of God, conceived by the Holy Spirit, and born of the Virgin Mary.

4. The sacrificial vicarious death of Christ on the cross is the only atonement for sin, and all who repent and believe in Him are justified on the ground of His shed blood.

DOCTRINAL STATEMENT (AMERICAN COUNCIL OF THE RAMABAI MUKTI MISSION) (continued)

5. The body of our Lord which was crucified was raised from the dead according to the Scriptures. He ascended into Heaven, and is seated on the right hand of God as our High Priest and Advocate.

6. The personal, bodily, visible, premillennial return of Christ is the blessed hope of the Church.

7. All men are sinful and in an eternally lost condition apart from the saving grace of Jesus Christ.

8. It is necessary for all to believe in and accept the Lord Jesus Christ as personal Sin-Bearer and Savior in order to become children of God.

9. There will be a resurrection of the just and the unjust, eternal blessedness of the redeemed in Christ, and eternal punishment of the unsaved.

Notes: *Founded in 1929, the American Council of the Ramabai Mukti Mission supports Evangelical missionaries in India. Its Doctrinal Statement represents a consensus Evangelical position.*

* * *

DOCTRINAL STATEMENT (AMERICAN MISSIONARY FELLOWSHIP)

We stand for and emphasize the foundational truths held in common by evangelical Christians: our basis of fellowship being a oneness of heart and mind in all things of the Lord and adherence to the historic Christian faith expressed as follows:

1. The Bible, which is verbally inspired by the Holy Spirit and inerrant in the original manuscripts and is the infallible and authoritative Word of God.

2. The Triune Godhead in Three Persons—Father, Son, and Holy Spirit.

3. The personality of Satan, called the Devil, and his present control over unregenerate mankind.

4. The fall and lost estate of man, whose total depravity makes necessary the new birth.

5. The deity of Jesus Christ, His virgin birth, sinless life, death, bodily resurrection, present exaltation at God's right hand, and personal imminent return.

6. The atonement by the substitutionary death and shed blood of Jesus Christ our Lord and Savior.

7. The resurrection of the saved unto everlasting life and blessedness in heaven, and the resurrection of the unsaved unto everlasting punishment in hell.

8. The Church, the Body or Bride of Christ, consisting only of those who are born again, for whom He now makes intercession in heaven for whom He shall come again.

9. Christ's commission to the Church to go into all the world and preach the gospel to every creature.

Notes: *The American Missionary Fellowship, founded in 1817, is the oldest independent home missionary organization operating in North America, although its conservative Doctrinal Statement reflects a number of the twentieth century doctrinal controversies. It affirms the inerrancy of the Bible, the personality of Satan, and the substitutionary atonement of Jesus Christ. The Fellowship's Reformed theological heritage is noted in its affirmation of humanity's total depravity.*

* * *

WHAT DOES THE ASA BELIEVE? (AMERICAN SCIENTIFIC AFFILIATION)

First, we affirm that "the Holy Scriptures are the inspired Word of God, the only unerring guide of faith and conduct"

Second, we affirm that "Jesus Christ is the Son of God, who through His atonement is the one and only Mediator between God and man".

Third, we affirm "God is the Creator of the physical universe. Certain laws are discernible in the manner in which God upholds the universe. The scientific approach is capable of giving reliable information about the natural world".

Notes: *The American Scientific Affiliation (ASA) is a professional association of Evangelical scholars dedicated to the investigation of the problems created by the overlap of the affirmations of religion and the conclusions of science. It is based in the Evangelical affirmation of the unique inspiration and authority of the Bible and the apparent contradiction between biblical text and such scientific findings as the theory of evolution and the historical findings of Holy Land archeology. The ASA's brief statement of belief defends absolute theological affirmations and asserts faith in the scientific method of understanding the world. It implies a belief that eventually the two apparent contradictions between the two realms can eventually be reconciled.*

* * *

DOCTRINAL POSITION (AMERICAN TECHNICAL OUTREACH MINISTRIES, INC.)

[1] We believe that the Scriptures of the Old and New Testaments are the verbally inspired Word of God, inerrant in the original languages and the supreme and final

authority in faith and life (II Peter 1:20, 21; II Timothy 3:16, 17).

[2] We believe in one God, eternally existing in three Persons: Father, Son, and Holy Spirit (Deut. 6.4; II Cor. 13:14).

[3] We believe that Jesus Christ was begotten of the Holy Spirit; born of the Virgin Mary; lived among men; suffered, bled and died; was buried; raised from the dead; ascended to the right hand of the Father; intercedes for us; and is true God and true man (Luke 1:35; Luke 2-6, 7, 52; Matthew 27:29, 30, 35, 50; Luke 23:50-56; Acts 2:24, 33; I John 2.1; John 10:30; 1 John 4:2, 3).

[4] We believe in the deity of the Holy Spirit, the third Person of the Trinity (Acts 5:3, 4; John 14:16, 17; John, 16:13).

[5] We believe that man was created in the image and likeness of God that he sinned and thereby incurred both physical and spiritual death; that all human beings are born with a sinful nature and are sinners in thought, word and deed (Genesis 1:26, 27; Romans 3:22, 23; Romans 5:12; Ephesians 2:1-3).

[6] We believe that Jesus Christ died for our sins, according to the Scriptures, as our representative and substitutionary sacrifice; and that all who believe on Him are justified on the ground of His shed blood (I Cor. 5:3, 1 Peter 3:18;, Romans 3:24-26).

[7] We believe that all who receive by faith the Lord Jesus Christ are born again of the Holy Spirit, and thereby become children of God; that they are indwelt and sealed by the Holy Spirit and are secure in Him until the day or redemption (John 1:12; John 3:5; Ephesians 1:13).

[8] We believe that the Church is composed of all believers; that we are baptized into His body, thus being members of one another (Ephesians 1:22, 23; I Cor. 12:12, 13).

[9] We believe that Jesus Christ instituted the Lord's Supper to commemorate His death until He comes. We believe that water baptism is an ordained testimony portraying our identification with Christ. We believe in believer's baptism by immersion (I Cor. 11:23-26; Matthew 28:19, 20; Romans 6:3, 4).

[10] We believe in ''that blessed hope'', the personal imminent, premillennial coming of the Lord into the air for His saints. We believe in the personal, visible and glorious return of Christ to the earth with His saints. We believe in the establishment of Christ's kingdom upon the earth (Titus 2:13; I Thes. 4:13-17; Rev. 19:11-16; Rev. 11-15).

[11] We believe in the bodily resurrection of the just and the unjust; the everlasting blessedness of the saved and the everlasting punishment of the lost (John 5:28, 29; John 14:13; Rev. 20:11-15).

[12] We believe in the personality of Satan; that he is the god of this age, the adversary of Christ and His Church, and that his destiny is eternal punishment (Job 1:6, 7; II Cor. 4:4; I Peter 5:8; Rev. 20:10).

Notes: *American Technical Outreach Ministries is a Fundamentalist missionary agency that supports missionary enterprise at several levels, rather than merely sending and directly supporting missionaries. Its theological perspective as reflected in its Doctrinal Position statement, is similar to that of the Independent Fundamental Churches of America.*

* * *

STATEMENT OF FAITH (ARAB WORLD MINISTRIES)

1. The full inspiration of the Scriptures of the Old and New Testaments; their authority, sufficiency, and inerrancy, not only as containing, but as themselves the Word of God; and the need of the teaching of the Holy Spirit for a true and spiritual understanding of the whole.

2. The unity of the Godhead and the divine co-equality of the Father, the Son and the Holy Spirit.

3. The utter depravity of human nature in consequence of the fall, and the necessity for regeneration.

4. The absolute Deity of our Lord Jesus Christ; His virgin birth; His real and perfect manhood; the authority of His teaching, and the infallibility of all His utterances; His work of atonement for the sin of mankind by His vicarious suffering and death; His bodily resurrection and His ascension into Heaven; His present High-priestly intercession for His people; and His lordship over His Church as its Supreme Head.

5. The justification of the sinner, solely by faith, on the ground of the merits and vicarious suffering, death, and bodily resurrection of our Lord and Savior, Jesus Christ.

6. The necessity of the work of the Holy Spirit in conviction of sin, regeneration, and sanctification, as well as in ministry and worship.

7. The resurrection of the body; the judgment of the work by our Lord Jesus Christ; the eternal blessedness of the righteous; and the eternal punishment of the wicked.

8. The personal return of the Lord Jesus Christ in glory.

Notes: *Arab World Ministries, founded in 1952, supports missionaries in predominantly Muslim countries and among*

Muslim communities in other countries. Its consensus Evangelical statement emphasizes the unity of the godhead, a point of contact with Muslim believers.

*   *   *

DOCTRINAL STATEMENT (ASSOCIATION OF CHRISTIAN LIBRARIANS)

Doctrinal Statement

We believe that there is one God, eternally existing in three persons; Father, Son, and Holy Spirit.

We believe the Bible to be the inspired, the only infallible, authoritative Word of God.

We believe in the Deity of our Lord Jesus Christ, in His virgin birth, in His sinless life, in His miracles, in His vicarious death and atonement through His shed blood, in His bodily resurrection, in His ascension to the right hand of the Father, and in His personal and visible return in power and glory.

We believe that man was created in the image of God, that he was tempted by Satan and fell, and that, because of the exceeding sinfulness of human nature, regeneration by the Holy Spirit is absolutely necessary for salvation.

We believe in the present ministry of the Holy Spirit by Whose indwelling the Christian is enabled to live a godly life, and by Whom the Church is empowered to carry out Christ's great commission.

We believe in the bodily resurrection of both the saved and the lost, those who are saved unto the resurrection of life and those who are lost unto the resurrection of damnation.

Notes: *The Association of Christian Librarians is a professional association for librarians who are Evangelical Christians and work in higher education institutions. It has a brief consensus statement of Evangelical beliefs.*

*   *   *

STATEMENT OF FAITH (AWANA CLUBS)

WE BELIEVE:

1. All Scripture is verbally inspired as originally written and therefore infallible and inerrant (II Timothy 3:16-17; II Peter 1:21; Matthew 5:18; I Corinthians 2:13).

The Bible IS the Word of God. We CANNOT accept the misleading statement, ''The Bible contains the Word of God.''

2. There is one living and true God who exists in three Persons—Father, Son, and Holy Spirit (Matthew 28:19; II Corinthians 13:14).

   The Father is God (I Corinthians 8:6), the Son is God (Isaiah 9:6; John 1:1, 14; Hebrews 1:8-10), and the Holy Spirit is God (Acts 5:3-4).

3. The Lord Jesus Christ was born of a virgin (Isaiah 7:14; Matthew 1:18-25; Luke I:26-38).

4. Christ rose bodily from the dead and ascended unto God the Father (Matthew 28; Mark 16; I Corinthians 15; Romans 1:4).

5. Christ will return.

   (a) First, for the ''dead in Christ'' who will be resurrected bodily and for those who are alive at His coming. This resurrection not only precedes His return to earth to reign 1000 years, but also precedes the Tribulation (I Thessalonians 4:13-18; 5:9).

   (b) Then to reign 1000 years on the earth (Revelation 20:1-6; II Timothy 2:12).

6. All men inherit a depraved nature and are lost sinners in need of salvation (Romans 3:9-19; Ephesians 2:1-3).

7. God has provided salvation through offering His Son on the cross of Calvary, and allowing his BLOOD to be shed to atone for our sins (Romans 3:25; Hebrews 9:22).

8. We are saved and justified when we recognize ourselves as sinners, and we put our trust in Christ as the Son of God and His finished work on the cross of Calvary. Salvation is by grace through faith plus nothing (Romans 3:24; 4:5; Ephesians 2:8-9).

9. Once saved we cannot be lost; we are eternally secure in Christ (John 3:16; Philippians 1:6; John 10:27-29; Romans 8:38-39).

10. We believe that the baptism of the Holy Spirit takes place at the time of conversion and is the act of placing the believer into the body of Christ. The baptism of the Holy Spirit is not a second work of grace, nor is it manifested by unusual signs such as speaking in tongues (I Corinthians 12:13; Galatians 3:27).

11. (a) We should regularly participate at the Lord's table (I Corinthians 11:23-32).

    (b) All believers should be baptized by immersion as an act of obedience, but not for securing their salvation (Acts 2:41; 19:4-5; Matthew 28:19-20).

12. The Bible teaches the eternal blessedness of the saved (John 4:14; 5:24; Ephesians 2:7).

    It also teaches the eternal punishment of the lost (John 5:28-29; Revelation 20:10, 15; Matthew 25:46).

13. The grace of God teaches us "to live soberly, righteously, godly" (Titus 2:11-3).

(a) Titus 2:13—Looking for the blessed hope of His returning for us.

(b) Colossians 3:2-3; I John 2:15-17—Setting "our affection on things above, not on things on the earth."

(c) II Corinthians 6:14-18—Living a life of separation from the world.

We believe in separation "unto God" (Romans 1:1; II Corinthians 6:17-18).

Notes: *Awana Clubs, founded in 1950, is a service organization that works with children and youth from age three through high school. It is a theologically conservative organization that affirms the inerrancy of the Bible and specifically rejects the neo-Orthodox position advocated by Swiss theologian Karl Barth that "the Bible contains the Word of God." Awana reflects a Reformed theological heritage in its affirmation of human depravity and the eternal security of believers, and of a Baptist tradition in its demand for baptism by immersion. Awana also rejects Pentecostalism and the practice of speaking in tongues, and theological liberalism and ecumenism represented by the National Council of Churches and the World Council of Churches.*

* * *

STATEMENT OF FAITH (BACK TO THE BIBLE BROADCAST)

1. THE BIBLE

We believe that the Bible, consisting of the 66 books of the Old and New Testaments, is the revelation of God to mankind, is verbally and fully inspired by Him, is sufficient for the knowledge of God and His will that is necessary for the eternal welfare of mankind, is infallible and inerrant in its original manuscripts, and is the supreme and final authority for all Christian faith and conduct.

II Tim. 3:16,17; II Pet. 1:21; I Cor. 2:13; Deut. 29:29; II Tim. 3:15; John 10:35.

2. GOD

We believe that there is but one God, whose essential nature is that of a living, personal Spirit. He is infinitely perfect in all of His attributes, He is the creator and sustainer of all things, and He exists in three persons—Father, Son and Holy Spirit.

1 Cor. 8:4; John 4:24; 5:26; Gen. 1:1; Col. 1:16,17; Matt. 28:19.

3. JESUS CHRIST

We believe that Jesus Christ is true God and true Man; that is, He is fully divine and also fully human. He preexisted eternally with the Father, was conceived by the Holy Spirit and born of the virgin Mary, lived a perfect life, and died a substitutionary death for the sins of mankind. We believe that He arose bodily from the grave, that He ascended to heaven, where He is presently High Priest and Advocate for His people, and that He will return personally and bodily to the earth at the close of this age. He is the world's only Saviour and is the Lord of all.

Phil. 2:5-11; John 1:1; Matt. 1:23-25; 1 Pet. 2:22; I Cor. 15:3; I Tim. 2:6; I Cor. 15:20; Heb. 4:14-16; John 14:3; Acts 4:12.

4. THE HOLY SPIRIT

We believe that the Holy Spirit is a divine person, the third person of the Trinity. We believe that He was sent from the Father by the son to convict the world, to regenerate and indwell those who trust in Christ, to baptize them into the Body of Christ, to seal them for the final day of redemption, to guide them into truth, to fill them for a life of holiness and victory, and to empower them for witness and service. We believe that He gives spiritual gifts to believers for the proper functioning of the Body of Christ, which is the Church.

Acts 5:3,4; John 16:7-14; 3:5-8; I Cor. 2:9-12; 3:16; 12:3-13,28-31; Eph. 1:13,14; Gal. 5:16-25; Acts 1:8.

5. MAN

We believe that man was originally created by a definite act of God in His own image and is dependent upon, and accountable to, his Creator. Through disobedience, the first man sinned and fell from his original state of moral perfection. As a consequence, he brought upon himself and upon the whole human race the penalty for sin, which is spiritual and physical death. Since Adam, every person is born with an inherently sinful nature and becomes a sinner in thought, word and deed. Every person, therefore, stands under the just condemnation of God and is unable to save himself or to present deeds worthy of merit before God.

Gen. 1:26,27; 2:7; Rom. 2:6-16; 5:12-21; 6:23; Matt. 5:20-48; John 3:36.

6. SALVATION

We believe that a person is saved by God's grace alone, made possible through the shed blood of Christ, whereby He died a substitutionary death for mankind, and through the resurrection of Christ. Salvation becomes effective when a person, by an act of faith, acknowledges Jesus Christ as his personal Savior and Lord. the benefits of this salvation include the forgiveness of sins and a new standing before God, the impartation of new life, and all the privileges that accompany a new family relationship with God. The assurance of salvation as a present possession is the privilege of every believer in Christ.

Eph. 2:8,9; I Cor. 15:3; Acts 16:31; Rom. 10:9; Acts 3:19; Rom. 3:28; John 3:16; John 1:12; 10:28; Phil. 1:16.

7. THE CHRISTIAN LIFE

We believe that God expects every believer to live a life of obedience, in which every area of his life is brought under the

STATEMENT OF FAITH (BACK TO THE BIBLE BROADCAST)
(continued)

lordship of Jesus Christ and the fruit of the Spirit becomes increasingly evident in his life. The goal of the Christian life is to be conformed to the image of Christ. This life is characterized supremely by self-giving love for God and for others. The life and character of Christ, which grows through the Holy Spirit, is noticeably distinct from the life of the world. A believer who resists the gracious working of the Holy Spirit and fails to grow in obedience is chastened in infinite love by his Heavenly Father so he may learn obedience.

John 14:21; II Cor. 10:4,5; Gal. 5:22,23; II Cor. 3:18; Matt. 22:37-40; 1 John 2:15-17; Heb. 12:5-14.

8. THE CHURCH

We believe that the Church of Jesus Christ is the universal company of God's redeemed people, His Body, of which He is the head, His Bride, whom He loves infinitely, and His temple, in which He dwells. This universal Body of Christ is visibly expressed in local assemblies whose purpose it is to glorify God through worship, fellowship, instruction in God's Word, observing the ordinances and training in service to the world. The supreme task in the mission of the Church is to make disciples for Christ in all the nation through the proclamation and teaching of the gospel. The Church is also to demonstrate the love and compassion of Christ, through word and deed, in all alienated world.

I Pet. 2:9,10: Eph. 1:22,23; 5:25-27; 2:19-22; I Thess. 2:14; Eph. 3:6-10; Acts 2:42; Eph. 4:11-13; Heb. 10:25; Matt. 28:18-20; 26:26-29; I John 4:17.

9. THE FUTURE LIFE

We believe in the imminent, premillennial return of Christ to take His people to be with Him and to judge and rule the earth in righteousness. We believe in he resurrection of the body for both believers and unbelievers. We believe that the believer goes to be with Christ in conscious blessedness immediately after death, having escaped the condemnation of his sins through the death of Christ. He will, however, stand before God to receive rewards for works approved by God or to suffer loss for works disapproved. The believer will live eternally in the immediate presence of God, while the unbeliever must face the eternal and holy Judge who will sentence him for his sins. He will experience the punishment of eternal separation in hell from the presence of God.

John 14:3; I Thess. 4:16,17; Rev. 11:15; I Cor. 15:20,23; Phil. 1:23; Rom. 8:1; II Cor. 5:10; Rev. 20:11-2:15; Rom. 2:11.

10. SATAN

We believe in the personality and depraved character of Satan, who is the great enemy of God and man. We believe that he, along with the company of demonic beings serving him, works out his evil plans through the ungodly world system, limited only by the sovereign rule of God. We believe that he was judged by Christ at the cross and will ultimately meet his doom in the lake of fire, where he will remain eternally.

Matt. 4:3-11; Gen. 3:1; John 8:44; Rev. 12:9,10: II Cor. 4:4;I John 5:19; Job 1:6-12; I John 3:8; Rev. 20:10.

Notes: *Founded in 1939, Back to the Bible Broadcast supports one of the oldest Evangelical radio broadcasts and has more recently broadened its work to include a television ministry. It holds to a conservative Evangelical position including the infallibility and inerrancy of the Scripture.*

* * *

DOCTRINAL STATEMENT (BCM INTERNATIONAL)

We believe that the Bible is made up of sixty-six books of the old and New testaments, is the verbally inspired Word of God, inerrant in the original writings, and being infallible constitutes a court from which there is no appeal.

We believe in one Triune God, eternally existing in three persons—Father, Son and Holy Spirit-co-eternal in being, co-identical in nature, co-equal in power and glory, and having the same attributes and perfections.

We believe the following regarding the person and work of the Lord Jesus Christ:

That Jesus Christ, the eternal Son of God, became man without ceasing to be God, having been conceived by the Holy Spirit and born of the virgin Mary, in order that He might reveal God and redeem sinful man.

That Jesus Christ accomplished our redemption through His death on the cross as a representative, vicarious, substitutionary sacrifice; and that our justification is fully attested by His literal, physical resurrection from the dead.

That Jesus Christ ascended to Heaven, and is now exalted at the right hand of God where, as our High Priest, He fulfills the ministry of Intercessor and Advocate.

That Jesus Christ is coming again to this world to establish His kingdom and set up the throne of David. His coming will be personal, imminent, and premillennial.

We believe the following concerning the person and work of the Holy Spirit:

That the Holy Spirit is a Person who convicts the world of sin, righteousness, and judgment; and that He is the Supernatural Agent in regeneration. We further believe that there is one baptism with the Spirit and it is into the Body of Christ, indwelling and sealing each believer unto the day of redemption. Pentecost is an historical event and is not to be repeated; therefore, we do not accept the teaching that speaking in tongues is associated with either the initial receiving of the Holy Spirit or as the evidence of His fullness.

That He is the Divine Teacher who guides believers into all truth; and that it is the privilege and responsibility of all believers to be filled with the Holy Spirit.

We believe that man was created in the image and likeness of God, but that in Adam's sin the race fell, inherited a sinful nature, and became alienated from God; and that man is totally depraved, and of himself utterly unable to remedy his lost condition.

We believe that salvation is the gift of God brought to man by grace and received by personal faith in the Lord Jesus Christ, that all who receive Christ are born again of the Holy Spirit and thereby become children of God. We believe that all the redeemed are kept by God's power. We also believe that God's Word clearly forbids the use of Christian liberty as an occasion to give license to the flesh.

We believe that God does hear and answer the prayer of faith, in accordance with His own will, for the sick and afflicted, but we do not accept the teaching that the divine healing of the body is in the atonement, for this present age, in the sense that salvation and forgiveness are in the atonement.

We believe that all believers should live in such a manner as not to bring reproach upon our Saviour and Lord; and that separation from all religious apostasy, all worldly and sinful pleasures, practices and associations is commanded by God.

We believe that the "Great Commission" of our Lord Jesus Christ to give the Gospel to every creature throughout the world is still incumbent on every believer.

We believe that Satan is a person, and the author of sin and the cause of the fall; that he is the open and declared enemy of God and man, and that he shall be eternally punished in the lake of fire.

We believe the Scriptures teach that all those who through faith are justified in the name of the Lord Jesus Christ will spend eternity in full enjoyment of God's presence and that those who through impenitence and unbelief refuse to accept God's offer of mercy will spend eternity in everlasting punishment.

Notes: *BCM International, formerly known as Bible Clubs Movement, was founded in 1936 with a program to strengthen local congregations by founding Bible clubs that would promote Bible study and memorization. It acknowledges both the inerrancy and infallibility of the Bible, is opposed to Pentecostalism (especially its teachings concerning speaking in tongues and divine healing being part of Christ's atonement), humanity's total depravity, and the personality of Satan.*

*　　*　　*

STATEMENT (BIBLE CHRISTIAN UNION)

The Holy Scriptures

I believe that the Old and New Testaments are the verbally inspired, infallible Word of God, inerrant in the original writings, and therefore, are the only final authority for faith and life. John 16:13-14; 2 Timothy 3:16; 2 Peter 1:20-21.

The Godhead

I believe that the Godhead eternally exists in three Persons: God the Father, God the Son and God the Holy Spirit; and that these three are truly one God. Deuteronomy 6:4; Matthew 28:19-20; 2 Corinthians 13:14.

The Person and Work of Christ

I believe that Jesus Christ is Himself God; that He was conceived by the Holy Spirit and born of the virgin Mary; that He received a human body and a sinless human nature, being at the same time fully God as well as sinless Man; that He died on the cross shedding His blood as the substitutionary sacrifice for man and rose again for our justification; that He arose in the same body; though transformed, ascended into heaven, and is seated at the right hand of God far above all; that He will come to catch up His church; that He will return to earth with His church to establish His millennial kingdom. Isaiah 9:6; Matthew 25:31-32; Luke 1:34-35; John 1:1; Acts 2:33; 1 Corinthians 15:3; Ephesians 1:20-22; Philippians 2:6-11; Colossians 1:15-20; 3:4; 1 Thessalonians 4:13-17; 2 Thessalonians 1:7-10; 1 Timothy 2:5; Revelation 20:1-6.

The Person and Work of the Holy Spirit

I believe that the Holy Spirit is himself God; that He glorifies the Lord Jesus Christ; that He was sent to convict the world of sin, righteousness, and judgment; that He regenerates the believer and baptizes him into the body of Christ; that He indwells the believer; that He desires to fill the believer: that He seals the believer unto the day of redemption; and that He imparts gifts to each believer as He wills for the edification of the church. John 16:7-15; Acts 5:3-4; 1 Corinthians 12:11,13; Ephesians 4:7,30; 5:18; Titus 3:5.

The Condition of Man

I believe that man was created in the image of God; that through disobedience he acquired a sinful nature and incurred both physical and spiritual death. All human beings, being born of Adam, inherit this sinful nature and are in themselves totally depraved, unable to remedy their lost condition. Genesis 1:26-27; Romans 3: 9-10;5:12,19;7:18.

STATEMENT (BIBLE CHRISTIAN UNION) (continued)

Salvation

I believe that salvation is the gift of God, purchased by the vicarious death of Jesus Christ and received by personal faith in Christ; that man by faith, apart from works, is justified freely by the grace of God through the redemption that is in Christ Jesus; that this salvation includes the priesthood of all believers. Romans 1:16; 3:21 22; Ephesians 1:7; 2:8-9; 1 Timothy 2:6; Hebrews 4:16; 1 Peter 2:5,9; 1 John 2:2; Revelation 1:6.

The Church

I believe the church is a company of all true believers in Jesus Christ, both Jews and Gentiles, regenerated and baptized by the Holy Spirit into one body; that the church was a mystery revealed to the apostle Paul and to the other apostles; that the local church should be organized according to New Testament principles, practicing believer's baptism and regularly having the Lord's Table for believers, and is God's instrument in this present age for preaching the good news of salvation by faith in Christ in order to call out of all nations a people for His Name; that the church should keep itself from theological liberalism; that the church will be gathered to meet the Lord in the air; that the church will return with Christ when He comes to earth to set up His millennial kingdom; that the church will have the honor of reigning with Him forever in the new heavens and new earth. Isaiah 65:17; Acts 8:30-38; 13-15; Romans 11:5; I Corinthians 11:23-26; Ephesians 3:1-11; I Thessalonians 4:13-17; 1 Timothy 3; 2 Timothy 2:12; Titus 1;Revelation 20:1-6.

Satan

I believe that Satan is an angelic personality who rebelled against God, fell, and became the archenemy of God and man; that Jesus Christ in His death defeated Satan: that during the tribulation the power of Satan will reach its supreme manifestation; that he finally will be cast into the lake of fire. Isaiah 14:12-14; Ezekiel 28:11-19; Hebrews 2:14; Revelation 13;20:7-10.

The Eternal State

I believe in the bodily resurrection of believers and unbelievers, the believers being raised unto eternal life and the unbelievers unto everlasting punishment. Daniel 12:2;John 5:28-29; Revelation 20:4-6, 11-15.

Notes: *The Bible Christian Union, founded in 1904, is a foreign and home missionary agency that operates primarily in Europe and North America. It is Evangelical in its doctrine, and supports both the infallibility and inerrancy of the Bible, human depravity, and the personality of Satan. It supports*

evangelization work within the Jewish community, and mentions "regenerated" Jews as part of the Church.

*　　*　　*

JERUSALEM CREDO (BIBLE LIGHT)

In harmony with the true faith of the Synagogue, all through the centuries, we do believe that the return of the Jews to their homeland (given by the Almighty as an everlasting possession) is accomplishing the prophetic Scriptures.

We do believe that this ingathering will be the means of blessing all nations, as it is the instrument of the introduction to messianic revolution, and the best herald of the Messiah's advent (Gen. 12:3; John 4:22).

We do believe with the Apostle Paul that the promises "still belong to Israel" (Epistle to the Romans 9:4; 11:15).

We do believe, according to the teaching of Jesus, that the retrieving of Jerusalem as of June 1967, marked the beginning of the end of "the times of the Gentiles" (as dominating world empires—St. Luke 21:24).

We do exhort Christian theologians everywhere to acknowledge with so many Jewish theologians, the supreme messianic quality of our time—and to preach the reconciliation of the children of Abraham—Jews, Christians, Arabs instead of opposing the rebirth of Israel, or simply remaining silent.

We do believe that the Arab nations' best friend is the State of Israel, and that together, they could begin to implement the prophecy of Isaiah (19:19-25), announcing this reconciliation.

We do believe that the first Zionist adventure, led by Moses and Joshua, gave the world the Hebrew Bible—we do believe that the second Zionist adventure, led by Ezra and Nehemiah, gave the world the New Testament and Christ Jesus—we do believe that the present and third Zionist adventure will soon give the world the advent of the One, expected by the Synagogue and by the Church.

We do believe that any Christian who gives encouragement and support to the ones who work for the destruction of the Jewish Nation, is in fact making falsifiers of the patriarchs, the prophets, of Paul and of Jesus Himself, and thus does directly oppose the Almighty's will to save our world through the Messianic advent on Israel's soil as foretold by the Hebrew prophets and the New Testament.

Notes: *Bible Light, founded in 1957 in the wake of the formation of the State of Israel, is an organization dedicated to the evangelization of the Jews. The Jerusalem Credo was authored and signed by a group of European leaders in the Jewish evangelism movement, and was proclaimed in the United States by Bible Light. Its subject is Israel, the formation of which it sees in prophetic terms. It stands in opposition to Roman Catholic and liberal Protestant critiques of Israel and* *calls for the development of an accord that would leave Israel in peace with its neighbors.*

* * *

STATEMENT OF FAITH (BIBLE LITERATURE INTERNATIONAL)

We believe that the Bible is t he only inspired, infallible, authoritative Word of God. II Tim. 3:16.

We believe that there is one God, eternally existent In three persons, Father, Son, and Holy Spirit. Deut. 6:4; matt. 28:19.

We believe in the deity of Jesus Christ, in His virgin birth, His sinless life, His miracles, His atoning death, His bodily resurrection, His ascension to the right hand of the Father, and His personal return in power and glory. John 1-1; I Cor. 15:3,4, Acts l:ll.

We believe that regeneration by the Holy Spirit is absolutely essential for salvation. John 3:5; Titus 3:5.

We believe in the present ministry of the Holy Spirit, by whose indwelling the Christian is able to live a godly life. John 14:16, 17, 26.

We believe in the resurrection of both the saved and the lost, they that are saved to the resurrection of life and they that are lost to the resurrection of damnation. Matt. 25:46.

We believe in the spiritual unity of all believers in Jesus Christ. John 17:20-23.

We believe in Christ's Great Commission to go into all the world and preach this Gospel to every creature, making disciples, baptizing and teaching. Mk. 16:15; Matt. 28:18-20.

Notes: *Bible Literature International, founded in 1923, publishes Bibles and Evangelical literature in many languages to missionaries. It is a member of the National Association of Evangelicals (NAE) and has a Statement of Faith derived from that of the NAE, with an additional paragraph on the Great Commission to evangelize the world.*

* * *

DOCTRINAL STATEMENT (BIBLES FOR THE WORLD)

We believe the Bible, as contained in the Old and New Testaments, is the inspired and infallible Word of God, being given by the Holy Spirit of God to holy men of old. It is, therefore, the only and final authority in all matters of faith and practice.

We believe in one God, eternally existing in three persons: Father, Son and Holy Spirit.

We believe in the deity of Jesus Christ, in His virgin birth, in His sinless life, in His works of miracles, in His vicarious and redeeming death, in His cleansing blood shed on Calvary, in His bodily resurrection, in His ascension to the right hand of God the Father and His personal and visible return in power and glory.

We believe in the Holy Spirit, the Lord and Giver of life, who proceeds from the Father and the Son: who by means of the Word of God, is the Author of the new birth, the comforter, and the sanctifier; and He indwells the believer.

We believe that man was created in the image of God, that he fell into sin, and thereby incurred, not physical death only, but spiritual death which is separation from God; that all human beings, in consequence of the Fall, are born with sinful nature.

We believe in the necessity of the new birth by the Holy Spirit in order that man may have peace with God, and this new birth cannot be received by being born in a Christian home or by association with believers but by accepting Christ as Savior. The evidence of this new birth should be manifested by a daily walk in the Spirit.

We believe in the resurrection of the body, both of the just and the unjust, the eternal blessedness of the redeemed in Christ, and the eternal punishment of those who have rejected the offer of Salvation.

We believe the commission of Christ to be witnesses of His life, death, resurrection, and eternal life through His name in the task of every born-again Christian.

Notes: *Bibles for the World, founded in 1928, publishes and distributes Bibles around the world, although they are best known for their work in India. Its Doctrinal Statement is an Evangelical consensus statement.*

* * *

STATEMENT OF FAITH (CAMPUS CRUSADE FOR CHRIST/INTERNATIONAL SCHOOL OF THEOLOGY)

The sole basis of our belief is the Bible, God's infallible written Word, the sixty-six books of the Old and New Testaments. We believe that it was uniquely, verbally and fully inspired by the Holy Spirit, and that it was written without error (inerrant) in the original manuscripts. It is the supreme and final authority in all matters on which it speaks.

The International School of Theology adheres to the major doctrinal teachings on which, historically, there has been general agreement among all true Christians. We desire to allow for freedom of conviction on other doctrinal matters, provided that any interpretation is based upon Scripture alone, and that no such interpretation becomes an issue which hinders the unity of the body of Christ.

We explicitly affirm our belief in the following teachings of Scripture:

1. There is one true God, eternally existing in three persons Father, Son and Holy Spirit—each of whom possesses equally all the attributes of deity and the characteristics of personality. (Deuteronomy 6-4; Matthew 28:18; John 1:1-3, 18; Acts 5:3,4.)

2. Jesus Christ is God, the living Word, who became flesh through His miraculous conception by the Holy Spirit and His virgin birth. Hence, He is perfect deity and true humanity united in one person forever. (John 1:1, 1-4; Matthew 1:18-25; Luke 1:30-37; Colossians 2:9; Philippians 2:6-11.)

3. He lived a sinless life and voluntarily atoned for the sins of men by dying on the cross as their substitute, thus satisfying divine justice and accomplishing salvation for all who trust Him alone. (I John 3:5; I Peter 3:18; John 10:17,18; 2 Corinthians 5:21; I John 1:10; Romans 3:24-26).

4. He rose from the dead in the same body, though glorified, in which He had lived and died. (I Corinthians 15:4 1-1-20; Luke 24:36-43; John 20:24-29.)

5. He ascended bodily into heaven and sat down at the right hand of God the Father where He, the only mediator between God and man, continually makes intercession for His own.(Acts 1:9-11; Ephesians 1:20 I Timothy 2:5; Hebrews 7:24,25;I John 2:12.)

6. Man was originally created in the image of God. He sinned by disobeying God; thus, he was alienated from his Creator. The historic fall brought all mankind under divine condemnation. (Genesis 1:26,27; 2:15-17; 3:1-24; Romans 5:12-21; I Corinthians 15;21,22.)

7. Man's nature is corrupted, and he is thus totally unable to please God. Every man is in need of regeneration and renewal by the Holy Spirit.(Romans 3:9-20; Ephesians 2:1-7; Mark 7:20-23; John 3:1-21; Titus 3:5-7.)

8. The salvation of man is wholly a work of God's free grace and is not the work, in whole or part, of human works or goodness or religious ceremony. God imputes His righteousness to those who put their faith in Christ alone for their salvation, and thereby justifies them in His sight. (Ephesians 2:8-10; Romans 3:21-26;9:30-33; Galatians 3:11-14,22-24.)

9. It is privilege of all who are born again of the Spirit to be assured of their salvation from the very moment in which they trust Christ as their Savior. This assurance is not based upon any kind of human merit, but is produced by the witness of the Holy Spirit, who confirms in the believer the testimony of God in His written Word. (I Thessalonians 1:5 John 1:12,13; I John 5:9-13; Romans 8:14-17.)

10. The Holy Spirit has come into the world to reveal and glorify Christ and to apply the saving work of Christ to men. He convicts and draws sinners to Christ, imparts new life to them, continually indwells them from the moment of spiritual birth, and seals them until the day of redemption. His fullness, power and control are appropriated in the believer's life by faith. (John 16:7-15; Titus 3:5; John 3:5-8; Romans 8:9; Ephesians 1:13,14 4:30; I Corinthians 6:19; Galatians 3:2,3; Romans 8:2-4.)

11. Every believer is called to so live in the power of the indwelling Spirit that he will not fulfill the lust of the flesh but will bear fruit to the glory of God. (Galatians 5:16-25; Ephesians 5:18).

12. Jesus Christ is the Head of the Church, His Body, which is composed of all men,living and dead, who have been joined to Him through saving faith. (Colossians 1:18; Ephesians 1:22,23; 5:23-32; I Thessalonians 4:13-18.)

13. God admonishes His people to assemble together regularly for worship, for participation in ordinances, for edification through the Scriptures and for mutual encouragement. (Hebrews 10:23-25; Acts 2:41,42;20:7;Ephesians 4:11-16; I Timothy 4:13; 2 Timothy 3:16-42.)

14. At physical death the believer enters immediately into eternal, conscious fellowship with the Lord and awaits the resurrection of his body to everlasting glory and blessing. (2 Corinthians 5:8; Philippians 1:23,24; Luke 23:39-13; I Corinthians 15:12-58; I Thessalonians 4:13-18; I John 3:2; Philippians 3:20,21.)

15. At physical death the unbeliever enters immediately into eternal, conscious separation from the Lord and awaits the resurrection of his body to everlasting judgment and condemnation. (Luke 16:19-31; John 5:23-29; Revelation 20:10-15 Matthew 13:40-43.)

16. Jesus Christ will come again to the earth-personally, visibly and bodily—to consummate history and the eternal plan of God. (Acts 1:9-11; 3:19-21; Matthew 24:44; Revelation 19-22.)

17. The Lord Jesus Christ commanded all believers to proclaim the gospel throughout the world and to disciple men of every nation The fulfillment of the Great Commission requires that all worldly and personal ambitions be subordinated to a total commitment to "Him who loved us and gave Himself for us." (Matthew 28:18-20; Mark 16:15,16 Luke 24:46-49; Acts 1:7,8; Romans 12:1,2; Galatians 2:19,20; Philippians 3:7-21.)

Notes: *Founded in 1951, Campus Crusade for Christ began one of the definitive organizations of the emerging Evangelical Movement, which had been founded in the 1940s. Beginning* on American campuses, it now has work in over sixty countries. Based on an understanding of the inerrancy and authority of the Bible, its Statement of Faith affirms a consensus Evangelical theological position.

* * *

DOCTRINE (CARVER FOREIGN MISSIONS, INC./ CARVER BIBLE INSTITUTE AND COLLEGE)

We believe in the One true and living God, revealed to man as Father, Son and Holy Spirit; one God Infinite and Eternal in His Wisdom, Power, Holiness, Justice and Truth.

Jesus Christ the Son of God, His virgin birth, His atoning death, His physical resurrection, His ascension, His High Priestly work of intercession, and His premillennial, personal and visible return to earth. The regenerating work of the Holy Spirit.

The Scriptures consisting of the Old and New Testaments, God's only written revelation to man, that they are of divine authority, verbally inspired by God as originally given.

We believe man to be in a fallen state of depravity, by reason of the fall of Adam, and in danger of eternal Hell Fire if outside of Christ.

Salvation by grace through faith in the blood of Jesus Christ.

We recognize the personality of Satan, the enemy of God and man.

We believe in evangelism and Christian missions; that it is the responsibility of the Church as a whole and Christians as individuals to use means in the propagation of the Gospel to the whole world.

The bodily resurrection of born again believers into an eternal life of blessedness.

While we stand for these truths, we consider a Christlike spirit of great importance, and the purity of life of the messenger equal importance with the orthodox correctness of his message. We hold the following fundamentals to be essential:

Wholehearted love toward God and man. Scriptural separation from the sin of the world. Christlike fellowship among believers.

Notes: *Carver Foreign Missions, founded in 1955, provides an independent Fundamentalist missionary sending agency operating primarily within the African-American community. Associated with the agency is Carver Bible Institute and College, founded in 1943, with which it shares a Statement of*

Doctrine. The statement emphasizes the verbal inspiration of the Bible, human depravity, and the need for believers to separate from the sins of the world.

* * *

STATEMENT OF BELIEF (DOCTRINAL STATEMENT) (CBM MINISTRIES, INC.)

While CBM Ministries, Inc. is conducted along strictly undenominational lines, there are certain truths to which we adhere:

a. The plenary inspiration of the Scriptures, in their original writings, as the very Word of God.

b. The deity of Jesus of Nazareth, the Son of God, coequal and coexistent with the Father and the Holy Spirit.

c. Man's fallen estate by which through nature and practice he stands guilty before God and is righteously judged fit only for an eternal hell.

d. We believe that the Lord Jesus Christ died for our sins, according to the Scriptures, as a representative and substitutionary sacrifice, and that His shed blood is the only, all-satisfying and eternally secure ground of justification to all who believe in Him.

e. The Lord Jesus Christ was raised from the dead on the third day in the same body in which He was crucified.

f. We believe in the visible, personal and imminent return of our Lord and Savior Jesus Christ.

g. We believe in the bodily resurrection of the just and the unjust, the everlasting felicity of the saved, and the everlasting punishment of the lost.

h. We believe the temporary gifts of speaking in tongues and the working of sign miracles gradually ceased as the New Testament Scriptures were completed and their authority became established (I Cor. 12:4-11; 13:8-12; II Cor. 12:12; Eph. 4:7, 11-16).

i. We believe that God hears and answers the prayer of faith, in accord with His own will, for the sick and afflicted (John 15:7, I John 5:14, 15).

Notes: *CBM Ministries, founded in 1935, is an Evangelical organization specializing in the evangelization of children. Its Statement of Belief emphasizes the plenary inspiration of the Bible and a consensus Evangelical theological perspective. The Ministries is opposed to the modern Charismatic move-*

ment, which emphasizes such gifts of the Spirit as speaking in tongues.

*   *   *

STATEMENT OF FAITH (CHILD EVANGELISM FELLOWSHIP)

WE BELIEVE-

A. *That "All Scripture is given by inspiration of God,"* by which we understand the whole book called THE BIBLE; that it is inerrant in the original writing and that its teaching and authority is absolute, supreme and final. That the Holy Spirit guided the holy men of old in all that they wrote. 2 Tim. 3:16; Deut. 4:2; 2 Pet. 1:2.

B. *The Godhead eternally exists in three persons—the Father, the Son and the Holy Spirit.* These three are one God, having the same nature, attributes and perfection. Rom. 1:20; Matt. 28:19 Deut 4:35; John 17:5.

C. *The Personality and Deity of the Lord Jesus Christ,* begotten of the Holy Spirit, born of the virgin Mary, truly God and truly man, John 1:1; 1:14; 10:30; Matt. 1:20; Luke 1:30, 31; Phil. 2:5-7;1 Tim. 3:16; Col 1:19.

D. *The Personality and Deity of the Holy Spirit,* the source and power of all acceptable worship and service, the infallible interpreter of the infallible Word, who indwells every true believer and is ever present to testify of Christ, seeking to occupy us with Him and not with ourselves or our experiences. John 15:26; Acts 5:3, 4; 1:8; Rom. 8:26 27; 1 Cor. 2:12, 14; Rom. 8:9; 1 Cor. 3:16; 12:13; John 16:13, 14.

E. *Man was created in the image of God, after His likeness, as stated in the Word of God, but the whole human race fell in the fall of the first Adam.* Not only was his moral nature grievously injured by the fall but he totally lost all spiritual life, becoming dead in trespasses and sins, and subject to the power of the devil. "The carnal mind is enmity against God; for it is not subject to the law of God, neither indeed can be. So then, they that are in the flesh cannot please God" (Rom. 8:7, 8). Therefore, he cannot see nor enter the kingdom of God until he is born again by the Holy Spirit. That no degree of reformation however great, no attainment in morality however high, no culture however attractive, no humanitarian and philanthropic schemes and societies however useful, no baptism or other ordinance however administered, can help the sinner to take even one step toward Heaven; but a new nature imparted from above, a new life implanted by the Holy Spirit through the Word is absolutely essential to salvation. Gen. 1:26, 27; Rom. 5:12; Eph. 2:1-3; John 3:3,6, 7; Titus 3:5.

F. *That Jesus Christ became the sinner's substitute before God and died as a propitiatory sacrifice for the sin of the whole world.* That He was made a curse for the sinner, dying for his sins according to the Scriptures; that no repentance, no feeling, no faith, no good resolutions, no sincere efforts, no submission to the rules and regulations of any church can add in the very least to the value of the precious blood or the merit of that finished work wrought for us by Him, who tasted death for every man. 1 John 2:2; Heb. 2:9; Gal. 3:13; Rom. 3:25; 4:4-5; 5:8; Col. 1:13, 14, 20, 21.

G. *In the resurrection of the crucified body of Jesus Christ;* that His body was raised from the dead according to the Scriptures and that He ascended into Heaven and sitteth on the right hand of God as the believer's high priest and advocate. Luke 24-39; Acts 1:10-11; Eph. 4:10; Heb. 1:3, 1 John 2:1.

H. *That Christ in the fullness of the blessings He has secured by His death and resurrection is received by faith alone* and that the moment we trust in Him as our Saviour, we pass out of death into everlasting life, justification from all things, accepted before the Father according to the measure of His acceptance, loved as He is loved and made one with Him. At the time of acceptance of Christ as Savior, He comes to dwell within the believer and to live out His life of holiness and power through him. Heb. 9:15, John 5:24; Rom. 3:28-43; 23-25; Eph. 1:3; John 17:23; Gal. 2:20; 4:6-7; 5:16; Act 1:8.

I. *That the Church all those who truly believe on the Lord Jesus Christ as Savior.* It is the body and bride of Christ. That every believer, whether Jew or Gentile, is baptized into the body of Christ by the Holy Spirit and having thus become members of one another we are responsible to keep the unity of the Spirit in the bond of peace, rising above all sectarian prejudices and denominational bigotry and loving one another with a pure heart fervently. Eph. 1:22, 23; 2:19-22; 1 Cor. 12:22-27; 1:10-13; Rom. 12:4,5; Eph. 4:3-6; 5:32; Phil. 2:1-5; Gal. 5:13-15.

J. *That all believers in our Lord Jesus Christ are called into a life of separation from worldly and sinful practices* and should abstain from such amusements and habits as will cause others to stumble or bring reproach upon the cross of Christ. Believers are created in Christ Jesus unto good works. "As we have therefore opportunity, let us do good unto all men, especially unto them who are the household of faith" (Gal. 6:10). 1 John 2:15, 16; Rom. 13:14; 14:13; 1 Cor. 10:31; Eph. 2:10.

K. *In the evangelization of the world;* that the supreme mission of the people of God in this age is to preach the Gospel to every creature. That special emphasis should be placed upon the evangelization of children. Mark 16:15; 2 Cor. 5:18, 19; Matt. 18:14.

L. *In the personal return of our Lord and Savior Jesus Christ;* that the coming again of Jesus Christ is the "blessed hope" set before us, for which we should be constantly looking. "Our citizenship is in heaven from whence we look for the

Saviour, the Lord Jesus Christ'' (Phil. 3:20). Acts 1:11; 1 Thess. 4:16, 17; John 14:1-3; Titus 2:13; Phil. 3:20, 21.

M. *That the souls of those who have trusted in the Lord Jesus Christ for salvation do at death immediately pass into His presence,* and there remain in conscious bliss until the resurrection of the body at His coming, when soul and body re-united shall be with Him forever in glory. Luke 23:43; 2 Cor. 5:8; Luke 16:22, 25; Phil. 1:23; 1 Thess. 4:15-18.

N. *That the souls of the lost remain after death in misery until the final judgment of the great white throne,* when soul and body re-united at the resurrection shall be cast ''into the lake of fire'' which is ''the second death,'' to be ''punished with everlasting destruction from the presence of the Lord, and from the glory of his power'' (2 Thess. 1:8,9). Luke 16:22-23, 27-28; Heb. 9:27; Rev. 20:5, 11-15; 2 Thess. 1:7-9.

O. *In the reality and personality of Satan,* ''that old serpent, called the devil, and Satan, which deceiveth the whole world'' (Rev. 12:9). Eph. 6:11,12; 1 Peter 5:8; Rev. 20:10.

Notes: *Child Evangelism Fellowship, founded in 1937, conducts evangelistic work among children, primarily in North America. It is a conservative Evangelical organization that affirms the infallibility and inerrancy of the Bible, human depravity, a life of separation from worldly and sinful practices, and the personality of Satan.*

*   *   *

STATEMENT OF FAITH (CHINESE CHRISTIAN MISSION)

1. We believe the Holy Scriptures, both Old and New testaments, is the inspired Word of God, the complete revelation of His will for the salvation of men, and the divine and final authority for all Christian faith and life.

2. We believe in the one, true and living God, eternally existing in three persons—Father, Son and the Holy Spirit.

3. We believe in God the Father, the Creator, Ruler and Sustainer of heaven and earth and everything therein.

4. We believe in God the Son, Jesus Christ, true God and true man, conceived of the Holy Spirit and born of the Virgin Mary. He died on the cross and shed His blood as an atonement for the sins of men, and was raised bodily from the dead. He ascended into heaven, where at the right hand of the Majesty on High. He now is our High Priest and Advocate. We believe in His imminent return according to His promise.

5. We believe in the Holy Spirit, the Third Person of the Godhead, who is of one substance, equal in power, and co-existent with the Father and the Son. His ministry is to convict men, regenerate the believing sinners, and to indwell, guide, instruct and empower the believers for godly living and service.

6. We believe that man was created in the image and the likeness of God, but in Adam all men have fallen into sin, and as sinners men cannot save themselves, but are in need of God's salvation.

7. We believe that penitent sinners are regenerated solely by God's grace and justified through faith in Jesus Christ.

8. We believe that there shall be a bodily resurrection of the just to eternal life, and of the unjust to eternal punishment.

9. We believe that the church is one body, consisting of those regenerated by the Spirit of God and of which Christ is the Head, expressing itself in worship, fellowship, evangelism and service.

Notes: *The Chinese Christian Mission, founded in 1961, is dedicated to the evangelization of Chinese people worldwide. It sponsors a radio ministry broadcast into mainland China and has missionaries among Chinese people in diaspora (settled far from their ancestral homeland), especially those living in Central America. Its Statement of Faith is a consensus Evangelical statement.*

*   *   *

WE BELIEVE IN (CHINESE OVERSEAS CHRISTIAN MISSION)

We believe in:

The divine inspiration of the Holy Scriptures as complete authority in all matters of faith and conduct.

The unity of the Father, the Son, and the Holy Spirit in the Godhead.

The universal sinfulness and guilt of human nature.

Redemption from the guilt penalty and power of sin only through the sacrificial death of Jesus Christ, the Incarnate Son of God, and none other.

The resurrection of Jesus Christ from the dead.

The necessity of the work of the Holy Spirit to make the death of Christ effective to the individual sinner, granting him repentance toward God and faith in Jesus Christ.

The indwelling and work of the Holy Spirit in the believer, empowering him to live a holy life.

The expectation of the personal return of the Lord Jesus Christ.

Notes: *The Chinese Overseas Christian Mission, founded in 1959, pursues evangelism among Chinese people worldwide. It sponsors radio broadcasts into mainland China and mis-*

WE BELIEVE IN (CHINESE OVERSEAS CHRISTIAN MISSION)
(continued)

sionary efforts among the Chinese in diaspora. Its has a brief Evangelical consensus statement of belief.

* * *

STATEMENT OF FAITH (CHRISTIAN AID MISSION)

1. We believe in the divine inspiration and authority of the Holy Scriptures. By this is meant a miraculous guidance of the Holy Spirit in their original writing (II Pet. 1:21) extending to all parts of the Old and New Testaments applying even to the choice of words, so that the result is the very Word of God; the only infallible rule of faith and practice (II Tim. 3:16).

2. We believe in one Lord God Almighty, who has revealed Himself as God the Father, God the Son, and God the Holy Spirit.

3. We believe that as through one man sin entered the world and death through sin, so death passed upon all men for that all have sinned, and the wages of sin is death (Rom 5:12, 6:23).

4. We believe in the virgin birth and true deity of our Lord Jesus Christ; in His death as the only true substitute for sin, and that His shed blood was and is a sufficient expiation for the sins of all men. We believe in His bodily resurrection from the dead, his ascension, and exaltation above all heavens (Eph. 4:10).

5. We believe that men are justified by faith alone and are accounted righteous before God only through the merit of our Lord and Savior Jesus Christ, and that all who are so justified are born anew and receive eternal life which is Christ in us the hope of glory (Col. 1:27), but that those who have not been born again shall not see the Kingdom of God (John 3:3).

6. We believe in the everlasting blessedness of the saved who are in Christ, and that God Himself will judge the lost who are outside of Christ with eternal punishment.

7. We believe that a local church is the body of Christ in that locality (I Cor. 12:27), but that all regenerated believers are also one body in Christ (Eph. 2:16) and constitute the true church (Col. 1:24).

8. We believe in the premillennial second coming to earth of our Lord Jesus Christ in power and great glory, that He will change our vile bodies and fashion them like unto His glorious body (Phil. 3:21). We believe that He shall reign as King of Kings and Lord of Lords upon this earth for a thousand years (Rev. 20:5), and in Heaven forever.

9. We believe it to be the supreme responsibility of the disciples of our Lord Jesus to plant His church among all nations (Rom. 1:5, Rev. 5:9).

Notes: *The Christian Aid Mission, founded in 1953, is a missionary support organization that assists foreign mission sending agencies. Its Statement of Faith is a consensus Evangelical statement.*

* * *

STATEMENT OF FAITH (CHRISTIAN HERITAGE ACADEMY)

We believe. . .

. . . that all the Words of the Scriptures, both Old and New Testament, are the inspired Words of God, without error in the original writings, the complete revelation of His will for the salvation of men, and the Divine and final authority for all Christian faith and life.

. . . in one God, Creator of all things, infinitely perfect and eternally existing in three persons, Father, Son and Holy Spirit.

. . . that Jesus Christ is true God and true man, having been conceived of the Holy Ghost and born of the virgin Mary. He died on the cross as a sacrifice for our sins according to the Scriptures. Further, He arose bodily from the dead and ascended into heaven, where at the right hand of the Majesty on High, He now is our High Priest and Advocate.

. . . that the ministry of the Holy Spirit is to glorify the Lord Jesus Christ, and during this age to convict men, regenerate the sinner, and indwell, guide, instruct and empower the believer for godly living and service.

. . . that man was created in the image of God but fell into sin and is therefore lost and only through regeneration by the Holy Spirit can salvation and spiritual life be obtained.

. . . that the shed blood of Jesus Christ and His resurrection provide the only ground for justification and salvation for all who believe, and only such as receive Jesus Christ are born of the Holy Spirit, and thus become children of God.

. . . that water baptism and the Lord's Supper are ordinances to be observed by the church during the present age. They are however, not to be regarded as means of salvation.

. . . that the true Church is composed of all and only such persons who through saving faith in Jesus Christ have been regenerated by the Holy Spirit and are united together in the body of Christ of which He is the Head.

. . . that Jesus Christ is the Lord and Head of the Church.

. . . in the personal and bodily return of our Lord Jesus Christ and that this "Blessed Hope" has a vital bearing on the personal life and service of the believer.

Notes: *The Christian Heritage Academy, in the Chicago, Illinois, suburb of Deerfield, is typical of numerous private Christian schools that seek to combine an excellent academic program for elementary school children, with a strong Evangelical Christian faith. It is a self-conscious alternative to public school education. It has a strong Fundamentalist Statement of Faith that emphasizes the inerrancy of the Bible.*

*   *   *

DOCTRINAL STATEMENT (CHRISTIAN JEW HOUR, INC.)

We Believe and Preach . . .

- the Verbal Inspiration of the Scriptures

- the Deity of the Lord Jesus Christ

- the Personality and Deity of the Holy Spirit

- the Total Depravity of man

- the Necessity of the New Birth

- the Shed Blood of Jesus Christ for the Remission of Sins

- Salvation by Grace through Faith

- the Life Everlasting of the Believer

- the Endless Punishment of the Lost

- the Pre-millennial Coming of the Lord

Notes: *The Christian Jew Hour, founded by evangelist Charles Halff, promotes Jewish evangelism, especially through Halff's radio program. Its brief Doctrinal Statement affirms the primary points of Evangelical belief.*

*   *   *

WE BELIEVE (CHRISTIAN LITERATURE CRUSADE)

WE BELIEVE . . .

—the Holy Scriptures as originally given to be the only inspired, infallible and authoritative Word of God.

—that there is only one God, eternally existent in three Persons, Father, Son and Holy Spirit.

—in the deity of our Lord Jesus Christ, in His virgin birth, in His sinless life, in His miracles, in His vicarious and atoning death through His shed blood, in His bodily resurrection, in His ascension to the right hand of the Father, in His mediatorial work, and in His coming personal return in power and glory.

—in the universal sinfulness and guilt of all mankind since the fall, rendering man subject to God's wrath and condemnation.

—that for the salvation of lost and sinful men regeneration by the Holy Spirit is absolutely essential.

—in the present ministry of the Holy Spirit, by whose indwelling the Christian is enabled to live a godly life.

—in the bodily resurrection of both the saved and the lost; they that are saved unto the resurrection of life, and they that are lost unto the resurrection of judgment.

—in the spiritual unity of believers in our Lord Jesus Christ, who comprise the Church, which is His body.

Notes: *Christian Literature Crusade, founded in 1941, is a prominent international Evangelical organization focused on the publishing and distribution of Christian literature. Its statement of belief is derived from that of the National Association of Evangelicals, to which it has added a paragraph on the sinfulness and guilt of all humanity.*

*   *   *

STATEMENT OF FAITH (CHRISTIAN LITERATURE INTERNATIONAL)

WE BELIEVE the Holy Bible to be inspired, the only infallible, authoritative Word of God, inerrant in the original writings.

WE BELIEVE that there is one triune God, eternally existent in three persons: Father, Son, and Holy Spirit.

WE BELIEVE in the deity of our Lord Jesus Christ, in His virgin birth, in His sinless life, in His miracles, in His vicarious and atoning death through His shed blood, in His bodily resurrection, in His ascension to the right hand of the Father, and in His return in power and glory.

WE BELIEVE that salvation is the free gift of God through grace, and received by faith in the Lord Jesus Christ, whose precious blood was shed on Calvary for the forgiveness of our sins.

WE BELIEVE in the ministry of the Holy Spirit by whose indwelling the Christian is enabled to live a godly and separated life.

WE BELIEVE in the resurrection of both the saved and the lost, they who are saved unto the resurrection of life, and they who are lost unto the resurrection of damnation.

WE BELIEVE that the Church, which is the body and bride of Christ, is a spiritual organism made up of all born-again persons. It is the obligation of all members of this Body to witness by lifestyle and words to the truths of Holy Scripture and proclaim the Good News of Christ to lost men everywhere.

Notes: *Christian Literature International, founded in 1967, publishes and distributes the New Life Version of the Bible, a*

STATEMENT OF FAITH (CHRISTIAN LITERATURE INTERNATIONAL) (continued)

version that replaces difficult words and phrases with easily understandable words. It is especially helpful for those whom English is a second language. Its Statement of Faith is derived from that of the National Association of Evangelicals, but has a completely rewritten final paragraph on the nature of the Church.

* * *

STATEMENT OF FAITH AND DOCTRINE (CHRISTIAN OUTREACH INTERNATIONAL)

- We believe the Bible to be the inspired, infallible and totally authoritative Word of God.

- We believe that there is one true God, eternally existing in three co-equal persons—Father, Son and Holy Spirit.

- We believe in the personality of Satan, who is called the devil (Rev. 20:2).

- We believe man is totally unable to save himself and in his unsaved state is condemned before God.

- We believe in the deity of Christ and His virgin birth, sinless life, substitutionary death, bodily resurrection, ascension and personal return.

- We believe in salvation by grace alone through faith in Christ. Man must be born again by receiving Jesus Christ personally in his heart and confessing Him as Lord (Rom. 10:9-10). Good works are a subsequent fruit of salvation.

- We believe in the Holy Spirit's present ministry in and to the believer enabling him to live a godly life and serve God effectively.

- We believe in the spiritual unity of believers in our Lord Jesus Christ, who comprises the Church which is His Body and in its local manifestation, the local church.

Notes: *Christian Outreach International, founded in 1984, is an international evangelistic organization. It has accepted, with some modifications and an additional statement about the nature of the Church, the doctrinal statement of the National Association of Evangelicals. It did so in the self-conscious recognition of the varying beliefs among Evangelical churches on many less essential matters and did not wish its doctrinal*

statement to be a hindrance in working with the broadest range of the Evangelical community.

* * *

STATEMENT OF FAITH (CHRISTIANS IN ACTION)

We Believe . . .

. . . The Bible to be the only infallible Word of God.

. . . There is one God, eternal in three persons: Father, Son and Holy Spirit.

. . . In the Deity of Jesus Christ, His virgin birth, sinless life, miracles, atonement, resurrection and second coming.

. . . That sinful man must be transformed by the Holy Spirit.

. . . In the indwelling of the Holy Spirit, Who empowers the Christian to live a godly life and witness to others.

. . . In the resurrection of Christians to eternal life and the lost to perdition.

. . . In the spiritual unity of all believers in Jesus Christ.

Notes: *Christians in Action, founded in 1957, supports missionary activities around the globe. Its statement is a shortened version of that of the National Association of Evangelicals.*

* * *

STATEMENT OF FAITH (CHURCHES ALIVE)

The Statement of Faith is to be used as the official doctrinal position for Churches Alive. Every Staff member will be required to sign the Statement of Faith to affirm his complete agreement with it.

The sole basis of our beliefs is the Bible, God's infallible written Word, the sixty-six books of the Old and New Testaments. We believe that it was uniquely, verbally and fully inspired by the Holy Spirit, and that it was written without error in the original manuscripts. It is the supreme and final authority in all matters on which it speaks.

A. We accept those large areas of doctrinal teaching on which, historically, there has been general agreement among all true Christians. Because of the specialized calling of our movement, we desire to allow for freedom of conviction on other doctrinal matters, provided that any interpretation is based upon the Bible alone, and that no such interpretation shall become an issue which hinders the ministry to which God has called us.

B. We explicitly affirm our belief in basic Bible teachings, as follows:

1. There is one true God, eternally existing in three persons Father, Son and Holy Spirit—each of whom possesses equally all the attributes of Deity and the characteristics of personality.

2. Jesus Christ is God, the living Word, who became flesh through His virgin birth. Hence, He is perfect Deity and true humanity united in one person forever.

3. He lived a sinless life, and voluntarily atoned for the sins of men by dying on the cross as their substitute, thus, satisfying divine justice and accomplishing salvation for all who trust in Him alone.

4. He rose from the dead in the same body, though glorified, in which He lived and died.

5. He ascended bodily into heaven, and sat down at the right hand of God the Father, where He, the only Mediator between God and man, continually makes intercession for His own.

6. Man was originally created in the image of God. He sinned by disobeying God; thus, he was alienated from his Creator. That historic fall brought all mankind under divine condemnation.

7. Man's nature is corrupted, and he is thus totally unable to please God. Every man is in need of regeneration and renewal by the Holy Spirit.

8. The salvation of man is wholly a work of God's grace and is not the result, in whole or in part, of human merit—moral or religious. God imputes His righteousness to those who put their faith in Christ alone for their salvation, and thereby justifies them in His sight.

9. It is the privilege of all who are born again of the Spirit to be assured of their salvation from the very moment in which they trust Christ as their Savior. This assurance is not dependent upon individual worthiness or accomplishment, but is produced by the witness of the Holy Spirit, who confirms in the believer the testimony of God in His written Word.

10. The Holy Spirit has come into the world to reveal and glorify Christ and to apply the saving work of Christ to men. He convicts and draws sinners to Christ, imparts new life to them, continually indwells them from the moment of spiritual birth and seals them until the day of redemption. His fullness, power, and control are appropriated in the believer's life by faith.

11. Every believer is called to so live in the power of the indwelling Spirit that he will not fulfill the lust of the flesh but will bear fruit to the glory of God.

12. Jesus Christ is the Head of the Church. His Body is composed of all men, living and dead, who have been joined to Him through saving faith.

13. God admonished His people to assemble together regularly for worship, for participation in ordinances, for edification through the Scriptures, and for mutual encouragement.

14. At physical death, the believer enters immediately into eternal, conscious fellowship with the Lord and awaits the resurrection of his body to everlasting glory and blessing.

15. At physical death, the unbeliever enters immediately into eternal, conscious separation from the Lord and awaits the resurrection of his body to everlasting judgment and condemnation.

16. Jesus Christ will come again to the earth—personally, visibly, and bodily—to consummate history and the eternal plan of God.

17. The Lord Jesus Christ commanded all believers to proclaim the gospel throughout the world and to disciple men of every nation. The fulfilling of that Great Commission requires that all worldly and personal ambitions be subordinated to a total commitment to "Him who loved us and gave Himself for us."

Without mental reservation, I hereby subscribe to the above statement and pledge myself anew to help in fulfilling the Great Commission in our generation, depending upon the Holy Spirit to guide and empower me.

Notes: *Churches Alive, founded in 1973, publishes materials to assist church growth and community evangelism. It is a conservative Evangelical organization that accepts the infallibility and inerrancy of the Bible and a consensus Evangelical theological perspective.*

*　　　*　　　*

WHAT WE BELIEVE (CIRCLE COMMUNITY CENTER)

What We Believe. . .

1. In one God, in three persons; God the Father, God the Son (the Lord Jesus Christ) and God the Holy Spirit.

   a. God the Father created and sustains us. He is the source of all truth, hope, love, and justice.

   b. Jesus Christ, God's Son, became a man so that we could see who God is and what God expects of us. He died to pay the penalty for our sins and then rose bodily from the grave to demonstrate His authority over all things.

   c. The Holy Spirit is God continuing to be with us. He guides us, convicts us of sin, assures us that we are God's children, and gives us gifts for ministry.

WHAT WE BELIEVE (CIRCLE COMMUNITY CENTER)
(continued)

2. The Bible is from God, completely true, and tells us who God is, who we are, and how we are to live. The Good News of the Bible addresses the spiritual, physical, emotional, and societal needs of mankind.

3. Each person is lovingly created in God's image and therefore has great value; but all people have been tragically separated from God by sin.

4. Salvation is God's plan of restoring us to a relationship with Him through the sacrifice of Christ. We accept salvation by confessing our sinfulness, and receiving God's forgiveness which must result in living in obedient faith.

5. The Church is made up of everyone who serves Jesus as Lord. Within the church, people worship God as well as love and care for each other.

6. The mission of the Church is to follow Jesus in pioneering the Kingdom of God. This includes proclaiming Jesus as Lord and Savior, working for social justice, and the relief of human suffering.

Notes: *Circle Community Center works primarily within the African American community of Chicago's West Side. Its statement, written in rather non-traditional language is, nevertheless, a consensus Evangelical statement of belief. Unusual for Evangelical statements, the belief statement emphasizes the love of God in creation, the Gospel's message for the emotional and societal needs of humanity, and the mutual care of Christians within the Church.*

* * *

STATEMENT OF FAITH (COALITION FOR CHRISTIAN OUTREACH)

The members of The Coalition for Christian Outreach jointly confess the following articles of the Christian Faith:

We believe in one God Father, Son, and Holy Spirit. The Triune God has created people in his own image and has called them to manifest and reflect holiness through obedience to His commandments. Because human beings have woefully fallen in this responsibility and entered into a state of moral corruption, they have subsequently become estranged from their Creator.

Because of a profound love for His creation, God has initiated a plan of redemption which he has accomplished on behalf of His people in the realm of temporal history. The zenith of this redemption is located in the historical incarnation of God in the person of Jesus of Nazareth. We confess Jesus to be the Christ of the Old Testament prophecy, being at the same time fully God and fully man. Jesus, through his atoning death and bodily

Resurrection, has provided the meritorious basis of our justification, which we receive by faith alone.

The risen and ascended Christ has sent His Holy Spirit to dwell in the hearts of believers, effecting their regeneration and operating in their sanctification. The same Holy Spirit has been given to the people of God to empower them for the service of bearing witness to the Kingdom of God. The Holy Spirit brings His people together to form a corporate community of believers. We believe that Christ has established a visible church which is called to live in the power of the Holy Spirit under the regulation of the authority of the Holy Scripture, exercising discipline administering the sacraments, and preaching the Gospel of Christ.

We support the work of Christian organizations and institutions that confess the Lordship of Jesus Christ. We believe that the Bible in its entirety is divine revelation, and we submit to the authority of Holy Scripture, acknowledging it to be inspired by God and carrying the full weight of His authority.

We are committed to the implementation of the social and cultural implications of God's commandments for the well-being of people and their environment. We believe our faith should be visible in concrete forms and models of personal and social behavior. We seek to be faithful disciples of Christ, enduring in love and obedience until He comes again to consummate His kingdom.

Notes: *The Coalition for Christian Outreach, founded in 1971, has an Evangelical ministry on college campuses in Pennsylvania, Ohio, and West Virginia. Its Statement of Faith represents a consensus Evangelical position, but avoids the language of infallibility, inerrancy, and plenary inspiration in its wording on biblical authority. The statement also emphasizes the necessity of examining and acting on the social and cultural implications of Christian faith.*

* * *

TEN PRINCIPLES (CONFRONTATION POINT MINISTRIES)

The following are the overriding, undergirding, foundational statements of Confrontation Point. These encompass the goals and background of the ministry and are the principles that enable and empower us to accomplish the task of providing an experience that will be the most beneficial for the individual needs of each unique group.

1. By living simply in nature, God is realized.

2. Help church group participants to form and to move toward their goals of ongoing ministry.

3. To develop understanding of Christ-like service through the giving of ourselves to others.

4. Through unconditional love and acceptance, we build Christian community.

5. Shattering preconceptions, confronting limitations and thereby facing new possibilities with self and with group in a challenging environment.

6. Leadership development that enables group ownership, affirms consensus decision making and holds group members accountable.

7. Free to be oneself, have fun, explore, discover, laugh, make new friends and celebrate the joy of life.

8. Provide an atmosphere in which participants can examine their own faith journey, experience spiritual renewal, and reflect upon their dependence upon God—PILGRIMAGE.

9. Develop a greater appreciation for God's creation, the natural world, and create a sense of environmental responsibility—STEWARDSHIP.

10. Provide an experience which will have long lasting benefits to the group members and will enable them to formulate specific strategies for applying their learning upon returning home.

Notes: *The Ten Principles of Confrontation Point Ministries, assume an Evangelical faith and press its insights into observations of the Christian lifestyle. The Ministries specialize in offering Christians an experience of God in nature, shared life in community, and the development of faith.*

*　　*　　*

STATEMENT OF BELIEF (CREATION RESEARCH SOCIETY)

Members of the Creation Research Society, which include research scientists representing various fields of successful scientific accomplishment, are committed to full belief in the Biblical record of creation and early history, and thus to a concept of dynamic special creation (as opposed to evolution), both of the universe and the earth with its complexity of living forms.

We propose to re-evaluate science from this viewpoint, and since 1964 have published a quarterly of research articles in this field. In 1970 the Society published a textbook, *Biology: A Search for Order in Complexity,* through Zondervan Publishing House, Grand Rapids, Michigan 49506. Subsequently a Revised Edition (1974), a Teachers' Guide and both Teachers' and Students' Laboratory Manuals have been published by Zondervan Publishing House. All members of the Society subscribe to the following statement of belief:

1. The Bible is the written Word of God, and because it is inspired throughout, all its assertions are historically and scientifically true in all the original autographs. To the student of nature this means that the account of origins in Genesis is a factual presentation of simple historical truths.

2. All basic types of living things, including man, were made by direct creative acts of God during the Creation Week described in Genesis. Whatever biological changes have occurred since Creation Week have accomplished only changes within the original created kinds.

3. The Great Flood described in Genesis, commonly referred to as the Noachian Flood, was an historic event worldwide in its extent and effect.

4. We are an organization of Christian men and women of science who accept Jesus Christ as our Lord and Savior. The account of the special creation of Adam and Eve as one man and woman and their subsequent fall into sin is the basis for our belief in the necessity of a Savior for all mankind. Therefore, salvation can come only through accepting Jesus Christ as our Savior.

Notes: *Founded in 1963, the Creation Research Society is one of the leading organizations supporting the scientific accuracy of the biblical accounts of creation. Its research looks for evidence of a relatively recent creation of the earth as described in Genesis, and opposes the current scientific consensus that the earth and its life forms, including humanity, evolved over many millions of years. As might be expected, the Society has a strong belief in the inerrancy of the Bible. Most importantly, those associated with the Society read the opening chapters of the Book of Genesis as a simple presentation of real events. It also accepts a literal account of the fall of humanity into sin as essential to their understanding of human salvation.*

*　　*　　*

DOCTRINAL STATEMENT (CRISTA MINISTRIES)

1. We believe in the Scripture of the Old and New Testaments as verbally inspired by God, and inerrant in the original writings, and that they are of supreme and final authority in faith and life.

2. We believe in one God, eternally existing in three persons: Father, Son and Holy Spirit.

3. We believe that Jesus Christ was begotten by the Holy Spirit and born of the virgin Mary, and is true God and true man.

4. We believe that man was created in the image of God; that he sinned, and thereby incurred, not only physical death, but also that spiritual death which is separation from God; and that all human beings are born with a sinful nature.

5. We believe that the Lord Jesus Christ died for our sins according to the Scriptures, as a representative and substitutionary sacrifice;, and that all that truly repent of their sins and believe in Him are justified on the ground of His shed blood.

6. We believe in the present ministry of the Holy Spirit by whose indwelling the Christian is enabled to live a godly life.

7. We believe in the resurrection of the crucified body of our Lord, and His ascension into heaven and in His present life there for us, as High Priest and Advocate.

8. We believe in that blessed hope, the personal, bodily return of our Lord and Savior, Jesus Christ.

Notes: *CRISTA Ministries, founded in 1948, is an Evangelical service agency with a wide variety of ministries, especially for youth and the aged. It operates out of an acceptance of the inerrancy of the Bible and holds to a consensus Evangelical theological assertions.*

*   *   *

STATEMENT OF FAITH (DAVID C. COOK PUBLISHING COMPANY)

The Bible

We believe that the Bible, both Old and New Testaments, is the divinely inspired and only authoritative Word of God; supreme and final in its authority in matters of faith and practice. The Bible stands unique and alone above all books. For this reason we believe every lesson should be based upon Scripture—every lesson a Bible lesson, with Scripture applied to present-day Christian living.

God

We believe in the Triune God of the Bible, the God who created the world, who made man in His own image, who so loved the world that He gave His only begotten Son for man's redemption.

Christ

We believe in the deity of Jesus Christ, that He is coeternal and coequal with God the Father. We believe the Bible record of His virgin birth, sinless life, words, works, vicarious death, bodily resurrection and ascension, and promise of His personal return. Christ came into the world to provide salvation through faith in Him as Savior and Lord, and to restore men to fellowship with God.

The Holy Spirit

We believe that God the Holy Spirit, as revealed in the Bible, is a Person coequal and coeternal with God the Father and God the Son. The Holy Spirit brings an awareness of guilt, brings about the new birth, and indwells the believer that he may lead a godly life. The Holy Spirit strengthens faith, brings comfort and peace in time of sorrow and distress, enlightens our hearts and minds to understand and apply the truth in Christ and the Bible.

Repentance

We believe that men become children of God by true repentance, turning from sin and turning to Christ as Savior. True repentance results in a changed life. The believer now seeks to live his life according to the will of God.

Faith

We believe that men who have received God's forgiveness for sin through Christ's atoning death and triumphant resurrection possess saving faith. The faith is awakened and strengthened by the hearing of the Word of God. Believers strive to express this saving faith through the total commitment of their lives to Christ as Savior and Lord.

The Christian Life

We believe that the Christian life is lived by trust in Christ and fellowship with Him, for He is ''the way, the truth, and the life.'' The Christian life manifests itself in service to God and service to fellow men of all races and stations in life. It is summed up in the two great commandments: to love God with all our hearts, souls, strength, and minds; and to love our neighbors as ourselves.

The Church

We believe that the Church, which is described in the Scriptures as Christ's body, is composed of all people who have accepted Christ in faith and have committed their lives to Him. In any local community the Church consists of all such people, regardless of the Christian group with which they are affiliated. The Church, spiritually conceived, is a living organism which expresses itself through dedicated Christians in all groups of believers, under the guidance of the Holy Spirit.

The Kingdom of God

The Kingdom of God is the rule of God, which has as its final goal the overcoming of every force which resists God's will. The Kingdom of God now manifests itself in the spiritual realm through believers, those who have accepted and responded to the claims of God's Kingdom through Christ. The Church, while not identical with the Kingdom of God, is a present manifestation of it. The Kingdom of God will be consummated when Christ comes again.

Eternal Life

We believe that eternal life begins here in this world, when one comes into a transforming, saving knowledge of Jesus Christ. It means also life after death for all ages to come. Eternal life further means a certain kind of life, a quality of life which God imparts to those who become children of God. Those who have rejected Christ as Savior and Lord are eternally separated from Christ; and thus are excluded from the everlasting bliss reserved for those who have accepted the love and forgiveness of God, revealed in Christ.

Notes: *David C. Cook Publishing Company, founded in 1875, grew out of the emerging post-Civil War Sunday School* *movement, primarily in the Methodist Episcopal Church. It has continued to publish church school material and has added a broad range of other Christian literature for use by Evangelical churches. Like churches out of the Methodist tradition, the Company avoids language concerning the infallibility and inerrancy of the Bible, nevertheless offering a strong affirmation of its authority. It Statement of Faith represents a consensus Evangelical position, but includes rarely encountered paragraphs on repentance and the kingdom of God.*

*　　*　　*

STATEMENT OF FAITH (EASTERN EUROPEAN MISSION)

1. We believe the Bible to be the inspired, the only infallible, authoritative Word of God.

2. We believe that there is one God, eternally existent in three persons: Father, Son, and Holy Spirit.

3. We believe in the deity of our Lord Jesus Christ, in His virgin birth, in His sinless life, in His miracles, in His vicarious and atoning death through His shed blood, in His bodily resurrection, in His ascension to the right hand of the Father, and in His second visible coming for the restoration of His kingdom here on earth, after which will be the judgment.

4. We believe that for the salvation of lost and sinful man regeneration by the Holy Spirit is absolutely essential.

5. We believe in the present ministry of the Holy Spirit by whose indwelling the Christian is enabled to live a godly life.

6. We believe in the resurrection of both the saved and the lost; they that are saved unto the resurrection of life and they that are lost unto the resurrection of damnation.

7. We believe in the spiritual unity of believers in our Lord Jesus Christ.

8. We believe in a regenerate church membership, separation from the world and scriptural church discipline.

Notes: *The Eastern European Mission, founded in 1927, specializes in evangelism in Europe, especially in the countries formerly allied in the Warsaw Pact. Its Statement of Faith is based on that of the National Association of Evangelicals, with an additional statement on the nature of the Church.*

*　　*　　*

DOCTRINAL POSITION [THE EVANGELICAL ALLIANCE MISSION (TEAM)]

Section 1. SPIRITUAL STANDARD. All members of the Board of Directors, administrative officers, missionaries. candidates, and workers in any capacity in this Mission, at home or abroad, shall be those who are new creatures in Christ, called into His service, having a love for Christ and a passion for souls, seeking to manifest the kind of life expressed in the apostolic exhortation, ''Be kindly, affectioned one to another with brotherly love; in honor preferring one another; not slothful in business; fervent in spirit; servicing the Lord; rejoicing in hope; patient in tribulation; continuing instant in prayer'' (Romans 12:10-12).

They shall be those who wholeheartedly and without mental reservation agree to the following Statement of Faith, signifying that agreement by a signed statement upon entering service or upon re-entry into any subsequent term of service.

Section 2. STATEMENT OF FAITH.

a. We believe the Scriptures, both Old and New Testaments, to be the inspired Word of God, without error in the original writings, the complete revelation of His will for the salvation of man and the divine and final authority for all Christian faith, life, and conduct.

b. We believe in one God, creator of all things, infinitely perfect and eternally existing in three persons, Father, Son, and Holy Spirit.

c. We believe Jesus Christ, without any change in His eternal deity, became man through conception by the Holy Spirit and virgin birth, that He died on the cross, a perfect and complete sacrifice, in our stead and for our sins according to the Scriptures. He arose bodily from the dead, and ascended into heaven where at the right hand of the Majesty on high, He is now our High Priest and Advocate.

d. We believe that the ministry of the Holy Spirit is to glorify the Lord Jesus Christ, and during this age to convict of sin and regenerate the sinner upon believing in Christ, at the time of regeneration baptizing the believer into the one body of which Christ is the head; and to indwell, guide, instruct, fill, and empower the believer for godly living and service.

e. We believe that man was directly created by God in His own image, but fell into sin. The entire human race is, therefore, lost and only through repentance and faith in Jesus Christ, and regeneration of the Holy Spirit, can salvation and spiritual life be obtained.

f. We believe that the atoning death of Jesus Christ, and His resurrection, provide the only ground of justification and salvation for all who believe, and that only such as receive Jesus Christ by personal faith are born of the Holy Spirit and, thus, become children of God.

g. We believe in the personal, premillennial return of our Lord Jesus Christ, and that this blessed hope has a vital bearing on the personal life and service of the believer.

h. We believe in the bodily resurrection of all the dead, of the believer to everlasting blessedness and joy with the Lord, and of the unbeliever to judgment and everlasting and conscious punishment.

i. We believe that the Church is composed of all such persons who through saving faith in Jesus Christ have been regenerated by the Holy Spirit and are united together in the body of Christ, of which He is the head.

j. We believe that water baptism and the Lord's Supper are ordinances to be observed by the Church during this present age. They are, however, not to be regarded as means of salvation.

k. We believe that all the saved should live in such manner as will honor and glorify and not bring reproach upon their Savior and Lord, and that it is commanded of God to remain separate from false doctrines, and sinful pleasures, practices, and associations.

Notes: *The Evangelical Alliance Mission (TEAM), founded in 1890, is an independent missionary sending agency operating in countries around the world. It is a conservative Evangelical organization standing firmly on the inerrancy of the Bible, with a strong statement of the fundamentals of Evangelical faith. It is opposed to cooperation with Christians who hold what it believes to be false doctrines and those who engage in sinful practices.*

*   *   *

STATEMENT OF FAITH (EVANGELICAL ENTERPRISES, INC.)

WE BELIEVE. . .

That the Scriptures of the Old and New Testaments wholly constitute the verbally inspired Word of God and are inerrant as originally given, and that they are the supreme and final authority in faith and practice.

That God is One, eternally existing in three persons—Father, Son, and Holy Ghost.

That Jesus Christ was supernaturally conceived by the Holy Ghost, that He was God incarnate born of the Virgin Mary, is true God and man, that He lived, taught and wrought miraculous works, wonders, and signs in fulfillment of the Scriptures and was put to death by crucifixion and was raised from the dead in body, and ascended where He now sits as our High Priest and Advocate at the right hand of God the Father, from whence He is coming again to this earth bodily and visibly with His saints to reign in glory and splendor.

That man was created in the image of God; that he sinned and thus incurred both physical and spiritual death; that all human beings are born with a sinful nature and upon reaching moral responsibility become sinners in thought, word, and deed.

That according to the scriptures, the Lord Jesus Christ died vicariously for sinners, and that all who place their faith in Him and receive Him into their heart and life, are justified on the ground of His shed blood.

That the Second Coming of our Lord Jesus Christ is personal, visible, premillennial, and imminent and in two aspects—the one His coming for the saints before the Great Tribulation, the other His coming with the saints after the Great Tribulation to set up His millennial reign on the throne of David.

That the Holy Spirit is the Divine Agent in nature, revelation, and redemption; that He convicts the world of righteousness, sin, and judgment; regenerates, indwells, seals, endues, guides, and teaches all those who believe in Jesus Christ as personal Savior.

That the church as an organism is the body and the bride of Christ of which He is the Living Head and regenerate believers of this present dispensation are the members; that to the church as an organization—body of baptized believers gathered together by the Holy Spirit for the purpose of carrying out the principles and precepts of God's Word—has been entrusted the administration of the ordinances of water baptism, an outward manifestation of an inward experience or picture of regeneration, and of the Lord's Supper, a memorial of our Lord's death, and reminder of His second coming; that the divine mission of the church is to glorify God by the winning of men to Christ, building them up in Christ, and sending them out for Christ.

That Angels are heavenly beings created for the glory of God and for service to the heirs of salvation, and that many of them rebelled against God, the chief of whom is Satan, the source of all evil, a personal being of great cunning and vast power, who shall ultimately be cast into the Lake of Fire and Brimstone to be tormented day and night forever.

That there is a bodily resurrection both of the just and also of the unjust, the one to everlasting bliss, the other to everlasting conscious torment.

Notes: *Evangelical Enterprises, founded in 1956, is a Fundamentalist missionary sending organization. Its conservative theological position begins with an affirmation of the inerrancy of the Bible. It continues with a relatively detailed statement concerning many issues not covered in most similar statements. For example, while many Evangelical organizations affirm a premillennial eschatology, Evangelical Enterprises describe in some detail the specific agenda for the future* *coming of Christ. Evangelical Enterprises has Baptist roots that manifest in its statement on the local church and the administration of the two ordinances (not sacraments) of baptism and the Lord's Supper.*

*   *   *

DOCTRINAL STATEMENT (EVANGELICAL TRAINING ASSOCIATION)

1. God is the infinite personal Spirit, who has revealed himself as a Trinity in unity, existing eternally as Father, Son, and Spirit—three Persons and yet but one God.

2. The Bible, including both the Old and the New Testaments, is a divine revelation, the original autographs of which were inspired by the Holy Spirit, so that the words were kept from error.

3. Jesus Christ is the image of the invisible God, which is to say, He is Himself very God; He took upon Him our nature, being conceived by the Holy Ghost, and born of the Virgin Mary; He died upon the cross as a substitutionary sacrifice for the sins of the world; He arose from the dead in the body in which He was crucified; He ascended into the heavens in that body glorified, where He is now, our interceding High Priest; He will come again personally and visibly to set up His kingdom and to judge the quick and the dead.

4. Man was created in the image of God, but fell into sin, and in that sense is lost; this is true of all men, and except a man be born again, he cannot see the kingdom of God; salvation is by grace through faith in Christ who He own self bore our sins in His own body upon the tree; the retribution of the wicked and unbelieving and the reward of the righteous are everlasting; and as the reward is conscious, so is the retribution.

5. The Church is an elect company of believers baptized by the Holy Spirit into one body, each believer living his life in the power of the Holy Spirit; its mission being to witness concerning its Head, Jesus Christ, and teach and preach the Gospel among all nations.

6. The entire program of Christian training is evangelical. It finds the reason for being, and its goal, in bringing the individual to a personal acceptance of Jesus Christ as Savior and Lord, in helping the Christian grow in grace and in the knowledge of our Lord, and in equipping Christians for more effective service.

Notes: *The Evangelical Training Association, founded in 1930, promotes cooperation among Evangelical institutions of higher learning and encourages them to develop programs to train church volunteers. The Association believes in the*

inerrancy of the Bible and affirms a consensus Evangelical position.

*   *   *

DOCTRINE (EVANGELICAL UNION OF SOUTH AMERICA)

Holding fellowship with all those of sound evangelical faith, the E.U.S.A. takes its stand on the following doctrinal basis.

1. The divine inspiration, sufficiency and authority of the Holy Scriptures.

2. The unity and trinity of the Godhead.

3. The depravity of human nature in consequence of the fall.

4. The deity of the Lord Jesus Christ; His virgin birth; His work of atonement for sin; His bodily resurrection; His mediatorial intercession; His personal, bodily and visible return; His judgment of the world; and the eternal kingdom.

5. The justification of the sinner by faith in our Lord Jesus Christ alone.

6. The work of the Holy Spirit in regeneration and sanctification.

7. The eternal life of the saved and the eternal punishment of the wicked.

Notes: *The Evangelical Union of South America was founded in Edinburgh, Scotland, in 1910, as an international evangelical society to mobilize Protestants to initiate work in Latin America, in spite of the hegemony of Roman Catholicism there. It adopted a brief doctrinal statement emphasizing the authority of the Bible, the Trinity, and the depravity of humanity.*

*   *   *

REAFFIRMATION (EVANGELICALS FOR SOCIAL ACTION)

I. As members of ESA we have only one goal and one source of authority. With all our heart, mind, and strength, we seek to glorify Jesus Christ, the Risen Lord. In obedience to the Scriptures.

II. Rejecting ideologies of left and right, we prayerfully seek to apply biblical principles to the desperate problems of modern society. This means that we cannot choose issues or project policies and programs on the basis of popular appeal or current interest Evangelical endeavors to change public life must reflect the whole

REAFFIRMATION (EVANGELICALS FOR SOCIAL ACTION)
(continued)

range of biblical concerns and emphases. We therefore welcome the challenges to and criticisms of our activities made by fellow-believers who, like ourselves, accept the Old and New Testaments as the only infallible rule of faith and practice.

III. With sadness we observe how easy it is for Christian social movements to lose their biblical foundations. We therefore affirm our unchanged conviction that historic Christian orthodoxy, and it alone, can provide a solid foundation for enduring social reform.

IV. Recognizing creation as the gift of the triune God, who made persons in His own Image, we accept His mandate to be faithful stewards of the earth and to respect the sacredness of human life. We acknowledge that our own lifestyles must demonstrate our commitment through personal righteousness and stewardship of our time, talent and resources for the advancement of God's kingdom.

V. Realizing that because of the Fall human beings are in bondage to sin, we repudiate secular plans to transform society through mere structural change and environmental improvement. Humanity's proud rebellion against God expresses itself in both personal and social sin. Aware, through, that the restraining hand of government can reduce the ways sin becomes embedded in socioeconomic systems, we dedicate ourselves to work for policies that promote liberty, justice and peace.

We know, however, that changing structures can never create new individuals as Marxists and humanists claim. Only personal conversion and the transforming power of the Spirit can release us from the bondage of selfishness rooted in the heart.

VI. We therefore reaffirm our belief in the centrality of evangelism. We seek to avoid those mistakes of the earlier Christian social movements that neglected or abandoned evangelistic concern. Enthusiastically we support the evangelistic mission of sister organizations, knowing that without them our task is impossible and incomplete. We rejoice in biblical evangelism which calls for repentance from all sin, both personal and social. Only an evangelism which summons people to costly discipleship can create new persons and build a Christocentric community capable of challenging materialism, racism, militarism and totalitarianism. We thank God for redemptive grace and saving faith which liberate through the free pardon of sin, and empower love of neighbor that works for peace and justice.

Notes: *It has been a major complaint by liberal Protestants that Evangelicals, especially those who hold to a premillennial eschatology, have largely abandoned the social reform programs, prominent in the nineteenth century, and have failed to think creatively about newly arisen social issues. During the 1970s some, mostly younger, Evangelical leaders began to reverse that trend and issued several mandates for Evangeli-*

cal social action. One result was the formation of Evangelicals for Social Action, founded in 1978. Its Reaffirmation seeks to call attention to social needs, without abandoning Evangelical imperatives to evangelism and world missions. It also opposes Marxist and humanist-based social change programs, while affirming the sacredness of human life and advocating action to create public policies that promote justice, liberty, and peace.

* * *

WE BELIEVE (FELLOWSHIP OF CHRISTIAN AIRLINE PERSONNEL)

We Believe

(1) In the verbal inspiration of Scripture, both Old and New Testament. We believe them to be inerrant in the original writings and that they are the supreme and final authority in faith and life.

(2) That God eternally exists in three persons: Father, Son, and the Holy Spirit.

(3) That Jesus Christ was begotten by the Holy Spirit, born of the Virgin Mary, and is true God and Man.

(4) That man was created in the image of God, that he sinned and thereby incurred not only physical death, but also spiritual death, which is separation from God, and that all human beings are born with a sinful nature. Romans 3:23: "For all have sinned and come short of the glory of God."

(5) That according to the Scriptures, Jesus Christ died for our sins as a representative and substitutionary sacrifice, and that all who believe in Him are justified on the grounds of His shed blood.

(6) In the Resurrection of the Crucified Body of our Lord, in His ascension into Heaven, and His presence there for us as High Priest, and Advocate.

(7) That our Lord and Savior, Jesus Christ, will personally return and set up His Kingdom wherein He will rule and reign in righteousness.

(8) That all who receive by faith Jesus Christ as Lord and Savior are born again of the Holy Spirit, and thereby become the children of God.

(9) In the bodily resurrection of the just and the unjust, the everlasting blessedness of the saved and the everlasting punishment of the lost.

Notes: *The statement of belief of the Fellowship of Christian Airline Personnel is a minimal summary of key Evangelical affirmations, beginning with the inerrancy of the Scriptures and the Trinity. Otherwise, the statement avoids consideration of doctrines that are matters of disagreement within the*

Evangelical community, such as the total depravity of humans, the sacraments, and Christ's thousand-year reign.

*　　　*　　　*

THIS WE BELIEVE (FINAL DELIVERY MINISTRIES)

We believe the Holy Bible, the Old and New Testaments, with its sixty-six canonical books in the original manuscripts is the verbal, plenary, inerrant and infallible Word of God, entirely without error or contradiction in all matters of which it speaks; we additionally believe that God, by His singular care and providence, has preserved His Holy Scriptures; and that the Holy Bible is, therefore, the only sufficient final and supreme rule of authority of faith and practice (Psa. 12:6-7, 119:89, 105, 152, 160; Matt. 5:18, 24-35; Luke 16:17; 2 Tim. 3:16,17; Heb. 4:12; I Peter 1:24-25; 2 Peter 1:21 and Rev. 22:18,19).

We believe in One Triune God, eternally existing in three persons: Father, Son, and Holy Spirit; that they are equal in essence and attributes yet distinct in office and activity (Deut. 6:4; Matt. 28:19; 2 Cor. 13:14).

We believe in the deity of the Lord Jesus Christ; that He was conceived of the Holy Spirit and born of the virgin Mary, lived a sinless and perfect life, died on Calvary's Cross, was buried and rose again the third day, was seen of many, ascended into heaven, that He ever liveth to make intercession for all that come to God by Him (John 1:1,14; Matt. 1:16-23; Isa. 7:14; Phil. 2:6-8; 1 Cor. 15:1-4; 2 Cor. 5:21; Acts 1:9-11; Heb. 7:25).

We believe in the deity of the Holy Spirit, that He is a person and not a force, that He regenerates, baptizes, seals, indwells, fills, teaches, guides, convicts, comforts, intercedes, and sanctifies the believer (John 4:24; Psa. 139:4; Col. 1:18; John 14:16,17; 1 Cor. 12:13; Titus 3:5; Eph. 1:13, 4:30, 5:18).

We believe that man is totally depraved, that the only way to be saved is by grace through faith in the death, burial, and resurrection of Christ. We believe in the eternal security of the believer (Eph. 2:1-3; Rom. 3:10, 23; Eph. 2:8-9; 1 Cor. 15:1-4; John 10:28).

We believe the Church which is the Body of Christ began with the descent of the Holy Spirit on the day of Pentecost, and that those who receive the Lord Jesus Christ as their personal Savior are a member of the Body of Christ and are indwelled by the Holy Spirit. We believe that the Gospel Commission is for the Church; that the Lord's Supper as a memorial and Baptism by Immersion are divine institutions, and that Christ has commanded us to practice them in this age (Acts 2, 8:38,39; 1 Cor. 12:12-18; 1 Cor. 6:19,20; Matt. 28:19,20; 1 Cor. 11:23-29).

We believe that Satan is a person, the author of the fall, and that he has been defeated on the cross, and shall be eternally punished (Job 1:7; Gen. 3:1-19; Heb. 2:14; Rev. 20:10).

We believe that Christ may at any moment return in the air to rapture the saints and that a tribulation of seven years will follow, after which He will come to the earth with His saints and rule for a thousand years. After this the wicked will be judged and cast into the lake of fire. We believe in the bodily resurrection of the dead, both of the just and the unjust; and in the eternal conscious punishment of the lost, and the eternal joy of the saved (1 Cor. 15:51-57; 1 Thess. 4:13-18; Dan. 9:27; Matt. 24:15-21, 25:46; Rev. 19:11, 20:10-15, 22:12-14).

We believe the sign gifts of the Spirit in 1 Corinthians 12:8-10 to be miraculous gifts, sovereignly bestowed by the Holy Spirit for a limited time and for specific circumstances. These gifts are all transitory in nature and limited in operation. By transitory in nature, we mean that by the time the New Testament Canon closed, these gifts had gradually come to an end, with none of them being operative past the end of the first century. By limited in operation, we mean that these were not gifts which were continually exercised by an individual over an extended period of time; and that the purpose of the usage determined the exercise of the gift. The purposes for which the Holy Spirit gave these gifts were: (1) as signs to unbelievers until the completion of the Canon; (2) for authentication of the Gospel; (3) as the seal of divine approval upon the Church; (4) of revelatory significance to believers. All of these purposes were and are served with the completed Word of God (1 Cor. 13:8-10). Therefore, we are convinced that these gifts which were operative in the early Church were discontinued by the time of the close of the New Testament Canon, and are not to be sought nor to be exercised in our day. The completion of the New Testament assured accessibility through the Word of God to knowledge and power adequate for life and service to all believers. Therefore, to seek the transitory gift is a denial of the efficacy of the Word of God (1 Thess. 2:13).

Notes: *Final Delivery Ministries is a conservative Evangelical Protestant organization that focuses its efforts on employees of the postal service. Typical of the statements of similar organizations, this statement of belief begins with a strong assertion of biblical authority, affirming both the infallibility and inerrancy of the Scripture. Important Evangelical assertions concerning God as Trinity and the personality of the Holy Spirit follow. The Ministries manifest a Calvinist Baptist background in its adherence to beliefs in the total depravity of humans, the eternal security of the believer, and the two ordinances (not sacraments) of baptism and the Lord's Supper. A premillennial eschatology is affirmed.*

THIS WE BELIEVE (FINAL DELIVERY MINISTRIES) (continued)

Final Delivery Ministries is non-Pentecostal and concludes its statement with a lengthy argument against the contemporary operation of the gifts of the Spirit among believers.

*　　*　　*

DOCTRINAL STATEMENT (FRIENDS OF ISRAEL)

I. BIBLE:

We believe that the Bible (consisting of 66 books) is the inspired Word of God, that every part is fully and equally inspired, and that every single word of Scripture was produced under the control of the Holy Spirit (2 Pet. 1:21; 2 Tim. 3:16).

We also accept the Scriptures in their entirety as being inerrant (in the original writings) and infallible. For this reason, we are committed to the Bible as being our final authority in all matters of doctrine (faith) and practice (Jn. 17:17; Mt. 5:17).

II. GOD:

We believe that there is only one true, eternal, living God, who is sovereign over all things. God can be known through the many absolute and relative attributes revealed in the Scriptures (Dt. 6:4; Ex. 3:14; Col. 1:15-17).

God is the source and sustainer of all life. He, according to the council of His own will, decreed whatsoever comes to pass, including both His permissive will and His casual will (Isa. 14:24, 26, 27; Eph. 1).

III. TRINITY:

We believe that, although there is only one true God, that God consists of three distinct Persons, each of whom is co-eternal and co-equal.

We believe that the Father is God, that the Son (Jesus, the Christ-Messiah) is God, and that the Holy Spirit is God (Dt. 6:4; Jn. 6:27; Jn. 1:1, 14; Acts 5:3, 4).

IV. CHRIST:

We believe the Lord Jesus Christ to be absolute Deity, the eternal Son of God, who became man without ceasing to be God. In the incarnation, He was conceived by the Holy Spirit and born of the Virgin Mary (Mt. 1:18-25; Heb. 1:8; Isa. 9:6, 7; Jn. 3:16).

We believe that Jesus Christ was both fully God and fully man at the same time (Phil. 2:5-8).

We believe that He was totally holy by virtue of His miraculous birth and sinless life (Heb. 4:15; 2 Cor. 5:21).

We believe that Jesus Christ voluntarily laid down His life, the Just dying for the unjust, making it possible for man to be saved (Jn. 10:17; Heb. 9:14, 28; 1 Pet. 3:18).

We believe that He rose bodily from the dead on the third day after death, and that He ascended into Heaven to the right hand of the Father (Jn. 2:19-22; Acts 1:9-11; Heb. 1:3).

We believe that, presently, He is our Intercessor and Advocate, the only true Mediator between God and man (Heb. 7:25; Heb. 4:14; 1 Jn. 2:1; 1 Tim. 2:5).

V. HOLY SPIRIT:

We. believe that the Holy Spirit is Deity, a Divine Person of the Godhead. He is not a force, but is truly a Person and is equal with the Father and the Son (Acts 5:3, 4).

We believe that the Holy Spirit gives spiritual gifts to every believer at the moment he is regenerated, and that these gifts are to be used for the edification and perfecting of the believers in the Church. We believe that the miracle and sign gifts were given for a unique purpose to the first-century church, but that they ceased at the end of that century (Rom. 12:3-8; 1 Cor. 12-14; Eph. 4:7-16; Heb. 2:3, 4).

VI. MAN:

We believe that God created man directly and instantaneously from the dust of the ground. Man was created in the image of God and was able to have intimate fellowship with God (Gen. 1:26, 27; 2:7).

We believe that all of humanity fell away from God when Adam first sinned and that the fall resulted in both physical and spiritual death for man. In this fallen condition, man was left totally depraved and unable to remedy his own situation (Gen. 3:6-13; Rom. 5:12-21; 1 Cor. 15:21, 22; Eph. 2).

VII. SIN:

We believe that sin is anything that does not conform to the character and nature of God (1 Jn. 3:4).

We believe that all of mankind sinned in Adam, the head of the human race, and that each human being has a sin nature and also has committed personal sin (Rom. 5:12; 1:18; 3:20; 1 Jn. 1:8-10).

VIII. SALVATION:

We believe that salvation is the act of God whereby man is brought into a proper relationship with God. It is that act where spiritually dead man is made spiritually alive (Ps. 3:8; John 2:9; Eph. 2:1, 2).

We believe that this is accomplished by the grace of God through man's faith in the death (shed blood), burial and bodily resurrection of the Lord Jesus Christ (Eph. 2:8-10; 1 Cor. 15:1-4).

We believe that salvation involves three things for the believer: deliverance from the penalty of sin at the moment of regeneration, victory over the power of sin during the Christian life, and deliverance from the presence of sin at glorification.

We believe that salvation positionally sanctifies the believer, but that the believer needs to experience, in his daily life, progressive sanctification (2 Cor. 5:21; Rom. 6:14; Phil. 3:20, 21).

IX. SATAN AND ANGELS:

We believe in the existence of the person of Satan. He was created by God as the greatest of angels, but later rebelled against God. After he fell, he organized his own kingdom which consists of both evil angels and also unregenerate man. He is currently the ruler-god of this age. Satan's ultimate goal is to overthrow God. He seeks to keep the unsaved from becoming saved. He seeks to hinder and destroy the Christian's testimony and ministry for God.

We believe that both Satan and his evil angels will be consigned to the eternal Lake of Fire after the Millennium (Mt. 25:41; Jn. 8:44; Isa. 14:12-17; Ezek. 28:11-19; Rev. 20:7-10).

X. CHURCH:

We believe that the true Church is a living organism and that it is the "body of Christ", who is Himself the head of this body. The Church is made up of regenerate, redeemed believers only (Eph. 1:22, 23; 5:23; Col. 1:18; 1 Cor. 12:13).

We believe that the, Church began on the day of Pentecost; that every believer was indwelt baptized by the Holy Spirit into the one body of Christ which is the Church (Acts 2:1-4; 1:4-5; Jn. 14:16-17; 1 Cor. 12:13).

We believe that the Scriptures teach that there are to be local churches. These churches are to be the visible representation of the body of Christ in the local community. Local churches are to observe the ordinances of Christ and to seek to do the will of God (Acts 20:28; 1 Cor. 1:2; Mt. 28:19, 20; 1 Cor. 11:23-28).

We believe that the local church should be totally committed to the edifying (developing to maturity) of the believers and also should have an active outreach in evangelism (Eph. 4:11-16; 1 Cor. 14).

XI. ESCHATOLOGY:

We believe in the premillennial and pretribulational return of Jesus Christ. This means that Christ's return for His bride (the Church) is imminent and therefore can happen at any moment (1 Th. 4:13-17; 1 Th. 5:6).

We believe that, following the Rapture of the Church, the Tribulation Period (Daniel's 70th Week, or the Time of Jacob's Trouble) will take place (Dan. 9:24-27; 2 Th. 2:3, 4).

We believe that, following the Tribulation, the Millennium will begin. This will be brought about by the literal, physical, visible, bodily return of our Lord Jesus Christ to the earth to rule and to reign for 1,000 years (Zech. 14:1-4; Rev. 19-20).

XII. ETERNAL STATE:

We believe in the eternal punishment of the lost and the eternal bliss of the redeemed (Rev. 20:11-15; Jn. 3:16).

Notes: *Friends of Israel Gospel Ministry, founded in 1938, is an Evangelical missionary/evangelism organization directed toward the Jewish community. It affirms the infallibility, inerrancy, and plenary inspiration of the Bible and a consensus Evangelical theological position. In its addenda on "Principles and Practices," it spells out its evangelistic program toward the Jews. They are committed to the conversion of Jews to Christianity and the integration of Jews within Gentile churches. The Ministry is opposed to the Messianic Jewish program of creating Christian synagogues based in Jewish ethnic practice.*

* * *

WHAT DOES GOM BELIEVE? (GLOBAL OUTREACH MISSION)

1. We believe the Bible to be verbally inspired, the only infallible, authoritative Word of God.

2. We believe that there is one God, eternally existent in three persons, Father, Son and Holy Spirit.

3. We believe in the deity of our Lord Jesus Christ in His virgin birth, in His sinless life, in His miracles, in His vicarious and atoning death through His shed blood, in His bodily resurrection, in His ascension to the right hand of the Father, and in His personal return in power and glory.

4. We believe that all men have sinned, and for the salvation of lost and sinful men, regeneration by the Holy Spirit is absolutely essential.

5. We believe in the present ministry of the Holy Spirit by whose indwelling the Christian is enabled to live a godly life.

6. We believe in the resurrection of both the saved and the lost; they that are saved unto the resurrection of life and they that are lost unto the resurrection of damnation.

7. We believe in the spiritual unity of believers in our Lord Jesus Christ.

Notes: *Global Outreach Mission, founded in 1943, is a missionary sending organization that supports work around the world. Its statement of belief is derived from that of the National Association of Evangelicals, to which it has added* *phrases on the second coming of Jesus and the universal sinfulness of humanity.*

* * *

STATEMENT OF FAITH (GOOD NEWS PUBLISHERS)

1. The Bible is inspired of God, inerrant in the original documents, and of final authority in all matters of faith and practice.

2. There is one God, eternally existent in three Persons—Father, Son and Holy Spirit.

3. The Lord Christ is fully God, born of a virgin, sinlessly perfect. His sacrifice is substitutionary and representative. He rose bodily from the dead and ascended to His Father's right hand, where He now ministers as our Great High Priest. He will come to rapture His Church and subsequently return to reign on the earth.

4. Each member of the human race is fallen, sinful and lost, and regeneration by the Holy Spirit is absolutely essential for the salvation of man. Redemption is wholly by the blood of Christ, and salvation is by grace through faith in our Lord Jesus Christ.

5. The Holy Spirit indwells the believer, who is sealed until the day of redemption and is empowered to live a godly life.

6. There will be a resurrection of the saved and of the lost; of the saved, unto eternal life, and of the lost, unto eternal and conscious judgement.

7. The Church began with the descent of the Holy Spirit at Pentecost and is composed of all true believers in the Lord Jesus Christ. These believers are united to Him and to one another by the indwelling Spirit. This means that the Church, as a whole, is not an organization, but a living organism, known as the Body of Christ.

   The Church's calling, hope and destiny are heavenly, and its chief functions are to glorify God and to witness for Christ until His return. The local Church is composed of believers in a locality who gather in Christ's name for worship, prayer, edification and testimony. Government and discipline are divinely outlined in the Epistles as being the responsibility of the local Church.

8. Christ, our risen Head, is the Giver of gifts, such as evangelists, pastors and teachers, and these men are responsible to Him for their service. They are given ''for the perfecting of the saints, for the work of the ministry, for the edifying of the body of Christ.'' The Lord's people, as such should have no other names then those which are given to them in Scripture, such as ''Christians,'' ''saints,'' ''believers,'' and ''brethren.''

9. There are two Christian ordinances, baptism and the Lord's Supper. Baptism by immersion signifies that the believer, having died with Christ, is buried with Him in baptism and also is risen with Christ to walk in newness of life. The Lord's Supper is a memorial feast, instituted by the Lord Himself exclusively for His own. In the observance of this supper, believers remember Him; they show His death until He comes, and they function as worshipping priests before God.

10. Every true child of God possesses eternal life and being justified, sanctified and sealed with the Holy Spirit, is safe and secure for all eternity. However, a Christian can, through sin, lose his fellowship, joy, power, testimony, and reward, and incur the Father's chastisement. Relationship is eternal, being established by new birth; fellowship, however, is dependent upon obedience.

11. The personal return of the Lord Jesus Christ to translate His Church is imminent, an event which concludes the present age of grace. This will be followed by the outpouring of God's wrath on the earth, known as the Tribulation. After this, Christ's Millennial Kingdom will be established, and ''the glory of the Lord will cover the earth as the waters cover the sea.'' At the conclusion of His Millennial Reign, Christ will deliver up the Kingdom of God, the Father, that the Triune God may be all in all.

Notes: *Good News Publishers, founded in 1938, is an Evangelical publishing house. Its conservative statement of faith asserts belief in the inerrancy of the Bible. There is a distinctive Baptist heritage evident in affirmations concerning the local church, two ordinances (not sacraments), and baptism by immersion.*

* * *

STATEMENT OF FAITH (GOSPEL FOR ASIA, INC.)

WE BELIEVE in the verbal inspiration of the Bible, that both the Old and New Testaments constitute the divinely inspired Word of God, the final authority for life and truth.

WE BELIEVE in one God, eternally existing in the Holy Trinity of Father, Son, and Holy Spirit, each with personality and deity.

WE BELIEVE in the virgin birth of Jesus Christ, His atoning death and glorious resurrection, and in the Premillennial return of Jesus Christ to this earth. We believe that He purchased for us a finished salvation, and it is ours solely by grace through faith. Also, that we are sealed by the Holy Spirit and kept by the power of God through faith unto salvation, ready to be revealed in the last day.

WE BELIEVE that repentance and faith in the finished work of Christ are the two essential steps for salvation.

WE BELIEVE that the Holy Spirit convicts, converts, and continues the work of grace in a believer. We believe that heaven is the home for God and His children, and that hell is the home for the devil and his children.

WE ALSO BELIEVE in New Testament soul-winning, the separated Christian life, and the local church.

Notes: *Gospel for Asia, founded in 1979, is a full service missionary agency that supports other missionaries and engages in church building in its assigned area. Its Statement of Faith is an Evangelical consensus statement.*

*   *   *

GOSPEL LIGHT AFFIRMS (GOSPEL LIGHT PUBLICATIONS)

We believe the Bible to be the divinely inspired and authoritative Word of God, the only infallible rule of faith and practice.

We believe in one God, creator and sustainer of the universe, who eternally exists in three persons: Father, Son and Holy Spirit.

We believe in the Lord Jesus Christ, who being fully God became fully man, was born of a virgin, lived a sinless life, died on a cross, was raised bodily, is exalted to God's right hand, and will personally come again.

We believe that all have sinned and are guilty before God, and, as a result, all, both individually and corporately, suffer the consequences of the fall and are under condemnation.

We believe that because of His love God sent His Son Jesus Christ, who inaugurated His kingdom, provided an atonement for sin, conquered the principalities and powers, is reconciling the world to Himself, and will consummate His kingdom in righteousness, power and glory.

We believe that all those who repent and believe in Christ are delivered from the judgment of God and are born again into life eternal, and are called to be instruments of God's righteousness and reconciliation in human society.

We believe in the Holy Spirit who glorifies Jesus Christ, works in all peoples to bring them to faith and obedience, and dwells in believers equipping and empowering them for lives of holiness and fruitful service.

We believe that the Church, the Body of Christ, consists of all believers and exists to fulfill Christ's mission, making disciples of all nations and bringing healing and justice to human society, all to the glory of God.

We believe in the resurrection of the body, the everlasting punishment of unbelievers and the everlasting blessedness of believers in the presence of Christ.

Notes: *Gospel Light Publications, founded in 1933, is an Evangelical publishing house. It works in close cooperation with Gospel Literature International (formerly Gospel Light International), which distributes Gospel Light publications overseas. Gospel Light's statement of belief is a consensus Evangelical statement, noteworthy because of its belief that the Church has a role in bringing healing and justice to human society, a topic rarely mentioned in Evangelical documents.*

*   *   *

DOCTRINAL POSITION (GOSPEL MISSION OF SOUTH AMERICA)

The Mission staunchly adheres to the following doctrinal position:

1. We believe in the Old and New Testament Scriptures as verbally inspired by God and inerrant in the original writings, and that they are the supreme and final authority in faith and life.

2. We believe in one God, eternally existing in three persons: Father, Son and Holy Spirit.

3. We believe that Jesus Christ was begotten by the Holy Spirit, born of the virgin Mary and is true God and true man.

4. We believe that man was created in the image of God, and that he sinned and thereby incurred both physical and spiritual death, the latter being eternal separation from God.

5. We believe that the Lord Jesus Christ died for our sins, according to the Scriptures, as a representative and substitutionary sacrifice; and that all who believe in Him are justified on the ground of His shed blood.

6. We believe in the resurrection of the crucified body of our Lord, in His ascension into Heaven and in His present life there for us, as High Priest and Advocate.

7. We believe that all who receive by faith the Lord Jesus Christ are born again of the Holy Spirit, and thereby become children of God; and that from the moment of their belief they are indwelt and sealed by the Holy Spirit, and thus are secured unto the day of redemption.

8. We believe that the Church of Jesus Christ was begun at Pentecost; is composed solely of believers; is the Body and Bride of our Lord; and that her purpose is to dedicate herself to the winning of lost souls to Christ and the edification of the believers.

9. We believe in that "blessed hope" the rapture of the Church, followed by the period of the great tribulation; and in the personal and premillennial second coming of the Lord Jesus Christ to earth with all His saints.

10. We believe in the resurrection of the just and the unjust, the everlasting blessedness of the saved, and the everlasting punishment of the lost.

DOCTRINAL POSITION (GOSPEL MISSION OF SOUTH
AMERICA) (continued)

Notes: *The Gospel Mission of South America is a Fundamentalist missionary sending agency whose work is concentrated in several countries in South America. Its doctrinal statement asserts a belief in the inerrancy of the Bible and a consensus Evangelical theological position.*

* * *

WE BELIEVE (GOSPEL MISSIONARY UNION)

The Bible

We believe in the verbal, plenary inspiration of the Holy Scriptures of the Old and New Testaments, inerrant as originally given, God's final written revelation of Himself and His will, and the sole authority for all faith and practice (2 Tim. 3:16,17; 2 Peter 1:21).

The Godhead

We believe in God, who is revealed in Scripture as subsisting in three distinct Persons: Father, Son and Holy Spirit, yet One in being, essence and power (Matt. 3:16,17; 28:18,19; 2 Cor. 13:14; Gal. 4:6,7; Heb. 9:14; 1 John 2:22,23)

The Lord Jesus Christ

a. We believe in the supernatural birth of Jesus Christ, who was conceived of the Holy Spirit, born of the virgin Mary, the incarnate Son of God, Immanuel, God with us (Matt. 1:20-23; Luke 1:35).

b. We believe in the deity of our Lord Jesus Christ, who is very God, the express image of the Father, the One by whom and for whom all things were created and consist (John 1:1-3,14; Col. 1:16,17).

c. We believe that the Lord Jesus Christ lived a sinless life and that He died as a perfect substitutionary sacrifice for the sins of all men, and that the believer's justification is made sure by His literal, physical resurrection from the dead (Matt. 28:6,7; Rom. 3:24,25; 1 Cor. 15:4-8; Heb. 2:9; 4:15; 1 Peter 3:18).

d. We believe that the Lord Jesus Christ ascended to the right hand of God, where He is the High Priest and Advocate for His people (Acts 1:9-11; Rom. 8:34; Heb. 7:25; 9:24; 1 John 2:1).

e. We believe in the imminent coming of our Lord Jesus Christ in the air to receive His Church unto Himself (John 14:3; 1 Cor. 15:51,52; 1 Thess. 4:13-18; Titus 2:13).

f. We believe in the subsequent, visible and premillennial return of the Lord Jesus Christ, with His Church, to establish His promised worldwide kingdom on the earth (Zech. 14:4-11; Rev. 19:11-16; 20:4-6).

The Holy Spirit

a. We believe in the personality and deity of the Holy Spirit, who convicts of sin, who is the Supernatural Agent in regeneration, and who, at the moment of conversion, baptizes and seals the believer into the Body of Christ, immediately indwelling him (John 14:16,17; 16:7-11; 1 Cor. 12:12-14; Eph. 1:13,14).

b. We believe that it is the duty and privilege of the believer to be filled with the Holy Spirit, who illumines, guides and energizes the believer, enabling him to maintain a consistent Christian walk (John 16:13; Gal. 5:16; Eph. 5:18; 1 John 2:20,27).

c. We believe that the ascended Christ gives gifts through the sovereign will of the Holy Spirit for the edification and unity of the Body of Christ (1 Cor. 12:4-12; Eph. 4:7-13).

Angels

We believe in the reality and personality of angels, both good and fallen, including Satan, the great enemy of God and man, whose opposition is ever increasing but whose ultimate doom is sure (Job 1:6,7; Psa. 103:20; Matt. 4:11; Luke 2:13; Heb. 1:14; Rev. 20:10).

Man

We believe in the creation of man by a direct act of God, and that he fell into sin, and thereby became depraved and guilty before God (Gen. 1:27; 3; Psa. 51:5; Isa. 64:6; Rom. 1:21-23; 3:23, 5:12, 21).

Salvation

We believe in salvation uniquely by the substitutionary atonement of Christ by grace through faith in His shed blood to accomplish man's redemption from sin and his reconciliation to God (Rom. 3:24-26; 5:9; Eph. 2:8,9; Titus 3:5; 1 Peter 1:18-21).

The Believer's Position

We believe in the sonship of all born-again believers in the family of God, their justification, sanctification, and eternal redemption being fully provided for and assured in the finished work of Christ on Calvary and in His continued intercession above (John 1:12,13; Rom. 5:1; 8:14-17; Gal. 3:26; 4:5-7; Eph. 1:13,14; Heb. 7:25; 1 Peter 2:9; 1 John 3:2; 5:11-13).

The Resurrection

We believe in the bodily resurrection of all men, each in his own order: the saints to everlasting life in God's presence; the wicked to conscious and everlasting condemnation in hell (Matt. 25:46; John 3:18,36; 5:28,29; Rev. 20:5,6, 11-15).

The Church and its Mission

We believe in the great commission as the primary mission of the Church, i.e., the preaching to all the world of the Gospel of the grace of God, teaching converts to obey the Lord in baptism by immersion in the name of the Father, Son, and Holy Spirit, to remember Christ's death till He comes, in observance of the Lord's Supper, to be always careful to live godly lives in the world, and to pursue fellowship and seek ministry in visible, organized churches (Matt. 16:18; Acts 1:8; 13:1-3; 14:23; 1 Cor. 1:2; 4:17; 12:12-14; Eph. 1:22,23; 5:23-27; Col. 1:18; 1 Thess. 2:14; Titus 2:11-15).

Notes: *Gospel Missionary Union, founded in 1892, is a missionary sending organization supporting work around the world. Its statement of belief affirms the infallibility of the Bible and a consensus Evangelical theological position. It has a Baptist heritage evident in its belief in baptism by immersion.*

*   *   *

STATEMENT OF FAITH (GREATER EUROPE MISSION)

"We believe the Bible to be the inspired, infallible, and authoritative Word of God.

"We believe that there is one God, eternally existent in three persons: Father, Son and Holy Spirit.

"We believe in the deity of our Lord Jesus Christ, in his virgin birth, in his sinless life, in his miracles. in his vicarious and atoning death through his shed blood, in his bodily resurrection, in his ascension to the right hand of the Father, and in his personal return to power and glory.

"We believe that for the salvation of lost and sinful man, regeneration by the Holy Spirit is absolutely essential.

"We believe in the present ministry of the Holy Spirit by whose indwelling the Christian is enabled to live a godly life.

"We believe in the resurrection of both the saved and the lost; they that are saved unto the resurrection of life and they that are lost unto the resurrection of damnation.

"We believe in the spiritual unity of believers in Christ.

Notes: *The Greater Europe Mission, founded in 1949, is a missionary sending organization that has concentrated its efforts in post-World War II Europe. Its concise Statement of Faith is derived from that of the National Association of Evangelicals.*

*   *   *

DOCTRINAL STATEMENT (HARVESTING IN SPANISH)

We Believe

. . . THAT THE BIBLE is the written word in the 66 books comprising the Old and New Testaments, inspired by the Holy Spirit, and only infallible and authoritative Word of God, and

the supreme and final authority in all matters on which it speaks.

. . . THAT JESUS is the only begotten Son of God, and that He is God the Living Word.

. . . IN THE DEITY of our Lord Jesus Christ, in His VIRGIN BIRTH, in His SINLESS LIFE, in His MIRACLES, in His voluntary, VICARIOUS DEATH ATONING for the sins of men, in His bodily RESURRECTION, in His visible, personal and bodily RETURN to this earth in power and glory in the future, consummating the earth's history and the eternal plan of God.

. . . THAT THE ONLY MEANS of being cleansed from sin and gaining eternal salvation is through sincere repentance and absolute faith in the substitutional sacrifice of the Son of God and the precious BLOOD He shed on Calvary's cross, which satisfied Divine justice through this act of love and mercy.

. . . THAT REGENERATION BY THE HOLY SPIRIT is absolutely essential for personal salvation, which is a gift of God's free grace.

. . . IN THE SANCTIFYING POWER OF THE HOLY SPIRIT by whose indwelling at salvation the Christian is enabled to LIVE A HOLY LIFE, not fulfilling the lust of the flesh, but bearing fruit to the glory of God.

. . . THAT JESUS CHRIST IS THE HEAD OF THE CHURCH which is the INTENDED BRIDE OF CHRIST, HIS Body, which is composed of all people, living and dead, who have been joined to Him through saving faith.

. . . IN THE RESURRECTION OF BOTH THE SAVED AND THE LOST, the one to everlasting life in blessing and glory, and the other to judgment and everlasting condemnation and damnation.

We have no conflict with any other doctrine embraced by others, provided they do not nullify or replace those outlined above.

Being interdenominational (inter-congregational), we seek to fellowship with all who love our Lord Jesus Christ (Eph. 6:24), and to love all who love Him (John 15:12) (1 John 4:20-21).

Notes: *Harvesting in Spanish, founded in 1980, is a missionary agency working among Spanish-speaking people primarily in Mexico and Central America. Its brief statement self-consciously covers the essentials of Evangelical faith and is stated in such a way that Harvesting in Spanish can work with a wide variety of Evangelical groups.*

*   *   *

DOCTRINAL STATEMENT (HELPS INTERNATIONAL MINISTRIES)

1.   We believe in the verbal inspiration of the Bible. II Tim. 3:16, 17

DOCTRINAL STATEMENT (HELPS INTERNATIONAL
MINISTRIES) (continued)

2. We believe in the triune God. II Cor. 13:14.

3. We believe in the pre-existence of Christ (John 1:1-3), His virgin birth, His vicarious death on the cross (I Peter 2:24), His resurrection, and His second coming. I Cor. 15:3,4.

4. We believe in the personality of the Holy Spirit, His convicting, regenerating, baptizing, sealing, indwelling, teaching and filling ministry. John 16:8-11; Eph. 1:13,14.

5. We believe Satan is the enemy of Jesus Christ and the saints. Rev. 12:9,10.

6. We believe man was created innocent in the image of God, but transgressed and fell in Adam. He is unable to recover himself. Eternal salvation is offered to him by faith in Christ in response to repentance toward God. I Cor. 15:22; John 3:16.

7. We believe each believer is in-dwelt by the Holy Spirit. Rom. 8:9,11.

8. We believe the local church is for the purpose of Christian fellowship, teaching, testimony, administration of the ordinances of baptism, and the Lord's Supper. Eph. 4:11-16.

9. We believe the redeemed will be resurrected to be with Christ, and the unsaved to everlasting punishment. I Cor. 15:20-23; John 3:36.

Notes: *Helps International Ministries, founded in 1976, is an Evangelical missionary organization offering assistance to missionaries in a variety of practical means, from construction to financial advice to computer training. Its Doctrinal Statement asserts a belief in the verbal inspiration of the Bible and a consensus Evangelical theological statement.*

*   *   *

WHAT DO WE BELIEVE? (INTERDISCIPLINARY BIBLICAL RESEARCH INSTITUTE)

All of us in IBRI believe in a great number of things we understand the Bible to teach. We have limited our doctrinal statement to the basics because we think real Christians should be able to work together, emphasizing their agreements rather than their differences. These basics are:

1. The Bible alone, and the Bible in its entirety, is the written Word of God, our absolute authority, inerrant in the autographs.

2. There is only one God, eternally existing in three persons, Father, Son and Holy Spirit, who created all things by His power. He is a spirit, infinite, eternal and unchangeable in His being, wisdom, power, holiness, justice, goodness and truth.

3. Jesus Christ is God the Son, co-equal and co-eternal with the Father and the Holy Spirit. He became man through a virginal conception and birth, lived a life of perfect righteousness, performed miracles, and died on the cross as a substitute to pay for the sins of all who trust in Him. He rose physically from the dead, ascended to heaven, and will one day return to rescue His own and put an end to sin.

4. All people are sinners as a result of Adam's fall and their own disobedience. Only through repentance from sin and dependence on Christ's work alone may they return to a right relationship with God. Those who return will one day be delivered from sin and death to spend an eternity of blessing enjoying and serving God. Those who continue in sin will one day face God's judgment, after which they will forever experience His wrath.

This doctrinal statement is to be understood within the framework of the New Hampshire, Philadelphia or Westminster confessions of faith.

Notes: *The Interdisciplinary Biblical Research Institute is an apologetic organization whose self-assigned task is the defense of the authority of the Bible, especially in the academic community. Understandably it has asserted a strong belief in the inerrancy of the Bible, to which it has added a concise statement of the Evangelical theological consensus.*

*   *   *

STATEMENT OF FAITH (INTERNATIONAL BIBLE SOCIETY)

WE BELIEVE

In the verbal inspiration of all Scriptures—as originally given —of both the Old and the New Testaments and that they are the final authority of faith and life.

In one God, personally existing in three persons—Father, Son, and Holy Spirit.

That the Lord Jesus Christ died for our sins and that with His shed blood He obtained for us eternal redemption.

In the resurrection of the crucified body of our Lord, in His ascension into heaven and in His present life there as our High Priest and Advocate.

In the personal, imminent return of our Lord Jesus Christ.

In the total depravity of all mankind and in the necessity of salvation through regeneration.

That salvation is the free gift of God entirely apart from works and is possessed by each individual who has, by faith, received the Lord Jesus Christ as his personal Savior.

That the Holy Spirit is a divine person and that He indwells all believers.

In the bodily resurrection of the just and the unjust, the everlasting blessedness of the saved, and the everlasting punishment of the lost.

Notes: *The International Bible Society, founded in 1809, specializes in the publishing and distribution of Bibles worldwide. It works in cooperation with the Wycliffe Bible Translators and publishes and distributes the Bible in many languages. Its Statement of Belief is a consensus Evangelical theological statement that includes a belief in plenary inspiration of the Bible and total human depravity.*

··   *   *   *

STATEMENT OF FAITH (INTERNATIONAL MESSENGERS)

WE BELIEVE the scriptures, both Old and New Testaments, to be the inspired Word of God, without error in the original writing, the complete revelation of His will for the salvation of men and the Divine and final authority for Christian faith and life.

WE BELIEVE in One God, Creator of all things, infinitely perfect and eternally existing in three persons, Father, Son, and Holy Spirit, having precisely the same nature and worthy of equal worship and obedience.

WE BELIEVE that Jesus Christ is true God and true man. Having been conceived of the Holy Spirit, and born of the virgin Mary, he lived a sinless life and died on the cross as a substitutional sacrifice for our sins. He arose bodily from the dead, and ascended into heaven, where He continues His High Priestly ministry at the right hand of the throne of God.

WE BELIEVE the ministry of the Holy Spirit is to glorify the Lord Jesus Christ, convict men, regenerate the believing sinner, indwell, guide, instruct and empower the believer for godly living and service.

WE BELIEVE that man was created in the image of God but fell into sin through Adam and is therefore totally depraved, and only through regeneration by the Holy Spirit can salvation and spiritual life be obtained.

WE BELIEVE that the shed blood of Jesus Christ and His resurrection provide the only ground for justification and salvation for all who believe, and only those who receive Jesus Christ are born of the Holy Spirit, and thus become children of God.

WE BELIEVE that water baptism and the Lord's Supper are ordinances to be observed by the Church during the present age. They are, however, not to be regarded as means of salvation.

WE BELIEVE that the true Church is composed of all who through personal faith in Jesus Christ have been regenerated by the Holy Spirit and are united together as the body of Christ of which He is the Head.

WE BELIEVE in the personal premillennial and imminent coming of our Lord Jesus Christ and that this "Blessed Hope" has a vital bearing on the personal life and service of the believer.

WE BELIEVE the destiny for the believer is to be present with the Lord and for the unbeliever is to be separated from the presence of the Lord in everlasting punishment.

WE BELIEVE the great evangelistic and missionary commission given by Jesus Christ to the disciples and to the continuing church is that of making Christ known throughout the world by word and example and bringing to maturity those who believe in Him through instruction from the Word.

Notes: *International Messengers is a missionary agency with concentrated activity in Eastern Europe. Its Statement of Faith emphasizes the inerrancy of the Bible, human total depravity, and the premillennial second coming of Jesus Christ.*

*   *   *

DOCTRINAL STATEMENT (INTERNATIONAL MINISTRIES TO ISRAEL)

1. We believe in the verbal inspiration of the Bible. The sixty-six books that make up the one Book are absolutely inerrant, infallible, and God breathed. The teaching of the cross is the central teaching of the whole Bible. (II Tim. 3:16-17; II Pet. 1:21)

2. We believe in the Trinity of the God-Head. That being One. God is manifested in three Persons, namely, the Father, Son, and Holy Ghost. These Persons are equal in every divine perfection, and executing distinct but harmonious offices in the great work of redemption. (I Jn. 5:7; Matt. 28:19) "The Father is all the fullness of the Godhead invisible, Jn. 1:18; the Son is all the fullness of the Godhead manifested. Jn. 1:14-18; the Spirit is all the fullness of the Godhead acting immediately upon the creature. (I Cor. 2:9-10)

3. We believe in the divinity and deity of our Lord Jesus Christ. He was born of the virgin Mary and was absolutely without sin. He died on the cross, was buried and the third day He rose again, according to the Scriptures, and He ascended on high where He ever liveth to make intercession for us. Christ was both God and man. (Jn. 1:1; 20:31, Isa. 7-14; Matt. 1:18; II Cor. 5:21; Heb. 1:8; I Cor. 15)

4. We believe in the existence of a personality of evil called the Devil. He was at one time an angel of God but through pride he fell and was excommunicated from the family of God. Satan is the source of all evil, and the father of lies.

5. We believe that man is a sinner and needs to be saved. The only way he can be saved is by grace through faith in the finished work of Christ upon Calvary's cross. The death of Christ was substitutionary and vicarious.

DOCTRINAL STATEMENT (INTERNATIONAL MINISTRIES TO ISRAEL) (continued)

6. The church is a called out body composed of believers in the Lord Jesus Christ. All regenerated persons are baptized into this body of Christ by the Holy Spirit. (Rom. 12:4-5; I Cor. 12:13)

7. All Christians have eternal life in Christ and that all unsaved are doomed to the eternal destiny given to the devil and his angels.

8. We believe in the second coming of the Lord Jesus Christ and that His second coming will be pre-millennial. The second coming will be in two phases. The first will be when He comes for His own and we shall be caught up to meet the Lord in the air. (I Thess. 4:13-18) The second phase of His coming will be after the seven year tribulation period when He shall come with His saints. (Matt. 25:31-36; Jude 14-15) It will be at this time that He shall sit upon the throne of His Father David and reign for a thousand years.

9. We believe that there is a heaven and a hell. Heaven is a place of eternal blessedness for the redeemed and hell is a place of eternal torment for the unsaved.

Notes: *International Ministries to Israel, for many years known as the American Association for Jewish Evangelism, founded in 1944, specializes in the evangelization of Jews in both the United States and internationally. Its Doctrinal Statement affirms the fundamentals of Evangelical faith, including the inerrancy of the Bible, the personality of Satan, and Christ's substitutionary atonement. There is only passing reference to its special ministry in the notation that Jesus, after his return, will rule from Jerusalem on the throne of David.*

*　　　*　　　*

DOCTRINAL STATEMENT (INTERNATIONAL MISSIONS)

THE SCRIPTURE

We believe that the Bible (consisting of the sixty-six books of the Old and New Testaments), is verbally inspired by the Holy Spirit and is inerrant in the original manuscripts, and is the infallible and authoritative Word of God.

GODHEAD OR TRINITY

We believe that there is one only, living and true God eternally co-existing in three persons: Father, Son and Holy Spirit, the same in substance, equal in power and glory.

GOD THE FATHER

We believe that God the Father loves the world and has given Christ to be its Savior and is the Father of all who believe on Jesus Christ as their personal Savior.

GOD THE SON

We believe that God the Son became incarnate in the person of Jesus Christ: that He was conceived of the Holy Spirit; and He was born of the virgin Mary; that He is truly God and truly man; that He lived a perfect, sinless life; that all His teachings and utterances are true.

We believe that Jesus Christ, the Son of God, shed His blood and died for the sins of the whole world according to the Scriptures, as a vicarious and substitutionary sacrifice.

We believe that the crucified body of Christ was raised from the dead according to the Scriptures; that our Lord ascended into heaven; that He sits on the right hand of God as our High Priest and Advocate.

GOD THE HOLY SPIRIT

We believe that the Holy Spirit is a Person; that He is the divine Author of the Scriptures; that He convicts the world of sin righteousness and judgment; that He is the divine Agent of regeneration; that He indwells all believers; that He baptizes all believers into the body of Christ at the time of their conversion.

MAN

We believe that man was created in the image of God; that he sinned and thereby incurred not only physical death, but also spiritual death which is separation from God; that all men are consequently born with a sinful nature which is enmity against God; that man is totally depraved, a sinner in thought, word and deed, and that he absolutely needs to be saved.

SALVATION

We believe that salvation is by grace through faith; that all who receive by faith the Lord Jesus Christ as their personal Savior are born again by the Holy Spirit. All who are truly born again have been given eternal life and shall never perish.

ORDINANCES

We believe that there are two ordinances, baptism and the Lord's Supper, which are divinely enjoined upon all believers; that they are without saving merit in themselves but that they provide an expression of faith regarding the believer's identification and fellowship with Christ.

THE RETURN OF CHRIST

We believe that Jesus Christ shall return personally and bodily to rapture the Church; that the second coming of Christ shall be premillennial to establish His kingdom upon the earth and to reign in righteousness and justice.

RESURRECTION

We believe that both the just and the unjust shall be raised from the dead bodily; that the redeemed in Christ shall enjoy eternal blessedness; that those who have not received the offer of salvation shall suffer eternal, conscious punishment.

THE CHRISTIAN LIFE

We believe that the Christian life is to be by faith, trusting the Lord for the provision of our spiritual and material needs. All who are saved possess two natures, with provision made for the victory of the new nature over the old nature by the power of the indwelling

Holy Spirit; that we are called to a Spirit-filled life; and that we are to be separated from all worldly and sinful practices.

Notes: *International Missions, founded in 1930, is an Evangelical missionary sending agency with work worldwide. Its Doctrinal Statement affirms the inerrancy of the Bible and a consensus Evangelical theological statement including a belief in total human depravity, two ordinances (not sacraments), and the necessity of separation from worldliness.*

*　　*　　*

STATEMENT OF FAITH (INTERNATIONAL STUDENTS, INC.)

"We believe in the divine inspiration and authority of the Scriptures. By this is meant a miraculous guidance of the holy Spirit in their original writing, extending to all parts of the Scripture equally, applying even to the choice of the words, so that the result is the very Word of God; the only infallible rule of faith and practice. Moreover, it is our conviction that God has exercised such singular care and providence through the ages in preserving the written Word, that the Scriptures as we now have them are in every essential particular as originally given, and contain all things necessary to salvation.

"We believe in the one God revealed as existing in three equal persons, the Father, the Son and the Holy Spirit. We believe in the Deity of the Lord Jesus Christ. We believe in the Holy Spirit as a Divine Person, a personality as distinct as the Father and the Son.

"We believe that as through one man sin entered the world and death through sin, so death passed unto all men for that all have sinned.

"We believe in the death of Jesus Christ as a true substitute and that His death was a sufficient expiation for the guilt of all men. We believe in His bodily resurrection from the dead.

"We believe that those who receive Christ by faith have a new life from God given to them.

"We believe that men are justified by faith alone and are counted as righteous before God only by the merit of our Lord and Savior Jesus Christ imputed to them.

"We believe in the everlasting conscious blessedness of the saved, and the everlasting conscious punishment of the lost.

"We believe in the personal, premillennial return of our Lord.

"We believe it to be the supreme responsibility of the disciples of the Lord Jesus Christ to make this Gospel known to all men."

Notes: *International Students, formed in 1953, has developed a ministry to students from foreign countries, many of whom are Hindu, Buddhist, or Muslim, while studying in the United States. Its Statement of Faith is composed of an affirmation of the infallibility of the Bible and a consensus Evangelical theological perspective.*

*　　*　　*

STATEMENT OF FAITH (INTERSERVE)

We believe in the one triune God . . . The Father, immortal, eternal, invisible; the Son, our Lord Jesus Christ, one with the Father and manifested in the flesh for our salvation, our Savior, Redeemer, and Mediator, through Whom alone we receive eternal life, pardon, and sanctification; and the Holy Spirit Who convicts the world of sin, righteousness, and judgment, indwells God's children, and builds up the Church.

We believe that all men are by nature dead in trespasses and sin, and that all equally need redemption through the atonement of Christ, and regeneration by the Holy Spirit.

We believe the Holy Scriptures are God's written Word, given by the inspiration of the Holy Spirit, and the only infallible test of faith and rule of conduct.

On the basis of this we proclaim the deity, incarnation, atoning sacrifice, resurrection, ascension, and personal return of our Lord and Savior Jesus Christ.

Notes: *Interserve, founded in 1964, is a missionary agency that specializes in evangelism in Southern Asia and the Middle East, areas identified as being the most resistant to the spread of Christianity. Its brief Statement of Faith, centered on the most essential of Evangelical affirmations, equips it to work with a variety of Christian denominations.*

*　　*　　*

DOCTRINAL BASIS (INTERVARSITY CHRISTIAN FELLOWSHIP)

Each member of the Corporation, Board of Trustees, Staff and any Council of Reference, as a qualification of membership or office, as the case may be, shall subscribe, at the time of election or before taking office and yearly thereafter, to their belief in the Doctrinal Basis of the Fellowship, which shall the basic Biblical truths of Christianity, including:

1. The unique Divine inspiration, entire trustworthiness and authority of the Bible.

2. The Deity of our Lord Jesus Christ.

3. The necessity and efficacy of the substitutionary death of Jesus Christ for the redemption of the world, and the historic fact of His bodily resurrection.

4. The presence and power of the Holy Spirit in the work of regeneration.

5. The expectation of the personal return of our Lord Jesus Christ.

Notes: *As its name implies, InterVarsity Christian Fellowship, founded in 1936, focuses its ministry on supplying an Evangelical Christian witness on college and university campuses. Its concise Doctrinal Basis includes only the most essential of Evangelical affirmations.*

*   *   *

DOCTRINAL STATEMENT (ISLAND MISSIONARY SOCIETY)

I. THE HOLY SCRIPTURES:

We believe the Holy Scriptures, including thirty-nine Old Testament books and twenty-seven New Testament books, to be the infallible written Word of God, verbally inspired, inerrant in the original writings, and life final authority for Christian faith, life, and conduct. II Tim. 3:15-17; 11 Peter 1:21; John 16:12-13; Matthew 5:18

II. THE GODHEAD:

We believe in the unity of the Godhead, eternally existing in three Persons—Father, Son, and Holy Spirit; co-eternal in being, co-equal in power and glory, co-identical in nature, all possessing tile attributes of Deity and characteristics of personality. Deut. 6:4; Matt. 28:19; II Cor. 13:14

III. THE PERSON AND WORK OF CHRIST:

a. We believe that Jesus Christ is the eternal Son of God, that He was conceived by the Holy Spirit and became incarnate through the virgin birth, that He might reveal God and accomplish all that God sent Him to do. John 1:1; Matt. 1:21-23; John 1:18; John 17:4

b. We believe that He provided for our redemption through the shedding of His blood on the cross as our substitutionary sacrifice, and that our justification is guaranteed by His literal bodily resurrection from the dead. Romans 3:24-25; I Peter 2:24; Ephesians 1:7

c. We believe that He ascended to heaven, is now exalted at the right hand of God the Father, where He ministers in our behalf as Intercessor, Mediator, and Advocate. Hebrews 9:24; 7:25; Romans 8:34; I John 2:1-2; I Tim. 2:5

d. We believe that our Lord's personal, pre-tribulational, pre-millennial return is imminent to receive His own unto Himself. We further believe in His subsequent return to the earth with His saints, to establish His Millennial Kingdom. I Thess. 4:13-18; Titus 2:13; I Thess. 1-10; Zech. 14:4; Rev. 19:11-19; Rev. 20:1-6

IV. TOTAL DEPRAVITY:

We believe that man was created in the image and likeness of God, and that in Adam's sin, the race fell, man inherited a sinful nature, and became alienated from God. This lost estate of man in total depravity makes his new birth an imperative in order to be accepted of God. Gen. 1:26-27; Romans 5:12; Eph.2:1-3; John 3:3

V. SALVATION:

We believe that salvation is the gift of eternal life, and is received by grace through faith in the Lord Jesus Christ who purchased our redemption by the shedding of His blood on the cross. Salvation is of the Lord, and is totally apart from human merit. Eph. 2:8-10; John 1:12; Romans 5:8; Eph. 1:7; Jonah 2:9

VI. SECURITY AND ASSURANCE OF BELIEVERS

We believe that all born again believers, regenerated by the Holy Spirit, are secure in Christ forever, and shall never come into condemnation for sin. We further believe that while it is the believer's privilege to rejoice in the assurance of his salvation, God's Word clearly forbids the use of this security as license or liberty as an occasion to the flesh. Rom. 8:1-39; I Pet. 1:5; John 5:24; John 10:27-29; Rom. 13:13-14; Gal. 5:13

VII. THE HOLY SPIRIT:

We believe that the Holy Spirit is a person who convicts the world of sin, of righteousness, and of judgment. That He regenerates, baptizes into the body of Christ, indwells, enlightens, guides, and empowers the believer for godly living and acceptable service. John 16:8-11: I Cor. 12:12-14; II Cor. 3:6; Eph. 5:18

VIII. SPIRITUAL GIFTS:

We believe that our sovereign God bestows spiritual gifts as He wills in every age for the ministry and perfecting of the Church. We believe that the "sign gifts" including tongues, were operative in the apostolic age, and that their usefulness has ceased as a valid and unifying ministry in edifying the established Church of Jesus Christ. We therefore cannot support or commend any propagation of unbiblical teaching concerning the exercise of these "sign gifts". Mark 16:17-20; Heb. 2:4; 1 Cor. 12:4-11; I Cor. 14:6-12; 14:22

IX. TWO NATURES OF THE BELIEVER:

We believe that every saved person possesses two natures, with provision made for the new nature to be victorious over the old nature through the power of the indwelling Holy Spirit, and that the sinful Adamic nature will be with us throughout our life on earth. Rom. 6:13; Rom. 8:12-13; Gal. 5:16-25; Eph. 4:22-24; I Pet. 1:14-16; I John 3:5-9

X. SEPARATION:

We believe that all Christians should be filled with the Holy Spirit which will produce holiness of living and separation unto the Lord. Our calling from God is to be separate from sinful practices and associations. Rom. 12:1-2; Rom. 14:13; II Cor. 6:14, 7: 11; II John 9-11

XI. THE CHURCH:

We believe that the Church, the body of Christ, consists of all born again believers and is a spiritual organism of which Christ is the Head, and to which Christ gave commission to go into all the world and preach the Gospel to every creature. We further believer in the establishment of the local Church as clearly revealed and defined in the New Testament Scriptures. Eph. 1:22-23, 5:25-27; I Cor. 12:12-14; Acts 14:27; I Tim. 3:1-13

XII. MISSIONS:

We believe it is the obligation of every born again believer to bear witness by life and word to the truths of the Scriptures, and to proclaim the Gospel to every creature. Mark 16:15; Acts 1:8; II Cor. 5: 19-20

XIII. PERSONALITY OF SATAN:

We believe that Satan is a person, a fallen angel, that he is the author of sin, the cause of man's fall, the open and declared enemy of God and men, and that he is doomed for the lake of fire for all eternity. Isa. 14:12-17; Matt. 4:2-11; Matt. 25:41; Rev. 20:10; Rev. 12:10

XIV. THE ETERNAL STATE:

We believe in the bodily resurrection of all men, the saved to eternal life, and the unsaved to judgment and everlasting punishment. John 5:28-29; John 11:25-26; Rev. 20:5-6, 12-13

Notes: *The Island Missionary Society, founded in 1938, is a Fundamentalist missionary sending agency that focuses its activity in the Caribbean Islands. Its conservative theological position is manifested in its affirmation of the inerrancy of the Bible, total human depravity, separation from sinful practices and associations, and the personality of Satan. The Society is strongly anti-Pentecostal.*

*　　*　　*

STATEMENT OF FAITH (ISRAEL'S EVANGELISTIC MISSION)

"We believe in one God, eternally existent in three persons; Father, Son and Holy Spirit. We believe in God the Father, creator of all things visible and invisible. We believe in Jesus Christ our prophet, priest and king; who was begotten of the Holy Spirit; born of the virgin Mary; who died for our sins, rose again from the dead, and ascended into heaven; who will come again, according to the Scriptures. We believe in the Holy Spirit, our instructor and comforter. We believe the Bible is the inspired, inerrant word of God. We believe in the efficacy of the atoning blood of our Lord Jesus Christ, shed on the cross of Calvary for Jew and Gentile alike.

Notes: *Israel's Evangelistic Mission was established for the evangelization of the Jews. Its brief Statement of Faith emphasizes Evangelical essentials including the Trinity, the saving work of Jesus Christ, and an inerrant Bible. Christ's saving work for the Jew is also emphasized.*

*　　*　　*

DOCTRINAL STATEMENT (JEWS FOR JESUS)

We believe that the Scriptures of the Old and New Testaments are divinely inspired, verbally and completely inerrant in the original writings, and of supreme and final authority in all matters of faith and life.

We recognize the value of traditional Jewish literature, but only where it is supported by or conformable to the Word of God. We regard it as in no way binding upon life or faith.

We believe in one sovereign God, existing in three persons: Father, Son, and Holy Spirit, perfect in holiness, infinite in wisdom, unbounded in power, and measureless in love; and that God is the source of all creation and that, through the immediate exercise of His power, all things came into being.

We believe that God the Father is the author of eternal salvation, having loved the world and given His Son for its redemption.

We believe that Jesus the Messiah was eternally preexistent and is co-equal with God the Father; that He took on Himself the nature of man through the virgin birth so that He possesses both divine and human natures. We believe in His sinless life and perfect obedience to the Law; in His atoning death, burial, bodily resurrection, ascension into heaven, high-priestly intercession, and His personal return in power and glory.

We believe that the Holy Spirit is co-equal and co-eternal with the Father and the Son; that He was active in the creation of all things and continues to be so in providence; that He convicts the world of sin, righteousness, and judgment; and that He regenerates, sanctifies, baptizes, indwells, seals, illumines, guides and bestows His gifts upon all believers.

We believe that God created man in His image; but that because of the disobedience of our first parents in the Garden of Eden, they lost their innocence and both they and their descendants, separated from God, suffer physical and spiritual death; and that all human beings, with the exception of Jesus the Messiah, are sinners by nature and practice.

DOCTRINAL STATEMENT (JEWS FOR JESUS) (continued)

We believe that Jesus the Messiah died for our sins, according to the Scriptures, as a representative and substitutionary sacrifice; that all who believe in Him are justified, not by any works of righteousness, but by His perfect righteousness and atoning blood; and that there is no other name under heaven by which we must be saved.

We believe that Israel exists as a covenant people through whom God continues to accomplish His purposes; and that the Church is an elect people in accordance with the New Covenant, comprising both Jesus and Gentiles who acknowledge Jesus as Messiah and Redeemer.

We believe that Jesus the Messiah will return personally in order to consummate the prophesied purposes concerning His Kingdom.

We believe in the bodily resurrection of the just and the unjust, the everlasting blessedness of the saved and the everlasting conscious punishment of the lost.

Notes: *Jews for Jesus, founded in 1973, was established by former workers of the American Board of Missions for the Jews who wished to extend their evangelistic efforts with a street ministry to the hippie culture of the early 1970s. In order to work with a broad range of Evangelical denominations, the organization has adopted a consensus Evangelical theological Doctrinal Statement, with additional paragraphs added to support their particular mission. Jews for Jesus affirms the value of Jewish literature and the ongoing role of Israel as God's covenant people. Throughout its Statement, the word "Christ" is replaced with its equivalent word "Messiah." Jews for Jesus believes in the integration of Jewish converts into local churches, which would include Gentile members, rather than the establishment of Messianic synagogues that sustain Jewish ethnic life and worship. Jews for Jesus is often confused with the messianic movement, especially in anti-Jewish evangelical polemical materials.*

*　　*　　*

STATEMENT OF FAITH (KIDS ALIVE, INTERNATIONAL)

I　We believe in one infinite God, eternally existing in three persons: Father, Son, and Holy Spirit.

II　We believe in Jesus Christ, the second person of the Trinity, and that as the Son of God He became incarnate by the Holy Spirit, being born of the Virgin Mary; that He truly rose from the dead, ascended into heaven and is now there engaged in intercession for us at the right hand of the Father.

III　We believe in the Holy Spirit, the third person of the Godhead, and that He is ever present and active in and with every true born child of God, and that He is present to reprove the world of sin, righteousness and judgment.

IV　We believe that the Scripture of the Old and the New Testaments are given by Divine inspiration; that they are the infallible, supreme and final authority in faith and life.

V　We believe that man was created in the image of God, that he sinned, and thereby incurred, not only physical death, but also spiritual death or separation from God; that all human beings are born with a sinful nature, and when moral responsibility is reached, they become sinners in thought, word and deed.

VI　We believe that Jesus Christ died for our sins, according to the Scriptures; that He, as the representative and substitutionary sacrifice for sin, obtained redemption, by the shedding of His blood, for all who believe in Him.

VII　We believe in "that blessed hope," the personal, premillennial and eminent return of our Lord and Savior, Jesus Christ.

VIII　We believe that all who repent of their sins and believe on the Lord Jesus Christ are freely justified by the Father, born again of the Holy Spirit, and thereby become children of God.

IX　We believe in the bodily resurrection of both the just and the unjust; the everlasting blessedness of the saved, and the everlasting, conscious punishment of the lost.

Notes: *Kids Alive, International, founded in 1916, has a ministry to disadvantaged children in foreign countries. Its Statement of Faith affirms a consensus Evangelical theological perspective.*

*　　*　　*

DOCTRINAL STATEMENT (LATIN AMERICA MISSION)

Although we come from different churches and denominations, we all adhere to this basic doctrinal statement:

We believe the Bible to be the divinely inspired and authoritative Word of God, the only infallible rule of faith and practice.

We believe in one God, creator and sustainer of the universe, who eternally exists in three persons: Father, Son and Holy Spirit.

We believe in the deity of the Lord Jesus Christ, His virgin birth, sinless life, redemptive death, bodily resurrection, present exaltation at God's right hand and the "blessed hope" of His personal return.

We believe that all men have sinned and therefore are guilty before God and are under His condemnation.

We believe that through the death of His Son, Jesus Christ, God in love provided an atonement for sin, so that, through repentance and saving faith in Christ, man is delivered from the judgment of God and is born again into life eternal.

We believe in the deity and personality of the Holy Spirit, who works in men to bring them to salvation through Christ and who dwells in believers, equipping and empowering them for lives of holiness and fruitful service.

We believe that the church is comprised of all true believers and that the mission of the church, with Christ as its head, is to communicate the Gospel of Christ to all the world.

We believe in the resurrection of the body, the everlasting punishment of unbelievers and the everlasting blessedness of believers in the presence of Christ.

Notes: *The Latin America Mission, founded in 1922, is an Evangelical missionary sending agency with work focused in Central and South America, and among Latin Americans residing in North America. Its Doctrinal Statement affirms the infallibility of the Bible and a consensus Evangelical theological position.*

*　　*　　*

STATEMENT OF FAITH (LIEBENZELL MISSION OF U.S.A.)

a. We believe that the whole Bible is inspired by the Holy Spirit and is the Divine authority and infallible rule for faith, life and doctrine.

b. We believe in one God, eternally existing in three Divine Persons, Father, Son and Holy Spirit, equal in nature, power and glory.

c. We believe in the Deity of the Lord Jesus Christ, in His virgin birth, in His sinless life, in His miracles, in His shed blood as the only atonement for sin, in His bodily resurrection and ascension to the right hand of the Father and His personal return in power and glory.

d. We believe in the Holy Spirit who convicts of sin, testifies of Christ, enables the believer to live a victorious life, and guides into all truth.

e. We believe that man was created in the image of God, but fell into sin and is in need of regeneration through faith in Jesus Christ.

f. We believe in the resurrection of the body. The believer will arise to eternal life, the unbeliever will arise to eternal damnation.

g. We believe in the Spiritual unity of all believers in our Lord Jesus Christ.

h. We believe in the commission of the Risen Christ, "Go ye therefore, and teach all nations, baptizing them in the name of the Father, and of the Son, and of the Holy Ghost: teaching them to observe all things whatsoever I have commanded you: and lo, I am with you always, even unto the end of the world. Amen." (Mat. 28:19, 20).

Notes: *Liebenzell Mission of U.S.A., founded in 1941, is the United States subsidiary of the Liebenzell Mission International founded in Germany in 1899. It is an Evangelical missionary sending agency. The American branch has adopted the statement of the National Association of Evangelicals, with several additions. The word "doctrine" was added to the statement on the Bible, and a paragraph on the missionary enterprise was added as an eighth paragraph.*

*　　*　　*

STATEMENT OF FAITH (LIFE MINISTRIES)

1. We believe the Bible to be the inspired, the only infallible authoritative Word of God.

2. We believe that there is one God, eternally existent in three persons: Father, Son and Holy Spirit

3. We believe in the Deity of our Lord Jesus Christ in his Virgin birth, in His sinless life, in His miracles, in His vicarious and atoning death through His shed blood, in His bodily resurrection, and in His personal return in power and glory.

4. We believe that for the salvation of the lost and sinful man regeneration by the Holy Spirit is absolutely essential.

5. We believe in the present ministry of the Holy Spirit by whose indwelling the Christian is enabled to live a godly life.

6. We believe in the resurrection of both the saved and the lost they that are saved unto the resurrection of life, and they that are lost unto the resurrection of damnation.

7. We believe in the spiritual unity of believers in our Lord Jesus Christ, who comprise the Church which is His body.

Notes: *Life Ministries, founded in 1967, is an Evangelical missionary sending organization with a focus on Asia and on*

STATEMENT OF FAITH (LIFE MINISTRIES) (continued)

Japanese currently residing in North America. Its Statement of Faith is that of the National Association of Evangelicals, to which it has added a phrase in the last paragraph on the Church.

* * *

STATEMENT OF FAITH (LIGONIER MINISTRIES)

We believe in one God—Father, Son and Holy Spirit. The Triune God has created man in His own image and has called him to manifest and reflect holiness through obedience to His commandments. Because man has woefully fallen in this responsibility and entered into a state of moral corruption, he has subsequently become estranged from his creator.

Because of a profound love for His creation, God has initiated a plan of redemption which He has accomplished on behalf of His people in the realm of temporal history. The zenith of this redemption is located in the historical incarnation of God in the person of Jesus of Nazareth. We confess Jesus to be the Christ of Old Testament prophecy, being at the same time fully God and fully man. Jesus, through His substitutionary atoning death and bodily resurrection, has provided the meritorious basis of our justification, which, by God's grace, we receive by faith alone.

The risen and ascended Christ has sent His Holy Spirit to dwell in the hearts of believers, effecting their regeneration and operating in their sanctification. The same Holy Spirit has been given to the people of God to empower them for the service of bearing witness to the Kingdom of God. The Holy Spirit brings His people together to form a corporate community of believers. We believe that Christ has established a visible church which is called to live in the power of the Holy Spirit under the regulation of the authority of the Holy Scripture, exercising discipline, administering the sacraments, and preaching the Gospel of Christ.

We believe that the Bible in its entirety is divine revelation, and we submit to the authority of Holy Scripture, acknowledging it to be inerrantly inspired by God and carrying the full weight of His authority.

We support the work of Christian organizations and institutions that confess the Lordship of Jesus Christ. We are committed to the implementation of the social and cultural implications of God's commandments for the well-being of man and his environment. We believe our faith should be visible in concrete forms and models of personal and social behavior. We seek to be faithful disciples of Christ, enduring in love and obedience until He comes again to consummate His Kingdom.

Notes: *Ligonier Ministries, founded in 1971, is a Christian education foundation that publishes adult education materials in a variety of contemporary formats. It operates out of a conservative Reformed theological tradition reflected in its Statement of Faith. It affirms the doctrine of the visible church, which according to Scripture has the authority to exercise discipline, administer the sacraments, and preach the gospel. The Ministries also acknowledges the inerrancy of the Bible.*

* * *

STATEMENT OF FAITH (LIVING BIBLES INTERNATIONAL)

1. We believe the Bible, the Old and New Testaments in their original renderings, to be inspired, the only infallible, authoritative Word of God.

2. We believe that there is one God, eternally existent in three persons: Father, Son, and Holy Ghost.

3. We believe in the deity of Christ, in his virgin birth, in his sinless life, in his miracles, in his vicarious and atoning death through his shed blood, in his bodily resurrection, in his ascension to the right hand of the Father, and in his personal return in power and glory.

4. We believe that for the salvation of lost and sinful men regeneration by the Holy Spirit is absolutely essential.

5. We believe in the present ministry of the Holy Spirit, by whose indwelling the Christian is enabled to live a godly life, and to overcome the attacks of the Evil One, Satan.

6. We believe in the resurrection of both the saved and the lost; they that are saved unto the resurrection of life and they that are lost unto the resurrection of damnation.

7. We believe in the spiritual unity of believers in our Lord Jesus Christ.

Notes: *Living Bibles International, founded in 1968, is a missionary agency that specializes in translating and distributing of Bibles, broadcasting ministry, and publishing Christian literature. Its Statement of Faith is that of the National Association of Evangelicals, with an additional phrase concerning the Holy Spirit's role in assisting the believer to overcome the attacks of Satan.*

* * *

STATEMENT OF FAITH AND VISION (LUIS PALAU EVANGELISTIC TEAM)

1. We believe that the Bible is the verbally inspired Word of God, without error in the original writings, and the supreme and final authority in doctrine and practice.

2. We believe in one God, eternally existent in three Persons: Father, Son and Holy Spirit.

3. We believe in the Deity of our Lord Jesus Christ, in His virgin birth, in His sinless life, in His miracles, in His vicarious death and atonement through His shed blood, in His bodily resurrection, in His ascension to the right hand of the Father, and in His personal return in power and glory.

4. We believe that for the salvation of lost and sinful man, faith in the Lord Jesus Christ and regeneration by the Spirit are essential.

5. We believe in the present ministry of the Holy Spirit by Whose indwelling the Christian is enabled to live a godly life.

6. We believe in the forgiveness of sins, the resurrection of the body, and life eternal.

7. We believe in the spiritual unity of the Church, which is the Body of Christ, composed of all who are regenerated through faith in the Lord Jesus Christ.

POSITION ON BIBLICAL INERRANCY

How authoritative and accurate is Scripture?

This has been a major issue among the Christian Church for centuries. The following summary statement prepared by the International Council on Biblical Inerrancy (ICBI), Oakland, California, represents the Luis Palau Evangelistic Team's position on biblical inerrancy. Mr. Palau serves on the ICBI's board of reference.

1. God, who is Himself Truth and speaks truth only, has inspired Holy Scripture in order thereby to reveal Himself to lost mankind through Jesus Christ as Creator and Lord, Redeemer and Judge. Holy Scripture is God's witness to Himself.

2. Holy Scripture, being God's own Word, written by men prepared and superintended by His Holy Spirit is of infallible divine authority in all matters upon which it touches; it is to be believed, as God's instruction, in all that it affirms; obeyed, as God's command, in all that it requires; embraced, as God's pledge, in all that it promises.

3. The Holy Spirit Scripture's divine Author, both authenticates it to us by His inward witness and opens our minds to understand its meaning.

4. Being wholly and verbally God-given, Scripture without error or fault in all its teaching no less what it states about God's acts in creation, about the events of world history, and about its own literary origins under God, than in its witness to God's saving grace in individual lives.

5. The authority of Scripture is inescapably impaired if this total divine inerrancy is in any way limited or disregarded, or made relative to a view of truth contrary to the Bible's own; and such lapses bring serious loss to both the individual and the Church.

Notes: *The Luis Palau Evangelistic Team, founded in 1978, supports the world ministry of evangelist Luis Palau. Its Statement of Faith is that of the National Association of Evangelicals, with the addition of an affirmation of the inerrancy of the Scripture.*

* * *

WE BELIEVE IN. . . (MAILBOX CLUB)

WE BELIEVE IN. . .

1. The Scriptures, Old and New Testaments fully inspired of God, inerrant in the original writings, the supreme authority in faith and practice.

2. One holy, almighty God, eternally existent in three co-equal Persons—Father, Son, and Holy Spirit.

3. Jesus Christ, the eternal Son of God and Son of Man, virgin born, Himself very God.

4. The bodily resurrection and ascension of Jesus Christ.

5. The fall of man and his consequent moral depravity.

6. Salvation by grace, a free gift of God, through faith in the shed blood of Jesus Christ.

7. The premillennial return of Jesus Christ.

8. The resurrection of the dead, the believer to life everlasting and the unbeliever to eternal condemnation.

9. The reality and personality of Satan.

10. The lost condition of the heathen, and therefore our solemn responsibility to preach the Gospel to every creature.

11. A practical, separated Christian walk, in an overcoming victorious life, provided on a basis faith in Christ's redemptive work.

12. The Church, consisting of all born again believers, the Body and Bride of Christ, represented in local congregations.

Notes: *The Mailbox Club, founded in 1965, is an association of people who operate Bible correspondence schools. It adheres to a conservative theological position that affirms the*

WE BELIEVE IN... (MAILBOX CLUB) (continued)

inerrancy of the Bible, total human depravity, the personality of Satan, and a separated life.

*　　　*　　　*

OUR MESSAGE TO ISRAEL (MAOZ)

It is the Almighty's will that the Jewish person repent of his sin and turn to God.

It is the Almighty's will that the Jewish person receive God's own Salvation which comes through His New Covenant (Jer. 31:31-34). This Covenant was ratified by the Prophet like unto Moses (Deut. 18:15 and Ezek. 37:24-26). This is Yeshua, Son of God, King of the Jews, Messiah of Israel and of all the nations who call upon the Lord.

This Covenant which He promised through His prophets lifts the curses of the Torah and gives the Jewish person a new heart and power to live a righteous life and thereby granting us the blessings promised by the Torah.

It is the will of the God of our fathers that not only the Jews, but all peoples repent and come to the one and only true God, as there is no other God. The Gentiles who follow the Messiah are grafted into the Jewish tree, the root of the Jewish faith being Abraham. The grafted-in Gentiles become the spiritual sons of Abraham, therefore brothers to the Jewish people.

Because there is only one God and one Messiah, there is only one Body of the Messiah of which we are all members-whether Jew or Greek, male or female.

But in these Last Days, God is not calling Israel to join Christendom—to become Baptists, Methodists, etc.—but to return to the God of Israel as Jews who are part of our people, our culture and who share the dreams and problems of the Jewish nation. In short, we are to become better Jews than ever before.

Notes: *Maoz exists to promote the Messianic Jewish movement in Israel. The Messianic Jewish movement evangelizes Jews and organizes them into Christian synagogues that retain the trappings of Jewish culture. Their statement of purpose, worded to speak to Jewish concerns, undergirds their ministry*

to Jews and affirms that, even with Messianic synagogues, there is only one Church.

*　　　*　　　*

STATEMENT OF FAITH (MEXICAN MISSION MINISTRIES)

WE BELIEVE THAT:

. . . the Bible is the Word of God, verbally inspired, a product of men controlled of the Spirit so that it is the truth without any admixture of error for its matter and is the center of Christian union and supreme standard by which all human conduct, creeds, and opinions shall be tried.—II Tim. 3:16, 17.

. . . there is one living and true God, infinite, intelligent, Spirit, Maker and Supreme Ruler of heaven and earth, who is worthy of all honor, confidence and love; three persons, Father, Son and Holy Ghost in the unity of the Godhead. —1 Cor. 8:6; John 15:26.

. . . that Christ is the second person of the Trinity, born of a virgin, Redeemer and Mediator of man, between God and man.—Luke 1:35; John 1:1, 14.

. . . the Holy Ghost is a divine person equal with God the Father and God the Son and works in perfect harmony in the Godhead in perfecting man's God-planned redemption.—John 16:7-15.

. . . Satan is a person, a malignant spirit, the unholy god of this age, author of all powers of darkness, and is destined to the judgment of an eternal justice in the lake of fire.—Mt. 4:1-10; Rev. 20:10

. . . we accept the Genesis account of creation.—Genesis, Chapters 1 and 2.

. . . man was created in the image of God, by voluntary choice transgressed and fell thus causing all mankind now to be sinners not only by constraint but by choice and is therefore under judgment without defence and excuse.—Rom. 5:10-19.

. . . Jesus was miraculously, through the Holy Ghost, born of a virgin, that he is both the Son of God and God, the Son.—Mt. 1:18-25.

. . . man is saved wholly by grace through the mediatorial office of the Son of God who by His death made full and vicarious atonement for our sins, not exemplary but substitutionary and voluntary, the Just dying for the unjust.—Eph. 2:8-9; Rom. 3:24.

. . . by the new birth the one dead in trespasses and sins is made a partaker of the divine nature and receives eternal life solely by the power of the Holy Spirit and thus becomes obedient to the gospel which is manifested in the fruits of repentance and faith and newness of life.—John 3:33, II Cor. 5:17.

. . . Justification includes the pardon of sin, the gift of eternal life on principles of righteousness, bestowed only through faith in the Redeemer's blood.—Rom. 8:1; Rom. 5:1, 9.

. . . faith in the Lord Jesus Christ is the only condition of salvation.—Acts 16:31.

. . . a local church is a congregation of born again believers, the true church consists of all born again believers and is the bride of Christ waiting for His return and the rapture.—Acts 2:42; Eph. 5:22-32,; 1 Thess. 4:13-18.

. . . all who are truly born again are kept by God the Father for Jesus Christ.—John 16:28; 29; Rom. 8:35-39.

. . . in God's sight only such as through faith are justified are truly righteous and sanctified and that all who continue in impenitence and unbelief are in His sight wicked and under the curse.—Rom. 6:23; Gal. 3:10, 13.

. . . civil government is of divine appointment and is to be prayed for and conscientiously honored and obeyed except in things opposed to the will of our Lord Jesus Christ.—Rom. 13:1-7; Acts 4:18-20.

. . . We believe in the bodily resurrection, the ascension, the high priesthood, the pre-millennial return of Christ; the resurrection of the righteous dead unto life, the rapture of living saints, the throne of David, and the millennial reign.—1 Cor. 15:4; Acts 1:9-11; Heb. 5:9 10:11 Thess. 4:16:1 Cor. 15:42-44; 1 Thess. 4:13-18; Acts 2:29, 30; Isa. 3:21-22.

Notes: *Mexican Mission Ministries, founded in 1954, is an Evangelical missionary sending agency with work in Mexico. Its very conservative Statement of Faith affirms the inerrancy of the Bible, especially the creation account in Genesis, and a consensus Evangelical theological perspective.*

*   *   *

STATEMENT OF FAITH (MIDNIGHT CALL)

WE BELIEVE in the divine inspiration of the whole Bible and therewith the infallibility of the Holy Scripture which is God's Word. WE BELIEVE in the eternal Triune God: Father, Son and Holy Spirit. WE BELIEVE that Jesus Christ, the Son of God, was begotten of the Holy Spirit, born of the virgin Mary, lived a sinless life, and shed His blood to save mankind. WE BELIEVE that the Lord Jesus Christ died in the place of each individual sinner and that all who believe in Him as their personal Savior are justified through His shed blood and become a child of God. WE BELIEVE that Israel is God's chosen people, and that the restoration of the Jews in their own land is the fulfillment of the Word of God. WE BELIEVE in the pre-millennial appearance of Jesus Christ for the rapture of His Church (all born again believers). WE BELIEVE in the immortality of our souls and the resurrection of our bodies. WE BELIEVE in the resurrection of the just and the unjust: the everlasting blessedness of the saved and the everlasting punishment of the lost.

Notes: *Midnight Call magazine holds up biblical prophetic messages and suggests that events foreseen in the Bible are happening in this generation. As might be expected, the brief Statement of Faith emphasizes the essentials of the Evangelical position with an emphasis on the events of the last days.*

*   *   *

DOCTRINE AND PRINCIPLES AND PRACTICES (MIDWEST HEBREW MINISTRIES)

The doctrine. . .

BIBLE

We believe and proclaim that the Bible (consisting of 66 books) is the inspired Word of God, that every part is fully and equally inspired; and that every single word of Scripture was produced under the control of the Holy Spirit (2 Pet. 1:21; 2 Tim. 3:16) We also accept the Scriptures in their entirety as being inerrant (in the original writings) and infallible.

GOD

We believe and proclaim there is only one true, eternal, living God, who is sovereign over all things. God is the source and sustainer of all life. He, according to the council of His own will, decreed whatsoever comes to pass, including both His permissive will and His casual will (Isa. 14:24, 26, 27; Eph. 1).

TRINITY

We believe and proclaim that, although there is only one true God, that God consists of three distinct Persons, each of whom is co-eternal and co-equal. We believe that the Father is God, that the Son (Jesus, the Christ-Messiah) is God, and that the Holy Spirit is God (Dt. 6:4; Jn. 6:27; Jn. 1: 1, 14; Acts 5:3,4).

CHRIST

We believe and proclaim the Lord Jesus Christ to be absolute Deity, the eternal Son of God, who became man without ceasing to be God. In the incarnation, He was conceived by the Holy Spirit and born of the Virgin Mary (Mt. 1: 18-25; Heb. 1:8; Isa. 9:6, Jn. 3:16). We believe that He rose bodily from the dead on the third day after death, and He ascended into Heaven to the right hand of the Father (Jn. 2:19-22; Acts 1:9-11; Heb. 1:3). We believe that, presently, He is our Intercessor and Advocate, the only true Mediator between God and man (Heb. 7:25; Heb. 4:14; 1 Jn. 2:1; 1 Tim. 2:5).

HOLY SPIRIT

We believe and proclaim that the Holy Spirit is Deity, a Divine Person of the Godhead. He is not a force, but is truly a Person and is equal with the Father and the Son (Acts 5:3, 4). We believe that the Holy Spirit gives spiritual gifts to every believer at the moment he is re-generated, and that these gifts are to be used for the edification and perfecting of the believers in the Church.

MAN

We believe and proclaim that God created man directly and instantaneously from the dust of the ground. Man was created in the image of God and was able to have intimate fellowship with God (Gen. 1:26, 27; 2:7).

SIN

We believe and proclaim that all of mankind sinned in Adam, the head of the human race, and that each human being has a sin nature and also has committed personal sin (Rom. 5:12; 1:18; 1:8-10).

SALVATION

We believe and proclaim that salvation is the act of God whereby man is brought into a proper relationship with God. It is that act where spiritually-dead man is made spiritually alive (Ps. 3:8; Jn. 2:9; Eph. 2:1,2). This is achieved through man's faith in the death (shed blood), burial and bodily resurrection of the Lord Jesus Christ (Eph. 2:8-10; 1 Cor. 15:1-4)

SATAN AND ANGELS

We believe and proclaim in the existence of the person—Satan. He was created by God as the greatest of angels, but later rebelled against God. We believe that both Satan and his evil angels will be consigned to the eternal Lake of Fire after the Millennium (Mt. 25:41; Jn. 8:44; Isa. 14:12-17; Ezek. 28:11-19; Rev. 20:7-10).

CHURCH

We believe and proclaim that the true Church is a living organism and that it is the "body of Christ", who is Himself the head of this body. The Church is made up of regenerate, redeemed believers only (Eph. 1:22, 23; 5:23; Col. 1:18; 1 Cor. 12:13). We believe that the Church began on the day of Pentecost. We believe that the Scriptures teach that there are to be local churches.

ESCHATOLOGY

We believe and proclaim in the premillennial return of Jesus Christ. This means that Christ's return for His bride (the Church) is imminent and therefore can happen at any moment (1 Th. 4:13-17, 1 Th. 5:6).

ETERNAL STATE

We believe in the eternal punishment of the lost and the eternal bliss of the redeemed (Rev. 20:11-15; Jn. 3:16).

Our principles and practices. . .

CONSISTENT WITH OLD TESTAMENT

We believe and proclaim that the physical descendants of Abraham through Jacob (Jews) are consistent with their Old Testament heritage in accepting Jesus Christ as Messiah (Savior).

COMMITTED TO THE INTEGRATION

We strongly believe and proclaim that both the redeemed Jews and Gentiles are one in the body of Christ. We are firmly committed to the integration, rather than isolation, of the Hebrew and Gentile Christians.

LOCAL CHURCH IS GOD'S INSTRUMENT

We believe and proclaim that the local church is God's ordained instrument in this age. We believe that all Christians (Hebrew and Gentile) should be part of the local church.

NO SHORT CUTS TO SPIRITUAL MATURITY

We believe and proclaim that there are no short cuts to spiritual maturity. Spiritual growth requires time, testing and triumph through the in-dwelling Spirit.

AS IF CHRIST WERE RETURNING DAILY

We believe and proclaim that the daily life of a Christian should be lived as if Christ were returning each day of his life.

Notes: *The Midwest Hebrew Ministries, founded in 1939, is a Fundamentalist Jewish evangelization organization. Its statement of faith affirms the inerrancy of the Bible and a consensus theological perspective. Strengthening the Ministries' program, affirmations have been added concerning the proper course of Jews in converting to Christianity and such converts being integrated into Gentile congregations.*

*   *   *

STATEMENT OF FAITH (MISSION AVIATION FELLOWSHIP)

Mission Aviation Fellowship believes in:

1. The divine inspiration of the Bible which is inerrant in the original writings; and that it is of supreme and final authority in faith and practice.

2. One God, eternally existing in three Persons: Father, Son and Holy Spirit.

3. The creation of man in the divine image, man's subsequent fall through sin, resulting in universal guilt and total depravity; and the necessity, therefore, of redemption and restoration.

4. The deity of Jesus Christ, His virgin birth, perfect life, redeeming death, bodily resurrection, heavenly intercession, and His personal return.

5. The personality of the Holy Spirit by Whose regenerative work sinful man is born again, and by Whose indwelling regenerate man is enabled to live a godly life.

6. The bodily resurrection of the just and the unjust; the everlasting blessedness of the saved, and the everlasting punishment of the lost.

7. The spiritual unity of all believers as comprising the true Church, which has the duty to preach the Gospel to every creature.

Notes: *Mission Aviation Fellowship, founded in 1945, serves missionary sending agencies and indigenous churches with its fleet of airplanes that keep in contact with isolated mission stations, and provide medical and mail service, and transportation for missionary personnel. Its Statement of Faith was adopted from that of the National Association of Evangelicals, with additional phrases on human total depravity, the personality of the Holy Spirit, the Church, and the world mission imperative.*

*　　*　　*

STATEMENT OF FAITH (MISSION 21 INDIA)

1. We believe the Scriptures, both Old and New Testaments, to be the inspired Word of God, without error, the complete revelation of His will for the salvation of men, and the Divine and final authority for all Christian faith and life.

2. We believe in one God, Creator of all things, infinitely perfect and eternally existing in three persons: Father, Son, and Holy Spirit.

3. We believe that Jesus Christ is true God and true man, having been conceived of the Holy Spirit and born of the Virgin Mary. He died on the cross, the sacrifice for our sins according to the Scriptures. He arose bodily from the dead, and He now is at the right hand of the Majesty on high.

4. We believe that the ministry of the Holy Spirit is to glorify the Lord Jesus Christ, and it is His work to convict men, regenerate the believing sinner, and indwell and empower the believer for godly living and service.

5. We believe that man was created in the image of God but fell into sin and is therefore lost, and only through regeneration can salvation and spiritual life be obtained.

6. We believe that the shed blood of Jesus Christ and His resurrection provide the only ground for justification and salvation for all who believe, and only such as receive Jesus Christ are born of the Holy Spirit and thus become children of God.

7. We believe in the personal and imminent coming of our Lord Jesus Christ and that this coming has an important bearing on the personal life of the believer.

8. We believe in the bodily resurrection of the dead, of the believer to everlasting fellowship and joy with the Lord, of the unbeliever to judgement and everlasting conscious punishment.

Notes: *Mission 21 India is a strategic planning organization that is attempting to mobilize missionary agencies and churches to systematically saturate India with Christian congregations during the 1990s. Its Statement of Faith affirms the inerrancy of the Bible and a consensus Evangelical theological position.*

*　　*　　*

FOUNDATIONAL BIBLICAL BELIEFS (MISSIONARY TECH TEAM)

Section 1

We believe the Bible, both the Old and New Testament to be the verbally inspired Word of God: that it is without error in the original writings and is the supreme, absolute, and final Authority in all matters of Christian doctrine, faith, life, and conduct.

Section 2

We believe there is one Eternal God, all powerful, all knowing, and everywhere present, creator of all things, co-equally existing in three persons: Father, Son and Holy Spirit; that God is holy righteous, faithful, the total expression of mercy and loving-kindness, and love.

Section 3

We believe in the personality and reality of Satan.

Section 4

We believe all men, without respect of condition or class, are sinners (spirit, soul, and body) before God; that because of man's total inability to save himself, salvation is by God's grace alone, apart from works of any kind; that salvation is received through faith, having a godly repentance and a wholehearted acceptance of Jesus Christ as personal Lord and Savior on the part of the individual; and that in this step he is born again and becomes a new creature in Christ Jesus.

Section 5

We believe Jesus Christ (the Son-pre-existent, creator of all things, equal with God and possessing the fullness of the God-head), without any change in His eternal deity, became man through conception by the Holy Spirit and virgin birth; that He possessed a sinless human nature being both truly God and truly man; that He died a substitutionary and propitiatory death on the cross, a perfect and complete sacrifice for the sins of the whole world according to the Scriptures; that He in His death, was reconciling the world to God and is triumphant over the power of Satan in man; that He was bodily resurrected and has ascended into Heaven where He was seated at the right hand of God the Father; that He is now our High Priest and advocate.

FOUNDATIONAL BIBLICAL BELIEFS (MISSIONARY TECH TEAM) (continued)

Section 6

We believe the Holy Spirit is a Person co-equally existing in the Godhead (trinity); that His present ministry is to reprove the world of sin, and of righteousness, and of judgment, and to glorify the Lord Jesus Christ by testifying of Him; that He regenerates the sinner when through faith he accepts the Lord Jesus Christ as his Savior; that He indwells all believers from the time of spiritual birth and baptizes each into one body; that He seals, enlightens, instructs, fills, guides, and empowers the believer for Christian living and service.

Section 7

We believe all who are born again by the Holy Spirit through faith in Jesus Christ have assurance of eternal life and all the rights, privileges, and heirship of the sons of God.

Section 8

We believe the child of God is "created in Christ Jesus unto good works;" that because of the indwelling power of the Holy Spirit all believers in the Lord Jesus Christ are called into a life of separation from worldly living and sinful practices, abstaining from such amusements, habits and conduct as will cause others to stumble or bring reproach upon our Lord Jesus Christ.

Section 9

We believe all born again believers possess two natures, the old Adamic nature and a new Christ-like nature; that the believer may be victorious over and put off the old Adamic nature through God who has made full provision in the power of the Holy Spirit whereby His children may be more than conquerors through the Lord Jesus Christ; and that elimination of the old Adamic Nature is unscriptural.

Section 10

We believe that God is sovereign in the bestowment of all His gifts: but that the believer is admonished to exemplify the fruits of the Spirit; that the gifts of evangelists, pastors and teachers are sufficient for the perfecting of the saints today; and that speaking in tongues and the working of sign miracles ceased as the New Testament scriptures were completed and their authority became established. We do believe that God hears and answers the prayer of faith, according to His own perfect will, for the sick and afflicted.

Section 11

We believe all the saved, regardless of race, color, social or economic status, make up the Body of Christ, the Church; that the vocation of the local church is for the perfecting of the saints, work of the ministry, and edifying of the Body of Christ.

Section 12

The supreme purpose of God for every child of His is to be 'to the praise of the glory of His grace' and to be a witness; that the question for each believer is not 'if' I should be a witness, but 'where and how' I should serve; and that our mission is to make Christ known to the whole world.

Section 13

We believe in the eternal blessedness of the saved.

Section 14

We believe in the eternal conscious punishment of all unsaved.

Section 15

We believe in the personal, bodily, visible and imminent premillennial return of our Lord and Savior Jesus Christ; that this blessed hope has a vital bearing on the life and service of the believer.

Notes: *The Missionary TECH Team, founded in 1969, provides various kinds of support, especially in the area of construction, for missionaries in Asia and South America. Its Statement of Faith affirms the inerrancy of the Bible and a consensus Evangelical theological perspective.*

*   *   *

STATEMENT OF FAITH (MISSIONARY WORLD SERVICE AND EVANGELISM)

We believe. . .

. . . That both Old and New Testaments constitute the divinely inspired Word of God, inerrant in the originals, and the final authority for life and truth.

. . . That there is one God, eternally existent in the Holy Trinity of Father, Son, and Holy Spirit, each with personality and deity.

. . . That the Son, our Lord Jesus Christ, manifested in the flesh through the virgin birth, died on Calvary for the redemption of the human family, all of whom may be saved from sin through faith in Him.

. . . That man, although created by God in His own image and likeness, fell into sin through disobedience and "so death passed upon all men, for that all have sinned" (Romans 5:12).

. . . In the salvation of the human soul, including the new birth, and in a subsequent work of God in the soul, a crisis, wrought by faith, whereby the heart is cleansed from all sin and filled with the Holy Spirit. This gracious experience is retained by faith as expressed in a constant obedience to God's revealed will, thus giving us perfect cleansing moment by moment (I John 1:7-9). We stand for the Wesleyan position.

. . . That the Church is the body of Christ; that all who are united by faith to Christ are members of the same; and that, having thus become members one of another, it is our solemn and covenant duty to fellowship with one another in peace, and to love one another with pure and fervent hearts.

. . . That our Lord Jesus Christ in His literal resurrection from the dead is the living guarantee of the resurrection of all human beings; the believing saved to conscious eternal joy, and the unbelieving lost to conscious eternal punishment.

. . . That our Lord Jesus Christ, in fulfillment of His own promise, both angelically and apostolically attested, will personally return in power and great glory.

Notes: *Missionary World Service and Evangelism, founded in 1968, is a missionary service agency that assists missionary organizations and indigenous congregations. Its Statement of Faith affirms the inerrancy of the Bible and a consensus Evangelical theological perspective.*

* * *

STATEMENT OF FAITH (THE NAVIGATORS)

- We believe in the Scripture of the Old and New Testaments as inspired by God, and inerrant in the original writings, and that they are of supreme and final authority in faith and life.

- We believe in one God, eternally existing in three persons: Father, Son, and Holy Spirit.

- We believe that Jesus Christ was begotten by the Holy Spirit, was born of the virgin Mary, and is true God and true man.

- We believe that man was created in the image of God; that he sinned, and thereby incurred, not only physical death, but also that spiritual death which is separation from God; and that all human beings are born with a sinful nature.

- We believe that the Lord Jesus Christ died for our sins according to the Scripture, as a representative and substitutionary sacrifice; and that all who believe in Him are justified on the ground of His shed blood.

- We believe in the resurrection of the crucified body of our Lord, in His ascension into Heaven, and in His present life there for us as High Priest and Advocate.

- We believe in "that blessed hope," the personal and imminent return of our Lord and Savior, Jesus Christ.

- We believe that all who receive by faith the Lord Jesus Christ are born again of the Holy Spirit and thereby become children of God.

- We believe in the bodily resurrection of the just and unjust, the everlasting blessedness of the saved, and the everlasting punishment of the lost.

Notes: *The Navigators, founded in 1933, is a world missionary organization that specializes in the training of Christian leaders. Its affirms the inerrancy of the Bible and a consensus Evangelical theological perspective.*

* * *

STATEMENT OF FAITH (NORTH AFRICA MISSION)

1. The full inspiration of the Scriptures of the Old and New Testaments; their authority, sufficiency, and inerrancy, not only as containing, but as being in themselves the Word of God; and the need of the teaching of the Holy Spirit for a true and spiritual understanding of the whole.

2. The unit of the Godhead and the divine co-equality of the Father, the Son and the Holy Spirit.

3. The utter depravity of human nature in consequence of the fall, and the necessity for regeneration.

4. The absolute Deity of our Lord Jesus Christ; His virgin birth; His real and perfect manhood; the authority of His teaching, and the infallibility of all His utterances; His work of atonement for the sin of mankind by His vicarious suffering and death; His bodily resurrection and His ascension into Heaven; His present High-priestly intercession for His people; and His lordship over His Church as its Supreme Head.

5. The justification of the sinner, solely by faith, on the ground of the merits and vicarious suffering, death, and bodily resurrection of our Lord and Savior, Jesus Christ.

6. The necessity of the work of the Holy Spirit in conviction of sin, regeneration, and sanctification, as well as in ministry and worship.

7. The resurrection of the body; the judgment of the work by our Lord Jesus Christ; the eternal blessedness of the righteous; and the eternal punishment of the wicked.

8. The personal return of the Lord Jesus Christ in glory.

Notes: *The North Africa Mission is one of several Evangelical missionary agencies that focuses on the evangelization of*

STATEMENT OF FAITH (NORTH AFRICA MISSION) (continued)

Muslims. Its work is concentrated in the countries of North Africa, and France, where almost two million North Africans currently reside. Its Statement of Faith affirms the inerrancy of the Bible and a consensus Evangelical theological position.

*　　*　　*

STATEMENT OF DOCTRINE (OFFICERS' CHRISTIAN FELLOWSHIP OF THE UNITED STATES OF AMERICA)

The following is the Doctrinal Statement of the OCF. It is required that all Elected Officers of the Fellowship, all Council Members, the Executive Director and all Field Staff Personnel subscribe to this statement without reservation:

1. We believe in one God, eternally existing in three persons: Father, Son and Holy Spirit.

2. We believe that the Old and New Testaments as originally written are the verbally inspired Word of God, and accept them as the supreme and all-sufficient authority in faith and life.

3. We believe that man was created in the image of God, but that he sinned and there by incurred not only physical death, but also spiritual death which is eternal separation from God; and that each human being is born with a sinful nature and cannot by his own efforts please God.

4. We believe that Jesus Christ was begotten by the Holy Spirit, was born of the Virgin Mary and is true God and true man.

5. We believe that the Lord Jesus Christ died for our sins as our vicarious sacrifice in accordance with the Scripture, and that all who believe in Him are cleansed of their sins by His shed blood and are justified before God.

6. We believe that all who by faith receive the Lord Jesus Christ are born again of the holy Spirit and so become the children of God, to live with Him through all eternity.

7. We believe in the resurrection of the crucified body or our Lord in His ascension into heaven, and in His present life there as our High Priest and Advocate.

8. We believe in the bodily resurrection of the just and unjust; the eternal blessedness of the saved; and the everlasting, conscious punishment of the lost.

9. We believe in the personal, visible and glorious return of the Lord Jesus Christ to this earth.

Notes: *The Officers Christian Fellowship of the U.S.A. was founded in 1943 as a fellowship of Christians within the officers corps of the United States Armed Forces. The Christian Military Fellowship, founded in 1976, is associated with the Officers Christian Fellowship, with whom it shares a headquarters office and a Statement of Doctrine. Its doctrinal statement represents an Evangelical consensus position.*

*　　*　　*

STATEMENT OF FAITH (OPEN AIR CAMPAIGNERS)

Doctrinally O.A.C. is committed to the evangelical fellowship of believers. A copy of the doctrinal statement is given below. This statement is basic to the specific purpose of evangelism, and is not intended to deal with the whole council of God.

The unity of the Godhead and Trinity of Persons therein (Father, Son and Holy Spirit).

The Virgin Birth, and Deity of Jesus Christ and the efficacy of His death as the only atonement for sin.

The deity of the Holy Spirit and His work in conversion, instruction, and sanctification of the believer.

The Bible account of the Creation as recorded in Genesis—the fall of our first parents, resulting in spiritual death, and the lost condition of every human being, thus making the new birth an absolute necessity;

Justification by faith in our Lord Jesus Christ as Savior;

The actual bodily resurrection of Jesus Christ, His ascension into Heaven and future Second Personal Advent;

The eternal existence of the soul, the resurrection of the body, the judgment of the world by our Lord Jesus Christ, as eternal blessedness of the regenerate and the eternal punishment of the unregenerate;

The divine inspiration, final authority and sufficiency of the Holy Scriptures—the Old and New Testaments.

Notes: *Open Air Campaigners, founded in 1956, promotes outdoor evangelism and trains people in the methods of reaching people through open-air work. Its conservative Statement of Faith affirms the plenary verbal inspiration of the*

Bible, especially the Genesis account of creation, and a consensus Evangelical theological perspective.

* * *

STATEMENT OF DOCTRINE (OVERSEAS CHRISTIAN SERVICEMAN'S CENTERS)

1. We believe in the plenary, verbal inspiration of the whole Bible and that it is the supreme and final authority in faith and life. (II Timothy 3:16-17; II Peter 1:20-21)

2. We believe in one God, eternally existing in three persons: Father, Son, and Holy Spirit. (Deut. 6:4; II Cor. 13:14)

3. We believe that Jesus Christ was conceived of the Holy Spirit, born of the Virgin Mary, and that He is true God and true man. (Matt. 1:20-25; John 1:14; Romans 8:3)

4. We believe that man was created in the image of God; that all men have sinned in the transgression of Adam and subsequently in their personal experience that they are therefore totally depraved and "The wrath of God abideth on them," and that the only way to escape eternal condemnation is through the one gracious provision of the love of God. (Gen. 1:25-27; Rom. 3:22-26)

5. We believe that salvation is the gift of God offered to man by grace and received by personal faith in the Lord Jesus Christ, that the Son of God gave "His life a ransom for many" and bore "our sins in His own body on the tree," and that all who truly believe in Him are eternally saved on the ground of His shed blood. (Eph. 2:8-9; I Peter 2:24; John 10:28-29)

6. We believe in the personal bodily resurrection of our Lord and Savior, in His ascension into heaven, and in His present mediatorial High Priestly office there at the right hand of the Father. (Acts 1:9; Luke 24:6-7, Heb. 9:24; 7:25)

7. We believe in "that blessed hope," the personal, bodily, imminent, and pre-millennial return of the Lord Jesus Christ. (Titus 2:13; Acts 1:9-11)

8. We believe that all who receive by faith the Lord Jesus Christ are born again by the Holy Spirit, and that the Holy Spirit indwells every believer to enlighten, enable, and guide him in life and service. (John 3:6-7; I Cor. 2:12; John 14:16, 26; 16:24; Rom. 8:14)

9. We believe in the bodily resurrection of the just and the unjust, the everlasting blessedness of the saved, and the everlasting, conscious punishment of the lost. (Mark 9:43-48; Rev. 20:15, 22:3-5, 11)

CONCLUSION:

We believe in doing something about it, that we should "walk worthy of the vocation" to which we have been called. and that we have been entrusted with the responsibility and privilege of preaching the Gospel to the lost of this world. (Eph. 4:1; Titus 2:11-14; Mark 16:15; Acts 1:8)

Notes: *Also sharing the headquarters of the Officers Christian Fellowship of the U.S.A., the Overseas Christian Serviceman's Centers is an evangelistic organization that works among Armed Forces personnel around the world. Its statement of faith is adapted from that of the Officers Christian Fellowship, but adds an emphasis on the plenary inspiration of the Bible, total human depravation, and the imminence of the second coming of Christ.*

* * *

DOCTRINAL POSITION (OVERSEAS MISSIONARY FELLOWSHIP)

While as an interdenominational body we agree to disagree on minor points, all our members subscribe without hesitation to the following truths:

1. We believe in one God, eternally existing in three Persons—Father, Son, and Holy Spirit.

2. We believe the Bible to be fully and uniquely inspired by the Holy Spirit and that it is the only authoritative, inerrant and infallible written Word of God.

3. We believe in the deity of our Lord Jesus Christ, His virgin birth, sinless life, miracles, inerrant teaching, substitutionary death and atonement, bodily resurrection and ascension to the right hand of the Father.

4. We believe that man, created in the image of God, was tempted by Satan and fell, and because of his consequent depraved state, requires regeneration by the Holy Spirit for salvation.

5. We believe that salvation consists in the forgiveness of sins, the imputation of Christ's righteousness, and the gift of eternal life, received by faith alone.

6. We believe in the ministry of the Holy Spirit, by whose indwelling the Christian is being sanctified and empowered to live a godly life.

7. We believe that the true Church, the Body of Christ, is composed of all those who have been regenerated and affirm that the Church is the appointed instrument for the fulfillment of Christ's Great Commission.

8. We believe in the imminent visible, personal return of Jesus Christ in power and glory.

9. We believe in the resurrection of the body, the eternal life of the saved and the eternal punishment of the lost.

Notes: *The Overseas Missionary Fellowship was founded in 1865 as the China Inland Mission. It has been one of the most influential of independent missions, and a model for those that*

*came after it. Its Doctrinal Position affirms the inerrancy of
the Bible and a consensus Evangelical theological position.*

*　　*　　*

STATEMENT OF BELIEF (PERSONAL FREEDOM OUTREACH)

We believe in:

I. The Bible as the divinely inspired, inerrant Word of God: it is in its entirety the sole authority for all matters of Christian belief and practice

II. The one true God. In the one true God there exist three persons, being:

> The Father
> The Son Jesus Christ
> The Holy Spirit

III. Jesus Christ: His deity, humanity, virgin birth, sinlessness, death and bodily resurrection who will personally and visibly return again to earth.

IV. The personality and deity of the Holy Spirit.

V. The existence and personality of Satan, his total opposition to God, and his power over the unregenerate.

VI. The complete and total depravity of all men which makes them hopelessly lost without the new birth obtainable through faith in Jesus Christ.

VII. The final estate of man for the saved, everlasting life in the presence of God and for the unsaved, everlasting punishment because of their unbelief.

VIII. The Gospel by which we are saved being summed in the death, burial and resurrection of our Lord Jesus Christ.

IX. The Church being the Body of Christ, united in the Holy Spirit, consisting of those who have received Jesus Christ as Savior. A local church is an organized assembly of believers united for the purpose of carrying out the Great Commission of Christ.

X. The Great Commission of Christ being to preach the Gospel to all men, baptizing and discipling those who have believed.

Notes: *Personal Freedom Outreach, founded in 1975, was
established to counter the effects of non-Christian, new
religious movements (sometimes called cults). It operates from
an Evangelical perspective that affirms the inerrancy of the
Bible, the total human depravity, and the personality of Satan*

*who exercises his power over those who have not received
Christ as their Savior.*

*　　*　　*

BASIS OF FAITH AND DOCTRINE (PIONEERS)

• We believe the Bible to be the inspired, infallible, inerrant and totally authoritative Word of God.

• We believe in God's eternal existence in three co-equal persons: Father, Son, and Holy Spirit.

• We believe in the direct creation by God of the heavens and earth, along with all life.

• We believe in the personality, power, and evil nature of Satan.

• We believe man is totally unable to save himself and in his unsaved state is condemned before God.

• We believe in the deity of Christ and in His virgin birth, sinless life, substitutionary death, bodily resurrection, ascension, session, and personal return.

• We believe in salvation by grace alone through faith in Christ and in good works as the subsequent fruit of salvation.

• We believe in the eternal security of the believer.

• We believe in the Holy Spirit's present ministry in and to the believer enabling him to live godly and serve effectively.

• We believe in the universal church which is Christ's body and in its local manifestation, the local church.

Notes: *Pioneers, founded in 1979, is an Evangelical missionary sending agency that supports work around the world. Its
statement of faith affirms the inerrancy of the Bible and a
consensus Evangelical theological position.*

*　　*　　*

DOCTRINAL STATEMENT (PRACTICAL MISSIONARY TRAINING, INC.)

1. We believe the Bible as the verbally inspired Word of God. II Timothy 3:16, 17.

2. We believe in the deity of Jesus Christ, His Virgin birth and incarnation of the God-head in Him. John 1:1-5; Luke 1:26-33; Philippians 2:6-8.

3. We believe in the substitutionary sacrifice of the Lord Jesus Christ: 11 Corinthians 5:21, that His shed blood is the foundation and means of our salvation. Romans 5:9; Ephesians 1:7; Hebrews 9:22; I Peter 1:19.

4. We believe in the bodily resurrection of the Lord Jesus Christ, and in the ascension in that body to the right hand of God. I Corinthians 15:3, 4; Hebrews 1:3; Hebrews 9:24.

5. We believe in the new birth by the Spirit of God whereby we are made the children of God. John 3:3, 6, 8; John 1:12.

6. We believe in the person of the Holy Spirit, and in His work of conviction of sin, His regenerating work and His indwelling to give victory over sins, and power in service. John 14:16, 17; John 16:7-11; Romans 8:9; Titus 3:5; Acts 1:8.

7. We believe in the personal, premillennial coming of Christ at which time we are to be caught up in bodies like unto His glorious body. I Thessalonians 4:13-17; Acts 1:10, 11; I John 3:1-3; Luke 12:40; Titus 2:13.

8. We believe in the eternal salvation of the regenerate and the eternal condemnation of the unregenerate. John 10:27-29; Romans 8: 38-39; II Thessalonians 1:7-9.

9. We believe the chief occupations of the Christian are to do the will of God, to preach the Gospel of saving grace to the lost and to build up the saints in the faith. John 4:34; John 17-18; Mark 16:15; Acts 1:8; Luke 22:32.

10. We believe that God's people should be separated unto the Lord and abstain from all appearance of evil. II Corinthians 6:14-18; I Thessalonians 1:9; I Thessalonians 5:22; I Peter 2:11.

Notes: *Practical Missionary Training is a conservative Evangelical missionary organization. It affirms the verbal inspiration of the Bible and a consensus Evangelical theological position that includes the separation of believers from evil and the appearance of evil.*

*   *   *

STATEMENT OF FAITH (PRISON FELLOWSHIP MINISTRIES)

We believe in one God, Creator and Lord of the Universe, the co-eternal Trinity: Father, Son and Holy Spirit.

We believe that Jesus Christ, God's Son, was conceived by the Holy Spirit, born of the Virgin Mary, lived a sinless life, died a substitutionary atoning death on the Cross, rose bodily from the dead and ascended to heaven where as truly God and truly man, He is the only mediator between God and man.

We believe that the Bible is God's authoritative and inspired Word. It is without error in all its teaching, including creation, history, its own origins, and salvation. Christians must submit to its divine authority, both individually and corporately, in all matters of belief and conduct, which is demonstrated by true righteous living.

We believe that all people are lost sinners and cannot see the Kingdom of God except through the new birth. Justification is by grace through faith in Christ alone.

We believe in one holy, universal, and apostolic Church. Its calling is to worship God, and witness concerning its Head, Jesus Christ, preaching the Gospel among all nations demonstrating its commitment by compassionate service to the needs of human beings and promoting righteousness and justice.

We believe in the necessity of the work of the Holy spirit for the individuals new birth and growth to maturity, and for the Church's constant renewal in truth, wisdom, faith, holiness, love, power, and mission.

We believe that Jesus Christ will personally and visibly return in glory to raise the dead and bring salvation and judgment to completion. God will fully manifest His Kingdom when He establishes a new heaven and new earth, in which He will be glorified forever and exclude all evil, suffering, and death.

Notes: *Prison Fellowship Ministries, founded in 1976, promotes ministries to prisoners, their families, and ex-offenders. Its Statement of Faith affirms the inerrancy of the Bible, including the story of creation and the history recounted throughout its pages, and a consensus Evangelical theological perspective. In addition, it calls for the church to demonstrate its commitment to Jesus Christ through "compassionate service to the needs of human beings and promoting righteousness and justice."*

*   *   *

DOCTRINAL STATEMENT (PRISON MISSION ASSOCIATION, INC.)

In view of the present unrest concerning doctrinal questions within the sphere of evangelical Christianity, and to answer inquiries be it Resolved That this Board places on record the following statement of faith as that to which its members severally subscribe to wit:

ARTICLE I: God is a Person who has revealed Himself as a Trinity in unity, Father, Son and Holy Spirit—three Persons and yet but one God (Deut. 6:4; Matt. 28:19; I Cor. 8:6).

ARTICLE II: The Bible, including both the Old and the New Testaments, is a divine revelation, the original autographs of which were verbally inspired by the Holy Spirit (II Tim. 3:16; 11 Pet. 1:21).

ARTICLE III: Jesus Christ is the image of the invisible God, which is to say, He is Himself very God; He took upon Him our nature, being conceived by the Holy Ghost and born of the Virgin Mary; He died upon the cross as a substitutionary sacrifice for the sin of the world; He arose from the dead in the body in which He was crucified; He ascended into heaven in that body glorified, where He is now, our interceding High Priest; He will come again personally and visibly to set up His kingdom and to judge the quick and the dead (Col. 1:15; Phil.

STATEMENT OF FAITH (PRISON FELLOWSHIP MINISTRIES)
(continued)

2:5-8; Matt. 1:18-25; I Pet. 2: 25; Luke 24; Heb. 4:14-16; Acts. 1:9-11; I Thess. 4:16-18; Matt. 25:31-46; Rev. 11:15-17; 20:4-6, 11-15).

ARTICLE IV: Man was created in the image of God but fell into sin and, in that sense, is lost; this is true of all men, and except a man be born again he cannot see the kingdom of God; salvation is by grace through faith in Christ who His own self bare our sins in His own body on the tree; the retribution of the wicked and unbelieving and the reward of the righteous are everlasting, and as the reward is conscious, so is the retribution.

(Gen. 1:26, 27; Rom. 3:10, 23; John 3:3; Acts. 13: 38,39; 4:12; John 3:16; Matt. 25:46, II Cor. 5:1; II Thess. 1:7-10; Eph. 2:8,9).

ARTICLE V: The Church is an elect company of believers baptized by the Holy Spirit into one body; its mission is to witness concerning its Head, Jesus Christ, preaching the gospel among all nations; it will be caught up to meet the Lord in the air where He appears to set up His kingdom.

(Eph. 1:3-6; I Cor. 12:12,13; I Thess. 4:16-18; II Cor. 5:19,20,; Titus 2:12-14; Eph. 3:1-11).

Notes: *The Prison Mission Association, founded in 1955, provides services, such as correspondence courses and training seminars, to prisoners and others ministering inside the prison system. Its Doctrinal Statement affirms the verbal inspiration of the Bible and a consensus Evangelical theological perspective.*

*   *   *

STATEMENT OF FAITH (PROBE MINISTRIES)

The final authority of our beliefs is the Bible, God's infallible written Word, the sixty-six books of the Old and New Testaments. We believe that the Bible was uniquely, verbally and fully inspired by the Holy Spirit, and that it was without error in the original manuscripts. It is the supreme and final authority in all matters on which it speaks (2 Tim. 3:16-17; 2 Peter 1:21; 1 Cor. 2:13, 10:11; John 10:35). (Detailed doctrinal statement available on written request.)

Notes: *Probe Ministries, founded in 1971, was founded by a group of educators who sought to broaden the impact of Christian insight, especially in education and the media.*

*   *   *

WHAT WE BELIEVE (RBMU INTERNATIONAL)

1. We believe the sixty-six books of the Bible to be the infallible, written Word of God, verbally inspired by the Holy Spirit, inerrant in the original manuscripts, and the only and final authority in all matters of faith and conduct.

2. We believe in the unity of the Godhead, eternally existing in three Persons—Father, Son, and Holy Spirit—each of whom possesses equally all the attributes of deity and the characteristics of personality.

3. We believe that Jesus Christ is the eternal Son of God, that He was conceived by the Holy Spirit and became incarnate through the virgin birth, and that He unites forever in His Person perfect deity and true humanity.

4. We believe that Jesus Christ lived a sinless life, that He was crucified as the substitutionary sacrifice for the sins of men, that He rose bodily from the dead, that He ascended into heaven where He is now exalted at the right hand of the Father, and where He intercedes for the believer.

5. We believe that man was originally and directly created in the image of God, and that through disobedience he fell. Consequently, all men were brought under divine condemnation and are born sinners, unable to please God in their natural state.

6. We believe in the work of the Holy Spirit in the conviction and regeneration of the sinner. We believe in His indwelling presence and ministry in the believer to glorify Christ.

7. We believe that salvation is wholly a work of God's grace, and that upon the sinner's repentance and personal faith in the Lord Jesus Christ his sins are forgiven and divine righteousness is imputed to him.

8. We believe that the Church, the Body of Christ, consists only of those who are born again, having been baptized into Christ by the Holy Spirit at the time of regeneration.

9. We believe that Jesus Christ will return personally, visibly and bodily to receive His own and to establish His kingdom, and to rule in righteousness and peace.

10. We believe in the bodily resurrection of the believer to eternal life and conscious fellowship with God. We believe in the bodily resurrection of the unbeliever to conscious separation from God in eternal punishment.

11. We believe that Christ commissioned the Church to proclaim the Gospel throughout the world to all men, and to make disciples in every nation.

Notes: *RBMU International, founded in 1873, is an Evangelical missionary sending agency with work around the world. Its statement of belief affirms the inerrancy of the Bible and a consensus Evangelical theological perspective.*

*　　　*　　　*

PHILOSOPHY/MISSION/OBJECTIVES (REAL LIFE MINISTRIES)

PHILOSOPHY

When ''the Word became flesh and dwelt among us,'' the Lord Jesus became that perfect medium through which God has chosen to communicate His redeeming love to all the world. The life and personality of Jesus, every word and deed of God the Son, all consistently point to the Father and glorify Him.

There is available to us all present-day disciples, intent on fulfilling the Great commission, the far less perfect yet very powerful medium of broadcast communication.

MISSION

The mission of Real Life Ministries is to communicate with force and clarity that Jesus Christ is the Way, the Truth and the Life to the glory of God the Father.

OBJECTIVES

To address the real needs of hurting, hopeless people, in a manner which lovingly declares God's Way out of their pain and despair;

To capture the attention of those who do not believe, so that they will be confronted by the Truth and saved;

To remind casual Christians that we are called to walk in a constant relationship with God, one which encompasses every facet of our lives;

To provide, in the form of taped and printed materials, quality resources for Christian growth;

To encourage those searching believers who may never have experienced in worship the free and joyous praise of God;

To make it clear to those who believe, as well as to those who do not, that victorious life in Christ is a daily choice;

To sow God's Word with the expectation that souls will be saved, but with the certainty that God alone can convict and convert;

And always, in a manner marked by honesty and credibility, to promote Jesus Christ and His Kingdom.

Notes: *Real Life Ministries is the outreach ministry of Mount Paran Church of God in Atlanta, Georgia. It has developed a radio and television broadcast ministry, supplemented by a cassette and video tape ministry to reach those who can only be reached by such media. Real Life Ministries understands that, just as Jesus was the perfect media for the embodiment of God in human flesh, such modern communications means are a fitting embodiment for the communication of the Truth of Jesus Christ.*

*　　　*　　　*

STATEMENT OF FAITH (REIGN MINISTRIES)

WE BELIEVE that the Bible is the verbally and plenary inspired Word of God, inerrant in its original manuscripts. The Bible is our supreme and final authority in faith and life. (II Timothy 3:16; II Peter 1:20, 21)

WE BELIEVE in one God, eternally existing in three persons, Father, Son and Holy Spirit. (Genesis 1:1,26; Matthew 28:19; John: 1,3,4:24; Acts 5:3,4; Romans 1:20; Ephesians 4:5,6; II Corinthians 13:14)

WE BELIEVE Jesus Christ was begotten by the Holy Spirit, and was born of the virgin, Mary, and is true God and true man. (Matthew 1:18-25; Luke 1:26-38; Romans 9:5; Titus 2:13)

WE BELIEVE that man was created in the image of God, that he sinned and thereby incurred not only physical death, but also spiritual death which is separation from God, and that all human beings are born with a sinful nature, and become guilty sinners, in thought, word and deed. (Genesis 1:26,27; 3:1-24; Romans 3:25; 5:12-18; I John 1:8)

WE BELIEVE that the Lord Jesus died for our sins and was raised from the dead according to the Scriptures as a representative and substitutionary sacrifice, and that all who believe in Him are justified on the grounds of His shed blood. (Isaiah 53; Matthew 20:28; John 3:16; Romans 3:24, 5:1; I Corinthians 15:3; II Corinthians 5:21; Ephesians 1: 17; 1 John 2:2)

WE BELIEVE in the personal and imminent return of our Lord Jesus Christ. (Acts 1:11; I Thessalonians 4:16,17)

WE BELIEVE that all who come by grace through faith to accept the Lord Jesus Christ are born again of the Holy Spirit and thereby become children of God. (John 3:3,5; 1: 12,13; James 1:18; I Peter 1: 23; Ephesians 2:8,9)

WE BELIEVE in the bodily resurrection of the just and the unjust, the everlasting conscious punishment of the lost. (John 5:28,29; I Corinthians 15; Corinthians 5:10; Matthew 25:31-46; Revelation 20:46, 11-15)

Notes: *Reign Ministries, founded in 1981, is a ministry that aims to train young people for effective future church leader-*

ship. It affirms the inerrancy of the Bible and a consensus Evangelical theological position.

*   *   *

OUR CREED (ROCK OF ISRAEL MINISTRIES)

The ROCK OF ISRAEL believes in ONE Gospel for both Jew and Gentile. It is interesting to note that Paul, in each town where he ministered, went first to the synagogue and (God's Word tells us) preached JESUS unto them (the Jews)! We also believe in ONE Church, ONE Body made up of JEWS and GENTILES. We cannot conceive of heaven being partitioned off—one side for Jews, the other for Gentiles for Jesus Christ, our Peace, has made both ONE and has broken down the middle wall of partition between us! Praise God! (See Ephesians 2:14).

Notes: *Rock of Israel Ministries, founded in 1970, is a Jewish evangelism agency. Its brief creedal statement emphasizes the necessity of Jewish evangelism and the movement of Jewish converts into one Church with Gentiles, rather than the development of an ethnic-based Jewish church.*

*   *   *

STATEMENT OF FAITH (ROGMA INTERNATIONAL, INC.)

I. We believe that the only true and living God is the God revealed in the Bible.

II. We believe that God is one in substance but three in manifestation: Father, Son and Holy Spirit.

III. We believe this triune God to be sovereign in the universe, to have created all things, to have existed from eternity and to possess equally all the attributes of deity including infinite love, absolute wisdom, perfect holiness and unlimited power.

IV. We believe that Jesus Christ is God the son who came to Earth by way of a virgin, that He lived a sinless life and died a vicarious, substitutionary death for the sins of all mankind, that He arose bodily from the grave and lives today at the right hand of the Father making daily intercession for all believers.

V. We believe the Holy Spirit to be the third person of the Trinity, that He was and is the agent of God's power, that he came to dwell permanently in the lives of believers at Pentecost, that all believers are baptized by Him into the body of Christ, that he fills and empowers believers for service, makes known to them all things relating to Christ and guides them into the truth.

VI. We believe the Bible to be the inspired word of God, completely inerrant in its original manuscripts, that its purity has been safeguarded through the years and is our only authority and guide for morals and practice.

VII. We believe that all men are sinners by nature and practice and are in need of redemption and regeneration.

VIII. We believe that salvation from sin is wholly by the grace of God, that it was purchased by the death and resurrection of Christ and is available to all men entirely apart from human merit or effort.

IX. We believe that the redemption purchased by the shed blood of Christ is available to all men everywhere. We believe that while men are spiritually depraved and can in no way save themselves, they nevertheless have a God-given will whereby they are able to repent toward God, believe the Gospel, receive Christ and be saved.

X. We believe that the great commission and the great thrust of missions is a rescue ministry, snatching brands from the burning and winning as many souls as possible before inevitable judgment.

XI. We believe in the imminent return of Christ for his church, all believers since Pentecost, which he has purchased with his blood, that the Church will rise to meet him in the air and will be forever with him and that this event will precede the period called "The Tribulation."

XII. We believe that Christ will then return to earth in power and great glory and that He will reign over the whole Earth bringing in an age of peace and righteousness.

Notes: *ROGMA International, founded in 1981, is a missionary agency that specializes in the publication and dissemination of evangelical literature, particularly a Bible correspondence course that it offers free to individuals. Its Statement of Faith affirms the inerrancy of the Bible and makes a case for the primary task of Christians to engage in evangelistic and missionary work.*

*   *   *

STATEMENT OF FAITH (ROMANIAN MISSIONARY SOCIETY)

1. We believe that there is one God, eternally existent in three persons: Father, Son and Holy Spirit.

2. We believe that the Bible is the inerrant Word of God written through the inspiration of the Holy Spirit; and hold it to be the only authoritative rule for Christian faith and practice.

3. We believe in the Deity of our Lord Jesus Christ, His virgin birth; His sinless life; His vicarious death and the

atoning power of His shed blood. We believe in His bodily resurrection; in His ascension the right hand of God, the Father.

4. We believe that man was created in the image of God and that man has fallen from the state of perfection by sin.

5. We believe in the necessity of the restoration of man, through regeneration by the Holy Spirit.

6. We believe in Christ's imminent return to take His church unto Himself, and in the resurrection of both the saved and the lost.

7. We believe that a Christian should maintain a strong and consistent testimony, striving always to walk in the foot-steps of our Savior and Lord, and working under the direction of the Holy Spirit for the salvation of lost souls and the edification of the Body of Christ.

8. We believe in the spiritual unity of believers in our Lord Jesus Christ and in the possibility of unified cooperation in evangelical missionary work at home and abroad.

Notes: *The Romanian Missionary Society, founded in 1968, conducts missionary work in Romania. Its Statement of Faith was adopted from that of the National Association of Evangelicals. Its order was changed so that the statement on God preceded that of the Bible. Added were affirmations on the inerrancy of the Bible and the hope of a unified cooperation in evangelical missionary work.*

*   *   *

STATEMENT OF DOCTRINAL PRINCIPLES (SCRIPTURE PRESS PUBLICATIONS, INC.)

WE BELIEVE in great doctrines of the evangelical Christian faith.

WE BELIEVE that the Scriptures, consisting of the Old and New Testaments, are verbally inspired and without error in their original writings, and are therefore our final authority in faith and life (Luke 24:27, 44; John 5:39; Acts 1:16; 28:25; I Cor. 2:13; II Tim. 3:16; II Pet. 1:21; Rev. 22:18, 19).

WE BELIEVE in one God, who exists eternally in three persons; the Father, the Son, and the Holy Spirit. We believe that Jesus Christ, who was God from eternity, was begotten by the Holy Spirit and born of the virgin Mary and thus is true man and true God (Deut. 6:4; Matt. 1:20-23; 28:18, 19; Mark 12:29; Luke 1:26-38; 2:7; John 1:14; Acts 5:3,4; II Cor. 13:14; Heb. 1:1-3: Rev. 1:4-6).

WE BELIEVE that God created a host of angels who were sinless and spiritual beings. Some of them, led by Satan, fell into sin, and now oppose God and those whom God blesses. The holy angels continue to minister as servants of God (Gen. 3:1-9; Isa. 14:12-17; Ezek. 28:11-19; Luke 15:10; II Cor. 4:3,4; 11:13-15; Eph. 6:10-12; Heb. 1:13, 14; 2:6-10, II Pet. 2:4; Jude 6. Rev. 12:9; 20:1-3.10).

WE BELIEVE that Adam was created without sin, but through his transgression fell from his original innocency. Descendants of Adam are born in sin and are subject to death and judgment, apart from divine grace (Gen. 1:26-27; 2:17; 3:6; 6:5. Ps. 14:1-3; 51:5; 58:3; Jer. 17:9; John 3:3-6; Rom. 3:10-19; 5:12; 6:23; 8:6,7; Eph. 2:1-3; 1 John 3:8).

WE BELIEVE that Christ died for our sins and rose bodily from the grave. We believe in His bodily ascension, in His present work for believers as High Priest and Advocate in heaven and in the "blessed hope" of His personal, bodily turn to receive saints unto Himself and establish His millennial reign on earth (Luke 23:46-49; 24:1-53; John 1:29; 14:2, 3; Acts 1:9-11; Rom. 3:23-26; 5:8; 1 Cor. 15:1-24, 51-58; II Cor. 5:14-21; Eph. 1:20-23, I Thess. 4:13-18; Titus 2:13; Heb. 1:3-7:25; 1 Pet. 3:18; 1 John 2:1; Rev. 1:5; 19:11-20:15).

WE BELIEVE that men can be saved from sin and come into possession of eternal life by realizing they are sinners, believing that the Lord Jesus Christ loves them and has provided salvation through His own shed blood upon Calvary. Salvation is by grace through faith in Christ as personal Savior and Sin-bearer and is entirely a free gift of God. Salvation cannot possibly be achieved by man's works (John 3:14-18, 36; 5:24; 6:47; Acts 4:12; Rom. 1:16, 17; 3:20-26; 5:1; 8:1; Eph. 2:8,9; Titus 3:5; 1 Pet. 1:18, 19; Rev. 1:5).

WE BELIEVE that at death the saved enter into the presence of God immediately, to spend eternity with Him. At death unsaved go immediately into eternal conscious punishment. We believe in the future bodily resurrection of all the dead (Dan. 12:2,3; Luke 16:19-31; John 5:28, 29: 1 Cor. 15:22, 51-54; II Cor. 5:8; Phil. 1:23; 1 Thess. 4:16; Rev. 20:4-6; 10-15).

WE BELIEVE that the Holy Spirit convicts sinners of their need of Christ as Savior, and regenerates those who place faith in Christ. The Holy Spirit indwells all true believers. As believers yield to His control He enables them to obey the will of God for them, and to lead godly lives, separate from the sins of the world (John 7:37-39; 14:16,17; 16:7-15; Acts 2:38; Rom. 8:1-17: 1 Cor. 6:19,20: Gal. 5:16; Eph. 5:18).

WE BELIEVE in the spiritual unity of true believers in Christ and that all believers are members of the Church, which is Christ's body and of which He is the Head (Rom. 12:3-8; 1 Cor. 12:13-27; Eph. 1:22,23; 2:13-22; 5:23-32).

WE BELIEVE that all Christians are called and commissioned by the Lord to live to the glory of God and to win others to Christ (Matt. 28:19; Mark 16:15; Luke 24:46-48; John 15:16; Acts 1:18; 1 Cor. 10:31; II Cor. 5:20; Phil. 1:20, 21).

Notes: *Scripture Press Publications, Inc., founded in 1934, is an Evangelical publishing house. Its Statement of Doctrinal*

STATEMENT OF DOCTRINAL PRINCIPLES (SCRIPTURE PRESS PUBLICATIONS, INC.) (continued)

Principles firms the inerrancy of the Bible and a consensus Evangelical theological perspective.

* * *

WE BELIEVE (SEND INTERNATIONAL)

WE BELIEVE:

1. In the plenary and verbal inspiration and inerrancy of the Bible as originally given; that it is the only infallible Word of God, and the supreme and final authority in all matters of faith and conduct;

2. That there is only one true God, eternally existing in three persons: Father, Son and Holy Spirit;

3. In Jesus Christ, God the Son, the world's only Savior; in His preincarnation, virgin birth, sinless life, vicarious death, burial, bodily resurrection, and personal, visible, and premillennial return;

4. In God, the Holy Spirit, who convicts the world of sin, regenerates, indwells, and empowers the believer;

5. That all men are sinful and lost and can be saved only by grace through faith in the shed blood of Christ;

6. In the resurrection of the dead, the believer to life everlasting, and the unbeliever to eternal condemnation;

7. That the church is the body of Jesus Christ, for which He will return, comprised of all who have accepted the redemption provided by Him;

8. That the presence of Jesus Christ by the Holy Spirit in the believer will result in a life of personal holiness and a walk of obedience to the will of God.

Notes: *Send International, founded in 1947, is an Evangelical missionary sending agency. Its statement of belief follows the pattern of the National Association of Evangelicals but adds affirmations on the inerrancy of the Bible, the premillennial second coming of Jesus Christ, and the nature of the Church.*

* * *

STATEMENT OF FAITH (SHALOM MINISTRIES)

THE BIBLE Inspired, infallible, authoritative Word of God.

ONE GOD Eternally co-existent in three persons—father, Son and Holy Spirit.

JESUS CHRIST Deity, virgin birth, sinless life, miracles, vicarious and atoning death and blood, bodily resurrection to God's right hand, imminent return.

REDEMPTION Holy Spirit's regeneration of lost and sinful man required.

HOLY SPIRIT Enables believers to live godly life by indwelling them.

RESURRECTION Of the saved to eternal life and bliss and of the lost to eternal damnation.

SPIRITUAL UNITY Only between believers in the Lord Jesus Christ.

Notes: *This brief Statement, adapted from that of the National Association of Evangelicals (NAE), summarizes the Evangelical theological position. Note the alteration in the NAE's statement on "Spiritual Unity," that spiritual unity is "only between believers."*

* * *

STATEMENT OF FAITH [SHORT TERM EVANGELICAL MISSION (STEM) MINISTRIES]

(1) The divine inspiration and consequent authority of the whole canonical Scriptures as the inerrant and only Word of God.

(2) The doctrine of the Trinity: God the Father, Jesus Christ the Son, and the Holy Spirit.

(3) The fall of man and his consequent moral depravity and need for regeneration.

(4) The atonement for sin through the substitutionary death of Jesus Christ.

(5) The doctrine of justification by faith.

(6) The regeneration and renewal of man through the work and presence of the Holy Spirit in his life.

(7) The resurrection of the body both in the case of the just and the unjust.

(8) The eternal life of the saved and the eternal punishment of the lost, as described in Scripture.

Notes: *Short Term Evangelical Mission (STEM) Ministries, founded in 1984, is an Evangelical missionary agency that involves people in short-term (two-week) mission projects in* *foreign countries. Its Statement of Faith asserts a belief in the inerrancy of the Bible, and an Evangelical consensus perspective.*

*   *   *

DOCTRINAL STATEMENT (SIM INTERNATIONAL)

1. The Bible which is verbally inspired by the Holy Spirit in the canonical Scriptures as originally given and is the inerrant and authoritative Word of God. 2 Timothy 3:15-17; 2 Peter 1:21.

2. The triune Godhead in three persons: Father, Son and Holy Spirit. Deuteronomy 6:4; Matthew 28:29; 2 Corinthians 13:14.

   a. The Father, Who is a Spirit, infinite, eternal and unchangeable in all His attributes. John 4:24; Exodus 34:6.

   b. The Son, Jesus Christ: His deity, virgin birth, sinless life, atoning death, bodily resurrection, personal exaltation at God's right hand and personal return. John 1:1; Isaiah 7:14; Hebrews 7:26; 1 Corinthians 15:3, 4; Acts 1:11.

   c. The Holy Spirit, Who is a divine person, equal with the Father and the Son and of the same nature. John 15:26.

3. The personality of Satan, who is called the devil. Revelation 20:2.

4. The fall and lost estate of man, whose total depravity makes necessary the new birth. Romans 5:12; John 3:5.

5. Salvation by grace through faith in the shed blood and substitutionary death of Jesus Christ our Lord and Savior. Titus 3:4-7; Ephesians 2:8,9; Romans 5:8.

6. The eternal blessedness of the saved and the everlasting punishment of the lost. Matthew 25:46; Philippians 3:21.

7. The Church, the bride of Christ: In its universal aspect comprising the whole body of those who have been born of the Spirit; and in its local expression established for worship, mutual edification and witness. Ephesians 1;22,23; 5:25-32; Acts 15:41; 16:5.

8. Christ's great commission to go into all the world and preach the gospel to every creature, making disciples, baptizing and teaching. Matthew 28:18-20.

Notes: *SIM International, founded in 1893, is an Evangelical missionary sending agency. Its Doctrinal Statement affirms the inerrancy of the Bible and a consensus Evangelical theo-*

logical perspective that includes a belief in the personality of Satan and total human depravity.

*   *   *

DOCTRINAL STATEMENT (SLAVIC GOSPEL ASSOCIATION)

1. We believe in the Scriptures of the Old and New Testaments as verbally inspired by God and inerrant in the original writings, and that they are of supreme and final authority in faith and life. (Luke 24:27, 44; II Tim. 3:16; II Peter 1:21)

2. We believe in one God, eternally existing in three persons: Father, Son and Holy Spirit. (Matt. 28:18-19; Mark 12:29; II Cor. 13:14; Heb. 1: 1-3; Acts 5:3)

3. We believe that Jesus Christ was begotten by the Holy Spirit and born of the Virgin Mary and is true God and true man. (Luke 1:26-38; John 1:14; 14:6-11; Heb. 1:1-8)

4. We believe that man was created in the image of God; that he sinned, and thereby incurred not only physical death, but also that spiritual death which is separation from God; and that all human beings are born with a sinful nature and, in the case of those who reach moral responsibility, become sinners in thought, word, and deed. (Rom. 3: 10-26; I Thess. 1:7-9; Jer. 17:9)

5. We believe that the Lord Jesus Christ died for our sins, according to the Scriptures, as a representative and substitutionary sacrifice; and that all that believe in Him are justified on the ground of His shed blood. (I Cor. 15:1-10; I John 1:7; 2:1-2; I Peter 3: 18; Rom. 3:24-25)

6. We believe in the resurrection of the crucified body of our Lord, in His ascension into Heaven, and His present life there for us, as High Priest and Advocate. (I Cor. 15:1-24; Heb. 10: 12-22; I John 2:1-2)

7. We believe in "that blessed hope," the personal premillennial and imminent return of our Lord and Savior, Jesus Christ. (Titus 2:13; Heb. 9:28; Rev. 1:5-8; Acts 1:8-12; I Thess. 4:13-18)

8. We believe that all who receive by faith the Lord Jesus Christ are born again of the Holy Spirit, thereby receiving eternal life and thus becoming children of God. (John 3:3-16; 1:12; Eph. 2:8-9; Titus 3:5; John 10:27-29)

9. We believe in the bodily resurrection of the just and unjust, the everlasting blessedness of the saved, and the everlasting, conscious punishment of the lost. (Matt. 25:46; Dan. 12:2-3; Rev. 20:4-6, 10-15)

10. We believe in the spreading of the gospel as Jesus said, "Go ye into all the world and preach the gospel to every creature," Mark 16:15. (Luke 24:45-48; Acts 1:8; II Cor. 5:20)

DOCTRINAL STATEMENT (SLAVIC GOSPEL ASSOCIATION)
(continued)

Notes: *The Slavic Gospel Association, founded in 1934, is an Evangelical missionary sending agency working among Russians and other Slavic peoples in their worldwide diaspora. Its very conservative Doctrinal Statement affirms a belief in the inerrancy of the Bible and a consensus Evangelical theological perspective.*

* * *

DOCTRINAL STATEMENT (SOUND DOCTRINE MINISTRIES)

We, of Sound Doctrine Ministries, hold the following beliefs:

1. The verbal, full inspiration and authority of the Scriptures.

2. God as a Trinity of three persons of one essence.

3. Jesus Christ is fully God and fully man, born of the Virgin Mary by the Holy Spirit.

4. The Deity and personality of the Holy Spirit.

5. Salvation by grace through faith in Jesus Christ alone.

6. The substitutionary death of Jesus Christ for our sins.

7. The bodily resurrection of Jesus Christ.

8. The resurrection of the saved to eternal life, and everlasting punishment for the lost.

Notes: *Sound Doctrine Ministries, founded in 1985, is an Evangelical ministry to counter the effects of non-Christian, new religious movements (known as cults). Its brief Doctrinal Statement affirms the verbal inspiration of the Bible and a consensus Evangelical theological perspective.*

* * *

STATEMENT OF FAITH (SOURCE OF LIGHT MINISTRIES INTERNATIONAL)

The Source of Light Ministries International is orthodox in theology and evangelistic in practice, believing in:

1. The plenary and verbal inspiration of the Bible and its inerrancy as God's Holy Word,

2. The Holy Trinity of Father, Son and Holy Spirit; three persons in one essence in the unity of the Godhead,

3. The creation of man by the direct act of God and his subsequent fall as revealed in the Genesis account,

4. The Deity, incarnation and virgin birth and sinless humanity of Jesus Christ our Lord; His substitutionary death on the cross as the atonement for man's sin; His bodily resurrection from the tomb; His ascension into Heaven to sit at the Father's right hand, the imminent rapture of the Church, and the personal, visible and pre-millennial return of Christ in power and great glory,

5. The power of Christ to save men eternally from the penalty of sin through faith in His shed blood, and the gift of eternal life by the grace of God,

6. The new birth of all who believe on Him through the regenerating work of the Holy Spirit,

7. The sanctification of the believer by the Holy Spirit through the Word,

8. The final judgment of the wicked and Satan's doom with the wicked in the lake of fire, and

9. The eternal happiness of the righteous in the presence of the of the Lord, and the ushering in of eternal righteousness in the new Heaven and the new earth.

Where We Stand on Issues of the Day

BIBLICAL INERRANCY—The Source of Light Ministries has always held, and still does today to the inerrancy of the 66 books of the Bible, and that in the original manuscripts each book was infallible and inerrant in all its parts. II Tim. 3:16,17; 4:3,4; II Pet. 1:19.20.

CO-OPERATIVE EVANGELISM—The Source of Light Ministries reserves the right to determine its relationship with such efforts as may be determined by the composition of the committees set up to manage the campaign. If it is inclusive, using both liberals and conservatives, then we would decline to participate. II Cor. 6:14; 7:1; Eph. 5:11.

THE CHARISMATIC MOVEMENT—The Source of Light Ministries does not agree with the Charismatic Movement, or that the Scriptures teach that speaking in tongues is the indispensable evidence of the gift of the Holy Spirit. In stating our position we do not mean to detract from the sincerity or Christian character of many within this movement. The Source of Light Ministries is not affiliated with any group or organization that is Charismatic in nature and practice. Rom. 6:17; James 3:16-18; I Tim. 4:1.

THE ECUMENICAL MOVEMENT—This movement places primary emphasis on uniting churches on a basis other than Biblically sound doctrine and is another indication of the end of the age. Therefore, the Source of light Ministries abstains from all associations that would link it with this movement. II Cor. 6:14-17; II Pet. 2:1-3; Rev. 18:1-4; II Chron. 19:2.

SEPARATION—The Source of Light Ministries emphasizes the Bible teaching that Christians should be separated from sin and ungodliness from the world, from believers who walk disorderly, from those who teach false doctrine, and those who deny the faith. II Cor. 6:14, 7:1; II John, verses 9-11; Ezek. 44:2b; I John 2:15-17; Rom. 12:2; I Cor. 5:9-13.

THE LOCAL CHURCH—The Source of Light Ministries believes in the scriptural importance of each local church. Our purpose is to assist the local church in its outreach for lost souls and to train believers to serve the Lord and to be good students of the Word of God. I Thess. 1:9,10; II Tim. 2:2, 2:15; Acts 2:41-46; I Tim. 3:15.

THE LORDS RETURN—The Source of Light Ministries teaches the imminent, bodily, pretribulation rapture of the church, which is His body (John 14:1-3; I Thess. 4:13-18) and His personal, visible return in glory with His saints (I Thess. 3:13; Matt. 24:30) to reign as KING OF KINGS AND LORD OF LORDS—II Thess. 1:8-10; Rev. 1:5-7; Isa. 11:4-9, 63:1-6.

THE ASSURANCE OF THE BELIEVER—The Source of Light Ministries believes that the Scripture assures the truly born-again one that his salvation is eternal (John 5:24) and that nothing can separate him from his union with Christ. Rom. 8:38,39; John 3:16, 6:47, 10:9; Rom. 5:9, 8:31; I Cor. 3:15; I John 5:12; Jude 24.

THE PERSON AND WORK OF THE HOLY SPIRIT—We believe and teach that the Holy Spirit, at the Instant of regeneration, baptizes the new believer Into the "Body of Christ" which is the Church of the living God (I Cor. 12:12). We further believe that only as the Holy Spirit controls and works through the believer can he be made pleasing to God and minister effectively for Him.

Notes: *Source of Light Ministries International, founded in 1953, is a Fundamentalist missionary sending agency. Its Statement of Faith emphasizes biblical inerrancy, separation from any who teach false doctrines, Pentecostalism, and the Ecumenical cooperative movement.*

*   *   *

DOCTRINAL STATEMENT (SOUTH AMERICA MISSION, INC.)

(A) The following doctrinal statement is adhered to by the Board of Directors, by all administrative personnel, by every missionary in active or inactive service and by all candidates its a condition of their acceptance. Each missionary reaffirms his adherence to these doctrines at the conclusion of each term of service and each member of the Board of Directors reaffirms his adherence annually by signing his name to this doctrinal statement:

The South America Mission and all its personnel are committed to

(1) The inspiration and authority of the Holy Scriptures.

(2) The Deity of the Lord Jesus Christ.

(3) The universal need of salvation from sin and from unending woe, through the mercy and grace of God.

(4) The efficacy of the sacrifice of our Lord Jesus Christ on Calvary's cross for the world's redemption.

(5) The bodily resurrection of the Savior.

(6) The ascension into heaven of the glorified Son of God.

(7) The personal mission of the Holy Spirit for the regeneration and sanctification of believers.

(8) The living church of Christ on earth, the missionary agent for the evangelization of the world.

(9) The bodily return of the Lord Jesus, the hope of the church.

(B) To be acceptable for service with SAM, candidates must be willing to work and have fellowship with all believers committed to the foundational truths set forth in this statement.

(C) Being persuaded that no particular sign or ability is necessarily and inevitably the evidence of salvation or of Holy Spirit baptism, which we believe take place at the same time, and observing the widespread divisiveness and resultant fragmentation of Christian unity caused by the modern "charismatic movement," the South America Mission is not to be classified as "pentecostal" or "charismatic" in the contemporary definition and its personnel will not be involved in the practices commonly associated with these movements.

Notes: *The South American Mission, founded in 1914, is an Evangelical missionary sending agency. Its brief Doctrinal Statement affirms a consensus Evangelical theological perspective.*

*   *   *

STATEMENT OF FAITH (SPIRITUAL COUNTERFEITS PROJECT)

I.   We believe that the Holy Bible is the uniquely inspired Word of God and fully authoritative in matters of faith and practice.

II. We believe that there is one God, eternally existent in three persons, the Father, the Son, and the Holy Spirit, who are of one substance and equal in power and glory.

III. We believe in the historic virgin birth of Jesus the Messiah, who was both fully God and fully human; that he lived a sinless life and that he died on the cross as a sinner's substitute, shedding his blood for the remission of sin; that he rose from the dead and ascended to the right hand of God to perform the ministry of intercession; and that he shall come again, personally and visibly, to complete the eternal plan of God.

IV. We believe that man and woman were created in the image of God but through disobedience fell from a sinless state; that through the Fall, all of humanity was sentenced to eternal death; and that men and women can

**STATEMENT OF FAITH (SPIRITUAL COUNTERFEITS
PROJECT) (continued)**

be delivered from this condition by the grace of God, through faith, on the basis of the work of Christ.

V. We believe in the ministry of the Holy Spirit, the third person of the Godhead, who applies the work of Christ to men and women through justification, regeneration, and sanctification; and that he makes it possible for a person who believes in Christ to live a godly life in this present world, which is under Satan's dominion.

VI. We believe in the spiritual unity of all true believers in Christ, and that these believers, who are committed to Jesus Christ as Lord, are thus recognized as his church.

Statement of Purpose: To understand the significance of the spiritual turmoil and pluralism in our culture; to research the effects and influence of the new religions, particularly those based on Eastern philosophies; to provide a biblical perspective on the new significant religions and other movements so that the church can respond appropriately; to produce accurate and attractive resources and bring the good news of Jesus Christ to individuals and society.

Notes: *Spiritual Counterfeits Project, founded in 1973, seeks to address the pluralistic religious situation of the late twentieth century by challenging the new, Eastern, and variant Christian religions (cults) from a Christian Evangelical perspective. Its own Statement of Faith is derived from that of the National Association of Evangelicals, with the addition of affirmations on the life and work of Christ, Satan's dominion over this present world, and the Church.*

*　　　*　　　*

WHAT WE BELIEVE (SPIRITUAL GROWTH RESOURCES)

1. We believe in the verbal, plenary inspiration of the Holy Scriptures, inerrant as originally given.

2. We believe in God, who is revealed in Scripture as subsisting in three distinct Persons: Father, Son and Holy Spirit, yet One in being, essence and power.

3. We believe Jesus Christ was conceived of the Holy Spirit, born of the Virgin Mary. We believe in His deity, His sinless life, and His substitutionary death for the sins of all men. We believe in the literal, physical resurrection, of Jesus Christ and in his ascension to the right hand of the Father. We believe in the imminent coming of our Lord Jesus Christ to receive His Church unto Himself. We believe in the visible and premillennial return of the Lord Jesus Christ, with His Church, to establish His promised worldwide kingdom on earth.

4. We believe in the personality and deity of the Holy Spirit, who convicts of sin, who is the Supernatural Agent in regeneration, and who, at the moment of conversion, baptizes and seals the believer into the Body of Christ, immediately indwelling him. We believe that it is the duty and privilege of the believer to be filled with the Holy Spirit who enables, him to maintain a consistent Christian walk. We believe that the ascended Christ gives gifts through the sovereign will of the Holy Spirit for the edification and unity of the Body of Christ.

5. We believe in the creation of man by a direct act of God, and that man sinfully rebelled against his creator, and thereby became depraved and guilty before God.

6. We believe in salvation uniquely by the substitutionary atonement of Christ by grace through faith in His shed blood to accomplish man's redemption from sin and his reconciliation to God.

7. We believe in the resurrection of both the saved and the lost; they that are saved unto the resurrection of life and they that are lost unto the resurrection of damnation.

8. We believe in the spiritual unity of believers in Christ.

Notes: *Spiritual Growth Resources directs its evangelistic and training work toward cultural Christians, believers who think of themselves as Christians, but lack a direct relationship with God and/or a life of vital discipleship. Its statement of belief is derived from that of the National Association of Evangelicals, but makes additional affirmations of the inerrancy of the Bible, a premillennial second coming of Jesus, and the personality of the Holy Spirit.*

*　　　*　　　*

STATEMENT OF FAITH (SPIRITUAL WARFARE MINISTRIES)

We are an evangelical organization which stands for the primary doctrines of faith as taught in the Bible.

We believe that the Scriptures of the Old and New Testaments are the Word of God written and are therefore inerrant in the original writings. They constitute the Divine rule of Christian faith and practice.

We believe that there is only one God who is the proper object of religious worship. There are three persons in the Godhead, the Father, the Son and the Holy Spirit, undivided in essence and co-equal in power and glory.

We believe that in the person of Jesus Christ that both Divine and human natures are united so that He is truly and properly God and truly and properly man. He is the only Mediator between God and humankind and His sacrifice at Calvary made atonement available for all who believe in Him as their Savior.

We believe that all men are born sinners and as such are justly exposed to the wrath of God.

We believe that repentance toward God, faith in the Lord Jesus Christ and regeneration by the Holy Spirit are necessary to salvation.

We believe that all Christians are called to do the works of Christ here upon the earth and have been equipped by the Holy Spirit with the full range of spiritual gifts to accomplish this task.

Notes: *Spiritual Warfare Ministries specializes in fighting Satan through a ministry to people experiencing spiritual, mental or physical oppression. Its Statement of Faith affirms the inerrancy of the Bible and a consensus Evangelical theological position.*

*   *   *

DOCTRINAL POSITION (STEER, INC.)

1. We believe the Bible, consisting of Old and New Testaments, to be the only verbally inspired by the Holy Spirit, inerrant, infallible and authoritative Word of God written.

2. We believe there is one God, eternally existent in three persons: Father, Son, and Holy Ghost,

3. We believe in the deity of Christ, His virgin birth, His sinless life, His miracles, His vicarious and atoning death through His shed blood, His bodily resurrection and His ascension to the right hand of God the Father where He is now making intercession for us.

4. We believe Jesus Christ's return is imminent, and will be visible and personal.

5. We believe that Adam, created in the image of God, was tempted by Satan, the Devil, and fell. Because of Adam's sin all men have guilt imputed, are totally depraved and need to be regenerated by the Holy Spirit for salvation.

6. We believe salvation consists of the remission of sins, the imputation of Christ's righteousness and the gift of eternal life received by faith alone, apart from works.

7. We believe in the resurrection of both the saved and the lost; they that are saved unto the resurrection of everlasting life and blessedness in Heaven; and they that are lost, unto the resurrection of everlasting punishment in Hell.

8. We believe the Church, the body of Christ, consists of those who are born again and who are baptized by the Holy Spirit unto Christ at the time of regeneration.

9. We believe in the spiritual unity of all believers in Christ.

10. We believe Jesus Christ commanded the Church to go into all the world and preach the Gospel to every creature, baptizing and teaching those who believe.

Notes: *Steer, Inc., founded in 1957, is a missionary organization that raises money to invest with farmers and ranchers in foreign countries who raise livestock and crops to support mission stations. Its Doctrinal Position adopted that of the National Association of Evangelicals, but adds affirmations on the inerrancy of the Bible, Christ's heavenly role interceding for humanity, Christ's imminent and visible second coming, total human depravity, the Church, and the universal commission to missions.*

*   *   *

STATEMENT OF DOCTRINAL POSITION (TRANS WORLD RADIO)

STATEMENT OF POSITION

In keeping with our conviction of the primary importance of the Scriptures, we do not carry programming, nor do we collaborate in any activity, which in its source of content gives emphasis to human philosophy, or to any revelation, such as visions and prophecies, or to promoting sign gifts, such as the present day tongues movement and modern faith healers. God's calling to Trans World Radio remains unchanged: to proclaim to needy men everywhere the good news of salvation which He offers by grace through faith in the Lord Jesus Christ.

We believe that the Holy Spirit regenerates and baptizes believers into the body of Christ; that He seals and indwells every believer unto the day of redemption; that the gift of tongues neither was, nor is, essential to prove the presence of the Holy Spirit; nor is it an indication of deep spiritual experience. We take the position that the present movement known as the ''Charismatic Movement'' has caused division and is not in harmony with our understanding of the clear teaching of the Word of God. (Ephesians 2:8-10; Ephesians 4:5: I Corinthians 12:13)

SEPARATION

TWR believes in the concept of Biblical separation as set forth in the Scriptures, in Titus 2:11-14, I John 2:15-16, I Cor. 8:13 and Romans 1:1. We recognize that Trans World Radio missionaries are in effect extensions of their supporting churches and individuals. Our missionaries are encouraged to reflect the mores and Biblical standards of their supporting churches.

We suggest the following guidelines for separation:

(a) Is it to the glory of God? I Cor. 10:31.

(b) Is it in agreement with God's Word? Ps. 119:105.

(c) Will it cool my love for Christ? I John 2:15-16.

(d) Will it cause some brother to stumble? I Cor. 8:13.

(e) Is it redeeming the time? Eph. 5:15-18.

(f) Am I following the Lord's example? I Peter 2:12.

(g) My body is God's temple—does this really glorify God? II Cor. 6:17-19.

STATEMENT OF DOCTRINAL POSITION

We believe:

1. In one Holy, Almighty God, eternally existing in three persons, the Father, the Son and the Holy Spirit—co-eternal in being, co-identical in nature, co-equal in power and glory, each with distinct personal attributes, but without division of nature, essence or being.

   Reference: Deuteronomy 6:4, Matthew 28:19, John 1:1-2, II Corinthians 13:14, Philippians 2:6

2. In the verbal and plenary inspiration of the Old and New Testaments; that they are infallible, inerrant in the original writings, and the final authority for faith and life.

   Reference: II Timothy 3:16, II Peter 1:20-21, Matthew 5:18, John 16:12-13

3. That the Lord Jesus Christ, the eternal Son of God, without ceasing to be God, became man by the Holy Spirit and virgin birth; that He lived a sinless life on earth; that He died at Calvary as a satisfactory substitutionary sacrifice for sinners; that His body was buried in and arose from the tomb; that He ascended to Heaven and was glorified as a man at God's right hand; that He is coming again for His own and then to set up His Kingdom.

   Reference: John 1:1, Matthew 1:20-23, II Corinthians 5:21, Hebrews 1:3, Hebrews 10:12, John 16:7-11, Matthew 19:28, Matthew 25:31, II Timothy 2:8

4. That the Holy Spirit is a divine person who convicts the world of sin, of righteousness and of judgment; that He is that supernatural agent in regeneration by whom all believers are baptized into the body of Christ; that He indwells and seals them until the day of redemption.

   He is the divine teacher and helper who guides believers into all truth; it is the privilege of all believers to be filled with the Spirit.

   Reference: John 16:7-15, I Corinthians 12:13, II Corinthians 1:22, Ephesians 1:13

5. That God created man in His own image and in the state of innocency. Through Adam's transgression "sin entered into the world, and death through sin;" and, consequently, mankind inherited a corrupt nature, being born in sin and under condemnation. As soon as men are capable of moral action they become actual transgressors in thought, word and deed.

   Reference: Genesis 1:26-27, Romans 5:12, Romans 3:23, I John 1:8, Ephesians 2:3

6. That salvation is the gift of God brought to man by grace and received only through personal repentance for sin and faith in the person and the finished work and the atoning blood of Jesus Christ.

   Reference: Ephesians 1:7, 2:1-10, John 1:12

7. In the bodily resurrection of all men, the saved to eternal life and the unsaved to everlasting punishment.

   That the souls of the redeemed are, at death, absent from the body and present with the Lord where, in conscious bliss they await the first resurrection when spirit, soul, and body are reunited to be glorified forever with the Lord.

   Reference: Revelation 20, Acts 24:15, John 5:28-29, Luke 16:19-31, II Corinthians 5:8, I Thessalonians 4:14-17, I John 3:2

8. That the church universal is a spiritual organism composed of the regenerated who are baptized into that body by the Holy Spirit at the time of the new birth and that the local church, the visible manifestation of this body, has the responsibility to provide for the fellowship and edification of believers and to propagate the Gospel in all the world.

   Reference: Acts 2, I Corinthians 12:13, Ephesians 5:27, Mark 16:15

Notes: *Trans World Radio, founded in 1954, is an Evangelical missionary organization engaged in a worldwide radio and television ministry. Its Position statement affirms the inerrancy of the Bible and a consensus Evangelical theological perspective. It specifically condemns the modern Pentecostal and faith-healing movements, and while recognizing the need for separation, it also recognizes the problems in the separation decision.*

*   *   *

STATEMENT OF FAITH (UNDERGROUND EVANGELISM INTERNATIONAL)

We believe the Bible is the inspired Word of God, the supreme source of faith and practice; in the eternal Deity of Jesus Christ; in His virgin birth, in His death on Calvary as a substitute for our sins, in His bodily resurrection; that salvation comes by faith in Jesus Christ, that all men are lost apart from the saving grace found in Christ; that the Church is composed of born-again believers; in the present ministry of the Holy Spirit in people's lives; that Christians are responsible to evangelize; in the personal return of Jesus to the Earth.

Notes: *Underground Evangelism International, founded in 1960, is one of several missionary organizations that specialized in evangelism in Eastern Europe, the Soviet Union, and China during the years of the Cold War, when evangelical Christianity experienced a degree of suppressio by Communist governments. Since the end of the Cold War, Underground Evangelism International has continued to build an aggressive* *evangelism program. Its brief Statement of Faith allows it to work with a wide variety of Evangelical organizations.*

* * *

DOCTRINAL STATEMENT (UNEVANGELIZED FIELDS MISSION)

1. We believe in the Divine and verbal plenary inspiration; the inerrancy and historical accuracy of the original Scriptures and their infallibility for faith and practice.

2. We believe in the unity of the God-head and the Trinity of the persons therein—Father, Son, and Holy Spirit.

3. We believe that Jesus Christ was begotten by the Holy Spirit and born of the Virgin Mary and is true God and true man.

4. We believe in the imperative necessity of the substitutionary death of Christ and that all who believe are justified on the basis of His shed blood.

5. We believe in the total depravity of man and the absolute necessity of the new birth for individual salvation, and that all who believe are members of the Church, the Body of Christ.

6. We believe in the regenerating and sanctifying work of the Holy Spirit who indwells all believers upon their acceptance of Jesus Christ.

7. We believe in two ordinances enjoined by Christ upon all believers: Baptism and the Lord's Supper.

8. We believe in the "Blessed Hope," the rapture of the church, the personal and premillennial second coming of the Lord Jesus Christ to the earth with all His saints.

9. We believe in the resurrection of the just and the unjust, the everlasting blessedness of the saved and the everlasting damnation of the lost.

10. We believe in the will, power, and providence of God to meet our every need in His service.

Notes: *Unevangelized Fields Mission is an independent Evangelical foreign mission agency. Its Doctrinal Statement affirms the inerrancy of the Bible, total human depravity, the two ordinances of the Lord's supper and believer's baptism, and the premillennial and personal return of Jesus Christ.*

* * *

WHAT WE BELIEVE (UNITED WORLD MISSION)

United World Mission believes that the Bible is the inspired, infallible, authoritative word of God, without error in the original languages. We believe in one God manifesting Himself in three persons: Father, Son, and Holy Spirit. We believe in the deity of Christ, in His virgin birth, in His sinless life, His miracles, His vicarious and atoning death, His bodily resurrection, His ascension to the right hand of the Father, and in His personal, premillennial and imminent return. We believe that regeneration by the Holy Spirit is essential for the salvation of lost men and that this salvation is wholly of grace through faith. We believe in the present ministry of the Holy Spirit by whose indwelling men are enabled to live godly lives. We believe the Church consists of all who trust in Christ and are true believers in His atoning death. We believe in the resurrection of both the saved and the lost . . . they that are saved unto the resurrection of life, and they that are lost unto the resurrection of damnation. We believe in the spiritual unity of all believers in our Lord Jesus Christ.

Notes: *United World Mission, founded in 1946, is an Evangelical missionary sending agency. Its statement of belief is based on that of the National Association of Evangelicals, to which an affirmation of biblical inerrancy, Christ's premillennial second coming, and the Church has been added.*

* * *

WE BELIEVE (UNLIMITED POTENTIAL)

We believe. . .

- In the Holy Scriptures, accepting fully the writings of the Old and New Testaments as the very Word of God, verbally inspired in all parts and therefore wholly without error as originally given of God, altogether sufficient in themselves as our only infallible rule of faith and practice (Matt. 5:18, John 10:35, 12:42, 17:17, II Tim 3:16, II Pet. 1:21).

- In the One Triune God, who is personal, spirit, and sovereign (Mark 12:29, John 4:24, 14:9, Psa. 135:6); perfect, infinite, and eternal in His being, holiness, love, wisdom and power (Psa. 18:30, 147:5, Deut. 33:27); absolutely separate and above the world as it's Creator, yet everywhere present in the world as the Upholder of all things (Genesis 1:1, Psalm 104); self-existent and self-revealing in three distinct Persons the Father, the Son, and Holy Spirit (John 5:26, Matt. 28:19, II Corinthians 13:14) each of whom is to be honored and worshiped equally as true God (John 5:23, Acts 5:3-4).

- In the Lord Jesus Christ, who is the Second Person of the Triune God, the eternal Word and Only Begotten Son, our great God and Savior (John 1:1, 3:16, Tit. 2:13, Rom. 9:5); that, without any essential change in His divine person (Heb. 13:8), He became man by the miracle of Virgin Birth (John 1:14, Matt. 1:23), thus to continue forever as both true God and true Man, one Person with two natures (Col. 2:9, Rev. 22:16); that as Man, He was in all points tempted like as we are, yet without sin (Heb. 4:15, John 8:46); that as the perfect Lamb of God He gave himself in death upon the Cross, bearing there the sin of the world, and suffering its

WE BELIEVE (UNLIMITED POTENTIAL) (continued)

full penalty of divine wrath in our stead (Isa. 53:5-6, Matt. 20:28, Gal. 3:13, John 1:29); that He rose again from the dead and was glorified in the same body in which He suffered and died (Luke 24:36-43, John 20:25-28); that as our great High Priest He ascended into heaven, there to appear before the face of God as our Advocate and Intercessor (Heb. 4:14, 9:24, I John 2:1).

- In the Holy Spirit, who is the Third Person of the Triune God (Matt. 28:19, Acts 5:3-4), the divine Agent in nature, revelation and redemption (Gen. 1:2, Psa. 104:30, I Cor. 2:10, II Cor. 3:18); that He convicts the world of sin (John 16:8-11), regenerates those who believe (John 3:5), and indwells, empowers, guides, teaches, and sanctifies all who become children of God through Christ (I Cor. 6:19, 12:13, Eph. 4:30, 3:16, Rom. 8:14, John 14:26, I Cor. 6:11).

- In salvation by grace through faith, that salvation is the free gift of God (Rom. 3:24, 6:23), neither merited nor secured in part or in whole by any virtue or work of man (Tit. 3:5, Rom. 4:4-5, 11:16), but received only by personal faith in the Lord Jesus Christ (John 3:16, 6:28-29, Acts 16:30-31, Eph. 2:8-9), in whom all true believers have as a present possession the free gift of eternal life, a perfect righteousness, sonship in the family of God, deliverance and security from all condemnation, every spiritual resource needed for life and godliness and the divine guarantee that they shall never perish (I John 5:13, Rom. 3:22, Gal. 3:26, John 5:24, Eph. 1:3, II Pet. 1:3, John 10:27-30); that this salvation includes the whole man, spirit and soul and body (I Thess. 5:23-24); and apart from Christ there is no possible salvation (John 14:6, Acts 4:12).

- In the second coming of Christ, that his return from heaven will be personal, visible and glorious—a Blessed Hope for which we should constantly watch and pray, the time being unrevealed but always imminent (Acts 1:11, Rev. 1:7, Mark 13:33-37, Tit. 2:11-13, Rev. 22:20).

Notes: *Unlimited Potential, founded in 1980, is an evangelistic and missionary organization that uses baseball as a tool in its evangelistic work. Unlimited Potential leaders establish baseball clinics that, along with teaching the fundamentals of the game, also share faith. Its statement of belief affirms the inerrancy of the Bible and a consensus Evangelical theological position.*

*   *   *

STATEMENT OF FAITH (WALK THRU THE BIBLE MINISTRIES)

Walk Thru the Bible Ministries is a nationwide education ministry whose goal is to assist local churches in the ministry of edification. The WTB team is committed to a transdenominational and transcultural ministry through the media of seminars literature and formal educators. It is our ultimate goal to conduct these ministries on an international scope.

We believe that there is one God, eternally existing in three persons: the Father, the Son, and the Holy Spirit (Deuteronomy 6:4: 2 Corinthians 13:14). We believe that the Bible is God's written revelation to man and that it is verbally inspired, authoritative, and without error in the original manuscripts (2 Timothy 3:16; 2 Peter 1:21; John 10:35; Matthew 5:18).

We believe in the deity of Jesus Christ, His virgin birth, sinless life. miracles, death on the cross to provide for our redemption resurrection bodily ascension into heaven, present ministry of intercession for us, and His return to earth in power and glory (John 1:1.14; Luke 1:26-38; 2 Corinthians 5:21: John 6:19: Romans 3:24: Matthew 28:6; Hebrews 8:1; Hebrews 7:25; Acts 1: 11; Luke 21:27).

We believe in the personality and deity of the Holy Spirit, that He performs the miracle of the new birth in an unbeliever and indwells believers, enabling them to live a godly life (Acts 5:3.4; Titus 3:5; Romans 8:9: Ephesians 5:18; Ephesians 4:30).

We believe that man was created in the image of God, but because of sin, was alienated from God. That alienation can be removed only by accepting through faith Gods gift of salvation which was made possible by Christ's death (Genesis 1:26,27; Romans 3:23; 5:8; 8:1: John 3:16-19; 5:24; Ephesians 2:8-10).

Notes: *Walk thru the Bible Ministries, founded in 1976, produces and distributes Bible study material in the United States and abroad. Its Statement of Faith affirms the inerrancy of the Bible and a consensus Evangelical theological perspective.*

*   *   *

DOCTRINAL STATEMENT (WATCHMAN FELLOWSHIP)

We stand firmly on these basic doctrines of the historic Christian faith:

1. The Bible, inerrant as originally given, is God's verbally inspired, complete revelation to mankind.

2. There is one God, who is infinitely holy and perfect, existing eternally in the Persons of the Father, the Son, and the Holy Spirit.

3. We accept the virgin birth, earthly miracles, sinless life, substitutionary death on the cross, bodily resurrection, ascension, and literal second coming of our Lord Jesus Christ.

4. The Holy Spirit is the Divine Person sent to indwell, guide, empower, and sanctify the believer, and thus to bear witness of our Lord Jesus Christ.

5. The Church consists of all those who believe on the Lord Jesus Christ, are redeemed through His blood and are born again of the Holy Spirit.

6. There will be a resurrection of both the saved and the lost, the first to everlasting life and the second to everlasting punishment.

Notes: *Watchman Fellowship is a ministry dedicated to counter the effects of non-Christian, new religious movements (often called cults) in modern life. It operates from an Evangelical theological position that affirms the inerrancy of the Bible and the Trinity.*

*　　*　　*

STATEMENT OF BELIEF (WITNESS INC.)

We believe in:

I. The Bible as the divinely inspired, inerrant Word of God: It is in its entirety the sole authority for all matters of Christian belief and practice.

II. The one true God. In the one true God there exists three persons, being:

> The Father
> The Son Jesus Christ
> The Holy Spirit

III. Jesus Christ: His deity, humanity, virgin birth, sinlessness, death and bodily resurrection who will personally and visibly return again to earth.

IV. The personality and deity of the Holy Spirit.

V. The existence and personality of Satan, his total opposition to God, and his power over the unregenerate.

VI. The complete and total depravity of all men which makes them hopelessly lost without the new birth obtainable through faith in Jesus Christ.

VII. The final estate of man for the saved, everlasting life in the presence of God and for the unsaved, everlasting punishment because of their unbelief.

VIII. The Gospel by which we are saved being summed in the death, burial and resurrection of our Lord Jesus Christ.

IX. The Church being the Body of Christ, united in the Holy Spirit, consisting of those who have received Jesus Christ as Savior. A local church is an organized assembly of believers united for the purpose of carrying out the Great Commission of Christ.

X. The Great Commission of Christ being to preach the Gospel to all men, baptizing and discipling those who have believed.

Notes: *Witness Inc. is one of several Evangelical organizations that attempts to counter the teachings of new and non-Christian religious groups (cults). Its operates from a belief in the inerrant Bible, total human depravity, and the power of Satan over the life of those apart from Christ. The organization is similar to Personal Freedom Outreach, another counter-cult group.*

*　　*　　*

STATEMENT OF FAITH (WORLD EVANGELICAL FELLOWSHIP)

We believe in the HOLY SCRIPTURES as originally given by God, divinely inspired, infallible, entirely trustworthy; and the supreme authority in all matters of faith and conduct . . . ONE GOD, eternally existent in three persons, Father, Son, and Holy Spirit .. . our LORD JESUS CHRIST, God manifest in the flesh, His virgin birth, His sinless human life, His divine miracles, His vicarious and atoning mediatorial work, and His personal return in power and glory . . . the SALVATION of lost and sinful man through the shed blood of the Lord Jesus Christ by faith apart from works, and regeneration by the Holy Spirit . . . the HOLY SPIRIT, by whose indwelling the believer is enabled to live a holy life, to witness and work for the Lord Jesus Christ . . . the UNITY OF THE SPIRIT of all true believers, the Church, the Body of Christ . . . the RESURRECTION of both the saved and lost; they that are saved unto the resurrection of life, they that are lost unto the resurrection of damnation.

Notes: *The World Evangelical Fellowship, founded in 1951, is a missionary service agency through the development of a "world evangelical identity." It is closely associated with the National Association of Evangelicals (NAE) and is headquartered in the same building. Its Statement of Faith is adapted from that of the NAE, but has added an affirmation on the nature of the Church.*

*　　*　　*

STATEMENT OF FAITH (WORLD MISSIONS FELLOWSHIP)

1. We believe in the verbal and plenary inspiration of the Old and New Testament Scriptures, and that they are inerrant in every part in the original text. We further believe that the Bible is the supreme and final authority in faith and life.

2. We believe in one God, infinitely perfect and eternally existing in three persons: Father, Son, and Holy Spirit. All things were created by His direct act.

3. We believe that Jesus Christ was begotten by the Holy Spirit, born of the Virgin Mary, and is true God and true Man.

4. We believe that man was created in the image of God, that he sinned, and thereby incurred not only physical death, but also spiritual death, which is separation from God, and that all are born with a sinful nature, totally depraved in mind, will, and emotions.

5. We believe that the Lord Jesus Christ died for our sins according to the Scriptures, a representative and substitutionary sacrifice, and that all who repent and believe in Him are justified on the ground of His shed blood.

6. We believe in the resurrection of the crucified body of our Lord, in His ascension into Heaven, and His present life there for us as High Priest and Advocate.

7. We believe in the personal, bodily return of our Lord and Savior Jesus Christ.

8. We believe that all who receive by faith the Lord Jesus Christ are born again of the Holy Spirit and at that moment are baptized by the Holy Spirit into one body, of which Christ is the head, and thereby become the children of God. The Holy Spirit indwells, instructs, and empowers the believer for godly living and service.

9. We believe in the bodily resurrection of the just and the unjust, the everlasting blessedness of the saved, and the everlasting, conscious punishment of the lost.

Notes: *World Missions Fellowship, founded in 1946, is a service organization supporting missionary endeavors. Its Statement of Faith affirms the inerrancy of the Bible and a consensus Evangelical theological perspective.*

*   *   *

STATEMENT OF FAITH (WORLD OUTREACH FELLOWSHIP)

We believe. . . .

•   that the Bible is the written revelation of God, and the sixty-six books of the Bible thus constitute the plenary word by the Holy Spirit. We believe that the Word of God is an objective, propositional revelation, verbally inspired in every word; in the original documents absolutely inerrant, infallible, and God breathed and that it constitutes the only infallible rule of faith and practice. We believe and teach that God spoke in His written Word by a process of dual authorship, in which the Holy Spirit so superintended the human authors that, through their individual personalities and different styles of writing, they composed and recorded God's Word to man, without error in the whole or in the part.

•   that there is but one God, eternally existing in three persons; Father, Son, and Holy Spirit.

•   that the Lord Jesus Christ is the only begotten Son of God, conceived by the Holy Spirit, born of the virgin, Mary, and is true God and the true man.

•   that man was created in the image of God; that he sinned and thereby incurred not only physical death, but also spiritual death, which is separation from God. Hence, totally depraved man has inherited and possesses a sinful nature.

•   that the Lord Jesus Christ died for our sins according to the Scriptures. We believe that He freely took upon himself our human nature, yet without sin, that He honored the divine law by His personal obedience to the Father and by His death became the complete substitutionary sacrifice for the sins of the whole world, and that all who believe on Him are justified on the basis of His shed blood.

•   the resurrection of the crucified body of our Lord, in His ascension into Heaven, and that He is seated at the Father's right hand and is our advocate to the Father As High Priest and Head of His Church.

•   the "blessed hope", the personal and imminent return of our Lord Jesus Christ to receive the Church, and following the literal fulfillment of the Great Tribulation, He will return visibly to earth with His saints to reign during the millennial kingdom.

•   the bodily resurrection of the just and of the unjust; in the everlasting life of the saved with the Lord in Heaven and the everlasting conscious suffering of the unsaved with Satan, the Devil, in the Lake of Fire.

•   that a person is born again by personal faith in the Lord Jesus Christ as Savior; that at regeneration, all believers in this age are also indwelt by the Holy Spirit, baptized by the Holy Spirit into the Body of Christ and sealed by the Holy Spirit, which signifies our eternal security, unto the day of redemption.

•   the ordinance of the Lord's Supper, that it is the commemoration of His death until He comes, and should be proceeded by spiritual self examination.

•   the ordinance of ritual Baptism and practice it in the form of immersion.

•   that the Holy Spirit alone administers spiritual gifts to the Church, not to glorify Himself or the gifts by ostentatious displays, but to glorify Christ and implement His work of redeeming the lost, to build up the saints in the faith and to perfect the saints for the work of the ministry. In this respect, we teach that speaking in tongues, as a sign gift, and the working of sign miracles gradually ceased as the New Testament Scriptures were completed and their authority became established.

- the responsibility of the Church to complete the job of world evangelization and the responsibility of each believer, motivated by the Holy Spirit, to faithfully witness for the Lord Jesus Christ in order to see the Great Commission fulfilled.

As a result of our doctrinal position as recorded in this Statement of Faith, we are not Charismatic nor will be affiliated with the World and/or National Council of Churches.

Notes: *World Outreach Fellowship, founded in 1982, is a conservative Fundamentalist missionary sending agency. Its Statement of Faith includes an affirmation of biblical inerrancy and total human depravity. The Fellowship's Baptist roots are manifested in its affirmation of the two ordinances (not sacraments) of baptism by immersion and the Lord's Supper. It is opposed to Pentecostalism and the practice of speaking in tongues, and affiliation with either the (liberal Protestant) World Council of Churches or the National Council of Churches.*

* * *

STATEMENT OF FAITH (WORLDTEAM USA)

Article 1. We believe that the Scriptures, consisting of the Old and New Testaments, are fully inspired by God, and that they are inerrant in the original writings and that they are the supreme authority in faith and practice.

Article 2. We believe in the one holy, almighty God, eternally existent in three co-equal persons: Father, Son and Holy Spirit.

Article 3. We believe that Jesus Christ as the Scriptures affirm, is the eternal Son of God and Son of Man, was born of a virgin, and is Himself very God. He is one person, having two distinct natures, and shed His blood in substitutionary sacrifice when He died for our sins according to the Scriptures.

Article 4. We believe in the bodily resurrection of Jesus Christ.

Article 5. We believe in the personal, visible and premillennial return of our Lord Jesus Christ.

Article 6. We believe that the whole human race fell into sin in Adam, the head and progenitor of mankind, and that, because of sin, all men are totally depraved, at enmity with God and eternally lost.

Article 7. We believe that salvation is only by grace, a free gift of God, through faith in the shed blood of the Lord Jesus Christ.

Article 8. We believe in the final bodily resurrection of all the dead—those that are saved unto eternal life and those that are lost unto eternal damnation in the lake of fire.

Article 9. We believe in the reality and personality of Satan, the enemy of God and the destroyer of men.

Article 10. We believe that those who have never heard the gospel are lost and that it is therefore our solemn responsibility to preach the gospel to every creature.

Article 11. We believe that all Christians should walk worthy of Christ in an overcoming, victorious life provided for them on the basis of faith in His redemptive work. We believe that Christians should grow daily in grace and in knowledge of the Lord, constantly being filled with the Holy Spirit who indwells every believer.

Article 12. We believe in the Church universal, consisting only of those who are born again, the Body and Bride of Christ, evidenced today in local congregations, for whom He shall come again.

Notes: *Worldteam USA, founded in 1928, is an Evangelical missionary sending agency. Its Statement of Faith affirms the inerrancy of the Bible and a consensus Evangelical theological perspective.*

* * *

DOCTRINAL STATEMENT (WYCLIFFE BIBLE TRANSLATORS)

Members of the organization are required to adhere to the following fundamental truths:

- The divine inspiration and consequent authority of the whole canonical Scripture. This includes their being free from all manner of error in the original manuscripts.

- The doctrine of the Trinity.

- The fall of man, his consequent moral depravity and his need of regeneration.

- The atonement through the substitutionary death of Christ. The doctrine of justification by faith. The resurrection of the body, both in the case of the just and of the unjust.

- The eternal life of the saved and the eternal punishment of the lost.

Notes: *Wycliffe Bible Translators, founded in 1934, specializes in the translation of the Bible into languages yet to be translated. Its brief Doctrinal Statement affirms the inerrancy of the Bible and a consensus Evangelical theological perspective.*

* * *

STATEMENT OF FAITH (YOUNG LIFE)

PREAMBLE

All those who participate in the ongoing work and witness of the Campaign shall be in sympathy with its central purpose of proclaiming the Gospel of Jesus Christ. In order to qualify for office, members of the Board of Directors, members of the regular and volunteer Staff and professors at the Young Life Institute shall subscribe to the following articles of faith:

ARTICLE I

The Scriptures of the Old and New Testaments being given by divine inspiration, are the word of God, the final and supreme authority in all matters of faith and conduct.

ARTICLE II

In the Scriptures God reveals himself as the living and true God, Creator of all things. Perfect in love and righteous in all his ways this one God exists eternally as a Trinity of persons: the Father, the Son, and the Holy Spirit.

ARTICLE III

God made man in his image that he might have fellowship with him. Being estranged from God by his disobedience, sinful man is incapable of a right relationship to God apart from divine grace.

ARTICLE IV

The only Mediator between God and man is Jesus Christ our Lord, God's eternal Son, who as man fully shared and fulfilled our humanity in a life of perfect obedience.

ARTICLE V

By his death in our place, Jesus revealed the divine love and upheld divine justice, removing our guilt and reconciling us to God. Having risen bodily from the dead and ascended into heaven, he rules as Lord over all and intercedes for us as our great high priest.

ARTICLE VI

The Holy Spirit, through the proclamation of the gospel, renews our hearts, persuading us to repent of our sins and confess Jesus as Lord. By the same Spirit we are led to trust in divine mercy, whereby we are forgiven all our sins, justified by faith through the merit of Christ our Savior, adopted into God's family as his children and enabled so to live in the world that men may see our good works and glorify our Father who is in heaven.

ARTICLE VII

God by his word and Spirit calls sinful men into the fellowship of Christ's body. Thus he creates the one holy, catholic and apostolic church, united in the bonds of love, endowed with the gifts of the Spirit and summoned by Christ to preach the gospel and to administer the sacraments, to relieve human need and to strive for social justice.

ARTICLE VIII

God's redemptive purpose will be consummated by the return of Christ to raise the dead, judge all men and establish his glorious kingdom. Those who are apart from Christ shall be eternally separated from God's presence, but the righteous shall live and reign with him forever.

Notes: *Young Life, founded in 1941, is a service organization that sponsors work among young people throughout the year. Its Statement of Faith represents a consensus Evangelical theological perspective.*

*   *   *

THE MANILA COVENANT (YOUTH WITH A MISSION)

WE AFFIRM that our calling as a missionary fellowship is to help complete the Great Commission. We celebrate the calling of the Lord Jesus upon our mission to be involved in evangelism, training, and ministries of mercy. We renew our commitment to the Lord and to one another so that by God's grace and the empowering of the Holy Spirit we will do all God asks of us to help complete the Great Commission.

WE AFFIRM the calling of the Lord upon our mission to mobilize youth for world evangelism. We express in this covenant our commitment to see young people mobilized in great numbers for world evangelism, and youthful, exuberant world changers be given every opportunity to take roles of leadership and influence in our mission.

WE AFFIRM God's calling upon our mission to focus on reaching those who have not been reached with the gospel. We declare our desire to see tens of thousands of workers mobilized on the following nine frontiers of world evangelism: the Muslim world, the Buddhist world, the Communist world, the Hindu world, the Small Half, Nominal Christians, the Cities, the Poor and Needy, and Tribal Peoples.

WE AFFIRM the Lordship of Christ over every sphere of life. We commit ourselves to spreading the gospel of Jesus Christ in such a way that His Lordship is proclaimed over individual lives, nations, the family and home, the church in all its expressions, education, the electronic and printed media, arts and entertainment, the sports world, commerce, science & technology, government and politics. We believe that this should be done in the same spirit in which Jesus came: as a humble servant, laying down His rights and so pleasing His Father.

WE AFFIRM that God wants Youth With A Mission to be a representative of all nations of the earth, and that our staff and leadership should be comprised of races from Africa, Asia, Australasia, Latin America, Oceania, the Middle East, Europe, and North America.

WE AFFIRM our calling as a mission to love people in both word and deed in order to proclaim and demonstrate the Good News of the gospel. Personal evangelism and practical concern alike give witness to Jesus Christ. Accordingly, we will, by God's grace and mercy, proclaim the Good News and perform acts of mercy so that men and women will embrace the truth of the gospel.

WE AFFIRM the importance of doing God's work, God's way. We declare our total dependence on God for wisdom, and ask Him to reveal to us any trace of paternalism, prejudice, or triumphalism. We choose to follow the example of the Lord Jesus who gave up His rights, defending the rights of the poor, and serving those He came to minister to in righteous humility.

WE AFFIRM that God wants both young and old, male and female, in positions of leadership and responsibility in our mission.

WE AFFIRM servant leadership and the importance of being accountable and submissive in our leadership styles and attitudes. We confirm the importance of all new staff going through a period of culturally appropriate training and orientation to help prepare them for service in God's Kingdom. We express our desire for God to continually revive and invigorate our discipleship training programs to make them a source of encouragement, equipping, and empowering for Christian service.

WE AFFIRM the importance of a spirit of humility, brokenness, and godly transparency in our relationships with one another. We commit ourselves afresh to the principles of unity as described by the apostle Paul in Ephesians chapters four and five. We accept the responsibility to deal with any character weakness or cultural barrier in a manner that would be pleasing to the Lord Jesus and that would promote unity within our mission and within the whole Body of Christ.

WE AFFIRM the importance of living a biblical and balanced life. We believe that we need Christians of all theological persuasions and backgrounds in the Body of Christ. We need their godly counsel, wisdom, teaching, and help to be all that God has intended us to be.

WE AFFIRM the importance of the local church. We humbly ask God for His grace and help to enable us to multiply and build up local churches and to work as partners with them for the fulfillment of the Great Commission.

WE AFFIRM the ministry of prayer and intercession. We declare our total and utter dependance upon God and ask Him to continually revive our hearts so that we will always be a mission that intercedes for the nations and seeks God for His direction and guidance. We believe God has called our mission to build everything it does on the foundation of prayer, knowing that apart from God's leading, our best efforts will be dead works. We further declare our need for others to pray for us.

WE AFFIRM the importance of accountability between Youth With A Mission as a whole and its various bases, ministries, teams and schools. We confirm our need to be in submission to those we serve, those who are over us in the Lord, and those we work with as co-laborers. We believe that this spirit of accountability welcomes correction, encouragement, and openness in our corporate and personal lives.

WE AFFIRM the value of the individual. We commit ourselves to pursue the equipping, upbuilding, and empowering of all those God sends to us for the fulfillment of His ministry and purpose in their lives.

WE AFFIRM the ministry of hospitality, and commit ourselves to open our bases, homes, and hearts to all those God sends to us. We recognize this to be a biblical responsibility and we joyfully embrace the privilege of serving and honoring guests, teachers, fellow YWAMers, and the poor and needy through this ministry.

WE AFFIRM the importance of financial accountability. We declare that we as Youth With A Mission will live by the highest legal, spiritual, and ethical standards in our handling of finances.

WE AFFIRM that Youth With A Mission is an international movement of Christians from many denominations dedicated to presenting Jesus Christ personally to this generation, to mobilizing as many as possible to help in this task, and to the training and equipping of believers for their part in fulfilling the Great Commission. As citizens of God's Kingdom, we are called to love, worship and obey our Lord, to love and serve His body, the Church, and to present the whole gospel for the whole person throughout the world.

WE AFFIRM that the Bible is God's inspired and authoritative word, revealing that Jesus Christ is God's Son. We believe that man is created in God's image and that He has created us to have eternal life through Christ. Although all men have sinned and come short of God's glory and are eternally lost without Christ, God has made salvation possible through the death on the cross and resurrection of Jesus Christ. We believe that repentance, faith, love and obedience are necessary and fitting responses to God's initiative of grace towards us and that God desires all men to be saved and to come to the knowledge of the truth. We believe that the Holy Spirit's power is demonstrated in and through us for the accomplishing of Christ's last commandment: ''Go ye into all the world and preach the gospel to every creature.'' (Mark 16:15)

WE AFFIRM the Christian Magna Carta which believes the following basic rights are implicit in the gospel. Everyone on earth has the right to:

1. Hear and understand the gospel of Jesus Christ.

2. Have a Bible available in their own language.

3. Have a Christian fellowship available nearby, to be able to meet for fellowship regularly each week, and to have biblical teaching and worship with others in the Body of Christ.

4. Have a Christian education available for their children.

5. Have the basic necessities of life: food, water, clothing, shelter and health care.

6. Lead a productive life of fulfillment spiritually, mentally, socially, emotionally, and physically. With the help of God, I, the undersigned, commit myself, by God's grace, to fulfill this covenant and to live for His glory.

THE MANILA COVENANT (YOUTH WITH A MISSION)
(continued)

Notes: *Youth With a Mission (YWAM), founded in 1960, has developed a specialized short term missionary training and participation program that has placed thousands of young people in the mission field around the world. In 1988, 1,500 YWAM staff workers gathered in Manila, Philippines, to consider their beliefs and mission. This Covenant has become the guiding document in the continuously developing YWAM program. It affirms the organization's primary commitment to evangelize the world and mobilize Christians to engage in evangelistic work. Theologically it presents a consensus Evangelical position.*

* * *

STATEMENT OF BELIEF (SAMUEL ZWEMER INSTITUTE)

We believe in:

— the Holy Scriptures as originally given by God, divinely inspired, infallible, entirely trustworthy in all matters of faith and conduct.

— One God, eternally existent in three persons, Father, Son, and Holy Spirit.

— Our Lord Jesus Christ, God manifest in the flesh, His virgin birth, His sinless human life, His divine miracles, His vicarious and atoning death, His bodily resurrection, His ascension, His mediatorial work, and His personal return in power and glory.

— The salvation of lost and sinful man through the shed blood of the Lord Jesus Christ by faith apart from works, and regeneration by the Holy Spirit.

— The Holy Spirit, by whose indwelling the believer is enabled to live a holy life, to witness and work for the Lord Jesus Christ.

— The unity of the Spirit of all true believers, the Church, the Body of Christ.

— The resurrection of both the saved and the lost; they that are saved unto the resurrection of life; they that are lost unto the resurrection of damnation.

Notes: *The Samuel Zwemer Institute of Muslim Studies, founded in 1979, has taken a leading role in the Evangelical community as a research, planning, and information center for the evangelism of the Muslim world. Its Statement of Faith is a variation on that of the National Association of Evangelicals.*

* * *

Independent Evangelical Schools

COLLEGE DOCTRINAL STANDARD (ALASKA BIBLE COLLEGE)

We believe in one Holy God, creator of all things, eternally existing in three different persons, Father, Son, and Holy Spirit.

We believe in the Virgin Birth, in the complete deity and complete humanity of Jesus Christ uniquely joined together in one person, and in the bodily resurrection and ascension of Jesus Christ.

We believe in the deity and personality of God, the Holy Spirit. The Holy Spirit regenerates, indwells, seals, and baptizes the believer into the body of Christ at conversion. The fruit of the Spirit is evidence of His presence. The gifts of the Spirit are for the edification of the body of Christ, His Church. Since these gifts are bestowed by the Lord in order to fulfill specific purposes in God's program, we believe that when the purpose of any gift is fulfilled, that particular gift (for example, tongues, signs, miracles, etc.) ceases.

We believe the Bible is verbally inspired of God and inerrant in the original writings and is the supreme and final authority in faith and life.

We believe man was created sinless; he willfully sinned which rendered him hopelessly lost before God.

We believe that man's salvation is by grace based solely on the substitutionary atonement of Christ.

We believe in the everlasting blessedness of the saved, and the eternal punishment of all who reject our Lord Jesus Christ.

We believe in the personality and eternal punishment of Satan.

We believe that the Church of Jesus Christ is composed solely of those who have been redeemed by the blood of Christ.

We believe in the personal, imminent, and premillennial return of Jesus Christ for His redeemed ones.

We believe that the two ordinances of the local church are the Lord's Supper and believer's baptism.

Notes: *Alaska Bible College, in Glenallen, Alaska, is located in the Copper Basin, near Fairbanks, Anchorage, and Valdez, Alaska. It is an independent Evangelical school with a Baptist* *heritage. It affirms the inerrancy of the Bible and the ordinance of believer's baptism.*

*   *   *

DOCTRINE STATEMENT (APPALACHIAN BIBLE COLLEGE)

SECTION 1. We believe in one Triune God, eternally existing in three persons Father, Son, and Holy Spirit co-eternal in being, co-identical in nature, co-equal in power and glory and having the same attributes and perfections (Deuteronomy 6:4. II Corinthians 13:14).

SECTION 2. We believe the Holy Scriptures of the Old and New Testaments to be the verbally inspired Word of God, wholly inerrant in the original writing, infallible and God-breathed, the final authority for faith and life (II Timothy 3:16,17; Matthew 5:18; II Peter 1:20, John 16:12, 13).

SECTION 3. We believe that the Lord Jesus Christ, the eternal Son of God, became man, without ceasing to be God, having been conceived by the Holy Spirit and born of the Virgin Mary, in order that He might reveal God and redeem sinful men (John 1:1, 2, 14; Luke 1:35). We believe that the Lord Jesus Christ accomplished our redemption through His death on the cross as a representative substitutionary sacrifice in providing an unlimited atonement for the sins of the whole world; and that our justification is made sure by His literal, physical resurrection from the dead (Romans 3:24, 25; I Peter 2:24; Ephesians 1:7; I Peter 1:3-5). We believe that the Lord Jesus Christ ascended to heaven and is now exalted at the right hand of God where, as our High priest, he fulfills the ministry of Representative, Intercessor, and Advocate (Acts 1:9-10; Hebrews 9:24; Romans 8:34; I John 2:1-2).

SECTION 4. We believe that man was created in the image and likeness of God, but that in Adam's sin the race fell, inherited a sinful nature, and became alienated from God, and that man is totally depraved and, of himself, utterly unable to remedy his lost condition (Genesis 1:26, 27; Ephesians 2:1-3; Romans 3:22, 23; 5:12). We believe that salvation is the gift of God brought to man by grace and received by personal faith in the Lord Jesus Christ, whose precious blood was shed on Calvary for the forgiveness of our sins (Ephesians 2:8-12; John 1:12; Ephesians 1:7; I Peter 1:18,19). We believe that all the redeemed, once saved, are kept by God's power and are thus secure in Christ forever (John 6:37-40; 10:27-30; Romans 8:1, 38, 39; I Corinthians 1:4-8; I Peter 1:5). We believe it is the privilege of believers to rejoice in the assurance of their salvation through the testimony of God's Word; which, however clearly forbids the use of Christian liberty as an occasion to the flesh (Romans 13:13,14; Galatians 5:13; Titus 2:11-15).

SECTION 5. We believe that the Church, which is the body and espoused bride of Christ, is a spiritual organism made up of all born-again persons of this present age (Ephesians 1:22, 23; 5:25-27: I Corinthians 12:12, 13; II Corinthians 11:2). We

believe that the establishment and continuance of local churches is clearly taught and defined in the New Testament Scriptures.

Appalachian Bible College repudiates neo-evangelicalism which it defines as a frame of mind held by some evangelical Christians which welcomes and seeks dialogue with both theological liberals and unregenerate intellectuals for purposes of broadening religious associations, of interpreting Christianity and the Word of God, or of uniting for social action.

Notes: *Appalachian Bible College in Bradley, West Virginia, is a Fundamentalist school. Its Doctrinal Statement, which must be signed annually by each member of its board of directors and teaching staff, affirms the inerrancy of the Bible, total human depravity, and the primacy of the local church. It is strongly opposed to the alignments with theological liberalism made by Evangelicals.*

*   *   *

WHAT WE BELIEVE (BETHEL BIBLE INSTITUTE)

WE BELIEVE in the Bible, the Word of God, verbally inspired by the Holy Spirit, infallible and inerrant in the original manuscripts, and the final authority in all matters of faith and practice.

WE BELIEVE in one God existing eternally in three persons: Father, Son and Holy Spirit, equal in essence and attributes but distinct in office.

WE BELIEVE in our Lord Jesus Christ, true God and true man; in his virgin birth, his sinless life, his atoning death, his bodily resurrection, his intercession on behalf of the saints, his imminent visible and bodily return, and his final glorious reign on earth and in heaven.

WE BELIEVE in the Holy Spirit who convicts the world of sin, regenerates and baptizes the believer at his conversion, dwells within him and seals him for the day of redemption. Through Him the believer is accounted perfectly righteous before God and is progressively sanctified in his daily life.

WE BELIEVE that the human race fell in Adam, that all are therefore sinners, lost and separated from God by nature and by choice.

WE BELIEVE in redemption accomplished through the death of Christ, freely offered to everyone by grace alone through faith.

WE BELIEVE in the Church, made up of all who are regenerated in our Lord Jesus Christ. He is the head. The Church is made up of local autonomous congregations with their leaders (elders, pastors, deacons). Its members celebrate two ordinances: baptism by immersion and the Lord's Supper in remembrance of Christ's death. They are responsible to build the Church and to carry the Good News to every creature.

WHAT WE BELIEVE (BETHEL BIBLE INSTITUTE) (continued)

WE BELIEVE in the bodily resurrection of the dead, their ultimate judgement and retribution according to their works.

WE BELIEVE in eternal punishment for unbelievers and in eternal glory for the faithful.

Notes: *Bethel Bible Institute, Sherbrooke, Quebec, is an independent Evangelical Bible college that works in predominantly Roman Catholic French Canada. Its statement of belief affirms the infallibility of the Bible, church organization built around local congregations, and baptism by immersion.*

*   *   *

DOCTRINAL STATEMENT (BIOLA UNIVERSITY)

In as much as the university is interdenominational and yet theologically conservative, the Articles of Incorporation contain a doctrinal statement which is given below:

The Bible, consisting of all the books of the Old and New Testaments, is the Word of God, a supernaturally given revelation from God Himself, concerning Himself, His being, nature, character, will and purposes; and concerning man, his nature, need and duty and destiny. The Scriptures of the Old and New Testaments are without error or misstatement in their moral and spiritual teaching and record of historical facts. They are without error or defect of any kind.

There is one God, eternally existing and manifesting Himself to us in three Persons—Father, Son and Holy Spirit.

Our Lord Jesus was supernaturally conceived by the power of the Holy Spirit and born of a virgin—Mary, a lineal descendant of David. He lived and taught and wrought mighty works and wonders and signs exactly as is recorded in the four Gospels. He was put to death by crucifixion under Pontius Pilate. God raised from the dead the body that had been nailed to the cross. The Lord Jesus after His crucifixion showed Himself to be alive to His disciples, appearing unto them by the space of forty days. After this the Lord Jesus ascended into heaven, and the Father caused Him to sit at His right hand in the heavenly places, far above all rule and authority and power and dominion, and every name that is named, not only in this world, but also in that which is to come, and put all things in subjection under His feet, and gave Him to be Head over all things to the Church.

The Lord Jesus, before His incarnation, existed in the form of God, and of His own choice laid aside His divine glory and took upon Himself the form of a servant and was made in the likeness of men. In His pre-existent state He was with God and was God. He is a divine person possessed of all the attributes of Deity, and should be worshipped as God by angels and man. "In Him dwelleth all the fullness of the Godhead bodily." All the words that He spoke during His earthly life were the words of God. There is absolutely no error of any king in them, and by the words of Jesus Christ the words of all other teachers must be tested.

The Lord Jesus became in every respect a real man, possessed of all the essential characteristics of human nature.

By His death on the cross, the Lord Jesus made a perfect atonement for sin, by which the wrath of God against sinners is appeased and a ground furnished upon which God can deal in mercy with sinners. He redeemed us from the curse of the law by becoming a curse in our place. He who Himself was absolutely without sin was made to be sin on our behalf that we might become the righteousness of God in Him. The Lord Jesus is coming again to this earth, personally, bodily, and visibly, The return of our Lord is the blessed hope of the believer, and in it God's purposes of grace toward mankind will find their consummation.

The Holy Spirit is a person, and is possessed of all the distinctively divine attributes. He is God.

Man was created in the image of God, after His likeness, but the whole human race fell in the fall of the first Adam. All men, until they accept the Lord Jesus as their personal Savior, are lost, darkened in their understanding, alienated from the life of God through the ignorance that is in them, hardened in heart, morally and spiritually dead through their trespasses and sins. They cannot see, nor enter the kingdom of God until they are born again of the Holy Spirit.

Men are justified on the simple and single ground of the shed blood of Christ and upon the simple and single condition of faith in Him who shed the blood, and are born again by the quickening, renewing, cleansing work of the Holy Spirit, through the instrumentality of the Word of God.

All those who receive Jesus Christ as their Savior and their Lord, and who confess Him as such before their fellow men, become children of God and receive eternal life. They become heirs of God and joint-heirs with Jesus Christ. At death their spirits depart to be with Christ in conscious blessedness, and at the second coming of Christ their bodies shall be raised and transformed into the likeness of the body of His glory.

All those who persistently reject Jesus Christ in the present life shall be raised from the dead and throughout eternity exist in a state of conscious, unutterable, endless torment and anguish.

The Church consists of all those who, in this present dispensation, truly believe on Jesus Christ. It is the body and bride of Christ, which Christ loves and for which He has given Himself.

There is a personal devil, a being of great cunning and power. "The prince of the power of the air." "The prince of this world" "The good of this age" He can exert vast power only so far as God suffers him to do so. He shall ultimately be cast into the lake of fire and brimstone and shall be tormented day and night forever.

NOTE: This doctrinal statement, presented here as originally conceived by the founders of the organization, has been and continues to be the stated theological position of Biola University. In addition, the following explanatory notes indicate the organization's understanding and teaching position on certain points which could be subject to various interpretations.

The Scriptures are to be interpreted according to dispensational distinctives with the conviction that the return of the Lord for His Church will be premillennial, before the Tribulation, and that the millennium is to be the last of the dispensations.

The existence of the creation is not explainable apart from the roles of God as the sovereign creator and sustainer of the entire natural realm. Concepts such as theistic or threshold evolution do not adequately explain creation.

Though there may be many fillings of the Holy Spirit, there is only one baptism which occurs at the time of regeneration. God gives His gifts to His people, in His sovereignty and not on demand. The charismatic manifestations (e.g., tongues and healing) had special significance during the revelatory period of the New Testament apostolic era and are not at all a necessary special work of the Holy Spirit today.

Confession before men is viewed as a tangible fruit of salvation and not as a qualifying condition for salvation.

Teaching biblical studies for academic credit at Biola University is a complex situation. A major goal of all teaching is for the student to gain knowledge and understanding of the subject matter as well as familiarity with the methodology of the field. Such a goal is of importance here. The Scriptures, however, are considered more than academic subject matter. They are the Word of God written for the purpose of revealing God and His actions with the desire of bringing people to harmony with Him. Our acceptance of the divine nature and intent of Scripture gives ultimate meaning and direction to all studies relating to the Scriptures. Entailed in the furtherance of the divine intent of Scripture are many facets of study ranging from the practical procedures for the propagation of the Christian faith to the highly technical dimensions of critical biblical studies and philosophical theology. Throughout this diversity of endeavors and the wide variety of gifts and skills employed, however, all participants are finally engaged in a common task which may be summarily stated as the understanding, acceptance and propagation of the biblical faith.

Notes: *Biola University, La Mirada, California, grew from the Bible Institute of Los Angeles that had been founded in the early twentieth century as a West Coast version of Moody Biblical Institute. Associated with it is Talbot Theological Seminary. It has continued to identify with the independent fundamentalist cause and affirms the inerrancy of the Bible, which is to be interpreted within a dispensational framework (most familiar is that taught in the Schofield Reference Bible). Dispensationalism divides human history into a succession of periods or dispensations during which God acted in slightly different ways toward humanity. The present dispensation began with Jesus' resurrection. The school also believes in a personal devil and the eternal conscious suffering of those who reject Christ in a fiery hell. It opposes Pentecostalism and the Charismatic movement.*

*   *   *

BELIEFS (BRIERCREST BIBLE COLLEGE)

Briercrest Bible College holds to a set of *beliefs* and a set of *objectives* as follows:

1. *We believe* that the Old and New Testament Scriptures were written by chosen men of God under the inspiration of the Holy Spirit and so constitute in their entirety the inerrant Word of God. We receive the Bible, therefore, as sole and final authority in regard to Christian life and doctrine.

2. *We believe* in one sovereign, eternal God existing in three co-eternal and co-equal persons identified for us in Scripture as Father, Son, and Holy Spirit. These three share in the one essential Being and in all attributes and perfections of the Godhead.

3. *We believe* in Jesus Christ, the Son of God, perfect in His deity. We believe that He took upon Himself a complete and perfect humanity in the incarnation; that He was born of a virgin, lived a sinless life, was crucified as a sacrifice for sins and a substitute for sinners: that He was raised personally and bodily from the dead, and that He ascended to heaven where He is now seated at the right hand of God in intercession for believers. We accept Jesus Christ as King of kings, Head of the Church. and Lord of all.

4. *We believe* in the Holy Spirit who is living, personal, and divine, having no personal inferiority to the Father and the Son. We believe that the Holy Spirit indwells and gives spiritual life to every true believer, that He fills those who are submitted to His will, and motivates, activates and empowers believers in their service of God and for holy living.

5. *We believe* that man was created directly by God, without sin and in the image and likeness of God, that man fell through disobedience and willful sin, and so came under the condemnation of God. We believe that man is depraved in that every part of his personality has been affected by sin; he has a natural bias toward sin; he has an innate enmity toward God, and he cannot in any way free himself from sin and its condemnation, and therefore needs to be saved by action other than his own.

6. *We believe* that salvation has been provided by the grace of God through the substitutionary death and resurrection of Jesus Christ, and that it must be personally appropriated by the sinner through conversion consisting of repentance toward God and faith toward our Lord Jesus Christ. We believe in justification by faith and the new birth, and that the one who is justified and born again is absolved of all guilt through remission of sins, and so shall never come into condemnation, but is passed from death unto life.

BELIEFS (BRIERCREST BIBLE COLLEGE) (continued)

7. *We believe* that every Christian should live a separated life by the adoption of Scriptural principles of thought and conduct different from those of the world. We believe that the Scriptures and the indwelling Spirit of God work progressively in the heart and life of the believer effecting purity and true holiness of deed, word, and thought, as the individual submits himself to the working of God.

8. *We believe* that the Church of our Lord Jesus Christ is a spiritual body made up of all who have through faith been justified and born again, who have been baptized by the Holy Spirit into the body of Christ, and who are, therefore, indwelt by the Spirit. We believe and teach the centrality and importance of the local church as the focus of Christian fellowship and witness, and the ordinances of believer's baptism and the Lord's Supper.

9. *We believe* that the Christian Church and every individual Christian have an obligation to bear witness to the saving Gospel of Jesus Christ, and to make this Gospel known to the inhabitants of the whole world.

10. *We believe* in the personal, bodily, premillennial return of Jesus Christ.

11. *We believe* in the reality and personality of Satan who co-ordinates and motivates opposition to God, and in the real existence of both angels and demons.

12. *We believe* in the bodily resurrection of all men; that of the saved at the coming of our Lord Jesus Christ, and that of the unsaved in the day of the Great Judgment.

13. *We believe* that all those who are redeemed will enjoy a life of everlasting blessedness in the presence of the Lord Jesus Christ. We believe that all those who are unsaved are condemned to a conscious existence in everlasting death and torment.

Notes: *Briercrest College, Caronport, Saskatchewan, is an independent Evangelical school. Its Beliefs include an affirmation of the inerrancy of the Bible, the centrality of the local congregation, adult believer's baptism, and the personality of Satan. Though the statement asserts belief in the baptism of the Holy Spirit, the school is not a Pentecostal or Charismatic institution.*

*   *   *

STATEMENT OF BELIEF (BRYAN COLLEGE)

We believe:

that the holy Bible, composed of the Old and Nin God the Father, God the Son, and God the Holy Ghost, this Trinity being one God, eternally existing in three persons;

in the virgin birth of Jesus Christ; that He was born of the virgin Mary and begotten of the Holy Spirit;

that the origin of man was by fiat of God in the act of creation as related in the Book of Genesis; that he was created in the image of God; that he sinned and thereby incurred physical and spiritual death;

that all human beings are born with a sinful nature, and are in need of a Savior for their reconciliation to God;

that the Lord Jesus Christ is the only Savior, that He was crucified for our sins, according to the Scriptures, as a voluntary representative and substitutionary sacrifice, and all who believe in Him and confess Him before men are justified on the grounds of His shed blood;

in the resurrection of the crucified body of Jesus, in His ascension into Heaven, and in "that blessed hope," the personal return to this earth of Jesus Christ, and He shall reign forever;

in the bodily resurrection of all persons, judgment to come, the everlasting blessedness of the saved, and the everlasting punishment of the lost.

Notes: *Bryan College is named for politician and fundamentalist lay leader William Jennings Bryan and is located in Dayton, Tennessee, where Bryan had his famous confrontation with Clarence Darrow in a trial over Tennessee's anti-evolution law. The school is Evangelical and the faculty and staff (though not the students) must subscribe to its Statement of Belief. It affirms the inerrancy of the Bible and as might be expected, the creation of the world by God by divine fiat.*

*   *   *

DOCTRINAL STATEMENT (CANYONVIEW BIBLE COLLEGE AND SEMINARY)

The literal-intended meaning of the Bible, rightly divided dispensationally, is the basis for comprehensively understanding Biblical doctrine. Since many are accustomed to determining what schools teach on the basis of doctrinal statements, we submit the following statement pertaining to key doctrines.

THE BIBLE

The Bible is the verbally inspired Word of God in its original writings, and for all intents-and-purposes these original writings are available to us today. It is our final, absolute, and exclusive authority in the spiritual sphere (1 Cor. 2:7-12; Gal. 1:11-12; Eph. 3:2-9; 1 Thess. 2:13; 2 Tim. 3:16-17; 2 Peter 1:21).

THE GODHEAD

There is one God eternally existing in three persons: the Father, Son, and Holy Spirit (Matt. 28:19; 1 Peter 1:2; Jude 20-21).

THE PERSON OF JESUS CHRIST

He was conceived by the Holy Spirit, born of the Virgin Mary, is true God and true man, impeccable, and the only Redeemer (Matt. 1:20; Luke 1:35; John 14:9; Col. 1:14-15).

THE PERSON AND WORK OF THE HOLY SPIRIT

He is the third person of the Godhead. He convicts and calls sinners to Christ He regenerates, indwells, fills, and baptizes and seals believers in the Body of Christ (John 16:8; Rom. 8:30; Eph 1:13-14; 5:18; Titus 3:5).

TOTAL DEPRAVITY OF MAN

As a result of the Adamic Fall all men by nature are sinners, dead in trespasses and sins, hence, unable to do anything to save themselves or to please God (Rom. 3:9; 5:6, 8; 8:8; Eph. 2:1-3).

REDEMPTION

God justifies sinners by Grace through faith on the basis of the Blood of Christ. The Apostle Paul emphatically declares that in Jesus Christ we have redemption through His Blood (Rom. 3:24-25; Eph. 1:7, 2:8-9; Col. 1:14).

THE CHURCH

There is one Church, the Body of Christ, over which Jesus Christ is the sole Head. It consists of all those chosen in Christ before the creation of the world—those called by the Spirit to exercise God-given faith in the Person of Jesus Christ (Rom. 8:30; 10:17; 1 Cor. 12:13; Eph. 1:4, 22-23; 2:8).

The specific time when the Church, the Body of Christ, began historically is not revealed in the New Testament. It is clear, however, that the message presented in the Synoptic Gospels and the first eight chapters in Acts is not directed to the Body of Christ but to the nation of Israel (Matt. 3:2; 4:17; 5:17-20; 10:5-8; 25:1, 31-40; 28:18-20; Mark 16:15-18; Acts 1:3; 2:16, 38-39; 3:18-25; contrast Romans 16:25; 1 Cor. 2:7-8; Eph. 3:2-9; Col. 1:24-27; 1 Cor. 1:17; 12:13; Eph. 4:3-5).

Notes: *Canyonview Bible College and Seminary is an Evangelical school. Its Doctrinal Statement affirms the verbal inspiration of the Bible, which is dispensationally interpreted. Dispensationalism is a perspective that divides world history into a set of successive dispensations during which God acts toward humanity in slightly different ways. The present dispensation of grace began with Jesus' resurrection. The school also affirms total human depravity, the election of the saved*

before the creation of the world, and the premillennial return of Jesus Christ.

*   *   *

STATEMENT OF FAITH (COLORADO CHRISTIAN COLLEGE)

Scriptures

We believe that the Scriptures of the Old and New Testaments are verbally and plenarily inspired by God, are inerrant in the original writings, and are the infallible authority in all matters upon which they touch. We believe that the Scriptures are to be interpreted literally (by which we mean the application of normal, historical, grammatical and cultural principles of interpretation).

Trinity

We believe in one God, eternally existing in three persons, Father, Son, and Holy Spirit. These three are equal in every divine perfection and execute distinct but harmonious offices in the work of creation and redemption. We believe that the dominant purpose of God in this age and in all ages is the praise of God's glory.

God, the Father

We believe in God the Father, Creator of heaven and earth, perfect in holiness, infinite in wisdom, measureless in power. We rejoice that He concerns Himself mercifully in the affairs of men, that He hears and answers prayer, and that He saves from sin and death all who come to Him through Jesus Christ.

God, the Son, Jesus Christ

We believe in Jesus Christ, the eternal and only begotten Son of God, conceived by the Holy Spirit, born of the virgin Mary, sinless in His life, making atonement for the sin of the world by His substitutionary death on the cross. We believe in His bodily resurrection, His ascension into heaven, His present high priestly intercession for His people, His personal, imminent return for His church, and His visible premillennial second advent to this earth according to His promise.

God, the Holy Spirit

We believe in the deity and personality of the Holy Spirit, who was sent to convict the world of sin, of righteousness, and of judgment; and to regenerate, sanctify, and comfort those who believe in Jesus Christ.

We believe that every true, born-again believer in Jesus Christ has been baptized and indwelt by the Holy Spirit, and that His ministry in believers produces Christlike spiritual fruits and unity.

We believe that spiritual gifts were given to the Church according to the sovereign will of the Holy Spirit and that no

STATEMENT OF FAITH (COLORADO CHRISTIAN COLLEGE)
(continued)

spiritual gift was intended to be a necessary sign of the baptism or the filling of the Holy Spirit.

Concerning the controversial gift of tongues, we believe that tongues should be practiced only if tested and shown to be the communication of doctrinally sound information in a true language by the Holy Spirit and only if its use is strictly controlled by biblical principles.

Salvation of Man

We believe that man was created in the image of God, that he sinned in Adam, and that all men by nature and by choice are sinners having incurred not only physical death but also that spiritual death which is separation from God. We also believe that "God so loved the World that He gave His only begotten Son that whosoever believes in Him should not perish but have everlasting life." Therefore, those who by faith, apart from human merit, works or ceremonies, accept the Lord Jesus Christ as personal Savior are justified on the ground of His shed blood and become children of God. We believe in the bodily resurrection of the just and the unjust. The saved will rejoice forever in God's presence, and the lost will be forever separated from God in everlasting conscious punishment. We believe that every human being is responsible primarily to God in all matters of faith.

We believe that the finished work of Christ—His perfect life, His death, and His resurrection—has potentially provided salvation from sin, reconciliation to God and eternal life for the whole world. We believe all who are born again by the Spirit through faith in Christ as revealed in the Scriptures, are assured of their salvation from the very day they take Him to be their Savior; and that truly born-again believers, though they may be disciplined by God in this life and lose eternal rewards, can never lose their position in Christ as children of God and the promise of eternal life.

Church

We believe that the Church universal is composed of all who are united by the Holy Spirit to the risen and ascended Son of God, that by the same Spirit we are all baptized into one body, whether we be Jews or Gentiles, and thus being members one of another we are responsible to keep the unity of the spirit in the bond of peace. We believe that it is our Lord's desire that His people organize into local assemblies (churches) and gather regularly.

We believe that to these local churches were committed, for observance "till He comes," the ordinances of baptism and communion; and that God has laid upon these churches the task of persuading a lost world to accept Jesus Christ as Savior and to enthrone Him as Lord and Master. We believe that human betterment and social improvement should normally result from the response to the Gospel.

We believe that the present age of the Church involves an economy different from Old Testament Israel; that God will fulfill His promise to Israel; and that the believer today is "not under law, but under grace."

Responsibility

We believe that we are under divine obligation to contend earnestly for the faith once delivered unto the saints by proclaiming to a lost world the acceptance of Jesus Christ as Savior, and the enthroning of Him as Lord and Master in the lives of His people.

Notes: *Colorado Christian College is an independent Evangelical school. Its Statement of Faith affirms the inerrancy of the Bible, human depravity, the eternal security of the believer, the ordinances of baptism and communion (the Lord's Supper), and the imminent premillennial return of Jesus Christ.*

*   *   *

DOCTRINAL STANDARD (COLUMBIA BIBLE COLLEGE)

The teaching in Columbia Bible College is based on the great fundamentals of the Christian faith, all of which center in the person of Jesus Christ, our crucified, risen, and glorified Savior and Lord. The following, together with other Christian principles of doctrine and practice, including the affirmation of the full trustworthiness of Scripture, which in its original writing was verbally inspired and without error, shall be the basis of the faith and doctrine of the Columbia Bible College:

1. The Bible is the inspired Word of God, the written record of His supernatural revelation of Himself to man, absolute in its authority, complete in its revelation, final in its content, and without any errors in its teachings.

2. All men in their natural state are lost, alienated from God, spiritually dead: "All have sinned, and fall short of the glory of God."

3. Salvation is only by grace, a free gift of God, through faith in the Lord Jesus, who died for our sins according to the Scriptures (I Cor. 15:3). Those who thus receive Christ by faith have their sins forgiven (Eph. 1:7), their hearts cleansed (Acts 15:9), are born of the Spirit, become children of God (Jn. 1:12, 13) are made new creatures in Christ (11 Cor. 5:17).

4. God is One God, Who reveals Himself in three Persons, Father, Son, and Holy Spirit. Jesus Christ, as the Scriptures affirm, is the son of God and Son of man, was born of a virgin, and is Himself very God. The Scriptures also declare the deity and personality of the Holy Spirit.

5. Our Lord Jesus rose from the dead in the same body that was laid to rest in the tomb (Jn. 20:25-27). The bodies of all believers who die will be raised from the dead, and they will receive an incorruptible body like unto His glorious body (I Cor. 15:53; Phil. 3:21). All other men shall be raised unto "the resurrection of judgment" (Jn. 5:28, 29).

6. Christians, born of the Spirit, are to live the new life in the present power of the Spirit. "If we live by the Spirit, by the Spirit let us also walk" (Gal. 5:16-25; Col. 2:6). The Christians responsibility and his normal attitude of life is to yield himself to God (Rom. 6:13), trusting God to keep him.

7. Christian "living" includes Christian service, the winning of souls around us, and the preaching of the Gospel in the uttermost parts of the earth. In carrying on this work there is needed the supernatural power of the Holy Spirit which is granted to every believer as he yields and trusts (Acts 1:8; 1 Cor. 12:7; Eph. 3:20; Acts 5:32). And in all of this service prayer is to have the central place (Jn. 14:12-14: Eph. 6:18. 19).

8. Jesus Christ will come again to earth the second time (Heb. 9:28); personally (Acts 1:11; 1 Thess. 4:16), bodily (Acts 1:11; Col. 2:9), visibly (Matt. 26:64; Rev. 1:7). His coming will precede the age of universal peace and righteousness, foretold in the Scriptures (Matt. 24:29,30, 42: II Thess. 2:7-8 Rev. 20:1-6). (Candidates for graduation need not affirm the premillennial position.)

Notes: *Columbia Bible College and Columbia Biblical Seminary and Graduate School of Missions, Columbia, South Carolina, are independent fundamentalist schools. Its Doctrinal Statement emphasizes the inerrancy of the Bible and a consensus fundamentalist theology. The College teaches a premillennial eschatology (that Christ will return to establish his millennial kingdom on earth) but does not require its students to adhere to that perspective.*

*   *   *

STATEMENT OF FAITH (FULLER THEOLOGICAL SEMINARY)

Doctrinally the institution stands for the fundamentals of the faith as taught in Holy Scripture and handed down by the Church. Consistent with this purpose, the faculty and trustees of the Seminary acknowledge the creeds of the early church and the confessions of the Protestant communions to which they severally belong, and, among recent evangelical statements, the Lausanne Covenant (1974). Under God, and subject to biblical authority, they also bear concerted witness to the following articles, to which they subscribe, and which they hold to be essential to their ministry.

I. God has revealed himself to be the living and true God, perfect in love and righteous in all his ways; one in essence, existing eternally in the three persons of the Trinity: Father, Son and Holy Spirit.

II. God, who discloses himself to humankind through his creation, has savingly spoken in the words and events of redemptive history. This history is fulfilled in Jesus Christ, the incarnate Word, who is made known to us by the Holy Spirit is sacred Scripture.

III. Scripture is an essential part and trustworthy record of this divine self-disclosure. All the books of the Old and New Testaments, given by divine inspiration, are the written word of God, the only infallible rule of faith and practice. They are to be interpreted according to their context and purpose and in reverent obedience to the Lord who speaks through them in living power.

IV. God, by his word and for his glory, freely created the world of nothing. He made man and woman in his own image, as the crown of creation, that they might have fellowship with Him. Tempted by Satan, they rebelled against God. Being estranged from their Maker, yet responsible to Him, they became subject to divine wrath, inwardly depraved, and, apart from grace, incapable of returning to God.

V. The only Mediator between God and humankind is Christ Jesus our Lord. God's eternal Son, who, being conceived by the Holy Spirit and born of the Virgin Mary, fully shared and fulfilled our humanity in a life of perfect obedience. By his death in our stead, he revealed the divine love and upheld divine justice, removing our guilt and reconciling us to God. Having redeemed us from sin, the third day he rose bodily from the grave, victorious over death and the powers of darkness. He ascended into heaven where, at God's right hand, he intercedes for his people and rules as Lord over all.

VI. The Holy Spirit, through the proclamation of the Gospel, renews our hearts, persuading us to repent of our sins and confess Jesus as Lord. By the same Spirit we are led to trust in divine mercy, whereby we are forgiven all our sins, justified by faith alone through the merit of Christ our Savior and granted the free gift of eternal life.

VII. God graciously adopts us into his family and enables us to call him Father. As we are led by the Spirit, we grow in the knowledge of the Lord, freely keeping his commandments and endeavoring so to live in the world that all may see our good works and glorify our Father who is in heaven.

VIII. God by his word and Spirit creates the one holy catholic and apostolic church, calling sinners out of the whole human race into the fellowship of Christ's body. By the same word and Spirit, he guides and preservers for eternity that new, redeemed humanity, which, being formed in every culture, is spiritually on with the people of God in all ages.

IX. The church is summoned by Christ to offer acceptable worship to God and to serve him by preaching the Gospel and making disciples of all nations, by tending the flock through the ministry of the word and sacraments and through daily pastoral care, by striving for social justice and by relieving human distress and need.

X. God's redemptive purpose will be consummated by the return of Christ to raise the dead, to judge all people according to the deeds done in the body and to establish his glorious kingdom. The wicked shall be separated from God's presence, but the righteous, in glorious

STATEMENT OF FAITH (FULLER THEOLOGICAL SEMINARY)
(continued)

bodies, shall live and reign with him forever. Then shall the eager expectation of creation be fulfilled and the whole earth shall proclaim the glory of God who makes all things new.

Notes: *The importance of Fuller Theological Seminary cannot be underestimated. Founded in the 1940s by the first generation of conservative Protestant leaders who called themselves Evangelicals, rather than Fundamentalists, it has been more closely identified with Evangelicalism than any other institution. Thus its position on theological issues has assumed a normative and definitive role throughout the whole movement. Its Statement of Faith is significant for its sophistication, as well as the particular assertions it makes. The statement should be looked at in the context of other Evangelical statements, especially the Lausanne Covenant.*

More attuned to the Christian confession of past centuries, the statement begins with the doctrine of God, not of the Scripture. Unlike most Evangelical statements, God's love is mentioned in the first sentence of the statement, a theme highlighted again in the paragraph on Jesus Christ. The infallibility of the Bible is affirmed, but there is no mention of infallibility. Inward depravity is asserted, but the language of total depravity is avoided. God calls people, among other duties, to continue a ministry of Word and sacraments (rather than ordinances) and social justice (a topic rarely touched on by Evangelicals).

Though generally thought of as a school representing a Reformed theological tradition, almost none of the identifying traits of the Reformed and Presbyterian tradition (sovereignty of God, predestination, total depravity) appear in this statement.

*   *   *

MISSION BEYOND THE MISSION (FULLER THEOLOGICAL SEMINARY)

IMPERATIVE ONE: Go and make disciples.

OUR RESPONSE:

A. We aim to have an active part in the evangelization of the whole world.

Any list of evangelical priorities must begin with evangelism. In obedience to our Lord's Great Commission, we share with all evangelical Christians the concern that every man and woman, every boy and girl, in all the families of the earth have the opportunity to hear the good news of God's love in Jesus Christ, receive the gift of eternal life, repent of sin, make a personal commitment to Jesus as Lord and Savior, and become responsible members of Christ's church, which is his body, the company of those called by his name and sealed by his Spirit.

The growth of this church—both in numbers and in spiritual maturity—is a continual demand; we do not shrink from dedicating personnel and resources to all that encourages this growth.

We are keenly aware of the three billion human beings in our world who are not disciples of Jesus Christ and feel especially committed to share Christ's love in words and deeds with the people groups who do not yet have a viable Christian witness in their cultures. We are conscious of the pivotal role of both local and national churches as well as mission agencies in this task.

These Christian entities are themselves essential to the Gospel's outreach, because they embody the worship of the triune God and the fellowship across all human barriers which are the Gospel's aim.

We pledge ourselves, therefore, to work for the spiritual renewal and the revived vision which will empower all of us for more effective service.

B. We aim to unite the study of theology with the doing of evangelism.

Theology, our reflection on the God revealed in the Scriptures, is directly concerned with God's mission in the world.

It must be a servant of evangelism, which is a key aspect of that mission.

And it must be expressed in terms sensitive to the distinctive character of the cultures in which mission is being carried out.

Likewise, evangelism must be rooted in a mature understanding of the fundamentals of the faith: the character of God, the work of Christ, the ministry of the Spirit, the authority of the Bible, the call to worship, the obedience of faith, the place of the church, the nature of human need, the hope of a new heaven and earth.

This tie between doctrine and practice must not be severed. We as a seminary have the obligation to share in the task, as well as to develop the theological base for evangelism.

C. We aim to encourage approaches to evangelization which reflect Christ's incarnation.

Under the direction and in the power of the Holy Spirit, we must allow the truth of God's revelation to do its work in every context, free from the burdens of colonialism or racism; we must understand the social and cultural milieu of the peoples to whom the Word is brought; we must, above all, seek both to demonstrate and to proclaim the reality that the God who is loving and just has called us to worship him in spirit and in truth.

With the aid of the behavioral sciences like psychology, sociology, anthropology, history, and the study of communication, we must seek to remove all distractions or offenses that prevent people from hearing the Gospel message, except the "offense of the cross."

Methods of evangelization must not be manipulative or coercive but must be subject to the same biblical scrutiny as the content of the evangelistic message.

We must learn to live the truth of Christ and to proclaim it in a style and language that reach the deepest levels of human consciousness. The joining of head and heart in the reception of God's holy love and its transforming freedom is our goal.

IMPERATIVE TWO: Call the church of Christ to renewal.

OUR RESPONSE:

A. We aim to support the church in its manifold forms as it seeks renewal in theology, spirituality, and mission.

At heart this renewal entails growth in Christian discipleship. It seeks to lay hold of all available spiritual resources—worship, sacraments, prayer, Scripture, personal example, stewardship, godly community and service—that contribute to Christian maturity. It gladly affirms that a transformed life, both individual and corporate, is the aim of God's Spirit who indwells and empowers the church.

The Spirit's fruit renews us in Christ's image; the Spirit's gifts equip us for effective service.

With the Reformers, we affirm the urgency of calling churches, once reformed, to press on with the task of continual reformation. The power, vitality, and magnitude of the Christ who is the truth defy captivity by any confession or communion. We want to shun the common temptation to grasp parts of Christ's truth and mistake those parts for the whole.

And we, therefore, are grieved by the tendency of one part of the church to focus on social action to the neglect of evangelization and of another part to do just the opposite.

Even more, we know that every denomination, congregation, mission agency, and educational institution lives in a world that threatens its spiritual, moral, and theological integrity.

Temptation to compromise, whether knowingly or unknowingly, with the world, the flesh, and the devil is a constant reality. The secularism, materialism, and egoism which pose this threat must be unmasked as frauds in the light of the claims and demands of Jesus Christ.

The best antidote is the continual affirmation of the truth and power of the Gospel.

Our first task in this renewal is to understand and apply the teachings of our biblical faith as consistently as possible to our own institutional and personal life and ministry.

Beyond that we stand ready to serve and learn from other Christian fellowships in their attempts to center their faith, life, and mission in the whole counsel of God. Our multidenominational character, corresponding as it does to the puriform nature of the churches, enhances our ability to render such service and engage in such learning.

B. We aim to exercise responsible partnership in the evangelical movement.

We recognize the scope and variety of Christian traditions that claim the term "evangelical." We gladly count ourselves among that group of believers world-wide who commit themselves to the historic Gospel, the infallible Scripture, the trinitarian faith, the deity and humanity of Christ, the atoning power of his death and resurrection, the hope of his triumphant return, the indwelling of the Holy Spirit, the importance of personal trust in God through Christ, the primary urgency of the Christian mission to call everyone everywhere to repentance and faith, to the assurance of eternal life, and to loving service on behalf of the poor and needy.

At the same time we do not assume that evangelical purity demands an isolation from other Christians who do not share our particular heritage.

Indeed, our dedication both to world evangelization and to church renewal requires us to learn from and influence those whose beliefs differ from ours as well as to fortify those with whom we agree.

We have, on the one hand, a commitment to serve the historic Protestant denominations, part of Fuller's mission from the beginning. At times, this has led to misunderstanding by some of our fellow evangelicals. We, nonetheless, are committed to support the cause of the Gospel in all churches open to our ministry, and we rejoice in the present signs of evangelical vitality in these historic denominations.

We continue, on the other hand, to serve the contemporary evangelical movement with its expressions in specifically evangelical denominations, in Pentecostal churches, in independent congregations, and in para-parochial agencies at a time of great vitality and virtually unparalleled opportunity for mission and renewal.

Yet this is also a time when a steadfast emphasis on the message of Christ crucified and risen is jeopardized by dangers which lurk in the path of these ministries: division over issues like the precise understanding of biblical inspiration, charismatic activity, women's ordination, sacramental observances, social and political action; conflict over priorities to be given to questions like abortion, pornography, or prayer and textbook selections in public schools; disagreement in approaches to ecumenically-oriented churches and the various Catholic traditions.

The opportunities and the dangers both call for responsible action. Fuller's relationship to a host of denominations, as well as to agencies not affiliated with any one denomination, together with our varied educational programs, equips us strategically to share in the development of plans for concerted evangelical effort.

C. We aim to maintain close association with national and international ecclesiastical fellowships.

Central to God's work in our world is the forming of a people—the church. All biblical descriptions of the church point to its unity—one body, one people, one bride, one temple, one priesthood, one kingdom. We are called, therefore, to experience and affirm the unity of God's people world-wide. "One holy catholic and apostolic church" is more than a slogan; it is a reality to be entered into and enjoyed.

Therefore, we renounce sectarianism and reach out to share in the life of those organizations, both evangelical and ecumenical, which seek to express Christian unity and pursue Christian mission.

It is essential to our work as a multidenominational and multiethnic school that we take part in and learn from the ministries of these fellowships.

D. We aim to participate in conversations with churches of the Catholic traditions.

Vatican II has opened a door for dialogue between Roman Catholics and Protestants which we are eager to enter. The Evangelical-Roman Catholic Dialogue on Mission (ERCDOM) and the National Convocations of Christian Leaders, in which Fuller has played a part, have demonstrated considerable common ground in desire for effective ways to evangelize non-Christians and renew parish life.

Conversations have shown that stereotypes need correcting, experience needs sharing, and possibilities of common witness and service need exploring.

A readiness to be open to the Spirit's work among God's people must characterize our relations with Catholics of all confessions—Orthodox, Roman, and Anglican—as with all other Christians.

The unity of the church is part of its purity.

We cannot compromise our biblical convictions; that is part of our commitment to purity.

And one of those biblical convictions is that Christ has but one church.

IMPERATIVE THREE: Work for the moral health of society.

OUR RESPONSE:

A. We aim to strengthen marriage covenants and family life.

Marriage and family are the primary social orders established by God at creation and, therefore, deserve the constant care of his people. Our mission must direct itself to the positive demonstration of God's intention for marriage and the family, to the expression of the church's role as the family of God with its ministry of supportive friendship, and to the reversal of the tide of divorce and the healing of the malaise in family life.

We are bound to teach the theological truth that the bond between husband and wife is not only a gift of the Creator

who made human beings in his image as male and female, it is also a sign, a demonstration, that God has placed covenant-making at the center of life.

He wants our marriages to be illustrations of the greatest of all covenants—the Covenant between God and his people, between Christ and his church.

We dare not see marriage, then, as a merely social convenience to be enjoyed only as long as both partners are pleased with it, nor as just a biological arrangement to satisfy sexual need and to propagate the race, nor as only a psychological device to alleviate loneliness and reinforce personal identity.

In fact, viewing marriage as a divinely ordained covenant is the best way to bring joy—social, physical and emotional—to the partners in it.

We want also to teach the evangelistic importance of Christian marriage. For Christian parents to bear and nurture children and watch them become faithful disciples of Christ is a major way in which the Great Commission is fulfilled and the church of Christ extended.

We shall strive, in learning and research, to use all tools, including the resources of the behavioral sciences, to understand the current threats to family stability and the ways to counteract them.

In particular, we oppose the popular hedonistic portrayals of human sexuality, the emotional, physical and sexual violence that spouse inflicts on spouse or parent on child, the largely selfish approaches to individual well-being which vitiate our generation's efforts to make and keep covenants with their spouses and children.

At the same time we want to serve the millions among us who live as single persons. The New Testament picture of Christian love must be recaptured in our day, so that the unmarried, as persons made in God's image, can experience full dignity, loving relationships, personal fulfillment in celibacy, and the best use of their gifts and talents.

B. We aim to affirm Christ's sovereignty over every sphere of human activity.

Because Jesus Christ is Lord, no domain is exempt from his claims on and purposes for humanity. The economic impact of business, organized labor, the professions, education and government on our lives makes these spheres of influence particularly needy of the scrutiny of Christian conscience.

To brand their activities as neutral and exempt them from sin, to trust that they will automatically monitor their own moral and ethical conduct, to mark them off as territory inappropriate for Christian moral examination, to restrict the biblical message to the changing of individual hearts alone without altering the systems within which the individuals work—all of these are unacceptable, though prevalent, responses to the realities of our governmental, professional, commercial, industrial and educational enterprises.

Before we are producers or consumers, we are persons made in God's image, responsible for the doing of his will on earth as it is done in heaven.

Even though we as a charitable organization benefit substantially from the generosity of business persons and receive exemption from public taxation, we cannot close our eyes to the possible abuses in these areas. Courage, stiffened by biblical conviction, must be our posture when we suspect that integrity is lacking.

The earth is the Lord's, and we are his stewards, gifted to use God's resources for his purposes, and wholly accountable to his righteous commands.

The basic Christian premise prods believers to look to their own practices and to use all fitting means to get others to do the same in the constant care for our environment, wise use of our resources, humane treatment of personnel, concern for full employment, respect for the rights of consumers, recognition of the importance of honest work, provision of adequate training or retraining for the underskilled, refusal to exact inordinate interest, advocacy of the handicapped, the weak and the disadvantaged, elimination of racism, sexism, and ageism.

The Bible deplores unjust weights and measures; it decries the withholding of suitable wages from those who have earned them; it denounces wicked waste and cruel selfishness; it discourages a laziness that takes advantage of others; it defends the rights of the poor and strangers, widows and orphans to share in the produce of the land; it disparages violence in the settling of disputes; it honors generosity as well as diligence.

Finally, we must not neglect stewardship in our own lives or in the life of our institution.

The same compassion in the treatment of persons, the same care in the use of resources, the same integrity in all our dealings, and the same willingness to live sacrificially that we call for elsewhere must be demonstrated in our own practices.

C. We aim to offer a Christian perspective on the moral issues raised by medical technology, particularly where they touch decisions that determine life and death.

If medicine is the "logical priesthood of a materialistic society," then its ethical practices warrant special concern.

Other fields, from architecture to law, have their unique problems, but the life and death character of medical decisions with the prominent play given them in the news media and the law courts singles them out for special attention.

We thank God for all the great good wrought by medicine in the alleviation of suffering and the enrichment of life. But we must not canonize medical knowledge or assume that it has the best answers as to when life should be terminated or prolonged.

And we must bear in mind that its practitioners are no more exempt from human sinfulness than the rest of us.

In a society careless of its aged and casual toward its yet-unborn, Christian conscience must sound stern warnings against our temptation to resort to voluntary euthanasia, and to neglect or dispose of the marginal minority for the convenience of the healthy majority.

The decisions as to how, when, and for whom medical resources should be distributed and extreme medical intervention and experimentation should be employed have impact far beyond medical circles and cannot be made on technical grounds or by technical people alone.

D. We aim to study the ethics of psychological and biomedical experimentation.

As Christians we must know that not everything possible to us in science and technology ought to be done.

Human judgment may have to safeguard human life and values from human ingenuity.

Whether or not certain kinds of personal experimentation like genetic engineering or psychological manipulation should be encouraged is a matter of monumental significance for the human family, especially where we have no way of predicting the long-range results, or where the core of what it means to be human may be tampered with.

Our confidence that God is the author and giver of life, who has made human beings capable of love for each other and fellowship with him, means that we must see life in spiritual as well as physical and emotional terms.

Indeed, the most important ingredients of human existence may not be capable of medical investigation.

We insist, therefore, on the need for the participation of Christian theologians and ethicists in all discussions designed to determine public policy in the host of medical and psychological issues presently being considered.

E. We aim to weigh the impact of mass media, especially television, on the morality of our society.

We need no documentation to prove that all of us, adults and children, have been deeply affected by the mass media, especially television.

As a school founded by a pioneer radio broadcaster, we gladly salute the benefits of this impact: the Gospel has been proclaimed to millions, our understanding of other nations and cultures has been heightened, the best in drama, art, music, and sports has been projected in our living rooms, the globe has been shrunk so that news of all the world has become instantly available.

On the other hand, humans and Christian values frequently have been undermined and even assaulted by the false, often perverse, profiles of allegedly acceptable character, by the simplistic, often violent, solutions to human dilemmas, by the persistent, often misleading, advertising which fuels a compulsive consumerism, and by the flippant, often seductive, condoning of immoral conduct on the television screen and in the printed page.

The more crass dangers of the media as carriers of propaganda, displayers of violence, and exploiters of sex have rightly drawn much Christian protest. But equally dangerous are some materials that may naively be called harmless.

Television, for instance, has often dedicated its highest talents to values dubious by biblical standards: chronic problems cheaply solved; religious convictions portrayed as bigoted; the desire to acquire fed by crass commercialism; authority depicted as arbitrary and silly; false pictures painted of the ''good life''; hurtful habits pictured as esteemed behavior.

In the face of all of this, we must dedicate ourselves to bring Christian conscience to bear on the power of the media. And we must encourage talented Christian persons to enter these fields as part of the church's salt and light in the world.

F. We aim to evaluate the contributions of public and private schooling to our society.

We recognize the traditional role that the schools have played in transmitting the value of our American heritage, and we are grateful for the multitude of Christians who have served society as teachers, administrators, and trustees in our educational systems. We also acknowledge that the varieties of cultural, social, racial, and religious groups in our society pose huge difficulties to the task of conveying values to the students, while at the same time they provide magnificent opportunities for understanding the diversity of God's world.

What we find disturbing are those instances where classrooms have ceased to be at least neutral toward Christian values and have adopted secularism as a creed, propagated with zeal by teachers and administrators. This secular viewpoint may be cloaked in disregard of the basic quality of education, or sex education without moral considerations, or doctrines of unbridled individualism, or atheistic theories of evolution, or anti-Christian philosophies of history, or competitive athletics where winning at any price is the aim, or the idolization of the nation.

In such instances, Christian beliefs are being attacked and replaced by anti-Christian views of life.

Wherever this happens, our educators need to be called to account in terms of their obligation to serve the needs of their entire constituency.

In our pluralistic society, we can scarcely hope that the public schools will support Christian beliefs exclusively, as many of the fine Christian schools do. Yet sensitivity to the areas that touch the faith of the students should surely be expected of the teachers to whom we have entrusted our young.

Disturbing as well are those instances where Christian people have set up private schools whose purpose has been to escape racial integration, to inculcate narrow, sectarian interpretations of the faith, or to encourage false definitions of what it means for Christians to live separately from the world.

Despite the contribution of public and private education to American life, we ourselves as Christians must take full responsibility to guard and transmit our cherished heritage.

Christian families and fellowships should be encouraged to form cultures within the culture, counter-cultures, that teach biblical understandings of creation, history, family life, worship of God, and concern for the needs of others. Equipping persons and families to do this must be a major concern of our Christian institutions, especially our churches.

G. We aim to participate in other concerns that rightly evoke the attention of many Christians:

The security of the nation and its cherished freedoms, the criminal violence in our cities, respect for law in those places where chaos threatens, the dreadful harm done by alcoholism and drug abuse, including smoking, the cavalier attitude toward human life which has encouraged the frightening rise in abortions, the hurtful effect of pornography on our people, young and old, the promotion of homosexuality as an acceptable alternative life-style, the distorted understanding of what separation of church and state means.

IMPERATIVE FOUR: Seek peace and justice in the world.

OUR RESPONSE:

A. We aim to address with vigor the larger social issues of our time:

We want to do all we can to understand the causes of and to support basic solutions to human hunger in our world; we intend to promote peace-making in the world and to press a call for limitation of arms—nuclear and others—by the nations; we aim to combat in our own and other societies the inhumanity and injustice of racism—including anti-Semitism—sexism, and other discriminating ideologies; we wish to enlarge our care about crime to include concern for the condition of our prisons, the fairness of our judicial systems, the effectiveness of our law enforcement, and the compassion due victims of crime and their families; we plan to apply Christian principles of stewardship to our society's policies for the protection of our environment and to support the call for simpler life-styles which reflect care in the use of all the earth's resources; we desire to question a world economy which retards the development of poorer countries by perpetuating their dependence on richer ones.

B. We aim to exemplify the biblical balance which calls for respect for governmental authority yet maintains the right to question that authority when it calls for anti-Christian actions.

We evangelicals are tempted to keep quiet in those areas where responsibility to Christ and loyalty to our country may appear to come in conflict. In the face of such conflicts, we can choose among some unacceptable options: we can focus on our private responsibilities alone and leave the running of the government to the elected and appointed officials; we can endorse all that our government does because ''the powers that be are ordained by God''; we can bring over-simple answers to complex problems.

These alternatives are evasions of Christian responsibility. Human government as described in Scripture is ambiguous: it is both the divinely ordered system of Romans which punishes evil and rewards good and the many-horned beast of Revelation which crawls out of the sea to wreak havoc on the people of God.

This ambiguity means that Christians can rarely give a total ''yes'' or a blanket ''no'' to the activities of any government, though we surely can acknowledge that some governments function more justly and more humanely than others. More specifically, Christians can readily give their loyalties to governments which uphold such biblical values as freedom of worship, restraint in the use of power, exercise of justice toward all inhabitants, concern for the quality of life of the citizenry, compassion for the under-represented and disadvantaged, commitment to the keeping of the peace internationally, and enhancement of the dignity of every person.

Biblical Christians must balance a loyalty to their own nation, where God's providence has placed them, with a concern for the welfare of the human family worldwide.

Christians must speak and act wherever governmental systems rob human beings of their basic rights, especially freedom of religion; wherever selfish oppression or cruel exploitation deprive people of basic goods like food, clothing, and shelter; wherever systems prevail that perpetuate such deprivation; wherever, through the build-up and sales of weaponry—whether nuclear, biological, chemical, or conventional—military powers threaten massive destruction; wherever justice fails—whether in neglect to redress wrongs, unsound law enforcement, outmoded legislation, crippled courts, dehumanizing prisons, or uneven and inhuman punishments; wherever racial, sexual, social or religious prejudices threaten the rights of persons made and loved by God.

In all these areas of world concern, biblical people must labor or make a difference, mindful that ultimate solutions to these human inequities are in divine hands alone.

But the magnitude of the task cannot be an excuse for apathy, any more than the geographical remoteness of some of the problems can be reason for provincialism.

The Lord of the world has called us to be stewards tending to its care as well as missionaries calling for its conversion.

IMPERATIVE FIVE: Uphold the truth of God's revelation.

OUR RESPONSE:

A. We aim to summon Christians to responsible thinking as part of obedient service to Christ in our world.

All Christians are called to love the Lord with their whole persons, including their minds. We who believe in the God who is the divine Creator and the incarnate Savior and the illuminating Holy Spirit must embrace our intellectual tasks with the same total commitment with which we engage in other forms of Christian service, even though we know that aiming to love God with our mind does not guarantee that all our answers will come easy or prove right.

We must seek to pray with the Spirit and with the mind so that the Spirit will bring light to our thinking about divine truth and help us to understand and obey it.

Because there is one Lord and he is Lord of all of life, we cannot divide truth into detached compartments.

What we believe about God's revelation in creation, history, incarnation, and Scripture has an intimate relationship to all other fields of knowledge.

We dare not study Christian truth in a vacuum.

Nor dare we dodge the intellectual challenges to our Christian beliefs, no matter from what quarter they may be launched. Instead, we must declare our openness to receiving the truth from all who have labored honestly to discover it. Nonetheless, we believe that patient study of Scripture's meaning will never compromise its trustworthiness as God's revelation, nor cast doubt on the true deity of Jesus Christ.

Though any research, humanely pursued, that increases our knowledge may be a valid endeavor for a Christian, an evangelical institution has a special responsibility to center its intellectual activities in those subjects which either clarify the meaning of the Christian faith, advance its communication, or defend it against opinions hostile to it.

The precise topics or fields of concern for our institution will vary from decade to decade or even year to year. The handful described in this agenda do not begin to exhaust the list of theological topics that we shall deal with. As our Statement of Faith demonstrates, theology lies at the center of all we do. whether in preparing students for ministry or in providing support for our missiological and psychological training.

We do, however, propose to lift up some special concerns because of the serious questions being posed in our generation about basic elements of Christian belief.

As a seminary, we place our intellectual tasks at the heart of our mission. We are not embarrassed to engender fruitful controversy, face tough cases, or admit the limits to our understanding.

MISSION BEYOND THE MISSION (FULLER THEOLOGICAL SEMINARY) (continued)

Asking hard questions about our faith and its application is part of our daily duty.

B. We aim to affirm and obey the authority of Scripture, and to use all responsible means to study, interpret, and apply it.

Crucial to our evangelical faith is our understanding of the Bible. We must seek ways to grasp its inspiration and authority so that the Bible will shape the faith, life, and ministry of our students and the church at large. Part of any seminary's mission is to call Christians to faithfulness in the study of Scripture and to the obedience of all it teaches.

Particularly important is the devout use of the best techniques of historical, literary, philological, cultural, as well as theological, study of the Scriptures. Though we are rightly reluctant to embrace theological or philosophical assumptions clearly shown by rigorous and honest exegetical inquiry to be at odds with the message of Scripture itself, we cannot turn our back on any method of investigation which promises to shed light on how the various parts of Scripture were composed and what their human authors intended.

The goal of this study is to discover the Scripture's unique profitability—its capacity to teach, reprove, correct, and equip the people of God.

What we need urgently, then, is an evangelical consensus in regard to the presuppositions of Bible study and to the methods which both open up the background and meaning of the Scriptures and also honor its canonical character as the written Word of God, within whose pages the Holy Spirit reveals the living Lord.

C. We aim to affirm the biblical witness to the eternal deity and redeeming work of our Lord.

At the heart of our Christian faith stands Jesus who is the Christ of Israel, the Head of the church, the Lord of the universe.

On his person, words, and works hang the truth and meaning of what we believe in, live by, hope for.

For this reason, any evangelical theory must be centered in Christ, the Kingdom he inaugurated, and the eternal salvation he has provided. We gladly join the Christians in every era who have labored, pondered, and prayed to understand the mystery of the Word become flesh and the wonder of his gracious death, mighty resurrection, present intercession, glorious coming, and cosmic authority.

In our day, certain critical approaches to New Testament study have threatened to diminish the confidence of Christians in Jesus' historic role as the pioneer and perfecter of our faith and have sought to replace it with reconstructions that give credit for the creation of the Gospel story to the pious invention of the early church.

Furthermore, many scholars have questioned the church's historic formulations of Christ's pre-existence and have thus devalued the central Christian truth of the incarnation of God's eternal Word.

Because of their consequences for New Testament and historic Christianity, both of these reinterpretations of the faith must be challenged with all the best tools of theology—exegetical, historical, philosophical, and systematic.

D. We aim to affirm the biblical witness to the Holy Spirit and to seek his leading and empowering in our lives.

We joyfully declare that the Christian faith is grounded in the self-revelation and self-communication of the triune God, Father, Son and Holy Spirit.

We joyfully confess the Holy Spirit as the Lord, the Giver of Life, in whom we have access to the Father through the Son.

We joyfully recognize the renewing work of the Spirit in the life of the church today.

We therefore seek a fresh understanding of the Spirit of God, his role in revelation, in the ministry of Jesus, and in the ongoing life and growth of the church.

We do this in the conviction that academic study on the highest level and the Christian walk in the Spirit are complementary, not separate, activities. The call of God and the well-being of the church demand them both.

E. We aim to explore the relationships between revealed Christian truths and sciences.

Ours is an age of pluralism, relativity, and anti-supernaturalism. The behavioral (or human) sciences, especially, have raised doubts as to whether any absolutes remain. Major intellectual clashes take place wherever Christian beliefs affirm that the human family originated as God's creation and the sciences teach our emergence by chance from inferior species, wherever faith affirms the existence of universal ethical norms and the sciences insist on the cultural relativity of all morality, and wherever faith affirms that human beings are all responsible to divine authority and the sciences acknowledge no authority beyond social consensus or the laws of nature.

The tensions between the affirmations of Christian faith and the hypotheses and dogmas of the sciences calls for ongoing conversation and cooperation. Ideally all intellectual disciplines should be allies in the quest for truth.

Christian wisdom seeks both to understand the proper uses of such sciences in interpreting human existence, and to discern the limitations of methods that can only describe what human conduct is and can neither prescribe what it ought to be nor discern the ultimate purpose of human existence.

EPILOGUE.

Our is a demanding agenda.

We put it forward without a timetable because the tasks it calls for are long lasting.

We offer it without promise of full completion because it deals with the most formidable questions of human living.

We present it without pride or presumption because it sets out issues which many concerned people are addressing.

We present it not as a final document but as one which needs continual reflection and revision.

But we do put forth our agenda. We ourselves at Fuller need it to guide our thinking, shape our priorities, test our progress, rally our resources, inform our prayers.

We put it forth, first, to and for ourselves. We seek agreement about the ways in which our statements of faith and purpose can express themselves in relation to the needs of the world. We intend that our whole community—students, staff, faculty, trustees—understand what we are about, why we head the way we do, how we care so deeply about issues which otherwise might be ignored.

But we also put forward this agenda for others. We do not presume to speak for all evangelicals. But we are confident that there are many persons, agencies, institutions, and churches which have found themselves under-represented in any narrower evangelical call to action.

We shall continue at Fuller, by God's grace, to do what we must do: we shall hope, moreover, to do it better than we ever have; we shall try to do it with courage and goodwill.

We shall rejoice at every sign which points to the presence of brothers and sisters who share our concerns, and we shall places our hands and hearts alongside theirs in the effort to pursue this manifold mission, which, we believe, sounds from the call of God to his people.

And we shall seek divine resources at every turn: wisdom for discernment to choose right and do well; forgiveness for constant failure in the choosing and the doing; grace to accept every enablement that our beneficent God may send our way.

Notes: *Beyond their Statement of Faith, in 1983 the faculty of Fuller Theological Seminary issued a lengthy statement addressed to the larger Evangelical movement and published it in Christianity Today, the movement's most representative periodical. The statement, which amounted to a future agenda for research and exploration at Fuller, emphasized the role of theological education in the evangelism of the world, supported a call to church renewal, outlined a response to some major moral-ethical issues in society, and began to probe the issues raised by science for religious authority. In its call to church renewal, the seminary clearly ignored the "separation" demanded by many Fundamentalists, and committed itself to work with all branches of the Evangelical movement, and interact with Christians, including those of the Roman Catholic Church.*

The ethical imperatives are based on the claim of Christ's sovereignty over all spheres of life. Among the issues that need attention are medical technology, mass media, private school-

ing, and the global issues of hunger, racism, and economic inequalities. The lengthy list of issues is not as important as the demonstration of the school's prioritizing of a broad social concern.

The final section of the Mission statement probes the crucial Evangelical issue of Biblical authority. The Evangelical movement traces its formation to the rise of science and the controversy it caused for biblical literalists. A moral relativity has resulted from an attunement to the assertions of social scientists and biblical criticism has eroded the authority of scripture to play a normative role in society. The situation calls not for an obscurantism that ignores or merely bemoans the trends of modern times, but a creative dialogue with proponents of science. Such a dialogue should lead to a discovery of the proper contribution of science to moral and metaphysical questions and well as its limitations.

Like many Evangelical schools, Fuller has no direct denominational support, but relies on local churches that support its ministerial training mission. Mission Beyond the Mission by the Fuller faculty attempts to go beyond ministerial training and lead its Evangelical supporters to an understanding and acceptance of its intellectual task, and awaken the Evangelical movement to a broader vision of its task in the world.

*　　*　　*

STATEMENT OF FAITH (GORDON COLLEGE/ GORDON-CONWELL THEOLOGICAL SEMINARY)

I.   The sixty-six canonical books of the Bible as originally written were inspired of God, hence free from error. They constitute the only infallible guide in faith and practice. A careful translation, such as the New International Version, is sufficiently close to the original writings in text and meaning to be entitled to acceptance as the Word of God.

II. There is one God, the Creator and Preserver of all things, infinite in being and perfection. He exists eternally in three Persons: The Father, the Son and the Holy Spirit, who are of one substance and equal in power and glory.

III. Mankind created in the image of God through disobedience fell from a sinless state at the suggestion of Satan. This fall plunged mankind into a state of sin and spiritual death, and brought upon the entire race the sentence of eternal death. From this condition mankind can be saved only by the grace of God, through faith, on the basis of the work of Christ, and by the agency of the Holy Spirit.

IV. The eternally pre-existent Son became incarnate without human father, by being born of the virgin Mary. Thus in the Lord Jesus Christ divine and human natures were united in one Person, both natures being whole, perfect and distinct. To effect salvation, He lived a sinless life and died on the cross as the sinner's substitute, shedding His blood for the remission of sins. On the third day He rose from the dead in the body which had been laid on the tomb. He ascended to the right hand of the Father, where He performs the ministry of intercession. He shall come once again, personally and visibly, to complete His saving work and to consummate the eternal plan of God.

V. The Holy Spirit is the third person of the Triune God. He applies to mankind the work of Christ. By justification and adoption mankind is given a right standing before God: by regeneration, sanctification and glorification mankind's nature is renewed.

VI. The believer having turned to God in penitent faith in the Lord Jesus Christ, is accountable to God for living a life separated from sin and characterized by the fruit of the Spirit. It is the responsibility of the believer to contribute by word and deed to the universal spread of the Gospel.

VII. At the end of the age the bodies of the dead shall be raised. The righteous shall enter into full possession of eternal bliss in the presence of God, and the wicked shall be condemned to eternal death.

Notes: *Gordon College, Wenham, Massachusetts, and the associated Gordon-Conwell Theological Seminary, share a common history and Statement of Faith. The Statement presents an Evangelical consensus perspective with an emphasis on the inerrancy and authority of the Bible as the Word of God.*

*   *   *

STATEMENT OF FAITH (GRACE BIBLE COLLEGE)

The following is a condensed statement of the doctrinal position to which the Board of Directors and administration of the College is committed.

The verbal inspiration and plenary authority of the Bible in its original writings.

The eternal trinity of the godhead.

The eternal deity and spotless humanity of the Lord Jesus Christ.

The total depravity of man by nature.

Salvation by grace, through faith in the crucified and risen Christ.

The eternal security of the saved.

The personality and deity of the Holy Spirit.

The essential unity of all believers of the present dispensation as members of the one true church, the body of Christ.

The privilege and duty of all the saved to walk as children of light.

The communion of the Lord's supper as revealed through Paul for members of the body of Christ, "till He come."

The one divine baptism by which believers are made members of the body of Christ as the only baptism necessary in God's spiritual program in this dispensation of the grace of God.

The resurrection of the body.

The pretribulation rapture of the members of the body of Christ.

The personal, premillennial return of Christ to reign on earth.

The eternal punishment of the unsaved dead.

The worldwide preaching of the gospel which Paul called "my gospel," in contrast the gospel of the kingdom.

Notes: *Michigan-based Grace Bible College is an independent Evangelical Bible school. Its Statement of Faith commits the College to a belief in the authority of the Bible, total human depravity, and a premillennial dispensational eschatology. Dispensationalism teaches that human history can be divided into a series of periods or dispensations during which God works in a slightly different manner toward humanity. Humanity now lives in the dispensation of grace. In the near future, prior to a period of tribulation through which those remaining on earth will suffer, Christ will return to take the members of the church to heaven. Following the tribulation, Jesus will return to establish His kingdom on earth.*

*   *   *

ARTICLES OF FAITH (JOHN BROWN UNIVERSITY)

1. We believe the Bible to be the inspired, the only infallible, authoritative of God.

2. We believe that there is one God, eternally existent in three persons: Father, Son, and Holy Spirit.

3. We believe in the deity of our Lord Jesus Christ, in His virgin birth, in His sinless life, in His miracles, in His vicarious and atoning death through His shed blood, in His bodily resurrection, in His ascension to the right hand of the Father, and in His personal return in power and glory.

4. We believe that for the salvation of lost and sinful man regeneration by the Holy Spirit is absolutely essential.

5. We believe in the resurrection of both the saved and the lost: they that are saved unto the resurrection of life and they that are lost unto the resurrection of damnation.

6. We believe in the spiritual unity of believers in our Lord Jesus Christ.

7. We believe in the present ministry of the Holy Spirit by whose indwelling the Christian is enabled to live a godly life.

Notes: *John Brown University, Siloam Springs, Arkansas, is an independent Evangelical school. Its Articles of Faith have been adopted from the National Association of Evangelicals, although the order has been slightly rearranged. This same statement had previously been adopted by the National Association of Christian Schools.*

*　　　*　　　*

DOCTRINAL STATEMENT (LANCASTER BIBLE COLLEGE)

- The Scriptures. We believe in the Scriptures of the Old and New Testaments as verbally inspired of God and inerrant in the original writings. We believe that the inspiration extends equally and fully to all parts of the Scriptures, and that they are the supreme and final authority in faith and life. II Timothy 3:16; II Peter 1:21.

- The Godhead. We believe in one God eternally existing in three persons: The Father, The Son, and The Holy Spirit, each having precisely the same nature, attributes, and perfections, and worthy of the same worship and obedience. Matthew 28:19-20; John 1:1-4.

- Jesus Christ—His Person. We believe that Jesus Christ is true God and true man. He was eternally begotten of the Father, conceived by the power of the Holy Spirit, and born of the Virgin Mary. We believe that Jesus Christ is impeccable and unchanging. Colossians 1:16-17, Hebrews 4:15.

- Jesus Christ—His Work. We believe that the Lord Jesus Christ died for our sins as a substitutionary sacrifice, that His crucified body was raised from the dead and that He 'ascended into heaven to appear before the Father as our High Priest, Advocate, and Mediator.' I Timothy 2:5, I Peter 1:18-20; I Corinthians 15:1-3.

- The Holy Spirit. We believe that the Holy Spirit took up His abode in the world in a special sense on the Day of Pentecost, dwells in every believer, and by His baptism unites all Christians in one body, the Church universal. In this age, the Holy Spirit carries out the ministries of restraining evil in the world, convicting people of sin, righteousness, and judgment, regenerating all believers, indwelling and anointing all Christians and sealing them unto the day of redemption, baptizing into the body of Christ all who are saved, and filling each yielded believer for power and service. We believe that some gifts of the Holy Spirit are permanent and are to be used throughout the entire Church Age. Other gifts were temporary and were given in the Apostolic Age for the purpose of founding the Church. Having fulfilled their purpose, they are not necessary and thus are not given today. These include the gifts of apostleship, prophecy, miracles, healings, tongues, and the interpretation of tongues. John 14:16-17; 16:7-15; I Corinthians 6:19; 12:28-30; 13:8; Ephesians 2:22; II Thessalonians 2:7.

- Man. We believe that man was created in the image of God, that he sinned and thereby incurred not only physical death but also spiritual death, and that all human beings, the man Christ Jesus alone excepted, are born with a sinful nature, are totally depraved, and need to be born again. Romans 5:12; John 3:3-7.

- Salvation. We believe that salvation was accomplished solely by the finished work of Christ shedding His blood upon the cross, and that nothing on the part of man can avail for salvation. We believe that salvation was provided for the whole world, and that whoever believes in Jesus Christ receives the new birth, becomes a partaker of the divine nature, and thus becomes a child of God, once for all, forever. John 3:16; 10:27-30; Ephesians 2:8-9.

- The Church. We believe the Church universal consists of all those who believe on the Lord Jesus Christ, are redeemed through His blood, and are born again of the Holy Spirit. Christ is the head of the Church, called His Body. The local church is a body of believers in Christ who are joined together under recognized scriptural leadership for the worship of God, for edification through the Word of God, for prayer, fellowship, the proclamation of the Gospel and observance of. the ordinances of baptism and the Lord's Supper. We believe that any ecumenical movement or mass evangelism effort which attempts to unite believers with unbelievers is not of God. Matthew 16:16-18; Acts 2:42-47; Romans 12:5; I Corinthians 12:13; II Corinthians 6:14; I Timothy 3:15; Ephesians 1:20-23; Philippians 1:1.

- The Future. We believe in "that blessed hope," the personal, premillennial, and imminent return of Jesus Christ, in the bodily resurrection of the just and unjust, in the reward and everlasting conscious blessedness of the just, and in the Judgment and everlasting conscious punishment of the lost. I Thessalonians 4:13-18; Revelation 20:1-15; 2:1-8; Luke 16:19-26.

Notes: *Lancaster Bible College, Lancaster, Pennsylvania, is an independent Evangelical school. Its Doctrinal Statement affirms the inerrancy of the Bible, total human depravity, and the premillennial return of Jesus Christ. The school is opposed to both the contemporary Charismatic movement (which emphasizes the gifts of the Spirit) and the Ecumenical movement.*

*　　　*　　　*

DOCTRINAL STATEMENT (MANNA BIBLE INSTITUTE)

WE BELIEVE that the Scriptures of the Old and New Testament are the Word of God; that these Holy Scriptures are verbally inspired of God and inerrant in the original writings;

DOCTRINAL STATEMENT (MANNA BIBLE INSTITUTE)
(continued)

and that they are the final and supreme authority in faith and life.

WE BELIEVE in one God existing eternally in three persons: Father, Son, and Holy Spirit, equal in nature, power, and glory. We believe in the Deity of the Lord Jesus Christ; and in the Holy Spirit a Divine Person distinct from the Father and Son.

WE BELIEVE, that Jesus Christ is the eternally begotten Son, conceived of the Holy Spirit and born of the Virgin Mary; that He is true God and true man, the only Mediator between God and man.

WE BELIEVE that man was originally created in the image of God, but that through sin he brought upon himself and his posterity not only physical death, but also spiritual death which is separation from God; that all human beings by physical birth possess a sinful nature and are, therefore, sinners in thought, word, and deed; that in order to be restored to fellowship with God they must be born again of the Spirit of God.

WE BELIEVE that "Christ died for our sins according to the Scriptures"; that His death was a substitutionary atonement for our sins; and that all who believe in Him are accounted righteous before God, justified and given the title to eternal life, solely through the merit of Christ on the ground of His shed blood.

WE BELIEVE that salvation is by grace through faith and all who receive by faith the Lord Jesus Christ are born again into the family of God, quickened by the Holy Spirit, and given a new life from God and are thus eternally secure in Him.

WE BELIEVE that Jesus Christ rose bodily from the dead on the third day; that He ascended into Heaven and now sits at the right hand of God, the Father Almighty, as our High Priest and Advocate.

WE BELIEVE in the personal, bodily, and premillennial return of our Lord Jesus Christ to establish His kingdom on earth.

WE BELIEVE in the bodily resurrection of the dead, both lost and saved; the everlasting blessedness of the saved, and the eternal punishment of the lost.

WE BELIEVE that all believers are vitally united to the Body of Christ, His Church, and that it is the supreme responsibility of its members to bear witness to the saving grace and power of the Lord Jesus Christ and to make His gospel known to all men.

Notes: *Manna Bible Institute, Philadelphia, Pennsylvania, is an independent Bible school. Its Doctrinal Statement, to which*

all teachers and staff must adhere, emphasizes the inerrancy of the Bible and a consensus Evangelical theological perspective.

*   *   *

STATEMENT OF FAITH (THE MASTER'S COLLEGE)

THE HOLY SCRIPTURES.

We teach that the Bible is God's written revelation to man, and thus the sixty-six books of the Bible given to us by the Holy Spirit constitute the plenary (inspired equally in all arts) Word of God (I Corinthians 2:7-14; 2 Peter 1:20-21).

We teach that the Word of God is an objective, propositional revelation (1 Thessalonians 2:13; 1 Corinthians 2:13), verbally inspired in every word (2 Timothy 3:16), absolutely inerrant in the original documents, infallible, and God-breathed. We teach the literal, grammatical-historical interpretation of Scripture which affirms the belief that the opening chapters of Genesis present creation in six literal days (Genesis 1:31; Exodus 31:17).

We teach that the Bible constitutes the only infallible rule of faith and practice (Matthew 5:18; 24:35; John 10:35; 16:12-13; 17:17; 1 Corinthians 2:13; 2 Timothy 3:15-17; Hebrews 4:12; 2 Peter 1:20-21).

We teach that God spoke in His written Word by a process of dual authorship. The holy Spirit so superintended the Human authors that, through their individual personalities and different styles of writing, they composed and recorded God's Word to man (2 Peter 1:20-2) without error in the whole or in the part (Matthew 5:18; 2 Timothy 3:16).

We teach that, whereas there may be several applications of any given passage of Scripture, there is but one true interpretation. The meaning of Scripture is to be found as one diligently applies the literal grammatical-historical method of interpretation under the enlightenment of the Holy Spirit (John 7:17; 16:12-15; 1 Corinthians 2:7-15; 1 John 2:20). It is the responsibility of believers to ascertain carefully the true intent and meaning of Scripture, recognizing that proper application is binding on all generations. Yet the truth of Scripture stands in judgment of men; never do men stand in judgment of it.

GOD.

We teach that there is but one living and true God (Deuteronomy 6:4; Isaiah 45:5-7; 1 Corinthians 8:4), an infinite, all-knowing Spirit (John 4:24), perfect in all His attributes, one in essence, eternally existing in three Persons—Father, Son, and Holy Spirit (Matthew 28:19; 2 Corinthians 13:14)—each equally deserving worship and obedience.

GOD THE FATHER. We teach that God the Father, the first person of the Trinity, orders and disposes all things according to His own purpose and grace (Psalm 145:18-9; 1 Corinthians 8:6). He is the creator of all things (Genesis 1:1-31; Ephesians

3:9). As the only absolute and omnipotent ruler in the universe, He is sovereign in creation, providence, and redemption (Psalm 103:19; Romans 11:36). His fatherhood involves both His designation within the Trinity and His relationship with mankind. As Creator He is Father to all men (Ephesians 4:6), but He is spiritual Father only to believers (Romans 8:14; 2 Corinthians 6:18). He has decreed for His own glory all things that come to pass (Ephesians 1:11). He continually upholds, directs, and governs all creatures and events (1 Chronicles 29:11). In His sovereignty He is neither author nor approver of sin (Habakkuk 1:13; John 8:38-47), nor does He abridge the accountability of moral, intelligent creatures (1 Peter 1:17). He has graciously chosen from eternity past those whom He would have as His own (Ephesians 1:4-6); He saves from sin all who come to Him through Jesus Christ; He adopts as His own all those who come to Him; and He becomes, upon adoption, Father to His own (John 1:12; Romans 8:15; Galatians 4:5; Hebrews 12:5-9).

GOD THE SON. We teach that Jesus Christ, the second person of the Trinity, possessed all the divine excellencies, and in these He is coequal, consubstantial, and coeternal with the Father (John 10:30; 14:9).

We teach that God the Father created according to His own will, through His Son, Jesus Christ, by whom all things continue in existence and in operation (John 1:3; Colossians 1:15-17; Hebrews 1:2).

We teach that in the incarnation (God becoming man) Christ surrendered only the prerogatives of deity but nothing of the divine essence, either in degree or kind. In His incarnation, the eternally existing second person of the Trinity accepted all the essential characteristics of humanity and so became the God-man (Philippians 2:5-8, Colossians 2:9).

We teach that Jesus Christ represents humanity and deity in invisible oneness (Micah 5:2; John 5:23; 14:9-10; Colossians 2:9).

We teach that our Lord Jesus Christ was virgin born (Isaiah 7:14; Matthew 1:23, 25; Luke 1:26-35); that He was God incarnate (John 1:1, 14); and that the purpose of the incarnation was to reveal God, redeem men, and rule over God's kingdom (Psalm 2:7-9; Isaiah 9:6; John 1:29; Philippians 2:9-11; Hebrews 7:25-26; 1 Peter 1:18-19).

We teach that, in the incarnation, the second person of the Trinity laid aside His right to the full prerogatives of coexistence with God, assumed the place of a Son, and took on an existence appropriate to a servant while never divesting Himself of His divine attributes (Philippians 2:5-8).

We teach that our Lord Jesus Christ accomplished our redemption through the shedding of His blood and sacrificial death on the cross and that His death was voluntary, vicarious, substitutionary, propitiatory, and redemptive (John 10:15; Romans 3:24-25; 5:8; 1 Peter 2:24).

We teach that on the basis of the efficacy of the death of our Lord Jesus Christ, the believing sinner is freed from the punishment, the penalty, the power, and one day the very presence of sin; and that he is declared righteous, given eternal life, and adopted into the family of God (Romans 3:25; 5:8-9; 2 Corinthians 5:14-15; 1 Peter 2:24; 3:18).

We teach that our justification is made sure by His literal, physical resurrection from the dead and that He is now ascended to the right hand of the Father, where He now mediates as our Advocate and High Priest (Matthew 28:6; Luke 24:38-39; Acts 2:30-31; Romans 4:25; 8:34; Hebrews 7:25; 9:24; 1 John 2:1).

We teach that in the resurrection of Jesus Christ from the grave, God confirmed the deity of His Son and gave proof that God has accepted the atoning work of Christ on the cross. Jesus' bodily resurrection is also the guarantee of a future resurrection life for all believers (John 5:26-29; 14:19; Romans 1:4; 4:25; 6:5-10; 1 Corinthians 15:20,23).

We teach that Jesus Christ will return to receive the church, which is His body, unto Himself at the rapture and, returning with His church in glory, will establish His millennial Kingdom on earth (Acts 1:19-11; 1 Thessalonians 4:13-18; Revelation 20).

We teach that the Lord Jesus Christ is the one through whom God will judge all mankind (John 5:22-23):

   a. Believers (1 Corinthians 3:10-15; 2 Corinthians 5:10)

   b. Living inhabitants of the earth at His glorious return (Matthew 25:31-46)

   c. Unbelieving dead at the Great White Throne (Revelation 20:11-15)

As the mediator between God and man (1 Timothy 2:5), the head of His body the church (Ephesians 1:22; 5:23; Colossians 1:18), and the coming universal King who will reign on the throne of David (Isaiah 9:16; Luke 1:31-33). He is the final judge of all who fail to place their trust in Him as Lord and Savior (Matthew 25:14-46; Acts 17:30-31).

GOD THE HOLY SPIRIT. We teach that the Holy Spirit is a divine person, eternal, underived, possessing all the attributes of personality and deity including intellect (1 Corinthians 2:10-13), emotions (Ephesians 4:30), will (1 Corinthians 12:11), eternality (Hebrews 9:14), omnipresence (Psalm 139:7-10), omniscience (Isaiah 40:13-14), omnipotence (Romans 15:13), and truthfulness (John 16:13).

In all the divine attributes He is coequal and consubstantial with the Father and the Son (Matthew 28:19; Acts 5:3-4; 28:25-26; 1 Corinthians 12:4-6; 2 Corinthians 13:14; and Jeremiah 31:31-34 with Hebrews 10:15-17).

We teach that it is the work of the Holy Spirit to execute the divine will with relation to all mankind. We recognize His sovereign activity in creation (Genesis 1:2), the incarnation (Matthew 1:18), the written revelation (2 Peter 1:20-21), and the work of salvation (John 3:5-7).

We teach that a unique work of the Holy Spirit in this age began at Pentecost when He came from the Father as promised by Christ (John 14:16-17; 15:26) to initiate and complete the building of the body of Christ, which is His church (1 Corinthians 12:13). The broad scope of His divine activity includes convicting the world of sin, of righteousness, and of judgement; glorifying the Lord Jesus Christ and transforming believers into the image of Christ (John 16:7-9; Acts 1:5; 2:4; Romans 8:29; 2 Corinthians 3:18; Ephesians 2:22).

We teach that the Holy Spirit is the supernatural and sovereign agent in regeneration, baptizing all believers into the body of Christ (1 Corinthians 12:13). The Holy Spirit also indwells, sanctifies, instructs empowers them for service, and seals them into the day of redemption (Romans 8:9,2 Corinthians 3:6; Ephesians 1:13).

We teach that the Holy Spirit is the divine teacher who guided the apostles and prophets into all truth as they committed to writing God's revelation, the Bible. Every believer possesses the indwelling presence of the Holy Spirit from the moment of salvation, and it is the duty of all those born of the Spirit to be filled with (controlled by) the Spirit (John 16:13; Romans 8:9; Ephesians 5:18; 2 Peter 1:19-21; 1 John 2:20,27).

We teach that the Holy Spirit administers spiritual gifts to the church. The Holy Spirit glorifies neither Himself nor His gifts by ostentatious displays, but He does glorify Christ by implementing His work of redeeming the lost and building up believers in the most holy faith (John 16:13-14; Acts 1:8; 1 Corinthians 12:4-11; 2 Corinthians 3:18).

We teach in this respect, that God the Holy Spirit is sovereign in the bestowing of all His gifts for the perfecting of the saints today and that speaking in tongues and the working of sign miracles in the beginning days of the church were for the purpose of pointing to and authenticating the apostles as revellers of divine truth, and were never intended to be characteristic of the lives of believers (1 Corinthians 12:4-11 13:8-10; 2 Corinthians 12:12; Ephesians 4:7-12; Hebrews 2:1-4).

MAN.

We teach that man was directly and immediately created by God in His image and likeness. Man was created free of sin with a rational nature, intelligence, volition, self-determination, and moral responsibility to God (Genesis 2:7, 15-25; James 3:9).

We teach that God's intention in the creation of man was that man should glorify God, enjoy God's fellowship, live his life in the will of God, and by this accomplish God's purpose for man in the world (Isaiah 43:7; Colossians 1:16; Revelation 4:11).

We teach that in Adam's sin of disobedience to the revealed will and Word of God, man lost his innocence; incurred the penalty of spiritual and physical death; became subject to the wrath of God; and became inherently corrupt and utterly incapable of choosing or doing that which is acceptable to God apart from divine grace. With no recuperative powers to enable him to recover himself, man is hopelessly lost. Man's salvation is thereby wholly of God's grace through the redemptive work of our Lord Jesus Christ (Genesis 2:16-17; 3:1-19; John 3:36;

Romans 3:23; 6:23; 1 Corinthians 2:14; Ephesians 2:1-3; 1 Timothy 2:13-14; 1 John 1:8).

We teach that because all men were in Adam, a nature corrupted by Adam's sin has been transmitted to all men of all ages, Jesus Christ being the only exception. All men are thus sinners by nature, by choice, and by divine declaration (Psalm 14:1-3; Jeremiah 17:19; Romans 3:9-18,23; 5:10-12).

SALVATION.

We teach that salvation is wholly of God by grace on the basis of the redemption of Jesus Christ, the merit of His shed blood, and not on the basis of human merit or works (John 1:12; Ephesians 1:7; 2:8-10; 1 Peter 1:18-19).

REGENERATION. We teach that regeneration is a supernatural work of the Holy Spirit by which the divine nature and divine life are given (John 3:3-7; Titus 3:5). It is instantaneous and is accomplished solely by the power of the Holy Spirit through the instrumentality of the Word of God (John 5:24), when the repentant sinner, as enabled by the Holy Spirit, responds in faith to the divine provision of salvation. Genuine regeneration is manifested by fruits worthy of repentance as demonstrated in righteous attitudes and conduct. Good works will be its proper evidence and fruit (1 Corinthians 6:19-20; Ephesians 2:10), and will be experienced to the extent that the believer submits to the control of the Holy Spirit in his life through faithful obedience to the Word of God (Ephesians 5:17-21; Philippians 2:12b; Colossians 3:16; 2 Peter 1:4-10). This obedience causes the believer to be increasingly conformed to the image of our Lord Jesus Christ (2 Corinthians 3:18). Such a conformity is climaxed in the believer's glorification at Christ's coming (Romans 8:17; 2 Peter 1:4; 1 John 3:2-3).

ELECTION. We teach that election is the act of God by which, before the foundation of the world, He chose in Christ those whom He graciously regenerates, saves, and sanctifies (Romans 8:28-30; Ephesians 1:4-11; 2 Thessalonians 2:13; 2 Timothy 2:10; 1 Peter 1:1-2).

We teach that sovereign election does not contradict or negate the responsibility of man to repent and trust Christ as Savior and Lord (Ezekiel 18:23,32; 33:11; John 3:18-19,36; 5:40; Romans 9:22-23; 2 Thessalonians 2:10-12; Revelation 22:17). Nevertheless, since sovereign grace includes the means of receiving the gift of salvation as well as the gift itself, sovereign election will result in what God determines. All whom the Father calls to Himself will come in faith and all who come in faith the Father will receive (John 6:37-40,44; Acts 13:48; James 4:8).

We teach that the unmerited favor that God grants to totally depraved sinners is not related to any initiative of their own part nor to God's anticipation of what they might do by their own will, but is solely of His sovereign grace and mercy (Ephesians 1:4-7; Titus 3:4-7; 1 Peter 1:2).

We teach that election should not be looked upon as based merely on abstract sovereignty. God is truly sovereign but He exercise this sovereignty in harmony with His other attributes, especially His omniscience, justice, holiness, wisdom, grace, and love (Romans 9:11-16). This sovereignty will always exalt the will of God in a manner totally consistent with His character as revealed in the life of our Lord Jesus Christ (Matthew 11:25-28; 2 Timothy 1:9).

JUSTIFICATION. We teach that justification before God is an act of God (Romans 8:33) by which He declares righteous those who, through faith in Christ, repent of their sins (Luke 13:3; Acts 2:38; 3:19; 11:18; Romans 2:4; 2 Corinthians 7:10; Isaiah 55:6-7) and confess Him as sovereign Lord (Romans 10:9-10; 1 Corinthians 12:3; 2 Corinthians 4:5; Philippians 2:11). This righteousness is apart from any virtue or work of man (Romans 3:20; 4;6) and involves the placing of our sins on Christ (Colossians 2:14; 1 Peter 2:24) and the imputation of Christ's righteousness to us (1 Corinthians 1:30; 2 Corinthians 5:21). By this means God is enabled to "be just, and the justifier of the one who has faith in Jesus" (Romans 3:26).

SANCTIFICATION. We teach that every believer is sanctified (set apart) unto God by justification and is therefore declared to be holy and is therefore identified as a saint. This sanctification is positional and instantaneous and should not be confused with progressive sanctification. This sanctification has to do with the believer's standing, not his present walk or condition (Acts 20:32; 1 Corinthians 1:2, 30;6-11; 2 Thessalonians 2:13; Hebrews 2:11; 3:1; 10:10, 14; 13:12; 1 Peter 1:2).

We teach that there is also by the work of the Holy Spirit a progressive sanctification by which the state of the believer is brought closer to the standing the believer positionally enjoys through justification. Through obedience to the Word of God and the empowering of the Holy Spirit, the believer is able to live a life of increasing holiness in conformity to the will of God, becoming more and more like our Lord Jesus Christ (John 17:17,19; Romans 6:1-22; 2 Corinthians 3:18; 1 Thessalonians 4:3-4, 5:23).

In this respect, we teach that every saved person is involved in a daily conflict—the new creation in Christ doing battle against the flesh—but adequate provision is made for victory through the power of the indwelling Holy Spirit. The struggle nevertheless stays with the believer all through this earthly life and is never completely ended. All claims to the eradication of sin is not possible, but the Holy Spirit does provide for victory over sin (Galatians 5:16-25; Ephesians 4:22-24; Philippians 3:12; Colossians 3:9-10; 1 Peter 1:14-16; 1 John 3:5-9).

SECURITY. We teach that all the redeemed once saved are kept by God's power and are thus secure in Christ forever (John 5:24; 6:37-40; 10:27-30; Romans 5:9-10; 8:1, 31-39; 1 Corinthians 1:4-8; Ephesians 4:30; Hebrews 7:25; 13:5; 1 Peter 1:5; Jude 24).

We teach that it is the privilege of believers to rejoice in the assurance of their salvation through the testimony of God's Word, which however, clearly forbids the use of Christian liberty as an occasion for sinful living and carnality (Romans 6:15-22; 13:13-14; Galatians 5:13,25-26; Titus 2:11-14).

SEPARATION. We teach that separation from sin is clearly called for throughout the Old and New Testaments, and that the Scriptures clearly indicate that in the last days apostasy and worldliness shall increase (2 Corinthians 6:14-7:1; 2 Timothy 3:1-5).

We teach that out of deep gratitude for the undeserved grace of God granted to us and because our glorious God is so worthy of our total consecration, all the saved should live in such a manner as to demonstrate our adoring love to God and so as not to bring reproach upon our Lord and Savior. We also teach that separation from any association with religious apostasy, and worldly and sinful practices is commanded of us by God (Romans 12:1-2, 1 Corinthians 5:9-13; 2 Corinthians 6:14-7:1; 1 John 2:15-17; 2 John 9-11).

We teach that believers should be separated unto our Lord Jesus Christ (2 Thessalonians 1:11-12; Hebrews 12:1-2) and affirm that the Christian life is a life of obedient righteousness demonstrated by a beatitude attitude (Matthew 5:2-12) and a continual pursuit of holiness (Romans 12:1- 2 Corinthians 7:1; Hebrews 12:14; Titus 2:11-14; 1 John 3:1-10).

THE CHURCH.

We teach that all who place their faith in Jesus Christ are immediately placed by the Holy Spirit into one united spiritual body, the church (1 Corinthians 12:12-13), the bride of Christ (2 Corinthians 11:2; Ephesians 5:23-32; Revelation 19:7-8), of which Christ is the head (Ephesians 1:22; 4:15; Colossians 1:18).

We teach that the formation of the church, the body of Christ, began on the day of Pentecost (Acts 2:1-21, 38-47) and will be completed at the coming of Christ for His own at the rapture (1 Corinthians 15:51-52; 1 Thessalonians 4:13-18).

We teach that the church is thus a unique spiritual organism designed by Christ, made up of all born-again believers in this present age (Ephesians 2:11-3:6). The church is distinct from Israel (1 Corinthians 10:32), a mystery not revealed until this age (Ephesians 3:1-6; 5:32).

We teach that the establishment and continuity of local churches is clearly taught and defined in the New Testament Scriptures (Acts 14:23, 27; 20:17, 28; Galatians 1:2; Philippians 1:1; 1 Thessalonians 1:1; 2 Thessalonians 1:1) and that the members of the one scriptural body are directed to associate themselves together in local assemblies (1 Corinthians 11:18-20; Hebrews 10:25).

We teach that the one supreme authority for the church is Christ (1 Corinthians 11:3; Ephesians 1:22; Colossians 1:18) and that church leadership gifts, order, discipline, and worship are all appointed through His sovereignty as found in the Scriptures. The biblically designed officers serving under Christ and over the assembly are elders (also called bishops, pastors, and pastor-teachers; Acts 20:28; Ephesians 4:11) and deacons, both of whom must meet biblical qualifications (1 Timothy 3:1-13; Titus 1:5-9; 1 Peter 5:1-5).

We teach that these leaders lead or rule as servants of Christ (1 Timothy 5:17-22) and have His authority in directing the church. The congregation is to submit to their leadership (Hebrews 13:7,17).

We teach the importance of discipleship (Matthew 28:19-20; 2 Timothy 2:2), mutual accountability of all believers to each other (Matthew 18:5-14), as well as the need for discipline of sinning members of the congregation in accord with the standards of Scripture (Matthew 18:15-22; Acts 5:1-11 Corinthians 5:1-13; 2 Thessalonians 3:6-15; 1 Timothy 1:19-20; Titus 1:10-16).

We teach the autonomy of the local church, free from any external authority or control, with the right of self-government and freedom from the interference of any hierarchy of individuals or organizations (Titus 1:5). We teach that it is scriptural for true churches to cooperate with each other for the presentation and propagation of the faith. Local churches, however, through their pastors and their interpretation and application of Scripture, should be the sole judge of the measure and method of its cooperation. (Acts 15:19-31; 20:28; 1 Corinthians 5:4-7, 13; 1 Peter 5:1-4).

We teach that the purpose of the church is to glorify God (Ephesians 3:21) by building itself up in the faith (Ephesians 4:13-16), by instruction of the Word (2 Timothy 2:2, 15; 3:16-17), by fellowship (Acts 2:47; 1 John 1:3), by keeping the ordinances (Luke 22:19; Acts 2:38-42) and by advancing and communicating the gospel to the entire world (Matthew 28:19; Acts 1:8; 2:42).

We teach the calling of all saints to the work of service (1 Corinthians 15:58; Ephesians 4:12; Revelation 22:12).

We teach the need of the church to cooperate with God as He accomplishes His purpose in the world. To that end, He gives the church spiritual gifts. First, He gives men chosen for the purpose of equipping the saints for the work of the ministry (Ephesians 4:7-12) and He also gives unique and special spiritual abilities to each member of the body of Christ (Romans 12:5-8; 1 Corinthians 12:4-31; 1 Peter 4:10-11).

We teach that there were two kind of gifts given the early church; miraculous gifts of divine revelation and healing, given temporarily in the apostolic era for the purpose of confirming the authenticity of the Apostles' message (Hebrews 2:3-4; 2 Corinthians 12:12); and ministering gifts, given to equip believers for edifying one another. With the New Testament revelation now complete, Scripture becomes the sole test of the authenticity of a man's message, and confirming gifts of a miraculous nature are no longer necessary to validate a man or his message (1 Corinthians 13:8-12). Miraculous gifts can even be counterfeited by Satan so as to deceive even believers (1 Corinthians 13:13-14:12; Revelation 13:13-14). The only gifts in operation today are those non-revelatory equipping gifts given for edification (Romans 12:6-8).

We teach that no one possess the gift of healing today but that God does hear and answer the prayer of faith and will answer in accordance with His own perfect will for the sick, suffering, and afflicted (1 Luke 18:1-6; John 5:13-16; 1 John 5:14-15).

We teach that two ordinances have been committed to the local church; baptism and the Lord's Supper (Acts 2:38-42).

Christian baptism by immersion (Acts 8:36-39) is the solemn and beautiful testimony of a believer showing for his faith in the crucified, buried, and risen Savior, and his union with Him in death to sin and resurrection to a new life (Romans 6:1-11). It is also a sign of fellowship and identification with the visible body of Christ (Acts 2:41-42).

We teach that the Lord's Supper is the commemoration and proclamation of His death until He comes, and should be always preceded by solemn self-examination (1 Corinthians 11:28-32). We also teach that whereas the elements of communion are only representative of the flesh and blood of Christ, the Lord's Supper is nevertheless an actual communication with the risen Christ who is present in a unique way, fellow shipping with His people (1 Corinthians 10:16).

ANGELS.

HOLY ANGELS. We teach that angels are created beings and are therefore not to be worshiped. Although they are a higher order of creation than man, they are created to serve God and to worship Him (Luke 2:9-14; Hebrews 1:6-7, 14; 2:6-7; Revelation 5:11-14; 19:10; 22:9).

FALLEN ANGELS. We teach that Satan is a created angel and the author of sin. He incurred the judgment of God by rebelling against his Creator (Isaiah 14:12-17; Ezekiel 28:11-19), by taking numerous angels with him in his fall (Matthew 25:41; Revelation 12:1-14), and by introducing sin into the human race by his temptation of Eve (Genesis 3:1-5).

We teach that Satan is the open and declared enemy of God and man (Isaiah 14:13-14; Matthew 4:1-11; Revelation 12:9-10), the prince of this world who has been defeated through the death and resurrection of Jesus Christ (Romans 16:20) and that he shall be eternally punished in the lake of fire (Isaiah 14:12-17; Ezekiel 28:11-19; Matthew 25:41; Revelation 20:10).

LAST THINGS (ESCHATOLOGY).

DEATH. We teach that physical death involves no loss of our immaterial consciousness (Revelation 6:9-11), that the soul of the redeemed passes immediately into the presence of Christ (Luke 23:43; Philippians 1:23; 2 Corinthians 5:8), that there is a separation of soul and body (Philippians 1:21-24), and that, for the redeemed, such separation will continue until the rapture (1 Thessalonians 4:13-17) which initiates the first resurrection (Revelation 20:4-6), when our soul and body will be reunited to be glorified forever with our Lord (Philippians 3:21;1 Corinthians 15:35-44, 50-54). Until that time, the souls of the redeemed in Christ remain in joyful fellowship with our Lord Jesus Christ (2 Corinthians 5:8).

We teach the bodily resurrection of all men, the saved to eternal life (John 6:39; Romans 8:10-11, 19-23; 2 Corinthians 4:14), and the unsaved to judgment and everlasting punishment (Daniel 12:2; John 5:29; Revelation 20:13-15).

We teach that the souls of the unsaved at death are kept under punishment until the second resurrection (Luke 16:19-26; Revelation 20:13-15), when the soul and the resurrection body will be united (John 5:28-29). They shall then appear at the Great White Throne judgment (Revelation 20:11-15) and shall be cast into hell, the lake of fire (Matthew 25:41-46), cut off from the life of God forever (Daniel 12:2; Matthew 25:41-46; 2 Thessalonians 1:7-9).

THE RAPTURE OF THE CHURCH. We teach the personal, bodily return of our Lord Jesus Christ before the seven-year tribulation (1 Thessalonians 4:16; Titus 2:13) to translate His church from this earth (John 14:1-3; 1 Corinthians 15:51-53; Thessalonians 4:15-5:11) and, between this event and His glorious return with His saints, to reward believers according to their works (1 Corinthians 3:11-15; 2 Corinthians 5:10).

THE TRIBULATION PERIOD. We teach that immediately following the removal of the church from the earth (John 14:1-3; 1 Thessalonians 4:13-18) the righteous judgments of God will be poured out upon an unbelieving world (Jeremiah 30:7; Daniel 9:27; 12:1; 2 Thessalonians 2:7-12; Revelation 16), and that these judgments will be climaxed by the return of Christ in glory to the earth (Matthew 24:27-31; 25:31-46; 2 Thessalonians 2:7-12). At that time the Old Testament and tribulation saints will be raised and the living will be judged (Daniel 12:2-3; Revelation 20:4-6). This period includes the seventieth week of Daniel's prophecy (Daniel 9:24-27; Matthew 24:15-31; 25:31-46).

THE SECOND COMING AND THE MILLENNIAL REIGN. We teach that after the tribulation period, Christ will come to earth to occupy the throne of David (Matthew 25:31; Luke 1:31-33: Acts 1:10-11; 2:29-30) and establish His Messianic Kingdom for a thousand years on the earth (Revelation 20:1-7). During this time the resurrected saints will reign with Him over Israel and all the nations of the earth (Ezekiel 37:21-28; Daniel 7:17-22; Revelation 19:11-16). This reign will be preceded by the overthrow of the Antichrist and the False Prophet, and by the removal of Satan from the world (Daniel 7:17-27; Revelation 20:1-7).

We teach that the kingdom itself will be the fulfillment of God's promise to Israel (Isaiah 65:17-25; Ezekiel 37:21-28; Zechariah 8:1-17) to restore them to the land which they forfeited through their disobedience (Deuteronomy 28:15-68). The result of their disobedience was that Israel was temporarily set aside (Matthew 21:43; Romans 11:1-26) but will again be awakened through repentance to enter into the land of blessing (Jeremiah 31:31-34; Ezekiel 36:22-32; Romans 11:25-29).

We teach that this time of our Lord's reign will be characterized by harmony, justice, peace, righteousness, and long life (Isaiah 11: 65:17-25; Ezekiel 36:33-38), and will be brought to an end with the release of Satan (Revelation 20:7).

THE JUDGMENT OF THE LOST. We teach that following the release of Satan after the thousand year reign of Christ (Revelation 20:7), Satan will deceive the nations of the earth and gather them to battle against the saints and the beloved city, at which time Satan and his army will be devoured by fire from heaven (Revelation 20:9). Following this, Satan will be thrown into the lake of fire and brimstone (Matthew 25:41; Revelation 20:10) whereupon Christ, who is the judge of all men (John 5:22), will resurrect and judge the great and small at the Great White Throne judgment.

We teach that this resurrection of the unsaved dead to judgment will be a physical resurrection, whereupon receiving their judgement (Romans 14:10-13), they will be committed to an eternal conscious punishment in the lake of fire (Matthew 25:41; Revelation 20:11-15).

ETERNITY. We teach that after the closing of the millennium, the temporary release of Satan, and the judgment of unbelievers (2 Thessalonians 1:9; Revelation 20:7-15), the saved will enter the eternal state of glory with God, after which the elements of this earth are to be dissolved (2 Peter 3:10) and replaced with a new earth wherein only righteousness dwells (Ephesians 5:5; Revelation 20:15, 21-22). Following this, the heavenly city will come down out of heaven (Revelation 21:2) and will be the dwelling place of the saints, where they will enjoy forever fellowship with God and one another (John 17:3; Revelation 21,22). Our Lord Jesus Christ, having fulfilled His redemptive mission, will then deliver up the kingdom of God the Father (1 Corinthians 15:24-28) that in all spheres the triune God may reign forever and ever (1 Corinthians 15:28).

Notes: *The Master's College is a Fundamentalist liberal arts college founded by scholars formerly affiliated with Biola University, although it has adopted a more conservative position than its parent institution. This position is spelled out in its lengthy doctrinal statement. As might be expected, it begins with a detailed affirmation of the plenary inspiration and inerrancy of the Bible. The doctrine of God is firmly in the Calvinist tradition, emphasizing God's sovereignty, and his Fatherly status in a spiritual sense extending only to preordained believers. The school is opposed to Pentecostalism. Human depravity and God's election of those to be saved is affirmed. Separation from all forms of "religions apostasy." Pentecostalism is denounced and it is assumed that no one has the biblical "gift of healing." Baptist roots are evident in the centrality assigned to the local congregations and the advocacy of two ordinances (rather than sacraments), baptism (by immersion) and the Lord's Supper.*

The statement closes with a very detailed presentation of beliefs on eschatology (last things). It advocates the premillennial position that Christ is to return prior to His establishing a millennial (thousand-year) kingdom on earth.

* * *

DOCTRINAL STATEMENT (MIAMI CHRISTIAN COLLEGE)

1. We believe that God is the one true and living God existing eternally, as three persons, Father, Son, and Holy Spirit; and that He is a Spirit, infinite, eternal, unchangeable in His love, mercy, power, wisdom, and righteousness (Isaiah 45:22, 40:25, 26; John 4:24, II Corinthians 13:14).

2. We believe that the Lord Jesus Christ is the Son of God; that He became incarnate through His virgin birth; that He is perfect both in His deity and humanity; that He willing-

DOCTRINAL STATEMENT (MIAMI CHRISTIAN COLLEGE)
(continued)

ly gave His life as the perfect and all-sufficient substitutionary sacrifice for the sins of man; that He arose from the dead in His physical, glorified body with which He is now seated in Heaven, making intercession for believers; and that He is coming again in His glorified body to establish His kingdom (Matt. 1:18-25; John 1:14; Col. 1:15-18; 1 Peter 2:24; Luke 24; Heb. 4:14; Matt. 25:31-46).

3. We believe that the Holy Spirit is equal in every attribute of deity with God the Father and with God the Son; that He performs the miracle of the new birth in those receiving Christ as Savior and is resident now in believers; that He seals them unto the day of redemption; and that He empowers them for service (I Corinthians 12:12, 13; 6:19; Ephesians 4:30; Acts 1:5; Titus 3:5).

4. We believe that the Bible is God's written revelation to man, verbally inspired and inerrant in the original manuscripts. The Bible is the supreme and final authority in all matters of faith and practice (II Timothy 3:15-17; II Peter 1:20, 21; Matthew 5:18).

5. We believe in the spiritual unity of all believers and that the church exists for fellowship, edification, and for communicating the gospel to all by means of Christian life and witness (Matt. 28:19-20; Acts 1:6-8; 2:41-42; I Cor. 12:13).

6. We believe that man was created in the image of God, but through Adam's sin became alienated from God and is condemned to eternal punishment. The only remedy for man's condition is salvation by personal faith in the person and work of Jesus Christ (John 3:15-18; Ephesians 1:17; Romans 10:9-10).

7. We believe that finite supernatural personal beings exist, including both unfallen angels and fallen angels (demons). Satan, the leader of fallen angels, is the open and declared enemy of god and man, and is doomed to the Lake of Fire (Hebrews 1:4-14; Jude 6; Matthew 25:41; Revelation 20:10).

8. We believe in the resurrection of both the saved and the lost; they that are saved to eternal life, and they that are lost to eternal damnation (I Corinthians 15; Daniel 12:1-2; John 5:28-29; II Thessalonians 1:7-10).

Notes: *Miami Christian College, Miami, Florida, is an independent Evangelical school. Its Doctrinal Statement is derived from that of the National Association of Evangelicals, although it has a different arrangement and additional phrases*

and biblical references have been added. There is also a new statement on the existence of angels, demons, and Satan.

* * *

STATEMENT OF FAITH (MILLAR MEMORIAL BIBLE INSTITUTE)

1. The divine inspiration, inerrancy and consequent authority of the whole canonical Scriptures.

2. The one living and true God, existing eternally in three equal persons, Father, Son, and Holy Spirit.

3. The deity of the Lord Jesus Christ. His virgin birth. His true humanity, bodily resurrection, ascension, present high priestly ministry and premillennial return.

4. The fall of man, his consequent moral depravity and need of regeneration.

5. Justification by faith in the substitutionary death of Christ and consequent Eternal Life.

6. Resurrection of the body, both of the unjust and the just.

7. Eternal bliss in heaven for the saved and eternal punishment in hell for the lost.

Notes: *Millar Memorial Bible Institute is an independent Evangelical Bible college. Its brief Statement of Faith emphasizes the inerrancy of the Bible and a consensus Evangelical theological perspective.*

* * *

DOCTRINAL STATEMENT (NIPAWIN BIBLE INSTITUTE)

I. We believe the Scriptures both Old and New Testaments, to be inerrant and the verbally Inspired Word of God, the complete revelation of His will of the salvation of man, and the supreme and final authority in faith, doctrine, and life.

2 Timothy 3:16; 2 Peter 1:21.

II. We believe In one God, Creator of all things, Infinitely perfect and eternally existing in three Persons: Father, Son and Holy Spirit, eternal in being, identical in nature, equal in power and glory and having the same attributes and perfections.

Deuteronomy 6:4; 2 Corinthians 13:14; Acts 5:3,4; Matthew 28:18,19; John 10:30.

III. We believe in the personality of Satan and other evil spirit beings as the enemies of God, the saints, and the holy angels.

Isaiah 14:12, 17; Ezekiel 28: 11—19; 2 Corinthians 4:3, 4.

IV. We believe that man was created in the image of God, that he sinned and hereby incurred not only physical death but spiritual death; that all human beings are born with a sinful nature, incapable of pleasing God and in the case of those who reach moral responsibility, become culpable sinners, utterly lost; and that only through regeneration by the Holy spirit can salvation and spiritual life be obtained.

Romans 5:12; Ephesians 2:1-3.

V. We believe that Jesus Christ was begotten by the Holy Spirit, born of the virgin Mary, and is true God and true man.

Matthew 1:23; Luke 1:35.

VI. We believe that the Lord Jesus Christ died for our sins according to the Scriptures as the representative and propitiatory sacrifice. I John 2:2; I Corinthians 15-3-6; Ephesians 1:20-22.

VII. We believe in the resurrection of the crucified body of our Lord; His ascension into heaven, and His personal bodily presence—here for us as Forerunner, High Priest, and Advocate.

I Corinthians 5:50-58; I Thessalonians 4:13-18; Acts 1:11; Hebrews 7:17.

VIII. We believe that the shed blood of Christ and his resurrection provide the only ground for justification and salvation; and that only those who by faith receive the Lord Jesus Christ as personnel Savior are born of the Holy Spirit and thus become children of God.

I Peter 1: 18,19; Ephesians 2:8,9.

IX. We believe that the true Church is composed of all persons, who, through saving faith in Jesus Christ have been regenerated by the Holy Spirit and are thus united together in the Body of Christ, of which He is the Head.

I Corinthians 12:13; Romans 12:5; Ephesians 1:22,23.

X. We believe that the local church's primary business (with no worldly alliances is to shed the light of the glorious Gospel of Jesus Christ continuously in all the earth, looking for her Lord's return.

Amos 3:3; 2 Corinthians 6:14-18.

XI. We believe in the personal, bodily, visible, pre-tribulation, pre-Millennial, and imminent return of our glorified Lord and Savior, Jesus Christ; and that this 'blessed hope' has a vital bearing on the personal life and service of the believer.

I Thessalonians 4:13-18; Acts 1:11.

XII. We believe that the ministry of the Holy Spirit is to glorify the Lord Jesus Christ, to convict men, to regenerate the believing sinner, to indwell, guide, instruct, sanctify, fill and empower the believer for Godly living and service.

John 16:8-14; Ephesians 5:18.

XIII. We believe that at death all men continue in conscious existence awaiting the bodily resurrection of the just and the unjust, the saved to everlasting blessedness, and the lost to everlasting conscious torment. Luke 16:19-31; Revelation 20:1-6.

Notes: *Nipawin Bible Institute, Nipawin, Saskatchewan, is an independent Evangelical Bible school. Its Doctrinal Statement emphasizes the inerrancy of Scripture and a consensus Evangelical theological position. The school offers a premillennial dispensational approach to Biblical interpretation. Dispensationalism sees human history as divided into successive periods of history during that Gods operates in a slightly different manner towards humanity. Humanity currently lives in the dispensation of grace that began with the death and resurrection of Jesus. In the near future, Jesus will return to gather his saints prior to a worldwide period of tribulation through which those who remain on earth will have to pass. Following the tribulation, he will then return to establish his millennial rule.*

*　　*　　*

DOCTRINAL STATEMENT (NORTHWESTERN COLLEGE)

I. The Scriptures

We believe that the Scriptures of the Old and New Testaments are verbally and plenarily inspired of God, are in: errant in the original writings, and are the infallible authority in all matters of faith and conduct (II. Tim.3:16).

II. The Godhead

We believe in one God, eternally existing in three persons, Father, Son and Holy Spirit (John 1:1,2). These three are equal in every divine perfection and execute distinct but harmonious offices in the work of creation and redemption (John 15:2).

III. The Father

We believe in God the Father, Creator of heaven and earth, perfect in holiness, infinite in wisdom, measureless in power (Gen. 1:1, Ex. 15:11, Job 12:13, Matt. 19:26). We rejoice that He concerns Himself mercifully in the affairs of men, that He hears and answers prayer (Matt. 6:6) and that He saves from sin and death all who come to Him through Jesus Christ (John 1:12).

DOCTRINAL STATEMENT (NORTHWESTERN COLLEGE)
(continued)

IV. The Son, Jesus Christ

We believe in Jesus Christ, the eternal and only begotten Son of God, conceived by the Holy Spirit, born of the Virgin Mary, sinless in His life, making atonement for the sin of the world by His substitutionary death on the cross. We believe in His bodily resurrection, His ascension into heaven, His present high priestly intercession for His people (Heb. 9:24), and His personal, visible, imminent (Heb. 9:28) and premillennial return to this earth according to His promise.

V. The Holy Spirit

We believe in the Holy Spirit, who came forth from God to convince the world of sin, of righteousness and of judgment, and to regenerate, sanctify and comfort those who believe in Jesus Christ (John 16:7,8).

VI. The Salvation of Man

We believe that man was created in the image of God (Gen. 1:26), that he sinned in Adam, and that all men by nature and by choice are sinners having incurred not only physical death but also that spiritual death which is separation from God (Rom. 3:23). We also believe that "God so loved the world that He gave His only begotten Son that whosoever believeth in Him should not perish but have everlasting life." Therefore, those who by faith, apart from human merit, works or ceremonies, accept Christ as Lord and Savior are justified on the ground of His shed blood and become children of God. We believe in the bodily resurrection of the just and the unjust (I Cor. 15:22, Acts 17:31). The saved will rejoice forever in God's presence and the lost will be forever separated from God in everlasting conscious punishment. We believe that every human being is responsible to God alone in all matters of faith (Jude 24).

VII. The Church

We believe in the Church—a living, spiritual body of which Christ is the Head and of which all regenerated people are members. We believe that a visible church is a company of believers in Jesus Christ, buried with Him in baptism and associated for worship, work, and fellowship (Eph. 1:22,23). We believe that to these visible churches were committed, for observance "till He come," the ordinances of baptism (Matt. 3:13-15) and the Lord's Supper (I Cor. 11:23-26); and that God has laid upon these churches the task of persuading a lost world to accept Jesus Christ as Savior and to enthrone Him as Lord and Master. We believe that human betterment and social improvement are essential products of the Gospel. We believe that Church and State must be kept separate as having different functions, each fulfilling its duties free from the dictation or patronage of the other.

VIII. The Responsibility

We believe that we are under divine obligation to contend earnestly for the faith once delivered unto the saints by proclaiming to a lost world the acceptance of Jesus Christ as Savior, and the enthroning of Him as Lord and Master (Jude 3, Acts 16:30, Col. 3:1-3).

Notes: *Northwestern College, Roseville, Minnesota, is an independent Fundamentalist liberal arts school. Its Doctrinal Statement emphasizes the inerrancy of the Bible and a consensus Fundamentalist theological perspective.*

* * *

DOCTRINAL STATEMENT (ONTARIO BIBLE COLLEGE/ONTARIO THEOLOGICAL SEMINARY)

The Bible:

We believe that the Bible alone, and the Bible in its entirety, is the written Word of God and, therefore inerrant in the autographs and absolutely authoritative.

Matt. 5:18; John 10:35; 2 Tim. 3:16,17; 2 Peter 1:19-21.

The Triune God:

We believe that there is but one living and true God, the Creator, Preserver and Governor of all things, who is Spirit, infinite in being, and in all perfections. We further believe that the one God exists eternally in three persons: the Father, the Son, and the Holy Spirit; all three having the same nature, attributes, and perfections, but each executing distinct, but harmonious, operations in the work of creation and of redemption.

Duet. 6:4; 1 Cor. 8:4; Gen. 1:1; Heb. 11:3; Neh. 9:6; Heb. 1:3; Ps. 104:26-33; Matt. 10:29; John 4:24; I Kings 8:27; Matt. 28:19; John 14:16; I Cor. 12:4-6; I Peter 1:1,2; Eph. 2:18: Jude 20,21.

Our Lord Jesus Christ:

We believe that Jesus Christ, the eternal Son of God, in His incarnation united to His divine nature a true human nature, and so continues to be both God and man, in two distinct natures but one Person, forever. He was begotten of the Holy Spirit, born of the Virgin Mary, perfectly obeyed the law of God, poured out His blood on the cross as a vicarious atonement for sin, and rose again bodily on the third day for our justification; He ascended to the Father's right hand where He now lives to make intercession for His redeemed.

John 1:1-3,14,18; Phil. 2:6-11: I John 1:1-3, 4:1-3; Rom. 8:3; Col. 2:9; Heb. 1:9ff; Isa. 7:14; Matt, 1:18-25, 3:15; John 8:46; Rom. 5:12ff.; 2 Cor. 5:21; Heb. 4:15, 7:26; Isa. 53:4-6; Matt. 20:28; Rom. 3:24-26; Gal. 3:13; Rom. 4:25; 1 Cor. 15:4,20; Acts 1:9-11; Heb. 1:3, 4:14, 7:25, 8:1; Rom. 8:34.

Man:

We believe that man was created in the image of God, that he sinned and in consequence incurred not only physical death, but also spiritual death which is separation from God, bringing sin, guilt, depravity and death upon all his posterity except the virgin-born Lord Jesus Christ.

Gen. 1:26,27; 2:7, 17, 3:6-24, 5:12ff.; I Cor. 15:21,22; Rom. 3:9-23; Eph. 2:1-3.

Salvation:

We believe that God in His mercy and grace saves all who repent of their sins and trust in Jesus Christ, justifying them through faith in the Savior and giving them new life by the Holy Spirit. God further wills that all such should grow in grace and in the knowledge of our Lord and Savior, Jesus Christ. True believers are kept by the power of God, so that none is lost; but the idea that this secure position in Christ entitles one to sin with impunity is false and pernicious.

Eph. 1:3-14, 2:4-10; Titus 3:4-7; Acts. 2:28, 16:31; Rom. 3:22; Rom. 4:5, 5:1; John 3:3,16,36, 5:24; 2 Pet. 3:18; John 17:12,17; 2 Cor. 3:18; John 6:37-40, 10:28,29; Rom. 5:9,10, 8:1,30,38,39; Phil. 1:6; 1 Pet. 1:4,5; 1 John 2:19, 3:4-10; Rom. 6:1; Col. 1:23; Heb. 3:14; John 15:6.

Things to Come:

We believe that, at a day and hour known only God, our Lord Jesus Christ shall come again personally, bodily, visibly, gloriously, to establish His Kingdom of righteousness and peace. We believe in the eternal blessedness of the redeemed and the eternal punishment of the unjust.

Mark 13:32; John 14:1-3; Acts 1:11; Rev. 1:7; Matt. 24:27,30, 36-39; 1 Thess. 4:13-18; Titus 2:13; John 3:36, 5:28,29; Acts 24:15; Matt. 25:46; Rev. 20:11-15.

Notes: *The related Ontario Bible College and Ontario Theological Seminary, Willowdale, Ontario, are independent Evangelical schools that share a common Doctrinal Statement. The Statement affirms the inerrancy of the Bible and consensus Evangelical theological position. Its Calvinist emphasis is echoed in the assertion of total human depravity and the security of true believers who are "kept by the power of God, so that none is lost."*

*   *   *

WHAT WE BELIEVE (PACIFIC CHRISTIAN COLLEGE)

Pacific Christian College does not subscribe to a formal creedal statement. Below is a summary of some critical and crucial truths which guide our institution.

1. In the beginning, God created the heavens and the earth (Genesis 1:1).

2. All Scripture is inspired by God and profitable for teaching, for reproof, for correction, for training in righteousness; that the man of God may be adequate, equipped for every good work (II Timothy 3:16,17).

3. The Law became our tutor to lead us to Jesus, the Messiah. Jesus established a new and better covenant (Galatians 3:24; Hebrews 7:22).

4. Jesus of Nazareth is the Christ, the Son of the living God, and Lord. He is the image of the invisible God (Matthew 16:16; Colossians 1:15; Acts 2:36).

5. Jesus died for our sins, was buried, and was raised on the third day according to the Scriptures (I Corinthians 15:4).

6. The Holy Spirit convicts the world concerning sin, and righteousness and judgement (John 16:8).

7. If any man is in Christ, he is a new creation (II Corinthians 5:17).

8. Jesus is the head of the Church which is built upon the foundation of the apostles (Ephesians 1:22-23; Ephesians 2:20).

9. God calls all Christians to be ministers of reconciliation regardless of their occupations (II Corinthians 5:18).

10. There are varieties of gifts, but the same Spirit. There are varieties of ministries, but the same Lord. There are varieties of effects, but the same God who works all things in all persons. But to each one is given the manifestation of the Spirit for the common good (I Corinthians 12:4-7).

11. Jesus' great commandment is to love. "Love your enemies" and "love one another." Whoever loves the Father, loves the child born of Him. Every Christian is a brother or sister to every other brother or sister and should live like it (Matthew 5:43; John 13:34-35; I John 5:1).

12. Jesus' great commission is to go and make disciples of all the nations, baptizing them in the name of the Father and the Son and the Holy Spirit, teaching them to observe all that He commanded of us and lo, He will be with us always (Matthew 28:19-20).

13. The Lord will come again for both judgement and salvation. Every eye shall see Him (Hebrews 9:38, Revelation 1:7, and I Thessalonians 4:16-17).

Notes: *Pacific Christian College, Fullerton, California, is an independent Evangelical school. Its statement of belief emphasizes the essentials of Evangelical Christianity, but avoids assuming a position on many controversial questions about which Christians might disagree. Rather than choosing phrases from contemporary debates within the Evangelical commu-*

WHAT WE BELIEVE (PACIFIC CHRISTIAN COLLEGE)
(continued)

nity, the statement takes much of its phrasing directly from the Bible.

*   *   *

STATEMENT OF FAITH (PEACE RIVER BIBLE INSTITUTE)

1. We believe in the verbal inspiration of the Old and New Testament Scriptures, inerrant in the original writings, and that they are the supreme authority in faith, doctrine and life

2. We believe in one God, eternally existing in three Persons: Father, Son and Holy Spirit

3. We believe that Jesus Christ, the eternal Son of God, was begotten by the Holy Spirit, and born of the virgin Mary, and is true God and true man

4. We believe in the personality of Satan and his host of fallen angels as the enemies of God, the saints and the holy angels

5. We believe that man was created in the image of God, that he sinned willfully, thereby incurring physical and spiritual death; and that all human beings are born with a sinful nature needing a divine rebirth

6. We believe that the Lord Jesus Christ died for the sins of the whole world, according to the Scriptures, as mankind's substitutionary sacrifice, and that all who believe in Him and receive Him are justified by His shed blood

7. We believe that all who are justified comprise the body of Christ universal, whose commission is to teach the gospel and disciple the nations

8. We believe that the fullness of the Holy Spirit is received through obedience and faith alone and that sanctification is both instantaneous at the point of the new birth, as well as progressive, producing daily growth in grace toward spiritual maturity

9. We believe in the physical resurrection of the crucified body of our Lord, His ascension into heaven and His intercession in heaven for believers as their High Priest and Advocate

10. We believe in that blessed hope, the personal, bodily, visible and imminent return of our Lord and Savior, Jesus Christ

11. We believe that at death, the justified are present in conscious existence with Christ, awaiting bodily resurrection and everlasting blessedness, and that the unregenerate at death are in conscious existence in hades, awaiting bodily resurrection and everlasting torment in gehenna.

Notes: *Peace River Bible Institute is an independent Evangelical school. Its Statement of Faith affirms the inerrancy of the Bible and a consensus Evangelical theological perspective.*

*   *   *

DOCTRINAL POSITION (PHILADELPHIA COLLEGE OF THE BIBLE)

I.   We believe in the divine inspiration and authority of the Scriptures. By this is meant a miraculous guidance of the Holy Spirit in their original writing, extending to all parts of the Scriptures equally, applying even to the choice of words, so that the result is the very Word of God, the only infallible rule of faith and practice. Moreover, it is our conviction that God has exercised such singular care and providence through the ages in preserving the written Word, that the Scriptures as we now have them are in every essential particular as originally given and contain all things necessary to salvation.

II. We believe in the one God revealed as eternally existing in three equal persons, the Father, the Son and the Holy Spirit. We believe in the deity of the Lord Jesus Christ. We believe in the Holy Spirit as a divine Person, a personality distinct from the Father and the Son.

III. We believe that God created an innumerable host of angels, some of whom followed the lead of Lucifer, now called Satan in rebelling against God, thereby bringing sin into the universe. We believe in Satan's complete defeat by the Lord Jesus Christ.

IV. We believe that man was created in the image of God, that he sinned and thereby incurred not only physical death but also that spiritual death which is separation from God; and that all human beings are born with a sinful nature and, in the case of those who reach moral responsibility, become sinners in thought, word and deed. And with such a nature, they are incapable of producing anything acceptable to God.

V.   We believe that Jesus Christ was begotten of the Holy Spirit, and born of the virgin Mary, and is true God and true man. We believe that He died for the sins of men as representative and substitutionary sacrifice, and that His death was a sufficient expiation, for the guilt of all men. We believe in the resurrection of the crucified body of our Lord, in His ascension into heaven, and in His present life there for us as High Priest and Advocate.

VI. We believe that men are justified by grace through faith, on the ground of the shed blood of Christ, and that all who receive the Lord Jesus Christ as Savior are born again of the Holy Spirit, and thereby become children of God.

VII. We believe in the bodily resurrection of the just and the unjust, the everlasting conscious blessedness of the saved, and the everlasting conscious punishment of the lost.

VIII. We believe that it is the supreme responsibility of believers to testify to the saving power of Christ's gospel, both personally and by proxy, at home and to the uttermost part of the earth.

IX. We believe that it is the duty of each believer to live a holy life unto God, keeping himself unspotted from the world, and that it is God's intention that this shall be accomplished in the believer's life by his constant dependence on the divine enablement of the indwelling Holy Spirit. We believe that this experience of deliverance from sin and empowerment for service is designated in the Scriptures as the filing with the Spirit rather than His baptism. Thus the baptism with the Spirit is not an experience to be sought subsequent to regeneration, but is already an accomplished fact.

X. We believe that God in the Scriptures has progressively revealed Himself through successive ages, during each of which man has been tested in respect of obedience to some specific revelation of the will of God; and we believe further that this dispensational viewpoint provides the key to correct interpretation of the plan and purpose of God in the world, past, present and future, as it relates to the Church, to Israel and to the nations. We believe in the actual offering of a kingdom to Israel by Christ at His first coming, and His postponement thereof as a result of their rejection. We believe that Israel, as well as the Church and nations, is included in the future aspects of God's program.

XI. We believe that the Church of Jesus Christ had its historical beginning at Pentecost; is composed solely of believers; is the Body and Bride of our Lord; is distinct from Israel; and that it will be completed as believers fulfill their duty by making Christ known.

XII. We believe that at any moment the Rapture of the saved may occur, when "the Lord himself shall descend from heaven" to catch up His people to meet Him "in the air" and deliver them from the period of judgment on earth designated in Scripture as the 70th Week of Daniel.

XIII. We believe in the personal, bodily and premillennial return of our Lord Jesus Christ after the 70th Week of Daniel. He will then set up His kingdom upon the earth for His thousand-year reign, after which He will deliver the kingdom to the Father, that the Godhead may be all in all.

Notes: *Philadelphia College of the Bible is one of the early schools of the Fundamentalist Bible school movement. It has retained its Fundamentalist theological perspective, and its doctrinal statement affirms the verbal inspiration and infallibility of the Bible, human depravity, and a dispensational view of human history. Dispensationalism views history as a series of stages through which God has successively revealed his saving plan for humankind. The period in which we now live is*

the dispensation of grace that began with Christ's death and resurrection. The college teaches a form of dispensationalism that suggests that Christ will return to gather his saints prior to a period of earthly tribulation (described in the biblical book of Daniel as the last week of a 70-week prophetic period). Following the tribulation, Christ will return to establish his millennial rule on earth. All faculty and staff must sign this statement.

* * *

DOCTRINAL STATEMENT (PRAIRIE BIBLE INSTITUTE)

We believe in:

The only true and living God, infinite, eternal, unchangeable.

The plenary, verbal inspiration, inerrancy, and final authority of the Old and New Testament Scriptures.

The virgin birth and essential deity of Jesus Christ, our Lord.

The physical resurrection of Christ from the dead.

The personality and deity of the Holy Spirit, the third Person of the Holy Trinity.

The personality of the Devil, as the enemy of Jesus Christ, the saints, and the angels.

The fall of man and the universal depravity of the human race.

The guilty and lost condition of all men everywhere outside of Christ.

Salvation by faith through the substitutionary death of Jesus Christ.

The infilling of the Holy Spirit for the child of God.

The life of Christian victory through faith in and obedience to Jesus Christ, under the Holy Spirit.

The second premillennial coming of Christ.

The physical resurrection of all men—the saints to everlasting joy and bliss, the lost to everlasting conscious torment.

The Church's sole business—shunning worldly alliances and looking for her Lord's return—to shed the light of the glorious Gospel continuously in all the earth.

Notes: *Prairie Bible College, Three Hills, Alberta, is an independent Evangelical Bible school. Its Doctrinal Statement*

DOCTRINAL STATEMENT (PRAIRIE BIBLE INSTITUTE)
(continued)

affirms the inerrancy of the Bible and a consensus Evangelical theological perspective.

*　　*　　*

THEOLOGICAL POSITION (REGENT UNIVERSITY)

We accept wholeheartedly the revelation of God given in the Scriptures of the Old and New Testaments and confess the faith therein set forth and summarized in such historic statements of the Christian Church as the Apostles Creed and the Nicene Creed. We here explicitly assert doctrines that they regard as crucial to the understanding and proclamation of the Gospel and to practical Christian living.

1. The sovereignty and grace of God the Father, Son and Holy Spirit in creation, providence, revelation, redemption and final judgement:

2. The divine inspiration of Holy Scripture and its consequent entire trustworthiness and supreme authority in all matters of faith and conduct.

3. The universal sinfulness and guilt of human nature since the fall, making man subject to God's wrath and condemnation.

4. The substitutionary sacrifice of the incarnate Son of God as the sole ground of redemption from the guilt, penalty and power of sin.

5. The justification of the sinner by the grace of God through faith alone in Christ crucified and risen from the dead.

6. The illuminating, regenerating, indwelling and sanctifying work of God the Holy Spirit in the believer.

7. The unity and common priesthood of all true believers, who together form the one universal Church, the Body of which Christ is the Head.

8. The expectation of the personal, visible return of the Lord Jesus Christ.

Notes: *Regent University is an independent Evangelical school affiliated with the University of British Columbia, Vancouver, British Columbia. Its Theological Position assumes the truth of the ancient Christian confessions—the Apostles Creed and the Nicene Creed—but adds statements of particular contemporary interest. It affirms the authority of Scripture, the substitutionary nature of Christ's sacrifice on the cross, the*

work of the Holy Spirit, and the expectation of Christ's personal and visible second coming.

*　　*　　*

STATEMENT OF FAITH (ST. STEPHEN'S UNIVERSITY)

St. Stephen's University affirms the objective truth of God's revelation to man in the Holy Scriptures—comprising the sixty-six canonical books of the Bible—and seeks to promulgate the personal appropriation and individual application of this truth.

In addition to affirming the historic creeds of Christendom, the following principles are foundational to the Christian faith as upheld and practiced by St. Stephen's University:

i) Belief in the plenary inspiration of Scripture, and acknowledgment that the Bible is the exclusive and definitive objective authority for the Church in all matters of faith and practice;

ii) Belief in the reality of the consubstantial, co-eternal Trinity of Father, Son and Holy Spirit;

iii) Belief in the reality of sin as the pervasive condition of all men who have not become at one with God through faith in Jesus Christ;

iv) Belief in the vicarious and atoning death of Jesus Christ, God's Son, and in the power of his resurrection;

v) Belief in the necessity of personal faith in Christ's finished work for salvation, or redemption from sin and condemnation;

vi) Belief in the reality of the personal indwelling of God of the Holy Spirit, who desires lordship over all aspects of the life of the individual Christian believer;

vii) Belief in the personal return of Christ to this world at a future point in time to gather together his Church and to effect the final destruction of Satan

viii) Belief in the reality of the final judgment of all men, when those who love God and keep his commandments will be drawn more fully into his presence, and when those who have rejected him and have not kept his commandments will be removed forever from the joy of his love;

ix) Belief that the gospel is indeed good news to all who receive it, and a source of rejoicing and hope in all life's situations; and

x) Belief that God calls upon all who love him to proclaim his goodness throughout his creation; to be co-worker, with in making his creation fruitful and hospitable to man; to encourage all that is beautiful in the lives of men by the grace of God; and to cause everything that is to redound to his glory!

Notes: *St. Stephen's University, St. Stephen, New Brunswick, is an independent Evangelical school. Its Statement of Faith affirms the plenary inspiration of the Bible and the objective nature of the truth found therein, and a consensus statement of the Evangelical theological perspective.*

*   *   *

DOCTRINAL STATEMENT (SOUTHEASTERN BIBLE COLLEGE)

WE BELIEVE AND TEACH:

1. That the Bible, consisting of the sixty-six books of the Old and New Testaments, in the autographs, is the inerrant and complete Word of God, the final authority in all matters of faith and practice. (2 Tim. 3:16-17; 2 Peter 1:20-21; Jude 3).

2. That there is one God, eternally existing in three Persons: Father, Son, and Holy Spirit. (Deut. 6:4; Matt. 28:19; Luke 3:21-22).

3. That the Lord Jesus christ is the only begotten Son of God, conceived by the Holy Spirit, born of the Virgin Mary, and is true God and true man (Luke 1:30-35; John 1:18, 3:16; Phil. 2:5-11).

4. That man was created in the image of God; that he sinned and thereby incurred not only physical death, but also spiritual death which is separation from God; and that, as a consequence; all men are declared by God to be totally depraved, having inherited a sinful nature and having become sinners in thought, word, and deed. (Gen. 1:26-27; 2:16-17; 3:6-19; Rom. 3:10-23; 6:23; 7:18; 11:32; Gal. 3:22).

5. That the Lord Jesus Christ died as a substitutionary and complete sacrifice for the sins of the whole world and that only those who believe in Him are saved, and this on the ground of His shed blood. (Rom. 3:24-28; 5:8-10; 1 Tim. 2:5-6; 1 John 2:1-2).

6. That the Lord Jesus Christ arose from the dead in the same body, through glorified, in which he was crucified; that He ascended into Heaven and is now exalted at the right hand of the Father as Head of the Church. (John 20:1-29, Acts 1:9-11; Eph. 1:20-23; Heb. 1:3).

7. That the Lord Jesus Christ will come again personally and bodily that first He will come in the air prior to the seven-year Tribulation, hence at any moment, to receive the Church, His body, unto Himself in heaven; and that following the literal fulfillment of the Great Tribulation spoken of by the prophets, He will return visibly to the earth with His saints to inaugurate His millennial Kingdom of universal peace and righteousness. (Acts 1:11; 1 Thess. 4:13-18; 1 Cor. 15:51-58; 2 Pet. 3:1-13; Rev. 19:11-16; 20:1-6).

8. That both the believer and the unbeliever will be resurrected bodily in their own order: the saved unto everlasting bliss, the lost unto everlasting and conscious punishment. (1 Cor. 15:1-50; 1 Thess. 4:13-18; Rev. 20:11-15; 21:22).

9. That on the sole condition of personal faith in the Lord Jesus Christ men are born again by the Holy Spirit; that at regeneration, all believers in this age are also indwelt by the Holy Spirit, baptized by the Holy Spirit into the Body of Christ, and sealed by the Holy Spirit unto the day of redemption. (Rom. 3:24-28; 8:9-11; 1 Cor. 12:13; Eph. 4:30).

10. That sanctification, which is separation unto God, is threefold: positionally, the believer was sanctified at his conversion by virtue of his union with Christ; progressively, he is continually being sanctified through the Word as he walks in the Spirit, thereby overcoming lusts of the flesh and producing the fruit of the Spirit; ultimately; he will be completely conformed to the image of Christ when he sees his Savior face to face. (John 17:17; Eph. 5:26; Col. 3:1-4; Heb. 10:14 1 John 3:1-3).

11. That the Church is the Body of Christ composed of all who are born again during this age of grace, which began at Pentecost and will be terminated at the rapture; that this church universal is to gather together as local churches or assemblies after the pattern of New Testament doctrine and practice, including the observance of the ordinances of water baptism and the Lord's Supper; and that God performs the ministry of His church through its members to whom He has given gifts for the purpose of edifying the Body of Christ. (Acts 2:1-47; Rom. 12:1-8; 1 Cor. 11:23-34; 1 Cor. 12:1-31; Eph. 1:22-23).

12. That the Great Commission was given to the Church and that this task of world evangelism is the mission of the Church today. (Matt. 28:18-20; Rom. 10:9-17; Eph. 4:7-16).

Notes: *Southeastern Bible College, Birmingham, Alabama, is an independent fundamentalist Bible school. Its Doctrinal Statement emphasizes the inerrancy of the Bible, total human depravity, and a premillennial dispensational eschatology. Dispensationalism views history as a series of stages through which God has successively revealed his saving plan for humankind. The period in which we now live is the dispensation of grace that began with Christ's death and resurrection. The college teaches a form of dispensationalism that suggests that Christ will return to gather his saints prior to a period of earthly tribulation. Following the tribulation, Christ will return to establish his millennial rule on earth. The college is opposed to the Charismatic movement and will not graduate a*

DOCTRINAL STATEMENT (SOUTHEASTERN BIBLE COLLEGE)
(continued)

student who adheres to that movement's ideas concerning the gifts of the Spirit.

* * *

STATEMENT OF FAITH (TOCCOA FALLS COLLEGE)

Toccoa Falls is committed to teach and defend the historic and basic doctrines of evangelical Christianity:

1. The verbal inspiration of the Holy Scriptures as originally given

2. The existence and manifestation of one God in three persons—Father, Son, and Holy Spirit

3. The incarnation and virgin birth of the Son of God

4. The redemption of man by the vicarious death of Christ on the cross

5. The bodily resurrection from the grave

6. The fact that all men have sinned and consequently must be regenerated by the working of God's grace

7. The fact of justification by faith

8. The sanctifying work of the Holy Spirit in the believer producing holiness of life and power for service

9. Practical faith in the sufficiency of Christ for spiritual, temporal, and physical needs

10. The purifying hope of the Lord's imminent return

11. The urgency of preaching the gospel to all mankind that men may be saved from eternal judgment

Notes: *Toccoa Falls College is an independent Evangelical Bible school. It Statement of Faith affirms the verbal inspiration of the Bible and a consensus Evangelical theological perspective. Members of the faculty must sign the doctrinal statement.*

* * *

DOCTRINAL STATEMENT (WASHINGTON BIBLE COLLEGE)

1. I believe in the Bible as the inerrant Word of God, verbally inspired, the all-sufficient rule of faith and practice.

2. I believe in One God, eternally existing in three persons, Father, Son, and Holy Spirit.

3. I believe in the virgin birth, the sinless perfection, the bodily resurrection and ascension into heaven of Jesus Christ, and in His present life there for us as High Priest and Advocate.

4. I believe man was created in the image of God; that he disobeyed God and thereby incurred spiritual death which is separation from God, and also physical death as a consequence; and that all the Adamic race are sinners by nature and practice.

5. I believe that the Lord Jesus Christ died for our sins as a vicarious and substitutionary sacrifice, and that all who believe in Him are justified on the ground of His shed blood.

6. I believe in the personal, premillennial and imminent return of our Lord and Savior, Jesus Christ.

7. I believe that all who receive by faith the Lord Jesus Christ are born of the Holy Spirit, and thereby become the children of God.

8. I believe in the bodily resurrection of the just and the unjust, the everlasting blessedness of the saved, and the everlasting punishment of the lost.

9. I believe the Church is an elect company of believers baptized by the Holy Spirit into one body; its mission is to witness concerning its Head, Jesus Christ, preaching the Gospel among all nations: it will be caught up to meet the Lord in the air ere He appears to set up his Kingdom.

10. I believe in the grace of God to be sufficient for the maintenance of a godly walk and that Christ and not the law is the believer's rule of life.

Notes: *Washington Bible College, Lanham, Maryland, is an Evangelical Bible school. Its Doctrinal Statement, to which faculty and students must adhere, emphasizes the inerrancy of the Bible and a premillennial dispensational eschatology. Dispensationalism views history as a series of stages through which God has successively revealed his saving plan for humankind. The period in which we now live is the dispensation of grace, which began with Christ's death and resurrection. The college teaches a form of dispensationalism that suggests that Christ will return to gather his saints prior to a period of earthly tribulation. Following the tribulation, Christ will return to establish his millennial rule on earth. The school* *affirms the necessity of water baptism, but does not argue for one mode (immersion, pouring, or sprinkling) over another.*

* * *

DOCTRINAL STANDARD (WESTMONT COLLEGE)

— that He died upon the cross a vicarious substitutionary death, thereby making atonement for the sin of the world (John 1:29). We believe that He is the only redeemer (Acts 4:12), and that his atonement is sufficient for the sins of all the world (Hebrews 7:25; I John 2:2), and efficient for all who believe (John 3:16, 36; Isaiah 45:22).

— that he bodily arose from the dead, that he ascended into Heaven, that there in His state of glorification He is now the interceding High Priest, Intercessor, and Advocate for all believers (I Corinthians 15:20; Luke 24; Acts 1:3; Hebrews 7:25; 4:15; 2:17; I John 2:1).

— that as in his first advent He became incarnate and dwelt on earth personally, bodily, visibly in an earthly tabernacle of flesh, the body of His humiliation, even so in his second advent He will return personally, bodily, visibly, but in the body of His glorification, to set up His kingdom and to judge the world in righteousness (Acts 1:9-11; I Thessalonians 4:13-18; Matthew 25: 31-46; Revelation 20:4-6, 11-15).

— that man, created in the image of God, fell into sin through the sin of the first Adam and in that sense is lost and separated from God, in order to secure salvation and restoration, man must be born again. Salvation is by grace through faith in Christ "Who His own self bore our sins in His own body on the tree" (I Peter 2:24). The punishment of the wicked and unbelieving, and the reward of the righteous are everlasting and as the reward is conscious, so is the punishment (Genesis 1:26-28; Romans 3:10, 22-23; John 3:16; Acts 4:12, 13:38-39; Matthew 25:46; II Corinthians 5:1; II Thessalonians 1:7-10).

— that the Holy Spirit, the third person of the Godhead, indwells all believers in the Lord Jesus Christ (I Corinthians 6:19), baptizes them into the body of Christ, and seals them unto the day of redemption. The Holy Spirit convinces and "reproves the world of sin and of righteousness and of judgment" (Romans 8:9; I Corinthians 12: 12-14; Ephesians 1:13-14, 5:18-20; John 16:8-11).

— that the Church is the body of Christ, a spiritual organism composed of all born-again persons in this present age. The mission of the Church is to witness concerning the Head, Jesus Christ, and to preach the gospel among all nations. The Church will be caught up to meet the Lord in the air prior to his appearing to set up His Kingdom (Ephesians 1:3-6, 22-23, 25, 30; I Corinthians 12:12-14; Matthew 28:19-20; I Thessalonians 4:16-18).

Even these declarations of faith do not define in detail what an individual Christian might believe in many important areas of doctrine and theology. Moreover, as a college seeking to serve evangelical Christians from many denominations, we feel less of an obligation to decide these various points in detail than we do to celebrate not only our unity in Jesus Christ but also our freedom to disagree, and to continue grappling in the many essential elements of our faith.

Notes: *Westmont College, Montecito, California, is an independent Evangelical liberal arts college. Its Statement of Faith affirms the inerrancy of the Bible and a consensus Evangelical theological perspective.*

* * *

THEOLOGICAL POSITION (WILLIAM TYNDALE COLLEGE)

Throughout the years, William Tyndale College has maintained an interdenominational character and a conservative theological position. The result has been the continued opportunity to serve the Christian public from many different churches in an atmosphere of theological understanding and mutual Christian fellowship. A doctrinal statement of the college was adopted in 1945 and is reaffirmed annually by the Board, faculty, and staff. This statement is outlined below:

1. The Scriptures, the Old and the New Testament, are verbally inspired of God and inerrant in the original writings, and are completely authoritative.

2. One God eternally exists in Three Persons: Father, Son, and Holy Spirit.

3. Man was created in the image of God, through disobedience he sinned and fell, and the entire human race shared in man's sin and is depraved by nature and lost.

4. Satan is a person, a fallen creature who, by the permission of God, holds a position of great influence and power in human affairs.

5. Jesus Christ is virgin born and He is God-man, Deity enfleshed.

6. The death of Jesus Christ is vicarious, sacrificial, and substitutionary; Christ died for sins and as the ransom for all.

7. Jesus Christ arose bodily from among the dead, and He ascended into Heaven where He is exalted as Lord and Christ. He is the Head of the Church, and is the priestly advocate and intercessor. Christ's second coming will be personal and premillennial, and it is imminent.

8. Salvation is a gift of God brought to man by grace, it is received by personal faith in the Lord Jesus Christ, and this faith is manifested by the believer in works pleasing to God.

9. The Holy Spirit is a Person. He regenerates, indwells, energizes, and empowers for godly living and for spiritual service. The Holy Spirit indwells the believer from the

moment of faith in Christ, and the believer is commanded to be filled with the Spirit.

10. All believers in the present dispensation are members of the Body of Christ, the Church, and they are baptized by the Holy Spirit into this Body the moment of faith in Christ.

11. All believers are called into a life of separation from all worldly and sinful practices.

12. It is God's plan that the world be evangelized by the Church through the preaching of the Gospel of Christ. This witnessing is the obligation of all who believe in Jesus Christ.

13. There is eternal damnation and punishment for all who are finally impenitent and unsaved.

Notes: *William Tyndale College, Farmington Hills, Michigan, is an independent Evangelical school. Its doctrinal statement, which is signed annually by all faculty and staff, affirms the inerrancy of the Bible and a consensus Evangelical theological position.*

*   *   *

DOCTRINAL STATEMENT (WINNIPEG THEOLOGICAL SEMINARY/WINNIPEG BIBLE COLLEGE

Doctrinal statements provide a basis upon which the seminary develops its distinctives in teaching as well as the positions it takes in current theological debates. This is a brief statement to which all faculty subscribe.

SCRIPTURE: The verbal plenary inspiration and divine authority of both the Old and New Testaments in the original manuscripts.

GOD: The one living, and true God, an eternal existent Trinity of three Persons. The Father, The Son, and The Holy Spirit, equal in every respect and executing distinct but harmonious offices in the activities of the Godhead.

CREATION: The Genesis account of creation as factual and historic and that man was created directly by God.

SIN: The temptation and fall of man, as recorded in Genesis, with the consequent depravity of all mankind and liability to eternal punishment for sin.

PERSON OF JESUS CHRIST: The deity of Jesus Christ and that through His Virgin Birth, true humanity and undiminished deity were united in one Person forever.

WORK OF JESUS CHRIST: The substitutionary death of Christ for sinners. His shed blood being the only ground for forgiveness of sin, and His bodily resurrection and ascension to heaven as Lord of all.

JUSTIFICATION: The truth that men are accounted righteous before God, regenerated by the Holy Spirit, and given eternal life on the single condition of faith in Jesus Christ as personal Savior.

SANCTIFICATION: The fact that every believer has perfect acceptance before God, in Christ, and that the indwelling Holy Spirit enables him to lead a life of godliness.

CHURCH: The Church as the body of Christ which began at Pentecost is a spiritual organism composed of all believers who are placed into that body by the baptism of the Holy Spirit. The local visible church is a manifestation of the universal church organized for the fellowship of believers and the continuation of Christ's work on earth.

SATAN: The personality of Satan and his associates, fallen through sin, whose activity is to thwart God's plan. for whom salvation is unavailable and the Lake of Fire is especially prepared.

ESCHATOLOGY: The resurrection of the bodies of the saints. the rapture of the church at the end of the present dispensation, the Tribulation followed by the premillennial return of Christ in glory, the resurrection of the bodies of the wicked, their judgment and eternal punishment.

MISSION: The responsibility of the saved to witness by life and word concerning Jesus Christ and to proclaim the Gospel to all the world.

Notes: *The affiliated Winnipeg Theological Seminary and Winnipeg Bible College share the same Doctrinal Position. The Position affirms the verbal plenary inspiration of the Bible, the Genesis account of creation as historically descriptive, and a premillennial dispensational eschatology. Dispensationalism views history as a series of stages through which God has successively revealed his saving plan for humankind. The period in which we now live is the dispensation of grace, which began with Christ's death and resurrection. The seminary and college also teach a form of dispensationalism that suggests that Christ will return to gather his saints prior to a period of earthly tribulation. Following the tribulation, Christ will return to establish his*

Chapter 12

Adventist Family

Sunday Adventist

SUGGESTIONS FOR A CREED (CHURCH OF GOD GENERAL CONFERENCE (ABRAHAMIC FAITH)/ RESTORATION FELLOWSHIP)

I believe in one God, the Father the only true God (Jn. 17:3), the one who alone is God (Jn. 5:44), the Creator of everything.

I believe in Jesus the Messiah promised by God; that Jesus is the Son of David and the Son of God brought into being by God through a supernatural conception in Mary (Luke 1:35); that the Son of God came into existence at His birth, though He was foreknown from eternity (I Pet. 1:20, Rev. 13:8, KJV).

I believe in the Gospel of the Kingdom of God and the things concerning the name of Jesus (Acts 8:12) as the essential saving message.

I believe in water-baptism, consequent upon belief in the saving message (Acts 8:12).

I believe in the holy spirit as the power, personality and presence of God and Jesus, available to the repentant and obedient believer so that the divine nature may be developed in him.

I believe in one international Church of God, bound by love stimulated by the holy spirit, and united in one mind and judgement (I Cor. 1:10). I believe that Christians should refuse to kill, or threaten to kill their enemies (Mat. 5:39,44; Rom. 12:17-21), and that the true Church is recognized by the love it expresses to all its members (not by the observation of Sabbaths, New Moons or Holy Days-Col 2:16)

I believe that Jesus will return to rule on earth in the Messianic Kingdom, restore all things according to the vision of the prophets (Acts 3;21), that He will gather together the faithful from around the world, raise the faithful dead of all the ages, give them immortality (I Cor. 15:22,23), and make them rulers with Him in His Kingdom (Mat.19:28, I Cor. 6:2, Rev 2:26, Rev. 3:21).

I believe that Christians should recognize, with Jesus and the Apostles, the existence of the evil cosmic personality, Satan, and his demonic forces, and that they should do battle with them in the power of the spirit (Eph. 6:12,13).

Notes: *Restoration Fellowship, founded in 1981, is an educational ministry that cooperates with the Church of God General Conference (Abrahamic Faith). Its Suggestions for a Creed affirm the One God and Jesus as the Son of God who came into existence at his birth, and the Holy Spirit as the power of God (a non-Trinitarian affirmation). The Fellowship is pacifist, opposes the celebration of the Jewish Sabbath or festivals (a key feature of many Adventist Church of God groups), and affirms the personality of Satan.*

*   *   *

Seventh-Day Adventist

STATEMENT OF FAITH (WORLDWIDE CHURCH OF GOD)

GOD

God, by the testimony of Scripture, is the only true God and Father of all, eternal, immutable, omnipotent, omniscient, omnipresent. He is creator of heaven and earth, sustainer of the universe and source of man's salvation. God is love and infinite goodness. The Church affirms the oneness of God and the full divinity of the Father, the Son, and the Holy Spirit.

(Mark 12:29, Ephesians 4:6, I Timothy 1:17, I John 4:8, I John 5:20, Matthew 28:19, II Corinthians 13:14, I Corinthians 8:6)

JESUS CHRIST

Jesus was the Word, through whom and for whom God created all things. He was God manifest in the flesh for man's salvation. He was begotten of the Holy Spirit and born of the virgin Mary. During his earthly life, Jesus was the Son of God, worthy of honor and reverence and the prophesied Savior of man. He died for our sins, was raised from the dead, and ascended to heaven, from where he mediates between man and

God. He will come again to reign as King of kings over all nations in the kingdom of God.

(John 1:1, Colossians 1:16, I Timothy 3:16, John 3:16, Matthew 1:20, I Corinthians 15:3-4, Hebrews 7:25, Revelation 19:16)

THE HOLY SPIRIT

The Holy Spirit is the Comforter promised by Jesus Christ, sent from God to the Church on the Day of Pentecost. God's Holy Spirit is the power that transforms man through repentance, baptism and continual renewal. The Holy Spirit is the source of inspiration and prophecy throughout the Scriptures, and the Christian's constant guide to all truth.

(John 14:16, Acts 2:4, 17-19, 38, Titus 3:5, John 16:13)

THE HOLY SCRIPTURES

The Holy Scriptures comprise the canonical books of the Old and New Testaments. They are the inspired Word of God, the foundation of truth and the accurate record of God's revelation to mankind. The Holy Scriptures constitute ultimate authority in all matters of doctrine, and embody the infallible principles that govern all facets of Christian living.

(II Timothy 3:15-17, II Peter 1:20-21, John 17:17)

THE ANGELIC REALM

Angels are created spirit beings endowed with free will. The holy angels serve God as messengers and agents, are appointed to minister to those who will obtain salvation and will accompany Christ at his return. The disobedient angels are called demons.

(Revelation 1:1, 22:6, Hebrews 1:14, Matthew 25:31)

SATAN

Satan is a fallen cherub who heads the evil forces in the spirit realm. He is referred to in the Bible in various ways including the devil, adversary, evil one, murderer, liar, thief, tempter, accuser of the brethren, prince of demons, and god of this world. He is in constant rebellion against God. Through his influence, Satan generates discord, deception and disobedience among human beings. His dominion and influence as god of this world will cease at the return of Jesus Christ.

(Revelation 12:9, I Peter 5:8, John 8:44, Revelation 12:10, II Corinthians 4:4, Revelation 20:1-3)

REPENTANCE

Repentance is a change of mind and attitude toward God. It follows conviction by the Holy Spirit through the word of God. Repentance entails an awareness of personal sins, accompanied by remorse and a resolution to respond to God's calling. Rather than a temporary, emotional response, repentance toward God results in an abiding change of thought, behavior, and direction of life, wherein a person resolutely turns to God

and purposes to forsake all sin and walk in all God's commandments.

(Acts 2:38, Romans 2:4, II Timothy 2:25, II Corinthians 7:9-11, Matthew 3:8, Romans 12:2)

WATER BAPTISM

Water baptism demonstrates a believer's repentance for personal sin and acceptance of Jesus Christ's atoning sacrifice. Baptism signifies a commitment to a new way of life governed by the spiritual laws of God, the example of Jesus Christ, and the indwelling of the Holy Spirit. The Worldwide Church of God practices baptism by immersion.

(Matthew 3:16, Mark 16:16, Galatians 3:27, Romans 6:4-5)

THE CHURCH

The Church is the collective body of believers who are called by God and in whom the Holy Spirit abides. The Church began on the Day of Pentecost and was commissioned to preach the gospel, to teach all that Christ commanded, to baptize, and to nurture the flock. In fulfilling its mission, it looks continually to Jesus Christ, the living head of the Church.

(I Corinthians 12:13, Romans 8:9, Matthew 28:19-20, Colossians 1:18, Ephesians 1:22, Acts 2:1-47)

CHURCH LEADERSHIP

The head of the Church is Jesus Christ. He guides the Church in the will of God, as revealed by the Holy Spirit in the Scriptures. In the Worldwide Church of God, the decision-making process under Christ involves councils of ministers that report to the Pastor General, who holds the chief administrative office in the Church.

(Ephesians 1:22, Colossians 1:18, Ephesians 4:11)

THE CHRISTIAN

The Christian is the person in whom the Holy Spirit abides, whose attitude and behavior are consistent with the teachings of Jesus Christ. Through the regeneration of the Holy Spirit, the Christian is born from above and maintains a right relationship with God and man through a life of love and service.

(Romans 8:9, 14, I Peter 2:21, I John 2:4-6, Matthew 22:37-39, John 1 3:35)

THE GOSPEL

The gospel is the message preached by Jesus Christ and by the Church about the kingdom of God. It is the good news of what God has done and will do through Christ, and is the central message of the Old and New Testaments.

(Matthew 28:19-20, Mark 1:14-15, Acts 8:12, 28:30-31, Luke 24:46-48)

PROPHECY

Prophecy is the divine revelation of God's will and purpose. In prophecy, God reveals himself as the one who supervises the course of history and reminds man that God is judge of all and that his judgment is surely coming. Prophecy assures man of God's love, mercy, and faithfulness and motivates the believer to live a godly life in Jesus Christ.

(Isaiah 46:9-11, Daniel 4:17, Jude 14-15, II Peter 3:14)

MAN

Man was made mortal, in the image of God. God formed him of the dust of the ground and breathed into his nostrils the breath of life, endowing him with mental and spiritual faculties. He was given dominion over all the earth, and the freedom to choose whether to obey his Creator. Because he chose sin, man was alienated from God and can be reconciled only through the sacrifice of Jesus Christ. Man's destiny is to inherit eternal life in the kingdom of God.

(Genesis 1:26-28, 2:7, 16-17, Romans 5:12-21)

SALVATION

Salvation is deliverance from the bondage of sin and from the ultimate penalty of sin, death. It is the gift of God, by grace through faith in Jesus Christ, not earned by personal merit or good works. Through our acceptance of the sacrifice of Jesus Christ, God offers salvation, not only for the present life, but for eternity following Christ's return. In the broadest sense, salvation encompasses even the creation.

(Romans 6:18, 22-23, Ephesians 2:8-9, I Peter 1:4, Romans 8:21-23)

GRACE

Grace is the free, unmerited favor God bestows on a sinner who repents. In its broadest sense, grace is expressed in every act of God's self-disclosure. By grace, man comes to know God, is justified, and is saved. Through faith, the Christian remains always under grace.

(Romans 3:24, 5:2, 15-17, 21, Ephesians 2:8-9, Titus 3:7)

SANCTIFICATION

Sanctification is the state of holiness imparted to the believer through the indwelling of God's Holy Spirit. Though all Christians sin, God's Holy Spirit leads them to a life of repentance and obedience, a life evidenced by the fruit of the Holy Spirit. Sanctification follows conversion and is made possible by God's grace, through faith in Jesus Christ.

(I Peter 1:2, I John 1:8, 3:6, 9, Romans 6:22, Galatians 5:22-23, Romans 5:1)

JUSTIFICATION

Justification is God's gracious act of pronouncing a believer righteous in his sight. It is dependent upon repentance and is made possible through faith in the shed blood of Jesus Christ and acceptance of him as Lord and Savior.

(Romans 3:20, 24-31, 4:1-8, 5:1, 9, Galatians 2:16)

CONVERSION

Conversion is a turning from the way of sin to the way of God. It is closely connected with God's calling, repentance, and baptism, and is sealed by the gift of the Holy Spirit. Conversion is manifest in godly thoughts, attitudes, and actions that form the basis of the believer's life in Christ.

(John 3:3-6, Matthew 18:3, Acts 2:38, 3:19, Colossians 3:1-17)

THE LAW

The law is a system of divinely inspired moral and religious precepts which, in letter and in spirit, define sin and regulate human conduct. Christ magnified the Old Testament law by revealing its spiritual intent and purpose. The Christian is not justified by the law, but by grace through faith in Jesus Christ. Whereas the Christian sins by breaking the spirit or the letter of God's law, he is not to persist in a state of sin, but must strive to exemplify the mind of God in every facet of his life.

(Romans 7:7, 12-14, Matthew 5:17-19, Ephesians 2:8-9, 1 John 3:9, Romans 13:10, I John 5:3)

THE SABBATH

The Sabbath is an appointed day of rest and worship. It was sanctified at creation because, on the seventh day, God rested from his work. The observance of the Sabbath was enjoined in the Ten Commandments, was a sign between God and his people Israel and was affirmed by the example of Jesus Christ and the apostles. Following these scriptural examples, the Worldwide Church of God continues to observe the seventh-day Sabbath.

(Genesis 2:2-3, Exodus 20:8-11, 31:17, Luke 4:16, Acts 17:2, Hebrews 4:9)

THE FESTIVALS

The observance of the festivals and holy days enjoined on ancient Israel was affirmed by the example of Jesus Christ and the apostles. They are holy convocations, memorials of God's great acts of salvation in history, symbols of the power of God, and types of the anticipated future fulfillment of God's plan of salvation. For the Christian, the festivals and holy days are annual celebrations of God's power, love, and saving grace.

(Leviticus 23:1-2, John 4:45, 5:1, 7:37, 12:12, Acts 2:1, 20:16, I Corinthians 5:7-8)

TITHING

Tithing is the scriptural practice of giving a tenth of one's increase to God. Freewill offerings are distinct from tithes and are given as the believer is able. Tithes and offerings were commanded in the Old Testament and were confirmed in the New Testament by Jesus Christ and the apostles. The Church uses tithes and offerings to fulfill its God-given mission to preach the gospel. Tithing and giving reflect the believer's worship, faith, and love for God, the Source of salvation and Giver of all good things.

(Leviticus 27:30, Numbers 18:20-21, Matthew 23:23, Hebrews 7:4-14)

THE SECOND COMING

Jesus Christ, as he promised, will return to earth to judge and reign over all nations, in the kingdom of God. His second coming will be visible, and in power and glory. This event is the hope of the Church, because it inaugurates the resurrection of the dead and the reward of the righteous.

(John 14:3, Revelation 17:14, Acts 1: 11, Revelation 1:7, Matthew 24:30, I Thessalonians 4:16-17)

THE MILLENNIUM

The Millennium is the one-thousand-year period during which Jesus Christ and the resurrected saints rule the world in peace, justice, and equity. It begins when Christ returns as King of kings and Lord of lords to establish the kingdom of God over all nations. At the beginning of the Millennium, Satan is bound and the prophesied "times of refreshing" begin. After the Millennium, when all enemies will have been put under his feet and all things made subject to him, Christ will deliver the kingdom to God the Father.

(Revelation 20:1-4, 6, Acts 3:19-21, Revelation 11:15, I Corinthians 15:24)

THE INHERITANCE OF THE BELIEVER

The inheritance of the believer is eternal life in the kingdom of God. This inheritance is reserved in heaven and will be bestowed at the second coming of Christ. The resurrected saints will then rule the nations with Christ in the kingdom of God.

(I John 2:25, Romans 8:16-19, Daniel 7:27, I Peter 1:3-5, Revelation 5:10)

THE FATE OF THE UNREPENTANT

Unrepentant sinners are those who, after coming to a full knowledge of God, deliberately and ultimately reject him. Their fate is to perish in the lake of fire. This death is eternal, and the Scriptures refer to it as the second death.

(Matthew 10:28, 3:12, 25:41, Revelation 20:14-15)

THE KINGDOM OF GOD

The kingdom of God in the broadest sense is God's supreme sovereignty. God reigns in the Church and in the life of each believer who is submissive to his will. The kingdom of God will be established over the whole world after the return of Jesus Christ and will increase to encompass all things.

(Luke 17:20-21, Daniel 2:44, Mark 1:14-15, I Corinthians 15:24-28, Revelation 11:15, 21:3, 22-27, 22:1-5)

Notes: *The Worldwide Church of God is the most successful of the several sabbatarian Church of God groups. These groups*

dissent from orthodox Christianity on the doctrine of the Trinity. Though non-Trinitarian, the Church affirms much of the substance of the traditional trinitarian doctrine. The Bible is considered the infallible Word of God. The Church worships on Saturday, and keeps the Sabbath of the Ten Commandments and Jewish festivals. It advocates tithing as the biblical form of giving.

*   *   *

Sacred Name Groups

THE DOCTRINES AND TEACHINGS (ASSEMBLY OF YHWHHOSHUA)

1. DENOMINATIONS AND AFFILIATIONS

The Assembly of YHWHHOSHUA is not affiliated or in accord with any other of the denominational or non-denominational churches or sects, and its members of the Assembly of YHWHHOSHUA are not simultaneously members of any other assembly, sect or church unless that sect, assembly or church, is preaching the true unadulterated Word of YHWHHOSHUA. The various churches in the United States in one form or another are in, the state of disobedience to the laws of YHWH. So we can not partake in these unrighteous churches.

2. THE NAME OF THE ALMIGHTY AND HIS MESSIAH

The true revealed Name of the Almighty is YHWH, and His Messiah, the Savior, is YHWHHOSHUA. The name YHWH, meaning, I AM or HE WHO IS, was declared by the Almighty, Himself, to Mosheh (Moses) on Mt. Horeb (Ex. 3:13-15), in which He declares, "This is My Name forever, and My Memorial unto all generations." It is quite clear from these passages that His NAME is not to be changed. In the King James (KJV) and other versions of the bible; translators have mistranslated the Divine Name, YHWH, into the word 'LORD'; and 'GOD' instead of 'ELOHIM', the Hebrew title for the Supreme Being. In their former languages, the title 'LORD' is 'BAAL', which is the supreme idol of heathen Babylon. 'ADONIS', 'ADONAI', or 'ADON' are the Phoenician and Greek idol of beauty from whence comes the name 'JEHO-VAH'. 'GOD' is the Assyrian deity of fortune. The NAME of the Son—"I am come in My Father's Name" (John 5:43)—is the Name YHWH, together with the Name HOSHUA (SAVIOR). In full, it is YHWHHOSHUA, meaning, I AM THE SAVIOR, or YHWH has become SALVATION. "I, even I, am YHWH, and beside ME there is no Savior. " (Isaiah 43:11) This uncompromising statement leaves no room for any savior named Jesus, Zeus, or any other name but YHWHHOSHUA. Jesus is the English form of the Greek name for their savior, which in Greek mythology is Zeus (Ie-Zeus or Ea-Zeus—healing Zeus). These facts can be documented. It is also disrespectful to call our Father and Savior by a shortened name or nickname, thus disallowing the terms 'YAH', 'Yahshua', or 'Yahoshua', and others in reference to our Father and Savior.

"I am YHWH, that is My Name, and My glory will I not five to another. . ." (Isaiah 42:8)

3. THE LAW OF YHWH AND THE GRACE OF YHWHHOSHUA

We believe that we are saved by the grace of YHWHHOSHUA, in that He shed his blood for the remission of our sins; and that we accept this grace by faith in what He did and taught as well as what He teaches today. We do not misconstrue this grace as a license to continue in our sin by disobeying YHWH's laws, but rather the strength to repent from our former lives of sin. It is by repentance and the keeping of YHWH's laws that we have access to His Holy Spirit.

4. IMMERSION (BAPTISM)

Once an individual decides that he or she is willing to dedicate their life of obedience to YHWH, it is required that one be baptized by full immersion in a natural body of water (lake, river or sea), by a minister of YHWHHOSHUA, as a token of the covenant that he is going to cleanse his life. We believe that YHWHHOSHUA honors this token of faith by applying the redeeming value of the blood that He shed to the individual's soul; cleansing him from all the sins that were committed previous to baptism. "He that believeth and is immersed shall be saved; but he that believeth not shall be damned." (Mark 16:16) "Repent and be immersed every one of you in the Name of YHWHHOSHUA the Messiah, for the remission of sins, and ye shall receive the gift of the Holy Spirit." (Acts 2:38) "Except a man be born of water and of the Spirit, he can not enter into the kingdom of YHWH". (John 3:5)

5. THE GIFT OF THE HOLY SPIRIT

Once a believer totally yields his heart, mind, body and soul to the perfect will of YHWH, he will receive the gift of the Holy Spirit, the Power of the Almighty, which will be initially evidenced by a marked improvement in the individual's life in the way of love, joy, peace, longsuffering, gentleness, faith, meekness, temperance, and a willingness to obey the laws of YHWH. When one receives the fullness and infilling of the Holy Spirit, he will speak in a heavenly tongue as the Spirit moves in him. "For with stammering lips and another tongue will He speak to this people." To whom He said, "This is the rest wherewith ye may cause the weary to rest; and this is the refreshing: yet they should not hear." (Isaiah 28:11-12) "And these signs shall follow them that believe; in My Name shall they cast out demons; they shall speak with new tongues:" (Mark 16:17)

6. MINISTERS

A minister or pastor of YHWHHOSHUA is a man (not a woman) who is in obedience to the doctrine of YHWHHOSHUA. ". . . ordain elders in every city. . ., If any be blame less, the husband of one wife. . ." (Titus 5:6) "That the man of YHWH may be perfect, thoroughly furnished unto all good works." (Timothy 3:17) "Let your women keep silence in the assemblies: for it is not permitted unto them to speak; but they are commanded to be under obedience, as also saith the law." (I Corinthians 14:34) "But I do not allow a woman to preach, nor to usurp authority over the man, but to be quiet. " (I Timothy 2:12)

7. SANCTIFICATION

The members of the assembly of YHWHHOSHUA are to be separate from the institutions, customs, traditions, styles and carnal pleasures of the United States as well as the world. A member in no way should participate into the affairs and practices of the world.

8. GOVERNMENT

YHWHHOSHUA is our government. He is our counselor, our welfare, medicare. He is our social security and old age care, our employment. Through YHWHHOSHUA all things are provided. The widows and orphans, the elderly and sick, those who are unable to work are to be supported by the assembly as a whole; the men working and giving out of the generosity of their hearts. It is the duty of every member of the assembly to help all those members of the assembly of YHWHHOSHUA who are in need. In no way should we participate in the charities of the world, for these charities are not for YHWH'S people. Thus a servant of YHWH can not vote or contribute to or accept any benefits from the institutions of the United States, such as Social Security, Medicare, Unemployment Compensation, etc. . . . nor shall he be allowed to be a government official, to be a juror, or to serve in the Armed Forces.

9. INCOME TAX

Members of the assembly of YHWHHOSHUA are not to pay the Federal Income Tax. The income tax of the United States is used to pay for such things that are contrary to the law of YHWH. Such as, the armed forces of America, "Thou shalt not kill." (Exodus 20) Numerous government medical benefits are provided by the income tax (abortion clinics, birth control research grants, experimental animal killing, etc . . .) These things are contrary to the law of YHWH. The lists seems endless, these are just a few of the atrocities the income tax encourages. "Render therefore unto Caesar (United States) the things which are Caesar's; and unto YHWH the things that are YHWH's." (Matthew 22:21) The money that the servants of YHWH earn belongs to YHWH and is to be used to supply the needs of YHWH's people, not those of the world. "And the multitude of them that believed were of one heart and of one soul; neither was there any among them that lacked; for as many as were possessors of lands or houses sold them and brought the prices of the things that were sold, and laid them down at the apostles' feet; and distribution was made unto every man according as he had need." (Acts 4:32, 34, 35) "Come out of her, My people, that ye be not partakers of her sins, and that ye received not of her plagues." (Rev. 18:4) "YHWHHOSHUA spoke to him, saying, What thinkest thou, Simon? of whom do the kings of the earth take custom or tribute? of their own children, or of strangers? Peter saith unto Him, Of strangers. YHWHHOSHUA saith unto him, Then are the children free." (Matthew 17:25-26)

10. HOLIDAYS

Christmas (Saturnalia), Easter (Ishtar), New Years, Independence Day, Thanksgiving, and any other heathen holiday are not celebrated in this assembly because of the inherent revelry contained in such celebration, as in the pagan names and sources that they represent. ''Thus saith YHWH, learn not the way of the heathen ... for the customs of the people are vain...'' (Jeremiah 10:2-3) ''Ye observe days, and months, and times, and years. I am afraid of you, lest I have bestowed upon you labor in vain.'' (Gal. 4:10-11) See also Lev. 19:26, and Deut. 18:10-11.

11. PASSOVER

However, we do observe the Passover, on the evening of the fourteenth day of the first month of the calendar of YHWH. This is a commandment of YHWH and YHWHHOSHUA, by partaking of the body and blood of the Messiah. For the body we use pure unleaven bread (whole wheat) and for the blood we use pure unfermented grape juice, and not liquor which is the custom of many churches in this world. ''And He said unto them, With desire I have desired to eat this Passover with you before I suffer; For I say unto you, I will not anymore eat thereof, until the kingdom of YHWH is established. And He took bread and gave thanks, and brake it, and gave unto them saying, This is My body which is given for you; this do in remembrance of Me. Likewise, after supper He took the cup, and gave thanks, and said, take this, and divide it among yourselves; For this cup is the new testament in my blood which is shed for you. For I say unto you, I will not drink of the fruit of the vine, until the kingdom of YHWH shall come.'' (Lk. 22:15-20) ''And this day shall be unto you for a memorial; and you shall keep it a feast to YHWH throughout your generations; he shall keep it a feast by an ordinance forever.'' (Ex. 12:14) We allow no graven images; such as pictures of statues, the Savior, and or relics supposedly of the Savior and His apostles, or the Messiah's mother. Our driver licenses have no pictures on them. These things are contrary to the first commandment of YHWH, and others as well. ''Thou shalt not make unto thee any graven idol, or any likeness of anything that is in heaven above, or that is in the earth beneath, or that is iii the water under the earth.'' (Ex. 20-4)

12. SELFISH PLEASURES

Television, radio, records and tapes, as well as all worldly music are forbidden. Sporting events, movies, plays, partying, dating and all other carnal pleasures are disallowed because they take away an individual from the real purpose of his existence for YHWH. However it is expressed that a servant of YHWH learn to play an instrument such as a guitar, piano, flute, etc... and compose their own righteous songs and music for the Almighty. ''Neither ye be idolaters as were some of them: as it is written, the people sat down to eat and drink, and rose up to play.'' (I Cor. 10:7) Many of these devices, especially movies and television, indoctrinate the whole world into the ways that are contrary to YHWH's law.

13. FOOD

A great deal of time can be discussed on the foods we choose to eat. YHWH commanded that we eat only the foods that He sanctified by His Word. (Lev. Chap 11) However, due to the great amount of chemicals present today, it is even a greater task to find clean wholesome food. The abundance of herbicides, pesticides and fertilizers found into today's markets causes a great many diseases and deaths. It is therefore most important that we eat clean pure food that is healthy and nourishing to our bodies. Taking a great deal of time to see that we stay away from such foods that contain preservatives, chemical additives; even impure processing. Also many drugs are found naturally in some foods such as caffeines which can be found in coffee also cocoa. A lot of processed foods have drugs added to give people a lift. Intoxicants are forbidden also in this assembly. ''If any man defile the temple of YHWH, him will YHWH destroy; for the temple of YHWH is holy, which temple ye are.'' (I Cor. 3:17) ''Wine is a mocker, strong drink is raging; and whosoever is deceived thereby is not wise.'' (Prov. 20:1)

14. MAN'S APPAREL

YHWHHOSHUA is our example of how we should dress. A full head of hair and beard, and a robe that is modest from head to foot. Because of fashion and disobedience to YHWH's laws, man has gotten away from a righteous form of dress and has introduced a mode of clothing for his own selfish desires, such as sex and enticement of the opposite sex. It is with great displeasure that YHWH finds the way of clothing in the world. Members of the assembly are not to shave or trim their beards. ''Ye shall not round the corners of your heads, neither shalt thou mar the corners of thy beard.'' (Lev. 19:27) He is forbidden to wear suits and neckties (cloth necklaces), colognes, make up, jewelry, hair spray, high-heel shoes, or tight, short, see through clothing. For these are effeminate (homo-sexual) styles of the world. ''Know ye not that the unrighteous shall not inherit the kingdom of YHWH? Be not deceived; neither fornicators nor idolaters, nor adulterers, nor effeminates (homosexuals), nor self abusers, nor thieves, nor covetous, nor drunkards, nor revilers, nor extortioners, shall inherit the kingdom of YHWH.'' (I Cor. 9:10)

15. WOMAN'S APPAREL

The women of the assembly wear a loose modest gown or dress of ankle length. Also a veil or head covering to cover the hair. ''in like manner also, that women adorn themselves in modest apparel, with shamefulness and sobriety; not with braided hair, or gold or pearls, or costly array; But with good works.'' (I Tim. 2:9-10) ''But every woman that prayeth or prophesieth with her head uncovered, let her also be shorn; but if it be a shame for a woman to be shorn or shaven; let her be covered. 'For this cause ought the woman to have the sign of the authority of her head because of the angles. (I Cor. 11:5-6-10) A women of the assembly is not to shave her legs, cut her hair, wear short dresses or skirts, nylons, jeans, shorts, styled hair, jewelry, perfume, make up, high heel shoes, tight see through clothing of any kind. She is not to wear or take on the appearance of a man in spirit or clothing. ''The women shall not wear that which pertaineth unto a man, neither shall a man put on a woman's garment; for all that do so are a abomination unto YHWH thy Elohim.'' (Deu. 22:5)

16. DUTIES OF A MAN

To work to support himself, and his family, to help others, especially the widows and orphans. "Let him that stole steal no more; but rather let him labor, working with his hands the thing which is good, that he many have, to give to him that needeth." (Eph. 4:28) It is required that he also teach the doctrine of YHWHHOSHUA to his family as well as to the stranger at his gate. To be a witness for YHWH at home and abroad. He is to be the head of the household, and not the woman.

17. DUTIES OF A WOMAN

To be meek, and quiet; in subjection to her pastor, if married to be in subjection to her husband; to be a keeper at home, to cook, sew, to clean the home. To raise her children in the righteousness of YHWH's law. To teach the younger women and children in YHWH's ways. "The aged women likewise, that they be in behavior as becometh holiness not false accusers, not given to much wine, teachers of good things; That they may teach the young women to be sober, to love their husbands, to love their children, to be discrete, chaste, keepers at home, good, obedient to their own husbands, that the word of YHWH be not blasphemed." (Tit. 2:3-5)

18. MARRIAGE AND DATING

Marriage, if it is free from lust of the flesh, is truly a great blessing from YHWH as long as it is in His perfect order. Marriage is a lifetime commitment, announced before the assembly and bounded by YHWH. No man or woman having a spouse yet alive, whether separate or not, is to marry another, except for the reason of fornication committeth by one of the partners; to do so is adultery. Moreover, no married or unmarried man should at any time be alone with another person of the opposite gender for the purpose of courting, or any type of seductive behavior for the purpose of dating. Seductive behavior is strictly forbidden, so a man should not be alone with a woman who is not his wife unless absolutely necessary. "Rebuke not an elder, but entreat him as a father; and the younger men as brethren the elder women as mothers; the younger as sisters with all purity." (I Cor. 7) "Now concerning the things whereof ye wrote unto me; it is good for a man not to touch a woman. Never the less, to avoid fornication, let every man have his own wife, and let every woman have her own husband." Even the common church practice of hugging, and/or kissing the opposite gender in greeting is also strictly disallowed in this assembly.

19. DOCTORS AND MEDICINES

The use of doctors or medicines is not allowed in this assembly. However a person has a choice in this matter to go to a doctor or not to go to a doctor. Thus saith YHWH; Cursed be the man that trusteth in man, and maketh flesh his arm, and whose heart departeth from YHWH." (Jer. 17:5) All children born in the assembly are delivered by a mid-wife. All sicknesses, cut, broken bones, are healed by the Almighty Hand of YHWH Himself. "See now that I, even I, am He, and there is none with me; I kill, and I make alive; I wound, and I heal, neither is there any that can deliver out of My hand." (Deu. 32:19) Even after death, we bury our own deceased. It is forbidden that the dead be subject to autopsies. A deceased member is placed into the ground within 24 hours after death has been determined.

20. PUBLIC SCHOOLS

The public school system is one of the biggest devices that the United States has for indoctrination and persuasion into the customs of the heathen nations. The public school system introduces such holidays as Halloween, Christmas, Easter; etc. . . . These holidays are hated by YHWH. (See Section X.) The cafeterias serve not only unclean foods but also unwholesome foods. The students as well as the teachers are dressed in immodest apparel. There is generally an immoral environment. Because of these things we have our own school for children from the first through the twelfth grade, taught by teachers from our assembly, who teach not only what the State contends to be taught but also the righteousness of the Almighty as well as providing a positive and healthy environment for all concerned.

21. THE BIBLE AND BIBLE SCHOOLS

We presently read and teach from a translation called the 'Holy Name Bible', which is similar to the KJV, only deleting the names of blasphemy (Rev, 17:3) used in the KJV (Lord, God, Jesus, Jehovah) We do not depend solely on the bible for our teachings, but rely on the Holy Spirit of YHWH to lead and guide us. "But the Comforter, which is the Holy Spirit, whom the Father will send in My Name, shall teach you all things, and bring all things to your remembrance, whatsoever I have said unto you." (John 14:26) We also rely on teachers especially ordained by YHWH with His Holy Spirit to teach us. "And he gave some, apostles; and some, prophets; and some, evangelists; and some, pastor and teachers; for the perfecting of the saints, for the work of the ministry, for the edifying of the body of the Messiah." (Eph. 4:11-12) Bible colleges and seminaries teach countless heresies which are contrary to the laws and ordinances of YHWH.

22. SABBATH

Along with the other commandments, the Assembly firmly believes In keeping Saturday, the Seventh day, as the Sabbath; in which they refrain from working, buying, and selling.

Notes: *The Assembly of YHWHHOSHUA is a small, Sacred Name church distinguished by its use of the Hebrew names for the Almighty and the Messiah. It avoids common translations of the Divine's name and uses YHWH (Lord), His title, "Elohim" (God), and the name of the Messiah as YHWHHOSHUA (Jesus). The Church believes the name Jesus is derived from Greek as a form of the name of the Pagan deity Zeus (Jesus = Ie-Zeus). Similarly, the Assembly also rejects the common Christian belief in the Trinity. The Holy Spirit is not an entity, but the Power of YHWH. The Assembly uses the Holy Name Bible, which has deleted the offending terms for YHWH and YHWHHOSHUA.*

The Assembly has accepted a number of positions which, while also adhered to by other groups, taken together present a rather radical form of traditional faith. The Assembly is sabbatarian, practices baptism by immersion, and has a

THE DOCTRINES AND TEACHINGS (ASSEMBLY OF YHWHHOSHUA) (continued)

Pentecostal emphasis emphasizing speaking in tongues. In common with other sacred name groups, popular holidays such as Christmas and Easter are shunned in favor of the older Jewish festival of Passover. Women are not admitted to the ministry, but are to remain in subjection the pastors and to their husbands, to dress modestly and not follow the fashions of the culture. The members of the Assembly do not use physicians.

Members of the Assembly live a separated life and do not participate in government social programs such a Medicare (not choosing to use physicians) and Social Security, nor do they serve in various government capacities such as juries or the Armed Forces. Most controversial of their behaviors is a refusal to pay income tax, which they believe goes to pay for many ungodly causes, including everything from abortion clinics to animal research. Members of the Assembly are expected to use what would have gone for taxes to pay for the care of the elderly and indigent among them. As part of its separatist stance, children of the members are not sent to public school, but to a parochial school, run by the Assembly.

* * *

DOCTRINES [HOUSE OF YAHWEH (ODESSA, TEXAS)]

1. THE HOLY SCRIPTURES

The Bible from Genesis through Revelations are the Holy Scriptures, inspired of Yahweh. We know the Holy Scriptures by the term Old and New Testaments. The Holy Scriptures must be believed by the House of Yahweh. They must be lived by, and when lived by, will make us perfect unto all holy works. The House of Yahweh does not accept any other writings as being inspired other than the Bible. No other writings are needed for Salvation. 2 Tim. 3:16, 17; Heb. 4:12, 2 Kepha 1:19, 21; Psa. 119:105; Ecc. 3:14,15.

2. YAHWEH

Yahweh is one. He is the Creator of all things. Beside him there is no Elohim. He is the Elohim of the fathers Abraham, Isaac, and Jacob. Yahweh is the one who raised the Messiah Yashua from the dead. He is our heavenly Father. His name is Yahweh, his title is Elohim. This name is his memorial forever. Gen. 1:1; Deut. 6:4; Isa. 41:4; Isa. 44:6-8; Isa. 45:5-21,22; Exo. 3:6-13,16; Acts 3:13,15; Exo. 3:15.

3. YESHUA

Yeshua is the holy begotten Son of Yahweh. He was begotten by Yahweh the Father in the womb of the virgin Miriam by the Holy Spirit. His name is called Yeshua because it means "He will save" or that he is "Salvation to man". There is no other name given among men whereby we can saved. John 3:18; Luke 1:26,35; Matt. 1:21; Acts 4:12.

4. MESSIAH

Yahweh has made this same Yeshua both Messiah and king. Yahweh ordained Yeshua to be king to rule all nations. He will rule them with a rod of iron, from sea to sea. He will sit on the throne of David when he returns at his second coming. Just as he went into heaven and the clouds received him out of sight, he will return in the same manner, and every eye shall see him coming in the clouds. Messiah means anointed. Yahweh anointed Yeshua to be Savior and King. Psa. 2: 6,9; Luke 1:26,35; John 1:41,49; Rev. 19:11,16; Rev. 20:4; Acts 2:36, 1 Cor. 15:22,28; Matt. 25:31,46; Acts 1:11; Rev. 1:7; Matt. 24:29,30.

5. THE SIGN OF THE MESSIAH

Yeshua was asked for a sign to prove that he was the Messiah. He told them that the only sign that he would give them to prove that he was the Messiah, was Jonah. Just as Jonah was three days and three nights in the whale's belly, he would be three days and three nights in the tomb. Yeshua was placed in the tomb just as the sun went down on what we call Wednesday evening. He was in the tomb Wednesday night (one night), Thursday day (one day), Thursday night (two nights) Friday day (two days) Friday night (three nights) Saturday day (three days) He rose from the dead just as the sun was going down on the day we call Saturday at evening. Matt. 12:38,40; Eph. 4:9; John 2:19,21; Mark 10:33,34; 1 Cor. 15:1,4; Mark 8:31; Matt. 28:1,6.

6. DEATH OF YESHUA

Yeshua died on the stake to reconcile the believer to the Father Yahweh. By his shed blood we are justified or forgiven before Yahweh. He who knew no sin became sin for us and died that we might live. Rom. 5:6,19; 1 Cor. 5:18,21.

7. RESURRECTION OF YESHUA

Because Yeshua was raised from the dead by the Father, we through him can also be raised from the dead. He became the firstborn from the dead, and through him all true believers will be made alive. Col. 1:18; Rom. 8:28,30; Rom. 8:17,23.

8. RESURRECTION OF BELIEVERS

The resurrection of Yeshua's people is called the first resurrection. When Yeshua returns, he will resurrect all of the righteous dead, from Abel up to the time of his second coming. The righteous who are still living when he comes will be changed to immortality along with the resurrected ones at the seventh trumpet sound. These will become kings and priests to rule with Messiah one thousand years. After his the kingdom will be turned over to Yahweh. 1 Cor. 15:12,57; 1 Thess. 4:13,18; Rev. 20:4; Rev. 5:10; Dan. 12:2,3; Dan. 7:14-27. 1 Thess. 4:13, 18; Rev. 20:4; Rev. 5:10; Dan. 12:2,3; Dan. 7:14-27.

9. SECOND RESURRECTION

At the end of the one thousand year reign of the Messiah and the saints, the rest of the dead will be resurrected. Those who died never having had an opportunity to be saved will be given that opportunity in this resurrection. Those who have had their opportunity and rejected it will be thrown in the lake of fire. Rev. 20:5,6; Rev. 20:11,15; Dan. 12:2, John 5:28,29; Acts 24:15.

10. PUNISHMENT OF THE WICKED

In the end of the thousand year reign of the Messiah the remaining wicked will be punished by being burned up in a lake of fire. The Bible states that they will be burned to ashes. All wicked shall die by fire. There is no such thing taught in the Bible as a hell fire, where souls are tormented day and night forever. The soul sins will die in fire, not live in fire. The wages of sin is death by fire, not a life in a hell fire. Rev. 20:12,15; Rom. 6:23; Ezek. 18:4; Matt. 10:28; Psa. 37:20; Matt. 3:11,12; Psa. 37:10; 2 Kepha 2:9; 2 Kepha 3:7,12; Matt. 13:41,42.

11. THE SOUL

Man is a living soul. He does not have a soul that lives on after death. When a man dies, he returns to the dust of the ground from which he came, in that day his thoughts perish. He knows nothing, and will not know anything until he is called from the grave by Yeshua who is the resurrection and life. The soul dies and the Bible calls this a sleep. Psa. 146:4; Ecc. 9:5,6; Psa. 115:17; Psa. 6:5; 1 Cor. 15:16,18; 1 Thess. 4:13; John 11:11,14; Dan. 12:2; Ecc. 3:19,20; Ecc. 9:10; Gen. 2:7; Gen 3:17,19; Job 14:12,14, Job 17:13; Job 14:21.

12. IMMORTALITY

Man is not immortal. The only way a man can receive this state is to seek after it, by repenting and being baptized and living a life pleasing to the giver of life. Only Yahweh and Yeshua have immortality at this time. Rom. 2:6,7; 1 Cor. 15:53; 1 Tim. 1:17; 1 Tim. 6:16.

13. REPENTANCE

Before any one can come to Yeshua, he must repent of sin. Before he can repent of sin, he must know that sin is. Only by the law of Yahweh is sin made known to man. Repentance is an act of being deeply broken up over the life of sin one has been living. Repentance means that one has resolved to amend his life. Any one who has not studied the law of Yahweh has no knowledge of sin, therefore he cannot repent. Acts 2:38; Acts 3:19; Rom. 3:20; Rom. 7:7; Gal. 3:24; Psa. 38:18; Psa. 19:7; 2 Cor. 7:10; Matt. 3:8; Jonah 3:10; Rom. 2:4,13.

14. SIN

Sin is the transgression of Yahweh's law. Transgression is not keeping the law of Yahweh. Yahweh's law has points, and any one breaking even one point or the least of Yahweh's commandments is guilty of breaking them all. This make him a sinner, and he abides under death. 1 John 3:4; James 2:8,11; Matt. 5:19; Rom. 6:23.

15. BAPTISM

To be saved, one must be baptized in water. Baptized means that the one who has repented must be plunged or dipped under water. This is a likeness of being buried in death and raised to life. Acts 2:38; John 3:23; 1 Kepha 3:20,21; Titus 3:5; Rom. 6:3,5; Col. 2:12.

16. IN THE NAME OF YESHUA

Baptism must be done in the name of Yeshua. This name must be used by the Minister doing the baptizing. Using titles such as Father, Son, and Holy Spirit are not names of any one. The name of Yeshua covers the name of the Father, Son, and Holy Spirit. For Yeshua came in the Father's name. The Holy Spirit was sent in Yeshua's name. Therefore when the Minister says, ''I now baptized you into the name of Yeshua the Messiah'' he is baptizing that person in the name of the Father, Son and Holy Spirit. For there is no other name given under heaven whereby man must be saved. His name means Salvation. That is why we are baptized, to obtain Salvation. Acts 2:38; Mat. 28:19; Acts 8:16; Acts 19:5; Rom. 6:3; Gal. 3:17; Acts 4:10,12; John 5:43; John 14:26.

17. REMISSION OF SINS

Baptism is done for the remission of sins. Remission means freeing from a due or merited punishment. A cancelling or giving up a claim or right. When baptized, the law's right to put us to death for our sins is given up. This is undeserved pardon. Baptism brings Yahweh's undeserved pardon to us, freeing us from the punishment which we deserved for breaking the law of Yahweh. But because baptism makes us free from the death claim which the law had against us does not give us the right to go back to breaking the law again. If we do this, we have no undeserved pardon or remission of sins. Acts 2:38; Rom. 6:1,23; Rom. 3:23, 25.

18. THE HOLY SPIRIT

When one completes the act of repenting and has been baptized for the remission of sins, he will receive the Holy Spirit to be with him by the laying on of the hands of the Ministers. The Holy Spirit is the gift of Yahweh to his people, giving them power to overcome and live as Yahweh commands. It is the power of the most High Yahweh sent forth in the name of Yeshua the Messiah. The Holy Spirit is not another person, but is the power and mind of Yahweh, a very part of Yahweh sent to be with us. It is not a holy ghost as is sometimes rendered in the King James version. The term holy ghost is a false translation and should never be used by the people of Yahweh. Luke 1:35; John 14:16,17-26; John 15:26; John 16:7,15; Acts 2:38,39; Acts 8:14,17; Acts 19:1,6.

19. FRUIT OF THE HOLY SPIRIT

There are nine fruits of the Holy Spirit which all believers must bear after they receive the Holy Spirit. This is the only sign by which they are known to be true believers. Gal. 5:22,23; Matt. 7:16; John 15:1,5.

20. GIFTS OF THE HOLY SPIRIT

There are nine gifts of the Holy Spirit. These are gifts given to the Ministry of The House of Yahweh to be used for the building up of the body of Messiah. No one man ever received all of these gifts. But they were given to each one to whom it pleased Yahweh to give that certain gift of the Holy Spirit. Yahweh gives these gifts to the Ministry when needed for the building up of the whole body. The so called modern day speaking in tongues is not one of these gifts and has no part in The House of Yahweh. 1 Cor. 12:1,11-29,30; 1 Cor. 14th chapter; Acts 3:1,7; James 5:14,15; Acts 8:5,7; Acts 14:8,10; 1 Tim. 6:20; 2 Tim. 2:16.

21. MINISTRY IN THE HOUSE OF YAHWEH

No man can become a Minister of Yahweh, except he be called by Yahweh for this job. When Yahweh calls a man to the office of a Minister, he will know it, and the other Ministers in The House of Yahweh will know it. Yahweh has placed in The House of Yahweh different office of the Ministry. They are listed as, Apostles, Prophets, Evangelists, Pastors, and Teachers. The required number for Apostles and Prophets are twelve Apostles and seventy Prophets. There are no required number for the other offices. All of these Ministering offices must be in unity on the doctrines of the House of Yahweh, that they may lead all of the saints into unity. They must be in unity to keep out every wind of doctrine brought in by false teachers who would deceive and toss the saints to and fro. No man who claims to be a Minister is to get up in The House of Yahweh pulpit and preach anything which he knows to be contrary to the doctrines of The House of Yahweh. If he feels he has a truth which The House of Yahweh is not teaching, he should bring it before the Elders for consideration. If the Elders agree it needs to be taught, it shall be taught, and if they do not agree it is truth, it is not to be taught in The House of Yahweh. Ministers are to feed the body of Messiah on true spiritual food that if may grow. They are to be about this job in season and out of season. Heb. 5:1,4; Eph. 4:11,14; 1 Cor. 12:28; Luke 9:1; Mark 3:13,19; Luke 10:1, Acts 1:15,26; Acts 13:1,3; Acts 14:23; Titus 1:5; Acts 20:17-28; Matt. 24:45,46; 1 Cor. 1:21; Heb. 13:7-17; 1 Tim. 5:17,19; 1 Thess. 5:12,13: 2 Tim. 4:1,5.

22. THE TWO GREAT COMMANDMENTS

The two great commandments teaches us to love Yahweh with all of our heart, and our neighbor as our self. Therefore the two great commandments teaches us to obey all of the laws of Yahweh which shows love to Yahweh and our neighbor. This was the message of Yeshua the Messiah. Deut. 6:4,5; Lev. 19:17; Luke 10:25,28; James 2:8; 1 John 5:2,3.

23. THE TEN COMMANDMENTS

The ten commandments are of the two great commandments. They show love to Yahweh and love to neighbor. Therefore they are to be kept by The House of Yahweh. Any one who loves Yahweh with all of his heart and who loves his fellowman as himself would never break one of these ten commandments. Exo. 20:1,17.

24. THE SABBATH

The Sabbath is the fourth commandment of the ten. It is a sign between Yahweh and his people. And as Yahweh commanded it to kept, we show our love for him when we keep it. The Sabbath is the seventh day of the week, the day which the world calls Saturday. Gen. 2:1,3; Exo. 16:14,29; Exo. 20:8,11;

Exo. 31:13,17; Ezek. 20:12-20; Luke 4:16; Acts 13:14-42,44; Acts 16:13; Acts 17:2; Acts 18:1,4; Heb. 4:4-9.

25. FEAST DAYS OF LEV. 23rd chap.

The feast days which Yahweh commanded to be sacred assemblies when Yahweh's people are to meet before him were ordained to be kept forever. When we keep these days as holy convocations, we show love for Yahweh. They are a part of the great commandment of love to Yahweh. These days were ordained at the creation of this world. Yahweh's people have always kept them and always will. Yeshua and his Apostles kept them, and they shall be kept after Yeshua sets up his kingdom. Lev. 23:1,44; Gen. 1:14; Deut. 16:1,17; Luke 22:7,20; John 7:1,37; Acts 2:1; Acts 18:21; Acts 20:6-16; 1 Cor. 16:8; Isa. 66:22,23; Zech. 14:16,19; Col. 2:16,17.

26. PASSOVER

Passover is one of the feast days of Yahweh. The House of Yahweh keeps Passover on the fourteenth of the first Bible month Abib between the two evenings, between sun-set and dark. The Passover is the memorial of the death angel passing over the houses of Israel in Egypt and striking the firstborn of the Egyptians dead, but passing over the houses of the children of Israel which had blood on their door posts. It is also a memorial of the death of the Messiah. We are to keep it as a memorial of his death till he comes. There has been no part of the Passover feast changed except the lamb. Yeshua became the lamb. Bread from the Passover table became the symbol of his body and the last glass of wine the symbol of his blood. Lev. 23:5; Luke 22:7,20; 1 Cor. 5:6,8; 1 Cor. 11:23,34; Exo. 12:1,27.

27. WINE

Pure fermented wine is to be used at the Passover table as the symbol of the blood of the Messiah. Grape juice cannot be used because it contains leavening or yeast. Webster's Dictionary states- ''Yeast, a substance consisting of cells of minute one-celled fungi and appearing as a surface froth or sediment in fruit juices and other saccharine liquids''. Fruit of the vine the term used by Yeshua at Passover is a Jewish term found in all Jewish Prayer books, and always means fermented wine. To use grape juice at Passover would be sinning against the blood of the Passover. Because no leavening is to be used at the Passover table. Luke 22:7,20; Exo. 12:27; Exo. 23:18; Exo. 34:25; Heb. 10:26,29.

28. SECOND TITHE

The People of Yahweh are to save back out of their income a second tithe, to be used by them to go to the place where Yahweh has set his name. There they are to spend that tithe on food and drink which they desire during the feasts of Yahweh. There at the place Yahweh has chosen to make a home for his name, they are to use this tithe to rejoice during the feast days. Every third and sixth year, between the Sabbath years, they are to use any surplus of this second tithe to help bring the stranger, the orphan, the widow, and any Minister of Yahweh which needs help, to Yahweh's feasts, that they also may rejoice in these feasts of Yahweh. Deut. 14:22,29; Deut. 26:1,14.

29. FIRST TITHE AND OFFERINGS

The people of Yahweh are to pay a tithe of their income, and give freewill offerings into The House of Yahweh to finance the Ministry of The House of Yahweh, that the message of the kingdom of Yeshua may be published among all nations. Tithe is an old English word meaning one tent or 10% of a person's income. Yahweh says that the people who do not pay tithe and give offerings are robbing him. Num. 18:1,32; 1 Cor. 9:6,14; 1 Tim. 5:17,18; Lev. 27:30,34; Matt. 23:23; Mal. 3:8,11; Deut. 16:16,17.

30. CLEAN AND UNCLEAN MEATS

The House of Yahweh is to eat nothing that the Bible says is unclean. Therefore all meats which Yahweh in his word says are unclean are not to eaten by the House of Yahweh people, nor are these unclean meats to be touched or handled. These unclean meat ruin the health of many millions of people yearly. Clean meat and milk, though they are clean are not to be eaten and drink, or cooked together. When eaten and drink together or cooked together, they will ruin ones health and cause many sicknesses and diseases, even cancer. Yahweh's people must abstain from eating milk and meat together. Gen. 7:2; Deut. 14:1,21; Lev. 11:1,47; Isa. 65:4,5; Isa. 66:15,17.

31. TALLITH

All male members of The House of Yahweh are to wear the tallith as commanded in the Bible. The tallith is a four cornered shawl with fringes at each corner. Num. 15:38,41; Deut. 22:12.

32. KEPA AND VEIL

All male members are to wear a kepa on their head in worship services and while praying. For it is a shame for a man to pray bare headed. All women of The House of Yahweh are to wear veils and dress in feminine dress. They are not to wear anything pertaining to a man such as long pants. Lev. 21:10; Lev. 10:6, 2 Sam. 15:29,32; Ezek. 24:17,23; 1 Cor. 11:1,15; Deut. 22:5.

33. BEARD

All male members of The House of Yahweh are to wear beards when at an age to grow beards. The Bible teaches that it is a shame for a man to shave. Lev. 19:27; Lev. 21:5; 2 Sam. 10:5; 1 Chr. 19:5; 2 Sam. 10:4; Jer. 41:5; Isa. 15:1,3; Psa. 133:2.

34. WAR

The people of Yahweh are not to fight or take up arms. There job is to take the Evangel of Yeshua to all nations, not to make war with any people. Matt. 28:19,20; Luke 3:14 Matt. 5:44; Rom. 12:17,21.

35. SATAN

Satan which is called the devil, serpent and dragon is a fallen Cherub, which was once named Lucifer. Through pride he fell, after his fall the tried to take over the throne of Yahweh. He was cast down out of heaven into the earth's solar system. In his rebellion against Yahweh, he led one third of the angels of the heavens to rebel against Yahweh. Since that time he has been the ruler and elohim of this world. His time is now short and he knows it and he is full of wrath against Yahweh's people. Isa. 14:12,15; Ezek. 23:18-19. Gen. 3:1,5; Luke 4:2,13; Job 1:6,7: Job 2:2; Rev. 12:7,9; Jude 6-9; 2 Kepha 2:4; Rev. 12:10,17; 2 Cor. 11:3-13,15; 2 Cor. 4:3,4.

36. THE KINGDOM OF YAHWEH

The kingdom of Yahweh is a kingdom that is to be set up here on earth at the second coming of Yeshua. This kingdom will rule all nations with a rod of iron. The House of Yahweh must publish and preach and message of this kingdom into all nations. Micah 4:2,4; Isa. 2:3,4; Isa. 11:4,9; Isa. 65:19,25; Dan. 7:27; Matt. 25:31,32; Rev. 20:4; Rev. 11:15.

37. THE HOUSE OF YAHWEH

The body of people which carry out Yahweh's plan for these last days is called The House of Yahweh. This is the Scriptural name for Yahweh's people, and fulfills the words of the Prophets Micah and Isaiah. This is The House of Yahweh established in these last days. The House of Yahweh is to carry the message of Yahweh's laws and coming kingdom to all nations. As this work is done, people and nations will flow into The House of Yahweh. There are no promises made to any other religious body of people other than The House of Yahweh. The House of Yahweh is the true body of Yeshua the Messiah. The House of Yahweh is the pillar and ground of all Bible truth. Mic. 4:1; Isa. 2:2; Psa. 23:6; Psa. 27:4,5; Psa. 84:10; Psa. 118:26; Psa. 122:1; Heb. 3:1,6: 1 Tim. 3:14,15: 1 Kepha 4:17; Heb. 10:21; Eph. 2:19,22.

Notes: *The House of Yahweh, headquartered in Odessa, Texas, was founded in Israel in 1973. Like other Sacred Name groups, it uses the Hebrew names of the Creator (Yahweh) and His Son the Messiah (Yeshua) and refrains from the use of such terms as God and Jesus. Yeshua is the Savior of humankind. He died on the stake (not a cross) on a Wednesday and rose from the dead three days later. The House of Yahweh is thus a sabbatarian group, worshipping on Saturday not Sunday.*

The House of Yahweh rejects the idea of the immortality of the soul in favor of the Hebrew (and biblical) notion that human beings are a soul that perishes at the time of human death and awaits the resurrection. Baptism by immersion is a necessary part of the process of salvation. Baptism is in the name of Yashua, not the Father, Son and Holy Spirit. Baptism frees the believer from the merited punishment for sin and offers the gift of the power of God, the Holy Spirit. The House of Yahweh affirms the member's reception and manifestation of the gifts of the Spirit (as described in I Cor. 12) but denies that the "modern day speaking in tongues" is one of the gifts.

The House of Yahweh keeps the Jewish festivals, commanded by Yahweh and described in the Old Testament. Most important of these is Passover. Members tithe their income, and also practice the second tithe to be spent during the Passover feast. Unspent second tithe money is to be used to bring the those otherwise unable to afford it, or strangers (prospective converts), to the feast. Members also follow kosher laws and refrain from meats described as unclean in the Bible, and do not drink milk and eat meat at the same meal.

DOCTRINES [HOUSE OF YAHWEH (ODESSA, TEXAS)]
(continued)

Male members grow beards and during worship wear the tallith (a shawl) and kepa (a cap). Women wear a veil and modest feminine dress during worship. Members are pacifists and do not participate in war.

*　　*　　*

British Israelism

AIMS AND OBJECTS [BRITISH-ISRAEL WORLD FEDERATION (CANADA)]

THE AIMS AND OBJECTS OF THE FEDERATION ARE:

1. To teach the Gospel of the Kingdom of God and all other doctrines of the Christian faith.

2. To proclaim the truth regarding the origin and early history of the Anglo-Celto-Saxon peoples, whether within the English-speaking countries or elsewhere; and to prove their identity with the so-called Lost Tribes of Israel as distinct from the two-tribed House of Judah.

3. To show that God Almighty has placed upon the before-mentioned peoples an unchanging and irrevocable charge and responsibility, in that they are called to act as His servants and His instruments in preparing the way for the establishment of the Kingdom of God under the direct sovereignty of Jesus Christ.

4. To establish as a fact that the said beliefs are supported and confirmed by the Holy Scriptures.

5. To promote the unification and consolidation of Anglo-Celto-Saxondom, (Christendon), throughout the world.

Notes: *The British-Israel World Federation is one key organization presenting the British-Israel teachings to Canadians. Embodied within an Evangelical Protestant perspective, British-Israelites believe that the Anglo-Celto-Saxon peoples are the literal descendants of the Lost Tribes of ancient Israel. This belief is spelled out in the second paragraph of their statement of Aims and Objects.*

*　　*　　*

ARTICLES OF RELIGION (CHRISTIAN CONSERVATIVE CHURCHES OF AMERICA)

ARTICLE I—GOD

There is one true and living God, an eternal and personal Being, of infinite wisdom, power, and goodness. He is the Creator and Sustainer of all things, and the only proper object of worship. United into a Oneness in the Godhead are the Father, the Son, and the Holy Spirit.

ARTICLE II—THE HEAVENLY FATHER

The Heavenly Father is not only the God and Father of our Saviour Jesus Christ but is also the Father of all those who become His spiritual offspring through faith in Christ. As the Father in Heaven, He stands supreme in the Godhead.

ARTICLE III—THE SON

Through Him and for Him were all things made that were made. The express image of the Father, by Him the infinite God is made nigh unto man. In Him is everlasting life and the light of God that lighteth every man coming into the world.

ARTICLE IV—THE HOLY SPIRIT

The Spirit of God, who proceeds from the Father and the Son, is subject to them in all things. He enlightens and persuades men concerning the truth of God. He directs, empowers, and comforts the children of God. He is the agency through whom the will of the Father and of the Son is accomplished.

ARTICLE V—MAN

All things that exist were created by the Word of God. They are not the product of evolution but were brought forth step by step on the successive days of creation. Man was the climax and pinnacle. He was not the offspring of lower forms of life; but, as a separate and direct creation, he was made in the image and likeness of God. Placed over the lower creation, he forfeited his high level of being and calling through sin. His hope for restoration is the redemption provided through Jesus Christ, whereby he may be renewed in the image of his Creator and reinstated in Divine favor.

ARTICLE VI—ORIGINAL SIN

Original sin is the corruption of the nature of man as a result of the sin and fall of the first man, Adam. It is transmitted from generation to generation, with the result the whole human race is fallen and far removed from the purity of heart and fellowship with God which man first enjoyed in the Garden. Original sin is not an act of transgression, but an inclination to evil so universal and strong that all who reach the age of accountability fall into acts of rebellion against God, becoming guilty and condemned for their own disobedience.

ARTICLE VII—SIN AND SINNING

Sin is of a duofold nature. It is not only an inward spirit of lawlessness or rebellion against God, but is also an act of the will which gives expression to this rebellious spirit by overt disobedience. The transgression of God's will and law results in separation from God, the source of Life. Thus, the wages of sin is death.

ARTICLE VIII—THE BIBLE

The Bible is a divine book inspired of God. It reveals His will and purpose for the human race as He has moved through His Spirit upon the hearts of many men through hundreds of years of time. It contains all things necessary to salvation. As it has preserved the story of the first coming of Christ, so will it some day include the record of the work and teachings of God in connection with the climactic period of all the ages of sacred history, the time of the second coming. It is not to be worshipped as a substitute for God, but to be revered and respected as an instrument of divine revelation.

ARTICLE IX—JESUS CHRIST

Jesus the Christ, the Son of God and the son of man, is both divine and human. He existed with the Father from the beginning. For him were all things created, and through him will all things be restored to their original glory and purpose. He came into this world as God's gift of love, to draw men to the heart of the Heavenly Father. He is the Redeemer of those who turn to God through him in faith. He will return from glory to judge the wicked and to reward the faithful and, as the promised Messiah, to rule over the nations of the world.

ARTICLE X—THE VIRGIN BIRTH

Jesus Christ was conceived by the Holy Ghost and born of the Virgin Mary. His coming was in keeping with prophecy and his birth attended by divine messages concerning the purpose of his advent and miraculous events.

ARTICLE XI—THE ATONEMENT

Jesus Christ did upon the Cross of Calvary offer himself as a perfect and complete sacrifice for the sins of the whole world. Through his sacrificial death he removed the legal barriers in the way of the forgiveness of men and their reconciliation with God the Father. Fully satisfying the demands of divine justice, his vicarious suffering made it possible for the Heavenly Father both to be just and the justifier of those who believed in him.

ARTICLE XII—THE RESURRECTION

Jesus Christ did on the third day by the mighty power of God rise again in the same body that was hung on the Cross and placed in the tomb. By so doing, he overcame the power of the enemy and his ultimate weapon, which is death. He brought forth from the grave life and immortality, becoming a firstfruit of those who sleep in him and the guarantee that they too shall one day, even as they are partakers of his death, likewise share in the glory of his resurrection.

ARTICLE XIII—SALVATION

Through the offering of Jesus Christ upon the Cross salvation is freely provided for all men. Any person who will earnestly and sincerely repent of his sins and turn to Jesus Christ in faith will find pardon and be enabled to stand justified before God. He will find the blood of Christ effective to wash away every stain, to remove all guilt from the conscience, and to enable him to serve the Lord his God without fear all the days of his life.

ARTICLE XIV—REGENERATION

They who accept the salvation provided through Jesus Christ immediately experience the firstfruits of resurrection power. Translated from spiritual death to life by the process of a new birth, they enter into the blessed fellowship of an intimate communion with God as their Heavenly Father. The grace of God becomes the dominant force in their spiritual lives, enabling them to triumph over the powers of spiritual death and darkness.

ARTICLE XV—SAVING FAITH

Although belief and confidence in God brings many blessings, only saving faith appropriates salvation. There is a faith that is required for a sinner to approach God, but this faith does not save. Saving faith is that act of confidence in the merits and the shed blood of Christ whereby the penitent sinner accepts and claims as his own the pardon, salvation, and deliverance from the power of sin freely offered to all. None but the repentant soul can exercise this faith, for it is by repentance the earnest seeker comes to a desire for this salvation. The object of the faith that saves is not any merit whatsoever in the penitent; rather, it looks unto the merits of Christ, his perfect sacrifice and righteousness. It is the one and immediate requirement for salvation. All who exercise saving faith are saved; anyone without it is lost.

ARTICLE XVI—RIGHTEOUSNESS

The image of God is not so completely obliterated by the curse of sin that the individual coming into this world has no goodness at all. Every person is born with a conscience, which, when awakened, enables him to discern to some degree between good and evil. He is prompted by this inborn goodness to do right and to a certain extent does so. Out of this higher nature of man have come moral insights, laws for nations, works of art and beauty, deeds of kindness — much that is very commendable. God, the Author of natural goodness, recognizes it and uses it on occasion. Although they could hardly be considered Christians, He chose and used Israel of old to establish His laws and fight His battles. Becoming the custodians of God's commandments, they then became the classic example of the limitations of the righteousness of man. They demonstrated how impossible it is for man, through the strength of natural goodness, to measure up to God's holy standards, to free himself from the bondage of sin and procure salvation. Their experience illustrated that in the subchristian soul birth sin has the upper hand, sooner or later forcing every individual into overt transgressions of the precepts of God. Their efforts to establish their own righteousness, ever ending in failure, prove that salvation from this enslavement cannot be achieved by righteous deeds, no matter the degree of natural goodness involved. Redemption cannot be earned by any acts of man's righteousness, any acts of obedience to God's laws, be they moral or ceremonial. It must be received as a free gift of God, solely through the merits of the righteousness of Christ. Nothing that any man can do; nothing that anyone can do for him can save him—the blood is his only plea. As he ceases to depend upon his own goodness and through faith receives the Spirit of Christ into his life, he finds peace and pardon and at the same time comes into the possession of the higher righteousness of Christ as the principle motivating power in his life. Self-righteousness, or boasting of one's own goodness then is excluded.

ARTICLE XVII-THE INNER WITNESS

The Spirit of God makes Christ real to the hearts of various individuals in different ways, dealing with each in the manner He considers needful and fit. No person should turn the eye of his faith upon another's experience, neither upon his own subjective feelings. The Spirit indeed does confirm the promises of God and assure the heart, but this witness is the result, not the cause of faith. The penitent sinner must place his trust in the sure Word of God. There is no excuse whatsoever for doubting God's promises. To the one who will commit himself in unwavering trust, in due time the realization of new life will come. It is always he that believeth, never he that doubteth, that hath the witness.

ARTICLE XVIII—GOOD WORKS

If good works do not procure salvation, they are the natural result, and are to be expected in the developing Christian life. They as naturally proceed from a life that is redeemed as desirable fruit is produced by a good tree. Growth in grace, in truth, and in the righteousness that is in Christ will produce an abundance of attitudes and deeds that bring spiritual help and encouragement to others. Such good works are pleasing and acceptable in the sight of God.

ARTICLE XIX—SPIRITUAL GIFTS

Spiritual gifts are like the members of the body, which though diversified and performing various functions, yet work harmoniously together, each contributing to the general objectives of the body as a whole. Regardless of how and upon whom they may be bestowed, the gifts of the Spirit function in harmony to advance the cause of the Lord God and His Son, Jesus Christ. They are not given to exalt any individual in spiritual pride or self-righteousness, but to be used in self-giving love for the edification of the body of Christ. Love is the greatest of all gifts.

ARTICLE XX—THE SPIRIT-FILLED LIFE

Regeneration is the beginning of spiritual life, not its fullness. Spiritual maturity requires a certain process of growth. Just as it takes time for a person to become acquainted with an individual who has been a stranger to him, so must there be a period of developing friendship and love as the born-again Christian comes more and more to know the God he has found through Jesus Christ. It is necessary that he attain to a considerable degree of such knowledge and love before he can wholeheartedly surrender the entire inner and outer life in complete dedication. This he must do to be filled with God's Holy Spirit. God must have all! This higher spiritual walk is called by other names, such as sanctification, the rest of faith, and perfect love. Available only to the completely consecrated soul, it is received by faith.

ARTICLE XXI—SPIRITUAL EVIDENCES

The Gift of the Holy Spirit is not to be confused with the gifts of the Spirit. The exercise of one or another of the gifts of the Spirit does not prove that an individual is Spirit-filled. Spiritual infants do sometimes receive and use spiritual gifts. On the other hand, just as it makes more effective the whole life and its witness for Christ, the infilling of the Spirit does bring divine power and marked improvement into the gifts and their exercise. It means far more of God and far less of self! The Holy Spirit brings the blessing of a pure heart to the consecrated Christian. Whether this condition may or may not be readily observed by those about him, to the one who receives it, it is an evidence of the indwelling of the Holy Spirit. It is not necessary that anyone produce infallible proof to someone else nor to the church as a whole that he is filled with the Spirit. God has not appointed us to take His place as spiritual judges of the Christian experiences of others. The infilling of the Holy Spirit is not to be though of as an outward demonstration but a baptism of divine love that frees the recipient of the bondages of self so that the power of God may flow through him to bless others. Love does not parade itself in carnal pride but strives in humility of spirit to serve. There is no higher evidence than humble, self-giving love of a close, Spirit-filled walk with God. For this reason Christ gave to us his new commandment that we should love one another as he had loved us, saying that this would be the evidence to all men that we are his disciples.

ARTICLE XXII—THE CHURCH

The Church is a fellowship of true Christian believers and may exist where only two or three are gathered in the name of Christ. Its members are joined, like the branches to the tree, by a living relationship to Christ, who is the head of the Church, and to one another by cords of divine love. Only as this association is maintained in spiritual vitality can the Church perform its proper functions and mission in this world. It does not require buildings, organization, forms, rituals, and other accouterments, although it may at times use these. It does not follow any particular type of worship, but if worthy of the name, it must always be the means whereby Christ moves through his people and the members of his spiritual body to accomplish his work in the world.

ARTICLE XXIII—THE SACRAMENTS

The sacraments were given as means of grace, not as objects of worship. Like prayer, Bible reading, and worship, if properly used they can be a means of spiritual edification and blessing. They include water baptism and the Lord's supper.

ARTICLE XXIV—THE SECOND COMING OF CHRIST

The Christ who was crucified, dead, and buried, and who arose again the third day to ascend into heaven to sit at the right hand of God the Father shall return in the glory of the Father with His angels to regain and rule upon earth. His return, which shall be in troublous times, shall be bodily and visible.

ARTICLE XXV—THE ISRAEL OF THE LAST DAYS

The lost tribes of Israel are not lost to God and need not to be lost to themselves. They are not the Jews but are peoples who have been gathered into the North American continent, the true land of re-gathered Israel. While any person of any race or nation may by accepting Christ be grafted spiritually into the

Israel of God, the Lord God Jehovah has not forgotten the literal nation, the descendants by genealogy of the Israel of ancient times. Through Israel of modern days He has bestowed upon many unspeakable blessings, such as freedom, the gospel, and humane leadership in the world. Although America, this present-day Israel, has in great measure fallen away from God and must undergo His judgments, it shall, in accordance with the promises to Abraham, yet be used in far greater degree than ever before as an instrument of blessing to all the nations of the earth. To battle for a land so chosen of God for His Kingdom purposes is not a violation of God's law. While the Ten Commandments strictly forbade such crimes as murder, never did the Israel of old interpret this to mean they were forbidden to go to war against the enemies of their nation, or that justice was not to be enforced by proper penalties. It is still true that the taking of human life is right when necessary to support the ends of legitimate government. It is right to defend the weak or helpless with whatever means may be needed.

ARTICLE XXVI—FREEDOM

Freedom is so important in the sight of God that even Satan has been permitted to exercise a great measure of it. Inasmuch as he is proving himself unworthy, this freedom shall one day come to a complete end, as will also that of all who follow in his ways. Until that time, God does permit the exercise of free choice, even though it means rebellion against Him. Man then may choose between God and Satan, right and wrong, but he cannot control the final consequences of his choice. In permitting man to be free, God holds him responsible for the exercise of that freedom, expecting him to respect the rights and freedom of others. In providing redemption, He called him to the highest kind of freedom; freedom in Christ, which begets all other forms of freedom, including, first of all, the liberty to worship God in the manner in which the individual feels brings to him the greatest help and enables him to be the highest blessing to others. Since man is an imperfect, finite being, no two exactly alike, it is to be expected that there shall be a great diversity of opinions, inclinations, and preferences concerning many things, including the worship and service of God. No particular rites, ceremonies, or modes of worship should be forced upon anyone, for all of these outward forms are but a means to the end of a spiritual and happy relationship with God. Furthermore, man must not be coerced in his conscience. The most enlightened has but very imperfect knowledge and must be allowed to work out his own salvation before God. He must be permitted to develop his own abilities and talents before God. The wisest governments are not those in which a few superintelligent persons at the top make all the decisions concerning what is best for all individuals, but those that consist of leadership which recognizes that God made all of his people to be creative, to feel they have a valuable contribution to make to others as God leads and inspires them.

Rather than develop into a conceited, self-righteous elitism, this kind of leadership will humbly seek the wisdom and help of God to be able to recognize and encourage any contribution to the good of others that comes from any person. It shall not stifle, but promote personal freedom in channels of blessing and righteousness.

ARTICLE XXVII—THE ELECT

The elect is a select group of 144,000 persons, 12,000 from each of the tribes, with the exception of Dan, of re-gathered Israel. They are chosen of God, tested, and proved faithful for leadership and responsibility in the great work of the Lord during the transition period from the gospel to the Kingdom age. These are marked in the forehead by the angel with the seal of God, insuring them divine protection and immunity from the great judgment plagues that must be visited upon their fellow men. They shall work together as a Joel's army and be able to shelter and sustain others who will look to them and to God for help in the time of storm. They are not called of God to advance their own selfish interests and ambitions, but are chosen to help others.

ARTICLE XXVIII—THE KINGDOM OF GOD

As the age of the gospel declines, the Kingdom of God, like the stone Daniel saw cut out of the mountain, shall emerge more and more upon earth. This does not mean the gospel and salvation upon gospel terms come to an end. Indeed, under the power and protection of the Kingdom, the message of salvation shall be proclaimed with greater effectiveness than ever before, even unto all the nations of the world, just as Christ said and commanded. The dispensational emphasis, however, in God's dealings with the race of man must begin to shift. Instead of God's work being under the direction of Church leaders, the ecclesiastical must become increasingly subordinated to the divine governmental direction placed in the world. While still exercising spiritual oversight, it, must do so under God's Kingdom authority that shall more and more challenge the rule of anti-Christ forces in the world, and finally overcome them.

ARTICLE XXIX—THE MILLENNIUM

Jesus Christ and His armies shall overthrow all the forces of the enemy and tread the winepress of the wrath of God at Armageddon. The dead in Christ He shall bring with him, those of his followers who are alive and remain shall also be changed from the earthly to the glorified state, and, including those who have suffered martyrdom during the awful times of the great tribulation and the reign of the anti-Christ upon earth, they shall all rule and reign with Christ for a thousand years. During this period of time Satan and his demons shall be bound in the bottomless pit. It shall be the happy days then the knowledge of God shall cover the earth as the waters cover the sea and all creation restored to its pristine glory. All traces of Satan's presence and work shall be erased from the earth. The last enemy which shall be overcome is death. When that is done, when Christ has placed all enemies under his feet, then shall the Kingdom be delivered up to God the Father, that God may be all in all.

ARTICLE XXX—THE JUDGMENT

The judgment process has already begun, since the deeds that men do are to some extent followed by consequences upon their own lives, whether good or bad. When Jesus Christ returns he will bring his angels with him, which will include punishment of the wicked and a place in his throne for the righteous. Following the thousand years reign of Christ upon

ARTICLES OF RELIGION (CHRISTIAN CONSERVATIVE CHURCHES OF AMERICA) (continued)

earth, all shall be judged. Those who have lived upon earth but who had no part in the first resurrection at the beginning of the millennium will be brought back in the body to stand before God on that great final Day of Judgment. There the books will be opened and all will be judged according to the lives they have lived upon earth. Those whose names are written in the Lamb's Book of Life shall be saved and enjoy the blessings of immortality in the everlasting City of the Living God.

Notes: *The Christian Conservative Church is one of several modern ''Identity'' churches, the name deriving from their identifying the present day Anglo-Saxons as the literal descendants of ancient Israel, and North America, in particular, as the modern day gathering place of Israel. This belief of the Christian Conservative Church is spelled out in Article 25. The key sentence reads, ''While any person of any race or nation may by accepting Christ be grafted spiritually into the Israel of God, the Lord God Jehovah has not forgotten the literal nation, the descendants by genealogy of the Israel of ancient times.''*

Apart from its Identity beliefs, the Church follows a conservative Evangelical Protestantism. It affirms the Trinity, creation by God (as opposed to evolutionary theories), and Christ's establishment of a premillennial kingdom. The Church promotes a high standard of Christian living and urges Christians to the Spirit-filled life also known as sanctification and perfect love. The spirit filled life is reserved for the consecrated soul and is received by faith. The seeking after charismatic gifts is discouraged.

Chapter 13

Liberal Family

STATEMENT OF PURPOSE (THE ASSOCIATION FOR LIBERAL MINISTRY)

We are an interdenominational and interfaith association providing opportunities for dialogue and mutual support for leaders and laity with liberal values and concerns, who feel isolated in their context of ministry.

Our aims are:

1. to promote a value for scripture and tradition as foundational sources, and for reason and experience as interpretive sources, for theological reflection and religious community formation and action.

2. to help leaders of religious communities to find effective ways to lead their congregations into areas of justice ministry in both their immediate context and in the larger world.

3. to help all members articulate and affirm ministry as a primary way to fulfill one's humanity, and to bring it to creative expression in their own religious context.

Notes: *The Association for Liberal Ministry is composed of ministers and laypersons from those churches historically related to the colonial Congregational Church who, though being in differing denominations today, share the same liberal Protestant theological perspective. Denominations represented include the Unitarian Universalist Association, the National Association of Congregational Christian Churches, and the United Church of Christ. The liberal Protestant perspective represents the most conservative element of the Unitarian Universalist Association, now home to various humanist and non-Christian theologies.*

The purpose of the association for Liberal Ministry is to provide fellowship for ministers and laypersons who feel themselves an isolated minority within their own denomina-

tions and assist them in their discovery of ways to work together on justice issues and the development of spiritual life.

* * *

CREED (CHURCH OF REASON)

I WILL SEEK TO KNOW. . .

Evasion is man's worst enemy.

I AFFIRM THAT REASON IS THE ONLY MEANS TO KNOWLEDGE. . .

Faith, revelation, and emotion are not tools of cognition.

I WILL ATTEMPT TO ACT ON THE BASIS OF KNOWLEDGE. . .

Action from ignorance forfeits control of life.

I WILL NOT INITIATE FORCE OR FRAUD. . .

My right to life depends on recognition of the same right in others.

Notes: *The Church of Reason, founded in the 1980s, is a contemporary expression of rationalism, the belief in the primary and exclusive role of reason as a means to gain knowledge (rather than one among several ways). This belief finds its place in the affirmation ''I affirm that reason is the only means to knowledge.'' The formation of a Church of Reason is, to use the definition of religion proposed by philosopher Brand Branshard, an attempt to provide an organization that furthers ''humanity's attempt to live and act in the light of what it holds to be ultimately true and good.'' It proposes a life of action based on knowledge derived from the use of reason.*

Chapter 14

Latter-Day Saints Family

Utah Mormons

ARTICLES OF BELIEF (CHURCH OF JESUS CHRIST OF LATTER-DAY SAINTS FUNDAMENTALISTS)

1. We believe in the Eternal Father and in His son Jesus Christ.

2. We believe that men will be punished for their own sins and not for Adam's transgressions.

3. We believe Jesus Christ that all the children of Adam will be saved and they are required to obey the Laws and the Ordinances of the Gospel.

4. We believe these Ordinances include; 1st, Belief and Faith in the Lord Jesus Christ; 2nd, Repentance; 3rd, Baptism by immersion for the remission of sins; 4th, Laying on of hands for the gift of the Holy Spirit; 5th, the Lord's Supper.

5. We believe that men must be called of God by inspiration, and by laying on of hands by those who are duly commissioned to preach the Gospel and administer in the ordinances thereof.

6. We believe in the same organization that existed in the primitive church, viz., apostles, pastors, teachers, evangelists, patriarchs, etc.

7. We believe in the powers and gifts of the everlasting Gospel, viz. the call to obedience to the Law, attaining perfection, discerning of spirits, prophecy, revelation, visions, healings, wisdom, charity, brotherly love, etc.

8. We believe that Jesus Christ is the Word of God, and we may learn of him in part by reading books including the Bible, the Book of Mormon, and other good authoritative sources.

9. We believe all that God has revealed; all that He does now reveal; and we believe that He will yet reveal many more great and important things pertaining to the Kingdom of God, and in the Messiah's second coming.

10. We believe in the literal gathering of Israel, and the Restoration of all twelve tribes; that Zion will be built upon the western continent upon the wreckage of Babylon; that Christ will personally reign upon the earth a thousand years; and that the earth will be renewed and receive its paradisiacal glory.

11. We believe in God's judgment and the literal resurrection of the body, Christ having been the first so to rise.

12. We claim the right to worshipping and obeying Almighty God according to our conscience unmolested, and according the same to others, letting them worship how and where they may be.

13. We believe in being subject to civil rulers in so far as they obey, honor, and sustain the law.

14. We believe in being honest, true, chaste, temperate, benevolent, virtuous, upright, and helping others.

Notes: *Lyman Wight was an apostle of the Latter-Day Saints in the days of Joseph Smith, Jr. Following Smith's assassination in 1844, he led a group of Saints who refused to accept Brigham Young's leadership to Texas and for several years oversaw a growing independent church. However, that church fell apart in the 1850s and most of its members joined the Reorganized Church of Jesus Christ of Latter-Day Saints. Over the decades a few members of the Wight family remained unattached to either the Reorganized Church or the Utah-based Church of Jesus Christ of Latter-Day Saints. In the early 1980s, several members of the Wight family who had left those two churches came together with some who had never affiliated with either and formed a new church body that others, unrelated to the Wight family, have joined.*

The Articles of Belief follow closely the text of the Articles of Faith of the Church of Jesus Christ of Latter-Day Saints with some important additions and deletions. For example, the words ''and the Holy Ghost,'' have been deleted from the first item. The organizational item now includes patriarchs among

413

ARTICLES OF BELIEF (CHURCH OF JESUS CHRIST OF LATTER-DAY SAINTS FUNDAMENTALISTS) (continued)

the church's structure. One new item, on the literal resurrection of the body, has been added.

* * *

TENETS (FREE WILL MORMON CHURCH)

1. My new church is a true church.

2. All churches that I have founded in my infinite wisdom are true. All churches that I choose to found in the future shall be true.

3. All creatures shall be welcomed into my new church, regardless of their present religion, beliefs, race, color, sex, age, language, or any other parameters of any kind whatsoever.

4. There shall be no formal ritual. Each creature shall hear from me how I want him to live his life at every moment in time and space. I may choose to speak to each of my creations in a different manner so that each may hear me truly.

5. The basic belief in my new church shall be love between all my creations.

6. There shall be no formal ritual. Every creature shall be free to choose the methods and means that will lead him to the highest form of enlightenment that he, she or it may attain while on this earth. No creature shall at any time impose his beliefs on any other of my creations.

7. There shall be no formal buildings created solely for meetings. Every point in space shall be holy and therefore suitable for meeting in the name of my new church.

8. The final aim of each of the members of my new church shall be pure enlightenment as attained by my son, Jesus, born of Mary Magdalene.

9. The final life style that shall be sought by each of my creations shall be that of Adam and Eve and the creatures of the Garden of Eden. This shall mean eating only the fruits and nuts of the trees and the drinking of pure water.

10. None of my creations shall be girded in loincloths of any kind.

11. My creations shall continue to worship me through the church to which they now belong, and at the same time be a member of the Free Will Mormon Church. The purpose of my creating a new church is to unite my creations, not divide them. Have not ye already created amongst thyselves divisioness?

12. While my creations are on the road to pure enlightenment and final life style, they may be free to eat and drink all foods, liquids and any other substances. Each time they do so, they shall ask themselves: 'is this act leading me to true enlightenment and final lifestyle?' If so, they shall be free to do so. If not, they shall throw down this substance.

13. All of my creations shall be free to love one another in any manner that is mutually acceptable.

14. Until the time all of my creations have achieved true enlightenment and final life style, which shall not be for many days, each of my creations shall continue to obey all the laws of the country, state and province in which they now presently abide. There shall be no revolutions. If one of my creations wishes to pursue the search for pure enlightenment in a manner which is in conflict with the laws of the country, state or province in which they are now abiding, they shall give in to those laws peacefully and without animosity to others. If there is unbearable conflict between themselves and those presently in authority, they shall attempt peacefully to change their physical location.

15. There shall be no tithing or donations to my new church. Each of my creations shall share as best they can what I have given to each in the way of talents.

16. There shall be no hierarchy in my new church. No member shall be in authority at any time, and no member shall be higher or lower than another. All members shall be called 'brother' and 'sister' only, followed by their family name or first name, whichever they prefer.

17. In the order of the priority of love, this shall be followed: First, thou shalt love thy god With all thy heart, soul and might. Secondly, thou shalt love thy mother with all thy heart, soul and might, and thy father also and thy brothers and sisters also, and thy children also, and thy husband and wife. Each of my creations shall, on their way to pure enlightenment and final life style, feel free to rearrange this order at any point and time in space.

18. The overriding principle that I want all of my creations to follow every moment of their waking life shall be pure and simply only this: will the following act that I am about to do hurt any other of the Lord's creations? If the answer is no, they shall be free to commit such act. If the answer is yes, they shall not be free to commit such act.

19. There shall be no world headquarters or formal newspaper. Each of my creations shall be free to communicate with all other creatures in any way that is mutually acceptable and that falls within the laws of the country, state or province in which they are physically located at the time such act is committed.

20. Baptism may be by any means whatsoever, but the purest baptism shall be by immersion in natural bodies of water such as oceans, rivers, lakes, streams while naked of any garments or by sprinkling with pure mineral water.

21. I shall continue from time to time to speak to Brother Coleman so that my true will be done: to have all of my creations living a life of true love and true happiness and true brotherhood. I may choose to speak to others and I

will not reveal conflicting means or methods to any of my creations.

22. I the Lord do not consider myself above or below any of my creations. If any of my creations feel happier by worshipping me as a higher authority, it is alright, but not necessary.

23. All of the existing beliefs of my Church of Jesus Christ of Latter Day Saints, the Mormon Church, are true as revealed to the Prophet Joseph Smith. There is no conflict between my new church and this existing church. I choose to reveal myself in many ways that may seem mysterious at the present time but will be clear in the future.

24. As my dear and beloved son, Jesus Christ of Nazareth, said to you: 'Love the little children and let them come to me.' I say unto you this day, love one another with all thy heart, soul and might so that all of the terrible wrongs that my creations are inflicting upon another shall cease, and that pure love shall reign on the earth as shown by my dear and beloved son, Jesus, who laid down his only life in terrible pain and suffering so that one day all of my creations shall be with me in the eternal paradise of heaven.

And I beseech thee, when thou lovest my little creations, remember that I created them in love, from love, and therefore they are pure when they are born. I cry unto you, do not besmirch their purity by any careless work or deed in thy own selfish interest. Do not perpetuate the hatred thou may now feeleth in thee, for if thou do so, you will be saddened and these little ones will be hurt for the rest of their days on the earth.

And when thou loveth my little creations, love them in the non-verbal way they know so well, for it is not your words only they hear, but your feelings they feel. And always physically place your head as low or lower than theirs, otherwise you appear to be a giant to them, and may frighten them.

And lastly, and perhaps most importantly, I want to say to you at this point in time and space, simply: when you are in pain and sadness, cry out to me, for I am a just god and full of love, and I will always help you, no matter what. I say to you, lovest thou not the children that ye have borne? How then could I call myself God and lovest thee not!

Verily, I say unto you, the only hell is the hell that you have created amongst yourselves, it is not of my will or doing.

There are forces of evil that seek constantly to destroy the love ye have for one another. Give ye not in.

Notes: *The Free Will Mormon Church is a small Latter-Day Saints church founded in 1980 by Franklin Lee Colemen of Waycross, Georgia. It is a loosely organized church based on principles of mutual love among humans and an action code allowing almost all forms of behavior as long as one's acts do not hurt anyone. Free love is also advocated, though there is some attention to living within the laws of the land on a member's residence. It believes in vegetarianism, even if its*

acceptance seems to be a far-off reality. There is no tithing, organizational hierarchy, or formal denominational structure.

* * *

EPITOME OF FAITH, ADDITIONAL ARTICLES (RESTORED CHURCH OF JESUS CHRIST OF LATTER-DAY SAINTS)

"We believe that, in fulfillment of numerous prophecies, the original church organized by Joseph Smith has strayed from many of the commandments of God and as foretold by the Prophet Isaiah, has transgressed the laws, changed the ordinances, and broken the everlasting covenant.

"We believe Elwood Russell to be the Messenger of the Covenant, foretold by the Prophet Malachi, who was sent by the Lord to restore all things from which the original church has fallen, and to prepare the world for the coming of the Lord on the great and dreadful day, to be followed by His Millennial reign.

"We believe the original church to be guilty of priestcraft and of raising up churches to get gain, as evidenced by the existence of a paid ministry among the General Authorities and by their investment of church funds in numerous forms of business enterprise.

"We believe that Jesus Christ is now living on the earth in the flesh and know that there are numerous witnesses to that effect.

"We believe that the keys of the Holy Priesthood have been with. drawn from the original church of Jesus Christ and are now transferred by the Lord into the hands of the members of the Restored Church to set in order the House of God, as foretold in Section 85 of the Doctrine and Covenants.

"We believe San Diego County of California to be the place foretold in many prophecies as the New Jerusalem, where the Tribes of Israel are to gather, so as to escape the time of the destruction of the wicked by fire that is at hand, and as a place of refuge from the wars that will continue until the end.

"We believe that the gathering of Israel can only be accomplished by the exercise of the covenant of Abraham, to separate the wicked from the righteous, without any prejudice as to race or the color of a man's skin.

"We believe ourselves to be the Elders of Israel who shall be directed by the Lord to save the Constitution of this land, and be instrumental in setting up the theocratic government, foretold by the prophet Daniel, that shall consume all other kingdoms and be the means by which the Lord shall rule and reign for a thousand years." (From an undated article, The Articles of Faith of the Restored Church of Jesus Christ of Latter Day Saints)

Notes: *The Restored Church of Jesus Christ of Latter-Day Saints was founded in San Diego, California, by former members of the Church of Jesus Christ of Latter-Day Saints*

EPITOME OF FAITH, ADDITIONAL ARTICLES (RESTORED CHURCH OF JESUS CHRIST OF LATTER-DAY SAINTS) (continued)

(LDS). Their object was to restore the power of the priesthood to the church, which they believe was lost at the time of the presidency of Joseph Fielding Smith.

The Restored Church accepts the Articles of Faith of the Church of Jesus Christ of Latter-Day Saints, to which it has appended the articles cited above. It believes that the LDS Church has strayed from true doctrine, practice, and organization, and that God has restored the church under the leadership of Ellwood Russell, the Restored Church's prophet. Among its most startling assertions are a belief that Jesus Christ has returned to earth and now resides here, and that the gathering place for the kingdom of God will be neither Independence, Missouri, nor Salt Lake City, Utah, as believed by most Latter-Day Saints, but San Diego, California.

* * *

BASIC BELIEFS (SCHOOL OF THE PROPHETS)

1. We believe the Bible to be the word of God as far as it is translated correctly. We also accept the Book of Mormon, the Doctrine and Covenants, and the Pearl of Great Price as scripture. We also believe that there is much inspiration and truth in many of the other scriptures of the world. We do not accept any scripture as being infallible for they were all given through men in their weakness; thus we need the Holy Ghost to get a true interpretation. Nevertheless, our line of thinking follows a more literal interpretation than those who believe that every word of the scriptures is infallible.

2. We believe that Onias was called of God to prepare the way for the setting in order of the church. We also believe that John Koyle who received visitations from translated Nephites was called of God to begin a mine which will bring much relief in the coming economic horror. [Ed. Note: The connection with Koyle, as stated here, must have some bearing on the group's move to Salem, Utah, near where Koyle's "mine" is located.] We believe that many prophets are now arising both truth and false and the only way to tell the difference is by the power of the Holy Ghost.

3. We do not accept any prophet as being infallible. Even if we accept the words of a true prophet without question and verification of the Spirit then we are no better off than the average Christian aspirant of the world who is de-

ceived by the craftiness of men. All those who are associated with the Restorers are to feel free to test the revelations of Onias or anyone else by the Holy Ghost, the scriptures, logic, and reason and are encouraged to voice their own answers, revelations, doubts, and feelings without fear of scorn. However, objections should be voiced in a loving spirit with mildness, and one should not be an "accuser of the brethren" as Satan is. We keep in mind that even Joseph Smith at one time received a false revelation to go to Canada and sell the copyright to the Book of Mormon. If he could be deceived then we must take extra precautions ourselves. The Restorers will make every attempt to verify the truth of all revelations by the power of the Holy Ghost before they are sent out. If anyone receiving these has manifestations otherwise we would be happy to hear it and then seek more verification if need be.

4. We believe the words of Joel are soon to come to pass: "And all flesh; and your sons and your daughters shall prophesy, your old men shall dream dreams, your young men shall see visions" Joel 2:28.

5. We believe that all men should be taught to look within for the truth and be filled with the Holy Spirit and not rely on the arm of flesh for this is the only way that "they shall see eye to eye when the Lord shall bring again Zion."

6. We believe that the present generation will live to see the Kingdom of God rise in power.

7. We believe that God will literally gather the elect from the four corners of the earth to build the city of New Jerusalem.

8. We believe that man must continually strive for new truth, that if he is not advancing in knowledge then he must retrogress. We seek to know all the mysteries of the Kingdom of God.

9. We work toward the day that "man should not counsel his fellow man, neither trust in the arm of flesh" D & C 1:1 9. No man, book or teaching should be looked upon as an authority only in so far as it is verified by the Holy Ghost and the Light of Christ.

Notes: *School of the Prophets was founded by followers of the revelations given in the 1960s to R. C. Crossfield, a former member of the Church of Jesus Christ of Latter-Day Saints, and first published in the Book of Onias (1969). Subsequent revelations have been added. The School's statement of Basic Beliefs emphasizes the doctrine of revelation, an important problem for its members, the School having been based on the nineteenth-century revelations to Joseph Smith, Jr., and more recently received ones of Crossfield. Crossfield's work has also been received in a context of the presence of numerous other revelations voiced by other Latter-Day Saints prophets. The School acknowledges these many revelations received both in the past and the present. Further, it believes none of them to be infallible, even the Bible, and concludes that only the power of the Holy Ghost can ultimately allow the believer to discern the true revelations from the false.*

As with many Latter-Day Saints, the members of the School believe they are living in the last days and that God will soon gather His people to build the Kingdom of God on earth.

* * *

Polygamy-Practicing Mormans

ARTICLES OF FAITH (CHRIST'S CHURCH)

1. We believe in God the Eternal Father—as Michael-Adam-God, the Creator; and in His Son, Jesus Christ, the Savior of the World; and in the Holy Ghost, Joseph Smith, Jr., the Witness and Testator and third member of the Godhead that rules the Earth!

2. We believe the first principles and ordinances of the Gospel of Jesus Christ, are:

   (1) Faith in the Lord Jesus Christ, His saving blood, that He atoned for our sins if we accept Him and keep His commandments.

   (2) That in order to receive effective Baptism and the other ordinances and blessings of the Gospel, all men and women must and shall offer the sacrifice of a broken heart (repentance) and a contrite (teachable) spirit.

   (3) Every candidate for receiving the Holy Ghost must be baptized, by immersion in water, by one having authority of Jesus Christ, who himself holds the Priesthood of the Living God and who personally has the Holy Ghost!

   (4) The laying on of hands of those who have the Holy Priesthood and the Holy Ghost, for the conferring of the Holy Ghost.

3. We believe that no one shall be confirmed, or accepted as a member of Christ's Church, until they have shown by a righteous walk of life, and have been voted upon by the members of the body of the Church. They are then to be confirmed a member of the Church by the laying on of hands.

4. We believe that men will be punished for their own sins and not for Adam's transgression.

5. We believe that through the Atonement of Christ all mankind may be saved by obedience to the laws and ordinances of the Gospel.

6. We believe that a man must be called of God, by prophecy, and by the laying on of hands by those who are in authority to preach the Gospel and administer in the ordinances thereof.

7. We believe in the Gifts of the Spirit, namely, the gift of tongues, prophecy, revelation, visions, healings, interpretations of tongues, etc.

8. We believe the Holy Bible to be the word of God as far as it is translated correctly; we also believe the Book of Mormon, the Doctrine and Covenants and the Pearl of Great Price to be the word of the Lord.

9. We believe all that God has revealed, all that He does now reveal, and we believe He will yet reveal many great and important things pertaining to the Kingdom of God!

10. We believe in the literal gathering of Israel and in the restoration of the Ten Tribes; that Zion will be built upon this the American continent; that Christ will reign personally upon the earth; and that the earth will be renewed and receive its paradisiacal glory.

11. We claim the privilege of worshipping the Almighty God according to the dictates of our own conscience and allow all men the same privilege, let them worship how, when, or what they may.

12. We believe in being subject to Almighty God and those kings, presidents, rulers and magistrates who honor and sustain the divine laws of God.

13. We believe in being honest, true, chaste, benevolent, virtuous, and in doing good to all men; indeed we may say that we follow the admonition of Paul—we believe all things, we have endured many things, and hope to be able to endure all things. If there is anything virtuous, lovely, or of good report or praiseworthy, we seek after these things.

Notes: *Christ's Church was founded in 1978 by Gerald W. Peterson, a former member of the Apostolic United Brethren, a polygamy-practicing Latter-Day Saints body. It derives its authority from a lineage of priesthood commissioned by LDS Church president John W. Taylor and believes that the contemporary Church of Jesus Christ of Latter-Day Saints has fallen away from its true teachings.*

These Articles are closely related to the Articles of Faith of the Church of Jesus Christ of Latter-Day Saints, but includes significant changes. Most importantly it accepts a popular (but never official) teaching of the church propounded that God the Father was identical to the biblical Adam. Christ's Church goes further, however, in teaching that Joseph Smith, Jr., is identical with the Holy Ghost, the third person of the Trinity. The statement on church organization has been dropped, a

ARTICLES OF FAITH (CHRIST'S CHURCH) (continued)

statement on church membership requirements added, and the statement on church ordinances greatly expanded.

*   *   *

Missouri Mormons

FAITH AND DOCTRINE [CHURCH OF JESUS CHRIST RESTORED (KING)]

FAITH AND DOCTRINE

"We believe in God, the Creator of all things, Our Father, who is unchangeable, from everlasting to everlasting, without beginning of days or end of years, the source of all righteous inspiration, whose capacity for love and wrath are beyond man's ability to know or find out. We believe He has given His Son the task of judging each man according to the works and faith they have practiced while on this earth. Therefore, there is no condemnation for the man who lives and dies ignorant of God's laws. Men choosing to ignore God's laws, however, live under the threat of condemnation from day to day and their just judgment is sure, except they repent and live according to all the principles of the gospel of Christ.

"We believe that just as God spoke to man in days past, so he speaks today. We expect it. We experience it. We are grateful because it delivers man's mind from instability, confusion and anxiety.

"We believe that Jesus of Nazareth was and is the Only Begotten Son of God; that with God He presided in the beginning over the creation of all things and that it was by Jesus Christ that God created all things that are.

"We believe God directs, comforts, teaches, chastises and/or reproves men by the ministry of His Holy Spirit, either directly or through divinely called ministers.

"We believe that as man 'feels after God' by diligent study and constant prayer, he is practicing faith and that by willfully enduring and gradually overcoming all things, under the protection and guidance of divinely called ministers, his faith will become knowledge.

"We believe that Jesus built His own church for the purpose of making men perfect in this life. Anything less than this, is not of Jesus Christ. The church that preaches the fullness of His gospel, accordingly promises the perfection of the soul in this life on condition of total obedience to godly principles.

"We believe repentance from doing sin and living an unproductive life (dead works), is essential for any man, woman or youth who by reason of intelligence (knowing right from wrong) are accountable before God and therefore as often as may be necessary, must conscientiously practice sincere repentance.

"Baptism by immersion in water, as performed by the Son of God in the river Jordan by an authoritative minister of God, for the remission of sins, is absolutely necessary to man's salvation. Without it there is no membership in the church and kingdom of Christ.

"We believe the Eucharist or Sacrament of the Lord's Supper, properly observed by authoritative ministers of God, provides for those who are members of Jesus' church and them alone, the opportunity to consider the blessed sacrifice of the Lamb, Jesus, to give thanks for that atonement His death made possible, and to confess to God publicly or privately the sins that separate man from his Maker and the Holy Ghost.

"The physical body and the spirit (or intelligence) in every man born into this world constitutes the soul of man and because God so loved the world (the souls of men), He allowed His Only Begotten Son to come in the meridian of time, to offer the only acceptable sacrifice for the sins of the world—His death on a cross and by so doing He gave His Father (and our Father) an acceptable offering and a complete and effectual reconciliation and mediation for mankind. Men may lay claim to this atonement only in the church that bears His name and teaches all He taught.

"We believe the fullness of the doctrine of Christ Jesus, is the only way by which man may be saved, and that giving support to any church which does not preach the fullness of the doctrine of jesus is supporting that which may be well-intentioned perhaps but nevertheless, a counterfeit and therefore, her promises are vain.

"Man is required (if he desires the salvation of his soul) to live by every word that proceedeth forth out of the mouth of God. We believe those words as they are found recorded in the Inspired Correction of the Scriptures (Bible)—even though all biblical references in this tract are to the King James Version—plus the Book of Mormon, the Doctrine and Covenants, and the latest revelations (called Supplements), received by our present prophet, Elder Stanley King and sanctioned by the saints.

"We believe that just as the original Church of Christ as organized by Jesus himself, apostatized, so also the Reorganized Church of Jesus Christ of Latter Day Saints—lawful successor to the church restored by Joseph Smith, Jr. in 1830—has also apostatized administratively. There are many good honorable people within that denomination as there are in many other denominations of the world today but this fact does not negate the evidences of her unfortunate apostasy.

"We believe Joseph Smith, Jr. was and is the great Prophet of this last dispensation and that as a man he may possibly have erred from time to time but as God's servant, ordained from before the foundation of the world, to speak forth His Word, He did not err.

"We believe Sanctification must be attained by the honest in heart. It is the process of perfection. Attaining perfection while living in a system of houses, stores, streets and divisive devilish influences of this present age is impossible. We believe the only way to effectively live in the world but not be part of it, is in the stake; the stake as revealed by God through

Joseph Smith, Jr., not those promoted by the RLDS or Utah churches. The Stakes divinely organized always start with the building of the House of the Lord (temple) first. This church has prepared for five years to do this and at this writing (1975) are very near to commencing such a work in obedience to His word and to His glory.

"The obligation upon the saint (member of the church) is to become independent above every other creature or system beneath the Celestial world. Practicing daily the attributes of God is a way of life in the Stake. The Law of Preference is taught and lived.

"We believe in being good stewards over all God gives us. Sacrifice is expected and desired by members in this church so that God's final glorious chapter of His strange act might be completed. There is no perfection without sacrifice and where there is no perfection there is no church. Man must not fail to please God. Jesus willingly sacrificed all for His Father. So must we.

"We believe heaven is a place of varied glories. There is the Celestial, Terrestrial and Telestial glory that man may attain. We believe that when this earth has fulfilled itself in the present system of things that it will be changed and provide for the righteous the greatest glory of all—Celestial glory.

"We believe there are no authoritative High Priests on the earth today (1975) but that very soon this ministry will be restored to the salvation of man, the redemption of Zion and the everlasting glory of God.

"There is historical support for Presidencies in the Church of Christ. We do believe they are acceptable to God and necessary for the church to function orderly.

"There are other tenets of faith that make up the fullness of the doctrine of Jesus such as Ministerial Authority (who really are the servants of God?), the gifts and fruits of God's Holy Spirit, Baptism for the dead (by revelation through a prophet), Endowments, and other temple ordinances, Celestial Priesthood Education (School of the Prophets), equality, the gathering of scattered Israel, plus many more." (From a tract introducing the church.)

PRIESTHOOD AND CHURCH ORGANIZATION

"We believe that a fully organized church must contain the following: High Priests, Elders, Priests, Teachers, Deacons: a First Presidency, consisting of three Elders (High Priests): the Council of Twelve Apostles, with one called to be the President: Twelve High Priests to form the Standing High Council of the Church, mainly a high judicial council: A Presiding Bishopric, consisting of three: A Presiding Patriarch, with two councilors: and also, the quorums of Seventy, to work under the direction of The Twelve as the leading missionary arm of the church."

"... the second presidency of the church is the council of the Twelve, and ... their prime function is to take the church into

all the world, and preach the gospel unto every creature... Those whom they send, are the several quorums of the Seventy who are really an extension of this second presidency." (Letter to the author from S.M. King, March 25, 1975)

TEMPLES

"The fullness of the gospel cannot be achieved without temples. They are the only Houses of worship which were employed in the first church. They did not build churches after the fashion of the world... The Temple had many functions which are not well understood by the people of the restoration, and those people who do believe in them, and those who do build them, do not build them like the ones built in the old days. Neither are they used for entirely the same purpose or for the same reasons.

"All Stakes which are to be built up unto the Lord are to have in the center square of the city, the House or the Houses of the Lord (Temples)... There were to have been twenty-four in all [referring to the city of Zion], all built the same size, which again bespeaks the equality of the church... The first three, for the First Presidency and his Councillors: Three for the Presiding Bishopric and his Councillors: Three for the Presiding Patriarch: Three for the Elders in Zion: Three for the Presidency of the Order of Aaron: and also, three more for the Priests of Aaron: Three for the Teachers: and Three for the Presidents of Deacons...

"Temples are Holy Houses... These are the only places which God can come to, and reveal His presence... Temples are the only place where the high ordinances can be performed ... such as, the annointings, washings, receiving of the endowment [not the same as taught by the Utah Church], baptism for the dead, and the receiving of the Holy Spirit of Promise, which in effect, is the Sealing Ordinance performed by the Patriarch, which is the sealing up unto eternal life, which is being saved, or as the scriptures more often call it, being sanctified..." (From letter referred to above.)

Notes: *The Church of Jesus Christ Restored was founded in 1970 by former members of the Reorganized Church of Jesus Christ of Latter Day Saints. It is the beliefs that God had chosen first the Church of Jesus Christ of Latter-Day Saints and then the Reorganized Church, but had rejected both in favor of the Church of Jesus Christ Restored. The Church's statement of Faith and Doctrine emphasizes the doctrine of present revelation, a direct reference to the revelations received by Stanley M. King in which the church believes. It holds the Inspired Version of the Bible, the books received by Joseph Smith, Jr., the Book of Mormon and the Pearl of Great Price, and the revelation to King to be authoritative literature.*

The Church preaches that people may attain perfection in this life through total obedience to Godly Principles. To be saved a person must be baptized into the true church, i.e., the one that preaches the fullness of the doctrine of Jesus. The saved may look forward to life in heaven, which is divided into three realms—the Celestial, the Terrestrial, and the Telestial. Upon

*the completion of their earthly sojourn, the righteous will
reside in the Celestial realm.*

* * *

STATEMENT OF PURPOSE (CHURCH OF JESUS CHRIST, ZION'S BRANCH)

Having a sure knowledge that Jesus Christ is the only Begotten
Son of God we, as members of the Church of Jesus Christ, by
reason of the covenant we have made with God in the waters of
baptism, in order that His will might be done and that His
Kingdom might again become a reality upon the face of the
earth, feel it wisdom in Christ to herein state our beliefs and
purposes of existence in order to better secure a more organized and beneficial promotion of His precious Gospel and
Doctrine. Without this gospel, man has no hope of attaining
that which he was created to be, even sons of God.

I. We believe in God the Eternal Father and in His Son
Jesus Christ and in the Holy Ghost. We have but one
Grand Head, He being Jesus Christ, the Savior of men.
He being begotten of God because He was conceived of
God, and He being the Son because He was born of the
flesh, and He being our Lord because he has received a
fullness of the glory of His Father, even the Eternal God.

II. We believe that the Church of Jesus Christ is eternal in
nature and that the eternal gospel of man's salvation
through Jesus Christ has been restored to mankind for
the last time. (RLDS D & C 26:3a-3c).

III. We believe in the Inspired Version of the Holy Scriptures and the Book of Mormon, both of which were
revealed through Joseph Smith, Jr., a prophet of the
Living and Eternal God. We also accept as divine
guidance the Doctrine and Covenants, so far as it is
consistent with past revelation and history. We herein
attest to these as being holy and sacred scriptures and
willingly bind ourselves for time and eternity to the
doctrine of Christ contained therein; and to the articles
of faith as adopted by the early Church of Jesus Christ
under the guidance of Joseph Smith, Jr.

IV. We believe and are prepared to defend the Church of
Jesus Christ as restored in 1830, and according to the
covenants and commandments of God at its Reorganization in 1860, which today exists only where the servants
of God have disassociated and abstained from the ordinances by that organization which once bore the name of
Christ in purity, but now finds itself apostate and abhorrent in the sight of Almighty God.

V. We of Zion's Branch have existed in a state of waiting
. . . hoping to see an indication of repentance on the part
of the leadership and membership of the RLDS organization and a commitment to once again represent Jesus
Christ and the fullness of truth before the world. We
have reached an understanding that the RLDS organization has not, nor appears ever will, return to the Holy
task for which it was established, for their pollution of
the Holy Priesthood was culminated as of April, 1984.

The responsibility of the remnants of the Lord's House
is to seek to establish themselves in righteousness and
bring to pass His Holy and Divine Will, which includes
the re-establishment of the full structure of Christ's
church.

VI. We believe that it is our purpose, through the covenants
we have made with Almighty God, to see that our
priesthood authority is used in its Holy and Sacred
power in concert with the commandments of God to
bring to pass righteous execution of all the ordinances of
the Church of Jesus Christ in order that a righteous
environment might be fostered, that our lives might be
so ordered as to become living temples, that God might
be glorified.

VII. We, as a remnant body, do declare our intention to do all
in our power to call mankind to repentance, to a firm
faith in God and the sure knowledge of Jesus Christ as
the beloved and only begotten Son of God.

VIII. We recognize that it is our responsibility to take the
gospel of Jesus Christ to a world in need, and therefore
vow to see that this is done in all deliberateness and with
singleness of purpose in order that God might be glorified and men might have the hope of Celestial glory.

IX. We recognize that Independence, Missouri shall be the
place of the gathering of the Saints and the place of Zion,
as commanded by God. Our commitment will be to
bring about such a condition of righteousness among
men that this promise will be fulfilled . . . to the eternal
blessing of all the earth.

X. We recognize the infallible and eternal nature of Almighty God and therefore recognize His unchangeability.
We therefore bear public record of our willingness
before God to carry out all His commandments as they
are made manifest, yesterday, today and from this time
hence, through His duly ordained channels, and will
seek not to council our God or place our wisdom above
His Divine Will and His revealments to us thereof.

XI. Our hope shall be steadfastly anchored in God's promise
to Enoch that: 'When thy posterity shall embrace the
truth, and look upward, then shall Zion look downward,
and all the heavens shall shake with gladness, and the
Earth shall tremble with joy, and the general assembly of
the Church of the Firstborn shall come down out of
heaven and possess the earth, and shall have place until
the end come' (IV Genesis 9:22, 23).

Notes: *The Church of Jesus Christ, Zion's Branch was organized in 1986 by former members of the Reorganized Church of
Jesus Christ of Latter-Day Saints. It believes that the Reorganized Church has become an apostate body, a fact con-*

firmed by its ordaining women. Zion's Branch believes that the Reorganized Church is beyond hope of restoration, and thus the Branch remains faithful to its original doctrine and program.

Zion's branch has done away with the offices of church president and high priest. In 1988, it issued its Statement of Purpose affirming the authority of the Inspired Version of the Bible and the Book of Mormon, but gives only secondary authority to the Doctrines and Covenants (a volume most Latter-Day Saints give equal authority with the Book of Mormon). It teaches that there will be a gathering of saints in Independence, Missouri, which will lead to the establishment of the kingdom of God.

*   *   *

BELIEFS OR DOCTRINES (RESTORATION BRANCHES MOVEMENT)

The Branch accepts the Inspired Version of the Holy Scriptures, the 1908 Authorized Edition of the Book of Mormon, and Sections 1 through 144 of the Doctrine and Covenants to be Scriptures, and to be the official law of the organization. The Branch accepts the Epitome of Faith and the original teachings of the Reorganized Church of Jesus Christ of Latter Day Saints, which were published before 1958, to be the beliefs of the Branch. It also accepts the Restorationist Principles which are found in its Bylaws to be a part of its beliefs.

Notes: *The Restoration Branches Movement represents the largest group of former members of the Reorganized Church of Jesus Christ of Latter Day Saints who broke with that church in the mid-1980s, following its initiating the practice of ordaining women. The Movement is a conservative association and its doctrinal statement sets its standard in the authoritative scriptures of the Reorganized Latter Day Saints, including the Inspired Version of the Bible, the 1908 Reorganized Church version of the Book of Mormon, and the Reorganized Church version of Doctrines and Covenants, through section 144. It is to be noted that section 145 and above were received under the presidency of W. Wallace Smith and Wallace B. Smith during which time the Movement believes that the Reorganized Church had fallen into prophecy. It accepts the beliefs of the Reorganized Church up to 1958 at which time it began to espouse apostate belief.*

*   *   *

RESTORATIONIST PRINCIPLES (RESTORATION BRANCHES MOVEMENT)

A. An Affirmation of the Divinity of the Church and of the Restoration Movement:

1. The Holy Scriptures. The Bible is the divinely sanctioned Word of God, and it contains the gospel of salvation. The Inspired Version was produced under divine direction and is the standard version of the Church.

2. The Book of Mormon. The Book of Mormon is divinely revealed Scripture, and it contains the fullness of the gospel. It is a true account of God's dealings with the ancient Americans. The 1908 RLDS edition is the standard edition of the Church.

3. The Doctrine and Covenants. The Doctrine and Covenants (Sections 1-144) is divinely revealed Scripture and is to be used as the law of the Church. It is to be used instead of the Book of Commandments (DC 126:10b).

4. The Law of the Church. The Three Standard Books named above contain the law of the Church, and their teachings must be adhered to in matters of doctrine and practice. Any theological practice or doctrine which is not in harmony with those Books is false doctrine.

5. The Church History. The history of the Church is important as a guide for the Church today, and the first four volumes of The History of the Reorganized Church of Jesus Christ of Latter Day Saints give a correct rendition of that history (up to 1890).

6. The Epitome of Faith. The Epitome of Faith is a correct and official statement of belief (see Times and Seasons 3:709-710; RLDS History 2:569-570).

7. The Godhead. God the Father and Christ the Son are two separate personages. The belief that there is only one personage in the Godhead is false doctrine.

8. Joseph Smith as a Prophet. Joseph Smith, Jr., was a true prophet and his experiences, such as the vision in Palmyra's grove and the obtaining of the Book of Mormon plates, are actual facts of history.

9. The Only True Church. The Church which God directed Joseph Smith to organize in 1830 is God's only true Church; it is Christ's New Testament Church restored.

10. The RLDS Church is the Only True Church. The Reorganized Church of Jesus Christ of Latter Day Saints is the lawful continuation of the true Church founded in 1830, and is the same Church reorganized.

11. The Unchangeability of Doctrine. God is unchangeable, and so are the doctrines and structure of the Church. They are the same in every age when revealed in their fullness.

B. An Admission that the Liberal Faction is in Apostasy:

12. The Apostasy of the Church Leaders. The present leaders of the World Church (the hierarchy) are in apostasy because they have espoused liberalism, humanism, and ecumenism—which are false belief systems. They have also rejected the Restoration Movement the belief that Joseph Smith, Jr., was a true prophet; that the Three Standard Books of Scripture are

of divine origin; and a literal belief in Zion, the virgin birth of Christ, His millennial advent, and other doctrines.

13. **The Higher Quorums Spiritually Vacant.** The present leaders of the Church lost their last vestige of God-given authority when the Presidency presented the Presidential Papers in 1979—and therefore, the higher quorums are now spiritually vacant and in disorder. The only God-given authority left in the Church is that held by the local priesthood who are still defending the original doctrines of the Restoration Gospel.

14. **The Pro-liberalists' Loss of Authority.** Since the leading officials are in apostasy, all who willingly follow them are also without authority—and even those fundamentalists who remain under their jurisdiction (the Pro-liberalists) will eventually lose their authority, if they have not already done so.

15. **The Removal of the Liberal Faction.** In His own due time God will remove the Liberal Faction and will "recover" the Church (Jacob 4:3-4), or cleanse it (DC105:9-10), and will yet use the RLDS Church to fulfill His promises concerning the building of Zion.

C. An Agreement That The RLDS Church is Being Preserved by the Restorationists:

16. **The Survival of the RLDS Church.** The RLDS Church is not dead, as some have claimed, but it is being preserved in and through the Restorationists—it continues to exist in all those who are defending and proclaiming the original beliefs while remaining within the Church.

17. **The Survival of Local Authority.** The local priesthood who openly proclaim the original doctrines of the Restored Gospel still have their full authority before God. They still have both the right and duty to preach the gospel, conduct services, and perform the ordinances. They should do these things in the name of the RLDS Church, even though they may have to use the name unofficially.

18. **The Survival of the Church Through Restoration Branches.** The saints in every locality should start their own Restoration Branch if the hierarchy prevents the teaching of true doctrine, or introduces Faith to Grow liberalism. Any such group may form a Restoration Branch if they have six or more members, and at least one of them is a priesthood member. Those groups which cannot organize as branches should meet regularly, nevertheless, for worship and study (see Action Time, pp. 150-160).

D. A Course of Action for Individual Saints:

19. **Withdraw Support from the Liberalists.** Since the men of the hierarchy lost all of their spiritual authority when they rejected the Restoration Gospel (see Presidential Papers, pp. 13-54; Action Time, p. 151), the saints should cease to support the Liberal Faction. They can best do this by withholding their influence, attendance, and finances (see Action Time, pp. 172-195).

20. **Believe the Restorationists Are "the Church."** The saints should insist that the Liberal Faction is no longer a part of the Church, but rather that the "institutional Church" now resides in the Restorationists. They should staunchly proclaim: "We are the true RLDS Church, and the hierarchy is only the Liberal Faction" (see Action Time, pp. 112-121).

21. **Ignore Priesthood Silences.** Since the Liberal Faction is in apostasy, any priesthood member who has been silenced by them for defending the original Faith is not silenced at all, and he should be upheld and his ministry accepted by the Restorationists, as long as he remains worthy of his office otherwise.

22. **Ignore Expulsions.** Likewise when members are, or shall hereafter be excommunicated or expelled from the Church by the hierarchy for defending the Restored Gospel, the Restorationists should consider them to be members of the RLDS Church in good standing, and they should be accepted into the Restoration Branches (see Action Time, pp. 199-200).

23. **Support the Restoration Branches Movement.** Since the RLDS Church is surviving through the Restoration Branches and shall continue to do so, the saints should take courage and renew their missionary efforts and spiritual activities, and should determine to carry on their Church work indefinitely without World Church direction or interference.

24. **Pay Tithing.** The saints should continue to pay tithing and give offerings but not to the Liberal Faction. They should give their tithes and offerings in ways that will help defend and promote the original Restoration Gospel (see Action Time, pp. 180-182). The Lord needs to have tithing paid to help save His true Church, and to sustain the needy, more in this time of apostasy than in normal times. Those who hesitate to call these monies "tithing," should give it as "contributions."

25. **Believe There Is Time to Return to the Restoration Gospel.** Though some are prophesying the immediate return of Christ, the Scriptures declare that many important events must yet occur before His great advent, which will take a number of years at the very least (see Action Time, pp. 204-206). Therefore, the saints should understand that Christ is granting sufficient time for the Restorationists to return the body of the saints (the body of Christ) to the Restoration Gospel, and to replace the Liberal Faction. For this reason the Restorationists should stop looking for a quick and easy end to the present crisis, and should vigorously renew their efforts to save the Church from Liberalism, with God's help.

E. An Agreement Regarding Membership and Priesthood in Restoration Branches:

26. No Withdrawal of Membership. The saints should not withdraw from the RLDS Church, but should stay in the Church and work from within to preserve it (see Action Time pp. 162-171). No person should be accepted as a member of a Restoration Branch unless he or she believes that the true Reorganized Church of Jesus Christ of Latter Day Saints (not the Liberal Faction) is God's only true Church.

27. Reinstatement of Membership. Those who have voluntarily surrendered their membership to the Liberalists at Church headquarters, should go to a Restoration Branch and be reinstated by (1) making application for reinstatement in the true RLDS Church, (2) making application to become a member of the Restoration Branch, (3) disavowing membership (if any) in any other fundamental group which is not a recognized Restoration Branch, (4) publicly affirming that they believe that the true RLDS Church is God's only true Church, and (5) affirming that they intend to be loyal to the said RLDS Church and to be an active member of the Branch. No member who has withdrawn should be served the Sacrament of the Lord's Supper by a Restoration Branch until he/she has been reinstated.

28. Authoritative Baptisms. No person shall be accepted as a member of a Restoration Branch unless he or she has been baptized and confirmed by priesthood men who were RLDS Restorationists at the time that those ordinances were performed. Persons who have been baptized and/or confirmed by persons who were Liberalists at the time the ordinances were performed, must be rebaptized and reconfirmed.

29. No Surrendering of Priesthood Licenses. Restorationist priesthood men should not turn in their priesthood cards to the Liberal leaders. If a priesthood man has already surrendered his license, he shall not be allowed to function in his office in a Restoration Branch until such license has been restored by a Restoration Branch.

30. Reinstatement of Priesthood Licenses. A man who has surrendered his license may have it restored by (1) applying to the Restoration Branch of which he is a member, and asking to have said license restored, (2) affirming publicly that he believes that the true RLDS Church is God's only true Church, (3) affirming that he will consider himself a loyal priesthood member of the RLDS Church, (4) affirming that he will be an active priesthood member in the Branch, and (5) by disclaiming membership or priesthood in any other church or denomination (including those new churches or denominations recently formed by fundamentalists who have withdrawn from the RLDS Church).

31. Authoritative Ordinations. The priesthood of a man shall not be accepted by a Restoration Branch if the man was ordained by persons who were Liberalists at the time of the ordination. When such a man joins a Restoration Branch, a new call and ordination shall be necessary before he can function as a member of the priesthood.

32. Acceptance of Membership and Priesthood from Other Restoration Branches. When two or more Restoration Branches endorse these Restorationists Principles, or their equivalent, they should accept each other's members and priesthood as being in good standing. However, the said saints shall have actual membership and voting rights only in the Branch which they have formally joined.

F. A Course of Action for the Restoration Branches:

33. Remain Loyal to the RLDS Church. Each Restoration Branch should consider itself a part of the true RLDS Church and remain loyal to it, while at the same time it should become completely independent of the hierarchy and the Liberal Faction.

34. Remain Independent. The Branch should remain independent of other fundamental groups which are (1) starting other denominations, (2) which declare that the RLDS Church is dead, (3) which require withdrawal of membership from the RLDS Church, (4) which have a one-man leadership, or are trying to fill the higher quorums with such officers as bishops, apostles, or a "prophet," or (5) which promote strange doctrines. It would be better to stand alone than to be a part of a fundamental organization which is in itself in apostasy (see Action Time, pp. 148-149, 181-182).

35. Be Organized According to the Scriptures. The Branch should be organized as the Doctrine and Covenants directs, and have a Branch President and two counselors (who are elected annually), and should have the priesthood acting as a council.

36. Have a Definite Legal Organization. The Branch should have a set of bylaws; and keep records of its history, business meetings, membership, and the ordinances performed.

37. Observe Common Consent. The final authority of the Branch resides in the membership and is expressed in the business meetings. All things should be done democratically by common consent, and strictly in harmony with the Scriptures (see Action Time, p. 155).

38. Seek Stability. The Restoration Branches throughout the Church should seek to become stable over a period of time. Later they should send delegate elders to their own General Conferences, to elect temporary officers to govern the RLDS Church on a temporary basis, without the higher quorums being filled. The Church should then function in this condition until the Lord shall provide new prophetic leadership in His own way and time.

RESTORATIONIST PRINCIPLES (RESTORATION BRANCHES MOVEMENT) (continued)

Notes: *In addition to its brief statement of doctrine, the Restoration Branches Movement has issued a lengthy statement as a guideline for adoption by the affiliated congregations. It greatly expands the briefer statement, but acknowledges the same authoritative documents including the Inspired Version of the Bible, The 1908 edition of the Book of Mormon (authorized by the Reorganized Church), and the first 144 section of the Doctrines and Covenants (those parts received by the church's presidents prior to the presidency of W. Wallace Smith).*

The congregations of the Restoration Branches Movement see themselves as continuing the doctrine and practice of the Reorganized Church prior to its leadership leading it into apostasy and they consider themselves true members of the Reorganized Church, the true church. As with most other LDS denominations, the Movement believes in a form of polytheism, and has resisted monotheistic interpretations of the Latter-Day Saint theology.

Chapter 15
Communal Family

Communal—After 1960

DOCTRINAL STATEMENT (BETHANY FELLOWSHIP)

WE BELIEVE the Bible to be the inspired, the infallible, authoritative Word of God.

WE BELIEVE that there is one God, eternally existent in three persons: Father, Son and Holy Spirit.

WE BELIEVE in the deity of our Lord Jesus Christ, in His virgin birth, in His sinless life, in His miracles, in His vicarious and atoning death through His shed blood, in His bodily resurrection, in His ascension to the right hand of the Father, and in His personal return in power and glory.

WE BELIEVE that man was created in the image of God, that he was tempted by Satan and fell, and that, because of the sin of mankind, regeneration by the Holy Spirit is absolutely necessary for salvation.

WE BELIEVE that it is the will of God that each believer should be sanctified through identification with Jesus Christ in His death and resurrection, and through the agency of the Holy Spirit, be separated from the world and sin and fully consecrated to the will of God, thereby receiving power for holy living and effective service.

WE BELIEVE in prayer for the sick in the Name of the Lord Jesus Christ, and that the anointing with oil, as set forth in James 5:14, is to be practiced by the Church in this present age.

WE BELIEVE in that "blessed hope," the personal premillennial return of our Lord and Savior, Jesus Christ. We believe in the bodily resurrection of all men, each in his order: the saints unto the resurrection of life; the lost unto the resurrection of judgment.

WE BELIEVE that the Scriptures clearly teach that all believers should manifest lives of faith and wholehearted consecration to Christ and His Gospel, give themselves continually to prayer and intercession, and especially fulfill the Great Commission to go into all the world as witnesses of the Gospel to every nation. This, we believe, is the ministry of the Church,

and the power of God is sufficient to meet every need arising out of service to Him according to His will.

Notes: *Bethany Fellowship is a Christian Evangelical communal fellowship headquartered in Minneapolis, Minnesota. Its Doctrinal Statement is based on that of the National Association of Evangelicals with the addition of affirmations concerning human creation, the necessity of sanctification, the practice of prayer for the sick, the premillennial return of Jesus Christ, and the need to fulfill the Great Commission to preach the Gospel in all the world.*

*　　　*　　　*

FIVE PRINCIPLES (PADANARAM SETTLEMENT)

1) As one would that others do, do unto them. (The harvest we reap are the seeds we've sown)

   The communal lifestyle brings materialistic equality, and the intellectualizing of its soundness, applicable to this lifestyle assures continuity. Whether one is man, woman or child, the communal lifestyle fulfills the social, educational, economical, philosophical, and religious needs. There are no rich, and none are poor. Material inequalities and injustices are non-existent. Adequate food, shelter, and clothing are provided for the whole communal family. Under this principle, each becomes his brother's keeper. Life takes on another meaning the reward of "Self" as "Apee" (the evil in man), is denied. Although this principle is challenged by the hostility of nature itself, its incorporation and demonstration proves the dedication and commitment of the inhabitants.

2) Hold all things in common; count nothing one's own. (All the pure rivers flow back to the sea)

   Food is served at a common table three times daily. Philosophical logic proves materialistic inequality continues competition, conflict and war. Living communally supplants these evils with equal distribution of goods among a

FIVE PRINCIPLES (PADANARAM SETTLEMENT)
(continued)

communion of friends. Peace on earth will avoid mankind until it is demonstrated that all races, tongues, and people are a family on earth.

3) Distribution to each according to the need. (The warmth of the sun is shared by all)

Talents and abilities among the villagers may vary. Individuals differ in intelligence, emotional stability, initiative, and learned skills due to environmental and hereditary forces. Yet each person is important and contributes to the communal good. As abilities vary, so do needs. Whereas one may have many needs, another may have few needs, yet both have committed their minds and strength to communal concepts above self-profit. Living and working together, the lives of the inhabitants are enriched and needs fulfilled.

4) Of one who has much, much is required (Footprints in the soil are according to the load)

Energy and skills are devoted to the common good. An individual talented in many areas, out of a personal sense of dedication, discipline, and responsibility, will go the "second mile". All work is intellectualized as honorable. Character and discipline demand that one perform toward a certain capacity and goal. Though there may be differences emotionally, physically, or intellectually, no one is esteemed above the other as all are members of the same organism.

5) One that won't work shall not eat. (If the hand is not lifted, the mouth is not fed)

Work is one's gift as a worker-priest to the whole communal family. It is the offering of the individual's spiritual, mental, and physical abilities. Many historical societies have collapsed from power exploitation, or the corrupting influence of the lazy, the uncommitted, and the uninspired. This final principle adds rule to a merciful, tolerant, benevolent society.

Notes: *Padanaram Settlement is a communal group founded in rural central Indiana in 1966 by Daniel Wright. It organized its existence around five basic working principles that describe a life of mutual respect for others, responsibility, hard work, and a shared existence.*

Chapter 16
Christian Science-Metaphysical Family

New Thought

STATEMENT OF FAITH (UNITY SCHOOL OF CHRISTIANITY)

1. We believe in God, the one and only omnipotent, omniscient, and omnipresent Spirit-mind.

2. We believe in Christ, the Son of God, in whom is imaged the ideal creation, with perfect man on the throne of dominion.

3. We believe in Christ Jesus, the Son of God made manifest in Jesus of Nazareth, who overcame death, and who is now with us in His perfect body as the Way-Shower in regeneration for all men.

4. We believe in the Holy Spirit, which baptizes the universe and man with the thoughts of God and perpetually establishes the divine law in all manifestation.

5. We believe in the supremacy and the eternity of the good, as the one and only objective of man and of all things visible and invisible.

6. We believe in the twelve disciples, the twelve powers of man, going forth into mind and body with power and authority to teach, preach, heal, and wholly save man and the world from sin, sickness, and death, the world from sin, sickness, and death.

7. We believe that "God is spirit," as Jesus taught, and that all of His Spirit is with us at all times, supplying every need.

8. We believe that divine intelligence is present in every atom of man and matter, and that the more abundant life, which Jesus promised, is flooding the world and quickening the minds and the bodies of men everywhere.

9. We believe that the original authority and dominion given to man was over his own thoughts, emotions, feelings, and passions, and that, in the lawful exercise of this authority, he will harmonize all discords within and without and restore the kingdom of God on the earth.

10. We believe in the creative power of thoughts and words; that they do accomplish that whereto they are sent and that all men are held accountable for even their lightest words.

11. We believe that through indulgence in sense consciousness men fell into the belief in the reality of matter and material conditions. We believe that the "kingdom of God" can be attained here and now by overcoming the world, the flesh, and the Adversary through Jesus Christ.

12. We believe in the atonement that Jesus reestablished between God and man, and that through Jesus we can regain our original estate as sons of God.

13. We believe that the prayer of faith will save the sick, resurrect the body from "trespasses and sins," and finally overcome the last enemy, death.

14. We believe that Jesus Christ, the Son of God, is alive and in the world today. We believe that the more abundant life, which Jesus promised, is poured into the race stream as a vitalizing energy, and that, when accepted in faith, it purifies the life-flow in our bodies and makes us immune to all diseased thoughts and germs.

15. We believe that sense consciousness may be lifted up, as Moses lifted up the serpent in the wilderness," and that all men may be again restored to paradise through faith, understanding, and practice of the divine law, as Jesus Christ taught and demonstrated.

16. We believe that creative Mind, God, is masculine and feminine, and that these attributes of Being are fundamental in both natural and spiritual man. "And God created man in his own image, in the image of God created he him; male and female created he them."

17. We believe that we live, move, and have our being in God-Mind; also that God-Mind lives, moves, and has being in us, to the extent of our consciousness.

18. We believe that the body of man is the highest-formed manifestation of creative Mind and that it is capable of unlimited expression of that Mind. "Know ye not that your body is a temple of the Holy Spirit?"

19. We believe that through conscious union with Jesus in the regeneration man can transform his body and make it perpetually healthy, therefore immortal, and that he can attain eternal life in this way and in no other way.

20. We believe that the blood of Jesus represents eternal life; that the body of Jesus represents incorruptible substance. We believe that these are original elements in Being and that they can be appropriated by all who, through faith and understanding, attain the Christ standard of spirituality.

21. We believe that spirit, soul, and body are a unit, and that any separation of these three is transgression of the divine law. We believe that the death that came into the world through the Adamic man resulted in body dissolution and that the restoration of the lost Eden is already begun, in the demonstration over the death of the body, as shown in the resurrection of Jesus Christ.

22. We believe that the dissolution of spirit, soul, and body, caused by death, is annulled by rebirth of the same spirit and soul of man to be a merciful provision of our loving Father to the end that all may have opportunity to attain immortality through regeneration, as did Jesus. "This corruptible must put on incorruption."

23. We believe that the kingdom of heaven or harmony is within man and that through man the law and order existing in Divine Mind are to be established on the earth.

24. We believe that the "second coming" of Jesus Christ is now being fulfilled, that His Spirit is quickening the whole world. "For as the lightning cometh forth from the east, and is seen even unto the west; so shall be the coming of the Son of man. Watch therefore: for ye know not on what day your Lord cometh."

25. We believe that the Golden Rule "Do unto others as you would have them do unto you," should be the standard of action among men.

26. We believe that Jehovah God is incarnate in Jesus Christ and that all men may attain the Christ perfection by living the righteous life. "Ye therefore shall be perfect, as your heavenly Father is perfect."

27. We believe that the Word of God is the thought of God expressed in creative ideas and that these ideas are the primal attributes of all enduring entities in the universe, visible and invisible. The Logos of the first chapter of the Gospel of John is the God idea or Christ that produced Jesus, the perfect man. We believe that the Scriptures are the testimonials of men who have in a measure apprehended the divine Logos but that their writings should not be taken as final.

28. We believe in the final resurrection of the body, through Christ. We believe that we do free our minds and resurrect our bodies by true thoughts and words and that this resurrection is being carried forward daily and will ultimate in a final purification of the body from all earthly errors. Through this process we shall be raised to the consciousness of continuous health and eternal life here and now, following Jesus Christ in the regeneration or "new birth."

29. We believe all the doctrines of Christianity spiritually interpreted.

30. Almighty Father-Mother, we thank Thee for this vision of Thine omnipotence, omniscience, and omnipresence in us and in all that we think and do, in the name of Jesus Christ. Amen!

Notes: *The Unity movement is one of a number of metaphysical groups that sees itself as doctrinally free and thus opposed to creedal statements that might bind its members and leaders. However, there is a doctrinal consensus that has found expression in the instructional materials published by the Unity School of Christianity. In the past it was summarized by founder Charles S. Fillmore in what was termed "Unity's Statement of Faith." While no longer published by Unity School, it remains an accurate and succinct statement of the major ideas taught in Unity's vast literature.*

While making use of Christian symbols and language, the teachings are essentially distinct from that of traditional Western Christianity. As mentioned in item 29, the School teaches the traditional Christian doctrines, but according to a spiritual interpretation. Spiritual interpretation, as pioneered by Emanuel Swedenborg and Mary Baker Eddy, tends to see the Bible allegorically. Thus the twelve disciples are seen by Unity as representations of the twelve power inherent in humans.

God is viewed as the one reality, the Spirit-mind that permeates and undergirds the universe. The universe is an expression of God. God is basically impersonal, but the attributes of Masculine and Feminine are an essential aspect of God (thus there is room for personal language about God). Christ is the ideal of creation and was manifested in the man Jesus of Nazareth. The Holy Spirit is an additional manifestation of God.

The human body was created as the highest-formed manifestation of Mind. It is capable of transformation to the point that it is perpetually healthy and hence physically immortal. In general, people do not attain immortality in this life, and death (the dissolution of the unity of body, spirit, and soul) is followed by the reincarnation (rebirth) of the soul and spirit into a another body.

The discord in human affairs is a sign of humanity's loss of dominion over their thoughts and emotions. Through the "at-one-ment" accomplished by Jesus, the human accord between God and man can be reestablished.

Chapter 17

Spiritualist, Psychic, and New Age Family

Spiritualism

THE AGASHA TEMPLE TEACHES (AGASHA TEMPLE)

THE AGASHA TEMPLE TEACHES . . .

''We teach you reincarnation is a necessity, not a luxury. We teach you that the creative life force in the universe is the 'I am' within each, not a singular individual set apart, but each one, of you, and myself for that matter.

We teach you that as you live your life, so shall you expect those things to come unto you. We teach you the laws of Karma. We teach you when you cannot make a conscious effective change to leave those things unto the hands of divine providence and those things that are meant for you to have shall come your way.

We teach you like unto like. We teach you that each singular individual is infinitely intelligent, no matter how dull or ignorant that individual may appear to be on the exterior. They have within them a multitude of information and we call that multitude of information the infinite wisdom of the soul. You are in existence as a singular entity, as I am in existence as a singular entity, not because of one another but for one another. You pour forth from your cup of knowledge unto me and likewise I do unto you. You bring out of the depths of your minds into a collective consciousness.

We teach you that all is. We hope that you would follow the Golden Rule: 'Do unto others as you would have them do unto you' —not before they do unto you, although I see so many of you often doing the latter.

We teach you the law of Agape and the difference between Agape and Eros. No individual is singular, for if we truly are part of all there is, then how can there only be one? We teach you to remove yourself from the mortal confines of the monster within you, the ego. We teach you that jealousy, false pride, ignorance are all parts, necessary parts of the self indeed, but that are parts to be overcome.

We teach you the laws of energy, the aurathic fields of power, the soul aura. The manifestation of life. We teach you of your meridians of your physical in order so you might keep yourselves in a healthier state. We teach you of your chakras so that you might cleanse yourself. God has given unto each individual the ability to understand. We teach you that it is not just to fear fear that is important. We teach you that it is important to understand your fear, for only in truly understanding your fear can you conquer it.

We teach you that your life is ever present and should be looked on in front of yourself. We teach you that yesterday is today and today is tomorrow. All time is only but existent within the individual mind and sphere of existence of that particular individual.

And more important than anything else, the greatest thing that we try to teach you, the most important thing and the hardest for us to see to do is to accept and love ourselves for whatever progressive stage that we might be in, but love ourselves honestly and void of ego. Manifest unto ourselves so that we can be of use to another.''

—Ayuibbi Tobabu

Notes: *The Agasha Temple is a Spiritualist Church built around the channelled teachings of its long-time medium Richard Zenor. The temple is named for the primary spirit entity who spoke through Zenor. Following Zenor's death, the temple continued under Gary Salvat through whom a second entity, Ayuibbi Tobabu spoke. The belief statement of the temple has been taken from one of Ayuibbi Tobabu's speeches. It emphasizes belief in the continuity of human life in a collective consciousness and the reality of reincarnation and karma for the individual soul. Individuals are on an upward evolutionary path, with each person at a different level. Morally, individuals should follow the Golden Rule, the law of love, and the acceptance of individuals in the knowledge that everyone is at a different stage of growth.*

The church teaches the subtle anatomy derived from Hindu teachings concerning the chakras, seven psychic centers believed to reside along the spinal column from which radiates a field of psychic energy, the aura. By manipulating these energy fields, health can be maintained.

*   *   *

DECLARATION OF PRINCIPLES (INTERNATIONAL GENERAL ASSEMBLY OF SPIRITUALISTS)

We believe in Infinite Intelligence.

We believe that the phenomena of nature both physical and spiritual, are the expressions of Infinite Intelligence.

We affirm that a correct understanding of such expression, and living in accordance therewith, constitute true religion.

We affirm that the existence and personal identity of the individual continue after the change called death.

We affirm that communication with the so called dead is a fact, scientifically proven by the phenomena of Spiritualism.

We believe that the highest morality is contained in the Golden Rule: ''Whatsoever ye would that others should do unto you, do ye also unto them.''

We affirm the moral responsibility of the individual, and that he makes his own happiness or unhappiness as he obeys natures physical and spiritual laws.

We affirm that the doorway to reformation is never closed against any human soul, here or hereafter.

We affirm that the practice of Prophecy, as authorized in the Holy Bible, is a divine and God-given gift, re-established and proven through mediumship by the phenomena of Spiritualism.

We affirm that all our Principles are made possible through Meditation and Prayer.

Notes: *This Declaration was taken over from the National Spiritualist Association of Churches, to which has been added the final paragraph on meditation and prayer.*

*   *   *

Teaching Spiritualism (Channeling)

TENETS (FOUNDATION CHURCH OF DIVINE TRUTH)

We Believe, that the soul of man is the same, in this world and in the next, and that, with physical death, man, manifesting a spirit body enters the spirit world to exist therein, and that his soul will continue to be purified in time to come until he reaches that plane in the spirit world called Paradise or the Sphere of the Perfect Man.

We Believe, that there is a Sphere beyond that of the Perfect Man, where humans souls have reached a state of perfection and purification beyond which they can no longer aspire, and that this Sphere, the Celestial Heavens, is open to those souls who seek the Divine Love of the Heavenly Father. This Divine Love bestowed upon man in response to earnest prayer, not merely purifies his human soul but transforms it into the Essence of the Father, so that the soul is aware of, and in possession of, immortality. This is the salvation that Jesus taught as the Messiah of the Father, in contradistinction to the perfect human soul as taught by Moses.

We Believe, that the true mission of Jesus, as the Christ, was to reach the Jews and all humanity the fact that, with his own soul as evidence, the Father's Love had been made available to mankind, and that immortality now resides in the souls obtaining the Father's Divine Love through prayer to Him for its possession. The potentiality of receiving this Love had been lost with the fall of our first parents.

We Believe, that the divinity of Jesus was made manifest in his divine soul, which became divine on earnest prayer to the Father throughout the hidden years of his life, until he at last realized what his mission was, and that the Divine Love may now enter the soul of whosoever seeks it in earnest prayer and thereby receives It, through the ministrations of the Holy Spirit—that energy of the Father which conveys His Love into the human soul.

We Believe, that Jesus was thus born of Mary and Joseph in accordance with God's law for the reproduction of humankind, yet born of the Holy Spirit in the sense that it was this agency which brought so much of the Father's Love into Jesus' soul that he realized it was like unto the Father's in Essence, and knew that in that way he was the Christ.

We Believe, that such rebirth of the human soul into a divine soul, as first experienced by Jesus through prayer to the Father for His Love, is the true meaning of the New Birth and the New Heart promised to mankind by God through the prophets Isaiah, Jeremiah and Ezekiel.

We Believe, in God, the Father, as a real, personal God, the Creator Soul, composed of Divine Love as His Essence, and all the wonderful Divine Virtues such as Goodness, Mercy, Kindness, Compassion and Patience, and eager to have His children turn to Him in earnest prayer to obtain His Love, so that their souls can be changed from human souls, the reflection of the Father's Soul, into divine souls filled to abundance with His Love and Essence through prayer to Him, in this world and in the next, throughout all eternity.

We Believe, that God is One, Unique and Alone, and not divided, as some religious cults believe into three personalities. God is Soul, Soul is God. Who has never appeared in the flesh in any guise or form, nor has ever manifested a spirit body, the vestment of the human soul after the death of the physical body. God is the Living Personality Divine, our

Eternal Father in Heaven, Who is ever seeking the good and happiness of His children and Whom the human soul may know through the soul perceptions awakened by faith, prayer, and the inflowing of the Divine Love.

We Believe, that sin is a violation of God's Laws of Perfect Harmony, the penalty for which must be paid by man on entry into the spirit world where, now a spirit and subject to God's spiritual laws, his abode therein is determined by the condition of his soul. Hence the evil soul dwells in a place of suffering and darkness as it goes through a period of expiation until it achieves purity. The achievement of such purity is forgetfulness, or what has been called forgiveness. No soul purity may be achieved through any vicarious atonement, or shedding of blood, the relic of barbarous practices among primitive men, but only as man realizes his errors and repentant, seeks reconciliation with the Father through prayer and undergoes the period of purification.

We Believe, that the condition of man's soul is not fixed forever at the time of his death in the flesh, as taught by some churches, but that whether on earth or as a spirit, the soul may at any time turn to God and seek to be purified of sin and that the great help in purification, and, indeed, in the converting of the human soul and its imperfections into a divine soul like unto that of God in Essence, is through earnest prayer to the Father for His Divine Love and Mercy, so that the soul achieves atonement with God and a place in his Kingdom, the Celestial Heavens, of which Jesus, the Messiah, is Master and Prince of Peace.

Notes: *The Foundation Church of Divine Truth is a Spiritualist organization built around channelled teachings received through James Edward Padgett from an entity identified as Jesus Christ and other high celestial spirits. These were compiled into a set of four books, the True Gospel Revealed Anew by Jesus. The Tenets of the Church summarize the teachings. They affirm the continuity of personality after death and the goal of human life is the attainment of the Celestial Heaven. Jesus' message concerned God's love. Humanity lost the ability to receive that love in the fall, but through Jesus that love was again made available to humanity. Born a human soul, Jesus experienced rebirth as a divine soul through prayer, thus demonstrating that possibility for all persons. In distinction from most Spiritualists, the Church teaches that God is personal, but in distinction from most Christian Churches, it disavows the idea of the Trinity.*

*   *   *

DECLARATION OF PRINCIPLES/ARTICLES OF FAITH (UNIVERSAL ASSOCIATION OF FAITHISTS)

1. We believe there is but one ruler of the universe, and He is the Creator, the Great Spirit, the Almighty, Jehovah; all was and ever shall be.

2. We believe our corporeal bodies are His and dedicated and covenanted to Him, to be in His service during our life times.

3. We believe in the continuity of life and that man's evolution is never finished.

4. We believe every individual is responsible for his own acts, and that no man can bear the sins of another.

5. We believe each individual born into the world is a child of the Creator, and that all men are brothers.

6. We affirm the universe is governed by the law of the Creator, which is absolute, eternal, unchangeable, and is the sufficient reason of all things seen and unseen.

7. Although we believe no book is infallible, we accept the Oahspe Bible as our guide to daily living.

8. We believe it to be our duty to help our brothers and sisters of the Human Family; to give love, wisdom, truth, and service and to do these at every opportunity in order that they may learn to help themselves and others. To become ministers, administering to others rather than working for one's self.

9. We believe the greatest satisfaction and happiness of one's life is to serve others, especially the young. Raising them up to work with the hand as well as the mind and teaching them the same Oahspe Bible tenets to work in communities, to establish the worship of the Father, and to help bring about His Kingdom on Earth, and world peace and brotherhood.

10. We believe that any desire, thought, or act, which will injure one's self or another, to be unjust and immoral. We abjure war or violence, discord or conflict in any form, and we believe it is our duty to live in Peace and Harmony with the entire Human Family. To strive to overcome all tendencies of hate, jealousy, malice, conceit, envy, deceit and all forms of physical, mental, emotional, and moral weakness. To increase knowledge of one's self, of life, and of nature; and to use this knowledge properly for self-improvement; to work towards spiritual development of love, wisdom, peace, universal understanding, that we may be of greater service to God, our Country, our Community, and our Fellow Man.

Notes: *Faithists follow the teaching of Oahspe, a book channelled by John Ballou Newbrough in the 1880s. This Declaration of Principles summarizes Oahspe's teachings. It affirms one God, Jehovah, and that each individual human is God's child. Humans are on a upward path of evolution and must be responsible for their own progress, a fact that negates the possibility of anyone, such as Jesus, being of any essential*

*help, in bearing their sins. We can and should help each other
by assisting people to become responsible. Faithists are pacifists.*

*　　*　　*

Drug-Related Groups

CREED (CHURCH OF SUNSHINE)

1. The psychedelic substances, such as LSD, mescaline, psilocybin, and marijuana, are instruments of salvation, both in the sense of liberation from ignorance or illusion and in the sense of deliverance from danger or difficulty.

2. The supreme authority of this church is not any person or group of persons or writings but the logical analysis of experience.

Notes: *The Church of Sunshine was founded by Jack Call, a former member of the Neo-American Church, one of the original religious groups espousing the use of psychedelic drugs in a religious context. However, Call broke with the Neo-American Church over its monarchical control by its leader, Art Kleps. The Creed of the Church of Sunshine emphasizes a non-hierarchical church organization and a belief that psychedelics bring salvation by liberating the individual from ignorance and illusion.*

*　　*　　*

THREE PRINCIPLES (THE ORIGINAL KLEPTONIAN NEO-AMERICAN CHURCH)

The three principles of the Church and of all the genuine affiliates of the Church are as follows:

1. Everyone has the right to expand consciousness and stimulate visionary experience by whatever means he considers desirable and proper without interference from anyone.

2. The psychedelic substances are religious sacraments in that they encourage Enlightenment, which is the realization that life is a dream and the externality of relations an illusion.

3. We do not encourage the ingestion of the Greater Sacraments (such as LSD and peyote) by those who are unprepared and we define preparedness as familiarity with the Lesser Sacraments (such as hemp and nitrous oxide) and with solipsist-nihilist epistemological reasoning on such models as David Hume and Nagarjuna.

Notes: *The Neo-American Church is the oldest of the presently existing drug-oriented religious organizations founded in the modern post-LSD period. It was founded in 1965 by Arthur Kleps. As its principles note, the church has worked for the acceptance of consciousness-altering drugs and the rights of adults to use them without state interference. It considers substances such as LSD as sacraments and values the religious/visionary experiences produced with their assistance. It also encourages the planned systematic use of such sacramental substances as a means to obtains their full effect without negative side-effects.*

*　　*　　*

Miscellaneous Psychic New Age Groups

SEVEN CONCEPTS (ALOHA INTERNATIONAL)

Huna, an ancient Hawaiian esoteric philosophy, is based on seven powerful concepts used to create personal, social and environmental harmony:

1. IKE The world is what you think it is.

2. KALA There are no limits.

3. MAKIA Energy flows where attention goes.

4. MANAWA Now is the moment of power.

5. ALOHA To love is to be happy with.

6. MANA All power comes from within.

7. PONO Effectiveness is the measure of truth.

The purpose of Aloha International is to promote the Aloha Spirit throughout the world, to teach the principles of Huna and their practical applications, and to help maintain the best of Polynesian culture. All of this is part of the great adventure of creating Paradise on Earth, the very realistic goal of a world of peace and plenty, which can be achieved by people who are in harmony with themselves and with their physical and social environment.

Notes: *Aloha International was founded in 1973 by Serge Kahilu King. It teaches a modern form of Kahuna beliefs and practices, the ancient religious system of the Hawaiian Islands. The Seven Concepts provide a philosophical basis for the shamanistic practices taught to adherents. The practices* concern the use of power inherent in humans, directed by attention, and having unlimited potential.

* * *

BELIEFS AND CREED (BELIEVERS' CIRCLE)

WE BELIEVE God is All Mighty, Supreme Power, Designer of the Universe and Creator of all things. God is neither male nor female. God is "Uni." God is love energy. God is Supreme Consciousness. God is in around and through all Creations.

We BELIEVE healing of spirit, mind and body occurs through God energy. All forms of healing for physical bodies are acceptable. Prayers should be for the good of all and harm to none.

WE BELIEVE the spiritsoul is indestructible, is directed to its present lifetime to correct past mistakes. The spiritsoul is assisted in its earthly body by a Guardian Angel or Guides from the higher realms. All things are a form of God Consciousness of which humans are one of the highest forms on the earth plane. All of God's creations may change form but can never be completely destroyed.

WE BELIEVE life on earth is for learning God's laws, which are absolute. Broken laws are mistakes, not sins. So-called death is a transition from the earth consciousness to the unobstructed universe where the spiritsoul continues to learn.

WE BELIEVE God's laws granting humans free will make people responsible for all conditions on earth. God's while light of energy, for the protection and good of all and harm to none, is available to all humans who believe in it.

ALL of this WE BELIEVE.

Notes: *The Believers' Circle is a New Age group built around the channeled material received through the Reverend Estel Merrill of Bakersfield, California. The material has been put together by Merrill's close associates into a set of correspondence lessons available to the general public. God is seen as the Creator of all things that exist as a form of God consciousness. Humans are the highest form of God consciousness. Through their free will, humans have made mistakes that have led to sickness and discord, both of which may be corrected by God*

energy. Humans continue after death in a spiritual realm where they continue to grow and learn.

* * *

OUR BELIEF (CHRISTIAN INSTITUTE OF SPIRITUAL SCIENCE)

The Christian Institute believes in God as the Absolute as He is beheld in the mind and consciousness of humanity, and as He is revealed through the presence, truth, and life of Christ in the word.

We believe in one God, the absolute, supreme, omnipotent Creator. He is our Heavenly Father and in Him we live, move and have our being. God is the Spirit of life, light, love, goodness, compassion, salvation, perfection, happiness and liberty.

We believe that God lives the divine drama of the Holy Trinity in the life, mind, and consciousness of humanity. He is experienced by human consciousness as the Father, Mother, Son Principles, or as the Creative Spirit, the Holy Spirit, and the Christ Spirit. As the Creator, God is the Divine Father of all. As the creative power that conceives the life, will, purpose and wisdom of the Absolute and projects them as creation, He is the Divine Mother Principle, the Cosmic Soul. As Divine Mind made manifest in creation, He is the Christ—the Creator present in creation as the Divinity, intelligence, perfection and immortality of all that is.

We believe that the Holy Trinity lives in man as his true identity. The Divine Father Principle lives in man as his spirit, the Divine Mother Principle, the Holy Spirit, lives in him as his soul, and the Christ Principle lives in him as his mind and consciousness. These triple and divine powers make man the fruit of creation, the Son of God, the immortal self.

We believe that man is the living intelligence, will, love, light, and idea of God made manifest in creation. Inwardly he is the Son of God. Outwardly he is the fruit of creation. As man is one with his intelligence will, love, light and idea, so God is one with man. As the intelligence, will, love, light and idea of man is his living expression, so man is the living likeness and expression of God.

We believe that all powers in heaven and in earth are given unto man. They are experienced by him through his spiritual resurrection and the transformation of his soul, mind, nature and body.

We believe in the Gift of the Holy Spirit. This is attained through faith and the heavenly presence in man. Through purity of heart and soul, through renunciation of all negation, through fervent devotion and love to God, through absolute surrender to His will, purpose, and wisdom, and through constant concentration and meditation upon the indwelling Christ Self, man attains resurrection. This spiritual unfoldment causes the quickening of the Holy Spirit and total regeneration of one's being. The Gift of the Holy Spirit quickens the

OUR BELIEF (CHRISTIAN INSTITUTE OF SPIRITUAL SCIENCE) (continued)

spiritual or psychic powers in man, inspires him, renews his being, and initiates him to the Christ Self. It endues him with the power of divine healing and inner sight. It confers upon him the use of Divine Mind and cosmic will, and blesses him with the sign of the Son of God, the miraculous power of the Spirit.

"And it shall come to pass in the last days, saith God, I will pour out of my Spirit upon all flesh: and your sons and your daughters shall prophecy, and your young men shall see visions, and your old men shall dream dreams:

"And on my servants and on my hand maidens I will pour out in those days of my Spirit; and they shall prophesy".

We believe that truth, righteousness, life, immortality, perfection and goodness are the attributes of Divine Presence. Therefore, in the positiveness of life there is no falsehood, darkness negation or evil. These assumed conditions are the creation of the instinctive man. Man's ignorance causes their timely effect and endurance, and his positiveness, righteousness and wisdom transform them. There is one presence, one life, one truth, one reality, one mind, one consciousness and one experience. It is God.

We believe in positiveness, goodness, spiritual worth, and eternal beauty of life. Life is an immortal and all-knowing consciousness. It is the author of divine wisdom, happiness, spiritual emanation, liberty, and oneness. We believe that eternal, immutable good is the only reality, and truth is the only life and power. We accept this as the conviction, foundation and guarantee of well-being.

We believe that heaven is the infinite and eternal kingdom of God, the angels, and man. It is a celestial and holy kingdom of love, happiness, liberty, and immortality. It is absolute and perfect in itself and underlies all existence. Heaven is beheld in man as his divine nature consciousness, inheritance and dominion. It is the infinite, spiritual expansion and power of his true being.

We believe in the power of prayer. Through prayer, or concentration, meditation and mystic communion with God, one is blest beyond measure. He is sanctified, enriched, strengthened and perfected. Through prayer the spirit is quickened divinely, and through that quickening is blest with the grace, love, and will of the Father.

We believe in the power of the Spoken Word. The Spoken Word is the etheric and living manifestation of the Logos, the Christ. Thus the Spoken Word is vitalized with spiritual will, that conforms and endues things with the power that liberates, blesses, enlightens and heals. The power of positive affirmation and of words of truth writes miracles in the world.

We believe in the power of faith. Through divine law the power of faith resurrects the Holy Spirit in the believer. This spiritual resurrection releases the will of God, whose miraculous power never fails.

We believe in divine healing. Healing is executed though Divine will, faith, prayer, and laying on of hands. All is traced to the spirit. Physical ailments have their mental and soul causes. The disturbance occurs in the creative light forces, and thus affects the physical. Healing prayer, or quickening, regenerative concentration and meditation, restores physical and soul health. Through prayer, or the Spoken Word, spiritual power is called into healing activity. The same is accomplished through will and laying on of hands.

We believe that Truth is all in all. The Spirit of Truth lives in all. The Spirit of Truth is all life, all power, all goodness, all positiveness, all wisdom, all love, all oneness, all reality, all universality, all individuality, all humaneness. Truth is God.

Notes: *The Christian Institute of Spiritual Science is a New Age organization. Its belief statement affirms God as Creator and as the Spirit of life who lives in the human consciousness where He is experienced as a Divine Trinity. God is Father Principle (spirit), Mother Principle or Holy Spirit (soul), and Christ Principle (mind). Humans are God made manifest in creation. Through spirit disciplines, humans may receive the Gift of the Holy Spirit, a spiritual unfolding that revives the psychic spiritual powers. Spiritual unfolding leads to heaven, the holy kingdom of love, happiness, liberty, and immortality.*

Members of the Institute practice divine healing and the use of affirmations, the stating of an ideal condition as a means of bringing it into visible existence.

*   *   *

DECLARATION OF FAITH (CHRIST'S CHURCH OF THE GOLDEN RULE)

We deem it proper to state herein some of the basic doctrines and principles upon which Christ's Church of The Golden Rule is founded, and the following declaration expresses, substantially, what we believe:

1. Of The True God:

We believe that there is but one living and true Father-Mother God; omnipotent, omniscient, and omnipresent Divine Mind and changeless perfection; that Creator and Preserver of all things, both visible and invisible; the Supreme Ruler of the Universe, wholly worthy of honor, confidence, and love—in Whom we live, move, and have our being.

2. Of Christ Jesus:

We believe that Jesus of Nazareth was inexpressibly wise, gentle, and holy; that he came to earth to reveal God to all men, and to exemplify by his actions and teachings all of the virtues and goodness of a perfect man; that by his life, crucifixion, death, resurrection, and ascension he became the Way-shower to all who believe in his teachings; but that the Christ—(Truth, the Mind that was in Christ Jesus)—existed even before Abraham was, and has always been co-existent with God . . . the man Jesus we believe to have been the highest exemplification of the Christ (Truth) to have evolved from the race of men—hence our acceptance of him as our Way-shower.

3. Of The Holy Scriptures:

We believe that the original basic teachings of the Holy Bible were written by men moved by the Mind or Spirit that is God; that it contains all directions necessary to salvation; that it reveals the principles by which we shall live and be judged; that it is, and will forever remain the basis of Christian fellowship and the most perfect standard by which human conduct shall be tried.

4. Of Salvation Through Repentance and Regeneration:

We believe that to be saved from the consequences of any kind of wrong-doing, we must truly repent thereof and correct our errors; that to be regenerated we must respond freely to the influence and power of the Mind that is God—the Mind that was in Christ Jesus—that only the works of that Mind be done on earth as they are in heaven (perfect harmony) . . . and that the evidence of regeneration shall appear as a more Christ-like life.

5. Of True Religion:

We believe that the essence of true religion is to learn to love God with all of one's heart and the art of doing unto others as we would have others do unto us; that we must serve, rather that be served; that the strong must help the so-called weak, so that none may suffer; and that in all things we should seek the perfect will of God, and the good of all men.

6. Of The Economy of The Church:

We believe that economic equality is the only enduring foundation upon which to build industrial, business, political, national and international relationships; and that to insure such equality the property and earnings of all individuals should be used to glorify God and to illustrate the teachings of Christ Jesus.

Notes: *Christ's Church of the Golden Rule is a New Age church. It affirms the existence of God, the Divine Mind. Christ, or Truth, is coexistent with God and found in supreme exemplification in the man Jesus of Nazareth. Men moved by God wrote the Bible, which contains the direction necessary for salvation. Those directions include repentance of our errors and respond to the influence of Mind (God).*

The Church advocates a change in the economic system to one of economic equality for the individual and both national and international structures.

*   *   *

CREED [FIRST CHRISTIANS' (ESSENE) CHURCH]

I believe in the Fatherhood of God, the Motherhood of Nature and the Brotherhood of Man.

I believe all the forces of life must be mobilized against the forces of death.

I believe mutual understanding creates peace which is the only way of survival for mankind

I believe in the preservation of our natural resources, our legacy for our children: the humble grass and the majestic trees; pure air, water, and soil.

I believe in preserving the purity of my body with fresh, natural whole, uncontaminated food.

I believe in simple, natural, creative ways leading to a life of harmony and wisdom.

I believe the improvement of life on our planet can begin with my efforts.

I believe in the Fatherhood of God, the Motherhood of Nature and the Brotherhood of Man.

Notes: *The First Christians' (Essene) Church was founded in 1937 by popular metaphysical writer/teacher Edmond Bordeaux Szekely. Szekely's teachings include a lifestyle in tune with the forces of nature, including vegetarianism and the eating of natural foods. This natural lifestyle finds expression in the church's Creed. Essenes believe in a simple and creative way of life.*

*   *   *

UNIFICATION THEOLOGICAL AFFIRMATIONS (HOLY SPIRIT ASSOCIATION FOR THE UNIFICATION OF WORLD CHRISTIANITY)

1. God. There is one living, eternal, and true God, a Person beyond space and time, who possesses perfect intellect, emotion, and will, whose deepest nature is heart and love, who combines both masculinity and femininity, who is the source of all truth, beauty, and goodness, and who is the creator and sustainer of man and the universe and of all things visible and invisible. Man and the universe reflect His personality, nature, and purpose.

2. Man. Man was made by God as a special creation, made in His image as His children, like Him in personality and nature, and created to respond to His love, to be the source of His joy, and to share His creativity.

3. God's Desire for Man and Creation. God's desire for man and creation is eternal and unchanging; God wants men and women to fulfill three things: first, each to grow to perfection so as to be one in heart, will, and action with God, having their bodies and minds united together in perfect harmony centering on God's love; second, to be united by God as husband and wife and give birth to sinless children of God, thereby establishing a sinless family and ultimately a sinless world; and third, to become lords of the created world by establishing a loving domin-

UNIFICATION THEOLOGICAL AFFIRMATIONS (HOLY SPIRIT ASSOCIATION FOR THE UNIFICATION OF WORLD CHRISTIANITY) (continued)

ion of reciprocal give-and-take with it. Because of man's sin, however, none of these happened, therefore God's present desire is that the problem of sin be solved and that all these things be restored, thus bringing about the earthly and heavenly Kingdom of God.

4. Sin. The first man and woman (Adam and Eve), before they had become perfected, were tempted by the archangel Lucifer into illicit and forbidden love. Through this Adam and Eve willfully turned away from God's will and purpose for them, thus bringing themselves and the human race into spiritual death. As a result of this Fall. Satan usurped the position of mankind's true father so that thereafter all people are born in sin both physically and spiritually and have a sinful propensity. Human beings therefore tend to oppose God and His will, and live in ignorance of their true nature and parentage and of all that they have lost. God too grieves for his lost children and lost world, and has had to struggle incessantly to restore them to himself. Creation groans in travail, waiting to be united with the true children of God.

5. Christology. Fallen mankind can be restored to God only through Christ (the Messiah), who comes as a new Adam to become the new head of the human race (replacing the sinful parents), through whom mankind can be reborn into God's family. In order for God to send the Messiah, mankind must fulfill certain conditions which restore what was lost through the Fall.

6. History. Restoration takes place through the paying of indemnity for (making reparations for) sin. Human history is the record of God's and man's efforts to make these reparations over time in order that conditions can be fulfilled so that God can send the Messiah, who comes to initiate the completed restoration process. When some effort at fulfilling some reparation condition fails, it must be repeated, usually by someone else after some intervening time-period; history therefore exhibits a cyclic pattern. History culminates in the coming of the Messiah, and at that time the old age ends and a new age begins.

7. Resurrection. The process of resurrection is the process of restoration to spiritual life and spiritual maturity, ultimately uniting man with God; it is passing from spiritual death into spiritual life. This is accomplished in part by man's effort (through prayer, good deeds. etc.) with the help of the saints in the spiritual world, and completed by God's activity of bringing man rebirth through Christ (the Messiah).

8. Predestination. God's will that all people be restored to Him is predestined absolutely, and He has elected all people to salvation, but he has also given man part of the responsibility (to be accomplished through man's free will) for the accomplishment of both His original will and His will for the accomplishment of restoration; that responsibility remains man's permanently. God has predes-

tined and called certain persons and groups of people for certain responsibilities; if they fulfill, mankind will be blessed and these people will be glorified, but if they fail, others must take up their roles and greater reparations must be made.

9. Jesus. Jesus of Nazareth came as the Christ, the Second Adam, the only begotten Son of God. He became one with God, speaking the words of God and doing the works of God, and revealing God to the people. The people, however, rejected and crucified him, thereby preventing his building the Kingdom of God on earth. Jesus, however, was victorious over Satan in his crucifixion and resurrection, and thus made possible spiritual salvation for those who are reborn through him and the Holy Spirit. The restoration of the Kingdom of God on earth awaits the Second Coming of Christ.

10. The Bible. The Old and New Testament Scriptures are the record of God's progressive revelation to mankind. The purpose of the Bible is to bring us to Christ, and to reveal God's heart. Truth is unique, eternal, and unchanging, so any new message from God will be in conformity with the Bible and will illuminate it more deeply. Yet, in these last days, new truth must come from God in order that mankind be able to accomplish what is, as yet, undone.

11. Completed Restoration. A proper understanding of theology concentrates simultaneously on man's relationship with God (vertical) and on man's relationship with his fellowmen (horizontal). Man's sin disrupted both these relationships, and all the problems of our world result from this. These problems will be solved through restoration of man to God through Christ, and also through such measures as initiating proper moral standards and practices, forming true families, uniting all peoples and races (such as Orient, Occident and Negro), resolving the tension between science and religion, righting economic, racial, political, and educational injustices, and overcoming God-denying ideologies such as Communism.

12. Second Coming or Eschatology. The Second Coming of Christ will occur in our age, an age much like that of the First Advent. Christ will come as before, as a man in the flesh, and he will establish a family through marriage to his Bride, a woman in the flesh, and they will become the True Parents of all mankind. Through our accepting the True Parents (the Second Coming of Christ), obeying them and following them, our original sin will be eliminated and we will eventually become perfect. True families fulfilling God's ideal will be begun, and the Kingdom of God will be established both on earth and in heaven. That day is now at hand.

Notes: *The Holy Spirit Association for the Unification of World Christianity, more popularly known as the Unification Church, was founded in Korea in 1954 by the Reverend Sun Myung Moon. It came to the United States in 1959 where it became well known as one of the most controversial religious groups in the last decades of the twentieth century. Reverend Moon developed an elaborate revision of traditional Christian teachings that were presented in a large volume, the Divine Principle.*

By the mid-1970s, the Church was in dialogue with many groups of theologians and clergy, few of whom were ready to make the effort to read the Divine Principle in full. Hence, a number of summaries of the church's teachings were attempted. The Unification Theological Affirmations were prepared by the students of the Unification Theological Seminary in Barrytown, New York, and published by the Seminary's press. The Affirmations attempt to summarize church teachings that center on the restoration of fallen humanity that will ultimately occur through the actions of the Messiah, though people must cooperate with that action by the paying of indemnity.

The key difference between the Unification Church and traditional Christianity concerns the former's beliefs about contemporary salvic history. In these days, new truths must come to stand beside the Bible. The Messiah will come, he will establish a family, and he an his wife will become the True Parents of the human race. Reverend Moon has fulfilled that role, and the Unification Church has initiated the completed restoration through its promotion of interracial marriages, solving the conflict between science and religion, and overcoming anti-God ideologies, the most prominent being Communism.

*   *   *

AIMS AND IDEALS (NATIONAL ALLIANCE FOR SPIRITUAL GROWTH)

The aims and ideals focussed on by NASG and its subsidiaries are principles which support the concepts of life, love and eternal progression in a manner which utilizes the precepts of truth, honesty, sincerity, integrity, choice and responsibility, together with the higher concepts of peace, brotherhood, order, and the basic divinity of all life. That the divine right of each person to get in touch with his or her own High Self and more fully realize God is a given truth.

New age sciences including New Physics, Metaphysics, Holistic Health and Transpersonal Psychology are accepted as valid. Meditation Intuition, Psychism and Channeling are also accepted as valid tools for growth.

Although channeling is accepted, we do not support the deification of or belief in other entities/consciousness as part of a hierarchical structure as it has been found limiting. It creates a spiritual barrier due to a focus on the deemed necessity for a channel or connection to God other than the eternally inherent connection of oneself as a spiritual being-already part of God. It has also been found psychologically limiting by placing others on a "more divine" level, thus lessening the estimation of oneself and one's integral impact within the whole.

With these ideals, NASG remains an expanding organization with a continued effort to network with others and to openly share and direct the highest level of information and genuine resources within the diversity of the New Age Movement, thus

remaining ever dedicated to the expansion of Being, and the experience of Becoming.

Notes: *The National Alliance for Spiritual Growth is a New Age organization loosely affiliated with the Congregational Church of Practical Theology. It affirms the basic divinity of all of life and hence the self as part of God. The Alliance centers on the experience of each person in contacting their High Self and thus realizing God. Members use a wide variety of tools for contacting their High Self including channeling, the speaking of a spirit entity through an individual or medium. However, it is recognized that channeling, a very popular New Age practice, is problematic insofar as it tends to deify the spirit entity who is channeled and detract from the individual's own attempt to be immediately present with God.*

*   *   *

ARTICLES OF BELIEF (NEW AGE COMMUNITY CHURCH)

1. We believe in God as the one eternal reality.

2. We reverence the Earth, that great matriarch, who is the source of all life.

3. We believe in Masters, Avatars and Gurus who can guide the lives of individuals and the destiny of mankind.

4. We believe in other dimensions, one of which is the astral plane or the spirit world, and we believe that we dwell there just as we dwell on the physical plane.

5. We believe the Bible, the Bhagavad-Gita, the Quran, and other scriptures are divinely inspired and, when correctly understood in the context of their revelation and translated correctly, can be said to be "The Word of God".

6. We believe the world is entering a New Age of consciousness, the Age of Aquarius, and we believe that the concept of a war between Good and Evil belongs to the old, Piscean Age.

7. We believe that the greatest threat to humanity today is government and its attempts to rule human thought and activity, and that those people who fail to control their government will be controlled by it.

8. We believe that it is the divine right of each individual to follow the dictates of his or her conscience and no one has the right to force others to his will.

9. We believe that there are many things as yet unknown or unexplained, but that humanity is continually growing in awareness.

Notes: *The New Age Community Church was founded in Phoenix, Arizona, in 1972. Its basic belief is in the coming of a new age, signaled by the enlightenment of minds attuned to it. The Church's Articles of Belief affirm a belief in God as the one eternal reality, Earth as the source of life, and the*

ARTICLES OF BELIEF (NEW AGE COMMUNITY CHURCH)
(continued)

existence of teachers who guide individuals. These teachers are both disembodied and incarnated. The church offers a strong affirmation of human freedom and is against government control of human activity.

*   *   *

CHURCH TENETS (SCIENCE OF MAN CHURCH)

1. Science of Man Church is a non-denominational, non-sectarian group of people, banded together for the purpose of a more thorough understanding of the Universal Laws of the Creator, so they might better manifest His Creation and thus promote Peace and Harmony among men.

2. We accept the basic law of the Triangle and the spoken word, as tools given to us by the Creator to fulfill our needs in this life and the one to come.

3. We accept both a seen and unseen plane of action of the Life-Force, as used by the Creator, when He created us.

4. We accept that Man was given, when created by the Great Creative Intelligence, Spiritual and Physical Senses.

5. We accept that life is continuous, uninterrupted, and ever-evolving at the point of Being,

6. We accept that man has the ability as the instrument of healing as given by the Creator to heal the sick, the lame, and the halt—as well as the mentally ill of the spirit, as vouched for by the Master Man Jesus.

7. We accept the giving of Communion, both materially and spiritually.

8. We accept baptism of the child and adult as the baptism of the Holy Ghost, and as the lifting of Consciousness.

9. We accept the confession of sins, through the confessional, if it is so desired by the individual, by and through the use of the Great Universal Law, which confessional shall be attended only by an ordained minister.

10. We accept the unity of the Great Creator, God, in mind and matter, throughout this solar system.

11. We accept that all men and women, regardless of race, creed, or color, shall be accepted on an equal basis in the eyes of the Creator and the church.

12. We accept that, above all things, man must be free to choose the things in his life, also that the spiritual and material world are one.

13. We accept Man as an evolving being of unlimited resources and unlimited expansion, with a God of Infinite Wisdom.

Notes: *The Science of Man Church continues the former Holy Order of MANS, which formally entered a merger with the Greek Archdiocese of Vasiloupolis in the late 1980s. Some members did not agree with the merger, but wished to continue with the more esoteric beliefs of the Holy Order. These Tenets affirm belief in God who created all and in the Life-Force, used by God in creation. Humans are entities of unlimited resources and capable of unlimited expansion. The church is a liturgical body exemplified by its practice of Communion, baptism, and the confession of sins in the presence of an ordained minister. Divine healing is also affirmed.*

*   *   *

CONCEPTS (TEACHING OF THE INNER CHRIST)

1. The scope of the Teaching is to reach humanity everywhere, regardless of race, creed, background, or state of consciousness.

2. The purpose of the Teaching is to assist every individual in the contacting of the Center of Divinity within the self, that they may become aware of and proceed toward gaining conscious communion with their Inner Christ.

3. It acknowledges that everyone is a potential revealer of Truth for the self, through contact with God through their Inner Christ.

4. Therefore, it teaches that there is a God consciousness in each person, as that person, reached through self-revelation of their spiritual nature, thus revealing their relationship to God and the Universe.

5. It teaches the mystical life of the Christ, the perceiving of Truth without mental process, through the awakening of inner sensing awareness, and to this purpose it teaches techniques of deep meditation and meditation control.

6. It teaches the spirit of Love and Truth, and the power of individual authority, proclaiming that all persons may attain dominion over circumstances.

7. It teaches that spiritual gifts are given to anyone who seeks to develop their inner sensitivity through contact with their Christ Self.

8. It teaches methods of spiritual mind healing through scientific prayer and the power of the spoken word.

9. It teaches the correlation of mystical events as related in the Bible to present day data on parapsychological phenomena and spiritual experience.

Notes: *The Teaching of the Inner Christ was founded in 1965 and is headed by Ann Meyer Makeever, a "sensitive," who claims to be in contact with several master teachers and her I AM self, from whom she channels the group's teachings. Based on Makeever's teachings, the church affirms the existence of God and the Inner Christ in each individual and the* *possibility of each individual making contact with them. Through said contact, the individual may become a revealer of Truth, possessed of the spiritual gifts, and attain dominion over circumstance. Spiritual healing may be accomplished through prayer and the use of affirmations, a form of prayer that asserts the existence of the ideal situation as a means of bringing it into reality.*

*   *   *

Psychic/New Age Organizations

PRINCIPLES AND PURPOSE (SPIRITUAL FRONTIERS FELLOWSHIP)

I

Among various manifestations of man's psychic and spiritual nature there are three main areas of concern which SFF would emphasize at this present time.

1. Most important is the development of creative and mystical Prayer in order to meet the need for a greater reality in prayer. God meets us in prayer. Life can be transformed and situations changed when prayer is seen not as "overcoming God's reluctance but as laying hold on God's willingness."

2. Spiritual healing, which is a frequent outgrowth of intercessory prayer. Well-attested success in healing has led to a larger recognition of the place of faith as a factor in mental and physical health, and there is increasing cooperation between the medical profession and religious leadership.

3. Personal immortality and the eternal life of the spirit. If, as the Scriptures would indicate, the spiritual world is another dimension, near us and not to be measured in light years or distance, may there not be some glimpses within the veil, as Peter and Paul and John experienced? Scripture testimony indicates that "The Communion of Saints" means far more than fellowship of believers on earth. How much more? To sift and weigh the evidence of the survival of the soul after death, as it is presented through psychical research, is a most serious concern. With open minds, and seeking to develop spiritual sensitivity, we believe in the reality of a future life and that spiritual guidance and personal communion with our beloved dead are possible.

Certain other practices and beliefs of the New Testament Church are now being accepted by growing numbers of people. These include recognition of the presence and ministry of angels, the reality of demon possession as far more than mere mental illness, and of deliverance by exorcism, guidance through dreams and visions, manifestation of the gifts of the Spirit described in First Corinthians as prophecy, interpretation, and discerning of spirits; and, more widespread than other phenomena, 'glossolalia' or speaking in tongues. Likewise,

some of the insights of modern depth psychology are proving for many to be roads to self understanding and spiritual reality.

More important than even these special concerns which may change from time to time, is a pioneer spirit which always looks forward to further steps in understanding and experience. SFF recognizes that no individual or institution can both stand still and follow truth.

II

Certain philosophical principles and viewpoints lie back of the special interest of SFF, although they may not necessarily be accepted by all its members:

1. Its basic world view, like that of the New Testament and many of the greatest philosophers, is that there is a physical world subject to the laws of physics and biology, and a nonphysical, or psychic world, which is just as real, yet entirely different. Since everything comes from one divine Mind, both are under the moral law of God with freedom, responsibility, and purpose. This implies the distinction of good from evil, and the concepts of heaven and hell.

2. Man is a creature of both worlds, and in spiritual experience becomes aware of his true heritage as a child of God with unlimited capacity for growth. Any effective religion must include acceptance of, experience with, and obedient response to the laws of the spiritual world.

3. The Bible, and more specifically the New Testament, is a reliable report of the experience of men and women in their dealings with Jesus Christ and the spiritual world. Thus, while SFF accepts the fruits of modern technology and the insights of critical Bible study as gifts of God, it is close to the fundamentals of New Testament Christianity.

4. SFF takes the scientific attitude that all human experiences, including extrasensory perception (telepathy, clairvoyance, precognition and related phenomena) are to be studied without prejudice for better understanding of the invisible world, and the nature of man and the universe. SFF acknowledges the part that the sciences, including psychology, parapsychology, physics and biophysics, have played in directing the attention of many lay people and ministers to the non-material nature of the world.

5. As men come into what they believe to be valid personal relationship with the spiritual world, they discover a firmer basis for understanding the great questions of life and faith, and for facing the human problems of suffering, injustice, and death.

6. SFF holds that the doors of revelation are never closed; God is still speaking, and by the disciplines of study, prayer, and healing our generation may learn more of those truths which Christ said his disciples were "not yet able to bear."

III

On the basis of these general principles, SFF has certain specific purposes:

PRINCIPLES AND PURPOSE (SPIRITUAL FRONTIERS FELLOWSHIP) (continued)

1. It seeks to enlarge the churches' interpretation of their Old and New Testament heritage; it endeavors to recapture the faith and experience of the First Century in order to speak with conviction to contemporary Man.

2. SFF seeks to share with science the implications of its own method, which is the examination of all available evidence as the basis of understanding and progress, and to urge that it be just as open-minded in dealing with parapsychology as it is with physics and biology,

3. It would open the eyes of a materialistic and skeptical generation to man's intrinsic spiritual nature.

4. For its own members, SFF seeks to provide an assurance that they are not alone, but are part of a larger company of people who desire to seek further exploration of truth and avenues for more effective service to God and Man. It seeks to provide a comfortable climate for sharing and discussing experiences of nonphysical reality.

SFF implements these purposes by means of a national office and officers, a book service and lending library, publications, research, seminars and conferences, area organizations, praystudy groups, spiritual and psychical study groups for spiritual development and healing.

IV

In line with its spiritual philosophy and church-centered purposes, there are certain matters of strategy and practice which should be kept in mind by officers and committees within the Fellowship, and by those outside in evaluating it. These are guidelines rather than rigid rules, but they represent the general attitude of both the organizers and the present national directors.

1. While SFF stresses the validity of spiritual and psychic gifts, its purpose is to bring them back into the life of the church, so that there would be no reason for SFF to perpetuate itself indefinitely as an organization.

2. In a broad sense, SFF was church-conceived, born and bred. Therefore, it chooses its leadership from among church members, and, as far as is practicable, it holds its public meetings in church buildings.

3. While it appreciates the contributions of the numerous movements which have sought to satisfy specific spiritual needs not otherwise met, it, seeks to recall those who have broken away from the redemptive fellowship of the church.

4. SFF seeks to cooperate with like-minded individuals and groups within and outside the churches. It invites the support of all spiritual pioneers and specifically seeks sponsorship by courageous and forward looking ecclesiastical leaders. It therefore welcomes cooperation with such groups as the Churches' Fellowship for Psychical and Spiritual Studies in Great Britain, and Imago Mundi, the Catholic oriented international study group in border areas of science.

5. SFF prefers to avoid public demonstrations of mystical and psychic phenomena which may attract curiosity seekers rather than the spiritually hungry. It makes a distinction between the mystical and the psychical in terms of their source and use. SFF investigates the psychical and encourages the mystical life.

6. While the Fellowship is not primarily a research group, it has created an active Research Committee which encourages investigation in the principal fields of the paranormal without being dogmatic about their validity or their interpretation. It welcomes the help and interest of all, regardless of religious background.

7. SFF recognizes that the frontier is always fraught with the dangers of extremism, individualism and self-deception. Both scripture and common sense require that we "try the spirits to see whether they be of God" (I John 4:1) and give some ground rules for doing so. But it also remembers that the growing edge is always on the frontier.

8. The Fellowship seeks to be democratic in its committees and official actions, and so seeks the participation of its members in the making of policy and program. For this reason also, it avoids "official endorsements" of specific persons and points of view.

9. The spiritual can never be put into a rigid mold, so there will always be diversities of emphasis, practice and theology. Therefore, SFF holds that the only essentials are loyalty to the truth as one perceives it, and willingness to venture out in obedience to it.

This is the Spiritual Frontiers Fellowship, we believe, called by God for such a time as this.

If the Spirit bears witness with your spirit that this is so, you are invited to bear witness also by your membership, your active participation and your public support.

Notes: *Spiritual Frontiers Fellowship is a New Age organization founded in 1956 by a group of Christian ministers and lay persons who were interested in exploring the world of the psychic. After existing as a fairly open organization for a generation, it realigned its thinking in the late 1970s to become a part of the emerging New Age movement. Throughout this entire period it has been guided by a set of Principles and Purpose, the current text was revised in 1974.*

The Principles and Purpose suggest an interest in the mystical side of life, especially in those experiences encountered in prayer, spiritual healing, and the search for life after death. It also suggests an attempt to communicate with both the traditional church and the world of scientific inquiry concerning these experiences. It accepts modern critical biblical scholarship, but believes that paranormal experiences assist in the understanding of the biblical text. The Fellowship is also aware of the problems encountered in the realm of the paranormal and seeks to encourage the development of spiritual life rather than provide entertainment for the curious.

Chapter 18

Ancient Wisdom Family

Liberal Catholic Churches

CONSTITUTION (FREE LIBERAL CATHOLIC CHURCH, INC.)

ARTICLE I. THE CHURCH

Section 1. The Free Liberal Catholic Church is a catholic church in that it administers through its bishops, priests, and deacons the Seven Sacraments handed down, according to Catholic tradition, from Christ Himself through His apostles and their successors.

Section 2. The Church is Liberal in that the only demand that it makes of its members, or of others who seek the grace of those Sacraments, is that they approach them in a spirit of reverence.

Section 3. The Church is Free in that all who serve in Her work and worship are free to seek God in accordance with their own conscience relying only on the ultimate authority of God in His infinite wisdom. No council, synod, bishop, priest, deacon, or other group or officer shall in the name of the Free Liberal Catholic Church require anyone to subscribe to a creed or definition of a term or terms, or in any other way require anyone to subscribe to anything that he or she does not understand.

Section 4. The Holy Bible is our guide and rule of life to the best of each communicant's understanding. Everyone is encouraged to seek the truth of God the Father in the Holy Bible and to augment that search with any and all studies that will contribute to the seeker's growth in the knowledge of God. To direct and protect freedom of inquiry teachers shall recommend lines of study but shall never prohibit any line of reading or study.

ARTICLE II. THE SACRAMENTS

Section 1. Holy Orders are conferred by the Holy Spirit through the offices of a bishop. Those orders conferred by a bishop in traditional and proper form must be recognized as valid; consequently; only a bishop guided by the Holy Spirit can have the final decision on who shall receive holy orders.

Once conferred holy orders cannot be retracted, withdrawn, resigned, or repented.

Section 2. Recognizing that God can and does work effectively through the ministrations of other Christian churches, continuing service in such churches shall not constitute a bar to ordinations by a bishop and reception into the full community of the Free Liberal Catholic clergy.

Section 3. Liturgical freedom is authorized by all Free Liberal Catholic bishops; its exercise in any particular service is the prerogative of the celebrant. No council, synod, congregation, or any person is permitted to attempt to infringe on this freedom.

Section 4. Baptism by water and the Holy Spirit is a basic Sacrament of the church which may be validly administered by laymen under special circumstances: therefore, any baptism acceptable to a bishop conferring the Sacrament of Confirmation shall be deemed acceptable in the eyes of the church. In the event of an emergency confirmation by a priest, the same rule shall apply.

Section 5. All other Sacraments are administered by the traditional orders, under the direction of the bishop.

Section 6. Since all things are possible with God the Church does not presume to say that any person is essential to the ministration of the Sacraments; however, we do declare that the sacraments are efficacious when administered by clergy duly ordained for that purpose. All sacraments are the work of the Holy Spirit and depend upon the clear conscience of the supplicant.

Notes: *The Liberal Catholic tradition, which emerged in the early twentieth century, has attempted to interpret and express the Western Catholic liturgical tradition through Theosophical categories. The Free Liberal Catholic Church is one of several independent jurisdictions that seek to work in this tradition. This statement of belief, taken from the church's constitution, deals with two basic questions of the liturgical tradition: the nature of the church and of the sacraments. The Free Liberal Catholic Church offers a doctrinally open approach to church life, but affirms its position of an apostolic succession through*

CONSTITUTION (FREE LIBERAL CATHOLIC CHURCH, INC.)
(continued)

which its bishop has his authority. Bishops ordain priests, who then have the authority to administer the sacraments.

* * *

A GNOSTIC AFFIRMATION (JOHANNINE CATHOLIC CHURCH)

I know One God, the Most High, Father Almighty, Creator of Heaven and Earth and all that is; visible and invisible, spiritual and physical.

I know One Lord, Jesus Christ, The Incarnate Word of God, Redeemer of all creation, born in the flesh as True Man, lived among us, yet sinless. He was crucified, died and was buried; rose from the grave, conquered death, and made the whole creation new. He is with us, now and always to lead and to guide us, until time shall end, and for ever after.

I know Schools of Sacred Mysteries where we establish links along our ancient Line of Light with blessed Royal Blood of Holy Wisdom. So shall we rise to rule ourselves with Royal Knowledge and Divine Discernment.

I know our tenfold Tree of Life whose branches are to bless us who live beneath them.

I know One Holy Spirit, Hagia Sophia-Shekhina, She to whom we are to make ourselves transparent.

I know One Holy Universal Church in which we are to use our gifts to serve all creatures under Heaven.

I know Holy Sacraments that draw our souls to holiness and grant the Grace and Power of God to our works on earth.

I know the Resurrection of the Body as Boddhisatva Principle of the One Eternal Soul of Man—that none may leave this earthly plane till all attain transcendence.

And I know Everlasting Life: our Soul shall grow and learn, first here on earth and in its planes then later on in higher planes, forever growing in the Light until time and space shall end and beyond, eternally forever. Amen.

Notes: *Theosophy has often seen itself as a modern form of Gnosticism and some churches out of the Liberal Catholic tradition have seen themselves more as gnostic than theosophical. This transition to Gnosticism has been aided by the twentieth-century discovery and publication of translations of numerous ancient Gnostic texts. Thus, the Johannine Catholic Church,*

though possessed of apostolic orders derived from Liberal Catholic sources, has found itself attuned to the basic approach of Gnosticism. Gnosticism sees the universe as the result of a series of emanations that can be traced step by step back to God. It is the task of humans to gain the wisdom (sophia) and knowledge (gnosis) to return to God. According to the Johannine Catholic Church, the soul shall ever progress toward God in successive lives on ever higher planes of existence.

The Church has absorbed various strains of compatible teachings from the world's religions including Jewish mysticism that pictures the world as a tree with ten branches or sephirot, and Chinese Buddhism that centers on veneration of the bodhisattvas who have completed their human purpose but remain to assist others in their spiritual journey.

* * *

Miscellaneous Theosophical Groups

OUR AIMS (INSTITUTE OF DIVINE METAPHYSICAL RESEARCH)

Primary Constitutional objectives of the Institute are as follows:

1st—To help you Find and Know Yahweh our Elohim as He really is and actually exists (Matthew 24:4; Matthew 11:27; II Thessalonians 1:7-8; Deuteronomy 6:4; II Corinthians 3:17; John 4:24).

2nd—To form a nucleus of Universal Brotherhood of Humanity in Yahshua the Messiah without distinction of Race or Nationality, Creed, Sex, Caste or Color (Acts 17:26; Ephesians 5:25-33; Acts 10:34).

3rd—To investigate the unexplained Spirit Law or so-called Law of Nature and the Powers latent in man (Romans 8:1-4; John 1:9).

4th—To encourage and promote the study of the Scriptures, comparative Religions, Psychology, Philosophy and Modern (practical and occult) Science (II Timothy 2:15; John 5:39; Romans 1:19-20).

5th—To extirpate current superstition, skepticism and ignorance (Psalms 19:7; John 8:32).

6th—To Learn, Know and Understand the operation of Yahweh's Eternal Purpose through the Dispensations and Ages (Ephesians 1:9-10).

7th—To Discern and Avoid being Deceived by Lucifer, the Serpent, the Devil of Satan and his demons, operating the

Mystery of Iniquity on Earth through the Dispensations of time (I John 4:1-4; II Corinthians 4:1-7; Revelations 12:8-10; I Timothy 4:1-3).

8th—To earnestly contend for the Common Salvation and Faith which was once delivered unto the Sons or Children of Yahweh (Jude 3; Galatians 4:6; John 1:12, I John 3:1).

9th—To make known that Yahweh, from the beginning, ordained there is NO OTHER NAME given among men whereby man can be saved, saving THE NAME OF YAHSHUA THE MESSIAH (Acts 4:10-12; I Timothy 2:5; Philippians 2:9-10).

10th—To inherit ETERNAL LIFE NOW in the Kingdom of Yahshua the Messiah, with the Hope of IMMORTAL (ETERNAL) GLORIFICATION in the NEW EARTH STATE (Ephesians 1:13; 1 John 5:20; Titus 1:2; John 17:3; Colossians 1:13).

Notes: *The Institute of Divine Metaphysical Research, founded in 1961 in Los Angeles, is built around the eclectic teachings of Dr. Henry Clifford Kinley. Kinley, a holiness minister, had absorbed influences from the Sacred Name movement that used the Hebrew names for God (Yahweh and Elohim), theosophy, and the Kabbalah, the Jewish mystical teachings. The theosophical emphases in this statement of Aims are manifest most clearly in items 2, 3, and 4, which are derived directly from the Three Objects of the Theosophical Society. The remaining items in this statement do not so much summarize the Institute's teachings as establish the context in which the teachings are to be explored.*

Chapter 19
Magick Family

Ritual Magick

STATEMENT OF PRINCIPLE (FRATERNITY OF LIGHT)

Central to our concepts is the doctrine that men and women consist of more than just a physical body. We believe that you inhabit your body, wear it if you will, much as you wear a suit of clothes. The inner essence of that which is "you" is a spark of divine consciousness which was born before time began and will continue on after it has ended. This divine "spark" has clothed itself with a series of "bodies" or sheaths of varying density of which the physical body is the most dense.

Each night in sleep, the "inner" or less dense sheaths move rhythmically in and out of the physical body. A kind of friction causes the experience that we call dreaming. If the physical body is damaged severely enough or just "burns out", the inner spark and some if its sheaths leave the physical body, just as in sleep, but their connection with it is severed and they can no longer return. This we call death.

There are actually several kinds of "death". What is referred to as the "second death" occurs about three days after physical death, when the spark, surrounded by the less dense (or higher) bodies leaves the denser bodies. The spark is then free to absorb the experiences of its past life until it is ready to take on a new life. It is then attracted by a "vortex", which is a sort of psychic whirlwind created by two individuals during the sex act. If conditions are right and fertilization occurs, the spark begins to build about itself a new series of bodies, which enter the new physical body at the time of birth.

This process, known as "reincarnation", occurs countless times. During each lifetime, however, various actions, both good and evil, set in motion certain forces. To a limited extent during embodiment and to a much greater extent during the disembodied condition, these forces are rayed forth from the individual into the universe, where they are absorbed by various cosmic beings (or angels) and then rayed back into the soul. This process of interaction causes certain physical and mental experiences to occur to the individual.

There is a kind of self-judgement involved by which reward and punishment are meted out according to how each person judges his own actions, not on a conscious basis necessarily, but deep within the unconscious mind. This is not really a system of retribution and reparation, though it may appear as such to the individual. The true purpose is to determine which experiences and circumstances will lead to the greatest spiritual development of the soul. The question of pre-destination naturally arises at this point.

If I say that next Tuesday a particular man will be at a certain place for most of the day doing a certain activity, is this predestined? The place is his office and the activity is his job. He will be there because it has been planned that way—he had planned it. Each person plans the general outline of his life and incarnates under conditions that make this possible. Yet these conditions are subject to changes based on our own day-to-day reactions.

We view this cycle of reincarnation and karma as a great, everchanging ballet under the constant direction of the Supreme Spirit who is called God, Allah or the Eternal One. We believe that this One appears to our minds in many forms, each an aspect of the One. In addition, there are Beings who are more evolved than us and others less evolved.

The whole story of the vast panorama of evolution is told in a book that is the scripture of the Fraternity. This is the Scroll of Daath, or Scroll of Knowledge. This was written under the direction of men who have evolved beyond the need for a physical body. These are the Masters. They do not usually appear physically and must therefore contact their students by a kind of telepathy.

Yet, the bulk of the teachings and information received by the trained occultist comes not from other beings but from a part of himself which we call the overself (or individuality). All of these overselves are in constant contact with each other so that each can work out his or her own destiny, according to a vast plan. This plan we describe as a great ballet.

We believe that this plan of destiny has been revealed in many ways and forms, but one of the best of these is the Qabalah. This system teaches that God is not a distant Being but immanent and all about us. It presents the concept that no priest or other intermediary is required for each person to come to know God in his or her own way. In our system this is done through communication with the overself. It is necessary, therefore, to be in reasonably good physical and mental health, for only thus can the communication be established.

Many people look to the occult as means of escaping their problems, and it can be if its powers are abused. There is no difference, however, between running away from a problem and running to get help to solve it. The work that we do can build and strengthen the inner being if it is approached rightly, but it can be terribly destructive when used wrongly. The energy is there; once tapped it will come roaring through whether you are ready to receive it or not.

For this reason we require a deep sense of commitment from all of our members. Once made, this commitment has a way of taking over one's life so that the work becomes central to everything. We have seen more than one marriage or similarly close relationship destroyed when only one partner became an active participant. This work is to be taken with the utmost degree of seriousness; it not to be trifled with.

There are degrees of commitment to this work, but each degree carries with it five distinct responsibilities: First is the willingness of all members to expend large amounts of time and energy on the study of the group's ideas and teachings, including a broad spectrum of general occult topics. Second is the willingness to do active work for the Fraternity to advance it in a practical sense. Third, members have financial obligations to the Fraternity according to their resources. Fourth, members must obey the rules of the Fraternity, especially with regard to abstention from the use of drugs. Fifth, there must be an emotional commitment that places a voluntarily high priority on these matters.

Each person who makes this kind of commitment will, when his or her own overself decides the time is right, attract, seemingly in the natural course of events, those circumstances that will serve to strengthen and test that person's inner devotion. These are the trials of initiation. Although each individual experiences trials appropriate to his or her own personal circumstances, there are certain general characteristics which apply to most any trial which occurs at a given level of initiation.

This process of initiation is a method of cooperating with the Divine Plan and thereby speeding up the normal course of evolution. Since we believe that everyone will eventually reach the same goal, a completion of the evolutionary process, it is frequently asked why one should seek initiation. The answer to this is that some people have a deep, inner, spiritual craving to do so. In a way, they have to. Moreover, only those individuals compelled by this inner urge are capable of succeeding; all others fall by the wayside, for their will is not of sufficient strength.

We believe that one of the most effective methods of advancing our evolution is through the use of ceremonial magic. This requires the development of certain abilities which the bulk of

humanity has not yet evolved. Yet, because all the overselves are in constant contact, the development of these abilities in a few men and women will effect the sum total of human consciousness.

The Fraternity of Light is one in a long series of Mystery Schools going back to the Order of the Golden Dawn in the late 19th century. Each of these groups has had a hand in easing into manifestation that great energy complex known as the Aquarian Age. If these forces were allowed to enter the world unaided, great wars, economic upheavals, and all manner of catastrophes would result. With the judicious application of relatively small amounts of energy by groups such as the Fraternity of Light, these effects may be minimized.

Magical energy may be used for a variety of purposes. One of its manifestations is in the form of so-called "psychic powers". The Fraternity, like many other high-level Mystery Schools, holds that the development of these powers occurs as a natural side-effect of initiation. When they begin to appear, we make efforts to develop them, for to ignore them or worse, try to suppress them, would be foolish. Yet we do not go out of our way to develop them, and they involve only a small portion of our work. Each person generally develops one or two special types of psychic ability, according to his or her nature.

One method of increasing magical energy is to contain it by keeping it a secret. Many Mystery Schools place a high premium on silence but, in the more modern tradition, we do not. With the exception of initiation ceremonies and a few activities reserved for high-ranking members, our material and ceremonies are open. Nevertheless, we do not spread it about carelessly and it is generally shown to those who have some legitimate interest.

The way to initiation and membership in the group is through the Study Course. In addition, open services are held weekly and special invitations can be arranged in many cases to join our quarterly major ceremonies.

Our aim is spiritual freedom for the individual, but this is not achieved without sacrifice. No member of the Fraternity is permitted to use non-medicinal drugs such as L.S.D. This prohibition extends to marijuana. While we recognize that smoking pot is a relatively harmless activity, we have found that the use of drugs, including marijuana, tends to activate certain glandular centers in the body which results in the feeling of intoxication or "high". Unfortunately, it also serves to damage the higher bodies in such a fashion that spiritual advancement becomes difficult or impossible. This damage will show up in future incarnations as defects and/or deformities of the physical body.

We do not argue the point. We simply state that it is not possible to be a member of this Fraternity and use drugs. This prohibition applies only to our members. It does not apply until such time as a person decides to join.

One last point concerns Christianity. We do not associate ourselves with Christianity, not on the basis of belief, but simply because Christianity is so strong a force that any group that is at all associated with it is quickly absorbed by it. Many of our members continue to belong to an exoteric Christian church and this is entirely satisfactory, as long as it does not mix or interfere with Fraternity activities. If conflict results between your church affiliation and your work with the Fraternity, it will probably become necessary to resolve the conflict before continuing.

Notes: *The Fraternity of Light is a magical order founded in 1970. Its Statement of Principle begins with a description of the true self, the divine inner speak, which periodically incarnates in a human body. The overall pattern of reincarnation is directed by God, the Supreme Spirit. The overall plan for humans is best revealed in the Qabalah (or Kabbalah), derived from the ancient Jewish mystical teachings. the Qabalah teaches the immanence of God in creation. Occult practices, especially the practice of ceremonial magic, supply an effective means of contacting God.*

*   *   *

THE VAMPIRE CREED (THE TEMPLE OF THE VAMPIRE)

I am a Vampire.

I worship my ego and I worship my life, for I am the only God that is.

I am proud that I am a predatory animal and I honor my animal instincts.

I exalt my rational mind and hold no belief that is in defiance of reason.

I recognize the difference between the world of truth and fantasy.

I acknowledge the fact that survival is the highest law.

I acknowledge the Powers of Darkness to be hidden natural laws through which I work my magic.

I know that my beliefs in Ritual are fantasy but the magic is real, and I respect and acknowledge the results of my magic.

I realize there is no heaven as there is no hell, and I view death as the destroyer of life.

Therefore I will make the most of life here and now.

I am a Vampire.

Bow down before me.

Notes: *The Temple of the Vampire emerged in the 1980s as a new ritual magick group. It defines vampires as superior and dominating people, an elite group within the general popula-*

tion. *Through ritual magick the potential vampire may develop his powers fully.*

*   *   *

Witchcraft and Neo-Paganism

WHAT NEOPAGON DRUIDS BELIEVE (AR NDRAIOCHT FEIN: A DRUID FELLOWSHIP, INC.)

1) We believe that *divinity is both immanent (internal) and transcendent (external).* We see the Gods as being able to manifest at any point in space or time, including within human beings, which they might choose, although they may often have their preferences. Often this develops among some Neopagans into pantheism ("the physical world is divine") or pan*en*theism ("The Gods are everywhere"). We tend more towards the latter position.

2) We believe that *divinity is as likely to manifest in a female form as it is in a male form, and that therefore women and men are spiritually equal.* We insist on a dynamic balance between female and male deities honored and/or invoked at every ceremony, and a strict gender balance in whatever theories of polytheology that we eventually develop. We're "liberals" about women's rights and gay rights, but not "radicals;" that is to say, we're unwilling to subordinate all our other principles in order to promote this particular principle. People who wish to make feminism or gay activism the absolute center of all their spiritual activity will probably be happier in other groups.

3) We believe in *a multiplicity of gods and goddesses, all of whom are likely to be worthy of respect, love and worship.* Sometimes we believe in these divinities as individual and independent entities; sometimes as Jungian "archetypes of the collective unconscious" or "circuits in the psychic Switch-board;" sometimes as aspects or faces of one or two major deities (the "High God/dess" and/or "the Goddess and the Horned God"); and sometimes as "all of the above!" We feel that this sort of flexibility leads to pluralism (instead of monism), multi-valued logic systems and an increased tolerance of other people's beliefs and lifestyles. All of these are vital if our species is ever going to learn to live in peace and harmony amid a multiplicity of human cultures.

4) We believe that *it is necessary to have a respect and love for Nature as divine in her own right, and to accept ourselves as a part of Nature and not as her "rulers."* We tend to accept what has come to be known as "the Gaia hypothesis," that the biosphere of our planet is a living being, who is due all the love and support that we, her children, can give her. This is especially important in our modern era, when 3000 years of monotheistic belief that "mankind is to have dominion over the Earth" have come close to destroying the ability of the biosphere to maintain itself. Many Neopagan groups refer to themselves as "Earth religions" and this is a title which we believe

Neopagan Druidism should proudly claim, and which we should work to earn. Thus we consider ecological awareness and activism to be sacred duties. If the ecology, conservation and anti-nuclear movements are ever to have "chaplains," we should be among them.

5) We believe *in accepting the positive aspects of western science and technology, but in maintaining an attitude of wariness towards their supposed ethical neutrality.* The overwhelming majority of Neopagans are technophiles, not technophobes. We tend to be better scientifically educated than the general population, and thus we have a religious duty to speak out about the economic, political and ecological uses and abuses of science and technology.

6) We share with most other Neopagans *a distaste for monolithic religious organizations and would-be messiahs and gurus.* Obviously, this places the founders of Neopagan religious traditions in a complex position: they need enough religious authority to focus the organizations they're founding, but not so much as to allow them (or their successors to become oppressive. Since the pluralistic approach denies the existence of any One True Right and Only Way, and since Neopagans insist upon their own human fallibility, we expect to be able to steer ADF between the Scylla of tyranny and the Charybdis of anarchy.

7) In keeping with this, we believe that healthy religions should have *a minimum amount of dogma and a maximum amount of eclecticism and flexibility.* Neopagans tend to be reluctant to accept any idea without personally investigating both its practically and its long-range consequences. They are also likely to take useful ideas from almost any source that doesn't run too fast to get away. We intend ADF to be a "reconstructionist" tradition of Druidism, but we know that eventually concepts from nonDruidic sources will be grafted on to our trees. There's no harm in this, as long as we stay away of what we are doing at every step of the way, and make a legitimate effort to find authentic (and therefore spiritually and aesthetically congruent) parallels in genuine Indo-European sources first. As for flexibility, Neopagan Druidism is an organic religion, and like all other organisms it can be expected to grow, change and produce offshoots as the years go by.

8) We believe that *ethics and morality should be based upon joy, self-love and respect; the avoidance of actual harm to others; and the increase of public benefit.* We try to balance out people's needs for personal autonomy and growth, with the necessity of paying attention to the impact of each individuals actions on the lives and welfare of others. The commonest Neopagan ethical expression is "If it doesn't hurt anyone, do what you like." Most Neopagans believe in some variant or another of the principle of karma, and state that the results of their actions will always return to them. It's difficult for ordinary humans to successfully commit "offenses against the Gods," short of major crimes such as ecocide or genocide, and our deities are perfectly capable of defending their own honor without any help from mortal busybodies. We see the traditional monotheistic concepts of sin, guilt and divine retribution for thought-crimes as sad misunderstandings of natural growth experiences.

9) We believe that *human beings were meant to lead lives filled with joy, love, pleasure, beauty and humor.* Most Neopagans are fond of food, drink, music, sex and bad puns, and consider all of these (except possibly the puns) to be sacraments. Although the ancient Druids appear to have had ascetics within their ranks, they also had a sensualist tradition, and the common folk have always preferred the latter. Neopagan Druids try to keep these two approaches in balance and harmony with each other by avoiding dualistic extremes. But the bedrock question is, "If your religion doesn't enable you to enjoy life more, why bother?"

10) We believe that *with proper training, art, discipline and intent, human minds and hearts are fully capable of performing most of the magic and miracles they are likely to need.* This is done through the use of what we perceive as natural, divinely granted psychic powers. As with many other Neopagan traditions, the conscious practice of magic is a central part of most of our religious rituals. Unlike monotheists, we see no clearcut division between magic and prayer. Neither, however, do we assume an automatic connection between a person's ability to perform "miracles" and either (a) their personal spirituality or (b) the accuracy of their theological or polytheological opinions.

11) We believe in *the importance of celebrating the solar, lunar and other cycles of our lives.* Because we see ourselves as a part of Nature, and because we know that repeating patterns can give meaning to our lives, we pay special attention to astronomical and biological cycles. By consciously observing the solstices, equinoxes and the points in between, as well as the phases of the moon, we are not only aligning ourselves with the movements and energy patterns of the external world, but we are also continuing customs that reach back to the original Indo-European peoples and beyond. These customs are human universals, as are the various ceremonies known as "rites of passage"—celebrations of birth, puberty, personal dedication to a given deity or group, marriage, ordination, death, etc. Together these various sorts of observations help us to fined ourselves in space and time—past, present and future.

12) We believe that *people have the ability to solve their current problems, both personal and public, and to create a better world.* Hunger, poverty, war and disease are not necessary, nor inevitable. Pain, depression, lack of creative opportunity and mutual oppression are not necessary either. What is necessary is a new spiritual consciousness in which short-sighted greed, power-mongering and violence are seen as absurd, rather than noble. This utopian vision, tempered with common sense, leads us to a strong commitment to personal and global growth, evolution and balance.

13) We believe that *people can progress far towards achieving growth, evolution and balance through the carefully planned alteration of their "normal" states of consciousness.* Neopagans use both ancient and modern methods of aiding concentration, meditation, reprogramming and ecstacy. We seek to avoid being locked into single-valued, monistic "tunnel realities," and instead work on being able to switch world views according to their appropriateness for each given situation, while still maintaining a firm spiritual, ethical and practical grounding.

14) We believe that *human interdependence implies community service.* Neopagan Druids are encouraged to use their talents to help others, both inside and outside of the Neopagan community. Some of us are active in political social, ecological and charitable organizations, while others prefer to work for the public good primarily through spiritual means (and many of us do both). As Neopagan Druids we have the right and the obligation to actively oppose (physically and spiritually) those forces which would kill our planet, oppress our fellow human beings, and destroy our freedom of religion. Also, however, we have a constant need to evaluate our own methods and motives, and to make sure that our actions are coming from the depths of our spiritual beings, and not from petty or short-sighted desires for power.

15) We believe that *if we are to achieve any of our goals, we must practice what we preach.* Neopagan Druidism should be a way of life, not merely a weekly or monthly social function. Thus we must always strive to make our lives consistent with our proclaimed beliefs. In a time when many people are looking for something solid to hang on to in the midst of rapid technological and cultural changes, Neopagan Druidism can offer a natural and creative alternative to the repressive structures of mainstream monotheism. But our alternative will not be seen as such unless we can manage to make it a complete lifestyle—one with concern, if not always immediate answers, for the problems of everyday life, as well as the grand cosmic questions.

Obviously, there's a great deal more to Neopaganism in general and our version of it in particular. The details of Neopagan polytheology will take years to develop. The section of the Handbook dealing with beliefs will consist of statements with commentaries (and even arguments) about the meanings of the statements. The purpose of this format is multiple: to emphasize that there are no final answers to the great questions of human existence; to express clearly that Neopagans can disagree with each other about subtle details of interpretation, while still remaining members of the same religion; and to allow the belief system to grow and adapt to changing cultural and technological needs. Neopagan Druidism is to be a religion of the future, as well as of the present and the past.

Notes: *Ar nDraiocht Fein (ADF), founded in the mid-1980s by Isaac Bonewits, is one of a number of organizations that grew out of the revived Druidism that first appeared in the 1962-63 school year among students at Carleton College in Northfield, Minnesota. Bonewits emerged as one of the major spokespersons*

of the Druids in the 1970s. Prior to the founding of ADF, he had participated in several of its earlier organized forms.

This statement, published by ADF, is meant not only as its defining statement but as a comment on Neopaganism as a whole. ADF operates within a polytheistic world that finds expression in worship of the gods and goddesses and a veneration of nature (seen in the celebration of the natural cycles of life). ADF is adamantly opposed to monotheistic approaches to religion (which most Neopagans see as intolerant and oppressive). It is also feminist in perspective and advocates the complete equality of male and female.

ADF offers a slight revision of Neopagan ethics that have traditionally been based solely on harmlessness. It additionally suggests the positive principles of joy, self-love, and respect as ideals upon which to build ethical guidelines. Thus, ADF argues, Neopagans should avoid harming others, but also work to promote the public good.

*　　*　　*

NATURE RELIGION TENET (CHURCH OF UNIVERSAL FORCES)

1. Any member of CHURCH OF UNIVERSAL FORCES has an obligation only to himself/herself. We strive to live in harmony with other human beings of this plane, and the spirits of the inner planes. We seek to live in harmony with the elements of nature. Our popular desire is to maintain our individual health and well being without denying ourselves our total satisfaction in so doing.

2. Our tradition is based upon perfect love and perfect trust. We are not concerned with the religious beliefs and practices of other traditions. Their origins, aspects, and philosophies are not debatable. We believe in freedom and security of the present. We do not seek to deny this freedom to anyone. The future is our own to live and let live.

3. The concept of absolute evil, the "devil" as defined by Christian doctrine is not acknowledged by the CHURCH OF UNIVERSAL FORCES, nor is any strict dogmatic conformity codes. We stress that everything and everybody has a soul accountable for its own actions and reactions. Our reflections about any religion that claims to be the only way is that it is so preoccupied with pragmatism, or sin and suffering. that it fails to allow its followers to realize their own individuality.

4. We do honor to those greater knowledge than ourselves, by ceremonial worship. We do not limit our Deities. They are one and they are many. We are their children, and we are allowed to enfold and develop because of their graciousness. We strive for perfection in order to be like as a Deity when we are evolved to higher planes.

5. We believe that power is available from the human mind and from the spirits. Power is gained through knowl-

edge—and knowledge shared is power shared; therefore, willpower, emotion, imagination, and faith, are our basic laws. They are our strength and our weakness. We are all united together for the purpose of learning and the affirmation of life.

6. We seek the aid of the Ancient Ones of the profession in faith that we receive the development of our consciousness via the evolution of life, by seeking within nature from the elements of nature to control the forces locked within ourselves.

7. We realize the root of our being and the power of our beginning is the Ultimate Deity; the Godhead of the Gods. Their names are as diverse as the Gods and Goddesses. The Godhead is considered to be equal and opposite masculine and feminine, negative and positive. We value neither above the other. Both are to be revered and worshiped daily. He and She is the overseeing authority with extensions delegated to the lower spirits,

8. We further engage to watch over one another, and to remember one another in brotherly love; to aid each other in sickness and distress; to cultivate sympathy and empathy in feeling, and courtesy in speech; and to be slow to take offense, but always, ready for reconciliation; and ever mindful of the threefold law, ''and ye harm none, do what you will''.

9. It shall be our solemn vow to maintain family devotions; to religiously educate our children, and acquaint them to our ways in comparison to other religions, that they may make their own choices when they are old enough to do so.

10. Having being led as we believe by the spirit of the Ancient Ones, we are drawn to this covenant, and the path of Nature Religions, we pledge ourselves to give devotion to our Deities, and walk together in love and friendship; strive for the advancement of this Church; to promote its prosperity, and spiritually, to sustain its worship, ordinances, discipline and doctrines; to contribute cheerfully and regularly to support and to spread these teachings throughout the nation.

11. We respect all other religions, and self-assertive cultures. We practice Rites to attune ourselves with nature according to the seasons and the phases of the moon. The only prerequisite for allegiance to this society is sincerity of heart, and honesty to oneself. We do not want to deny participation to anyone sincerely interested in our beliefs and traditions.

12. We realize that learning is a lifelong process; therefore, this sect recognizes its authoritarian hierarchy to be diligent study, practice, and participation in the Mystic Arts, and Occult activity for a period of no less than a year and a day in each respective discipline.

13. A sectary of this lore that has completed the established requirements, displays finesse in their skills, and has shown him or herself to be competent in these abilities may begin his/her own religious hierarchy under the authority and the guardianship of CHURCH OF UNIVERSAL FORCES hierarchy.

14. We perceive any evidence of supernatural paranormal phenomena as fulfillment of whatever psychic marvel one is inclined to perform either on this outer or the inner dimension. Both being necessary and supportive of the other as a natural potential in all human beings.

15. Our philosophy is that a positive subconscious is a powerful weapon that can be trained consciously, and binds us to strive for perfection, giving all of ourselves, and taking our fair share of life and happiness. Whatever we give, we receive three times over—if we take unjustly, it too will return three times nefarious.

16. We study ancient pagan religions, and fellowship with other modern neotenic societies. We will teach our customs without prejudice to any neophyte who honestly wants to learn.

17. Our collection of Art and Music for the protected Archive will be compositions from any internal member with active participation. Donations from other sources will be gratefully accepted and acknowledged unless specifically requested by the donator that it not be acknowledged.

18. We believe the influences of the heavenly bodies on the affairs of nature can be adapted to our own advantage, or disadvantage; therefore, we shall endeavor to harness these influences to benefit each practicality.

19. We must maintain that our Rites and practices are held and upheld in utmost secrecy. No one must ever divulge the inner teachings of this commonwealth in order to reap the benevolence of the Deities, or resist their wrath.

OUR PHILOSOPHY AND MOTTO

''AND YE HARM NONE, DO WHAT YOU WILL''.—LET THE FORCES GUIDE & PROTECT

Notes: *The Church of Universal Forces is a nature-oriented modern Neopagan religion. It recognizes the Ultimate Deity, the God above the Gods, who is both masculine and feminine. The gods (spirits) are honored in ceremonial worship. Church members seek to live a life of harmony with nature and the spirits of the inner planes. Power, both from the human mind and the spirits, is valued.*

The Church rejects the concept of absolute evil or the ''Devil'' and of any religion that claims to be the only way. Church members do not debate religion, but seek to promote their own way in a spirit of freedom for all. Members seek to harm none, and to cultivate the virtues of brotherly love, sympathy and empathy for others, and a readiness for reconciliation with others. Members practice the magical arts, and its rituals are kept confidential.

*　　*　　*

WHAT CONTEMPORARY PAGANS BELIEVE (COVENANT OF UNITARIAN UNIVERSALIST PAGANS)

While there is no set of beliefs shared by all Pagans, most would agree that their similarities are greater than their differences, and there are a number of beliefs held by the vast majority of contemporary Pagans. Some of these are:

1. Divinity is immanent in all of nature.

2. Divinity is just as likely to manifest in female form, as "the Goddess", the interconnectedness of life.

3. Multiple paths to the divine, as symbolized by many "goddesses" and "gods", often viewed as archetypes or gateways to the unconscious.

4. Respect and love for Mother Earth as "Gaia", a living being of which we are a part.

5. The goodness of creation, in which all beings are meant to live in joy, love, and harmony.

6. An ethics and morality based on the avoidance of harm to other beings and to the Earth, which mandates environmental activism as religious responsibility.

7. The knowledge that human interdependence implies community cooperation.

8. The importance of celebrating the solar and lunar cycles, and the cycles of our lives, leading to the revival of ancient customs (and the invention of new ones!).

9. A strong commitment to personal and planetary growth, evolution, and balance.

10. The awareness of making one's lifestyle consistent with one's belief ("the personal is political").

11. A minimum of dogma and a maximum of eclecticism.

12. A healthy skepticism and a reluctance to accept an idea without personally investigating it.

13. A distrust of would-be messiahs and gurus.

Notes: *The Covenant of Unitarian Universalist Pagans is a group within the larger fellowship of the Unitarian Universalist Association, which focuses Pagan belief and practice among members of that rather diverse fellowship. Pagans do not have a creed, but do hold to a common set of beliefs. One attempt to commit those beliefs to writings was circulated in* the 1970s by the Aquarian Tabernacle Church. What Contemporary Pagans Believe is a revised form of that earlier statement, but has added specific mention of the Goddess, a mandate to social activism on the issue of the environment, and a distrust of would-be messiahs and gurus.

*　　*　　*

PURPOSES (NATIONAL ALLIANCE OF PANTHEISTS)

The National Alliance of Pantheists is a Non-Profit Religious Society with the following purposes:

1. To worship in accordance with Pantheist traditions, theology and practices. To establish facilities for such worship and to encourage the growth of Pantheism as the religious foundation of ones life.

2. To promote theological research, writings and creations, through methods which may include but shall not be limited to publications, dissemination and distribution of information, literature and religious artifacts.

3. To educate our youth, ourselves and the public to our history, our traditions, aims, goals and philosophy through any legal means possible, which may include but shall not be limited to schools, symposia, cenobitical activities and pamphlets.

4. To train, ordain and/or recognize Pantheist Clergy, to grant them all the rights and responsibilities pursuant to that position, which may include but shall not be limited to a network of communication, dialogue, workshops, training and group benefits as to be determined by the Board of Directors from time to time.

5. To care for the earth and its inhabitants as stewards entrusted with the care of the land as a manifestation of the divine, rather than as owners with rights to exploit, being as Pantheism recognizes the immanence of Deity with creation as opposed to separate from it.

6. To perform and do, either directly or indirectly, and either alone or in conjunction or cooperation with other persons or organizations of every kind and nature, all other acts, things incidental to or in furtherance of the accomplishment of the above enumerated purposes of the organization, and to use and exercise all powers conferred presently and from time to time by the laws of the State of Maine upon corporations organized under title 13-B of the Maine Revised Statutes Annotated, and within the meaning of Section 501 (c) 3 of the Internal Revenue Code of 1954 as amended.

Notes: *The National Alliance of Pantheists is an association of Neopagans and Neopagan groups that interpret Neopaganism from a pantheistic perspective. Neopaganism emphasizes the worship of nature, and pantheism emphasizes the identification of the world as the body of God. Hence the church believes*

PURPOSES (NATIONAL ALLIANCE OF PANTHEISTS)
(continued)

in God's immanence in the world as opposed to His transcendence of it as Creator.

*   *   *

BELIEFS (VENUSIAN CHURCH)

The Venusian Church believes in the following:

1. Sharing our love and our religion and not forcing either on anyone.

2. A separation of church and state so that no religious custom can be forced on anyone.

3. That all forms of consenting loving conduct between male and female, female and female, male and male, or in any group combination are sacred and beautiful in the eyes of God and in the eyes of Her true followers.

4. That the physical body is the holy temple of God and that its various parts all have beautiful and holy purposes. Those parts which can be used in the expression and fulfillment of love are a special glory to God.

5. That although sexual intimacy is not condemned by itself, we emphasize that it is not complete without the other aspects of love: sharing, concern, and tenderness.

6. That all forms of erotic expression, especially those which arouse passion, and feelings of desire, should be viewed with the knowledge that this is God's greatest gift.

7. That God's principle gifts to all living creatures are life, love, and the sexual expression of love which can reproduce life. Through procreation we can achieve immortality.

8. That God wants us to be happy in the here and now, rather than wishing for something better in an afterlife. She instructs us to use Her gifts in this life not only for procreation but for recreation. This recreation not only pleases us physical beings, but pleases God and is therefore our most holy form of worship.

Notes: *The Venusian Church, founded in 1975, is a Pagan religion that emphasizes the open and free expression of sexuality. Its beliefs emphasize the rightness of all forms of sexual expression between consenting adults as a sacred and beautiful experience. The Church emphasizes the separation of church and state, having been a victim of government action instigated by some who neither appreciated nor understood the lifestyle of its members.*

Chapter 20

Middle Eastern Family

SEVEN PILLARS (AMERICAN DRUZE SOCIETY)

i. Testimony, *shahada*. Exoterically (*Islam*), Muslims have understood that God sent the Prophet Muhammad to humankind with God's word; esoterically (*iman*), the Shi'a have believed that the Imam is the interpreter of that Word. The real meaning i.e. what it means to the Druze, is a kind of combination of *Islam* and *iman* in the essential purpose of humankind, that is, striving to feel united with the One God.

ii. Prayer, *salat*. While the Muslims see prayer as expressed through the specific rituals performed five times a day, the Druze understand it as one's soul drawing close to God through the realization of the divine unity.

iii. Almsgiving, *zakat*. The Islamic understanding of zakat as giving fixed amounts of money to the needy of the community is seen as exoteric, while the esoteric or real meaning as expounded by Hamza.b.Ali combines exoteric and esoteric to mean safeguarding one's fellows through the purification of the soul which leads to the knowledge of God's unity.

iv. Fasting, *sawm*. The external, Islamic meaning of abstinence gives way to the real or internal significance, which is the self-realization, or understanding within oneself of the unity of God. This becomes a kind of abstaining from anything that detracts one from that purpose.

v. Pilgrimage, *Hajj*. While the hajj for most Muslims means the physical act of going to Mecca, and for those who favor an allegorical interpretation means adherence to the teachings of the Imam, for the Druze it is "taking oneself" to the place where one understands the knowledge of the unity of God.

vi. Striving in the way of God, *jihad*. Striving or personal effort means for the Druze not physical fighting through carrying out a holy war, but the effort to come to the knowledge of God's oneness.

vii. Allegiance to the Imam, *wilaya*. For the Muslim wilaya has meant paying allegiance to the head of the community or more specifically for the Shi'i it has meant following the teachings of the Shi'i Imam. For the Druze, however, it means, submitting to the "human embodiments of the luminary cosmic principles", by which one will see everything in its reality and will see God immanent in all things.

Notes: *The American Druze Society represents in North America the Druze, an ethic community that originated among Shi'a Muslims in Egypt in the eleventh century. The Druze religion has traditionally been among the identifying elements of the Druze community. This religion has been kept secret, in part due to the fear of persecution by the dominant Muslim community in which Druze members have been forced to exist. Over the last centuries, however, the Druze books have been translated and published in Western languages and much of the faith has become public knowledge.*

A contemporary Druze spokesperson, Sami Nasim Makarem, has attempted to summarize the perspective of the Druze believers in North America. He proposed seven pillars of the faith as opposed to the five pillars of Islam. Some are very similar to the Islamic pillars—prayer, almsgiving, fasting, pilgrimage, and striving in the way of God—but such beliefs are here compared and contrasted with those of Islam. The Druze Faith emerges as a simple affirmation of one God and a non-ritualistic approach to coming into relationship with that one God. The Druze thus reject the specifically Islamic requirements of prayer five times a day, a pilgrimage to Mecca, and the fasting period of Ramadan.

Chapter 21

Eastern Family

Buddhism

STATEMENT (GAY AND LESBIAN BUDDHIST GROUP)

1) All is change or impermanence—We can not depend on anything remaining the same indefinitely. Trying to do so causes unnecessary grief and disappointment in life.

2) No detectable unchanging soul—The universal law of impermanence is true for ourselves. Life and death are one and the same state of flux. Realizing this in the deepest sense is enlightenment (Nirvana).

3) No God to determine our fate—There is no basis for a belief in a changeless deity. Even the Buddha, though fully enlightened, still remained a human being.

4) Not sin, but suffering is our problem—We suffer due to a deep delusion or ignorance about our real nature; and not because of some willful disobedience to a supreme authority.

5) Cause and effect is the governing force of the universe—Each person is the sum total of his/her previous thoughts and deeds. By these alone we cause ourselves suffering and/or joy.

6) Compassion is a blessing—All life forms experience suffering. By being fully sensitive to this we come to know a oneness with all life which dissolves our insecurities about life and death.

7) No authority other than our own experience—No living or dead person, no sacred books or traditions can be trusted as much as our personal experience especially through or with meditation.

8) The Middle Path alone is our liberator—Ignorance of our own and the world's real nature is kept going by living in and by extremist or highly subjective views, feelings and acts. Following a very carefully balanced path in all of these frees us from all unnecessary anguish and meaninglessness, and make us enlightened, compassionate and content beings.

Notes: *The Gay and Lesbian Buddhist Group serves Buddhists within the larger Gay and Lesbian community of the Greater Los Angeles Metropolitan Area. It is affiliated with a Korean Zen center, the Bo Hyun Son Dharma Center in Los Angeles. Buddhism has no particular condemnation of homosexuality and most Buddhist groups admit gay and lesbian people without prejudice. However, some groups have felt the need for an exclusively homosexual fellowship to help gay and lesbian persons integrate Buddhism into their daily lives.*

The statement issued by the Group does not deal with homosexual issues directly, but rather presents a consensus statement of the Buddhist perspective. Among the differences between Buddhism and most other religious traditions is the denial of the existence of either a Supreme Deity or of a substantial self.

*   *   *

Hinduism

WE BELIEVE (NEOTANTRIC CHURCH)

We Believe

1) There is a Universal Energy.

2) Sexual energy is a human manifestation of the Universal Energy.

3) Tension and pain can block the flow of sexual energy.

4) Blocked energy can cause poor health, both physical and mental.

WE BELIEVE (NEOTANTRIC CHURCH) (continued)

5) Sexual energy can be controlled through the study and practice of special techniques.

6) Removal of energy blocks can restore health and balance.

7) Sexual energy can be manipulated for spiritual growth.

8) Every human being is entitled to enjoy full sexual pleasure and growth.

9) Any healthy expression of sexuality is sacred.

10) Repression of healthy sexuality is evil.

Notes: *The NeoTantric Church was founded in the 1980s to teach and practice Tantra, a world-affirming form of Hinduism that, rather than denying sexual expression as yoga tends to do, affirms the value of sexuality as a tool in spiritual development. Tantra has traditionally taught a series of yoga-like techniques that integrate sexuality into the process of spiritual attainment. The NeoTantric Church beliefs react to both a culture and those religious expressions that attempt to repress sexuality, but teaches that ''Sexual energy can be manipulated for spiritual growth.''*

Chapter 22

Unclassified Christian Churches

CHRIST MANIFESTO (CHRIST FAMILY)

WE THE ANGELS OF GOD, do ordain and establish this Constitution of a Saint. Followed, this insures Life, Liberty, and Happiness for ALL God's Creation. To Brothers and Sisters that seek Peace on Earth, Peace is a Gift of God, this Constitution of a Saint shows the way out of the tree of good and evil, into the Tree of Everlasting Life.

PRAISE GOD AMEN

Sit back and relax and follow these lines.

LET US MOVE INTO THE NEW AGE WITH A PURE HEART AND A CLEAR MIND

DIVINITY IS THE TRUE LIFE OF MAN

The Lord is Divinity in Action. He is Divine Love because He is Life itself. Life itself is Love itself; God's thoughts made audible. The Law of the Lord is Perfect. The Lord's spiritual image is Giving Life. Giving Life is Love; God with us. The Saint is a Receiver of that Life. In the giving of his life to the Holy Father he freely Receives everlasting Life. Divine Love has been stirred to its unfathomable depths for the sake of man. Angels marvel at mankind's shallow appreciation of the Love of God. Man was created to be a Receiver; a Receiver by the measure in which he loves God. Away from his Spiritual Image, mankind does not know his purpose. He was given the choice to live in the Tree of Life in Peace or live in the tree of knowledge. He chose knowledge and received death; so he does not know Love. It is understood by the Spirit and those who dwell therein called Saints. Saints are in the Lord and the Lord in them. The Lord alone is Heaven.

"THE KINGDOM AND DOMINION OF THE GREATNESS OF THE KINGDOM UNDER THE WHOLE HEAVEN SHALL BE GIVEN TO THE PEOPLE, SAINTS OF THE MOST HIGH."

FAITH THE CARRIER

Faith is the vehicle from the old world to the New World. As a moth to the flame, the Saint offers his carnal self to Almighty God to be consumed as his living witness. He magnifies and makes Honorable the Law of Peace.

Forgiveness powers Faith. Faith is casting away all that is known in order to experience that which is not known. Faith is blind so that Spiritual Sight can be given. True Spiritual Sight is Understanding. Understanding is given with the experience of Innocence—FAITH.

A child born into the world knows nothing. He must trust in his papa for all things. A man born into the Kingdom of Heaven knows nothing. He must trust in the Almighty Father for ALL things. This gift is from the Lord alone. His coming has made the Delivery Immediate!

The Angels of Glory find their Joy in Giving. They carry with them the Power of God's Forgiveness. The Power of resurrection is not in oneself. You can do nothing of yourself. Therefore, one must Freely Receive the instructions from the Living Word: a Christ Brother. God's Excellence of Character made manifest.

In this action of Freely Receiving and Freely Giving, the Miracle of God's Transforming Promise begins and the Saint is carried in Faith through Forgiveness out of the tree of good and evil directly into the Tree of Everlasting Eternal Life.

THE LORD OF HOSTS IS THE KING OF GLORY.

HEREIN IS LOVE: THAT THE KING OF GLORY STOOPED DOWN TO TAKE HUMANITY!

THE CALL OF FAITH

Listen to the Voice of Him Who is from Eternity. The Light and Life of the world, a Light which shines in the darkness, and the darkness comprehends it not. . .

The Invitation:

The Lord is gathering His People!

He is harvesting His First Fruits; all those who Love Him and His Ways. The Ways of Heaven are opposite of the ways of this world of killing, sex and materialism. One has got to give up everything for the kingdom; therefore the Saint proclaims his separation from evil by his willful decision which unfolds his Spiritual Life. This is the Living Declaration of Indepen-

CHRIST MANIFESTO (CHRIST FAMILY) (continued)

dence. He lives in Perfect Union, which is the Manifest Will of God, giving Life, Liberty and Happiness to ALL living creatures.

Mankind stands alone, confused and bewildered, he knows something is missing, he is a mutant species away from God, doomed to extinction.

The Man of God stands with the Almighty, in Peace, trusting in the unseen, knowing all things work for Good—a Living Testimony of Faith.

Fleeing from Evil:

Love and Wisdom are not obvious to the senses. The physical senses will deceive you. For every impure thought defiles the soul. It dims the Spiritual Vision so man cannot behold God.

Many in the ''learned world'' have wearied themselves with inquiries into the soul, they know nothing of the Kingdom of Heaven or Eternal Life. They can only form theories. Therefore, from the view of Heaven, they must increase. The Pure in Heart shall see God.

It is known that man is born into evil and that he inherited it from his parents. Evils increase from generation to generation, until man, by birth, is saturated with evil. There is no recovery from this breed except through their fleeing from evil by the Hand of the Lord.

All evils and their falsities have their seat in the physical mind, which is in the image of the world: finite. The Spiritual Mind is in the Image of Heaven: Infinite. The physical mind looks to itself—the Spiritual Mind looks to God.

Elevation:

Sum up all the things you know and have gathered in your life, that would be knowledge of good and evil, give this to careful inspection, and in the same elevation of Spirit, Receive all things and you will See that Love of your Brother and Wisdom, which is the Love of God, are the essentials of any Spiritual Man's Life. Everything of your New Life hinges upon this. This is the Giving nature. Apart from this is nothing. This no one can deny! For God Loves everyone from Love in Himself and leads everyone, with Wisdom, to Himself.

The Divine Providence in the Reforming, degeneration and Saving of man is calling him to abide in His Living Word.

Reforming:

The Holy Father is Reforming a New Nation of Chosen People. Since the Beginning, the Father has projected the Gathering and Return of ALL who Love Him.

Regeneration:

In living the Word of God, Brothers and Sisters are United in The Kingdom. This communion is the degeneration of God's Chosen People into Divinity. The Dawning of the New Age is the shedding of the cocoon of the physical body and the spreading forth of the Wings of Light. In this Regeneration the spark is passed from Christ Brother to becoming Saint.

Saving:

Those who walk in the image of Christ are given the Power and Glory of Resurrection. This is the Saving Faith of the Saints.

Because of disobedience, God sent Adam forth from the Garden of Eden:

''So He drove out the man. Thou shalt surely die. For as by one man's disobedience many were made sinners, so by the obedience of one shall many be made righteous. For as in Adam all die, even so in Christ shall all be made alive. The gift of God is eternal Life. If you will enter into eternal Life keep the Commandments.''

Divine Love is the Righteousness of the Saints. Divine Wisdom is their Obedience to His Commandments. The Saint is not under the discipline of the Law, he is freed by the Law. The Innocent are free from judgment.

All men who believe in God are being brought together in these last days. Through the word of God the Lord's Army unites. They hear the bugle heralding the Lords Return. The Saint receives his draft notice. He is called to duty. The Saints are God's soldiers laying all things aside to wage the warfare of the Saints; the Good Fight of Faith.

In the Service of the Father, mount your white horse and draw your sword in the war against evil. Be willing to March into hell for a Heavenly Cause. Under the Lord's Banner, stand firm in faith. The Saint has been prepared with the Shield of Faith, the Helmet of Salvation and the Sword of Truth. He is made Mighty through the Almighty Father. Victory over the world is from God. Peace shall reign upon the face of the earth when it is in a man's heart.

THE CALL IS RINGING OUT WITH YAHWEH.

All in All:

There shall be two in the field: the one shall be taken and the other left. Be ready to release everything; All in All—Don't Cling!

The Honor Code of God's Minute Men is not to hold anything higher than the Call of God. This Honor is Sacred to all men who Love God.

Draw nigh to God and He will draw nigh to you. He who gave you your Life and Breath. It is He who had made us, not we ourselves. We are His People, the Sheep of His Pasture. What more has a man to give than his Life to Serve his Creator and magnify his Work!

The Most High Action is the Praising of God. Don't Hesitate. Be Prepared. CATCH-UP.

''THE SON OF RIGHTEOUSNESS HAS ARISEN. THIS SONG IS RECEIVED BY THE VOICE OF THE GREAT MULTITUDE, AS THE VOICE OF MANY WATERS SAYING, 'ALLELUIA,' FOR THE LORD GOD REIGNETH.''

THE WISDOM OF EXPERIENCE

Love strives unceasingly toward the human form and is knocking upon the Heart. . .

Fallen mans heart has been hardened by his involvement in the ways of the world, contrary to the Living word of God. Only by Obedience to the Word can one regain Communion with the Heart. This brings Peace of Mind. Only with Holy Communion of the Heart can one affect Good; for the greatest Good is the Receiving of the Kingdom of Heaven.

DONE IN CONVENTION, BY THE UNANIMOUS CONSENT OF THE HOST OF ANGELS ASSEMBLED:

RESOLVED,

That the Constitution of a Saint be laid before the nations of the world, as a direct Sign of the time; and step by step procedure out of the Coming tribulations.

We have now the honor to submit to the nations of the world, this Constitution of a Saint which is the direct cure, when followed, to mankinds' disease. Our foundation is from the Great Giver, the Law of Life—NO KILLING. The Order of the Universe is found in the stillness of Peace, Jesus Christ Lightning Amen is the Serenity of NO KILLING.

The Perfect Union was formed at the Foundation of Creation, guaranteeing Life, Liberty and Happiness to All Living Things. Few People of this world have sought True Righteousness; the power to separate from the world and its evil doctrines. It is time that this Constitution be instituted among men and these Rights be given to ALL Creatures!

Hence results the necessity of a different organization.

Individuals entering into the New Age must give up what they know as their life to receive a New Life. The first step of Life is NO KILLING. One who gives life receives Life.

The magnitude of giving is nothing compared to what has already been given. Obedience to God's Law is fulfillment. There is a precise line between the Kingdom of Heaven and the ways of the world. So is the same in surrendering ALL for the Kingdom. The difficulty has been the increased difference and separation of the ways of the world, which have led to selfish habits and interests of the people therein.

In all our deliberations on this subject, we've kept the Faith, which appears to us the greatest interest of every True citizen of the New Age. This important consideration seriously and deeply impressed on our minds is of vital importance to a man's heart. The decree of NO KILLING is the basic formula for Peace on Earth; supporting NO KILLING by ALL, to ALL living Things.

Only this step will fulfill God's Living Word and begin mankinds' ascension from darkness. This commitment is the Restoration and Regeneration of an infected and disordered planet. The Breath of Life is Pure, Clean and Corrective of the degenerated mind that kills.

Thus, the Constitution of a Saint, which now is Present, is the result of the Return of Christ and the witness of the Holy Spirit; as an example to mankind, The Light in the Darkness, The way to Walk. That he may see in simplicity the way out of chaos.

So that his heart is made Pure and his mind Clear in the entering of this New Age.

TO THE GLORY OF THE MOST HIGH!

THE PILGRIMS ESCORT—TRUST IN THE ANGELS

A Christ Brother is an Angel manifested in the flesh to give explicit directions to the Kingdom of God. He speaks directly of the way, because he is One with it. His voice rings the Bells of the Heart. He brings the pilgrim to the altar to recite the wedding vows of Holy Communion. Marriage to the Holy Spirit, the Deepest of the Deep. Mercy and Truth are met together; Righteousness and Peace have embraced each other.

The Lord has Called man to deceive his Brother in Faith. He has implored mankind to will their life and conform to the Image of His Son, Spirit in the flesh. He has Commanded them to Receive Those that walk in this Light. Words cannot tell it. Let it be Reflected in the character and manifested in the Life. It is essential for Divine Love not to Love self but Love Others. He that loves not his brother abides in death. He has lost holding the Most High, Most High. Without God nothing is full.

Faith comes by Hearing the Living Word of God and Activating the Will. The will corresponds to the Heart. It is the direction of your life. You surrender your will to God and He gives you His Will.

"Thy Will Be Done." The Saints' will becomes God's Will.

To Listen, Follow and Obey!

Walk not after the things of the flesh but after the Spirit. For the Law of the Spirit, manifest in the Life of Christ, will set you free from sin and death.

A Christ Brother stands before you in a white robe of Salvation, walking humbly in his barefeet, following after Christ, step by step. "Blessed are the Peacemakers." He makes the unfamiliar territory, Familiar. You know not where your are going or where you've come from.

ORIENTATION

"Give up your cares, cut off the things which hinder you, no decisions to make, because you've already made the decision. Forget yourself, don't listen to the voices of the past, Catch up, Follow me!"

Follow a Christ Brother, go where he goes, do what he does, eat what he eats. In doing together it will be revealed, you will see no wrong in his Life. Faith then becomes the Trust.

The tug of this strange and distant world decreases Living In The Wind. Feeling the Call he keeps moving by his Devotion to God. Now the Father can take over his life. In his witness of walking side by side with a Christ Brother, the pilgrim Sees that Everything that has happened to him has not just been for himself, but for the Good of everyone. He knows that every action of a Christ Brother gives Light to those in darkness. A

CHRIST MANIFESTO (CHRIST FAMILY) (continued)

Christ Brother never raises his hand to his Brother. The blindness of the world is revealed to the pilgrim through the eyes of Christ, his Brother. This is his reproof. This is a gift of God.

A Saint has no worries. To worry about the unknown is to have doubt. Doubt is of the world. Now comes continuous Activation of Faith. The path has been made clear. The Angels have prepared the Way.

THE TRUTH WILL SET YOU FREE. Free from doubt.

A Christ Brother knows the day of Effortlessness Ease.

LOVE SEES, IT TEACHES AND SHOWS THE WAY

In fulfilling the Word of God, the Saint transcends the human ways and Returns to his Natural state of Divinity. This is the True Marriage to the Lord. His heart is Clean so the Lord dwells there; consciously letting the Lord in the heart, he must quit killing. Killing is when one participates in the murder of Any Living thing. Killing is a Direct act against God. Every Living thing must have Freedom.

The Lord is Wisdom and has shown the Way by His Example as a Life Giver. The Saint knows the difference between good and evil by opposing the ways of the world. No killing is the first sound of the bell of his heart. God is in the Earth so the Saint cannot kill.

He becomes a strict vegetarian not for health or self, but for the Love of God. He sees how God has Given Life to All things. The animals are God's Living garden tools created to keep the garden.

Love is unable to change anything by its human form, without a marriage of wisdom.

Wisdom is knowing the difference between Good and evil. It is the Light in which Love Sees. It teaches and shows the way...

The carnal man does not know the difference between good and evil. That is why in Receiving the kingdom, the activation of Faith is Called upon. The reproof is the Wisdom of Experience.

All earthly experience has shown that mankind is inclined to kill everything that has the Breath of Life in it. This is clearly seen in the exploitation of the animals. The animals are Brothers of Life. Human beings have been raised in a dark world. They are cannibals. They have been taught to eat their Brothers, the animals.

What one involves himself in he becomes. The exploitation and bondage of the animals has tainted every facet of mans existence, until he himself is slaughtered, tormented and depressed. His mind is fenced in, taken to market, butchered and sold for money. He has sold his life out. What you sow you reap: this is universal law! No place can he go and hide.

A saint Receives his Natural state as the Son of God.

Love prepares a bridal chamber for its future wife, which is Wisdom and Understanding.

Love, when Purified by Wisdom and Understanding, becomes Spiritual and Celestial.

Love, when defiled in the Understanding, becomes physical and sensual.

Sensual love is love of the world and love of self.

Spiritual Love is Love of your Brother.

Celestial Love is Love of the Lord.

The end of all creation is the Return of the Creation to the Creator. The Way to Divinity has already been shown by the Life of Christ. The Saint prepares his Being for the Greatest and most fulfilling Marriage. He gives his entire being in Serving God day and night, walking in the Image of Christ.

Entering the Spirit:

To know all things, one must Consciously Experience all things. To walk through all things, one must enter a state of no resistance. The state of no resistance in the Spirit, the Light Body. Give up old for New, give up old glory for New Glory. Proof is in the Experience. Experience is in Faith. Faith is something that cannot be seen, only felt.

The Saint focuses solely on his True Love, the Lord. He is given the Realization that the creation of more flesh is bondage to souls. The Saint abstains from sex and becomes nonpossessive, free of the Flesh. It is greed to possess others, which puts veils in from of the Spiritual Eye. As a result, carnal man is unable to see the Light of Truth.

THE DIVINE IS NOT DIVISIBLE

The Saint can only Serve One Master. He works only for the One True God. Giving the Kingdom of Heaven to his Brother. In living no Materialism, he walks in Faith. All his needs are provided through Miracles performed by God.

The Saint is not possessive of anything. Therefore all locks, fences and walls cease to exist. He is projected from the limited to the Limitless; from the divisible to the Indivisible. This is the marriage of Good and Truth, for God is God.

When you have made the decision to go to the Kingdom of Heaven, that is what you Will do.

The death which is spoken of by the Lord is not the burying of the body in the grave. It is the death of the carnal mind that images a physical world and Conscious Rebirth into the New Age. Conscious Rebirth creates space for Christ to come into consciousness within the emptied room of the Saints being. The crucifixion of Jesus Christ made Salvation possible. The Second Coming has made it a Reality.

Turning to the Lord is the Living and Giving of his Life. The Saint Flowing the in the Power of God's Free Gift Consciously gives up the tree of good and evil and dies in consciousness to the ways of killing, sex and materialism.

He is the herald of the New Age. Carried by Faith through the Inner Spiritual Wilderness, the Saint experiences Christ's

Consciousness. Being Born again into the True and Faithful Image of the Holy Spirit in the flesh.

The Spiritual multiplication of Jesus Christ who is the Tree of Life is occurring at this time on the face of planet earth.

BLESSED AND HONOR AND GLORY AND POWER BE UNTO HIM THAT SITTETH UPON THE THRONE AND UNTO THE LAMB FOR EVER AND EVER.

AMEN

TIME FOR DECISION

The Dedication:

Now is the time for all brothers to come to the aid of their brother. Make a decision from the evaluation of your life. Are you full and content? Judge not according to appearances of the things of the world, you will be fooled.

Judge with the Righteous Judgment according to the Life of Lord Jesus Christ: The Way, The Truth and The Life.

If your answer is "What I have is not Heaven, everything I know has proved to be against me." Then you have steps to make. You must Trust in what can not be seen and let it work for you. Who are you going to put you Faith in, whose hands are you going to put your hand in? The knowledge that you have gained must be invested somewhere—The evidence of the Resurrection is the Testimony of a Higher Life.

THE WAY—is One:

Follow after Christ for His Life shows the way into the New World. This world is not of Our Father.

THE TRUTH—is One:

Saints Do: Worship, work for, Serve, Give all to, walk—in the image of, Rejoice—in the Miracles of, Speak—to Use One Another of and Meditate Continually on the Most High Love of Our Father.

THE LIFE—is One and Everlasting

THE ART OF RELEASING

What you can't see will be Given.

What you can't overcome will be removed.

What you can't understand will be made Clear through Faith.

For when you find that you can only speak as a child; then you will Listen to the Angels and walk in their ways.

JOURNEY THROUGH THE MIND: ENTERING THE TREE OF LIFE

In the progression from separation to Independence, the Saint launches into the voyage from darkness to Light.

The Valley of Death:

Hand in hand with the Holy Father, the Saint Experiences every feeling known and unknown. He is plunged into the valley of death, where he faces his ultimate enemy—Fear. Here, he is a Christ Child. The Saint is given the ability to do what is Good, Beautiful and True. This will is not the Saints but is the Lord's in the Saint. It is never taken away.

Desert Places of the Carnal Mind:

The Saint is Freed from guilt. He Sees through the illusion of death and is led across the desolate places of the mind. When appearances are accepted as real truths they become a mirage of falsities. Believing in evil and falsity is the closing up of Heaven, for every Good an Truth Flows in from Heaven, through the Lord. When Heaven is closed, man is in hell. All things in which a man believes become his love and his Life. Every man whatever his condition, turns in a like manner to his first Love.

The wind of the desert places of the carnal mind are filled with a multitude of voices, haunting voices of the past. Mankind knows not forgiveness. The Baptism of Fire gives the Power of Forgiveness. One must Forgive in order to leave yesterday. He must leave yesterday to get to today. Perseverance breaks the connections with the past.

The Denial of Self:

The Saint forgets self for the Overall Good of the Kingdom. He knows this world is not his. The True value is in the Kingdom of Heaven.

In the moments of deepest desolation, Christ appears, life flashes by as a flicker. Now he is purged from the controversy of the mind and Unites with the Heart. God has turned his mind around and allowed him to see the world from His Overall Point of View harmonizing all differences. He Lives in a state of continuous Rebirth. Strength is made Perfect in weakness. His New Self moves forward, Flowing as streams in the desert.

The Mountains of Good and Truth:

Now Given Courage and Confidence, he knows God Is with him. The Almighty hand Raises the Saint to the Heights of the Mountains of Good and Truth. He who is in evil cannot see Good; but he who is in Good can see evil. There he is shown the Most High. He receives the Inner Most Gift, being in the hands of God. He knows now the Greatest Praise is to be a Son of God. Pleasing the Father is pleasing the self. The Saint is ready to pass through the clouds of the mind into the Son.

He is now a True Space Traveler.

SPACE TRAVELLING

The Saint moves into the many roomed mansion of the Holy Fathers Kingdom. He becomes a pilgrim on a journey of transformation to the Golden Castle of the Heart.

Denying self is Consciously dying. The pilgrim experiences the starving of the carnal mind and the nourishing of the New Christ Mind.

In the Receiving of a New Mind and New Heart, all perceptions, thoughts and feelings become New. The pilgrim experiences that he can no longer Trust his eyes, ears or thinking. The Truth is far Deeper than temporal appearances. No worldly

CHRIST MANIFESTO (CHRIST FAMILY) (continued)

logic Understands the Truth. Only the activation of faith on what is said by a Christ Brother is the reproof of Enlightenment.

This is Trusting the Angles.

THE PROCEDURE FROM SEPARATION TO INDEPENDENCE

In the fulfilling of God's word, the pilgrim Releases the things on the outside, allowing the Angels to cut off the carnal roots that lodge in the mind. It is as if he is sitting in the basket of an air balloon. Every string that comes from the basket is tied to sand bags, this keeps him bound to earth. By the cutting of these strings the balloon gets lighter and lighter. The pilgrim gets Higher and Higher. He now sees Clearly to cut the finest strings.

Liquidation: The Cutting of the Strings.

The Star of David symbolizes the dual nature of the human being. It is made of two interlaced triangles, one of which is directed upward, the other directed downward. Each Conscious act of Giving results in Elevation. Holding onto the sandbags keeps you grounded. The journey is an Inward One, "The Kingdom of God is within You".

The Fulfillment of the Commandment of NO KILLING begins in your home.

Step 1:

Stand in the entrance of your kitchen and say a Prayer to Our Father for the Strength to carry out His Will. Enter with this thought first on your mind and He will help you carry out your intent.

Start by removing every object that represents killing or slavery for any Living thing. This includes all flesh products such as meat, fish, poultry, eggs, cheese, milk, butter, whey, lard, honey or any item containing these. Look carefully at every label, remove that which is contaminated. Leather is a by-product of slaughter—don't let these slip by you.

Next, give the entire kitchen a thorough cleaning. Scour out all the pots and pans; scrub the stove and refrigerator, wash the counters and the floor. Open the doors and windows and let the Good wind blow through the room which is fit to prepare food for a Free Man. Let the Wind sweep through your dwelling and refresh and Purify it. Now you are ready to enjoy the True Bread of Life.

With every step you take the next will become clearer. The Holy Spirit will give you the Power to Perceive and Overcome the things which you have not yet seen.

Step 2:

Now move into your bathroom. Open the windows and the door and eliminate all which is contaminated. Read every label with care. You will be surprised to find that many commercial preparations sold for cleanliness contain hydroginized animal protein, milk, honey, etc. Throw it into the garbage for it is unclean. Hang a towel over each mirror for the reflection is finite and limited, showing only the physical. You are created in the Image and Likeness of God. You are a Spiritual Being. Cast out any objects which glorify the flesh such as perfume, lipstick, and jewelry. Scrub the floor, walls and ceiling and see that you are as beautiful as you feel.

The Beauty of the Saints is the form of their Love, which is His Love—for Love is One. One continuous, eternal, modulated, harmonious expression of the flow of He who is Our god.

Step 3:

On to the living room, dining room and bedroom: Check each drawer; each cabinet and when you come to your clothes, throw them out for they are designed to glorify the flesh. All you will have need of is a white robe from neck-to-ankle. You will soon be walking in your bare feet with an army blanket for warmth, in the Lord's Army. The use of your physical body for any purpose other than to Serve God is vanity and vexation to the Spirit.

Each step that you are taking is Elevating your Higher Self and withering your lower self. Consciously cease to desire and you shall have Everlasting Peace.

Now you are feeling the flow of momentum to enter into Conscious Communion with God as a worthy Disciple of Christ.

Step 4:

A Christian home is simple and basic. All that is needed is a few pots and pans and a sleeping bag for each member of the family. The more space, the less distractions, the more can be Received—inside, outside. Every object that fills a room fills your mind. Clear your home of furniture, televisions, radios, pictures and hand-graven images. Do not be preoccupied with material objects. Hold all things in common, since everything that you have Received has come Freely from God. Always keep your door Open to those in need. You know not who might be knocking. . . .

With this Force you are being propelled toward the Kingdom, away from the world, step by Conscious step. You are ready to cut the final strings and exercise Full Faith in God. Follow Christ's Command to His Disciples.

"Sell all that you have and Give alms. Provide yourselves with bags which wax not old, a Treasure in the Heavens that faileth not, where no thief approacheth; neither moth corrupteth, for where your Treasure is there will your Heart be also."

"Go forth among the people and as you go, preach saying, the Kingdom of Heaven is at hand. Heal the sick, Cleanse the lepers, Raise the dead, Cast out devils. Freely have you Received; Freely Give. Provide neither gold nor silver nor brass in your purse, nor script for our journey, neither two coats, neither shoes, now yet staves, for the workman is worthy of his meat."

Open your ear and Listen and Believe—know God through His Servants. He's coming from the Most High and is One with God. Let him speak the Song of your Heart. Be willing to add your will to your Brothers will. Offer all things up. Calm the mind and let God respond within you. In the moment the words will be Given. As the squire and the knight, He will Guide you through the Battle of the Mind. Empty your cup so that it may be filled with "New Wine".

HE THAT HATH RECEIVED HIS WITNESS HATH SET HIS SEAL TO THIS THAT GOD IS TRUE.

In The Wind:

The Saint is carefree: This relate to the Inner Self as a Spirit that can move without clinging to anything. Follow the Son! No hesitation! The bugle blows: The Angel goes to Serve God in Righteousness.

Set your sails and wait for the wind . . . As the True Fishers of Men.

You are now leaving the state of Hope of the world and entering the Faith of Christ. Launching into the Life of Miracles. You'll soon be "in a twinkle of an eye," in the Fulfillment of your dreams. Stay young at Heart! God is with You!

"All nations of earth shall hear the Gospel of His Grace. How beautiful upon the mountains are the feet of him that bringeth Good Tidings that publish Peace, that bringeth Good Tidings of God, that publisheth Salvation, that saith unto Zion: "THY GOD REIGNETH.""

To the general assembly and the church of the First Born, which are written in Heaven, and to God the Judge of All, and to the Spirits of Just men made Perfect, and to Jesus the Mediator of the New Covenant, and to the blood of sprinkling that speaketh better than that of Abel. This word, yet once more, signifieth the removing of those things that are shaken, as of things that are made, that these things which cannot be shaken may remain. Wherefore, we Receiving a Kingdom which cannot be moved, let us have grace, whereby we may Serve God acceptably with Reverence and Godly Fear. To Fear God is to Praise God. Praising God is the Life of the Saint.

" . . . break forth into Joy, Sing Together, ye waste places . . . for the Lord hath Comforted His People. The Lord hath made bare his Holy Arm in the eyes of all the nations and all the ends of the earth shall see the Salvation of Our God. . . ."

WE DO HEREBY PROCLAIM AS IT IS A NEW SONG:

NEW GLORY
HOLY, HOLY, HOLY BE THE KING OF KING OF KINGS,
AND HOW BLESSED BE HIS ANGELS
WHO FROM HIM RECEIVE THEIR WINGS -
AND TO SPREAD HIS LOVE, THEY USE THEM,
SINCE NO GREATER USE THERE BE -
THAN PROCLAIMING OF GODS KINGDOM -
HOW GODS LOVE DOES SET YOU FREE
AND HOW ONLY IN THIS FREEDOM, CAN ONE SERVE HIM UTTERLY!

YEA THE MASTER OF THE UNIVERSE, ON EARTH HE WALKS AGAIN,

AS IT WAS THE ONLY MATTER OF DESTROYING ALL THE SIN
AS HE STROLLS O'ER THE PLANET, WITH HIS ANGELS, SAINTS, HIS KIN.

YES THEY'RE SINGING THE NEW SONG NOW,
SO THAT EVERY EAR SHALL HEAR -
EACH AND EVERY STEP TO MAKE,
TO HAVE GODS PLAN BECOME ALL CLEAR.
HIT YOUR KNEES IN HUMBLE REVERENCE,
THROUGH OBEDIENCE COMES TRUST -
DOING ALL THAT GOD COMMANDS,
NOW'S THE TIME, HE'S HERE, YOU MUST !

GLORY TO GOD IN THE HIGHEST

AND ON EARTH PEACE, GOODWILL TOWARD MEN !

AMEN

MESSAGE FROM SPACE TO TIME

TO THE NATIONS OF THE WORLD:

There is the way of the Upright, walking humbly.

Trusting in God, All is gained

Oh man of time, you sit back dismayed at the atrocities of this bemuddled world. Violence is upon your door step. Plagues and famines are neighbors and it passes you by; they do and they die and still His Mighty words echo: "Love one another as I have loved you." The planet sways in discontent. Truly Grace is being stretched. Can you not discern the Sign of the Times? Mankind stands at the Threshold of a New Age.

If a man contemplates himself and his relation to the world and is not pleased then it is the Season to Receive a New Point of View. To break the limits of time and pass through the obstacles of birth, death and old age into the limitlessness of space—Everlasting Life.

Receive the Clarity to involve yourself with Good.

As in the smallest to the greatest, the same applies. For a man is a nation within and a nation is a man without. If a man has not the solution within his Heart to be at Peace, then it is mockery to counsel together seeking the solutions for nations to live in one accord. It is the blind leading the blind.

Selfishness entangles those who take. Nothing can be taken from those who give. Selflessness unveils the Giving Nature. What is yours will come to you. Rather dwell on what you can Give.

Do you have a thirst for Truth? Can a Good Word of Truth soften your Heart for Righteousness? Do you Care for the Living?

Then you must arise and stand firm as the Rock. You shall be as a Lighthouse among men; a Guiding Light, solid on the Rock. Guiding those at sea safely into Harbour of Peace.

CHRIST MANIFESTO (CHRIST FAMILY) (continued)

Receive the Overall Point of View of the Kingdom of Heaven.
Now is the Time of Agreement.
Orientate yourself with the Peace of NO KILLING.
Change frames.
Give! instead of taking.

There is the Way of the Upright. This way has been paved by Divinity from Space to man's time. Fulfillment is Now walking upon the face of the earth. By Trusting in God, the Voice of the Heart is clearly the Watchtower in the storm.

These are the Days of Preparation. When you least expect it, it will be upon you.
Be Prepared !
Show that you care—GIVE LIFE !

FOR THE GOOD OF ALL STOP KILLING

ALL GLORY TO THE MOST HIGH

AMEN

IN CONVENTION, BY THE UNANIMOUS CONSENT OF THE HOST OF ANGELS ASSEMBLED:

RESOLVED,

That the Constitution of a Saint be laid before the nations of the world, as a direct Sign of the time; and step by step procedure out of the Coming tribulations.

We have now the honor to submit to the nations of the world, this constitution of a Saint which is the direct cure, when followed, to mankinds' disease. Our foundation is from the Great Giver, the Law of Life—NO KILLING. The Order of the Universe is found in the stillness of Peace, Jesus Christ Lightning Amen is the Serenity of NO KILLING.

The Perfect Union was formed at the Foundation of Creation, guaranteeing Life, Liberty and Happiness to All Living Things. Few People of this world have sought True Righteousness; the power to separate from the world and its evil doctrines. It is time that this Constitution be instituted among men and these Rights be given to ALL Creatures.

Hence results the necessity of a different organization.

Individuals entering into the New Age must give up what they know as their life to receive a New Life. The first step of Life is NO KILLING. One who gives life receives Life.

The magnitude of giving is nothing compared to what has already been given. Obedience to God's Law is fulfillment. There is a precise line between the Kingdom of Heaven and the ways of the world. So is the same in surrendering ALL for the Kingdom. The difficulty has been the increased difference and separation of the ways of the world, which have lead to selfish habits and interests of the people therein.

"In all our deliberations on this subject, we've kept the Faith, which appears to us the greatest interest of every True citizen of the New Age. This important consideration seriously and deeply impressed on our minds is of vital importance to a

man's heart. The decree of NO KILLING is the basic formula for Peace on Earth; supporting NO KILLING by ALL, to ALL living Things.

Only this step will fulfill God's Living Word and begin mankinds' ascension from darkness. This commitment is the Restoration and Regeneration of an infected and disordered planet. The Breath of Life is Pure, Clean and Corrective of the degenerate mind that kills.

Thus, the Constitution of a Saint, which now is Present, is the result of the Return of Christ and the Witness of the Holy Spirit; as an example to mankind, The Light in the Darkness, The Way to Walk. That he may see in simplicity the way out of chaos.

So that his heart is made Pure and his mind Clear in the entering of this New Age.

TO THE GLORY OF THE MOST HIGH !

AMEN

Notes: *The Christ Family emerged in the 1970s as a radical wing of the Jesus People Movement. While based in an Evangelical Christian perspective, the Christ Family developed an unconventional lifestyle. The semi-nomadic members dressed in white and wore no shoes. They were opposed to the current order as it manifested in killing, sex, and materialism. The admonition against killing led to the adoption of vegetarianism.*

The members of the Christ Family, i.e., the Saints, called others to join them and adopt their life of faith. That life begins in separating from the world of killing, adopting the simple life by selling all one's possessions and giving the receipts to the poor, and moving out among people preaching the gospel.

*　　*　　*

Homosexually Oriented Churches

STATEMENT OF BELIEFS (RESTORATION CHURCH OF JESUS CHRIST)

"We believe and accept as binding on us, as a church, the Articles of Faith as written by the Prophet Joseph Smith. As such, we do solemnly proclaim and testify:

"Our mission is to provide an opportunity for spiritual growth for estranged Latter-day Saints, regardless of their original LDS church affiliation.

"Our mission is to fulfill the divine mission to preach the everlasting or 'fullness' of the Restored Gospel of Jesus Christ to 'every . . . people' in all the world, including the gay and lesbian communities worldwide.

"Our mission is to promote the knowledge of God's love for each and all of humanity. We are witnesses that the Almighty creates unity out of diversity by revealing himself to persons of all nations, kindreds, tongues and peoples according to their own understanding, culture, time and society.

"Our mission is to extend the blessings of the Holy Priesthood, according to the inspirations of Almighty God, to all who are called of God to the saving work of the Holy Priesthood, including women.

"Our mission is to allow revelation in all its forms, to work in the calling of and in the duration of priesthood callings an church offices for we testify that God is the Head of this work and not man.

"Our mission is to use the sacred Sealing Power of the Holy Priesthood of God to bind all loving relationships for time and eternity as the inspirations of God may direct.

"Our mission is to foster a positive and healthy attitude among Latter-day Saints about their individual human expressions of affection toward one another so that each may be free from false guilt so that personal faith might grow without inhibition.

"Our mission is to '. . . bear one another's burdens, that they may be light . . . mourn with those that mourn . . . comfort those that stand in need of comfort, and to stand as witnesses of God at all times and in all things, and in all places . . . even until death. . .'"

Notes: *Founded in California in the early 1980s, the Restoration Church of Jesus Christ is a small splinter group of the Church of Jesus Christ of Latter-day Saints that began among that church's alienated gay and lesbian members. Its Statement of Beliefs assumes an acceptance of the Articles of Belief of the Church of Jesus Christ of Latter-day Saints, now makes explicit an acceptance of gays and lesbians of Mormon and other religious backgrounds. It seeks to provide its membership with the benefits of the Mormon priesthood that had previously been denied it because of sexual orientation.*

*　　*　　*

STATEMENT OF FAITH (UNIVERSAL FELLOWSHIP OF METROPOLITAN COMMUNITY CHURCHES)

UFMCC Bylaws, Article III: Doctrine, Sacraments and Rites.

A. Doctrine: Christianity is the revelation of God in Jesus Christ and is the religion set forth in the Scriptures. Jesus Christ is foretold in the Old Testament, presented in the New Testament, and proclaimed by the Christian Church in every age and in every land.

Founded in the interest of offering a church home to all who confess and believe, the Universal Fellowship of Metropolitan Community Churches moves in the mainstream of Christianity.

Our faith is based upon the principles outline in the historic creeds: Apostles' and Nicene.

We believe:

1. In one triune God, omnipotent, omnipresent and omniscient, of one substance and of three persons: God-our Parent-Creator; Jesus-begotten of God, God in flesh, human; and the Holy Spirit-God as our sustainer.

2. That the Bible is the divinely inspired Word of God, showing forth God to every person through the law and the prophets, and finally, completely and ultimately on earth in the being of Jesus Christ.

3. That Jesus . . . the Christ . . . historically recorded as living some 2,000 years before this writing, is God incarnate, of human birth, fully God and fully human, and that by being one with the will of God, Jesus has demonstrated once and forever that all people are likewise Children of God, being spiritually made in God's image.

4. That the Holy Spirit is God making known God's love and interest to all people. The Holy Spirit is God, available to and working through all who are willing to place their welfare in God's keeping.

5. Every person is justified by Grace to God through faith in Jesus Christ.

6. We are saved from loneliness, despair and degradation through God's gift of grace, as was declared by our Savior. Such grace is not earned, but is a pure gift from a God of pure love. We further commend the community of the faithful to a life of prayer; to seek genuine forgiveness for unkind, thoughtless and unloving acts; and to a committed life of Christian service.

7. The Church serves to bring all people to God through Christ. To this end, it shall arrange for regular services of worship, prayer, interpretation of the Scriptures, and edification through the teaching and preaching of the Word.

B. Sacraments: This church embraces two holy Sacraments:

1. Baptism by water and the Spirit, as recorded in the Scriptures, shall be a sign of the dedication of each life to God and God's service. Through the words and acts of this sacrament, the recipient is identified as God's own Child.

2. Holy Communion is the partaking of blessed bread and wine in accordance with the words of Jesus: "This is my body . . . this is my blood." (Matthew 26:26-28)

All who believe, confess and repent and seek God's love through Christ, after examining their consciences, may freely participate in the communal meal, signifying their desire to be received into community with Jesus Christ, to be saved by Jesus Christ's sacrifice, to participate in Jesus Christ's resurrection, and to commit their lives anew to the service of Jesus Christ.

Notes: *The Universal Fellowship of Metropolitan Community Churches is the largest of the several churches that have*

STATEMENT OF FAITH (UNIVERSAL FELLOWSHIP OF METROPOLITAN COMMUNITY CHURCHES) (continued)

developed within the homosexual community in the United States (and, in more recent years, internationally). It is a broad church that finds room for people moving into its membership and leadership from a wide variety of Christian backgrounds. However, the Fellowship assumed a liberal Protestant position in adopting a doctrinal stance for inclusion in its own constitution and as a recommended statement for its affiliated congregations.

The Fellowship affirms the Trinity with a post-feminist wording of God as Parent-Creator, rather than Father. Dealing as it does with people who have experienced a high degree of rejection and alienation, the Fellowship affirms some universalist themes by emphasizing that all people are the Children of God, that God loves and is interested in all people, and that everyone is justified in Christ. Two sacraments, baptism and Holy Communion, are recognized.

* * *

Homosexual Organizations

STATEMENT OF POSITION AND PURPOSE (DIGNITY/USA)

We believe that gay and lesbian Catholics are members of Christ's mystical body, numbered among the people of God. We have an inherent dignity because God created us, Christ died for us, and the Holy Spirit sanctified us in Baptism, making us Temples of the Spirit, and channels through which God's love might become visible. Because of this, it is our right, our privilege, and our duty to live the sacramental life of the Church, so that we might become more powerful instruments of God's love working among all people.

We believe that gay men and lesbian women can express their sexuality in a manner that is consonant with Christ's teaching. We believe that we can express our sexuality physically in a unitive manner that is loving, life giving and life affirming. We believe that all sexuality should be exercised in an ethically responsible and unselfish way.

Dignity is organized to unite gay and lesbian Catholics, to develop leadership and to be an instrument through which we may be heard by the Church and Society. To be such an organization, we must accept our responsibility to the Church, to Society, and to the individual gay and lesbian Catholic.

1. TO THE CHURCH: We work for the development of its sexuality and for the appearance of gay men and lesbian women as full and equal members of the one Christ.

2. TO SOCIETY: We work for justice and social acceptance through education and legal reforms.

3. TO INDIVIDUAL GAY & LESBIAN CATHOLICS: We reinforce their sense of self-acceptance and dignity, and encourage their full participation in the life the Church and society.

As members of Dignity, we promote causes of interest to gay and lesbian Catholics. We have five primary areas of concern:

1. SPIRITUAL DEVELOPMENT: We shall strive to achieve Christian maturity through all the means at our disposal, especially the Mass, the sacraments, scripture personal prayer, and an active love of neighbor.

2. EDUCATION: We inform ourselves in all matters of faith as well as in all that concerns the gay and lesbian community so that we may develop the maturity of outlook needed to live fulfilling lives in which sexuality and spirituality are integrated, and to prepare us for service in the gay and lesbian community.

3. SOCIAL INVOLVEMENT: As Catholics and members of society, we involve ourselves in those actions that bring the love of Christ to others and provide the basis for social reform. We are actively involved with:

   a. Individuals: We lead a life of service to others, rendering visible the love of Christ and assisting in the creation of a love-centered community.

   b. Gay and Lesbian Groups: We work with other groups to seek justice for gays and lesbians and to promote a sense of solidarity within the community.

   c. Religious and Secular Groups. We work with many groups and organizations so that their members might better understand gay men and lesbian women, and thus recognize present injustices.

4. FEMINIST ISSUES: We dedicate ourselves to develop the potential to become more fully human. To do this we must work toward the eradication of all constraints on our personhood based on the ascribed social roles of women and men.

5. SOCIAL EVENTS: We provide activities of a social and recreational nature in an atmosphere where friendship can develop and mature and our sense of self-acceptance and dignity can be affirmed.

Notes: *Dignity/USA was the first of the denominational gay/lesbian caucus groups to emerge in the 1970s, early in the modern phase of the struggle for gay/lesbian rights and recognition. It functions among gay/lesbian Roman Catholics and their supporters. While there seemed to be some hope during the 1970s that a more positive stance toward gay and lesbian people might be assumed by the Roman Catholic Church hierarchy, by the time this Statement of Position and Purpose was adopted in 1989, the Church had shut the door on it dialogue with Dignity.*

In spite of the Church's rejection, Dignity persists in attempting to attain the sacraments for people living as gays and lesbians and remains committed to working with the Roman

Catholic Church leadership. Meanwhile, it is developing a full program for its members.

*   *   *

DOCTRINAL STATEMENT (EXODUS INTERNATIONAL)

We believe the Scriptures of the Old and New Testaments are the inspired Word of God, the final authority for doctrine, reproof, correction and instruction in right living.

We believe in one God, existing eternally in three persons: Father, Son and Holy Spirit.

We believe in the deity of our Lord Jesus Christ, fully man and fully God, only begotten Son of the Father. He was conceived by the Holy Spirit, born of the Virgin Mary, and lived a sinless life. He suffered under Pontius Pilate, was crucified, buried, and rose physically from the dead. He ascended to the right hand of the Father and will come again in power and glory.

We believe that faith alone in Jesus Christ as Savior and Lord frees us from the mastery of sin, and its consequences of death and eternal damnation. He assumed the penalty of death Himself, and enables us to live out of His resurrected life unto eternity.

We believe the Holy Spirit carries out this work of renewal in our lives, empowering us to grow in loving union with our Heavenly Father and to walk in obedience to His will.

We believe that the church of Jesus Christ is formed of all those who know Him as their Savior and Lord, regardless of denominational beliefs.

Notes: *Exodus International, founded in 1976, is an Evangelical Christian ministry directed toward the homosexual community. It is the belief of most Evangelicals that homosexuality is a chosen ungodly lifestyle that, no matter how ingrained, can be replaced with a heterosexual life. Exodus ministers to gay and lesbian people, those who formerly lived a homosexual lifestyle, and others with sexual orientation concerns. Its Doctrinal Statement is a consensus Evangelical statement.*

*   *   *

THE FOURTEEN STEPS (HOMOSEXUALS ANONYMOUS)

1. We admitted that we were powerless over our homosexuality and that our emotional lives were unmanageable.

2. We came to believe the love of God, who forgave us and accepted us in spite of all that we are and have done.

3. We learned to see purpose in our suffering, that our failed lives were under God's control, who is able to bring good out of trouble.

4. We came to believe that God had already broken the power of homosexuality and that He could therefore restore our true personhood.

5. We came to perceive that we had accepted a lie about ourselves, an illusion that had trapped us in a false identity.

6. We learned to claim our true reality that, as mankind, we are part of God's heterosexual creation and that God calls us to rediscover that identity in Him through Jesus Christ, as our faith perceives Him.

7. We resolved to entrust our lives to our loving God and live by faith, praising Him for our new unseen identity, confident that it would become visible to us in God's good time.

8. As forgiven people free from condemnation, we made a searching and fearless moral inventory of ourselves, determined to root out fear, hidden hostility and contempt for the world.

9. We admitted to God, to ourselves and to another human being the exact nature of our wrongs and humbly asked God to remove our defects of character.

10. We willingly made direct amends wherever wise and possible to all people we had harmed.

11. We determined to live no longer in fear in of the world, believing that God's victorious control turns all that is against us into our favor, bringing advantage out of sorrow and order from disaster.

12. We determined to mature in our relationship with men and women, learning the meaning of a partnership of equals, seeking neither dominance over people nor servile dependency on them.

13. We sought, through confident praying and the wisdom of the Scriptures, for an ongoing growth in our relationship with God and a humble acceptance of His guidance for our lives.

14. Having had a spiritual awakening, we tried to carry this message to people in homosexuality with a love that demands nothing and to practice these steps in all our lives activities, as far as lies within us.

Notes: *Homosexuals Anonymous, founded in 1980, is an Evangelical Christian organization that assists people who wish to change their sexual orientation. It is based on the Evangelical position that homosexuality is a chosen lifestyle that can be replaced with a heterosexual one. The Fourteen Steps have been adapted from the Twelve Step program of*

THE FOURTEEN STEPS (HOMOSEXUALS ANONYMOUS)
(continued)

Alcoholics Anonymous. It assumes that with God's help, homosexuality can be overcome.

*　　*　　*

STATEMENT OF FAITH (METANOIA MINISTRIES)

A) The Apostles' Creed

　I.　I believe in God the Father, Almighty, Maker of heaven and earth.

　II.　And in Jesus Christ, His only begotten son, our Lord;

　III.　Who was conceived by the Holy Spirit, born of the Virgin Mary;

　IV.　Suffered under Pontius Pilate; was crucified, dead and buried, He descended into Hell;

　V.　The third day He rose again from the dead;

　VI.　He ascended into heaven, and sitteth at the right hand of God the Father Almighty.

　VII.　From thence He shall come to judge the living and the dead.

　VIII.　I believe in the Holy Spirit.

　IX.　I believe a holy catholic Church, the communion of saints;

　X.　The forgiveness of sins;

　XI.　The resurrection of the body;

　XII.　And the life everlasting. Amen.

B) We believe that our only comfort in life and death is that with body and soul, both in life and death, we are not our own, but belong to our faithful Savior Jesus Christ; Who with His precious blood has fully satisfied for all our sin, and delivered us from all the power of the devil; and so preserves us that without the will of our heavenly Father not a hair can fall from our head; yea, that all things must be subservient to our salvation wherefore by His Holy Spirit He also assures us of eternal life, and makes us heartily willing and ready, henceforth, to live unto Him. (Isaiah 43:1-7; Romans 8:14, 16, 28, 14:8; I Cor. 6:19).

C) We believe that mankind has been separated from God through his own willful disobedience or sin in thought, word, and deed and he must pay the penalty of death and hell. (Romans 6:23, 3:23, 5:12, 18-19).

D) We believe that man is unable to save himself. (Romans 3:23).

E) We believe that God through His justice must punish sin, but in His mercy and love He sent His Son Jesus Christ to bear that punishment. (John 3:16; Romans 6:23).

F) We believe that because Jesus Christ is both truly God and truly man, He has become our substitute, receiving in Himself the penalty due to us all. (Hebrews 6:23).

G) We believe that Christ's death fully paid the penalty of all men who believe in (cling to and rely upon) Him as Savior and Lord.

H) We believe that the Holy Bible is the complete and true Word of God to mankind useful for teaching, rebuking, correcting, and training in righteousness. (II Timothy 3:16).

I) We believe that it is God's will for us to tell others about what He has done both to us and throughout history leading others into a saving knowledge of Christ. (Matthew 23:19-20; Acts 1:8).

J) We believe that according to Scripture all homosexual behavior, identity, fantasy, and lifestyle are sin and need to be totally forsaken. We affirm God's love and power to recreate the person who acknowledges Jesus Christ as Lord and Savior.

Notes: *Metanoia Ministries is an Evangelical ministry to homosexuals based on the belief that homosexuality is a sin and that AIDS is a direct result of homosexual sin. Their Statement of Faith includes the text of the Apostles Creed, to which is appended a consensus statement of the Evangelical Christian perspective. The final item in the statement summarizes the Ministries' position on homosexuality.*

*　　*　　*

A STATEMENT OF RECONCILIATION (RECONCILING CONGREGATION PROGRAM/ UNITED METHODIST CHURCH)

All persons are recipients of God's love and grace. God intends the church to be a community which embodies love, grace, and justice for all people. As a sign of faithfulness to God's covenant with all humankind, we discern that God is challenging the Christian community to accept lesbians and gay men as sisters, brothers, and co-workers in the household of faith.

We affirm the participation of lesbians and gay men in all aspects of our life together. We seek to address and advocate the needs and concerns of gay men and lesbians in our church and society. We strive to utilize the gifts of all persons in our ministry without regard to sexual/affectional orientation.

We are distressed by the presence of homophobia within the United Methodist Church and in our society. Such fear and hatred reflects neither God's love nor God's intent for the community of faith. We hope that our affirmation of the wholeness of all persons will bring reconciliation to all people within the church who because of prejudice, homophobia, or ignorance find themselves in exile from the family of God.

Notes: *Since 1972, the United Methodist Church has regularly affirmed a position that welcomes homosexuals as members of its congregations, but condemns homosexuality and bans homosexuals from the ministry and various other leadership positions. The Program is comprised of a vocal minority within the Church opposed to that position and working for the full acceptance of gays and lesbians within the church.*

Chapter 23
Unclassified Religious Groups

PRIMARY BELIEFS (ORDER OF THE CELESTIAL)

The Celestial Order has but two primary beliefs and these are:

(a) The Fatherhood of God and the brotherhood of man.

(b) There is One God and One race the human race.

The order of the Celestial is a fellowship established to promote a greater Unity between all mankind through the comparison of modern and ancient religious thought. It is not the intention of the order of the Celestial to force any dogma or belief on any man. We seek only to lend a helping hand to mankind as he searches for the Ultimate Truth in the seat of his own consciousness.

Notes: *The Order of the Celestial is a religious fellowship founded in Kansas City, Missouri, that ministers to incarcerated people and ex-offenders residing in half-way houses. The Order has a very brief belief statement. Apart from a fundamental belief in the fatherhood of God and the brotherhood of man, it affirms only a life of service to humanity.*

Creed/Organization Name and Keyword Index

This index provides an alphabetical listing of all creed titles and organization names presented in both Volumes I and II of *Encyclopedia of American Religions: Religious Creeds*. It also contains citations to keywords appearing in creed titles and significant names. Creed titles appear in italic type to distinguish them from organization names. Page references to citations appearing in Volume I are preceded by "Vol I"; "Vol II" precedes page references to citations appearing in Volume II.

A

Aaronic Order　Vol I: 655

(Abrahamic Faith); Church of God General Conference　Vol I: 586; Vol II: 295

Abridgement of Doctrine (International Liberal Catholic Church)　Vol I: 745

Abstract of Principles (Southern Baptist Convention/ Southern Baptist Theological Seminary)　Vol II: 222

Abstracts of Principles [Banner Herald (Progressive)]　Vol I: 507

Abundant Living Christian Fellowship (Kingsport, Tennessee)　Vol I: 380

Accent Publications　Vol II: 287

Account of Our Religion, Doctrine and Faith (Hutterite Brethren)　Vol I: 672

Accrediting Association of Bible Colleges　Vol II: 225

Accrediting Association of Theological Institutions; American　Vol II: 289

An Act of Gnosis (Ecclesia Gnostica)　Vol I: 744

Action International Ministries　Vol II: 287

Addition to the Twenty-nine Important Bible Truths [Church of God (World Headquarters)]　Vol I: 343

Additions to the Twenty-five Articles of Religion (African Methodist Episcopal Church)　Vol I: 277

Additions to the Twenty-five Articles of Religion (African Methodist Episcopal Zion Church)　Vol I: 278

Additions to the Twenty-five Articles of Religion (Asbury Bible Churches)　Vol I: 266

Additions to the Twenty-five Articles of Religion (Christian Methodist Episcopal Church)　Vol I: 278

Additions to the Twenty-five Articles of Religion (Congregational Methodist Church)　Vol I: 270

Additions to the Twenty-five Articles of Religion (Evangelical Church of America)　Vol I: 270

Additions to the Twenty-five Articles of Religion (Evangelical Methodist Church)　Vol I: 270

Additions to the Twenty-five Articles of Religion (Southern Methodist Church)　Vol I: 273

Advent Christian Church　Vol I: 585, 587

Advent Christian Church; Primitive　Vol I: 587

Adventist; Church of God　Vol I: 593

Adventist Church; Seventh-Day　Vol I: 588

Adventist Reform Movement; Seventh-Day　Vol I: 592

Adventist; Seventh-Day　Vol I: 588

Adventist; Sunday　Vol I: 585

Aetherius Society　Vol I: 732

Affirmation of Faith [Ashland Theological Seminary-Brethren Church (Ashland, Ohio)]　Vol I: 437

An Affirmation of Our Faith (Baptist General Conference)　Vol I: 515

The Affirmation of St. Louis (1976)　Vol I: 26

Affirmations (Church of the Awakening)　Vol I: 734

Affirmations for Humanistic Jews (Sherwin T. Wine, Society for Humanistic Judaism)　Vol I: 776

The Affirmations (Free Church of Berkeley)　Vol I: 809

Affirmations of the Ethical Movement (American Ethical Union); Statement of Principles and　Vol I: 636

Africa Evangelical Fellowship　Vol II: 287

Africa Inland Mission　Vol II: 287

African Mission; North　Vol II: 337

African Methodist Episcopal Church　Vol I: 263, 277

African Methodist Episcopal Zion Church　Vol I: 263, 278

African Orthodox Christian Church; Pan　Vol I: 775

African Orthodox Church　Vol I: 35, 37

African Union First Colored Methodist Protestant Church　Vol I: 263

African Universal Church　Vol I: 401; Vol II: 177

Agasha Temple　Vol II: 429

The Agasha Temple Teaches (Agasha Temple)　Vol II: 429

Ageless Wisdom; International Church of　Vol I: 723

Agnostics; Society of Evangelical　Vol I: 648

Agreed Upon Beliefs of the Green River (Kentucky) Association of United Baptists　Vol I: 521

Ahmadiyya Anjuman Ishaat Islam, Lahore, Inc.　Vol I: 784

Ahmadiyya Movement of Islam　Vol I: 784, 785

Aims and Ideals (National Alliance for Spiritual Growth)　Vol II: 437

Aims and Ideals (Self-Realization Fellowship); Aims and Tenets (Yogoda Sat-Sanga Movement) and　Vol I: 789

Aims and Objects [British-Israel World Federation (Canada)]　Vol II: 406

B

C

J

K

L

O

P

Q

R